The Baltic Sea and Approaches

The Baltic Sea and Approaches

Germany, Denmark, Sweden, Finland, Russia (including Kaliningrad), Poland, Lithuania, Latvia, Estonia

 RCC PILOTAGE FOUNDATION

Imray Laurie Norie & Wilson

Published by
Imray Laurie Norie & Wilson Ltd
Wych House The Broadway
St Ives Cambridgeshire PE27 5BT England
www.imray.com
2017

All rights reserved. No part of this publication may be reproduced, transmitted or used in any form by any means – graphic, electronic or mechanical, including photocopying, recording, taping or information storage and retrieval systems or otherwise – without the prior permission of the Publishers.

First edition 1992
Second edition 2003
Third edition 2010
Fourth edition 2017

© Text: RCC Pilotage Foundation 2017
© Plans: Imray Laurie Norie & Wilson Ltd 2017
© Photographs as credited 2017

ISBN 978 184623 689 1

British Library Cataloguing in Publication Data.
A catalogue record for this title is available from the British Library.

The plans have been reproduced with the permission of Sjöfartsverket (Swedish Maritime Administration), Liikennevirasto (Finnish Transport Agency) and BSH Bundesamt für Seeschifffahrt und Hydrographie (Federal Maritime and Hydrographic Agency of Germany), licence number 11123/2012-15.
This product has been derived in part from products owned by the Danish Geodata Agency, licence number G10-2002.

The last input of technical information was July 2017

Printed in Croatia by Zrinski

CAUTION

Whilst the RCC Pilotage Foundation, the author and the publishers have used reasonable endeavours to ensure the accuracy of the content of this book, it contains selected information and thus is not definitive. It does not contain all known information on the subject in hand and should not be relied on alone for navigational use: it should only be used in conjunction with official hydrographical data. This is particularly relevant to the plans, which should not be used for navigation. The RCC Pilotage Foundation, the authors and the publishers believe that the information which they have included is a useful aid to prudent navigation, but the safety of a vessel depends ultimately on the judgment of the skipper, who should assess all information, published or unpublished. The information provided in this pilot book may be out of date and may be changed or updated without notice. The RCC Pilotage Foundation cannot accept any liability for any error, omission or failure to update such information. To the extent permitted by law, the RCC Pilotage Foundation, the author and the publishers do not accept liability for any loss and/or damage howsoever caused that may arise from reliance on information contained in these pages.

Positions and Waypoints
All positions and waypoints are to datum WGS 84. They are included to help in locating places, features and transits. Do not rely on them alone for safe navigation.

Bearings and Lights
Any bearings are given as °T and from seaward. The characteristics of lights may be changed during the lifetime of this book. They should be checked against the latest edition of the UK Admiralty *List of Lights*.

Updates and Supplements
Corrections, updates and annual supplements for this title are published as free downloads at www.imray.com. Printed copies are also available on request from the publishers.

Find out more
For a wealth of further information, including passage planning guides and cruising logs for this area visit the RCC Pilotage Foundation website at www.rccpf.org.uk

Feedback
The RCC Pilotage Foundation is a voluntary, charitable organisation. We welcome all feedback for updates and new information. If you notice any errors or omissions, please let us know at www.rccpf.org.uk

Contents

The RCC Pilotage Foundation	*vi*
Foreword	*vii*
Acknowledgements	*vii*

Introduction — *1*
- Early History of the Baltic — *2*
- Reaching the Baltic — *5*
- Berthing systems — *10*

1. Germany — **14**
- 1a. Approach to the Baltic via the Kiel Canal and River Eider — *21*
- 1b. Kieler Förde to Flensburg Förde — *29*
- 1c. Kieler Förde to Mecklenburger Bucht — *37*
- 1d. Darsser Ort to the Polish border — *53*

2. Denmark — **66**
- 2a. Eastern Danish ports — *72*
- 2b. The Danish side of The Øresund — *78*
- 2c. Approach to the Kattegat through the Limfjord — *87*
- 2d. Danish harbours and anchorages of the Kattegat — *92*
- 2e. Approach to The Baltic by the Lille Bælt — *106*
- 2f. Approach to The Baltic by the Store Bælt — *116*
- 2g. Bornholm and Christiansø — *126*

3. Sweden — **130**

West coast of Sweden — *138*
- 3a. The Swedish side of the Øresund — *139*
- 3b. Southwest coast (Södra västkusten) — *146*
- 3c. The Bohuslän coast – Northwest coast — *157*
- 3d. Göta Alv, Trollhätte and Göta Kanals — *167*

South coast of Sweden — *177*
- 3e. Gislövs Läge to Utklippan — *177*

East coast of Sweden — *187*
- 3f. Utlangan to Landsort, including Öland and Gotland — *187*
- 3g. Stockholm - the Archipelago and surrounding area — *204*

The Gulf of Bothnia — *225*
- 3h. The Swedish coast of the Gulf of Bothnia — *226*

4. Finland — **244**
- 4a. The Finnish coast of the Gulf of Bothnia — *252*
- 4b. The Archipelago Sea — *264*
- 4c. Gulf of Finland - western part — *287*
- 4d. Gulf of Finland - eastern part — *300*
- 4e. The Russian channel, Saimaa Canal and Lake — *313*

5. Russia — **318**

6. Poland — **334**
- 6a. Zalew Szczeciński to Berlin — *341*
- 6b. Coast of Poland — *349*

7. Kaliningrad — **368**

8. Lithuania — **372**

9. Latvia — **378**
- 9a. Baltic Sea Coast — *382*
- 9b. The Gulf of Rīga — *387*

10. Estonia — **392**

Appendix — **418**
- I. Suppliers of charts and publications — *418*
- II. Abbreviations used on Russian charts — *419*
- III. Firing practice areas — *420*
- IV. Search and Rescue — *421*
- V. Radio communications and weather information — *423*
- VI. Chart coverage in Russia, Estonia, Latvia and Lithuania — *430*

Index — **434**

The RCC Pilotage Foundation

The RCC Pilotage Foundation was formed as an independent charity in 1976 supported by a gift and permanent endowment made to the Royal Cruising Club by Dr Fred Ellis. The Foundation's charitable objective is 'to advance the education of the public in the science and practice of navigation'.

The Foundation is privileged to have been given the copyrights to books written by a number of distinguished authors and yachtsmen. These are kept as up to date as possible. New publications are also produced by the Foundation to cover a range of cruising areas. This is only made possible through the dedicated work of our authors and editors, all of whom are experienced sailors, who depend on a valuable supply of information from generous-minded yachtsmen and women from around the world.

Most of the management of the Foundation is done on a voluntary basis. In line with its charitable status, the Foundation distributes no profits. Any surpluses are used to finance new publications and to subsidise publications which cover some of the more remote areas of the world.

The Foundation works in close collaboration with three publishers – Imray Laurie Norie & Wilson, Bloomsbury (Adlard Coles Nautical) and On Board Publications. The Foundation also itself publishes guides and pilots, including web downloads, for areas where limited demand does not justify large print runs. Several books have been translated into French, Spanish, Italian and German and some books are now available in e-versions.

For further details about the RCC Pilotage Foundation and its publications visit **www.rccpf.org.uk**

PUBLICATIONS OF THE RCC PILOTAGE FOUNDATION

Imray
Arctic and Northern Waters
Atlantic France
Atlantic Islands
Atlantic Spain & Portugal
Black Sea
Cape Horn and Antarctic Waters
Channel Islands, Cherbourg Peninsula and North Brittany
Chile
Corsica and North Sardinia
Islas Baleares
Isles of Scilly
Mediterranean Spain
North Africa
Norway
South Biscay
The Baltic Sea and Approaches

Adlard Coles Nautical
Atlantic Crossing Guide
Pacific Crossing Guide

On Board Publications
South Atlantic Circuit
Havens and Anchorages for the South American Coast

RCC Pilotage Foundation
Supplement to Falkland Island Shores
Guide to West Africa
Argentina

RCCPF website www.rccpf.org.uk
Supplements
Support files for books
Passage Planning Guides
ePilots - from the Arctic to the Antarctic Peninsula

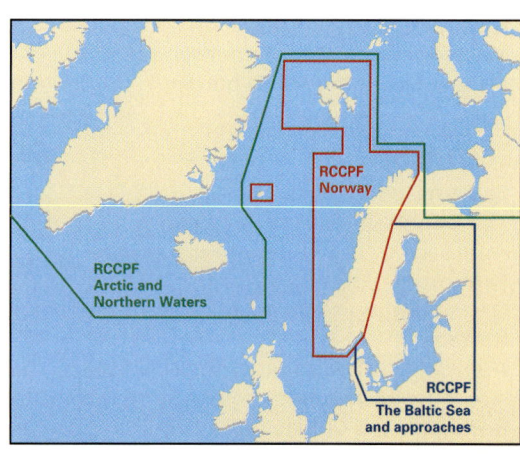

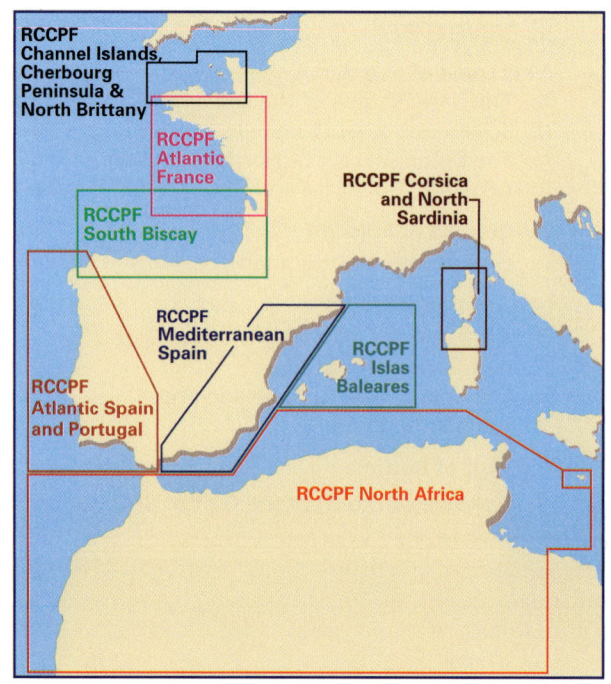

Foreword

The area covered by *The Baltic Sea and Approaches* encompasses unlimited places to tie up or anchor in a number of diverse cruising grounds, including the densest archipelago in the world. It would be impossible for one book to provide in depth coverage of every region and this book does not pretend to supplant the detailed pilot books available for each country or coastline. Instead the hope is that *The Baltic Sea and Approaches* gives a valuable overview to the whole area, with sufficient pilotage detail to enable the reader to passage plan effectively, either for a single season or for multiple seasons. Further pointers are given towards the sources of more detailed cruising information for each region, available either in book form or electronically.

It would be a herculean task to produce a book of this coverage without a dedicated team of authors, each of whom have spent time cruising the Baltic, some of them for many, many years. The RCC Pilotage Foundation is immensely grateful to the following people who have worked so hard to bring this edition up to date:

Germany Miranda Delmar-Morgan

Denmark (excl. Bornholm) Annette Ridout

Bornholm Nicholas Hill

Sweden
　Introduction Nicholas Hill
　West Coast Annette Ridout
　Gota Canal Annette Ridout
　South and East Coasts Nicholas Hill
　Gulf of Bothnia Nicholas Hill

Finland (incl. Aland Islands) Madeleine Strobel and Jan Horhammer

Russia Graham and Fay Cattell & Vladimir Ivankiv

Poland Miranda Delmar-Morgan

Kaliningrad Graham and Fay Cattell & Vladimir Ivankiv

Lithuania Graham and Fay Cattell

Latvia Graham and Fay Cattell

Estonia Graham and Fay Cattell

The RCC Pilotage Foundation is also hugely indebted to Nigel Wollen who has worked closely with the team to pull this edition together so effectively.

The team at Imray, led by Lucy Wilson, have spun their usual magic in turning an enormous and complex bundle of text and images into such an attractive and well-presented treasure trove of information. We are all extremely grateful to them for their hard work and expertise.

The RCC Pilotage Foundation continues to depend on all of the yachtsmen and women who cruise the Baltic to help to keep this book up to date by contributing information based on their own experience of the region. If you have some information or photographs for us we would love to hear from you at info@rccpf.org.uk. Any feedback will be published on our website at www.rccpf.org.uk and annual correctional supplements to the book will be available via the Imray website at www.imray.com.

Jane Russell
Editor in chief
June 2017

Acknowledgements

This fourth edition has built on the work of previous authors and contributors and we remain very grateful to them all for this firm foundation. Mike and Liz Redfern and Michael Lewin-Harris deserve a special mention in this regard. Nigel Wollen and the current team of authors would also like to thank the following contributors who have been so generous in sharing Baltic information for this edition, whether in the form of photographs, updates to chart information, or sections of text: Tom Aitken, Lennart Andreasson, Jake Backus, Arnis Berzins, Stuart Carnegie, Max Ekholm, Anthony Fawcett, Andrew Fleck, John Langdon, Rolf and Cornelia Massow, Dirk Neubert, David Ridout, Stephan Strobel, John Sadd, Dr Horst Saforovic, Janet Saforovic, Arabella Sprot, Kalevi Westersund, Dr John Wilson, Alison Wilson and Bindy Wollen. Individual photographs are credited with each image. The book would not have been possible without this valued input from so many fellow cruisers. The authors are also very grateful to Lucy Wilson, Elinor Cole, Isabel Eaton and the rest of the team at Imray for deciphering all of their submitted information and converting it all, so beautifully, into a coherent whole.

Nigel Wollen
June 2017

The Cruising Association (CA) provides an invaluable further resource of Baltic Sea information to its members and the team of authors recommend CA membership to anyone planning a Baltic cruise.

West Finland

Introduction

Compiled by Nigel Wollen

The Baltic has much to offer the cruising yachtsman. Incorporating nine countries, each with their own distinctive features, it provides a fascinating variety of scenery, pilotage, traditions and history.

This fourth edition of *The Baltic Sea and Approaches* owes much to the groundwork, research and effort that has formed the basis of previous editions, but has been completely revised to cover the many changes that have taken place, including a number of new harbours and anchorages. Each country has been researched by different editors with first hand knowledge and who have been able to draw on the experiences of many others.

The overall objective of the book is to provide a general introduction to the Baltic Sea and its adjoining countries, to capture the flavour of the places and the people, and to act as a reference to the more detailed pilot books, charts and other sources of information. It is therefore intended to be a useful planning guide to what is, at first sight, quite a confusing cruising ground. It is not possible to cover such a large and varied area in one volume, and it does not pretend to be a comprehensive pilot book. However, it is hoped that it includes sufficient detail of the main harbours and approaches for it to have a place in the cockpit or at the chart table as well as an aid to passage planning.

There is always some debate as to where the Baltic Sea begins and ends, with purists arguing that the island of Bornholm marks its western extremity. However, for the purposes of this book, it is deemed to include Denmark (other than the west coast) and the whole of Sweden, as well as the other countries referred to, and references to 'the Baltic countries' should be interpreted accordingly. The sequence of chapters runs in a northerly arc between Germany and Russia, then from Poland to Estonia along the southern shore.

Why go to the Baltic?

The attractions of the Baltic to the cruising yachtsman are very varied, and really include something for everyone.

- Although subject to the normal vagaries, the summer weather is governed by continental weather patterns and is generally far warmer than one might expect in those latitudes.
- The days are long during the main season, and there is little need for night sailing. For the Scandinavians, the season starts late (on or around midsummer on 21 June), and the harbours are less crowded in the earlier and later parts of the season. The holiday season ends by mid-August but it is perfectly possible to continue cruising well into September or even later.
- There is no tide, so no need to crawl out of one's bunk in the early hours. There are, however, some currents, which may be used to good effect. These are generally wind driven and are dealt with in more detail on page 6.
- There are hundreds of anchorages, and a huge variety of harbours with well developed facilities. The latter tend to become busy during the holiday season but it is nearly always possible to find a quiet anchorage.
- In the sheltered waters of the archipelagos there is relatively flat water and very little swell, with short distances between anchorages. This makes it ideal for sailing with young children or less experienced crew.

Busy children *Bindy Wollen*

INTRODUCTION

Kalmar Castle, Sweden *C.N.Hill*

Typical fish menu, Ålö, Sweden *Bindy Wollen*

Smørrebrød in Copenhagen *E. Redfern*

- All the Baltic countries have a rich and eventful history, which is evidenced by the number of great castles and churches as well as beautiful historic towns and cities which provide plenty to do if the weather turns nasty. (For more details of Baltic history see below, and the introductory section for each country).
- Each country has its own distinctive choice of food, such as the famous Scandinavian smörgåsbord. Fish dishes feature strongly, with excellent fish smokeries operating in many harbours.
- There are plenty of places to leave a yacht, or to lay up for the winter, but early booking is strongly advised. See further information below.

Early history of the Baltic

Contributed by John Langdon

Geologically, the Baltic first became recognisable as a region when it broke away from the super-continent Concordia in the southern hemisphere 1,800 million years ago. It then drifted around on its own tectonic plate as other super-continents came and went, before reaching its current position between the Eurasian and North American plates. The land remains low lying except for the mountains of Norway that were created by pressure from the North American plate.

Evidence of the earliest known Baltic inhabitants has been found in Wolf Cave in west Finland and dated to 125,000BC. By then humans had evolved in Africa, but Europe and the near east were Neanderthal territory. Then came the last ice age glaciation in 110,000 BC, which continued until 10,000 BC. Scandinavia was covered by 2km of snow and ice, with even more over Canada. Sea levels correspondingly fell by 120m (nearly 400ft), leaving considerably more dry land around the world than today, and the ice-covered lands were crushed lower into the earth's magma. Even now the north Baltic countries are still "rebounding" at a rate of a metre per century, leaving harbours from as recently as Viking times well inland.

EARLY HISTORY OF THE BALTIC

It was half way through the ice age that at most 5,000 humans left Africa steadily to populate the world. After 15,000 years some had reached Australia, a journey that at that time would have only crossed 40 miles of water. Only then did humans head for Neanderthal Europe, and for whatever reason, 5,000 years later the Neanderthals were extinct.

From 10,000BC humans could follow the now rapidly receding ice from north Germany and northwest Russia into the Nordic countries. The forests, lakes and marshlands, however, kept them in small, isolated communities of hunter-gatherers until quite late on. There is little sign of planted crops or domesticated farm animals much before 2,000BC.

The early human civilisations developed in warmer climes. Even the Romans, who had successfully colonised France and Britain, could make little progress through the cold, wet forests of Germany, let alone any further north. Indeed, even the medieval Teutonic Knights sometimes had to squeeze their armies in single file through the forests of Latvia. Alexander Nevsky's great set-piece battle against them had to be fought on the winter ice.

There was, however, still plenty of contact between the Baltic peoples and the more sophisticated south. The Baltic Sea and its rivers, just like the Mediterranean, soon became the most convenient highway. Baltic amber was found in Tutenkamen's tomb, for example, and the Roman historian Tacitus speaks very highly of the tall, fine-looking Baltic people, their noble way of life and their longboats.

It was the Vikings who put the Baltic firmly on the world map. Their heyday was between 800 and 1,100AD when as raiders, traders or settlers, they sailed further and further from home. Norwegian Vikings followed the north Atlantic to Scotland and Ireland and then on to Iceland, Greenland and Canada. The Danes went to England, France, Spain and the western Mediterranean. The Swedes headed east along the Gulf of Finland and south through the rivers to the Caspian, the Black Sea and the eastern Mediterranean and were connected to the Middle East and Asia via the old trade routes.

'Going a-Viking' was usually a small, local, freelance affair. The Vikings never made any attempt to co-ordinate and merge their conquests into a single great empire. Indeed the Danish Norsemen, or Normans, who conquered northern France and then England, soon adopted the language of their subject peoples and lost all ties with their original homeland. Similarly the Swedish Vikings, or Rus, who created Russia, were soon defending their territory against their fellow Swedes.

By the later Middle Ages, having seen for themselves what the more advanced Roman, Byzantine and Islamic civilisations had achieved, local Baltic leaders were slowly conquering or merging with their neighbouring tribes to create nations with similar prosperity and stability.

Source: Bogdan Giuşcă / Wikipedia 2005

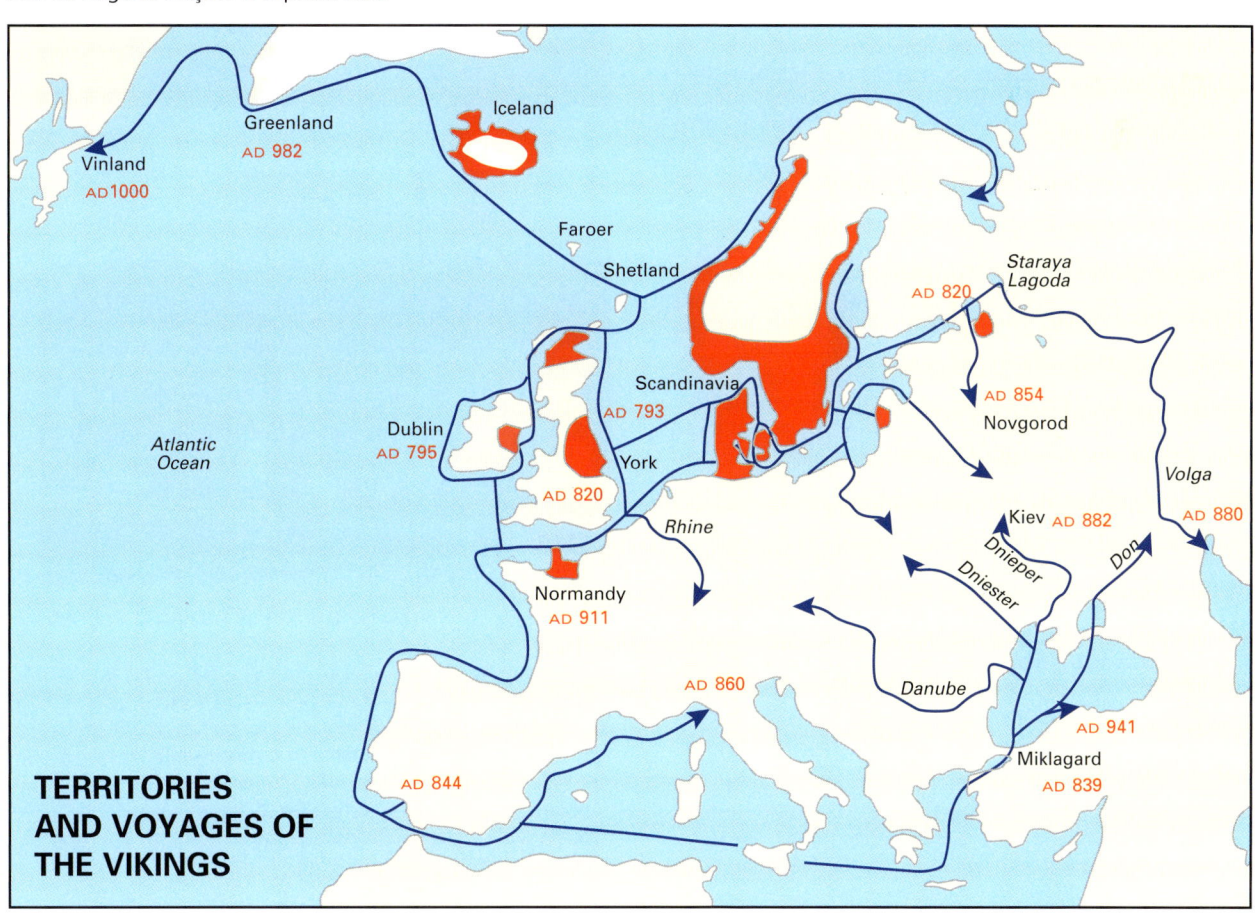

TERRITORIES AND VOYAGES OF THE VIKINGS

INTRODUCTION

They also sought to exploit their Baltic trade as Europe's main supplier of grain and ship-building materials, with first Denmark, then the German Hanseatic League, then Sweden and then Russia dominating the region. At the end of WWII, the Soviet Union occupied all of the southern and eastern Baltic, leaving only Denmark, Sweden and Finland independent. Then at last came the break up of the Soviet Union in 1991. Now all of the Baltic countries are free market democracies and all but Russia (including Kaliningrad) are members of the EU.

More detailed histories from the Middle Ages onwards are to be found in the sections on the individual countries which follow.

Useful sources of information

Contact details and websites for sources of information in specific countries are listed in the text for each country. The internet is a valuable resource when planning a Baltic cruise, and is also an excellent source of weather information, as summarised in the Appendix on page 429.

The Cruising Association (CA) deserves a special mention as its Baltic Section provides its members with an outstanding source of information, including pilot books for each of the Baltic countries, newsletters and access to 37 local representatives as well as seminars and social events. Its Cruising Almanac, published anually by Imray, also contains a section on the Baltic (www.theca.org.uk).

The Royal Yachting Association will advise on a wide range of issues, including the International Certificate of Competence, VHF Operators Certificate, and VAT (for further details see www.rya.org.uk).

The sauna experience

Contributed by John Dare, sauna enthusiast

For many people a wonderful extra to cruising in the Baltic is the sauna experience. Almost everywhere one goes – hotels, marinas, yacht clubs and even fairly remote islands – one will find a sauna to enjoy. After a few days at sea, particularly if the weather has been a little unfriendly, there are few things more pleasant than a relaxing sauna bath. It is a great delight to get warm, clean and relaxed all at the same time.

So what happens? The sauna experience varies from the well-organised facility with showers, jacuzzis and swimming pools adjacent, to the little sauna hut in the woods with a simple, wood-burning stove. The latter are perhaps the most enjoyable, particularly if they are on the edge of the water with a lovely view as they often are. In any case the experience is basically the same. First, wash yourself in the shower, sea, pool or other available water. Then sit and relax in the sauna and the heat (most likely between 60°C and 90°C) should have you perspiring freely in five minutes or so. A first stay of around ten minutes serves most people, but step out for a break if you feel at all uncomfortable. During the break the most traditional thing to do is to enter the sea, which you will find remarkably refreshing. Then return to the sauna for some more heat and repeat as you wish. Also, during the break, especially where you have the sauna to yourself, it is very relaxing to simply sit outdoors enjoying a snack or perhaps a cold beer. Remember, the essence of the experience is to relax and take your time – a hurried sauna is a waste of time.

There are no hard and fast rules about sauna etiquette, but a few general guidelines should be observed. Drinking and eating in the sauna is not done. Traditionally saunas are mixed, but in busy or more public places you will come across designated hours for men and women, or even different saunas for each. Normally saunas are taken naked, but if modesty dictates you can certainly wrap a towel around yourself or even wear a swimsuit - and you should, of course, respect the privacy of others using the sauna before you. If you are using a wood-burning sauna you will doubtless find wood and wood-cutting tools close to hand, and you are expected to replace the wood you have used. Saunas by definition are clean places, and you should certainly leave the area as clean as you found it. In some marinas use of the sauna is included in your harbour dues while in other places a charge is made, and it may sometimes be necessary to book, usually for one hour. The situation varies and one simply has to enquire.

Above all, saunas are social places to be enjoyed with friends and/or family. The sauna experience is an essential part of the Baltic cruise, so relax and enjoy it!

A typical Finnish sauna *P. and G. Price*

Enjoying post-sauna chat *Bindy Wollen*

Reaching the Baltic

The three main routes into the Baltic are:
A via Kiel Canal
B via Limfjord/Kattegat
C via Skagerrak/Kattegat

For the more adventurous, there is a fourth route from the White Sea via the Baltic Canal, which connects the White Sea to St Petersburg. This is outside the scope of this book, but would require careful research of the formalities prevailing at the time and its viability (see RCCPF *Arctic and Northern Waters*, Imray).

The entrance to the Kiel Canal can be reached in a few days from the English Channel, whilst the Limfjord or Skaggerak routes are alternatives if crossing from northern England or Scotland.

The Göta Canal can be a useful and interesting route across Sweden if entering or returning from a Baltic cruise.

Full details of the Kiel Canal, Limfjord and Göta Canal are included in the text.

The detail of passages to and from the Baltic is outside the remit of this book but extensive details can be found on the RCC Pilotage Foundation website (available to all) at www.rccpf.org.uk and to members of the Cruising Association on their website www.theca.org.uk

Travel

By sea

For those who leave their yachts in the Baltic, it can make sound economic sense to drive out with a laden car at the beginning of each season. Unfortunately, the Harwich to Esbjerg ferry has closed, and the only direct ferry from the UK is now a freight ferry from Immingham to Göteborg. It is, of course, possible to take a car through the Eurotunnel or via one of the many ferries to France or Holland, and there are then a host of ferry options into the Baltic from one of the German, Danish or Polish ports, with numerous different ferry operators. See www.ferrylines.com for up to date news on services, closures and new routes. There is a very comprehensive ferry service between the Baltic countries, and within each country. Some of them are huge vessels, and their sudden appearance is enough to keep the unwary yachtsman on his toes.

Ferries have right of way *Bindy Wollen*

Brightly-painted houses at Degerby in the Åland Islands
E. Redfern

By air

All the Baltic countries are well served by both national and budget airlines, as well as internal flights. Individual country details are given in the text, but the following resumé of airports may be helpful when planning crew changes or visits home.

Germany	Hamburg, Lübeck and Berlin
Denmark	Esbjerg, Billund, Århus, Ålborg, and Copenhagen
Sweden	Göteborg (Landvetter) and Malmö in the West. On the East coast, Stockholm (Arlanda, Skavsta or Västerås), Karlskrona (Ronneby), Kalmar, Gotland (Visby), and, further north, Örnsköldsvik, Umeå and Luleå
Finland	Helsinki, Vaasa, Mariehamn, and Turku. On the Saimaa lakes, Lappeenranta and Savonlinna
Russia	St Petersburg (Pulkovo-2 for international flights and Pulkova-1 for domestic flights), and Kaliningrad (via Copenhagen or Hanover)
Poland	Warsaw, Gdansk and Kraków
Lithuania	Vilnius, Palanga, and Kaunas
Latvia	Rīga, Liepaja
Estonia	Tallinn, Kärdla, Roomassaare, Parnu

By land

Details for individual countries will be found in the text. Both rail and bus services are generally very good throughout the Baltic countries and most of the major ports mentioned in this book are on national rail networks or can be reached by bus or ferry. The European Rail Timetable is an invaluable guide for planning rail travel in Europe or Scandinavia.
www.europeanrailtimetable.eu

INTRODUCTION

Navigation

Search and rescue

The Global Maritime Safety System (GMDSS) is fully established in the Baltic and the Baltic countries communicate and coordinate in maritime rescue. Area A1 (20-30 NM off the coast) is covered by VHF Channel 70. Area A2 (up to 150 NM off the coast) MF-DSC 2187.5 kHz. Otherwise, communication is on Channel 16 or MF 2182 kHz. In practice, the maritime services monitor VHF channels 16 and 70.

> **Emergency phone numbers**
>
> All countries ☏ 112
> (this number applies to all EU countries, together with Russia and Kaliningrad, and can be dialled from mobiles. It is free)
>
> Germany ☏ +49 124124
>
> Finland ☏ +358 (0)204 1000
>
> Latvia ☏ +371 673 23103
>
> Russia ☏ +7 8123274146

Buoyage

The IALA System A has been adopted by all countries. In Finland and Sweden the cardinal and lateral marks may not have topmarks, so it is important to be able to identify by colour alone (which, in turn, may be faded and can be difficult to see if sailing towards the sun). Many of the buoys are small by UK standards, and a good pair of binoculars is essential. Transits are also common, usually taking the form of a vertical yellow stripe against a red background, or occasionally a less visible black and white.

Waypoints/positions

Positions of lights and other marks given in this book have been taken from a variety of sources and will not necessarily agree exactly with GPS positions. The positions given beneath each harbour name (or on the chartlets or plans) are intended purely to facilitate planning, and are NOT intended as a waypoint unless specifically stated.

Tides and currents

There is no appreciable tide within the Baltic, but prolonged winds in one direction and changes in atmospheric pressure can produce significant variations in depth. The datum of charts of the Baltic is generally mean sea level, not the lowest astronomical tide.

Because the Baltic collects more fresh water than evaporates from its surface, there is a weak but steady surface outflow of less dense, less saline, water through the Kattegat into the North Sea, partially balanced by a return flow of more saline water at a lower level. Within the Baltic, surface currents are weak and tend to run towards Denmark, parallel to the associated coastline. Wind patterns can produce their own surface currents. Currents can flow in almost any direction, even upwind, since their direction is influenced not only by the wind but also by the shapes of the basins. Following a blow which upsets sea levels, surface and underwater currents may be markedly different.

Long term prediction is not possible, and the best course is to consider the effect of the weather pattern of the previous days on the surface of the water. Ask locally when in doubt.

Charts/pilot books

British Admiralty charts are useful for passage planning, notably charts 259 (the Baltic Sea), 2816 (the Baltic Sea – Southern Sheet) and 2817 (the Baltic Sea – Northern Sheet) and possibly 2252 (Gulf of Bothnia).

However, it is essential to carry the detailed large scale charts published in each country, and details of these (and of local pilot books) are given in the chapters covering the individual countries and in the Appendix. In complex areas where each island looks much like its neighbour, as do the buoys on the chart, it is vitally important to be able to find your place at a glance and a supply of small removable adhesive markers or arrows may help.

Electronic chartplotters

There has been very rapid development and improvement of electronic charts and their associated equipment, with iPads or even smart phones performing a useful role. These are useful for passage-making provided that the user is aware of the need to scroll in to a large enough scale to see the detail. They are also useful for planning purposes but this is limited by the loss of detail when you scroll out to a smaller scale. They should not be regarded as a substitute for detailed paper charts.

Traffic separation schemes (TSS)

There are a number of TSS in the Baltic, all of which are shown on the charts. They are monitored closely and the regulations should be strictly observed.

Weather forecasts

There is extensive weather information for most of the Baltic countries. See main text for each country and the Appendix for details. Many forecasts give wind speeds in metres per second; multiply by two for the approximate equivalent in knots, and divide by two for Beaufort.

Formalities

General

Note In June 2016 the UK voted by referendum that it should leave the EU. It is impossible to predict the impact this will have on the formalities required for UK passport holders travelling within the EU once it has ceased to be a member (or, indeed, on British registered yachts that are kept in the Baltic for more than one season). However, the UK will remain an EU member until negotiations are complete, and the summary below sets out the current position. All visitors to the Baltic countries should check for any changes before departure.

Customs and immigration

The individual requirements of each country are set out in the relevant chapters.

All countries require a valid passport for each person aboard. Visitors are advised to check visa or other requirements before departure, but at the time of publication only Russia required a visa (see page 320).

All the countries except Russia are members of the EU and passage between those countries should be free from customs formalities for EU citizens in boats on which VAT has been paid or exempted. Holders of non EU passports should check the position. Customs and Immigration requirements are quite distinct from Schengen clearance, which is dealt with in the next paragraph.

Schengen area

All the Baltic countries except Russia are parties to the Schengen agreement, which allows citizens of those countries freedom to travel between member countries without formality. It is important to understand that the UK and the Republic of Ireland are not members of the Schengen area (and never have been). Skippers arriving from the UK or another non Schengen area country are required to check in or out. Skippers should enquire of the harbourmaster, Police or Customs at the first Schengen port of entry, and be prepared to present a crew list containing name, nationality, date of birth and passport number for each. In practice this requirement seems to have been applied with a light touch in the past, but it should be noted that, at the time of publication, the whole future of Schengen was being called into question, with some member countries (Scandinavian and others) starting to assert more control over their borders. Readers are advised to check the up to date position well before departure (see www.schengenvisainfo.com).

Ship's papers

All yachts should carry a registration document (either under Part I of the Merchant Shipping Act 1995 or the Small Ships Register (SSR), or the national equivalent, together with a VAT receipt or exemption (the EU Single Administrative Document), evidence of marine insurance (specifying the areas covered and period of cover), and a VHF Ships Radio Licence.

Restrictions on duration of visits

A VAT-paid yacht registered in an EU country can be kept in any other EU country indefinitely. Non EU registered yachts can be kept in the EU (and moved between EU countries) for a period of up to 18 months and this period can be extended to allow for lay-up periods or similar, after which they must clear out of the EU and clear back in. The regulations are subject to frequent change, and owners should check before arrival. In the UK details are available from HM Revenue and Customs (www.hmrc.gov.uk).

Courtesy flags

A courtesy flag for the country being visited should be flown from the starboard spreader. (Note that the Åland islands have their own flag).

Ensigns

The national ensign of the visiting yacht should be flown. The red ensign is widely recognised, whilst the blue or the white can lead to some entertaining but sometimes exhausting attempts to explain the niceties of British ensign etiquette.

Skipper and crew

VHF Operator's Certificate

At least one person aboard should hold a VHF Operator's Certificate of Competence, with GMDSS endorsement if appropriate.

International Certificate of Competence

There is no general requirement for skippers of visiting yachts to hold a certificate of competence, but in practice it is desirable for skippers to hold an ICC (or equivalent), especially if visiting Poland, Lithuania, Latvia, Estonia or Russia. Although skippers of boats registered in the Baltic States require a certificate, this does not apply to skippers of boats whose flag state does not require them to have such qualifications (such as the UK). In practice, the crew should carry whatever certificates they do hold.

EHIC cards / health insurance

EU nationals should carry a European Health Insurance Card, which entitles them to free medical treatment under reciprocal agreements with the health services of the home country. It should be noted that EHIC cards must be renewed every 5 years (see www.gov.uk/european-health-card for details as to how to apply or renew). Appropriate health insurance is also advisable, but be alert for restrictions on the duration of visits or policies that restrict or exclude pursuits such as sailing.

INTRODUCTION

Health risks

Tick bites
Visitors should be aware of the health risk from tick bites. Ticks are most prevalent in, but not confined to, areas of woodland and long grass. Ticks may be infected with TBE (Tick Borne Encephalitis) and/or Lyme Disease. TBE is the most serious and can lead to death in rare cases. A course of injections with annual top-ups will give immunisation. Injections can only be obtained privately in the UK and can be arranged via a GP surgery. The risks are taken very seriously by the locals and there is a travelling vaccination facility on a yacht in the Stockholm archipelago (www.vaccinkliniken.se). Lyme disease is less serious but there is no immunisation available against it. Both diseases can show similar symptoms at the beginning, including fatigue, aching limbs, fever and (in the case of Lyme Disease) a red ring around the bite. If there is any sign of such symptoms medical advice should be sought without delay.

Mosquitoes
Can be a nuisance in certain areas, especially in late evening. Netting is available from most camping shops and can be draped over open hatches like a wedding veil, or fitted nets can be made. Mosquito repellent should be carried.

Algae
This sometimes forms in the main part of the Baltic, particularly during hot summers. It forms into a crust on the surface, and can be toxic. Swimming should be avoided if and when it appears (especially for children and pets). It is believed to be caused by unsustainable farming methods, and every effort is being made to eradicate the problem. Details of algae coverage can be found at www.SMHI.se/weather.

Tick bite vaccination yacht, Nynashamn, Sweden
Bindy Wollen

Preparing and equipping the boat

Motor/sailing cone
To be displayed in the foretriangle when motor sailing: this is mandatory and strictly enforced in Germany (and in Holland if visiting that country en route to the Baltic).

Holding tanks
The regulations differ between the various countries, but are becoming stricter each year. Sweden, for instance, now imposes an absolute prohibition on the discharge of sewage from pleasure craft within 12 miles of the shore, regardless of nationality or flag status, and all countries impose regulations concerning the discharge of sewage in harbours or in close proximity to the land. It is therefore becoming increasingly difficult to cruise in the Baltic without fitting a holding tank capable of discharge at a pump-out facility. Given the fact that the sea is almost tideless, and given the Scandinavian love of swimming, the regulations are entirely understandable. It may be possible to comply by using a portable chemical toilet ('porta potty') or composting toilet (C-Head), if an owner wishes to avoid fitting a holding tank. Pump out facilities are becoming more generally available.

Mobile phones
In general, mobile coverage in the Baltic is excellent. All the Baltic countries except Russia are in the EU, which since June 2017 has abolished 'roaming' charges. The new rules mean that citizens travelling within the EU are able to call, text and browse the internet on mobile devices at the same price they pay at home. Mobile users should check the detail of their tariffs with their phone providers to avoid being caught out by surprise charges. It will be up to a future UK government to decide whether to have the EU price restrictions on roaming or not after the UK leaves the EU.

Internet access
WiFi is widely available in Scandinavia, in café's, tourist offices and marinas. The signal in marinas is sometimes weak, especially when moored some distance from the aerial, and there is often a charge to use it. One increasingly popular device is the MiFi, a relatively cheap and simple device which creates a local WiFi 'hotspot' via the local mobile network, with its own (usually local) SIM card.

Bottled gas
This is a complex muddle. Butane gas is not widely available in the north or east Baltic because it remains liquid at low temperatures but both butane and the popular Camping Gaz are widely available in Germany and Denmark, and in certain harbours in Sweden (Kalmar, Visby, Trosa, Vastervik, Nyköping, Oxelösund, Nynashamn, Stockholm (Wasahamn), Furusund, Bullandö, Saltsjöbaden, Ystad and probably others) and Finland (Mariehamn East, Hanko, NJK Helsinki and HSK

8 THE BALTIC SEA AND APPROACHES

PREPARING AND EQUIPPING THE BOAT

Helsinki). Supplies are often limited and expensive.

Calor Gas is not available as either butane or propane outside the UK and EU safety regulations preclude refilling of bottles (although there may still be facilities to refill propane cylinders at Stenungsund and Kalmar in Sweden). On no account should butane bottles be refilled with propane because propane stores at a higher pressure and could cause the bottle to explode. Note that the British 'colour code' of blue bottles for butane and orange bottles for propane does not hold good around the Baltic.

The alternative is to purchase a local bottle and connecting regulator (but refills may only be available in the country of origin), or the solution may be to buy a set of worldwide connectors (see www.gasboat.net).

Gas consumption can be reduced by the use of a pressure cooker, or by cooking over an open fire (but never light a fire on bare rock which may crack, nor on grass where fire may spread). Portable barbecues are very popular in Scandinavia, and are in use quite regardless of the weather.

Electricity

A 220volt electricity supply is available in most yacht harbours throughout the Baltic, usually with the familiar circular blue European standard connectors. However, older facilities still have continental 2-pin plugs and other variations will occasionally be encountered. It is advisable to carry a very long connecting cable, as berths are often some distance from the nearest socket. A residual current device (RCD) to trip the supply if any leakage occurs to earth may provide an additional safety measure if the yacht is connected to an aged harbour circuit.

Fuel

Diesel fuel is readily available throughout the Baltic, other than in Kaliningrad. However, a few yacht harbours do not have diesel pumps on site and so a few 20 litre containers may be useful. In Sweden, many fuel points are either card or banknote operated and instructions are generally given in English as well as Swedish. Tax-free fuel is not available. If there is red diesel in the tanks, skippers should carry receipts showing that tax has been paid. Red diesel should only be in the boat's tanks and not in cans.

Skippers need to be aware of the risk of 'diesel bug' caused by fuel containing a Bio component, which can cause blockages of filters and fuel lines. This can be countered by the use of a biocide to discourage bug growth. At the present time, it is understood that marine diesel sold in Denmark, Sweden, Poland, and Russia contains no biofuel, but care is needed if the station also sells fuel for road use (in which case it may all come from the same tank). Storage time of the fuel is a compounding factor.

Water

Water is available on the pontoons in most of the Baltic yacht harbours, and where this is not the case it is noted in the text. Quality is generally good, except in Russia (both the St Petersburg and Kaliningrad regions) where visitors are advised to boil tap water before drinking, or to arrive with tanks already full. It will often be necessary to provide your own hose, with a variety of different connectors.

Chandlery

Where possible, details of chandlers are given for individual countries. There has been a trend towards chandlery becoming more of a mail order/internet business but, although chandlery shops are quite scarce, they are generally available in the main yacht harbours. The best are to be found in Sweden, Finland, Germany and Denmark, but they are also becoming more common in Poland, the Baltic States, and St Petersburg. They have very variable ranges of stock, but if they do not stock a particular item, they can usually obtain it within 24 hours or so.

Laundry

Many yacht harbours have on-site launderettes, which may need to be booked in advance. The machines are often operated on eco-cycles at low temperatures and can take two hours or more for a standard wash.

Maypole in Åland islands *Bindy Wollen*

THE BALTIC SEA AND APPROACHES   9

INTRODUCTION

A rocky foreshore on the coast east of Helsinki *E. Redfern*

Provisioning and alcohol

All the main towns and cities are well served with supermarkets and stores, and open markets can be found in many places. However few, if any, shops will be found near the more remote anchorages. It is therefore necessary to plan ahead, and stock up when the opportunity arises.

If, having transited the Kiel Canal, you are headed towards Denmark, Sweden and Finland, considerable savings are to be made by provisioning the boat before leaving Germany.

It should be noted that midsummer (21 June) marks the start of the holidays, and many of the shops and restaurants in the smaller communities remain closed until then. Midsummer's Day is cause for great celebrations, usually around the maypole.

Alcohol prices are often the subject of concern for visiting yachts and the situation varies from one country to another. In Sweden and Finland, alcoholic drinks can only be purchased from government owned shops, known as *Systembolaget* in Sweden (where minimum age for purchase is 20 years old) and *Alko* in Finland, although beer not exceeding 3.5% alcohol is available in supermarkets. These shops are only to be found in the larger towns or shopping centres. These restrictions do not apply in the other Baltic countries. As a general comment, alcohol is expensive in Sweden and Finland, less so in Denmark, and even less in Germany, Poland and the Baltic States.

Laying up

There are a great many excellent yards where yachts may be laid up for the winter. They are too numerous to list in detail, and it is important to obtain up to date information as standards can change very quickly upon a change of ownership. If possible, seek personal recommendation, or obtain details via yacht clubs or marinas. The Cruising Association provides a very useful directory which is reviewed at regular intervals.

Prices in Sweden, Finland and Denmark tend to be higher than in Germany and the south and east (and remember that VAT rates are higher than in the UK for all of the countries concerned except Germany). The price also depends on whether the yacht is stored in a shed (heated or unheated), or outside.

The cold winter temperatures mean that it is important to drain all systems unless in a heated shed, and electrical equipment should be disconnected.

Above all, it is very important to book early, as space in the good yards is reserved several months ahead.

Berthing systems

Baltic mooring

There is little or no tide in the Baltic, and so floating pontoons are the exception rather than the rule. Instead, there are a variety of moorings techniques described below, some of which may take a bit of getting used to.

One essential for many of these Baltic moorings is to be able to climb off the yacht from the stern or the bow. Most yachts based in the Baltic have a split pushpit but those with easy stern access will often berth stern first. The jetty (or shore) is often well below the level of the bow, and a bow ladder will avoid the need for a potentially dangerous gazelle-like leap ashore.

Alongside

Mooring alongside is possible in many harbours, and no allowance needs to be made for tides. Some quaysides may be protected by large motor tyres, or be rather rough or damaged, in which case a fender board is useful. Be prepared for yachts to raft up.

Box moorings

These are particularly prevalent in Denmark and Germany, but are also found in the other Baltic countries, and provide an interesting challenge, especially in a cross wind. They are formed with a series of vertical posts, usually of timber but

Rock mooring is much easier with a bow ladder *David Ridout*

10 THE BALTIC SEA AND APPROACHES

BERTHING SYSTEMS

Box berths both occupied and vacant *David Ridout*

increasingly of steel, piled into the harbour bed and separated from the quay by a distance of 8 to 15 metres (sometimes more).

To moor in these, the yacht is steered in between two posts, with long lines (20m minimum is recommended) attached to the stern cleat. These lines should have large bowline loops at the end. The loops are dropped over the posts as the boat passes between them. When the boat reaches the staging or jetty, a crew member leaps off the bow with lines and ties them off. He should also be calling the distance from the jetty back to the helmsman. The lines from the stern can then be tightened to hold the boat in place.

Fenders should be hung either side so as to protect your boat from those in adjacent boxes. If the adjoining berth is occupied by another yacht it is perfectly acceptable to lie alongside it during the berthing process, and there is much to be said for selecting a box that lies to windward of an occupied berth, so as not to be blown downwind.

It is important to select a box which is not too narrow, and to have the fenders tied on but left on deck until the widest part of the yacht has passed the posts.

This is not an easy manoeuvre to carry out in a strong crosswind. To avoid being blown sideways, concentrate on securing the windward lines first, and sort the others out afterwards. If you get the opportunity, it is a good idea to practise your technique in an empty harbour on a quiet day.

Stern buoy

A row of mooring buoys is laid 2 to 3 boat lengths off a jetty or pontoon. Most buoys have a ring on a stalk, to which a long stern line is secured on

Stern buoy mooring *C.N. Hill*

INTRODUCTION

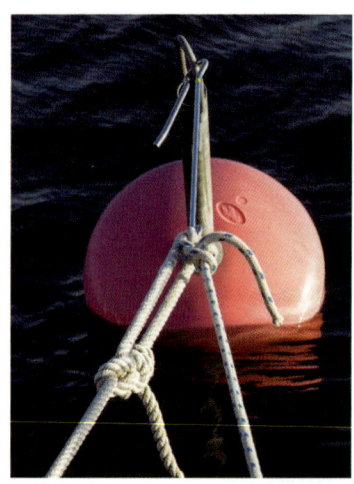

Left **Stern buoy**
Miranda Delmar-Morgan

Below **Examples of devices to attach to a stern buoy mooring: commonly found in Baltic chandleries**
C.N. Hill

Stern line on reel *Miranda Delmar-Morgan*

approach and then lines from the bow are made up ashore. It is best to approach to windward of the chosen buoy. There are various devices which can help, including having a stern line on a reel, and using a Scandinavian buoy hook. Once the bow is made fast, the line back to the buoy can then be tightened to hold the boat away from the jetty.

It is common practice for stern buoys to be shared if all are in use.

Stern anchor

This system involves deploying a stern anchor 3 to 4 boat lengths out, and taking a bow line to the jetty or shore. As with the stern buoy system, it can help to have the stern line or tape on a reel attached to the pushpit.

Yachts frequently use this technique to moor direct to the rocky shores in the sheltered waters of the archipelagos, in which case the anchor is dropped on the approach and a crew member has to jump ashore and make fast to convenient trees or rings or hammer in rock pegs. This should only be attempted where the shore is sufficiently steep-to, and it is always advisable to reconnoitre the chosen place first to ensure that there are no shallow areas or hidden rocks.

Booms

These are narrow (perhaps only 10cm wide) finger pontoons laid at right angles to the main pontoon, and often only 5-6m long. Lines have to be attached from the yacht to the outer (and sometimes the inner) end of the boom and to the main pontoon. Use of sheet winches can help. Access the shore via the bow as the boom will not take your weight. Do not try it!

Generally there is space for two yachts between each set of booms, but sometimes they are individual slots.

Lazy line

In this case, a line is tied to the jetty and runs to a heavy weight some distance from it. Approach the jetty, pick up the line, preferably with a boat hook, and take it back to the stern and secure it to a stern cleat. At the same time, a member of crew should have jumped ashore and secured the bow lines.

The line will have spent all season in the water, and may well be muddy and weedy. A pair of waterproof gloves might be useful.

Care should be taken to determine whether this system is in use, since dropping a stern anchor could lead to it becoming seriously fouled on the ground chains. Harbours which employ this particular system may well have a sign (an anchor with a red line across it: see illustration). This is not intended to forbid mooring, but means 'Do not use a stern anchor'.

Warning sign: do not anchor, lazy lines in place
C. N. Hill

12 THE BALTIC SEA AND APPROACHES

BERTHING SYSTEMS

Rock mooring with stern anchors *Bindy Wollen*

Boom berthing, not to be walked on!
C. N Hill

Lazy line mooring, Vaxholm Stockholm *C.N. Hill*

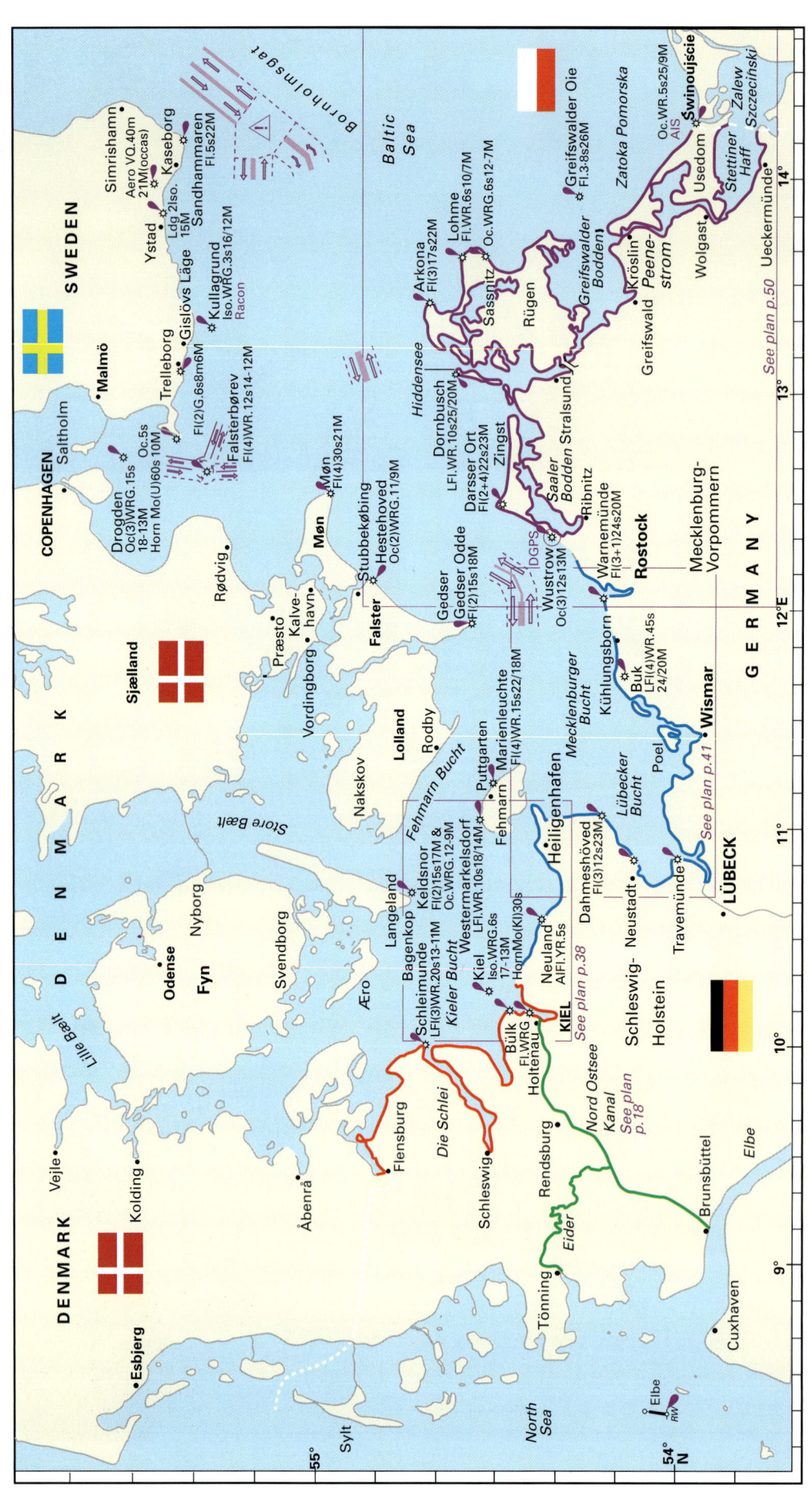

14 THE BALTIC SEA AND APPROACHES

1a. Approach to the Baltic via the Kiel Canal and the Eider river, 21
1b. Kieler Förde to Flensburg Förde, 29
1c. Kieler Förde to Mecklenburger Bucht, 37
1d. Darsser Ort to the Polish border, 53

1. Germany

Germany's Baltic coastline falls naturally into two parts – the former West German province of Schleswig-Holstein and the former East German province of Mecklenburg-Vorpommern. Neither has any dramatic physical feature, but they are both very interesting in many other respects, and have much to offer the cruising yachtsman.

The western segment, from Flensburg to Travemünde, has excellent yachting centres. It is an agricultural country with scattered farms, hillocks, small valleys, lakes and estuaries leading to important ports such as Kiel and the historic and beautiful city of Lübeck.

In the eastern part, although there has been much redevelopment since reunification since 1990, one can still enjoy large areas of countryside which remains untouched and where wildlife has been protected and left undisturbed. The coast has spits, bars and islands enclosing irregular inland seas known as Bodden, often backed by sand dunes planted with Norwegian spruce. There are a number of historically significant towns, each with its own character.

Economically, Schleswig-Holstein depends largely on agriculture and service industries, including the maintenance of a considerable volume of shipping in transit. The mainstays of Mecklenburg-Vorpommern are agriculture, fishing and tourism, together with shipbuilding at Rostock and Wismar. There is very little manufacturing industry apart from that associated with shipping. The tourist industry has been established since the end of the 19th century when the extensive beaches of the province became popular.

Throughout the whole area, major restoration work continues to be undertaken to preserve the many historic buildings and towns, and there has also been massive investment in the infrastructure such as roads and railways. English is widely spoken throughout this part of Germany, especially among the business community, but there are still some areas, especially in Mecklenburg-Vorpommern, where it may not be encountered.

Key information

Rescue/Safety services

Emergency ☎ 112
Police ☎ 110
MRCC Bremen Rescue Radio monitors VHF 16 and 70, DSC MMSI 00 211 1240, ☎ 124 124 (without prefix).
This is operated by the German national lifeboat organisation DGzRS and coordinates rescues in both the German North Sea and the Baltic.

Charts and chart packs

UKHO Admiralty charts, or their German equivalents, are excellent for yachts on passage. However for more leisurely cruising, and particularly to explore the area between Darsser Ort and the Polish border, three series of chart packs are available – the BSH Sportschiffahrtskarten 3000 series published by the German Hydrographic Office, the NV Sportschiffahrtskarten series and the Delius Klasing Sportbootkarten series. These are also sold digitally.

All of the above are available to order from Imray. www.imray.com

The German Hydrographic Office (BSH) Sportschiffahrtskarten 3000 Series covers all of the German Baltic Coast but the sets for Rugen (3006), the Peenestrom and Stettiner Haff (3007) and the Zalew Szczecinski and Szczecin (3020) are particularly useful.

There are two excellent series of chart packs (size A2). They are published annually and come with electronic versions on CD and complementary pilot books:

Nautische Veröffentlichung (NV)

Serie 1 Fünen – Kiel
Serie 2 Lübeck – Bornholm – Kopenhagen
Serie 4 Rügen – Bodengewässer – Stettin
Serie 6 Poland – Litauen – Lettland
NOK Nord-Ostsee Kanal. A chart (A2) of the Kiel Canal.

Delius Klasing Sportbootkarten

Satz 1: Kieler Bucht, Mecklenburger Bucht, Schlei – 12 charts and 78 harbour plans covering the coast as far east as Warnemünde.

Satz 2: Mecklenburg, Vorpommern, Bornholm – 10 charts and 85 harbour plans covering the coast from Darsser Ort to the Polish border.

The advantages of the series type of chart are that one pack covers a large area and many harbour plans are included. The charts include a combination of large and small scales which can take a little getting used to.

Pilots and cruising guides

In English
The Baltic Pilot Volumes I and II (NP 18 and 19) are useful for reference, but they are not ideally suited to the needs of the yachtsman.
The Cruising Almanac Imray/Cruising Association www.imray.com
Admiralty List of Lights and Fog Signals, Vols. B and C NP75 and 76
Admiralty List of Radio Signals, Vols 1,2,3,5, and 6
Admiralty Maritime Communications United Kingdom and the Baltic, NP291

1. GERMANY

Admiralty Sailing Directions North Sea (East) Pilot No. 55 and Baltic Pilot No 18

Cruising Association Skipper's Guide: Hamble to Helsinki, Fay and Graham Cattell

Cruising Guide to Germany and Denmark, Brian Navin (Imray, 2012) is very useful.

Yachtsman's Ten Language Dictionary, Barbara Webb & Michael Manton, (Adlard Coles Nautical)

Wie erreich ich wen in Allen deutsche Häfen, (How Do I Reach Whom in all German Harbours) (Storck Verlag 2014, 56th edition)

The Cruising Association publishes an excellent guide *Cruising in Baltic Germany* (available to non-members), which includes the Kiel Canal and many harbours as well as general information.

An organisation called ADAC (rather similar to the UK's AA car rescue service) has a useful website, with a marina index of roughly 600 ports in Germany and Europe. www.marinafuehrer.addac.de/haefen/

In German

There are several pilot books available in German covering the Baltic coast, including:

Ostseeküste Travemünde bis Flensburg by Jan Werner published by Delius Klasing as companion to their Satz 1 chart series, and *Ostseeküste Travemünde bis Stettin* by Jan Werner published by Delius Klasing as companion to their Satz 2 chart series.

The NV Nautische Veröffentlichung chart series (NV Ostsee) include their *Hafenlotse* guides which complement the charts and contain harbour plans.

The Delius Klasing-Sportbootkarten series also has excellent supplements with harbour plans and aerial shots.

Sejlerens Marina Guide Volume 4, Ostsee, Nordsee, Elbe and Weser covers both North Sea and Baltic marinas. Revised annually and available free at marina offices.

Hafenhandbuch Vols Ostsee 1 and Mecklenburg-Vorpommern und Polen (Delius Klasing)

Guidance for Pleasure Craft in the Kiel Canal - *Merkblatt für Spoortbootfahrer* obtainable at the canal or download from www.wsa-kiel.wsv.de

See the Appendix, page 418, for sources.

Time

Germany uses UT+1 in winter and UT+2 in summer.

€ Money

Germany uses the Euro. Cash dispensers are widespread. Credit cards are often not accepted, but the Mastercard Maestro debit card is quite widely used.

Formalities

Germany is a member of the EU and of the Schengen Area (see main Introduction page 7 for general details of Schengen formalities, and see below).

EU passport holders do not require visas. Passports, yacht registration and insurance documents and radio licence must be carried. The International Certificate of Competence is desirable but not compulsory except where required by the country of registration. The German ColRegs (Seeschiffahrtsstrassen-Ordnung) must also be carried (whether you understand them or not!) and maintenance of a daily log (passage plan, log and position readings) is also mandatory.

Customs clearance is not necessary when coming from another EU country, unless non-EU nationals are aboard. Yachts arriving from a non-EU country must report to Customs (*Zoll*) at one of the ports of entry. Border patrol or Customs vessels on the German/Dutch border in the North Sea will sometimes board transiting yachts and ask for passports and the yacht's papers.

There are customs clearance and immigration (*Bundespolizei*) posts at Holtenau and Brunsbüttel in the Kiel Canal and at Laboe, Flensburg, Neustadt, Rostock, Warnemünde and Stralsund on the Baltic coast. In the North Sea use Cuxhaven.

Schengen Area formalities

If you arrive direct from a non-Schengen country (such as the UK or Ireland) then you need to check in. This has to be done at a Bundespolizei Office (see above). Passports and two crew lists must be produced. One crew list will be stamped and should be shown when signing out of Germany at your last port.

Small ports may not have an office (check with Head Office in Hamburg ✆ +49 40 66995050 if in doubt). However, in many yacht harbours you will see a blue sign stating that the harbour is an official *Grenzuebergangstelle* i.e. a 'checking-in' port. Heikendorf, Laboe, Kieler Yacht Club are examples, and Cuxhaven and Brunsbüttel are convenient if arriving direct from the UK. Here you can acquire the Schengen form, which should be filled in and put it in the letterbox supplied for this purpose. The form 'Schiffsdaten-und Crewlist' can be downloaded from the internet (www.bundespolizei.de) and completed in advance, with details of ship and crew. Keep a copy.

If you arrive in a *Grenzuerbergang* harbour and cannot find an officer you are assumed (by some curious anomaly) to have complied with Schengen assuming you fulfill the requirements, i.e. you have passports for all crew, no contraband, and you have created a crew list. If you arrive in a non-immigration port you can apply for clearance if you ask the Bundespolizei Bad Bramstadt in advance. If you have come to Germany from Belgium or the Netherlands it is assumed that you cleared into Schengen there and nothing further is required. However, you may be required to produce passports, and a crew list.

Keep a copy of the stamped (carbon) copy with your Ship's papers as proof of your compliance with Schengen requirements.

Other regulations

- Children under 15 are not permitted to steer a vessel in German waters. In certain rivers the age limit is 21 or 23.
- Animals microchipped, blood tested, with a passport, current health certificate and Rabies vaccination, issued by a recognised vet prior to entry, are allowed in under the Pet Travel Scheme (PETS).
- Vessels over 15 tons are treated as merchant ships and must carry a pilot through most state waterways unless the skipper has a Master's Certificate. However, in practice, this does not seem to be applied to yachts. Some inland waterways require special permission before entry for power vessels and sometimes sailing yachts.
- Motor/sailing cones are taken seriously and failure to display one when required can lead to an immediate fine.

There should be no difficulty in keeping a VAT-paid yacht in Germany indefinitely. It does not matter in which country the VAT has been paid, but proof of payment may be needed. Non EU-registered yachts can stay in the EU for a maximum of 18 months.

Customs enquiries ✆ +49 (0)351 44834 530, enquiries.english@zoll.de

Germany Embassy 23 Belgrave Square, London SW1X 8PZ ✆ 020 7824 1300 consularl@german-embassy.org.uk

GERMANY - KEY INFORMATION

The Consulate General (to which visa enquiries should be addressed) is round the corner at 1–6 Chesham Place, Belgrave Mews West, London SW1X 8PZ
☏ 020 7824 1463
pass@lond.diplo.de
The website for both is www.london.diplo.de
British Embassy Wilhelmstrasse 70, 10117 Berlin
☏ +49 (0)30 204570
www.gov.uk/government/world/organisations/british-embassy-berlin.de
Honorary Consul 11–14, 24159 Kiel
☏ +49 431 331971.

From November 2015 the Visa Information System VIS has been introduced. Every applicant aged 12 years and over must apply in person in order to have fingerprints taken. Appointments have to be booked in advance.

☼ Public holidays

Official public holidays in Germany include:
1 January, Good Friday, Easter Sunday and Monday, 1 May (Labour Day), Ascension Day (May), Whit Sunday and Monday (May or June), 3 October (German Unification Day), 24–26 December, 31 December. A number of regional holidays are also held.

☏ Communications

The country code for Germany is 49. Telephone communication facilities are excellent. To make an international call, dial 00 followed by the country code, area code (omitting any initial 0) and number. Phone boxes are mostly card-operated although some are dual card/cash. Phone cards are readily obtainable. There is good mobile phone coverage and internet cafés are widely available. WiFi is now installed at most larger marinas. German prepaid SIM cards or else dongles known as Surfsticks can be inserted into a laptop and avoid data roaming charges.

✈ Travel

There are major **airports** serving the Baltic coast area at Hamburg, Lübeck and Berlin and Rostock.

There are good **train** services throughout Germany and on to Poland, and excellent express coach services from London to Hamburg and Travemünde.

Ferry services operate on the following routes: Kiel – Klaipeda, Kiel – Oslo, Kiel – Göteborg, Puttgarden – Rødby; Travemünde – Trelleborg ; Travemünde – Helsinki; Travemünde – Rlga; Rostock – Gedser; Rostock – Trelleborg, Rostock – Helsinki, Rostock – Ventspils, Sassnitz/Mukran – Trelleborg; Sassnitz/Mukran – Baltysk, Sassnitz/Mukran – Klaipeda.

🚻 Holding tanks

Toilets must not be discharged within 12M of the shore. Holding tanks are not compulsory for foreign yachts which are staying in Germany for one season. Yachts built before 1980 or less than 10.5m LOA/2.8m beam built before 2003 are also exempt.

💻 Websites

www.germany-tourism.de The German National Tourist Office. All the usual links, weather information etc. Includes pages on both Schleswig-Holstein and Mecklenburg-Vorpommern. English version.

www.visits-to-germany.com A general tourist site, but with attractive graphics and much of interest. English version.

www.dwd.de The German Meteorological Office. Useful forecasts in English.

www.bsh.de The German Hydrographic Office. Includes an (apparently complete) listing of German charts and official publications. Impeccable English version.

www.kiel-canal.de The (commercial) United Canal Agency. Some history, webcams etc. English version.

www.wsa-kiel.wsv.de Kiel canal site with guidance for pleasure craft.

www.luebeck-tourism.de Tourist guide to Travemünde and Lübeck, with full English translation.

www.all-in-all.com An excellent site covering the Mecklenburg-Vorpommern region, with English translation and many useful links.

www.warnemuende.com Warnemünde/Rostock city.

www.ycstr.de The Yacht Club of Strelasund. In German only.

www.ruegen.de A very useful website covering Rügen island, with links to many of its towns and villages. Full English translation.

www.peenemuende.de The Peenemünde museum. In German only.

www.stettiner-haff.de The Stettiner Haff (Zalew Szczeciński). In German only.

www.wattenschipper.de/Aktuelles.htm German Wattenschipper service. LW water depth soundings on all seegats together with tips on entrance channel usage.

📻 Radio communications and ☁ weather information

The coast has continuous **VHF** coast radio station coverage which is run by a private company, DP07 (Delta Papa Null Sieben). Areas: Kiel Bay north, Ch 67, Kiel Bay south, Ch 23, Lübeck Bay, Ch 24. Rostock transmits on Ch 60 and Arkona on Ch 66. Weather forecasts in slow German are issued on these channels at 0745, 0945, 1245, 1645 and 1945 statutory country time, add an hour for March to October. Vital navigational warnings are broadcast on VHF Ch 16 every Hour and H+30 until cancelled. Coastal areas covered are Flensburger Forde to Fehmarn, East of Fehmarn to Rugen, and East of Rugen. Sea areas are: Belte und Sund (Belts and Sound), Westliche Ostsee (Western Baltic), Sudliche Ostsee (Southern Baltic) and Boddengewasser Ost (Boddengewasser East).

NAVTEX, 518kHz is perhaps the best and most reliable method of receiving weather information in English. See Appendix on page 423.

The German Met Service, DWD (Deutscher Wetter Dienst) provides forecasts in English for the North Sea and Baltic Sea, www.dwd.de. It also has a useful 3-day forecast for winds and wave heights. There is an English translation button.

Marina Offices are another good source of weather forecasts.

Todendorf Firing Range – Radio Naval Todendorf Naval ☏ +49 4385 59 1313
VHF Ch 16 and Ch 11, see text for times.

Note Wind speeds are sometimes given in metres per second. As a very approximate guide, double them to convert to knots and halve them to convert to Beaufort.

The German Hydrographic Office (BSH) offers GRIB files which can be downloaded from
ftp://ftp.bsh.de/Stroemungsvorhersagen/

1. GERMANY

THE BALTIC SEA AND APPROACHES — 17

1. GERMANY

History

Contributed by John Langdon

From the days of Charlemagne until the 19th century, Germany was a loose federation of dukedoms and principalities, nominally under the Holy Roman Emperor. The Germanic states only started to have real influence on the Baltic from the 12th century.

As the Viking age declined, piracy in the Baltic continued to have a crippling effect on trade. It was the German Hanseatic League that first managed to organise some stability. A Hansa was a guild of German shipping merchants operating from a trading port. The Hansa ports increasingly worked together, coordinated by their *Diet*, or council, in Lübeck. At its height, the Hansa included 200 trading ports between the Netherlands, England, Norway and Russia. They dramatically increased trade and prosperity across the whole region until the 16th century when national governments had become strong enough to replace them.

Rome had finally separated from the Orthodox Church in the Great Schism of 1057, making Christian Russia a Crusading target as well. In 1201 the German Bishop Albrecht landed his army in Rīga, where the Hanseatic League were already building a trading port. In 1202 he formed the 'Livonian Brothers of the Sword', named after the particular Latvian tribe that lived there, in order to convert the locals.

Soon afterwards came the Teutonic Knights, a formidable German military Crusading Order who had recently left Acre when the Holy Land was recaptured by the Moslems. The Knights were invited by Poland in 1226 to help subdue and convert Prussia, northeast of Poland. Once subdued, Prussia was to become the Teutonic Knights' crusading base. The Livonian Brothers were eventually defeated in 1236 when they tried to invade Lithuania. Their survivors were reassigned by the Pope to form the Livonian Order within the Teutonic Knights. After years of ferocious fighting, Latvia and Estonia, still jointly named 'Livonia', were run by immigrant German landowners, albeit as a Polish fiefdom.

As time went on, much of the Catholic world became increasingly disillusioned with the perceived greed and materialism of church management. In 1517 Germany's Martin Luther gave voice to these criticisms in his 95 proposed reforms. Rome's response was total intransigence. Most of the north German states and the Baltic countries declared for Luther, nationalising Church property and publishing the Bible in the local language. In 1525 the Grand Master of the Teutonic Knights himself also became a Lutheran with the new title of Grand Duke of Prussia.

Rome eventually tried to regain control of the Protestant states, leading to a prolonged period of religious wars across Europe. In Germany it was the Thirty Years War from 1618-48, between the Holy Roman Emperor and the German protestant states, progressively supported by Denmark, then Catholic France for its own reasons, and finally Sweden. The war changed very little, but thirty years of starving armies trying to live off the land, left Germany in ruins, particularly in the north.

The Duke of Prussia was of the same Hohenzollern family as the Duke of Brandenburg, who had his capital in Berlin. By the end of the century the two states had united, although still with a piece of Poland in between.

Meanwhile Poland had united with Lithuania, both of whom expanded to form the largest state in Europe, spreading from the Baltic to the Black Sea and from Germany almost to Moscow. Towards the end of the 18th century, to reduce their perceived threat, Prussia, Austria and Russia joined forces to fight a series of three Wars of Partition against Poland-Lithuania. By the end of the third war, Poland and Lithuania ceased to exist as independent states. German Prussia now ruled all the land between itself and Brandenberg, together with Poland's entire Baltic coast.

Prussia was now rivalling Austria, the home of the Holy Roman Emperor, in its ability to unite all the German-speaking peoples into a single nation. In the event it was Prussia in the 19th century that prevailed under Bismarck's guidance. In 1871 the Prussian Hohenzollern King William was crowned Kaiser of the 'German Empire' - all of Germany, but without Austria.

At the end of WWI, the Treaty of Versailles at last recreated Poland as an independent democracy with a corridor through Germany to its only Baltic port of Danzig (Gdansk). After WWII, having united Germany, Prussia was dissolved. Poland was extended westwards over most of West Prussia, gaining a much wider Baltic coast in the process. East Prussia, became the Russian enclave of Kaliningrad. Eastern Germany became part of the Warsaw Pact: nominally independent, but under the political and military control of the USSR. Not until the Soviet Union was collapsing in October 1990 did Germany at last reunite as an independent democracy.

Compared with Prussia, Germany's current Baltic states of Mecklenburg and Schleswig-Holstein may have seemed remarkably quiet. Schleswig-Holstein, however, had been an intractable problem for over three centuries. Lord Palmerston famously said that only three people ever really understood the issues. The first was dead, the second went mad and the third was himself, and he had forgotten. Suffice to say that it was finally settled by a plebiscite in 1920 that gave Denmark north Schleswig and Germany the rest.

GERMANY - CRUISING

Practicalities

Yacht services and chandlery

Mooring fees are considerably lower than in the UK, and in ports with few facilities there may well be no charges at all for overnight mooring.

Berthing will usually be in box berths, or sometimes bows-to with the stern secured to a buoy, or alongside a jetty or, in recently-built marinas, against a finger pontoon (see main introduction for details of berthing systems, page 10). The concept of visitors' berths is uncommon, and a vacant berth will usually be indicated by a green plaque at its head. A red one indicates that it is reserved and that its owner will soon be returning. Communication with marinas is generally conducted over the telephone rather than by VHF.

In Schleswig-Holstein yachts are well provided for. Chandlery, fuel and bottled gas (including Camping Gaz) are readily available.

In Mecklenburg-Vorpommern facilities have improved significantly with the development of many new marinas. Obtaining fuel and bottled gas is no longer a problem and chandlery is available in the major harbours.

Shopping

The availability and choice of consumer goods in Schleswig-Holstein is as extensive as anywhere in Europe. The facilities in Mecklenburg-Vorpommern have been greatly improved in recent years and are now excellent.

Most shops are closed on Saturday afternoons and on Sundays.

As prices throughout Germany are lower than in Scandinavia, yachts bound in that direction might well consider stocking up with non-perishable stores before leaving Germany. This applies particularly to beer, wines and spirits as these are expensive in Denmark and even more so in Sweden and Finland.

Diesel

Non-bio red diesel is not available, and any that is bought in the UK should be kept in the main tank (not cans) and the receipt retained. At the time of publication German diesel contains a 7% bio component.

Gas

Gas cylinders, including Calor Gas, can be refilled in northern Germany, see www.faerbergas.de

Health

See main Introduction page 7 concerning EHIC cards Some prescription drugs may be banned so it is best to keep a doctor's note on board confirming your need for particular medicines. See German Customs website for up to date information in English. www.zoll.de/EN/Private-individuals/ Travel

Cruising

The cruising areas

The area between Flensburg and Kiel has well-developed yachting facilities. Flensburg and the Schlei are rewarding and will intrigue readers of Erskine Childers *The Riddle of the Sands* as the area where the heroes of that classic spy story, Davies and Carruthers, began their adventure in the Dulcibella.

The coast east of Kiel is low-lying and well populated. Yachts aiming for the Mecklenburg area will sail past the mammoth Heiligenhafen yacht harbour before passing under the impressive Fehmarnsund bridge (clearance 23m, but winds from north or east can raise sea level by up to 1·5m) connecting Fehmarn island to the mainland. Those heading for southern Sweden will skirt the northern coast of Fehmarn. Neither route holds much of shore interest, but Travemünde and particularly Lübeck are well worth a visit.

East of Wismar the coast features hills and woods for some 6M but then flattens out. Further east it is again wooded between Warnemünde and the promontory of Darsser Ort. Inland lies the Mecklenburg lake district. It is densely wooded and has over a thousand lakes. This unspoilt region is ideal for walking, cycling or indeed exploring by boat, via a system of shallow canals linking major lakes.

The coastline is low lying and seemingly featureless from seaward, but behind the tree-lined spits and sandbars which form much of this coast lie the Bodden. These large unspoilt lagoons, often bordered by immense expanses of reeds, are remarkable for their birds, isolation, shoal waters and small fishing ports. Local ferries run day-trippers out to them and they have become popular tourist destinations, but they still have a special ambience derived from their isolation and tranquillity.

For navigation in the Bodden, German charts (and perhaps one of the German pilot books) are necessary, and the small craft folios, which are increasingly available in electronic form as well as on paper, are clear and accurate.

Behind the coasts of Darss and Zingst the three Boddens of Barther, Bodstedter and Saaler may be entered from the eastern end. Dredged, buoyed channels to 25m wide are maintained with depths of 3·2m up to Barth and 2·4m beyond (the offshoot to Prerow carries 2·1m, that to Wustrow 1·5m and that to Ribnitz 1·6m). But it must be remembered that, depending on the winds and atmospheric conditions, sea levels may change by as much as +2m to –1m.

The coastal islands of Hiddensee, Rügen and Usedom, have long, wide, sandy beaches alternating with steep cliffs. Away from the resorts there are secluded fishing villages and large nature reserves full of birdlife. Hiddeensee has no cars and lovely bike riding. Vitte has good facilities, and the view from the Dornbusch lighthouse is worth the walk up the hill from Kloster.

1. GERMANY

THE BALTIC SEA AND APPROACHES   19

1. GERMANY

Behind the western and northern coasts of Rügen is another area of Bodden which can be entered from the north or the south, with depths of 3m in the dredged channels, but very shoal and sometimes stony outside them.

At the southern tip of Hiddensee, approached via The Gellenstrom, lies the entrance to the Strelasund, a buoyed channel separating Rügen from the mainland. Just inside the entrance is a major breeding ground for wild geese and swans, which may be seen in their thousands. The clearly-marked channel winds past the small yacht and fishing harbour of Barhöft (where the SAR vessel is stationed). Darsser Ort regularly silts up, and cannot be relied on for entry. It gets dredged occasionally, but it is now designated as an 'emergency only' haven and yachts are not welcome. The local SAR vessel is sometimes based here.

The Libben Channel to the NE of Hiddensee is a useful alternative approach in strong onshore winds, giving access to sheltered waters. It saves continuing on to the more distant Sassnitz if the Gellenstrom passage is felt to be untenable.

The Strelasund leads to the charming town of Stralsund, which is undergoing considerable restoration and is also an excellent shopping centre. It has impressive churches with far reaching views, an award winning aquarium (the Ozeanum) and direct trains to Berlin. The double lifting road and rail bridge, the Ziegelgrabenbrücke, leads through to the Strelasund south, which meanders through marshes and meadows to Stahlbrode and Palmer Ort where the comparatively deep (8m) Greifswalder Bodden begins.

The small islands of Ruden and Greifswalder Oie lie off the eastern entrance of the Greifswalder Bodden, the shores of which hide a number of small harbours tucked into inlets.

To the south the Peenestrom, a well-buoyed, landlocked channel, leads through green countryside past Peenemünde (of wartime V1/V2 'Doodlebug' fame) and inside the island of Usedom. There are two opening bridges, at Wolgast and Zecherin, to negotiate en route. The opening times of these bridges appear to vary from year to year, but can be obtained from the harbour office at Stralsund or the harbourmasters of most of the smaller ports in the area. Dredged depths are 6m as far as Wolgast which has a big ship building facility, and 2·5m beyond. South of Wolgast, on the east side of the Peenestrom lies the Achterwasser, an extensive area of water with several small attractive harbours.

The seaward side of Usedom, from Peenemünde to the approaches to Swinoujscie, is generally low – less than 60m – and featureless, with no harbours. The best marks are the churches of Zinnowitz, Heringsdorf and Ahlbeck (the border lies about 1·5M southeast of Ahlbeck church).

At the southern end of the Peenestrom yachts emerge into a large inland sea known as the Stettiner Haff in German or the Zalew Szczeciński in Polish. The border is marked with the red and white Haff buoy. This attractive and sheltered area (depths 3-5m) is festooned with nets and they are a major hazard (see diagrams page 65). If you deviate from the buoyed routes you can become mired in them. Off the headlands nets will be marked with posts and withies with an outer diamond mark (*stell netz*). Further out they resemble a suspended tennis court net with double flag markers on each end. They may be very close together with a mere 30m passage between them. The difficulty lies in establishing which end you have encountered and where the clear water lies. These are unlit, and uncharted and make tacking across the Haff hazardous.

1a. Approach to the Baltic via the Kiel Canal and the River Eider

The Kiel Canal

The Nord-Ostsee Kanal (NOK), also known as the Kiel Canal, is one of the major routes from the North Sea into the Baltic, and is a formidable feat of engineering. Built so that the German fleet could move between the Baltic and the North Sea without having to pass through the Kattegat, it was opened in 1895. It is just over 53M (98·5km) long with a minimum bridge clearance of 39·6m (130ft). It is very wide, and dredged to 11m. Near Rendsburg, roughly halfway along the canal, is one of the last remaining transporter bridges in the world. Its moving section crosses the canal at a height of 12m.

There are two pairs of locks at each end – the western at Brunsbüttel, at the entrance from the Elbe, and the eastern at Holtenau (a suburb of Kiel) where the canal enters Kiel Hafen. At Brunsbüttel yachts are usually directed to the southern lock, and at Holtenau to the northern lock, except in winter.

If approaching from the west, the waiting area is to the southeast of the moles (see plan), where you stem the tide, which can run very hard here, until you are allowed to enter.

A confusing array of lights may be displayed from the locks. See table below.

Yacht relevant signals at locks

Fixed single white light	No entry
White over red	Prepare to enter
One white occulting light on the signal mast at the lock island	Entry for pleasure craft permitted into the approach area
One white occulting light on the signal mast at the lock	Entry for pleasure craft permitted into the outer harbour and the locks
White over green	Entry permitted for vessels exempt from pilotage

Lock and canal communications

Lock area and approaches in Brunsbüttel	VHF Ch13, call Kiel Canal 1
Canal stretch between Brunsbüttel and Breiholz	VHF Ch 02 call Kiel Canal 11
Canal stretch between Breiholz and Kiel-Holtenau	VHF Ch 3, call Kiel Canal 111
Lock area and approaches in Kiel-Holtenau	VHF Ch4, call Kiel Canal 1V
Kiel Lock master can also be contacted by phone	☏ 0431-3603-152

Kiel Canal websites

wsa-kiel-holtenau@wsv.bund.de
www.wsa-kiel.wsv.de
www.wsv.de
www.kiel-canal.org Click on Pleasure Craft. This links you to the WSV website where you fill find an English version of *Merkblatt für di Sportschiffahrt* (Instructions for pleasure craft).

A loudspeaker also instructs yachts regarding entry. The lock keepers are very busy, so avoid calling them if possible. Yachts caught in sudden fog or poor visibility may moor inside the dolphins on the mooring rings. Pleasure craft drawing over 3.1m are subject to mandatory pilotage. Pleasure craft of 20m or more must operate a class A or B AIS transponder during their transit, rentable at the canal entrance locks if necessary. Recreational multi hulls up to 12m wide and under 20m long are exempt from the mandatory pilotage requirement.

In the locks, mooring is to very low floating wooden rafts, so fenders need to be at water level, preferably weighted, (a small covered tyre which does not float is invaluable). The rise and fall is very small at both ends and there is no turbulence – indeed, it is generally not even possible to distinguish whether the lock is being filled or emptied. Be prepared to share the lock with ships and expect associated propeller wash.

It is essential to keep well clear of commercial shipping whilst in the canal, generally by keeping to the starboard side. Even so it is wise to keep well clear of the bank, as passing ships can create a great deal of wash which may even ground a yacht. A good watch should also be kept for the many ferries which cross the canal along its length, and have right of way over yachts. Should three vertical red lights be seen all yachts should keep to starboard and stop, usually to allow a large vessel to pass.

Sharing the locks... Fenders need to be kept low! *John Sadd*

1A. APPROACH TO THE BALTIC VIA THE KIEL CANAL AND THE RIVER EIDER

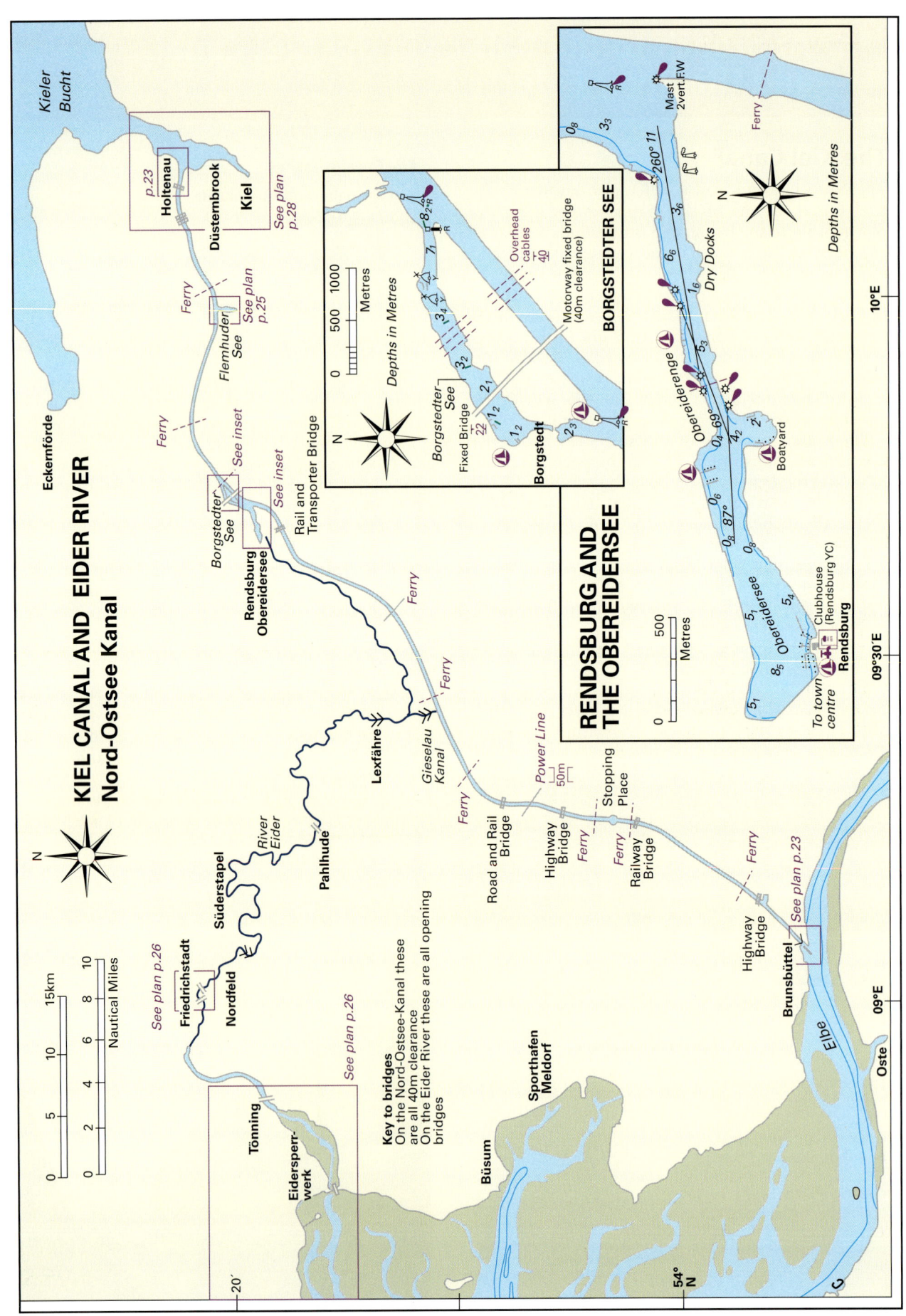

KIEL CANAL

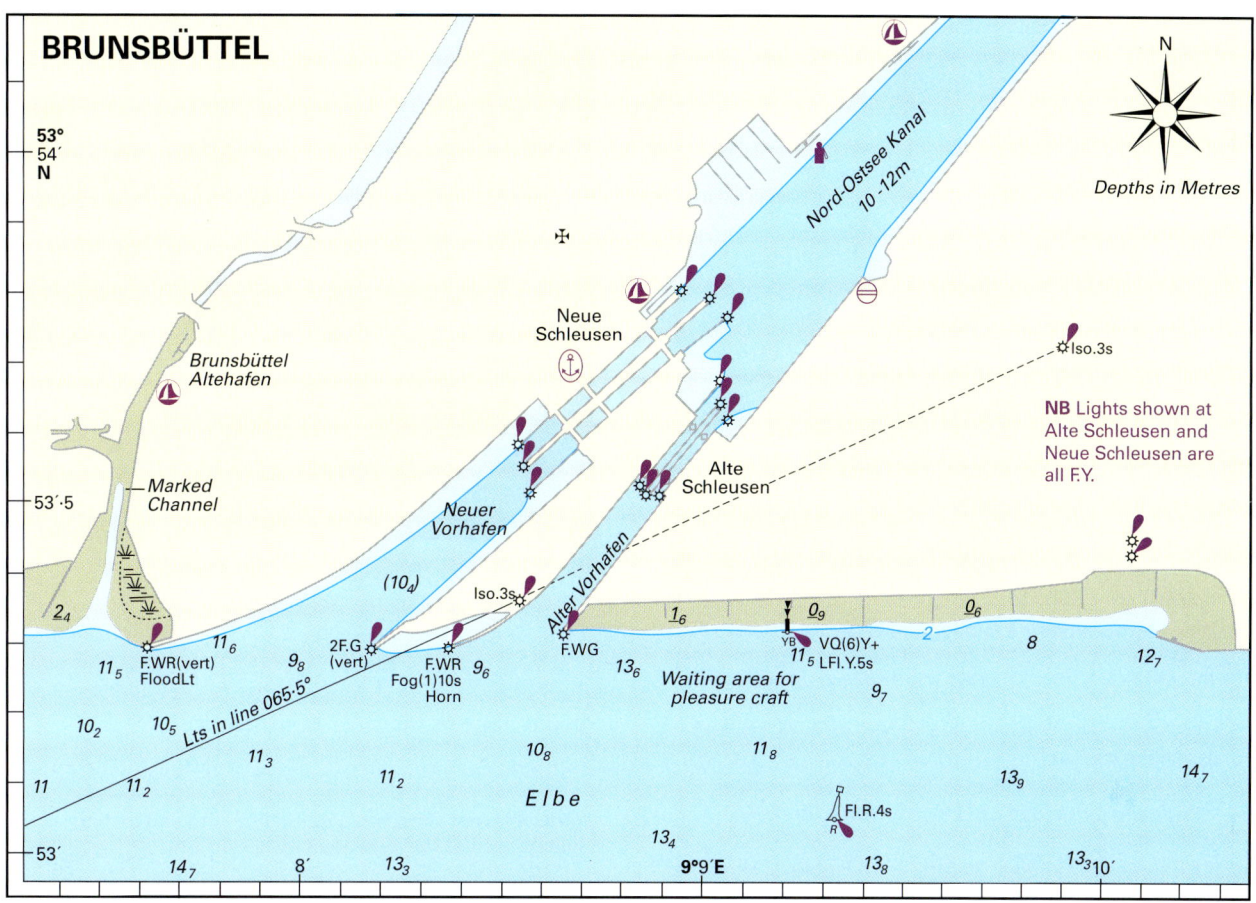

The modest canal dues are payable at Holtenau. New cash/card machines will be located (late 2017) at the new waiting area to the north, and also on the Tiessenkai. Charts can be bought at Holtenau at Kapitän Stegmann's office which is on the south side of the locks. Unfortunately it is forbidden to cross the canal on foot across the locks so that it is necessary to moor alongside the quay at Tiessenkai just east of the locks and walk back to the foot ferry.

Although the canal can be traversed in one day at a speed of five knots (the maximum speed is 8·1 knots or 15km/h), it is quite an effort to do so as hand-steering is required throughout. Shorthanded yachts will find it easier to stop overnight (see below).

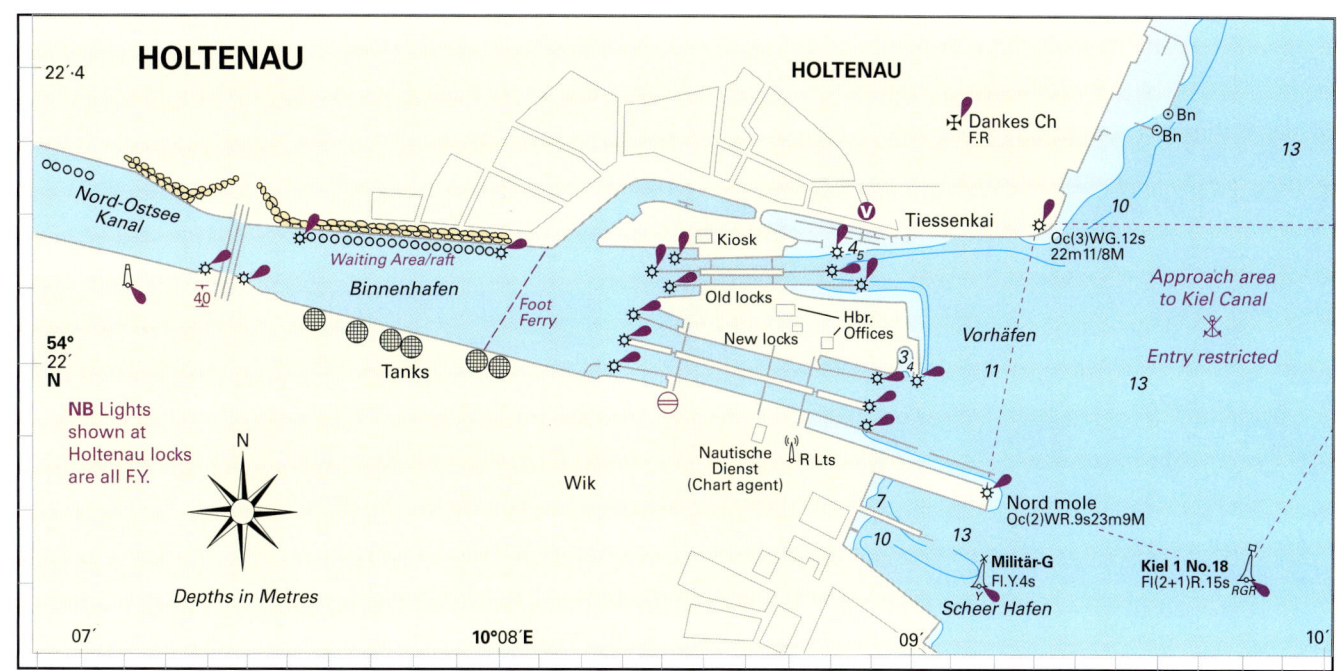

THE BALTIC SEA AND APPROACHES

1A. APPROACH TO THE BALTIC VIA THE KIEL CANAL AND THE RIVER EIDER

Motorsailing is permitted, providing a speed of at least 3·25 knots (6km/h) is maintained. Pure sailing and tacking are not permitted. When motor-sailing the regulation downward-pointing cone must be displayed.

Yachts are not permitted to proceed through the canal between sunset and sunrise or in bad visibility, and will not be locked in unless there is time to reach one of the authorized mooring places, marked by yellow buoys. Kilometre markers standing on the banks of the canal indicate the distance from Brunsbüttel. Lockmasters will provide details of the latest permitted mooring places but there are currently the following options for an overnight stay:

A Brunsbüttel either just inside the locks on the north side (but this is rather noisy and can get very busy) or 1km further east on the same side in more rural surroundings but with no facilities. (Between the two is a fuel berth for yachts).

B The best facilities are to be found in Rendsburg, at Km66 (see chartlet page 22). The yacht harbour, Regatta-Verein Rendsburg ☏ + 43 31 23961 is at the head of the bight, near the Rendsburg Yacht Club www.regatta-verein-rendsburg.de and convenient for the town centre and mainline station.

It has good marina facilities, fuel, a restaurant, food shops and a chandlery and is convenient for crew changes.

C Dückerswisch Siding at 20·5km, or Oldenbüttel Siding at 40·5km.

D A peaceful spot is the entrance to the Gieselau Kanal on the waiting pontoon just before the lock at 40·5Kms.

E The Marina Schreiber Borgstedt at 67·5km (the latter has a pontoon berth and diesel is available).

F There is an attractive anchorage in the entrance to the Flemhuder at Km 85·5 (48M from Brunsbüttel and 7M from Holtenau) where the anchorage carrying about 2·5m depth is marked out by four yellow buoys.

Peaceful berth at Gieselau Lock *Nigel Wollen*

When exiting the sidings and rejoining the canal the lights on signal masts must be obeyed in case a ship is approaching, see table below.

Yacht relevant signals regarding entering and exiting sidings such as the Gieselau Canal

One red quick flashing light on siding signal mast	Entry is prohibited
Three occulting red lights above each other, on siding signal	Exit is prohibited
Two isophase white lights one above the other, on siding exit signal mast	Exit prohibited for vessels of a speed less than 15km/h or 8.1kn
Two fixed red lights side by side on signal mast near turning basin at Brunsbüttel oil harbour	Proceeding is prohibited
Three vertical red lights in the main canal	Everybody stop and await instructions

Brunsbüttel marina looking NE *John Sadd*

Rendsburg guest house with interesting carvings! *Miranda Delmar-Morgan*

APPROACH TO THE BALTIC VIA THE RIVER EIDER

Rendsburg Transporter Bridge
Miranda Delmar-Morgan

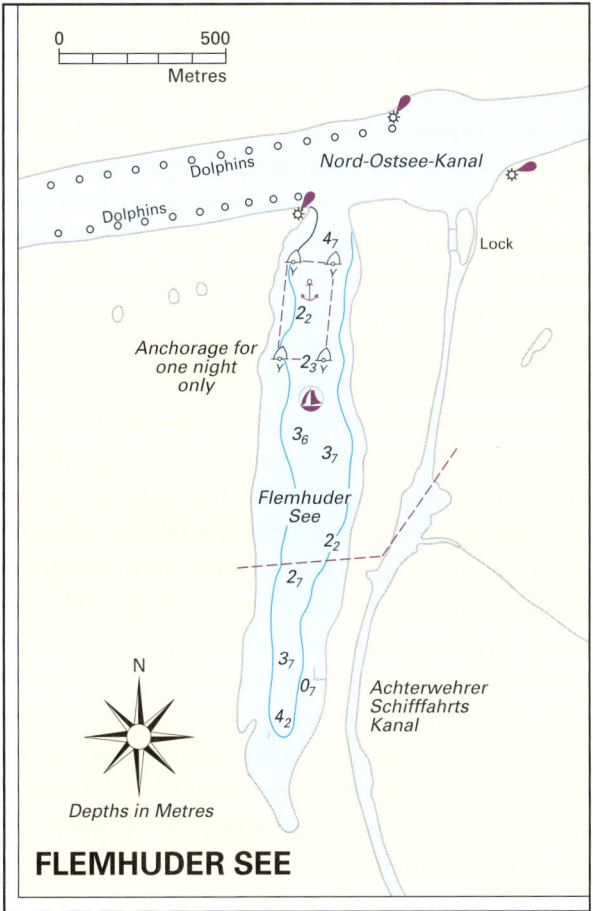

FLEMHUDER SEE

Approach to the Baltic via the River Eider

The slow-flowing and meandering River Eider is an alternative mast-up route to the Baltic for those with time to spare. It does not by-pass the Kiel Canal entirely as one has to join the Kiel Canal just past the 40km mark via the mile-long Gieselau Kanal. However it is a very attractive route which includes the charming towns of Tönning and Friedrichstadt. It is 85M from the entrance to the river to Holtenau as opposed to 54M from Brunsbüttel to Holtenau. There are four locks and four opening bridges and apart from the Eidersperrwerk lock (Eiderdamm), which is manned continuously, they are not manned at night and only at set times on Sundays and public holidays. See box below for Eider bridge and lock times. The river is tidal as far as the lock at Nordfeld.

It is 21M from Helgoland to the River Eider landfall buoy at 55°14'·5N 08°27'·6E and from there another 16M along the shallow buoyed channel to the lock at Eiderdamm. There is a waiting basin on the seaward side and a quay on the landward side of the lock. The lock is open 24h but currents of 2-5kn run seaward when the sluices are opened (HW+0230) It is essential to arrange to tackle the buoyed approach channel during the second half of the flood and to avoid the route altogether in strong onshore winds because of the bar (1·5–3m). HW at Eiderdamm is HW Helgoland +0120.

Eidersperrwerks (Eiderdamm) ☎ +49 4833 45350, VHF Ch 14
Lock open 24h
For bridge and lock opening times see
www.wsv.de/wsa-toe/service/schleusen/index.html

Tönning HM ☎ +49 157 7829 0741

River Eider charts
German Hydrographic (BSH) 104, Bundesamt für Seeschifffahrt und Hydrographie
NV charts Series 10
Delius Klasing Satz 1, Kieler Bucht und Rund Fünen

1. GERMANY

THE BALTIC SEA AND APPROACHES   **25**

1A. APPROACH TO THE BALTIC VIA THE KIEL CANAL AND THE RIVER EIDER

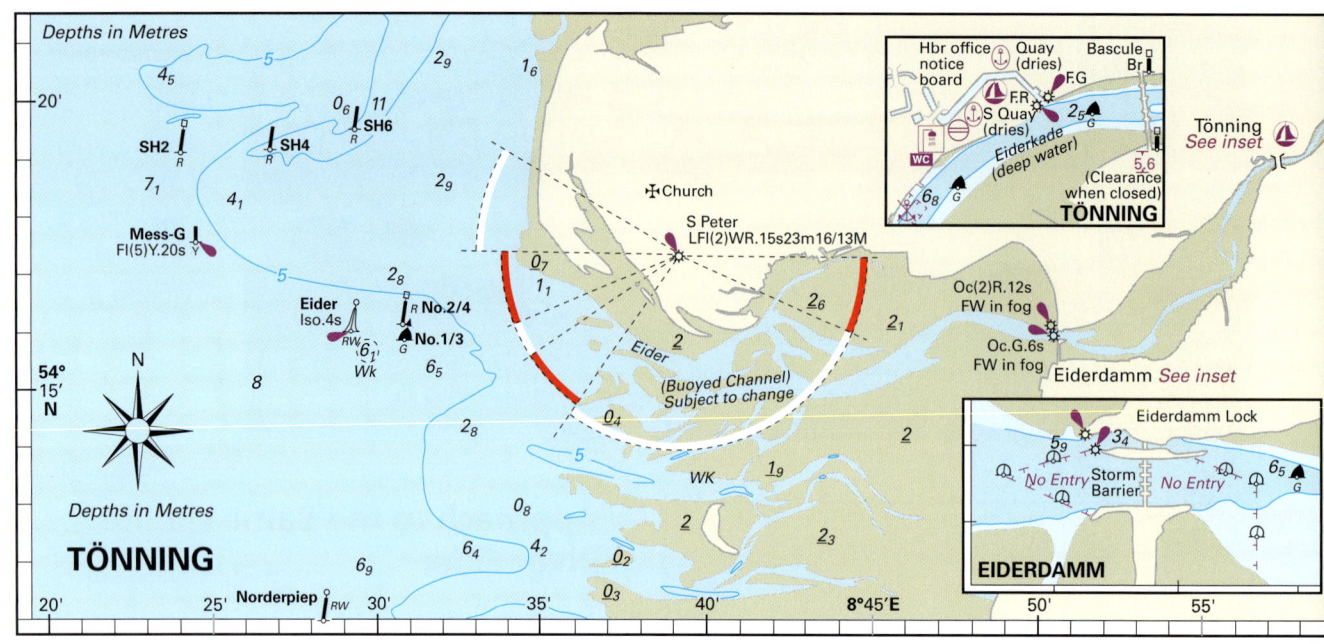

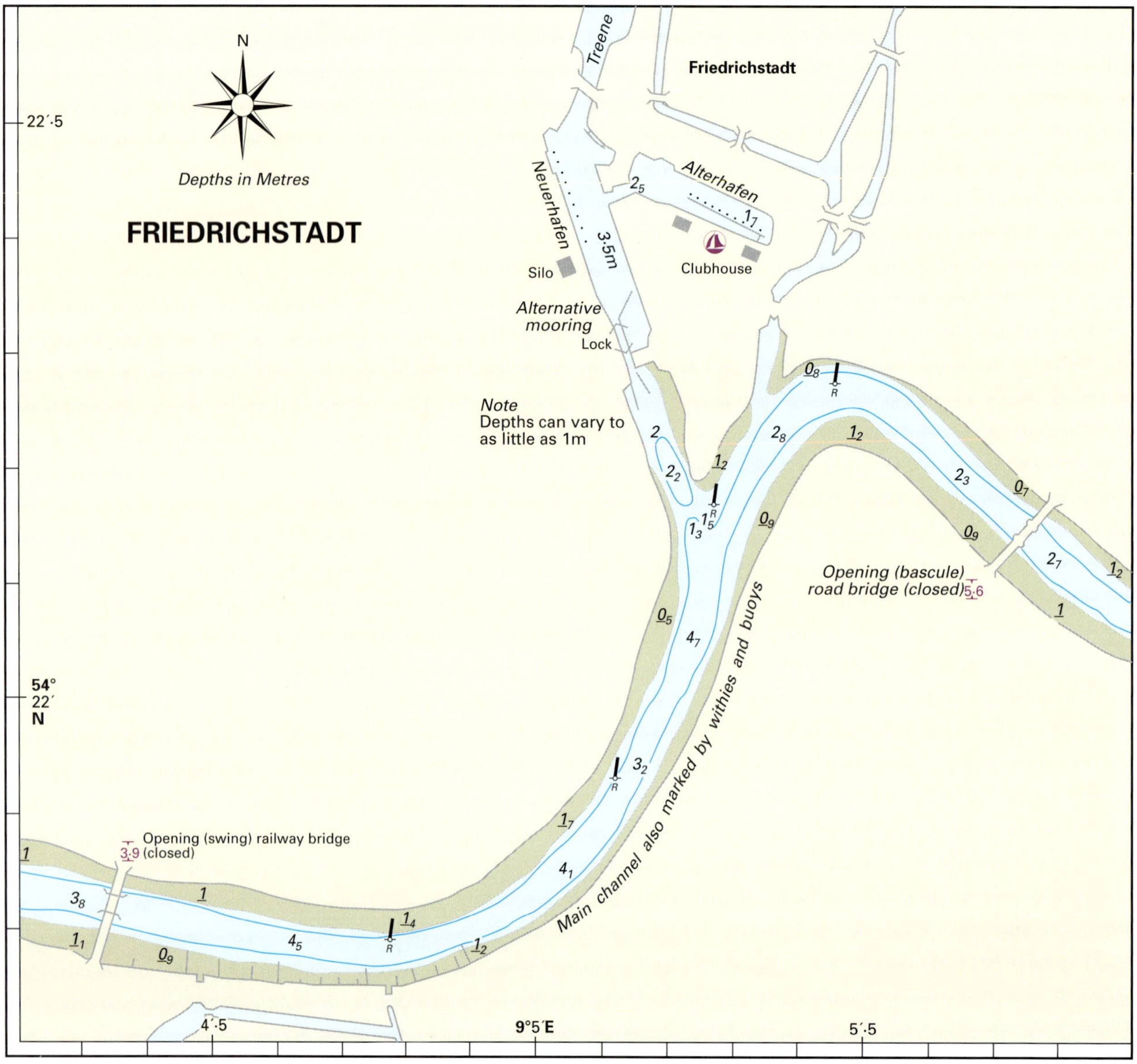

26 THE BALTIC SEA AND APPROACHES

APPROACH TO THE BALTIC VIA THE RIVER EIDER

The quays at Tönning Miranda Delmar-Morgan

Once through the Eiderdamm lock it is another 5M to Tönning by unlit buoyed channel but if it is getting late there is a good anchorage in the river between red buoys No. 62 and 64. No anchoring is permitted within 2km of the dam. Westbound from Tönning you should leave before HW in order to allow for arrival at the Eiderdamm locks near HW for best of use of the ebb and tidal height into the North Sea.

Tönning

This is an attractive old fishing town and berthing is possible alongside in the river. The quays in the inner harbour channel mostly dry at LW. Basic facilities but no fuel berth.

Friedrichstadt

This charming town was built by the Dutch when they were brought in to sort out the drainage problems of the area in the 17th century. Consequently the town has a very Dutch appearance with a network of canals, bridges and gabled houses. Berth in the Neuerhafen in 3m or the Alterhafen in 1·7m by going through the lock, but the approach to the lock can carry as little as 1m at LW. Basic facilities.

Friedrichstadt façade Miranda Delmar-Morgan

THE BALTIC SEA AND APPROACHES   27

1. GERMANY

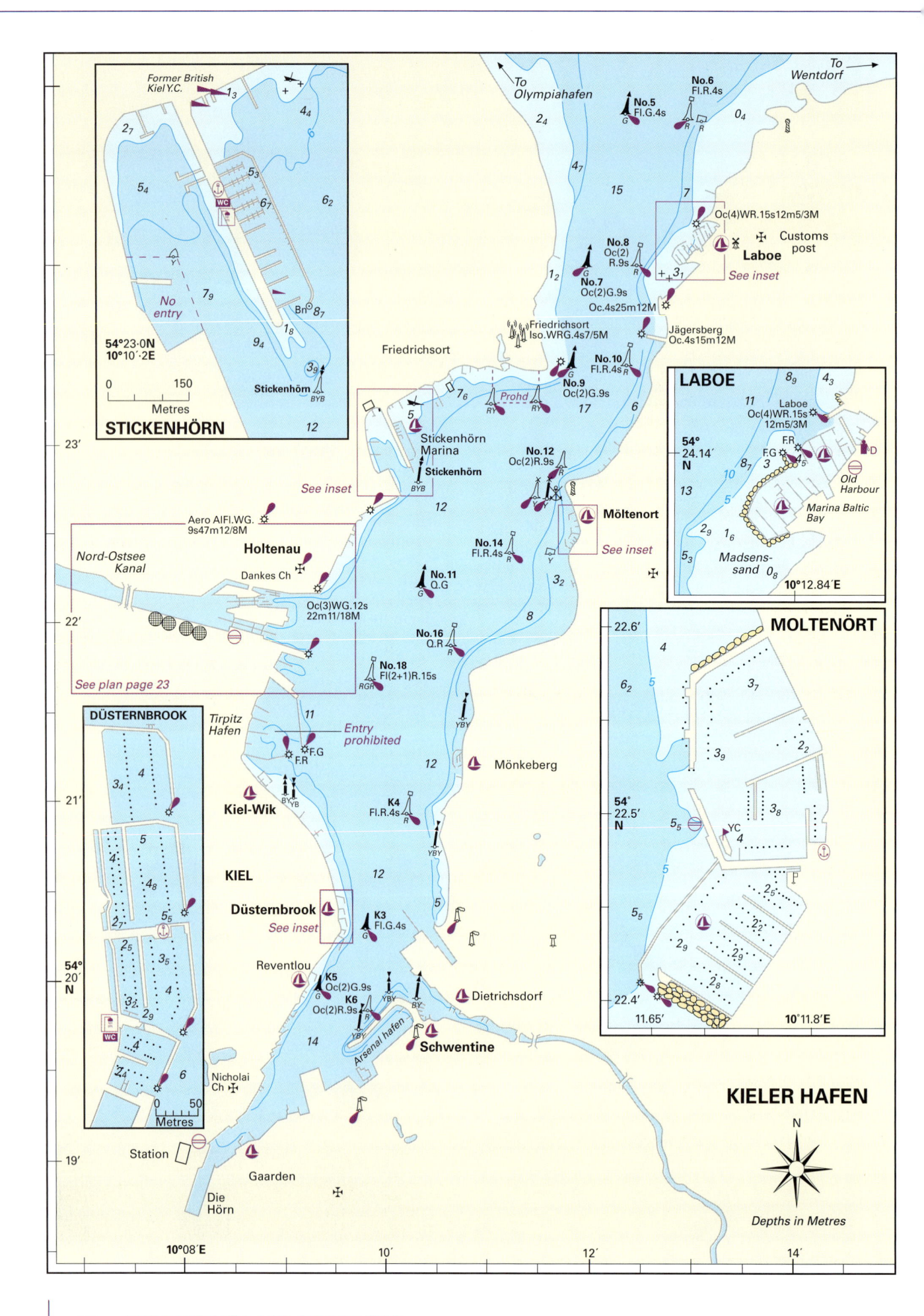

1B. KIELER FÖRDE TO FLENSBURG FÖRDE

28 THE BALTIC SEA AND APPROACHES

KIELER FÖRDE

1b. Kieler Förde to Flensburg Förde

Kieler Förde including Kiel

54°21′N 10°10′E

Distances (from Kiel)
Heiligenhafen 35M, The Schlei 25M, Flensburg Förde 50M, Travemünde 65M, Gislövs Läge 130M, Copenhagen 145M, Stubbekøbing 85M

Charts
UKHO 2341, 2344, 2469, 2942
German 30, 32, 33, 34

Lights
Kiel light tower 54°30′N 10°16′·5E Iso.WRG.6s29m17–13M
071°-R-088°-W-091·3°-G-148·5°-W-220°-R-246·5°-W-295°-R-358°-W-025·5°-G-056° Horn Mo(KI)30s Racon
Red round tower, white band on grey base 33m. Floodlit
Friedrichsort 54°23′·4N 10°11′·6E Iso.WRG.32m7–5M
171·5°-G-196°-W-202° 209°-R-224°-W-280°-G-300°-W-032°-G-090° + F.Y. 019°-vis-039° 188°-vis-209° + F.W.6M 202°-vis-209° White round tower, green bands on gallery and base 32m. Floodlit
The marina breakwater south head, 1M southwest, is lit
Scheerhafen (Holtenauer Schleusen, S side) 54°21′·8N 10°09′·1E Oc(2)WR.9s23m9M
159°-R-192°-W-214°-R-288°-W-003° Red beacon, white band, grey lantern, masonry base 20m
Nord-Ostsee Kanal (Holtenauer Schleusen, N side)
54°22′·2N 10°09′·2E Oc(3)WG.12s22m11/8M
217°-G-224°-W-270°-G-354°-G(unintens)-012°-W(unintens)-039° Red round tower 20m

Communications
Port Office ✆ +49 4319 011173, VHF Ch 11 (0730–1600 LT),
✆ +49 1716 497373 (outside office hours)
www.port-of-kiel.de
Kieler Förde/Kiel Canal Vessel Traffic Service
✆ +49 4313 603456, VHF Ch 22

General

Kieler Förde (also referred to as Kieler Bucht on Danish charts) is the approach to Kieler Hafen, with Kiel, a major naval base, a commercial port and easily the largest yachting centre in the Baltic, at its head. Holtenau, the eastern end of the Kiel Canal, lies on the western side of Kieler Hafen, and there are numerous yacht harbours around its shores.

Kiel has a superb shopping centre – modern, busy and with great variety. For yachts entering the Baltic it is an excellent place to store ship for the whole Baltic cruise or to have repairs carried out and, having first-class travel facilities, it is an ideal place for crew changes.

The spectacular Kiel Week (Kielerwoche) takes place during the last full week in June, when the entire waterfront will be packed with tall ships and other vessels, so book a berth well in advance.

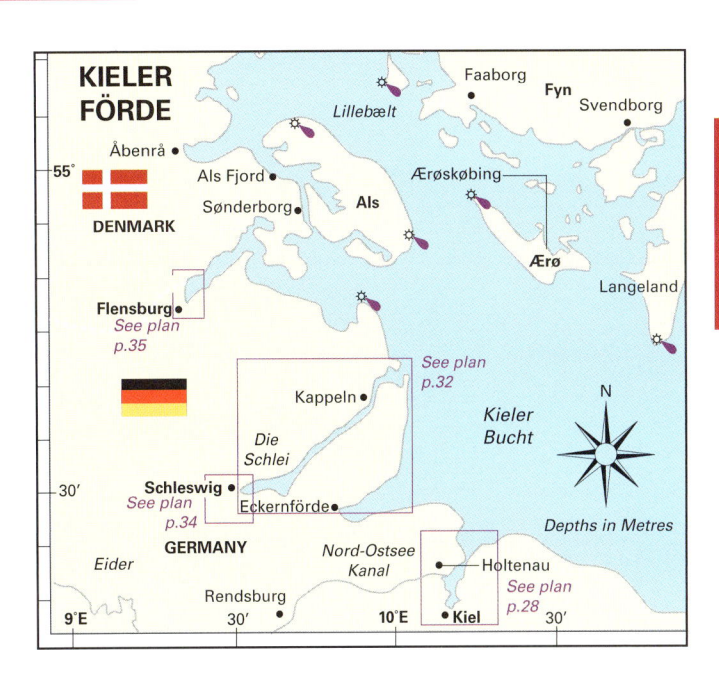

Approach

From north and northwest 54°30′N 10°15′E
From east or northeast 54°28′N 10°20′E

It should be noted that there are military firing ranges (Todendorf and Putlos) between Kieler Förde and Heiligenhafen. They are likely to be in use on weekdays, but not at weekends. When in use AlFl.YR.5s lights are shown on towers on the shore at 54°26′N 10°19′E and 54°23′N 10°56′E and at five other locations in between. Range control boats are stationed at the east and west ends of the range in use to intercept yachts and pass instructions to them on VHF Ch 16. A situation broadcast by Todendorf Naval Coastal Radio Station is broadcast at 0730, 1100, and 1530 LT Mon–Fri (and exceptionally at 0730 and 1100 on Saturdays) on VHF Ch 11 announced five minutes beforehand on VHF Ch 16. The range is crossed by the Kiel-Fehmarnsund route

The port-hand of the two Kieler Bucht light structures, marking the Baltic approach to Kiel A. and A. Fleck

THE BALTIC SEA AND APPROACHES 29

1. GERMANY

1B. KIELER FÖRDE TO FLENSBURG FÖRDE

Holtenau Lighthouse Miranda Delmar-Morgan

and it is a long way around the outermost buoys. NATO exercises use the extended area.

Major landmarks at the entrance to Kieler Förde are the Kiel light tower and (in daylight) the impressive German Navy war memorial just north of Laboe. The förde is very well buoyed throughout, but there is a large area of shoal water extending from the shore near the naval war memorial. Friedrichsort light is a prominent landmark when approaching Stickenhörn Marina. The entrance to the canal is about 1M further south.

Formalities

Yachts arriving from the North Sea will, if necessary, already have cleared customs at Cuxhaven or Brunsbüttel. Those coming from Scandinavia or the Baltic do not normally require clearance, but will have to use Brunsbüttel if necessary.

For yachts leaving Germany, outward clearance is also obtainable at Brunsbüttel or Laboe, but it is only necessary if sailing to a country outside the EU.

Anchorage, berthing and facilities

There are no restrictions on anchoring in Kieler Hafen, but because of the heavy volume of commercial traffic it is strongly recommended that yachts should seek a berth at one of the many yacht harbours.

In view of the extensive choice of yacht harbours and associated facilities to be found in the Kieler Förde area, this section merely highlights a selection.

Communications and travel

The nearest international airports are Hamburg and Lübeck. There are good train and coach services to all parts of Europe.

Tiessenkai at Holtenau
54°22′N 10°09′E

Tiessenkai is a small yacht harbour on the north bank immediately outside the Holtenau entrance to the canal (see plan page 23). Mooring is mostly rafted alongside staging. Although there are few facilities apart from two small chandleries, there are a couple of restaurants near the quay in Holtenau, outside the lock gates, and this is a convenient place from which to observe the canal. Customs post. The chart agent, Kapitän Stegmann, is to be found on the south side of the Holtenau locks (see under Holtenau in the section on the Kiel Canal) in a small trading estate, together with Elna, a marine electronics company. Water and electricity available and showers with a key from the lockmaster.

British Kiel Yacht Club (BKYC)
54°22·7′N 10°10·1′E

The BKYC has closed. The site's future is currently unknown, but it is likely that a marina will remain there in some form.

Stickenhorn Marina
54°22·8′N 10°10·2′E
℡ + 49 431/260484-24
www.sporthafen-keil.de

This marina, adjacent to the erstwhile British Kiel YC, is about a 20 minute walk from Friedrichsort which has all the usual shops, banks, supermarket and restaurants. It also has petrol and diesel supplies. Friedrichsort has ferries to Laboe. See www.sfk-kiel.de (Kiel Tug and Ferry Company) for ferry routes across the Kieler Förde. Camping Gaz can be bought from some nearby petrol stations.

Laboe monument Miranda Delmar-Morgan

DIE SCHLEI

Düsternbrook
54°20.4′N 10°09.5′E outer mole
Situated about 1·5M south of the canal entrance.
Düsternbrook Sporthafen ☎ + 49 (0)431 260 484 26/21/22
Mobile + 49 172 8024 352
www.sporthafen-kiel.de

This is the nearest harbour to the excellent shopping centre of Kiel, which can be reached on foot via the promenade and the Oslokai. Constructed for the 1938 Olympics, it has 288 berths in 2–4m and all normal marina facilities including WiFi. It is a good base from which to stock up or change crews. Large yachts berth in the northernmost basin. The Kieler Yacht Club ☎ + 49 4431 85021 www.kyc.de, has its headquarters on the other side of the main road and welcomes (well dressed!) visiting yachtsmen. There is a very large and well-stocked chandlery in Kiel town centre.

Laboe
54°24.1′N 10°12.8′E east mole

Laboe is a pleasant small town with an old fishing and yacht harbour ☎ +49 4343 427556 and a new Marina Baltic Bay ☎ +49 4343 421151 built immediately south of it on the eastern side of Kieler Förde. Beware the frequent ferry traffic from the inner side of the outer mole of the old harbour. It is best not to round the molehead too closely. The fuel berth is in the old harbour to port as you enter but closes at 1400 daily. There are engineers, a marine electrician and sailmaker on site and Camping Gaz is available. Laboe is the closest place from which to visit the conspicuous U-Boat Memorial. It is one of the Grenzuebergangstelle (border crossing) ports offering Schengen clearance facilities. Complete yacht service, new build and repairs. Bikes for hire.

Strande
54°26.1′N 10°10.3′E
☎ +49 4349 8988, (0800–1200 and 1600–1800 LT)
VHF Ch 11
www.hafen-strande.de
Olympiahafen Schilksee marina ☎ +49 4313 71021 or 431 260484 *Mobile* +49 172 8024352

Strande is situated on the western side of Kieler Förde, about 4M north of Holtenau. Like Laboe, it is a good place to obtain fuel as well as being worth considering in its own right as a pleasant first or last night stop in the Baltic. Good bathing beach. Close by is the Olympiahafen Schilksee marina built for the 1972 Sailing Olympics. It has all facilities.

Die Schlei

54°40′.1N 10°03′.3E (SW mark)

Distances
Flensburg 35M, Sønderborg 20M, Eckernförde 19M, Kiel 22M, Marstal 22M

Charts
German Small Craft Chart Set 3003, German 41, Danish 195

Lights
N Mole Hd 54°40′.3N 10°02′.2E LFl(3)WR.20s14m14M White round tower, green band
Ldg Lts 107·5 *Front* 54°40′.4N 10°02′E Oc.W.4s6m9M White mast Rear 90m from front Oc.W.4s8m9M White Mast

Communications
Marina Olpenitz/Lotsinsel Marina ☎ +49 4622 912
Schleimünde Marina ☎ +49 4642 4972
 Mobile ☎ +49 172 721 5366
 www.schleimuende-hafen.de
Maasholm Marina ☎ +49 4642 6571
 www.maasolm.de
Kappeln Stadthafen ☎ +49 4642 3156
 +49 1724 106702 and VHF Ch 11
 www.kappeln.de
Kappeln Yachtzentrum ☎ +49 4642 1563
 Mobile +49 170 451 7172
 www.yachtzentrum-kappeln.de
Arnis Wassersportgemeinschaft ☎ +49 4642 4421
 www.wsg-arnis.de
Lindaunis Marina ☎ +49 01578/2040608
 www.sportboothafen-lindaunis.de
Brodersby Marina ☎ +49 4622 2188
 www.marina brodersby.de
Schleswig Wiking Yachthafen ☎ +49 4621 35666
 www.wiking-yachthafen.de
Schleswig Stadthafen ☎ +49 4621 801 450
 www.hafen-schleswig.de

General
This beautiful fjord is 20M long and offers sheltered sailing in lovely surroundings. There are many choices of marina, some urban, some with yacht yard facilities and some in very rural surroundings with few facilities. All tastes are catered for within short distances. And there are many anchoring opportunities out of the buoyed channel but depths must be closely watched as there is much shallow water and depths can vary suddenly and unpredictably (see below).

Depending on wind conditions there may be quite strong currents up to four knots in the narrows in extreme conditions and depths and clearances can also be affected by 1–2m. This can make berthing problematical in some places.

There is a double road and rail bridge at Kappeln (closed clearance 3·3m). It opens 15 minutes before every hour from 0545 to 2145 (April–October). The electric cables just north of Kappeln have a clearance of 26m. And there is another lifting bridge at Lindaunis. which opens on request. In Germany and Denmark vessels fly international code flag 'N' in the rigging to indicate that they are waiting for a bridge to open.

1. GERMANY

THE BALTIC SEA AND APPROACHES   **31**

1B. KIELER FÖRDE TO FLENSBURG FÖRDE

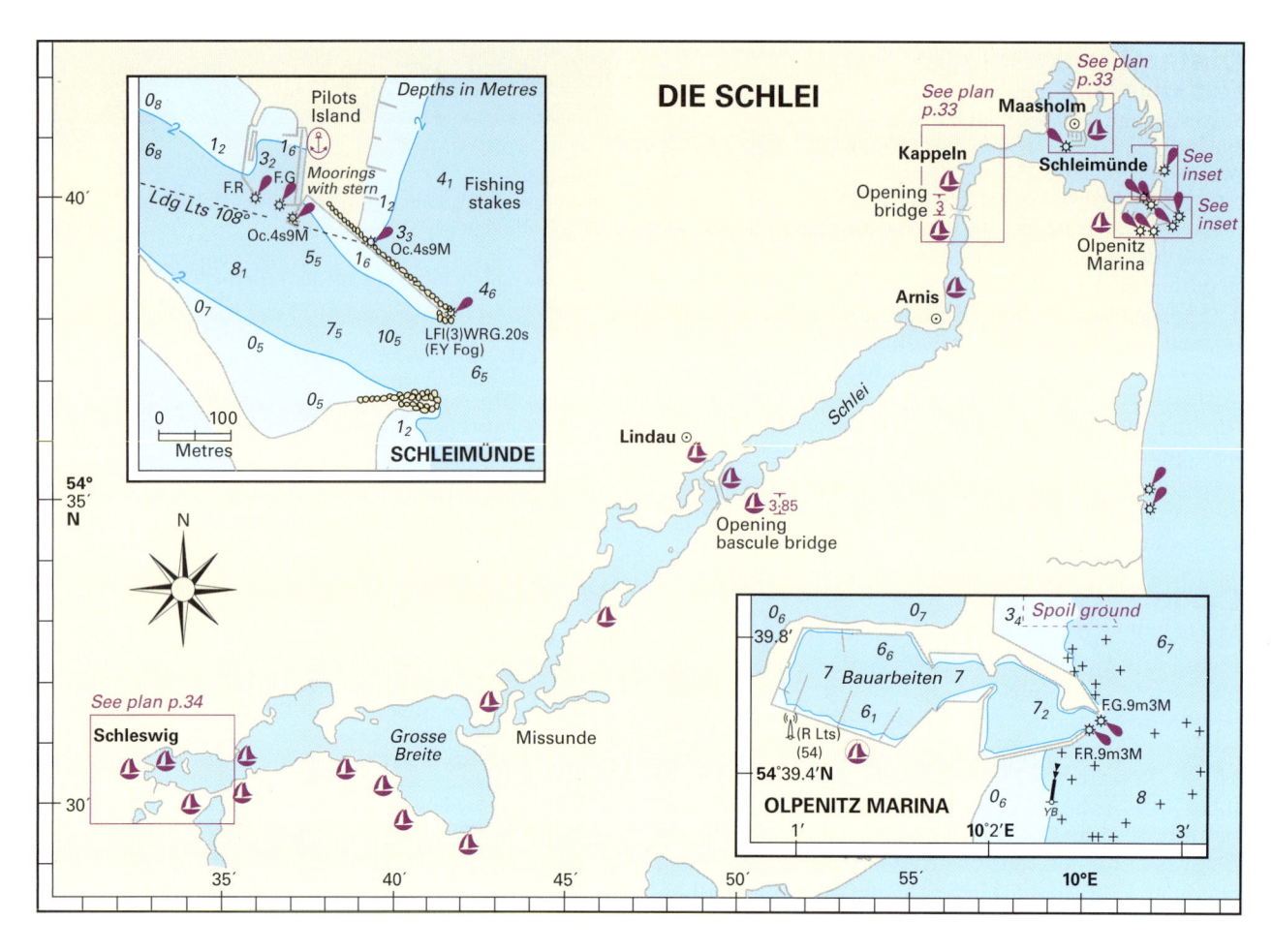

Approach

The approach is straightforward on 287° from the Schlei landfall RW buoy Oc.4s at 54°40'·05N 10°03'·4E and follow the buoyed channel through the narrow entrance between the piers. The channel is dredged to 5m. Do not confuse the entrance to the Schlei with the more prominent entrance to the erstwhile Olpenitz naval harbour, 0·75M further south. The latter has just undergone major redevelopment as Marina Olpenitz, part of a new holiday resort, with prominent new buildings, with FR and FG lit beacons at the mole ends.

Approaching the Schlei and Olpenitz, beware the 'No Entry' sector marked with seven yellow special buoys to the SE of Olpenitz.

Port Olpenitz Marina

54°39.58'N 10°02.57'E
Distances Maasholm 4M, Keppeln 6M, Kiel 26M
Communications ☎ +49 4053 800485
HM ☎ +49 172 404 150
Lights North Mole 54°39·'58N 10°02'·57E
    Mast Flood Lt F.WG.3M
South Mole 54°39'·53N 10°02·49'E Mast F.WR.3M

New marina opened in 2016. It has a 75-ton travel-lift and offers berthing for boats up to 80m.

Berthing in Die Schlei

Once through the entrance, the first of many marinas is at Schleimünde immediately inside the northern entrance mole. This small harbour is for temporary overnight berthing only, with few

Kappeln Bridge
Miranda Delmar-Morgan

DIE SCHLEI

Maasholm harbour looking NE *Miranda Delmar-Morgan*

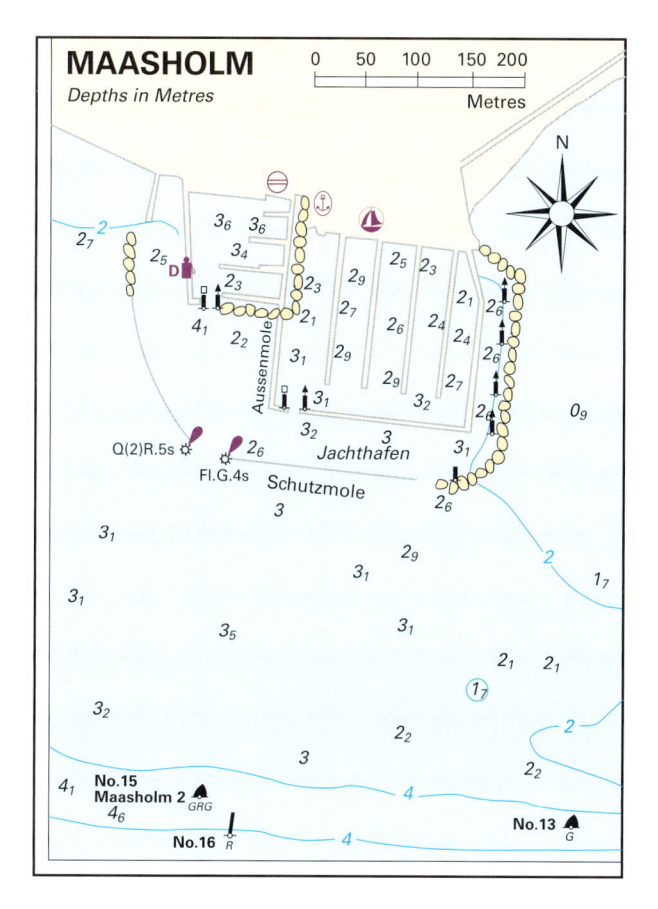

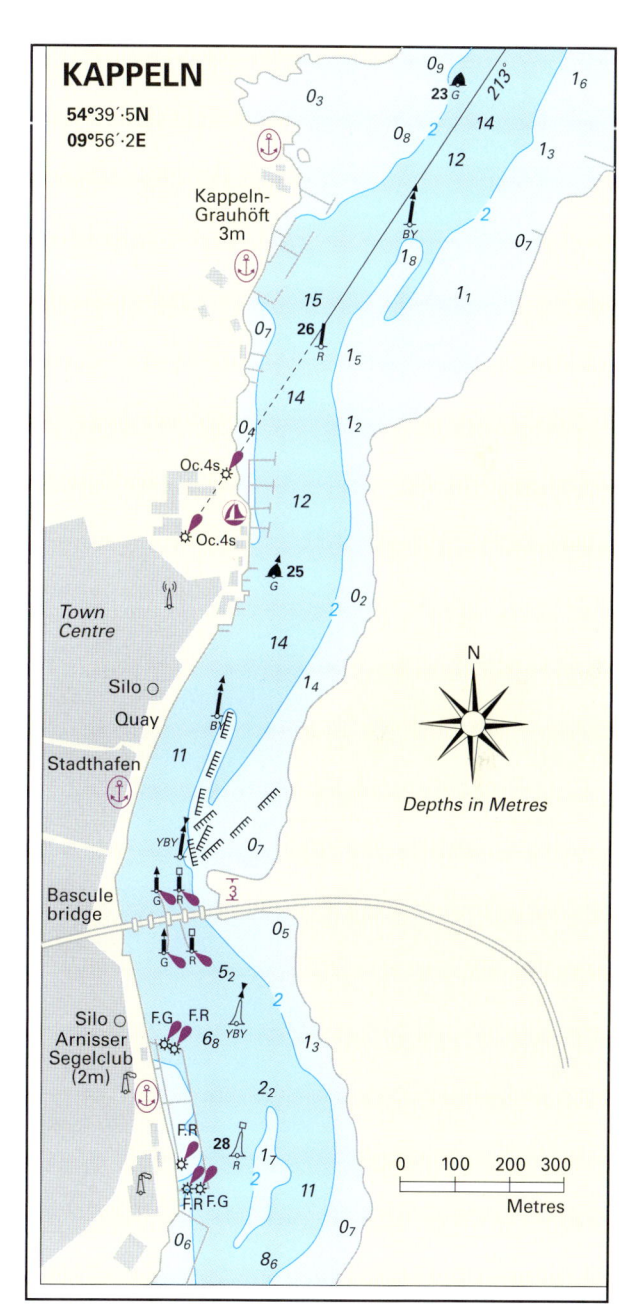

1. GERMANY

facilities and is exposed to E/SE winds. A much larger marina with all facilities and again on the northern side is 1·5M from the entrance at Maasholm. Berth in box berths in the yacht hafen on the starboard side of the entrance or larger yachts can berth on the outside of the southern jetty of the yacht basin. Fuel berth, and Customs office.

The first major town on the passage up-river is Kappeln which has a big choice of marinas but the most convenient for visitors is the Stadthafen; box berths with bow to a pontoon on the west side of the river just before the bridge. It has basic facilities and a fuel berth close by. An average speed of 8kn is needed if you wish to make the openings of both the Kappeln and Lindau bridges in one passage.

Upriver of Kappeln the scenery becomes more rural but continues to have a wide choice of marinas right up to Schleswig where the main marina is the Wiking Yachthafen which has all facilities. It is dominated by a huge octagonal apartment block. On the north side of the river at Schleswig is the

THE BALTIC SEA AND APPROACHES 33

1B. KIELER FÖRDE TO FLENSBURG FÖRDE

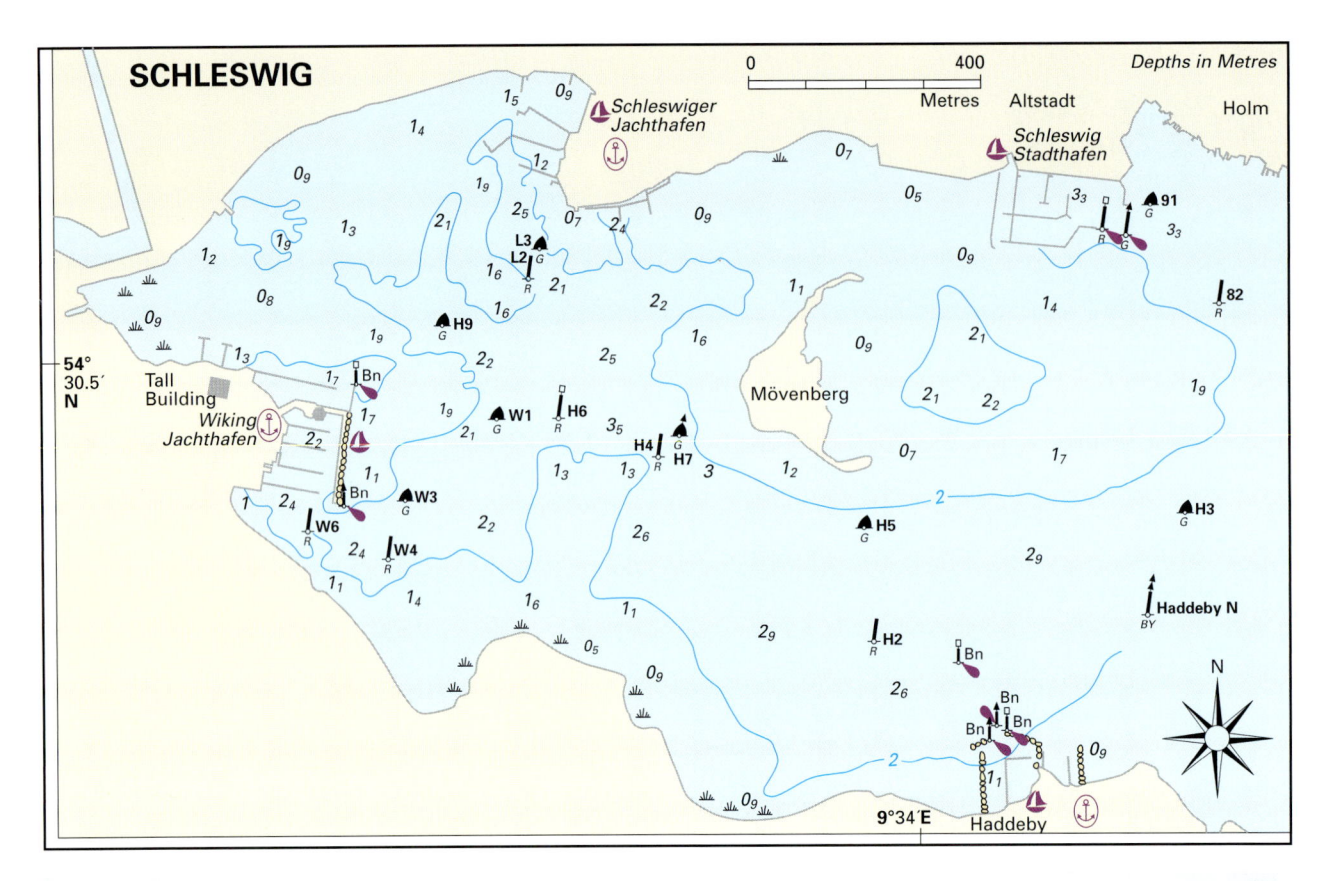

Kappeln, looking across at town quay
Miranda Delmar-Morgan

Schleswiger Yachthafen and the much smaller Stadthafen further east.

Facilities

All the marinas have basic facilities but several are attached to yacht yards such as the Yachtzentrum at Kappeln and several have been considerably upgraded. Schleswig has an interesting Viking Centre at Haddeby as it was from here that the Vikings used to haul their longships overland to the North Sea. There is a local ferry to Haddeby from Schleswig Stadthafen.

34   THE BALTIC SEA AND APPROACHES

FLENSBURG FÖRDE

Flensburg Förde including Flensburg

54°47'N 09°26'E

Distances (from Flensburg)
Sønderborg 21M, Fåborg 56M, Schlei entrance 36M, Kiel 56M

Charts
UKHO 2942, 2532, 919
German Small Craft Chart set 3003, German 26
Danish 152, 154, 155

Lights
Gammel-Pøl 54°52'·9N 10°04'·2E Oc(3)WRG.15s20m11–8M White column, red band. 166·5°-W-320°-R-008°-G-036·5°-W-049°-R-136·5°
Kegnaes 54°51'·2N 09°59'·3E Oc.WRG.5s32m12–9M 217°-R-266·5°-G-273°-W-289·5°-R-337°-G-026°-W-044°-R-050·5°-G-075°-W-080°-R-102·5
Kalkgrund 54°49'·5N 09°53'·3E Iso.WRG.8s22m14–12M Red round tower, two white bands, three galleries 012°-W-062°-R-084°-W-100°-R-120°-W-131·5°-G-157°-W-164°-R-190°-W-252·6°-G-258°-W-265°-R-292°-W-308°-R-012°. Horn Mo(FS)30s
Holnis 54°51'·7N 09°34'·5E Iso.WRG.6s32m13–11M Red tower and gallery, white band. 053°-R-060°-W-066·5-G-091·5-W-189°-R-196°-W-203°-R-208° 283°-R-289°-W-294·5°-R-302°
Skodsbøl Ldg Lts 028° *Front* 54°53'·6N 09°38'·4E Iso.W.2s11m10M White round tower with red band. Rear 900m from front Iso.W.4s24m12M Red diamond shape on white metal framework tower
Lågemade Ldg Lts 048° *Front* 54°54'·1N 09°36'·9E Iso.R.2s13m14M Red triangle on white round tower, red band. Rear 700m from front Iso.R.4s26m14M Red inverted triangle on white metal framework tower W, red top
Rinkenaes Ldg Lts 289·5° *Front* 54°53'·4N 09°34'·6E Iso.WG.2s10m11/8M White round tower with red band 227°-W-312°-G-004° Rear 0·55M from front Iso.W.4s30m11M White diamond on white framework tower
Kielseng 54°48'·3N 09°26'·8E Oc.WRG.4s32m10–3M Mast 193°-G-195°-W-199°-R-201°
Flensburg Ldg Lts 299° *Front* 54°48'·2N 09°26'·1E Iso.G.4s15m12M White metal framework tower Rear 80m from front Iso.G.4s19m13M White metal framework tower

Communications
Stadthafen im-jaich Marina ✆ +49 (0) 46 11 74 99
 Mobile + 49 174 746 7508
 www.im-jaich.de
Werftkontor Marina ✆ +49 4611 609104
 www.marina-werftkontor.de
Kielseng Marina (Industriehafen) WSF ✆ +49 4612 1631
 www.wsf/flensburg.de
Kielseng FYS (Flensburger Yacht-Service)
 ✆ +49 461 1772716 or +49 461 177270
 www.fys.de
Sonwik Marina ✆ +49 4615 050450
 www.sonwik.de
WSV Galwik ✆ +49 4614 3555
 wsv.galwik.de
Niro Petersen ✆ +49 461 5003333
 www.niro-petersen.de

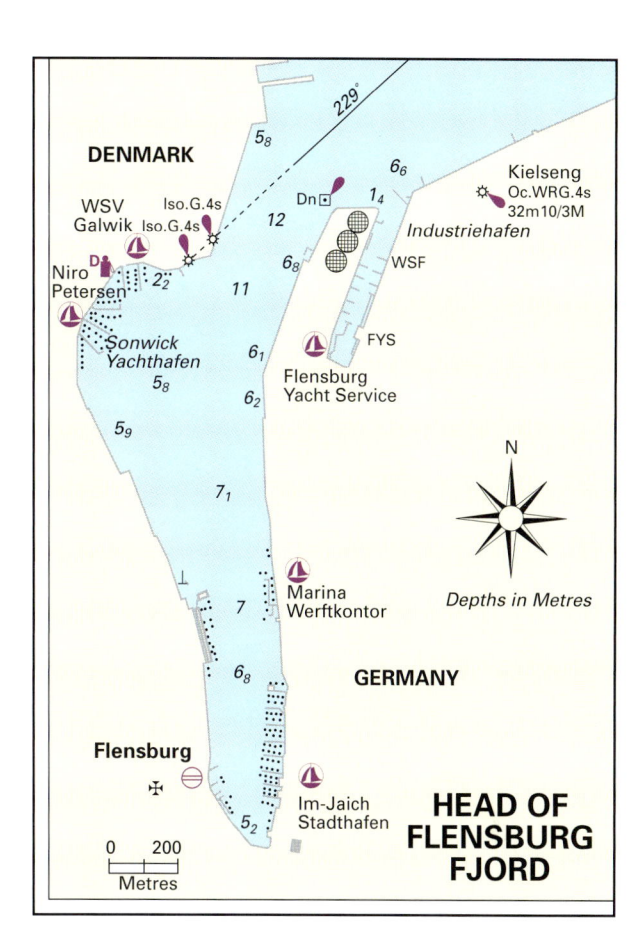

General

This lovely fjord forms the boundary between Germany and Denmark and in fact the boundary line runs along the middle of the shipping channel in such a way that the porthand buoys are in Germany and the starboardhand ones are in Denmark. There are numerous small towns, harbours and opportunities for anchoring along its shores and at its head is the attractive city of Flensburg nearly 28M from the open sea.

Flensburg Stadhafen marina *Miranda Delmar-Morgan*

THE BALTIC SEA AND APPROACHES 35

1. GERMANY

1B. KIELER FÖRDE TO FLENSBURG FÖRDE

Flensburg *J. Parkinson*

Approach
From north and northeast 54°50'·5N 10°07'E
From south and southeast 54°45'N 10°05'E

From these waypoints appropriate courses lead to Kalkgrund Lt which is left to port and from there a westerly course leads to the start of the channel buoys which eventually lead to Flensburg.

Berth
The nearest marina to the city is the Stadthafen, now run by Im-Jaich Marinas which has box berths for 168 yachts, depths of 1·5-6m, and all facilities. It can be very crowded but sometimes guests may berth on the pontoons reserved for the Fishcerei Verein (Fishing Club/Union) if there is space. There is a form you fill in and an honesty box for payment. Depths at Flensburg can increase up to 4m in prolonged easterly gales and reduce by up to 2m in similar conditions from the west. There are other marinas nearby and one can usually find a berth somewhere but this may necessitate motoring round to look for an empty space with a green plaque at its head. On the west shore of the harbour are the Watersports Club marina (WSV Galwik), the Niro-Petersen marina, Sonwick and opposite the Stadthafen is a small marina for traditional yachts. Niro-Petersen specialises in stainless steel fabrication and has diesel. Tall ships berth at the quay just to the north of them. Kielseng has major yacht facilities, (Flensburg Yacht Services (Nautor Swan), Baum & Konig) repairs and riggers and over wintering sheds. Flensburg has a plethora of facilities, restaurants, and of course, their own Pilsener brewery.

Facilities
The Stadthafen has water/electricity on the jetties and showers/toilets near the office. There is a restaurant and laundry. All other services are available somewhere.

North of Flensburg
For continuation north from Flensburg in the Lille Bælt, see pages 106-115.

1c. Kieler Förde to Mecklenburger Bucht

Heiligenhafen

54°23′N 11°00′E

Distances
Kiel 35M, Travemünde 33M, Wismar 38M, Warnemünde 43M

Charts
UKHO 2117
German 43, 31

Lights
Heiligenhafen (S side of Heiligreede) 54°22′·2N 11°01′·2E
Oc(2)WRG.9s16m13–9M 100°-G-206°-W-212·2°-R-250°
Red tower, platform, white lantern, red and white dwelling 13m
Outer Ldg Lts 268·5° *Front* 54°22′·4N 10°59′·6E
Oc.4s13m17M White g with red border on white mast 11m
Rear 312m from front Oc.4s19m17M White v with red border on grey warehouse
Inner Ldg Lts 279·2° *Front* 54°22′·6N 10°59′·1E
Iso.3s13m17M Red g on white mast 14m
Rear 195m from front, Iso.3s13m17M Red v on white mast 16m

Communications
Heiligenhafen Harbourmaster ☎ +49 4362 5034 24
www.marina-heiligenhafen.de
Marina Heiligenhafen ☎ +49 174 586 68 71
www.marina-heiligenhafen.de

General

See notes regarding Firing Ranges under Kieler Förde on page 29–30.

Heiligenhafen is a major yacht and fishing harbour strategically placed for yachtsmen making eastwards from Kieler Förde. In strong northeasterly conditions the approach may become unpleasant, and in these circumstances it may be preferable to seek a harbour on Fehmarn Island such as Orth (54°27′N 11°03′E), or Burgtiefe (54°25′N 11°12′E) and Burgstaaken (54°25′N 11°11′E) in the Burger See to the east of Fehmarnsund bridge (see plan page 40). Burgtiefe has a useful set of 'boxes' in a circular pattern to accommodate berthing in any wind direction.

Approach and entrance

Approach is made in the white sector of Heiligenhafen light on a bearing of approximately 210° to pick up the outer leading lights in the vicinity of Heiligenhafen No. 1 buoy. By day a useful guide to the entrance is the 134m radar tower about a mile south-southwest of Heiligenhafen light. By night this tower has red lights. After following the outer leading lights for about 0·7M the inner leading lights will be picked up.

Anchorage and berthing

It is possible to anchor off Heiligenhafen light in 5 or 6m in suitable conditions but most yachts will wish to continue to the main yacht harbour. It may be possible to find an alongside berth in the old harbour to the south of the yacht harbour and if the charter fleet is out their berths may be unofficially available.

Heligenhafen entrance from east *Miranda Delmar-Morgan*

1C. KIELER FÖRDE TO MECKLENBURGER BUCHT

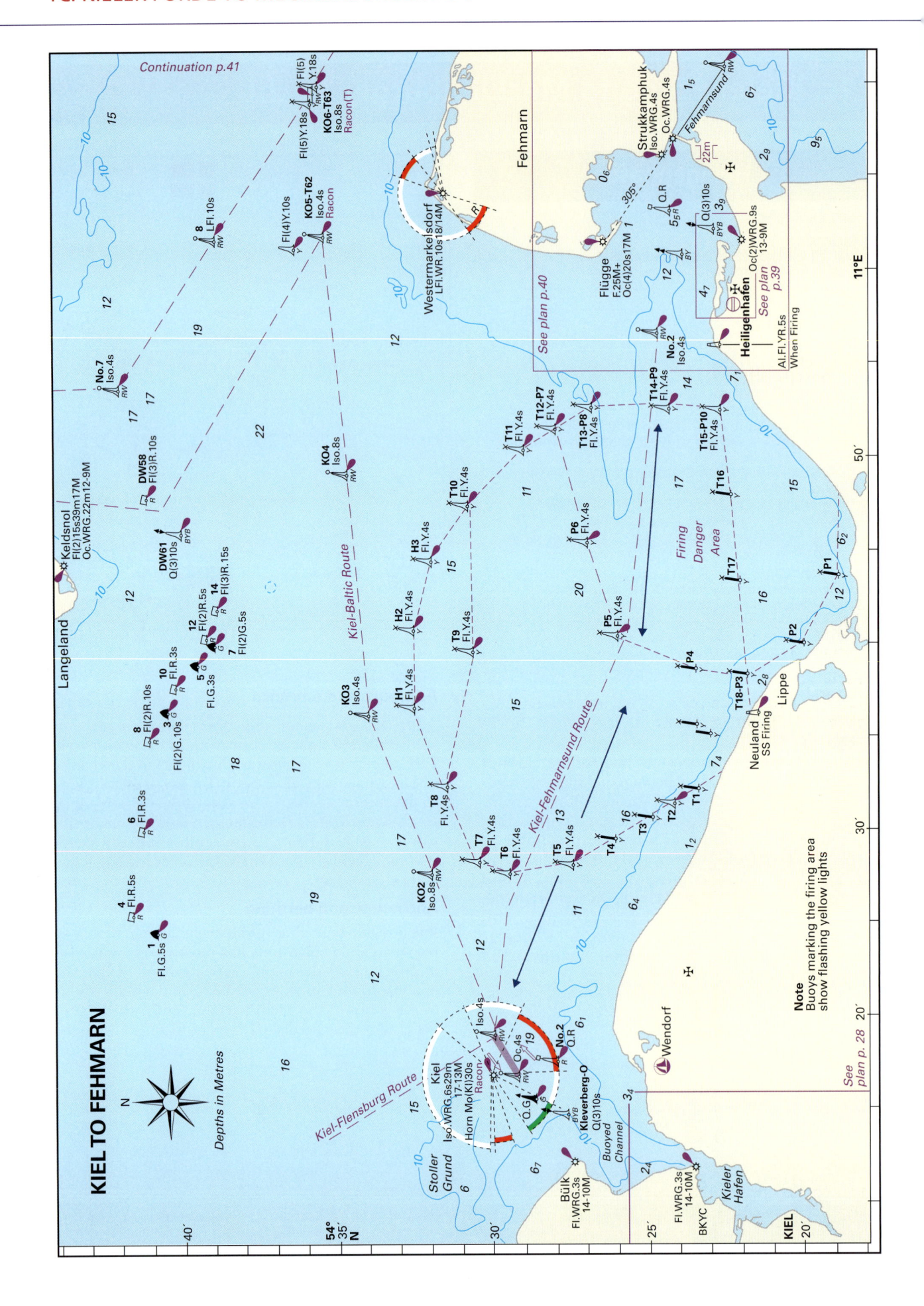

HEILIGENHAFEN

[Chart: HEILIGENHAFEN, 54°22'·1N 10°59'·0E to 11°01'·0E, Depths in Metres. Features labelled include: Yacht Harbour, Graswarder, Warder Eck, Fishing Hbr, Silos, Heiligenhafen-0 Q(3)10s BYB, Heiligenhafen 1 Q.G, Heiligenhafen Oc(2)WRG.9s 16m13-9M, Oc.4s17M, Iso.3s, Lts in line 268·5°, 279°.]

1. GERMANY

Formalities
The harbourmaster's office is between the yacht harbour and old harbour.

Facilities
Heiligenhafen is an attractive small holiday town with all shopping facilities convenient to the harbour. It has a sizeable charter fleet and a full range of yacht services, including chandlery, diesel and WiFi.

The Blue House, Graswarder
Miranda Delmar-Morgan

The yacht club sometimes has bikes for hire, and there are good restaurants and fresh fish. Excellent bird watching on the Graswarder nature reserve.

Communications and travel
There are regular buses to Grossenbrode where you can catch trains to Berlin and Fehmarn.

Fehmarnsund
This is the channel between the island of Fehmarn and the mainland. It is crossed by a combined rail and road bridge with a clearance of 22m. but this can vary by up to 2m depending on wind conditions. Clearance is indicated at water level on each side of the bridge. There are sometimes currents up to four knots if there have been persistent strong winds from the east or west.

The approach from the west is wide and straightforward but from the east the channel is very narrow and closely buoyed. It carries a depth of 5m. Neustadt, in the Lübecker Bucht, has a Schengen clearance facility, Ancora Marina, outer mole at 54°05'·59N 10°48'·4E has diesel.

Heligenhafen Graswarder looking seaward *Miranda Delmar-Morgan*

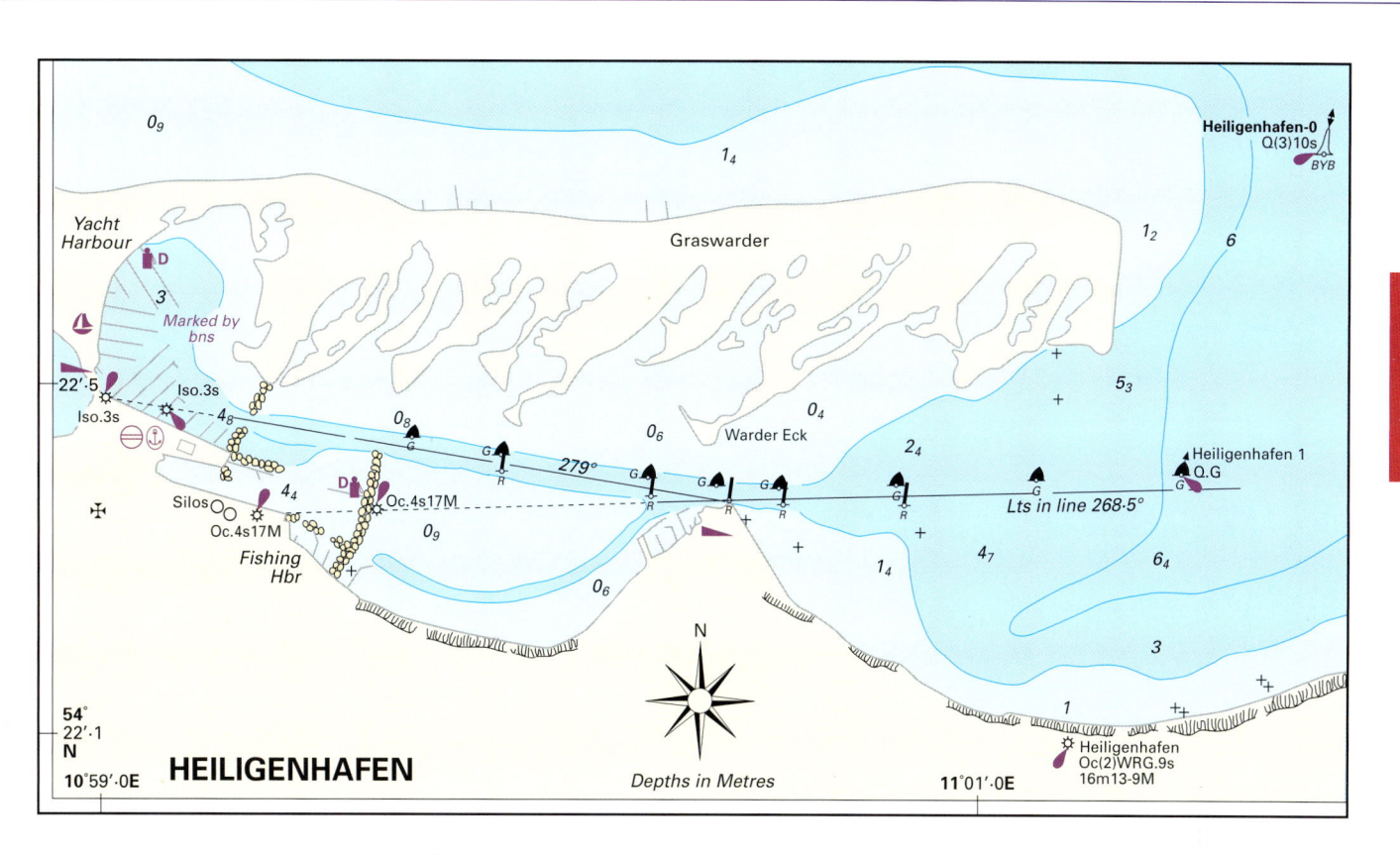

THE BALTIC SEA AND APPROACHES 39

1C. KIELER FÖRDE TO MECKLENBURGER BUCHT

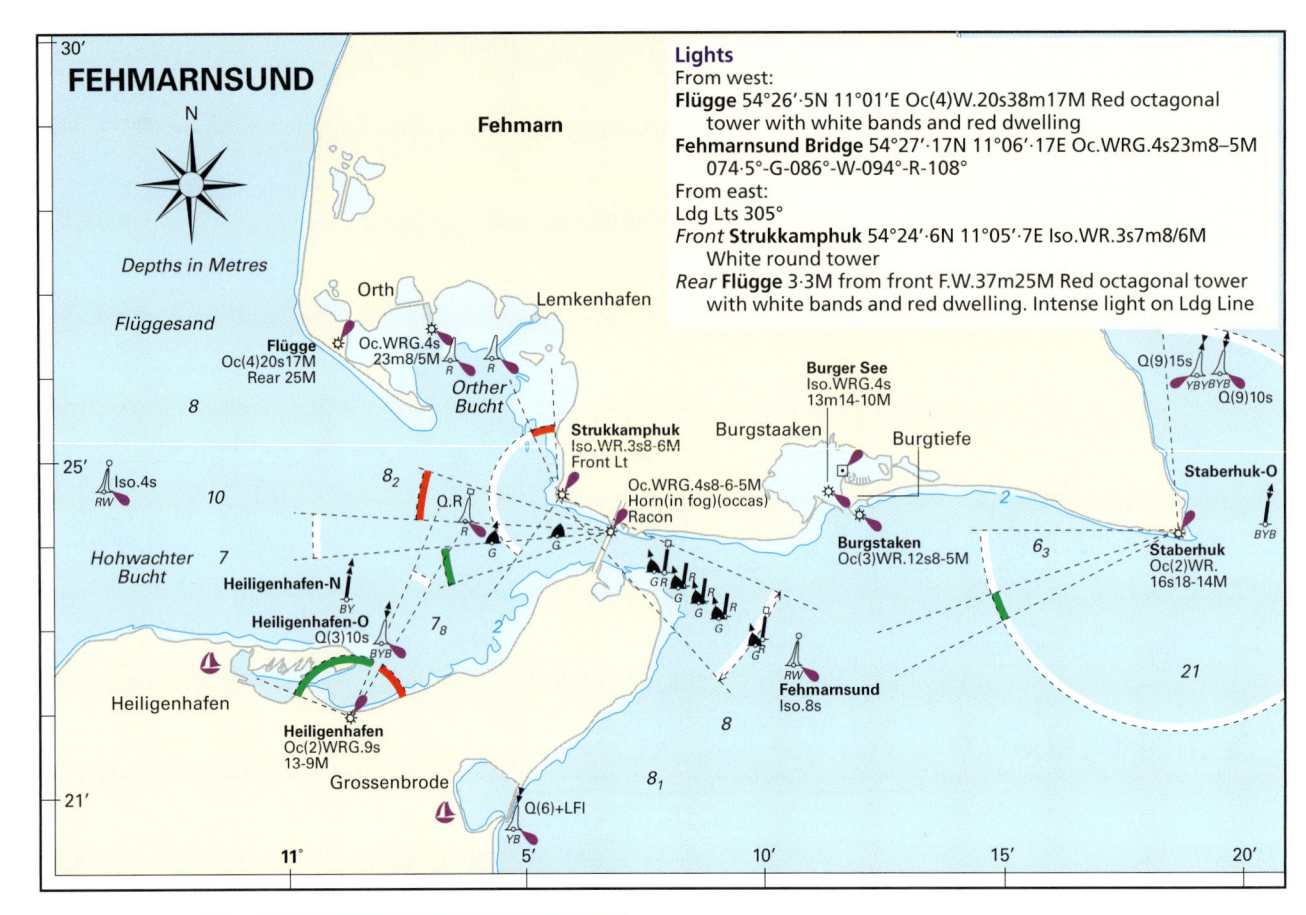

Lights
From west:
Flügge 54°26'·5N 11°01'E Oc(4)W.20s38m17M Red octagonal tower with white bands and red dwelling
Fehmarnsund Bridge 54°27'·17N 11°06'·17E Oc.WRG.4s23m8–5M 074·5°-G-086°-W-094°-R-108°
From east:
Ldg Lts 305°
Front **Strukkamphuk** 54°24'·6N 11°05'·7E Iso.WR.3s7m8/6M White round tower
Rear **Flügge** 3·3M from front F.W.37m25M Red octagonal tower with white bands and red dwelling. Intense light on Ldg Line

Travemünde (including Lübeck)

North mole 53°57'·7N 10°53'·3E

Distances (to Travemünde)
Kiel 65M, Heiligenhafen 35M, Wismar 25M

Charts
UKHO 2117, 2354, 2355
German 36, 37, 35, 51, 52

Lights
Travemünde (Hochhaus) 53°57'·8N 10°53'E
Fl.WR.4s114m19/15M 165°-R-214°-W-234°-R-245° Building 118m
Priwall Ldg Lts 215·9° *Front* 53°57'·5N 10°53'·2E
Oc(2)9s14m17M White ▲ with red border on white mast 13m
Rear 380m from front Oc(2)9s24m17M White ▼ with red border on white framework tower 21m
North molehead 53°57'·8N 10°53'·4E
Oc.RG.4s10m6/5M+F.Y in fog 123°-R-201°-G-066° White tower, black bands with glass bricks 9m Floodlit

Communications
Travemünde Port Authority ☎ +49 4502 74362
VHF Ch 16, 19
Travemünde/Lübeck Vessel Traffic Service ☎ +49 4502 84750, VHF Ch 13 (broadcasts every three hours from 0600–2100 LT)
Trave Bridge (Herrenbrüke) VHF Ch 13
Lübeck Hubbrucken VHF Ch 18
Passathafen Marina ☎ +49 4502 6396
Böbs Werft Marina ☎ +49 4502 5051
www.boebs-werft.de
Marina Baltica ☎ +49 4502 86010
www.marina-baltica.de
Eric Warburg Bridge summer opening times: 0930, 1200, 1730, 1930.

General
Travemünde is the outer port for Lübeck. It is a holiday resort and a busy ferry and commercial port with three major yacht harbours. Its shopping centre is adequate though not extensive. Travemünde is an ideal base from which to visit Lübeck by public transport.

Approach
The Trave RW SWM 53°59'·8N 10°56'·7E

The most prominent landmark, the Hotel Maritim, is a 37-floor tower block (with Travemünde light on the top) immediately north of the harbour entrance, visible from a considerable distance out to sea.

The fairway leading into the harbour is well buoyed, with powerful leading lights on a bearing of 216°. The frequent arrivals and departures of ferries also serve to indicate the harbour entrance, which is very narrow and controlled by International Port Traffic Signals (IPTS). Beware large shoal area to NW of approach channel.

Anchorage
Anchoring outside the entrance to the Trave is unwise because of the many large rocks left over from the ice age and anchoring in the river is impracticable because of the heavy commercial traffic but it is possible in the Potenitzer Wiek, from 1100 Saturday to 1100 Monday between the four yellow anchorage buoys (beware submarine cables). The Dassower See is a nature reserve and permission for entry is needed. Higher up the river towards Lübeck there are various bays on the south side and at Silk on the north after the river curves westward.

40 THE BALTIC SEA AND APPROACHES

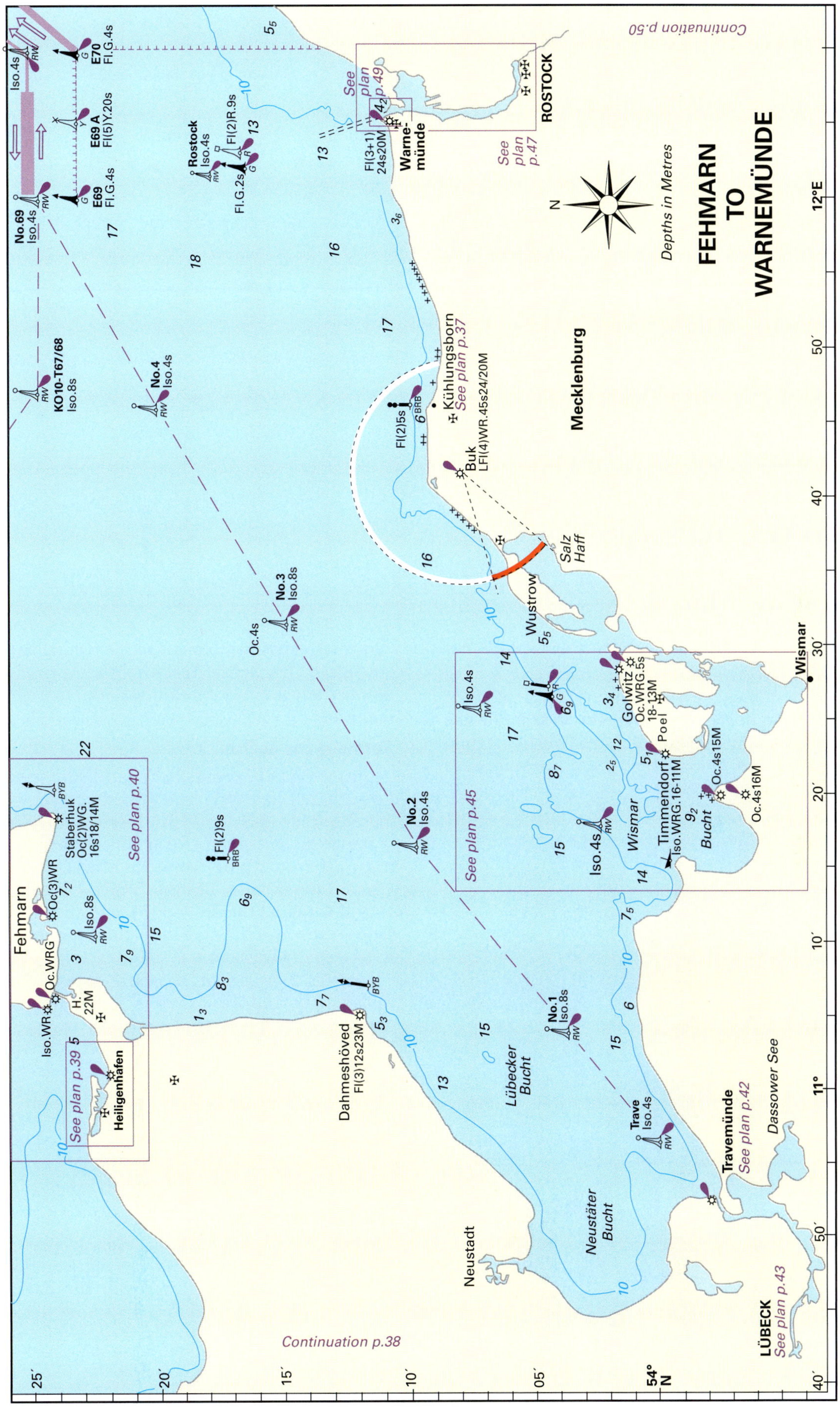
FEHMARN
TO
WARNEMÜNDE
Depths in Metres
Continuation p.50
Continuation p.38
Fehmarn
Staberhuk
Oc(2)WG.
16s18/14M
Heiligenhafen
See plan p.39
See plan p.40
Dahmeshöved
Fl(3)12s23M
Lübecker Bucht
Neustädter Bucht
Neustadt
Travemünde
See plan p.42
Dassower See
LÜBECK
See plan p.43
Wismar
Wismar Bucht
See plan p.45
Timmendorf
Iso.WRG.16-11M
Poel
Golwitz
Oc.WRG.5s
18-13M
Wustrow
Salz Haff
Buk
LFl(4)WR.45s24/20M
Kühlungsborn
See plan p.37
Mecklenburg
Warne-
münde
Fl(3+1)
24s20M
See plan p.49
ROSTOCK
See plan p.47
No.1
Iso.8s
No.2
Iso.4s
No.3
Iso.8s
No.4
Iso.4s
No.69
Iso.4s
KO10-T67/68
Iso.8s
E69
Fl.G.4s
E69 A
Fl(5)Y.20s
E70
Fl.G.4s
Rostock
Iso.4s
Trave
Iso.4s
1. GERMANY

1C. KIELER FÖRDE TO MECKLENBURGER BUCHT

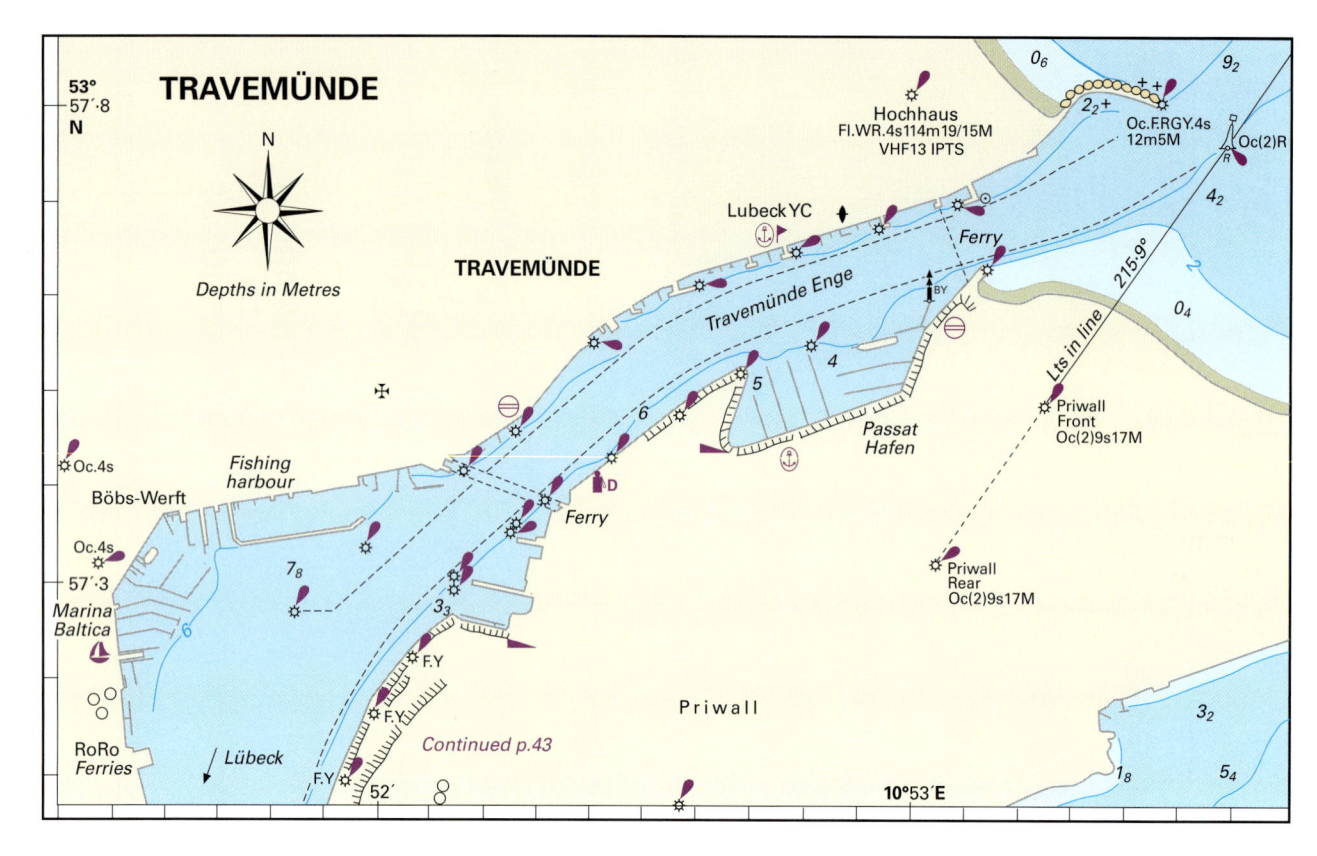

Berthing

There are three major yacht harbours – the Passathafen, immediately to port on entry behind the permanently-moored square-rigger *Passat*, or the Marina Baltica and adjacent Böbs Werft marina, both about half a mile further in on the starboard hand. All carry depths of up to 7m.

It is also possible to berth in the fishing harbour, to starboard just before reaching the Marina Baltica, where there is a more traditional ambience but fewer facilities.

Services for yachts

All three yacht harbours have excellent facilities. The Passathafen has WiFi and is perhaps slightly more attractive visually, but all are efficient. There is a crane at the Passathafen if it is necessary to step the mast after emerging from the Elbe-Lübeck Canal. On the north side, Lübeck YC halfway along the strand manages the box berths, and the HM office is below the yacht club. Berths operate on the red/green card system.

Marina Baltica can accommodate yachts up to 30m length and 5m draught. It has boat-building facilities with engineers and onshore storage.

Fuel can be obtained at the bunker station, on the Priwall side of the river close to the car ferry, and Camping Gaz can bought from the hardware store in the town centre. There is no full-scale chandlery shop, but there are several boatyards equipped for most repairs. Weather forecasts can be obtained from the yacht harbours or Lübeck Radio.

General facilities

There is a shopping centre on the north bank, about 10 minutes' walk from Marina Baltica and a short ferry ride across the river from the Passathafen. Banks, restaurants, hotels and a tourist information office will be found in the centre of the town. Customs post.

Travemünde, the *Passat* with Passathafen behind
Miranda Delmar-Morgan

UPRIVER TO LÜBECK

Travemünde, harbourside café *Miranda Delmar-Morgan*

Communications and travel

There are good bus and rail services to Lübeck and Hamburg, where there are international airports. Ferries to Trelleborg, Helsinki and Rīga.

Upriver to Lübeck

The Hanseatic city of Lübeck, 11M up the River Trave from Travemünde, is easily reached by bus or train from Travemünde, and should not be missed. The city has a population of 200,000 and it is full of historic buildings which have been painstakingly restored and maintained following the bomb damage of the Second World War. There is also an interesting historic-ship harbour, the Hansahafen, where a number of carefully preserved old ships lie.

The trip up the River Trave is interesting. It once formed the east/west German border. The undeveloped surroundings alter from rural to industrial as you progress and beyond the marinas at Herreninsel and Schlutup, the river becomes increasingly industrialized. There are ship turning circles to observe, before you pass through the Eric Warburg lifting bridge after which you may spot the *Lisa von Lübec*, a replica of a Hanseatic trading ship, which berths on the north side of the Hansahafen. You can step ashore into this magnificent UNESCO city but there is only one pontoon with scant facilities, and it is therefore easier to visit from Travemunde.

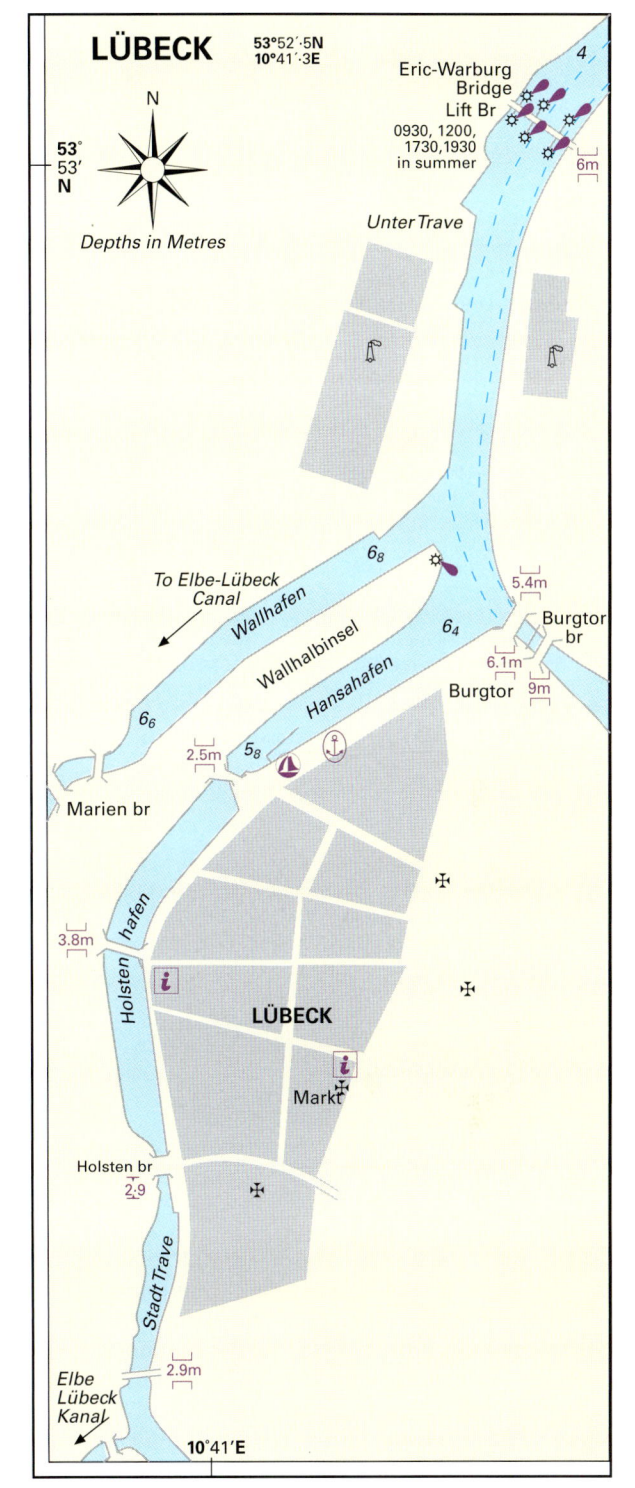

Lübeck, approach to Hansahafen
Miranda Delmar-Morgan

1. GERMANY

THE BALTIC SEA AND APPROACHES 43

1C. KIELER FÖRDE TO MECKLENBURGER BUCHT

Wismar

53°54′N 11°26′E

Distances
Travemünde 25M, Warnemünde 35M

Charts
UKHO 2217, 2359
German 1641, 37

Lights
Timmendorf 53°59′·5N 11°22′·6E Iso.WRG.6s21m16–11M 049°-W-054·5-G-073°-W-079°-R-125°-G-135°-W-137°-R-196°-G-202·5-W-211·5-R-220° White round tower, red and brown top, white lantern, red cupola, with white dwelling 21m
Gollwitz N 54°01′·4N 11°28′E Iso.WRG.4s13m19–14M 162·3°-G-164·5°-W-166°-R168·3° White tower with red and green lantern on white building
Hohen Wieschendorf Ldg Lts 180·3° Front 53°57′·6N 11°20′E Oc.4s20m15M White lattice mast 16m
Rear 1500m from front Oc.4s39m16M White v with red surround on white lattice mast 21m
Walfisch Ldg Lts 123·9° Front 53°56′·7N 11°25′·1E Oc(2)9s10m7M Red and white g on white tubular metal mast 10m
Rear 1·35M from front, Oc(2)9s30m7M Red and white tubular metal mast 30m
Wismar Ldg Lts 149·9° Front 53°54′N 11°27′·1E Oc.R.4s28m12M Framework tower on promontory on west side of harbour 26m
Rear 700m from front Oc.R.4s46m12M Framework tower 43m

Communications
Harbour Office ☎ +49 3841 224491 (0700–1530 Monday–Friday, 0800–1200 LT Saturday) *Mobile* +49 162/4720355
Wismar Vessel Traffic Service VHF Ch 12 (broadcasts on VHF Ch 12 every 3hrs from 0630–2130 LT in German or English on request)
Wismar Tourist office www.wismar-tourist.de
Wismar Alter Hafen ☎ +49 3841/2513260
Wismar Westhafen ☎ +49 3841 224491 or +49 1624 720355 *Mobile* +49 1624 720355 www.westhafen.net
Wismar Brunkowkai ☎ +49 3841 2513260

Wismar panoramic view *Miranda Delmar-Morgan*

General
Wismar, a historic town of some 60,000 inhabitants, is principally engaged in shipbuilding and repairs. The old town has remarkable baroque and Gothic architecture and the Alte Markt is a reminder of the greatness of the Hanseatic League. It is one of the largest squares in Germany, with many gabled houses including the 'Alte Schwede', built in 1380 though taking its name from the pub opened there in the late 19th century, a reminder that Wismar belonged to Sweden in the 17th and 18th centuries. The old town has a preservation order and much restoration has been carried out, though of the medieval fortifications only the Wassertor and bits of the town wall remain. The church of St Nicholas and the museum in the Schabbelhaus are worth visiting.

An attraction of Wismar from the yachtsman's viewpoint is that one berths within easy walking distance of the centre of this comparatively small and memorable town. The new Marina Westhafen has most modern facilities, a Netto supermarket a short walk to the SW, bike hire nearby, a petrol station and an ATM to the west up Lübsche Strasse about 300m away. There is also an Edeka supermarket in town (no credit cards). The Alterhafen is home to the fishing boat stalls with their fantastic array of smoked and fresh fish for sale. From Wismar, ships of the White Fleet (Weisse Flotte) take an hour to run to the island of Poel, which is popular for its beaches. Poel also has a museum showcasing the island. Schwerin, on the edge of the Mecklenburg Lake District, is some 30km by rail from Wismar. Its castle, inspired by Chateau Chambord, was the seat of the Dukes of Mecklenburg until they were thrown out in 1918 – it is both amazingly grand and unsatisfactorily dull, though its gardens and orangery are pleasant enough. Outside the town, Schweriner See is, at 65km^2, the largest of many lakes which contribute to a pretty countryside.

Approach
The Grossestief channel is entered about 3M north of the island of Poel on about 165° (in the white sector of Gollwitz N light) before swinging west at the second pair of channel buoys on to 230° south of Hannibal Shoal. Thereafter the channel is marked by buoys and leading lights. The vast ship-building shed of Nordic Yachts is clearly visible.

An alternative approach, from the Offentief landfall buoy with about 5m depth, crosses between the Hannibal and Lieps shoals northwest of Timmendorf light. It is marked by a pair of unlit buoys and is in a white sector of Timmendorf light.

Anchorage
Anchor outside the shipping channel (but display anchor ball and light as there is considerable commercial shipping in Wismarbucht). If visiting the attractive little village of Kirchdorf on the island of Poel do not consider anchoring in the dredged approach channel as the holding is bad in very soft mud and ferries take up most of the fairway. Visiting yachts can moor on the western pontoon in 2m at the outer end.

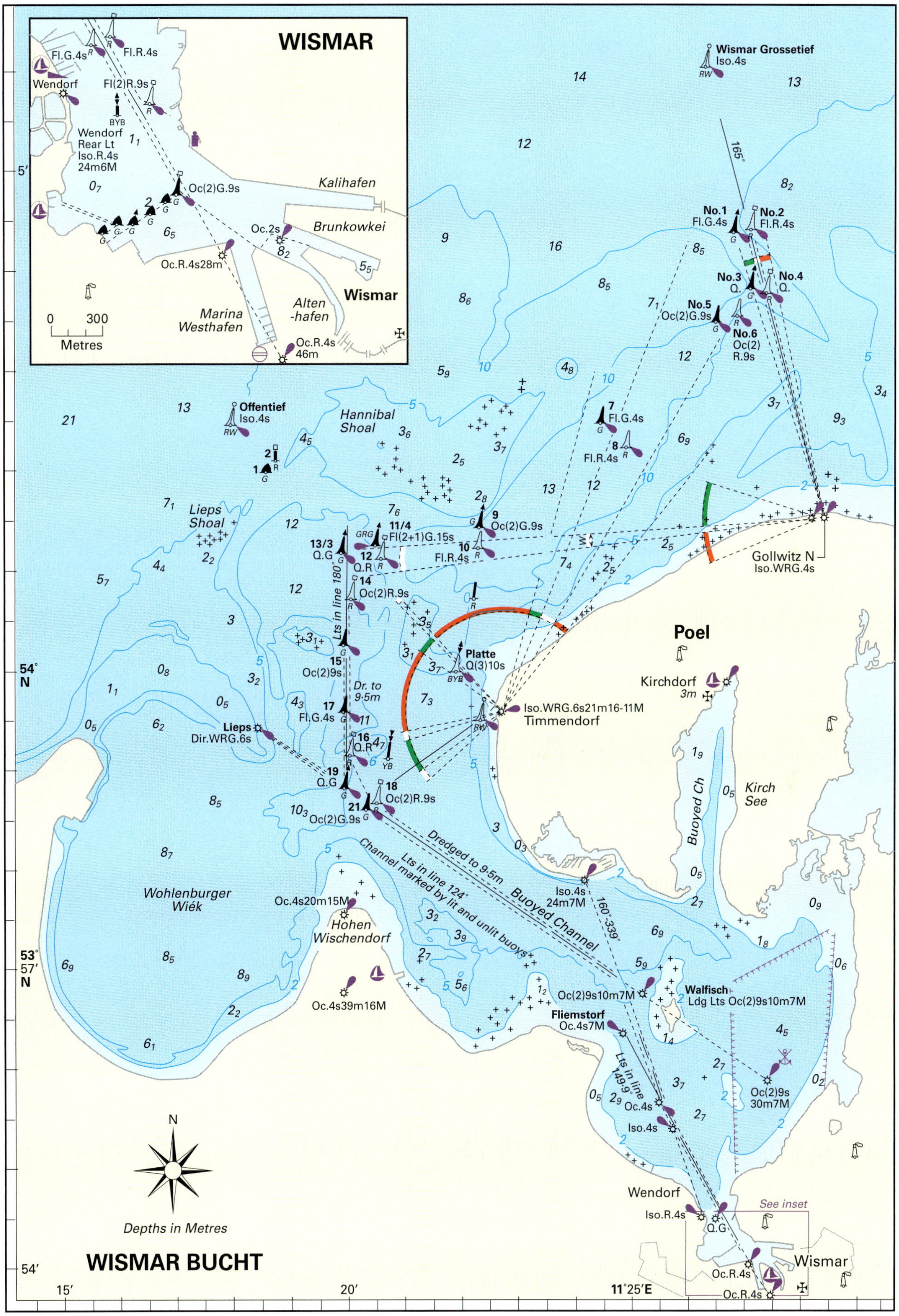
WISMAR
Fl.G.4s
Fl.R.4s
Wendorf
Fl(2)R.9s
BYB
Wendorf Rear Lt Iso.R.4s 24m6M
Oc(2)G.9s
Kalihafen
Brunkowkei
Oc.2s
Oc.R.4s28m
Marina Westhafen
Alten -hafen
Wismar
Oc.R.4s 46m
0 300
Metres
Wismar Grossetief Iso.4s
No.1 Fl.G.4s
No.2 Fl.R.4s
No.3 Q.
No.4 Q.
No.5 Oc(2)G.9s
No.6 Oc(2) R.9s
165°
Offentief Iso.4s
Hannibal Shoal
7 Fl.G.4s
8 Fl.R.4s
Lieps Shoal
9 Oc(2)G.9s
10 Fl.R.4s
11/4 Fl(2+1)G.15s
13/3 Q.G
12 Q.R
14 Oc(2)R.9s
Lts in line 180°
Gollwitz N Iso.WRG.4s
Poel
Platte Q(3)10s
15 Oc(2)9s
Dr. to 9·5m
Iso.WRG.6s21m16-11M Timmendorf
Kirchdorf
17 Fl.G.4s
16 Q.R
Lieps Dir.WRG.6s
19 Q.G
18 Oc(2)R.9s
21 Oc(2)G.9s
Buoyed Ch
Kirch See
Dredged to 9·5m
Lts in line 124°
Channel marked by lit and unlit buoys
Buoyed Channel
Iso.4s 24m7M
160°339°
Wohlenburger Wiek
Oc.4s20m15M
Hohen Wischendorf
Oc.4s39m16M
Oc(2)9s10m7M
Walfisch
Ldg Lts Oc(2)9s10m7M
Fliemstorf Oc.4s7M
Lts in line 149·9°
Oc.4s
Iso.4s
Oc(2)9s 30m7M
Wendorf
Iso.R.4s
Q.G
See inset
Wismar
Oc.R.4s
Depths in Metres
WISMAR BUCHT
N
5′
54° N
53° 57′ N
54′
15′
20′
11°25′E

1C. KIELER FÖRDE TO MECKLENBURGER BUCHT

Wismar old harbour, Alten Hafen, approaches
Miranda Delmar-Morgan

Berthing
In Wismar visiting yachts can berth alongside on the east side of the Alten Hafen but this is more suitable for larger vessels. Berthing for yachts is available at the Westhafen or Brunkowkei marinas which are not much further from the city centre.

Services
Water, electricity and shower/toilet facilities are available at both marinas although facilities at Brunkowkei are minimal. There are laundry facilities at Westhafen and there is a fuel station on the north side of the harbour basin between the oil jetty and the chemical works. Weather forecasts are available on request from the harbourmaster's office. There is a black water pump out station to starboard as you enter the Alter Hafen.

There is no yacht chandlery or sailmaker and no specialist facilities for yacht repairs, although the ship repair yard could no doubt be approached in connection with serious problems.

General facilities
Groceries, gas and most other supplies are available in the town centre, where there is a tourist information office and banks, restaurants and hotels abound.

Communications and travel
There are good train services to Hamburg, Berlin and Rostock.

Wismar channel marker *Miranda Delmar-Morgan*

Kühlungsborn

53°09'·2N 11°46'·4E outer mole

Distances
Wismar 27M, Heiligenhafen 30M,
Warnemünde 12M, Gedser 25M, Stralsund 64M

Charts
UKHO 2365, 2117
German 163, 1671

Lights
Buk 54°07'·9N 11°41'·6E LFl(4)WR.45s95m24–20M Red and brown round tower, red cupola
Kuhlungsborn E Mole Head FR.6m4M Red Mast
N Mole Head FG.6m4M Green Mast
Warnemünde 54°10'·9N 12°05'·1E Fl(3+1)W.24s 34M 20M White round tower with black bands, two galleries, copper cupola

Communications
Harbourmaster ☎ +49 38 2934 1055
 Mobile +49 151 12110565
 www.bootshafen-kuehlungsborn.de

General
A large new marina with several hundred berths just to the east of Kühlungsborn, the largest seaside resort in Mecklenburg, amongst much new housing development.

Approach
Straightforward by day or night from a northeasterly direction and around the eastern end of the north breakwater.

Berth
Berth at new pontoons in 3·0 to 3·5m.

Facilities
Water/electricity on the pontoons. Showers/toilets. Laundry, Diesel berth. Shops, restaurants and banks are all available in the town.

From Kühlungsborn the Molli, a steam railway, which has a gauge of only 90cm and is a great tourist attraction, runs through Heiligendamm and beautiful countryside into the centre of Bad Doberan, which has the Doberaner Munster, a great brick church built by the Cistercians between 1294 and 1368. It has never been bombed and remains beautifully intact and preserved.

Heiligendamm was established in 1793 as a spa, it is known as 'The White Town by the Sea' because of its white-painted, period buildings.

THE BALTIC SEA AND APPROACHES

WARNEMÜNDE

KÜHLUNGSBORN — Depths in Metres

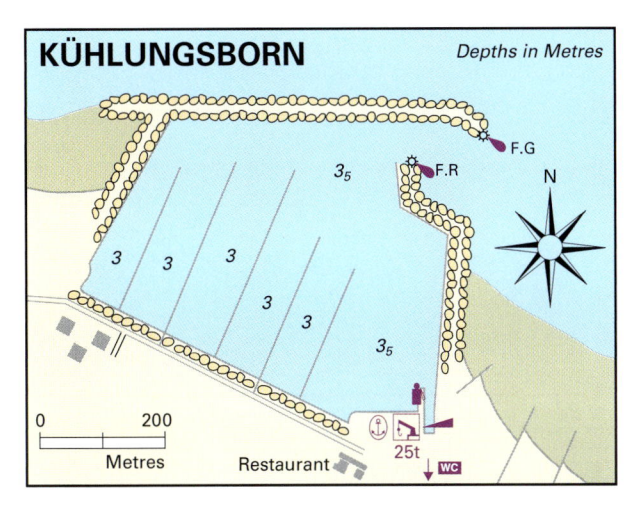

Kühlungsborn, Bad Doberan minster
Miranda Delmar-Morgan

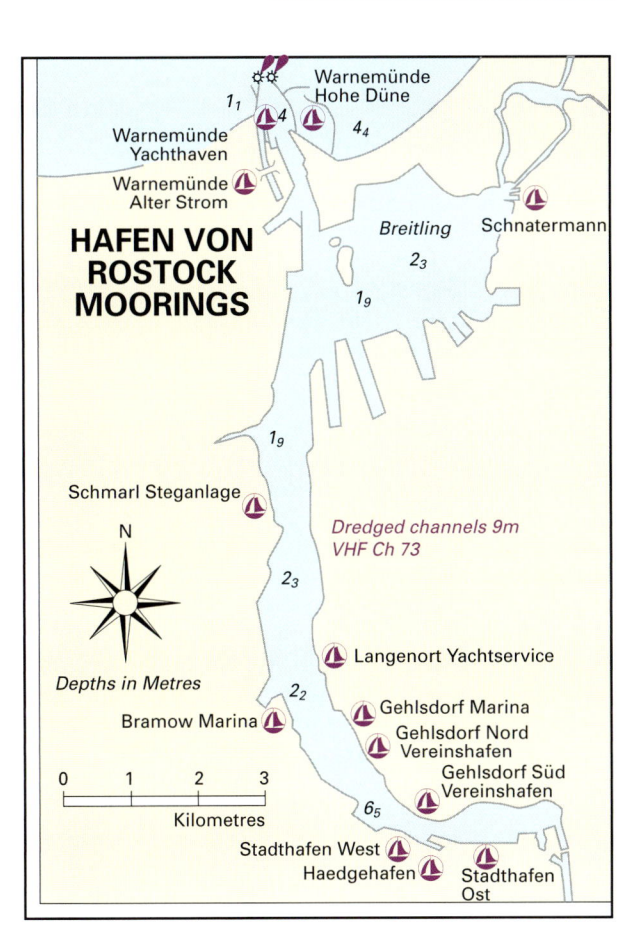

HAFEN VON ROSTOCK MOORINGS

Depths in Metres

Dredged channels 9m
VHF Ch 73

Warnemünde (with Rostock)

54°11'·2N 12°05'·2E west mole

Distances
Wismar 35M, Kühlungsborn 12M, Rostock 6M, Darsser Ort 30M, Stralsund 54M

Charts
UKHO 2370, 8026
German 163, 1671, 1672

Lights
Warnemünde, W side of entrance 54°10'·9N 12°05'·1E Fl(3+1)24s34m20M White round tower, black bands, two galleries, copper cupola 31m
Petersdorf Ldg Lts 161·6° *Front* 54°08'·7N 12°06'·8E Oc.R.4s24m12M Striped metal mast, red top 21m *Rear* 0·84M from front Oc.R.4s45m15M Striped metal mast, red top 33m
West mole head, E arm 54°11'·2N 12°05'·2E Iso.G.4s14m6M Green tower, white band, two galleries 12m Floodlit
East mole 54°11'·2N 12°05'·5E Iso.R.4s14m6M Red tower, white band, two balconies 12m Floodlit

Communications
Warnemünde/Rostock Vessel Traffic Service ℡ +49 381 2067 1141/2 *VHF* Ch 73, 16 (vessels must maintain a listening watch on VHF Ch 73 – broadcasts on VHF Ch 73 every two hours from 0515–2115 LT in German, English on request)
Rostock Port Authority ℡ +49 38 1381 3500 *VHF* Ch 10
Alter Strom ℡ +49 3815 1864
Hohe Düne Yachthafen ℡ +49 0381 5040 8080 www.yachthafen-hohe-duene.de
www.warnemunde.de

General
Warnemünde, a holiday resort and ferry terminal, still maintains an inshore fishing fleet which ties up with yachts in the Alter Strom alongside gabled houses. It lies at the entrance to the huge, commercial but ancient Hanseatic port of Rostock, whose docks and shipyards stretch for 15M due south from Warnemünde along the River Warnow. Warnemünde is a good base from which to visit Rostock by train.

Approach and entrance
54°13N 12°04'E

The harbour mouth is very obvious both by day and by night, and is equipped with powerful leading lights. There are no hazards outside the harbour, and there is a well-buoyed fairway extending some 7M out to the Rostock fairway buoy but beware of commercial traffic which must not be obstructed.

The harbour mouth is divided into two, the eastern side being the deep-water channel to the large and busy commercial port and to Rostock, whilst the western side leads to the yacht harbour and the fishing port. On the east side of the entrance the very grand Hohe Düne development has been built with its own large and well appointed marina. This has its own straightforward entrance as in the plan on page 49. Immediately inside the western entrance of the main harbour there are again two channels, the eastern one leading past the entrance to the yacht harbour before rejoining the deep-water

1. GERMANY

THE BALTIC SEA AND APPROACHES   **47**

1C. KIELER FÖRDE TO MECKLENBURGER BUCHT

Warnemünde old harbour Miranda Delmar-Morgan

channel, and the western one being the Alter Strom, which is much used by fishing boats and tourist vessels. At night, beware several unlit dolphins at the seaward end of the dividing wall between the yacht harbour and the Alter Strom.

Anchorage
Do not anchor in this busy waterway.

Berthing
The Alter Strom, which is much the most picturesque and convenient area in which to berth, is now very congested with fishing boats and tourist vessels. Yachts may have difficulty finding a berth and may have to raft up to a fishing boat. Maximum draught 3·1m. It is uncomfortable in onshore winds.

The Yachthafen to the east of the Alter Strom is fairly convenient but is subject to surge in onshore winds and from ships passing in the main channel. It has box berths and the entrance carries a depth of only 2·2m.

The Hohe Düne marina is more expensive but the berths (box berths bows-to-pontoon) are well sheltered. There are toilet facilities on some of the pontoons. Empty pontoons may indicate that those particular facilities are not in use. If you arrive out of office hours you can collect a key card from the 5 star spa hotel.

Services
Water, electricity, toilets and showers are available in the Alter Strom, Yachthafen and at Hohe Düne. Fuel berths in the Alter Strom and Hohe Düne. Camping Gaz from SchiffService Warnow Werkstatte Warnemünde (who are also Volvo Penta agents) in the Alter Strom. There is a crane capable of lifting 2·5 tonnes at the yacht harbour, and a larger one capable of handling 40 tonnes at Hohe Düne.

General facilities
Provisions are available from nearby shops, and there are stalls selling pancakes, hot dogs and other forms of fast food on the Alter Strom. Since this is a holiday resort, there is a very wide range of restaurants, hotels and banks to choose from. The Hohe Düne has a luxury hotel and a large choice of restaurants, cafés and bars on the marina-side.

A supermarket is on the other side of the river in the centre of town. It is a short walk and a ferry ride to reach the town. Trains to Rostock for onward journeys to Berlin and Hamburg.

Communications and travel
There is a regular ferry sailing to Gedser in Denmark, Trelleborg in Sweden and Ventspils in Latvia while the centre of Rostock is no more than 10 minutes by the S-bahn railway.

Warnemünde Alter Strom Miranda Delmar-Morgan

WARNEMÜNDE

Approach to Rostock Miranda Delmar-Morgan

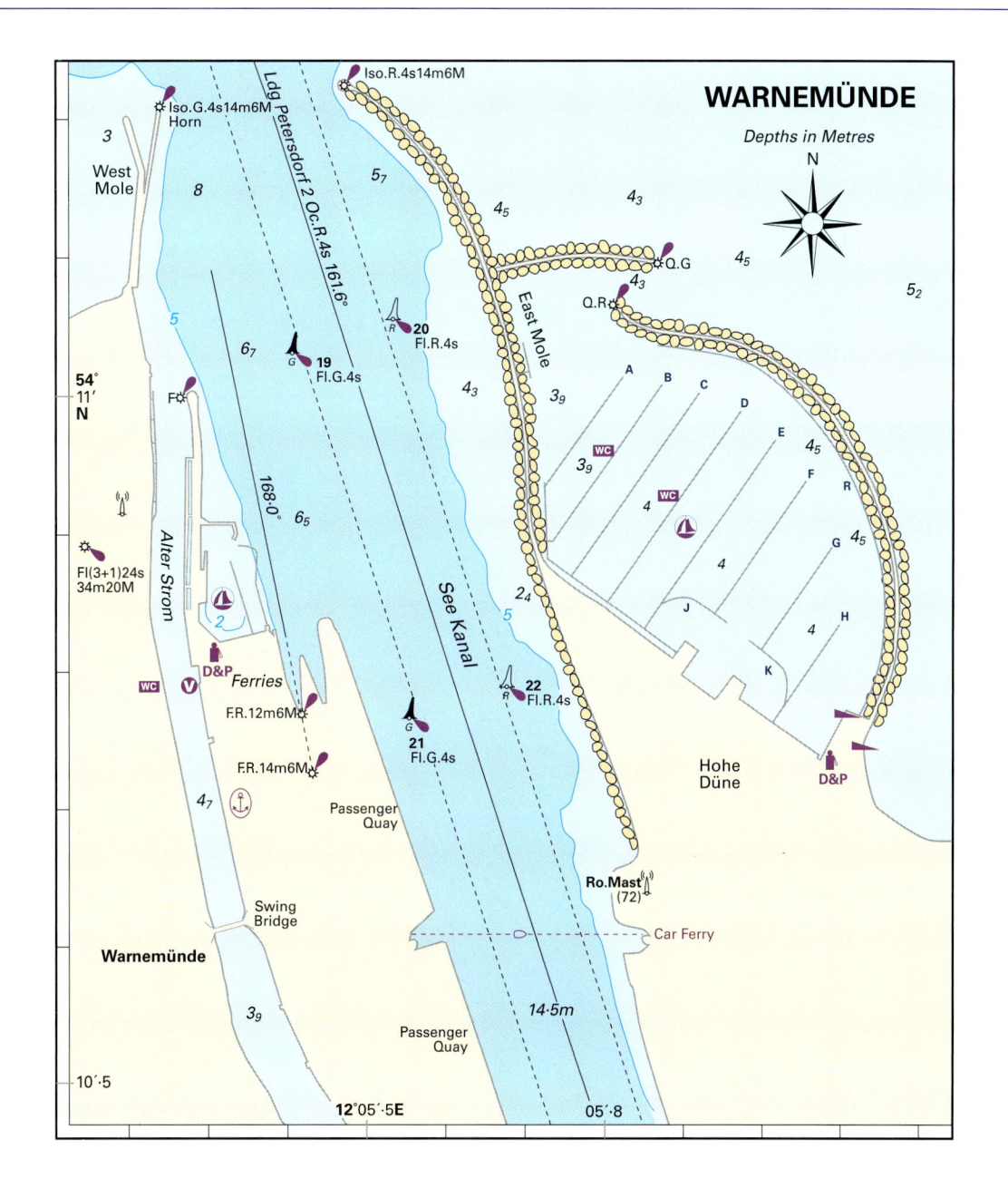

Upriver to Rostock

From Warnemünde yachts can take the well-marked main channel 6M upriver to Rostock, the largest town in the area and notable for its numerous fine buildings, many of which survive despite heavy bombing during the Second World War. The centrepiece is the Marienkirche, an immense gothic edifice built over a period of 400 years, which houses a late 15th-century astronomical clock and a famous baroque organ.

Pilotage is straightforward, past the shipyards and docks, though the passage is best made in daylight due to numerous unlit buoys and projecting wooden jetties. Around Gehlsdorf there are a number of small yacht harbours along the east bank of the river, but these are not well situated for exploring Rostock, (see plan on page 47). Beyond Gehlsdorf the river runs east/west and a variety of berthing options are available on the south (city) bank. The first is in the Haedge Hafen by the Rostocker Segelverein. Further upstream, between the conspicuous Volks Theater and A.G. Getreide buildings, there are more small marinas until one reaches the town quay (Stadthafen Ost). This is separated from the town by a very busy main road but the town is worth a visit. There is a BSH

THE BALTIC SEA AND APPROACHES   **49**

1. GERMANY

1C. KIELER FÖRDE TO MECKLENBURGER BUCHT

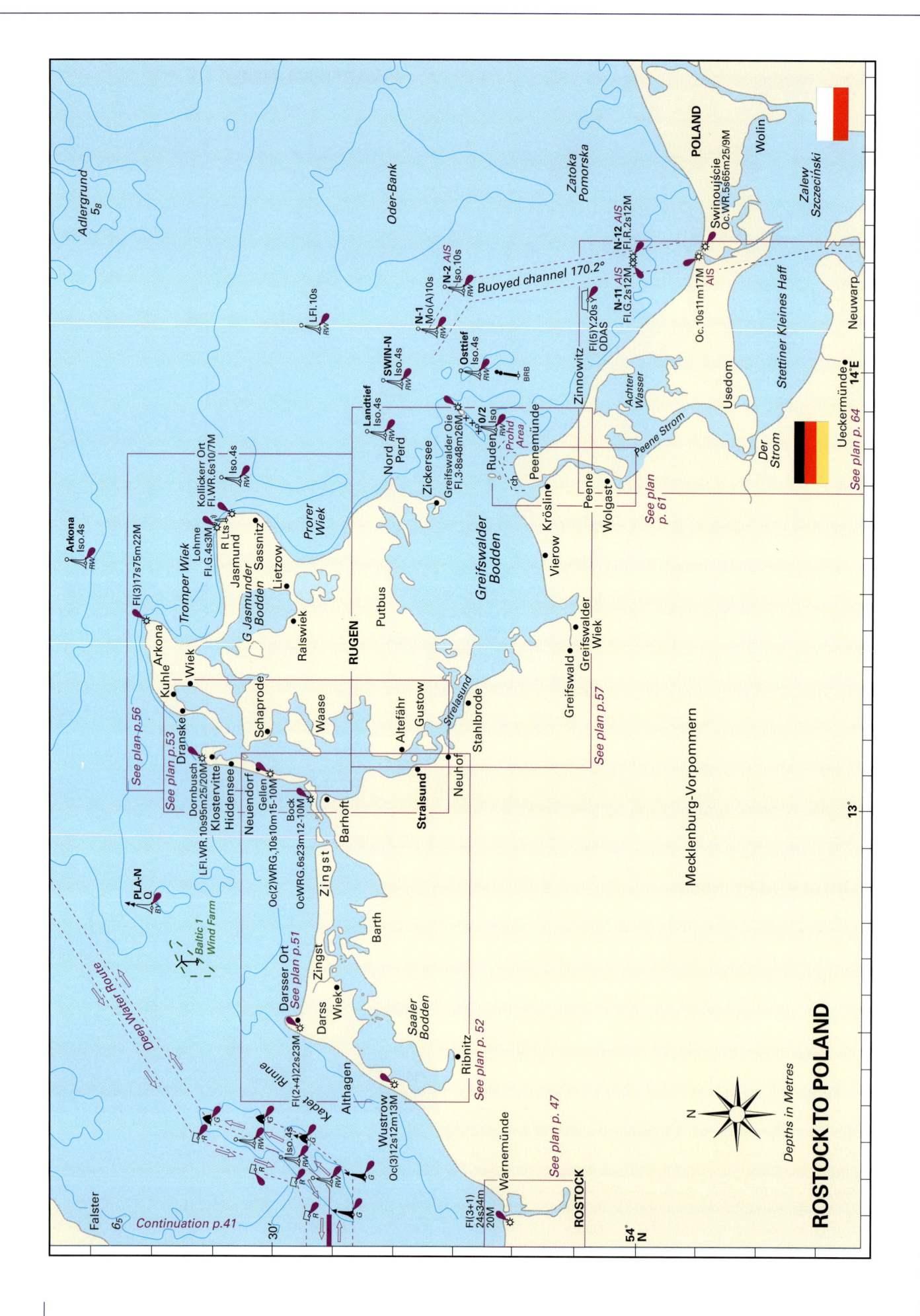

WARNEMÜNDE TO THE ENTRANCE TO THE STRELASUND

Rostock main square Miranda Delmar-Morgan

Hydrographic Office here, and a branch of Nautischer Dienst Kapitän Stegmann, Admiralty chart agents. The harbourmaster is in the ground floor of the local chandlery. Washing machines and good facilities.

All normal shopping facilities, hotels, banks and restaurants are available in the town centre, and the town has good rail connections with Berlin and Hamburg. Outside Rostock is the open air Klockenhagen Museum illustrating a regional farmhouse and farming. It is possible to take the train further afield, from Warnemünde to Rostock and on to Bad Doberan (see Kühlungsborn).

Smokehouse, Rostock Miranda Delmar-Morgan

Warnemünde to the entrance to the Strelasund

Mecklenburger Bucht Traffic Separation Scheme

It should be noted that there is a Traffic Separation Scheme between Falster (Denmark) and the German coast between Warnemünde and Darsser Ort (see plan opposite).

Darsser Ort

54°28'·3N 12°31'·5E Harbour groyne
Charts UKHO 2365, 2601; German 162

The harbour entrance frequently silts over and gets closed for long periods before it is re-dredged to 3m. The SAR vessel was relocated to Barhoft several years ago. The steg has had the cleats removed, some say by conservationists who do not want yachts in this nature resort, but the stern buoys remain in place. The wildlife is said to be spectacular but there is also a prolific mosquito population. It is retained in this book as an emergency stop between Warnemünde and Stralsund which are 54M apart. Anchoring is not allowed in the harbour. One might, in extremis, gain shelter by anchoring in 6m in the lee of the headland, to the south east to avoid westerlies, but bear in mind that it is a *Schutzzone* of the national park. The shoal off the point of Darsser Ort is marked by east and west cardinal buoys, but the narrow and silting entrance needs a cautious approach. When the harbour is closed the lights are extinguished. In 2015 the entrance was dredged and declared open for emergencies only. Call Stralsund harbourmaster for confirmation that it is open. There are plans for a marina on the Baltic side of Prerow.

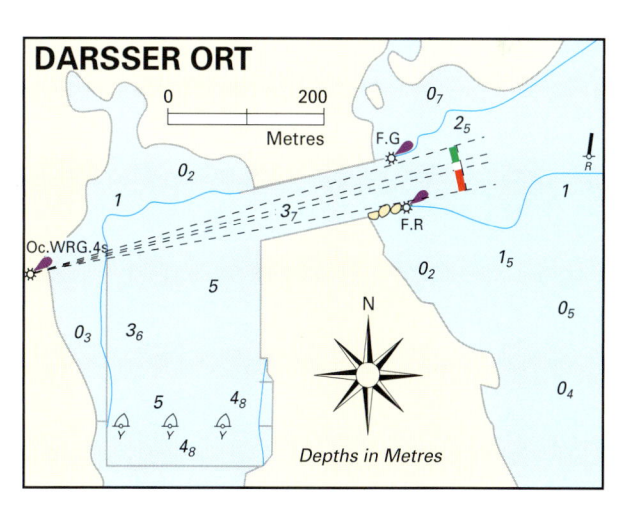

1. GERMANY

THE BALTIC SEA AND APPROACHES   51

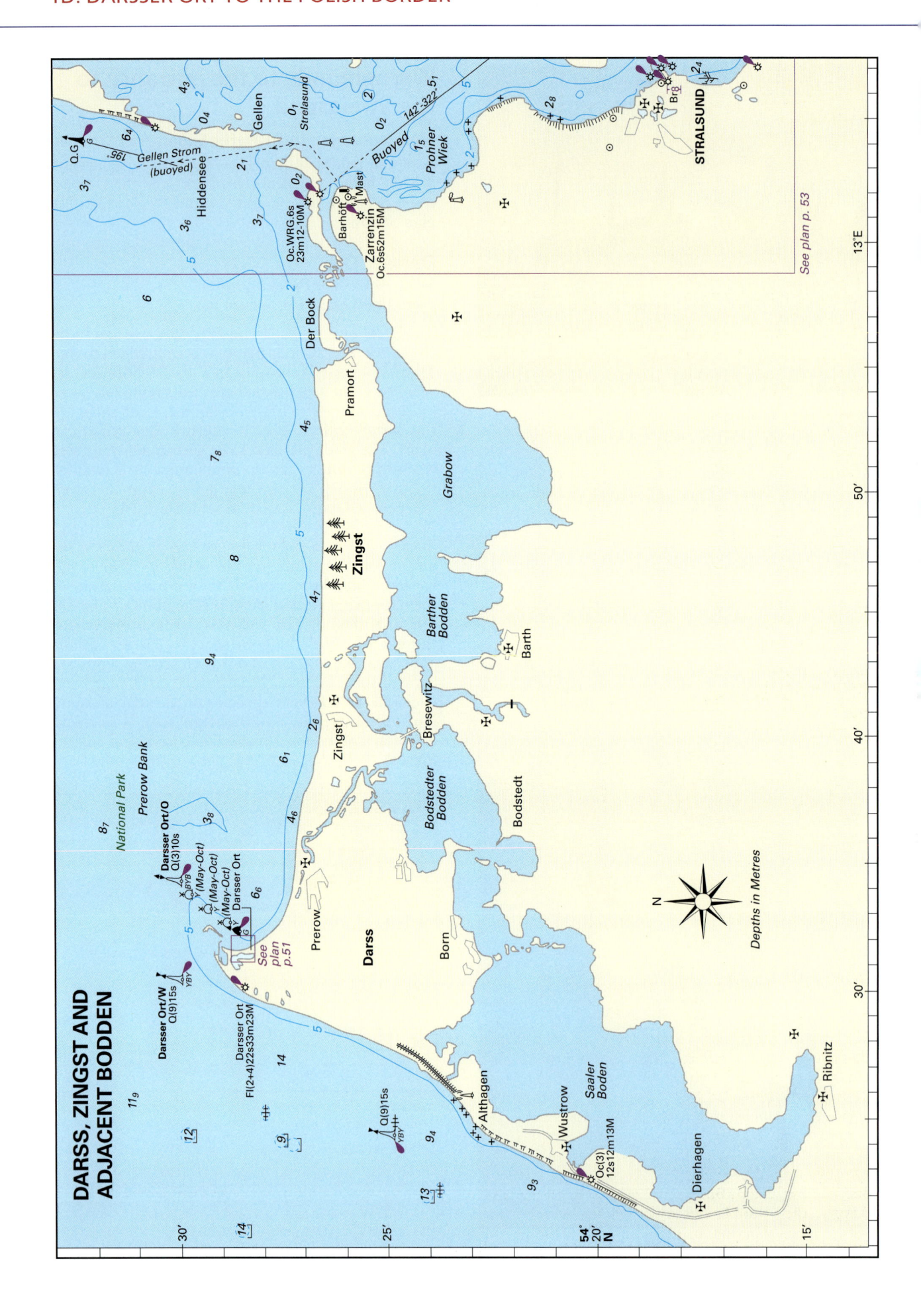

1D. DARSSER ORT TO THE POLISH BORDER

NORTHERN APPROACHES TO THE STRELASUND

1d. Darsser Ort to the Polish border

In order to get from Darsser Ort to Poland, the quickest route is probably to stay offshore and leave the island of Rügen to starboard. Since Darsser Ort is now an 'emergencies only' haven (see above) this involves a passage of around 100 miles from Warnemünde to Sassnitz, the first good harbour on the outer side of Rügen Island, with a further 40 miles to Świnoujście, the nearest port in Poland. Unless you are contemplating a long passage to the Gulf of Gdańsk this makes little sense, and would entail missing the Boddens and Haffs sheltered by the islands and sometimes likened to the Norfolk Broads on a grand scale.

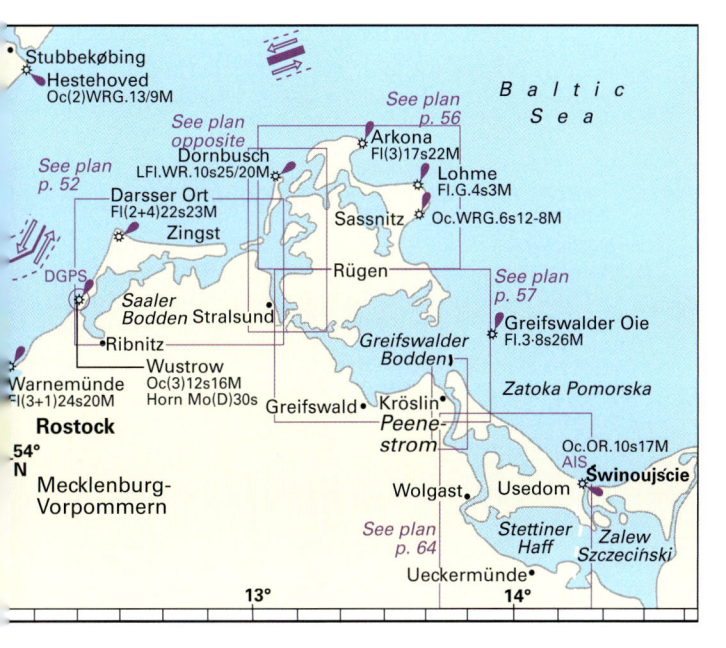

Barth
54°22′N 12°43′E

Yachtsmen wishing to sample this area might consider a visit to Barth at the head of the Barther Bodden, where there are a couple of well-equipped marinas, huge wintering sheds, a railway to Stralsund, and all the facilities of an interesting small town close at hand. It was home to Stalag Luft 1 PoW camp during the Second World War.

Northern approaches to the Strelasund

Saaler Bodden, Bodstetter Bodden, Barther Bodden and Grabow

Given the 'emergency only' access to Darsser Ort one must assume that there are no harbours between Warnemünde and the entrance to the Strelasund. The coast shields an extensive area of shallow Bodden, which are entered from the Strelasund just north of the small fishing and yacht harbour of Barhöft (54°26′N 13°02′E). The Bodden are well buoyed and contain a number of charming little harbours, but it is essential to have the large-scale charts of the area to get to them (e.g. BSH Sportschiffahrtskarten 3008). To access the western Bodden (Saaler and Bodstetter) it is necessary to pass through the swing bridge at Bresewitz, which from May to September opens daily at 0745, 0945, 1745 and 2045 LT, for a maximum of 15 minutes. It opens less often in winter.

THE BALTIC SEA AND APPROACHES 53

1. GERMANY

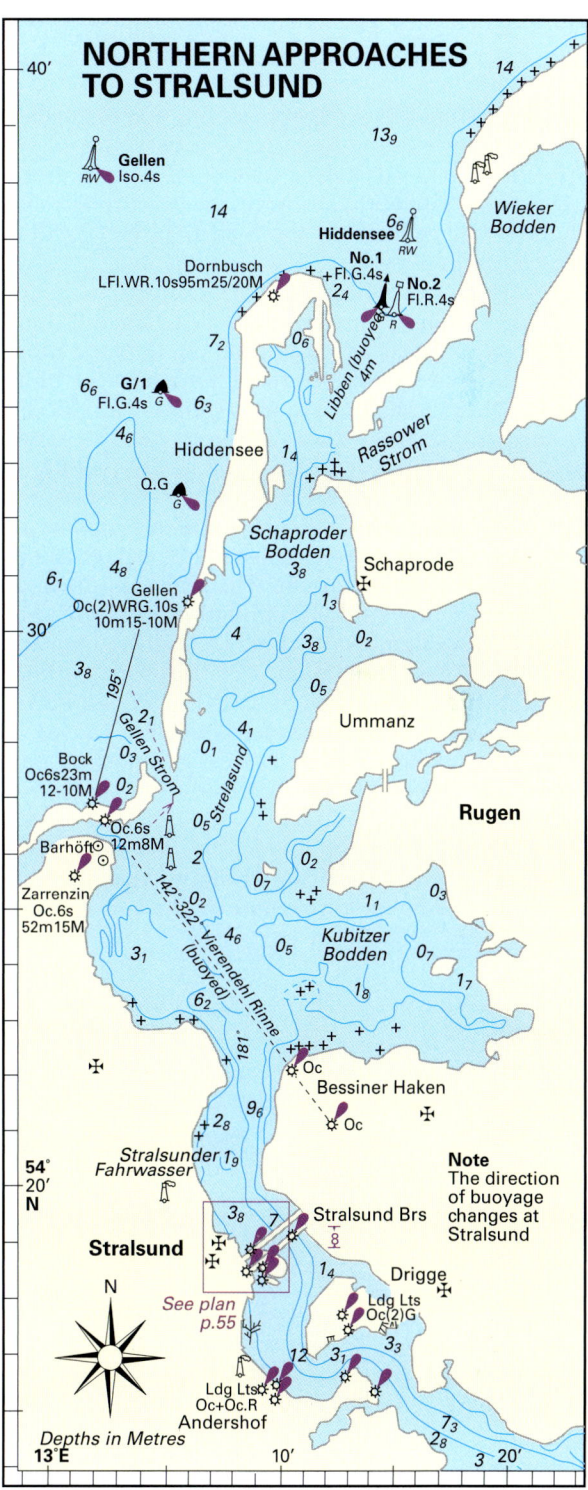

1D. DARSSER ORT TO THE POLISH BORDER

At sea off Hiddensee Miranda Delmar-Morgan

The Strelasund offers the opportunity for yachtsmen to take an interesting route inside Rügen island, via Stralsund, to Greifswalder Bodden. This is a shortcut to the northern entrance of the Peenestrom channel which leads to the Stettiner Haff (Zalew Szczeciński).

The northern approach via the Gellenstrom west of Hiddensee island, starts at the Gellen Landfall Buoy (54°38'·4N 13°02'·6E) although from the west it is more practical to enter the channel at No. 1 G buoy (54°33'·9N 13°03'·4E) or in quiet conditions at No. 3/5 G buoy (54°32'·1N 13°03'·9E) in the western W sector of the Gellen Light (54°30'·5N 13°04'·5E Oc(2)WRG.10s10m15–10M white round metal tower, red top, stone base) although it would be unwise to attempt this approach to Stralsund in the dark as not all the channel buoys are lit. The latter approach to No. 3/5 G buoy carries a minimum depth of 3m. There is a designated anchorage (*Reede*) between Barhöft and Bock near G buoy 29. In strong onshore winds it would be prudent to reach the Strelasund via the channels of the Schaproder Bodden in the lee of Hiddensee. These channels are well-marked and dredged to 2·5m and can be entered from the Libben to the northeast of Hiddensee at 54°36'N 13°10'·9E. Vitte and Kloster on Hiddensee are delightful. However, in the dark or in strong northerly winds course should be set for Sassnitz on the east coast of Rügen.

Hiddensee, Vitte yacht harbour Miranda Delmar-Morgan

Stralsund

54°19'N 13°06'E

Distances
Warnemünde 51M, Świnoujście 50M, Szczecin 85M

Charts
UKHO 2944, 2945
German 162, 1622, 1579, 1511

Lights
Approach
Darsser Ort 54°28'·4N 12°30'·2E Fl(2+4)22s33m23M Round red tower, brown cupola and building 35m
Zarrenzin Ldg Lts 195·1° *Front* 54°26'·9N 13°01'·4E Oc.WR.6s23m12M 089°-W-180°-R-191°-W-290°-G-308°-W-069° White framework tower, red lantern and gallery with white roof, grey stone base, white stripe 23m
Rear 1·3M from front Oc.6s52m15M White metal framework tower, red bands and lantern, white cupola 24m Visible on leading line only
Kap Arkona 54°40'·8N 13°25'·9E Fl(3)17s75m22M Red lantern on yellow round tower with two galleries 35m
Channel
Bock Ldg Lts 322·1° *Front* 54°27'N 13°02'E Oc.6s12m8M 302°-vis-342° White framework tower, red lantern and gallery with white roof, grey stone base, white stripe 13m
Rear 700m from front, as above. A back bearing on 322·1° can be used when heading south towards Stralsund

Communications
Stralsund North and Stralsund East Vessel Traffic Services ✆ +49 381 2067 1143, VHF Ch 16, 67 (vessels must maintain a listening watch on VHF Ch 16 or 67 – broadcasts on VHF Ch 67 every two hours 0635–2235 and at 0235 LT). (Office hrs 0700–2000 Monday–Friday, 0700–1300 and 1800–2000 LT weekends and holidays). Port Ops VHF Ch 11.
City Marina harbourmaster ✆ +49 38 3144 4978
www.rundtoern-marinas.com

Stralsund was founded in 1209 and joined the Hanseatic League in 1293. Like Wismar, it was under Swedish control in the 17th and 18th centuries and came under Prussian control in 1815. It was very badly damaged in British and US air raids during the Second World War. However the fine Town Hall survived, and over its windows on the market side can be seen the arms of Hamburg, Lübeck, Wismar, Rostock, Stralsund and Greifswald. The three parish churches of St Mary, St James (Jacobikirche) and St Nicholas demonstrate the prosperity of the town – especially the last, which was started in the 13th century and largely rebuilt after a fire in 1662. The award winning 'Ozeaneum' maritime museum has aquariums for the North and Baltic seas and the North Atlantic, and studies the life and biology of the Boddens.

This is an attractive port and holiday resort, full of old-world charm and with many historic buildings, cobbled streets and a lively open-air market. A vast amount of high-quality restoration work has been completed and more is being done. There are many good, modern shops. Direct trains to Berlin.

54 THE BALTIC SEA AND APPROACHES

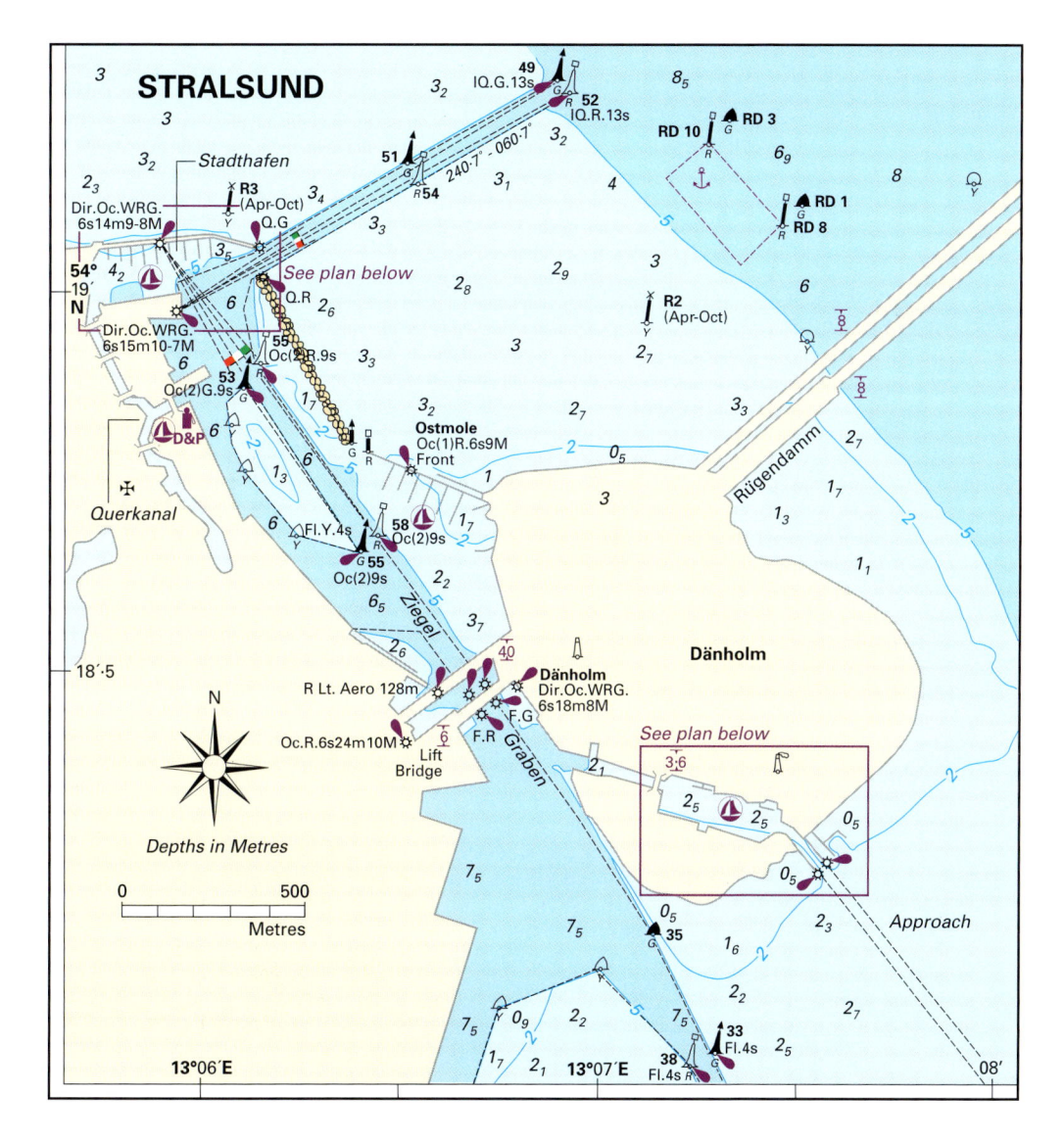

STRALSUND

Approach

The port lies on the west bank of the Strelasund, the narrow channel between the island of Rügen and the mainland, where the small island of Dänholm provided a convenient bridging point. Whether coming from the north or the south it is necessary to navigate through this channel, which is tortuous but very clearly marked and well lit. There is sometimes a small current in the Strelasund, with a direction and strength dependent on wind conditions over the southern Baltic.

The approach from the north is via the Gellenstrom (see above) and this leads eventually into the Strelasund via channels dredged to 4·5m. If intending to continue south to the Greifswalder Bodden, it will be necessary to enter Stralsund harbour to pass through the opening bridge, whether or not one stops at Stralsund itself. This bridge opens five times daily at 0520, 0820, 1220, 1720, 2130 but a check should be made at harbour offices or by calling *Stralsund Traffic* (VHF 16/67). City Marina has a printout of the times.

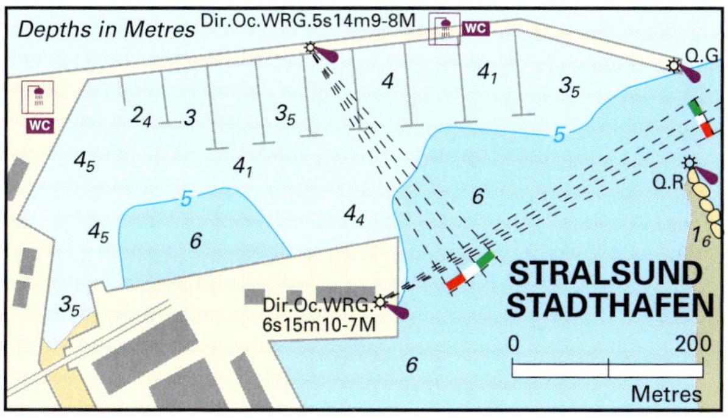

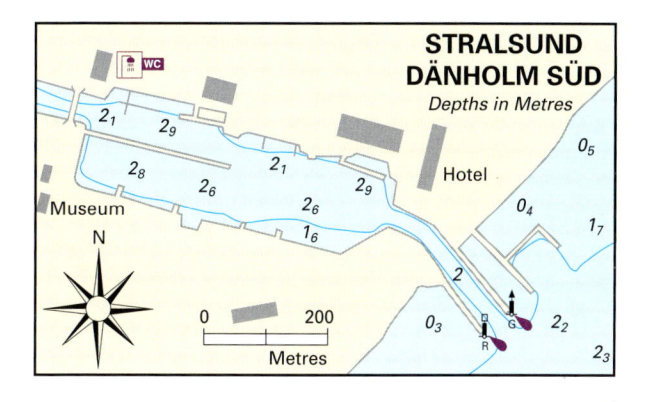

THE BALTIC SEA AND APPROACHES 55

1D. DARSSER ORT TO THE POLISH BORDER

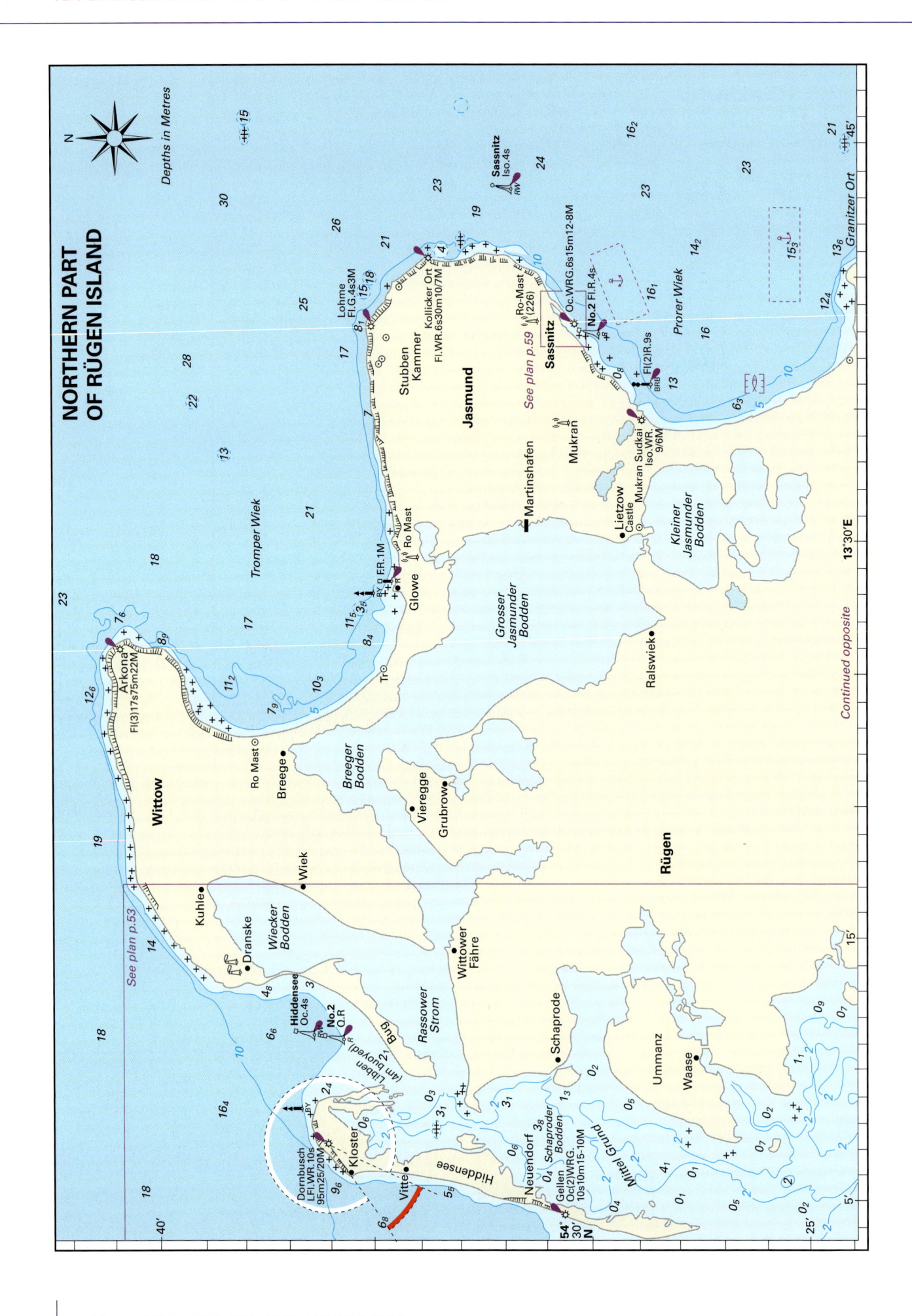

NORTHERN PART OF RÜGEN ISLAND

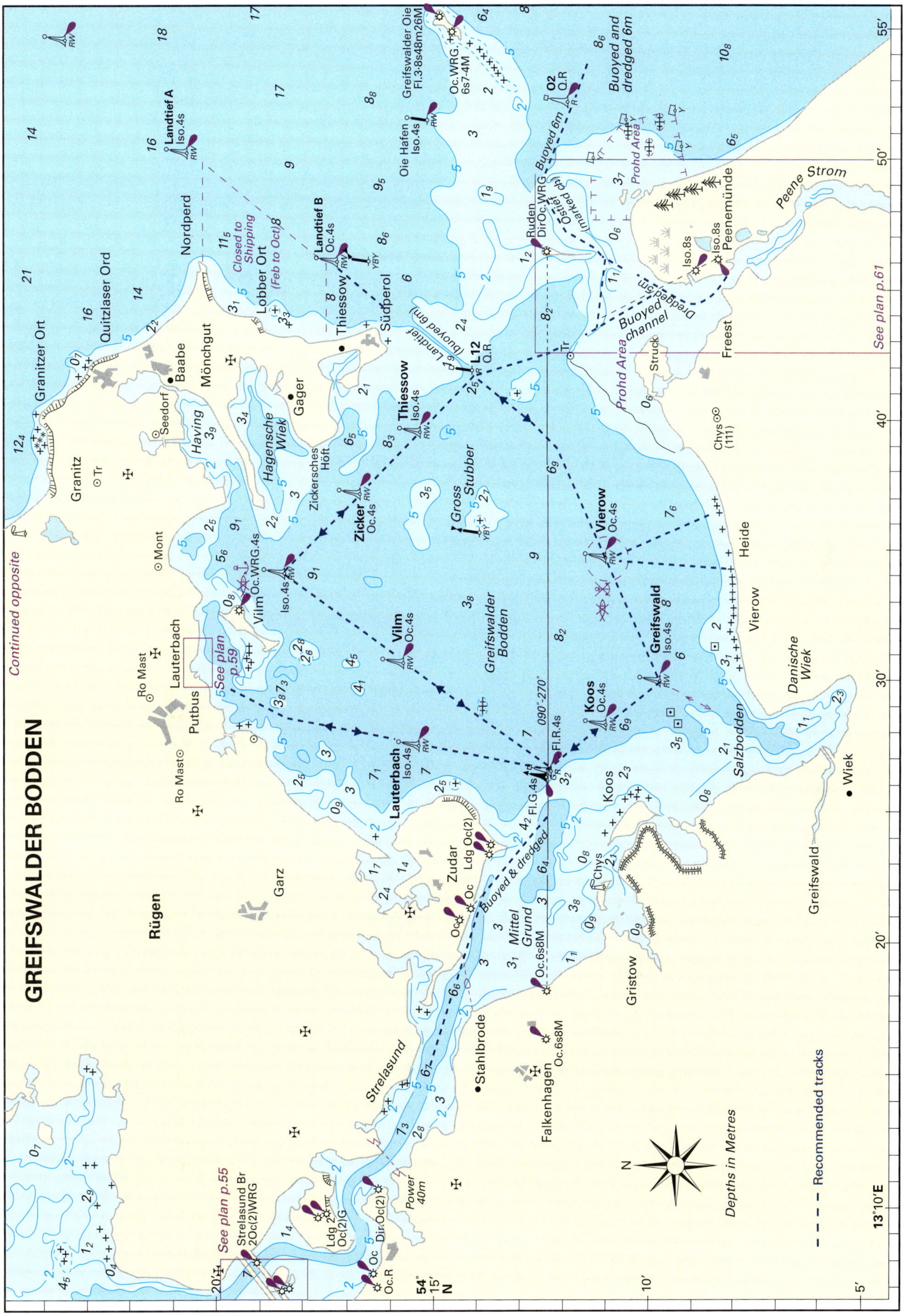
GREIFSWALDER BODDEN
Continued opposite
Rügen
Granitzer Ort
Quitzlaser Ord
Granitz
Nordperd
Lobber Ort
Closed to Shipping (Feb to Oct)
Landtief A Iso.4s
Landtief B Oc.4s
Baabe
Mönchgut
Seedorf
Having
Hagensche Wiek
Gager
Zickersches Höft
Thiessow
Südperol
Landtief (buoyed 6m)
L12 Q.R
Thiessow Iso.4s
Zicker Oc.4s
Gross Stubber
Mont
Vilm Oc.WRG.4s
Vilm Iso.4s
Vilm Oc.4s
Lauterbach
See plan p.59
Putbus
Ro Mast
Lauterbach Iso.4s
Greifswalder Bodden
Garz
Zudar
Ldg Oc(2)
Buoyed & dredged
Mittel Grund
Oc.6s8M
Fl.R.4s
Fl.G.4s
090°-270°
Koos Oc.4s
Koos
Chys
Gristow
Greifswald Iso.4s
Vierow Oc.4s
Vierow
Heide
Danische Wiek
Salzbodden
Wiek
Greifswald
Stahlbrode
Falkenhagen
Oc.6s8M
Strelasund
Strelasund Br 2Oc(2)WRG
See plan p.55
Ldg Oc(2)G
Dir.Oc(2)
Oc
Oc.R
Power 40m
Depths in Metres
Recommended tracks
Greifswalder Oie Fl.3·8s48m26M
Oc.WRG. 6s7-4M
Oie Hafen Iso.4s
O2 Q.R
Buoyed 6m
Buoyed and dredged 6m
Ruden DirOc.WRG
Ostief ch (marked)
Prohd Area
Peenemünde
Iso.8s
Peene Strom
Buoyed channel
Dredged 5m
Struck
Freest
See plan p.61
Chys (111)
54° 15′ N
13°10′E
20′
30′
40′
50′
55′

1D. DARSSER ORT TO THE POLISH BORDER

Stralsund, approach from north *Miranda Delmar-Morgan*

Approaching from the south, the channel divides around the island of Dänholm (see plan page 55), the western fork (the Ziegel Graben) leading to the town through twin lifting road and rail bridges (see above for opening times). There are no shoreside waiting berths. The new fixed motorway bridge just north of the lifting bridge has a clearance of 40m. The longer part of the railway bridge connecting Dänholm to the larger island of Rügen does not open, and has a fixed height of 8m.

The direction of buoyage changes at the bridges.

Anchorage
There are numerous anchorages outside the fairway, but appropriate signals must be displayed.

Berthing
Visiting yachts normally moor to pontoons in the Stadthafen which lies immediately to starboard after entering the harbour through the northern entrance. There are 240 berths, mostly alongside finger pontoons, but they are uncomfortable in southeasterly winds. Yachts may also be permitted to moor alongside the commercial quays midway between the north and south entrances, provided that no larger vessels are expected.

The basin at the south end of Dänholm island, which is accessed from the eastern fork (the main channel) of the Strelasund is quite small and usually full of local yachts. The yacht club at the northern end of Dänholm, to the north of the bridge might have berths, but it is quite exposed and both of these entail a long walk into the town centre. It is also possible to berth in the Querkanal close to the town centre but this has a depth of only 1·5m and has no facilities. Access is via an opening bridge which has fixed opening times.

Services
Water, electricity and WiFi are available on the City Marina pontoons, with showers and toilets on Pontoon 8 and near the harbourmaster's office. There is a chandlery on the quay north of the Querkanal, where Camping Gaz cylinders may be exchanged, and fuel from a jetty a little further south, near the Querkanal (operating times vary – enquire in advance).

General facilities
There are floating fish restaurants on the harbourside walls but otherwise all shops, banks and restaurants are in the town centre, within easy walking distance from the Stadthafen. There is an Edeka supermarket SW of the Rathaus, and various Nettos, Lidls and Aldis further out.

Communications and travel
There are good train services to Berlin and Rostock, but it should be noted that there are two railway stations, Hauptbahnhof to the west of, and for, the town centre, and Rugendamm for onward passage to Sassnitz, Mukran ferry port and Sweden.

Stralsund aerial view with Rügen in the background *Miranda Delmar-Morgan*

Stadthafen marina *Miranda Delmar-Morgan*

THE BALTIC SEA AND APPROACHES

GREIFSWALDER BODDEN

Rügen

For yachtsmen equipped with detailed German charts, Rügen offers numerous opportunities to discover a variety of small yacht harbours tucked away in the corners of the Bodden, on Hiddensee and the northern part of Rügen, all reached by closely buoyed and dredged channels.

Schaprode
54°30·84'N 13°09·6'E PHM 'Sch 6'
Charts UKHO 2365
German 64, 162,
☎ +49 383 0091209

Principal port for Hiddensee on the west coast of Rügen. Shallow approaches (2·5m channel) and busy with ferries. Floating pontoons beyond ferry berths. Small town with mediaeval church. Diesel. Facilities but no provisions. Many cars left here by visitors going to the car-free Hiddensee.

Sassnitz
54°30·3'N 13°38·2'E east mole
Charts UKHO 2365
German 162, 151, 1516
Port Authority ☎ +49 383 92 661 570, VHF Ch 69
Marina HM ☎ +49 162 23 70 864
www.stadhafen-sassnitz.de

The only harbour of any consequence on the 'outside' of Rügen is Sassnitz, which lies on the east coast. Although still an active fishing port, the major ferry activity has now transferred to a new ferry port at Neu Mukran some 3M to the southwest. A small local ferry runs trips to Cap Arcona. There is a new City Marina with many box berths and all facilities at this useful staging point. Diesel at the bunker station on the quayside.

Greifswalder Bodden

The southern end of the Strelasund leads into Greifswalder Bodden, a large body of mostly navigable water to the south of Rügen (see page 57).

From the eastern end of Greifswalder Bodden there are two alternatives:
- Via one of the two dredged channels through to the open Baltic, either northeast for Sweden and Bornholm or southeast for Świnoujście and the Polish coast;
- Or – more interestingly – via the Peenestrom channel through to the Stettiner Haff (Zalew Szczeciński), a lake some 30 miles long straddling the German/Polish border from which there is access back into the Baltic (see page 343).

Lauterbach
54°20·2'N 13°30·4'E south mole
Charts UKHO 2365
German 151, 1511, 1578
Im-jaich marina ☎ +49 38 301 8090 www.im-jaich.de

Lauterbach is on the north side of Greifswalder Bodden, on the south coast of Rügen island. The Im-jaich marina has 300 box berths on pontoons with 2·9 to 3·4m depths behind the eastern breakwaters, fresh bread rolls to order. Beware narrow entrance and tight turns inside the breakwaters. Fuel berth in the communal harbour where there are also some berths for visitors, WC €0.50, lovely walks and cycle rides. Putbus, about 1·5km inland, once a highly fashionable summer resort with a theatre, and Prince Putbus' palace are well worth a visit. Surviving from those days are a park and a circular terrace of fine houses. A narrow-guage steam train runs from beside the marina and will take you close to the palace (see Seedorf). A supermarket and other shops will be found a short walk along the road to Putbus. There is a large charter fleet here, and it is also the home of Vilm Yachts.

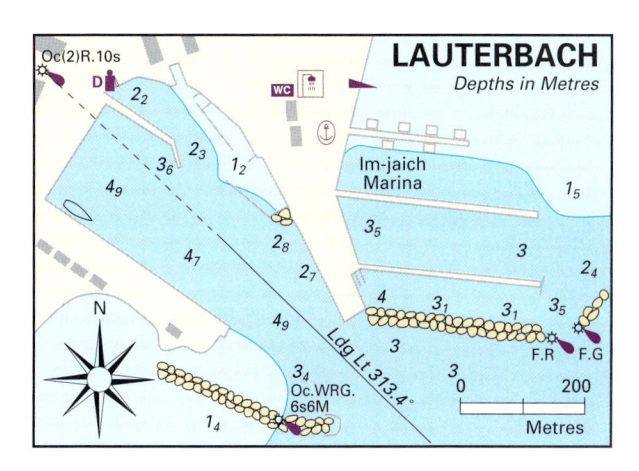

1. GERMANY

THE BALTIC SEA AND APPROACHES

1D. DARSSER ORT TO THE POLISH BORDER

Seedorf Fischräucherei Miranda Delmar-Morgan

Seedorf
54°21′N 13°39′E
Charts UKHO 2365
German 151, 1511, 1578
☎ +44 383 03736

Seedorf, also on the south coast of Rügen island, east of Lauterbach, is a beautiful natural harbour in unspoilt country, with some 40 berths amongst the reeds. It is approached by a buoyed channel with minimum depth of 2–6m. There are no facilities, but it is the harbour from which to visit the Jagdschloss, Prince Putbus' amazing hunting 'lodge' in the Granitz wood. Although a 4km walk, the schloss is well worth the effort. There are spectacular views if you can brave the open sided spiral staircase! On the way one may also encounter the steam train which runs in a loop around this part of the island. There is an excellent fish shop with pickled herring rolls and fish brötchen. A travelling van visits with basic provisions.

Gager
54°18·72′N 13°40·0′E mole end
Charts UKHO 2365
German charts 151, 1511, 1578
☎ +49 383 088210

A charming little place on the eastern edge of Greifswalder Bodden with a lovely walk up the hill onto the Mönchgut Peninsula. Newly extended breakwater with sternbuoys, depths of 4·5m, and improved facilities. Buoyed channel, unlit lateral buoys. Laundry facility at camp site. Biosphere reservation area.

Greifswald/Greifswald Wieck
54°05·8′N 13°27·4′E Wiek north mole
Charts UKHO 2150
German 151, 1511
Greifswald Yachtzentrum ☎ +49 383 457920

In the southwest corner of Greifswalder Bodden lies the attractive harbour of Greifswald Wieck, with simple facilities and shopping in Wieck on the north bank. At the top of the harbour a charming wooden drawbridge, which opens about every hour (times on the bridge), allows yachts to access the university town of Greifswald some 2·5M up the river Ryck. Beware raised sections of the bridge which do not open fully vertically, (cap shrouds have been known to get caught with the inevitable consequence!). At

Greifswald Wieck drawbridge with broken mast!
Miranda Delmar-Morgan

Right Greifswald Rathaus
Below Greifswald Wieck flood defences
Miranda Delmar-Morgan

60   THE BALTIC SEA AND APPROACHES

PEENEMÜNDE AND THE NORTHERN PEENESTROM

Greifswald, yachts lie alongside in the Museumhafen along with many historic boats close to the town centre. Diesel is available. The town has been much renovated and has a beautiful market square.

Ruden and Greifswalder Oie
54°12'N 13°46'E and 54°15'N 13°54'E
Charts UKHO 2365
German 151, 1511, 1512, 1578

Small island addicts may wish to visit Ruden and Greifswalder Oie in the eastern approaches to Greifswalder Bodden. Neither has any facilities. Ruden, now a nature reserve which can be walked around, still has the remains of missile tracking facilities which were installed to observe the trials of V1 and V2 missiles launched from Peenemünde. Greifswalder Oie is simply an unspoilt island which is also a nature reserve and subject to restrictions.

Peenemünde and the northern Peenestrom
Marina Kröslin ✆ +49 383 70 2510
Karlshagen marina ✆ +49 383 712 0066

The northern end of the Peenestrom passes Peenemünde, the German wartime research and development site for the V1 and V2 'Doodlebug' missiles, which some consider to be the birthplace of space flight. The site, now a museum of rocketry, is well worth a visit for those with an interest in military history or engineering. An old Russian submarine is berthed in the harbour which has basic facilities.

Opposite Peenemünde, on the west bank of the Peenestrom, is the large modern marina at Kröslin (54°07'N 13°45'E), with finger pontoons, good repair and servicing facilities and diesel. The marina is well sheltered and a yacht could safely be left there for an extended period. A small supermarket and other shops are to be found in the nearby village. Buses to Wolgast for trains to Berlin. Karlshagen, just south of Peenemünde, has a modern marina but it is a bit of a walk into town. There is a train to Peenemünde. Birdlife is abundant on the Peenestrom and one is unlucky not to see white-tailed sea eagles.

Peenemünde, old Luftwaffe tower with Ruden island in the background *Miranda Delmar-Morgan*

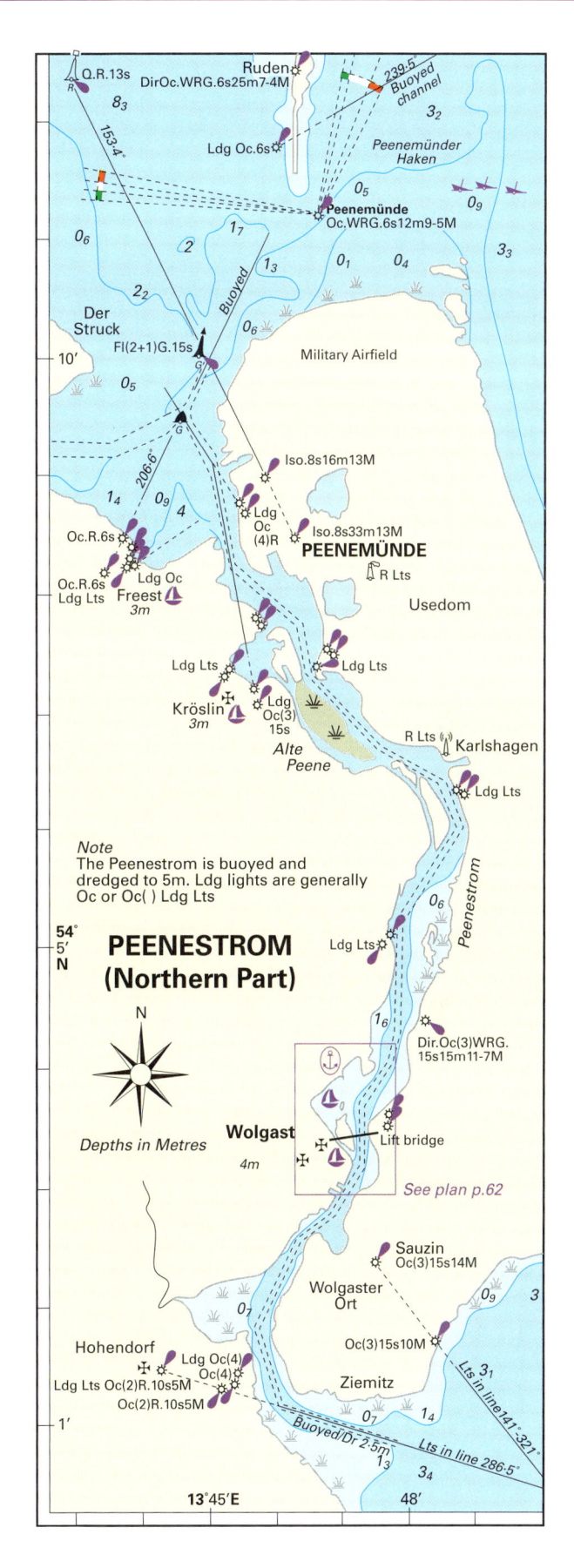

1. GERMANY

THE BALTIC SEA AND APPROACHES

1D. DARSSER ORT TO THE POLISH BORDER

Peenemünde, looking down the Peenestrom
Miranda Delmar-Morgan

Wolgast
54°03′N 13°47′E
Charts UKHO 2150
German 151, 1512, 1513
Wolgast Stadthafen ✆ + 49 383 3620 2238
Wolgast Bridge ✆ +49 3836 232 4458 or +49 755 773 610
Summer opening times 0545, 0745, 1245, 1645, 2045 and 2345 LT. Call ten minutes beforehand
Wolfgast VTS ✆ +49 381 2067 1144

Wolgast is an attractive small town, recently much restored. South of the bridge, yachts can berth on the town quay in about 3m on the south side of Schlossinsel, provided commercial vessels are not expected. It is only a short walk from the town centre. There are basic facilities with a chandlery nearby, Camping Gaz, as well as the usual domestic shops. A long electric cable is needed. North of the bridge there is a small marina also on Schlossinsel but further from the town. Diesel is available. There is a big shipbuilding facility here and associated shipping movements. Wolgast VTS transmits on VHF Ch 09 every two hours from 0515–2115 LT. Situation Reports are available on VHF Ch 14 in German and English on demand.

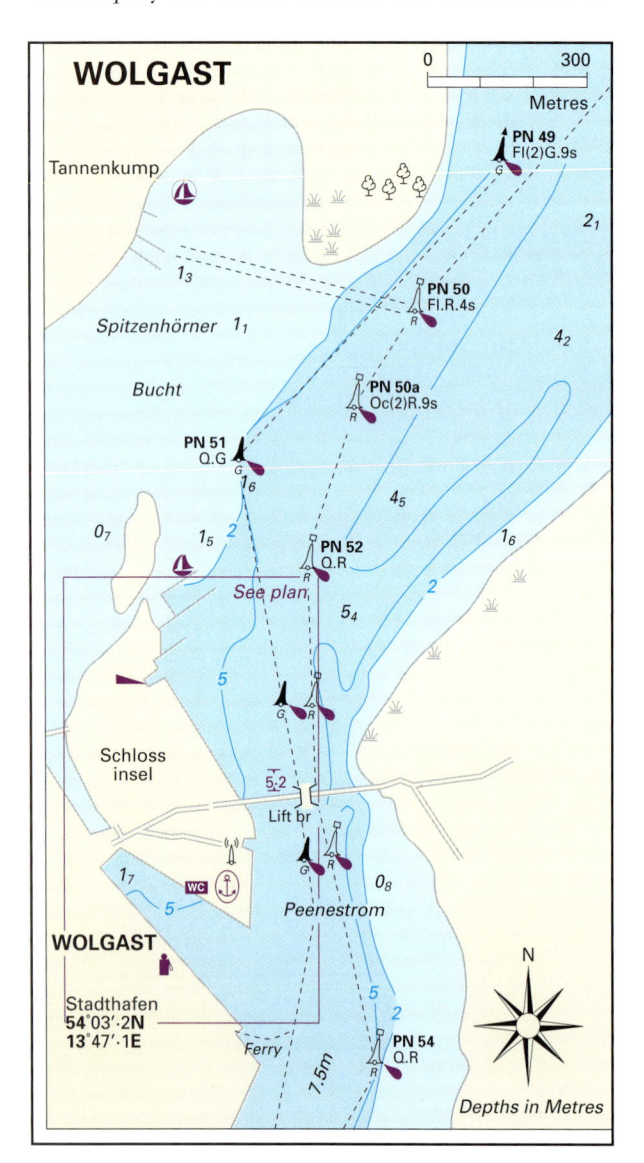

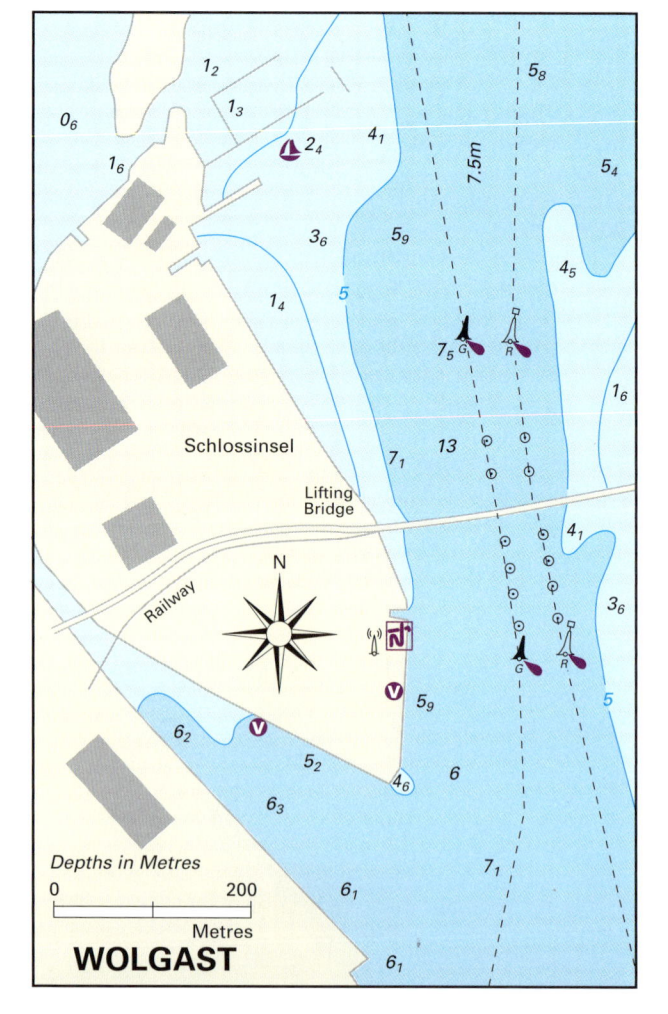

62 THE BALTIC SEA AND APPROACHES

THE SOUTHERN PEENESTROM

Wolgast town quay and Peenestrom *Miranda Delmar-Morgan*

Wolgast bridge
Miranda Delmar-Morgan

The southern Peenestrom
Zecherin Bridge ℡ +49 383 3727 0838 or +49 175 577 3609

From Wolgast southwards the well buoyed but very shallow channels are lit mainly by leading lights which are usually only operated when commercial traffic is expected. The dredged channel is narrow and the buoys are mostly unlit so that night navigation would undoubtedly lead to groundings. Far better to anchor in one of the many suitable places and wait for the dawn. The channel opens out into a lake, the Achterwasser, which can be explored with a large-scale chart and due care. The southern end narrows to a channel (The Moderort Rinne), dredged to 2·5m which is marked by unlit buoys, any deviation from the transits puts you instantly in soft, glutinous mud.

Zecherin Bridge summer opening times are 0545, 0940, 1145, 1645, 2045. Call them 10 minutes in advance. Times may vary slightly from year to year and should be checked.

Two miles below this bridge at Karnin is the derelict lifting span, now permanently raised, of the old railway spanning the Peenestrom. The approach spans were bombed during the war and no trace can now be seen. The main channel now passes south of the remains. Once past this old relic the way is clear into the Stettiner Haff (Zalew Szczeciński), where you can start your negotiation of the nets!

The remains of Karnin bridge from the north
Miranda Delmar-Morgan

1. GERMANY

THE BALTIC SEA AND APPROACHES 63

1D. DARSSER ORT TO THE POLISH BORDER

Stettiner Haff

There are several small picturesque harbours around the lake but it is a minefield of fishing stakes, and suspended nets resembling those on a tennis court. The lake is shallow so even if the latter are anchored close to the bottom you may still only have 1m clearance. Those suspended may be a mere 0·5m below the surface. There should be 30m passages between them but establishing whether you are looking through a genuine gap, or merely between the markers at each end can be difficult to ascertain.

PEENESTROM AND STETTINER HAFF

Depths in Metres

64 THE BALTIC SEA AND APPROACHES

STETTINER HAFF

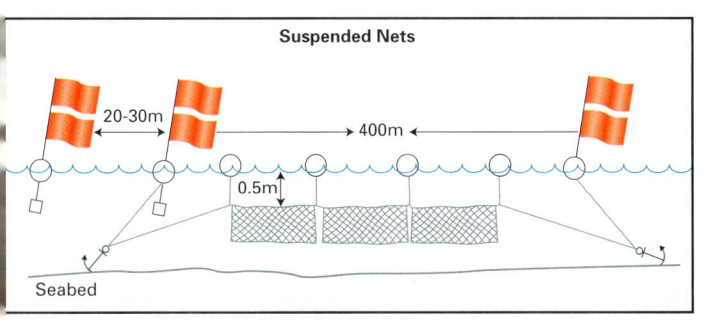

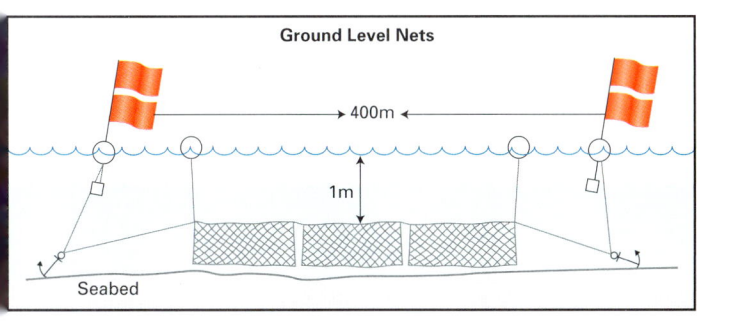

Suspended Nets (diagram: 20-30m, 400m, 0.5m, Seabed)

Ground Level Nets (diagram: 400m, 1m, Seabed)

Net stakes, Stettiner Haff Miranda Delmar-Morgan

They are unlit and uncharted. The stake markers are mostly in the shallows, particularly off the headlands. End stakes carry a red and white diamond, the white side points to clear passage and the red to the obstructed side. There are designated lines of passage across the Haff, and straying off them is at your own risk! The red and white 'Haff' buoy marks the Polish border but no formalities are required here.

Haff buoy on the Polish border
Miranda Delmar-Morgan

Ueckermünde
53°45′N 14°04′E
Charts German 1513
Port Control ✆ +49 39 771 3181, VHF Ch 14
Nuendorf Marina HM ✆ +49 171 622 2234

Ueckermünde, on the south side of Stettiner Haff, offers a good opportunity to obtain stores or yacht services close to the Polish border. Approaching vessels are requested to report to the Port Control by making contact 10 minutes before reaching the landfall buoy UE at 53°45′·4N 14°05′·9E and again before departure. No two way traffic is allowed in the canal entrance for vessels greater than 10m.

Neuendorf Marina
After an attractive tree-lined entrance Neuendorf Marina to port has diesel and a pump-out station. Tankstelle (fuel) ✆ + 49 151 1799 5917. It is associated with a housing development but is nearly 1·5km from the nearest shopping in Neuendorf/Ueckermünde Ost. Whilst more suited to locals it would probably be a safe place to leave your boat whilst using the connections to Berlin.

A mile further up the Uecker on the starboard hand lies a second yacht harbour carrying a depth of 1·8m where there are two sailing clubs with visitors' box berths some of which are on the west side of the river in deeper water. These berths are a short walk from the small town of Ueckermünde. Closer to town yachts can lie alongside the northern quay, with water and electricity, upriver of the ferry terminal. Facilities are behind the tourist office. Ueckermünde is a good place to stock up with gas before entering Poland as there is a large gas station on the far side of the town (beyond the Lidl supermarket) selling various types of gas including Camping Gaz.

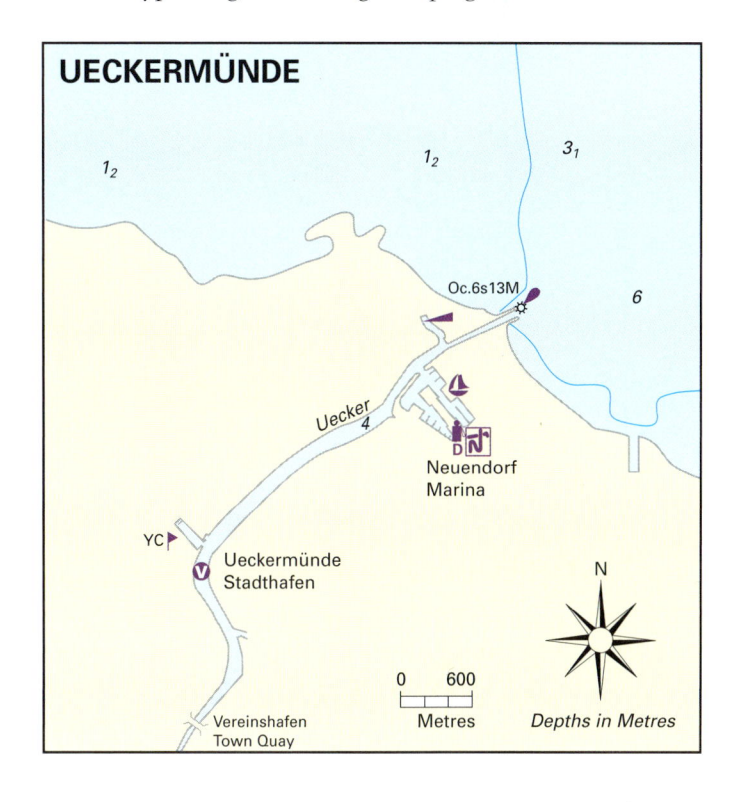

UECKERMÜNDE (chartlet showing Uecker river, Oc.6s13M, Neuendorf Marina, YC, Ueckermünde Stadthafen, Vereinshafen Town Quay; scale 0–600 Metres; Depths in Metres)

1. GERMANY

THE BALTIC SEA AND APPROACHES

2. DENMARK

2a. Eastern Danish ports, *72*

2b. The Danish side of the Øresund, *78*

2c. Approach to the Kattegat through the Limfjord, *87*

2d. Danish harbours and anchorages of the Kattegat, *92*

2e. Approach to the Baltic via the Lille Bælt, *106*

2f. Approach to the Baltic via the Store Bælt, *116*

2g. Bornholm and Christiansø, *126*

66   THE BALTIC SEA AND APPROACHES

2. Denmark

Denmark lies on the doorstep of the Baltic and has much to offer the cruising yachtsman, both in its own right and as an interesting stop for those on their way to or from the Baltic proper. It therefore enjoys a well earned place in this book.

It is not possible to cover all the harbours and anchorages in a single chapter, but full details are given for the principal harbours on the popular sailing routes. These are mainly situated approximately 30M sailing distance apart but at times closer where the harbour is thought to be of particular interest or well placed, and references are included for other places that deserve a visit.

Information is also included at the end of this chapter on the islands of Bornholm and Christiansø which are quite separate from the main Danish cruising areas but are, nonetheless, part of Denmark.

The selected harbours are described by reference to routes as follows: the majority of yachts visiting the Baltic Sea will approach it by the Kiel Canal and so the Danish harbours of the western Baltic are covered from southwest to northeast. The Sound (Øresund) is covered from south to north to the Göta Kanal. A minority will approach the Baltic through the Kattegat (including the Limfjord) and may continue through the Little Belt (Lille Bælt) or the Great Belt (Store Bælt) so these harbours are covered from north to south.

Key information

Rescue/Safety services

Emergency 112
(This is the emergency number for all EU countries).

Lyngby radio Call sign *OXZ*. Operates on MF and VHF. VHF Channel 16 (24/7)
+45 66 63 48 00.

Charts and chart packs

Available to order from Imray

UKHO Admiralty charts are excellent for the main channels around Denmark and for reaching all the passage harbours, and include details of the Traffic Separation Schemes, firing practice ranges, windfarms and other significant features both on the charts and in notes. Large-scale charts will be needed for exploration of the fjords and the Limfjord and for the approaches to Copenhagen.

Danish hydrographic charts give very good large-scale coverage (see www.kms.dk) and details of the relevant chart are set out at the commencement of each harbour description below.

There are two excellent series of German chart packs (size A2) both of which are readily available in Denmark and internationally. They are published annually and come with electronic versions on CD and complementary pilot books and the relevant packs are as follows:

NV Baltic Charts (published by Nautische Veröffentlichung):
Serie 1 Fünen – Kiel
Serie 2 Lübeck – Bornholm – København
Serie 3 Samsö – Sund – Kattegat
Serie 4 Rügen – Bodengewässer – Stettin
Serie 5 Schwedische Westküste

Delius Klasing Charts (published by Delius Klasing Verlag GmbH):
Satz 1 Kieler Bucht und Rund Fünen (includes the Kiel Canal)
Satz 2 Mecklenburg - Vorpommern - Bornholm
Satz 3 Westküste-Schweden
Satz 4 Grosser Belt bis Bornholm
Satz 5 Kattegat
Satz 6 Limfjord, Skagerrak, Danische Nordseeküste
Satz 11 Ostküste Schweden 1
Satz 12 Ostküste Schweden 2

The advantages of both these series are that one pack covers a large area and many harbour plans are included. They therefore represent very good value. The charts include a combination of large and small scales, which can take a little getting used to.

Navionics and iSailor provide excellent regularly updated electronic charts for plotters and iPads/tablets.

UKHO charts 2113, 2601, 2365, 2115, 902, 903, 2595, 2594, 2108, 2107, 426, 429, 894, 2591, 2592 2532, 2596, 923, 938, 2597.

Pilots and cruising guides

In English

Cruising Guide to Germany and Denmark, Brian Navin (Imray)

Cruising Almanac (Cruising Association/Imray)

Komma's Havnelods, Aschehoug Dansk Forlag. Comprehensive harbour information in Danish but with easily understood symbols for facilities available. Published twice per year.

In German

Dänemark I & 2, Jan Werner (DK Edition Maritim)

Hafenführer Dänemark (DK Edition Maritim)

Ankerplatz in Dänemark, Gerti and Harm Claussen (DK Edition Maritim)

Der Grosse NV Hafen Lotse, Volumes 1, 2 and 3 (Nautische Veröffentlichung) Complements Serie 1, 2 and 3 of their charts.

2. DENMARK

Hafenhandbuch Ostsee 1 covers all the harbours of Denmark apart from Jutland north of Grenå which are covered in the Nord See volume. Excellent harbour plans. (Delius, Klasing & Co). Complements DK chart series.

Baltic Pilot Volume I (NP 18) covers the Danish islands in great detail but is not the most convenient publication for everyday pilotage.

In Danish/Swedish

Havneguiden Danmark og sydvestlige Sverige, Per Hotvedt, Skagerak Forlag (Weilbach) covers harbours and anchorages. Excellent drawings and aerial photos. www.havneguiden.no

Additional reading

For more detail, Brian Navin's *Cruising Guide to Denmark and Germany* (Imray) is comprehensive. Another useful publication is Sejlerens Marina Guide newly published at the beginning of each season and available free at marinas. It is in Danish and German but has plans and aerial photos of marinas and easily understood symbols for the facilities available. Obtain a copy at the first Danish Marina you visit. Large scale charts are also essential.

See Appendix page 418 for suppliers of charts and publications

Time

Denmark uses UT+1 in winter and UT+2 in summer. The clocks change at the same time as UK.

Money

The unit of currency is the Danish krone (Dkr) divided into 100 øre. Although Denmark is a member of the EU, it voted not to join the Euro.

Cash points (ATMs) are numerous and all major credit cards are accepted in shops, at marinas and for fuel. In fact in many cases the credit card is the only method of payment.

Formalities

Customs

Denmark is a member of the European Union and the Schengen area (See main introduction, page 7, for more information). Visas are not required for EU passport holders but if arriving from a non-Schengen area country such as the UK you should enquire at the nearest HM or police station as to their requirements. Customs Offices are scarce and if one expects to need to report to customs it would be advisable to check availability before arrival. For enquiries telephone the head office in Copenhagen, ☏ +45 72 22 18 18 .

There are limits on the quantity of alcohol, tobacco or other goods that may be imported, and these vary according to whether you are coming from another EU country.

Full details of the current restrictions and regulations can be found on www.skat.dk

Immigration

Please refer to main Introduction page 7, with particular reference to the requirements of the Schengen Area.

Valid passports for all crew members are required. Visas are not required for citizens of EU countries, Scandinavian countries, the USA, Canada and many others. If in doubt check with any Danish Embassy. Visitors are advised to report to the harbourmaster at the first port of call.

Embassies

Royal Danish Embassy
55 Sloane Street, London SW1X 9SR,
☏ +44 (0)207 333 0200.
lonamb@um.dk, www.denmark.org.uk.

British Embassy
Kastelvej 36/38/40, DK-2100
Copenhagen, ☏ +45 35 44 52 00.
enquiry.Copenhagen@fco.gov.uk.

Public holidays

Official public holidays in Denmark include: 1st January, Maundy Thursday, Good Friday, Easter Sunday, Great Prayer Day (May), Whit Sunday and Monday (May or June), 5th June (Constitution Day), 25-26th December.

Communications

All card and coin telephones can be used for international calls – dial 00 followed by the country code, area code (omitting any initial 0) and number. The country code for Denmark is 45. There is reasonably good coverage of mobile phones (mainly 3G at the time of publication) but coverage does not extend very far out to sea. For international directory enquiries dial 113.

WiFi is available at most marinas (sometimes without charge), and is widely available in cafés and bars.

Travel

Denmark can be reached very easily from most parts of Western Europe by air, rail and road.

There are **ferries** between Denmark and Norway, Sweden and Germany but no longer to the UK.

Low cost airlines now operate to several **airports** including Esbjerg, Aarhus, Billund (in southern Jutland) and Copenhagen.

There is a large **train** network with regular trains. When booking your train ticket do make sure to book a seat number or you may have to stand! You can take bicycles onboard the trains. There are also many buses, especially useful in big towns.

If you have space, folding **bicycles** are very useful as there is excellent provision for cyclists with many cycle paths. Some towns and marinas have bicycles which you can pick up for a small deposit and either return or leave at another point (map on the bicycle).

Websites

www.sejlnet.dk Gives a short resume of harbour with plan and aerial photo plus contact details

www.havneguide.dk An app with aerial photo and contact details

www.MarinaBooking.dk A very useful website which enables you to book berths online in most of the main yacht harbours and marinas.

www.amblondon.um.dk/en Danish Embassy in London.

http://ukindenmark.fco.gov.uk/en/ British Embassy in Copenhagen.

www.visitdenmark.com Danish Tourist Board.

www.visitcopenhagen.dk Copenhagen city website.

www.lolland-falster.dk Tourist website for Lolland and Falster Islands.

www.visitvordingborg.dk Tourist website for Møn Island.

www.visitfyn.com Tourist website for Fyn Island.

www.bornholminfo.dk Tourist website for Bornholm Island (includes harbour plans)

www.dmi.dk Danmarks Meteorologiske Institut for weather forecasts and water levels

www.gst.dk Kort and Matrikelstyrelsen, national mapping and charting agency who do not sell direct to the public. Corrections to Danish charts are available on line.

www.skat.dk Danish Customs. Not very user-friendly, but does give phone numbers for enquiries.

www.weilbach.dk Chart and nautical book suppliers, see under Copenhagen.

Radio communications and weather information

There are no regular **VHF** weather forecasts but Lyngby Radio is monitored 24/7 and can be contacted with request for weather information. Gale warnings are however given in both Danish and English as well as navigational warnings

DENMARK - THE COUNTRY

on a very regular basis and the VHF coverage is excellent (they refer you to working channels, see page 423 to get right channel for the area relevant to you).

Five-day forecasts in English are available on the **Danish Meteorological Institute** (dmi) website, www.dmi.dk and they also have a section on water levels www.dmi.dk/hav/maalinger/vandstand (*maalinger* are measurements and *vandstand* is water level). Most marinas/harbours will post daily weather forecasts from dmi during the season.

A very useful weather app from fcoo.dk is sejladsudsigt.dk which gives you 48 hour forecasts updated hourly.

NAVTEX Denmark falls within Metarea 1-Baltic subarea. Details of Navtex stations can be obtained at www.weather.mailasail.com and from other sources.

In most harbours VHF is not used and any communication with harbour masters is normally by telephone.

◆ Tidal streams and depths

There is little tide as such in Denmark. The predominant current is north through the two Bælts and the Sound but the prevailing wind can vary this both in strength and direction to a marked degree, which makes it difficult to predict. The current is usually modest other than in the narrow parts of the channels of the two Bælts and the Sound north of Copenhagen. The NV chart packs include details of the prevailing north and south going currents.

Water levels can vary quite substantially by up to nearly 2m due to atmospheric and wind conditions. Strong offshore winds in particular can reduce the stated depth in the harbour. Depths generally are quite shallow and many of the harbours have depths around 2-2.5m so it is necessary to check charts and plan carefully before entering a new harbour. Mean level is used for chart datum. As a help Baltic sea levels are monitored every 30km in Denmark (see www.dmi.dk for updated water level information).

When sailing in shallower water close to the coast look out for fishing flags and buoys.

WC Holding tanks

Holding tanks are not mandatory for foreign yachts but toilets must not be discharged within 2M of the shore nor in harbour. Shore facilities should be used whenever possible. Danish registered vessels built after 1 January 2000 with a fixed toilet now have to be fitted with holding tanks with the means of being discharged through a deck fitting.

The country

Of the total land area of 43,000km² 65% is devoted to farming with a further 12% used for forestry. Environmental considerations are given high priority. The countryside is generally flat with the highest point only 173m above sea level. Motorways connect the main cities by means of high-level bridges or tunnels between the major islands. Bridges to the smaller islands are either of sufficient clearance or open to allow the passage of yachts and other small boat traffic.

The people, the church and the language

The Danes are friendly, tolerant and relaxed. They enjoy their pleasures and are happy to share them with visitors, but their harbours do become very busy during the main part of the sailing season.

Some 90% of the population of over 5 million are estimated to belong to the Lutheran Church which was established in 1536 and is the national church, under the direction of the state. Education has been compulsory since 1814 and there are several universities as well as various other institutions of higher education. A comprehensive social security system covers health, pensions, industrial accidents unemployment and certain other hazards.

Danish is one of the Scandinavian languages and is most closely related to Norwegian and Swedish. The Danish alphabet is the same as the Norwegian, consisting of the twenty-six letters of the English alphabet plus æ, ø and å at the end. English is widely spoken, especially by the young and in the cities.

A votive ship as found in many churches   E. Redfern

THE BALTIC SEA AND APPROACHES

2. DENMARK

History

The earliest tribes of Denmark that we know much about were the Jutes, large numbers of whom settled in England in the 5th century after the collapse of Rome's western Empire. Then came the Angles from southern Jutland, who with their Saxon neighbours were to replace the Celts as England's dominant race.

The Viking era started in the 9th century when Danish Vikings increasingly pillaged or settled in England, France, Portugal and Spain. In 966 Danish Norsemen, or Normans, under their leader Rollo were invited by the king of France to settle in the area to be called Normandy provided that they agreed to keep out any more Vikings.

Danish attacks on England culminated with Knut the Great arriving with an army of Danes in 1015 to become King of England as well as of Denmark and Norway. Then in 1066 the Norman Duke brought an invading army to England, thereby changing his epithet from 'William the Bastard' to William the Conqueror'.

Denmark itself now concentrated on the Baltic. Disunity amongst the Swedish nobility had made it easier for Denmark to control Sweden's coast and much of Finland's for several centuries. Rome's Northern Crusades gave Denmark an excuse in 1219 to capture Estonia's coast. Then in 1363 Denmark united with the rest of Sweden in a royal marriage, later formalized into the Kalmar Union of 1397 that included Norway as well. Denmark was by then by far the most powerful Baltic state.

In the 15th century, however, Denmark was in decline. First it sought to exploit its ownership of both sides of the Øresund, the entry channel to the Baltic between Denmark and Sweden by taxing trading ships passing through. The Hanseatic League defended its trading monopoly with a prolonged war and trade embargoes until the Danes finally had to accept a humiliating peace agreement.

Meanwhile the Swedes found that their union with Denmark simply meant ever increasing taxes to fund Denmark's defence of its southern border in Jutland. Periodic Swedish rebellions were suppressed, sometimes brutally. Then came the Stockholm Massacre of 1520 when the Danes captured and beheaded eighty nobles in a day. The public horror was such that Gustav Vasa was able to unite his fellow countrymen to drive the Danes out once and for all.

Denmark had officially been Catholic since King Harald Bluetooth's conversion in 965 AD. By Martin Luther's time, however, church revenue from tithes and fees had reached three times that of the government. Luther's proposed reforms gained huge popular support and in 1536 the government declared the nation Lutheran. The bishops were all put in prison until each of them promised to accept the reforms and to get married.

Over the 17th and 18th centuries, Denmark became more prosperous. The Hanseatic League had gone, so the Øresund tax brought in good revenue. Social and agricultural reforms produced increasing wealth at home. The Danish East India Company, founded in 1620 made a very comfortable living selling tea to the British.

Denmark was no longer a major power, however. Despite attempts to regain Swedish territory, Russia and its coalition victors of the great Northern War that defeated Sweden in 1721 were not going to allow any other nation to control access to the Baltic. During the Napoleonic wars Denmark had tried to maintain an 'armed neutrality' rather than fight the French. In the 1814 Treaty of Kiel, Denmark ceded Norway to Sweden. Norway was not to become independent until 1905.

The country struggled to recover economically and was in constant conflict with Germany over Schleswig-Holstein. Finally Germany resorted to force and following battles in 1864 Denmark ceded both territories. After WWI the present border was established giving some of the territory lost in 1864 back to Denmark.

Denmark sought to be neutral in the two world wars. As an agricultural and trading nation with few natural resources, WWI caused great hardship to the Danes and in WWII the Nazis occupied Denmark anyway. The Danes promptly scuttled their fleet to keep it out of Nazi hands.

Since the war, Denmark gave up its attempts at neutrality and was a founder member of NATO. The country is now a constitutional monarchy under Queen Margarethe II with an elected parliament (Folketinget). It is also a cautious member of the EU but not of the Eurozone.

Practicalities

Yacht services and chandlery

There are chandlers in most of the main towns, although items sometimes have to be delivered from Copenhagen. There are several sailmakers, and yacht clubs or harbour masters will be able to advise you where to get sails mended.

Gas

Re-filling non-Danish gas cylinders is likely to be extremely difficult. However, camping gas cylinders are widely available. (See 'Gas' section in main introduction.)

Diesel

Diesel can be obtained in many harbours but petrol is not so readily available and may have to be purchased at a filling station. Diesel at filling stations contains some bio fuel (See section on Fuel in main introduction for further detail on the associated problems), so try to use marine outlets only.

DENMARK - PRACTICALITIES

Shopping

Supermarkets in Denmark have a wide variety of foods. Prices are lower than Norway and Sweden but slightly higher than Germany, so if approaching Denmark via the Kiel Canal it is worth stocking up with non-perishable stores in Holtenau or other German ports.

Alcohol is widely available in supermarkets, without any of the restrictions on outlets that apply in Sweden or Finland. Alcohol prices are significantly lower than in Norway or Sweden, but higher than in Germany, and so, again, it pays to stock up before leaving Germany if possible.

Most shops, including hardware shops and some supermarkets, are closed on Saturday afternoons and many shops are closed on Sundays. However, bakeries are usually open on Sunday mornings, and these restrictions tend not to apply in tourist areas during the holiday season.

There some excellent fish shops or stalls to be found in many of the Danish harbours.

Hotels and restaurants

There are many hotels and restaurants in the major towns, catering for all tastes and budgets, and modest restaurants and bars are to be found in most harbours during the season. The Danes have a more relaxed attitude to alcohol than the other Scandinavian countries, with a correspondingly lively nightlife.

Laying up

There are a large number of boatyards where yachts can be laid up for the winter. Costs are generally reasonable but depend upon whether you require to be stored in a shed (heated or unheated) and other factors and you should seek local advice. Early booking is advised. See main Introduction page 10 for further details.

Berths

Danish harbours can be very busy during the peak summer months of July and August, as German and Swedish yachts join the ever expanding fleet of Danish yachts and motor boats. This is exacerbated by the numerous festivals which take place during the summer season. Be prepared to raft up several boats deep if berthing alongside a quay. However, there is usually a friendly welcome and willingness to fit you in if at all possible, and the periods before and after the main holiday season are relatively quiet.

Berthing is usually in box berths with bow to a quay or jetty and the stern moored to a post on each quarter. Some berths are very narrow and the width between the posts may be given. See section on Baltic mooring in the main Introduction on page 10. An unoccupied berth is marked by a green plaque at its head sometimes with the date on which its owner plans to return. A red plaque on the other hand indicates the berth is not to be used.

Free bicycle hire at Århus J. Parkinson

Berthing charges

Fees are generally very reasonable. The harbour office is often unmanned and payment is usually by a machine which may only take credit cards and no cash. The machine issues you with a sticker that must displayed on the boat (harbourmaster/student will come round and check when they are on duty, often only for an hour a day). The machine will also dispense a card which gives you access to shower and washing facilities as well as electricity, and give you the WiFi code. Many marinas have *sejlerstuer* (sailors' lounges) accessible with the card and these offer free cooking and washing up facilities and sometimes a fridge as well as seating areas. Any money not spent on the card will be refunded when you return the card.

Yacht clubs

Yacht clubs in Denmark are generally an association of local yachtsmen who are based in a particular yacht harbour. In many cases the club or association is responsible for the operation of the yacht harbour and the provision of the facilities. Visitors are usually offered temporary use of any club facilities during their stay.

Danish harbour names
The following terms are commonly used:

Lystbådehavn or Søsporthavn	yacht harbour or marina
Traffikhavn	commercial harbour
Fiskerihavn	fishing harbour
Gamle (Gammel) Havn	old port
Nordre Havn (Nordhavn)	north harbour/basin
Søndre Havn (Sydhavn)	south harbour/basin
Østre Havn (Østhavn)	eastern harbour/basin
Vestre Havn (Vesthavn)	western harbour/basin

THE BALTIC SEA AND APPROACHES

2a. Eastern Danish ports

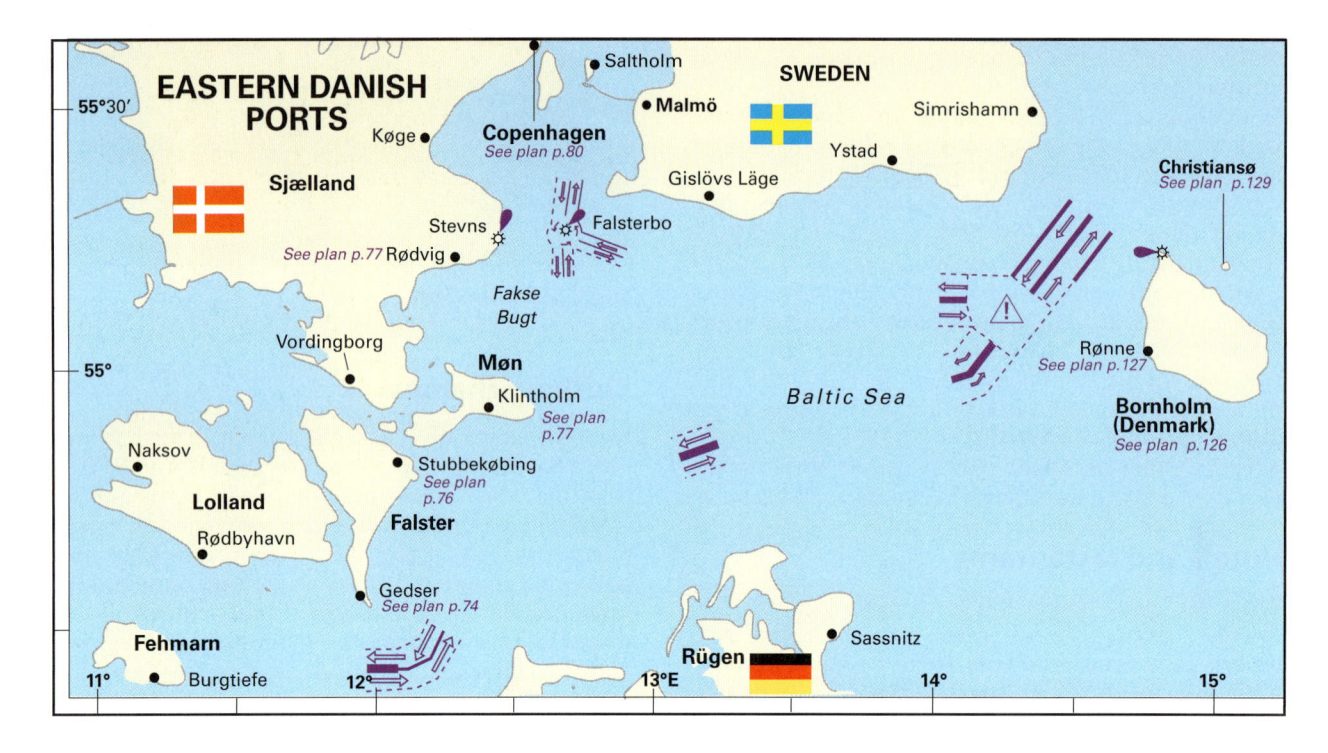

These harbours are listed here as convenient harbours on the southern Danish Islands on the quickest route from the Kiel Canal to Copenhagen or southern Sweden. They are chosen as being at approximately day sailing intervals. The route is relatively exposed, may require overnight passages and will be close to main shipping routes. The information given is designed to be used with passage charts – large-scale charts should not be needed.

On leaving Kiel and heading towards Copenhagen or Sweden there are two main options – either to head east to Heiligenhafen (35M) and pass through Fehmarnsund (see Germany, page 39) before crossing the shipping channels and heading for the Gedser peninsula, or to head northeastwards to Denmark, either to Rødbyhavn (45M) or Gedser (70M). In either case close attention to shipping lanes, practice firing ranges and crossing ferries will be needed.

Rounding Gedser Rev (shoal) requires due care to navigate safely between the shallows off the land and the major turning point in the shipping lanes some 9M offshore. Once round Gedser Rev the route north or east is straightforward.

Rødbyhavn

54°39′N 11°20′E starboard mole head

Distances
Kiel (Holtenau) 45M, Gedser 30M

Charts
UKHO 2942
Danish charts 196

Lights
Landfall buoy 54°38′·3N 11°19′·4E RW LFl.10s
Central pierhead Ldg Lts 045·2° *Front* 54°39′·2N 11°21′E Iso.R.2s17m6M Red triangle on red framework tower *Rear* 300m from front, Iso.R.4s26m6M Red inverted triangle on grey framework tower
West molehead 54°39′·1N 11°20′·8E F.R.8m5M Red framework tower 5m
East molehead 54°39′N 11°20′·8E F.G.8m5M Green framework tower on hut 5m

Communications
Harbourmaster ☎ +45 54 60 09 34
Port Control VHF Ch 74, havne@lolland.dk

General
Rødbyhavn, on the southwest coast of Lolland, is a busy port with a major ferry link to Germany. Access is straightforward with entry by day or night and, although not particularly yacht-friendly, it can be useful as a first stop in Denmark on passage from Kiel to Copenhagen or Sweden. Beware and keep clear of ferries on entry.

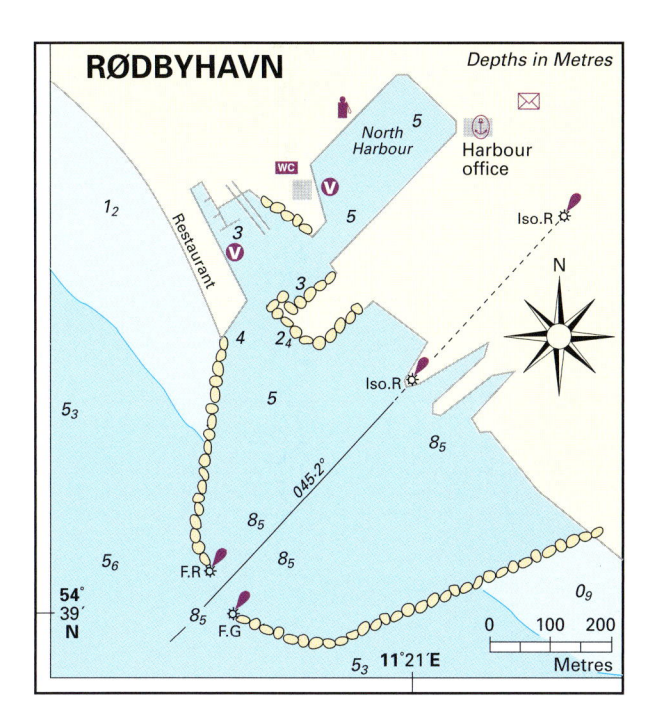

GEDSER YACHT HAVEN

RØDBYHAVN — *Depths in Metres*

Gedser Yacht Haven

54°34'·85N 11°55'·19E starboard mole head

Distances
Kiel 70M, Rødbyhavn 30M, Stubbekøbing 30M, Klintholm 35M, Copenhagen 85M, Gislövs Läge (Sweden) 70M, Rønne (Bornholm) 100M

Charts
UKHO 2601, 2944, 2945
Danish 197

Lights
Gedser Odde 54°33'·9N 11°57'·9E Fl(2)15s26m18M Racon (G) White hexagonal tower 20m
Gedser Odde S end 54°31'·7N 11°56'·2E Fl(3)R.10s13m10M Red pillar and lantern 14m Floodlit Horn(3)30s
Ldg Lts 350·5° *Front* 54°34'·3N 11°55'·7E Iso.2s17m9M 280·5°-vis-060·5° Red triangle on grey framework mast 15m
Rear 376m from front Iso.2s26m9M 280·5°-vis-060·5° Grey framework tower 30m
Note Buoyage in the entrance channel runs north to south (red buoys/lights to starboard on the approach from the South)
Yacht harbour N mole 54°34'·9N 11°55'·2E F.R.4m2M Grey post 2m
Yacht harbour S mole 54°34'·9N 11°55'·3E F.G.4m2M Grey post 2m

Communications
Gedser Yacht Haven ☎ +45 54 17 92 45
gk@guldborgsund.dk

Approach
From the landfall buoy follow the (lit) leading line on 045·2°. After passing between the breakwaters turn due north and head for the inner harbour.

Berthing
Tie up alongside on the NW side of the North Harbour or in one of the box berths (which are quite small) immediately to port when you enter North Harbour. There are also some box berths in West Harbour.

Facilities
All main harbour facilities are available including restaurant and diesel, with petrol at 500m. Ferries to Puttgarden (Fehmarn). Train connections with Copenhagen and Hamburg.

General
The Gedser peninsula on the south end of the island of Falster is about half way between the Kiel Canal and Copenhagen or southern Sweden, with a major traffic separation zone some 9M offshore. It is a major ferry port but the yacht harbour is quite separate from the commercial harbour.

Gedser looking SSE David Ridout

THE BALTIC SEA AND APPROACHES

2. DENMARK

2A. EASTERN DANISH PORTS

Approach

Approaching from the west, navigate to a position just east of the south cardinal buoy (54°30'·91N 11°50'·77E, unlit), keeping clear of the offshore wind farm. Approaching from the east, keep clear of the shoals which run some distance south-southeast from the tip of the peninsula.

As Gedser has a major ferry terminal, there is a buoyed and lit channel and a lit leading line – red buoys to starboard. Follow the channel until just before the entrance to the ferry harbour, then turn to port and follow the next part of the marked channel for about 0·75M, when the yacht harbour will be seen to starboard.

Berthing

Berth in box berths or alongside on starboard side after entering the harbour, just before the fuel station. The southernmost berths carry a depth of 3m and the others 2·5m.

Facilities

All basic facilities are available including a restaurant and a diesel berth. There is a 1km walk to the supermarket.

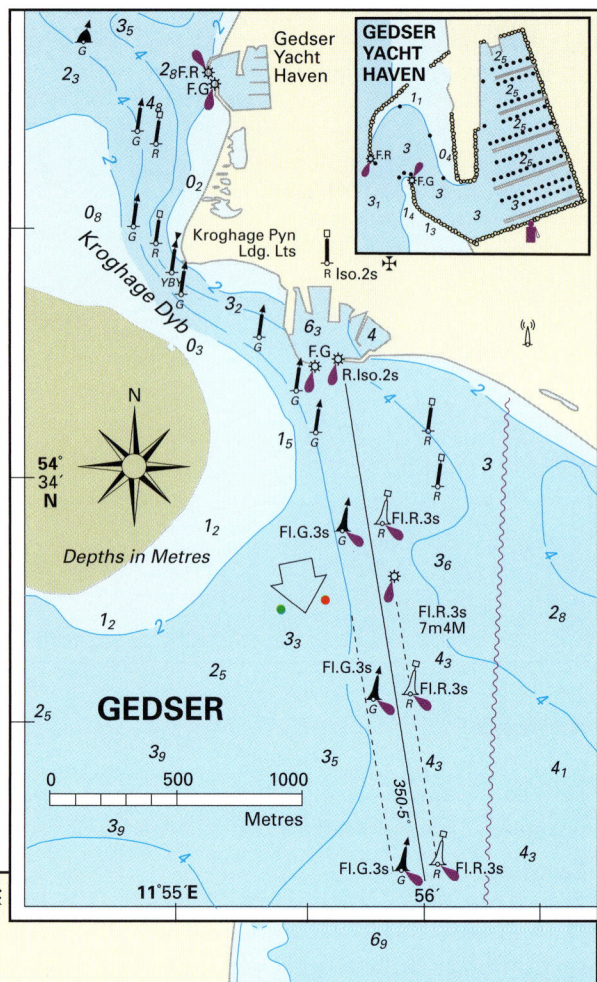

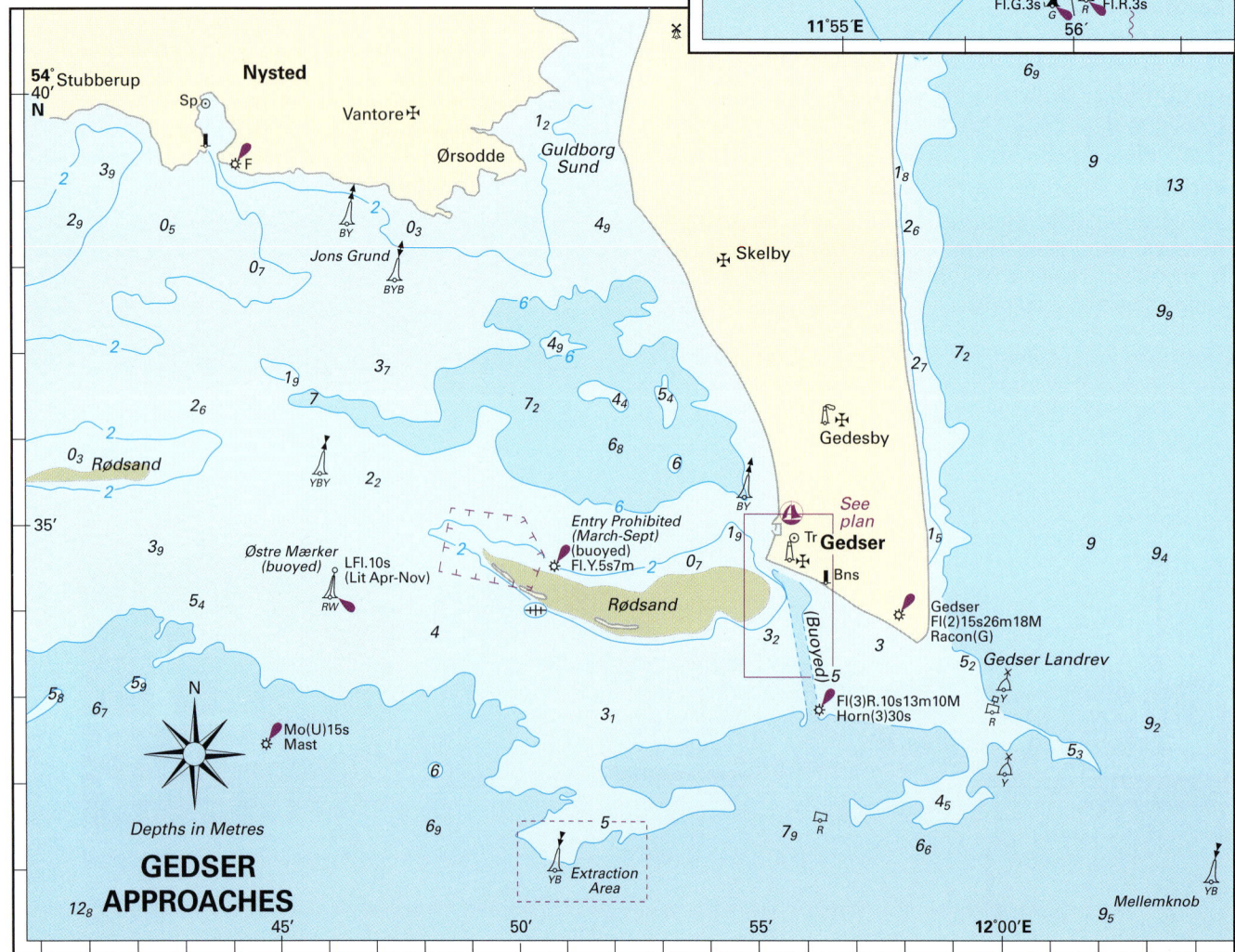

74   THE BALTIC SEA AND APPROACHES

STUBBEKØBING

Stubbekøbing

54°53'·68N 12°02'·65E East cardinal mark at entrance to channel into harbour

Distances
Kiel 95M, Gedser 30M, Klintholm 20M, Copenhagen 70M, Gislövs Läge 60M

Charts
UKHO 2115
Danish 198, 162

Lights
Hestehoved 54°50'·1N 12°09'·9E Oc(2)WRG.6s14m13–9M 216·5°-R-264°-G-290°-W-342°-R-007°-G-024° White house 4m
Red can buoy 54°49'·8N 12°11'·4E Fl(3)R.10s
Ldg Lts 324° *Front* 54°53'N 12°07'·2E Iso.2s12m9M 319°-intens-329° Red triangle on white tower 13m
Skansepynt *Rear* 520m from front, Iso.4s20m13M 319°-intens-329° Red inverted triangle, white bands, on grey framework tower 19m
Hårbølle Pynt Ldg Lts. 353·5° *Front* 54°53'N 12°08'·9E Iso.G.2s10m7M Red triangle, white bands on grey framework tower
Rear 480m from front. Iso.G.4s21m8M Red inverted triangle, white bands, on grey framework tower
Borgsted 54°54'·2N 12°06'·5E Oc.WRG.5s3m10–8M White house, red band. 317°-G-320°-W-323°-R-332·5
Hårbolle 54°53'·3N 12°08'·2E Oc.WRG.10s6m12–9M Red triangle, white bands, on framework tower. 064°-G-101·5-W-106·5°-R-117°
Stubbekøbing Ldg Lts 176° *Front* W molehead 54°53'·5N 12°02'·7E F.G.3m Post. *Rear* 130m from front F.G.7m Grey framework tower
Note Buoyage in the main entrance channels runs northwest to southeast (red buoys/lights to starboard). Into the harbour, green buoys are to starboard

Communications
Harbourmaster ☎ +45 51 74 01 09
stubhavn@guldborgsund.dk

General

Stubbekøbing is a useful stop on the way from Kiel to Copenhagen or southern Sweden especially if you choose to go through the Smålandsfarvandet (see page 123 and via Bøgestrømmen towards Copenhagen/Sweden). It is a very pleasant small town and commercial port, with a clubhouse and comfortable yacht harbour which is the easternmost of the three harbours.

Looking W with big box berths David Ridout

Approach

54°49'·8N 12°11'·4E red buoy Fl(3)R.10s marking the beginning of the buoyed channel

The dredged and well-buoyed approach channel – red buoys to starboard – with leading lights, starts to the east of Hestehoved light. The initial course is 324° from near the red can buoy noted above, thereafter see plan. Leave the main channel opposite the harbour entrance and follow the buoyed channel southwards towards the commercial harbour. Just before the entrance turn eastwards to follow the breakwater round to the yacht harbour entrance. Do not cut the corner. A sign directs you to the Lystbådehavn where there is now a floating pontoon by the entrance which you leave to starboard before entering the yacht harbour.

Berthing

The yacht harbour was redeveloped in 2013 and there are now new box berths along the north mole with the first on your starboard side having a width of up to 5m and length 15m. These berths then become smaller and narrower as you head further into the harbour. Depths between 2·5-2·7m.

Alternatively you may tie up alongside in the main harbour. The fuel facility is also there. This harbour is council run.

Facilities

All main harbour facilities are available including diesel, with petrol at 500m. There is a kiosk selling a limited selection of groceries and drinks beside the commercial harbour, and a shopping centre in the town some 500m further away, where there are the usual banks, restaurants and hotels, and a motor bike museum. Most types of repairs can be undertaken here. Bicycles can be borrowed from the harbourmaster.

Stubbekøbing aerial view
by kind permission of Stubbekøbing harbourmaster

THE BALTIC SEA AND APPROACHES

2A. EASTERN DANISH PORTS

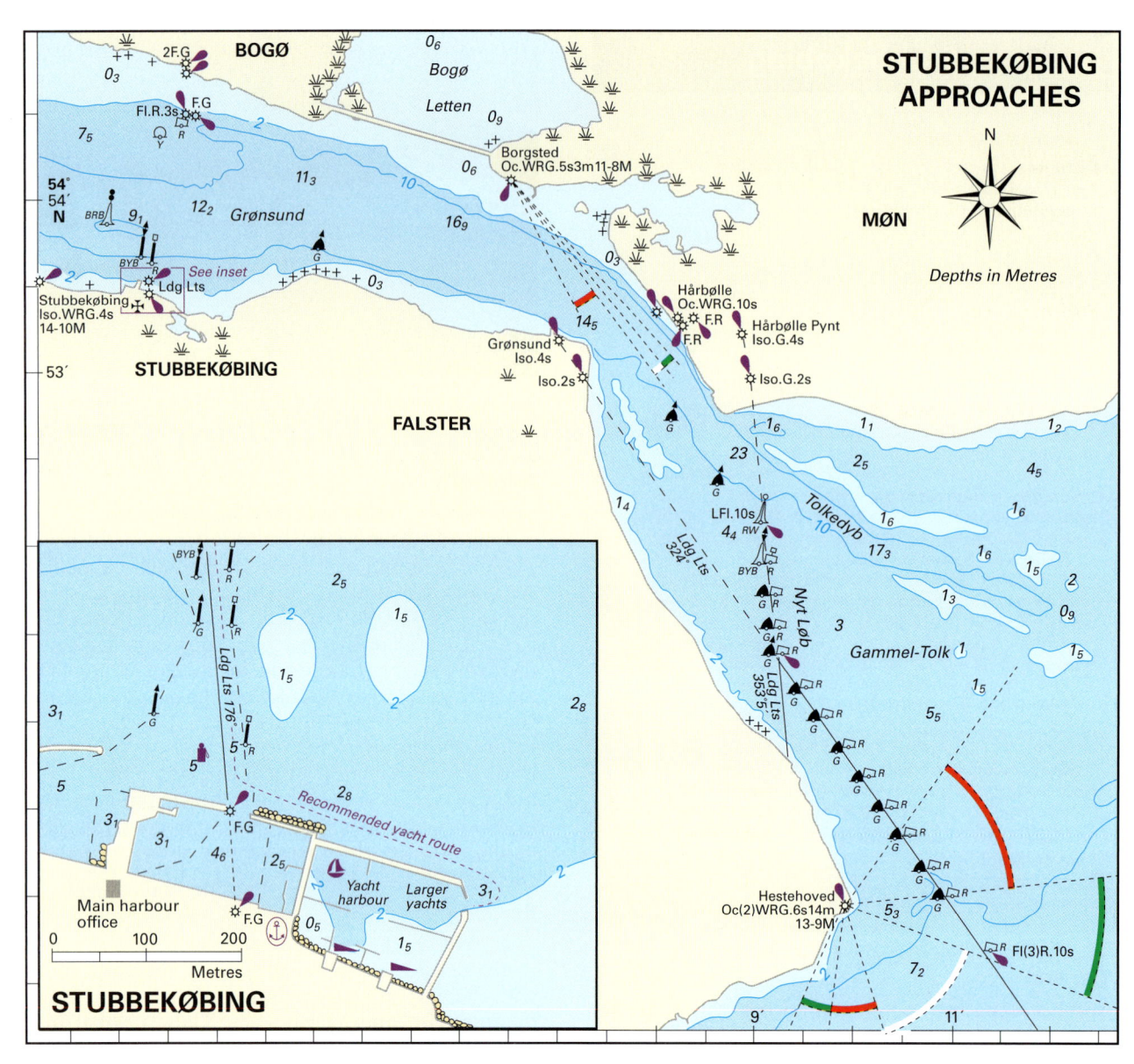

Klintholm

54°57'N 12°27'·79E starboard mole head

Distances
Gedser 35M, Stubbekøbing 20M, Rødvig 25M,
  Copenhagen 55M, Gislövs Läge 40M

Charts
UKHO 2115, 2944, 2945
Danish 198

Lights
Møn SE Point 54°56'·8N 12°32'·4E Fl(4)30s25m21M
  214°-vis°071° Yellow square tower 13m
North molehead 54°57'·2N 12°27'·9E Fl.R.3s4m4M Post
South molehead 54°57'·1N 12°27'·9E Fl.G.3s5m4M
  White pedestal 3m

Communications
Klintholm Harbourmaster +45 24 42 21 82
  micl@vordingborg.dk

General

Klintholm is an attractive harbour with excellent facilities for yachts. It is worth visiting in its own right, and also provides a good passage harbour as it is close to the direct route to Copenhagen and provides a good starting point for the leg to southern Sweden.

Approach

The approach is straightforward with no hazards when coming from the south. After passing between the breakwaters, bear to port for the yacht harbour.

Berthing

Berth in box berths either in the smaller basin to the north of the entrance or in the larger basin to the northwest. Both carry 2·5m depth. Large yachts can moor alongside the W mole in the fishing harbour.

Facilities

All main harbour facilities are available including diesel, with petrol at 200m. A sailmaker works locally and there are banks, a small grocer's shop and restaurants nearby and two good beaches.

76 THE BALTIC SEA AND APPROACHES

RØDVIG

Klintholm entrance *David Ridout*

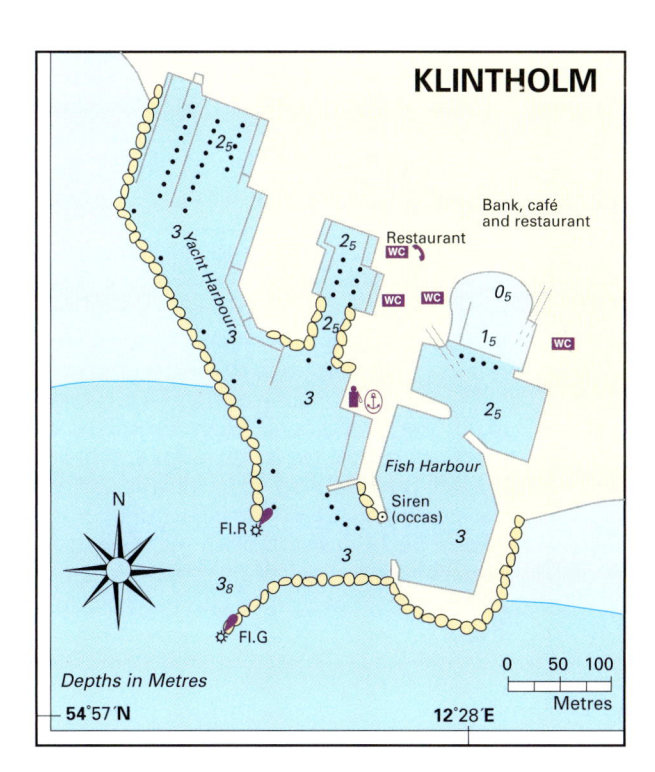

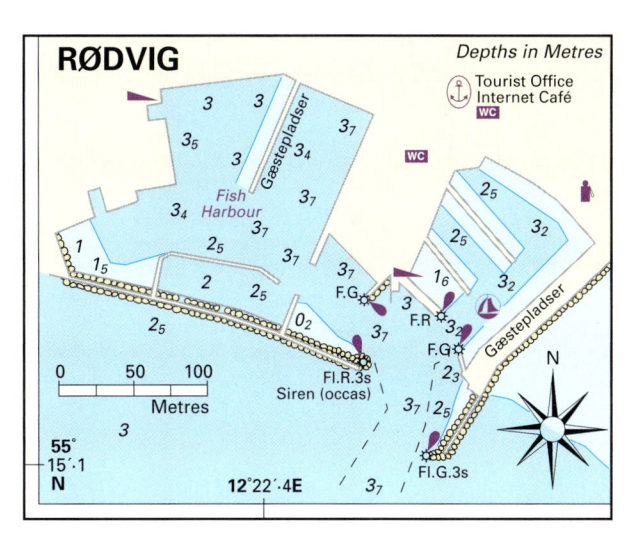

Rødvig

55°15'N 12°22'E starboard mole head

Distances
Gedser 55M, Klintholm 25M, Copenhagen 35M

Charts
UKHO 2115
Danish 198, 190

Lights
Stevns 55°17'·5N 12°27'·2E LFl.25s64m21M White round tower 26m
Landfall buoy 55°14'·1N 12°23'·6E LFl.10s Red and white pillar buoy
East molehead 55°15'·2N 12°22'·6E Fl.G.3s5m3M Red pedestal, white band
West molehead 55°15'·2N 12°22'·5E Fl.R.3s5m3M Grey conical concrete hut 3m

Communications
Rødvig Harbourmaster ☎ +45 56 50 60 07
stevns@stevnsingo.dk

General

Rødvig is a pleasant small harbour and a useful stop to break the journey from the south to Copenhagen. The yacht harbour to the northeast of the entrance is often congested. The fishing harbour to the west is relatively clear and has greater character, but no facilities.

Approach

The harbour entrance should be approached in a north-northeasterly direction to avoid the many fishing stakes just offshore. Entry at night is not recommended on a first visit.

Berthing

Berth in box berths in the yacht harbour to the north-northeast of the main entrance. The first two rows of berths carry a depth of 1·5m while the ones further in are deeper with 2·8m. If the yacht harbour is full there is alongside berthing for yachts in the fishing harbour to the northwest of the main entrance.

Facilities

All main harbour facilities are available including diesel and petrol in the main harbour. WiFi.

THE BALTIC SEA AND APPROACHES   77

2b. The Danish side of the Øresund (The Sound)

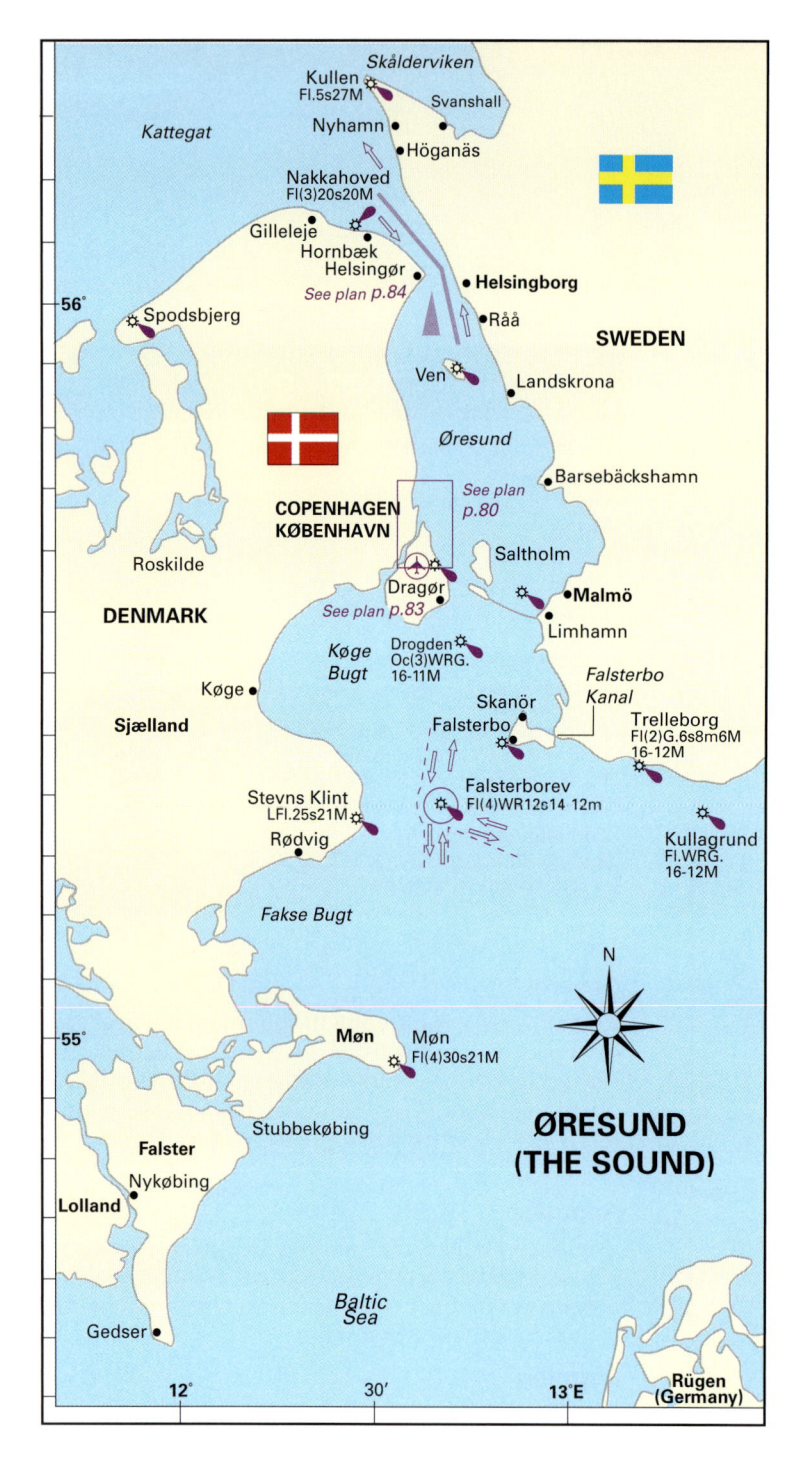

General notes

The Sound is the most direct route from the Kattegat into the main part of the Baltic and, as such, is a major shipping route. It is also narrow, being only three miles wide at its narrowest point. There is a traffic separation scheme off Falsterborev, and another in the narrows between Helsingør and Helsingborg. The hazard is from the size of some vessels using this route, rather than the sheer numbers such as in the Straits of Dover, but nevertheless yachts crossing the sound should pay close attention to the normal rules for such schemes. The waters between Copenhagen and Malmö are tortuous and shallow in places and crossed by the Øresund bridge, but there is a well-marked, dredged channel for large vessels. Currents in this area will vary with the wind in both strength and direction, and can run up to 2 kn in the narrower parts of the Sound. It therefore follows that close attention needs to be paid to navigation in this area. All this may make the area sound hazardous but in practice it is far less so than, for example, the English Channel. It is an interesting cruising ground, home to large numbers of yachts on both the Danish and Swedish sides. There are several guest harbours on the Swedish shore (see chapter 3, page 139).

Lighthouses, Helsingør

78 THE BALTIC SEA AND APPROACHES

COPENHAGEN

Copenhagen

55°41′N 12°36′E

Distances
Helsingør 22M, Klintholm 55M, Gedser 85M, Kiel 150M, Stralsund 85M, Falsterbo Kanal 21M, Gislövs Läge (Sweden) 35M, Rønne 90M.

Charts
UKHO 902, 903, 2115, 2595
Danish 131, 132, 133, 134

Lights
Middelgrunds Fort west 55°43′·3N 12°39′·9E
 Oc.WRG.5s11m12–10M 005°-R-069°-G-128°-R-173°-G-184°-W-193°-R-225° Red block
Middelgrunds Fort east 55°43′·2N 12°40′·1E
 Oc(2)WRG.12s11m12–10M 204·5°-W-245°-R-290°-G-346°-W-350°-R-056° Red block
Trekroner, east side 55°42′·2N 12°37′E
 Iso.WRG.2s20m17–13M 175°-R-195°-G-207°-W-210°-R-214°-G-219·8°-W-222·9°-R-255°-G-316·5°-W-320°-R-336° White round tower 12m
Prøvestenshavn oil jetty 55°41′N 12°38′·3E
 Oc(3)WRG.15s10m13–10M 160°-G-168°-W-171°-R-175°-G-178·2°-W-180·4°-R-182·2°-G-203° White framework tower, white hut, red band 8m
Nordre-Røse 55°38′·2N 12°41′·3E Oc(2)WRG.6s14m17–13M Racon (M) 140°-R-157·5°-G-176·5°-W-181°-R-186°-G-030·5° Round granite tower 17m
Drogden 55°32′·2N 12°42′·8E Oc(3)WRG.15s18m18–13M 009°-R-021°-G-028·5°-W-071°-R-256·5°-G-357·5°-W-009° Racon (X) White square tower, red bands, grey base 20m Horn Mo(U)30s (occas)

Communications
Copenhagen Port Authority ☏ +45 35 46 11 11
 VHF Ch 12, 16
 cmport@cmport.com www.cmport.com
Copenhagen Harbourmaster ☏ +45 35 46 11 38
Langelinie Harbourmaster ☏ +45 35 26 23 38
 havnefoged-llb@mail.dk
 www.langeliniehavn.dk
Svanemølle Harbourmaster ☏ +45 39 20 22 21
 (0900–1900 LT) info@smhavn.dk
 www.smhavn.dk
Tuborg Harbourmaster ☏ +45 20 13 37 87
 kdy@kdy.dk
Hellerup Harbourmaster ☏ +45 39 62 07 61
 havn@gentofte.dk
Margaretheholms Havn (Lynette Sailing Club)
 ☏ +45 32 57 57 78 www.lynetten.dk

General

Copenhagen is a friendly city with a strong feeling of history. There is much for the tourist, better described in one of the numerous shore-based guide books than here. Sightseeing in the centre of the city can be done on foot.

Approach

The approaches to Copenhagen are well marked and lit but a large-scale chart is recommended. From the south - locate the red and green channel buoy just north of the Drogden lighthouse and follow the channel northwards but beware: RED buoys and lights are left to starboard. To the northeast the Øresund Bridge to Sweden can be seen as it traverses Peberholm Island before entering a tunnel under the main shipping channel. After Nordre-Røse lighthouse is left to port, a branch of the channel (the Kongedybet) bears northwestwards on a leading line of 317·8° towards the city area and Trekroner light, leaving the pylons of the wind farm on Middelgrund to starboard. By day and in poor visibility, care should be taken in the vicinity of the off-lying islands of Saltholm and Peberholm, which are surrounded by shoal water and are very low-lying; so much so that it is very easy to misjudge distances. From the north the approach is straightforward.

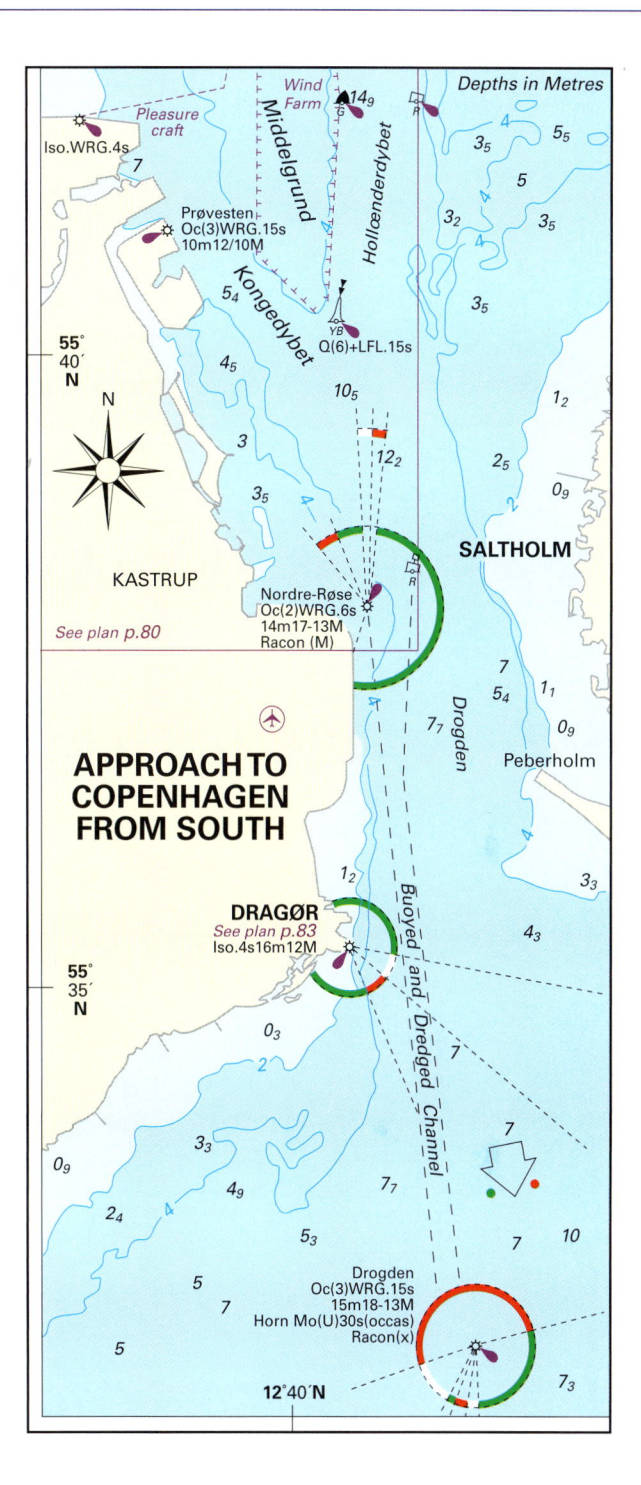

Pleasure craft are requested to enter the main harbour via Lynetteløbet and the northern marinas via Skudeløbet and there are buoys laid from 1 April to 15 November to mark the route.

A north or south-going current can be up to 4–5 knots in the Sound depending on wind conditions.

THE BALTIC SEA AND APPROACHES

2B. THE DANISH SIDE OF THE ØRESUND (THE SOUND)

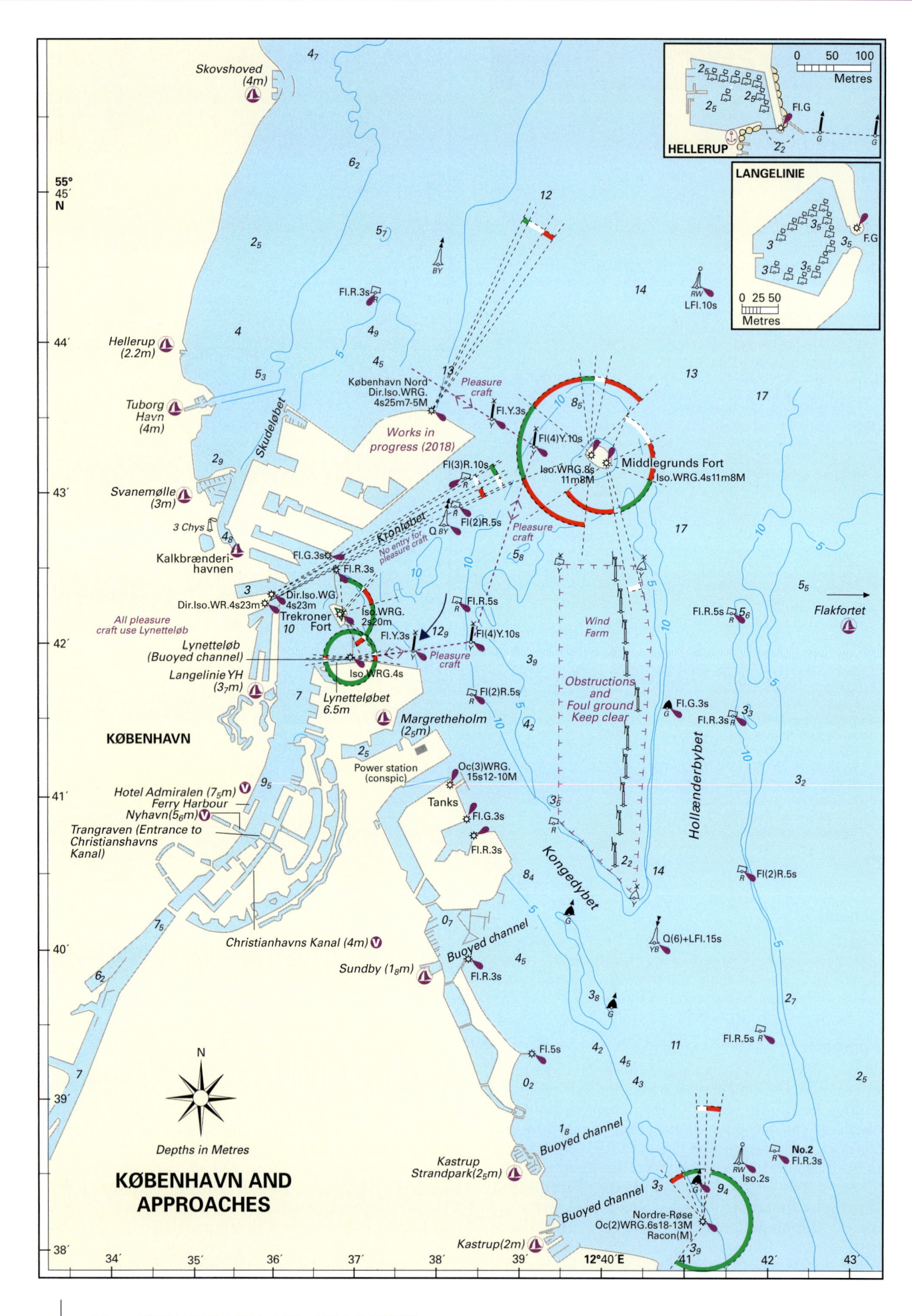

KØBENHAVN AND APPROACHES

Depths in Metres

HELLERUP

LANGELINIE

80   THE BALTIC SEA AND APPROACHES

COPENHAGEN

Anchorage

It is not advisable to anchor in the environs of Copenhagen due to the large amount of shipping and the difficulty of getting ashore.

Berthing

There are several yacht harbours close to the centre of Copenhagen and some details are given for Nyhavn, Christianshavns Kanal, Langelinie, Svanemølle, Tuborg, Hellerup and Dragør. The Christianshavns Kanal, on the southeast side of the main harbour, is also very convenient for sightseeing.

Nyhavn

HM ☏ +45 40 42 39 77 www.byoghavn.dk

The picturesque old harbour, close to the city centre, which frequently figures in publicity photographs. It is well worth a visit but now not very suitable for the average yacht. Large yachts over 15m and training ships may book a berth at Amaliehaven at Sdr. Toldbod and in Nyhavn east of Nyhavnsbroen (bridge) by calling the harbourmaster.

Christianshavns Kanal

HM *mobile* +45 40 96 37 72 www.marina.wilders.dk
marina@wilders.dk

Entered almost directly opposite Nyhavn, is a picturesque but crowded place. Mooring is between two poles with bow to quay on the starboard side with alongside mooring on port side and at a few other places. Easy access to the city centre. This area, with its bridges and gabled houses, is reminiscent of Amsterdam's inner canals. Local people recommend it as the place to moor for sightseeing but it is very busy and it would pay you to book a place through the harbourmaster. Office hours are Mon–Fri 0800–12.00 and 1600–1800, Sat 0900–1200 and 1600–1800. Sundays and bank holidays 0900–1200 during the summer season.

Langelinie

HM *mobile* +45 27 44 75 45

A circular basin about 1km from the city centre. It can be busy but is useful for its proximity to the city. It lies amongst the parks and gardens near the Little Mermaid, who sits on a rock at the water's edge near Langelinie promenade. Mooring is bows to the quay

The Little Mermaid *David Ridout*

Langelinie looking east *David Ridout*

Christianshavns Kanal berths *David Ridout*

THE BALTIC SEA AND APPROACHES   **81**

2B. THE DANISH SIDE OF THE ØRESUND (THE SOUND)

View of Frelsens Kirke Tower from Christianshavns Kanal
David Ridout

with stern line to a buoy. It is advisable to arrive at Langelinie early in the day to improve the chance of finding a vacant berth. There are basic facilities but no fuel is available. Payment is by card at the 'havnekontor'. Harbourmaster available Mon–Fri. 1600–1700 and Sat–Sun. 1200–1300. You have to vacate your berth by 1400 on the day you are leaving.

Svanemølle

☏ +45 39 20 22 21
info@smhavn.dk

The largest of the Copenhagen yacht harbours and normally has space for visitors. It is approached in a southwesterly direction via a buoyed channel leading from the northern end of the dock complex. It is 4km from the main shopping centre, but the excellent public transport system makes travelling there easy. No fuel and rather tired facilities (fuel is available at Tuborg marina just to the north). Payment by machine, harbourmaster sometimes there.

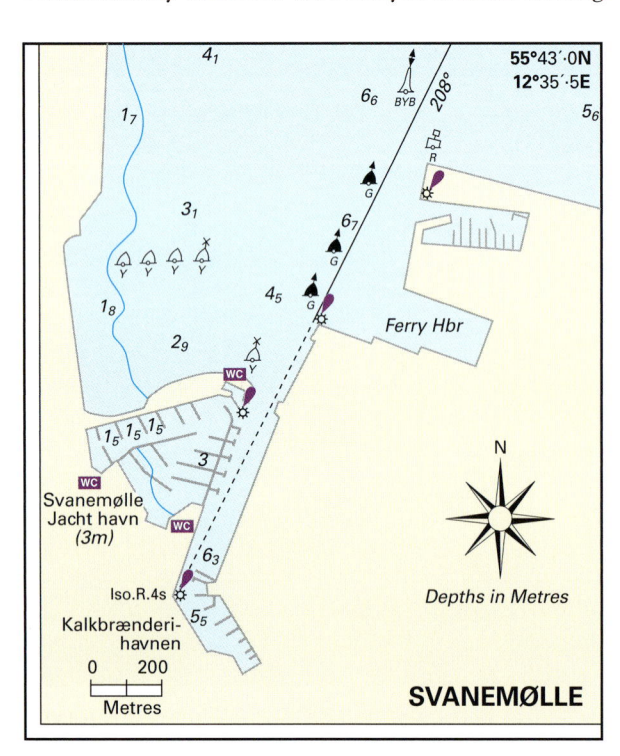

Tuborg marina

☏ +45 20 13 37 87, VHF Ch 13 (when manned)
kdy@kdy.dk

Lies just to the north of Svanemølle and has excellent modern facilities including water, electricity, showers, laundry, WiFi, diesel and petrol. Least depths 3m. It is the home of the Kongelige Danske Yacht Klub. As with Svanemølle there is excellent public transport to the city.

Hellerup

A small yacht harbour 6km from the city centre and 500m north of the Tuborg harbour. It is a small square basin flanked by trees and overlooked by the yacht club. There is an obvious buoyed channel leading to the south-facing harbour entrance. Mooring is bows-to with stern lines to posts. A new jetty to starboard before you enter the harbour offers additional mooring alongside when wind allows (not good in strong easterlies). Facilities include water and electricity on the quayside, toilets, showers and a sauna. There is no fuelling berth. The harbour office is on the port side as you enter the yacht basin and they will do their best to accommodate visitors. Hellerup shopping centre is about 300m away with a wide range of shops, banks, restaurants etc.

Dragør

HM VHF channels 12/13/16 or ☏ +45 32 89 15 70

On the west side of the southern end of the Drogden channel (see plan page 79) is a pretty mediaeval fishing village developed by the Dutch. There is easy access by bus into the city (30 minutes) and it is very convenient for the airport (15 minutes). There is a marina on the south side of the harbour complex but it is shallow. The harbour area once used for ferries is now available to yachts of 15m by prior

Hellerup looking SE *David Ridout*

82   THE BALTIC SEA AND APPROACHES

HELSINGØR

The old pilot station at Dragør, now a museum
David Ridout

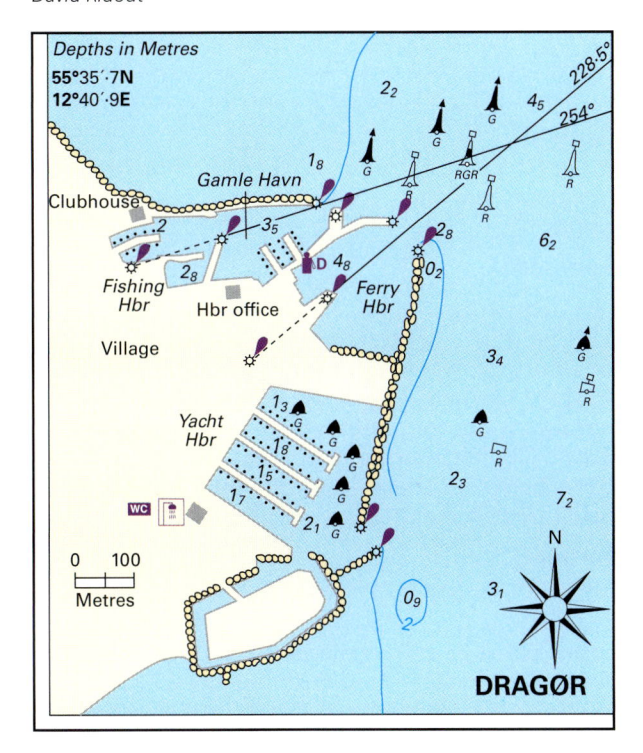

arrangement with the harbourmaster and there is a diesel pump here. The Gamle Havn is where most people moor and depths here are 2·5–3·5m. There are good facilities including laundry and WiFi and it is convenient for the little town with its excellent supermarket, as well as several cafés and restaurants. There is also a small boatyard.

Services for yachts

There are several chandlers in Copenhagen, and most repairs can be arranged. There are a number of sailmakers in and around the city.

Danish, Swedish, German and British charts and pilot books may be bought from:

Iver Weilbach & Co, Toldbodgade 35, DK 1253 København K ✆ +45 33 34 35 75
nautical@weilbach.dk www.weilbach.dk
Customs: Toldskat København, Tagensvej 135, 2200 København N ✆ +45 72 22 18 18

General facilities

The city provides many banks, restaurants and hotels. The main tourist information office is at Vesterbrogade 4A. Only Dragør and possibly Hellerup are close to shops for provisioning.

Note The yacht harbours to the southwest of Copenhagen (such as Brøndby) also give easy access to the centre of Copenhagen by train, are near the airport and offer winter lay-up facilities which may be of interest.

Tourist information ✆ +45 70 22 24 42
www.visitcopenhagen.dk

Helsingør

56°02′N 12°37′·2E south (port) pier head to main harbour
56°02′.6 N 12°37′.15 PHE starboard mole head for marina

Distances
Gilleleje 12M, Copenhagen 22M, Halmstad 43M.

Charts
UKHO 2108, 2115, 2594
Danish 102, 131

Lights
Kronborg 56°02′·4N 12°37′·3E Oc(2)WRG.6s34m15–12M NE tower of castle. 129°-G-137°-W-145°-R-161°-G-214°-W-311°-R-349°-G-352°-W-356°-R-017°-G-027°
Ldg Lts 257·8° *Front* 56°02′N 12°37′·1E FW.13m6M Grey mast. 337·8-vis-277·8. *Rear* 77m from front. FW.14m6M Square brick tower
S pierhead 56°02′·1N 12°37′·2E FR.7m6M Red round metal tower
N molehead 56°02′·1N 12°37′·2E FG.7m6M Green round tower

Communications
Harbourmaster ✆ +45 4928 1080
nordhavnen@helsingor.dk
www.nordhavn.helsingor.dk
Tourist information at the harbour office.

General

Overlooking the narrows, Shakespeare's Elsinore Castle (or to give it its correct name Kronborg Slot) dominates Helsingør. Originally built in the 15th century to enforce the collection of tolls from all ships sailing up or down the Øresund, it played a major part in the creation of Denmark's wealth. Helsingør has a large marina north of Kronberg Slot which is in the process of being modernised. The approach to the east facing entrance is straightforward.

Berthing

Helsingør Marina, Nordhavn 56°02′.61N 12°37′15E
Starboard mole head

There are visitor pontoons, asshown on the plan. These are stated to be for yachts 12–20m but the area can be used by other sized yachts if there is space. Elsewhere in the harbour the red/green availability notices apply. Depths are 2·5–3m.

Søndre Havn

The marina office also administers berths in the main commercial harbour, Søndre Havn, southwest

2. DENMARK

THE BALTIC SEA AND APPROACHES 83

2B. THE DANISH SIDE OF THE ØRESUND (THE SOUND)

HELSINGØR NORDHAVN

Gilleleje

56°08'N 12°19'E starboard mole head

Distances
Grenå 50M, Anholt 50M, Lynaes 22M, Falkenberg 48M, Lynaes 22M, Helsingør 12M, Copenhagen 34M.

Charts
UKHO 2108, 2115, 2594
Danish 102, 129

Lights
Nakkehoved 56°07'·2N 12°20'·6E Fl(3)W.20s54m20M
 White square tower
W Molehead 56°07'·8N 12°18'·7E Fl.G.3s7m4M
 Green round tower
E Molehead 56°07'·8N 12°18'·7E Fl.R.3s7m4M
 Red reflective post

Communications
Harbourmaster ✆ +45 48 30 16 63
 mobile +45 40 16 66 63

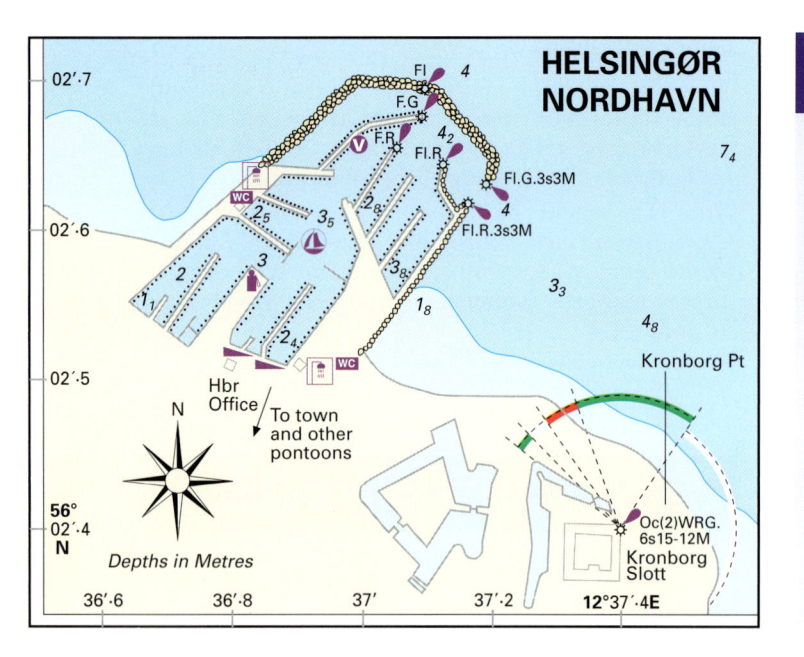

of the castle. Yacht berths are situated by the Kultur Værftet (a striking glass walled concert hall and theatre), just north of the ferry terminal. The approach to these is through the harbour entrance, then turn to starboard towards the Kultur Værftet. There are now three pontoons with electricity and water. Very large yachts can moor on the quay on the port-hand side. There is water and electricity but all other facilities are at the marina some distance away. These harbour berths are, however, very close to the town centre and railway station with a splendid view of the castle. At the entrance it states that this is for yachts of over 50' but in practice smaller yachts are allowed.

Facilities
All facilities are available including WiFi.

General
A busy fishing harbour, 12M to the northwest of Helsingør, which is gradually being taken over by yachts.

Approach
The area to the NNW of the entrance, known as Gilleleje Flak, is littered with shoals which cause uncomfortable seas in onshore winds. It is marked by three cardinal buoys, N, E and S. The harbour entrance is approx. 500m SSE of the south cardinal mark. The harbour approach has one red and one green buoy. All these buoys are unlit but the mole heads are lit red and green (see above).

Berthing
Berth in box berths at jetties running out from the east breakwater or alongside in the south fishing basin. Berth in any available space, but not in the North Basin which is reserved for fishing boats.

Kronborg Slot on approach to Helsingør with marina entrance to its right, looking north *David Ridout*

THE BALTIC SEA AND APPROACHES

GILLELEJE

Fishing gear by the village green, Gilleleje *David Ridout*

Facilites

All facilities are available. WiFi. All types of restaurant surround the harbour.

Isefjorden and Roskildefjorden

After leaving Gilleleje if you are heading west there are several anchorages and harbours that are worth considering:

Hundested, south of landfall buoy 55°59'.67N 11°51'E, is the first you will come to at the entrance to Isefjorden with **Lynæs** slightly further south, both on the eastern side. On the opposite side of the entrance you will find a good anchorage behind a spit of land, Skansehage, which is north of the entrance channel to another harbour, **Rørvig**. There are several places one can visit in the **Isefjorden** and **Roskildefjorden** with quite a few anchoring options. 16M west of Hundested, the yacht and fishing harbour at **Odden** (55°58'·4N 11°22'·4E) would also make a good stop.

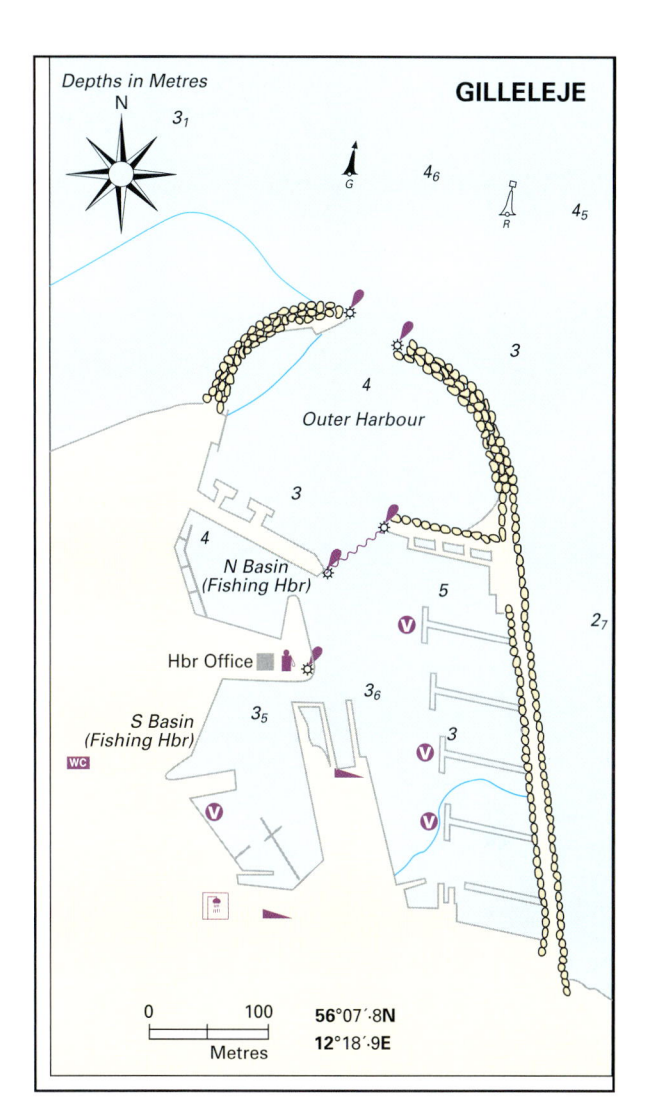

Gilleleje looking NE through entrance *David Ridout*

THE BALTIC SEA AND APPROACHES **85**

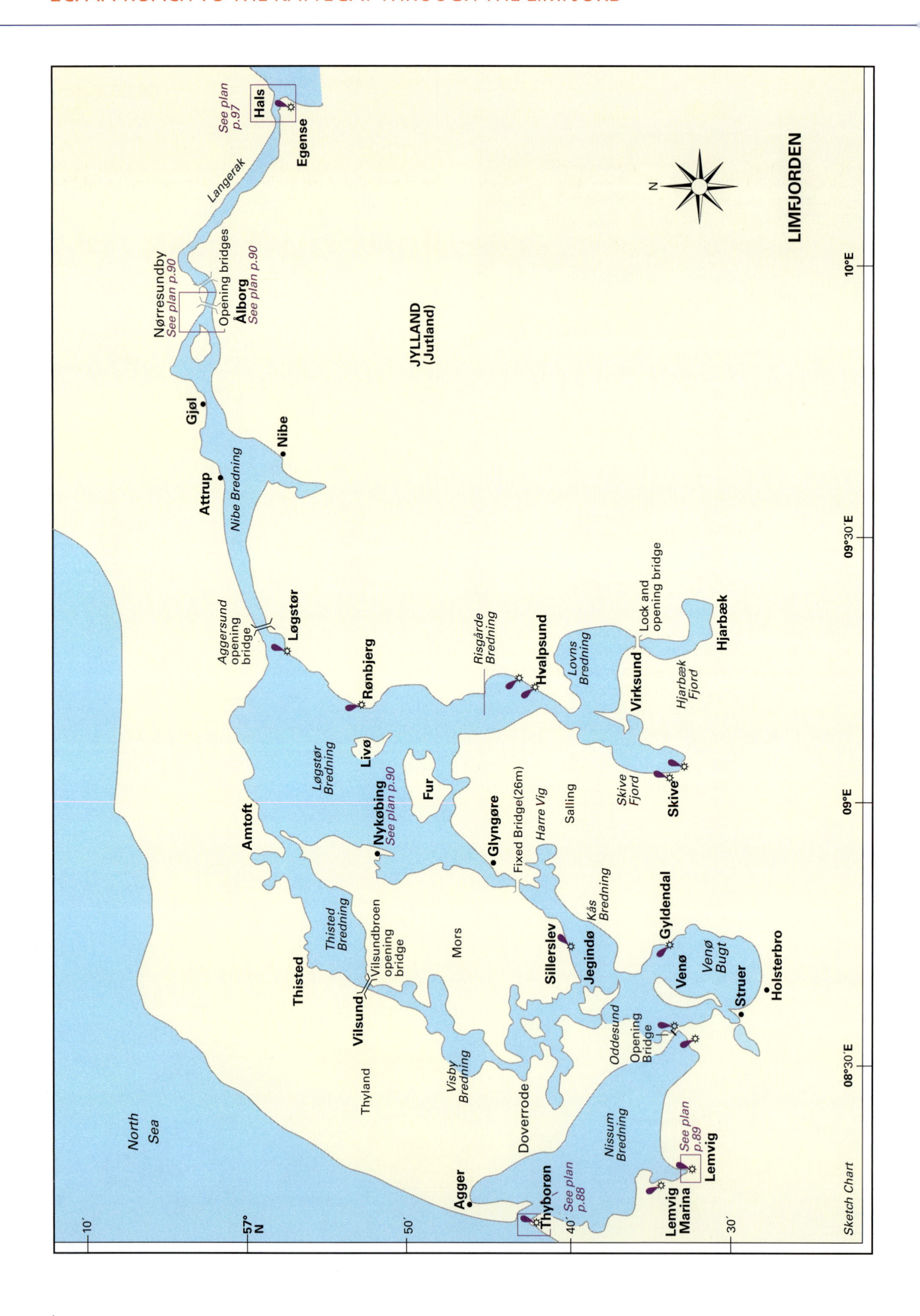

2C. APPROACH TO THE KATTEGAT THROUGH THE LIMFJORD

86 THE BALTIC SEA AND APPROACHES

THE LIMFJORD

2c. Approach to the Kattegat through the Limfjord

The Limfjord provides a very pleasant shortcut for yachts sailing to the Baltic from Scotland or further north. It saves the long sail round Skagen, where the seas can be unpleasant, and it provides sheltered sailing in beautiful surroundings in which to recover from the long passage across the North Sea. In fact one could spend a couple of weeks cruising in the area and still not see it all. Much of it is shallow but with a draught of less than 2m most of it is accessible. Minimum depth for the through route is 4m in the dredged channel west of Ålborg and maximum air draught 26m at the Sallingsund fixed bridge near Nykøbing.

Unfortunately the approach can be dangerous in onshore winds over Force 5 especially on the ebb when the current runs at up to two knots (but this can increase up to six knots in very strong winds) in which case diversion to Hanstholm, Hirtshals or round the Skagen may be necessary. If intending to enter the Limfjord the two large scale Danish charts *108* and *109* or their German equivalents are essential. Admiralty charts do not cover the Limfjord further west than Løgstør. The Danish charts are difficult to obtain west of Ålborg and need to be purchased before arrival. An alternative would be the German Chart *Set 6* published by Delius Klasing which covers the whole of the Danish North Sea coast, the whole Limfjord and some of the western Kattegat as well. Navionics and iSailor electronic charts cover the area.

Lemvig. Yachts in the fishing basin *J. Parkinson*

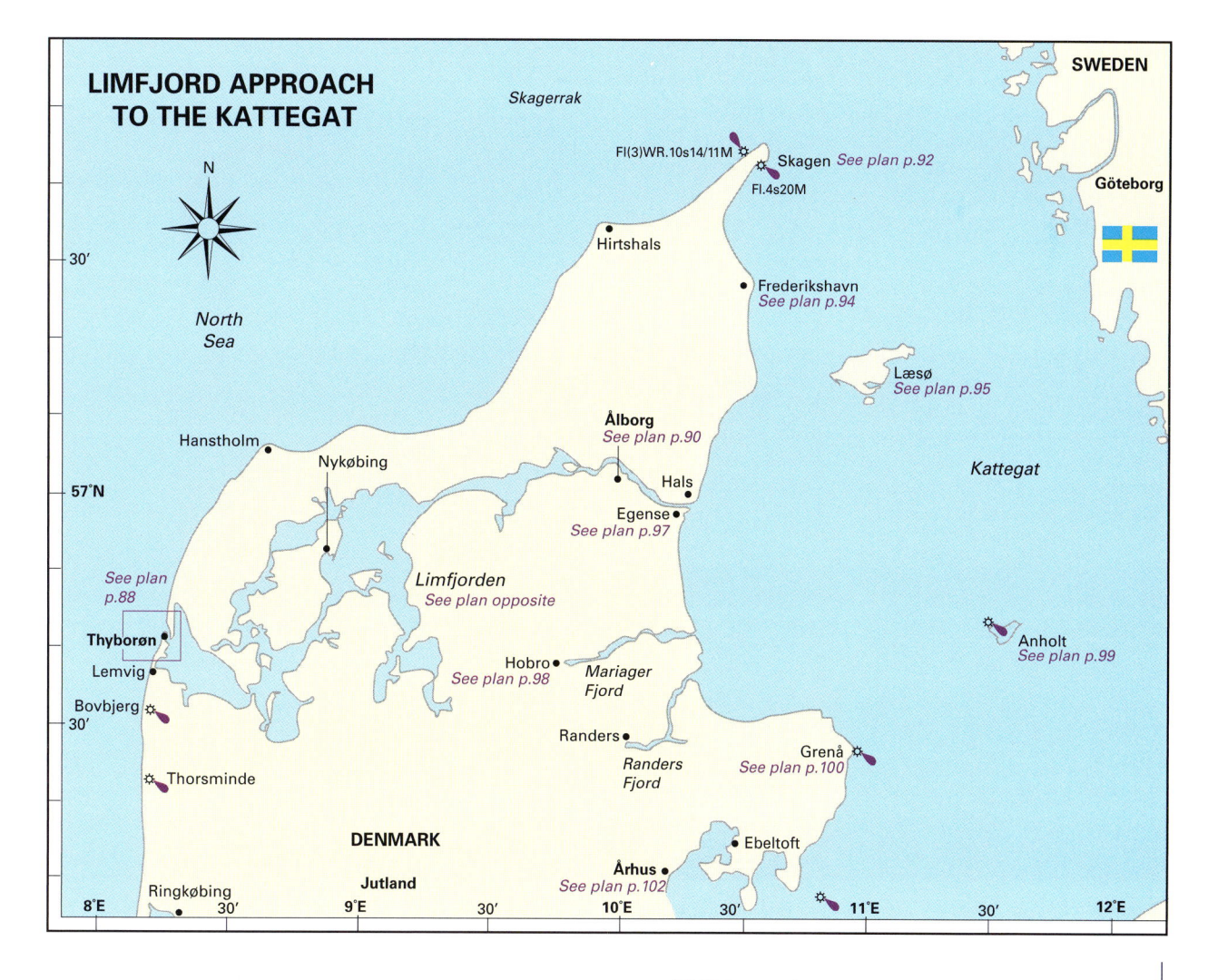

THE BALTIC SEA AND APPROACHES

2C. APPROACH TO THE KATTEGAT THROUGH THE LIMFJORD

Thyborøn

56°42′N 08°13′.52E starboard or north mole head of harbour

Distances
Edinburgh 400M, Den Helder 250M, Helgoland 170M, Ålborg 80M, Esbjerg 90M, Christiansand 85M.

Charts
UKHO 426
Danish 93

Lights
Hanstholm 57°06′.7N 08°36′E Fl(3)20s65m24M
Lodbjerg 56°49′.4N 08°15′.8E Fl(2)20s48m21M
Ldg Lts 082° *Front* 56°43′N 06°14′.1E Iso.WRG.4s8m10/8M
Rear 0·5M behind front Iso.4s17m11M
Landfall buoy 56°42′.53N 08°08′.65E LFl.10s Red and white buoy
Thyborøn 56°42′.5N 8°12′.9E Fl(3)10s12M
Bovbjerg 56°31′.7N 8°07′.1E Fl(2)15s62m16M

Tides
HW Esjberg +0120 – +0230 ML 0.0

Depths
Least depth in approach from seaward about 6m and inside the bar 5–8m.

Communications
Harbourmaster ☎ +45 97 83 11 88
port@thyboronport.dk
www.thyboronport.dk

General

This small town has quite a large harbour which is mainly concerned with fishing and the ferry across the Limfjord. It is situated just inside the western entrance to the Limfjord. Facilities for yachts have recently been improved and it would make a good stopover whether one has just arrived from the North Sea or is waiting to depart. There is room for all sizes of yachts.

Approach

Landfall buoy 56°42′53N 08°08′.65E

On arrival at the landfall buoy make 082° on the leading line into the entrance and there pick up the starboardhand channel buoys and follow them round to the SSE and the harbour entrance to starboard. Once inside the breakwater turn northwards to the northernmost basin where there are berths for yachts in 3·5m.

Thyborøn entrance looking out to sea in a NNW direction on a calm day *David Ridout*

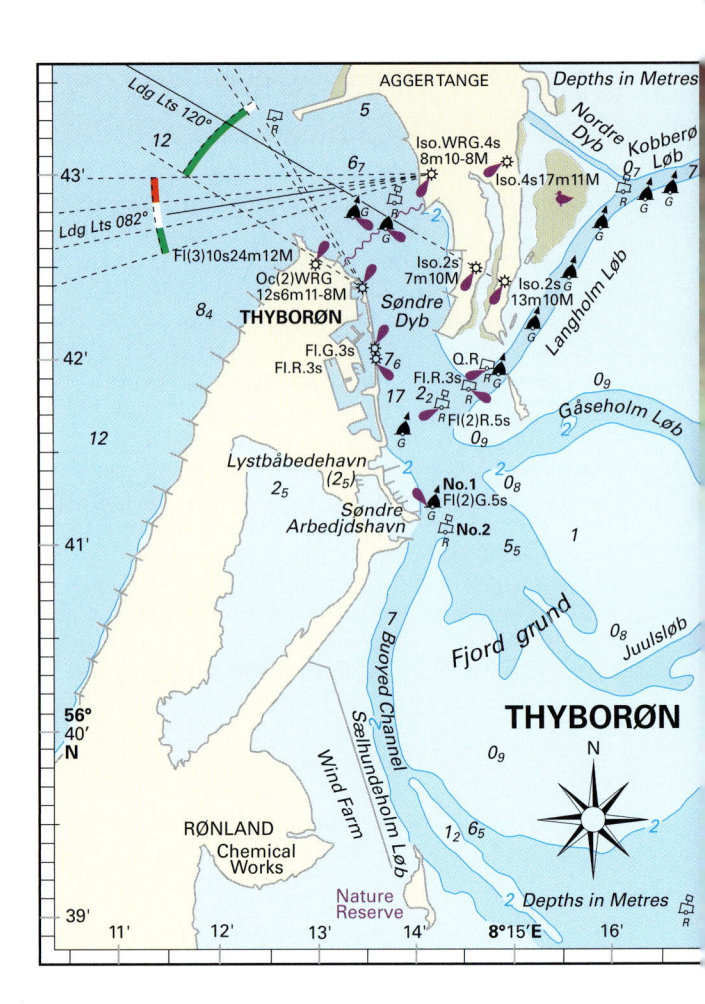

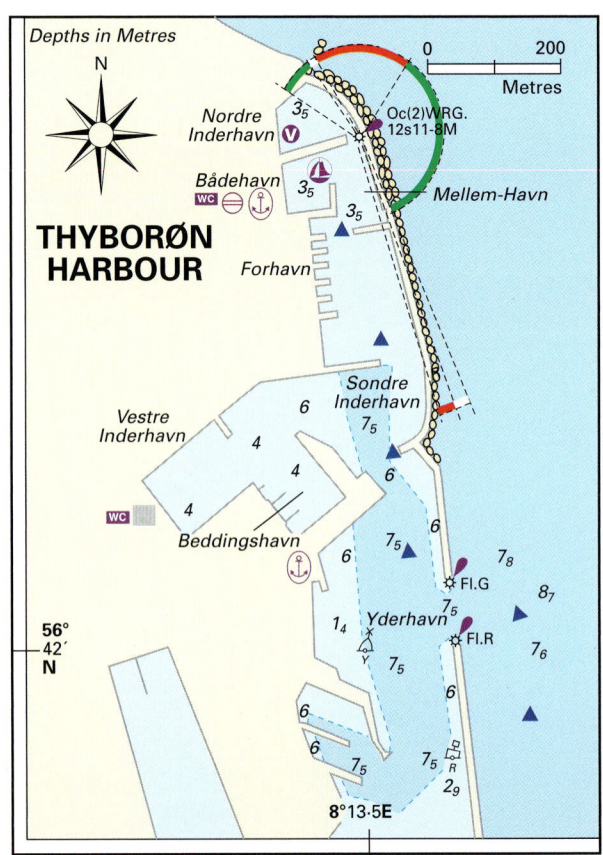

88 THE BALTIC SEA AND APPROACHES

NYKØBING

Thyboron yacht harbour looking SE *David Ridout*

The approach from the east involves picking up the narrow buoyed channel (some lit) which starts with a north cardinal mark at 56°37'·9N 08°17E and curves round northwards to join the main entrance channel past the harbour.

Facilities
All facilities are available including diesel which can be obtained from a barge in the main harbour.

Lemvig
56°33'N 08°18'·33E starboard mole head Lemvig Havn
HM ☏ +45 97 82 01 06, www.visitlemvig.dk

This is a small and attractive town in the creek on the south side of the westernmost lake of the Limfjord, the Nissum Bredning.

It is approached through a long buoyed channel which is dredged to 4·4m

The dredged channel leaves a marina to starboard but it is a long way from the town and it is better to continue further and berth in the main harbour either alongside one of the quays or in one of the many box berths which can accommodate quite large yachts. The harbour has been extended so now has plenty of space. The harbour has all facilities including diesel.

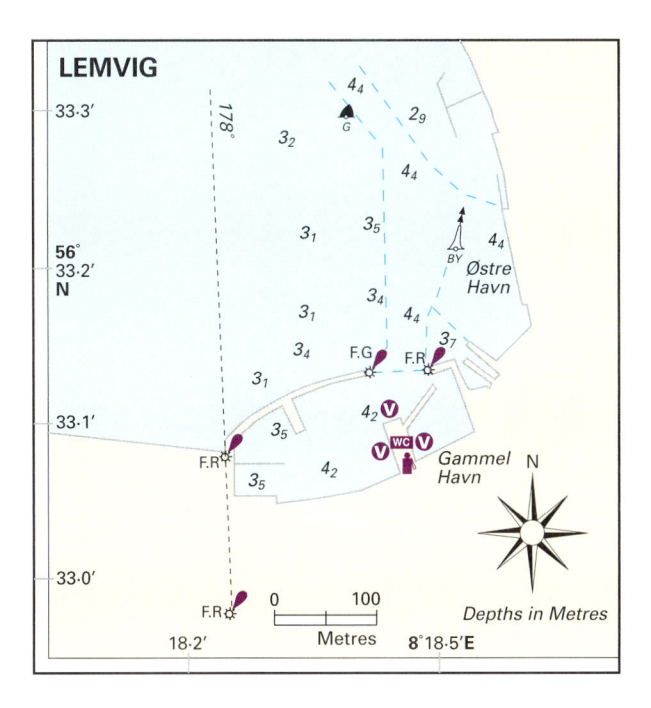

Oddesund Bridge
56°34'·5N 08°32'·5E
Bridge keeper ☏ +45 97 87 50 55 or ☏ +45 21 77 38 82
VHF Ch 16, 12, 13

This combined rail and road bridge opens on demand from 0600-1730 at a quarter to and quarter past the hour but remains closed for 15 minutes before a train is due. Contact the bridge keeper and hoist International Code Flag N in the rigging and wait. Information in *Komma's havnelods* (under Oddesund).

Once through the bridge the more direct route to Ålborg and the Kattegat continues in a northeasterly direction but one can divert south into Venø Sund to visit Struer or take the northern route to Ålborg via a series of small lakes to Thisted Bredning and Thisted.

Nykøbing
56°47'·53N 08°52'·13E port mole at entrance to harbour
HM ☏ +45 20 57 65 62

Nykøbing is a useful stop on the direct route to Ålborg as it is 30M from Thyborøn and 35M from Ålborg. 2M southwest of the entrance channel is a fixed road bridge with a clearance of 26m.

Nykøbing is an old fisheries town with many museums. It is entered by a buoyed entrance channel dredged to 4·4m. It starts at the East cardinal mark just west of the point which forms the eastern side of the bay. Follow the buoyed channel on 345° with 2F.R Lts in line bearing round on to 323·6° (2F.G Lts in line) through the harbour entrance. Then berth either at pontoons in the marina in 3m on the port hand (but observe the port hand buoy when entering and do not cut inside it) or continue into the

The Oddesund lifting road and rail bridge across the Limfjord will open for yachts even at rush hour *E. Redfern*

THE BALTIC SEA AND APPROACHES

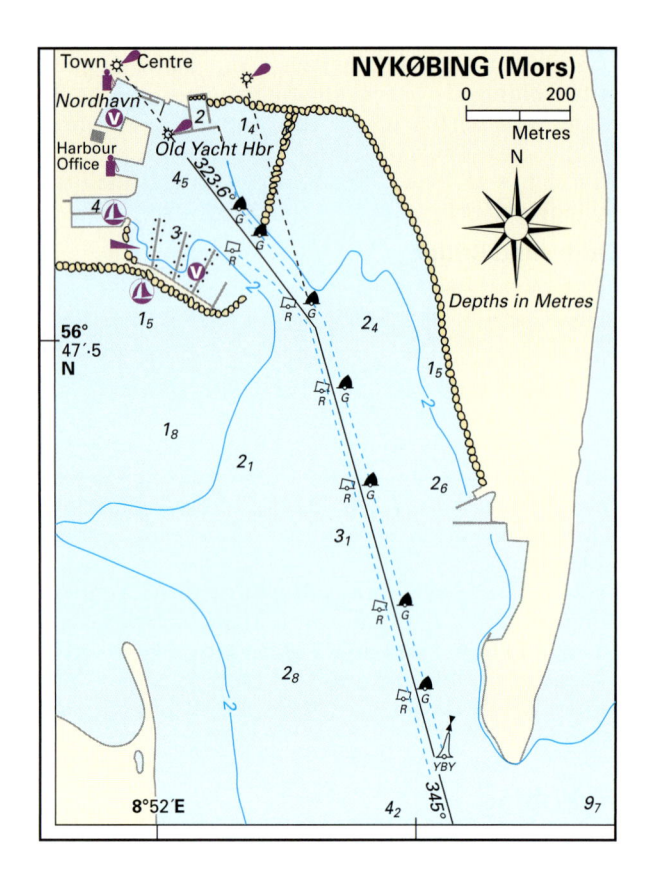

2C. APPROACH TO THE KATTEGAT THROUGH THE LIMFJORD

Ålborg

57°03′N 09°55′E

Ålborg is the capital of the region and the centre of communications as well as being a university town. It now has major industries but its original wealth came from the herring fisheries. The old part of the town, the Østerågade, is attractive and interesting. It is well known for Ålborg Akvavit!

Approach

The approach from the west by the Løgstør Bredning starts at the red port-hand mark Fl(3)R10s at 56°58′·5N 09°09′·3E some 26M west of Ålborg. Leading lights Iso.W.2s and 4s on 079·2° then lead up the channel to Løgstør where there is a marina with alongside berths in a canal which is entered just west of the main harbour.

The main channel to Ålborg then continues northeastward to the Aggersund Lifting Bridge, which opens on demand, in theory, but in practice seems to wait until there are a number of yachts waiting. At any bridge one can make one's wishes known by hoisting the N flag in the rigging and calling on VHF Ch 12 or 13.

The buoyed channel then continues for another 20 miles up to Ålborg. For the most part it is wide with depths over 4m but it is very narrow where it is dredged to 4m through the Drag Banke.

At Ålborg there is a choice of marinas but the most convenient ones for the shops and for a bus or train to the centre are Ålborg Skudehavn (which has plenty of room both in box berths and alongside and it now has a small wave barrier) and the Vestre Lystbådehavnen where there may be a box berth, or tie up along the quayside. All facilities are available and fuel may be possible in the Nordhavnen where the fishing boats are moored but the pump is reported to be old.

90 THE BALTIC SEA AND APPROACHES

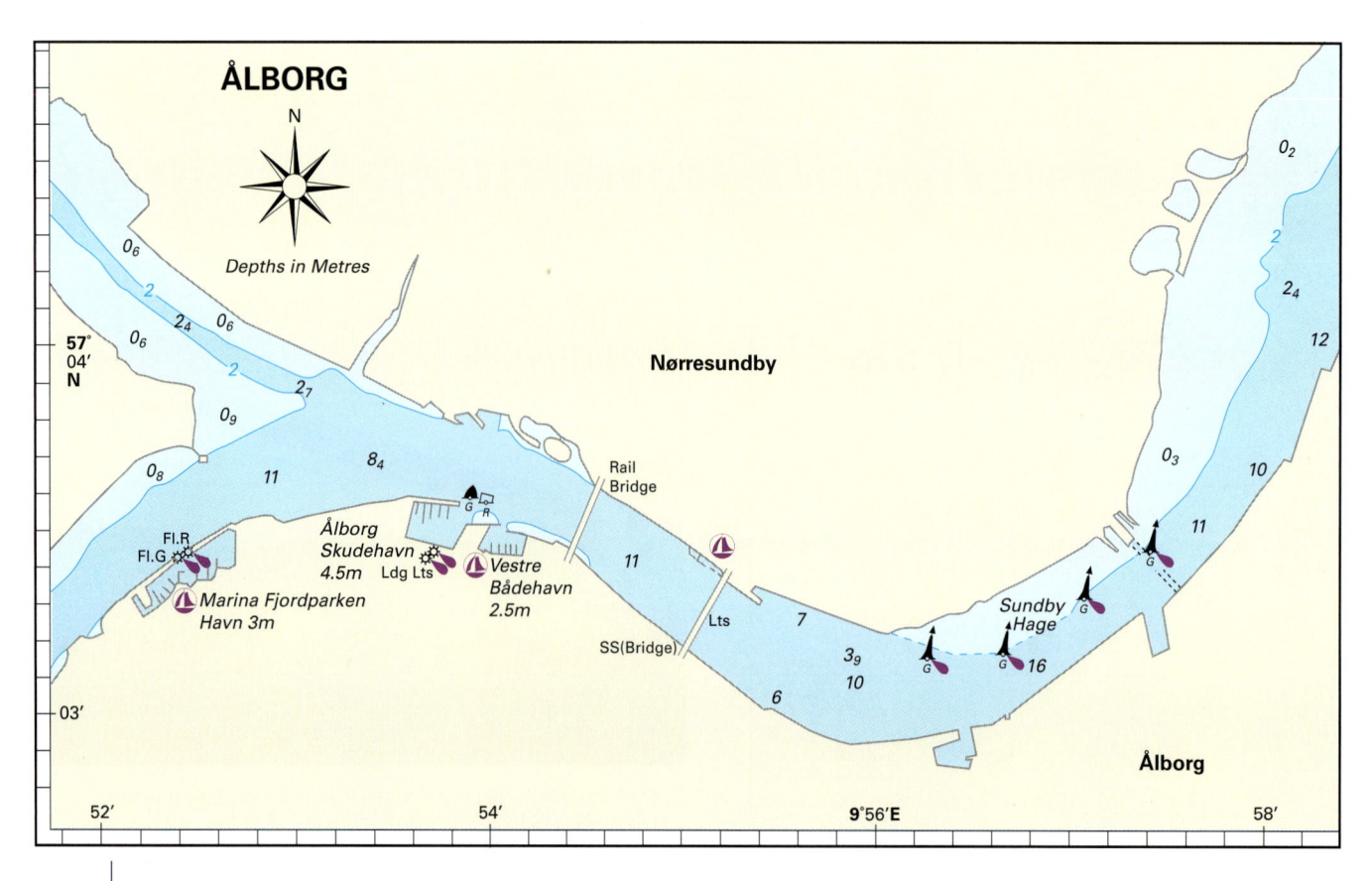

ÅLBORG

Bådehavn (which is the last one on the south side before the railway bridge). It has restaurants and all facilities as well as an excellent chandlery but it is often crowded and a berth that is wide enough can sometimes be hard to find, especially as the channels between the box berths are very narrow.

There are two lifting bridges in Ålborg. The western one is a railway bridge which seems to stay in a closed position most of the time. The bridge is operated by DSB and it is advisable to call up the

Ålborg Bridge with rail bridge beyond J. Parkinson

*Ålborg, end of Tall Ships Race, taken from the road bridge
David Ridout*

bridge (channels 12, 13 or 16) to find out opening times. The eastern bridge is the Limfjord Road Bridge which generally opens on the hour every hour, but this can change at busy times. Again contact on one of the aforementioned channels. Opening times for both bridges can be found on www.visitaalborg.com. The route east from Ålborg to the sea at Hals and Egense is well buoyed and straight-forward. See chapter on Limfjord East entrance.

Ålborg from the west with Ålborg Skudehaven - now with additional pontoon and wave barrier - and Vestre Bådehavn on south shore Patrick Roach

THE BALTIC SEA AND APPROACHES

2D. DANISH HARBOURS AND ANCHORAGES OF THE KATTEGAT

2d. Danish harbours and anchorages of the Kattegat

Skagen

57°42'·72N 10°36'E outer pier south

Distances
Kristiansand 100M, Göteborg 47M, Edinburgh 500M, Fredrikshavn 20M, Copenhagen 145M.

Charts
UKHO 2107
Danish 101

Lights
Skagen W 57°44'·9N 10°35'·7E Fl(3)WR.10s31m14/11M
  White round tower 053°-W-248°-R-323°
Skagen Shoal buoy 57°46'N 10°44'E NCM Q.Fl
Skagen 57°44'·1N 10°37'·8E Fl.4s44m20M
  Grey round tower
Skagen outer mole N 57°42'·92N 10°35'·92E Fl.G.3s5M
Skagen outer mole S 57°42'·72N 10°35'·99E Fl.R.3s5M
Skagen inner pier N 57°42'·87N 10°35'·65E Fl.G.5s3M
Skagen inner pier S 57°42'·84N 10°35'·55E Fl.R.5s3M
Hirsholm 57°29'·1N 10°37'·5E Fl(3).30s30m22M Round granite tower

Communications
Port Authority ☎ +45 98 44 13 46, VHF Ch 12
Lystbådehavn (Marina) Harbourmaster ☎ +45 98 44 33 41
lystbaadehavn@frederikshavn.dk

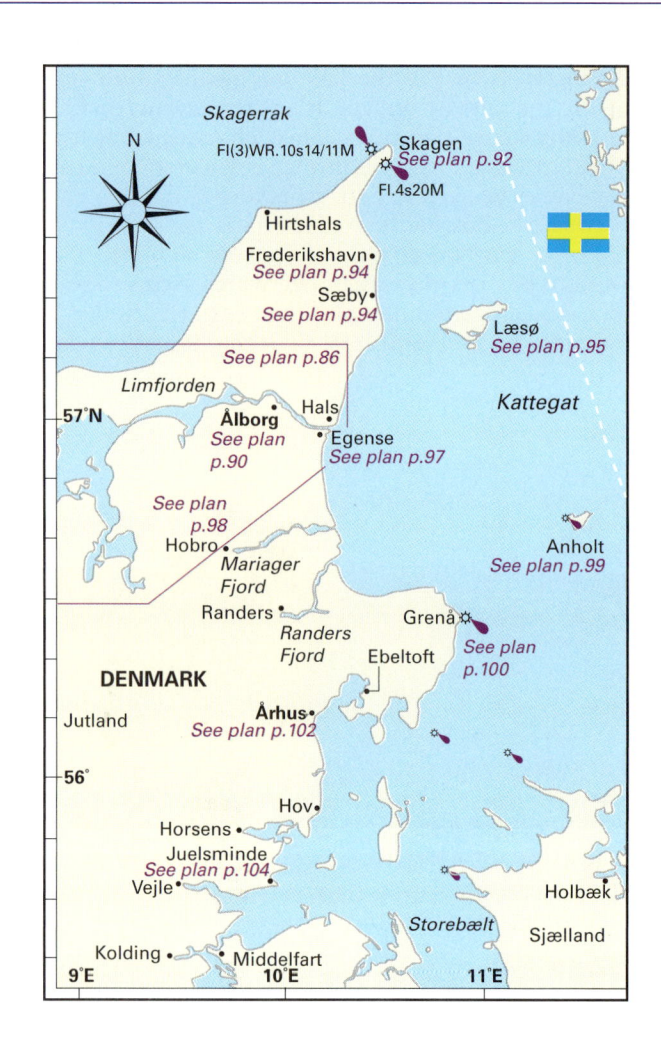

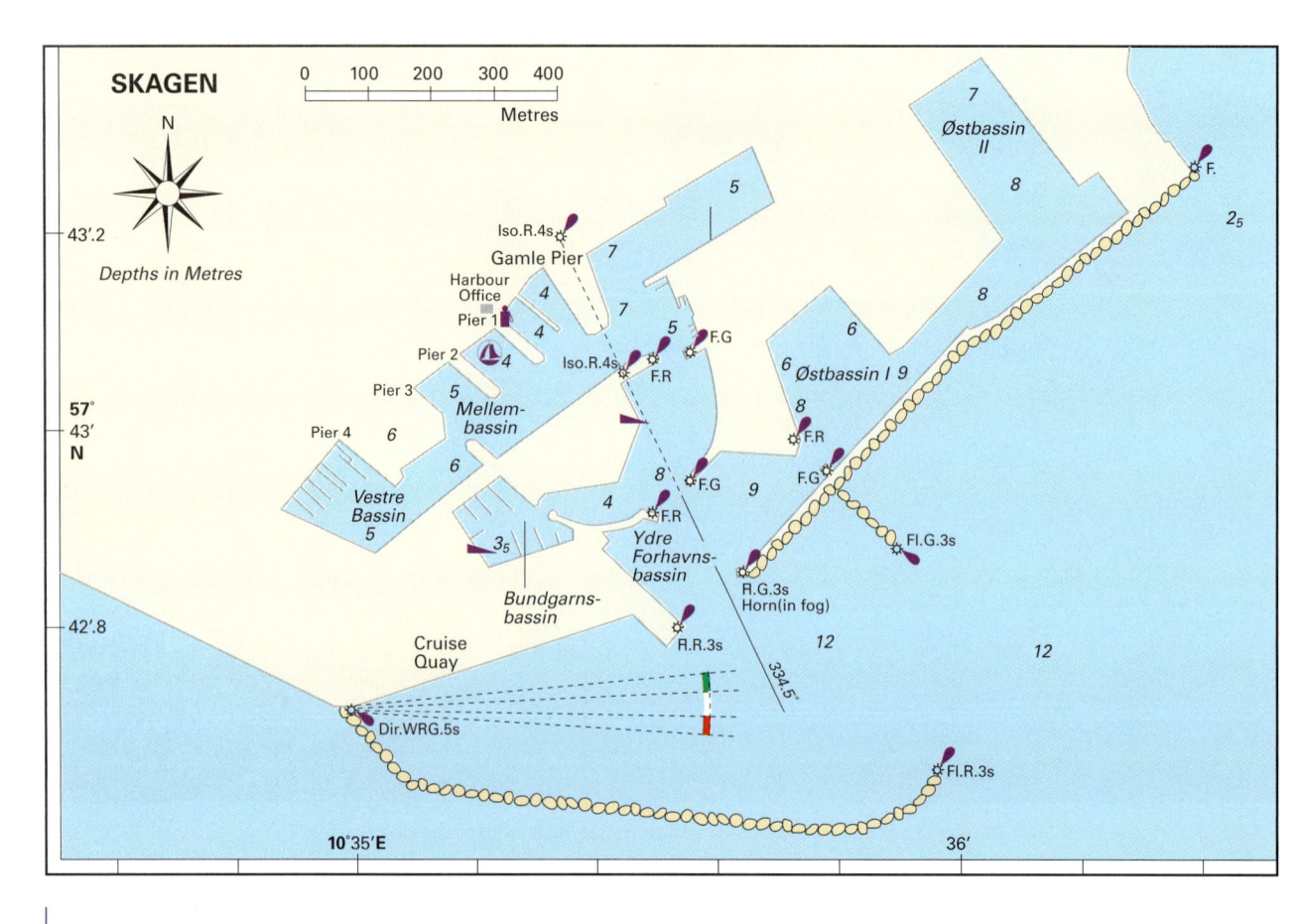

92 THE BALTIC SEA AND APPROACHES

FREDERIKSHAVN

General
Skagen is a busy fishing harbour and a thriving holiday resort. The area is a favourite with Danish artists. The harbour provides good protection.

Approach
The flat Skagen headland with its two lighthouses is extended for 2M in an east-northeast direction by a shallow reef marked by a North cardinal mark. In strong west and northwesterly winds the seas can be heavy and in addition there is usually much commercial traffic rounding the headland. Once rounded, course can be set for Skagen harbour entrance giving the shallows off the point a reasonably wide berth. New outer moles have been constructed (see Skagen lights opposite for details). From a position of approximately 57°42'·80N 10°36'·1E go on a heading of 280° to enter between these, aiming for the two inner pier heads marking the outer harbour. Alter course to 335° for a short distance for next piers (fixed red and green) then head due north through the next harbour basin before turning to port for the marina.

Berthing
Berth in the marina on pontoons between Gamle Pier and Pier 1 or between Piers 1 and 2 in 4m depths. Should these two areas be completely full, the basin immediately northeast of Gamle Pier is sometimes opened up for mooring.

Facilities
All facilities including fuel.

Skagen from the northwest before the new outer moles were built *Patrick Roach*

Frederikshavn
57°25'·61N 10°32'E north marina mole

Distances
Skagen 20M, Læsø Vesterø Havn 15M, Limfjord entrance 30M.

Charts
UKHO 2107
Danish 101, 123

Lights
Hirsholm 57°29'·1N 10°37'·5E Fl(3).30s30m22M Round granite tower Also FRW.30m 007·6°-W-013·5°-R-016·4°
Commercial Port NE Breakwater Hd 57°26'N 10°33'·2E Fl.G.3s7m7M Metal post, green band
Commercial Port Approach Light 57°26'·2N 10°32'·5E Oc.WRG.10s14m9M 305·8°-G-308·3°-W-310·3°-R-312·8°
Marina E Mole Hd 57°25'·6N 10°32'E Fl.R.3s4m3M Mast
Læsø Rende 57°13'·1N 10°40'·3E Fl(2)10s27m6M White round concrete tower, black base

Communications
Marina harbourmaster ☎ +45 98 43 28 56
www.Frederikshavnsejlklub.dk

General
Fredrikshavn Port is a very busy ferry and commercial harbour with ferries to Oslo, Larvik, Göteborg and Læsø. The *Søsporthavn* or marina is situated approximately 0·75M to the southwest of the entrance to the main port.

Approach
Approaching from the north the rocks and islands of Hirsholm, guarded by the Hirsholm Lt, must be left to starboard and the shallows to the east of Fredrikshavn, which are marked by north and south cardinal marks and a green starboardhand buoy, must be skirted in the same way. Head for the marina which has a red and green buoy just before entering between the moles. Enter between the north and south mole (which is quite narrow) into the marina. From the south the approach is straightforward although fish traps may be a hazard close to the shore.

There are depths of 2·5m in buoyed entrance channel but subject to silting.

Frederickshavn, new berths to port soon after entering the marina *David Ridout*

2. DENMARK

THE BALTIC SEA AND APPROACHES   93

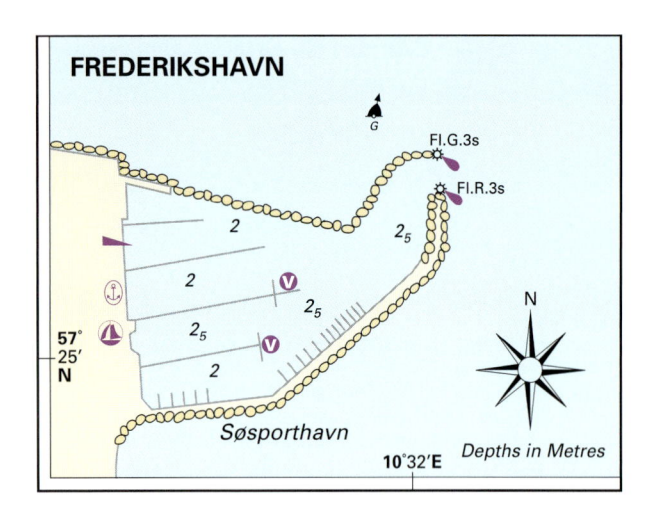

2D. DANISH HARBOURS AND ANCHORAGES OF THE KATTEGAT

Berthing
Moor in box berths with bow to staging. There are several berths for large yachts on the south mole, some of them alongside.

Facilities
All facilities are available but the marina is some way from the city centre. Local food shops nearby.

Sæby

57°19'·98N 10°32'·17E

Charts
UKHO 2107
Danish 101, 123

Lights
Nordre Rønner 57°21'·6N 10°55'·4E Fl.15s16m14M
   Round granite tower
Ldg Lts 136·1° *Front* Outer E mole Head
   57°17'·9N 10°55'·4E Iso.R.2s7m3M
   Red triangle on red framework tower.
   Rear 364m from front. Iso.R.4s14m3M
   Red inverted triangle on framework tower
Læsø buoy NW Rev 57°15'·7N 10°45'·4E Fl(2)R.5s
   Red can buoy
Læsø Rende 57°13'·1N 10°40'·3E Fl(2)10s27m6M
   White round concrete tower, black base

Communications
Harbourmaster +45 98 46 10 59

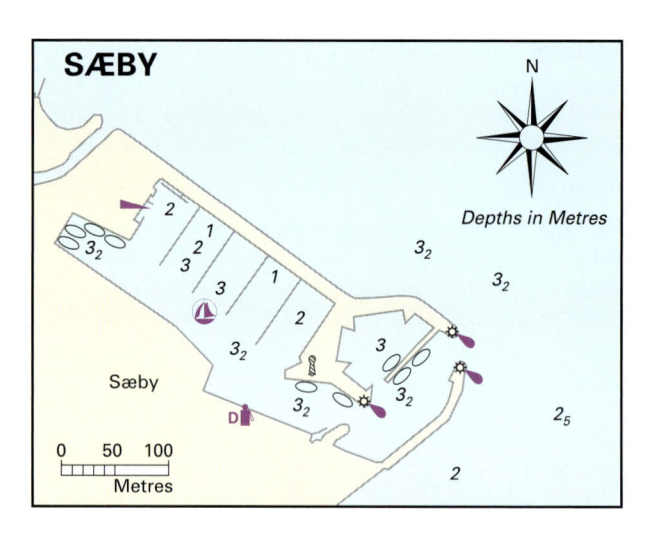

General
5·6 miles south of Frederikshavn, Sæby is a very charming harbour, which has recently been enlarged to accommodate many more yachts.

Approach
This is straightforward but, as the waters are shallow, care should be taken in strong onshore winds. Once inside the harbour moles there are various mooring options. A large mosaic sculpture (Lady of the Sea) is prominent near the entrance.

Berthing
Berthing is available alongside, immediately to starboard after entering between the moles. Alternatively, continue into the main section of the

The Lady of the Sea sculpture and church in background
David Ridout

Entrance to Sæby harbour looking W David Ridout

94   THE BALTIC SEA AND APPROACHES

VESTERØ - LÆSØ

harbour with fuel to port and some alongside mooring to starboard. Further in there are box berths to port along the main quayside and box berths to starboard (with red/green availability markers). At the head of the harbour there are moorings close to the harbour office - pay by machine.

Facilities
All facilities, free WiFi. Several restaurants. Supermarket nearby.

Beautiful church with very old chalk paintings, restored between 2006-09. Beaches and a pretty park north of the harbour.

Vesterø - Læsø

57°17'·89N 10°55'·29E starboard mole head

Distances
Frederikshavn 15M, Skagen 27M, Limfjord Entrance 30M, Göteborg 45M

Charts
UKHO 2107
Danish 123

Lights
Nordre Rønner 57°21'·6N 10°55'·4E Fl.15s16m14M
  Round granite tower
Ldg Lts 136·1° *Front* Outer E mole Head 57°17'·9N 10°55'·4E Iso.R.2s7m3M Red triangle on red framework tower. *Rear* 364m from front. Iso.R.4s14m3M Red inverted triangle on framework tower
Læsø buoy NW Rev 57°15'·7N 10°45'·4E Fl(2)R.5s
  Red can buoy
Læsø Rende 57°13'·1N 10°40'·3E Fl(2).10s27m6M
  White round concrete tower, black base

Communications
Harbourmaster ☎ +45 98 49 92 22
  http://havne.laesoe.dk
  vesteroehavn@laesoe.dk

General
Læsø is a quiet and attractive island with many sandy beaches. The island is unique in that it has several houses on which a thick layer of seaweed has been used for roofing. The main Museum is one such and is well worth a visit.

Approach
The leading line on 136·1° runs in from the northwest of the island with the Nordre Rønner reef with its light tower 2M to port and the northwest Læsø Reef (marked at its northwest corner by a red lightbuoy) 3·5M to starboard. The Nordre Rønner reef is extensively buoyed on the porthand but it is not until one is within 1M of the entrance that there are green starboardhand buoys. The entrance carries a depth of 3·4m.

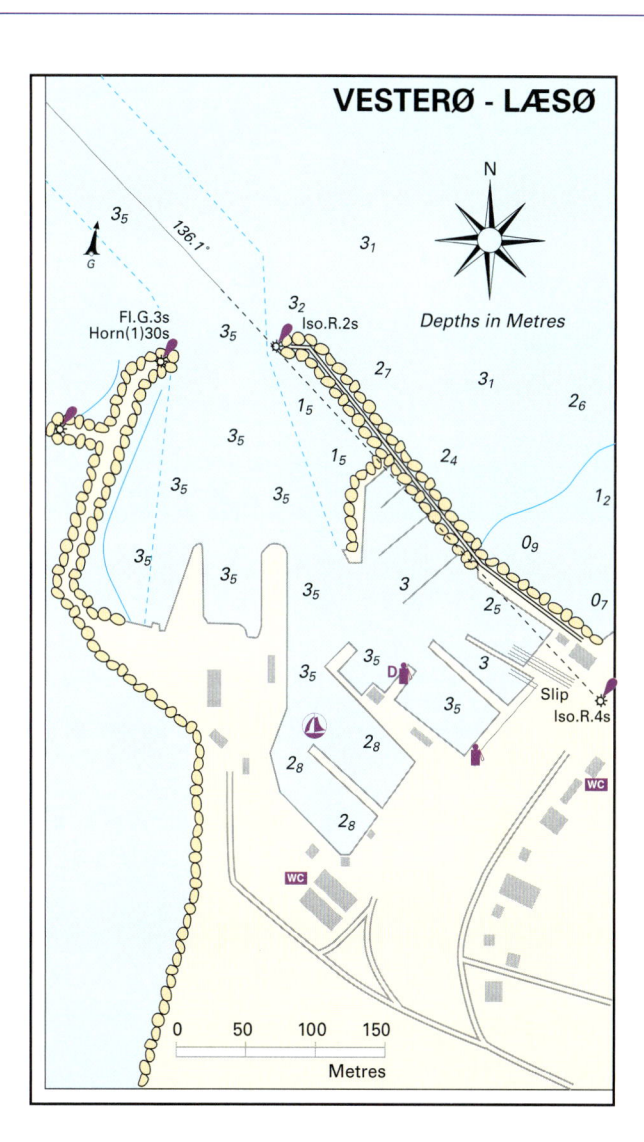

Berthing
Berth bow to the quay and pick up a stern line. Berth where space allows but not in the fishing harbour.

Facilities
All facilities. Webcam. Beaches both north and south of harbour. Cafés and grills along the quay side. Brugsen supermarket nearby. Hire of bikes and

Læsø, Vesterø harbour looking NW with entrance in the background David Ridout

THE BALTIC SEA AND APPROACHES 95

2D. DANISH HARBOURS AND ANCHORAGES OF THE KATTEGAT

Læsø, house with seaweed roof David Ridout

electric cars. During the high season there is a free bus running between Vesterø and Østerby calling at various places including the museum.

Østerby Harbour at the eastern end of Læsø is another popular and welcoming harbour with all facilities including bicycle and electric car hire plus an excellent fresh fish shop on the fishing quay and a well stocked grocer close to the fish shop. This harbour is particularly popular with the Swedes due to its proximity to Göteborg. In settled weather it is possible to anchor off in an area to the west of the harbour entrance.

Limfjord approach and entrance

The main shipping channel for entry to the Limfjord begins 23M out in the Ålborg Bugt near the Svitringen South Light Tower but smaller craft can enter the channel much closer in, between the Hals Barre Light Tower and the twin Red and Green Light Towers marking the entrance. (56°58′N 10°22′E.)

Egense and Hals

56°58′N 10°21·87′E Hals Barre N

Distances
Fredrikshavn 30M, Vesterø 30M, Ålborg 15M, Mariager Fjord 20M, Anholt 42M, Grenå 45M.

Charts
UKHO 2107, 894, 429
Danish 122, 107, 106

Lights
Læsø Rende 57°13′·1N 10°40′·3E Fl(2)10s27m6M
  White round concrete tower, black base
Hals Barre 56°57′·3N 10°25′·5E Iso.WRG.2s18m8M
  305°-G-313°-W-319°-R-323°
Svitringen Rende S 56°51′N 10°36′·3E Fl.W.3s13m8M
  Red tower, white stripes marked SV S
Korsholm Ldg Lts Egense N Front 294·3° 56°58′·4N
  10°20′·1E Iso.G.2s5m9M Red 8-sided concrete tower
  Secondary Lt FlR3s5m3M Vis 139·5°-290·5° S *Front*
  Iso.R.2s5m9M Vis 290·3°-298·3° *Rear* 1·2M from front
  Iso.W.2s20m15M Red inverted triangle on red framework tower.
  All synchronised

Communications
Hals harbourmaster ☏ +45 51 52 66 24
  post@halsbaadelaug.dk
  www.halsbaadelaug.dk
Egense YH and Sail Club ☏ +45 98 31 00 57

Approach

The channel continues with port and starboardhand buoys, some lit and some unlit, up to Ålborg. There is a succession of leading lights all the way up to Ålborg, 15M inland.

Berthing

Egense and Hals are on opposite sides of the entrance. Hals, on the north side, is a fishing harbour, lit and with 3m depth. It has all facilities and shops. Egense, on the south side, is smaller, unlit and has 2m depth. A small passenger ferry runs between the two harbours very regularly in the season.

Alternatively there is an anchorage with good protection from southwest through west to north and some protection from north through east to south in 2·3–3·1m in the area west of Korsholm. In the southernmost part of the anchorage is a narrow deeper part carrying 4m depth where a few yellow mooring buoys for visitors have been laid.

*Hals, looking north
David Ridout*

96   THE BALTIC SEA AND APPROACHES

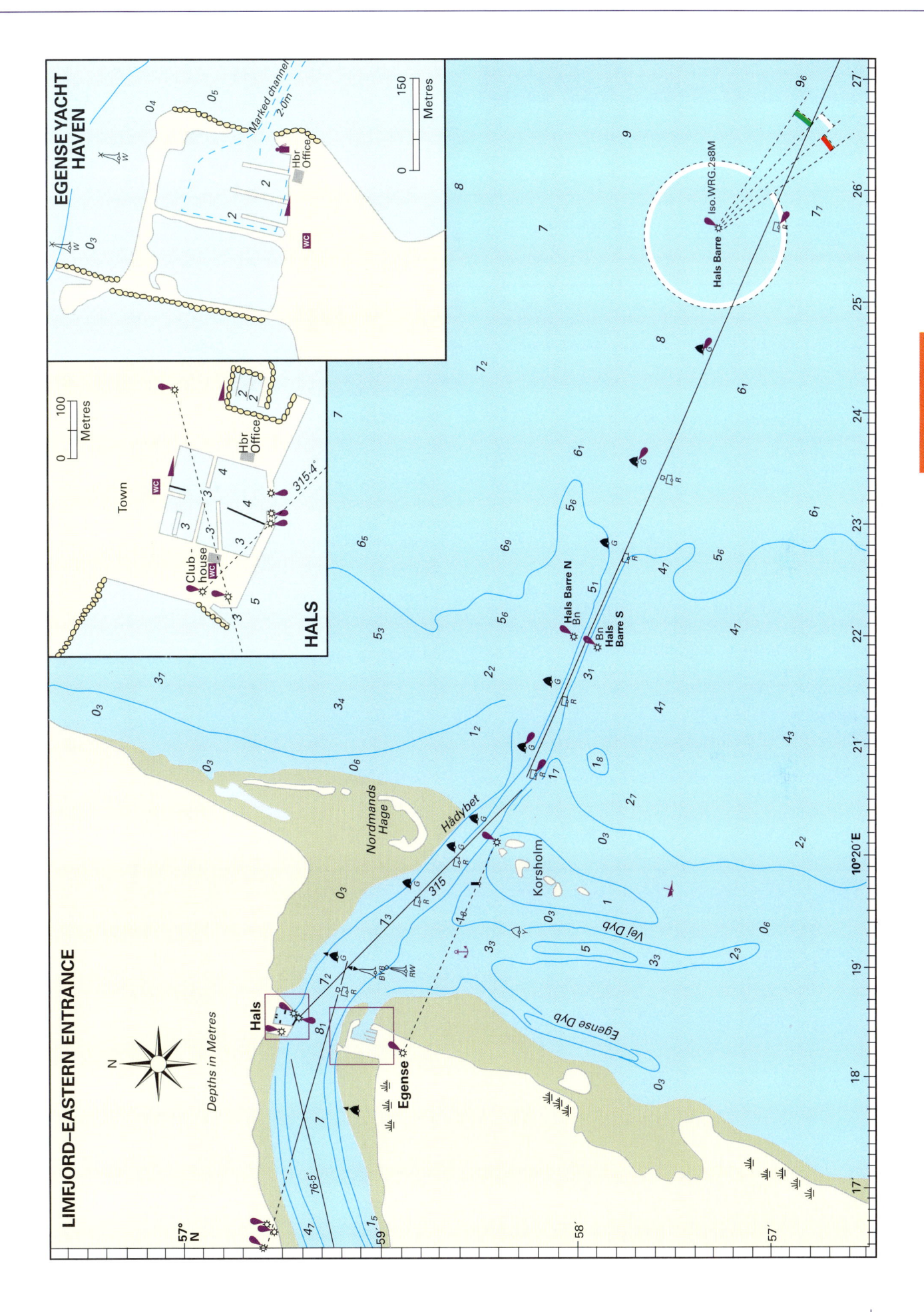

EGENSE AND HALS

EGENSE YACHT HAVEN

HALS

LIMFJORD – EASTERN ENTRANCE

2. DENMARK

THE BALTIC SEA AND APPROACHES 97

2D. DANISH HARBOURS AND ANCHORAGES OF THE KATTEGAT

Mariager Fjord

Distances
Limfjord Entrance 22M, Grenå 30M.

Charts
UKHO 894
Danish 122, 110

Lights
Hals Barre 56°57'·3N 10°25'·5E Iso.WRG.2s18m8M Red tower, white bands
Svitringen Rende S 56°51'N 10°36'·3E Fl.W.3s13m8M Red tower, white stripes marked SV S
Als Odde Ldg Lts 261·9° *Front* 56°42'·7N 10°20'·8E Iso.W.2s7m9M Red triangle on grey framework tower. *Rear* 1511m from front Iso.W.4s24m10M Red inverted triangle on framework tower
Udbyhøj, Elkaer Bakke 56°35'·4N 10°19'·2E Oc.WRG.5s33m15–12M White lighthouse, red band. 194°-G-228°-W-232°-R-254°-G-276°-W-279°-R-289°

Communications
Hadsund Lystbådehaven ☎ +45 98 57 24 39
Hadsund Bridge VHF Ch 12, 16
Hobro Havn Harbourmaster ☎ +45 98 51 02 67
Hobro Lystbådehavn ☎ +45 98 51 07 70

Mariager Fjord looking east from Hobro Patrick Roach

General
Mariager Fjord is reputed to be one of the most beautiful fjords in Denmark with reed-lined vistas in its lower reaches and wooded hills further west. It is 20M long and is included here as it is a reasonable distance between the Limfjord and Grenå and offers good anchoring opportunities in attractive surroundings. There is an interesting viking fortress, Fyrkat, 3km from Hobro.

Approach
56°43'N 10°25'·6E green light buoy marking beginning of buoyed channel

Pick up the buoyed entrance channel dredged to 5·7m and marked at its outer end by a green lightbuoy Fl(2)G.5s and make the approach on 262°.

There can be a two knot current in the entrance when entry and departure in strong easterlies can be very rough. There is an opening bridge at Hadsund (opens on the hour every hour in the season).

Berthing
Berth in Hadsund Harbour, Mariager Marina (midway along the south shore), Hobro Havn or at one of the smaller marinas. Hobro Sailing Club is adjacent to the marina at Hobro Havn and also has some berths.

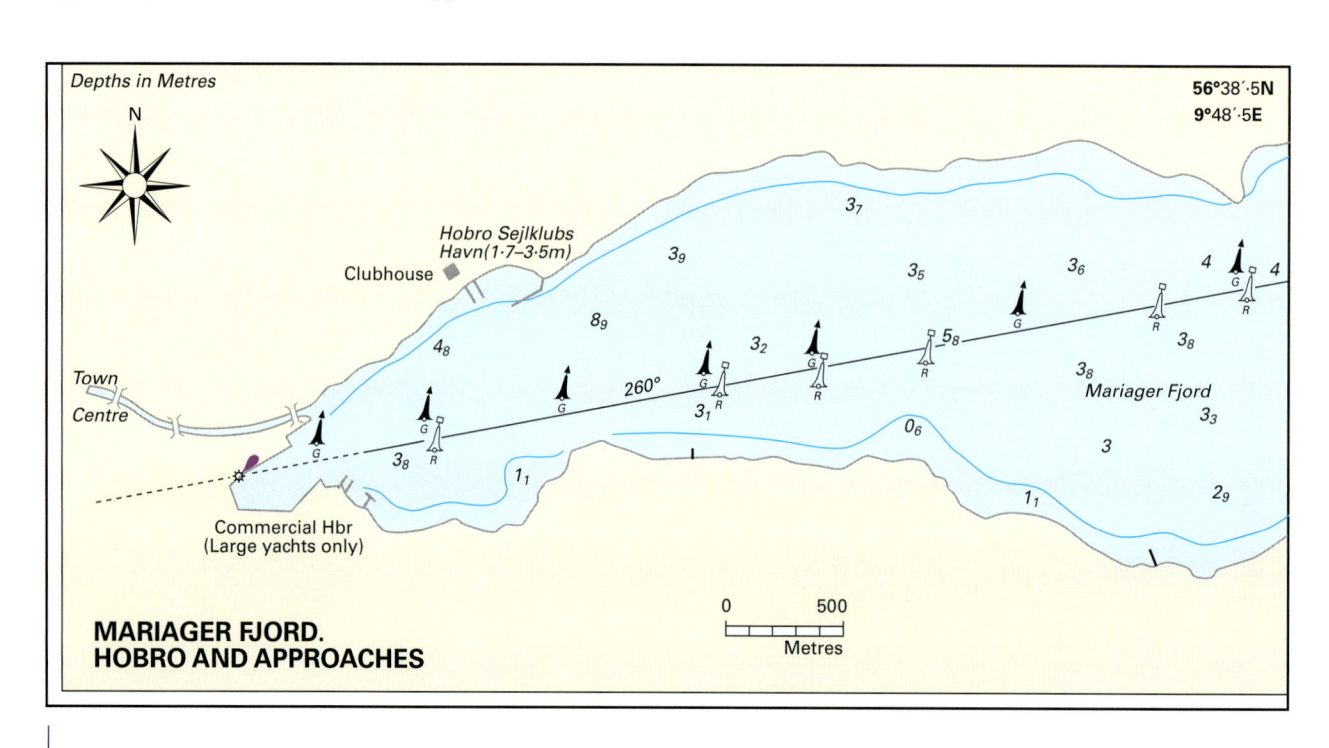

MARIAGER FJORD. HOBRO AND APPROACHES

98   THE BALTIC SEA AND APPROACHES

ANHOLT

Mariager Fjord marina, half way between Hadsund and Hobro, looking NW *David Ridout*

Deserted eastern beach on Anholt *David Ridout*

Anholt

56°42′·85N 11°30′·48E starboard mole head

Distances
Limfjord entrance 42M, Grenå 28M, Falkenberg 35M, Helsingør 55M.

Charts
UKHO 2107, 2108
Danish 102, 124

Lights
Anholt Near E end 56°44′·2N 11°39′E Fl.15s40m14M White round tower with upper part red
Anholt Harbour Outer N mole head 56°42′·9N 11°30′·5E Fl.R.3s8m4M Post

Communications
Harbourmaster ☏ +45 86 31 90 08
Mobile +45 20 30 07 08
anholt@anholtharbour.com

General
Anholt is a lovely little island 38M due east of Mariager Fjord. With good beaches, walking and cycling.

Approach
Easy approach from the west but the water is shallow for a long way out and is rough in onshore winds over Force 5. Beware shallow patches extending 3M northwest of the harbour and the 5M long Osterev Spit marked by an East cardinal mark extending from the eastern end of the island. The harbour entrance carries a depth of 3·5m.

Berthing
Berth bow to pontoons with stern buoys. Notices warn that berthing alongside will be charged double. This is not surprising as the harbour is very crowded in season. Anchoring is possible in the outer harbour but make sure the channel is clear for the ferry from Grenå.

Facilities
All basic facilities and fuel. Anholt is famous for its nightlife and music-making so don't forget to take your earplugs!

View over Anholt harbour, pre-season, looking west *David Ridout*

THE BALTIC SEA AND APPROACHES

2D. DANISH HARBOURS AND ANCHORAGES OF THE KATTEGAT

Grenå

56°24'·17N 10°55'·56E port mole of marina

Distances
Limfjord Entrance 42M, Mariager Fjord 30M, Anholt 28M, Ebeltoft 28M, Århus 38M

Charts
UKHO 2108
Danish 112

Lights
Fornæs 56°26'·6N 10°57'·4E Fl.20s32m21M Round stone tower
Grenå Harbour N approach 56°25'·07N 10°56'·12E Fl.G.3s10m5M Green mast 5m
Grenå Harbour S approach 56°24'·7N 10°55'·2E Fl.R.3s5m4M White pyramid, red top
Lystbådehavn N Breakwater Hd 56°24'·2N 10°55'·5E Fl.G.3s5m4M White pyramid green top. S Breakwater Hd Fl.R.3s5m4M White pyramid, red top
Hesselø 56°11'·8N 11°42'·6E Fl.15s40m13M White round tower
Hjelm Summit 56°08'N 10°48'·3E Iso.WRG.8s61m14–11M White round tower 016·5°-G-043°-W-051°-R-068°-G-088°-W-091°-R-110°-W-016·5°
Sjælland Rev N 56°06'N 11°12'·1E Iso.WRG.2s25m16–13M White colomn, red band, black pedestal. 025°-G-036°-W-039°-R062°-G-074°-W-077°-R-105°-G118°-R-141°-G-205°-W212°-R-235°-G-256°-W-283°-R-317°-G-350°-025°

Communications
Marina ☎ +45 86 32 72 55
havn@grenaamarina.dk

General
Grenå marina is 1M south of the entrance to the commercial port from which ferries go to Varberg in Sweden and Anholt.

Approach
If approaching from the north leave the Kalkgrund North cardinal mark and South cardinal mark to starboard before turning west towards the marina entrance. From the south leave the Naveren East cardinal mark to port. There is 3·5m in the entrance and 2·5m just outside.

Berthing
Yachts over 13m berth alongside on the inside of the east mole in 3·2m and smaller yachts in box berths at the other jetties. These size restrictions are strictly enforced. The berths get smaller (and the water shallower) the further one proceeds into the harbour.

Facilities
All facilities are available including restaurants, WiFi and fuel. The marina is some way from the town centre but there are basic shops quite close. Also close to the marina is the Kattegat Centre Oceanarium which specialises in sharks. Grenå has a ferry to Varberg.

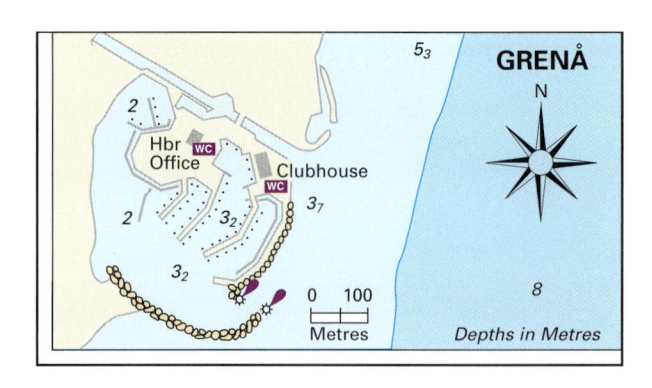

Ebeltoft

56°11'·47N 10°40'E Port mole for the marina
56°11'·82N 10°40'·1E Port mole head for the Traffikhavn

Distances
Grenå 38M, Juelsminde 33M.

Charts
UKHO 2108
Danish 124

Lights
Helgenaes Sletterhage SW end 56°05'·7N 10°30'·8E Oc.WRG.10s17m15–12M White round tower 250·9°-R-275°-G-297°-W-302·1°-R-320·5°-G-006·1°-R-060·2°-G-088·6°-W-117°-R-125·6°
Ebeltoft Vig 56°13·87'N 10°36'·44E Oc.WRG.5s13m12/9·5M White house, red band 355°-G-357°-W-358·5°-R-005°-G-008°-W-008·5°-R-010°
Øer mole head 56°08'·91N 10°40'·27E F.G.3m3M Round metal tower

Communications
Harbourmaster Traffikhavnen and the 'Museum' havn ☎ +45 86 34 31 24, VHF Ch 12, 13
Harbourmaster lystbådehavnen ☎ +45 86 34 30 08
Mobile +45 40 16 75 54
www.ebeltoftby.dk

General
This is a charming little town tucked away in a bay between Grenå and Århus. Although the first impression on entering is not particularly attractive, walk one street in and you are surrounded by old

The old town hall, now a museum *David Ridout*

100 THE BALTIC SEA AND APPROACHES

EBELTOFT

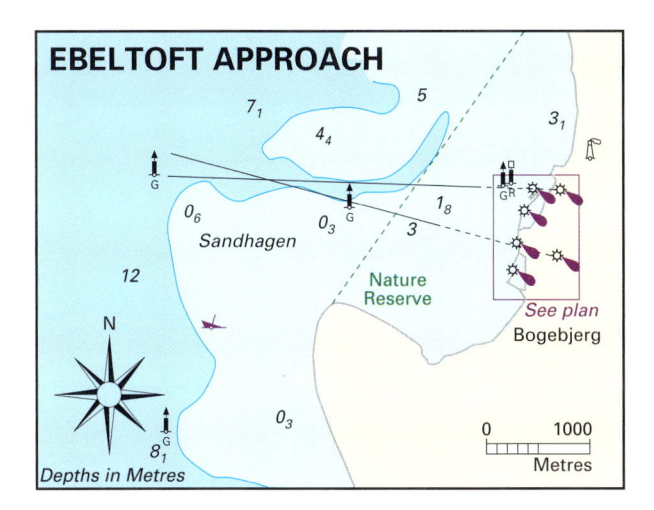

EBELTOFT APPROACH

Danish houses and an old town hall now functioning as a museum. In addition there is one of the world's longest wooden warships, the frigate *Jylland*, which includes another interesting museum. There are various shops, including 'Mols Bolsjer Fabrik' where you can see *bolsjer* (sweets) being made. There are three separate harbours, a marina (*lystbådehavn*), a fishing harbour, and the main harbour (*traffikhavn*) with two basins - the latter two are council owned and run.

Approach

Head into Ebeltoft Vig (Bay) on a northerly course, avoiding the Skadegrund and Øreflak shallows and leaving Øer Havn to starboard. Two green buoys mark a shallow area known as Sandhagen. From the second buoy (56°12'N 10°36·7'E) steer a course of 092° for the Traffikhavnen, Lystbådehavnen and Ebeltoft Fishing Harbour. At the next green buoy either alter course to 104° if heading for Lystbådehavnen or stay on 092° for Traffikhavnen. In daylight there is an aerial above the town which will lead you in on the 092° course. At night there is a leading light (green) towards the Traffikhavnen and a red leading light to the fishing harbour. Be careful of a 1·8m patch between the two leading lines.

Berthing

Traffikhavnen

After passing the red and green posts and the mole heads you will either turn into the Traffikhavnen on your starboard side where you can take any box berth with a green sign or moor alongside the south wall, or you can turn to port and moor alongside in the 'museum' harbour (the Kulturhavnen) where the frigate *Jylland* is situated. This part of the harbour is free of charge to wooden yachts. The box berths have a width of up to 4·6m and the harbours can handle boats up to 50m and have a depth of up to 4·5m, but less in the box berths.

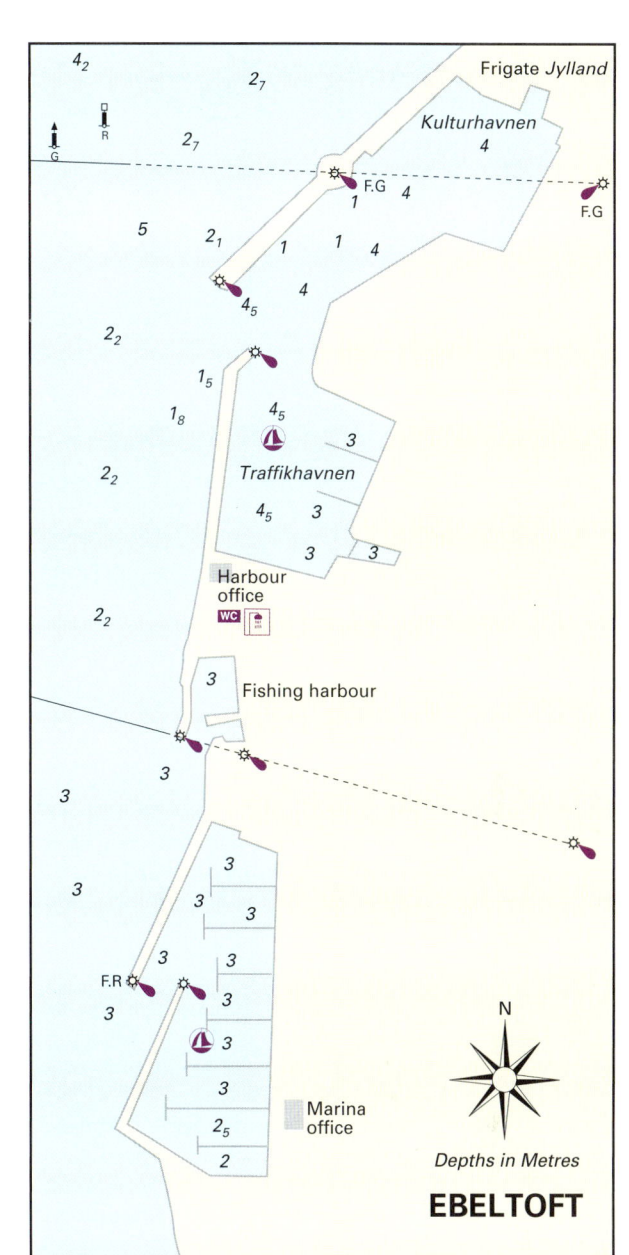

Traffikhavnen yacht harbour
by kind permission of Ebeltoft harbourmaster

THE BALTIC SEA AND APPROACHES

2D. DANISH HARBOURS AND ANCHORAGES OF THE KATTEGAT

Ebeltoft Kulturhavnen, with the frigate Jylland
David Ridout

Lystbådehavnen
This is privately owned, with all the facilities of a modern marina. Box berths (red/green availability notices) and depth of 2·5m. It is generally for boats not much longer than 40′. It is a bit further from the city centre and very similar to marinas elsewhere but it is immaculate.

Facilities
Electricity and water is available by the berths, toilets and showers. Diesel can be arranged or obtained in neighbouring Lystbådehavnen at certain times. The harbourmaster issues mooring tickets from an old English bus conductor's machine! Excellent chandlery nearby and a small supermarket and a fresh fish shop within easy walking distance with more shopping facilities in town, including a delicatessen which specialises in cheeses. Restaurants.

Buses from here to Århus and Randers.

Århus

56°09′·04N 10°17′·1E starboard hand buoy marking out limit Fl.G(3)10s

Distances
Grenå 38M, Juelsminde 33M.

Charts
UKHO 2108
Danish 112

Lights
Helgenæs Sletterhage SW end 56°05′·7N 10°30′·8E Oc.WRG.10s17m15–12M White round tower 250·9°-R-275°-G-297°-W-302·1°-R-320·5°-G-006·1°-R-060·2°-G-088·6°-W-117°-R-125·6°
Ldg Lts 295·1° *Front* 56°09′·8N 10°13′·8E Iso.2s37m7M Grey framework tower *Rear* 421m from front Iso.2s48m7M Grey framework tower. Synchronised with front
Tunø 55°57′N 10°26′·6E Oc.WRG.5s31m12–9M White church tower. 133°-G-157°-W-160°-R-175°-G-214°-W-220°-R-326°-G-345°-W-350°-R-045°

Communications
Commercial Port ☎ +45 98 12 27 77, VHF Ch 12, 13
Lystebådehavnen Marina HM ☎ +45 86 19 15 90
www.aarhuslystbaadehavn.dk
Marselisborg Marina ☎ +45 86 19 86 44
www.marselisborghavn.dk

General
Århus (European Capital of Culture 2017) has plenty of sights to see and things to do. There is an interesting open air museum of urban history, Den Gamle By, located in the Botanical Garden.

One of the great joys of this town, from a yachtsman's point of view, is the excellent free bicycle service run by the council. One can pick up a free bicycle (by inserting a 20DKr deposit in the handlebars to release the chain) from any of the rails round the city and leave it at a different one, where you chain it up again and get your money back.

On the north side of Århus Bay is an area of wooded bays and low hills with several small harbours and attractive anchorages.

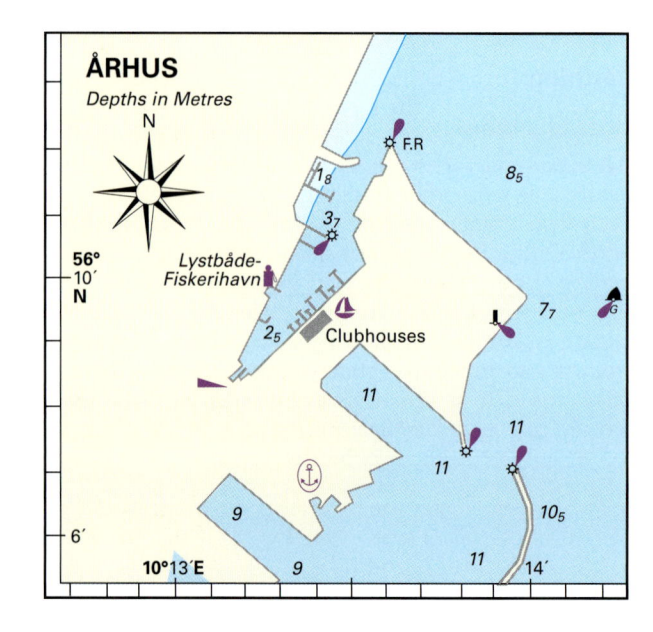

102 THE BALTIC SEA AND APPROACHES

ÅRHUS

Århus Lystebådehavn with commercial port in background
Patrick Roach

Lystbådehavnen (north Århus)

Approach
56°10′·18N 10°13′·54E port mole head

The entrance to the marina is 0·5M NW of the commercial harbour. It is open to the northeast. The whole area has now been built out and extended with tall new buildings. The entrance is straightforward.

Berthing
Berth in box berths anywhere there is a green sign but be aware that the facilities are on the eastern side of the harbour. Most box berths are for narrower boats but there are some alongside possibilities.

Facilities
All facilities available. Good rail communications. Ferry to Kalundborg. International airport via bus connection.

Marselisborg Marina (south Århus)

56°08′.21N 10°12′.91E Red and white safe water spar buoy

General
This marina will be the first you come to if approaching from the south/southeast and is easy to access. It is in an attractive location, about 1·5M southwest of the entrance to the commercial harbour, with excellent bicycle tracks and walking to the south through beech woods. The Danish Queen's summer castle, Marselisborg, is a short walk away and there is a pleasant beach nearby. Shopping and the town centre are an easy bicycle ride/walk/bus ride away. You can pick up Århus bicycles by the road just at the end of the marina complex. About 4 miles south of here is the very interesting Moesgård Museum. www.moesgaardmuseum.dk.

Approach
From the southeast the approach is straightforward to a red and white safe water buoy off the entrance. The starboard mole end is lit.

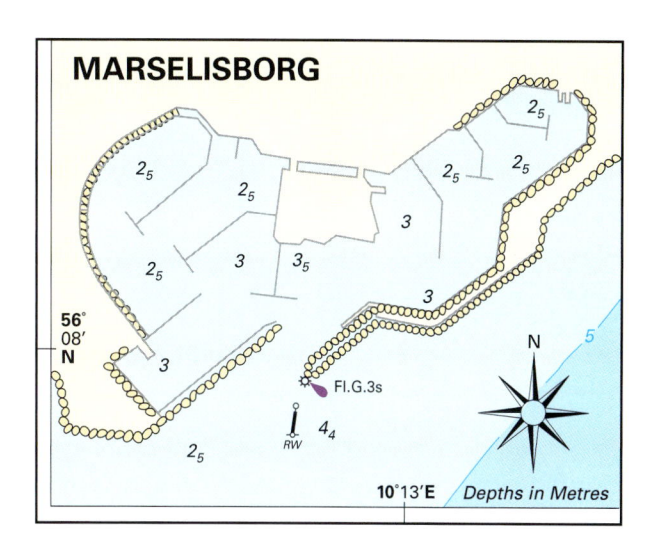

Berthing
Box berths, any marked with green can be taken provided they are wide enough for your boat. Some berths on the pier immediately in front of you on entry are for boats over 12m and large boats can also lie alongside in front of the harbour office.

Facilities
Water and electricity by berths. Showers and washing machines. Harbour WiFi. Diesel. 20 tonne crane.

Excellent chandlery where you can exchange your camping gas bottles. Several restaurants and cafes. In the summer season the harbour office is manned 0900–1200 and 1300–1800. Payment by machine or at the harbour office.

Marselisborg Marina *Photo courtesy of Marselisborg Marina*

THE BALTIC SEA AND APPROACHES 103

2D. DANISH HARBOURS AND ANCHORAGES OF THE KATTEGAT

Juelsminde

55°42'·98N 10°001'·96E port hand mole head (marina)

Distances
Århus 33M, Middelfart 20M, Bogense 10M, Horsens 16M, Velje 21M

Charts
UKHO 2591
Danish 114

Lights
E mole Head 55°42'·9N 10°01'·1E Fl.R.5s5m4M Red metal pillar
Æbelø NW Point 55°38'·8N 10°09'·8E Fl.W.15s20m14M Round granite tower
Trelde Næs 55°37'·5N 09°51'·5E Iso.WRG.2s26m9–6M Metal framework tower
Shore-G-124°-W-128°-R-136·5°-W-232°-R-256°-G-276·5-W-010°

Communications
Juelsminde harbour and marina ☏ +45 75 69 35 81
www.juelsmindehavn.dk

Juelsminde. Since the photo was taken a new marina, Sandbjerg, has been built to the NW and the Østhavn has also been added *Patrick Roach*

General
Juelsminde is a holiday town just north of the entrance to Vejle Fjord. Its three marinas are very busy in season.

Approach
55°43'N 10°00'·9E port mole head

From Århus Bay there are several shoals to be negotiated including the Søgrund north of Endelave. This carries a depth of only 3·5m and in strong weather from the northeast or southwest it would be wise to take the long way round the west coast of Samsø. From southwest the Bjørnsknude shallows extending south and east must be left to port.

Berthing
Juelsminde marina is to starboard on arrival; Østhavn marina is to port. Ahead is the Gamle Havn old harbour.

The Østhavn has now been extended to provide many more box berths, including some deeper ones for large yachts immediately to the left as you enter the harbour. The old harbour provides some alongside mooring and several box berths, as does Juelsminde marina (all using the red/green availability signs). Sandbjerg Marina 0·2M west of the entrance may also be able to accommodate you.

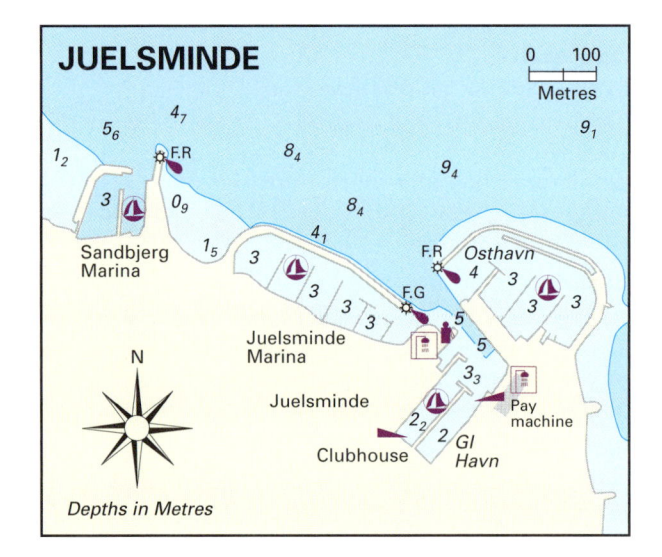

Facilities
The marinas have all facilities but no craneage.

Juelsminde, looking into entrance, Gamle Havn on right and Østhavn on left *David Ridout*

104   THE BALTIC SEA AND APPROACHES

Vejle

55°42'·25N 09°33'·6E by the last buoy opposite the entrance to the marina

Distances
Middelfart town 23M, Juelsminde 20M

Charts
UKHO 2591
Danish 114

Lights
Æbelø NW Point 55°38'·8N 10°09'·8E Fl.W.15s20m14M
  Round granite tower
Trelde Næs 55°37'·5N 09°51'·5E Iso.WRG.2s26m9–6M
  Metal framework tower
Shore-G-124°-W-128°-R-136·5°-W-232°-R-256°-G-276·5-W-010°
1st red spar buoy 55°41'·91N 09°40'·10E Fl(2)R.10s
2nd red spar buoy 55°41'·90N 09°37'·78E Fl(3)R.10s
3rd red spar buoy 55°41'·93N 09°35'·32E Fl(2)R.5s

Communications
Harbourmaster ☎ +45 75 82 59 42 or +45 20 28 39 90
http://marinaguide.dk/vejle-lystbaadehavn/

Looking SE over Vejle marina. The only entrance is the one on the left *Photo courtesy of the harbourmaster*

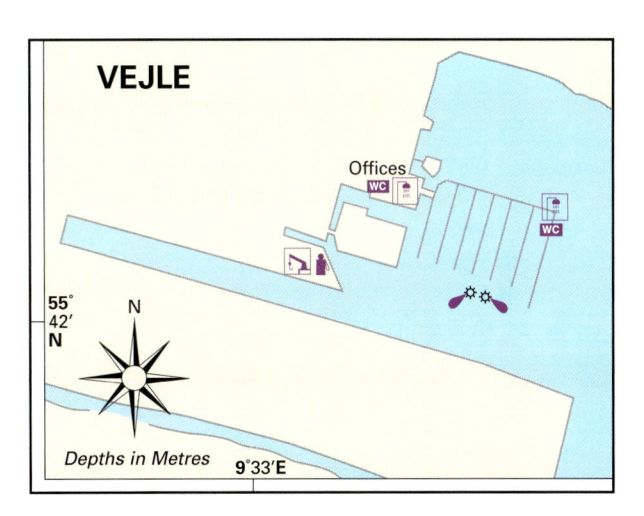

General

Vejle lies at the head of Vejle Fjord and has a commercial harbour and a large new marina. Vejle Fjord is a 12M inlet with some anchoring possibilities along the south shore as well as another smaller marina, Brejning about halfway. The town has good rail connections and makes an excellent base for changing crew or visiting Legoland and Jelling Burial Mounds. The railway/bus station is a 20 min walk away with good train connections to the rest of Denmark and there are bus connections to Billund Airport.

Approach

The big ship channel starts by the second spar buoy after which there are a series of port and starboard buoys. At the third red spar buoy come onto a leading line of 288°. The marina entrance is marked with red and green buoys and is just N of the channel, shortly after passing under the bridge. It is a modern marina and very well equipped.

Approaching Vejle with two ships leaving (looking west)
David Ridout

Berthing

Moor alongside pontoons of varying sizes but some are just small metal booms. The usual red/green plaques apply with some of them giving a date when they should be vacated.

Facilities

All facilities, water and electricity on pontoons. Fuel can be obtained from a jetty at the western end of the marina (outside the main marina area) near the white haul-out crane. Big well equipped *sejlerstue* with cooking and washing up facilities as well as barbecues and covered outside seating area. Areas for children to play and swim. Good WiFi.

There is an excellent chandler and also a big supermarket within easy walking distance. Various repair facilities.

The marina is very moderately priced and would be a good place to leave a boat temporarily.

THE BALTIC SEA AND APPROACHES **105**

2e. Approach to The Baltic by the Lille Bælt

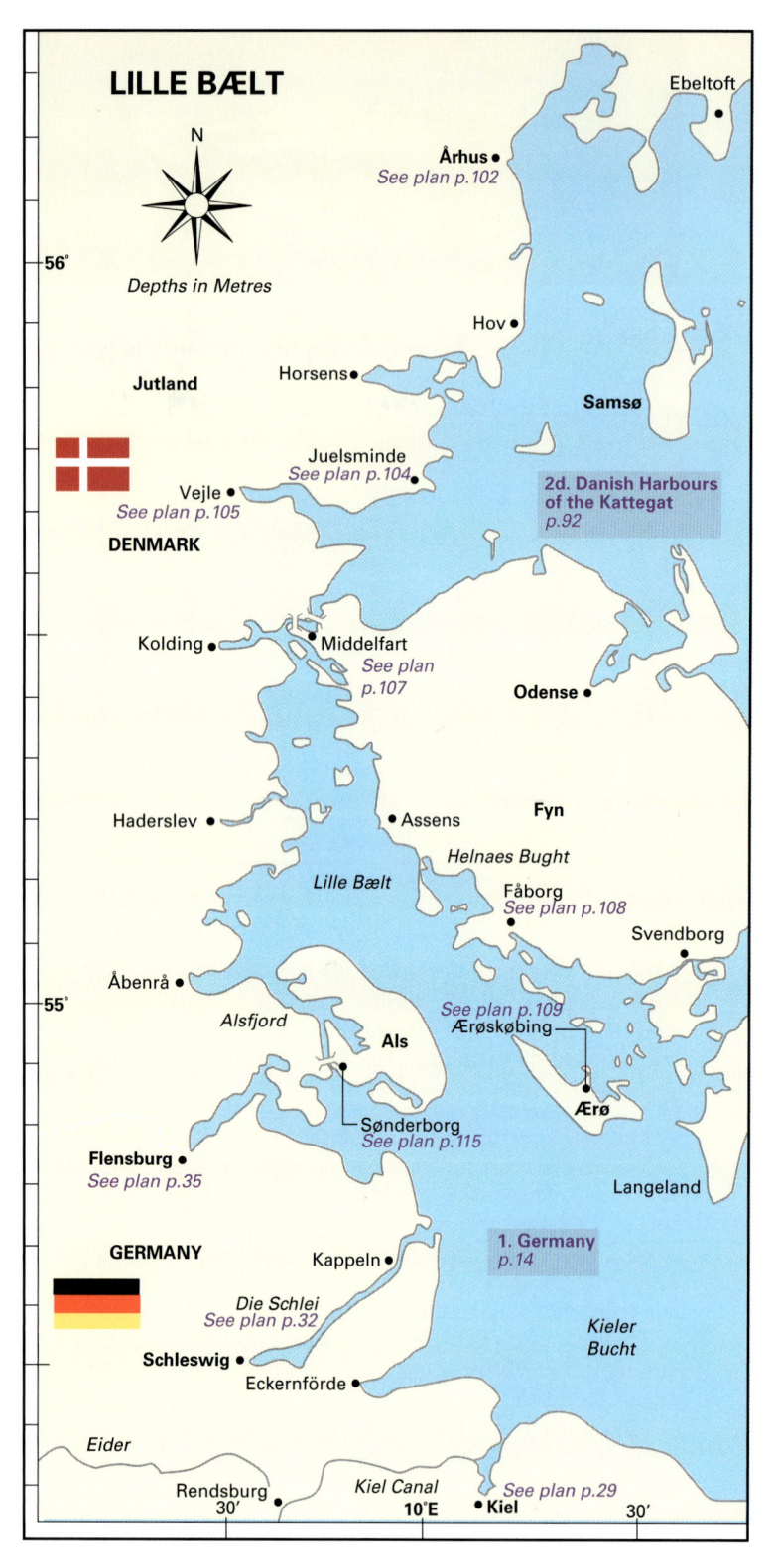

Middelfart

55°30'·49N 09°43'·51E port mole head for Gamle Havn
55°29'·51N 09°43'·40E starboard mole head Middelfart Marina

Distances
Juelsminde 22M, Assens 15M, Fåborg 38M, Svendborg 50M, Dyvig 35M, Sønderborg 40M

Charts
UKHO 2591, 2592
Danish 151, 158

Lights
Trelde Næs 55°37'·5N 09°51'·5E Iso.WRG.2s26m9–6M Metal framework tower Shore-G-124°-W-128°-R-136·5°-W-232°-R-256°-G-276·5°-W-010°
Strib 55°32'·6 09°45'·4E Oc.WRG.5s21m13–10M White square tower 351°-G-007·5°-W-013·5°-R-135°-G-232°-W-238°-R-shore
Fænø 55°28'·5N 09°42'·1E Fl.WRG.5s11m11–8M Gable of white house 338°-G-342°-W-346°-R-350°

Communications
Gamle Havn Harbourmaster ☎ +45 20 41 92 60
Middelfart Marina Harbourmaster ☎ +45 88 88 49 10
havnen@middelfart.dk
www.middelfart.dk

General

Middelfart lies on the northwest tip of the island of Fyn, at the Lille Bælt narrows. There are three small mooring basins on the Middelfart side, between the two fixed bridges (33m), plus a marina in Fænø Sund. Coming from the north, the first is the Tel-Ka marina, and a bit further along is the Gamle Havn and just before the second bridge is Kongebro Havn, all with a limited number of berths. The Gamle Havn is centrally positioned with a good fish shop on the quay.

Approach

Middelfart is at the narrowest part of the Lille Bælt and there is normally a two knot current flowing south, with north flowing eddies in the bays. This current can increase to four knots in strong northerlies but with strong winds from the south the currents will be reversed. Make allowances for the current in the approaches to the marinas.

Middelfart Marina is on Fænø Sund, to the south of the town, around the bend in the channel beyond the second bridge. Approach the marina on a NE heading, keeping relatively close to the east mole head where the water is deeper.

FÅBORG

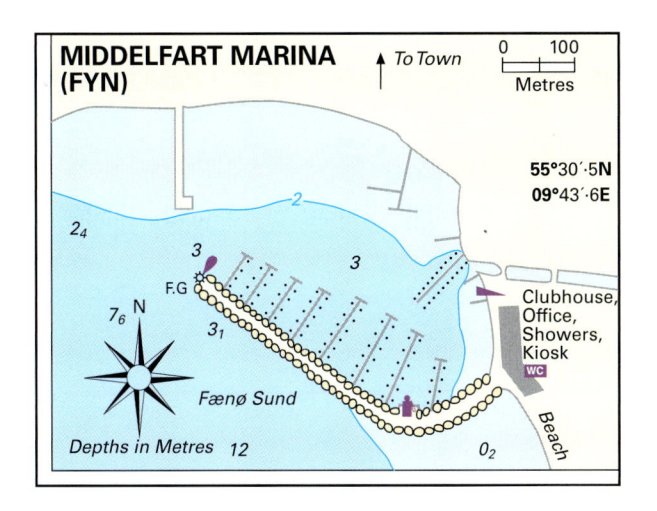

MIDDELFART MARINA (FYN)
55°30'·5N 09°43'·6E

Berthing
Berth alongside in 3–4m and probably rafted out in the Gamle Havn or in box berths in the marinas. Middelfart Marina in Fænø Sound now also has alongside berths at the end of each finger for boats too wide for the box berths. Some of the pontoons here state the width and length of the box berths on the end posts. The marina has 3m but less further in.

Middelfart Gamle Havn old harbour looking NE
David Ridout

Looking S towards Middelfart Marina   David Ridout

There may be a few small commercial vessels in the Gamle Havn but it makes a useful stop for stores after a night at anchor. Payment by machine.

There are nearby anchorages in Fænø Sund in the bay on the north side of Fænø and in Gamborg Fjord.

Facilities
Gamle Havn has basic facilities but is closer to shopping with a nice fish shop on the quay. Middelfart marina has all facilities, including WiFi and a lovely beach next to it. Buses go into town from here.

Fåborg

55°05'·56N 10°14'·27E starboard mole head for the old harbour

Distances
Middelfart 38M, Assens 23M, Svendborg 15M, Marstal 28M, Sønderborg 27M

Charts
UKHO 2532
Danish 152

Lights
Helnæs, Lindehoved 55°08'N 09°58'·7E
  Fl.WRG.5s30m13–10M White square tower
  302°-R-321°-G-330°-W-343°-R-030°-G-075°-W-125°-R-141°-G-179°
Bjørnø 55°03'·3N 10°15'·7E Iso.WRG.4s6m10–7M
  White hut, red band. 040°-G-052°-W-060°-R-971°.
Sisserodde 55°05'·7N 10°13'·7E Dir.Iso.WRG.2s8m16–14M
  White hut, red band 350·7°-G-352·2°-W-354·2°-R-355·7°
Leading light into Fåborg harbour F.R – 156.5°/336.5°
Munke 55°01'·4N 10°16'·3E Iso.WRG.4s10m15–11M
  White hut, red band 259°-G-264°-W-268°-R-273°
Nakkeodde 55°01'N 10°20'E Oc.WRG.5s9m11–8M
  White hut, red band 115·2°-G-123°-W-130°-R-143°
Skjoldnæs 54°58'·2N 10°12'·4E LFl.W.30s32m22M Round granite tower

Communications
Harbourmaster ☎ +45 72 53 02 60
  faaborghavn@fmk.dk
  www.fåborghavn.fmk.dk

General
Fåborg is a pretty little town on the southwest corner of Fyn, with old houses and cobbled streets. Yachts berth in either the old harbour or the new marina 400m further north. There is a ferry to Gelting in Germany. The ferry berth is just south of the old harbour and classic Baltic Traders lie alongside the southern quays.

Approach
The approach into Fåborg Fjord is either by the buoyed main channel to the west of Bjørnø or through the narrow and buoyed Grydeløb channel to the east of Bjørnø which carries a least depth of 3·4m. The main channel is covered by a succession of leading lights and lightbuoys but the Grydeløb is unlit.

THE BALTIC SEA AND APPROACHES

2E. APPROACH TO THE BALTIC BY THE LILLE BÆLT

Fåborg from the west. Note that the marina has been extended *Patrick Roach*

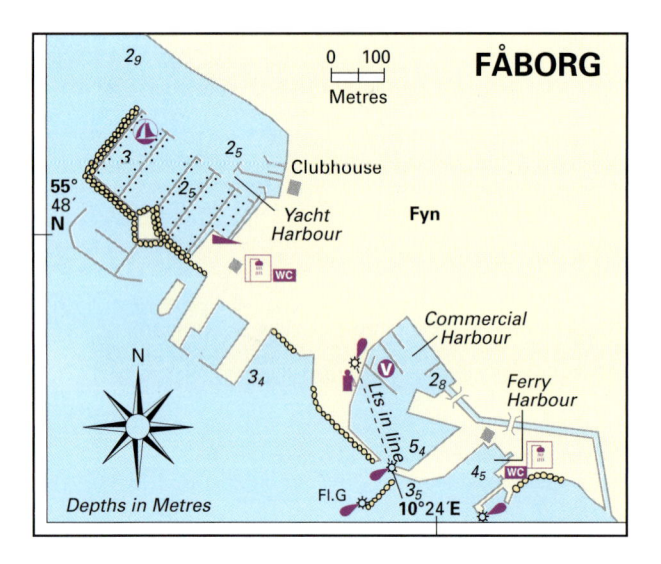

Once in the fjord by the main channel proceed on a course of 046° until the Højen porthand buoy is abeam when course can be altered to 336° for the harbour entrance.

Berthing

Berth in box berths either in the main harbour in 2·5–5m or in the marina which carries 2·5m in the approach and 3m inside. Vessels over 12m can berth alongside the south quay in the old harbour.

Facilities

Between them the two harbours provide all facilities including WiFi. There is a good chandler close to the marina.

Fåborg (Fyn) *J. Parkinson*

108　THE BALTIC SEA AND APPROACHES

ÆRØSKØBING

Ærøskøbing

54°53'·5N 10°24'·84E port mole head harbour
54°53'·65N 10°24'·65E port mole head marina

Distances
Fåborg 15M, Svendborg 12M, Sønderborg 30M, Kiel 45M

Charts
UKHO 2532
Danish 152

Lights
Skjoldnæs 54°58'·2N 10°12'·4E LFl.W.30s32m22M Round granite tower
Ærøskøbing Havn Ldg Lts 196·3° W Mole Head *Front* 54°53'·5N 10°24'·8E F.G.11m5M also Fl.G.5s4m4M Red triangle on green metal mast, white top. *Rear* 145m from front F.G.15m5M Red inverted triangle on white metal mast

Communications
Harbourmaster ☎ +45 30 53 47 49
(from 1 April – 30 October)

Looking NE towards the sea *David Ridout*

General

Ærøskøbing, on the northeastern corner of Ærø, is a very pretty little town that is well worth a visit, in spite of some difficulties in reaching it from the south. Its quaint streets and houses feature prominently in Danish tourist brochures and on the internet, and for good reason.

Approach

From the north the approach is straightforward and the leading line on 196° can be picked up just to the west of the landfall buoy. This takes one into the commercial harbour along a buoyed channel dredged to 3·8m. 0·3M from the commercial harbour entrance another buoyed channel, dredged to 2·5m, forks off SSW to the marina entrance.

From the south there are extensive shallows to be negotiated around the eastern end of the island. Dredged and well-buoyed channels with a charted minimum depth of 2·3m take you across the entrance to Marstal Harbour, then north for 0·7M before heading northeast to a RW safe water buoy from which one heads northwest to enter the Mørkedyb Channel at the Grenshage South cardinal mark. The Mørkedyb continues north-westwards for 5M leaving the Bredholm and Birkholm islands close to starboard. At the next RW safe water buoy course can be set (leaving the Egholm Flak north cardinal mark to port) for the RW safe water buoy marking the start of the channel into Ærøskøbing. If courage fails when contemplating the complexity of this southern approach there is always the long way round up the west coast of the island of Ærø, or stop off at Marstal which is another pretty place with a proud maritime history.

Typical pretty street with hollyhocks *David Ridout*

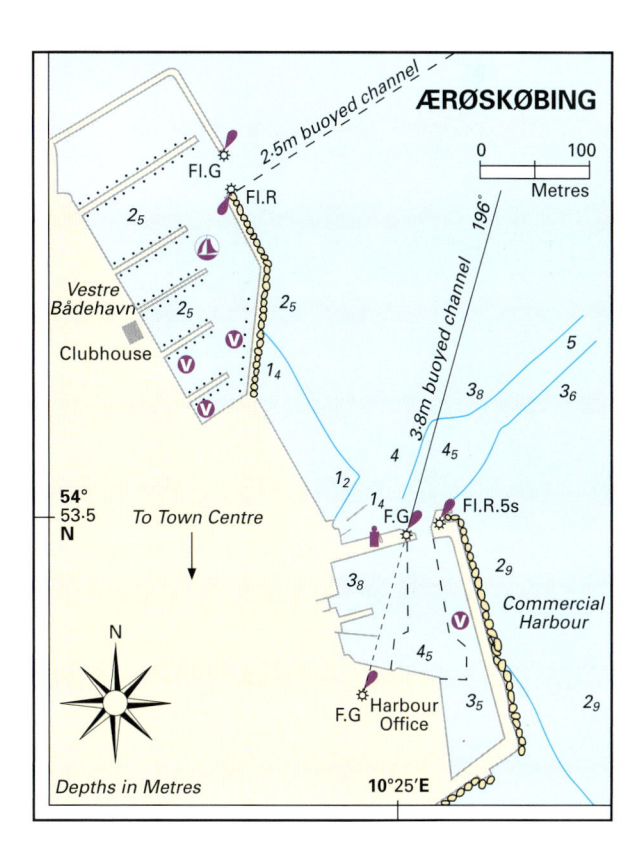

THE BALTIC SEA AND APPROACHES

2E. APPROACH TO THE BALTIC BY THE LILLE BÆLT

Looking ENE through the marina entrance *David Ridout*

Berthing
Either in box berths in the marina which has now been extended and also has a few alongside berths immediately to port on entry. In the old harbour you can moor alongside wherever there is a space or raft up and there are a few box berths immediately to port on entering the harbour. Large and classic vessels berth just inside the old harbour on the north pier. If the harbours are too crowded there is a good anchorage in the Revkrog, the bay just to the west of the isthmus that juts N of the town. Good protection from NE through S to W.

Facilities
All facilities are available. Ferry to Svendborg.

Svendborg

55°03'·5N 10°37'·28E light on port side entering Svendborg harbour just after colourful floating dock

Distances
Nyborg 24M, Ærøskøbing 13M, Fåborg 15M, Bagenkop 15M, Kiel 45M, Sønderborg 35M

Charts
UKHO 2532, 2597
Danish 152, 171

Lights
Buoy Thurø Reef SCM 55°01'·2N 10°44'E Q(6)+LFl.15s
Tåsinge. Ldg Lts 283° *Front* 55°01'·7N 10°39'·4E Iso.R.2s11m14M Red triangle on red framework tower, white stripes. *Rear* 223m from front Iso.R.4s15m14M Red inverted triangle on red post with white stripes
Vindebyøre Ldg Lts 061° *Front* 55°03'·2N 10°37'·4E Iso.W.2s4m12M White post, red band. *Rear* 203m from front Iso.W.4s10m12M White post, red band.
Gasværk 55°03'·3N 10°36'·8E Oc.WRG.5s8m9–7M White building 227°-G-232°-W-237°-R-252·5°-G-289°
St Jorgens 55°02'·9N 10°35'·8E Oc(2)WRG.6s8m12–9M White hut, red band, on wooden piles. 053·5°-G-058·5°-W-060·5°-R-066°
Bækkehave 55°01'N 10°32'·7E Oc.WRG.5s6m12–9M White hut, red band. 095°-G-100°-W-105°-R-107°

Communications
Harbourmaster ☏ +45 62 21 06 57

General
Svendborg is situated on a very beautiful sound on the SE corner of Fyn and is attractive, with a long history of old working sailing ships. The town has many shops, restaurants and a couple of chandleries and bus and train connections close to the north harbour. There is an excellent fish shop.

Svendborg Nordre Havn looking southeast *Patrick Roach*

110 THE BALTIC SEA AND APPROACHES

SVENDBORG

Nordre Havn
Østre Havn
Frederiksø
Shipyard
Søndre Havn
Ferry
Fl.R.3s
Q(6)+LFl.15s

Svendborg Sound from the west *C. Lassen*

55° 04′ N

SVENDBORG

N

Depths in Metres

Fyn

Svendborg Havn Gasværk
Oc.WRG.5s

Skanseodde

Svendborg YH
F.R

Vindeby Nor

F.G

Vindeby

61°

10°37′E

THE BALTIC SEA AND APPROACHES 111

2. DENMARK

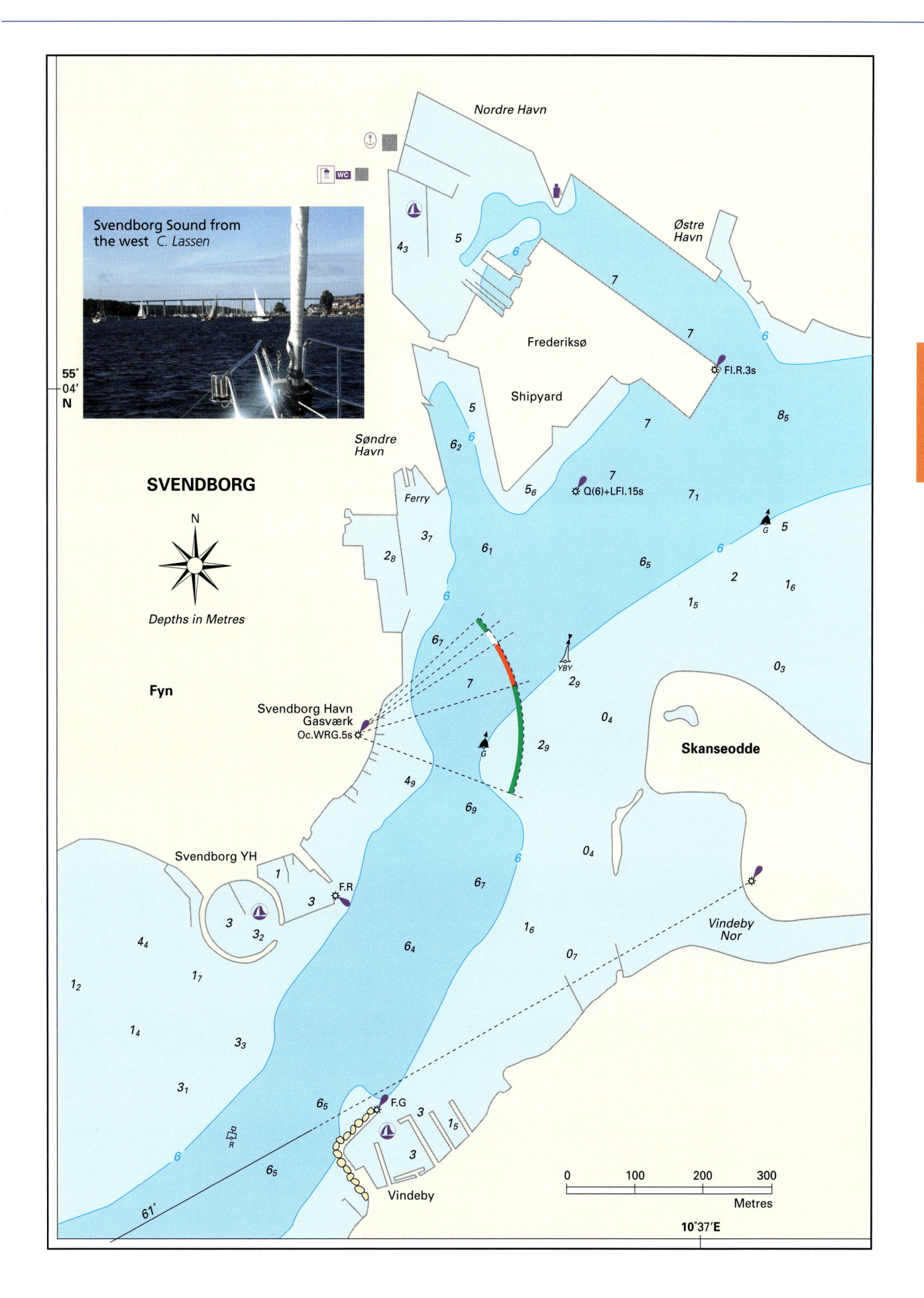

2E. APPROACH TO THE BALTIC BY THE LILLE BÆLT

Approach
The approach along Svendborgsund from the west is straightforward as long as one stays within the buoyed (unlit) channel. The fixed bridge just west of the town has a clearance of 33m. There is usually an east-going current of up to 2·5 knots in the sound.

On approaching the eastern entrance to Svendborg Sound from the north (see section 2f page 116) the Thurø Reef South cardinal mark must be left to starboard before turning westward on to the leading line on 283°. (Be warned that many experienced sailors have inadvertently cut the corner and hit rock). 283° leads into the sound which has a succession of leading lights and unlit buoys through the dog-leg which leads up into Svendborg.

Please note that buoyage for yachts traversing the sound changes at the north cardinal mark 55°03'·51N 10°37'·74E.

Berthing
Berth in one of several marinas on either side of the sound but the most convenient berth for the town is in the Nordre Havn. Yachts berth either in box berths or alongside in 4–5m but a strong current in the sound can sweep into the harbour and make it uncomfortable.

Svendborg (Lystbådehavn) is 10 min walk from the centre and has some box berths (red/green availability signs) and some alongside berths. Fuel and pump out facilities.

Facilities
Showers in the office block and at the south end of the main town quay. Most other facilities are available including a repair yard for traditional craft. There is a diesel berth on the north side of the basin. Most of the smaller marinas are served by a ferryboat into the town.

One of the many attractive cottages in Troense David Ridout

Troense
About 2 miles SSE of Svendborg is the charming little town of Troense on the island of Søby, where you can anchor off or tie up if there is an empty berth. Opposite is a long inlet on Thurø island, Thurø Bund, with the well-known boatyard, Walsteds, on its northern shore, just W of Gambøt. There are good anchoring possibilities in the inlet in the right winds. Valdemar's Castle lies just a little south of Troense and is well worth a visit.

Troense looking east David Ridout

112 THE BALTIC SEA AND APPROACHES

THE ALS FJORD AND SØNDERBORG

The Als Fjord and Sønderborg

54°54'·4N 09°46'·9E Lighthouse just west of Sønderborg Slot

Distances from northern entrance
Fåborg 25M, Middelfart 27M, Augustenborg 11M, Sønderborg 10M.

Charts
UKHO 2532
Danish 155, 159

Lights
Nordborg 55°04'·7N 09°42'·7E Oc.WRG.5s27m12–9M Yellow round tower. 065°-G-070°-W-073°-R-171°-G-184·5°-W-236°-R-254°
Ballebro 54°59'·8N 09°40'·4E Iso.WRG.2s11m10–7M White round tower, red band. 128°-G-140°-W-152°-R-253°-G-262·5°-W-274-R-283°
Sottrupskov 54°58'·3N 09°44'·6E Iso.WRG.4s9m6–4M White pedestal, red band. 151°-G-192·5°-W-201°-R-238°
Als. S Point. Kegnaes 54°51'·2N 09°59'·3E Oc.WRG.5s32m12–9M Yellow round tower 217°-R-266·5°-G-273°-W-289·5°-R-337°-G-026°-W-044°-R-050·5°-G-075°-W-080°-R-102·5°
Kalkgrund 54°49'·5N 09°53'·3E Iso.WRG.8s22m14–12M Red round tower, two white bands, three galleries. 012°-W-062°-R-084°-W-100°-R-120°-W-131·5-G-157°-W-164°-R-190°-W-252·6°-G-258°-W-265°-R-292°-W-308°-R-012°

Communications
Dyvig Bro Marina ⓘ +45 21 49 00 21
Dyvig Lystbådehavn ⓘ +45 27 51 80 33
Augustenborg Yachthavn ⓘ +45 74 47 15 62
Yachtyard ⓘ +45 74 47 10 86
Christian X Bridge ⓘ +45 74 32 39 39, VHF Ch 12, 13
Sønderborg Harbourmaster ⓘ +45 74 42 27 65
  Harbour office ⓘ +45 74 42 93 92
  http://sonderborg.sonderborg.dk/marina/
Marina ⓘ +45 74 42 93 92

General
West of Fyn and at the southern end of Lille Bælt, Als Fjord is an attractive, sheltered route through to Sønderborg and the Flensburg Fjord. At the northern end there is an almost totally enclosed anchorage at Dyvig. The Als Fjord then leads eastwards into the Augustenborg Fjord with Augustenborg at its eastern end. At the junction of the two fjords the Als Sund leads southwards to Sønderborg with its Christian X bridge where one usually has to wait for the next opening which is signalled by a digital clock on one side of the opening bridge.

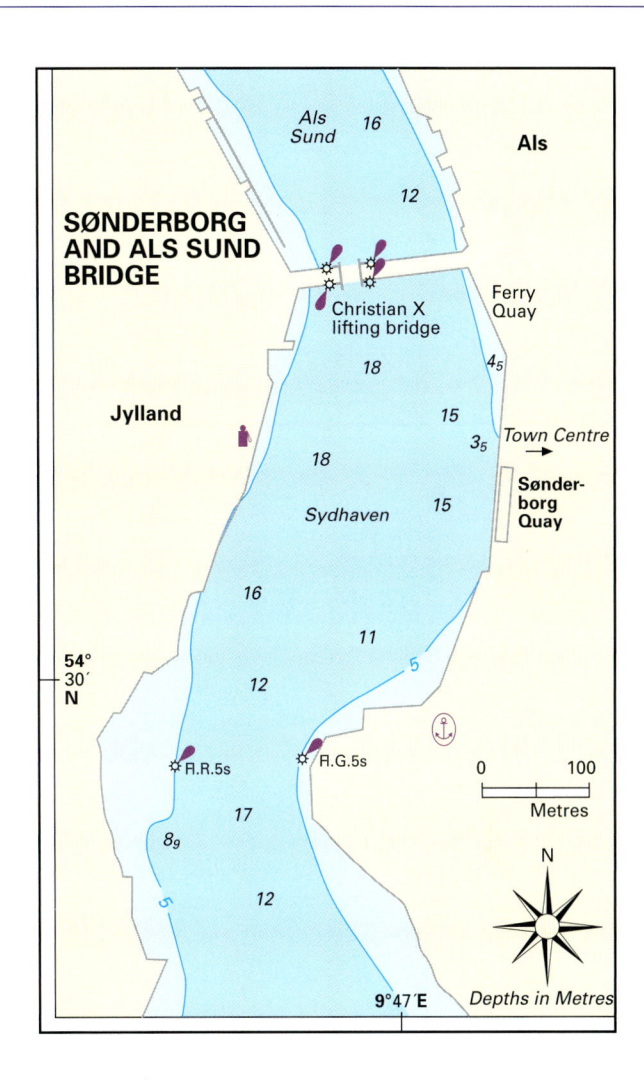

Approach
From the north the entrance into Als Fjord is straightforward. From the south a westerly cardinal and a port hand buoy mark the edges of the shallows at the entrance to Als Sund.

Dyvig anchorage
The narrow entrance to the Dyvig anchorage is on the east side at the northern end of Als Fjord. The buoyed entrance carries a least depth of 3·5m with 9·5m in the excellent anchorage beyond. There are

Looking west with Dyvig Bro Marina on the right
David Ridout

THE BALTIC SEA AND APPROACHES 113

2E. APPROACH TO THE BALTIC BY THE LILLE BÆLT

Christian X bridge looking NW on a busy day David Ridout

also two small marinas at Dyvig. Dyvig Bro Marina on the north side has 5m depth and accommodation for larger yachts. Dyvig Lystbådehavn on the south side has 3m. There are two restaurants at Dyvig Badehotel adjacent to Dyvig Bro Marina and all facilities at both. No fuel at either. Several free bicycles available and also a free tourist bus (yellow).

Augustenborg

Augustenborg is in the furthest southeast corner of Augustenborg fjord. It is reached by a buoyed channel dredged to 4m. On the west side of the fjord is an airfield and anchoring is forbidden within 600m of the west shore. Augustenborg has a large marina on the south side with a boattyard, fuel station and restaurant. On the north side there is a very friendly sailing club which has basic facilities and welcomes visitors. The very neat village and the grandiose castle, now turned into a nursing home, are also on this side.

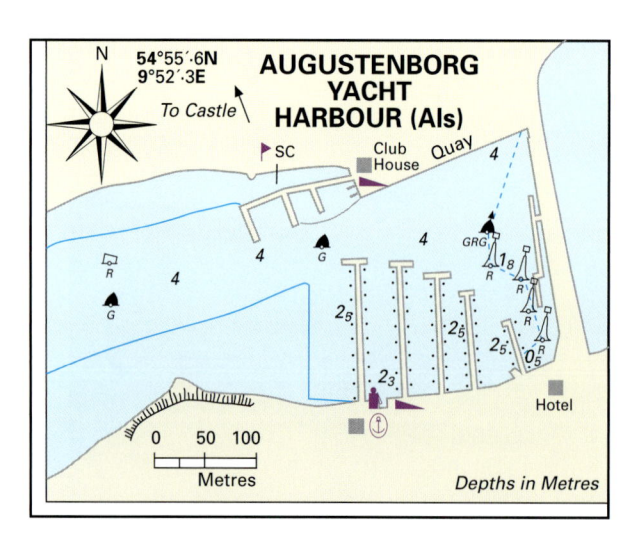

Sønderborg

Sønderborg is at the southern end of Als Sund and is dominated by the Christian X opening rail and road bridge. 1M further north is a fixed road bridge with a clearance of 33m. Opening times of the lifting bridge are displayed on a digital clock on one of the piers of the opening section of the bridge. The bridge opens on the hour and half hour during the busy season from 0830–2230. Keep to starboard and watch out for current.

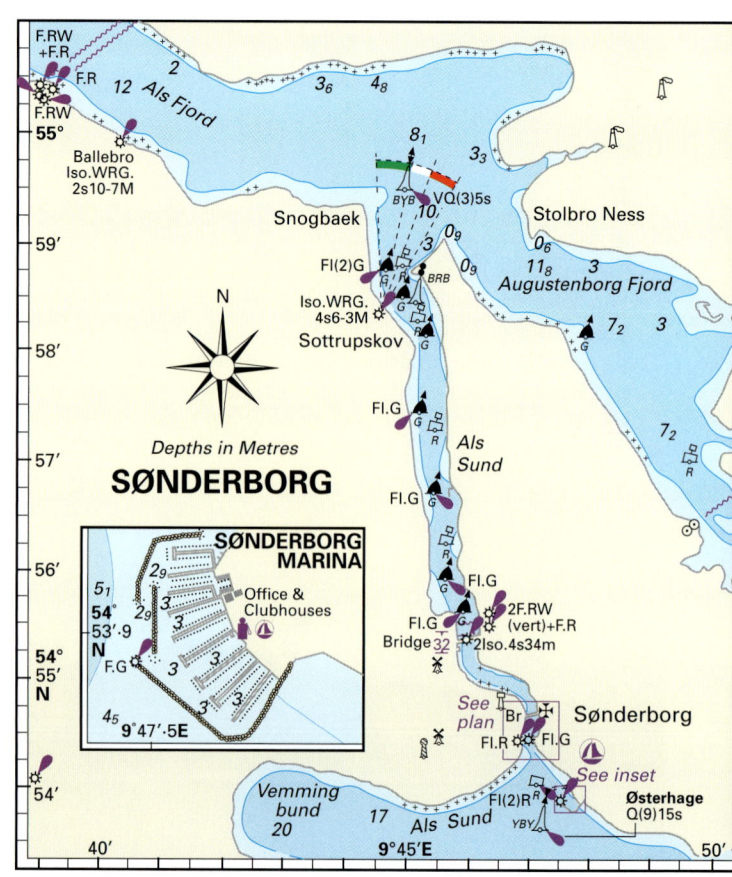

114 THE BALTIC SEA AND APPROACHES

THE ALS FJORD AND SØNDERBORG

Sønderborg from the northwest Patrick Roach

There is a large marina on the east side of the southern entrance to Als Sund, with box berths and all facilities but quite a long walk from the town. The more interesting berths are alongside the quayside staging on the east side, just south of the lifting bridge near the castle. A fender plank is useful as there are awkward piles. There are basic facilities and it is close to the shops and supermarkets.

A 3km walk over the bridge takes one up to the Dybbøl Mølle and the Battlefield Centre which commemorate the battle of 1864 when the Danes lost Schleswig-Holstein to Germany. The mill was twice destroyed first during the battle 1848-49 and again in 1864 after which it was again rebuilt.

There is a good anchorage outside the southern entrance to the Als Sund at Vemmingbund, 2M to the west.

Looking NNE to the quayside at Sønderborg David Ridout

THE BALTIC SEA AND APPROACHES

2f. Approach to the Baltic by the Store Bælt

At the northern approaches to Store Bælt (Great Belt) you have the charming little island of Sejerø with a small harbour on the south/west side where you could easily break your journey (55°52'·7N 11°08'·1E - port mole head). Alternatively the journey could be be broken at Ballen on Samsø - another attractive option (55°49'N 10°38'·5E - port mole head) but both these places are very busy in the season.

Kalundborg

55°40'·18N 11°04'·64E port mole head (Gisseløre)

Distances
Århus 45M, Grenå 50M, Lynaes 60M, Nyborg 33M.

Charts
UKHO 2596, 2108, 923
Danish 141, 145

Lights
Rosnæs Puller 55°45'N 10°50'·6E Fl(2).5s9m10M
    Red mast on granite base
Asnæs. NW point. 55°40'·3N 10°56'·1E Fl.3s12m4M
    White pedestal, red band
Anæsværket N Dir Lt 116·52° 55°39'·90N 11°04'·73E
    Dir.Oc.WRG.10s13m12-8M Grey framework tower.
    113·52°-G-115·52°-W-116·52°-R-118·52°
    Synchronised with 1507·4
Anæsværket S 55°39'·89N 11°04'·72E
    Dir.Oc.WRG.10s13m12-8M Grey framework tower
    114·52°-G-116·52°-W-117·52°-R-119·52°
    Synchronised with 1507·3

Communications
Harbourmaster ☎ +45 59 53 40 00
Port Control VHF Ch 12, 13

General
Kalundborg is a large town and ferry port on the west coast of Sjælland with good shops and an interesting 12th-century church.

Approach
A buoyed approach channel on 116·5° leads in to a coal-fired powerstation on the southern side, where course is altered on to 090·7° past the power station and then on to 020° towards the ferry terminal, between a red porthand buoy and a West cardinal mark. Off the end of the ferry terminal steer NW for a small red perch with a F.R light and solar panel, which is difficult to see from a distance in daylight but it marks the eastern end of a breakwater, some of which may be under water. The red perch must be left to port in order to enter the Vesthavn.

Berthing
Berth alongside the quays in the Vesthavn in 2·8m with 1·7m further in. There is limited space (even with rafting up) and these berths can be uncomfortable in strong onshore winds. The small yacht harbour at Gisseløre is a good alternative. There is 2·5m in the dredged approach channel and between the two outside jetties. It is run by the sailing club.

STORE BÆLT AND SMÅLANDSFARVANDET

116 THE BALTIC SEA AND APPROACHES

KALUNDBORG

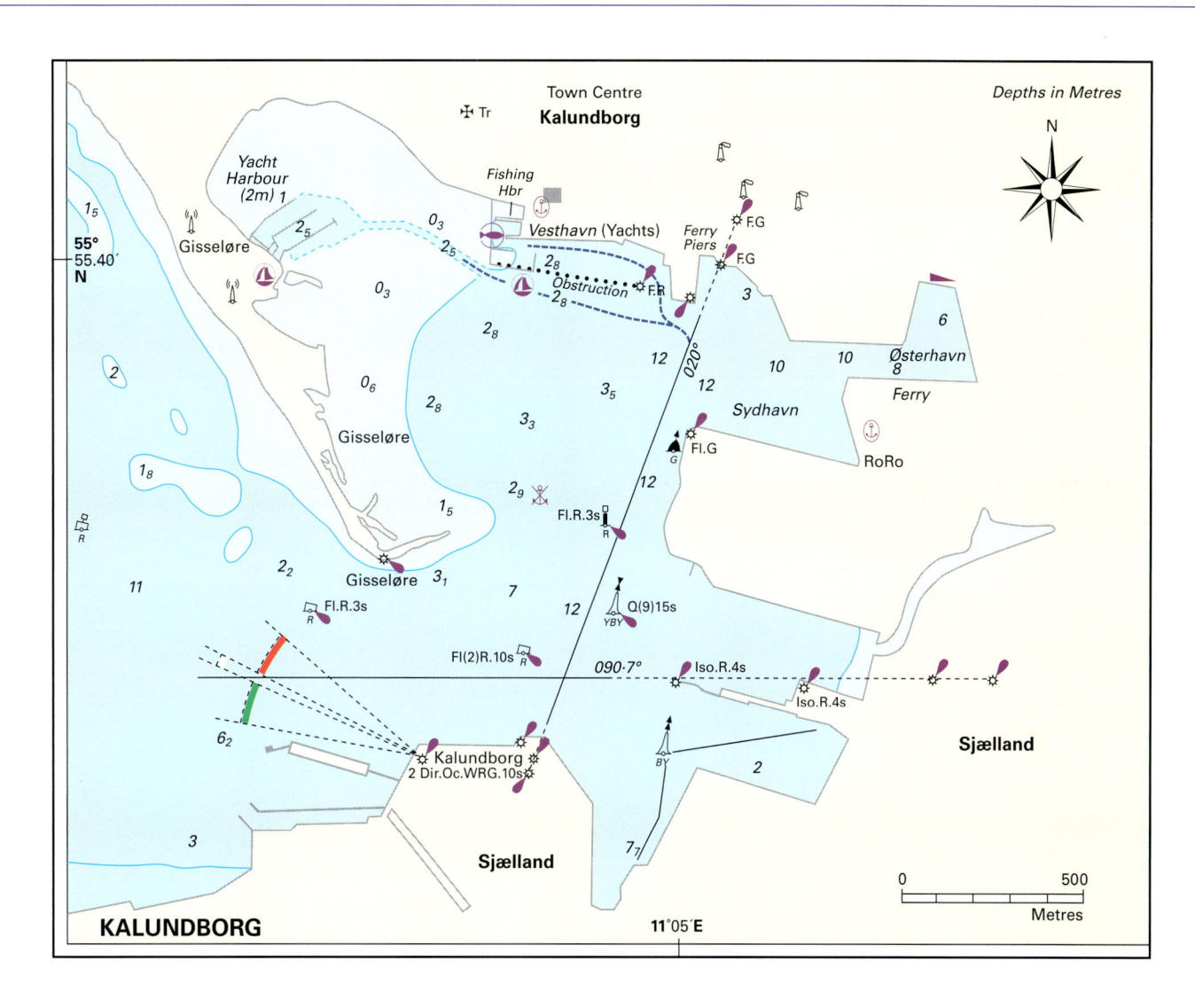

Facilities

Showers/toilets on the ground floor of the harbour office. Water/electricity on the pier. Fuel station in the fishing harbour, run by the Yacht Club which has to be phoned to arrange a time. The Yacht Harbour has good basic facilities but is a longer walk to town. Good rail connections with Copenhagen and ferry to Samsø.

Kalundborg from the northwest Patrick Roach

THE BALTIC SEA AND APPROACHES

2F. APPROACH TO THE BALTIC BY THE STORE BÆLT

Kerteminde (Fyn)

55°27'·05N 10°40'E port mole head to main harbour. Wave barrier and entrance to marina just north of here.

Distances
Juelsminde 30M, Kalundborg 25M, Nyborg 15M, Korsør 18M

Charts
UKHO 2596
Danish 141

Lights
Romsø Tue. No 24. 55°33'·5N 10°49'·2E
  Fl.WRG.3s10m8–7M Green tower 051°-G-132°-W-135°-R-150°-G-158°-W-169°-R-300°-G-325°-W-332°-R-051°
Ldg Lts 253° *Front* 55°27'N 10°39'·7E Iso.R.2s6m5M
  Yellow triangle on grey pillar. *Rear* 85m from front.
  Iso.R.4s7m5M Yellow inverted triangle on grey pillar
Storebælt Bridge, Vesterrenden, E Passage. W Dir Lt 333·3° 55°18'·56N 10°53'·90E Dir.Iso.WR.8s26m10–8M 331·8°-R-334·8°-R-341·8°. E Dir Lt 336·3° 55°18'·57N 10°53'·93E Dir.Iso.WG.8s26m10–8M 327·8°-G-334·8-W-337·8°
Storbælt Bridge, Vesterrenden, W passage W Dir Lt 157·2° 55°18'·51N 10°53'·60E Dir.Iso.WG.8s26m10–8M 148·7°-G-155·7°-W-158·7°. E Dir Lt 154·2° 55°18'·51N 10°53'·63E Dir.Iso.WR.8s26m10–8M 152·7°-W-155·7°-R-162·7°

Communications
Marina harbourmaster ☏ +45 65 15 15 37

General

On the western side of the Store Bælt, Kerteminde is a pretty holiday town which used to be the mediaeval port for Odense, Denmark's third city, and at one time harboured Fyn's largest fishing fleet. It has a large yacht harbour. The Danish version of the Nordic folk boat is built here.

Approach

Straight forward approach on 253° on the leading line which leads into the commercial harbour with a diversion northwards into the yacht harbour leaving the outer baffle breakwater to starboard.

Berthing

Berth in box berths with bow to jetties in 2–3m at outer ends and shallower further in. Larger vessels can berth on the north quay of the commercial harbour near the grain silo in 4·5m.

Kerteminde looking west Patrick Roach

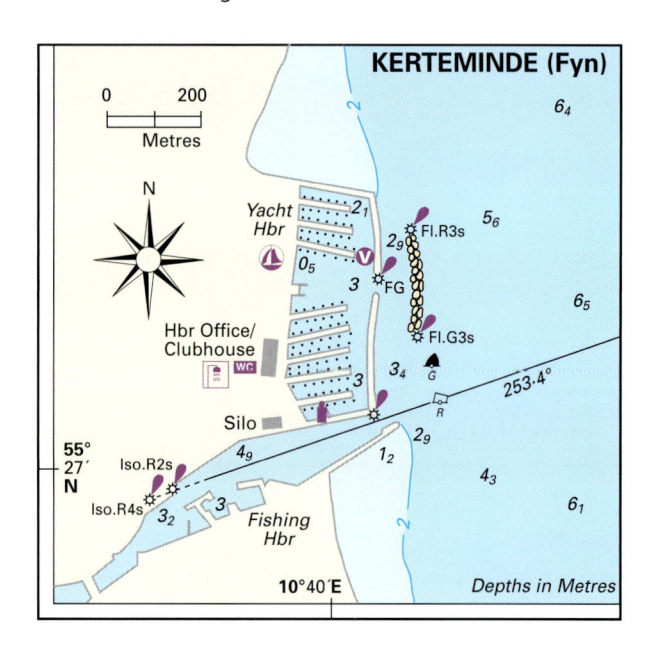

Facilities

The yacht harbour has all facilities including an excellent chandlery. Fuel in the commercial harbour next to the grain silo. Bus to Odense. Excavated Viking burial mound at Ladby 4km southwest.

Looking north from main harbour mole with wave barrier on the right

118 THE BALTIC SEA AND APPROACHES

STORE BÆLT BRIDGE

Store Bælt bridge

55°20'·5N 10°02'·17E

Distances
Juelsminde 46M, Kerteminde 13M, Korsør 3M, Nyborg 10M

Charts
UKHO 938
Danish 143

VTS Great Belt
The radar system guarding the area 12M north and south of the Great Belt Line. It is monitored from the VTS centre in Korsør day and night.

The East Bridge has a navigation span between pylons 16 and 17 (pylons are numbered 2-26 starting at Sjælland). Here a Traffic Separation Zone exists. The entrance to the northbound and southbound traffic separation zones is marked by a racon.

Østerrenden
55°22'·04N 11°01'·28E - W25A Conical green buoy Fl(2)G.10s first starboard hand buoy for Østerrenden approaching from the north

55°19'·1N 11°02'·82E - E28A can red Fl(2)R.10s first starboard hand buoy for Østerrenden coming from the south

Vesterrenden
55°18'·95N 10°53'·20E Conical green buoy FL.G first starboard hand buoy for Vesterrenden approaching from the north

55°18'·13N 10°54'·34E Red Can Fl.R first starboard hand buoy for Vesterrenden coming from the south

Lights
Vesterenden buoy 55°19'·85N 10°52'·5E Iso.4s
  Red and white vertical stripes
Vesterrenden, W passage W Dir Lt 157·2° 55°18'·51N 10°53'·60E Dir.Iso.WG.8s26m10–8M 148·7°-G-155·7°-W-158·7°
E Dir Lt 154·2° 55°18'·51N 10°53'·63E
  Dir.Iso.WR.8s26m10–8M 152·7°-W-155·7°-R-162·7°
Vesterrenden, E Passage. W Dir Lt 333·3° 55°18'·56N 10°53'·90E Dir.Iso.WR.8s26m10–8M 331·8°-W-334·8°-R-341·8°
E Dir Lt 336·3° 55°18'·57N 10°53'·93E
  Dir.Iso.WG.8s26m10–8M 327·8°-G-334·8°-W-337·8°
Buoy 55°17'·25N 10°54'·1E Iso.4s
  Red and white vertical stripes
Sprogø 55°19'·8N 10°58'·2E Fl.W.5s44m8M
  Red round masonary structure, yellow bands
Østerrenden buoy 55°22'·1N 11°02'·2E Iso.4s
  Red and white vertical stripes
W Channel Ldg Lts 180° N side. *Front* 55°20'·49N 11°01'·82E Iso.W.4s74m10M 164·3-vis-194·3.
  S Side *Rear* 3FW(vert)95m6M
E Channel Ldg Lts 000° S side. *Front* 55°20'·54N 11°02'·46E
  Iso.W.4s74m10M N side *Rear* 3FW(vert)95m6M
Østerrenden S E28 55°19'·5N Fl(3)R.10s10m8M Red mast with platform
Buoy 55°18'·88N 11°02'·2E Iso.4s Red and white vertical stripes

Communications
VHF working channels 10, 11, 16 and 74
☎ +45 58 37 68 68
www.forsvaret.dk

The impressive Store Bælt bridge *C. Lassen*

General

The bridge was opened in 1998 and is part of the motorway system which now connects Jutland with Sweden. The western end (Vesterrenden) connects Fyn with the island of Sprogø and is a combined rail and road bridge with multiple spans and a clearance of 18m in the marked navigation channels. The eastern end (Østerrenden) is a motorway suspension bridge connecting Sprogø with Sjælland. It has a clearance of 65m. The railway goes into a tunnel under the Østerrenden.

It is preferred, but not compulsory, that vessels able to do so use Vesterrenden (height restriction 18m) or navigate outside the Østerrenden TSS if possible or as near as possible to the starboard side. If in any doubt, discuss with Great Belt Traffic on VHF Ch 10, 11, 16.

2. DENMARK

THE BALTIC SEA AND APPROACHES

2F. APPROACH TO THE BALTIC BY THE STORE BÆLT

Nyborg

55°16'·28N 10°51'·05E safe water buoy

Distances
Kerteminde 17M, Kalundborg 35M, Korsør 14M, Svendborg 24M, Bagenkop 42M, Naksov 36M

Charts
UKHO 2596, 2597, 938
Danish 141, 142, 143

Lights
Sprogø 55°19'·8N 10°58'·2E Fl.W.5s44m8M
  Red round masonry structure, yellow bands
Knudshoved 55°17'·4N 10°51'·1E Oc.WRG.10s16m12–10M
  White square tower. 220°-G-269°-W-276°-R-305·5°-G-359°-W-003·5°-R-095° (Partly obscured 072°-080°)
Ldg Lts 306° *Front* 55°18'N 10°46'·9E Iso.W.2s4m9M
  White disc on beacon
  Rear 55m from front Iso.W.2s13m9M White disc on white beacon
Langelandsøre, Omø 55°09'·6N 11°08'E
  Oc(2)WRG.12s21m17–14M Yellow round tower 266°-G-271°-W-283°-R-291°-G-296°-W-304·5°-R-006°-G-101°-W-104°-R-118°-G-133°-W-138·5°-R-146°-G-162°-W-164·5°R-183°-G220°
Frankeklint 55°09'·6N 10°55'·9E Oc.RG.5s16m8M Gable of white house 039°-G-047°-R-151°-G-178°-R-219°
Hov 55°08'·8N 10°57'·3E Iso.WRG.4s12m16–13M
  White round tower, red band. 210°-R-226·5°-G-232·5°-W-237°-R-308·5°-G-341°-W-346°-R-010°

Communications
Harbour office ☎ +45 63 33 70 83 / +45 63 33 79 83
  Mobile ☎ +45 29 13 19 59
  ait@nyborg.dk

General

Before the Store Bælt Bridge was built Nyborg, which lies at the Fyn end of the bridge, was a busy ferry port full of train ferries for the crossing to Sjælland. It is now concentrating on tourism and trade. It is an attractive town with a fine castle and some old buildings dating from mediaeval times when it was the seat of the Danish Parliament and used to collect dues from ships sailing through the Store Bælt.

Approach

Approaching from the north the Store Bælt bridge must be negotiated and this is ideally done through the buoyed channel in the middle of the West Bridge 55°18'·5N 10°53'·7E where the clearance is 18m in the centre of the span and 16m at the sides. Otherwise use the East Bridge (see above under Store Bælt Bridge). Once south of the bridge, course can be altered to the SW towards Nyborg safe water buoy from which the fjord is entered on a bearing of 306° on the leading line into the harbour.

From the south the landfall buoy can be approached directly, taking care to avoid the low islands at Langesand and its surrounding shoals.

Store Bælt can have quite strong currents flowing either way depending on time of year and weather conditions.

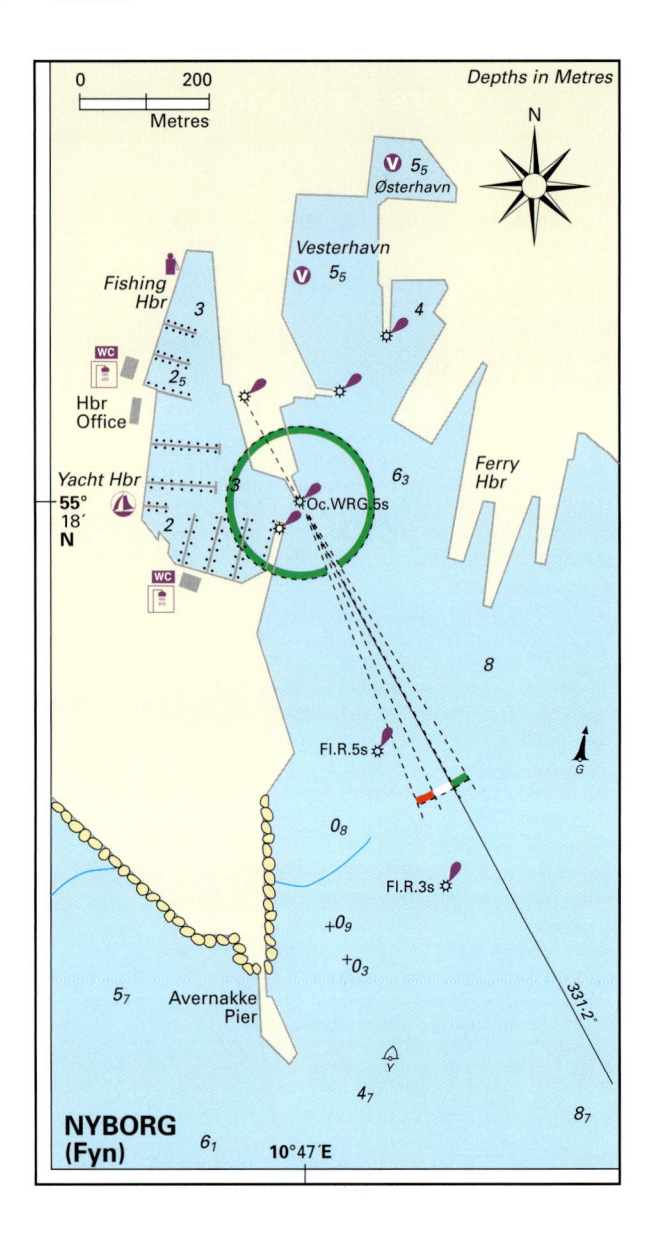

Nyborg looking northwest *Patrick Roach*

KORSØR

Østerhavnen guest harbour looking north *David Ridout*

Berthing
Berth in the yacht harbour in box berths in the southern part of the basin on the west side of the harbour with a maximum of 3m depth or alongside in the Vesterhavn in 7·5m or the Østerhavn in 5m (which is closest to the town).

Facilities
Nyborg has all facilities including several supermarkets and restaurants. Fuel is available in the fishing harbour in the northern part of the marina basin. Trains to Copenhagen, Odense and Hamburg.

Lundeborg Havn
This is a charming small yacht harbour 10M south of Nyborg if you do not want to be near a town.

Korsør
55°19'·94N 11°07'·16E starboard outer mole
55°19'·68N 11°07'·6E port mole head of marina

Distances
Svendborg 30M, Nyborg 14M, Kiel 73M

Charts
UKHO 2596, 938
Danish 141, 143

Lights
(For Store Bælt Bridge lights see page 119)
Sprogø 55°19'·8N 10°58'·2E Fl.W.5s44m8M Red round masonary structure, yellow bands
Commercial Harbour Ldg Lts 073·5° Front 55°20'·2N 11°08'·2E F.R.9m10M Orange triangle on grey column. 068°-vis-080° Rear 164m from front F.R.18m10M Inverted triangle on grey column
Yacht Harbour N Mole. S Head 55°19'·7N 11°07'·7E Fl.R.3s4M
Yacht Harbour S Mole. N Head 55°19'·7N 11°07'·8E Fl.G.3s4m2M Green mast
Egholm Flak 55°15'·3N 11°05'·8E Fl.RG.3s10m8M Red metal mast with platform marked 30 158°-G-345°-R-158°

Communications
Harbour office ☎ +45 58 37 59 30
Marina ☎ +45 21 18 59 30
korsoerlystbaadehavn@gmail.com
www.korsoerlystbaadehavn.dk

General
On the opposite side of Store Bælt to Nyborg is Korsør and a ferry used to run between the two towns until the arrival of the bridge. There is a large marina on the south side of a naval basin which is itself on the south side of the commercial harbour. The town is old and has some interesting mediaeval buildings. Visitors may berth in the marina or alongside in the Gamle Havn.

Korsør looking north *Patrick Roach*

THE BALTIC SEA AND APPROACHES

2F. APPROACH TO THE BALTIC BY THE STORE BÆLT

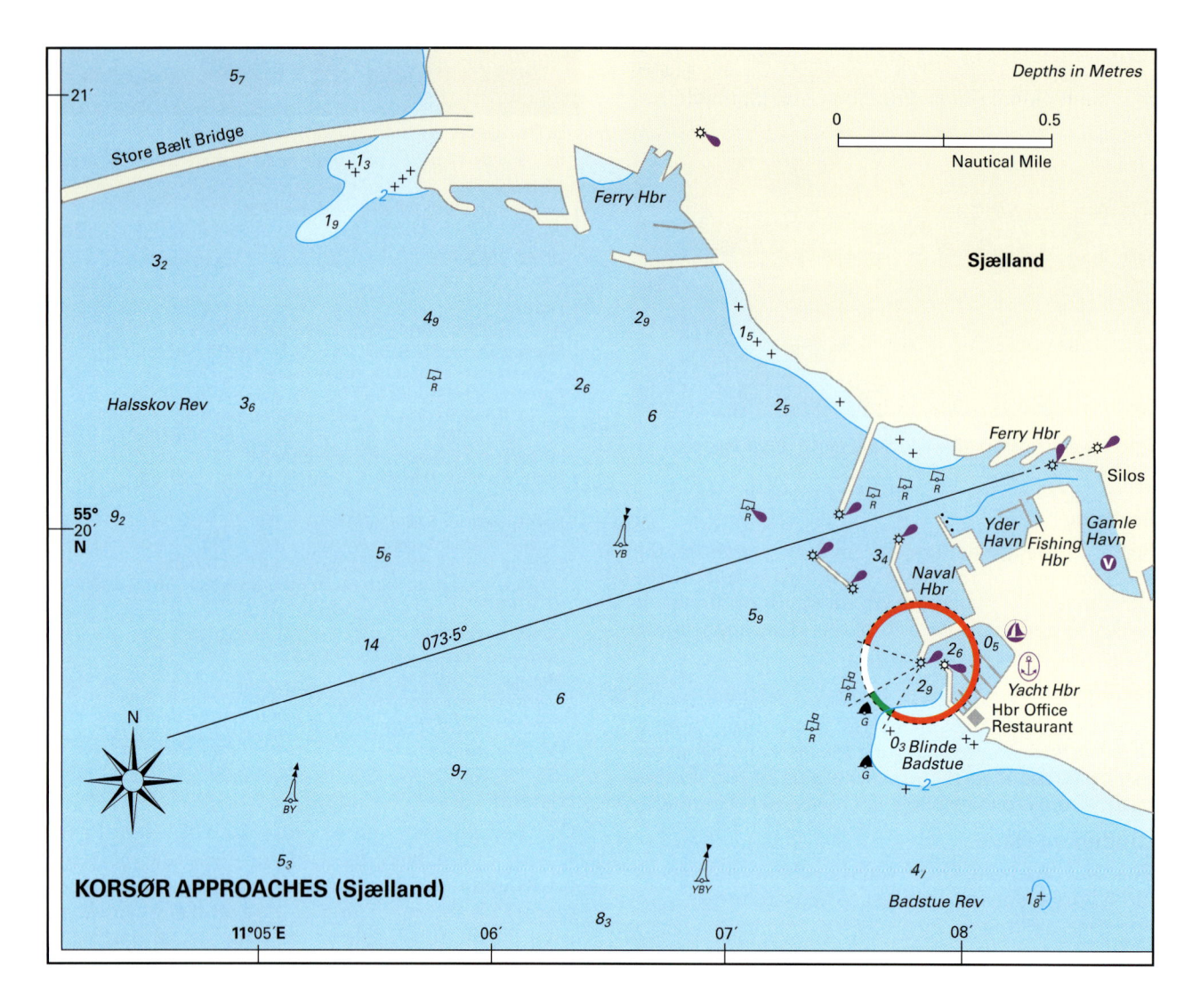

Approach
The leading line for the commercial harbour leads north of the Nygrund north cardinal mark and north of the detached outer breakwater and into the old harbour. If heading for the marina head east after the Nygrund north cardinal mark to pick up the buoyed entrance channel. If approaching from the south or from the Agersøsund leave the Badstue Shoal West cardinal mark to starboard. The entrance to the marina carries a least depth of 2·6m.

Berthing
Berth in the marina in a box berth in 2·4 to 2·6m (but visitors berths are limited so advisable to phone in advance). The alternative is to go alongside in the Gamle Havn but this has no facilities and is not recommended.

Facilities
All the usual facilities are available in the marina including a restaurant and fuel berth. The town centre is a short walk away. Trains to Copenhagen, Fyn and Jutland.

Southern Store Bælt and Langeland Bælt
Moving south through the Bælt and keeping to the western side you come to the island of Langeland. At the top of the island is the old ferry port of Lohals and on the east side of Langeland is another small yacht harbour, Spodsbjerg Turistbådehavn which is very sheltered in westerly winds. Both of these harbours have berths on the usual red/green basis and most facilities.

BAGENKOP

Bagenkop

54°45'·2N 10°40'·17E starboard mole head

Distances
Svendborg 22M, Nyborg 43M, Kiel 30M, Vordingborg 55M

Charts
UKHO 2942, 2597
Danish 142, 195

Lights
Vejsnæs Nakke 54°49'·1N 10°25'·5E Fl.5s23m12M White mast, red band
Ldg Lts 102·3° *Front* 54°45'·2N 10°40'·4E Iso.WRG.4s10m8–5M Red triangle on grey framework tower. 079°-G-099°-W-106-R-126° *Rear* Iso.W.4s13m6M red inverted triangle on grey framework tower. 077·3°-vis-127·3°
Kelsnor 54°43'·9N 10°43'·3E Fl(2)W.15s39m17M White square tower 200°-vis-116° and in Marstal Bugt. Obscured 098°-135° when close to Langeland

Communications
Harbourmaster ☎ +45 63 52 62 75

General

Although situated on the west side of the southern tip of Langeland, Bagenkop is a useful stop if headed from the Store Bælt towards Kiel and vice versa or from Kiel to the Smålandsfarvandet. Bagenkop is a fishing village but has a a marina and some holiday homes.

Approach

The approach is buoyed from the west on leading lights situated on the north pier on a bearing of 102°. Leave the western pierhead to starboard before heading southeast into the harbour.

Berthing

Berth in box berths in the northern basin or alongside where space allows.

Facilities

Most facilities are available together with small food stores and restaurants. There is a diesel berth in the fishing harbour.

Bagenkop looking SW *David Ridout*

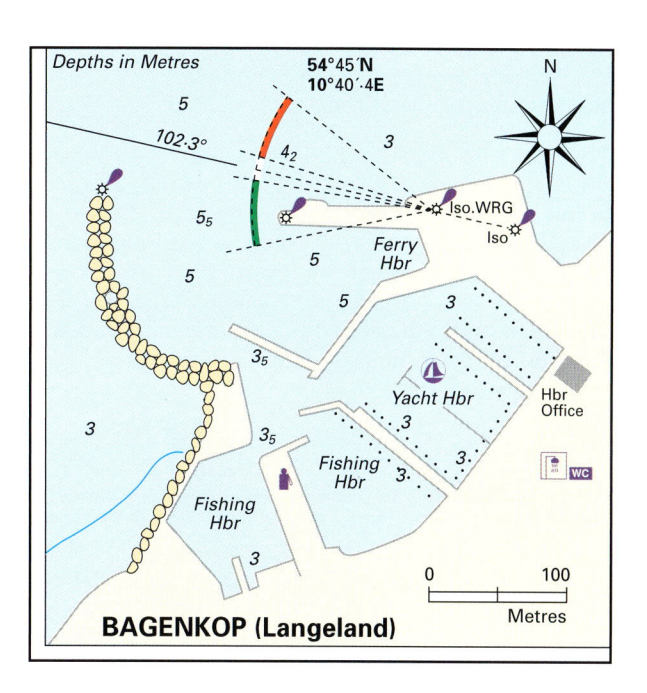

East of the Store Bælt – Smålandsfarvandet

This is a large area of water to the east of the Store Bælt and between the islands of Lolland and Falster in the south and Sjælland in the north. It provides a very attractive and interesting route which should not be missed by those wanting a more intimate glimpse of Denmark (albeit a little slower than the direct route from Kiel to Sweden and Finland). There are several islands, each with its own small harbour. Three of them in particular, Vejrø, Femø and Fejø, are interesting to visit. They are all surrounded by shallow water making for intricate pilotage. In the right conditions anchoring in the lee of an island is possible provided the yacht's draught allows a close enough approach.

In the east the Baltic Sea can be rejoined via the Storstrøm with Vordingborg on its Sjælland shore and then through the Grønsund between Falster and Møn with Stubbekøbing on its southern side. The Storstrøm has a fixed bridge with 26m clearance on its east-going channel and 25m on its west-going side. The Grønsund also has a fixed bridge with a clearance of 26m. For those wishing to visit Copenhagen there is a northeast passage, the Bøgestrøm, from the Ulvesund which leads on from the Masnedsund providing a shortcut to join the Sound but there are two fixed bridges (clearances 20m and 25·6m). The well-marked but unlit Bøgestrøm channel is shallow and intricate and should be avoided in strong easterly conditions (this was recently dredged to give a guaranteed depth of 2·2m but may well have more and that is of course also dependent on atmospheric pressure).

2. DENMARK

THE BALTIC SEA AND APPROACHES 123

2F. APPROACH TO THE BALTIC BY THE STORE BÆLT

Vejrø

55°02'·07N 11°22'·58E starboard mole for head of yacht harbour

www.vejroe.dk/havnen

This attractive island is privately owned. A yacht harbour on the NE corner has been developed in recent years to provide 85 berths with luxurious showers and other facilities (no fuel). Depths 3m in most of the harbour, and good shelter. Free bike hire and use of tennis court and for children a pirate play ship and rabbit mountain! Popular with weekenders from the mainland in season.

Vordingborg

55°00'N 11°55'E at end of approach to marina

Distances
Korsør 36M, Nakskov 45M, Klintholm 28M, Rødvig 28M, Copenhagen 60M

Charts
UKHO 2115
Danish 162, 161

Lights
Ore 55°00'·4N 11°52'·2E Iso.WRG.4s13m12–10M White square tower, red bands. 050°-G-091°-W-094°-R-108°
Vordingborg Ldg Lts 309° *Front* 55°00'·2N 11°54'·9E F.R.4m2M Mast on quay. *Rear* 103m from front. F.R.8m2M Mast

Communications
Vordingborg Nordhavn ☎ +45 40 49 44 25
Masnedø Bridge ☎ +45 55 77 70 28
VHF Ch 12, 13, 16

General

The Nordhavn is in an attractive and sheltered inlet off the Masnedsund. It is ten minutes walk from the town which is modern although it has an ancient history. But apart from the church the only remnant of that history are the remains of the 12th-century castle with its 26m tall Goose Tower and its golden goose near the harbour.

Approach

From the west, the former approach through the Masnedsund road and rail bridge is no longer available as the bridge was locked in July 2016. Yachts with an air draught of less than 25m and a draught of less than 2·5m can instead pass beneath the fixed Storstrøm Bridge and then cross the buoyed shallow Middelgrund to pick up the Trellegrund East cardinal mark and buoyed channel into Vordingborg.

From the Grønsund in the south, pass under the fixed Farø-Falster Bridge (clearance 26m) and head towards the southern tip of Masnedø to pick up the buoyed channel eastwards across the shallow Middelgrund (2·5m) to the Trellegrund East cardinal mark and buoyed channel to Vordingborg.

Looking south over Vordingborg marina *David Ridout*

124 THE BALTIC SEA AND APPROACHES

VORDINGBORG

Vordingborg *Patrick Roach*

Berthing
Berth in box berths in the marina or, if the marina is full, alongside near the boatyard just west of the marina. Beware that some berths in the marina are shallower than 1·5m and the deepest berths have a depth of max. 2m

Facilities
Water and electricity on the jetties, showers and toilets onshore. Fish shop and marina kiosk. Yacht yard and restaurant. Fuel and chandlery are available at the Masnedø Marinecentre, situated at the southern end of the Masnedsund bridge on its eastern side.

Masnedø Marinecentre ℡ +45 55 35 40 00

View over Vordingborg *E. Redfern*

2. DENMARK

THE BALTIC SEA AND APPROACHES   **125**

2g. Bornholm and Christiansø

The islands of Bornholm and neighbouring Christiansø are both Danish, although geographically much closer to Sweden. Bornholm is sometimes referred to as 'the pearl of the Baltic', with white sandy beaches to the south, rolling hills and a claim to have the highest number of sunshine hours in the Baltic.

It occupies a strategic position at the entrance to the Baltic, and has had an eventful history. Once a Viking stronghold, independent until the 10th century, it was then controlled by Sweden and then, in the 16th century, by Lübeck (a German Hanseatic League city), Awarded to Sweden by the Treaty of Roskilde in 1658, it was returned to Denmark in 1660. There are many historic buildings, including the famous 12th century round churches (fortress-churches) and the ruins of the imposing 13th century castle of Hammershus.

There are good connections from Rønne to Sweden by fast ferry to Ystad, with bus or rail connections to Copenhagen via the Øresund bridge. Currently there are also ferry services from Rønne to Sassnitz in Germany and Køge in Denmark, and from Kołobrzeg to Nexø. In addition, a ferry runs from Gudhjem to Christiansø.

All the harbours have a fairly straightforward approach, although there is usually an elaborate system of breakwaters once inside, to give protection

126 THE BALTIC SEA AND APPROACHES

to the inner basins. Access to some of the harbours on the east coast and to Christiansø will be dependent on the weather, and significant currents can be generated round the island by strong winds. Some harbours have gates which close off the inner basin in bad weather.

All berthing fees on both Bornholm and Christiansø are in the middle range.

It is a popular cycling destination, and bicycles can be hired at most of the harbours. There are bus services across the island, and cars can be hired in Rønne.

Rønne

55°06′N 14°41′E

Distances
Gedser 100M, Copenhagen 90M, Sassnitz (Germany) 50M, Gislövs Läge (Sweden) 55M, Simrishavn (Sweden) 30M, Karlskrona (Sweden) 75M

Charts
UKHO 958, 2014, 2015, 2018, 2040
Danish 189 (covers all Bornholm)

Lights
Fairway buoy 55°05′·1N 14°38′·6E LFl.10s
   Red and white pillar buoy Whistle
Ldg Lts 064·5° *Front* 55°05′·9N 14°41′·8E Iso.2s16m9M
   048°-vis-081° Framework tower 14m.
   Rear 229m from front Iso.4s24m9M 048°-vis-081°
   Red mast 12m
South shelter mole 55°05′·6N 14°40′·9E Fl.G.3s11m7M
   Horn20s (on request) Green tower 5m Floodlit
East molehead 55°05′·7N 14°40′·9E Fl.R.3s11m7M
   Red framework tower 5m Floodlit
Nørrekås 55°06′·4N 14°42′E Oc.WRG.5s5m6–4M 045°-G-090°-W-105°-R-180° White hut, two red bands 3m

Communications
Rønne Harbourmaster ✆ +45 56 95 06 78, *VHF* Ch 12, 13, 16
   (0800–1600 LT)
   roennehavn@roennehavn.dk
   www.roennehavn.dk
Nørrekås Harbourmaster ✆ +45 56 92 23 20 (0900–1000 and 1600–1700 LT)
   yachtroenne@mail.dk
   www.bornholm.org/noerrekaas/default.htm

General
Yachts are expected to use the Nørrekås yacht harbour (to the north of the main harbour) and should only use the main harbour if the yacht harbour is full or weather conditions dictate.

Approach
Position of breakwater end 55°06′·4N 14°4′·7E

Nørrekås should be approached on a bearing of approximately 100° in the white sector of the Nørrekås light. Leave the outer breakwater head with its green buoy to starboard. Beware the Hvidodde Reef 1M to the north marked by an East cardinal mark and a South cardinal mark. There is also an unmarked outlier on the south side of this reef with 3·7m over it, the Kasgaard Rev.

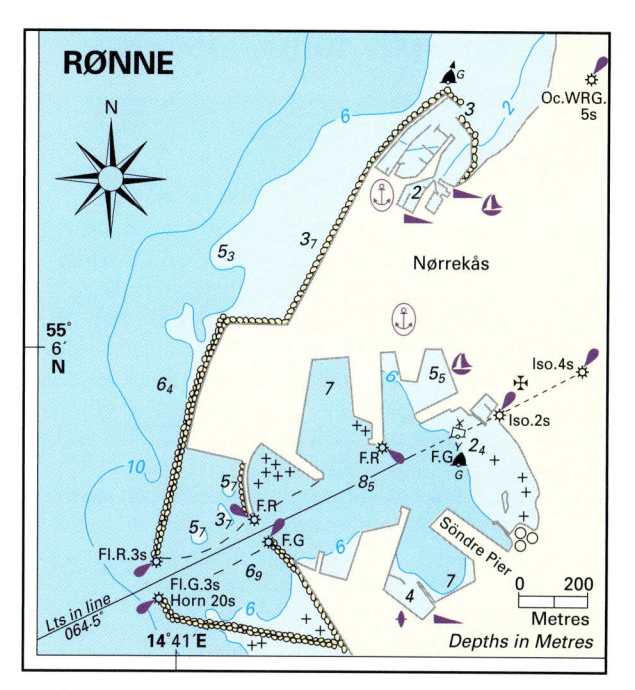

The approach to the main harbour is on 064·5° on the leading line.

Berthing
Berth in any vacant box berth not marked with a red plaque. Depths are 3m at the outer berths and 2m or less further in. The berths in the two small basins to the south of the main marina may be more comfortable in onshore winds and carry 2m depth but the approach to them needs care and is close to the starboard hand quay.

If it is necessary to enter the main harbour there is the possibility of alongside berthing for yachts on the southern quay of the northern basin or the western wall of the southern basin.

Facilities
All facilities are available at Nørrekås, including diesel and a sailmaker.

As the main town on Bornholm, Rønne has all amenities including a tourist office, supermarket, bicycle hire, bus tours etc. WiFi. Ferries to Ystad, Køge and Świnoujście and an airport 5kms away. However unless these features are required it is well worth considering one of the other smaller yacht harbours around the island, some of which are listed below.

Rønne C.N. Hill

2G. BORNHOLM AND CHRISTIANSØ

Other yacht harbours around Bornholm

Hasle
55°11'N 14°42'E on leading line close to breakwater
HM ☎ +45 56 92 23 22 haslehavn@brk.dk

This fishing and yachting harbour is 5M north of Rønne and makes a good alternative to it.

Approach the harbour mouth on a bearing of 097° in the white sector of Hasle Lt. Beware of a shallow patch with 3·7m just north of the leading line close to the harbour entrance.

Only Bassin IV is labelled clearly for Guests, but Bassin III can also used. Mooring is alongside to stone quays. For electric contact the harbourmaster.

Shopping facilities, restaurants in the town and buses to Rønne.

Hammerhavn
55°16'·75N 14°48'·2E between breakwaters of harbour entrance
HM ☎ +45 56 92 23 24

This bay on the northwest tip of the island is protected by breakwaters and makes a change from built-up areas. It is well placed for a visit to the ruins of Hammershus Castle or for walking in the Hammerknuden nature reserve. Approach the harbour mouth on a bearing of 075° in the white sector of Hammerhavn Lt. Berth alongside the jetties of the inner harbour in 3m decreasing to 2m. The facilities are fairly basic but fuel is available. The nearest village with shops and restaurants is Sandvig 2km away.

Allinge
55°16'·75N 14°48'·2E leading line by harbour entrance
HM ☎ +45 56 92 23 28

This picturesque ferry harbour on the northeast tip of the island provides sheltered alongside berthing in 3·9m in the inner harbour with most facilities, but the harbour may be closed by a shut gate between the outer and inner harbours in strong onshore winds. A black ball or three Vertical Red lights signal that the harbour is closed. Approach the harbour mouth on 208·9° on the leading line. Fuel is no longer available except at petrol station. Shore power and showers available. Free WiFi in café on quay. Easy passage to Christiansø (12M) and only 23M to Simrishamn in Sweden.

The harbour at Tjen is very well sheltered and offers good facilities, although it is less picturesque than some on the island C. N. Hill

Tjen
55°15·0'N 14°50'·E on leading line at harbour entrance

This harbour is rather less picturesque than many of the others along the northern coast of Bornholm, but offers excellent shelter in bad weather. The entrance should also be straightforward even in poor conditions.

There is a basin for yachts, but this is rather cramped. Available places are marked with a green marker. Normally, yachts can tie alongside in the main basin. Fuel is available. There is an excellent chandlers and sailmaker about 500 m away. A small supermarket is adjacent to the quay.

Gudhjem South
55°12'·9N 14°58'·4E on leading line close to harbour
HM ☎ +45 56 92 23 36

Another pleasant harbour offering most facilities including diesel. However access to the inner harbour is closed by a gate in onshore winds of more than 10m/s (20 knots). This is signalled by a red ball hoisted on a flagpole or extinguished leading lights (F.R). Approach on 202°. Berth alongside or bow to quay with stern anchor in the inner harbour. Frequent ferries to Christiansø.

Gudhjem South harbourmaster ☎ +45 56 92 23 36.

Svaneke
55°08'·14N 15°08'·8E leading line by north breakwater
HM ☎ +45 56 49 60 40

A charming and well preserved old market town with plenty going on and good bus connections to the rest of the island. Svaneke boasts Bornholm's largest fish smokery. The outer harbour gets rough in strong onshore winds and the inner harbour gate is closed in these conditions. Enter the bay on a course of 215° in the white sector of the sectored light at 55°08'·04N 15°08'·73E until the harbour mouth opens up and the leading line appears on 297°. Berth alongside or bow to quay with stern anchor in the inner harbour in 3·9m. All facilities available including diesel and a sailmaker.

Nexø
55°03'·9N 15°08'·5E on leading line by southern breakwater
HM ☎ +45 56 49 22 50

Nexø is a fishing and commercial port and has a summer ferry connection to Poland. It is an all-weather port and is a useful landfall if coming from Poland. Approach on the leading line (F.G) on 232° (church spire in line with entrance). Boats less than 10m in length can berth alongside or to stern buoys

128 THE BALTIC SEA AND APPROACHES

CHRISTIANSØ

The approach to the harbour at Gudhjem. Notice the prominent leading marks. There is not a great deal of room to manoeuvre within the harbour and berthing might be tight *C. N. Hill*

The visitors' berths in the small basin to your starboard side as you enter Nexø harbour. You can tie alongside or use the stern buoys provided. Alternatively, turn to port and moor in the first basin, using stern buoys *C. N. Hill*

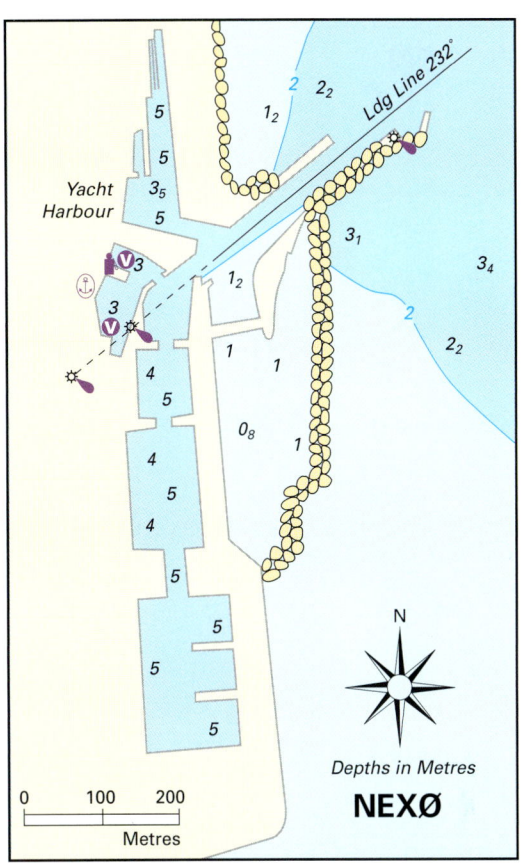

on the west quay of the old harbour (the second basin on the starboard side). Boats over 10m in length can use the next basin to the south. Moor to stern buoys. All facilities including fuel, WiFi and a sailmaker. Buses to other parts of the island.

Christiansø

55° 19.1N 15° 11.17E on southern approach to harbour (East of Snarken red can buoy)
HM ✆ +45 40 45 20 14

A gorgeous small island northeast (10M) from Bornholm and separated by a narrow sound between it and the adjoining island of Frederiksø. The sound forms two harbours, separated by a swing footbridge which only opens by prior arrangement with the harbourmaster. The south harbour affords berths in 2-3 metres. The north harbour is occupied by fishing boats and has very limited, if any, space. It has been a fortress and naval harbour since the 1600s.

Approach the southern harbour from the west on the leading line on 103°, leaving the red can buoy (marking a dangerous rock, Snarken) to port until the harbour opens up and enter in the white sector of the light on Frederiksø. A black ball or three red lights signal that the harbour is closed either because of bad weather or because the harbour is full. Mooring is either alongside the main quay (which often involves rafting up) or by stern buoy on the west side (which is more exposed). Facilities are limited but diesel is available.

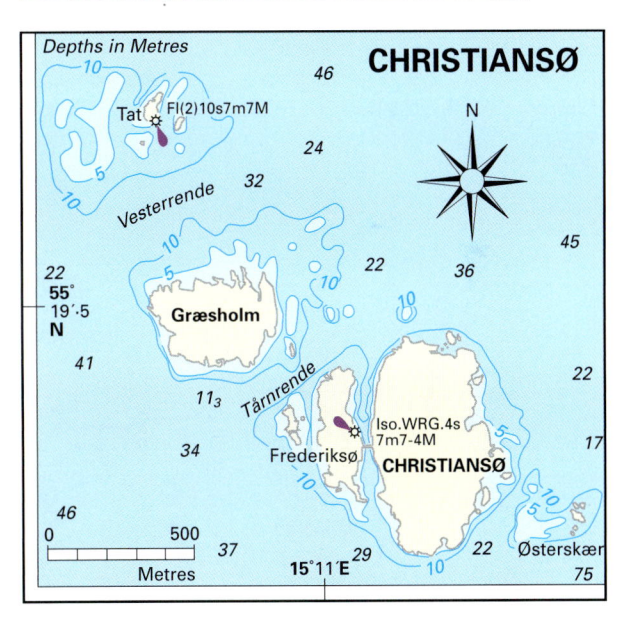

The harbour at Christiansø early in the year, it will become very crowded in the season *C. N. Hill*

THE BALTIC SEA AND APPROACHES 129

3. SWEDEN

3. SWEDEN

The Swedish coast is the longest and probably the most varied in the Baltic. The west coast runs north from the busy and heavily populated Øresund, passing the fertile shores north of Kullen until the Göteborg *Skärgård* is reached. After this come the wonderful cruising grounds of the Bohuslän before reaching the bare rocky foreshores backed by extensive forest towards the Norwegian border.

The southern coast is very different in nature. There are far fewer rocks, but instead long stretches of sandy beaches. Early in the season, some shoaling may occur in harbour entrances due to the shifting sand in winter storms. Rather than coming in close to the breakwaters, it is better to line up the entrance at least 200m out and follow the line in.

North and east of Simrishamn the geology begins to change to the more familiar rock-strewn coastline, with outlying archipelagos, or *skärgård*, of islands. The first major archipelago centres around Karlskrona.

The east coast from Kalmar to beyond Stockholm is largely a *skärgård* area. It demands careful navigation, but at the same time offers sheltered sailing in smooth waters dotted with hundreds of secluded anchorages and pretty visitors' harbours (*gästhamnar*). It is seldom crowded outside midsummer but a fair proportion of those who visit the Baltic with the intention of exploring north and east become so entranced with this area that they never progress further. The *skärgård* surrounding Stockholm is an immense cruising area in itself.

The Gulf of Bothnia has long been sailed by Swedes, Finns and Germans and is gaining in popularity with others. A glance at the invaluable *Gästhamns Guiden* (see pilots and cruising guides) reveals many small harbours and marinas. The season is necessarily shorter, with ice lingering into May, and those who venture north have the opportunity to experience an entirely different facet of Swedish cruising. This area includes the High Coast (Höga Kusten), which is a UNESCO World Heritage site. This can claim to be among the most beautiful of all the Baltic cruising areas.

Finally, in addition to its coastal waters, vast areas of central Sweden consist of interconnected lakes, many of them accessible to yachts with fixed masts. Lakes Vänern and Vättern are traversed by the hundreds of yachts which pass through the Trollhätte Kanal and Göta Kanal each year, while Lake Malaren, directly inland from the city of Stockholm, was cradle to some of the earliest Swedish civilisation and culture and has many of Sweden's oldest buildings dotted around its shores.

3a-d   West coast of Sweden (including the Göta Kanal) *138*

3e   South coast of Sweden *177*

3f   East coast of Sweden: Utlangan to Landsort, including Öland and Gotland *187*

3g   East coast of Sweden: Stockholm - the Archipelago and surrounding area *204*

3h   The Gulf of Bothnia *226*

THE BALTIC SEA AND APPROACHES   **131**

3. SWEDEN

Key information

⚓ Rescue/Safety services

Emergency ☏ 112 or VHF Ch16

National SAR agency is **Swedish Maritime Administration**. Communicate via **MRCC Göteborg**,
VHF DSC MMSI 002653000
☏ +46(0)31 699080
or in emergency +46(0)31 699050.
Stockholm SJD, VHF DSC MMSI 002652000
☏ +46(0)86 017906

Most emergencies will be referred to the Swedish Sea Rescue Society (SSRS). There are additional benefits if you join. See www.sjoraddning.se

⊕ Charts and chart packs

Admiralty charts give good general coverage of the Swedish coast, quite sufficient for passage-making or cruise planning. However for cruising the intricate Blå Kustens (Blue Coast) either side of Västervik, or Stockholm's superb *skärgård*, the Swedish publications are essential. These, produced by Sjöfartsverket, (the Swedish Maritime Administration), are divided into small-scale 'Coastal charts', medium-scale 'Archipelago charts' and large-scale 'Special and harbour charts'. More details will be found on their website www.sjofartsverket.se.

Of particular appeal to the yachtsman are the excellent Båtsportkort series of chart-packs, effectively a combination of 'Archipelago' and 'Special' charts, mostly at scales of 1:50,000 or 1:25,000. These have recently been revised and now come as 15 Spiral bound A3 sized booklets. However, the series does not cover the entire Swedish coast, and neither does it run in sequence.

There are also two useful series of German-published chart packs (size A2) which are readily available in Denmark. They are published annually and come with electronic versions on CD and complementary pilot books. These are the NV Baltic Charts and the Delius Klasing charts.

📖 Pilots and cruising guides

The *Svenska Kusthandbok* series which was produced by Sjöfartsverket (the Swedish Maritime Administration) aimed at the recreational market is no longer published, but copies are still available of two volumes only, *Mälaren and Hjalmälaren* and *Vanern and Trollhätte Kanal*. Further information can be found on the website www.sjofartsverket.se but only on the Swedish version.

Gästhamns Guiden (in Swedish only) is free of charge and widely available at harbours, hotels and restaurants. www.svenskagasthamnar.se

Arholma to Landsort (Stockholm Archipelago). Norstedts Förlagsgrupp AB. No English version currently available

Landsort to Skanor Published in English by Norstedts Förlagsgrupp AB. Available from Imray.

Norrlandskust by Erik Nyström (Bilda Förlag). Available only in Sweden, with no English version. However the excellent chartlets and photographs more than make up for this.

See the Appendix, page 418, for sources.

🕐 Time

Sweden uses UT+1 in winter and UT+2 in summer. The clocks usually change on the last Sundays in March and September.

kr Money

The unit of currency is the Swedish krona (usually abbreviated to SEK, plural kronor and often spoken of as crown), divided into 100 öre. It seems unlikely that Sweden will join the Eurozone in the foreseeable future.

Major credit and debit cards are widely accepted, both in payment for goods and services and by banks, nearly all of which have ATMs, known as *Bankomat*. Many businesses will now prefer a credit card to taking cash.

📄 Formalities

Sweden is a member of the EU and is part of the Schengen area, (see main Introduction page 7 for further details of Schengen requirements).

EU passport holders do not require visas. The British Embassy in Stockholm is located at Skarpögatan 6–8, Box 27819, 115 93 Stockholm, ☏ +46 8 671 3000. info@britishembassy.se.

If arriving from a non Schengen country, enquire at the HM or police station as to their requirements

EU citizens coming direct from another EU country do not need to seek customs or immigration clearance on arrival unless carrying items which must be declared. Alcohol and tobacco that has purchased elsewhere in the EU (duty paid) can be freely imported and it may be a good idea to stock up before arrival if possible.

☼ Public holidays

Official public holidays in Sweden include:

1 January, 6 January (Epiphany), Good Friday, Easter Sunday and Monday, 1 May (Labour Day), Ascension Day (May), Whit Sunday and Monday (May or June), Midsummer's Eve and Day (close to the summer solstice), All Saints Day (a Saturday in late October/early November), 24–26 December and 31 December.

☏ Communications

It may be taken for granted nowadays that almost every Swede under 50 speaks fluent English.

Mobile phones are widely used, although for the visiting yachtsmen there is always the problem of compatibility of SIM cards.

Almost all marinas will have WiFi, as will many shops and cafes. An alternative is to use a mobile broadband USB stick in a laptop. These are relatively inexpensive, and the Telia broadband can be topped up at any Coop or ICA supermarket by purchasing a coupon. They have the advantage they can still give a connection while sailing or at anchor.

✈ Travel

Sweden is well served by air, and some bus, rail and sea services from other parts of Europe.

Arlanda, approximately 42 kilometres from Stockholm, is the main international airport for the Stockholm region and places north. Gothenburg also has direct flights to the UK. Copenhagen is another alternative. It is also possible to drive direct from the UK using the Øresund bridge between Denmark and Sweden. Budget airlines use Västerås and Skavsta.

Internal bus, train and air services are exemplary. Various discounts are available to senior citizens on train services and some ferry routes. Note that on many bus routes, the driver will not accept cash; tickets need to be purchased in advance from a kiosk or elsewhere.

🖥 Websites

Sites directly connected with charts, pilot books and cruising guides are shown under that heading. Sites for harbours are shown under the harbour.

Many sites have English versions but often with only a summary of the content.

SWEDEN - KEY INFORMATION

sweden.se Describes itself as the 'Official Gateway to Sweden', with many useful links.

www.visit-sweden.com The Swedish Travel and Tourism Council.

www.sverigeturism.se The Swedish Tourism Trade Association, with links to tourist offices and on to marinas.

www.tullverket.se The Swedish Board of Customs. Includes regulations for 'Pleasure Boats' in English and links to other Swedish government sites.

www.gotakanal.se Göta Canal Company's excellent and very informative website.

www.stockholmtown.com Carries the excellent nine-language Stockholm Official Visitor's Guide.

www.stockholm.se The City of Stockholm's website, designed primarily for local residents, slightly more formal than the above but with interesting parts e.g. entertainment and theatres.

www.skargardsstiftelsen.se Skärgårdsstiftelsen (the Archipelago Foundation).

www.sjofartsverket.se/en/ Lock opening times, bridge heights and bridge opening times. Similar information for Stockholm at **www.portsofstockholm.com/stockholm/**

www.ksss.se The Kungl Svenska Segel Sällskapet, (the Royal Swedish Yacht Club) have marinas at Saltsjöbaden and Sandhamn.

www.sxk.se The Svenska Kryssarklubben (Swedish Cruising Club). In Swedish only.

www.promarina.se This company operates several marinas and bookings of berths can be made on-line. In Swedish only.

www.gasthamnsguiden.se Useful details of guest harbours. In Swedish only.

www.smhi.se Provides shipping forecast for all Baltic areas in English as well as Swedish.

Radio communications and weather information

Details of the above, including Search and Rescue, GMDSS, Coast Radio Stations, Weather Bulletins and Navigational Warnings, NAVTEX and Weatherfax transmissions, weather forecasts on the internet and Firing Practice areas will be found on pages 420.

Weather forecasts in (SHMI) Swedish and English are broadcast at 0800 and 2000 UT on the working channels of all the many VHF stations remotely controlled from Stockholm – see page 424 for details. Note that wind speeds are normally given in metres per second. As a very rough guide, halve this to get Beaufort; double it to get knots.

Since most harbours now have WiFi, and with other means of connecting to the internet, this is now undoubtedly the best source of weather information.

WC Holding tanks

A new law introduced in 2015 provides that no human waste, either solid or liquid, be discharged into Swedish waters – that is, within 12 miles of land. Although holding tanks are not compulsory, it will be very difficult to comply without a holding tanks or some other method of avoiding discharge. The law also requires harbours to provide a pump out station for a holding tank, but it may take some time for this to be achieved.

It is not yet clear as to how rigorously the new law will be enforced but yachtsmen should take all possible steps to comply.

Most marinas and harbours will of course have toilet arrangements, but at nature harbours, or in the more remote harbours, it may be found that the only facilities are the somewhat more primitive composting toilets.

The country

The varied nature of the cruising to be had around Sweden's coast is, to a large extent, a reflection of the country's geology. The country comprises four distinct zones, three of which are founded on ancient rocks. The northern two thirds of the country has mountains to the west, along the Norwegian border, while to the east it is boulder-strewn bare rock, with peat bogs and spruce, pine and birch stretching northwards until they are beaten by the climate. South of this the land slopes down to the central lowlands, which are more hospitable, with prosperous agriculture and deciduous trees among the conifers. Stockholm and Göteborg are in this region. Southern Sweden has a central raised area with the same feel as the rocky north, bordered by coastal lowlands given over to agriculture and fishing. The fourth region, Skåne, in the extreme southwest, has the most recent rock, often covered with boulder clay, with beech and oak rather than conifers.

The coast from north of Stockholm down to Kalmar is fringed by tens of thousands of islands – some inhabited, some not, some rocky and desolate and others green and fertile. It is a seductive area and immensely popular with both Swedish and foreign yachtsmen. The southern part of the Swedish coast, from Kalmar round to Malmö, is attractive, with an undulating coastline and a number of interesting harbours. There is another, smaller, archipelago centred around Karlskrona.

A major resource is timber, which covers more than half of the country. North of Stockholm, paper mills are conspicuous by the clouds of steam they produce. Fishing is much reduced, and it is rare to see fishing boats out at sea.

Even the smallest islands in the archipelagos have holiday homes, and the owners need boats to visit them. As a consequence, boat ownership in Sweden is higher than anywhere else in Europe.

THE BALTIC SEA AND APPROACHES   133

3. SWEDEN

History

While the Danish and Norwegian Vikings headed west, Swedish Vikings went east and then south along the rivers of Russia to the Caspian and Black Seas, reaching Constantinople by 838. They settled Novgorod as a trading centre under their leader Rurik. By 900AD Rurik's successors had their capital in Kiev and ruled all the Slavic tribes from the Caspian and Black Seas to the Baltic in what was then called Kiev-Rus, the embryo Russia. ('Rus' was the Viking word for an oar or oarsman, probably because of their red hair.) Emperor Basil II of Constantinople, capital of the surviving eastern Roman Empire, even employed Rus Vikings as his 'Varangian guard', his personal and most trusted bodyguard, a tradition that lasted for four centuries.

During the middle ages, Sweden's south and west coasts were ruled by Denmark. Then in 1397 a royal marriage led to the Kalmar Union which united all the rest of Sweden and all of Norway under Denmark. To the Swedes the Union simply meant ever increasing taxes for the Danes to fund their wars in southern Jutland. Periodic Swedish rebellions were brutally suppressed. Then came the Stockholm Massacre of 1520 when 80 Swedish nobles were arrested and publicly beheaded on a single day. The Swedes were so appalled that they united under Gustav Vasa to drive the Danes out of Sweden. Gustav Vasa was elected king of the newly independent Sweden (which still included Finland). During his reign, he consolidated the state and its treasury, laying the foundations for his later successor, Gustavus Adolphus.

Gustavus Adolphus (or Gustav II Adolf) was king from 1611 to 1632. He was both an enlightened ruler and an extraordinary military innovator. He was regarded as the founder of modern warfare by later generals such as Clausewitz, Bonaparte and Patten. During his reign he captured the whole of the Russian Baltic coast as well as Polish Livonia (i.e. most of modern Latvia and Estonia) where memory of his rule is still celebrated. He then fought with the German Protestant states in the Thirty Years War against the Holy Roman Emperor, reaching Bavaria before he was finally killed in battle. By the end of his reign, Sweden had become one of Europe's major powers, controlling nearly the entire Baltic coast and hence its trade as the main exporter of grain and shipbuilding materials to the rest of Europe.

Sweden was to remain a great power for the rest of the 17th century. Then in 1700 Denmark/Norway, Poland and Russia united to launch the Great Northern War to clip Sweden's wings. Charles XII of Sweden started well, but was routed when he tried to invade Russia and was later killed when he invaded Norway (still in union with Denmark). In the resulting peace treaty, Sweden kept most of Finland, but lost Karelia, in east Finland, and Estonia and Latvia to Russia, which under Peter the Great was now to become the latest nation to dominate the Baltic.

In the 18th century, Sweden, like most of Europe, settled down to the Enlightenment and improving democracy. Then at the end of the century came the French Revolution followed by the Napoleonic wars. Sweden initially sided with Napoleon, but fared badly, losing all of Finland to Russia in 1809. The Swedish parliament elected one of Napoleon's defecting generals, Jean-Baptiste Bernadotte, as their new king Charles XIV John. In 1813 Charles joined the allies against Napoleon and defeated Denmark, thereby gaining Norway for Sweden until 1905.

The impact of war had put an end to 18th century prosperity. About a million Swedes emigrated to America in the 19th century, although many returned bringing with them ideas about American industrial methods. Sweden's industrialisation was based on iron and steel, textiles and timber. The country had never had the deep class divisions that plagued other nations, and so was able to develop quietly as an economically successful liberal democracy with a model welfare state.

In World Wars I and II, Sweden remained neutral, although sometimes bowing to pressure from Germany. It continues to be a constitutional monarchy under King Carl XVI Gustav, is a member of the EU, but not the Eurozone, and has the 8th highest per capita income in the world.

The people

Sweden has a population of around nine million, and a political system which includes a hereditary monarchy and a parliamentary democracy with a universal franchise, proportional representation and a single chamber of 349 members elected every three years. The established national church is Lutheran – non-Lutherans (including 130,000 Roman Catholics) make up less than 1·5% of the population.

Early on in the modern period, attention was paid to the welfare of all sections of the society, not just to the upper layers. Free education and poor relief started in 1807, old age pensions in 1890, employment injury insurance in 1901, and basic and disability pensions in 1914. Further benefits were added until, by the 1990s, an income tax rate of 45% was required to fund them and social expenditure, including health and social assistance, comprised about a third of the gross national product. Monetary problems during the early 1990s resulted in some services being cut back, allowing taxes to drop by about a quarter. At the general election of 2006 the Social Democratic Party, which had governed Sweden for many years, was defeated by the Moderate Party in coalition with minor parties, thereby representing a swing to the right in politics. VAT is set at 25%, and Sweden remains a relatively expensive country for the visitor. The education system is excellent, one result being a well trained work force, another an appreciation of the arts, and a third, conveniently, widespread skill in the English language.

Friendly but sometimes formal, the Swedes have developed a regulated society which, from Gustav Vasa onwards, has looked after its environment and has avoided the worst squalors of industrialisation.

Practicalities

Shopping
The cost (and the standard) of living is higher than in much of Europe. All daily needs can be met with ease other than in some parts of the archipelagos – the *skärgårds* – where food stores may be few and far between. Throughout the country alcohol – other than beer at 2–3% – is expensive and available only from Systembolaget, the state-owned chain of liquor stores. www.systembolaget.se

The two main supermarket chains are the Coop Konsum and ICA (pronounced *eeka*).

Health
In July and August mosquitoes can be an irritation, and the risks posed by tick-borne Encephalitis should be taken seriously. See main Introduction page 8 for further details and precautions.

Alcohol
The blood alcohol concentration (BAC) limits are 20mg/100ml for drivers of boats over 10 metres or boats capable of over 15 knots. For boats less than 10 metres and boats capable of less than 15 knots, the BAC limit is 100mg/100ml. Penalties include fines or imprisonment, depending on the circumstances. The same requirements apply to visiting sailors.

Yacht services and chandlery
Visitors' marinas in Sweden are indicated by a gold anchor symbol on a blue background and the words *Gästhamn* or guest harbour.

Some harbours, especially those run by sailing clubs, are private, and although they will usually try to find you a berth, it is better to arrange this in advance rather than pitch up and hope for the best.

Harbours for visitors are called *gasthamnar*, or guest harbours, however, even within these, many of the berths will be private. It is considered bad form to take a private berth, even if empty – rather like parking in someone's driveway (the same is true in Finland). Having said that, some harbours or marinas also operate the red/green marker system – if you see a green, you may take the berth.

Usually there will be a set of moorings specifically set aside for visitors, and marked with the *gästhamnen* sign (see illustration). The moorings can be stern buoys, booms, stern anchor, alongside or lazyline, or a mixture of any of these!

Many of the smaller harbours, particularly north of Stockholm, may not have a harbour master available to take your mooring fee; instead there may well be an 'honesty box' in which you can place your payment.

It is possible to book berths on-line at several marinas, which can be useful during the busy holiday season. See www.dockspot.com

Automatic vending machines are also on the increase, where you type in your boat details, insert a credit card, and are then issued with a sticker for your boat, together with relevant codes for the toilets, showers and other facilities.

Flag indicating a guest harbour *C.N. Hill*

Moorings for visitors are clearly marked with *gästhamn* *C.N. Hill*

3. SWEDEN

Electricity sockets are usually the marina type, although in remote harbours the two pin continental sockets may be found, and it is wise to carry an adaptor.

Diesel is readily obtainable, often at a berth at which a holding-tank can also be emptied. An increasing number of fuel points are either card or banknote operated, usually (but not always) with instructions in English and German in addition to Swedish.

Bottled gas may be a problem, with butane increasingly difficult to obtain as one progresses north. Camping Gaz – and possibly Calor Gas – cylinders can be refilled at Kalmar, but north of this only propane is likely to be found. It may be possible to get British propane cylinders (such as those manufactured by Calor Gas) refilled, but a suitable adapter is likely to be required. If remaining in the Baltic for any length of time it may be worth buying one or more Swedish cylinders in the hope of reselling them on one's return south.

Buoyage

Very many cardinal marks do not have topmarks, and have to be identified only by their coloured stripes. This is not always straightforward, as the buoy may be silhouetted against the sun, or the paint may have become obscured or discoloured.

Similarly, red and green markers may be rather similar in shape, although their colours are usually more recognisable. Red and green markers will be found extensively in the channels through the archipelago, and they are almost invariably marking some particular hazard – a submerged rock or shoal.

It is therefore even more important than usual to keep on the correct side.

Further north, and early in the season, it is possible to find buoys which have been moved out of position by the ice during the winter. Care should be taken if you think a buoy is not in its correct position.

Berthing fees

Berthing fees vary considerably depending on location and time of season. Some marinas charge a flat rate per boat, some by length (usually by range of lengths (e.g. 9-12m), and some by beam; some charge extra for showers, electricity or WiFi while others are inclusive.

Nature harbours

The extensive chain of islands around the *skärgårds*, which in Stockholm's case extends up to 50 miles off shore, means there are an immense number of sheltered bays and inlets perfect for anchoring. These are known locally as 'nature harbours'. Many Swedish sailors tie up bow to the steep rocky shore with lines to convenient rocks/trees and secure the boat with a stern anchor. Alternatively, you can anchor in the middle of the bay and use a dinghy (but be careful not to obstruct the stern anchors of those who are rock mooring).

Facilities in these nature harbours are obviously very limited, but the point of them is to 'get away from it all'.

Coverage of such harbours is beyond the scope of this book, but there are pilot books which can be purchased in local chandleries. Even if they are

Typical cardinal mark (in this case with seagull topmark!) *C.N. Hill*

Buoys out of position by winter ice *C.N. Hill*

Port hand buoy marking submerged rock *C.N. Hill*

136 THE BALTIC SEA AND APPROACHES

A typical lighthouse along the Blue Coast near Loftahmmar *C.N. Hill*

A miniature lighthouse in the intricate passages of the Blue Coast archipelago *C.N. Hill*

available only in Swedish, the aerial photographs and chartlets are invaluable. See Appendix page 418 for more details.

The Right of Public Access

Swedes are justly proud of their *Allemansrätten* (Right of Public Access) legislation.

From the yachtsman's point of view this means that a boat can be anchored anywhere (though not secured to a private jetty), and that one can then swim or go ashore, provided one respects the privacy of people's homes and does not enter gardens, trample growing crops, etc. Elsewhere one may walk across private land, pick berries, flowers or mushrooms (not those of protected species, of course), and even pitch a tent.

Naturally this freedom brings responsibilities. Disturbing wildlife – particularly nesting birds – leaving litter and lighting fires other than on purpose-built barbecues is not acceptable. Neither is driving or riding any motorised vehicle off the road, though pedal cycles (and horses) are fine. Fishing is limited to rod and line. Basically, show consideration for the enjoyment of others and one will not go far wrong.

The Skärgårds

The archipelagos or *skärgårds* (pronounced *shair-gord*) are possibly the main attraction when cruising Sweden, with intricate passages through thousands of beautiful islands providing an absorbing and memorable experience. The Blue Coast, stretching from Oskarshamn to Arkosund, and the Stockholm Archipelago, as well as the Bohuslan coast on the west of the country, provide cruising grounds where one could wander for a month without ever repeating an anchorage, with rock mooring in remote corners an additional attraction. See further details of these areas on pages 157, 194 and 213.

However, when cruising in the *skärgårds* it is particularly important to take heed of the advice to carry adequate charts, and to be absolutely sure of your position at all times. You also need to be alert to the sudden appearance of huge ferries which can easily catch you on the hop, especially in the Stockholm *skärgård*.

Restricted areas

Notwithstanding the above, there are various areas which are off limits for all or parts of the year, normally due to being either Military or Conservation Areas. Both are clearly indicated on Swedish charts.

The regulations controlling the former have been relaxed, so that it is no longer forbidden for foreigners to enter or cross them during peacetime. If there are smaller areas or installations within them where entrance is forbidden to all, they will be clearly marked on the ground.

At certain times of the year landing is not permitted on wildlife sanctuaries, and in some cases approach within 100m of the shore is forbidden. In addition to being marked on the chart a line of linked buoys will sometimes be used to close off an inlet, but even in their absence all restrictions should be rigorously observed.

WEST COAST OF SWEDEN

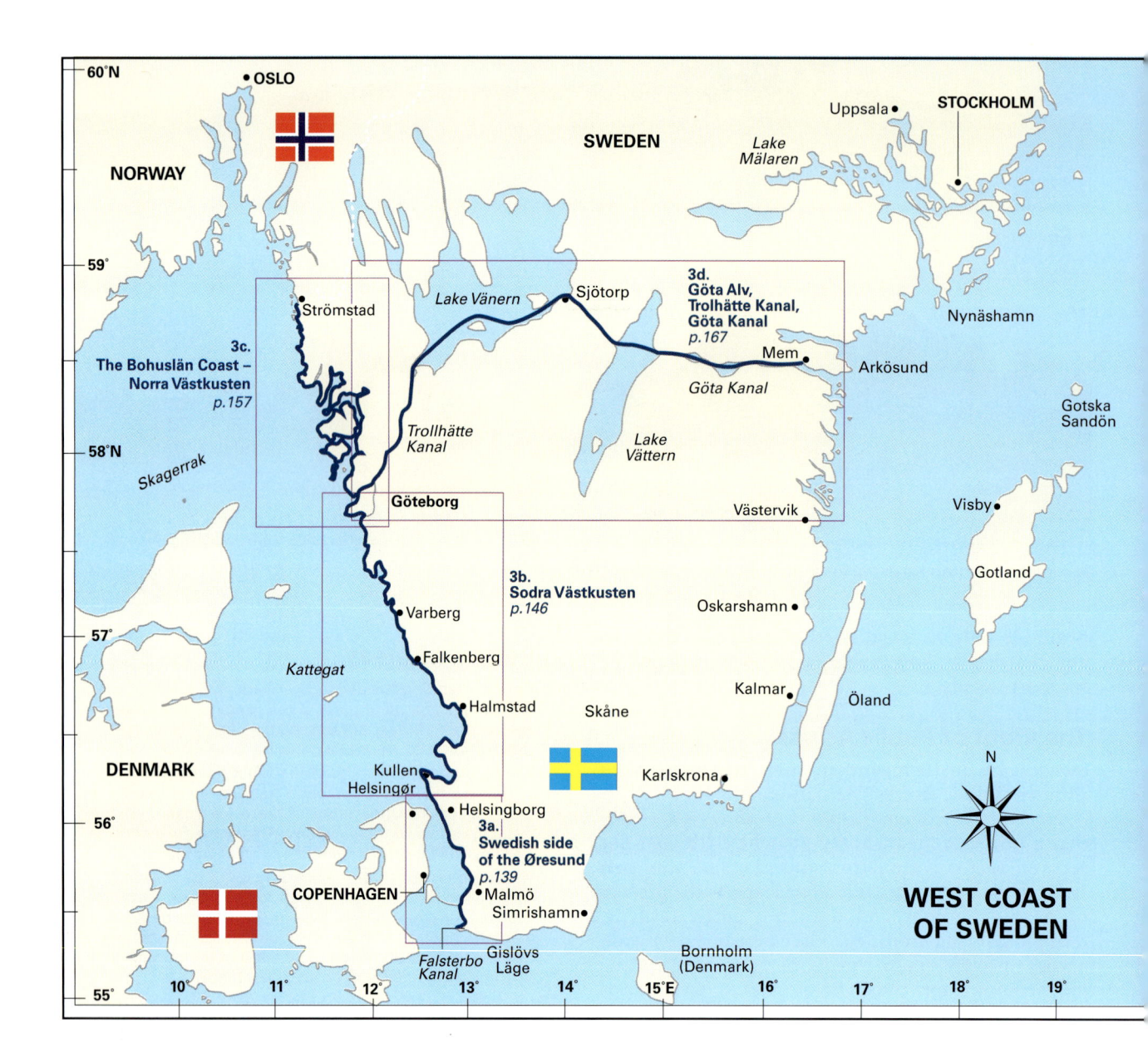

3a. The Swedish side of the Øresund, *139*

3b. Southwest coast (Södra Västkusten), *146*

3c. The Bohuslän coast – Northwest coast, *157*

3d. Göta Alv, Trollhätte and Göta Kanals, *167*

Outer *skärgård* on a windy day *D. and P. Thorne*

3a. The Swedish side of the Øresund

Øresund Bridge *E. Redfern*

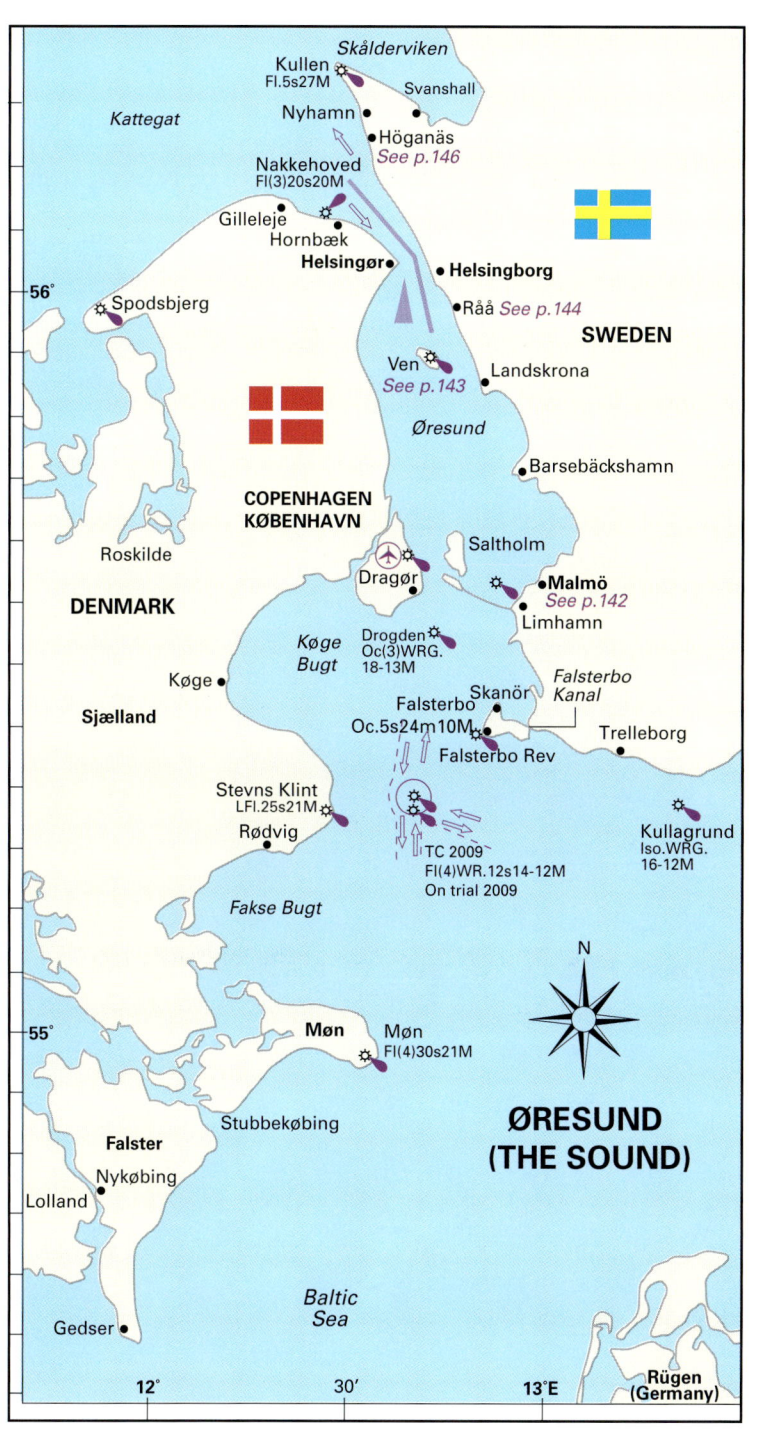

The Øresund (The Sound) is the most direct route from the Baltic into the main part of the Kattegat when coming from the east, and as such, is a major shipping route. It is also narrow, being only three miles wide at its narrowest point. There is a traffic separation scheme off Falsterbo Rev, the southwest corner of Sweden, and another in the narrows between Helsingør and Helsingborg. The hazard is from the size of some vessels using this route, rather than the sheer numbers, but nevertheless yachts crossing the sound should pay close attention to the TSS regulations, which are rigorously enforced. The waters between Copenhagen and Malmö are tortuous and shallow in places and crossed by the Øresund Bridge, but there is a well-marked dredged channel for large vessels. Currents in this area will vary with the wind in both strength and direction, and can run up to 2kn in the narrower parts of the Sound. It therefore follows that close attention needs to be paid to navigation. However, you should not allow these warnings to put you off, since they are in no way unusual and it is a very interesting and rewarding cruising ground. It is home to large numbers of yachts on both the Swedish and Danish sides and there are many guest harbours listed on the Swedish shore alone.

It is perhaps worth noting that the Swedish laws relating to alcohol consumption by a yacht's crew have been known to be particularly actively enforced in this area.

THE BALTIC SEA AND APPROACHES **139**

WEST COAST OF SWEDEN

Skanör

55°25'N 12°49.66'E West mole head

Distances
Stralsund 68M, Rostock 78M, Travemünde 110M, Kiel 125M

Charts
Swedish 921

Skanör is a popular holiday spot on the southwest corner of Sweden. The harbour, which can be crowded at times, has pile moorings with some space alongside a quay, and makes a useful stopping place on a route between the north German coast at Rügen and Copenhagen.

Falsterbo Kanal

55°24'·94N 12°55'·84E East Breakwater at beginning of canal, approaching from The Sound (NW)

55°23'·56N and 012°57'·98E NE Breakwater at beginning of canal approaching from the East

Distances (north end)
Copenhagen 21 M, Gislövs Läge 11 M

Charts
Swedish 921
UKHO 2014, 2015, 2018, 2040, 2115, 2595, 2816

Communications
☏ +46 40 20 43 80
VHF Ch 11 (Falsterbo Canal)
www.Falsterbokanalen.se

Looking NW from Falsterbo Kanal through outer breakwater
David Ridout

The mile-long Falsterbo Canal (pronounced *Fahlstehr-boo Kah-naal*) provides a convenient short cut from Øresund to the Baltic, particularly useful to yachts coming from Copenhagen or beyond. Depth is 4m. There are no locks, no dues and only one lifting bridge which opens every hour on the hour from 0600 to 2200 except 0800 and 1700 from April 15 to Sept 30. Outside that time it is open at 0630 and 1830. Signal light: fixed white and flashing red mean Stop, green means proceed. Both sailing and anchoring in the canal are forbidden.

Falsterbo Kanal looking SE *Lars-Erik Hansson*

140 THE BALTIC SEA AND APPROACHES

3A. THE SWEDISH SIDE OF THE ØRESUND

Höllviken
☎ +46 40 45 34 92

This is a small yacht harbour north of the bridge at the entrance to the canal. Pontoon moorings with piles or fingers, with green/red markers for availability. There are the usual facilities including bicycle hire and a cafe which is open from mid May till end August. WiFi and a webcam. Fuel at the coastguard dock on the porthand side of the canal coming from the north.

Malmö Dockan Marina
55°37·1'N 12°59'·19E North mole head (starboard on approach)
☎ +46 703 40 19 18
marinan@dockanmarina.se
www.dockan.se Go to 'Guest', click tiny English flag.

Approach is deep water directly from harbour entrance. Moorings are pile or finger. Use a vacant mooring with green sign and pay at the machine. Services are limited to power and fresh water, it is small and expensive, but it is well placed close to the centre of the city.

Malmö

Distances
Copenhagen 13M, Göteborg 136M, Falsterbo Kanal 13M, Stralsund 80M

Charts
Swedish 921, 8141, 9211

Malmö is Sweden's third largest city, and as such has every facility which would be expected, including some cutting edge architecture. It has excellent communications with the Øresund Bridge linking it to Denmark, as well as road, rail and air links to the rest of Scandinavia and beyond.

Three main yacht harbours serve the city.

Malmö marinas looking NE *Patrick Roach*

A sunset view of Dockan Marina, Malmö

THE BALTIC SEA AND APPROACHES **141**

WEST COAST OF SWEDEN

**MALMÖ
LIMHAMN-WEST AND LAGUNEN
YACHT HARBOURS (SWEDEN)**

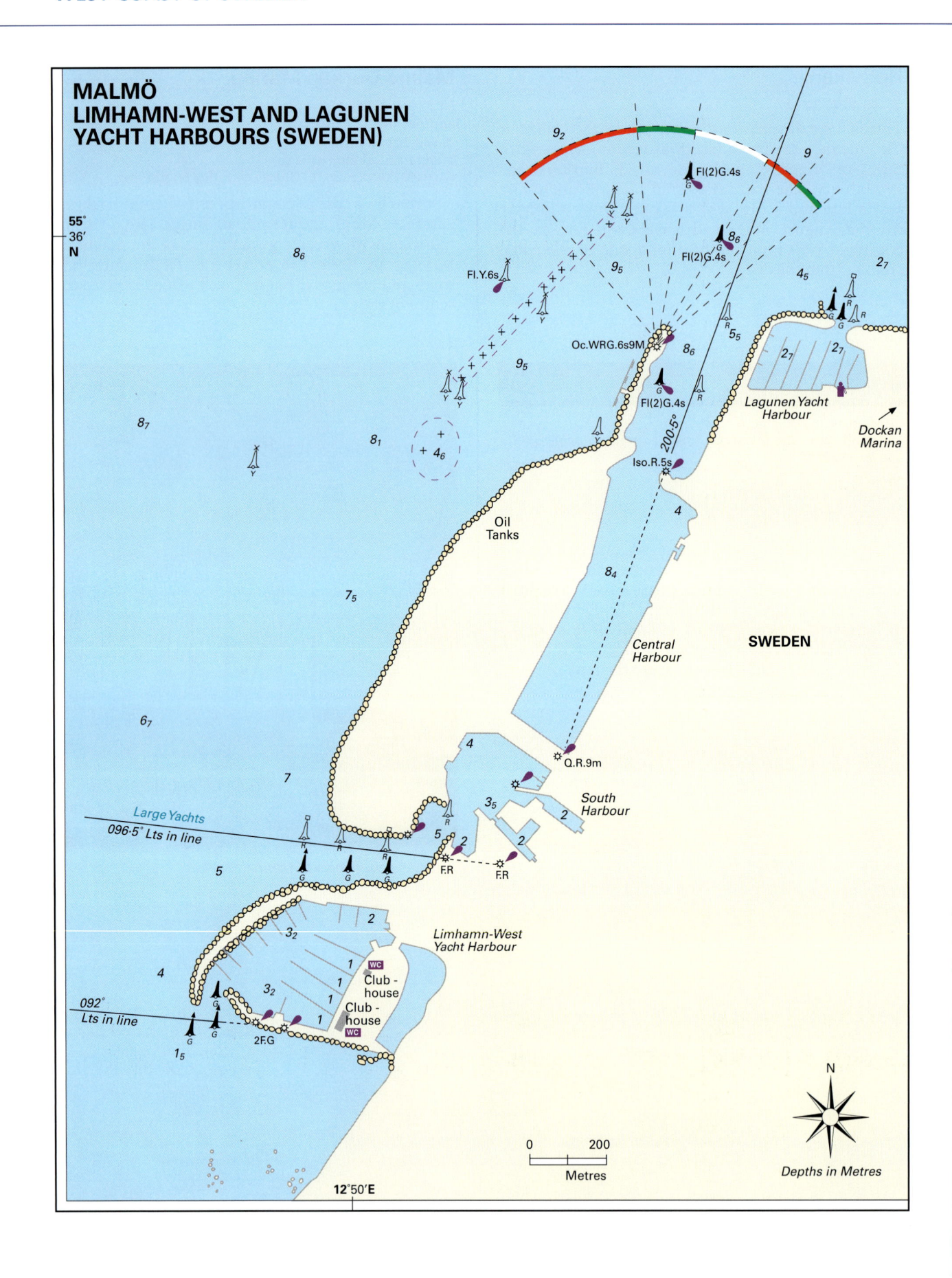

3A. THE SWEDISH SIDE OF THE ØRESUND

Malmö Lagunen

55°35'·9N 12°56'·26E North mole head
Harbourmaster ☎ + 46 40 16 04 30
Office ☎ + 46 40 16 04 18
kansli@lagunen.nu
www.lagunen.nu

This marina is home to many local boats, with all the usual facilities, and is particularly suitable for families with a nearby playground, beach and open surrounding fields. It is, however, nearly two miles from the city centre, but reportedly with a bus service. The approach is straightforward but with a well-marked reef, charted at 1·7m depth in places, just under half a mile offshore. The entrance to the marina is unlit. Depth in the marina is 2·7m. There are no dedicated berths for visitors, but they are welcome to use any vacant berth with a green sign. Payment is at the marina office.

Malmö Limhamn

55°34'·94N 12°54'·59E West mole head
Vågbrytarevägen 216 12 Limhamn
☎ + 46 706 15 20 25
info@gasthamnsguiden.se
www.smabatshamnen.nu

This is the best prepared marina for visitors, with all the usual facilities available, including WiFi, but has the disadvantage of being some three miles from the city centre. Approach is straightforward, with depth up to 3m, but beware of the pontoons on the east side, which shallow to 1m at the shore end. Visitors berths are at pontoon F, or use any vacant berth with a green sign and pay at harbour office. If the harbour office is closed, ask for help at the Harbour Grill. Bikes can also be hired from here.

Limhamn *Patrick Roach*

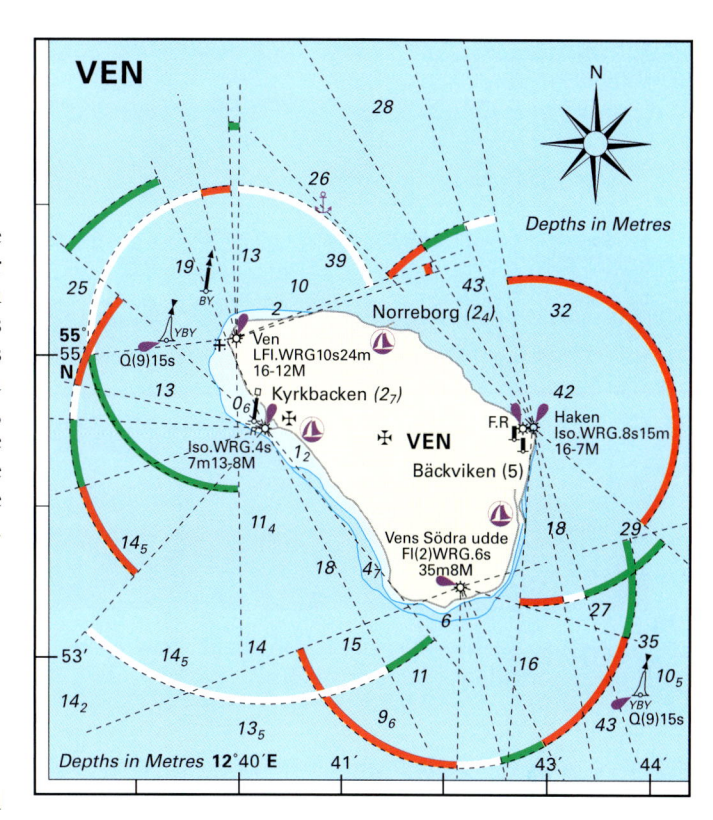

Ven Island

Charts Swedish 922

Ven is a small Swedish island 3M from Landskrona and 4½M off the Danish coast. It is a pleasant holiday island with two small and one slightly larger harbour. Ven is 2·3M long and 1·3M across, the highest spot being where Tycho Brahe built his castle, Uranienborg, 45m above sea-level. The island slopes from south to north, the new Western Lighthouse at the north western tip being 5m above the sea. Approach is simple from all directions, the only hazards being on the northwest corner of the island which are well-marked by cardinals.

Kyrkbacken

55°54'·59N 12°.40'·26E North mole head
☎ + 46 41872400
www.kyrkbacken.se

This is the best of the three harbours for visitors. Depth is 2·7m, and there are said to be 200 berths for visitors, both pile and alongside, with usual facilities, including fuel. Harbour dues must be paid at the office, under penalty of an extra payment if they have to come to find you! The harbour is popular with Danish boats.

Norreborg

North coast. This is a small harbour, depth 2m, with minimal facilities and mooring head to quay, stern to a pile or anchor.

Bäckviken

East coast. This is the main ferry harbour, which brings day visitors to the island from Landskrona. Depth is 1–2m and there are some pile moorings, or

THE BALTIC SEA AND APPROACHES 143

WEST COAST OF SWEDEN

Kyrkbacken harbour, Ven Island, looking west
David Ridout

alongside but the ferry berth must be kept clear. Power is available, but not much else.

Anchorage is also possible almost anywhere round the shore, depending on wind conditions. It may however be necessary to make a precipitate departure in the event of a sudden increase or shift of wind.

Shore facilities include a convenience store and bicycle hire. The Tycho Brahe museum, which during 2007 was nominated for the 'European Museum of the Year Award', is a must. Here you can follow the famous scientist's life and how his research made Ven a scientific meeting place during the 16th century. There are several other interesting places to visit as well as a golf course and good beaches.

Råå

55°59'·44N 12°44'·45E West mole head of northern entrance to marina

Distances
Copenhagen 22M, Malmö 29M, Falsterbo Kanal 40M, Stralsund 106M, Göteborg 103M

Charts
Swedish 922

Communications
Råå Port Association
☎ +46 42 26 16 35 0900–1300
raa.hamnforening@telia.com

This is an alternative yacht harbour for Helsingborg, about 3·5 miles south of the main port. Entrance is most easily made at the northern end, which is the mouth of the river Råå. Beware of possible strong currents in the entrance where depth is 3·5–4·0m and in the harbour is 2·5m. Berths are all between piles with bow to quay. Use any vacant berth, preferably with green tag. Harbour office in fishing harbour is manned 0900–1300.

Ashore it is a pleasant, if unremarkable, small town with a shopping centre close to the yacht haven. Also nearby is the fishing harbour with a fishery and shipping museum. There are several repair yards here.

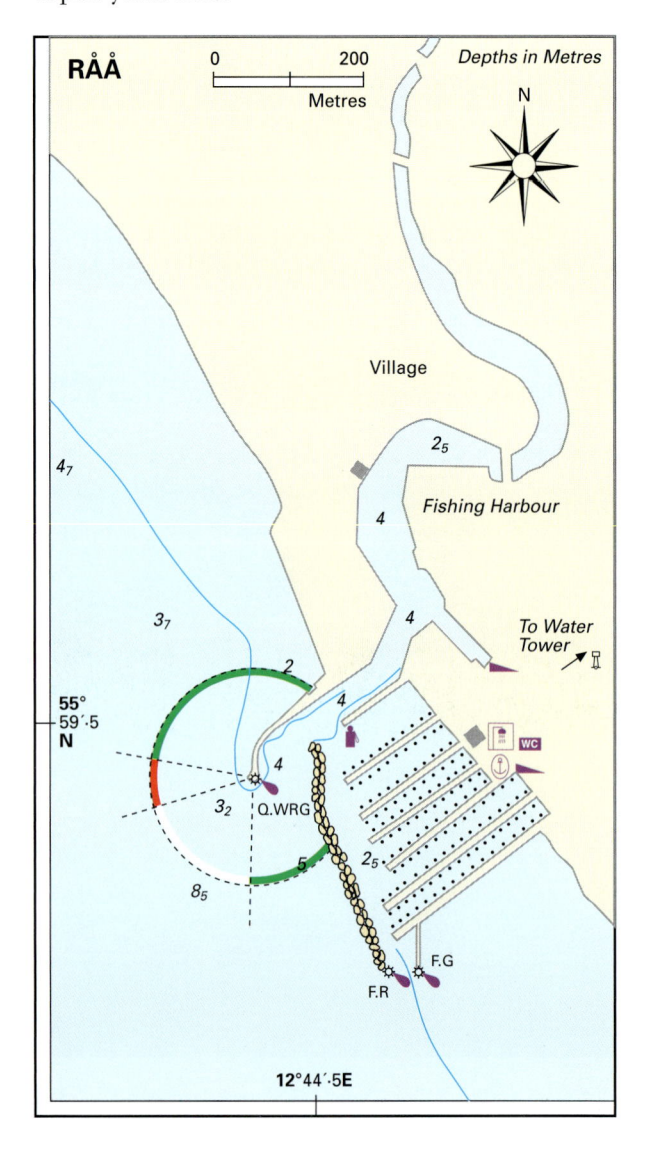

144 THE BALTIC SEA AND APPROACHES

3A. THE SWEDISH SIDE OF THE ØRESUND

Helsingborg (Norrahamnen)

56°03′N 12°41′E

Distances
Copenhagen 22M, Malmö 29M, Falsterbo Kanal 40M, Stralsund 106M, Göteborg 103M

Charts
Swedish 922, 9221

Communications
Harbourmaster ☏ +46 42 21 13 21
port@marinahelsingborg.se
www.marinahelsingborg.se

This modern marina is half a mile north of the main ferry entrance to Helsingborg and a distance of 2·5M across the Sound from Helsingør, and thus offers an alternative, should that popular harbour be overcrowded. All other Helsingborg harbour basins are closed to private yachts. Moor alongside the East Quay, or use any vacant berth with a green tag. Depth is stated to be 4m throughout, and maximum beam in the finger moorings is 4·2m. Fuel is available from an automatic dispenser near the harbour entrance. There is a sailmaker and a chandlery at the north end of the harbour.

Ashore, the half mile walk up to the ancient part of the city and the Karnän tower gives a good view over the area from the top. The Fredriksdal open-air museum and gardens are said to be worth a visit. The usual attributes of a major city are available, including a theatre and concert hall close to the marina.

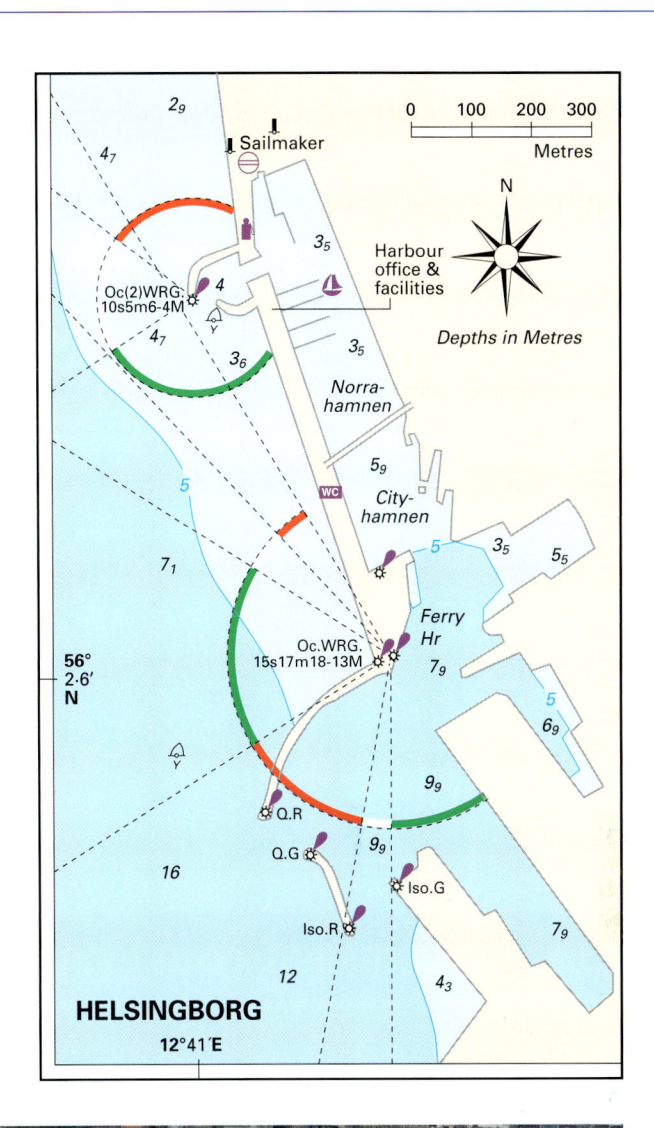

Helsingborg Marina looking N towards the marina entrance *Patrick Roach*

Helsingborg looking north *David Ridout*

THE BALTIC SEA AND APPROACHES 145

WEST COAST OF SWEDEN

Höganäs

56°11'·79N 12°32'·54E West mole head

Distances
Helsingør 10M, Göteborg 96M, Copenhagen 30M

Charts
Swedish 922
UKHO 2594

Communications
Harbourmaster ☎ +46 72 500 04 48
  hamnmastare@hbs.se
  www.hbs.se

Höganäs is seven miles south-southeast of Kullen Västra Point, the northern entrance to The Sound; a pleasant small town in attractive surroundings with a marina with 2·5m depth and the usual facilities, including fuel and WiFi. Berthing is stern to pile, and bow to quay. Use vacant berth with green tag. Öresundsmarin Boatyard has repair facilities. Shore facilities include good bathing close to the harbour, bicycle hire, and local museum. Several flights daily from Heathrow via Stockholm to Ängelholm airport (13 miles) and other direct flights are planned.

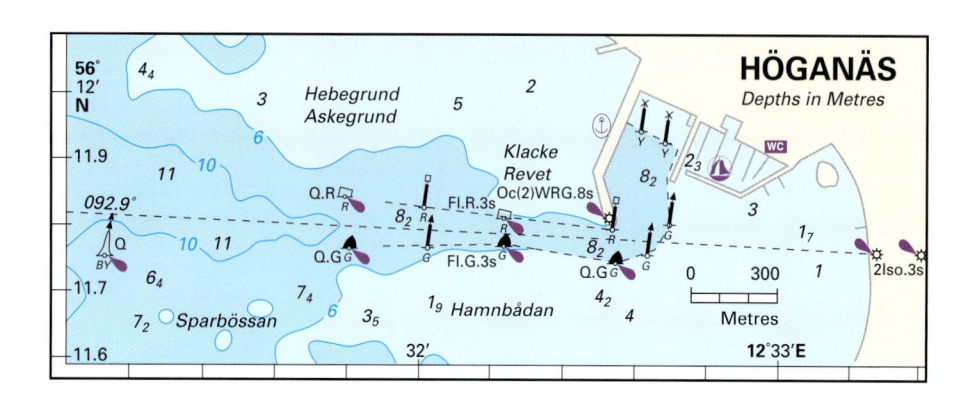

3b. Southwest coast (Södra västkusten)

The coast between Kullen, at the north end of the Sound, to the frontier with Norway, has two different and distinct aspects. Starting from the south, the coast is low-lying and rather featureless. There is good agricultural land and there are beaches, golf courses and summer resorts. The principal towns are Halmstad, the provincial capital of Halland with a population of around 65,000; Falkenberg with a population of around 20,000; and Varberg with a population of about 28,000. All three places are commercial ports. Then about 25 miles south of Göteborg, the scenery begins to change from pastoral to rugged and the coast becomes broken and studded with the islands and rocks of the *skärgård* and this continues to the border. The principal geological feature is that of gneiss intermingled with granite which forms extensive rock slabs.

Kullen to Göteborg

It is important to emphasise that the Kattegat is open water. The distance between the coast of Sweden and that of Jutland to the west varies from between 40 and 60 miles. A passage northwards is open to a very long fetch from the Skagerrak and likewise a southwards passage is subject to a long exposure to south or southwest winds. It follows that careful judgement must be made, particularly in unsettled conditions, as to when it is advisable to proceed. In favourable conditions, a non-stop passage either way between Kullen and the sheltered waters of the *skärgård* south of Göteborg, a distance of some 80 miles, can be made with ease. But in strong onshore winds, bear in mind that the open coast is liable to be a lee shore and that the approach to some of the harbours may be hazardous. It is also advisable to contact the harbour or marina in advance to check the availability of berths during the busy holiday season.

Surface water travels from the Baltic Sea towards the North Sea but the rate is insignificant, being less than 1kn in the open sea. The tidal range is also of little account being not more than 0·3m (1ft) in the north Kattegat decreasing towards the south. However, strong winds either from an easterly or a westerly direction may cause the sea level along this coast to fall or rise respectively by as much as 0·9m (3ft). The climate in the Kattegat and in the Skagerrak is affected by weather conditions prevailing in the north Atlantic.

Despite the caution given, it would be unreasonable to disregard the coast south of the *skärgård*. There are pleasant harbours for those wishing to break the journey and a selection of these is given below, proceeding from south to north.

146 THE BALTIC SEA AND APPROACHES

3B. SOUTHWEST COAST

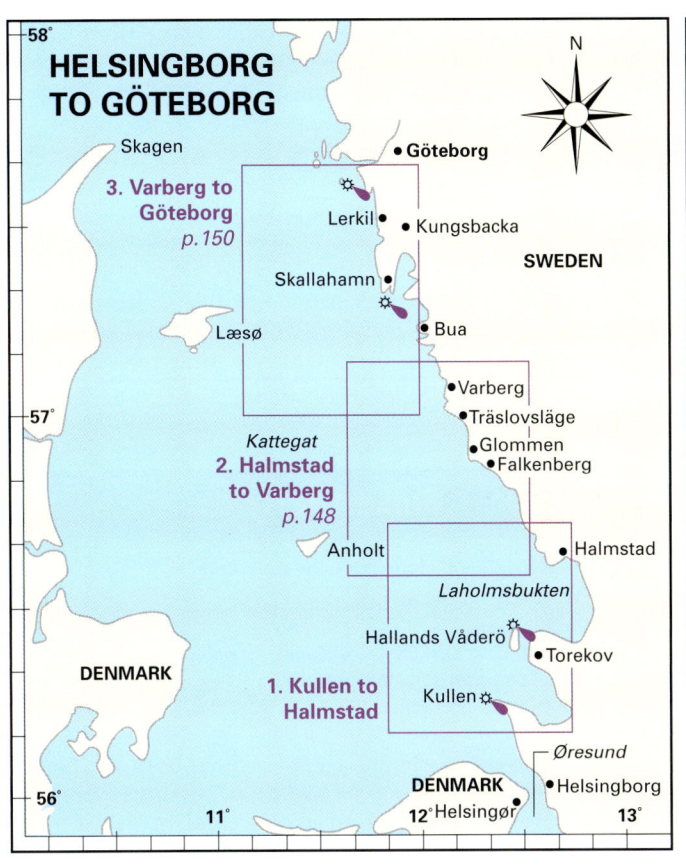

1. Kullen to Halmstad

Distance 25 miles

The promontory of Kullen is high and conspicuous. Approaching from the north it appears at first as an island until low-lying land to the east appears above the horizon. In 1941 the escape of the *Bismarck* from the Baltic was confirmed by the signalling station at Kullen

The coast trends to the north east and is indented by two large bays, Skälderviken and Laholmsbukten. For those wishing to make progress towards the north, it is more direct to proceed from Kullen towards Falkenberg or Varberg but these two bays are not without interest.

Torekov

56°25'·74N 12°37'58E North mole head
Charts
Swedish 923
UKHO 875, 2108

Communications ✆ +46 431 363 534,
info@torekovshamn.nu www.tbss.se

Torekov lies between the two bays and is a convenient place at which to stop, if going south, before rounding Kullen. The north wall gives good shelter but the pontoon berths may be subject to swell in northerly or north westerly winds. It is a pretty place but apt to be overcrowded. Diesel is available. Lying offshore is the only island in this

Torekov harbour looking north
C. Lassen

THE BALTIC SEA AND APPROACHES   147

WEST COAST OF SWEDEN

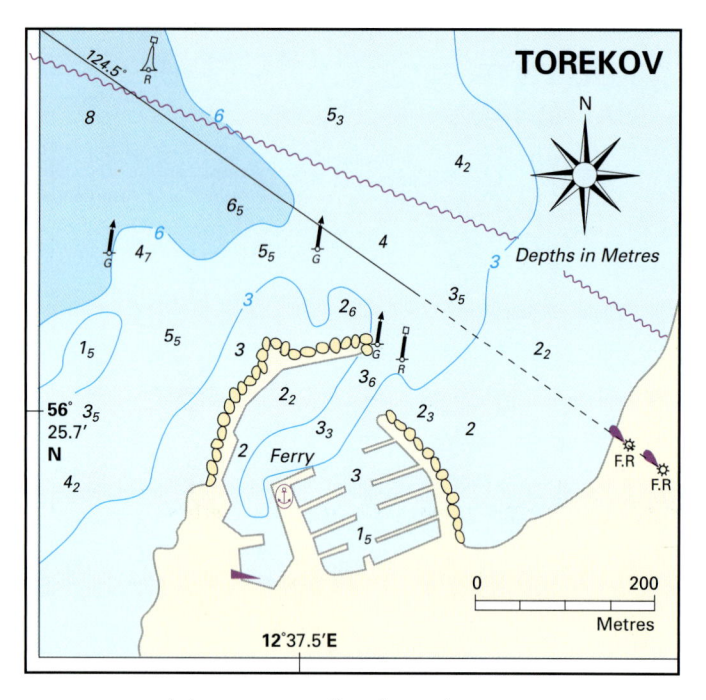

part of the coast, Hallands Väderö, a nature reserve with shelter from westerly winds on its eastern side.

Halmstad

56°38'·91N 12°50'·17E Outer breakwater head
Charts Swedish 923, UKHO 875, 2108
Communications ☎ +46 35 184 775
www.halmstadgasthamn.se

This was a Danish town until the middle of the 17th century. It lies at the mouth of the river Nissan. A buoyed channel leads into the river where there is shelter from all winds and berthing on the starboard side in pleasant surroundings. Depth 3–7m. The town has all the facilities expected of a provincial capital.

2. Halmstad to Varberg

Distance 38 miles

Leaving Halmstad and after passing Tylögrund lighthouse and the very popular resort of Tylösand, the coast trends in a north westerly direction. With shallow water extending some distance off shore it is advisable to give this stretch of coast a good offing.

Falkenberg

56°52'·89N 12°28'E South breakwater head
Charts Swedish 924
Communications
Sailing club ☎ +46 34 68 41 24 Evenings only
www.falkenbergs-batsallskap.se

This is a useful stopping place at the mouth of the river Atran. Protected by a series of moles and breakwaters there is good shelter and protection from any westerly swell caused by gales from the west or south west. Berthing is available at a small marina in the river on the south west side or possibly alongside the quay on the east side opposite silos. There may be appreciable current from the river in certain conditions and it may be risky to approach or leave the port in the event of strong winds outside.

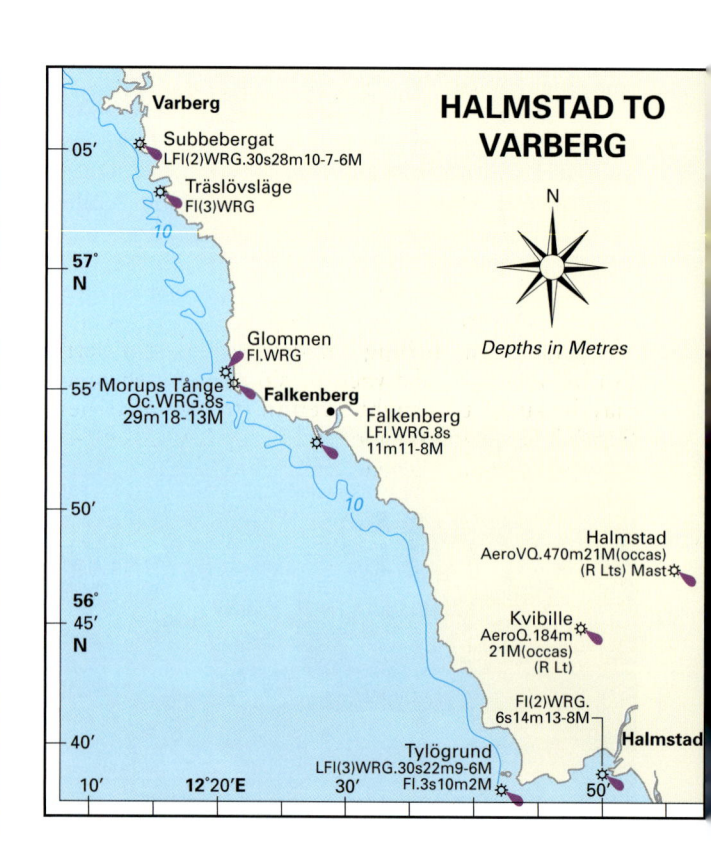

148 THE BALTIC SEA AND APPROACHES

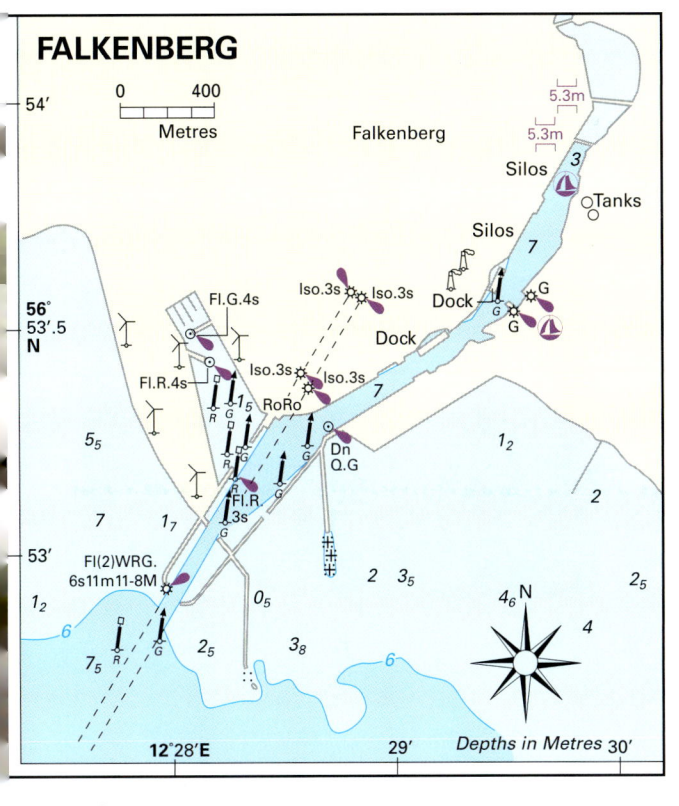

3B. SOUTHWEST COAST

Glommen

56°55′·74N 12°20′·89E North breakwater head
Chart Swedish 924

Glommen is a picturesque harbour on the coastal plain open to the winds but safe enough inside, either at the pontoon provided for yachts of moderate size or alongside the quays. It is typical of other local harbours along this coast which are small but safe with tricky entrances.

Träslövsläge

57°03′·43N 12°16′E South breakwater head
Charts Swedish 924
Communications Sailing club ☎ +46 340 67 07 07

This harbour, 14M north of Falkenberg, is a large fishing port and provides good shelter, especially alongside in the fishing harbour, provided a berth can be obtained. The yacht basin near the entrance may be subject to slight swell in strong westerlies. Depth is 2·4m and the moorings are pile with bow-to on fingers. Usual marina facilities and shops.

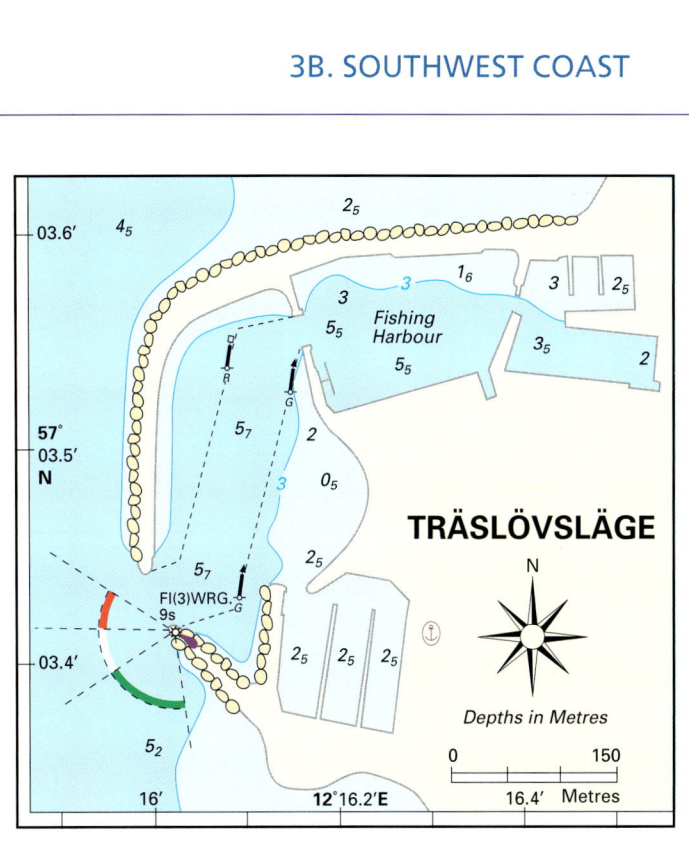

Varberg

57°06′·47N 12°13′·9E South outer breakwater head
Charts Swedish 924
Communications
Yacht club ☎ +46 34 08 49 80
 getteron@telia.com
 gasthamn@varberg.se

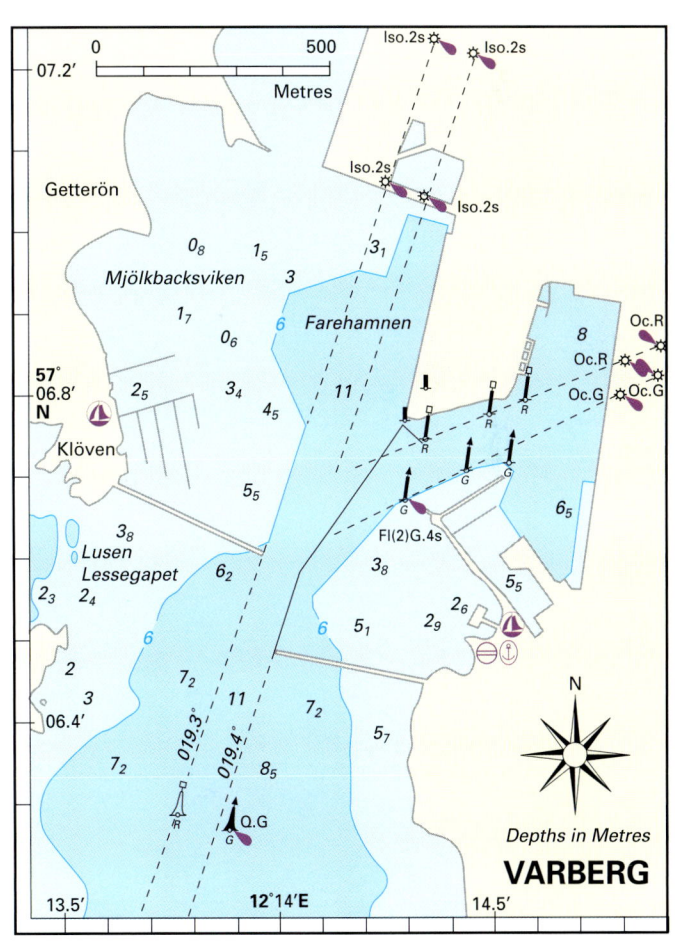

This historic town and spa built in the 17th century and dominated by a mediaeval fortress, is worth a visit, it is charming and has a wide selection of shops plus a vibrant café life. It is one of the most important harbours in Sweden for the export of timber. There is a ferry connection to Grenå in Denmark. On entering, a marina lies to port on Getterön. This has little connection to the town so yachts wanting to visit Varberg town should go to the inner harbour on the starboard side (57°06′·7N,

THE BALTIC SEA AND APPROACHES 149

WEST COAST OF SWEDEN

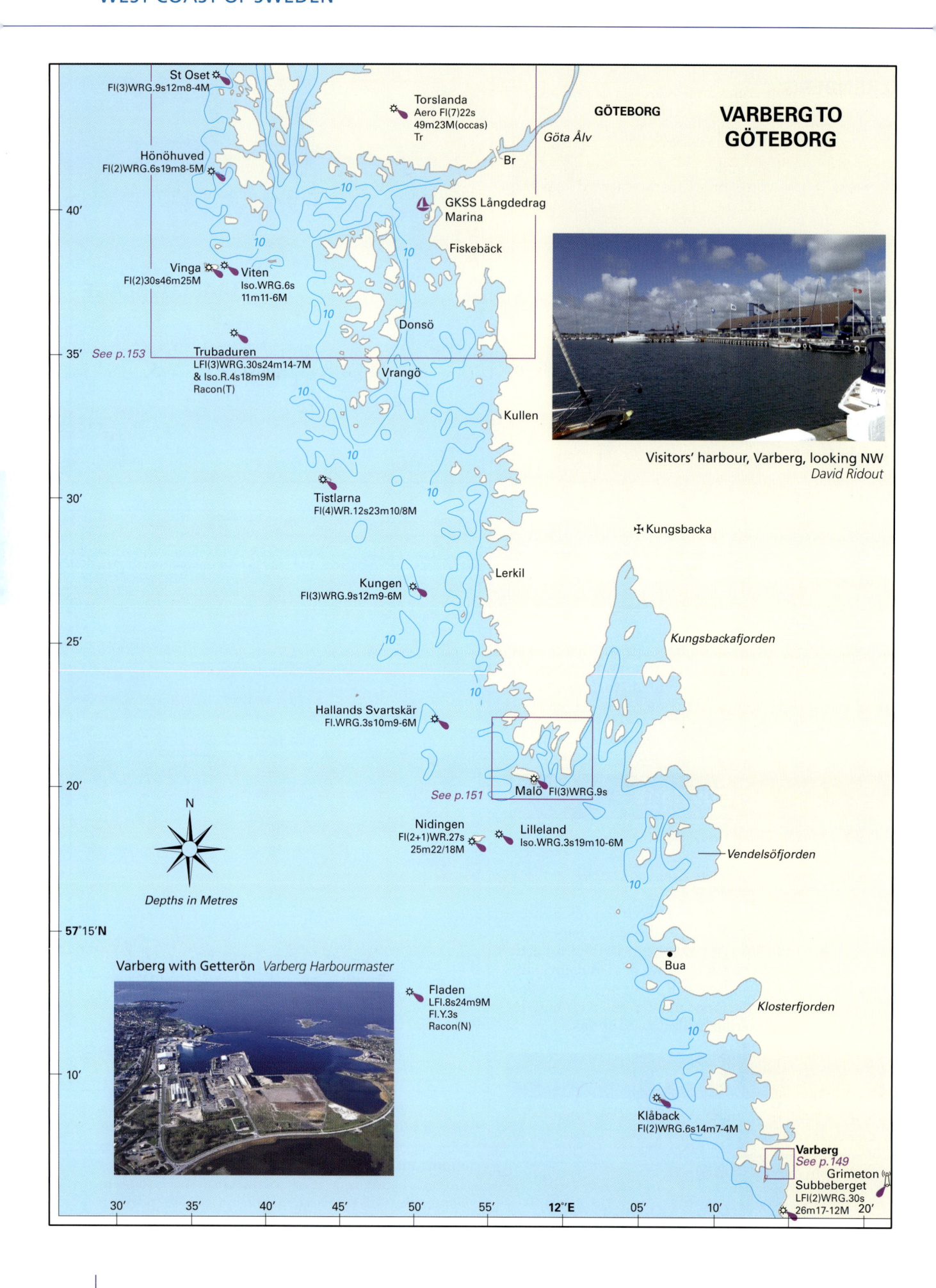

VARBERG TO GÖTEBORG

GÖTEBORG
Göta Älv

St Oset
Fl(3)WRG.9s12m8-4M

Torslanda
Aero Fl(7)22s
49m23M(occas)
Tr

Hönöhuved
Fl(2)WRG.6s19m8-5M

Br

GKSS Långdedrag Marina

Fiskebäck

40'

Vinga
Fl(2)30s46m25M

Viten
Iso.WRG.6s
11m11-6M

Donsö

35' *See p.153*

Trubaduren
LFl(3)WRG.30s24m14-7M
& Iso.R.4s18m9M
Racon(T)

Vrangö

Kullen

Visitors' harbour, Varberg, looking NW
David Ridout

30'

Tistlarna
Fl(4)WR.12s23m10/8M

⊕ Kungsbacka

Lerkil

Kungen
Fl(3)WRG.9s12m9-6M

25'

Kungsbackafjorden

Hallands Svartskär
Fl.WRG.3s10m9-6M

20'

N

See p.151
Malö Fl(3)WRG.9s

Nidingen
Fl(2+1)WR.27s
25m22/18M

Lilleland
Iso.WRG.3s19m10-6M

Vendelsöfjorden

Depths in Metres

57°15'N

Bua

Klosterfjorden

Varberg with Getterön *Varberg Harbourmaster*

Fladen
LFl.8s24m9M
Fl.Y.3s
Racon(N)

10'

Klåback
Fl(2)WRG.6s14m7-4M

Varberg
See p.149

Grimeton
Subbeberget
LFl(2)WRG.30s
26m17-12M

30'   35'   40'   45'   50'   55'   **12°E**   05'   10'   20'

150   THE BALTIC SEA AND APPROACHES

3B. SOUTHWEST COAST

12°14'·54E - mole head behind which is the visitors' harbour). Most berthing here is alongside. Varberg is arguably the best half way house between the Sound and Göteborg. It is also a good landfall when crossing the Kattegat from the Limfjord (distance approximately 60 miles). In clear weather, the fortress is visible 15 miles from seaward and the Grimeton aero light tower can be seen from over 20 miles away.

3. Varberg to Göteborg (Långedrag)

Distance 40 miles

North of Varberg the character of the scenery begins to change and the first of many natural harbours is to be found. The channel proceeds northwards on a well-marked passage south of Malö and inside (east of) the lights at Lilleland (57°18'·37N 11°56'·62E), Hallands Svartskär (57°22'·42N 11°51'·35E) and Kungen (57°26'·93N 11°49'·88E). Abeam Tistlarna (57°30'·56N 11°43'·57E – position of the Lighthouse on Tistlarna), the *skärgård* is entered with protection from the west and in another 12 miles the main channel into the port of Göteborg is reached.

Malö anchorages

Chart Swedish 925

For the north bound traveller, the bays just north of Malö will be the first experience of the scenery which will prevail in various forms thereafter. There are two possible anchorages. Skallahamn gives shelter in moderate depths apart from the risk of swell in strong south westerly winds. To the west of Skallahamn snug anchorage is to be found between Hästholmen and Mönster. However, in these places, as generally on this coast, the quality of the holding ground cannot be relied upon.

Donsö Island looking south. Guest berths to starboard on entering *John Sadd*

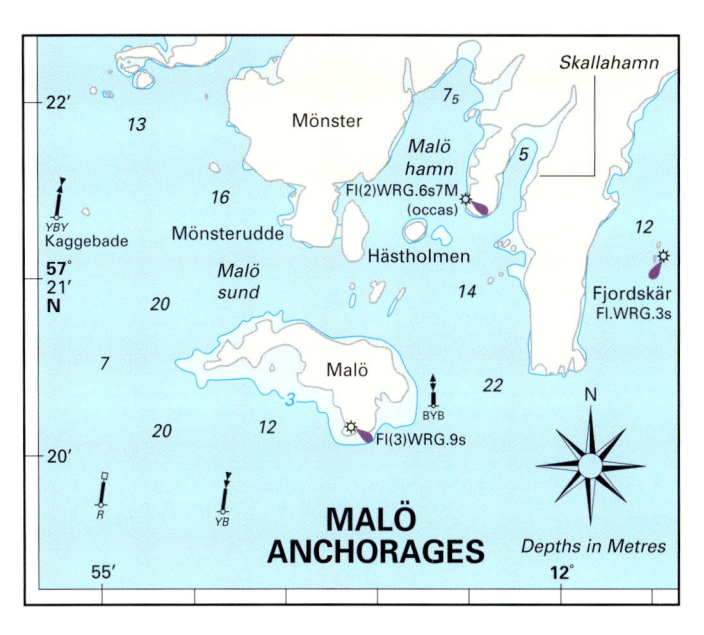

Donsö

57°36'N 11°47.5'E

An attractive island with guest harbour which is a convenient stop with all facilities together with a café and shops. There is a fast ferry to Saltholmen on the mainland from where there is an easy tram ride to Gothenburg City Centre.

Lerkil

57°27'·32N 11°54'·81E Outer mole head
Charts Swedish 925
Communications
Harbourmaster ☎ +46 30 02 79 39
info@lerkil.net

The last harbour before the shelter of the *skärgård*, Lerkil is a sizeable yacht harbour which gives good shelter, although the entrance may be difficult in strong north westerly winds. The harbour has recently been improved, and all the usual marina facilities are available.

THE BALTIC SEA AND APPROACHES

WEST COAST OF SWEDEN

Göteborg (Gothenburg)

57°41′N 11°50′E

Distances
Arkosund 210M (390km) by inland waterway, Stockholm 350M (650km) by road, Copenhagen 130M

Charts and guides
Swedish 92, 93, 931, 9313, 9312
Båtsportkort series: Västkusten (S)

Lights
Trubaduren 57°35′·7N 11°38′E LFl(3)WRG.30s24m14–7M
005·5°-W-131·6°-R-163·5°-G-214·4°-W-237·2°-R-247·5°-G-005·5° Racon Helipad
Iso.R.18m9M 064°-vis-131° Black tower, orange top, on grey base 25m
Buskärs Knöte 57°38′·3N 11°41′·1E Fl(3)WRG.9s12m7–4M
012·6°-W-029·5°-R-088°-(partially obscd 065°-080°)-G-182°-W-190·5°-R-212°-G-234·4°-W-239·1°-R-270·5°-G-012·6° Racon Orange tower 12m Floodlit
Vasskärsgrund 57°39′·2N 11°43′·4E
VQ(8).WR.8s11m13–10M Racon Red tower, white top, red roof on grey plinth 12m
Gäveskär 57°39′·7N 11°46′·1E QR.10m4M White tower 10m Floodlit but obscured
No. 29 Channel Marker 57°40′·7N 11°48′·9E Fl(2)G.6s

Communications
Göteborg Port Control ☏ +46 313 68 75 15,
VHF Ch 16; 12(24 hours)
www.portgot.se
VTS Göteborg ☏ +46 771 63 06 60,
VHF Ch 16, 13, (24 hours)
Marieholmsbron and Göta Älvbron bridges
VHF Ch 09 (24 hours)
Lilla Bommen Marina
Harbourmaster ☏ +46 31 15 40 05
info@goteborgsgasthamn.se
GKSS Långedrag Marina
☏ +46 703 39 93 98
hamnvakten@gkss.se
www.gkss.se

Red channel marker to Göteborg
C. Lassen

Among the islands of the *skärgård* are many harbours, both natural and artificial, particularly in the vicinity of Vrangö, Donsö, Styrsö and Brannö. It was in the roadstead north of these islands that a Royal Navy fleet, commanded by Admiral Sir James Saumarez in HMS *Victory*, was stationed for several years after 1808, guarding the British Baltic convoy system. The enterprising yachtsman can spend a leisurely time exploring the various nooks and crannies of the archipelago but, owing to the vicinity of Göteborg, the guest harbours are apt to be very busy. Apart from Vrangö, the islands mentioned above are within the commuter belt of Göteborg and frequent ferry traffic can create a disturbing wash.

General

Göteborg is the second largest city in Sweden, and is a working port with a wide and busy river. The city is friendly and vibrant with much to offer both culturally and recreationally. Much of it is very attractive, with many fine buildings, canals and tree-lined avenues in the downtown area, good shops, and many excellent restaurants.

Overlooking the central (Lilla Bommen) marina is the impressive opera house and, a few hundred metres downriver, the aquarium and Göteborg Maritime Centre, whose moored museum ships are

Approach to Lilla Bommen *M. Lewin-Harris*

THE BALTIC SEA AND APPROACHES

APPROACHES TO GÖTEBORG

claimed to form the largest floating maritime museum in the world. The Natural History Museum is situated at Slottsskogen, and further out (about 25 minutes by tram from the city centre) are the Liseberg Amusement Park with its huge funfair and the nearby Universeum, an environmental museum.

Visitors generally use either Lilla Bommen Hamnen, referred to above, or the Royal Göteborg Yacht Club (Göteborgs Kungliga Segel Sällskap or GKSS) Långedrag marina some 5M further downstream on the southern shore.

The Port of Göteborg maintains an interesting website at www.portgot.se.

Approach and entrance

From the sea the main approach channel from the southwest, leaving the Trubaduren tower to port, is wide, well buoyed and, where necessary, dredged. The main hazard for yachts is likely to be large commercial traffic. Other channels (all shown clearly on BA 858) lead in from northwest, west and south. All these channels converge south of the prominent Knippelholmen tower to continue up the Älvsborgsfjorden into the city centre. The Älvsborgsbron road bridge (clearance 45m), which lies some 2·5M east of the towers, is conspicuous from well out to sea. Sailing is forbidden east of the bridge, though motor-sailing is permitted, and all moored ships must be given at least 25m clearance.

The Lilla Bommen marina lies on the starboard hand about 250m short of a tall (19·5m) bridge, the entrance conveniently marked by a most distinctive red and white building (*see photo*). The square-rigged sailing ship *Viking* lies close by. It is now an hotel and restaurant.

THE BALTIC SEA AND APPROACHES

WEST COAST OF SWEDEN

If arriving from the canal system inland via the Göta Älv, the conurbation starts several miles upstream. Notice of imminent arrival is heralded by a rail bridge (swing bridge), the Marieholmsbron (clearance 5·9m). Opening times are displayed on a LED board. A bare 1·3M further downstream is the massive Göta Älvbron (centre span 19·5m, side span 18·5m) which opens on request when called on VHF Ch 09, or may respond to a sound signal. The Lilla Bommen marina lies on the port hand some 250m beyond the Göta Älvbron.

Anchorage

It is not possible to anchor in downtown Göteborg – the river is too busy and crowded. However there are numerous small islands in the western approaches to the city where anchoring would be perfectly feasible.

Berthing

Lilla Bommen

☏ +46 31 15 40 05, info@goteborgsgasthamn.se

Primarily a visitors marina with around 100 guest berths in depths of 2·5–3·5m, and is very popular due to its convenient location in the centre of the city. Enter with caution as passenger boats and small ferries berth on the east side of the basin and depart at speed. Movements are particularly intense in the morning between 0900 and 0930 and in the early evening. The marina basin should be exited slowly and carefully for the same reason. There are a few berths alongside but most are bows to pontoons with stern lines. It is also possible to moor alongside the quay just outside the marina, but there is constant wash from river traffic. Secure in any free berth on arrival and visit the marina office at the southeast corner, where the staff speak some English (open 0800–2200). Berthing fee – upper band.

GKSS Långedrag Marina

☏ +46 703 39 93 98, VHF Ch 68, www.gkss.se, hamnvakten@gkss.se

Situated several miles southwest of the city, beside the GKSS clubhouse and close to several other, larger, private yacht harbours. Its peaceful surroundings are connected to the city by a 40 minute tram ride – interesting in itself. There are 550 permanent berths, at least 100 of which are reserved for visitors. Berthing is between posts. There are areas in the approach with no more than 1·3m at chart datum, but the marina itself has 3–4m throughout. Any berth with a green sign may be used by a visitor – secure as appropriate and contact the harbour office. Berthing fee – middle band.

Formalities

Göteborg is in a *skyddsområde* (defence area), and yachts may occasionally be boarded as they approach from seaward. However on the whole Swedish customs and immigration authorities seem largely unconcerned about the movements of foreign yachts, particularly if EU registered. However if

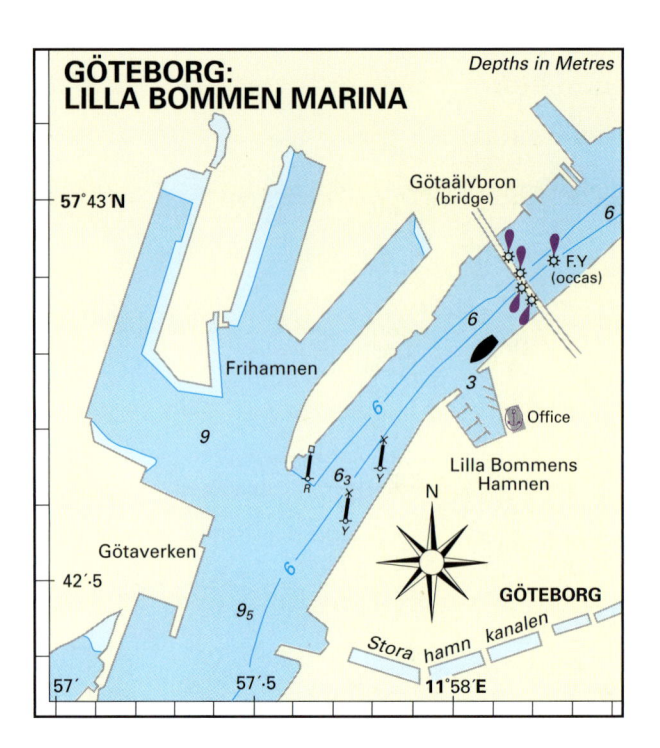

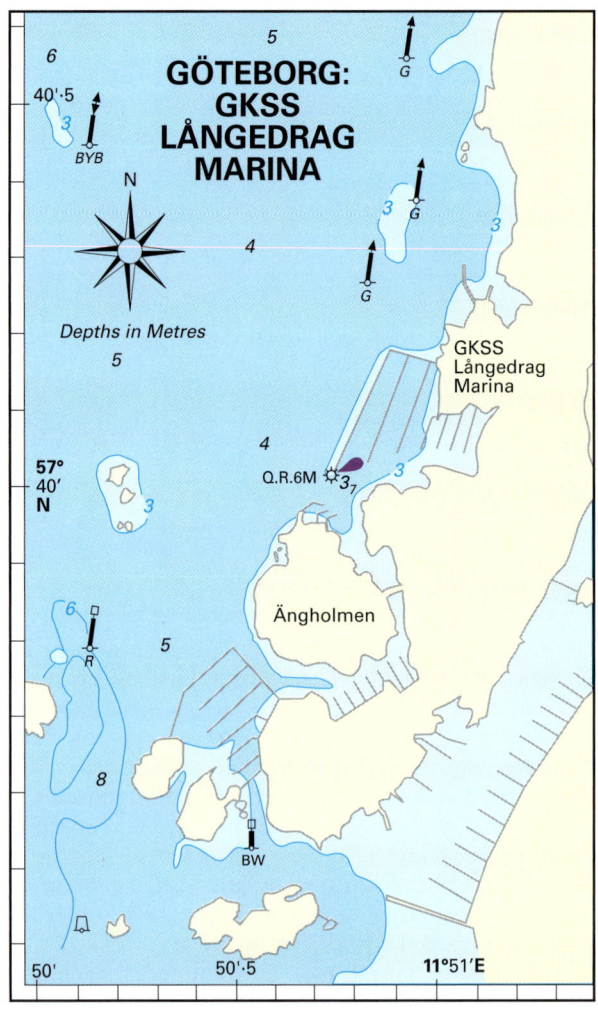

GÖTEBORG

Göteborg. The view from the office tower beside Lilla Bommen, clockwise from *The Viking* are the ferry berths and the guest harbour with the Opera House behind *E. Redfern*

arriving from outside the country the formalities should certainly be observed – enquire at the marina offices for the relevant telephone numbers.

Services for yachts
The Lilla Bommen marina complex offers the usual showers, toilets and launderette, plus cafés, small shops and a chandlery in the office building. There is water and electricity to all berths. The GKSS Långedrag marina has water and electricity to all berths, with laundry facilities at the GKSS clubhouse and a small shop close by. A weather forecast is updated daily. The yacht club is friendly, with a pleasant clubhouse and several good restaurants nearby.

Ask at Lilla Bommen marina office for the nearest available outlets of diesel, petrol and bottled gas. The nearest diesel pump to the GKSS Långedrag marina is at Wahlborgs Marine (open 0900–1800 weekdays, 1000–1500 weekends), on the south side of Saltholmen island. Bottled gas is available at the GKSS Långedrag marina, and both have facilities for emptying holding tanks.

There is a boatyard with travel-lift and engineers at the GKSS Långedrag marina. For electronic or radio repairs at either marina ☏ +46 31 69 51 00 or 90 96 00, and for sail repairs ☏ +46 31 29 00 21 or 29 11 52. There is a small onsite chandlery at Lilla Bommen marina, also at Wahlborgs Marine and both the Hinsholmskilen and Fiskebäck marinas. Charts, sailing directions and books are available from Nautic AB, Klangsfärgsgatan 16, 42652 Västra Frölunda, ☏ +46 31 10 08 85 and from most bookshops in the city.

General facilities
From Lilla Bommen marina an elevated walkway leads to the Nordstan shopping mall with banks, supermarkets, delicatessen, bookshops, Systembolaget etc, with the city's train and bus terminals a short distance beyond. Cafés and restaurants abound, many with views out over the river. The Cityakuten hospital ☏ +46 31 10 10 10, is about 1km distant.

If moored at the GKSS Långedrag marina and intent on major shopping, ride two stops on the tram to the Konsum supermarket (open 0900–2200), with a bank with cash machine located about 400m beyond.

Communications and travel
There are public telephones at both marinas and post offices in the city, though none very close to Lilla Bommen marina. WiFi is available but there is a charge.

The proximity of Lilla Bommen marina to the city's bus and train stations makes it particularly convenient for crew arrival or departure. The Långedrag marina is served by trams, which run to the city centre (about 40 minutes). In addition, taxis or car hire are easily arranged. Göteborg's Landvetter Airport is some 25km east of the city, while the City Airport is about 20km to the north, both with good bus connections. Passenger ferries from Denmark and Germany visit the port regularly.

The Göta Kanal – Göta Alv, Trollhätte and Göta Kanals see page 167.

3. SWEDEN

THE BALTIC SEA AND APPROACHES

WEST COAST OF SWEDEN

THE BOHUSLÄN COAST
Göteborg to Norway

RCCPF
Norway
Judy Lomax
(Imray)

NORWAY

SWEDEN

Halden
Kjerkøy
Trestenene
Fl(2)WRG.10s7-4M
59°N
Tisler
Nord-Hällsö
Q.WRG.10-5M
See plan p.165
Klövningarna
Iso.WRG.4s11-7M
Strömstad
Koster
Tjärnö
Ursholmen
LFl(2)WRG.15s10M
Rasso
Ramskär
Fl(3)WRG.9s8M

Otterö

Väderobod
LFl.8s6M
See plan p.165
Hamburgsund

See plan p.162
Sotekanalen
See plan p.160
Smögen
Uddevalla
Hällö
Fl.12s10M
Vänersborg
Lysekil
Trollhätten
Henän
Kungsviken
Vindön
Hättan
Fl(2)WRG.6s8M
Gullholmen
Ellös
Orust
Trollhätte
Kanal

**3d. Göta Älv,
Trollhätte Kanal
& Göta Kanal**
p.167

Måseskär
Fl(3)WRG.30s16M
Tjörn

Lake Vänern

58°N
Hakefjord
Marstrand
Hätteberget
Fl(2)WRG.12s21-16M
See plan p.158
Göta Älv
Kungälv

Stora Pölsan
LFl.WRG.8s8M
Nordre Älv
See p.153
Skagen West
Fl(3)WR.10s14-11M
Stora Oset
Fl(3)WRG.9s8M
Källö Knippla
See plan p.158
Göta Älv
Skagen
Fl.4s20M
Kattegat
Hönöhuved
Fl(2)WRG.6s8-5M
GÖTEBORG
(Lilla Bommen)
Viten
Iso.WRG.6s11-6M
11°E
12°E

156   THE BALTIC SEA AND APPROACHES

3c. The Bohuslän coast – Northwest coast

Göteborg to the Norwegian border

Charts Swedish 93 for general planning

This 80 mile stretch of coast between Göteborg and the Norwegian border, known as the Bohuslän, is a highly attractive and interesting cruising ground. It is deservedly popular, especially for Norwegians sailing south or east from their bases in Oslofjorden or on the southeast coast. Although the Skagerrak can be very rough in strong southwesterly weather, virtually the whole distance can be sailed inside the relative shelter of the *skärgård*. In lighter weather winds can be fickle and a number of places are too narrow to sail.

It was originally settled by hunters and communication between settlements was by sea. Until the middle of the 17th century, it was part of Norway and this is reflected in place names and the local dialect. In time fishing became an important industry and fishing villages were settled up and down the coast. Fishing still has a significant role but many of the houses in picturesque places have become holiday homes. Religion has played an important part in local life, and was strongly influenced by the early 19th-century Calvinist clergyman Henric Schartau (who believed that closed curtains were a sign of sin within, with the result that many houses are still curtain free) and there are many beautiful and striking churches dating from the early 1800s to the early 20th century.

There are useful landfalls for those approaching from the North Sea across the Skagerrak. The coastline of pink Nordic granite is rather reminiscent of the Åland Islands, albeit a little higher, with the smattering of houses in the south slowly giving way to trees as one approaches Norway.

A typical bows-to *skärgård* mooring *J. Backus*

Coast and harbours

The main towns, apart from Göteborg (population 550,000), are Uddevalla (population 32,000), Lysekil (population 8,000) and Strömstad (population 7,000). There are many sizeable villages or small towns of which the most notable is Marstrand, a well-known centre for sailing.

There are some 65 *gästhamns* listed in the *Gästhamns Guiden* and innumerable anchorages in the many fjords and sounds. To do justice to these would require a book on its own, so this one is confined to a few suggested places to allow a leisurely transit of the coast. It must be emphasised that the use of the largest available scale of chart is advisable for anything other than a purely offshore passage. Minimal tidal differences make for easy bows-to mooring or anchoring.

In season supplies and services are plentiful but before June and after the middle of August a little more planning is required as many of the smaller harbours may then close their facilities, particularly restaurants and fuel points.

During the season, and particularly at weekends, the coast (including the islands) is likely to be very crowded. This is a route south for Norwegians and Göteborg's maritime playground with thousands of holiday or weekend cottages all of which seem to have their own mooring or ready access to small marinas.

Routes north

To go north from Göteborg (see plan on page 153) there is a choice of routes, all clearly marked on both UKHO chart 858 and the Båtsportkort B. For the most direct and shortest route, leave the main ships' channel out of Göteborg after Red Channel Buoy No. 20 and head on a NW course leaving Skaddan to starboard with Måvholmnsskaren to port. Then pass south of Stora Porsholmen and between Stora Varholmen and Lilla Varholmen. This brings one to the Öckerö archipelago, and, if taking the passage on between Kalven and Grötö, beware of unmarked outlying rocks, some awash, particularly on the south side. The Kalvesund channel leading north-northwest is narrow, but clearly marked. This group of 10 notable islands and numerous islets is less than half an hour by car from the centre of Göteborg and readily accessible by all kinds of boats and ferry, so it is not surprising that in places there is no space for any more houses or boats. There are ten *gästhamns* many of which will still give you a feel for this wild and magnificent Bohus countryside.

WEST COAST OF SWEDEN

Källö-Knippla harbour *David Ridout*

Källö-Knippla harbour looking south-southeast
M. Lewin-Harris

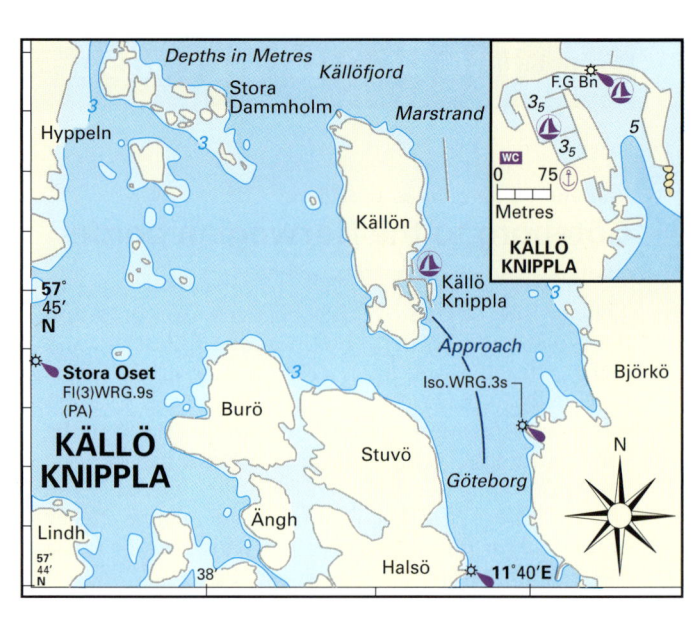

Källö-Knippla

57°44'·9N 11°39'·3E SE outer harbour limit
Charts Swedish 931 NW

Typical *gästhamn* in Ökeröarna.

Just 14M from the Lilla Bommen marina or 9M from the GKSS. Easily entered on a leading line from the south and just off the main route from Göteborg to Marstrand. Bows-to mooring from buoys and ample facilities for an overnight stop amid attractive, traditional Bohus houses.

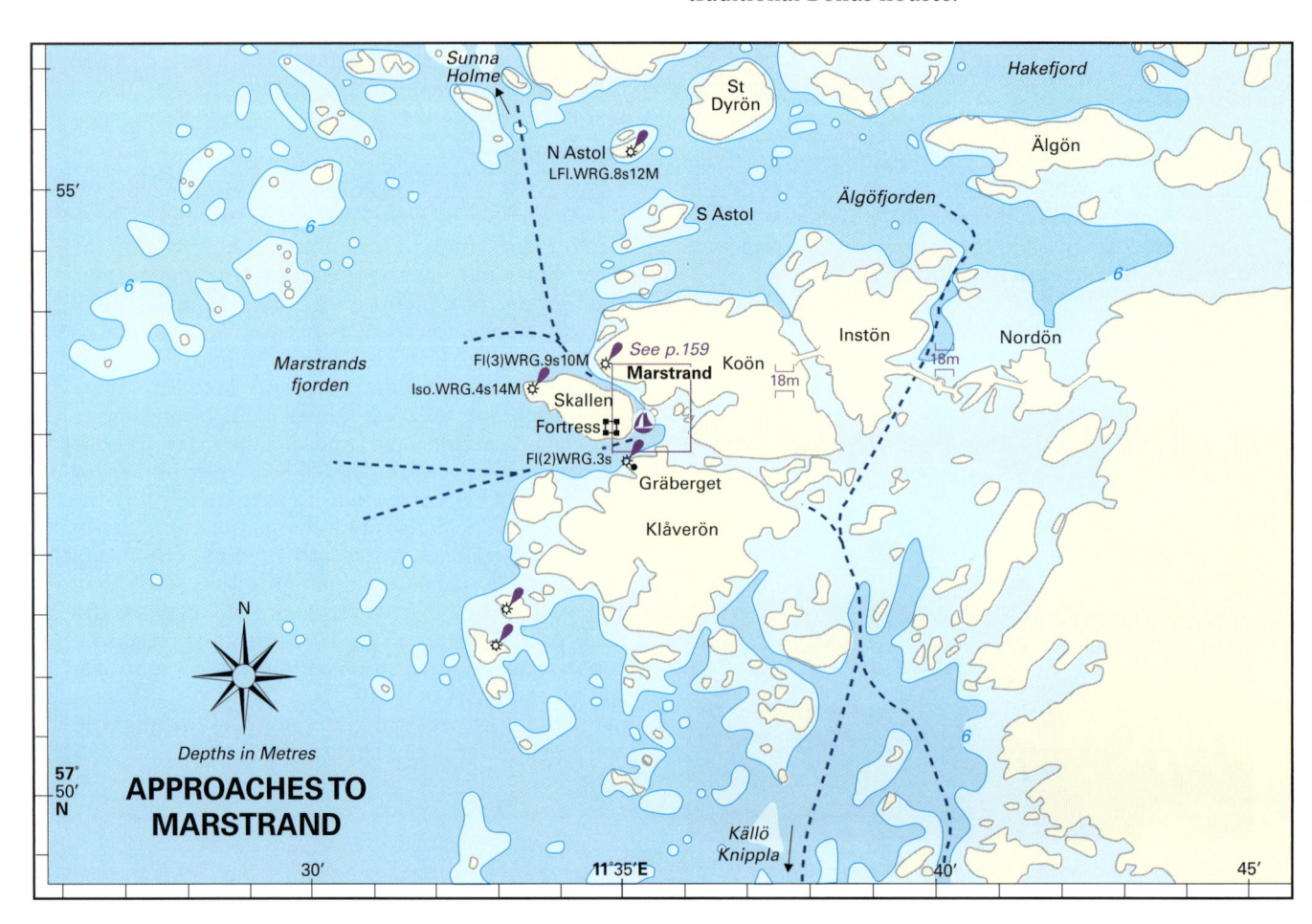

158 THE BALTIC SEA AND APPROACHES

3C. THE BOHUSLÄN COAST

Marstrand

57°53'N 11°35'·2E Off southern mole head
Charts Swedish 931 NW
Communications
Harbour office ☏ +46 30 36 10 53
   hamnkontoret@kungalv.se
   www.marstrandsgasthamn.se

This is a Mecca of west coast Swedish yachting, situated only 12M north of Källö-Knippla. The most attractive route is from the southeast through the narrow Albrektssunds kanal. Also there are well-buoyed entries from the open sea on the west and northwest. Mooring is bows-to with lazy lines. As most visitors will want to call here it is very crowded even during the week. Good services, restaurants and supplies with a small Watski chandlery and cash machine a short ferry ride away. Fuel is available from a self service pontoon by the fishing harbour. The harbour is dominated by the conspicuous Carlsten Fortress which is well worth a visit.

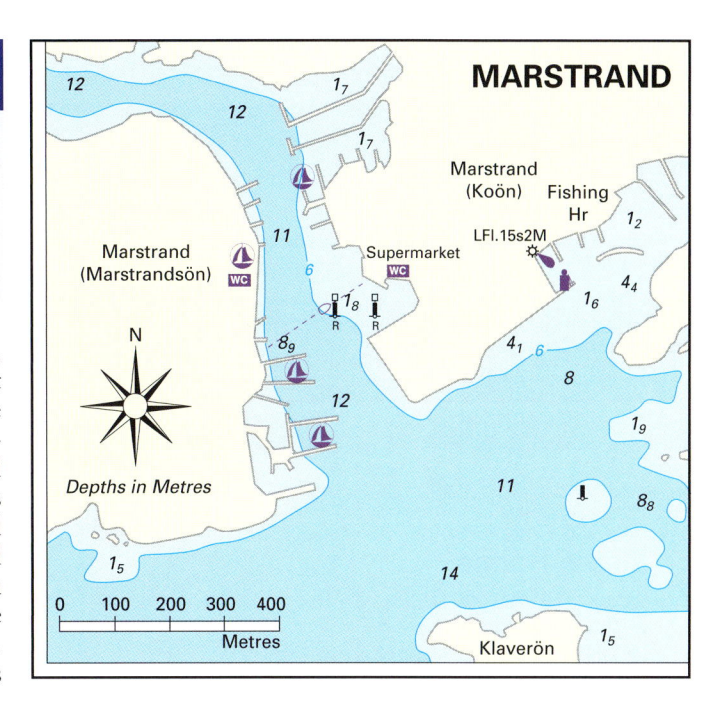

Looking NW with the Carlsten fortress in background *David Ridout*

View of Marstrand from fortress looking SE *David Ridout*

Marstrand new fuel dock *David Ridout*

THE BALTIC SEA AND APPROACHES 159

WEST COAST OF SWEDEN

Sunna Holme anchorage *John Sadd*

Sunna Holme

58°00'·3N 11°31'·3E Middle of entrance between two small headlands

Charts Swedish 9321 NW, UKHO 870, 873

A natural anchorage in beautiful surroundings, it lies 9M north of Marstrand in a lovely rock pool, typical of others along this coast. Shallow entrance from the south but with 6m inside and good holding. Anchor on either side as the centre is a little exposed to the south otherwise there are some rings for mooring bows to the rocks with a stern anchor. At busy times this is the more acceptable way to allow for extra boats.

Tjörn and Orust

Charts Swedish 932 SW, SE and NE, 933 SE and SW

From Marstrand you really have four choices:

1. Head NE (leaving Koön to starboard and Tjörn and Orust to port);
2. Work your way up the mainly protected leads on the west of the latter two islands;
3. Go out to sea, clear of all hazards;
4. Leave Marstrand by the east-southeast channel and take the route east of Koön and Inston which joins up with Hakefjord. Note there is a bridge with 18m clearance on this route. Then head up Hakefjord under either bridge (min 26m), past the island of Källön, to the Askeröfjorden where the twisting route round the top of Tjörn joins. Then north through Halsefjorden and the narrow 11M Svanesund to the top of Orust. Here in the Havstensfjord the important town of Uddevalla is found 4·5M to the northeast. If you turn to port just 3M to the west there are very capable yards at the Vindö bridge. There is excellent shopping at Henän only 5M further south. The route then heads southwest and through some narrow passages, passed Ellös to Gullholmen to the west or turn north 6M to the major tourist destination but useful town of Lysekil. Along this diversion of approximately 45M there are over 15 *gästhamns* and innumerable anchorages to explore for as long as time permits.

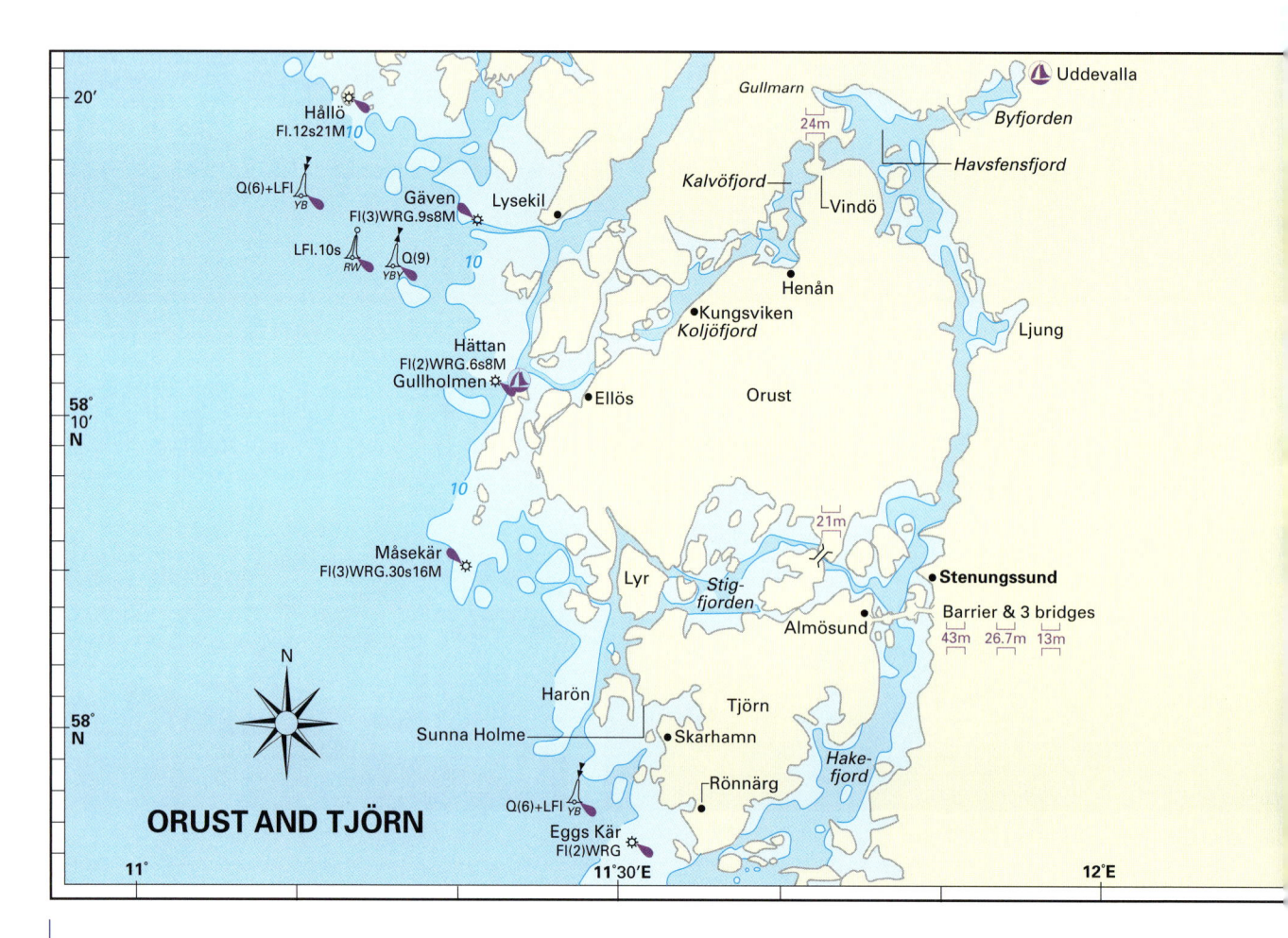

ORUST AND TJÖRN

160 THE BALTIC SEA AND APPROACHES

3C. THE BOHUSLÄN COAST

The boatyard and bridge at Vindo E. Redfern

Mollösund
58°04'·3N 11°28'·2E off fuelling pontoon

Delightful small village with harbour and has easy fuelling access.

Gullholmen

58°10'·57N 11°24'·25E Southern entrance
58°10'·69N 11°24'·34E Northern approx. mid entrance
Charts Swedish 932 NW   UKHO, 853, 869, 870

Island *gästhamn* and holiday village.

On the north of Härmanö and 3M west of Ellös on Orust. Well buoyed approaches from both north and south. The harbour lies between two islands and is completely sheltered. There are two entrances to guest harbour areas, the southern one (**58°10'·57N 11°24'·25E**) has the *gästhamn* sign by it (anchor). The northern entrance is at (**58°10'·69N 11°24'·34E** approx. mid entrance). Note: if approaching from the north, the first inlet you see between Gullholmen and Härmanö is not for visitors.

Moor alongside or bows-to with lazy lines. Good facilities including an ICA mini-market. Bracing walks to the top are rewarded with spectacular views. The permanent population mushrooms from 140 to about 4,000 in season when the harbour is also extremely crowded.

Gullholmen, looking into the northern harbour David Ridout

Southern guest harbour, looking NW David Ridout

3. SWEDEN

THE BALTIC SEA AND APPROACHES **161**

WEST COAST OF SWEDEN

Lysekil

58°16'·06N 11°26'·29E by port hand buoy

Chart Swedish chart 933

This is an old established resort town and as you approach it, the skyline is dominated by the church with a tall spire. It has a large marina with 4 entrances, all facilities including fuel. The harbour office is in the SW corner of the marina.

Lysekil, looking NNW David Ridout

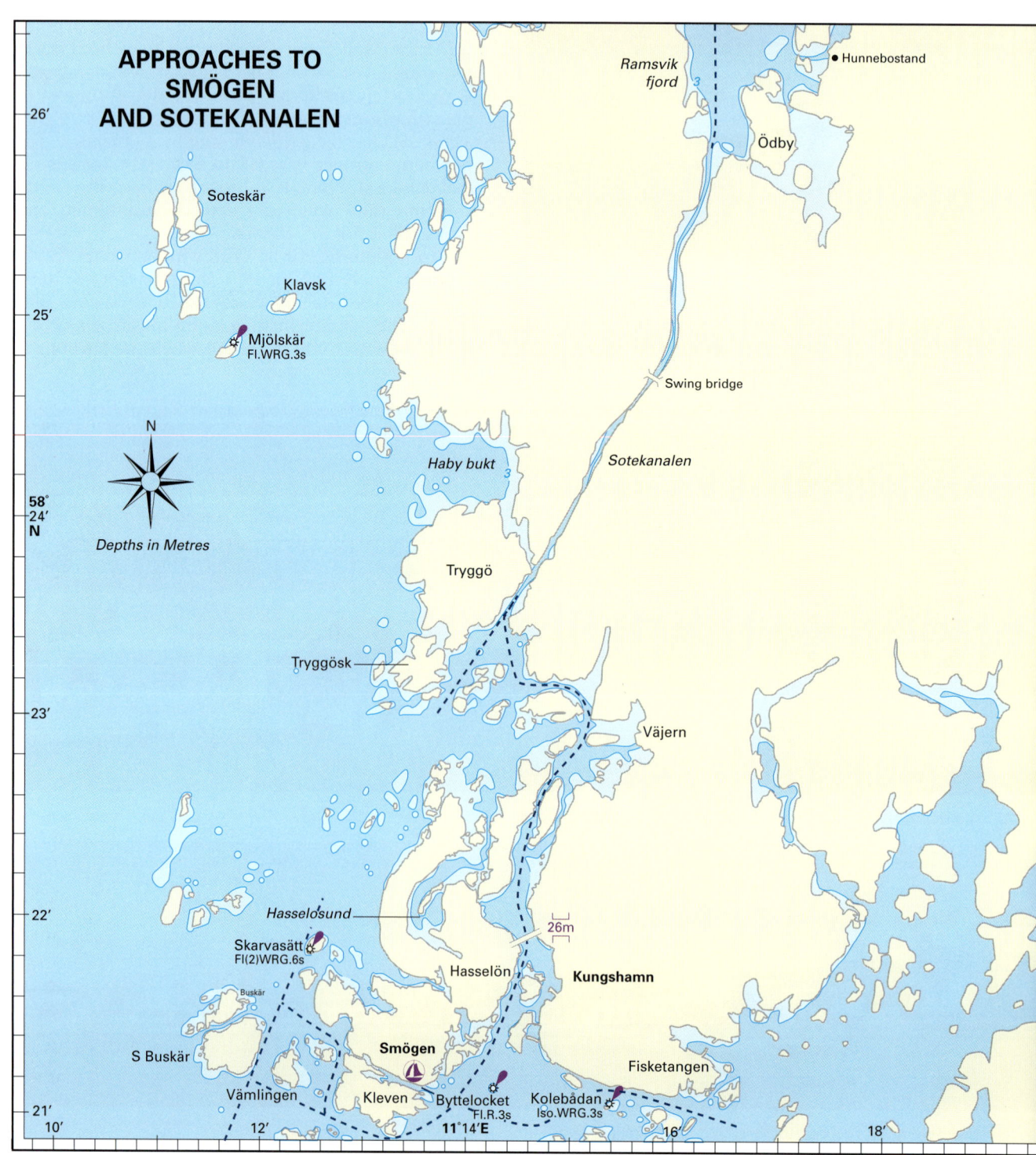

162   THE BALTIC SEA AND APPROACHES

3C. THE BOHUSLÄN COAST

The summer town of Smögen *David Ridout*

Smögen harbour *David Ridout*

Smögen

58°21'·16N 11°113'·79E Green buoy by entrance
Charts Swedish 933 NW

Lively tourist town and fishing port.

Much prettier than Kungshamn half a mile to its east, Smögen lies some 15m northwest of Orust and close to the open sea but exposed only to the east. There is a very long wooden quay against which you moor or raft alongside. Less crowded is a new marina to port but it is a long walk round to the town. However, in the high season a small ferry runs every 15 minutes from Smögen to the marina and to Kungshamn in an endless loop.

This is a picturesque and popular 'summer town' with many tourist shops in the wooden houses overlooking the quay. Good facilities but fuel only available at nearby Kungshamn, an important fishing harbour with fish market and large processing factories. Considerable modern development on its north side.

If time is short, it is only a day's sail of about 40M outside all the off lying islands and skerries to Strömstad, however that would be to miss much of the variety of this coast.

There are 16 *gästhamns* and countless anchorages between Smögen and Strömstad and various routes which may be taken, depending on your vessel's draught and air draught (mast height). These are clearly marked on the *Båtsportkort*.

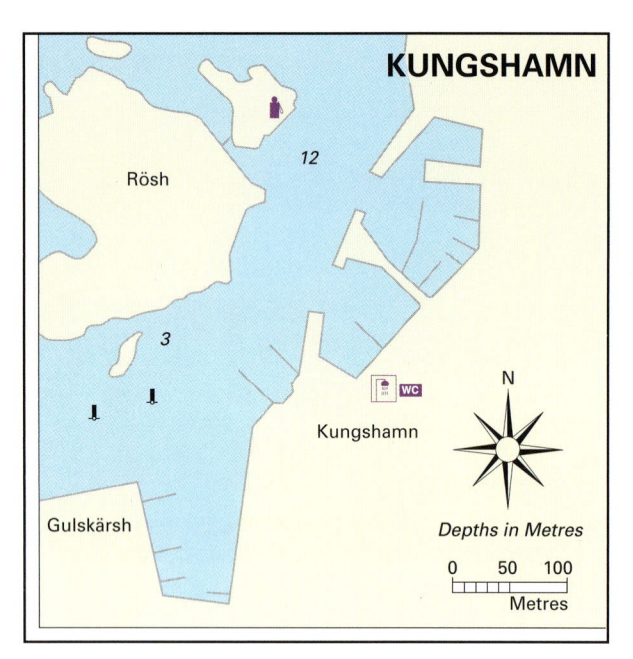

WEST COAST OF SWEDEN

Northern harbour, Hunnebostrand, looking SW David Ridout

Hunnebostrand, two harbours looking SW David Ridout

Kungshamn

58°21'66N 11°14'80E (middle of central quay)

A useful alternative to Smögen, especially if the latter is full. Berth in the old fishing harbour, part of which has been allocated for yachts.

Sotekanalen

58°23'·5N 11°14'·33E southern entrance
Chart Swedish 933 NW
http://kanaler.arnholm.nu/sotens

This partly artificial canal was opened in 1935 with the object of allowing local craft to avoid the exposed coast of the Sote peninsula which could be dangerous to small vessels in stormy southwest weather. Its length is just under three miles and passes through, typically, more gentle Bohus countryside with a few houses and farms. Today it makes a convenient shortcut to the 200 berth *gästhamn* of Hunnebostrand and is used by some 50,000 vessels of all sizes each year, the limitation being a beam of 15m and draught of 4·5m. It has one opening bridge, which usually opens as you approach between 0600 and 2200 local time. There is no charge for transit, nor are there any suitable stopping places. Sailing is forbidden.

Hunnebostrand

58°26'·52N 11°17'·58E north of starboard pier into the visitors' harbour
Chart Swedish 933NW

Hunnebostrand is divided into three harbours, the northern one being for visitors but the southern one has several shipyards and repair facilities. Granite was exported from here and there is a stone mason museum in the small town. It was one of the original fishing settlements on this coast. While still a centre of lobster fishing it is now a fairly genteel tourist and retirement town. It is the home of the Swedish Lobster Academy.

Hamburgsund

58°33'N 11°16'·2E South mole head
Chart Swedish 934 SE

The sound is a natural waterway which, because of its totally sheltered position has been a centre of commerce and shipping for over 200 years. Sailing is forbidden and today its use is almost entirely leisure with some fishing activity which has attracted many holiday homes and boats. Despite this it is attractive, and there is much history to be found in the area by those so inclined. There is a well set up *gästhamn* in

Sotekanalen bridge opening M. Lewin-Harris

164 THE BALTIC SEA AND APPROACHES

3C. THE BOHUSLÄN COAST

Hamburgsund marina *M. Lewin-Harris*

the centre which is popular in the season, and there is good basic shopping, including a supermarket.

There is a cable-operated vehicle ferry close to the marina which crosses at frequent intervals particularly at peak times and this needs care to pass safely. There are instructions on both approaches.

Resö

58°48'N 11°09'·7E

Chart Swedish 934 SE

A small, active fishing harbour, approximately 15 miles N of Hamburgsund, which makes its limited free spaces available to yachtsmen and is worth having a look at if time allows.

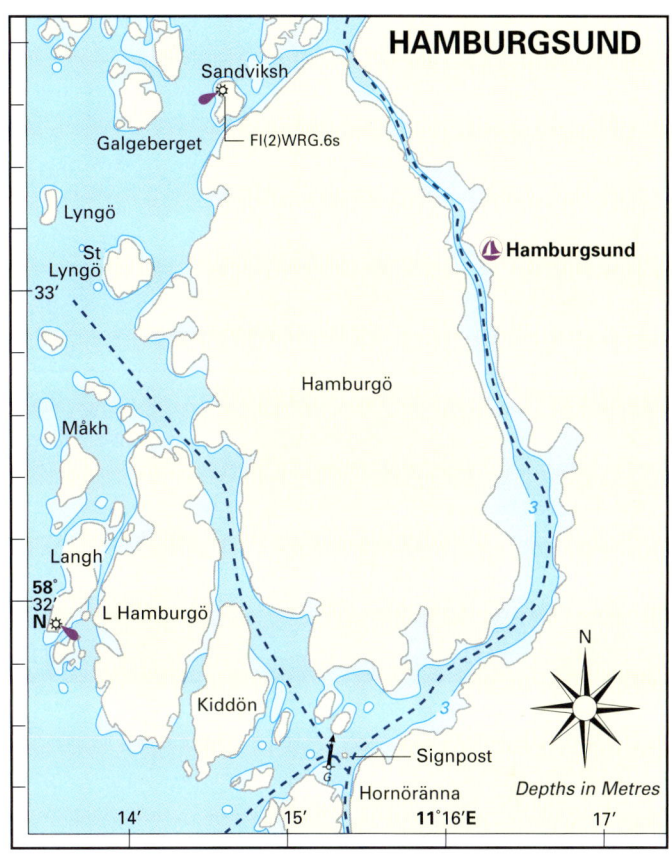

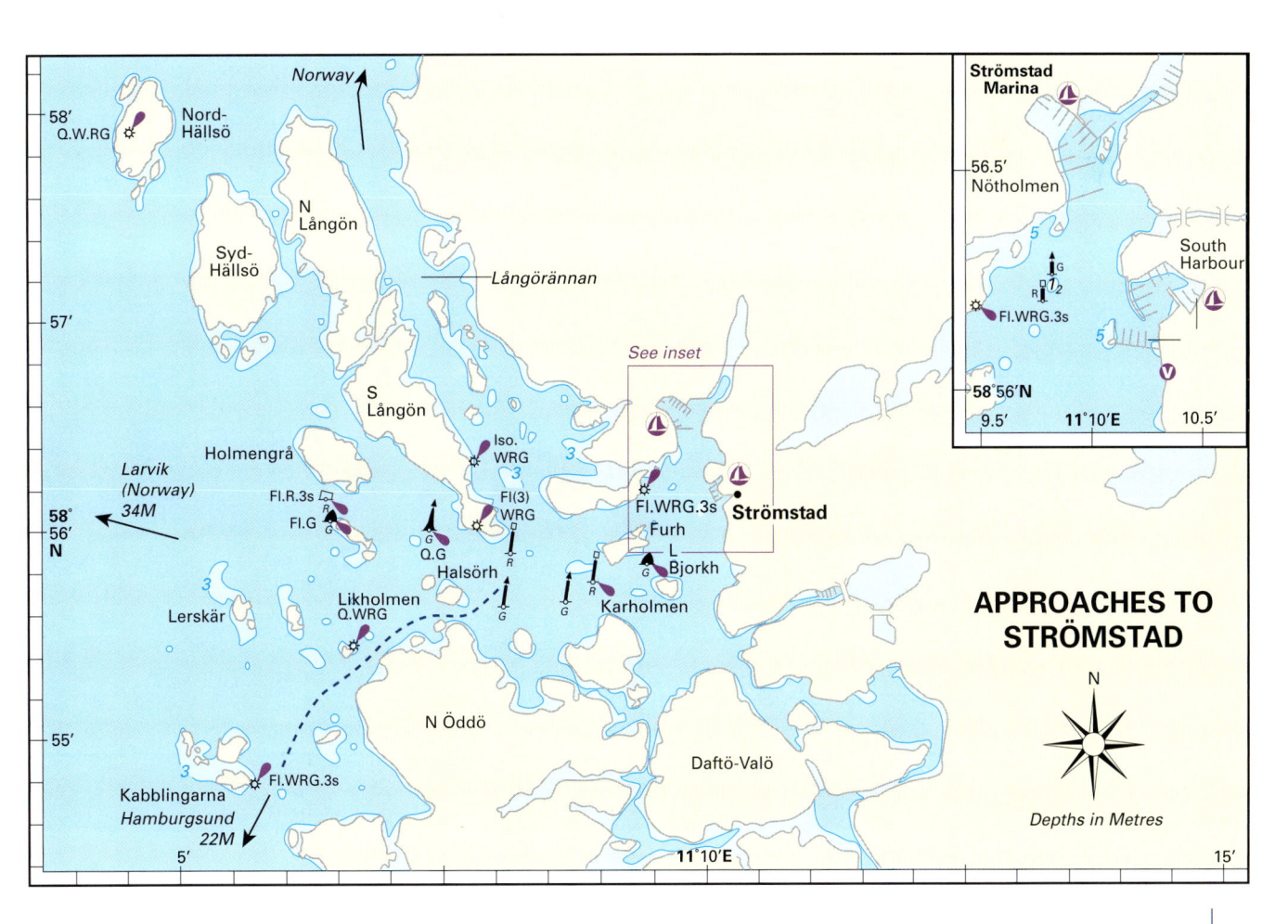

HAMBURGSUND

APPROACHES TO STRÖMSTAD

THE BALTIC SEA AND APPROACHES   165

WEST COAST OF SWEDEN

Southern harbour, Strömstad, looking NW *Janny Bernays*

Strömstad

58°56'·14 N 11°09'·96E North of the islet of Skurve
Chart Swedish 935 E
Communications
Stromstad Marina ☎ +46 526 13920
 Stromstadmarina.se
Southern Harbour ☎ +46 526 19050
 gasthamn@stromstad.se

Barely 5M from the border with Norway, this is the northernmost town on the Swedish west coast and is a popular yachting centre.

It has very well buoyed approaches from the north and west for the regular ferry to Larvik. There are also approaches from the south but these have restrictions on headroom and draught which are only clear on the detailed Swedish charts. The visitors' moorings are in the south harbour which is approached by leaving the islet of Skurve, which is now connected to the shore by marina berthing pontoons, to starboard. Berth on these or continue into the inner harbour which is more convenient to the shore facilities if space is available there. Otherwise use any vacant 'box' with a green label. The full facilities and services include an excellent Watski chandlery nearby. The community of 11,500 justify a first-class shopping centre and two large supermarkets plus Systembolaget which does a brisk trade with the many visiting Norwegians. This is a 10 min walk north of the marina.

Mooring fees can be paid at the chandlery on the southern edge of the harbour or at the harbourmaster's office on the northern edge of the harbour. Just beyond the harbourmaster's office there is an excellent tourist information office. Here one can obtain a ticket to operate the self-controlled cable ferry across to the marina lying to the NW of the main town.

This marina, Marieholm Strömstad Marina, has a large chandlery and haul out facility up to 50 tonnes and is a popular place for people leaving their boat. It is necessary to ring the marina and book a place. There is the ferry connection referred to above and a free bus to town, but the Strömstad Southern Harbour is more convenient for a short visit and shopping.

Strömstad to the Norwegian border

The route north to the Norwegian border is straightforward by way of the Långörännan channel giving access either up Oslo Fjord or towards Halden or Fredrikstad.

Strömstad Marina looking NW *David Ridout*

3d. Göta Älv, Trollhätte Kanal and Göta Kanal

The Göta Kanal
'Sweden's Blue Ribbon'

Charts and guides
Swedish charts 13, 121, 135, 134, 133, 132, 131, 1352, 1353, 1331
Svensk Kusthandbok series: Vänern – Trollhätte Kanal
Båtsportkort series: Vänern (E)
Båtsportkort series: Göta kanal (Mem–Sjötorp)
The Göta Kanal, Mem–Sjötorp (in English), Sjöfartsverket 1993
German/Swedish NV Sportschiffahrtskarten Binnen - Gota Kanal Trollhatte kanal
Gota Kanal App

Communications
① +46 141 20 20 50, info@gotakanal.se
www.gotakanal.se

The term 'Göta Kanal' is often used to describe the entire 210M (390km) route between Göteborg on the west coast and Mem on the Baltic coast of Sweden, but this is not technically correct. The westernmost stretch is in fact a river, the Göta Älv, which is connected by the Trollhätte Kanal to Lake Vänern (the largest lake in Sweden and one of the largest lakes in Europe). Between Lake Vänern and the smaller lake Vättern runs the 35M (65km) western section of the Göta Kanal proper, which includes the canal's highest point at almost 92m (302ft) above sea level. The eastern section between Lake Vättern and the Baltic Sea is some 50M (93km) in length. Thus only about half of the 'Göta Kanal' is actually canalised, and a good part of that is not the Göta Kanal at all.

In spite of its numerous bridges most yachts are able to pass through the entire system with masts in place, the minimum clearance being 22m at

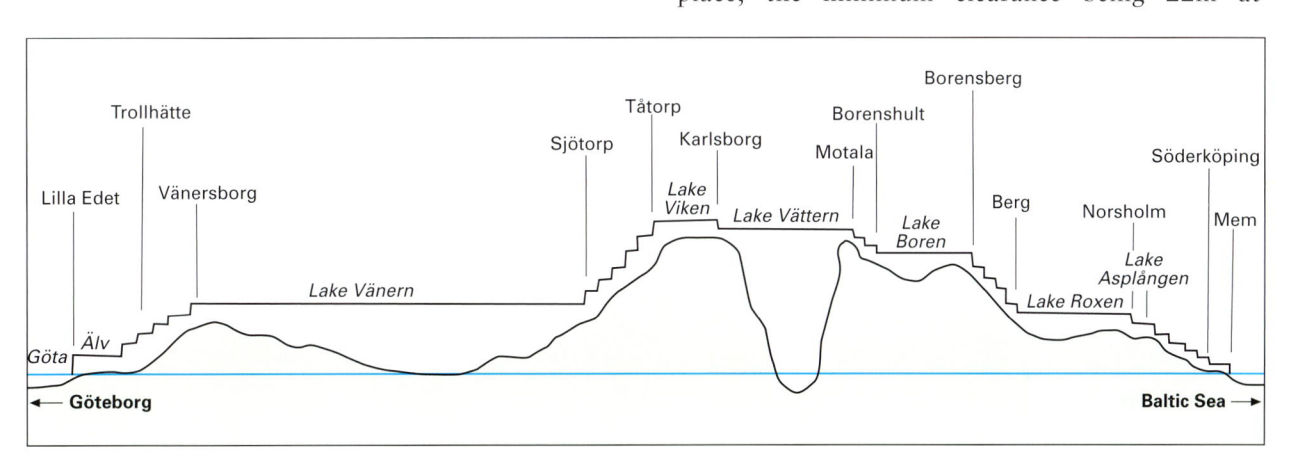

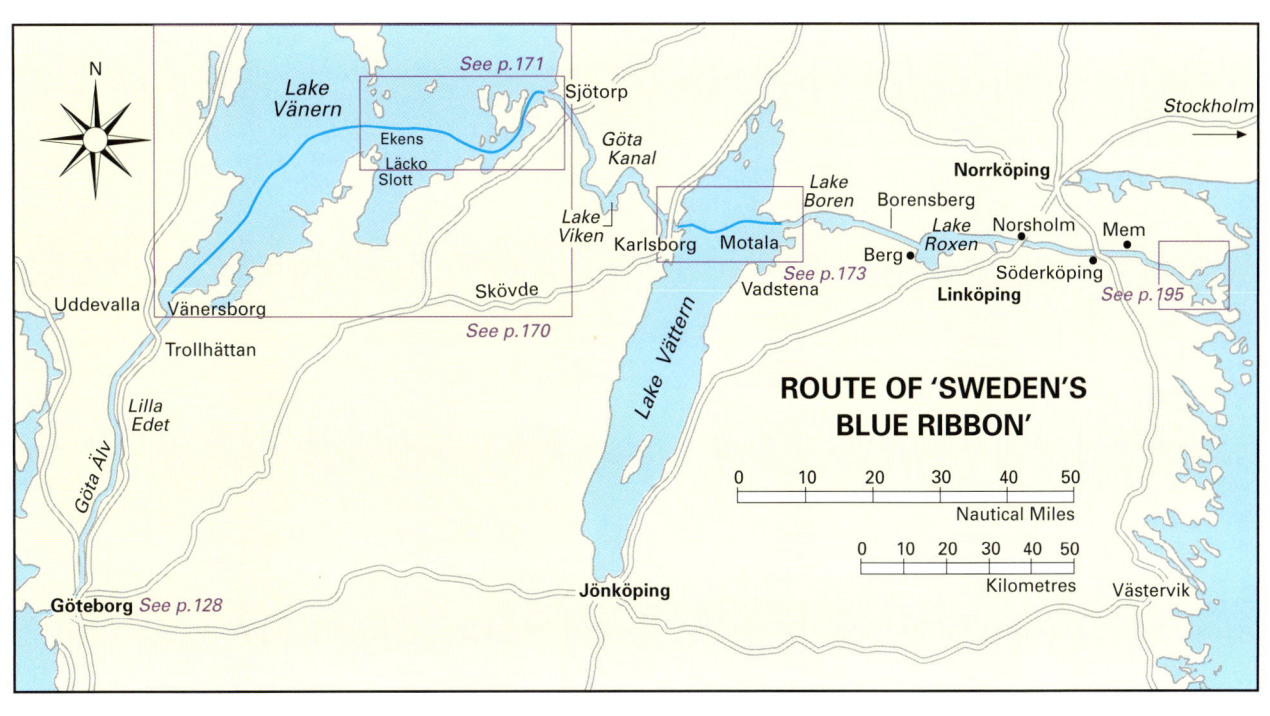

THE BALTIC SEA AND APPROACHES 167

WEST COAST OF SWEDEN

View from below Trollhättan Locks *E. Redfern*

Norsholm on the eastern stretch. The maximum allowable length is 32m and the controlling width is 7·2m. Depths are nominally no less than 2·5m.

If taken slowly the passage offers plenty of variety: peace and quiet, but also plenty of interesting little towns and historical buildings to visit, not to mention several museums featuring the canal's own history. Many of the small guest harbours are surrounded by fields and open countryside, and children almost invariably enjoy the passage.

History

The western part of the system was the first to be canalised, with the Trollhätte Kanal (bypassing the Trollhätte Falls) opening in 1800 to allow access for shipping to Lake Vänern. Work on the Göta Kanal section began in 1809, under the direction of Baron von Platen and the civil engineer Thomas Telford, and took 23 years to complete. It was finally opened in 1832. However, commercial traffic decreased markedly after the mainline railway link across Sweden was opened in 1862, but the potential for tourism was soon recognised, with several passenger steamers plying its length. Now, the waterway is a popular holiday destination, and home to three historic vessels of the Göta Canal Steamship Company in addition to many fleets of hire cruisers. Although originally in private hands, the entire complex now belongs to the Swedish Government.

Opening times

The Trollhätte Kanal is regularly used by seagoing commercial ships of up to 4000 tons and is open all year round except at times in the winter when lock maintenance is being carried out or the flow of the water is affected by ice.

The Göta Kanal and the Eastern section are generally open from May to September inclusive with small variations from year to year. Advance booking is required for May and Early June, and also from mid August to the end of September (check website for precise dates each year) but in the intervening high season the canal operates between 0900 and 1800 daily and booking is not required.

Practicalities

- Dues are payable in the upper lock of the Trollhätte Kanal. For the Göta Kanal they are paid at Sjötorp (if eastbound) or Mem (if westbound). It is worth booking your passage all the way through online as you receive a discount. You will be given a reference number which you present when entering the canal, and you will be issued with a package containing information and regulations. The dues may seem high, but they do include up to five nights berthing and services in each of the 21 guest harbours.

- Heads may not be used at any time unless a holding tank is installed. There are now pump-out stations at most of the guest harbours.

- Take careful note of the safety regulations, especially relating to sound signals. A horn should be sounded when approaching locks and bridges and at entrances to narrow sections.

- Locks can be crowded in season and constant vigilance is required. In general it is suggested that a minimum of three crew is desirable but for a vessel of moderate size two may suffice. Bear in mind that in the Göta Kanal a crew member has to lend a hand at each lock to handle lines.

- It is advisable to carry at least two lines of about 10m in length. Some of the older locks have uneven walls and an absolute minimum of four large fenders is recommended. A plank is also useful to hang outside the fenders.

- Delays can be expected at both locks and bridges, especially in season. The lifting road bridges at Töreboda, Karlsborg and Söderköping have fixed opening times, as do the railway bridges at Lyrestad, Töreboda, Motala and Norsholm, all listed in the information packs available on entering the system. Other bridges on the Göta Kanal are remotely controlled and will normally open within 10 minutes of a yacht appearing. The lock keepers and bridge masters do not monitor VHF.

- There is a five knot speed limit on both canals. With light traffic and an active crew it may be possible to complete the passage in five to seven days if in a hurry, but it is far more rewarding to allow more time. It can be very crowded during the Swedish holiday season which straddles the month of July and early August and there is much to be said for making the passage before or after that period. There is no obvious preferred direction of travel: the wind direction and strength can be significant when crossing the two lakes, and the current in the Göta Älv may be a factor after heavy rain.

3D. GÖTA ÄLV, TROLLHÄTTE KANAL AND GÖTA KANAL

The Göta Älv and Trollhätte Kanal

A sketch plan of this stretch is available from the Lille Bommen office.

The approach from the west is via the port of Göteborg, the first lock being encountered at Lilla Edet, 26M (49km) upstream. Below the first lock the stream in the Göta Älv can be strong, running at up to three knots in the Göta gorge 2M below the lock. The average over the whole distance decreases from around two knots in early summer to 1·5 knots until autumn.

On the Göta Älv and Trollhätte Canal the approach to bridges and locks is monitored by cameras, and they will normally be opened when a yacht approaches.

Between Göteborg and Trollhätte, there is limited opportunity for mooring. There is a small harbour north of the lock at Lilla Edet but for scenic beauty and natural surroundings, it is better to proceed to the small marina just after the Trollhätten staircase.

This stretch of the system carries large (90m LOA) freighters, and movement by small craft after dark or in poor visibility is firmly discouraged. All six of its locks have a rise of between 6 to 8m, in contrast to the locks of the Göta Kanal the majority of which are 2·5m. In busy periods they may be filled by yachts wall-to-wall. Both sides of these large locks are fitted with small, recessed bollards some 3–4m apart vertically, so that those alongside can move lines up or down as the water level changes. Even easier is to secure to one of the ladders, generally against the south or southeast wall (the smoother of the two). Despite their impressive size, the locks are gentle in operation due to an unusual system of filling (or emptying) the chambers through gratings in their floors, which produces little turbulence.

It takes around 45 minutes to pass through the four giant locks bypassing the Trollhättan falls – or more accurately the three locks, holding basin, and single upper lock – and if time permits it is well worth pausing in the guest harbour beside the upper lock to visit the Trollhätte Canal Museum (open 1100–1900 daily) and explore the two flights of disused locks – the original 1800 flight, and larger replacements opened in 1844. Those currently in use date back to 1916. The final lock is at Brinkebergskulle, just short of Vänersborg where the canal merges with Lake Vänern, some 44M (82km) from the open sea.

There are five official guest harbours between Göteborg and Lake Vänern:

Kungälv About 10 miles upstream from the centre on Göteborg below the ramparts of the fortress of Bohus where there are a few berths approached by a narrow and tortuous channel.

Lilla Edet

Åkerssjö Immediately above the Trollhättan locks, with 15 berths.

Spikön Between Trollhättan's two bridges, the first lifting and the second a bascule, and close to the centre of the town: 25 berths with water and electricity, laundry facilities, showers and restaurant.

Vänersborg An unassuming but pleasant town with a wide range of shops in the pedestrian precinct. The marina is beside the railway station and 10 to 15 minutes from the shops and a large supermarket. It has most facilities including fuel, toilets, laundry and a good chandlery.

Lake Vänern

Vänersborg – Sjötorp

From Vänersborg to the start of the Göta Kanal proper at Sjötorp, the course is initially in a north easterly direction for just over 30 miles when the island of Kallandsö is reached. Passing through the Ekens *skärgård*, yachts proceed in an easterly direction for about 20 miles until Mariestad is abeam thereafter turning northwards under the bridge (clearance 18m) connecting the mainland with Torsö. The land is generally low-lying, the principal landmark seen for many miles around being a table mountain, Kinnekulle (305m) (58°36'N 13°25'E) on the southeast shore. The lack of elevation means that care must be taken to sight the relevant buoys, specially the marks off the finger-like promontory of Hindens Rev and the marks at the approaches to the *skärgård*.

Between Vänersborg and Ekens *skärgård*, there are a number of inlets where shelter can be obtained. They include Sanneboviken (58°30'N 12°28'E), Dalbergsa (58°36'·4N 12°36'E), Jarlehusudden (58°37'N 13°1'E) and also in the bay to the east of Klitt island, a few miles north of Jarlehusudden. Within the *skärgård* itself there is a free choice of a number of anchorages in calm and beautiful surroundings.

The channel going from west to east divides in the middle of the passage through the *skärgård*, one branch heading north towards open water and the other proceeding between two lines of concrete blocks (once used for pulling through sailing vessels) in a south easterly direction. Both channels are very

Heading west with lock emptying. Note the smooth wall on the port side David Ridout

THE BALTIC SEA AND APPROACHES

WEST COAST OF SWEDEN

LAKE VÄNERN

0 — 15 Kilometres

Karlstad
Grums
Kristinehamn
Säffle
Arvika K
Amal
Tösse
Värmlandssjön
Gullspång
Dalbosjön
Pålgrunden LGl(2)WRG.12s Racon 13M
Lurön
Runnen Iso.WRG.4s8M
Sjötorp
Dalslands K
N Klasgrundet Fl(3)WR.10s7M
Lemongr Q.R
Torsö
Hjortgr Fl(2)WRG.6s7M Racon
L Milskär Fl.WRG.3s6M
Göta Kanal
Maken Q.WRG (occas)
Ekens Skägård
Hjortens udde Fl.5s13M
See p.172
Kållandsö
See p.171
Mariestad
Dalbergså
Jarlehusudden
Kinnekulle
Hindens rev
Klitt Kl
Läckö Slott
Sanneboviken Galleudde LFl(2)12s13M
Stefanskullen Iso.WRG.5s
Viken
Lidköping
Normansgr Fl.WRG.3s7M Racon
Vänersborg
Trollhätte K

170 THE BALTIC SEA AND APPROACHES

3D. GÖTA ÄLV, TROLLHÄTTE KANAL AND GÖTA KANAL

Above The rail and road bridges looking north from Vänersborg towards Lake Vänern *M. Lewin-Harris*

well marked. The southeast channel leads past the small marina of Spiken (58°41'·5N 13°12'E) to the imposing mediaeval castle and grounds of Läckö which is open to the public. There is a marina to the northwest of the castle and it is feasible to anchor in the bay to the east (see plan page 172).

The approach to Sjötorp passing Mariestad is by way of a winding buoyed channel which presents no difficulty provided a good lookout is maintained. The fine city of Mariestad has an early 17th-century cathedral said to be a copy of Stockholm Cathedral. Guest berths are to be found at the southwest wall of the harbour. Full facilities are available and there is a main line railway connection. Boats which cannot go under the bridge with 18m clearance can go between Brommö and Fågelö, then north east to find the way north of Sjötorps Svartskär before heading SE for Sjötorp

At Sjötorp there is a marina in the outer harbour which is often crowded and is exposed to strong winds from the west and north. To avoid discomfort in strong westerly winds shelter may be obtained in the lee of the promontory to the west of the canal entrance.

General information

Although the majority of yachts making their way across Sweden may be expected to take the direct route described above, Lake Vänern offers considerable scope for diversion. It is the largest expanse of fresh water in Sweden; from southwest to northeast is about 80 miles and from northwest to southeast is about 40 miles. The depths shown on the charts are subject to variation of up to one metre depending on the amount of melted snow and rain or the lack of either. There are wide stretches of open water where conditions can become very uncomfortable in bad weather but the shoreline is much indented and provides many places of shelter.

The lake is conveniently divided by two promontories into sections, namely, Dalbosjön to the southwest and Värmlandssjön to the northeast. The channel between these peninsulas is restricted by the Lurö *skärgård* but the passage is well marked.

Two canals are found in the western region of Dalsland:

Dalslands Kanal starts at Köpmannebro (58°46'N 12°31'E) and ascends by way of 31 locks and a series of lakes almost to the Norwegian frontier. Passage is restricted to vessels drawing not more than 1·8m, not more than 22m in length, and a masthead height of not more than 12m.

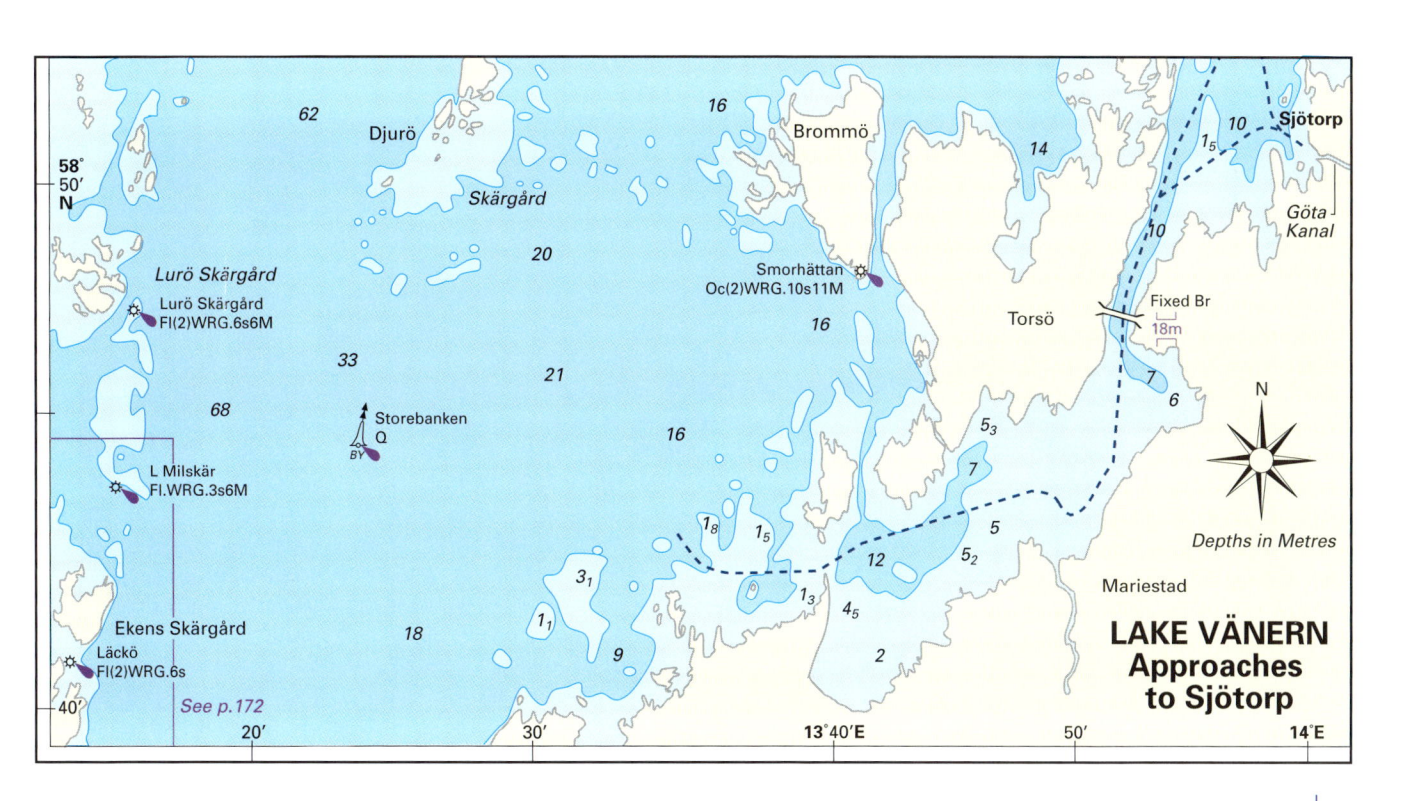

LAKE VÄNERN
Approaches to Sjötorp

THE BALTIC SEA AND APPROACHES

WEST COAST OF SWEDEN

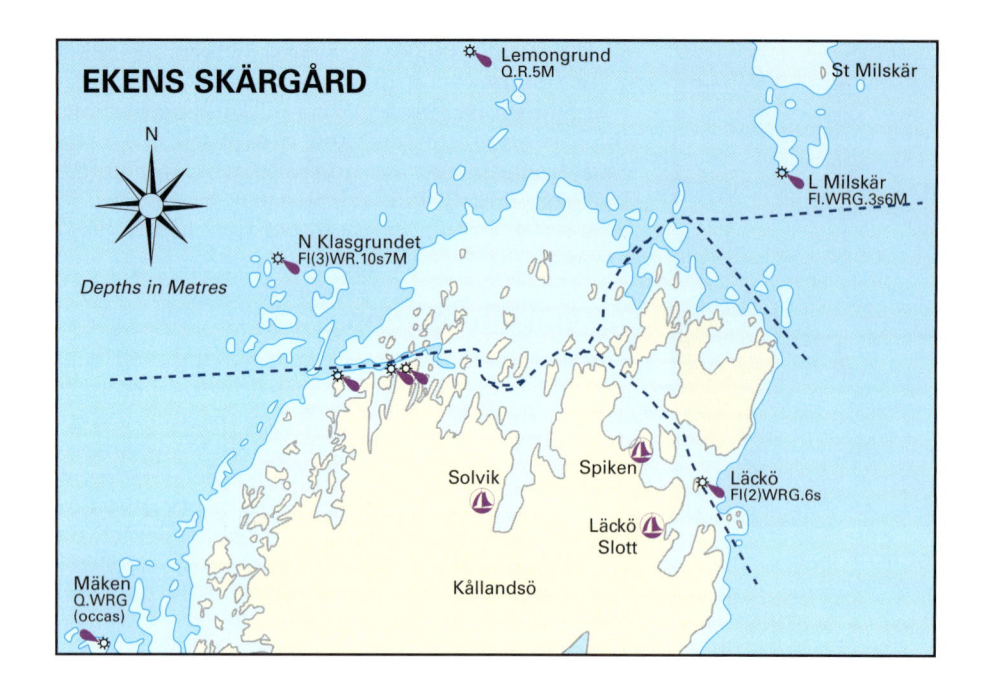

EKENS SKÄRGÅRD

Arvika Kanal, the longer of the two, leaves the lake just south of Säffle (59°08'N 12°55'E) and meanders north for about 40 miles through lakes and narrow channels. The maximum length, draught and masthead height are, respectively, 42m, 3m, and 16m. Maximum beam is 4·5m.

Both canals were formerly used for the transport of timber and other cargoes but this traffic has now ceased. They are used, when open in the summer, by pleasure craft and are of great scenic beauty.

The principal town in Dalsland is Åmål (population 12,800). This well laid out town, with a fine 17th-century church overlooking it, has a sheltered marina. A few miles to the south lies the Tösse *skärgård* with scenery resembling the islands of the Stockholm archipelago. The *skärgårds* of Djurö, Ekens and Brommö lying not far north of the direct route between Vanersborg and Sjötorp are also popular with those seeking natural surroundings, but during summer weekends and the holiday month of July, there is liable to be activity, sometimes noisy, and wash from fast power boats and the like.

At the north end of Värmlandssjon are two sizeable towns. The larger of these, Karlstad (population 80,000) is a commercial port and capital of the province of Värmland. There are all the facilities of a large town as well as a substantial guest harbour. In the northeast corner of the lake lies Kristinehamn where there is a small marina. Between the two towns and indeed along the entire north shore of Värmlandssjon the coast is much broken up and there are numerous sheltered anchorages.

Lake Viken, heading west *David Ridout*

172 THE BALTIC SEA AND APPROACHES

3D. GÖTA ÄLV, TROLLHÄTTE KANAL AND GÖTA KANAL

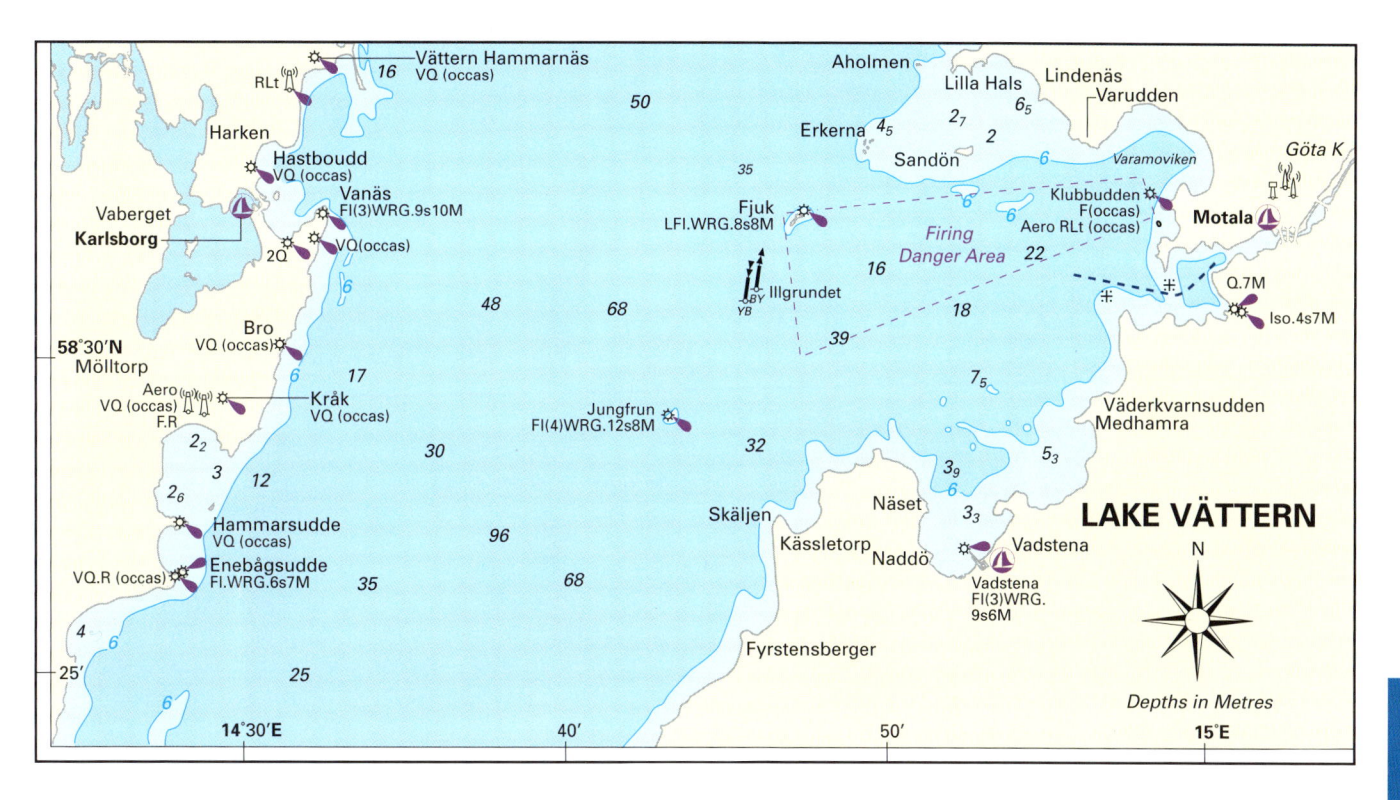

The Göta Kanal to Lake Vättern

This 35M section includes the route's highest point which is in the Berg Kanal. There is a small inlet with a pontoon for a few boats and an obelisk marks the point. This is a few miles before Tåtorp. The beautiful Lake Viken is almost 92m (302ft) above sea level. Eastbound vessels climb 20 locks in 9M to reach the angular lake, which accounts for some 11M of the section, then pass through their first descending lock just beyond its eastern exit. A further 15M through attractive agricultural countryside without locks takes vessels through to Lake Vättern. There are eight guest harbours on the stretch between the two lakes – Sjötorp, Lyrestad, Hajstorp, Töreboda, Vassbacken, Tåtorp, Forsvik and Karlsborg – all with water, toilets and showers, but most without fuel pumps. Of the guest harbours mentioned above, Töreboda and Karlsborg are recommended for their facilities. Töreboda has supermarkets, a bank and is convenient for a crew change, being on the main line from Stockholm to Göteborg. Karlsborg has a fuel station and it also boasts an enormous citadel built in the early 19th century. There are guest harbours both in the canal and at Stenbryggen just below the fortress. A good museum is situated within the fortress.

The stretch between Lakes Vänern and Vättern is the wildest and most remote part of the canal – a landscape of lakes and fir trees, very different from further east where the waterway runs through lush pastures and carefully cultivated farmland. Lake Viken is particularly beautiful, with an abundance of possible anchorages in small bays and between islands. The lock at the west end of the lake is manually operated. At its eastern end is Forsvik Sluss (lock), which is both the highest and the oldest lock on the canal, and boasts the oldest iron bridge in Sweden. The walls of this lock are uneven and vessels should beware of unexpected protrusions.

Lake Vättern

This lake is about 60 miles in length running approximately north to south. Vessels making the transit of the canal will normally proceed directly between Karlsborg and Motala. The 17 mile passage is straightforward and the islet of Fjuk (58°32'·3N 14°47'·5E) provides a landmark two thirds of the way across the lake. A good lookout should be kept in approaching Motala from the west for the marks at Kävernöns Bk showing the entrance to the channel.

An alternative landfall is Vadstena, about eight miles southwest of Motala. The 16th-century castle provides a conspicuous landmark. The guest

Moored at the visitors' berths just west of the bridge at Karlsborg E. Redfern

THE BALTIC SEA AND APPROACHES 173

WEST COAST OF SWEDEN

Lifting bridge opening automatically usually after short wait – yacht going west *David Ridout*

The Carl Johan flight of locks looking east *Kate Thornton*

harbour is in the castle moat and is approached by a narrow canal. It has 15 berths in depths of 1·5 and 2·5m with a range of facilities. The castle is impressive as is the peaceful old town with its 13th-century convent and 15th-century abbey.

In comparison with Lake Vänern, Lake Vättern provides less incentive to divert those proceeding through Sweden by the canal. The lake is long, deep and unindented for the most part and is noted for its sudden squalls. However, a group of islands at Djäknesundet, 10 miles north/northeast of Karlsborg (58°37'·5N 14°34'E) provides a number of attractive and sheltered anchorages. The archipelago and the channels at the north end of the lake consist of over 200 islands and for those with the time to spare is well worth a visit.

There are firing ranges on the lake and for information about firing times, ☏ +46 505 40460 or call VHF Ch 14.

Lake Vättern to the Baltic Sea

On the 50M stretch between Motala on the eastern shores of Lake Vättern and Mem, where yachts lock out into the Slätbaken, an inlet of the Baltic Sea, there are 37 locks, all 'downhill' if eastbound. The distance is served by six guest harbours – at Motala, Borensberg where the lock is manually operated, Berg, Norsholm, Söderköping and Mem itself – where, again, up to five free nights may be spent. The guest harbour beside the canal entrance at Motala has 65 berths and all facilities, including fuel pumps and a holding tank emptying station. The nearby canal museum includes a working model of a lock – much enjoyed by children of all ages.

3D. GÖTA ÄLV, TROLLHÄTTE KANAL AND GÖTA KANAL

Motala (charming motor museum just behind the quay) *Kate Thornton*

Less than three miles after leaving Motala, eastbound vessels reach a staircase of five locks at Borenshult. A wait of several hours may occur at this point. Lake Boren is six miles long and after Borensberg, a further 13 miles takes one through open agricultural country to Berg, where the canal descends four pairs of locks before reaching the small guest harbour, which has limited facilities but is handy for the small town's cafés and restaurants. Below the harbour basin is the spectacular Carl Johan flight – seven locks which lower the canal the 18·8m down to Lake Roxen. On summer days these locks are thronged with spectators who come to watch the yachts and river steamers pass up and down the flights. However waits can be long, and if one misses the 'traffic lights' it may be two hours or more before the direction of flow is reversed. Both Lake Boren and the 13·5M Lake Roxen are very pretty, and offer unhurried travellers the opportunity to anchor in unspoilt surroundings and off the beaten track.

Norsholm is at the east end of Lake Roxen. The busy main railway line from southern Sweden to Stockholm passes over the Canal at this point. At the lock beside the railway bridge, hanging warps are provided as the rise is only 0·9m. From Norsholm onwards a further 15M of canal (broken by the small and rocky Lake Asplången) and 15 locks connect to the Baltic Sea at Mem. East of Norsholm the canal is at its most rural, meandering along between cow pastures and past pretty cottages and gardens.

By Söderköping east-going yachts are almost at their journey's end, and many are tempted to stay for a day or two before heading out into the Baltic. The town is a favourite with the Swedes, and in July an almost Mediterranean atmosphere develops as people stroll in the sunshine. The canal is lined with tourist shops and restaurants (including a famous ice cream restaurant) many with live music, and some yachtsmen will find the 50 berth guest harbour, which lies along the canal just above the town's lock, both noisy and lacking in privacy. In compensation the town is most attractive with a fine 18th-century town hall and two mediaeval churches, both with beautiful interiors. Unlike Mem, Söderköping has many shops and is a good place for provisioning.

There are quays at Mem on both sides of the lock, with a 125m quay on the Slätbaken (Baltic) side where vessels entering the canal system wait to enter the lock and while dealing with paperwork. This berth can be uncomfortable in east or southeast winds. Inside the lock there is a second, longer quay with depths of 2·5–3m and space for about 20 visiting boats, with a further 10 bows-to berths on the (single) guest harbour pontoon (small). Showers and toilets, telephone, diesel pump and holding tank emptying station, café and restaurant are all to hand, but there is no town nearby. The warehouse just above the lock was the venue for the canal's official opening ceremony, carried out by King Karl XIV Johan in 1832. Today it houses a shop, café and youth hostel.

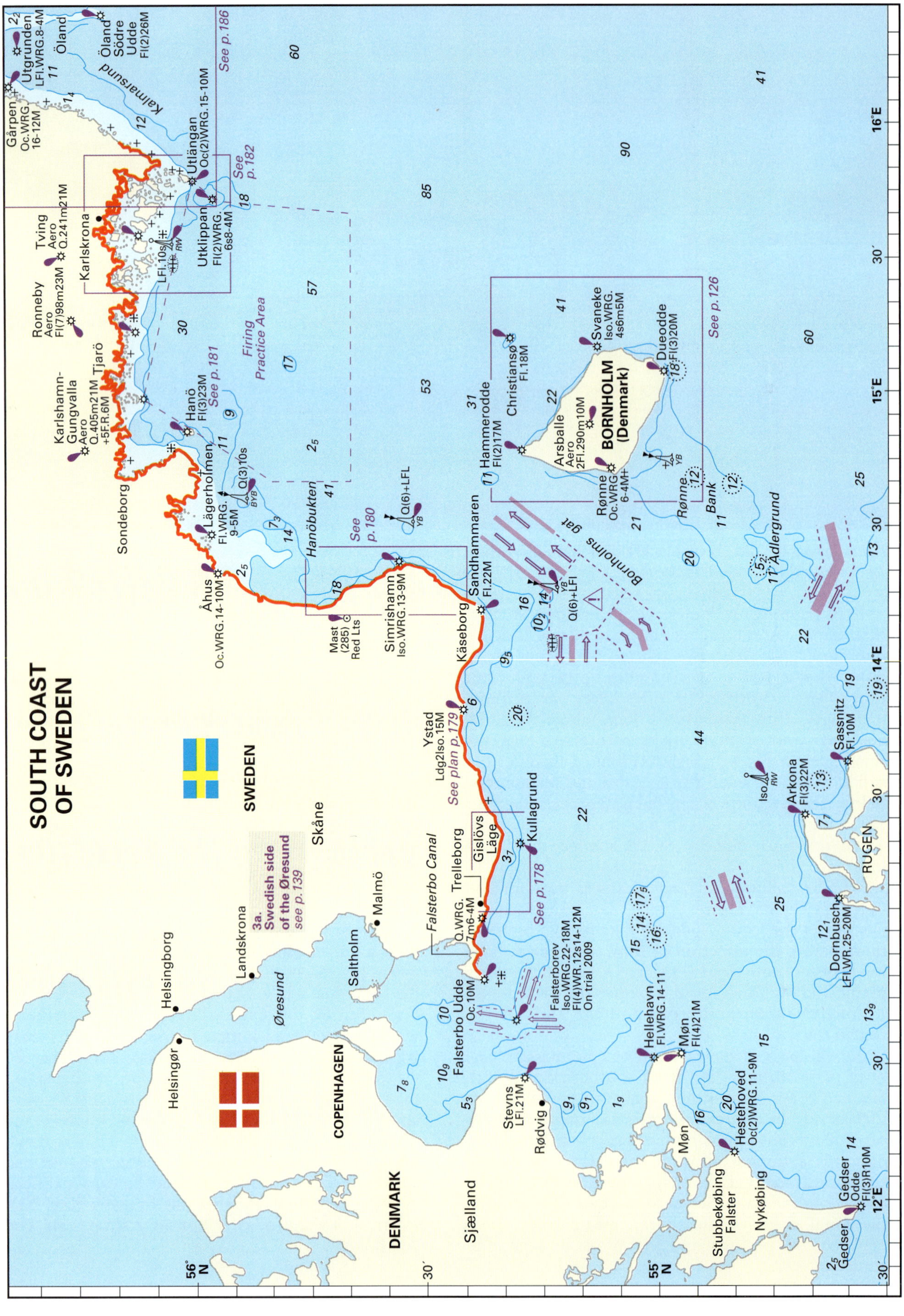

SOUTH COAST OF SWEDEN
SWEDEN
DENMARK
Skåne
Sjælland
COPENHAGEN
Helsingør
Helsingborg
Landskrona
Malmö
Saltholm
Øresund
3a. Swedish side of the Øresund see p.139
Falsterbo Canal
Falsterbo Udde Oc.10M
Falsterborev Iso.WRG.22-18M Fl(4)WR.12s14-12M On trial 2009
Trelleborg
Q.WRG. 7m6-4M
Gislövs Läge
Kullagrund
See p.178
Ystad Ldg2Iso.15M
See plan p.179
Käseborg
Sandhammaren Fl.22M
Simrishamn Iso.WRG.13-9M
Mast (285) Red Lts
See p.180
Hanöbukten
Åhus Oc.WRG.14-10M
Lägerholmen Fl.WRG. 9-5M
Q(3)10s
Q(6)+LFL
Sondeborg
Hanö Fl(3)23M
See p.181
Firing Practice Area
Karlshamn-Gungvalla Aero Q.405m21M +5F.R.6M
Tjarö
Ronneby Aero Fl(7)98m23M
Tving Aero Q.241m21M
Karlskrona
LFl.10s
Utklippan Fl(2)WRG. 6s8-4M
Utlängan Oc(2)WRG.15-10M
See p.182
Gärpen Oc.WRG. 16-12M
Utgrunden LFl.WRG.8-4M
Öland
Kalmarsund
Öland Södre Udde Fl(2)26M
See p.186
Hammerodde Fl(2)17M
Christiansø Fl.18M
Svaneke Iso.WRG. 4s6m5M
Dueodde Fl(3)20M
Arsballe Aero 2Fl.290m10M
BORNHOLM (Denmark)
Rønne Oc.WRG. 6-4M+
Rønne Bank
See p.126
Bornholms gat
Q(6)+LFl
Adlergrund
Iso
Arkona Fl(3)22M
Sassnitz Fl.10M
RUGEN
Dornbusch LFl.WR.25-20M
Stevns LFl.21M
Rødvig
Hellehavn Fl.WRG.14-11
Møn Fl(4)21M
Møn
Hesteoved Oc(2)WRG.11-9M
Stubbekøbing
Falster
Nykøbing
Gedser
Gedser Odde Fl(3)R10M
56° N
55° N
12°E
14°E
15°E
16°E

SOUTH COAST OF SWEDEN

3e. Gislövs Läge to Utklippan

The south coast of Sweden from Falsterbo as far as Simrishamn is largely low-lying, gentle, and with numerous sandy beaches. There are greater distances between significant harbours than on the rest of Sweden's coast line and the shore is open with few sheltered anchorages. Once past Simrishamn, the coastline starts to rise, and beyond Åhus it begins to assume the rocks and islands aspect, which is so typical of both the Kattegat and northeast coasts. There are firing ranges off this coast (see Appendix on page 420).

Gislövs Läge

55°21′N 13°14′E

Distances
Ystad 21M, Simrishamn 50M, Copenhagen 33M (by Falsterbo Kanal), Gedser (Denmark) 70M, Kiel 135M, Rønne (Bornholm) 55M

Charts and guides
Swedish 83, 839 UKHO 2115, 2360

Lights
Kullagrund 55°17′·9N 13°19′·5E Fl.WRG.3s18m16–12M
  181°-R-244°-G-271°-W-105°-R-120°-G-181° Racon
  Red tower with black band, white lantern 20m Floodlit
Trelleborg 55°21′·4N 13°09′·1E Fl(2)G.6s8m6M
Gislövs Ldg Lts 022·5° *Front* 55°21′·3N 13°13′·9E F.R.4m7M
  White ▲ with red border, on framework tower on inner east pierhead
  Rear 201m from front, F.R.11m7M White ▼ with red border, on framework tower. Inner pierheads Floodlit

Communications
Harbourmaster ☎ +46 410 73 33 77
Marina office ☎ +46 704 807 692
  VHF Ch 67 (Trelleborg commercial harbour)

Gislövs Läge (pronounced *Yeece-leuvs Lair-ge*) is a useful but somewhat featureless yacht harbour 3M east of the town of Trelleborg, itself a major ferry port and large commercial harbour but with no facilities for yachts. Several fishing boats are based at Gislövs Läge, but the harbour is mainly reserved for yachts and is administered as one of the civil amenities of Trelleborg.

Approach
On approach, the town of Trelleborg is very obvious from the sea, marked by the continual comings and goings of the ferries and other large vessels. Once within 3M of the coast, in normal visibility, the entrance to Gislövs Läge can be seen. Approach is on 022.5° with leading lights in line. Unlit channel markers indicate the last half mile of the approach. There is a small outer harbour with several small green and red buoys just inside the entrance showing the way to the inner harbour. The southwestern part of the inner harbour has depths of 2m or more, shoaling to the north and east and at times of low water have been known to be less than this. However the bottom is soft mud and it is usually possible to push through. Entrance should not be attempted in a strong southerly, when swell can penetrate the inner harbour.

Berthing
There are a total of some 30 guest berths – eight bows-on to a pontoon to port just inside the entrance with stern lines to posts, and a further 20 or so (rather narrow) slots at the outer ends of the two longer pontoons, again with stern lines to posts. Neither of the pontoons have hammerheads. Other available berths are marked by a green disc. It may also be possible to raft up alongside the western quay, provided yachts do not impede the working fishing boats.

Services
Water and electricity are on the pontoons. Toilets, showers and washing machines are in two small buildings between the clubhouse and a small café (tokens bought at the marina office required for washing machines can be a problem). WiFi is free. Fuel is available from a self service credit card pump on the west quay (check depth).

General facilities
Ashore, there is a small village, partly serving as a residential area for Trelleborg and partly as a quiet location for holiday homes, though there is a

The moorings at Gislövs Läge *E. Redfern*

SOUTH COAST OF SWEDEN

APPROACHES TO GISLÖVS LÄGE

(chart: Depths in Metres)

GISLÖVS LÄGE

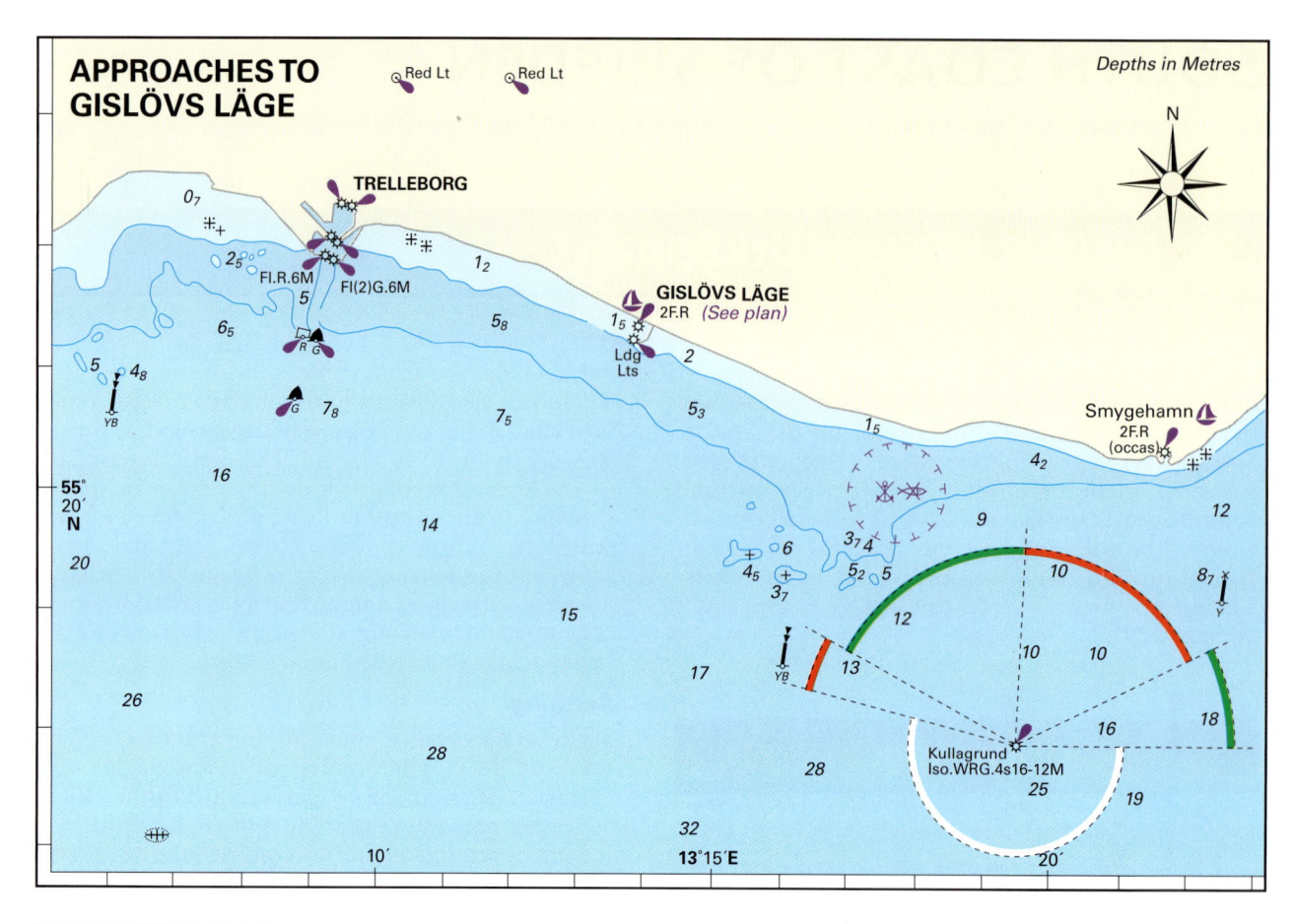

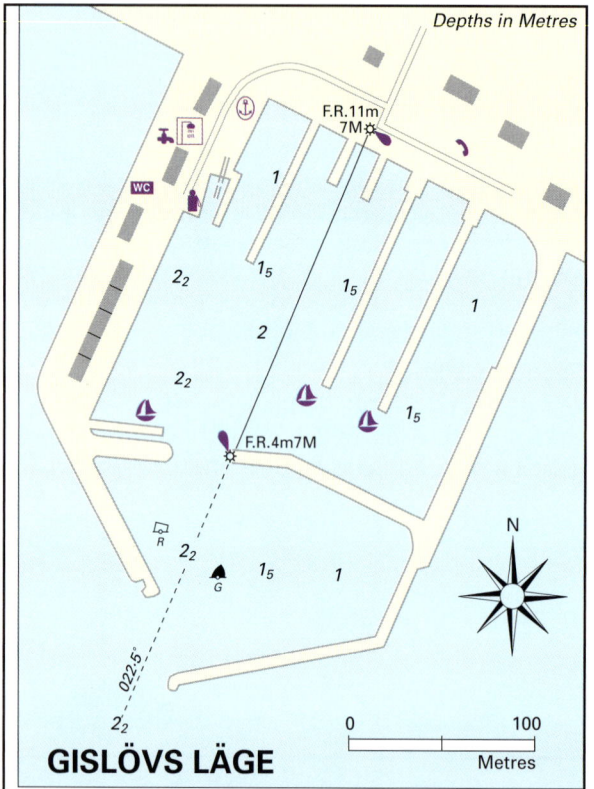

(harbour plan: Depths in Metres)

restaurant and a small grocery store about 10 minutes walk up the road. Frequent buses go to Trelleborg which has all the attributes of a city.

Ystad

55°25′N 13°49′E

Distances
Distances Gislövs Läge 21M, Simrishamn 28M, Copenhagen 58M

Communications
Marina office ☏ +46 704 807 692
kommunen@ystad.se

This is a busy ferry port to Bornholm in Denmark and Świnoujście in Poland with a separate yacht basin, depth 2·7m in entrance, to the west of the main harbour. These are protected from south to southeast by two outer breakwaters of rough boulders, the north one having been extended to provide improved shelter to the yacht harbour (which is generally well sheltered but susceptible to some surge in strong south westerlies). The yacht harbour entrance should be approached with

178 THE BALTIC SEA AND APPROACHES

3E. GISLÖVS LÄGE TO UTKLIPPAN

An early season photograph of the visitors' harbour at Ystad with the new pontoons. There is also alongside mooring to the left of the pontoons *C.N.Hill*

Tacker o Tag chandlery *Stuart Carnegie*

caution in strong southwest to west weather and the approach is prone to shoaling with the sands shifting in storms. The best approach is to align yourself with the entrance about 200m off.

In the approach the large green grain elevator on the west side of the main harbour stands out well from seaward. The outlying shallows are well buoyed and lit.

Berthing (up to 30 berths for visiting yachts) is now on walk ashore pontoons, with some alongside sections in addition. The *gästhamn* can be very full in the season. Electricity is paid for with a Tallycard, which also gives access to the ablutions. There is a washing machine and diesel pontoon. The berthing fee can be paid at a machine with a credit card, and the machine also provides Tallycards for late arrivals.

'Tacker o Tag' is an old-fashioned chandlery, an Aladdins cave with ancient and modern items including Camping Gaz exchange. Bike hire is available. Bus and train station is five minutes walk. The town with supermarkets, shopping, banks, plenty of pizzerias but not many good restaurants, is a 15 minute walk. It is a beautiful town with many interesting old buildings, and in particular St Mary's Church should not be missed.

Ystad to Simrishamn or Bornholm

The passage from Ystad to Bornholm will pass through the Bornholmsgat. This is the main route for deep-water shipping entering the Baltic, and is controlled by a major Traffic Separation Scheme (TSS). All small craft must keep well clear of vessels using the TSS and if crossing to Bornholm, cross at right angles as required by international regulations. The passage to Simrishamn is a straightforward coast hop. Check firing times with marina office for range south and west of Sandhammaren light.

For Bornholm see pages 126-129

THE BALTIC SEA AND APPROACHES

SOUTH COAST OF SWEDEN

Simrishamn

55°33′N 14°22′E

Distances
Gislövs Läge 50M, Rønne (Bornholm) 30M, Karlskrona 60M, Kalmar 100M

Charts and guides
Swedish 7, 74, 839 *Båtsportkort C: Hanöbukten*, UKHO 2014, 2015, 2018, 2040

Lights
Sandhammaren 55°23′N 14°11′·8E Fl.5s31m22M Red metal tower, framework base 29m
Simrishamn 55°33′·5N 14°22′E Iso.WRG.6s16m13-9M shore-G-160°-W-223°-G-238°-W-279°-R-285°-W-355°-R-shore White tower 15m
buoy **Långagrund** 55°32′·4N 14°30′·2E Q(6)+Fl.15s South cardinal pillar buoy, ⱶ topmark

Communications
Commercial harbour ☏ +46 414 89 12 02
Marina office ☏ +46 708 16 58 81
Info@simrishamn-marina.se
www.simrishamn-marina.se (Swedish only)
VHF Channel 11, 16

Simrishamn (pronounced *Sim-ris-hahmn*) is a pleasant town with a busy commercial and fishing harbour, leading to a well-equipped yacht harbour. It is a convenient stopping place on the way to or from the northern Baltic, though when the fishing fleet is active the harbour can be noisy and disturbed and particular care must be taken on entry and departure. The largely 19th-century town has pretty cobbled streets, painted houses and open market, and the 12th-century St Nicolai Kyrka (church) is particularly worth visiting.

Approach

Both Simrishamn lighthouse and the gabled red-roofed church are good landmarks from offshore. When closer in, fluorescent orange leading marks will be seen on a bearing of 250°, keeping vessels well south of the 2·7m Nedjan shoal, itself marked by cardinal buoys. The harbour should only be approached with extreme caution in strong onshore winds, and unpredictable currents may be created both inside and outside the entrance by prolonged easterlies. The yacht marina with all facilities is immediately to starboard after entering the main harbour. The entrance to the marina is marked by buoys. Do not stray outside the marked channel.

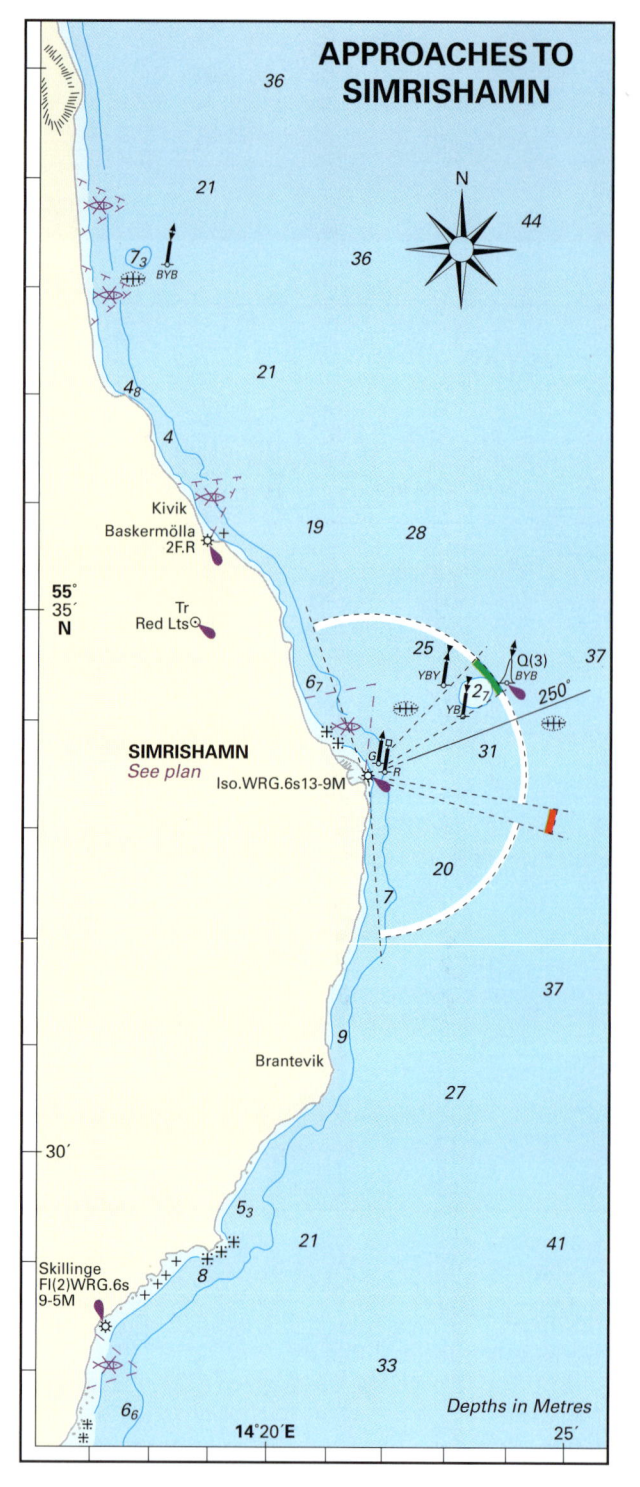

Simrishamn. The entrance is relatively straightforward. There are leading lines, but they are not particularly conspicuous. Once through the harbour entrance, turn to starboard for the entrance to the marina *C.N.Hill*

THE BALTIC SEA AND APPROACHES

3E. GISLÖVS LÄGE TO UTKLIPPAN

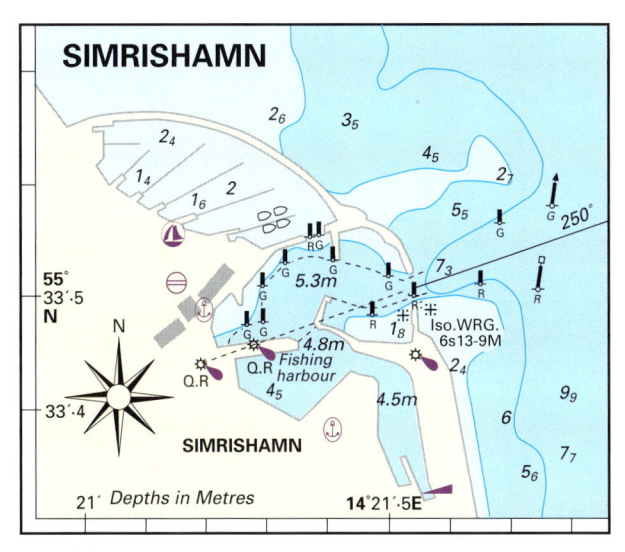

Berthing
The outer ends of the two southernmost jetties are reserved for visiting yachts, berths on the nearer jetty being alongside and reserved for those of more than 4m beam. The 26 visitors' berths on the second pontoon are step on pontoons, both depth and width being indicated on posts on the pontoon itself. Yachts which are too large to use the marina may be able to berth in the fishing or commercial harbours – contact the harbour office before arrival.

Services and facilities
Normal facilities including washing machine are behind the white clubhouse building. A Tallycard system is in use for electricity and access. Fuel, propane and holding tank pump out are available. Engine and electronics repairs can be arranged – either the marina office or the sailing club may be able to assist.

There is a large chandlery and sailmaker at Skillinge, 6M south of Simrishamn, Skeppshandel and Österlens Segelmakeri.
✆ +46 414 302 50, info@skepp.com, www.skepp.com

Simrishamns Segelsällskap is an active sailing club with a pleasant clubhouse and a busy summer programme of racing and social events.
✆ +46 414 107 70

All normal facilities of a medium-sized town are available with the helpful tourist office close to the harbour. Bus and rail stations are within 0·5km of the marina.

The coast from Hanö to Karlskrona and beyond
It is only eight miles north of Hanö that the east coast truly begins. This is an extraordinary coastline, consisting of thousands of islands with countless channels between them, many small harbours and myriad anchorages. Apart from Kalmarsund which runs inside the 70 mile long island of Öland, the *skärgård* runs to about 100M north of Stockholm. This provides a fascinating cruising ground which can take many years to explore to the full. A book such as this can only scratch the surface of what is available, and safe navigation demands the presence of the most detailed charts available.

Sailing in the *skärgård* requires constant attention. The main channels are marked on the charts as a dashed line, indicating that these are safe for navigation. You may choose to take your own shortcuts, but you do so at your own peril. The channels are buoyed with red and green markers, which are usually there for a specific purpose, marking shoals or submerged rocks.

Hanö
56°01'N 14°50'E

Distances
Simrishamn 32M, Rønne (Bornholm) 55M, Karlskrona 28M, Utklippan 29M

Communications
Marina office ✆ +46 456 53008, Mobile +46 768 993008

Hanö is a small artificial harbour on the west side of Hanö Island, and is a pleasant and convenient stopping place between Simrishamn and either Karlskrona or Utklippan. Approach is straightforward, but could be uncomfortable in northwest winds. Berthing alongside, or possibly rafting, particularly at weekends in the summer, where the harbourmaster will help. Depth is 2m anywhere, and 4m, alongside west or north piers. Basic marina facilities are available, also a shop, café and post.

There is an interesting walk up to the lighthouse and to the naval cemetery, where a cross was erected in 1973 in memory of the sailors of HMS Victory, who died there during the winter of 1810.

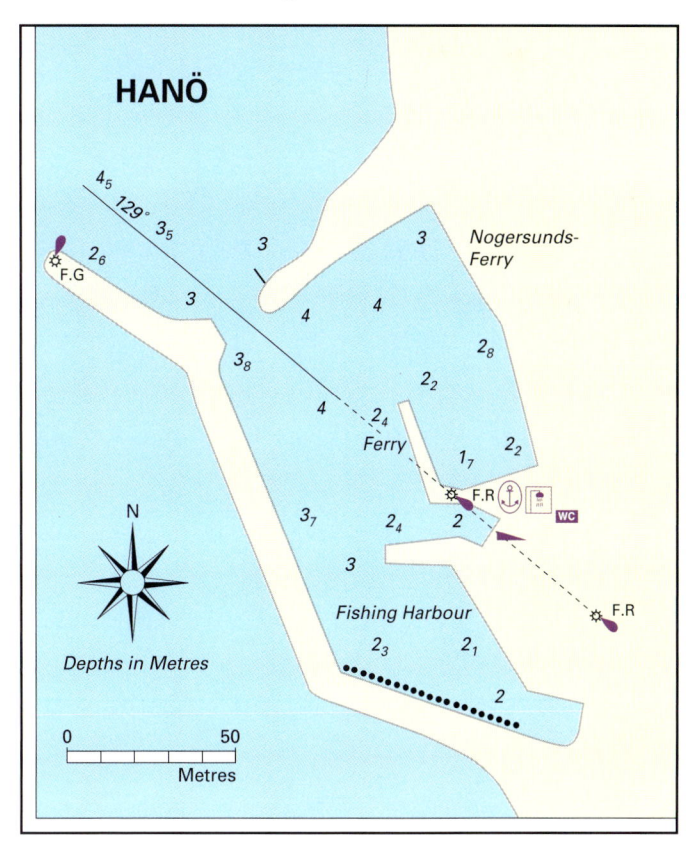

THE BALTIC SEA AND APPROACHES 181

3. SWEDEN

SOUTH COAST OF SWEDEN

The harbour at Hanö. It is rather open to northwesterly winds *C.N. Hill*

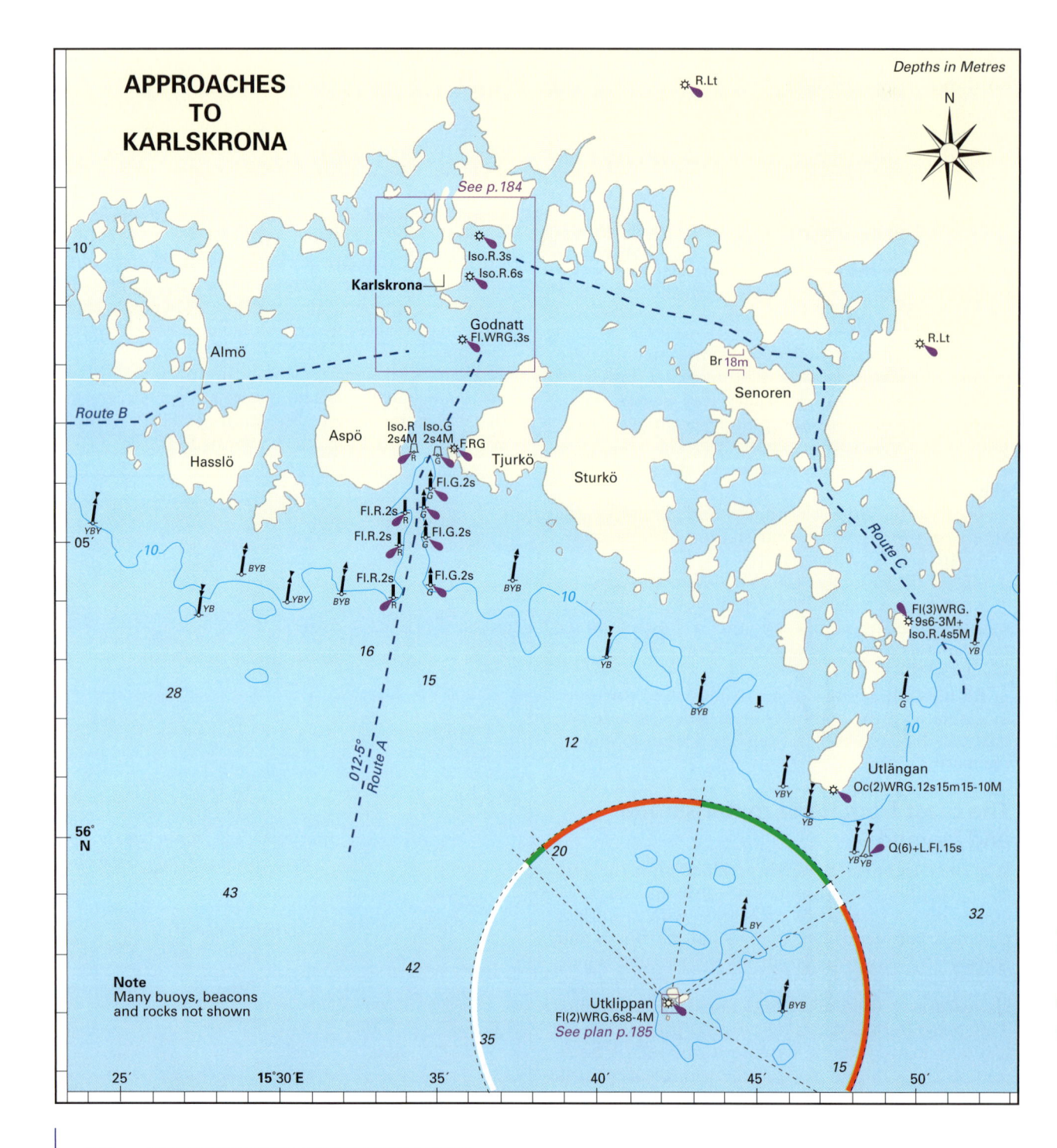

APPROACHES TO KARLSKRONA

Note Many buoys, beacons and rocks not shown

182   THE BALTIC SEA AND APPROACHES

3E. GISLÖVS LÄGE TO UTKLIPPAN

Karlskrona

56°10'N 15°36'E

Distances
Hanö 28M, Simrishamn 60M, Rønne 75M, Kalmar 50M, Utklippan, 13M

Charts and guides
Swedish 7, 74, 821 Båtsportkort C: Hanöbukten
UKHO 2014, 2015, 2018, 2040, 2816, 2857

Lights
Utklippan south rock 55°57'·2N 15°42'·2E Fl(2)WRG. 6s.31m W8/R5/G4M. Nov. to Mar. only. Red framework tower on old fort 30m
Karlskrona Ldg Lts 012·5° *Front* Stumholmen, 56°09'·5N 15°36'E Iso.R.6s22m16M White round concrete tower 24m
Rear 0·7M from front Iso.R.3s37m16M White round concrete tower 15m
Västra Försänkningen 56°06'·5N 15°34'·5E Iso.R.2s6m6M Racon White and red dolphin Floodlit
Godnatt 56°08'·5N 15°35'·8E
Fl.WRG.3s20m11–7M
003°-G-013·5°-W-017·5°-R-028·5°-G-056°-R-073·5°-G-079·5°-W-082·5°-R-125·5°-G-137°-W-139·5°-R-144°-G-189°-R-197°-G-234°-W-242°-R-302°-G-330°-R-003°
Grey fort

Communications
Karlskrona Port Authority ✆ +46 (0)455 303000, VHF Ch 14, 16
Karlskrona Harbourmaster ✆ +46 (0)455 21871, *Mobile* +46 70 930 3151, VHF Ch 14, 16

The principal naval base of Sweden, Karlskrona occupies an easily-defended island site connected to the mainland by road and railway bridges, with an interesting 20M approach through the *skärgård*. The approach from the southeast is restricted by an 18m bridge. In addition to an attractive, cobbled city centre, Karlskrona boasts a large maritime museum (www.marinmuseum.se) on Stumholmen island, where historic ships lie alongside the museum's own quay, the fortress of Kungsholmen and Drottningskär citadel on the island of Aspö. The naval port of Karlskrona is included in UNESCO's World Heritage list.

Approach and entrance

There are three principal channels, all of which require large-scale charts:

1. The main channel, which leads between the large islands of Aspö and Tjurkö on a bearing of 012·5° and is well buoyed and lit.
2. The southwest channel, which is entered at the Hyperionsgrund buoy (56°06'·7N 15°22'E) and is buoyed but not lit. There is a swing bridge between Almö and Hasslö islands at 56°07'·7N 15°27'·7E. Opening times are given at: www.sjofartsverket.se/en/Maritime-services/Hydrographic-Information/Opening-times-bridges-and-canals/Hasslobron/
c. The southeast channel, which is entered east of Långören island at 56°03'·7N 15°50'E and is elaborately buoyed but not lit. It passes first through a wide shoal area studded with grass-covered islands (mostly designated nature reserves), then via a narrower, dog-legged channel and under a high level (18m) bridge north of the large island of Senoren (56°08'·2N 15°45'E), and thence to Karlskrona. If leaving the port to head eastwards, this route offers some interesting pilotage and saves many miles.

Even using the large-scale chart some of the buoyage is confusing, and calls for caution.

Berthing

Tallebryggan Marina

56°10'N 15°35'·3E
Marina office ✆ +46 455 303150
info@karlskronastadsmarina.se

This is the main yacht harbour for Karlskrona, and lies in a basin north of the city. It is very convenient for the city, but a motorway with its inevitable lights runs close along the side and the surroundings are not particularly attractive. In the final approach, the buoys marking the channel must be followed carefully. The layout of the harbour has been changed recently, and the visitors' berths are clearly marked. They now consist of two jetties with walk on pontoons, and there is also some alongside mooring.

The area around the marina is currently being redeveloped, and the facilities renewed. Fuel is available from an automatic pump about 200m from the marina entrance. Bottled gas is available at the filling station, and the office building nearby also houses a restaurant and the Tallebryggans Båtklubb, and is open 0700–2200 daily.

Hässlo swing bridge, west of Karlskrona Martin Lunt

Karlskrona, Tallebryggan marina C.N. Hill

THE BALTIC SEA AND APPROACHES

SOUTH COAST OF SWEDEN

KARLSKRONA

The main downside to the Marina is a nearby busy motorway which is distinctly noisy.

The town itself is pleasant, with good shops, a fish market; the outstanding maritime museum is a short walk away and by it the fascinating traditional wooden boat building school (Litorina Folkhögskola). The bus and railway station is 200m away. There are regular car ferries to Gdynia in Poland.

Dragsö Yacht Harbour

56°10′·4N 15°33′·9E

Marina office ☎ +46 455 10596, Mobile +46 709 283788

Dragsö Yacht Harbour on Utkik island, administered by the Karlskrona Segelsällskap (sailing club), is quieter and much more scenic but is a long way from the city. Six of its 130 berths are reserved for visitors, but a red/green system is also used to indicate free berths.

From any of the approach channels, pass north of the conspicuous Godnatt tower and follow the buoyed channel south of Lindholmen island, south of the Arsenal and west of Saltö island. The small islet northwest of Saltö must also be left to

184 THE BALTIC SEA AND APPROACHES

3E. GISLÖVS LÄGE TO UTKLIPPAN

Utklippan basin *C.N. Hill*

starboard. Once past this islet a buoyed channel opens to the east. Follow it, and the marina's two pontoons will soon come into view to starboard beyond the clubhouse. Berthing is bows on, stern to a buoy, in depths of 2–2·5m, with visitors placed at the ends of the two outer (westernmost) pontoons. A little swell may find its way in during strong northwesterly winds. The yacht harbour is in an almost enclosed lagoon surrounded by countryside, though some noise may penetrate from the nearby campsite. There is a children's play area and a barbecue area for the use of guests. There is water to all berths and electricity to most, with showers, sauna and laundry facilities ashore, a clubhouse with seasonal café, but no restaurant, shop or fuel. Slipway (with pressure hose and plenty of vacant cradles in summer) – enquire at the office. A diver is also available.

The Saltö Varv boatyard, ☏ +46 455 15511, where minor repairs might be undertaken, is about 300m to the south (though further by water). They will be able to help locate other tradesmen. The harbour is not within walking distance of the city but is on a bus route and bicycles can be hired from the nearby campsite.

Utklippan

55°57'N 15°42'E

Distances
Karlskrona 13M, Bergkvara 29M, Kalmar 48M, Visby (Gotland) 135M, Christiansø 42M

Utklippan provides an interesting and convenient overnight stop for yachts on passage along the Swedish coast. It consists of two small skerries situated 4·5M southwest of Utlängan, the nearest land. Four breakwaters nearly join the two skerries on their east and west sides, thus nearly enclosing the lagoon between them. In the north skerry a basin 90m x 40m was originally excavated for the use of the lighthouse tender, with two entrances, on the southeast and southwest sides (the south west one is deeper). It is a delightful spot with perfect shelter and is capable – at a squeeze – of berthing up to 25 boats in 2·5–3m depths but be prepared to raft up. There is a lighthouse 30m high on the south skerry (you will need a dinghy to reach this) and an automatic fog horn. Shoals extend both north and south of the islands, which should be approached with care and a large scale chart.

Final approach from either direction (favour the lee side) is via rock-fringed channels and thence between low moles, where strong currents can be encountered. At night, approach in the white sector of the Södraskär light from the northeast, or the green from the northwest. Facilities are limited to chemical toilets and refuse bins in season, reportedly with electricity to a few berths in the southeast corner and WiFi, but the wild and attractive surroundings more than compensate. It is reported to be an outstanding spot for bird watching, though noisy in the nesting season when their young are vigorously defended.

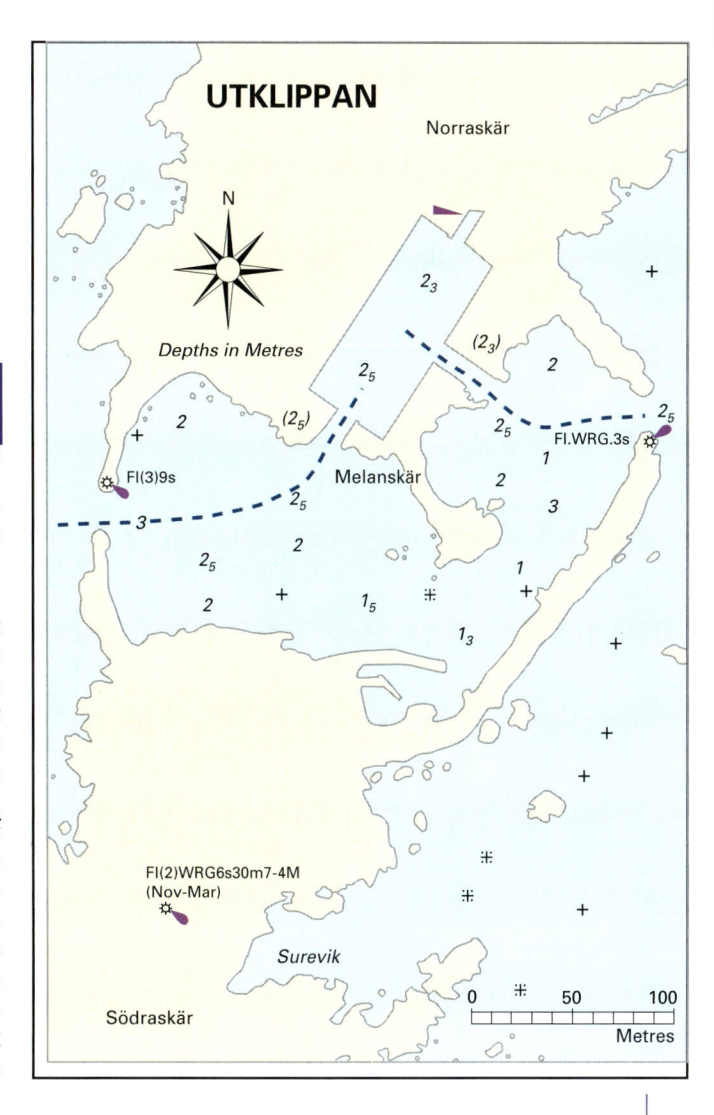

THE BALTIC SEA AND APPROACHES 185

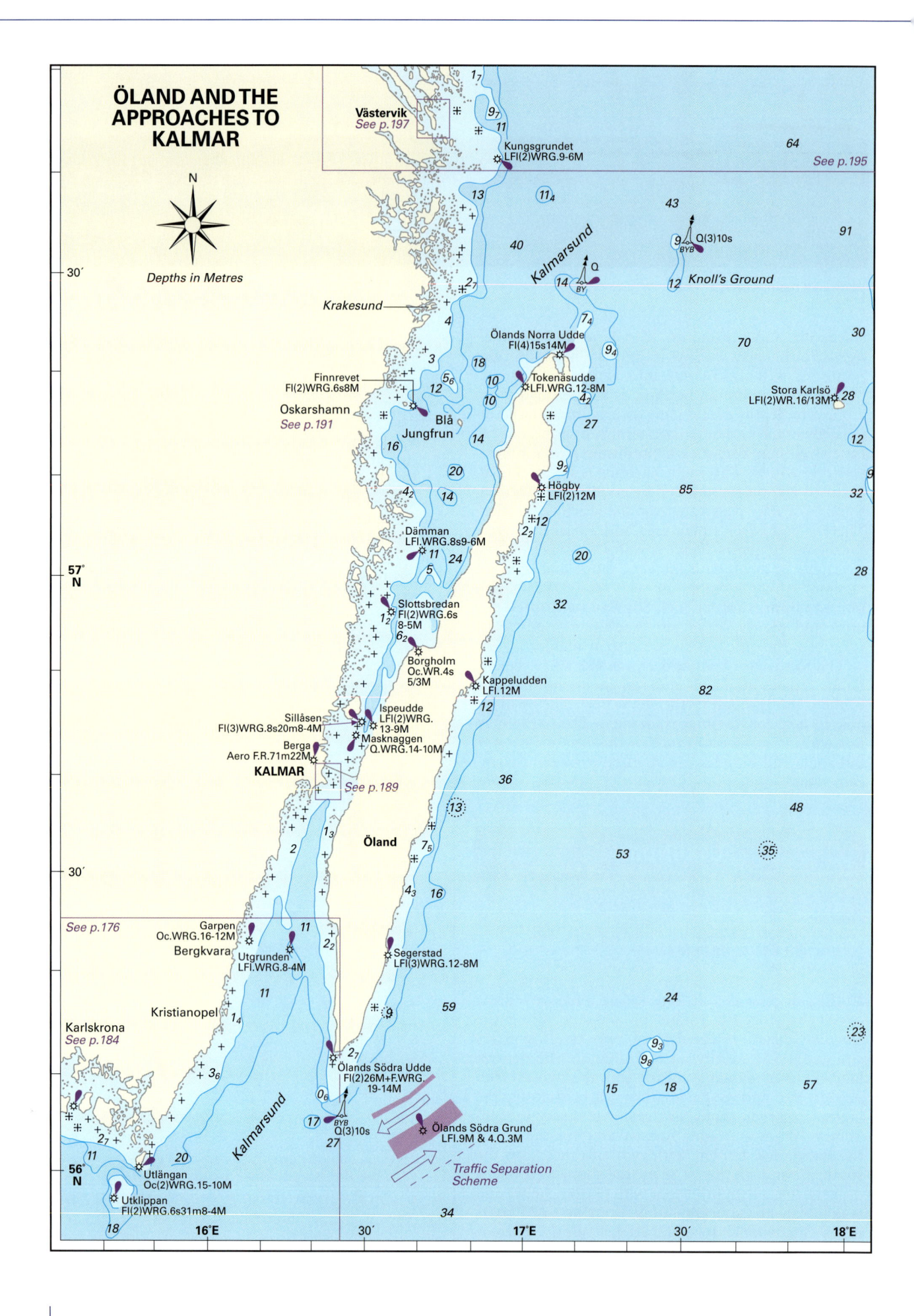

EAST COAST OF SWEDEN

ÖLAND AND THE APPROACHES TO KALMAR

Depths in Metres

Västervik See p.197

Kungsgrundet LFl(2)WRG.9-6M

See p.195

Q(3)10s

Kalmarsund

Knoll's Ground

Krakesund

Ölands Norra Udde Fl(4)15s14M

Tokenäsudde LFl.WRG.12-8M

Stora Karlsö LFl(2)WR.16/13M

Finnrevet Fl(2)WRG.6s8M

Oskarshamn See p.191

Blå Jungfrun

Högby LFl(2)12M

Dämman LFl.WRG.8s9-6M

57° N

Slottsbredan Fl(2)WRG.6s 8-5M

Borgholm Oc.WR.4s 5/3M

Kappeludden LFl.12M

Sillåsen Fl(3)WRG.8s20m8-4M

Ispeudde LFl(2)WRG. 13-9M

Berga Aero F.R.71m22M

Masknaggen Q.WRG.14-10M

KALMAR

See p.189

Öland

30'

See p.176

Garpen Oc.WRG.16-12M

Bergkvara

Utgrunden LFl.WRG.8-4M

Segerstad LFl(3)WRG.12-8M

Kristianopel

Karlskrona See p.184

Ölands Södra Udde Fl(2)26M+F.WRG. 19-14M

Q(3)10s

Ölands Södra Grund LFl.9M & 4.Q.3M

Traffic Separation Scheme

56° N

Utlängan Oc(2)WRG.15-10M

Utklippan Fl(2)WRG.6s31m8-4M

16°E — 30' — 17°E — 30' — 18°E

186 THE BALTIC SEA AND APPROACHES

EAST COAST OF SWEDEN

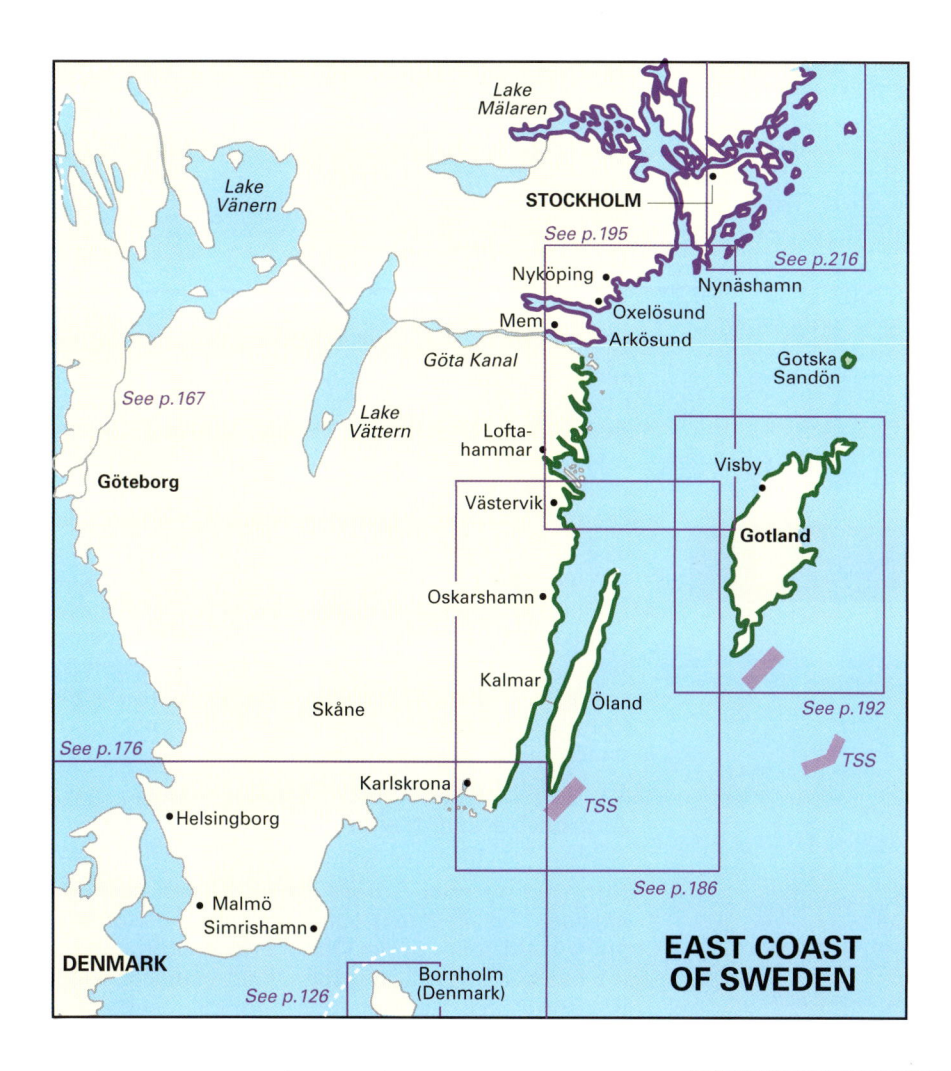

3f. Utlangan to Landsort, including Öland and Gotland, *187*

3g. Stockholm - the Archipelago and surrounding area, *204*

Sweden's East coast changes character as one moves north. For the first few miles it is open to the full width of the Baltic, and then comes under the influence of two major and one minor offshore islands. Öland, some 70 miles long is separated from the mainland by Kalmarsund, which is spanned by a bridge. Northeast of that lies Gotland, of similar length to Öland but wider, which is reputed to have some of the best summer weather in the Baltic. Visby is its only real harbour and is inclined to be busy during the peak months, but towards autumn the activity decreases and makes this an attractive time to visit. North of Gotland is the small island of Gotska Sandon which has no harbour, but is surrounded by superb sandy beaches off any of which one may anchor in suitable conditions.

North of Kalmarsund the *skärgård* begins with deep inlets and myriad offshore rocks and islands presenting a beautiful and interesting cruising area. The Göta Canal meets the Baltic at Mem, some 70 miles north of Kalmarsund, and the *skärgård* continues to Stockholm which is set between the lake and islands of Malaren to the west and the extensive Stockholm *skärgård* to the east and northeast.

There are firing practice areas on this coast – see Appendix page 420 for details.

3f. Utlangan to Landsort including Öland and Gotland

Kalmarsund

The Baltic coast of Sweden north of Utklippan offers superb cruising in relatively sheltered waters among islands. The first 20 miles or so is open until the entrance to Kalmarsund, the strait which runs for 70 miles inside the island of Öland. It narrows from about 10M wide at either end to 4M at its narrowest, and it can funnel the wind to provide some brisk sailing. The town of Kalmar is immediately south of its narrowest point, where it is crossed by a high level bridge with a clearance of 36m. The southern end of Gotland and Öland have a reputation for fog, but this tends to clear in summer as the sound is entered. There is a Traffic Separation Scheme off the southeast of Öland. There are numerous wind farms in Kalmarsund, and on Öland, not all of which are shown on the charts.

THE BALTIC SEA AND APPROACHES   **187**

EAST COAST OF SWEDEN

Once north of Kalmar the *skärgård* begins to assert itself and the number of small harbours and anchorages increases far beyond the compass of this book. It is unwise to navigate anywhere on this coast without large scale (1:50,000 or greater) Swedish charts; from here northwards they should be regarded as essential. It is also wise to carry at least one of the local pilot books (see page 132) on board.

There are three relatively small harbours along the mainland before arriving at Kalmar. These are Sandhamn (not to be confused with the harbour of the same name in the Stockholm archipelago), Kristianopel and Bergkvara. The passage from either Utklippan or Karlskrona to Kalmar is quite lengthy, and any of these would be a comfortable overnight stop.

Kalmar Castle is a World Heritage Site Stuart Carnegie

Kalmar is one of Sweden's oldest towns, and the scene of the Union of Kalmar in 1397. It was originally a Viking stronghold, and became one of the major ports of the Hanseatic League. The present town, with a population of around 50,000, has many historic buildings dating back to the 17th century, a fine baroque cathedral and a picturesque and very interesting castle, which is a World Heritage Site, in a dominant position overlooking Kalmarsund. The castle museum has an outstanding exhibition of articles from the sunken 17th-century warship Kronan, while the maritime museum in the old quarter at the east end of the town is also worth visiting. Kalmar has a very good shopping centre which, like all these attractions is within easy walking distance of the harbour.

Kalmar

56°40′N 16°21′E

Distances
Simrishamn 100M, Karlskrona 50M, Visby 95M, Västervik 65M

Charts and guides
UKHO 2054
Swedish 81, 712
Båtsportkort F: Sydostkusten – Kalmarsund.

Lights
Southern approach
Ölands Södra Udde 56°11′·8N 16°24′E Fl(2)30s41m26M
  Round white stone tower, black band 42m Floodlit
Utgrunden (north end of shoal) 56°22′·5N 16°15′·7E
  LFl.WRG.8s29m8–4M Racon
  019°–R–096°–G–153°–R–166°–G–185°–W–192°–R–265°–G–292°–R–316·5°–G–349°–W–019° Black tower, white band and lantern, grey conical base 28m
Skansgrundet 56°39′·1N 16°22′·7E
  Oc(2)WRG.20s18m15–11M
  008°–G–019°–W–024·5°–R–032°–G–058°–R–150°–G–197°–W–202·5°–R–215°–G–217°–R–249°–G–256°–R–008° Black tower, green band, grey conical base, white lantern 19m Floodlit
Northern approach
Dämman 57°03′·4N 16°41′·7E
  LFl.WRG.8s9–6M
  010°–G–021°–W–024·5°–R–120°–G–169°–W–209°–R–010°
  Orange tower, black band, grey base 21m
Slottsbredan 56°55′·7N 16°36′·3E Fl(2)WRG.6s20m8–4M
  018°–W–022°–R–048°–G–098°–R–184°–G–202°–W–208°–R–359°–G–018° Black tower, green band and lantern, grey conical base 21m
Krongrundet 56°41′·4N 16°24′·5E
  Oc(2)WRG.8s10m15–10M
  023°–W–031°–R–058°–G–104°–W–184°–R–214°–G–222·5°–W–226·5°–R–284°–G–023° White tower, green and black stripe 11m

Communications
VTS Oxelösund ☎ +46 480 10719, VHF Ch 09.
Kalmar Commercial Harbour ☎ +46 480 451450
  VHF Ch 09, 12, 16
  kalmar.hamn@kommun.kalmar.se
Kalmar Guest Harbour ☎ +46 480 417700
  gasthamn@turistbyra.kalmar.se
  www.kalmar.se. Click on Tourism – Travel – Marinas.

Approach and entrance

From either direction, follow the main north - south shipping channel which passes close past the harbour. The entrance leads off it to the west at a point 1·2M south of the Öland bridge. Berthing is in the old northwest basin, the Ölandshamnen, which is approached through the Gamlahamnen, itself directly opposite the harbour entrance. Mooring is mainly with bows to the quay and stern to a buoy, though a few alongside berths may be found on the starboard hand near the entrance. There are also some booms in the far left-hand corner; the width of the boom is indicated on a sign at the end. Depths vary from 4·5m near the entrance to 2m at the head of the harbour. As the basin is entirely reserved for

Kalmar approach to yacht harbour Stuart Carnegie

188   THE BALTIC SEA AND APPROACHES

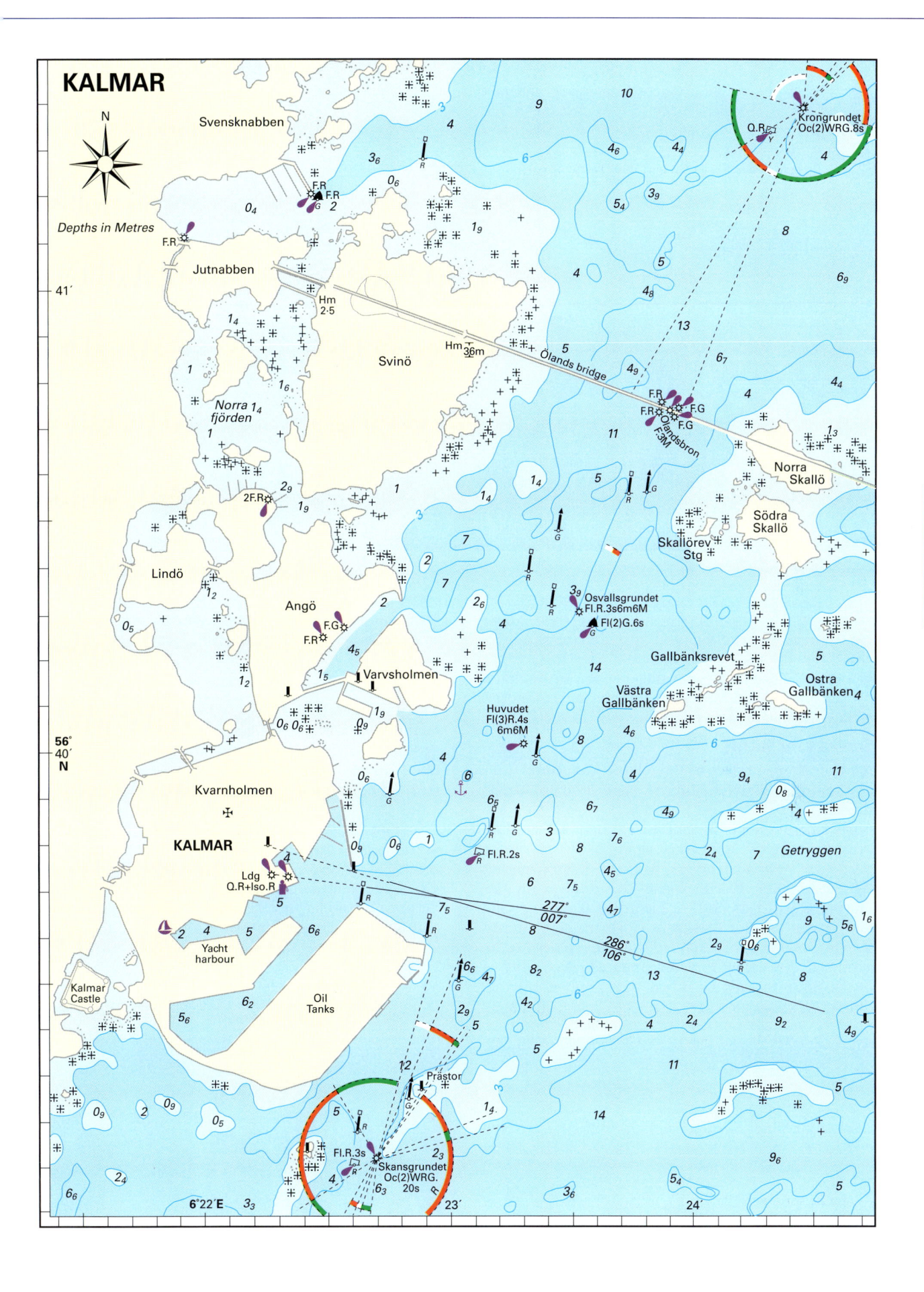

3F. UTLANGAN TO LANDSORT INCLUDING ÖLAND AND GOTLAND

THE BALTIC SEA AND APPROACHES

EAST COAST OF SWEDEN

Kalmar Gästhamn *C.N. Hill*

visitors, any free berth can be taken on arrival. There are some 120 berths; the office is in the tourist centre and the marina is fully operational May to October inclusive. Out of season arrangements can be made by telephone. Anchoring is not permitted in the vicinity of Kalmar harbour.

Services for yachts

All the usual services are available including WiFi and sauna. Launderette time slots must be booked at the harbour office. Fuel (diesel and petrol) is on the north side of the marina entrance. There is a holding tank pump-out station. Kalmar is home to a particularly good chandlery, Baltic Skeppsfournering AB, ☎ +46 480 10600, across the road from the marina basin. Gas bottles, including Camping Gaz and possibly Calor Gas, plus German, Danish and Swedish makes can be refilled. Engine repairs can be arranged. A weather forecast, updated twice daily, is displayed in the marina office, but is only accessible during office hours.

A company called Kalmar Marina offers winter storage and many other boatyard facilities, including a sailmaker.

General facilities

There is a very good shopping centre with excellent facilities adjacent to the harbour. A new and rather upmarket supermarket has opened here recently, and there is also a well stocked Clas Ohlsen department store. The town is well served with shops of all kinds.

The railway and coach stations are opposite the marina, providing easy access to the rest of the country. Car hire can be arranged by the chandlery. Taxis are readily available. The airport a short distance inland has several daily flights to Stockholm and Malmö. Altogether it is a good place for crew changes.

Ölands Bridge just north of Kalmar *B. Sheffield*

THE BALTIC SEA AND APPROACHES

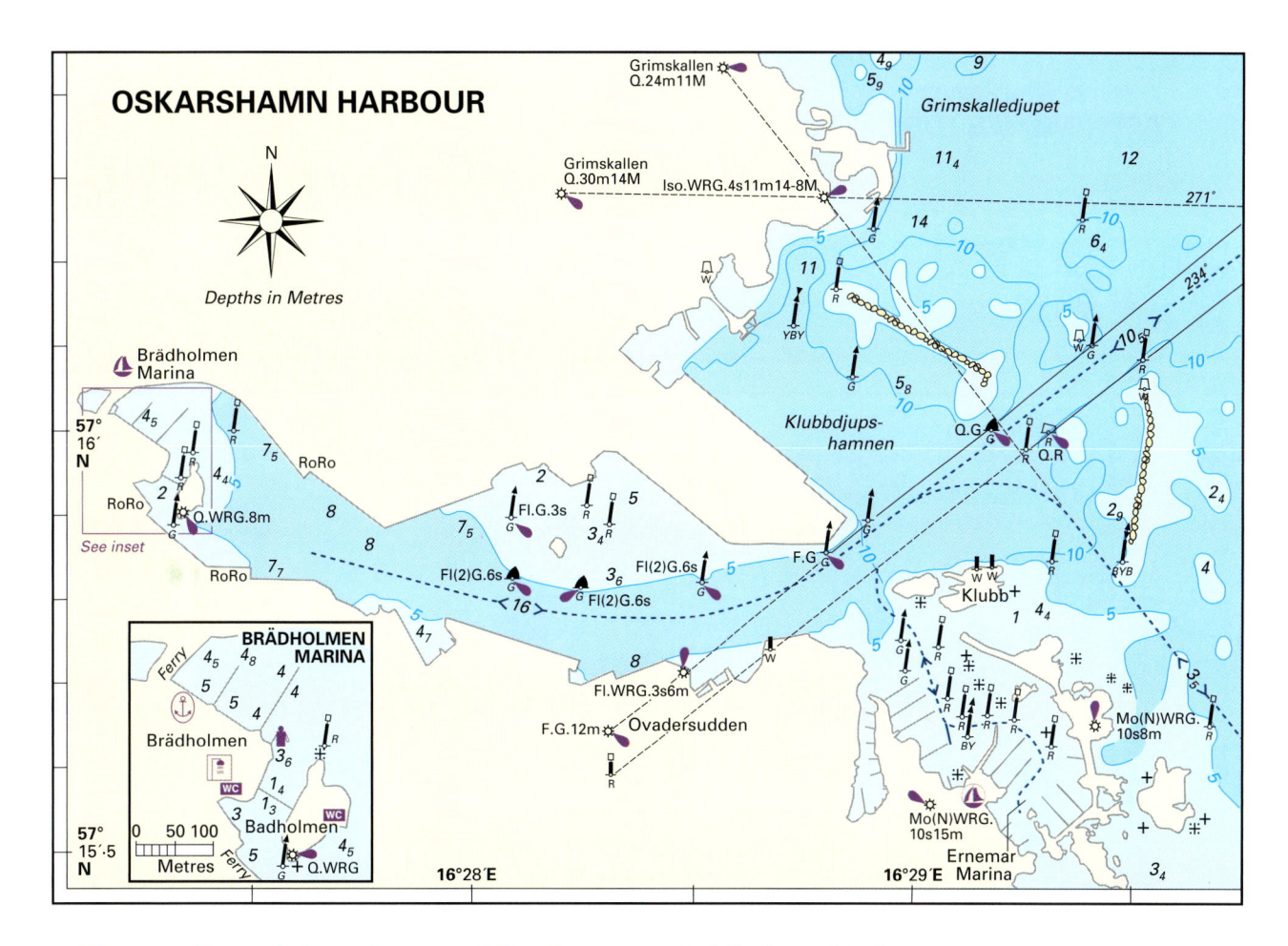

3F. UTLANGAN TO LANDSORT INCLUDING ÖLAND AND GOTLAND

Blå Jungfrun (The Blue Maiden)

56°40′N 16°21′E

Blå Jungfrun is a National Park island in the northern part of Kalmarsund. The island has dramatic granite slopes and varied flora with an ancient stone maze on the south coast, and plays an important part in Swedish folklore. There are daytime anchorages at Sikhamn in the northwest and Lervik in the northeast, where summer students act as welcoming wardens.

Oskarshamn

56°40′N 16°21′E

Distances
Kalmar 36M, Västervik 30M, Visby (Gotland) 63M

Communications
www.oskarshamn.se Click on Tourists – Marinas

This is a busy, shipbuilding port but nevertheless pleasant, clean and tidy. Approach may be made either north or south of Finnrevet lighthouse which is 5M east by north of the harbour and is well marked, presenting no difficulty, even at night. However beware of ferries in the narrow channels.

Brädholmen Marina

☎ +46 705 74 79 90

Most visitors' preferred harbour, at the head of the harbour, either side of the bridge to the island, mostly 3m, either bow to with stern anchor or with stern buoys, or larger yachts can go alongside. This marina has all the usual services available. Diesel available on adjoining pontoon. There are all the shops, post, banks of a fairly large town and a small Watski chandler 350m away. The boatyard to the south of the main harbour has been recommended by locals.

Ernemar Marina

57°15′·6N 16°29′·E
☎ +46 49 11 74 00,

At the east end of the harbour. This is a quieter place with less urban surroundings, most services, but more than a mile to the town facilities. There are 10 guest buoys, otherwise use a green marked space.

THE BALTIC SEA AND APPROACHES

EAST COAST OF SWEDEN

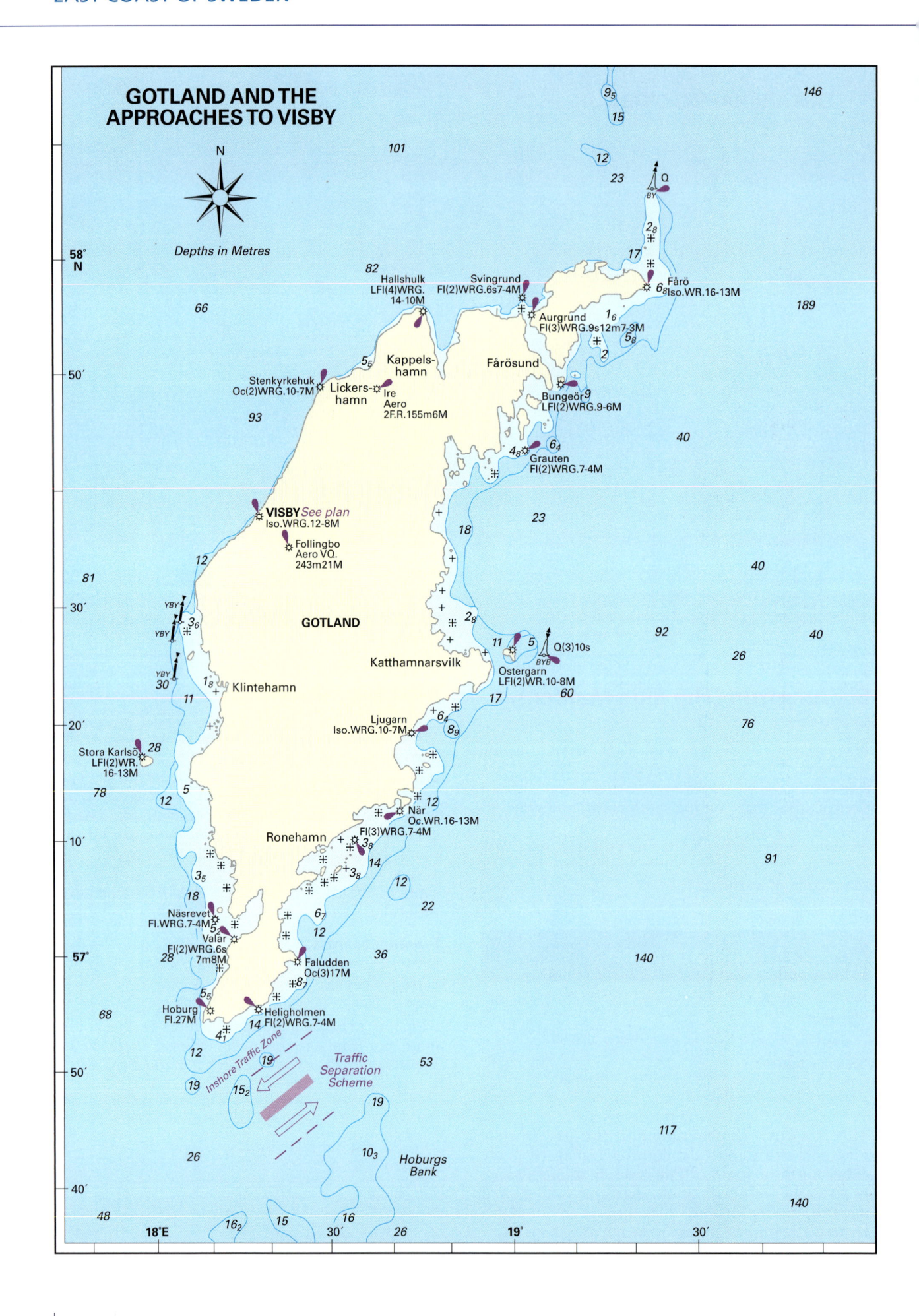

GOTLAND AND THE APPROACHES TO VISBY

3F. UTLANGAN TO LANDSORT INCLUDING ÖLAND AND GOTLAND

Visby (Gotland)

57°39'N 18°17'E

Distances
Kalmar 95M, Västervik 55M, Arkösund 65M

Charts and guides
UKHO 2054, 2055
Swedish 72, 73, 731

Lights
Follingbo 57°35'·6N 19°22'·6E Aero VQ.243m21M. Mast
 Note This light is 4M inland with obstructions
Stora Karlsö, west side 57°17'·5N 17°57'·8E
 LFl(2)WR.12s56m16–13M
 340°-W-193°-R-212°-W-233°-R-340° White tower on dwelling 18m
Visby, north breakwater 57°38'·1N 18°16'·2E Q.R.9m9M
 White tower, green band, 6m Floodlit
Visby, south breakwater 57°38'·1N 18°16'·4E
 Iso.WRG.4s11m12–8M 007°-R-044°-G-055°-W-087°-R-209°-G-239°-W-245°-R-296° White tower, red band 8m Floodlit

Harbour communications
VTS Oxelösund ☎ +46 855 42 45 50, VHF Ch 09
Visby pilots ☎ +46 498 21 01 38
Visby Guest Harbour ☎ +46 498 21 51 90
 Mobile +46 736 00 63 00
 VTS & pilots VHF Ch 09 (0600–2200 LT)
 info@visbygasthamn.se
 www.visbygasthamn.se

As will be seen from the distances above, getting to Visby from the mainland involves quite a lengthy journey. An alternative would be to stop for the night at a small harbour at the northern tip of Öland – Byxelkrok. From here to Visby is a distance of around 40 miles.

The approaches to Byxelkrok are quite straightforward, and there are moorings alongside on the central jetty or on the inside of the breakwater. The harbour is a little exposed to the southwest.

Visby (pronounced *Vees-bu*) is the only town of any size on Gotland, and is a pleasant mixture of old and new. Its position led to it becoming one of the most important trading centres of Europe in the 10th and 11th centuries, and later a principal depot of the Hanseatic League. This strategic position and wealth led to conflict, and the island of Gotland changed hands many times between the Swedes, the Danes and lastly the Russians, most recently in 1808. Visby's 13th-century towers and walls are a striking sight from the sea, and they and the ten early mediaeval churches stand witness to the city's former importance. A 'mediaeval week' is held in early August, particularly impressive on the Sundays at either end when many local people wear period costume. There is also an excellent museum. The island's website will be found at www.gotland.se.

Visby's harbour is deservedly popular with both yachtsmen and tourists. It can become very crowded and noisy on warm summer nights – particularly during the various festivals – with sidewalk cafés, a quayside amusement park and other yachts hosting cockpit parties late into the night. Gotland is claimed to have the best summer climate in Sweden, with only half the average rainfall of the mainland, but the south and west coasts may be subject to fog.

Approach and entrance
Both the water tower and the cathedral are conspicuous from offshore, as is the 343m Follingbo aero mast 4M southeast of the harbour. The entrance can be identified by the prominent oil tanks at its southern end, and often by the ferries berthed alongside. The outer harbour is large, with plenty of room to lower and stow sails once inside. After dark, approach using the sectored light on the end of the south breakwater, transferring to the two occulting red leading lights on 055° for final entry. The main north/south shipping lane runs some 4M offshore past Visby, carrying moderate to heavy traffic. A new pier and terminal for cruise liners was under construction outside the harbour in 2017.

Berthing
Visiting yachts normally use the 200 berth marina in the extreme northeast of the harbour, where mooring is bows to a pontoon and stern to a buoy in depths of 3–6m, but it is crowded in the season. Local yachts have their own basin behind the ferry berth opposite the harbour mouth, but sometimes the harbourmaster will allow its use. When full, yachts have berthed against the northwest sea wall in the Imre Hamn but the walk to the harbourmaster's office and showers becomes a trek. In strong southwest-west winds the fishing harbour offers better shelter from the swell. All are administered from an office overlooking the northeast basin, open 0900–2100 in season. There are no suitable anchorages near Visby.

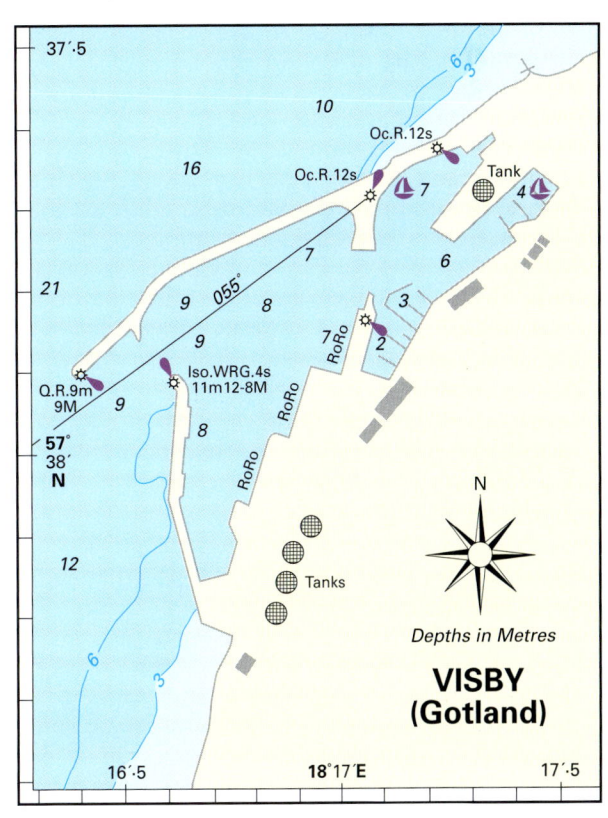

THE BALTIC SEA AND APPROACHES 193

EAST COAST OF SWEDEN

The guest harbour at Visby C.N. Hill

Services for yachts
The usual services and shops are available, including WiFi. Toilets and showers, crowded at times, plus a launderette, are near the marina office. Fuel (diesel and petrol with cash or credit card) is beside the large slipway at the north end of the northwest basin. The chandlery, Ljungs Skeppshandel, www.boatfittings.com, is conveniently near the harbour. Bottled gas and Swedish charts are available in addition to equipment. There are some excellent restaurants and a Systembolaget in town.

Communications and travel
Cars and bicycles for hire. Frequent air and ferry connections with the mainland (the latter to/from Oskarshamn and Nynäshamn), and buses to all parts of Gotland.

Other harbours on Gotland
The northern tip of Gotland is a useful jumping off point for either the Stockholm archipelago or for Latvia in the Baltic states. There are three harbours within easy sailing distance of Visby. From these, it is around 60 to 70 miles to Nynashamn at the southernmost part of the Stockholm archipelago. The harbours are Lickershamn, Kappelshamn and Lauterhorn on the island of Fårö, just to the north-east of Gotland. Of these, Lauterhorn is probably the most scenic. It lies in a bay which provides shelter from all directions, and in suitable weather conditions would make a good anchorage.

The passage between Fårö and Gotland is known as the Fårösund, and there are at least three harbours or marinas at the town of Fårösund. From here, it is 80 to 90 miles to Ventspils or Pavilosta in Latvia.

The small but well sheltered harbour at Lauterhorn on the island of Fårö C.N. Hill

Blå Kusten (The Blue Coast)
The Blå Kusten is an extremely attractive area, characterised by thousands of small islands, many with interesting harbours or anchorages which stretches some 60M from Oskarshamn in the south to Arkösund in the north. Whilst providing the main coastal conduit from the southern Baltic to the northern cruising grounds, it also constitutes an attractive sailing area in its own right where one may linger in perfect shelter amongst the hundreds of wild islands, or venture up long leads to the several large and sophisticated towns.

Approaching the *skärgård* from the south through the wide and well marked Kalmarsund, considerable mental adjustment is required before one gains confidence when sailing fast in flat water only yards from rocks, winding down leads which appear to be dead ends, and keeping check of one's position where the marks are unnamed. But these are the joys and skills of *skärgård* sailing, which can be safe and relaxing provided one obeys the rules. These are few and simple but absolutely vital – to have a detailed chart, to stay in the marked channels, and ALWAYS to know where you are. As so often, the key to safety and enjoyment lies in planning ahead. Decide where you are going and where you plan to stop. To explore the many delightful anchorages a copy of the Swedish book Naturhamnar på Ostkusten is invaluable and is available from the Svenska Kryssarklubben (Swedish Cruising Club or SXK) – see page 224).

The Blue Coast is an important area for nesting birds, and many sites are out of bounds during the breeding season. These are marked both on the Swedish large-scale charts and on the water, where floating signs give the dates of prohibition. These vary between February to August, and must be respected.

From the south, one enters the *skärgård* at Krakesund (see plan page 186). There are sheltered passages or leads running north from here for almost 60 miles. These have the advantage that they provide flat water no matter what wind is blowing. There are innumerable anchorages in sheltered bays. Fjords lead up to the towns of Blankaholm, Västervik and Loftahammar. At the northern end is the entrance to the Göta Kanal at Mem (see page 175).

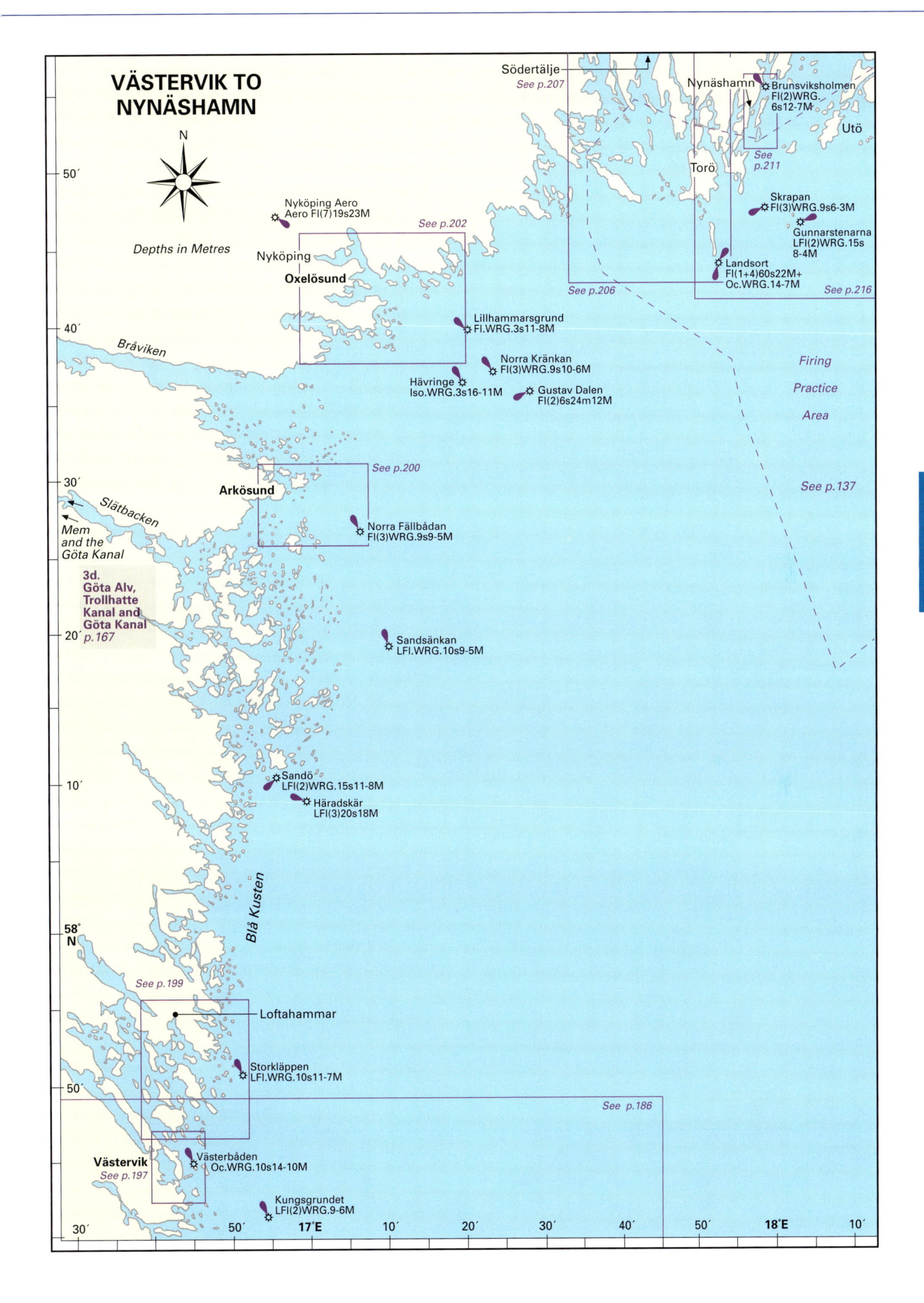

3F. UTLANGAN TO LANDSORT INCLUDING ÖLAND AND GOTLAND

VÄSTERVIK TO NYNÄSHAMN

Depths in Metres

Nyköping Aero Aero Fl(7)19s23M
Nyköping
Oxelösund
See p.202
Bråviken
Lillhammarsgrund Fl.WRG.3s11-8M
Norra Kränkan Fl(3)WRG.9s10-6M
Hävringe Iso.WRG.3s16-11M
Gustav Dalen Fl(2)6s24m12M

Södertälje
See p.207
Nynäshamn
Brunsviksholmen Fl(2)WRG.6s12-7M
Utö
Torö
See p.211
Skrapan Fl(3)WRG.9s6-3M
Gunnarstenarna LFl(2)WRG.15s 8-4M
Landsort Fl(1+4)60s22M+ Oc.WRG.14-7M
See p.206
See p.216

Firing Practice Area

See p.137

Slätbacken
Mem and the Göta Kanal

3d. Göta Alv, Trollhatte Kanal and Göta Kanal p.167

Arkösund
See p.200
Norra Fällbådan Fl(3)WRG.9s9-5M

Sandsänkan LFl.WRG.10s9-5M

Sandö LFl(2)WRG.15s11-8M
Häradskär LFl(3)20s18M

Blå Kusten

58° N

See p.199
Loftahammar
Storkläppen LFl.WRG.10s11-7M

See p.186

Västervik
See p.197
Västerbåden Oc.WRG.10s14-10M
Kungsgrundet LFl(2)WRG.9-6M

17°E   18°E

3. SWEDEN

THE BALTIC SEA AND APPROACHES   195

EAST COAST OF SWEDEN

Västervik

57°45′N 16°39′E

Distances
Kalmar 65M, Visby 55M, Oskarsham 33M, Mem 50M, Arkösund 55M, Södertälje 95M, Nynäshamn 85M

Charts and guides
Swedish 6, 72, 623, 6231 *Båtsportkort C: Ostkusten–Kalmarsund*
UKHO 2816, 2055, 2848

Lights
Västerviks angöring 57°44′·8N 16°55′·3E Q.Fl
  North cardinal pillar buoy, ↟ topmark
Kungsgrundet 57°41′·1N 16°54′·2E LFl(2)WRG.27m9–6M
  005°-R-048°-G-088·5°-R-122°-G-193°-W-005° Racon
  Black tower, red band, white lantern. Helipad
Västerbåden 57°44′·8N 16°44′·5E Oc.WRG.10s14m14–10M
  112°-G-133·5°-R-258·5°-G-268°-W-269·5°- R-309°-G-321°-R-011°-G-040° Racon Red tower, black base 15m
  Floodlit
Idö Stångskär 57°40′·3N 16°47′·1E Q.WRG.13m8–5M
  145°-G-150°-W-152°-R-302°-G-321°-W-324°-R-338°
  White lantern, red base
Stickskär Ldg Lts 236° 57°43′·3N 16°45′·3E
  Front Fl.WRG.1·5s10m7–3M White tower
  Rear Spårö 1M from front Iso.6s36m14M
  White tower 8m

Communications
Västervik Commercial Harbour ☏ +46 490 16920/10690
  VHF Ch 12, 16
Notholmen Yacht Harbour ☏ +46 490 12385 (0800–1200 and 1500–2000 LT)
Västerviks Gästhamn ☏ +46 490 36900,
  Mobile +46 70 459 3919 (0800–2000 LT)
Västerviks Marina ☏ +46 490 69800,
  Mobile +46 70 715 3200 (0800–1900 LT)

Västervik is a small industrial town with a modern harbour for small ships, many of them carrying timber. It is pleasant but unpretentious, with an attractive waterfront, some interesting old buildings and considerable charm. It has good shopping, including several large supermarkets and an open market, and a choice of three yacht harbours with several more in the approach. An outdoor song festival is held every July in the remains of Stegeholm Castle.

Västervik is an excellent base from which to explore the famous Blå Kustens archipelago to the south.

Approach and entrance

The approach to Västervik involves the negotiation of intricate, rock-fringed channels and a large-scale chart is essential. From seaward there are two main approaches, both well marked on the chart:

a. From the east, pass close to Västerviks angöring North cardinal buoy, which lies some 4M north of Kungsgrundet light, and head west towards Västerbåden light. Turn south-southwest and follow the buoyed and lit channel, turning west across Lusärnafjärden entrance.

b. From the southeast head towards Ido Stängskär light on a bearing of 323° and pass close northeast of it. Head for the beacon on Spårö Island, and pass north through the Spårösund, to join the approach (a). Turn west and cross the broad entry to Lusärnafjärden, to reach the port of Västervik.

There are no restrictions on anchoring in the area. It is also possible to continue through the lifting bridge to the Gamlebyviken.

Berthing

There are two yacht harbours on Lusärnafjärden both in quiet surroundings but at some distance from the town.

Solberg Udde

☏ +46 490 16291 Mobile +46 731 61 06 00

This is tucked behind a group of small islands on the south side close to the entrance. Around 20 of its berths are available for visitors, in depths of 2–5m, with a maximum beam of 3·5m and weight of 10 tonnes. The facilities are those of the nearby camping ground, restaurant and boatyard.

Gränsö Slott

☏ +46 490 37080 Mobile +46 706 99 25 15

This is just north of Ekholmen Island, near the entrance to the Gränsö canal. It is run by the hotel and has 30 visitors berths in 1·5–2·3m, and has good basic services, plus use of the swimming pool and WiFi. It is a pleasant stop

There are three yacht harbours near the town itself, which are reached by passing through the (very well marked) narrows close north of Lusärna island and across the Skeppsbrofjärden. Mooring in all three is bows-to, with stern to a buoy.

The narrow Sparösund which separates the islands of Grönö and Sparö on the southern approach to Västervik *C.N. Hill*

THE BALTIC SEA AND APPROACHES

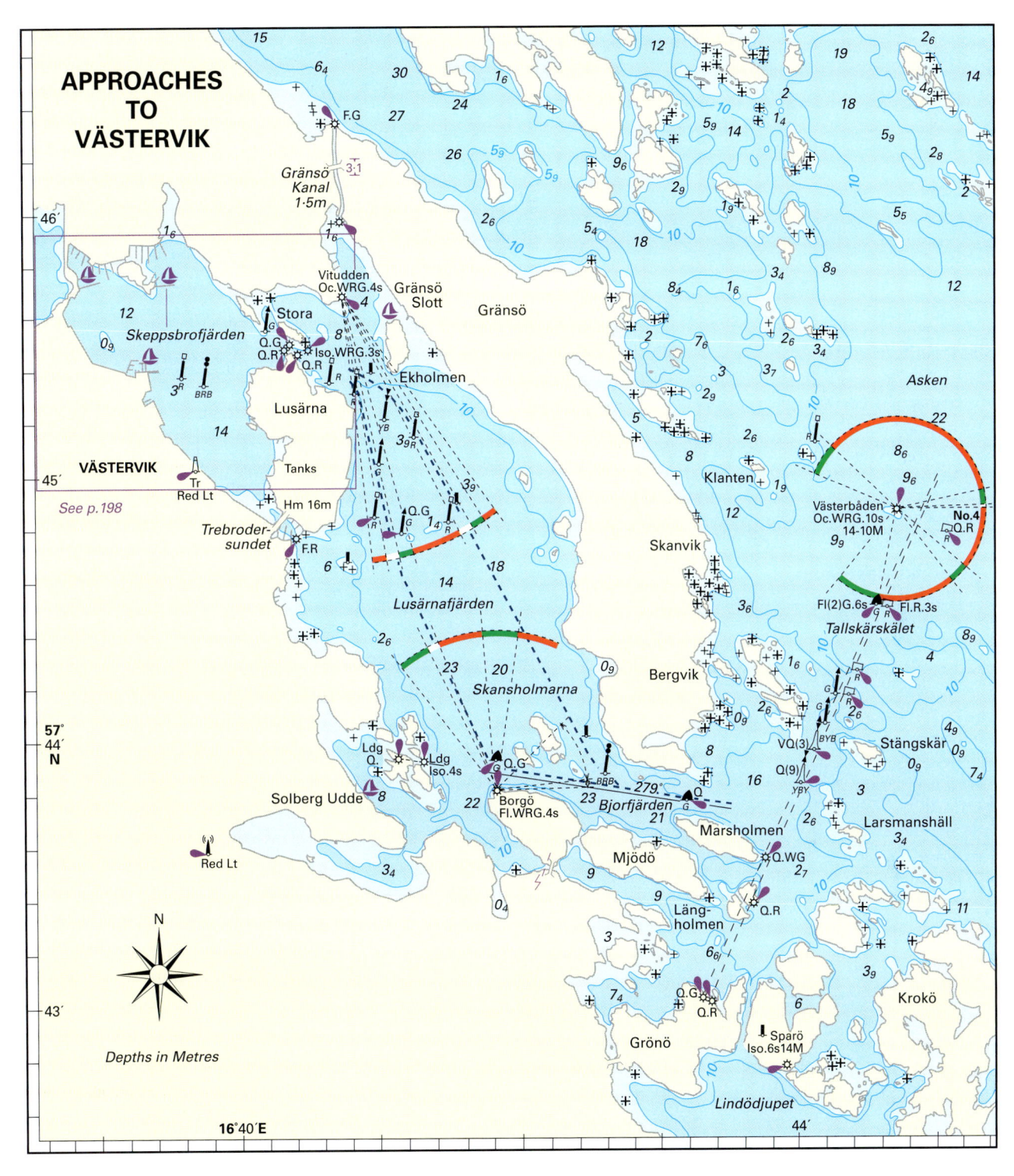

3F. UTLANGAN TO LANDSORT INCLUDING ÖLAND AND GOTLAND

These posts mark the narrow but well marked passage between the Lusärnafjärden and Skeppsbrofjärden on the final approach to Västervik *C.N. Hill*

THE BALTIC SEA AND APPROACHES   **197**

EAST COAST OF SWEDEN

Vastervik waterfront *C.N. Hill*

Västerviks Marina

This is on the south side of the harbour, has berthing for about 40 boats with the usual services and is more of a 'working' marina than those to the north, with a chandlery and boatyard ashore and a good electronics dealer nearby. The surroundings are industrial, and it is about 10 minutes walk from the town centre. It is possible to lie alongside (for free) whilst visiting the chandlery.

Västerviks Gästhamn

☏ +46 490 36900 *Mobile* +46 708 98 57 37
info@westervikwaterfront.se
www.westervikwaterfront.se

Sometimes known as the Blå Kustens marina, it is in the northwest corner of Skeppsbrofjärden and fills the space between the isthmus leading to the town and Notholmen peninsula. To add to the confusion, it is the one listed as 'Västervik Marina' in the *Gästhamnsguiden* free national guide! There is berthing for over 300 yachts, good shelter from all but strong south winds and a full range of facilities including swimming pool and chandlery Reception is at the fuel berth, open 0800–1900 daily. Boats over 12m are requested to telephone in advance of arrival.

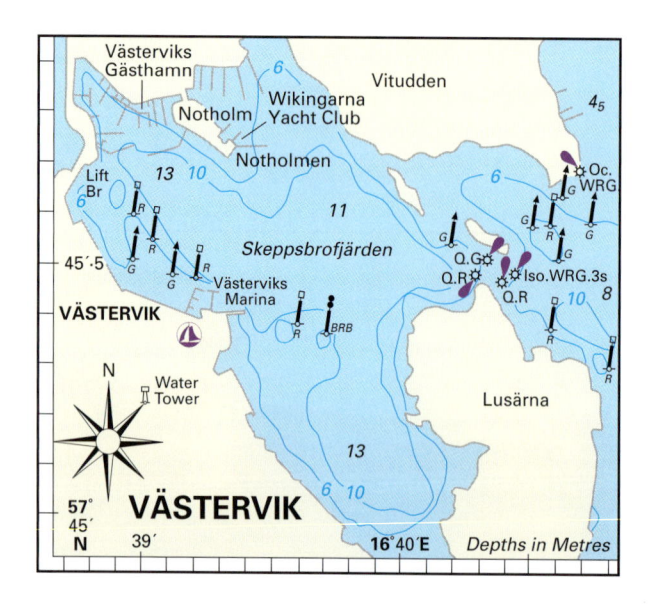

Westerviks Segelsällskap Wikingarna Yacht Club

☏ +46 490 12385
sekreterare@wikingarna.com
www.wikingarna.com

They are on the east side of the tip of the peninsula of Notholmen, east of Västerviks Gästhamn. Do not confuse with a small boat marina to its north which does not take visitors. This friendly club has three pontoons, and keeps a few guest moorings on pontoons; much quieter than the town *gästhamn* and there is more chance of finding a berth. It is worth telephoning in advance of arrival to ensure a berth is available.

General facilities

Västervik has all the facilities of a larger town, including good shopping, several large supermarkets, a wide variety of snack bars, restaurants and hotels, and an outdoor market in the square on Saturday mornings. For a short stay and quick shop, berth alongside the northwest end of the commercial quay in northwest corner of harbour. This is handy for the shops. The town centre is within walking distance of all three marinas, the path from the northern pair being across an attractive causeway complete with lifting bridge, next to which is the tourist office. Taxis are readily available if returning laden with shopping. Rail and coach services provide access to the rest of the country.

198   THE BALTIC SEA AND APPROACHES

3F. UTLANGAN TO LANDSORT INCLUDING ÖLAND AND GOTLAND

Loftahammar

57°54'·1N 16°41'·9E

Distances
Västervik 16M, Arkösund 43M

Charts and guides
Swedish 623 NW & NE

Communications
Värd ☎ +46 493 613 15 or +46 70 530 8912

The small passage harbour of Fyrudden *C.N. Hill*

A large landlocked basin at the head of a long fjord; worth a visit being tranquil and picturesque.

There are narrow, twisting and shallow routes from the west and east in addition to the main approach from the southeast.

The basin is approached by a very narrow buoyed channel 3m deep. As you come out of this channel, the marina can be seen to starboard. It has 50 guest berths with all facilities which are on a jetty marked with the guest harbour sign. The surroundings are very scenic, and there is a useful tourist bureau in the town near the church. There is also quite a well-stocked supermarket.

Fyrudden

Harbourmaster ☎ +46123 40160

This small passage harbour is located north from Loftahammar, and is a convenient stop for fuel, provisions and water. Mooring is either alongside or from a stern buoy.

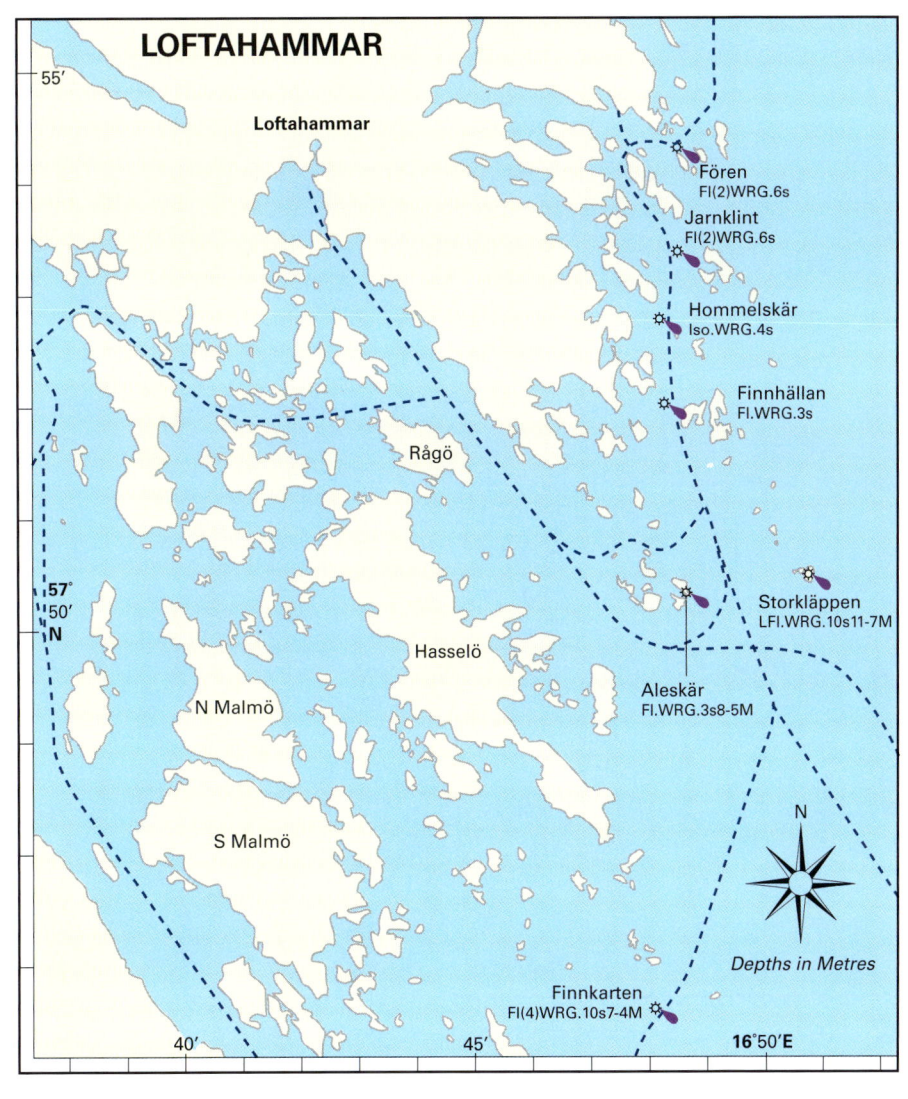

THE BALTIC SEA AND APPROACHES 199

EAST COAST OF SWEDEN

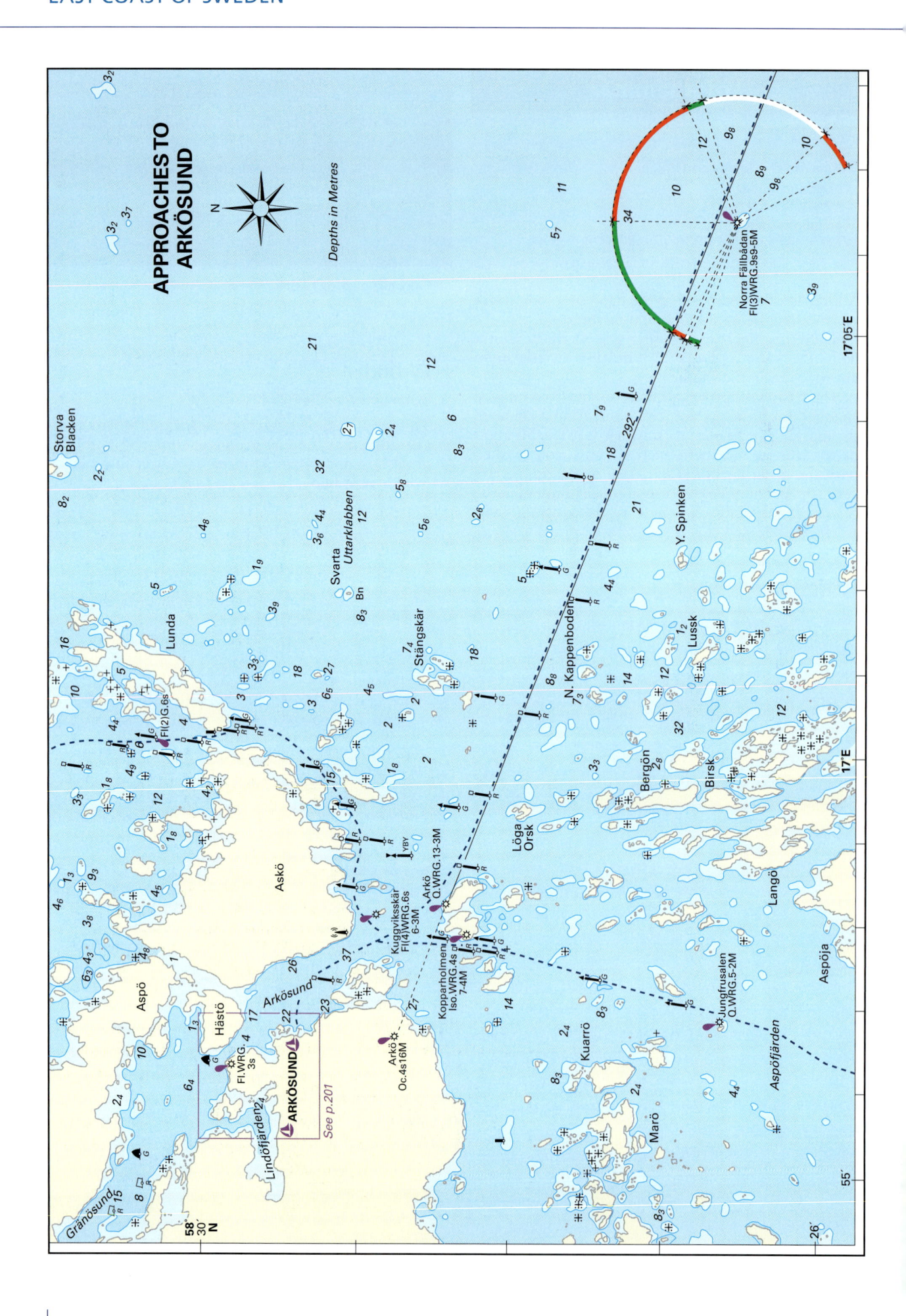

APPROACHES TO ARKÖSUND

3F. UTLANGAN TO LANDSORT INCLUDING ÖLAND AND GOTLAND

Arkösund

58°29'N 16°56'E

Distances
Visby 65M, Västervik 55M, Mem 20M,
Södertälje 60M, Nynäshamn 50M

Charts and guides
Swedish 72, 621 *Båtsportkort C: Ostkusten*
UKHO 2055, 2362, 3217

Lights
Norra Fällbåden 58°26'·5N 17°06'·2E
  Fl(3)WRG.9s16m9–5M
  108·5°-G-114·5°-W-116°-R-122°-G(unintens)-180°-
  R(unintens)-240°-R-245°-G-253°-W-315°-R-333·5° Black
  concrete tower, white top, yellow band, grey base 17m
  Wind generator
Arkö, Östra Kopparholm Ldg Lts 292° *Front* 58°28'·4N
  16°58'·4E Q.WRG.8m13–3M
  119°-G-149°-W-156·5°-R-188°-R(unintens)228·5° White
  intens on leading line. White lantern, red rectangle,
  white stripe
Kälebo *Rear* 0·9M from front Iso.4s27m14M
  White lantern, red column, white stripe
Kuggviksskär 58°28'·8N 16°58'·2E Fl(4)WRG.6s13m6–3M
  307·5°-R-331°-G-009·5°-W-019°-R-051°-G-058·5°-R-090°-
  G-129°-W-139°-R-253° White tower 12m

Communications
Norrköpings Segelsällskap ① +46 125 20555
Arkösund Quay ① +46 125 20036
**Badholmarna, Bäckmansviken and Nordanskog Yacht
  Harbours** ① +46 125 20684
  Mobile ① +46 706 86 74 50

In addition to being a popular yachting centre in an attractive rural setting, Arkösund is less than 20M from Mem, the eastern gateway to the Göta Kanal.

If heading up the long, narrow Slätbaken fjord which leads to Mem, allow time to combat the strong east-going currents which are sometimes encountered in the narrows at Ettersundet and Stegeborg.

Approach and entrance

From the open sea, pass close north of Norra Fällbåden lighthouse to enter the Arkö approach channel, marked at intervals with spar buoys on either side, on a course of 292°. The channel is also indicated by the Arkö leading marks, but these are not easily visible. However, the buoyage is clear in daylight, and once the Arkö light is reached the entrance becomes obvious.

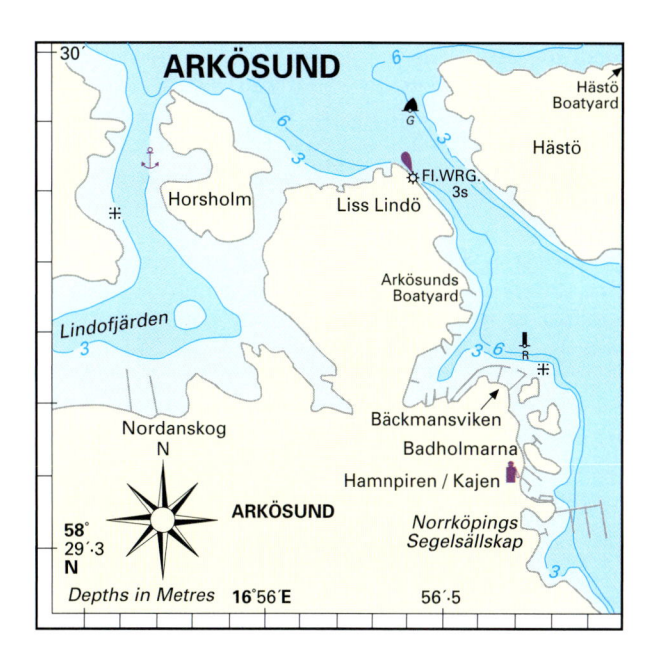

Entry is not recommended by night or in poor visibility. It is also possible to approach from the north, via one of several buoyed channels.

Berthing

There have been major changes to the berthing arrangements in Arkösund. The Badholmarna Marina is now entirely private. Instead, the facilities around the old quay have been extended. Three new jetties have been built out from the quay, with lazy line mooring, and the new arrangement should be able to accommodate a considerable number of visitors. The major drawback is that these are very exposed to the south east, and the outer berths would be very uncomfortable in a wind strength of more than around Force 5. If possible, try to find a lee berth.

Northwest of the three small, low islands lies Bäckmansviken guest harbour – effectively four pontoons set in a rough square, with a single narrow entrance and some 20 berths inside in depths of 1·5–3m. It is unsuitable for vessels of more than about 11m (unless exceptionally manoeuvrable), but larger yachts may find a bows-to berth on the pontoon just beyond. Shore facilities are shared with Kajen and

*The new jetties at Arkösund. Mooring is by lazy line.
However, this is very uncomfortable in strong southwesterly winds* C.N. Hill

THE BALTIC SEA AND APPROACHES 201

EAST COAST OF SWEDEN

Badholmarna. The red pillar buoy just off the guest harbour marks a rocky shoal and should be left to port on entry. Through the narrows between Liss Lindö and Hästö, and past the small island of Horshol, a channel to the southwest gives onto Lindöfjärden and the two long pontoons of Nordanskog yacht harbour. The 20 or so visitors' berths are at the outer ends of both pontoons in 2·5–3m, bows-to with the stern to a buoy. There is neither water nor electricity on the pontoons, though there are taps near their roots. Toilets and showers will be found at the nearby campsite Arkö Camp Strandgrillen where berthing fees are paid (open 0900–2100) and there is also a restaurant and small shop.

There are no restrictions on anchoring in this area. One recommended spot is west of Horsholm island.

Services

There is a fuel berth near the root of the old quay amongst the Hamnpiren/Kajen berths, the kiosk also contains a small shop. There are two boatyards in the area, the Arkösunds Båtvarv at Rökholmen on the Liss Lindö peninsula, and Hästö Båtvarv on the northern side of Hästö island. Arkösunds Båtvarv, ☏ +46 125 20053, open 0800–1630 weekdays only, can be reached on foot and has a 5·5 tonne crane and a small engineering workshop. Hästö Båtvarv, ☏ +46 125 20073, is larger if less accessible, though several buoys are available for visitors. It has an 8-tonne crane, open air and undercover storage, a diving service, large engineering workshop and GRP repair facilities.

General facilities

Arkösund is a very popular tourist spot, with several cafés and restaurants and at least one large hotel. The tourist office (open 1000–1200 and 1400–2000) is within the hotel grounds. A supermarket is situated near the root of the Bäckmansviken pontoon, but there is no bank or Post Office. There is a regular bus service to Norrköping, connecting with the railway system and convenient if changing crews.

The Göta Kanal

The eastern entrance to the Göta Kanal is at Mem (see page 175) which is reached through the Slätbacken. Allow a mimimum of 4hrs for the attractive but tricky 21M from Arkösund to Mem if having to meet a particular lock opening time.

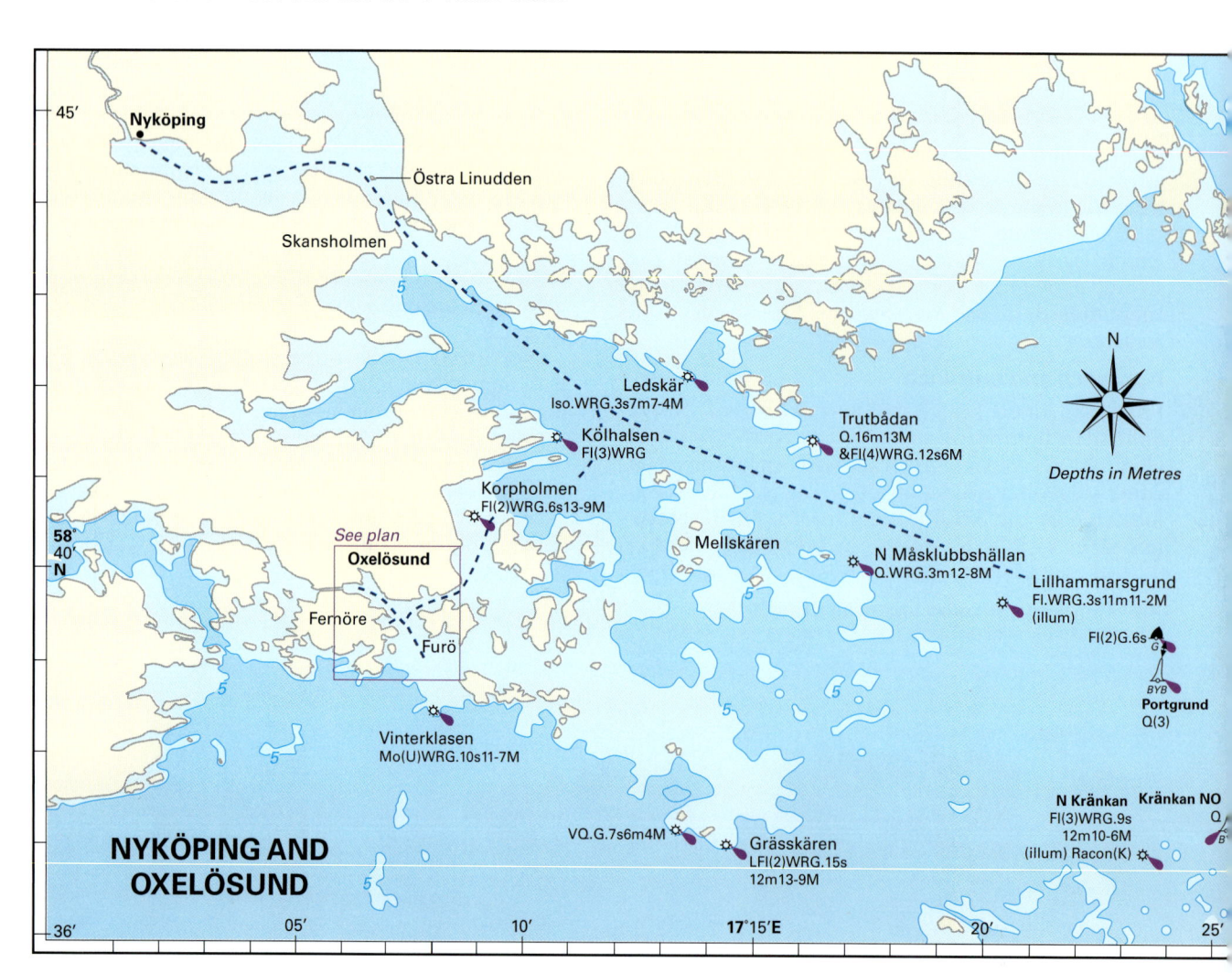

202 THE BALTIC SEA AND APPROACHES

3F. UTLANGAN TO LANDSORT INCLUDING ÖLAND AND GOTLAND

Oxelösund

58°39'·3N 17°06'·1E

Distances
Arkö Sund 14M, Nyköping 10M

Charts and guides
Swedish 16211 SW

A large town with a conspicuous ironworks on the east. Not the most attractive place but good for crew changes, stores and repairs.

Gamla Oxelösund is an island museum of restored buildings and there are well displayed remains of Cold War defences to the south of the entrance.

Approach and berthing

The prominent chimneys of the ironworks make a useful landmark, the entrance is very well buoyed and easy to follow to the two *gästhamns*.

First and to the south is the Fiskehamnen with 25 visitors' berths. Larger yachts will find greater depths of 2·5m to 4·5m here. Oxelösunds Båtvarv at the head of the Fiskehamnen offers all kinds of repair and has laying up facilities.

Half a mile to the north and closest to the town is the well laid out Badhusviken marina. This has been extended with three new large jetties, with mooring using stern buoys. However, this is very open to strong winds from the south-east, and the jetties offer little protection. If you can, find a berth on the jetty just inside the old harbour breakwater.

There is a good chandlery at the offices and both *gästhamns* have a full range of services.

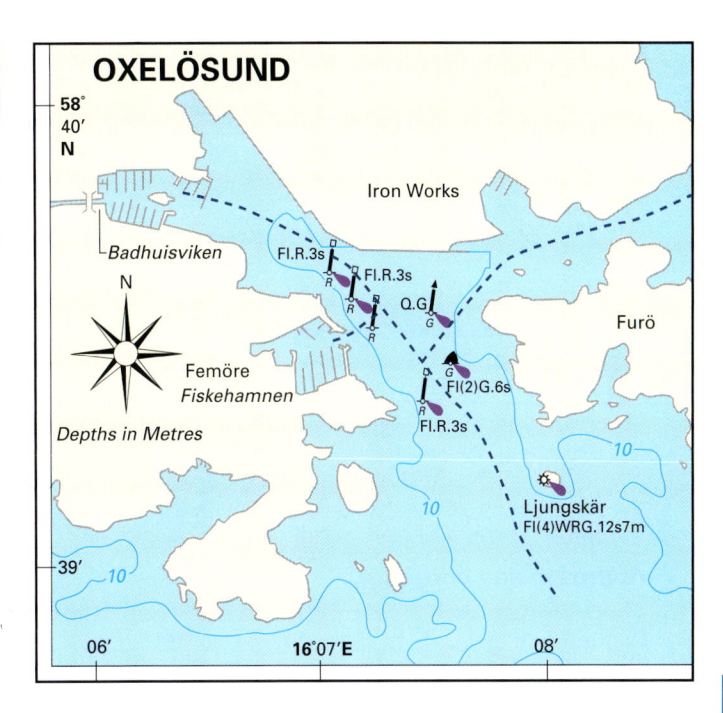

General facilities

Both marinas have their own restaurants and there is a tourist information office and excellent children's playground at Badhusviken. The shopping precinct has good shops, a very good supermarket and Systembolaget. A free 'Tuf-Tuf' train takes you the 1km up the hill to the town centre and back every half hour otherwise bicycles are an advantage. There is a very modern church on the hill in town.

It is less than half an hour by taxi to the airport at Skavsta.

New jetties at Oxelösund. These are open to the south and southeast, and uncomfortable in strong winds. The jetties do not provide much of a wave break *C.N. Hill*

EAST COAST OF SWEDEN

Nyköping

Distances
Oxelösund 10M, Landsort 30M

Harbour communications
Värd ☎ +46 155 21 72 30

An attractive small commercial and yachting harbour with the town marina on the west of the entrance and the large *gästhamn* and boat yard on the east.

The town itself is divided by a river and has a mediaeval castle. Although it is some distance from the harbour, it is an attractive town with a good shopping centre, and well worth visiting.

Approach and berthing.

There is a well marked approach from the Lillhammarsgrund light (58°39'·7N 17°20'·3E) approx 4M off shore. This shoals to a 4m dredged channel at the Skansholmen Narrows, turns west at the Östra Linudden marker where it bears to port again and is too restricted to sail unless you are lucky enough to have a favourable wind. The *gästhamn* provides 110 berths with the wider ones being first to starboard as you enter. The inside berths have a max width of 3·8m. Larger vessels can also tie up on the outside of the outside pontoons but passing high speed motor boats can create a tiresome wash. All the usual services are available and WiFi at some berths. The very capable boat yard and a chandlery are a little further east.

General

There is a substantial supermarket situated conveniently opposite the Systembolaget, and several good restaurants in the middle of the town. The *gästhamn* is only fifteen minutes by taxi from Skavsta airport which provides regular cheap flights to Stansted via Ryanair. Although a good place for crew changes or leaving one's boat it is further from the sea than Oxelösund.

3g. Stockholm - the archipelago and surrounding area

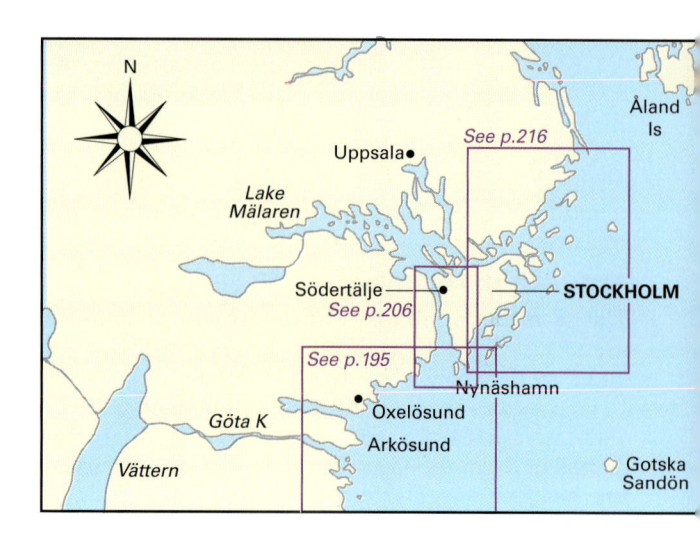

Stockholm itself is hidden deep in the rock strewn archipelago. The usual approach is from the south; the northern approach will be discussed later.

It is possible to sail from the northern tip of Gotland, but this may be a fairly lengthy passage of 60 miles or more. It is more likely that boats will be travelling from the neighbourhood of Arkosund or Oxelsund.

There are two possible routes from the south into Stockholm and its archipelago

a. Sail inside Landsort, through the Södertälje canal, into Lake Mälaren and then to central Stockholm. This route has the advantage that it is relatively sheltered and quite scenic.

b. Pass east of Landsort, in which case the first obvious port of call is Nynäshamn. From Nynäshamn there are a variety of routes around the archipelago and into central Stockholm.

204 THE BALTIC SEA AND APPROACHES

3G. STOCKHOLM - THE ARCHIPELAGO AND SURROUNDING AREA

Södertälje and the Södertälje Kanal

59°12′N 17°38′E

Distances
Västervik 95M, Arkösund 60M, Nynäshamn 40M, Lake Mälaren (from Mälarbron bridge) 5M

Charts and guides
UKHO 864, 2055, 3170, 3168
Swedish 11, 6172, 6181
Swedish *Båtsportkort:* Mälaren

Lights
Landsorts Bredgrund 58°43′·9N 17°51′·9E
 Iso.WRG.4s18m16–8M
 001°-R-013°-G-047·5°-W-053°-R-086°-G-127°-R-159°-G-177°-R-210°-G-217°-W-219°-R-224°-G-234°-R-273°-G-321·5°-R-345°-G-356·5°-W-001° Racon. Orange tower. Floodlit
Landsort, south point 58°44′·4N 17°52′·1E
 Fl(1+4)60s45m22M+Oc.WRG.27m14–7M
 323·5°-G-351°-W-358°-R-023° White tower, red top 25m
Asenskallen 58°47′N 17°42′·1E
 Fl.WRG.3s12m8–5M
 091°-G-106°-W-110°-R-238°-G-259°-W-267°-R-277°-G-294°-R-300° White tower, green band 9m
Granklubben 58°47′·9N 17°44′·9E Fl(4)WRG.12s13m13-9M
 225°-G-298°-R-312·5°-G-317·5°-W-320°-R-329·5°-G-011°-W-054°-R-075° White lantern

Harbour communications
Södertälje Kanal ℡ +46 8 554 22720/22730/1/2
 Traffic Information Centre VHF Ch 68
 Smallcraft VHF Ch 14
Södertälje Commercial Harbour ℡ +46 8 550 23740/23750
 VHF Ch 11, 14, 16
Södertälje Guest Harbour ℡ +46 8 550 64712
 Mobile 070 310 6449
 info@sghc.net, www.sghc.net
Järnvägs and Motorvägsbroarna bridges VHF Ch 16, 68
Slussbron lock and bridge VHF Ch 14, 16, 68
Mälarbron bridge VHF Ch 14, 16, 68
 www.sjofartsverket.se/en/Recreational-Boating/Sodertalje-Canal/Opening-Hours-for-the-Sodertalje-Lock-and-Bridge-Malarbron/

Södertälje (pronounced *Seu-dehr-tehl-je*) is a commercial port and town of about 25,000 inhabitants. A surprising tonnage of commercial traffic still uses the Södertälje Kanal each year but it is also very convenient as a route into Stockholm.

If heading northwards from the Nyköping area, the *skärgård* is entered at the Landsort light, where a lumpy sea can build in northerly winds. In such conditions, the well sheltered and interesting approach to Stockholm offered by the Södertälje Kanal may prove a real boon. The canal then takes you into Lake Mälaren.

However, depending on where you have come from, it is a fair way to get to Landsort, and Södertälje is a further 35 miles from there. The harbour at Trosa is a good place at which to break the journey.

Trosa

58°54′·4N 17°33′·1E

Distances
Oxelsund 45M, Södertälje 25M

Harbour communications
Harbour office ℡ +46(0)156-161 11
 (*Note* berths cannot be reserved)

Trosa is an attractive old town with an interesting history.

The *gästhamn* is on the east side with 140 bows to or alongside berths in 2–3m (watch out for depths due to silting). There are also a limited number of berths up the canal towards the town.

Full services, including a Watski's chandlery, are available and town facilities are within 500m. A good anchorage may be found in Lagnnöviken bay to the south west of the entrance channel.

Approach and entrance to Södertälje

The entrance to the channel up to Södertälje begins at Landsort, and the first few miles are rather intricate and rock strewn. It leads into the Himmerfjärden, a long and relatively straight fjord which trends northnorthwest for more than 30M before it reaches Lake Mälaren at Viksberg. Over its length the fjord changes its name several times before reaching Södertälje's two sections of canal, the Södra Kanalen and Norra Kanalen, separated by a single lock.

Södertälje lock as seen from the south *C.N. Hill*

EAST COAST OF SWEDEN

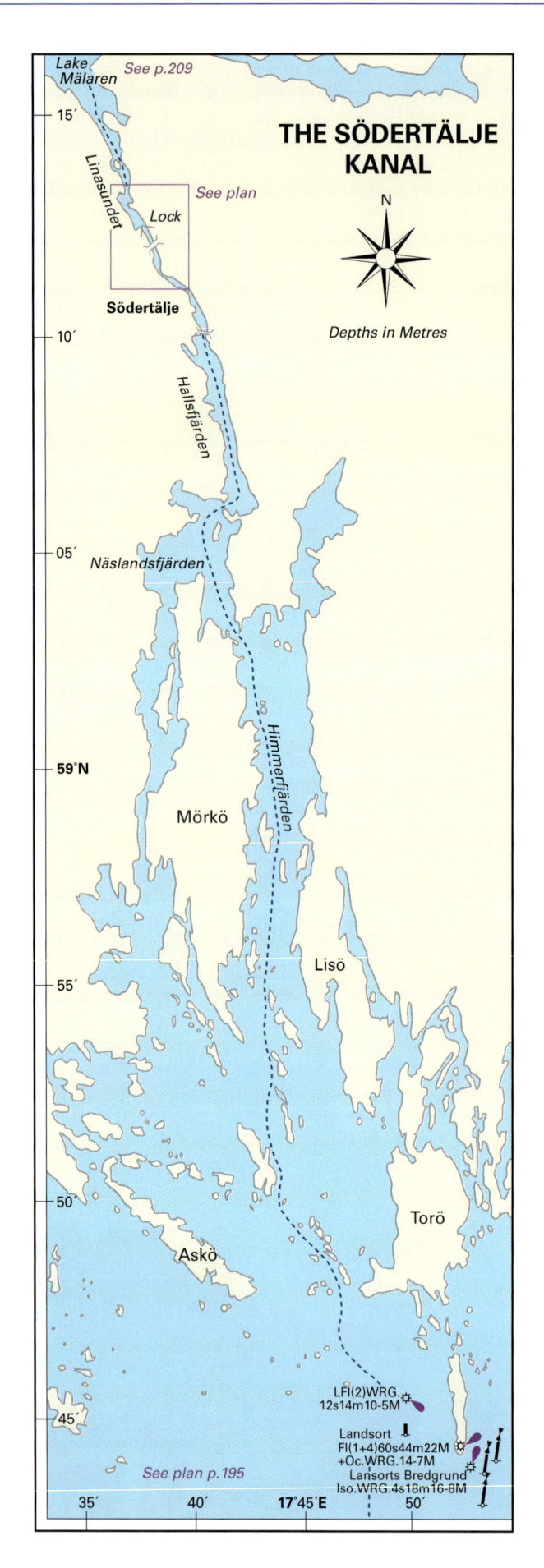

The Mälarbron bridge. Unfortunately, opening times do not always coincide with the openings of the lock C.N. Hill

Approaching from the south, as the waterway narrows, vessels pass under a railway bridge (40m clearance), before reaching the canal proper. Some 0·3M into the canal's narrow section lies a second railway bridge, with a motorway bridge just beyond (the Järnvägs and Motorvägsbroarna bridges, both clearance 25·9m), which open simultaneously. A request for opening, if required, should be made to Södertäjle VTS ☏ +46 8554 24500 or VHF Ch 68, who will advise times.

The guest harbour, lock and associated road bridge lie about 0·5M further on. The lock, which has a rise of less than 1m, accommodates vessels of up to 120m and 5·5m draught. It operates 0815–2115, opening southbound at 15 minutes past the hour and northbound immediately following the southbound lock, and is crossed by a low bridge which opens in conjunction with the lock gates. Payment has to be made by card if southbound but not if northbound; you pay to get out of the lake but not to go in.

A third road bridge, the Mälarbron bridge, is encountered some 0·4M beyond the lock, close to the northern end of the canal. This bridge (clearance 13·8m) opens at approximately 2hr intervals 0900–2100 weekdays and hourly 0800–2100 weekends.

It is advisable to check the opening times of the lock and the bridge if you are heading north, otherwise you might find you have to wait up to 90 minutes in a half mile length of canal with nowhere to tie up. It is possible to contact the lock and bridge on VHF Ch 14 to request an opening of the bridge soon after the lock. More details as to opening times etc can be found at www.sjofartsverket.se

From the Malarbron bridge it is only a few miles further into Lake Mälaren (see page 209) which is an extensive cruising area in itself. The passage from Lake Mälaren to central Stockholm is quite straightforward.

Regulations

Sailing in the canal is forbidden between the south end of the Södra Kanalen and Linasundet to the north, and commercial shipping takes precedence over leisure craft at all times. It is recommended, but not mandatory, that small craft monitor VHF Ch 16

THE BALTIC SEA AND APPROACHES

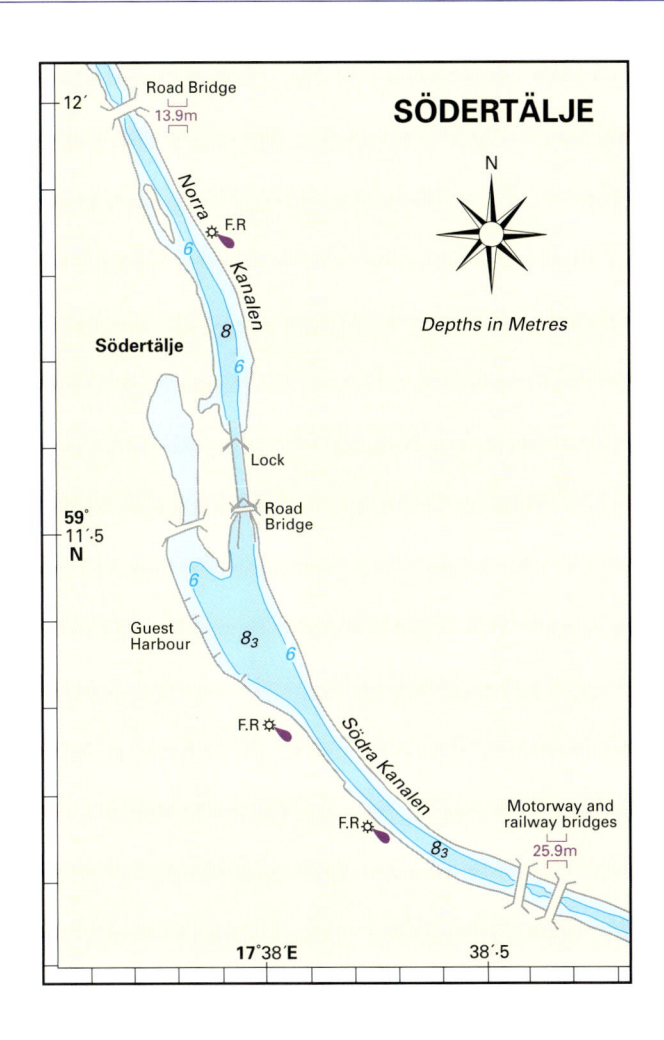

3G. STOCKHOLM - THE ARCHIPELAGO AND SURROUNDING AREA

and 68 whilst in the canal section. There is no space for even a small yacht to pass a ship in the canal or lock, so all vessels must obey the light signals situated on the east bank at each end of the canal and at the lock – 2Iso.R.3s signifies STOP or DO NOT ENTER. Yachts may not pass through the lock at the same time as commercial vessels – permission to enter is given on VHF Ch 68 or by loudspeaker.

Berthing

There are waiting berths (to starboard on approaching) both below and above the lock, but for a longer stay use the guest harbour on the west side of the channel just south of the lock. This has 90 visitors' berths in 2–8m depths, mostly bows-to between booms and step off pontoons. Enter any berth on arrival unless actually marked 'private' or 'reserved'. The harbour office, open 0730–2200 in summer, is situated in the café/shop about 50m south of the pontoons. Berthing fees are in the middle band (see page 136).

Services for yachts

Water and electricity are provided on the pontoons, with showers and launderette ashore. Fuelling berth (diesel and petrol) close south, near the café and shop.

General facilities

All the facilities of a good-sized town with an excellent shopping centre are within walking distance, with the bonus of an excellent swimming pool complex. The station, which has a frequent service to Stockholm, is only five minutes' walk from the harbour.

The guest harbour at Södertäjle *C.N. Hill*

EAST COAST OF SWEDEN

The Lilljeholmen lifting bridge *C.N. Hill*

Södertälje to Stockholm

To reach Stockholm from the Södertälje canal is a journey of around 25 to 30 miles, although having come this far, most visitors would probably prefer to spend some time exploring Lake Mälaren.

From the canal head due east into the city. There are various bridges, one of which is high (26m) and fixed, as well as four lifting bridges and a lock. Payment has to be made at the lock by card if leaving the lake, but not if you are entering it. Just past the final bridge, the channel leads into the main waterway in the centre of Stockholm, and it is just a short journey from here to the two marinas in the centre of the city.

In sequence from east to west (i.e. from Lake Mälaren to Stockholm. Reverse this if going out of Stockholm), you encounter the following:

Lilljeholmen (road bridge, clearance 13·7m; fixed span 15·5m)
☏ +46 8 508 27913, *Mobile* +46 70 770 2812,
VHF Ch 12, 16, 68
Open 0000–0615, 0900–1600, 1830–2400 LT weekdays
24 hours weekends and holidays
0000–0615, 0900–1200, 1430–2400 LT on days preceding holidays.

Årstabron north (rail bridge) now closed to marine traffic or Årstabron south (fixed rail bridge – clearance 26m).

Hammarbyslussen (lock)
☏ +46 8 670 2815,
VHF Ch 12, 16

Skansbron (rail bridge, clearance 11·7m)
☏ 08 508 27912, *Mobile* 070 770 2812,
VHF Ch 12
Open 0000–0630, 0700–0720, 0845–1630, 1800–2400 LT weekdays,
24 hours weekends and holidays,
0000–0630, 0700–0720, 0845–1200, 1430–2400 LT on days preceding holidays.

Danviksbron (rail bridge, clearance 11.7m)
☏ 08 508 27911, VHF Ch 12, 16
Open 0000–0613, 0700–0718, 0903–1200, 1430–2400 LT weekdays,
24 hours weekends and holidays.

More details are available here
www.portsofstockholm.com
It is possible to contact the bridges by VHF to check on the next opening time, and they may well open on request as you approach.

The Hammarby lock. Payment is made when leaving Lake Mälaren *C.N. Hill*

3G. STOCKHOLM - THE ARCHIPELAGO AND SURROUNDING AREA

Lake Mälaren

Charts and guides
Swedish 11, 111, 112, 113, 114, 1131
Båtsportkort D: Mälaren
UKHO 2055

Lake Mälaren, the third-largest lake in Sweden, stretches for some 70M to the west of Stockholm and provides a fine sailing ground in beautiful surroundings. Much of its charm lies in the fact that it is not one great sheet of water but is broken up by many large and small islands, forming a variety of channels through which to explore.

Water levels in Lake Mälaren are less than a metre above those in the Baltic, and it can be entered from the south via the Södertälje Kanal (see page 205) or from the east via the Hammarbyleden, just south of Stockholm. Prehistorically it was continuous with the sea. With the thawing of the ice sheet in the north of Scandinavia the whole country gradually rose, until the medieval settlements were cut off from the sea by the rapids which now separate Stockholm's Gamla Stan (old town) from the Södermalm.

Local interest

The lake is home to or visited by large numbers of wildfowl and other birds. You would be unlucky not to see at least one Osprey or Sea Eagle most days. Though not as many sailing yachts are to be seen on Lake Mälaren as in Swedish coastal waters it is nevertheless a very popular cruising ground. There are nearly 30 yacht harbours on the lake itself and another dozen or so on its various extensions, as well as limitless possibilities for anchoring. However the surrounding land rises to more than 30m in places and is well wooded, sometimes making the wind flukey or non-existent.

There are many interesting and historic places on Lake Mälaren's shores, and a month or more could easily be spent visiting them all. A selection of the most well-known follows

Björkö

59°20'N 17°32'·7E

Birka on this small island was the ancient Viking capital of Sweden and is now a World Heritage site. There are some supplies, an excellent museum, a good restaurant, lovely walks around the burial mounds and some reconstructed buildings. A fairly basic *gästhamn* with 40 visitors' berths (stern anchors with bows to the jetty) can become very busy during the season.

Björkö gästhamn *Bindy Wollen*

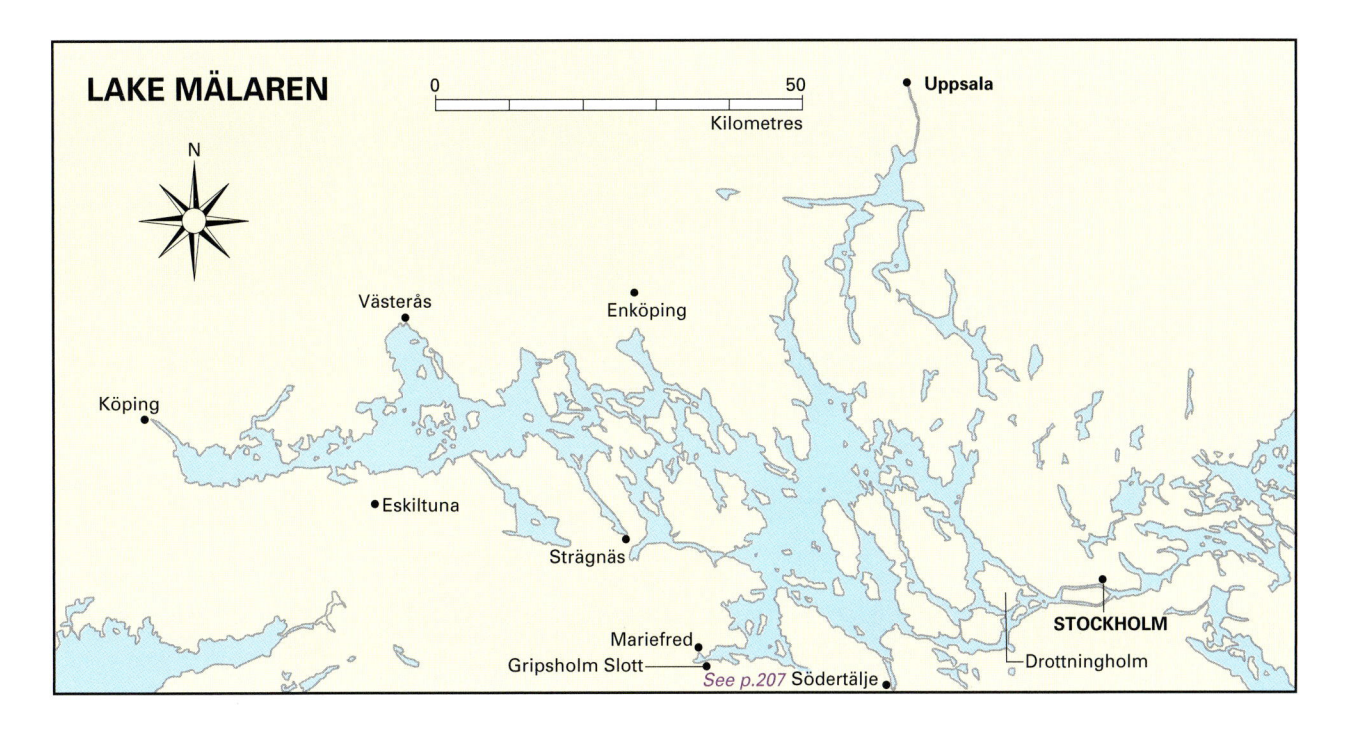

THE BALTIC SEA AND APPROACHES

EAST COAST OF SWEDEN

Drottningholm palace *Bindy Wollen*

Drottningholm
59°19'·5N 17°53'·5E

Home of the Swedish royal family. The palace and gardens are well worth a visit as is the unique wooden 18th-century royal theatre. It is possible to moor bows-to or anchor nearby. There is a good anchorage opposite the palace in the bay north of Högholmen. The bridge just north of the palace (1·3m) does not open.

Gröneborg
59°32'7N 17°06'E

There is a quiet anchorage in the bay on the west of this strategically placed island. Some stone remains of the 13th-century refuge citadel are still visible on the hill at the southern end.

Mariefred
59°15'·4N 17°13'·5E

The beautiful Gripsholm Slott, which houses the National Portrait Gallery, is within easy walking distance of the *gästhamn* and is certainly worth a visit. Limited depths but all facilities and 50 visitors' berths (stern buoys with bows to jetty) and good facilities. A delightful little town with a variety of shops and a systembolaget, which became established to service the royal castle.

Strägnäs
59°22'·7N 17°02'·5E

Although touristy this is a charming little Episcopal seat with a striking red brick cathedral. All the usual facilities are available at the 40 berth *gästhamn* just northwest of the Tosterbron swing bridge which opens on the hour for a maximum of 10 minutes.

Uppsala
59°51'·5N 17°55'E

There are 20 visitors' berths at the *gästhamn* but with restricted facilities although all services can be obtained nearby. This is Sweden's most famous university town and it also boasts the country's largest cathedral. See the Linnaeus Botanical Garden.

Västerås
59°36'·2N 16°33'·5E

Said to be Sweden's largest freshwater port. With many miles of cycle paths it is ideal for a cycling break. 13th-century cathedral and close to the airport. 30 visitors' berths at the *gästhamn* which is about 800m from the shopping centre.

Many passenger boats ply the routes around the Lake, most notably the Mariefred which has been steaming between Stockholm and Mariefred continuously since 1903.

Gripsholm Slott, Mariefred *Bindy Wollen*

Mariefred on the Mälaren Lakes *P. & G. Price*

210   THE BALTIC SEA AND APPROACHES

3G. STOCKHOLM – THE ARCHIPELAGO AND SURROUNDING AREA

Stockholm and its archipelago

Nynäshamn

58°54′N 17°57′E

Distances
Västervik 85M, Arkösund 50M, Södertälje 40M, Saltsjöbaden 35M, Stockholm (via the Baggensstäket) 45M, Stockholm (via the *skärgård*) 70+M, Sandhamn 45M

Charts and guides
Swedish 11, 61, 72, 616, 6171
Båtsportkort A: *Stockholm Södra*
UKHO 831, 836, 864, 872, 2055

Lights
Southern approach
Landsorts Bredgrund 58°43′·9N 17°52′·5E
Iso.WRG.4s18m16–8M
001°-R-113°-G-047·5°-W-053°-R-086°-G-127°-R-159°-G-177°-R-210°-G-217°-W-219°-R-224°-G-234°-R-273°-G-321·5°-R-345°-G-356·5°-W-001° Racon Orange tower Floodlit
Landsort, south point 58°44′·4N 17°52′·1E
Fl(1+4)60s45m22M+Iso.WRG.27m14–7M
323·5°-G-351°-W-358°-R-023° White tower, red top 25m
Gunnarstenarna 58°46′·5N 18°03′·3E
LFl(2)WRG.15s14m8–4M
000°-R-019°-G-038°-R-102°-G-142·5°-W-152·5°-R-180°-G-235°-W-000° White structure on red base
Måsknuv 58°51′·4N 18°01′·1E Mo(A)WRG.8s13m13–7M
008·5°-G-020°-W-024°-R-029°-W-156·5°-G-171°-W-182·5°-R-188°-G-195·5°-W-213°-R-217·5° White tower 10m
Trehörningen 58°53′·5N 17°56′·8E VQ(6).WRG.6s8m10–5M
315°-G-358·5°-W-359·5°-R-025° White square metal framework tower
Bedarö 58°53′·8N 17°56′·6E
Iso.WRG.4s3m7–4M 020·5°-G-033·5°-W-036°-R-043° 115°-G-163°-W-177°-R-195° White lantern
Strathmos Lts in Line 315° *Front* 58°54′·8N 17°57′·7E
F.R.8m2M Red ▲ on pillar
Rear 100m from front F.R.11m2M Red ▲ on pillar

Northern approach
Örngrund 58°53′·8N 18°01′·5E
Q.WRG.10m10–5M
010°-W-020·5°-R-105°-G-131·5°-W-147°-R-195°-G-232·5°-W-246°-R-290°-G-340°-W-344·5°-R-358°-G-010° Black GRP tower, red band on concrete base
Brunsviksholmen 58°55′·1N 17°58′·7E
Fl(2)WRG.6s8m12–6M
270°-R-279·5°-G-296·5°-W-306·5°-R-317°-G-323°-W-327°-R-000°-G-039°-R-043°-R-047·5° White tower 8m

Harbour communications
Nynäshamn Commercial Harbour ☏ +46 8520 10615, *VHF* Ch 11, 16
Nynäshamn Guest Harbour ☏ +46 8520 68888
info@nynashamn.se
www.nynashamn.se/gasthamn

Leaving Landsort to port, this is the first significant harbour of the archipelago to be encountered. A growing town with an attractive older centre near the large marina, the wide variety of shops and particularly good market make Nynäshamn (pronounced *Nu-nairs-hahmn*) a convenient place for storing up.

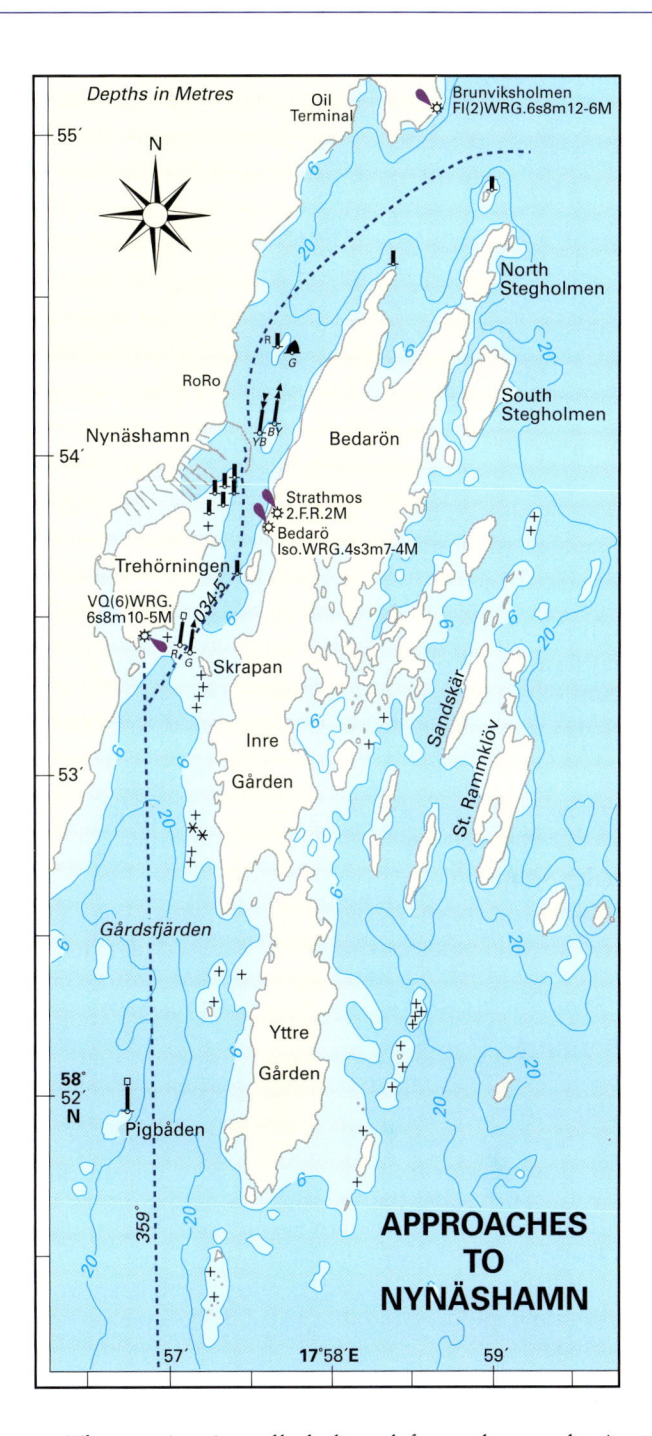

APPROACHES TO NYNÄSHAMN

The marina is well sheltered from the south. A large new wavebreak with 100 berths has improved shelter from the north.

Approach and entrance

The southern approach is straightforward, provided the red pillar buoy marking Pigbåden shoal is left well to port. The passage between Trehörningen and Skrapan islands is no more than 100m in width but is well buoyed and carries a minimum of 4m. The marina is approached around the north end of Trehörningen island, from which shoals extend nearly 400m to the northeast. No liberties should be taken with the buoyage.

From the north, approach can be made from the wide Mysingen passage which separates the island of Utö from mainland Sweden.

THE BALTIC SEA AND APPROACHES 211

EAST COAST OF SWEDEN

The guest harbour at Nynashamn C.N. Hill

There are some shoal areas close to the marina, and the buoyage is more than a little confusing. Navigate cautiously here.

From the outer *skärgård*, and armed with the necessary large-scale Swedish charts, it is possible to sail through the gap between Utö and Ornö, either north or south of Långbäling and Marbäling. At one time closed to yachts entirely, some restrictions remain and anchoring, scuba diving and fishing are still forbidden in the area. There is a firing range to the southeast of Utö which extends up to 12M offshore and this area may be temporarily closed to navigation – see page 363 for contact details.

Anchorage

There is too much traffic to anchor off Nynäshamn itself, with commercial ships including cruise liners and ferries berthing north of the marina, but plenty of possibilities exist amongst the nearby islands.

Berthing

Nynäshamn Gasthamn is a large marina with some 200 visitors' berths in 4–10m depths.

There is a new and very long jetty constructed in 2012 to the north of the marina. Berthing on this jetty is alongside, but elsewhere it is a mixture of booms and stern buoys. All berths, other than those very close to the shore, are available to visitors. Berthing fees are calculated by reference to beam and are in the middle band, but halve if the yacht is not occupied.

Services for yachts

Most, though not all, berths have access to water and electricity, with showers, a sauna and laundry facilities ashore. Fuel (diesel and petrol) from the Shell berth close north of the marina (℡ +46 8 520 11268, open 0900–2100 mid-season, otherwise 0900–1800) where bottled gas is also available in limited quantities. There is a boatyard near the marina, with an extensive chandlery. Charts are available from the chandlery as well as from the 'Appeltofts' bookstore in town. Dyk and Marin, ℡ +46 8 520 13928, provide a dive service and will refill scuba tanks.

General facilities

All the usual facilities of a medium sized town, including good shopping, the aforementioned market and a Systembolaget liquor store. Many pavement cafés and restaurants near the waterfront, including two in the marina itself. There is an excellent and famous fish smokery on the quay, and a van delivers fresh bread each morning.

Communications and travel

The marina is immediately adjacent to the railway station with a direct line to Stockholm (about one hour), making it a convenient spot for crew changes or from which to explore the capital. Ferries run to Ventspils in Latvia from berths north of the marina. There is a regular ferry running to the Gotska Sandon National Park about 40M north of Gotland during the season, weather permitting, and a ferry to the islands south of Utö (Nåttarö, Rånö and Ålö).

The marina office is happy to hold mail for visiting yachts (Nynäshamns Gästhamn, Fiskargränd 5, 14930 Nynäshamn, Sweden). There is WiFi at the marina.

Utö

Utö is an island on the edge of the *skärgård* with a popular harbour of the same name on its north-west coast at 58°58'3N, 18°19'6E. The harbour is approximately 15 miles from Nynäshamn. The final approach needs to be made with care, and there is a narrow but well buoyed entrance with conspicuous leading lines. Out of season, there would be room to tie alongside, but mooring at busier times is by stern anchor.

There is a sheltered anchorage at Utö Kyrkvik 58°57'72N 18°17'68E but be careful to keep clear of the ferry.

The island is popular for its unspoiled nature. There are several attractive anchorages among the islands to the south (Nåttarö, Rånö and Ålö) with the popular Båtshaket fish restaurant on the latter.

Kyrkvik anchorage, Utö Bindy Wollen

212 THE BALTIC SEA AND APPROACHES

3G. STOCKHOLM - THE ARCHIPELAGO AND SURROUNDING AREA

Approaches to Stockholm

Charts and guides
Swedish 11, 61, 616, 615, 613, 612, 611, 719, 6161, 6145, 6144, 6143, 6142, 6141
Swedish *Båtsportkort: Stockholm S, M and N.*
UKHO 811, 821, 831, 832, 836, 872, 881, 887, 888, 2055, 3155

Most yachtsmen working their way north along the east coast of Sweden will want to visit Stockholm, one of the most beautiful cities of northern Europe and offering a huge amount for all tastes. In particular, the incomparable Wasa museum must not be missed. There are two large marinas in the centre of the city. In the height of the season, they may be rather crowded but berths can be booked on-line. There is also a fair amount of wash from the small and large ferries which are used by local commuters. It is certainly worth going into the centre by boat, but there are also a number of harbours some way out which have good rail access to the centre. Two possibilities are Nynashamn and Saltsjöbaden.

There are a variety of different routes which lead to the city, the one through the offlying archipelago or *skärgård* being further subdivided into two major channels with potentially innumerable variations. The most southerly approach is the 'back entrance' via the Södertälje Kanal (see page 205). The southeasterly approach via the narrow Baggensstäket (see page 214) departs just north of Saltsjöbaden to emerge at Kungshamn less than 4M east of the city centre. The *skärgård* routes from the Baltic twist through a myriad of possible channels to pass close to Vaxholm and enter the city from the northeast.

The Skärgård

The Stockholm Archipelago or *skärgård* (pronounced *shair-gord*) is a vast area of islands stretching from Landsort in the southwest to Tjärven, on the edge of the Åland Sea, in the northeast. It is quite heavily populated, particularly during the summer, and is very popular with Swedish yachtsmen but, nevertheless, offers a most attractive cruising ground (see page 137).

The inner *skärgård* is dotted with small guest harbours, though there are few marinas of any size other than those at Sandhamn and Bullandö. The outer archipelago however, to the north and east of Sandhamn, presents a wild and challenging cruising ground. This area is well charted, though largely unbuoyed and quite heavily rock-encumbered, but with care can be navigated in safety to reach some of the most beautiful and remote anchorages in the whole of the Baltic. In the *skärgård*, as elsewhere on the Swedish coast, ensuring that one keeps a constant and accurate track of one's position among the numerous reefs and islands is vital. If following the well-charted routes, you should have few problems but if you go 'off piste' take particular care. Cruising in the archipelago can involve navigating within metres of rocks. Strong winds can blow up quite suddenly, kicking up short seas. A complete set of current, large-scale Swedish charts is essential.

A further potential hazard is posed by the large modern ferries and cruise liners which weave their way through the tortuous passages which characterise much of the inner approaches to Stockholm. At times a ferry's upperworks may be visible behind a nearby island, looking like a moving block of flats. It cannot be stressed too often that these ferries have absolute right of way AT ALL TIMES. Some of the 'pinch points' are so narrow that they do not allow room for a ferry to pass even a small yacht, and the vast difference in speeds should be taken into account whenever one of these gaps is approached – not forgetting to look astern as well as ahead!

Cruise liner leaving Stockholm. These will head northeast out through the archipelago *C.N. Hill*

EAST COAST OF SWEDEN

Saltsjöbaden and the Baggensstäket

59°16′N 18°19′E

Distances
Nynäshamn 35M, Stockholm (via the Baggensstäket) 10M, Sandhamn 25M

Charts and guides
Swedish 11, 61, 6145, 6142
Båtsportkort A: *Stockholms skärgård*
UKHO 831, 836, 872, 2362

Lights
Fjärdhällan 59°09′·3N 18°33′·3E
  Fl.WRG.3s7m7–4M 006°-R-031°-G-063·5°-W-069°-R-109°-G-177°-R-199°-G-202°-W-205°-R-208°-G-255°-W-006° White round tower, black base 7m
Grönö 59°12′·5N 18°34′E Iso.WRG.4s7m5–3M
  shore-G-246°-W-307·5°-R-331°-G-352°-W-358°-R-015°-G-053·5°-W-079°-R-092° Red tower, white top 8m
Boo 59°18′·6N 18°17′·8E Fl(2)6s2m6M White hut, green band
Kingshamn 59°20′·1N 18°12′·6E Fl.WRG.3s6m6-3M shore-G-058·5°-W-062°-R-076·5°-G-091°-W-098°-R-205°-G-219°-W-227·5°-R-shore White lantern

Harbour communications
KSSS Marina ② +46 871 70856
  ksss@ksss.se www.ksss.se
Pålnäsviken *Mobile* ② +46 707 18 93 87
  kontakta@saltsjobadensbatklubb.se
  www.saltsjobadensbatklubb.se

Saltsjöbaden (pronounced *Sahlt-sheu-bahd-ehn*) has long been a popular spa and summer holiday resort, surrounded by attractive countryside and only half an hour by rail from Stockholm. It is the mainland headquarters of the Kungl Svenska Segel Sällskapet (Royal Swedish Yacht Club, better known as KSSS), whose extremely helpful staff also administer one of the two marinas. The narrow Baggensstäket (pronounced *Bahggehns- stairck-eht*) forms the southeastern – and smaller – of Stockholm's two 'back entrances'.

Approach and entrance
The approach up the wide Ingaröfjärden, giving onto the Ägnöfjärden and the Baggensfjärden, is largely unbuoyed, but quite straightforward. Saltsjöbaden lies at the south end of the Baggensfjärden and 2M short of the narrow entrance to the Baggensstäket and the Skurusundet – a long, winding but very attractive gorge which runs for 5M between high wooded banks to Kungshamn, less than 4M from the city centre. Depths in the Baggensstäket are least at its southeastern end, with under 3m in some sections. The channel has no locks and is crossed by a single bridge with 30m clearance. The narrowest sections are controlled by sound signals shown on boards.

Berthing
Saltsjöbaden has two marinas – the Pålnäsviken (Saltsjöbadens båtklubb) and the larger KSSS marina to the west. The former is small with just five guest moorings but the KSSS marina reserves some three dozen berths for visitors (green stern buoys with green signs on the jetty) in depths of 2·5–12m, though it has on occasion fitted in as many as 80 visitors. Although the marina has several different sections, visitors should pass south of the small central island when the pontoons will be seen to starboard. Mooring is, as usual, bows-to with a buoy astern. The berths are close to a popular but quite noisy restaurant.

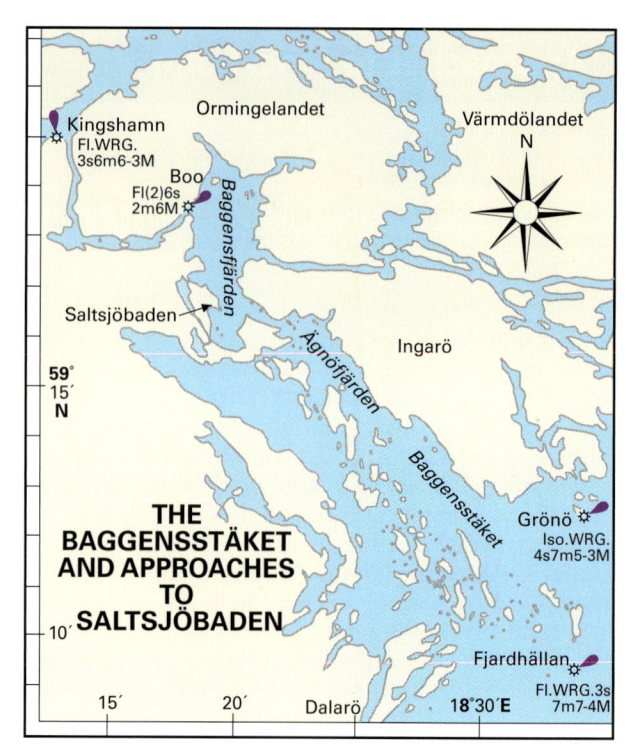

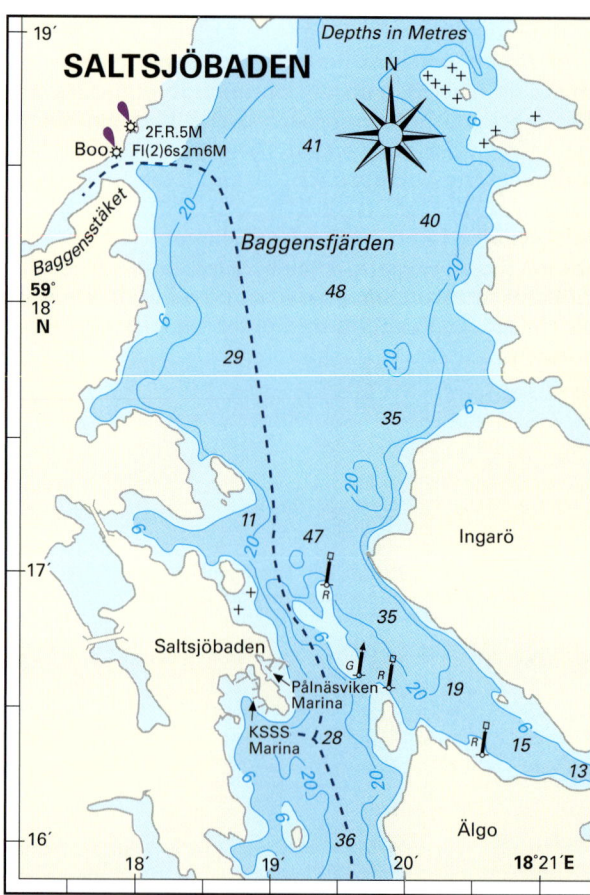

214   THE BALTIC SEA AND APPROACHES

3G. STOCKHOLM - THE ARCHIPELAGO AND SURROUNDING AREA

Narrow passage at east end of Baggenstaket *Bindy Wollen*

The marina is not obvious when you are coming up from the south, as it is concealed by the small island. However, the Grand Hotel is a very obvious landmark, and you head for that, leaving the island to starboard. You should take care here, as, unusually for Sweden, there are many mooring buoys in the bay with attached yachts. The visitors' moorings are very clearly marked.

Services for yachts

Water and electricity are provided on the KSSS pontoons, with a card phone, toilets, showers and launderette near the marina office. There is a small engineering workshop at their clubhouse, and the very helpful staff would doubtless assist in organising any other work which needed to be done. They will also advise regarding possible yards in which to lay up ashore. Fuel and bottled gas are available at the Pålnäsviken marina, east of the central island, and there are a number of boatyards in the area.

General facilities

Surprisingly, there are no food shops or stores within walking distance. A 20 minute walk inland or three stops on the train (ask for directions at the marina office) takes one to the large shopping mall at Tippen, which also has Post Office, bank, Systembolaget and much more. The imposing Grand Hotel overlooks the harbour and is apparently being restored to its former glory by new owners after several years of neglect. Fast trains run every 20 minutes to the centre of Stockholm – an attractive and interesting ride in itself which takes about half an hour. The station is only a few minutes' walk from the harbour.

Visitors' morings at KSSS, Saltsjobaden *C.N. Hill*

Grand Hotel, Saltsjobaden *C.N. Hill*

THE BALTIC SEA AND APPROACHES   215

STOCKHOLM AND THE SKÄRGÅRD
N
Depths in Metres
Vätö
Tjärven
Fl(4)12s15M
Graddö
Remmargrund
LFl.WRG.
8s13-9M
Norrtälje
Kapellskär
Fl(4)WRG.
12s11-7M
Lerskärsgrund
Fl(3)WRG.
9s13-8M
40′
Furusund
Yxlan
Blidösund
Blidö
Fl.WRG.3s
8-4M
Hundskär
Rodloga
N. Ljustero
30′
Morsken
Fl(3)WRG.
8s6-3M
For L Mäleren
see p.209
See
p.218
S. Ljustero
2a
2b
Björskärs-
fjärden
Stora
Möja
Q.WRG.
5-3M
Prästkobben
Vaderö
Vaxholm
Aero
VQ&Q.21M
+5 Aero F.R
Vindö
Karholms
fjärden
20′
See p.220
Sandhamn
Oc.WRG.30s13-5M
Varmdölandet
Horssten
Fl(4)WRG.12s6-3M
Nacka
See p.223
Aero VQ.21M+
8F.R.6M
Iso.WRG.
8-4M
Stockholm
Saltsjöbaden
See p.214
Ingarö
Runmaro
Q.WRG.12-7M
Sandhamn
Entrance
Revengegrundet
LFl(2)WRG.
18s16-12M
HornMo(R)60s
YB
Q(3)10s
BYB
3c
Rumarö
Baggensstäket
Namdö
3b
See p.214
10′
F.3M
Peskobben
Almagrundet
Fl(4)WR.12s29m13M
Dalarö
Ormsta
Aero Q.21M
+Aero F.R.6M
F
Skeppskobben
3a
Ornö
59°
N
Vindbådan
Fl.3s3M
Musko
Mysingen
Utö
VQ.R+VQ.Y.12M
Huvudskär
Mo(N)25s12M
See p.211
6M
9M
12M
Nynäshamn
Utö
Brunsviksholmen
Fl(2)WRG.
6s12-6M
May be temporarily closed to shipping
Skrapan
Fl(3)WRG.9s6-3M
Gunnarstenarna
LFl(2)WRG.
15s8-4M
Firing Practice Area
See page 420
Landsort
Fl(1+4)60s22M
Oc.WRG.14-7M
18°E
See p.195
10′
20′
30′
40′
50′
19°E
10′
20′

3G. STOCKHOLM - THE ARCHIPELAGO AND SURROUNDING AREA

Routes within the *skärgård*

Since the various routes through both inner and outer *skärgård*s are effectively limitless, the following brief descriptions barely scratch the surface of what is possible. The plan opposite outlines the routes being described. These are only suggestions, and there are innumerable variations.

Routes 1-3 are the routes which can be taken if coming from the south – Nynashamn or Üto. These routes diverge at Dalarö. Sandhamn is another entry point for the *skärgård* (the small island group at Huvudskär (58°58′N 18°34′E) is a useful stopping off point if heading to/from Sandhamn).

If approaching from the north, route 5 is the most obvious.

Route 1 Nynashamn to Vaxholm (the inner *skärgård*)

Route 2 Nynashamn to Tjärven at the northern end of the archipelago

Route 3 from the southwest into the *skärgård* and Sandhamn

Route 4 Sandhamn to Vaxholm

Route 5 Tjärven (at the northern end of the archipelago) to Vaxholm

Route 6 Sandhamn to Tjärven

These routes are all outlined on the chart opposite and should be studied in conjunction with this chart. The Swedish chart, Arholma-Landsort *Skärgård*skort, provides a very useful overview of the skägård and makes passage planning among the islands much easier.

Dalarö

This can be a useful jumping off point for the *skärgård* when coming from the south.

There are two guest harbours, but the Hotellbryggan has neither water nor electricity, and is distinctly exposed, not only to weather but to the wash of passing motorboats and ferries. The other harbour is Askfatshamnen, not far away. One jetty is reserved for visitors. This has quite widely spaced booms. There are the usual ablutions and a reasonable restaurant, although it is very remote. A useful stop off, but nothing more. It is rather exposed and may well be crowded in the summer.

Route 1 Nynashamn to Vaxholm (the inner *skärgård*)

This route, the latter parts of which are much used by both international and inter-island ferries, leads northeastwards up the main channel inside the islands of Nämdö (59°12′N 18°42′E), and Runmarö (59°16′N 18°44′E) before swinging west along the north coast of Vindö (19°21′N 18°41′E). It branches to pass either north or south of Kavlön and Västerholmen – via the Grindafjärden to the north or the Sandöfjärden to the south – but the two rejoin at the narrows south of Vårholma (59°25′N 18°29′E). It then continues west-northwest via the Lindalssundet to the tiny island of Brödstycket (59°25′N 18°24′E), where larger vessels turn southwest to follow the main channel to Stockholm. Smaller craft – though including some sizeable inter-island ferries – continue west towards Hästholmen (59°25′N 18°21′·5E) to take the very narrow passage between Hästholmen, Resarö and the small islands which lie between, to approach Vaxholm from the north. The entire passage measures some 35M, and for much of its distance follows major shipping channels, well buoyed and lit. (For details of Vaxholm itself, see page 221.)

There is a possible diversion from this route which takes one south of Djüro, passing under a fixed road bridge (20m) and then heads northwards up the very beautiful Älgöfjärd to rejoin the main route. This takes you past the Bullandö marina which purports to be the largest marina in the Baltic (see details on page 221).

The moorings at Dalarö are reasonably well sheltered. Be careful on the approach as the channel shallows very rapidly on the left-hand side – although the bottom is mainly mud and sand. Space is limited *C.N. Hill*

THE BALTIC SEA AND APPROACHES 217

EAST COAST OF SWEDEN

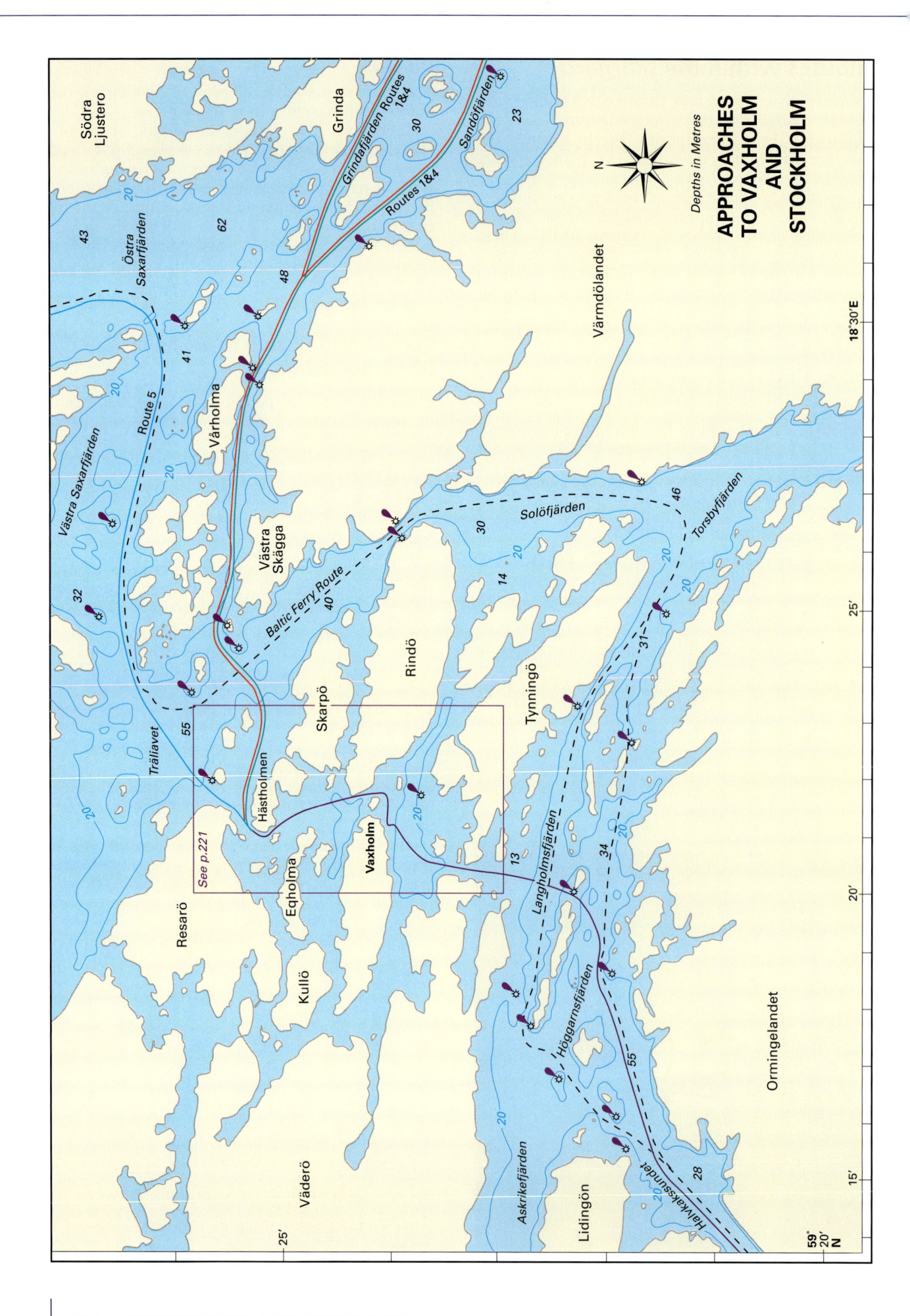

APPROACHES TO VAXHOLM AND STOCKHOLM

Depths in Metres

3G. STOCKHOLM - THE ARCHIPELAGO AND SURROUNDING AREA

Route 2 Nynäshamn to Tjärven at the northern end of the archipelago

From Nynäshamn northeastwards through the Stockholm *skärgård* to Tjärven where the Åland Sea begins, there is a choice of route. The early stages of both follow Route 1, diverging where that heads west around Vindö island. There is then a choice between inner and outer passages:

a. The inner route continues northeast across the Kanholmsfjärden to pass west of Södermöja (59°24'N 18°51'·5E) and Stora Möja (59°25'·5N 18°53'E), then north via an intricate but well-marked 8M passage between smaller islands to reach the south end of Blidösund (59°35'N 18°51'E), which separates Yxlan and Blidö islands. The north end of Blidösund gives onto the main Stockholm–Åland channel, known as the Söderarm. This route measures some 50M in total and includes some very attractive stretches, especially that between Stora Möja and Blidösund. It is well buoyed, but is not lit between Stora Möja and the northern end of Blidösund.

b. The outer route follows that above as far as the south end of Södermöja, but passes east of both it and Stora Möja. It then continues northeastwards through a more open passage than that of 2a, past Morsken (59°30'·9N 19°05'·4E) and Hundskärsknuv (59°35'·9N 19°07'·5E) light structures, and rejoins the above in the vicinity of 59°43'·5N 19°10'·5E. The total distance is some 52M, and it is well buoyed and lit throughout.

Route 3 from the southwest into the *skärgård* and Sandhamn

The outer *skärgård* is in many ways more interesting than the inner part, with deciduous trees – birch and oak scrub – which makes a change from the fir trees which are prevalent further inshore. However the pilotage is more challenging and demands great care. There are few floating marks – instead there are stone cairns, wooden triangles and marks painted on the rocks – but these are not always shown on the charts and their significance is not always apparent.

The best routes eastward to the outer *skärgård* are as follows:

a. Via the sound south of Gillinge (59°06'·5N 18°39'E).

b. South of Mörtöklubb (59°09'N 18°37'E) a high, conspicuous islet south of the larger Mörtö, and then in a general east-northeast direction passing south of Orrön (59°10'·5N 18°42'E) and north of Måsskär (59°11'·7N 18°48'E), after which turn southeast and south.

c. To reach Sandhamn (see page 220 for details of this major sailing centre) follow the above route as far as Måsskär, continuing northeast to pass close east of Stora and Lilla Melskär (59°12'·5N 18°49'·5E). The route then leads northwest for a short distance, and then northeast again to pass west of the very conspicuous Algkobb (59°14'N 18°53'E). It then continues northeast up the Stora *Skärgård*en between Hötterskär and Stora Hästskär, past Osterskär light (59°15'·5N 18°57'E), and finally approaches Sandhamn via the southeast entrance between Sandön and Korsö.

Route 4 Sandhamn to Vaxholm

Leaving Sandhamn by its narrow northwest entrance, this relatively straightforward route heads northwest between Getholmen (59°15'N 18°52'·5E) and Smörasken (59°15'N 18°52'·2E) and south of Hasselkobben to emerge into the Kanholmsfjärden north of Runmarö, where it joins Route 1 towards Vaxholm. The total distance is approximately 22M.

Route 5 Tjärven (at the northern end of the archipelago) to Vaxholm

The main approach to Vaxholm from the northeast follows the main channel used by the Åland and Helsinki ferries, which are likely to pose a considerably greater threat to the average yacht than the navigation. From the Tjärven light structure (59°47'·5N 19°22'·2E) the channels runs southwest and narrows to pass between Furusund and the north end of Yxlan island. It then splits either side of a group of small islands at 59°36'N 18°47'E, leaves the Södra Växlet shoal to the north, and continues southwest parallel to the mainland shore, north of the small islands of Långh (59°32'·2N 18°34'·4E), Huvön and beyond en route to the Trälhavet and Hästholmen (59°25'N 18°21'·5E) where it joins Route 1 for Vaxholm.

The scenery is less varied than that further south, consisting of long straight fjords fringed by long islands covered with fir trees, and there are fewer of the snug anchorages which are such a feature of the other routes. From Tjärven to Vaxholm is just over 40M.

Route 6 Sandhamn to Tjärven

The outer *skärgård* beyond Sandhamn is a fascinating and mysterious area. Within an area of 280M2 there are some 13 individual groups of islets, each of which affords at least one beautiful, remote anchorage. Stora Nassa is probably the most well known of these mini archipelagos, and is well worth a visit in reasonable weather. The soundings on the chart are much sparser than in the more frequented channels, but those shown can generally be relied upon. Dotted about between the main groups of islets are innumerable rocks just above or below water, so one has to pick one's way with caution. However given moderate weather and reasonable visibility the pilotage is not difficult – it simply requires great care and detailed charts.

The area may be entered either from Sandhamn, passing north of Högskär (59°17'·7N 19°01'·3E) and through the middle of the Björskärs *skärgård* (59°22'N 19°08'·2E), or from any convenient point on Route 2b northeast of Stora Möja.

EAST COAST OF SWEDEN

Sandhamn

59°17'N 18°55'E

Distances

Nynäshamn 45M, Saltsjöbaden 25M, Vaxholm 20M, Stockholm 30M

Charts and guides

Swedish 61, 615, 6143, 6144
Båtsportkort: Stockholm M
UKHO 2362, 832, 881

Harbour communications

KSSS marinas ☎ +46 857 15 32 85
   Mobile +46 702 13 20 68
   ksss@ksss.se
   www.ksss.se
KSSS Lökholmen ☎ +46 857 15 31 03
   Mobile +46 702 13 20 68

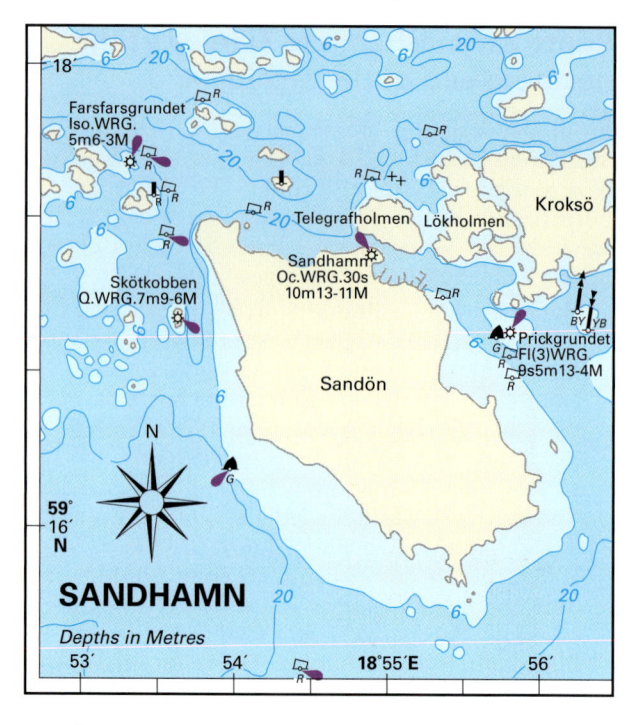

Sometimes described as the 'Cowes of Sweden', Sandhamn has been the offshore home of the Royal Swedish Yacht Club, the Kungl Svenska Segel Sällskapet (KSSS) for more than a century. Additional berthing space on the adjacent island of Lökholmen was acquired in 1946. The whole area becomes very crowded in high summer, particularly in July at the time of the annual Round Gotland Race, which regularly attracts up to 500 yachts. It can, not surprisingly, be very noisy at night, particularly at weekends.

The island of Sandön is picturesque in the extreme, with clapboard houses, sanded roads and several good beaches. There is a permanent population of about 100 which increases vastly in summer, and a hotel/restaurant, the Sandhamns Värdshus, which is said to have been open throughout the year ever since 1672. The old yacht club building adjoining the marina is now a hotel with good facilities.

Approach and entrance

See Routes 3 and 4 on page 216.

Berthing

Although in theory three separate marinas – the Västerhamn, the KSSS and the Österhamn – all are administered by the KSSS and share common shore facilities. Around 200 visitors berths are available on Sandhamn, in 2·5m or more, with a further 150 at Lökholmen, reached by water taxi. Berthing on one of the three marinas' six pontoons is mainly bows-to with a lazyline astern, preferably as directed by one of the KSSS staff. Water and electricity is available at most berths, with showers and other facilities ashore (the ablutions are distinctly inadequate for a marina of this size), and fuel from a jetty near the southeast end of the marina where holding tanks can also be emptied. Both mechanical and sail repairs can be carried out, but there would almost certainly be a considerable delay in the high season. There is a boatyard on the west side of Lökholmen but no chandlery on either island, the nearest (and that small) being close to the ferry berth at Stavsnäs.

General facilities

The island has adequate food shopping from two small supermarkets, a post office, numerous cafés, restaurants and boutiques, but no bank. There is an excellent, if expensive, bakery on the waterfront.

The waterfront at Sandhamn.
The reason for its name is obvious *C.N. Hill*

THE BALTIC SEA AND APPROACHES

3G. STOCKHOLM - THE ARCHIPELAGO AND SURROUNDING AREA

Bullandö

59°17'9N 18°39'1E

Charts Swedish 61, 6143, 6145 UKHO 821, 831, 2362

☏ +46(0)8571 45210

This large marina lies just a short distance off Route 1 detailed above. The approach from the east passes under a fixed road bridge with 20m clearance, but from the north there are no obstructions. It only has 30 visitors berths adjoining the harbour office and restaurant (on lazy lines from the quay) with a few more alongside a pontoon, but the harbour office can normally find you a space. Water, electricity and WiFi are available along with excellent showers, sauna and laundry. For such a large marina it has quite a small but well stocked food shop which also has a limited supply of chandlery (including camping gaz), and a popular restaurant. There is a large boatyard which can handle any kind of repair and has extensive laying up facilities. The bus stop is just outside the gates with a direct bus service to Stockholm.

Vaxholm

59°24'N 18°21'E

Charts Swedish11, 61, 6142, UKHO 2362, 3155

Guest harbour ☏ +46 8 541 33080

The *skärgård* approach to Stockholm contains innumerable possible routes, but all come together northeast of Vaxholm. The main shipping channel passes east of Rindö, but most yachts will take the very narrow passage between Hästholmen, Resarö and the small islands which lie between. On approaching Vaxholm from the north, yachts are directed to pass east of the forbidding castle – which occupies an island in the centre of the channel – so leaving the western channel for the inter-island ferries.

There is a guest harbour at the southeast corner of Vaxholm island which has some 100 visitors berths in depths ranging from 0·5–6m. Mooring is by lazyline. The narrow entrance faces east and is well protected, but considerable wash rolls in from all the ferry and motorboats outside. Not surprisingly the harbour becomes very crowded and is very noisy in high summer, particularly at weekends. Berthing fees are in the middle band. The marina has all the usual services, and there is a launderette nearby. Fuel is available at a jetty by the marina entrance or at a pontoon to the west of the castle which must be approached from the north. See page 224 for details of fuel outlets in or close to Stockholm.

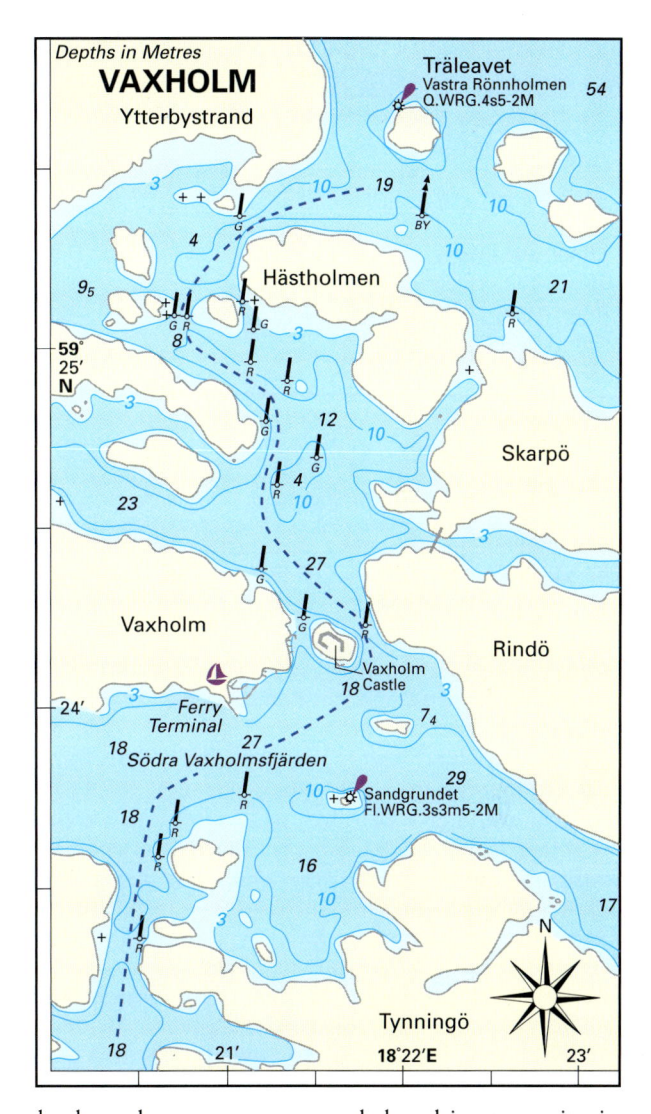

There is good shopping close to the harbour, including one of the few Systembolagets in the *skärgård*, a well-stocked Watski chandlers, and a good Coop supermarket. Frequent ferries run into central Stockholm or, for variety, take the bus over the bridges which link the island with mainland Sweden.

Vaxholm fortress *Bindy Wollen*

THE BALTIC SEA AND APPROACHES

EAST COAST OF SWEDEN

Stockholm

59°20′N 18°04′E

Distances
Vaxholm 10M, Nynäshamn (via the Baggensstäket) 45M, Sandhamn 30M, Mariehamn 70M, Öregrund 85M

Charts and guides
Swedish 61, 11, 6142, 6141
Båtsportkort: *Stockholm M*
UKHO 881, 887, 2362, 3155

Harbour communications
Stockholm Port Authority ☏ +46 867 02600
  VHF Ch 09, 12, 16,
  info@stoports.com
  www.stoports.com
VTS Stockholm ☏ +46 855 42 45 00
  VHF Ch 16, 73 (yachts have no obligation to report but should maintain a listening watch on VHF Ch 73)
Wasahamnen Marina ☏ +46 866 19187
  info@wasahamnen.se
  www.wasahamnen.se
Navishamnen Marina ☏ +46 866 21127
(Information relating to the locks and bridges on the Hammarbyleden can be found on page 208)

The incomparable *Wasa*, perhaps the greatest of Stockholm's many treasures   *P. & G. Price*

Stockholm, established where access to Lake Mälaren could be controlled, was founded as a town by Birger Jarl in 1250, and was especially concerned with the metalwork industry which had developed inland. It was an important trading centre during Hanseatic times, when half its population was German. The old town and royal palace remain on the central island, the Gamla Stan, which has medieval and renaissance street plans. Modern Stockholm, with a population now approaching two million, has spread across the waterways to the mainland. It is a friendly, relaxing city with tree lined squares and beautiful waterfronts blended with modern architecture, all intersected by busy waterways.

Stockholm has many places of cultural interest, including outstanding museums, palaces and churches. However for those of a nautical bent pride of place must go to the 17th-century man-of-war Wasa, raised in 1961 – seemingly almost undamaged – from the spot where she filled and sank within minutes of setting out on her maiden voyage more than 330 years earlier. The ship, together with the display of artefacts which surround her, are without equal anywhere in the world.

The website carrying the excellent nine-language Stockholm Official Visitor's Guide, with innumerable useful links, will be found at www.stockholmtown.com. The slightly more formal City of Stockholm website (also with English translation) is at www.stockholm.se.

Approaches
The three main approaches to Stockholm are detailed on pages 213–219.

Anchorage
Anchoring is not advisable in the main harbour area, though there are many possibilities in the approaches.

Berthing
There are several large yacht harbours in the Stockholm area, but only two which are both convenient for the city and accept visitors. There is also a public quay, normally used only by large yachts, with facilities geared to the requirements of sizeable vessels – contact the port authority before arrival. Visiting yachts of normal size have the choice of the Wasahamnen marina, sandwiched between the Vasa museum, the aquarium and the nearby Tivoli Gronalund, or the Navishamnen marina

A view of the waterfront at Stockholm   *C.N. Hill*

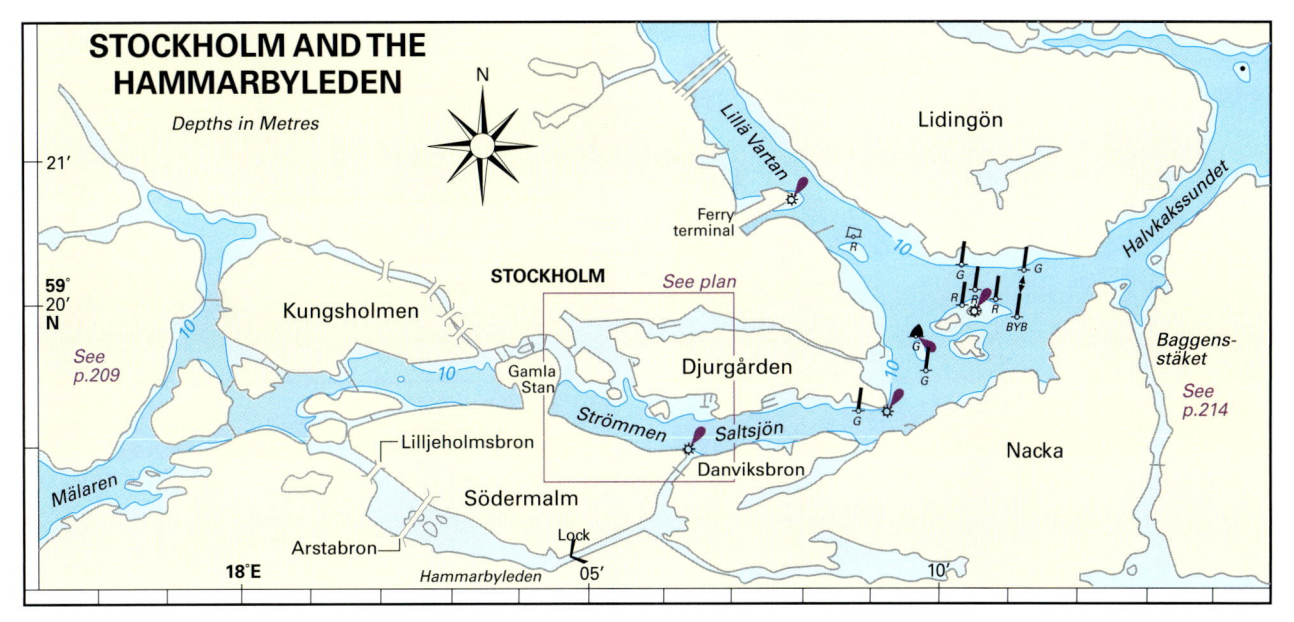

3G. STOCKHOLM - THE ARCHIPELAGO AND SURROUNDING AREA

further east. Both are on the Djurgården, on the north side of the channel and well within walking distance of the city centre. As might be expected, they become very full during the holiday season and it is best to arrive early or reserve a berth in advance by telephone or on-line (preferably on an inner pontoon, as the outer berths can be uncomfortable due to wash or strong winds). Berthing fees in both marinas are in the upper band.

Wasahamnen Marina

☎ +46 8 661 9187 (0800–1600),
info@wasahamnen.se www.wasahamnen.se

Has around 150 visitors berths in 2–6m, arranged on two long pontoons lying parallel to the shore. Most berthing is walk on pontoons one side with a boom on the other. On arrival, take any vacant space and report as soon as convenient to the harbour office on the inner pontoon.

Navishamnen Marina

☎ +46 8 662 1127

About 900m southeast, has some 60 visitors berths in 2–7m depths, though more yachts may be squeezed in at times. Again, all berths are bows-to. Entry is from the east and the marina can be masked by the various houseboats and other large craft on the outer pontoon, though these do afford the inner berths some degree of protection.

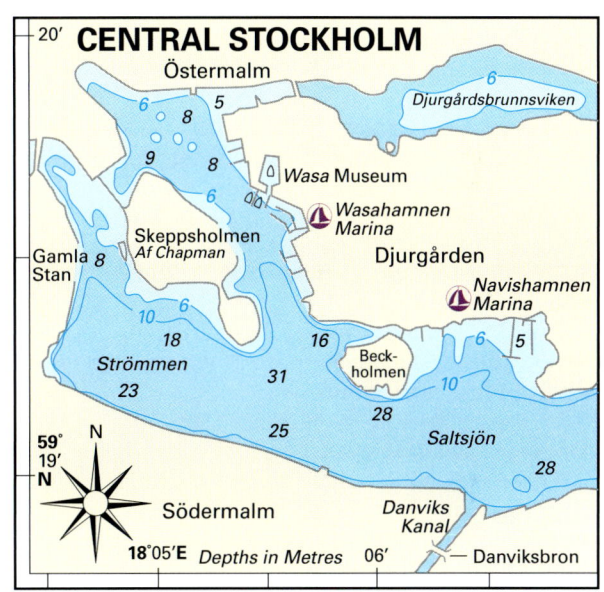

Services for yachts

The Wasahamnen marina has electricity and water throughout, with toilets, showers and laundry facilities (included in the mooring fee) ashore. WiFi is available in most berths. There is a small foodstore in summer and many cafés and restaurants nearby.

The Navishamnen marina has water and electricity on the pontoons, and toilets, showers and launderette ashore. There is a café and a small shop on site, and though there are no repair facilities as

The guest harbour at Wasahamn is very well placed for the centre of the city but can be subject to wash at times *C.N. Hill*

THE BALTIC SEA AND APPROACHES   223

The beautiful House of Nobility in central Stockholm with the distinctive steeple of the Riddarholmskyran (Royal burial church) on the right *E. Redfern*

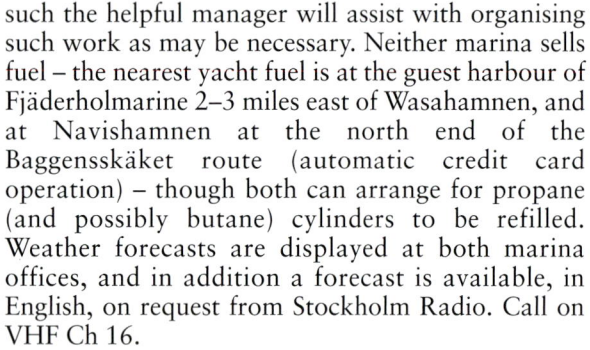

The rapids between Gamla Stan and Södermalm *E. Redfern*

such the helpful manager will assist with organising such work as may be necessary. Neither marina sells fuel – the nearest yacht fuel is at the guest harbour of Fjäderholmarine 2–3 miles east of Wasahamnen, and at Navishamnen at the north end of the Baggensskäket route (automatic credit card operation) – though both can arrange for propane (and possibly butane) cylinders to be refilled. Weather forecasts are displayed at both marina offices, and in addition a forecast is available, in English, on request from Stockholm Radio. Call on VHF Ch 16.

Royal Sails have a loft at Djurgården 46, directly behind the Wasahamnen marina, where all types of repair can be carried out.
☎ +46 8 660 5505 *Mobile* +46 70 589 5505, hans.segelmakaren@royalsails.se

There is a very well equipped chandlery called Captains at Kommendörsgaten 26, 114 48 Stockholm (about 10 minutes' walk north of Djurgården). This was formerly part of the Watski chain but is now independent. ☎ +46 8 663 7777

Swedish and foreign charts and other publications (including many books in English) are available from Nautiska Magasinet AB, at Slussplan 5 in the Gamla Stan (Box 15410, S-10465 Stockholm).
☎ +46 8 677 0000, nautiska@nautiska.com, www.nautiska.com.

More general maps are available from Kartcentrum Stockholm at Vasag 16 (opposite the Central Station).

Staff at the Svenska Kryssarklubben (Swedish Cruising Club) headquarters, at Augustendalsvägen 54, S–13127 Nacka Strand, ☎ +46 8 448 2880, info@sxk.se, www.sxk.se, are very helpful and the club has a good range of yachting publications and charts on sale.

General facilities
Stockholm has all the shopping opportunities one might expect of a major European capital, including many familiar British names, and top quality goods of all types can be bought – at a price. There is a particularly helpful tourist office on the Hamngatan.

Communications and travel
Travel within the city centre is made easy – even enjoyable – by the frequent buses and modern underground system (the same bus route serves both marinas, or one can get a waterbus across to the old town). Alternatively, as Stockholm is largely flat and appears to breed singularly considerate drivers, bicycles are a very practical way to get around. All three international airports can easily be reached by bus or train (but note that the main airport Arlanda is some 30 miles north of the city). Frequent rail, coach and ferry services run between Stockholm and other parts of Europe.

THE GULF OF BOTHNIA

Planning Charts
UKHO 2252, Swedish 5, 4, Finnish 5, 3

Note that many more lights, buoys and beacons exist than are shown on the plans which accompany this section.

During the winter storms and ice can cause considerable damage to buoys which are sometimes not replaced in the early part of the season. Buoys can also be moved out of place by the ice.

Guides to this part of the world are few. By far the best is *Norrlandskust* by Erik Nyström (Bilda Förlag). This is in Swedish without an English translation, but the many small charts and aerial photographs are invaluable. Even a small smattering of Swedish would go a long way to understanding much of the text. Unfortunately, the book is not available in the UK, but it is easily found in Sweden.

General

The Gulf stretches northeast for some 350 miles with the Swedish/Finnish border neatly bisecting its closed end. Commercial shipping carries mainly paper, timber and iron ore. There is little commercial fishing activity. There is considerable local yachting all along the coast, particularly in the vicinity of the main towns of Hudiksvall, Sundsvall, Harnösand, Umeå, Skellefteå and Luleå, but though the area is popular with German and Finnish yachtsmen it has been less frequently visited by cruisers of other nationalities. However, for those who wish to get away from the beaten track, the Gulf of Bothnia provides excellent sailing, often in *skärgård*s, and even in July when the southern cruising grounds are crowded, one can still enjoy a solitary night at anchor in the most idyllic surroundings.

For many it is natural to want to reach the top of the gulf. However, it is impossible for most cruising yachts to visit Haparanda on the Swedish side of the Tornio river because of the rock strewn approaches and fixed bridges, but the sheltered harbour at Haparandahamn is 18km southeast and is connected by bus. The northernmost point by water is at Töre, a little further west, which can be reached with care and detailed charts.

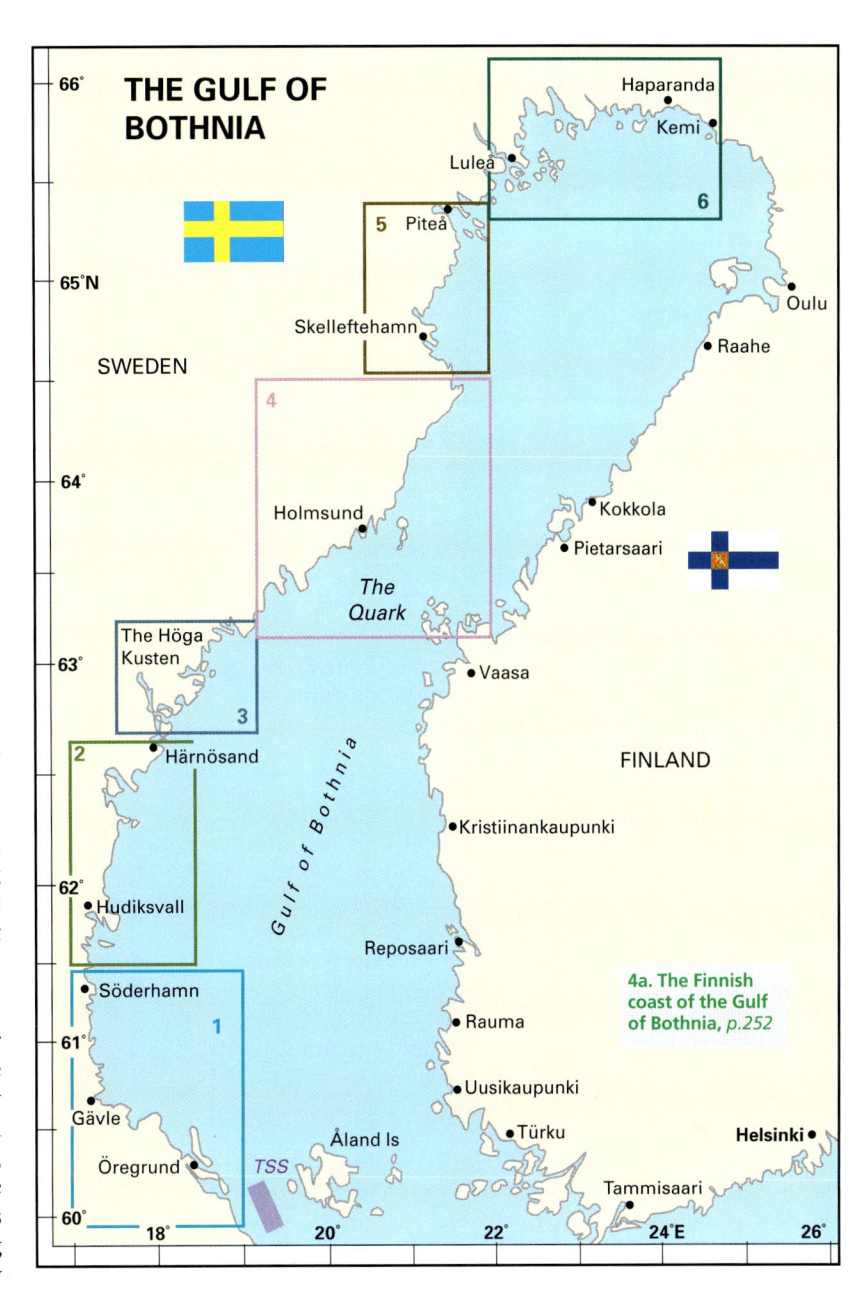

3h. Swedish coast of the Gulf of Bothnia, *226*

1. **Svartklubben to Soderhamn,** *226*
2. **Hudiksvall to Härnösand,** *229*
3. **The Höga Kusten,** *232*
4. **Husum to Bjuröklubb,** *235*
5. **Skelleftehamn to Luleå,** *238*
6. **Luleå to Haparanda,** *241*

Many of the smaller harbours will not have a harbour master or anyone else to come to collect your mooring fee, but instead have an 'honesty box' into which you can drop an envelope with your payment.

GULF OF BOTHNIA

3h. The Swedish coast of the Gulf of Bothnia

The coastline

The Swedish coast between Öregrund and Sundsvall is low lying, the only landmarks being the occasional factory chimney. North of Sundsvall the 'High Coast' (Swedish 'Höga Kusten') begins, and from here to Örnsköldsvik is a fascinating area where hills of about 250m come straight down to the water. Scenically this is perhaps the most beautiful part of eastern Sweden, with many possible anchorages and *gästhamns*. North of Örnsköldsvik, The Quark is a difficult area of shoal waters requiring intricate navigation and the coast becomes flat again. Inland there are low hills and fast flowing rivers with various tourist attractions, and it may well be worth hiring a car for a day or two if weather-bound. The *skärgård* restarts at Piteå and extends for some 90 miles, all the way to the Finnish border.

Route planning and weather

When making a round trip, most yachtsmen prefer to go north along the Swedish side of the Gulf and back south down the Finnish, possibly because in summer the sea breeze tends to become established from the southeast on the west side and from the northwest on the east side. However northerly winds are also quite usual and the worst weather can come from that quarter, often with little warning. Gales are unusual in July, but fog is not uncommon. However this is considered to be the best month for cruising, with the weather improving as one sails north.

The Gulf is icebound for a considerable part of the year and though normally ice-free after May can still be very cold in June. It is fed by rivers from Sweden and Lapland, giving the Gulf as a whole very low salinity. There is no tide, but there are some local currents and water level is subject both to wind direction and to changes in atmospheric pressure. Most harbours are very shallow and becoming more so due to continuing land rise since the last Ice Age.

Stockholm archipelago to Öregrund

The Väddö Canal, which used to provide a convenient shortcut if coming from the Stockholm *skärgård*, has been blocked to many cruising yachts by the construction of a fixed bridge with 17m clearance at approximately 60°03′N.

If leaving from the Stockholm archipelago, a good jumping off point is Gräddö, near Norrtälje, or from one of the small harbours around Arholma. From there, the route runs parallel to the coast and clear of the TSS to enter the channel which runs up to Öregrund. The channel can be entered at Svartklubben (60°10′·6N 18°48′·7E), but a more straightforward passage can be found approximately two miles north of this. It is not much more than 40 miles from Gräddö to Öregrund. Indeed, it is also not far to Mariehamn in the Åland islands (slightly less than 40 miles from Gräddö), and from Mariehamn to Öregrund is also an easy day's passage.

1. Svartklubben to Söderhamn

Distance 90M

The southwest gateway to the gulf and Gävleborg coast. Apart from the infrequent mill chimney, landmarks are rare and you will come across progressively fewer yachts outside the main centres.

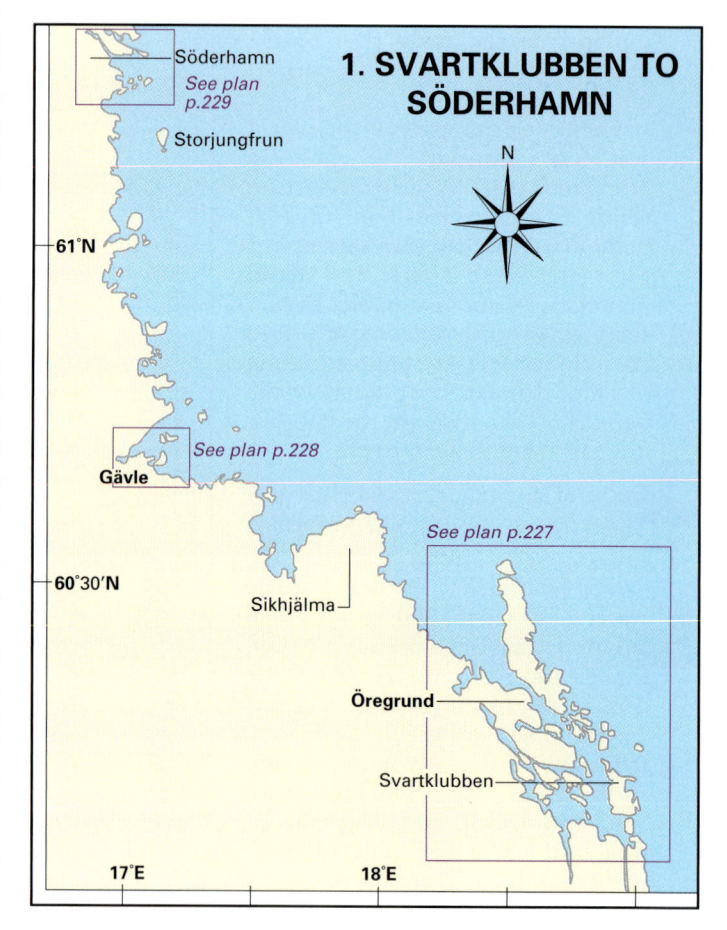

226 THE BALTIC SEA AND APPROACHES

3H. THE SWEDISH COAST OF THE GULF OF BOTHNIA

Öregrund harbour C.N. Hill

Öregrund
60°20'·5N 18°26'·8E
(Pronounced *Uhr-e-gruhnd*)

The southeast approach is via the well buoyed, sheltered and but straightforward *skärgård* route. From the northwest it is relatively easy through the Öregrunds Grepen.

A busy harbour, particularly in season, with 80 guest berths ranging from 1–7m depth. There is a long jetty at the harbour entrance, and the more sheltered berths are on the inner side. Mooring is by lazy line. There are some stern buoys on the outer side. The not unusual north winds can make the harbour uncomfortable when it is best to cross 1M to anchor, in clay, in the sheltered Kullbådaviken from where there is a nearby ferry back to town.

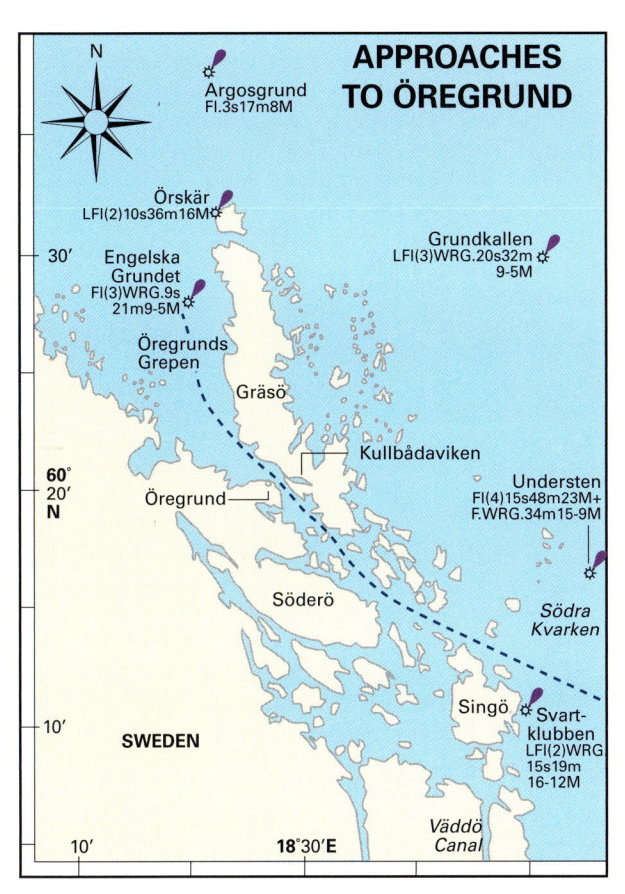

All the usual facilities are available from the *gästhamn* or quay with Öregrunds Båtvarv ☏ +46 173 30423 less than 1M to the south offering general boatyard engineering and lay up. Market on the quay, good shopping which includes a supermarket, Systembolaget and bookshop for Swedish charts. Wide selection of restaurants, interesting church and maritime museum.

Nearest station is Gimo, some 30km distant but accessible by ferry and bus. The latter also run direct to Stockholm.

There are few guest harbours between Öregrund and Gävle, although there are several nature harbours and anchorages. One possibility is Sikhjälma (60°34'·5N 17°49'E), which is a small holiday village 30M from Öregrund. There are very limited facilities and only four guest berths bows-to wooden staging from a stern anchor in 2·5m.

Gävle
60°40'·4N 17°13'·1E
(Pronounced *Yairv-leh*)

Large regional, commercial and shopping centre with docks, industry and a university.

The main channel from the northeast is very well marked for shipping. There is an alternative route for leisure craft from the east between the islands of Limön and Orana.

Visiting yachts generally berth in the large, sheltered marina at Fliskar just beyond and opposite the docks. However there is little more than 2m and a limited number of guest spaces between metal booms. There is a 10 minute walk to the No. 12 bus which then takes half an hour to reach the centre of town. It may also be possible to berth further west at the sailing club to port just short of the canalized river entrance. The Fliskar marina includes a yacht club, all the usual facilities and access to boatyard services.

GULF OF BOTHNIA

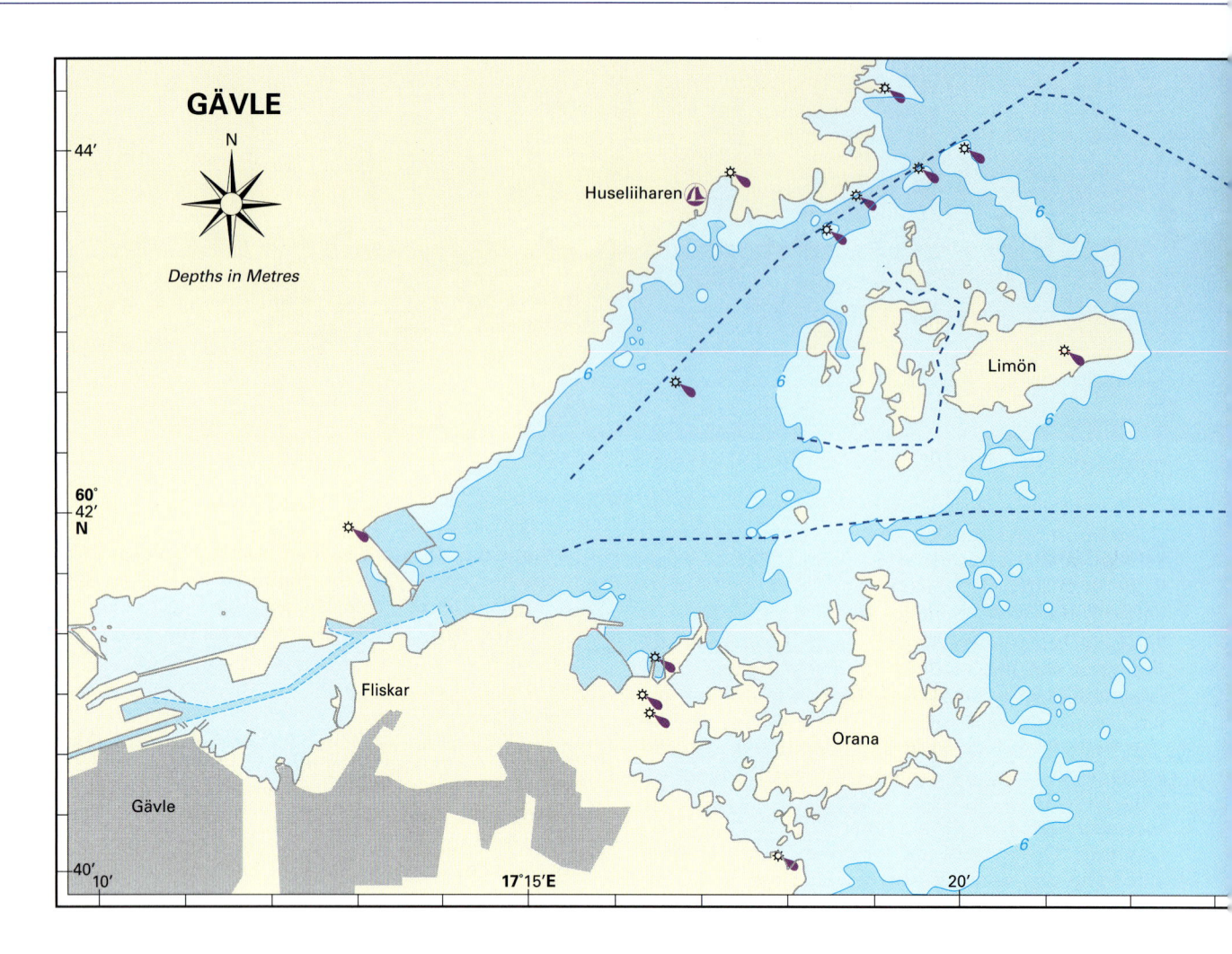

Gävle centre has excellent shopping and all services of a town of nearly 70,000. The most attractive part is of older wooden houses, close to the River Gavleän.

Norrsundet

60°57′·8N 17°15′·0E

This lies a few miles north of Gävle, and the harbour is a few miles down an inlet. Once past the now disused commercial quay, the channel narrows, and although the approach is straightforward, care needs to be taken. There are six stern buoys to a wooden staging. There is a small clubhouse with the usual facilities, and a supermarket 200m away. There is also a bus service to Gävle, which might be more convenient than stopping at Fliskar.

The harbour should be sheltered even in the worst weathers.

Heading north, there is an extensive archipelago containing several anchorages and natural harbours behind the island of Kusör. There is a small guest harbour at Axmar.

The guest moorings at Norrsundet C.N. Hill

Axmar

61°02′·9N 17°09′·6E

The approach to Axmar is at least 3m at the shallowest, but although the channel is well buoyed, it is somewhat complicated, and needs to be taken with some caution.

There is a restaurant with a long section of staging, and there are stern buoys provided. Keep to the section of staging where there are buoys – on the left-hand section as you face the staging, there is a submerged rock! There are no warning signs.

The restaurant is busy in the season, and there are the usual facilities of ablutions, electricity and water, but apart from that, this is a very remote spot.

228   THE BALTIC SEA AND APPROACHES

3H. THE SWEDISH COAST OF THE GULF OF BOTHNIA

2. Hudiksvall to Härnösand

Distance 85M

This section covers the coast north from the Hornslandet peninsula to the start of the 'Höga Kusten'.

There are a series of small fishing villages along the north Hälsingland and Medelpad coasts. The wide Sundsvallbukten leads into Sweden's largest river delta. There are useful anchorages in addition to the 20 *gästhamns* covering this area, mainly around Hudiksvall and Sundsvall. As you sail north the land starts to rise where the High Coast begins between Sundsvall and Härnösand.

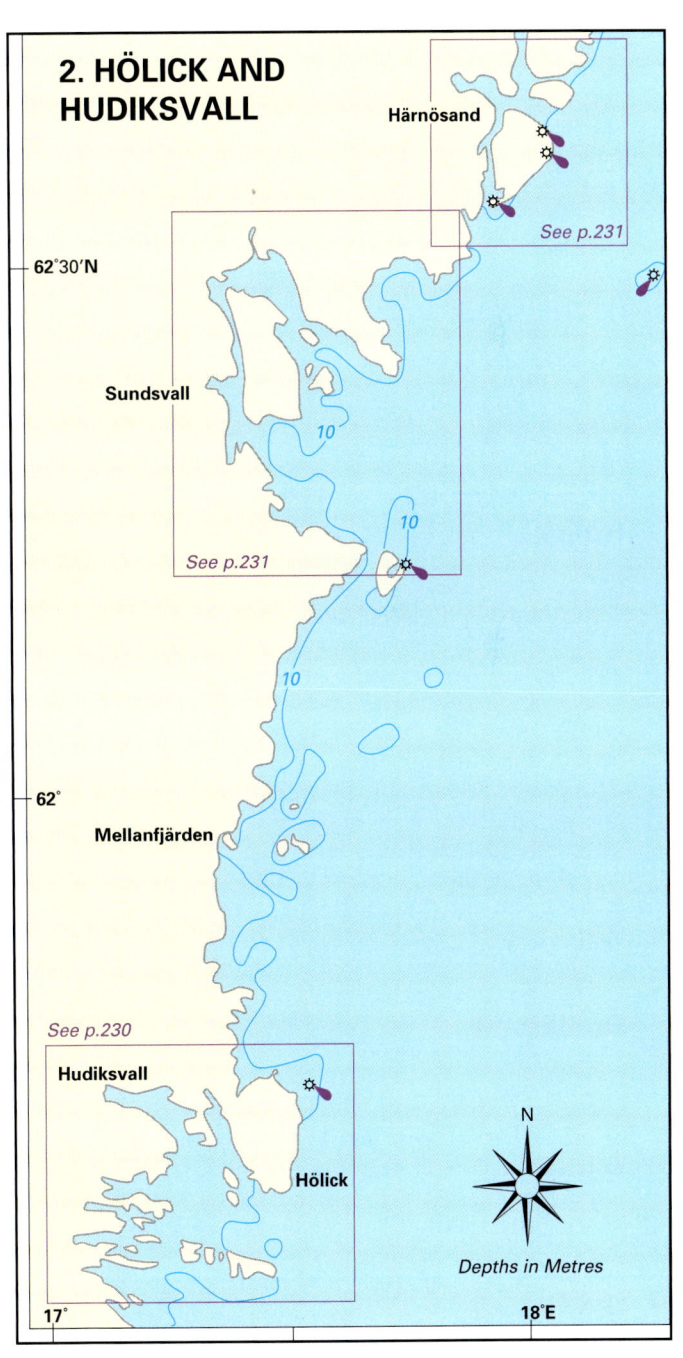

Moorings at the island of Storjungfrun *C.N. Hill*

Storjungfrun

61°10'·1N 17°20'·3E

Take care to avoid the well-marked Storgrundet shoal 2M to the east of the prominent black and white lighthouse just above the small *gästhamn*.

Mooring is by stern buoy to the inside of the breakwater wall in 2·4m, but it can be crowded at week-ends and in season. The harbour can be uncomfortable in a southeasterly but is nonetheless much more attractive than the mainland *gästhamns* at Vallvik or Ljusne. Excellent walks to the west side.

Here there are the first clear signs of rising land. The seaward side of the island is strewn with lichen covered, rounded rocks or large stones. Wood plank pathways have been laid to picturesque wooden houses and the delightful old chapel.

Söderhamn

61°17'·6N 17°04'·7E

Gästhamn in the centre of town with eight bows-to berths from stern buoys in 2m. Well serviced with all the facilities of a municipal centre nearby. The main railway and E4 highway pass through town.

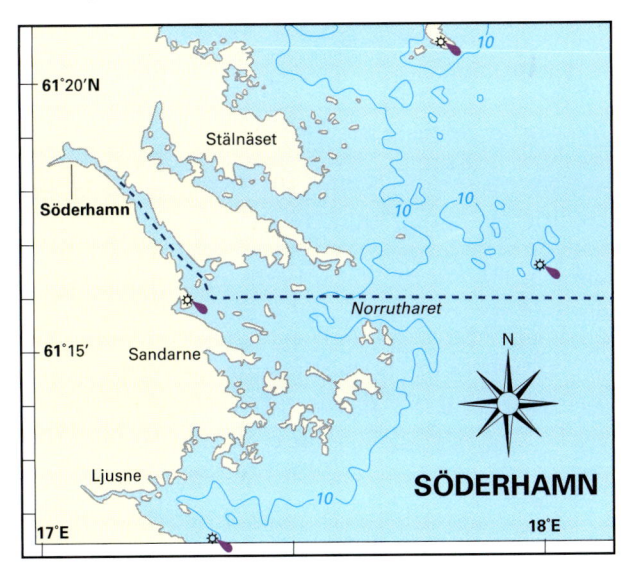

Agön

61°34'·2N 17°18'·2E

This small island is almost bisected by a deep inlet which runs from the south northwards. It is possible either to anchor or to tie up against a small jetty using a stern anchor. It is a picturesque and well sheltered spot.

THE BALTIC SEA AND APPROACHES 229

GULF OF BOTHNIA

The harbour at Hölick – convenient but lacking in facilities *C.N. Hill*

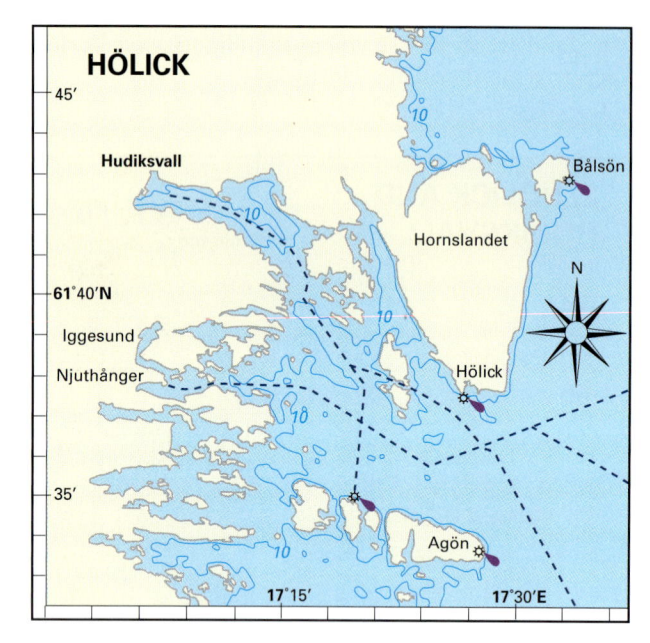

Hölick

61°37'·5N 17°26'·1E

This comprises a marina and holiday camp.

Having passed either side of the Olofsgrund shoal 1M north of Ago, Hölick is in an old fishing harbour on the southwest corner of Hornslandet 3M further north. Be sure to enter between the approach buoys outside the harbour breakwaters to the west of the lighthouse. Mooring is between the metal arms of booms, and larger yachts might struggle to fit in. There are few services apart from a café/restaurant across the harbour, as most facilities are 500m away at the camp site. Very attractive church high on the rocks above the village and excellent walks.

Road access only to Hudiksvall 14km away.

Hudiksvall

61°43'·5N 17°07'·1E

Large municipal centre with docks and deep-water berths. The harbour lies 15M from the sea along well marked channels from the open sea but with some shipping. As you enter there is a large marina to starboard with 12 guest berths with booms or stern buoys in 3·5–7m.

The usual guest services are to hand and there is useful shopping in the town centre some 10 minutes' walk away.

The E4 highway, mainline railway and airport all make this a good crew change harbour.

Mellanfjärden

61°57'·4N 17°20'·5E

Attractive old fishing village.

The easiest approach is from the south of Jättholmarna 5M to the east. There is a lit leading line and then unlit buoys to the *gästhamn* just past a local boat marina to port. Well sheltered with 20 berths, bows-to a wooden quay from stern buoys. In addition to the guest harbour, there is another large almost enclosed bay just to the east. This makes a good anchorage as an alternative to the guest harbour. The entrance to the bay is quite obvious, but there are also leading lines in the trees distant.

Village style facilities serve this attractive collection of red-painted wooden houses with an hotel on the quay.

Sundsvall

62°23'·6N 17°17'·8E

Rebuilt deep-water marina in neo-Renaissance town.

Follow the deep-water channel into town. A new motorway bridge has been built across this part of the harbour, but should provide no problems to yachts. Before this bridge was constructed, all the traffic along the coast went through the town.

The Båt-och *gästhamn* is on the port hand and has 40 berths in 3–12m to stern buoys but could be a little open to the east. There is a clubhouse with washing machine, dryer, cooker, television, all provided with the mooring fee, and there are all the facilities expected of a town of nearly 50,000, including a large chandlery a little less than a kilometre from the guest harbour. Situated at the head of its own fjord, the town has some richly ornamental buildings and nearby beaches.

Well served by the mainline rail network and E4 highway. It is closer to the local airport than Härnösand.

Härnösand

62°38'·1N 17°56'·2E

Bridges ☏ +46 611 15687 (pre 1600) or
+46 601 20184 (post 1600)

Regional and shopping centre with commercial port. (Pronounced *Hair-neu-sahnd*).

Deep water approaches from south, east and north all leading to the narrow fjord inside of Härnön island. Well placed lighthouses make this an easy landfall if sailing straight up from Öregrund or

230   THE BALTIC SEA AND APPROACHES

3H. THE SWEDISH COAST OF THE GULF OF BOTHNIA

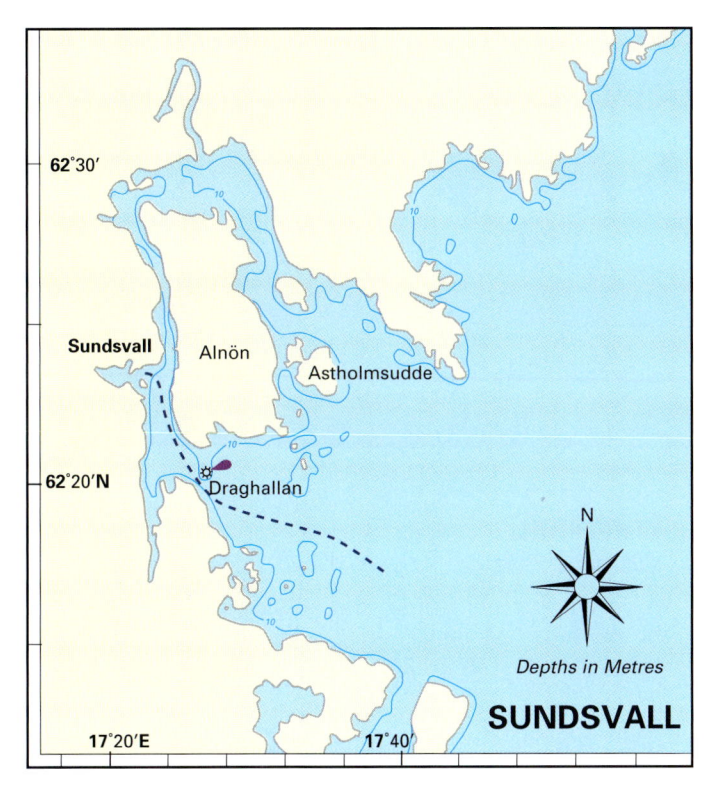

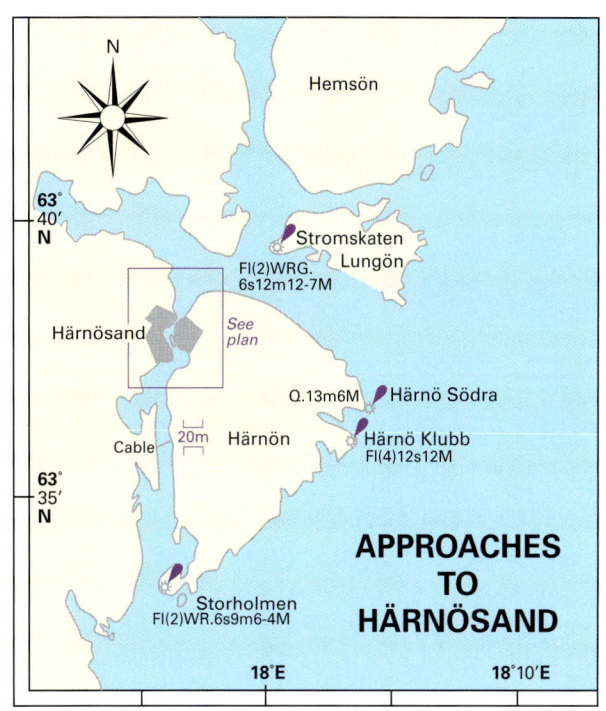

from the Åland Islands but note the 20m cable across the south entrance.

There are three *gästhamns* one of which will always be sheltered whatever the wind. Södra Sundet is below the lifting bridge, Norra Sundet is above the swing bridge and Nattviken between the two bridges. The north swing bridge is only 8m wide and is immediately north of a 90° turn to port. The bridges open at limited times by telephone request.

Each of the *gästhamns* has the usual facilities although fuel is perhaps most easily obtained from the fuel station on the mainland north of Norra Sundet. There is a helpful boatyard Dahlman Marin ☎ +46 611 5566 500m across the bay from Södra Sundet Gästhamn.

There is a large shopping centre spread across both banks of the fjord, a university and multi-faith cathedral.

The moorings at Härnösand on the northern side of the sound. The guest harbour is on the right *C.N. Hill*

GULF OF BOTHNIA

The small village of Bönhamn *C.N. Hill*

3. The Höga Kusten

Distance 45M

In the centre of Västernorrland this is, in many ways, the most attractive part of the whole of the Gulf of Bothnia. World Heritage Site status recognises the Höga Kusten (High Coast) as something special. If you are short of time, don't miss this area.

During the last ice age 3km of ice depressed the region by 800 metres. In the last 10,000 years the land has risen by over 400 metres and remains the fastest rising coast around the world. Currently rising at 9mm per annum it is expected to continue its upward trend for another 5,000 years. It is not unlike the west coast of Scotland but is lower and less austere. The steep tree clad hillsides stretch down to the water which is often fringed with pink Nordic granite among the red houses with white windows.

This makes for an ideal cruising ground with 20 *gästhamns* and many anchorages dotted along the 45M from Härnösand to Örnsköldsvik.

Bönhamn

62°53′N 18°27′·2E

A very pretty old fishing and holiday village, not to be missed. 1M inside the prominent Högbonden light (62°52′N 18°28′·8E) lies this most attractive harbour. The narrow southeast entrance is less easy than that from the north. It is difficult to argue with their claim to be the 'best kept *gästhamn* on this coast'. The berths off the new starboard breakwater are very shallow.

Out of season it may be possible to moor alongside, but the harbour is usually crowded in season, especially at weekends when mooring bows-to from stern anchors can produce crossed lines. Water, power, showers etc at the harbour. There is a café, kiosk, restaurant and art gallery in season. Good walks both north and south of the village giving wonderful views.

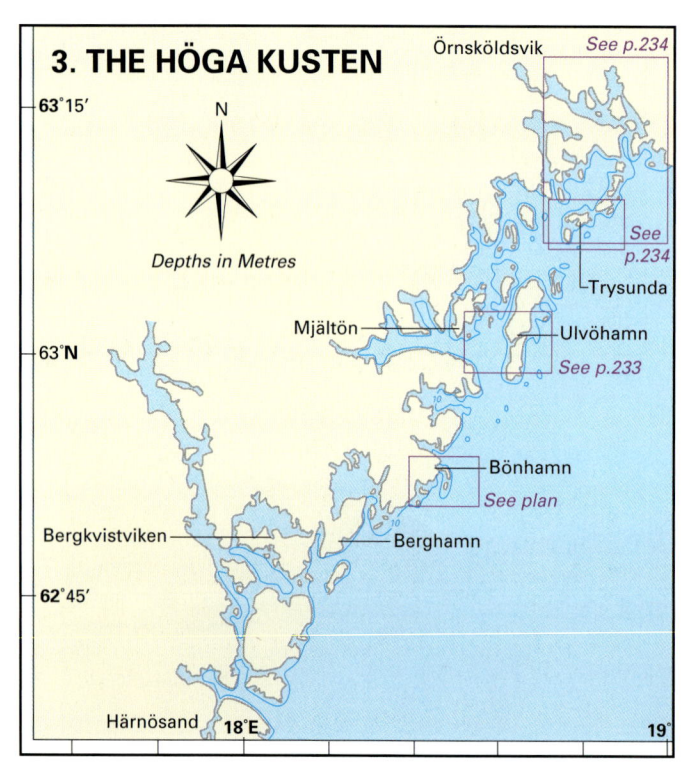

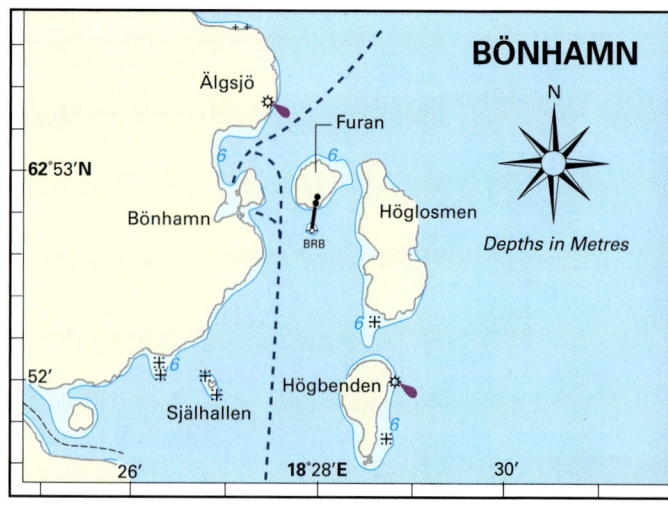

232   THE BALTIC SEA AND APPROACHES

3H. THE SWEDISH COAST OF THE GULF OF BOTHNIA

Norrfällsviken
62°58'·5N 18°31'·3E

Approach is through a fairly narrow channel which opens out into a large bay. At the end of the bay there is an hotel with moorings for visitors, either alongside or in booms.

Ulvöhamn
63°01'·4N 18°39'·6E

A picture-perfect village with a splendid natural harbour.

Between the islands of north and south Ulvö lies the generally sheltered Ulvösund. Entry via the shallow and twisting southwest route is enlivened by the regular Ulvö ferry which has little respect for other vessels! The northeast and south entrances are more straightforward. Very deep water in the sound makes anchoring off difficult but there are three *gästhamns* with bows-to mooring from stern buoys or anchors and some rock moorings near the southwest entrance.

The large and attractive village has a permanent population, shop, pharmacy, hotel and restaurants. The usual facilities and fuel are available. Try to see the ancient wooden chapel with painted interior and taste the local fermented herring speciality of Surströmming. Very popular in season but well worth a visit.

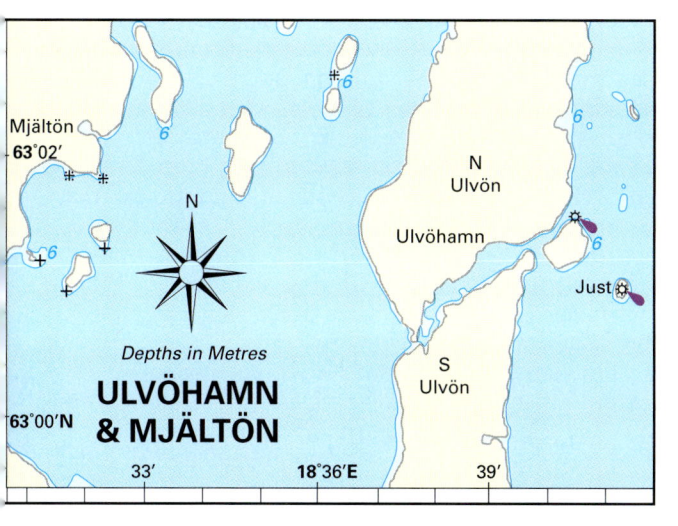

The natural lagoon at Mjälton *E. Redfern*

Mjältön
63°02'·3N 18°32'·3E

A natural lagoon. The narrow and shallow entrance reveals itself on the southeast side of the island. Totally protected and deep in the centre. Limited bows-to mooring to basic pontoons on the north side. If anchoring off, a trip line may be wise following extensive logging on the south side. Barbecue areas on the beach and latrine. Good walks into the nature reserve.

Set a new record by walking to the top of Sweden's highest island peak! Bastutoberger is about a 2km walk and reaches 236m above sea level, rising at 9mm per annum.

Trysunda
63°08'·4N 18°47'·4E

An enchanting holiday village in a nature reserve. Easy entrance from the southwest to moor bows-to a substantial jetty from stern buoys in 3–7m. Exposed to the south when it may be possible to anchor on the north of the island. Power, water, washroom etc at the *gästhamn*.

The picturesque town at Ulvöhamn *C.N. Hill*

THE BALTIC SEA AND APPROACHES

GULF OF BOTHNIA

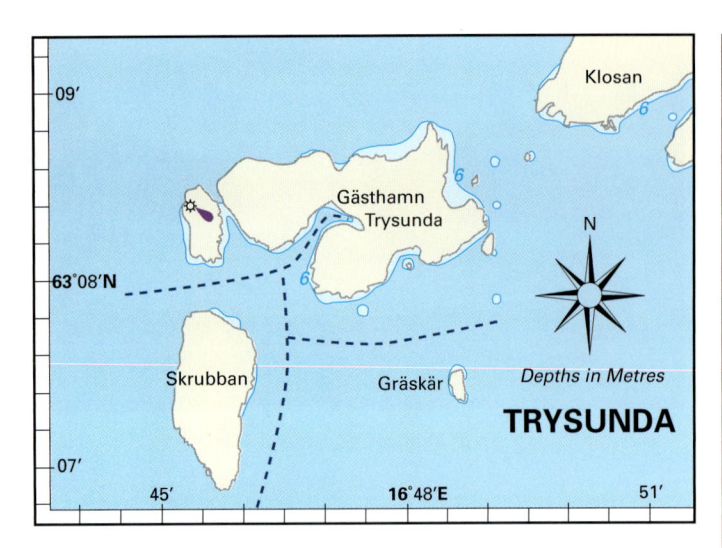

A view over the harbour at Trysunda, which is a little exposed to the south C.N. Hill

This former fishing village is now almost entirely holiday homes with very few permanent residents. Beautifully maintained but nothing open before midsummer when a small shop and restaurants appear for the season. Interesting wooden seamen's chapel with painted interior. Excellent walks around the island.

The route into the guest harbour at Örnöldsvik C.N. Hill

Örnsköldsvik

63°17'·2N 18°42'·7E

A regional centre and commercial port.

(Pronounced *Urn-sheulds-veek*). From the open sea the Skagsudde light (63°11'·3N 19°01'·4E) marks the start of a deep-water channel. After 4M this joins with the coastal route from the southwest from inside Trysunda. A sharp turn to port precedes 5M of well-marked and lit channel right up to the extreme northwest corner of the harbour. The *gästhamn* of 35 berths in 3m offers boom or alongside moorings with all the usual services. There are many nearby anchorages from which to choose but all are well away from town.

The large and modern town centre provides extensive shopping and services. The town is also Sweden's Ice Hockey centre. Well served by the E4 highway and buses but with no immediate rail link. There is an airport 20km away.

234   THE BALTIC SEA AND APPROACHES

3H. THE SWEDISH COAST OF THE GULF OF BOTHNIA

4. Husum to Bjuröklubb

Distance 110M

The Västerbotten coast and Norra Kvarken. Well served by the E4 highway which links most of the dozen *gästhamns*, but shallow midway and sometimes living up to its fearsome sounding name 'The Quark'. While signs of current or past industrial activities are spread along the coastline the island of Holmön just offshore claims to be Sweden's sunniest.

Husum

63°19'·8N 19°08'·5E

Safe harbour and commercial centre. Well-lit and buoyed entrance towards a dominating pulp mill.

This is a convenient first stop north of the Höga Kusten but the *gästhamn* is 3km away from the town. Six berths for alongside or bows-to from stern anchor moorings in 2–4m. Basic facilities as most services are in town.

E4 highway within 3km and airport 10km.

Järnäsklubb

63°26'·3N 19°40'·7E

Old pilot station. Situated 3M northeast of the Störbaden light (63°24'·5N 19°30'·36), which should be given a good offing. There is a leading line, but it is not easy to find. The narrow entrance opens out into a much larger bay, and the harbour itself cannot be seen until you are well inside. There is alongside mooring for five rafted in 1–3m. To accommodate the claimed 10 boats all would have to be less than 7m LOA. There is a small clubhouse and kiosk. Limited electricity points.

If the harbour is full, it is possible to anchor in the bay outside. Shelter in here should be good.

The small but perfectly formed harbour at Järnäsklubb. Like other similar harbours along this coast, this was once used by pilot boats *C.N. Hill*

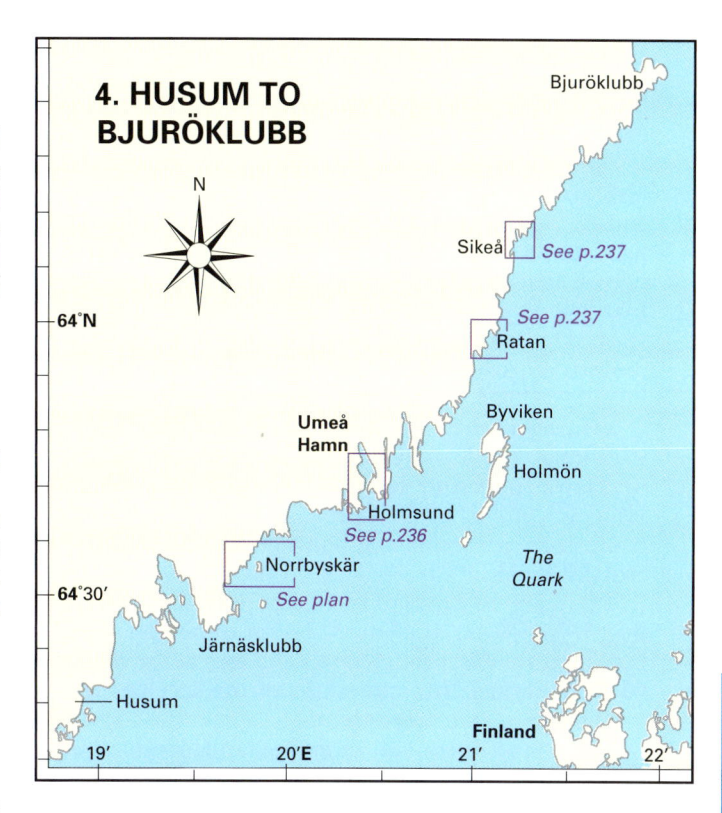

Norrbyskär

63°33'·8N 19°52'·5E

A fascinating island, the site of abandoned saw mill. The small *gastbrygga* at Kalmarn on the northern end has space for no more than three alongside unless rafting. Take great care to avoid the sunken timbers at either end. Basic facilities and a 1km walk down to the village. Here there are 20 bows-to visitors' moorings from stern anchors with better facilities but close to the ferry quay from Norrbyn and exposed to the east.

In the 19th century this became the largest saw mill company in Europe and was set up as a model society. The management and workers' houses lining the street are now holiday homes. There are remains of its previous use all over the island and a miniature reproduction of the mill draws many day visitors from the mainland.

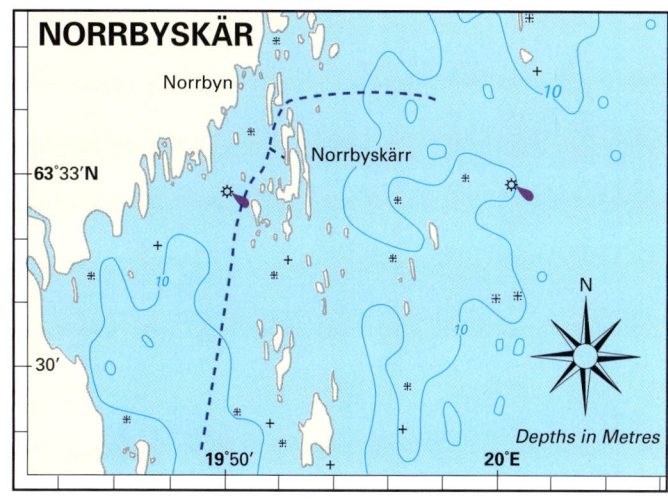

THE BALTIC SEA AND APPROACHES

GULF OF BOTHNIA

Holmsund, Umeå

63°49'N 20°16'E

Provincial capital, ferry port and yacht club marina.

The main entrance north-northeast from the Vaktaren light (63°36'·9N 20°25'·4E) is well buoyed and lit for the ferries to Finland. From the Lillbådan light (63°38'·9N 20°20'·8E) there is a straight forward deep water route to the north-northeast of the long Fjardgrund peninsula. This leads past the docks to starboard at Umeå Hamn but is then blocked by a 3·8m fixed bridge before going all the way 18km inland to Umeå.

Visiting yachts usually berth at the Holmsund, Patholmsviken Yacht Club and *gästhamn* to the east of Fjardgrund and north of the ferry terminal. However, north of the Lillbådan light can be very confusing with conflicting buoyage for different and cross channels.

There are 10 bows-to moorings from stern buoys in 1·5–6m. Water and limited power on the pontoon but there are excellent facilities and fuel at the Yacht Club boatyard, lift out and lay up services are available from the nearby yard.

There are adequate shopping and services at Holmsund 1km north and full services in a large shopping centre with a hospital and two universities 15km to the north by No. 124 bus at Umeå which is sometimes known as 'The City of Birches'.

The E4 highway, rail services and a busy local airport make this a good place to change crew.

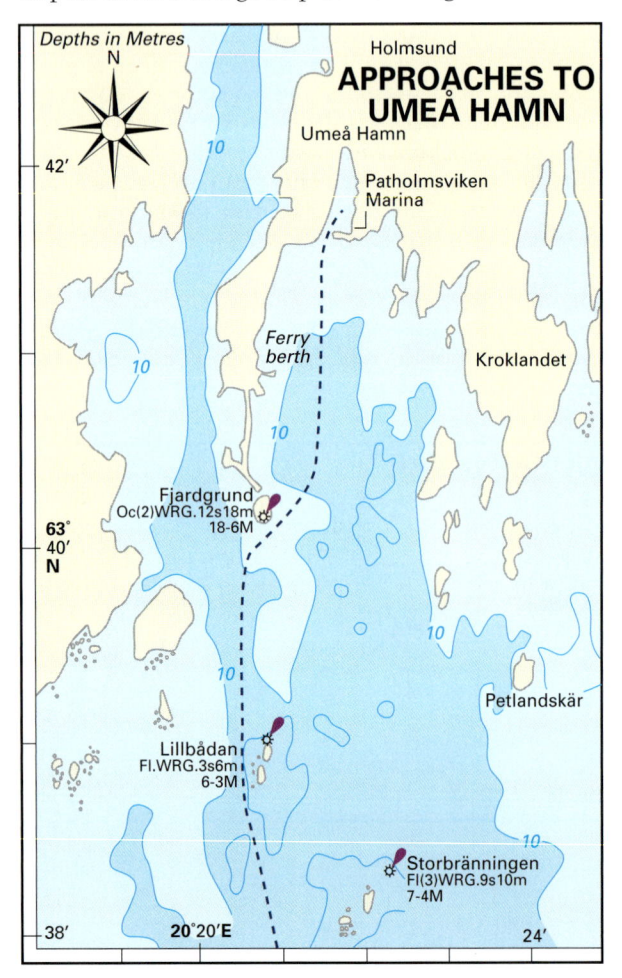

The Patholmsviken Yacht Club at Umeå Hamn *C.N. Hill*

Byviken

63°48'·4N 20°52'·5E

Small guest and ferry harbour on the north of Holmön.

A straight forward entrance from the north to moor bows-to from stern buoys behind the east breakwater. There is 3m near the fairway but quickly shoaling towards the shore. You need to turn immediately to port on entering, and watch the depth sounder carefully. Water and power on the quay with basic facilities nearby.

In season there are a café, kiosk, restaurant and the excellent boat museum between the ferry and prominent lighthouse on the west of the harbour. Small shop, chemist and Systembolaget 2km to the south.

Lying 6M off shore this is a popular weekend destination and good jumping off place for Finland just 45M to the east.

The very shallow harbour at Byviken on Holmön *E. Redfern*

236 THE BALTIC SEA AND APPROACHES

3H. THE SWEDISH COAST OF THE GULF OF BOTHNIA

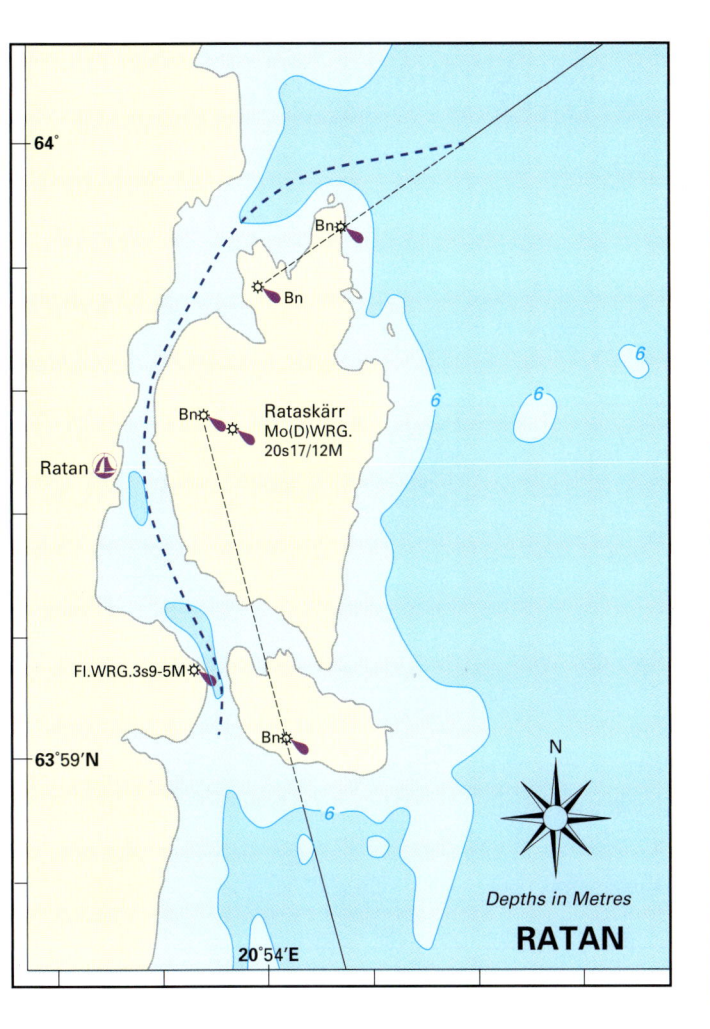

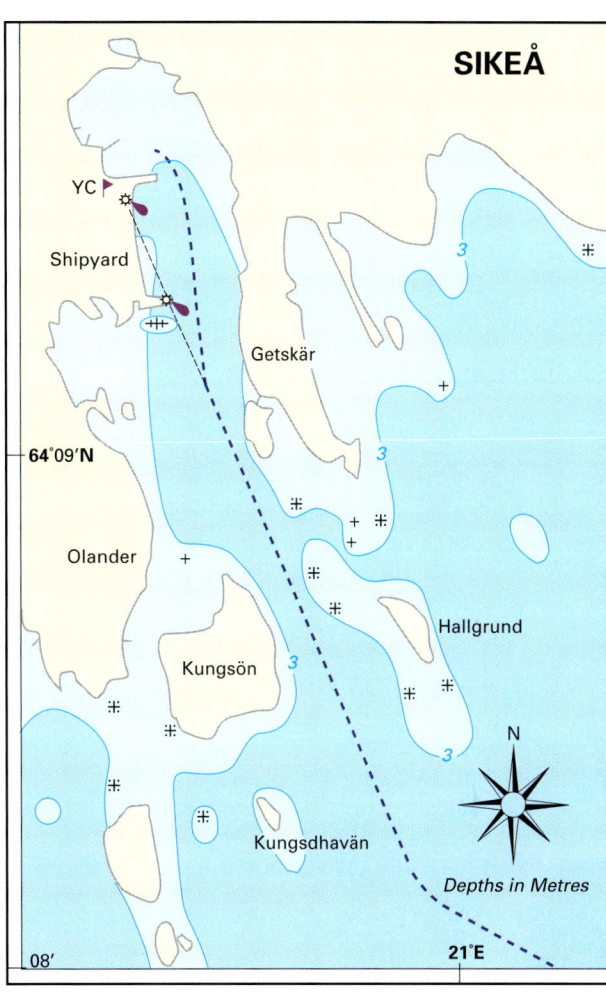

Ratan

63°59'·5N 20°53'·7E

The best natural harbour on this coast. Easy deep-water entrance from the southeast but more care is needed for the shallow north entrance. Mooring in 4·5m alongside or bows-to from stern anchors if crowded. Power, water and fuel on the quay with other facilities within 300m. Can be exposed to strong southeast winds when it is possible to anchor in the lee of Rataskar island further in.

Ratan was an important customs port and the site of a 'land uplift' experiment by Celsius and Linnaeus in the 19th century. The small building for their mareograph still stands. The excellent restaurant at Tullgårdens Gärtgifueri (closed Mondays) was previously a holiday home for worn-out housewives but was built for the Customs Chief Officer. Scene of a major battle with the Russians in 1809.

Go by dinghy for good walks on Rataskar.

Sikeå

64°09'·6N 20°58'·7E

Abandoned shipbuilding yard and port for ironworks, now a holiday camp.

A straight forward, well-marked entrance from the southeast. An operative leading light remains from previous usage. Moor in 2·5m bows-to from stern buoys at the outer end of the second jetty but it is very shallow beyond. Power and water on the quay with other facilities at the friendly yacht club 300m away. Some supplies at the campsite.

In the 18th century this was an important shipbuilding yard and trading port for the Robertfors Ironworks some miles inland.

Bjuröklubb

64°19'·8N 21°22'·5E

Tiny old pilot station. Buoyed from the southeast and easy approach from the north to inside of Bjuron point. Unless there are small boats moored bows-to there is alongside berthing for four in 1–4m. There have been reports of shoaling, and so care should be taken entering the harbour. In settled weather it is also possible to anchor off.

Basic facilities with a barbecue and free sauna but the invigorating walk up to the lighthouse is well worth the effort for spectacular views and the sunset.

In season there is a café near the lighthouse and fish for sale from a boat in the harbour.

THE BALTIC SEA AND APPROACHES

GULF OF BOTHNIA

5. Skelleftehamn to Luleå

Distance 70M

Norbotten and the north *skärgård*

The waters are often shallower but the islands become more frequent throughout this area which becomes progressively more attractive. *Gästhamns* are less common and usually smaller but the opportunities to anchor increase.

Skelleftehamn, Kurjoviken

64°41'·2N 21°13'·7E

Sailing Club marina and guest harbour.

Like Umeå, the town of Skellefteå is some 18km inland and cannot be approached by sailing yachts due to several low fixed bridges. Visiting yachts normally berth at the friendly Ursvikens Sailing Club at Kurjoviken.

From the south pass either side of Skötgrönnan beacon (64°35'·9N 21°30'E). From the north leave Gäsören light (64°39'·8N 21°19'·3E) to starboard. Then join the main buoyed channel just north of the Rakan light (64°38'·8N 21°18'E) and steer northwest to pass south and west of the prominent foundry on Rönnskär. Continue northwest approximately 2M through the buoys until the narrow entrance to Kurjoviken opens on the starboard beam. There is a leading line through this 2·7m channel to the marina which could be tricky in a strong on shore wind. A new *gästhamn* pontoon is immediately to port with bows-to mooring from stern buoys or anchors.

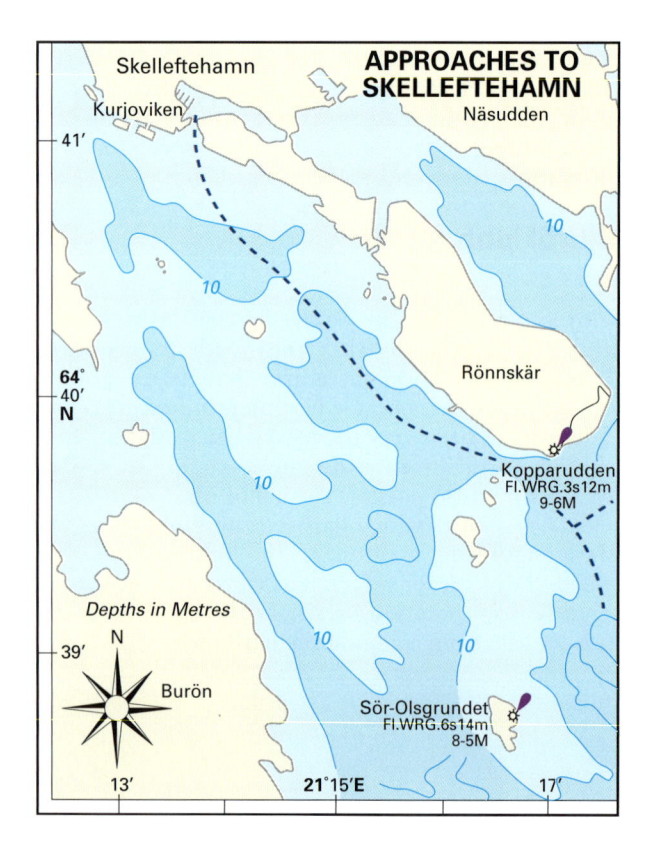

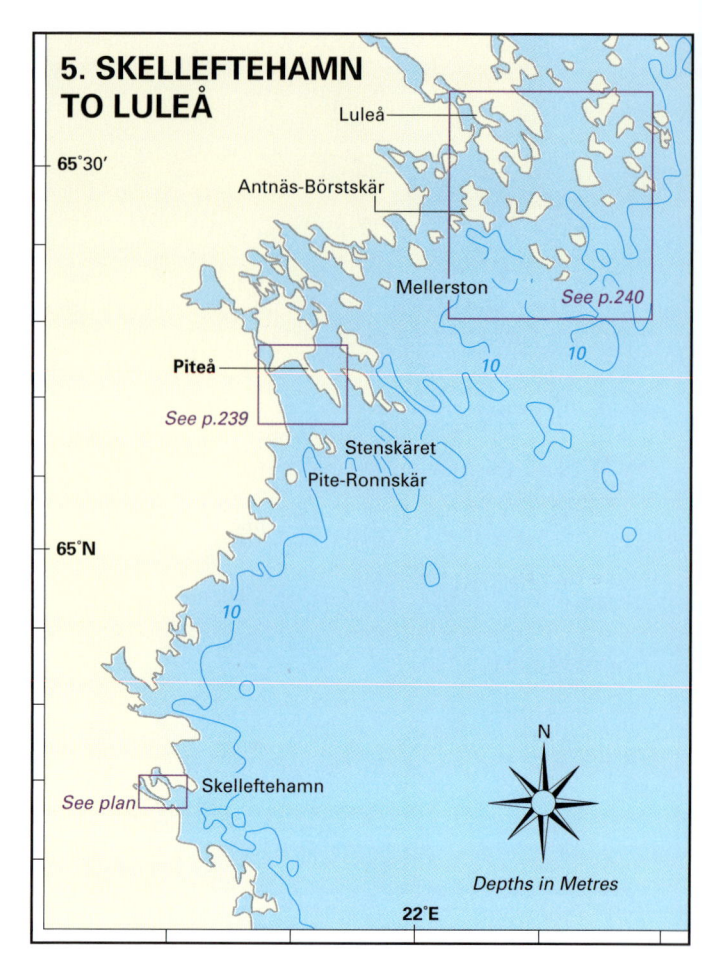

Water and power on this pontoon and all the usual facilities at the nearby clubhouse.

There is adequate shopping and some services within 2km and frequent buses to a large shopping centre in town. Boatyard, lift out services and lay up facilities at the marina. Pleasant walks around Kurjoviken.

Pite-Rönnskär

65°03'·2N 21°33'·4E

A prominent red lighthouse overlooks this old pilot station.

This little island lies 3·5M west of the Nygrån light (65°01'N 22°41'·5E). Even with a large scale chart

The iron lighthouse at Pite-Rönnskär
E. Redfern

238 THE BALTIC SEA AND APPROACHES

3H. THE SWEDISH COAST OF THE GULF OF BOTHNIA

Pite-Rönnskär from the lighthouse *E. Redfern*

the entrance looks unfriendly but round the buoy to it's north to pick up the leading line and creep into this spectacular spot. A small ferry from Piteå claims the immediate alongside berth leaving just enough space for six boats to moor bows-to from their own stern anchors in 2·5m. During the season and at weekends more than 10m LOA is likely to be too large. By July long weeds stream to the surface.

An ideal lunch stop with few facilities. Most of the wooden houses are now holiday homes handed down through the generations. Fishing nets used to be stored for the winter in the small wooden chapel. It is worth seeking out a guide to climb the unusual iron lighthouse for panoramic views.

Pite-Rönnskär beacon *M. Bowyer*

Stenskäret
65°07'N 21°43'E

Good anchorage and a small guest pontoon near an old fishing village.

Just 7M to the northeast of Pite-Rönnskär is this reverse L-shaped island. However approach from the north into a long gently shelving bay with the guest pontoon to port. You may moor bows-to from a stern anchor generally with many local boats but the rest of the bay is an easy anchorage open only to the northwest.

There are no facilities but extensive walks along sweeping sandy beaches backed by flowering sea peas, marram grass and wild flowers. Also large areas of multi-coloured stones cover the ground. On the seaward side these are coated with lichen. In the southwest corner behind the settlement are a number of fertility or good luck circles laid out by generations of fishermen.

Piteå, Haraholmen
65°14'·5N 21°37'·6E

Small marina beside commercial port. Well buoyed and lit routes lead to the port and the small sailing club marina is just to the northwest. There are no facilities apart from water on hand but this could be a useful place from which to reach the large town of Piteå which is beyond a low fixed bridge. Nearby sandy beaches at Pitsundet seem to attract many Norwegians for their holidays. The *gästhamns* on the north side of this peninsula are only suitable for boats drawing less than 1·2m and 1·5m.

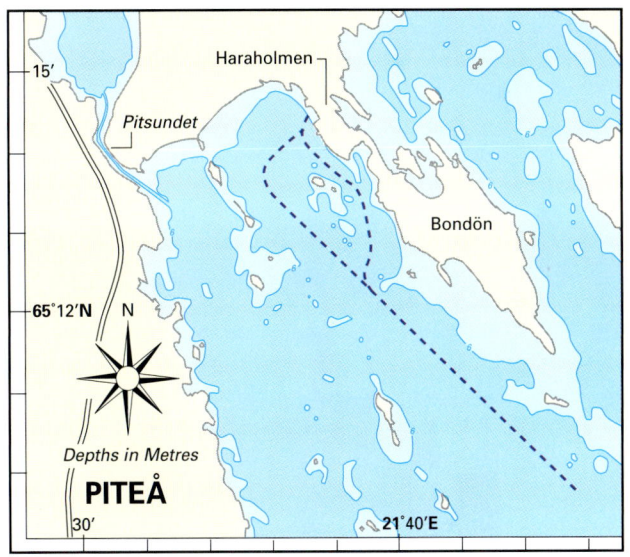

Mellerston
65°11'N 21°47'·4E

Lunch time anchorage. Another 7M north and to the east of Bondön is the large island of Mellerston. On its north shore are several anchorages the west of which has a small and shallow guest pontoon.

There are no facilities but this is a useful lunch time anchorage in 1·5–2m open only to the northwest.

THE BALTIC SEA AND APPROACHES   **239**

GULF OF BOTHNIA

Antnäs-Börskä

65°25'·7N 22°06'·5E

Small guest pontoon and anchorage by a friendly village. There is an easy relatively deep-water entrance from the northwest. The pontoon for 10 bows-to berths has some stern buoys in 2·5m and is straight ahead. Anchor in deeper water in the bay which is exposed only to the northwest.

The few facilities include a free sauna provided by the commune but please split replacement wood.

Luleå

65°34'·8N 22°09'·7E

Regional capital, industrial, commercial, shopping and yachting centre.

There are two main entrances to Luleå. Between the airport and Sandön into the 1M long, dredged Tjuvholmsundet canal is convenient for leisure boats from the south. The very well-buoyed commercial route from the open sea starts just north of the Farstugr whistle buoy (65°19'·8N 22°45'E). After 16M to the northwest the narrows at Likskarët (65°31'N 22°22'E) are reached. These two routes meet just north of Sandön 5M later but still 2·5M short of the marina. Pass the impressive icebreaker fleet to starboard and head for the west end of the marina for the Ettans Båthamn *gästhamn*. Berth bows-to the jetty between booms in 3·5m. Larger vessels can moor alongside further west on the town quay.

The *gästhamn* is fully equipped with good facilities and all the usual boatyard services. Dues are paid at the comprehensive Granek chandlers behind and there is a restaurant attached. The nearby major shopping centre will meet all needs.

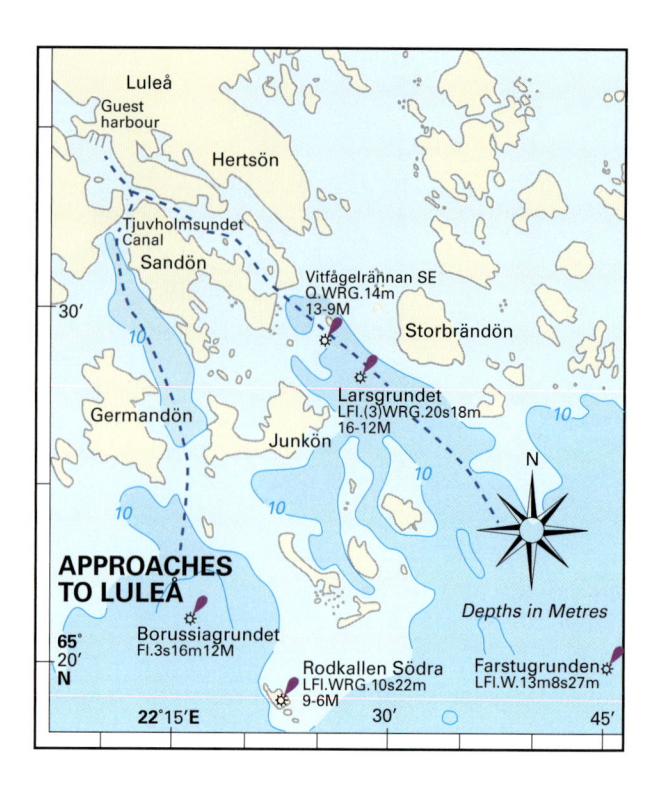

This town of nearly 75,000 is well served by road, rail and air communications to make it a first class crew change base.

The World Heritage site at Gammelstad Church Village 10km to the northwest is well worth a visit for its interesting history and good restaurants. Luleå is also an excellent place from which to hire a car for a short break to drive into the Arctic Circle, Lapland and even Norway. Don't miss the spectacular Storforsen falls en route.

The two icebreakers which keep the harbour clear in winter *C.N. Hill*

240   THE BALTIC SEA AND APPROACHES

3H. THE SWEDISH COAST OF THE GULF OF BOTHNIA

6. Luleå to Haparanda

Distance 65M

The top of the Gulf and border country. The *skärgård* which started around Piteå continues all the way round to the Finnish border. In places it is shallow but there are enough *gästhamns*, anchorages and deep water to make this an attractive cruising area in its own right. Don't expect to find many visiting yachts but this leaves space for abundant wildlife and waterfowl.

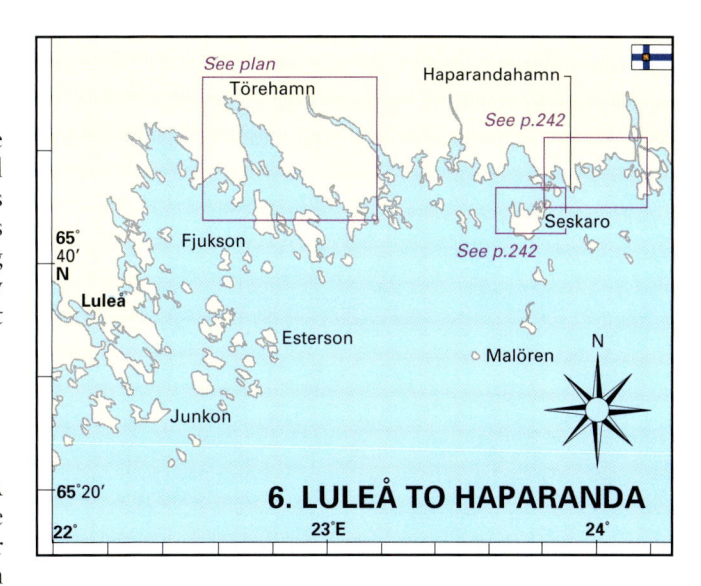

Junkon

65°27'·4N 22°24'·3E

Restored harbour with windmill and walks. A straight forward approach from the north to the west bay on the top of the island. 10 berths for alongside, bows-to from stern anchors or between booms in 1·9–2·5m.

Since being declassified as a defence area the harbour and buildings have benefited from a make-over financed by the EU. There are a small café, museum, windmill and good walks on the island which is visited by a day trip boat from Luleå. It is sometimes possible to buy fish from a local fisherman.

Esterson

65°32'·9N 22°47'·5E

Quiet natural anchorage. Enter either end of the channel between the two islands. From the northwest there is a leading line. From the southeast stay south of the rocky shallows and mind the regular fishing nets. There is an overnight anchorage just west of the house in good holding or a lunch time stop on the east in more doubtful holding. Exposed to the northwest and east.

Fjukson

65°40'·9N 22°37'·3E

Well placed overnight anchorage. Approach from the west and it is simple to anchor in 8m just west of the house on the north shore. Good mud holding but exposed to the west. Well positioned if visiting Töre 15M further north.

Törehamn

65°54'·1N 22°39'E

Gästhamn at the top of the gulf.

Follow the transits and well-buoyed channel past Törefors to the grain silos. There are six guest berths in 1·9m in the *gästhamn* or go alongside in deeper water outside. There are few facilities but a café serves the nearby camp site.

This is the most northerly point in the Baltic Sea so it may be quite busy in season. Close by is a large yellow buoy with a letter box on its side. If you fill in the form provided you will receive a certificate recording that you have reached this landmark.

Malören

65°31'·6N 22°33'·5E

Remote lighthouse island. A bow shaped island with two lights and a Racon. Enter from the south and anchor off on the southwest of the pier but because of land uplift do not expect to find more than 1·5m. Exposed but safe in all winds except from the southwest. This is a convenient but shallow stop if crossing the top of the gulf. Popular at the weekends during the season.

Seskaro, Leppaniemi

65°44'N 23°44'·5E

Small guest harbour on attractive agricultural island. Most yachts will have to approach from the northwest because of an 11·5m fixed bridge on the east side. There are several anchorages or harbours on the north side of this island. Leppaniemi is in the

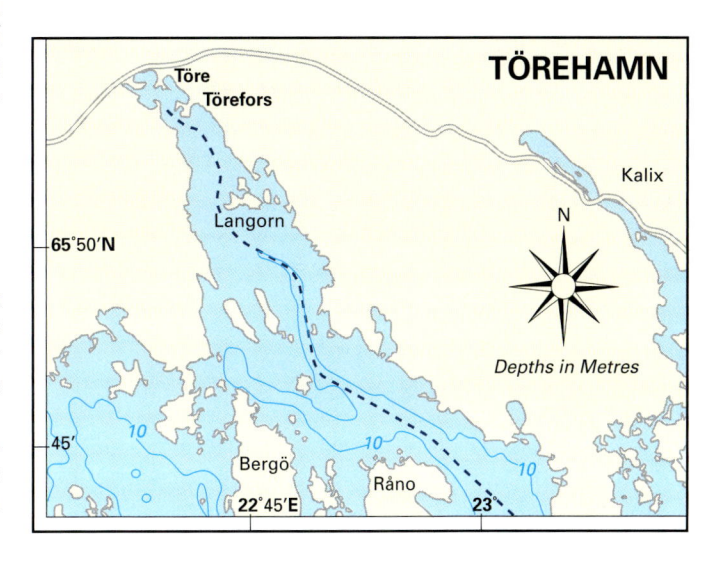

GULF OF BOTHNIA

centre and easily entered with good buoyage and a leading line. Berth alongside or bows-to from a stern anchor at the jetty to starboard just north of the log pool or anchor off in 7m. Good holding and well sheltered except from the north when it would be quieter to tackle the tricky entrance to the east bay. Some facilities, campsite and limited provisions but daily buses to Haparanda.

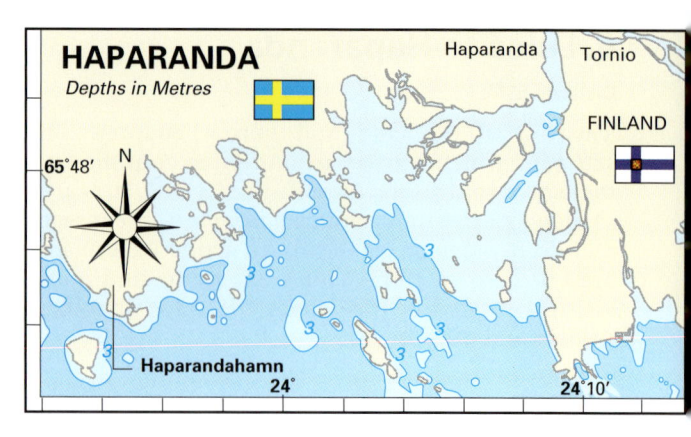

Haparandahamn

65°46'·3N 23°54'·5E

Guest harbour for the northern border town.

A sheltered *gästhamn* with ten berths in 3m and the usual facilities run by a friendly Sailing Club. Not the most interesting spot but convenient if visiting Haparanda some 18km to the northeast, access to which is restricted by rocky shallows and fixed bridges. Haparanda lies on the Swedish side of the River Tornio and is best visited by bus.

Båtskärsnäs

65°47'·15N 23°25'·7E

Said to be the largest boatyard in the Bay of Bothnia, with an 80 ton crane. There is a *gästhamn* with 40 visitors berths in 2–6m but few facilities and no public transport.

The clubhouse at Haparandahamn. Even as late as the end of May, the season has hardly started *C.N. Hill*

242   THE BALTIC SEA AND APPROACHES

3H. THE SWEDISH COAST OF THE GULF OF BOTHNIA

Vaxholm Fortress, strategically placed to defend Stockholm *C.N. Hill*

One of the many historic excursion boats in Stockholm archipelago *C.N. Hill*

Kalmar market square *C.N. Hill*

A lighthouse in the Blue Coast archipelago *C.N. Hill*

The 30m high bridge in Baggensstäket *C.N. Hill*

FINLAND – GULF OF BOTHNIA, ARCHIPELAGO SEA (ÅLAND AND ÅBO), GULF OF FINLAND

4a. The Finnish coast of the Gulf of Bothnia, *252*
4b. The Archipelago Sea: Åland Islands and Åbo Archipelago, *264*
4c. Gulf of Finland western part, *287*
4d. Gulf of Finland eastern part, *300*
4e. The Russian channel, Saimaa Canal and lake, *313*

244   THE BALTIC SEA AND APPROACHES

4. Finland

Cruising in Finland means meandering amid tree-clad islands, with clear, tideless and sheltered waters, colourful villages, well-run marinas, secluded anchorages, warm summer days, rich and fertile land, and fragrant forests carpeted with pine needles.

The people are extremely friendly and wildlife abounds – wild swans, eider, deer, sea trout, turbot and many other species. There is a special satisfaction in being able to navigate in complete confidence through myriad channels between the islands, often only a matter of feet from the rocks, with the use of the Finnish charts. In complex areas where each island looks much like its neighbour, a small, removable adhesive marker may be found useful to keep track of one's position on the chart
To the north, the Gulf of Bothnia extends almost to the Arctic Circle. The further north one goes, the less it is populated and the fir trees predominate.

The Åland Islands, a favourite cruising ground for yachtsmen from Sweden and Finland – not to mention further afield – are of particular interest, not only because of their beauty, but also because of their connection with the sailing traders. The Åland Sea, the stretch of water that separates Sweden from the Åland Islands is only about 19M wide if measured between the easternmost Swedish *skärgård* and the westernmost Finnish one and forms a well trodden path for yachts and ferries during the summer months but is not to be taken lightly in poor weather.

The boundary between the Åland Islands and the rest of Finland is marked by the Kihti (Skiftet), a long, narrow sound only 0·9M wide in its northern part becoming 20M wide in the south. It runs north–south on longitude 21°09′E. West of this boundary the language spoken is almost entirely Swedish. East of it Finnish speakers and place names gradually become more frequent. The waters between the western Åland islands and Hanko are said to be the densest archipelago in the world.

The beauty of remote anchorages *John Langdon*

THE BALTIC SEA AND APPROACHES   **245**

4. FINLAND

From the Åland Islands to Hamina, just short of the border with Russia, the coast is a saaristo or *skärgård* coast, that is to say there is a sheltered route in smooth water behind the fringe of islands. It is difficult to convey the fascination of this kind of sailing to those who have never experienced it. One sails for hundreds of miles in smooth water through a vast forest or rock garden, stopping almost at will. At first the pilotage may seem difficult, especially if it is blowing hard, but the waters are excellently marked by buoys, lighthouses and stone cairns, and by pairs of wooden transits on shore. These cairns, or kummel are the oldest marks in the islands, and very skilfully sited. They show the general direction of the route but not, of course, every isolated danger.

Yachtsmen who are new to these waters often expend a great deal of nervous energy looking for 'the next mark'. It should be borne in mind, however, that if there are no rocks there will be no marks, sometimes for several miles. Therefore, as a general rule, one is better off if one cannot see a mark than if one can – provided one is in the fairway, which means on the correct side of the relevant island. There are exceptions, of course…

An entirely separate cruising ground is the Saimaa Lake area, an immense landlocked complex of lakes entered through the Saimaa Canal. The Canal starts near Vyborg (see page 325), and runs through territory secured by the Russians in 1944 and leased back to the Finns in 1963 in return for the latter undertaking the upkeep of the canal. The Saimaa lakes are a favourite cruising ground for local yachtsmen, especially at the time of the Savonlinna Opera Festival in July, but are little visited by foreign yachts. The Board of Management of the Saimaa Canal issues a well-produced booklet of instructions for small-boat traffic in the Saimaa Canal.

There are many beautiful and interesting harbours in Finland and it is only possible in this guide to mention a small selection of them.

The country

The Finns call their country *Suomi*, 'the land of lakes and fens'. It has a narrow coastal plain, which supports most of the population and farming. Further inland there is a rocky, forested plateau some 100m above sea level where the wildlife is largely undisturbed. The plateau, also known as the Finnish Lakeland, contains about 188,000 lakes, which drain westwards into the Gulf of Bothnia and south into the Gulf of Finland. Lake Saimaa is the fourth largest lake in Europe. The Lappi uplands of the far north comprise a third of the total country. Life in Lapland is difficult to sustain because most of it is boggy in the summer and extremely cold in the winter. Reindeer herding and tourism support a limited population. The highly indented Baltic coastline is fringed with thousands of islands, including the remarkable Archipelago Sea, between continental Finland and the main island of Åland, and also the Kvarken (Quark(en)) which stretch more than half way across the Gulf of Bothnia towards Sweden.

Much of the geography of Finland can be explained by the Ice Age. The glaciers were thicker and lasted longer in this part of Europe. Having been compressed under the enormous weight of the glaciers, the land is still rising about 10mm a year in the Kvarken area and 4mm in the south of Finland due to 'post-glacial rebound'. In fact, the surface area of Finland is expanding by about 7 square kilometers annually.

With a population of around 5·5 million, the majority of whom live in the southern regions, Finland is the most sparsely populated country in the European Union. It is a parliamentary republic with a central government based in the capital, Helsinki. Since its independence from Russia in 1917, Finland has developed into a Nordic-style welfare state, resulting in widespread prosperity. It has one of the highest per capita incomes in the world. Finland today is a top performer in education, economic competitiveness, civil liberties, quality of life and human development. At the 2015 World Economic Forum, Finland was ranked top in the World Human Capital and the Press Freedom Index (http://reports.weforum.org/human-capital-report-2015/rankings/), and as the most stable country in the world according to the Fragile States Index.

The largest sector in the economy is services (66%), followed by manufacturing (31%), electronics, machinery, vehicles and other engineered metal products (21%), forest industry (13%) and chemicals (11%). Forests play a key role in the country's economy, making it one of the world's leading wood producers and providing raw materials for the crucial wood-processing industries.

Day mark *M. Strobel*

Transits and marks *M. Strobel*

FINLAND - KEY INFORMATION

Key information

⚠ Rescue/Safety services

Emergency ☎ 112 (no area code required). Applicable to all emergencies. Calls answered in English as well as Finnish or Swedish.

Maritime rescue alarm ☎ +358 294 1000

International distress frequencies:
VHF-DSC Channel 70
VHF Channel 16
MF-DSC Frequency 2187,5 kHz.

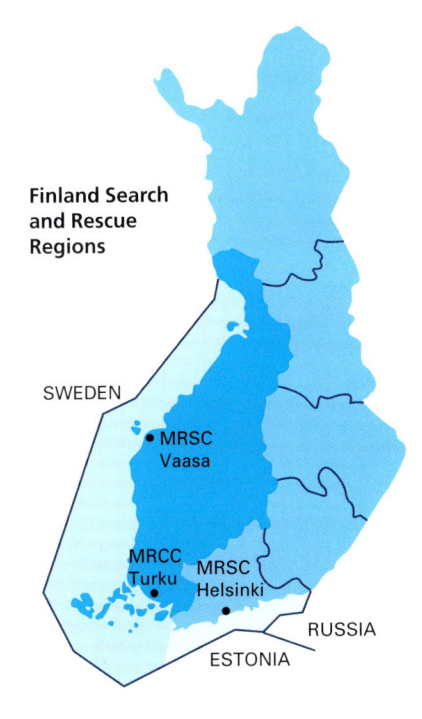

Finland Search and Rescue Regions

SWEDEN
• MRSC Vaasa
• MRCC Turku
• MRSC Helsinki
RUSSIA
ESTONIA

In Finland, the Border Guard is the lead SAR authority and responsible for coordinating all SAR activity. Finland's Search and Rescue Region (SRR) extends beyond Finland's territorial waters into international waters bordering the SRRs of Sweden, Russia and Estonia.

The SRR is divided into two so-called Search and Rescue Sub-Regions (SRS). The West Finland Coast Guard is responsible for maritime SAR operations in the West Finland Search and Rescue Sub-Region, with missions coordinated by the Turku Maritime Rescue Coordination Centre (MRCC), under the command of the Coast Guard Headquarters. The Gulf of Finland Coast Guard District is responsible for the Gulf of Finland Rescue Sub-Region (RSR), with missions coordinated by the Helsinki Maritime Rescue Sub-Centre (MRSC Helsinki).

In Finland, MRCCs receive distress messages by telephone and via the Global Maritime Distress Safety System (GMDSS). Contact between the MRCCs and both vessels in distress or danger and the subsidiary and maritime SAR units operating at sea takes place via the marine VHF radio distress and working channels, and digital selective calling (DSC).

Finland's Maritime Search and Rescue: www.raja.fi/sar/en/system

Other useful links: www.raja.fi/sar/en/links

Details of the above, including Search and Rescue, GMDSS, Coast Radio Stations, Weather Bulletins and Navigational Warnings, NAVTEX transmissions, weather forecasts on the internet and Firing Practice areas can be found in the Appendix page 420.

⊕ Charts and chart packs

UKHO Admiralty charts are useful for passage planning and offshore navigation, but the large-scale Finnish charts are essential in order to enjoy the delights of cruising inside the archipelago.

Finnish small-scale charts with a scale of 1:100 000 to 1:500 000 for Sea Areas around Finland

Gulf of Bothnia: 958 (Bay of Bothnia), 957 (Kvarken), 955 (Southern Sea of Bothnia), 956 (Northern Sea of Bothnia)

Archipelago Sea including Gulf of Finland: 950.

Archipelago Sea: 953, 935 (Sea of Åland).

Western Gulf of Finland: 952.

Eastern Gulf of Finland: 951.

Coastal charts at 1:50 000 scale

Gulf of Bothnia (chart numbers: 40 – 60)
Archipelago Sea (chart numbers: 22 – 37)
Gulf of Finland (chart numbers: 13 – 21)

Chart folios

Books with 25 pages, at 1:50 000 scale. These are also called the *Merikarttasarja* (Finnish) *Sjökortsserie* (Swedish) series and are less expensive than coastal charts. These are strongly recommended. Chart folios are updated approximately every 4 or 5 years according to a schedule. Besides the normal 1:50 000 chart sheets, there are many special charts included in the series. These are essential for navigation in the labyrinthine archipelago.

The chart folios have letters:

A Vyborg – Helsinki
B Helsinki – Parainen
C Åland Islands
D Turku Archipelago
E Sea of Bothnia
F The Kvarken
G Bay of Bothnia
S Saimaa Canal
L Lapeenranta – Savonlinna (Lake Saimaa)
M Savonlinna – Kuopio (Lake Saimaa)

http://portal.liikennevirasto.fi/sivu/www/e/transport_network/nautical_charts/editions/sea_areas/folios

http://sail-in-finland.info/2012/07/charts-for-the-finnish-waters/

Charts and publications can be obtained from John Nurminen Marine (See appendix page 418) and can be ordered on the internet www.johnnurminenmarine.com

📖 Pilots and cruising guides

Each harbour described in the Finland chapter has a reference number which corresponds to the harbour numbers in the books listed below.

Suuri Satamakirja (Stora Hamnboken) series in four volumes, shows over 450 anchorages and all the major and minor harbours. Much of the text in the Stora Hamnboken is in Finnish/Swedish but the book is still valuable because of the good chart drawings and photographs. Only one book is in English/German: *The Great Harbour Book IV*.
www.satamakirja.fi

SH1 *xxx*: Numbered harbours in *Vol 1 Turun Saaristo (Åbo Skägård)*

SH2 *xxx*: Numbered harbours in *Vol 2 Ahvenanmaa (Åland)*

SH3 *xxx*: Numbered harbours in *Vol 3 Suomenlahti (Finska Viken) (Gulf of Finland)*

SH Bottenhavet *xxx*: Numbered harbours in *Pohjanlahti (Bottenhavet)* (Gulf of Bothnia, Sweden and Finland)

GHB *xxx*: Numbered harbours in *The Great Harbour Book IV*. 145 natural and guest harbours from Sweden, Finland and Estonia published in English and German

FMA *xxx*: Numbered harbours in *Käyntisatamat-Besökshamnar*. Published yearly in mid May, it gives accurate, up-to-date information on all the harbours along the Finnish coastline (including the Archipelago Sea) and their services, presenting them in an easy-to-use, symbol-based format, which can be read in English, Finnish, Swedish and German. The numbers of the harbours in the book correlate to the numbers on the charts in the chart folios, increasing from east to west, making route planning and refuge seeking fast, easy and convenient. Distance diagrams of all the chart series are shown to help planning schedules and routes

SKS *xxx*: Numbered harbours in the *Saaiman Käyntisatamat Besökshamnar*, published yearly. It has the same format as above and covers the Saimaa Lake. It also gives instructions for small boat traffic in the Saimaa Canal in several languages including English.

4. FINLAND

THE BALTIC SEA AND APPROACHES   **247**

4. FINLAND

Åland Gasthafen, published by PQR, is available in Swedish, Finnish and German. It has excellent aerial photos and plans of most of the harbours and anchorages in the Åland islands. It is widely svailable for sale in most information offices and harbours and is very popular with the locals.
www.pqr.ax

See the Appendix, page 418, for suppliers of charts and publications.

⏲ Time

Finland uses UT+2 in winter and UT+3 in summer.

€ Money

Finland has used the Euro since January 2002. Major credit and debit cards are widely accepted, except in small shops in the archipelago. Nearly all banks have ATMs.

📄 Formalities

Finland is a member of the EU and is part of the Schengen area, so if you have already cleared in there are no further formalities. (See page 7 for further details of the Schengen requirements.) Visas are not required for EU passport holders.

The Frontier Guard (Finnish *Rajavartiolaitos,* Swedish *Gränsbevakningsväsendet*) is the national security agency which is responsible for border crossings and passport control. For current regulations on formalities such as clearance, immigration, customs and restrictions visit www.noonsite.com

A yacht coming directly from another Schengen country need not report to the passport control point nor is it required to sail within the official channels to the nearest Passport Control station.

All crew members must carry their passport or national ID card. A crew list signed by the captain is required if transiting the Saimaa Canal.

EU citizens coming direct from another EU country do not need to seek customs or immigration clearance unless carrying items that must be declared.

Foreign yachts arriving in Finland from a non-Schengen country must keep to the official Customs routes, and report to the nearest coastguard station or Port of Entry along the channel. The passport control station should be alerted by VHF Ch 68 or 16 or by telephone, approximately one hour before arrival.

When sailing between Finland and a non-Schengen country (eg Russia), a yacht always has to go to the passport control point and file a Customs declaration. A clearance declaration is issued on completion of formalities and this must be shown to the authorities at the port of departure.

Visas required for visitors from and to Russia (also Kaliningrad).
Finnish Customs ☎ +358 9 6141
www.tulli.fi

The Finnish Embassy in London is at 38 Chesham Place, London SW1X 8HW, ☎ 020 7838 6200. Visas by appointment only: appointment.lon@formin.fi.

As from 20 November 2015, all Schengen visa applicants will be requested to submit their biometric data, including fingerprints and a digital photograph.
sanomat.lon@formin.fi
www.finemb.org.uk/en

The **British Embassy** in Helsinki is located at Itäinen Puistotie 17, 00140 Helsinki, ☎ +358 (0)9 2286 5100.
www.gov.uk
info.helsinki@fco.gov.uk

In addition there are **Honorary British Consuls** in a number of the larger towns and cities, including Mariehamn (now a Consulate General), Turku, Kotka and Vaasa, Tampere, Rovaniemi, Oulu, Kuopio.

Finnish Border Guard
☎ +358 295 420000
www.raja.fi
(for Border crossing points information and telephone numbers)

For EU boats, proof of VAT status is required also Ship's Radio Licence. One member of the crew must have a radio operator's certificate of competence. An EU-registered boat on which VAT has been paid can be kept in Finland indefinitely. A non-EU registered boat can stay in the country for up to one year, but a bond may be payable whilst over-wintering and Customs should be notified before the yacht comes ashore.

The yacht is expected to carry standard safety equipment, but as of 2010 there is no requirement for the skipper to hold the International Certificate of Competence or any other formal qualification.

Sailing whilst under the influence of alcohol is an offence under Finnish law, and the authorities can (and do) stop a vessel at sea to check the alcohol levels of both the skipper and whoever is at the helm.

The Finnish flag is white with a blue Scandinavian cross; the Åland flag blue with a red cross on a yellow cross. Although the Åland Islands are administered by Finland they value their separate identity and the 'border' between the Åland islands and the rest of Finland is marked by the *Kihti* (Swedish *Skiftet*), a deep channel running north-south approximately along longitude 21° 07'E. The Åland flag should be flown in Finnish waters west of this line and the Finnish flag in the rest of Finland. Never fly the two flags together.

For more useful information on pleasure craft sailing in Finland, visit the Baltic Sea Cruising Network website: www.marinas.nautilus.ee

☼ Public holidays

Official public holidays in Finland include:

1 January, 6 January (Epiphany), Good Friday, Easter Sunday and Monday, 1 May (May Day), Ascension Day (May), Midsummer's Eve and Day (third weekend in June), 1 November (All Saints' Day), All Saints' Day (Saturday between October 31 and November 6), 6 December (Independence Day), 24–26 December (Christmas).

Local festivals and other events are held in many towns throughout the summer, listed in the Finland Festivals booklet and on line at www.festivals.fi

☎ Communications

The telephone country code for Finland is +358, and if dialling from abroad the initial 0 of the area code is not required.

The Finnish telephone system is excellent with extensive mobile coverage. Most telephone kiosks have been removed as old fashioned. For international calls dial +, followed by the country code, area code (omitting any initial 0) and number. Dialling within Finland only the area code (including initial 0) and number are required, or number only for a local calls.

Internet access is widespread, with free terminals in almost every public library. Other options are included in the text for each harbour. Letters normally take 2–3 days to or from the United Kingdom. It is essential to quote the correct postcode when addressing letters to Finland.

✈ Travel

Helsinki has good communications by **air** with all parts of Europe, and Mariehamn and Turku can be reached from Stockholm and Helsinki. There are many daily **ferry** services linking Helsinki with Turku, Mariehamn, Stockholm and many other destinations, including Tallinn in

FINLAND - KEY INFORMATION

Estonia. The rail/ferry and coach/ferry services to Europe are good, as is the rail service within Finland.

A **train** service links Helsinki to St Petersburg, for which **coaches** also depart several times each day. There are also five sailings weekly by **ferry** to St Petersburg.

Websites

Seemingly everyone in Finland has their own website, and this is certainly true of nearly all companies and government organisations. The following are just the tip of the iceberg and even brief use of an internet search engine will uncover hundreds more.

The following websites are of particular interest to sailors visiting Finland:

www.visitsaaristo.net
The harbour plans and numbers are the same as in the *Käyntisatamat-Besökshamnar* (see above).

www.ym.fi/en-US/Latest_news/Publications/Brochures/Everymans_right(4484 Everyman's right.

www.nationalparks.fi/en Information on National Parks.

www.visitfinland.com/article/the-finnish-sailing-experience
About sailing in Finland.

www.fmi.fi The website of the Finnish Meteorological Institute, containing everything from today's weather forecast to long term climate statistics.

www.visitfinland.com/about-us The homepage of the Finnish Tourist Board.

www.finland-tourism.com The Official Online Travel Guide to Finland, maintained by the Finnish Tourist Board and containing much of direct relevance to visitors, including travel information and many useful links.

www.festivals.fi The website of the Finland Festivals organisation, with details of thousands of local festivals and events, all with relevant email and/or website addresses.

www.visitaland.com The official Åland tourist gateway website.

www.finlandarchipelago.org A well-constructed website covering the Turku archipelago (the Turunmaan *saaristo* or Åbolands *skärgård*) – effectively those islands east of the Kihti (Skiftet).

www.yachtclub.com/europe/scandinavianyc.html A useful site providing links to the homepages of most yacht clubs in Scandinavia and beyond.

Holding tanks

In Finnish waters, the discharge of untreated sewage is prohibited at a distance of less than 12 nautical miles from the nearest land i.e. within their territorial waters. Although holding tanks are not compulsory for non-Finnish flagged yachts, it will be difficult to comply without this or some other method of avoiding discharge.

The availability of pump-out facilities compares well with other countries, and they can be found in most guest harbours and some anchorages.

www.hallskargadenren/roope-palvelut

Radio communications

Finland's VHF coast radio stations are extremely well organised and convenient to use, and all parts of the coastline have excellent coverage. All VHF stations are remotely controlled from Turku. (See the Appendix page 426.)

Weather information

Weather bulletins are broadcast in English at 0633 and 1833 UT, gale warnings on receipt and at 0233, 0633, 1033, 1433, 1833 and 2233 UT. (See Appendix page 426.)

Restricted areas

There are 17 military Restricted Areas in Finnish waters, some of which contain smaller Military Areas and all of which are marked on current Finnish charts. They range in size from a single island to an area west of Helsinki measuring, at its extremes, some 29 by 30·5 kilometers. Although movement within Restricted Areas is no longer forbidden or even limited, certain activities are, in particular scuba diving and bottom fishing (though use of a rod or a towed line appears quite acceptable). Pleasure craft under 24m can anchor where they wish. No Military Area may be approached within 100m unless within a marked fairway. These regulations apply to all, regardless of nationality. Further details can be found on the Finnish Defence Forces website at **www.mil.fi**

In addition to the military Restricted Areas, there are Conservation Areas – most often to ensure that breeding birds remain undisturbed – where limitations on movement and/or anchoring may be in force for part of the year. Like the military areas they are clearly marked on the Finnish charts and should be rigorously observed.

Log transport, Saimaa Lake *M. Strobel*

4. FINLAND

The people, church and language

Finnish and Swedish are the official languages in Finland.

Finland is home to several distinct ethnic groups and at least three major languages. The majority of Finns speak Finnish as their native tongue while Swedish is spoken in some coastal areas and mostly in the autonomous region of Åland. The Sami language is the official language in northern Lapland. In many places road signs, as well as names on street maps, will be in more than one language.

Finnish is an agglutinative language related to Hungarian and is very difficult to master. Lacking the common Latin or Teutonic origins of the majority of European languages it appears totally alien to most visitors – almost no words can be guessed, even when seen written. Fortunately the excellent Finnish educational system means that almost everyone, from marina executives through to bus drivers, speaks passable and often fluent English (and often German and/or French as well).

Swedish is somewhat easier to understand and, again, almost all Swedish-speaking Finns also speak excellent English. Although the national percentage is relatively small, a disproportionate number of Finnish yachtsmen come from this group and several of the major yacht clubs consider a good command of Swedish to be an essential requirement for membership. Even so, the visitor should be aware that Swedish-speaking Finns are very definitely Finns and not Swedes, even in the Åland islands where Swedish is the official language, spoken by up to 90% of the population.

The Samis (Lapps) live in the northern part of the country so are unlikely to be encountered by cruising yachtsmen unless travelling inland. The Lappish language (which has several distinct variants) is related to Finnish, as is their culture. Although the Samis of Finland now number no more than 7,000, they maintain close links with those resident in Norway, Sweden and Russia.

There are two national churches, Lutheran and Eastern Orthodox, with 75% of Finns belonging to the former.

History

The earliest inhabitants of Finland are the Sami people, previously called Laplanders, who are believed to have been living in the Arctic regions of Norway, Finland and Russia since the end of the Ice Age at around 10,000 BC. They continue to maintain their traditional way of life as fishermen or by herding reindeer as much as modern civilisation will allow.

The rest of Finland and all Estonia speak a Finno-Ugric language, related to Hungarian but otherwise unlike any other European language. They arrived around 3,000 BC and for much of their history had little contact with their Germanic or Slavic neighbours. By the Middle Ages, the huge areas of forest, lakes and marshlands kept them living as simple farmers in small self-regulating communities. There was no central power-base to coordinate the country as a whole.

Contact with Sweden had been growing since Viking times, as southern Finland was on the Swedish route through Russia to Constantinople. Christianity started to arrive in the 11th century and was consolidated in the Catholic Northern Crusades by the Swedes and Dominican monks who arrived in 1249. Many Swedes came to settle in Finland. Turku in the southwest became a larger Swedish city than any in Sweden itself. Meanwhile Russian Novgorod established its influence and its Orthodox church in Karelia in eastern Finland.

Finland was increasingly seen as a part of Sweden, and this was formally established in 1362 when Finnish representatives were invited to help elect a new Swedish king. In the following centuries, Finns paid Swedish taxes, provided soldiers for Swedish armies and became Lutheran when Sweden did. Many new cities were built, notably Helsinki in 1550 under the name Helsingfors. During the 17th century Sweden encouraged settlement of the empty wilderness of central Finland which came at the expense of the Sami nomads. The Lutheran requirement that everyone should be able to read the bible greatly increased literacy and education. The 18th century saw improved Finnish farming, increased trade and greater prosperity for most Finnish peasants.

Then in 1809 Sweden lost a war with Russia who took Finland as a Grand Duchy under the Tsar until the Russian Revolution of 1917. It was only under the Russians that Finns began to think of themselves as a nation, spurred on by the Tsar's 'Russification' policy. In 1835 the poem Kalevala was published and became the national epic, and by 1900 Sibelius had written Finlandia. But Russia also provided a market for Finland's developing industry and training for Finland's soldiers.

Following the 1917 Russian revolution, Finland declared its independence and this was accepted by the Bolsheviks. A substantial number of rural and industrial workers wanted Finland to follow Russia's socialist ideals, however, and there followed a bitter civil war that lasted a year before the 'Whites', proponents of a Finnish democratic mixed economy, prevailed.

Between the world wars there were a number of reforms to make Finland more egalitarian. By the 1930s Stalin had clearly changed his mind about Finnish independence. In 1939 the secret Molotov-Ribbentrop pact between Russia and Germany put Finland and the Baltic states under the Russian 'sphere of influence'. Stalin wanted to station troops in Finland. Marshal Mannerheim refused and led Finland in a heroic defence in the 1940 Winter War. Then Hitler offered to help. Mannerheim succeeded in walking the very narrow path required to keep the Russians out without being overrun by Germany or becoming involved in any of Hitler's other objectives. In 1944 Germany was clearly losing in Europe, and Mannerheim fought the Lapland War to remove the remaining German troops from north

Finland. Then as president he negotiated the peace with the USSR, giving as little away as possible while still maintaining trading relations.

In the 1990s Mannerheim was voted the greatest Finn ever. He was also a fastidious gourmet and inventor of the Marskyn ryyppy (Marshal's tipple) – aquavit, gin and Noilly Pratt, filling the glass to 1mm below the rim and to be drunk in three gulps without toasts or spillage.

Cruising and general information

Yacht services and chandleries

Throughout Finland, visitors marinas are indicated by a white anchor on a blue background and the words 'Vierassatama', 'Gästhamn' or 'Guest Harbour' – or occasionally all three. There are numerous good boatyards and a chandlery at most harbours of any size, though probably the largest and best-stocked ones are to be found at Uusikaupunki, Mariehamn, Turku, Hanko and, of course, Helsinki.

Gas

Propane gas (LPG) is the most widely available. Some suppliers will also have butane gas. International Camping Gaz (ICG) cylinders can be exchanged at Mariehamn East (at STI fuel station near harbour), at Hanko, at the NJK harbour in Helsinki, at HSK Lauttassaari, Helsinki, and at Kaasuvalu, Unioninkatu 45, 00170 Helsinki. The main problem that you will encounter is that Sweden, Norway and Finland all have different connectors. Swedish cylinders can be exchanged for Finnish cylinders at the STI fuel station in Mariehamn East, and at the NJK in Helsinki. It is virtually impossible to refill non-Finnish cylinders but OY Interenergy, near Lohja, might be worth a try. www.pressocenter.fi

Diesel

Diesel is obtainable at nearly all marinas, often together with a station at which a holding-tank can be emptied. There is a bio component additive of 6% on all diesel (for marine or road use)

Shopping

Food is plentiful, and there are many well-stocked supermarkets as well as small local shops throughout the coastal area of Finland. Prices are generally higher than in England.

Alcohol

Beer with an alcohol content of around 4·5% is available in supermarkets and other shops, but full-strength beer (5·2–8%), wines and spirits can only be purchased at branches of ALKO, the national alcoholic beverage retailing monopoly in Finland, which are only to be found in the main towns. In both cases prices are higher than in the UK.

Remote anchoring *T. Fooks*

Yacht clubs

The principal club is the Nylandska Jaktklubben (NJK), which has a fine clubhouse in Helsinki including a marina which welcomes visiting yachts. It also owns a number of islands and anchorages where its members enjoy their privacy.

The Finnish Cruising Club (Merikarhut, or Sea Bears) also owns islands and anchorages for the exclusive use of its members.

The cruising season

Finland has an even shorter cruising season than Sweden, and it should be noted that some services are only provided between mid-June and mid-August, if that. The numbers of Finnish cruising yachts are already falling off by the third week of July, and decrease markedly by early August. By late August most local yachts are sailing in local home waters or already laid up ashore.

Private islands

Most smaller islands in Finland and Åland are privately owned, many sporting one single house and most likely a sauna, and although anchoring off seems to cause no problems it is polite to do so out of sight of the house (and sauna). The owners of islands guard their privacy jealously and using a private jetty is not allowed.

It is important that you adhere to the Everyman's Right basic rules, which grant you the right to roam in the countryside. A very good article on anchoring and landing restrictions in Finland has been published online:

http://sail-in-finland.info/2015/01/anchoring-landing-restrictions-finland/

Even on private land, you do not need the landowner's permission, and there is no charge. However, you must not damage the environment or disturb others while exercising public access rights. For more information on the Everyman's Right consult:

www.ym.fi/en-US/Latest_news/Publications/Brochures/Everymans_right(4484

4A. THE FINNISH COAST OF THE GULF OF BOTHNIA

4a. The Finnish coast of the Gulf of Bothnia

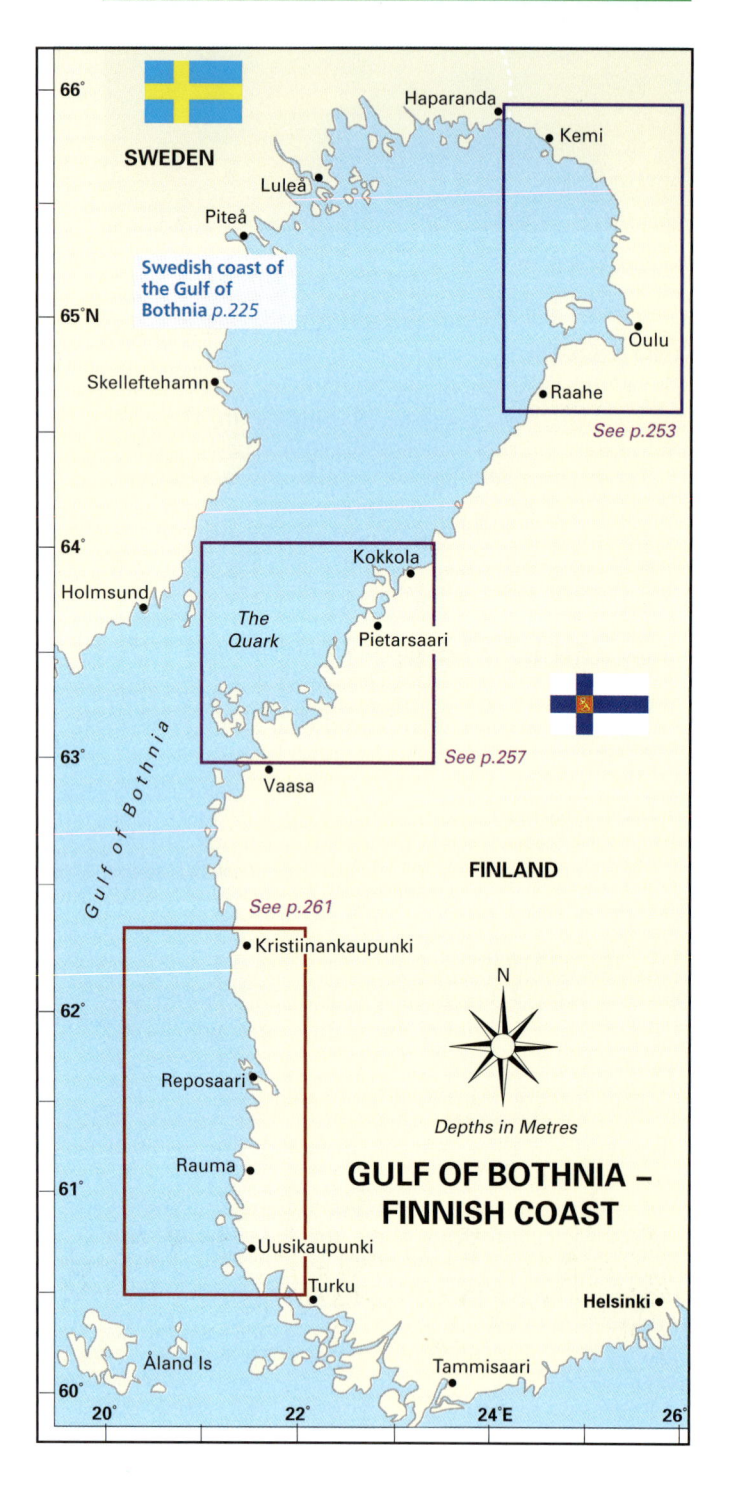

The following section has been arranged from north to south, assuming that most yachts in the Gulf of Bothnia will have sailed north along the Swedish coast. The Gulf of Bothnia on the Finnish side is divided into three areas:

- Bottenviken or Bay of Bothnia to the north between Tornio and Kalajoki
- Kvarken or (Quark(en)) between Kalajoki and Kaskinen
- Bottenhavet or the Sea of Bothnia in the south between Kaskinen and Uusikaupunki.

Heading south from Tornio there are many small harbours or *gästhamns* and several important towns of interest: Kemi, Oulu and Raahe in the north; Kokkola, Pietarsaari (home of Nautor and Baltic yachts) and Vaasa in the Kvarken; Kristiinankaupunki, Pori (with its world famous jazz festival), Rauma and Uusikaupunki further south. The coastline is mostly flat with shallow water necessitating careful passage-making at a considerable distance from the coast. There are many small skerries dotted around the northern part of the Gulf of Bothnia (Bottenviken) between Tornio and Kemi, around Oulu and Raahe.

In the Kvarken, extensive skerries reach almost all the way across to the Swedish coast. Many of them are nature reserves. Further south in the Bottenhavet, the skerries are close to the shore. These areas do not provide good shelter.

Navigational charts – harbour guides

Planning charts (1:250 000)
F958 (Perämeri) Bay of Bothnia
F957 (Merenkurkku) the Quark
F955 (Southern Sea of Bothnia)
F956 (Northern Sea of Bothnia)

Chart folios (1:50 000)
E-Selkämeri/Bottenhavet (Sea of Bothnia)
F-Merenkurkku/Kvarken (The Quark)
G-Perämeri/Bottenviken (Bay of Bothnia)

Harbour guides
The Great Harbour Book – Bottenhavet (**GHB** *xxx*)

Käyntisatamat/Besökshamnar guide to 511 harbours on the Finnish coast (the numbers of the harbours in the book correspond with the numbers on the charts, **FMA** *xxx*).

Note Each harbour described in this section has a reference number (*xxx*) which corresponds to the harbour guides above. However, some of the numbers may change over time.

Shallow, rocky coast NW of Kokkola *M. Strobel*

252   THE BALTIC SEA AND APPROACHES

1. BAY OF BOTHNIA: TORNIO TO RAAHE

1. Bay of Bothnia: Tornio to Raahe

Distance Tornio to Raahe: 120M
Charts Merikarttasarja–G Perämeri/Bottenviken
Rannikkokartat 59, 58, 57, 56, 55
www.visitfinland.fi

The northeast (Finnish) corner of the Gulf is a shallow area which can be inhospitable in bad weather. Extensive shoals often call for long diversions. However, this coast is very well mapped and the charts show recommended routes and the minimum depth to be expected. The many transits and buoys make navigation straightforward. Care should also be taken with the water depth in this area which is affected by the currents flowing between the North Sea and the Baltic Sea, atmospheric pressure and wind direction. Depending on the direction and strength of the wind, depths can vary by up to 2·0m. The strongest variations in water levels in the Baltic Sea are to be found in the Gulf of Bothnia and the Gulf of Finland.

Koivuluodonletto

65°45·9N 24°13'·7E (south mole)
Chart G855 and 59
SH Bottenhavet *117*

This is the first small harbour to the east of Tornio (the border between Sweden and Finland) deep enough for sailing boats up to 3·5m draught. There are new pontoons with water and electricity; six bows-to spaces from stern buoys and four finger pontoons in 3–3·5m; pumpout station and sauna. There are walks through the woods and marshlands.

Approach from the southeast on the transit at Kiuasletto to avoid a rock awash 0·2M southeast of the harbour entrance.

Kemi

65°43'·7N 24°33'·2E (south mole)
Distance Tornio 20M
Charts G855, 855.2 and 59
SH Bottenhavet *116* **FMA** *1964*
Communications
www.visitkemi.fi
www.kemi.fi
www.visitsaaristo.net

Kemi is a town near the city of Tornio in the Lapland region. It is at the mouth of the river Kemijoki and has a population of 22,000. The town was very severely damaged during World War II but was rebuilt during the Russian occupation. It now has a polytechnic university for applied sciences.

Kemi was founded in 1869 by decree of the Russian Emperor Alexander II because of its deep water harbour. This is kept open throughout the winter by icebreakers which service two paper and woodpulp mills, the timber trade and the only chromium mine in Europe.

The commercial and ferry port is on the peninsula of Ajos 6·5km to the south.

Two of the main winter attractions in Kemi are the snow castle (hotel, restaurant and chapel) which is reconstructed every year to a different design, and the Sampo, a former Finnish government icebreaker, stationed in Kemi, that offers cruises on the Gulf of Bothnia.

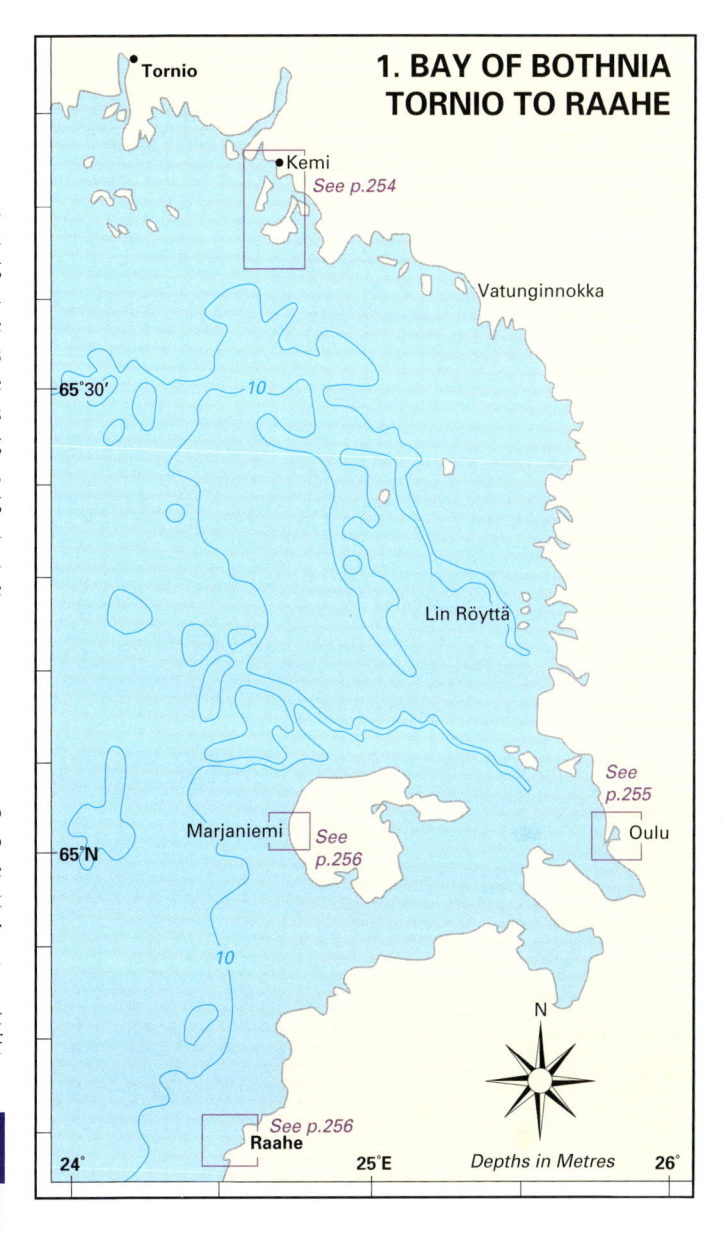

Koivuluodonletto *M. Strobel*

THE BALTIC SEA AND APPROACHES 253

4A. THE FINNISH COAST OF THE GULF OF BOTHNIA

Kemi M. Strobel

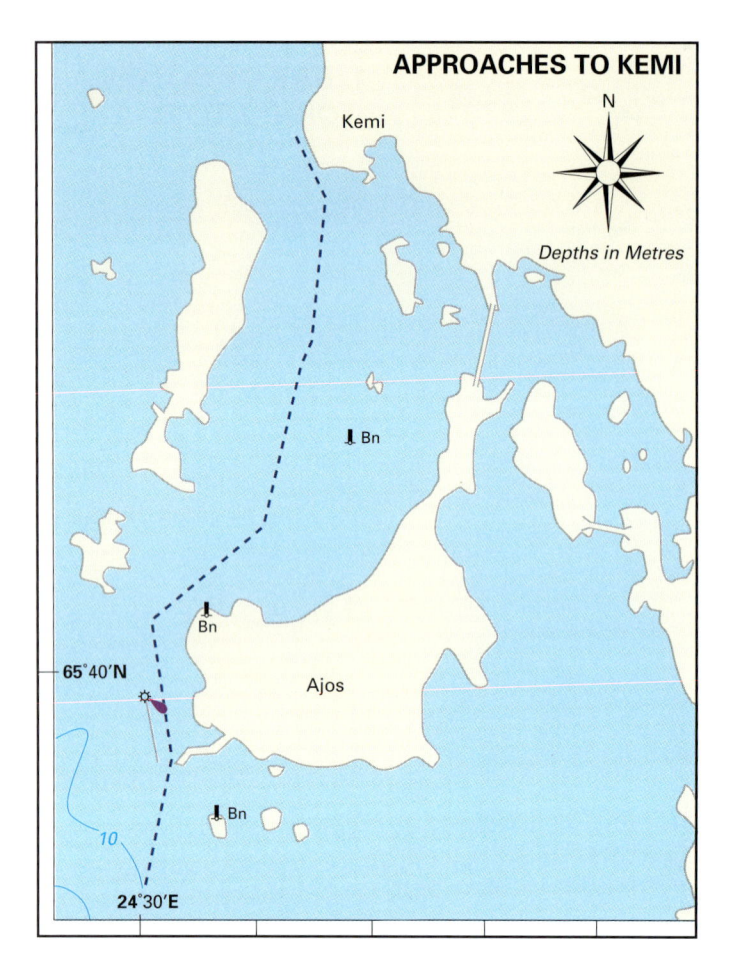

Sampo icebreaker stationed in Kemi M. Strobel

Kemi can be approached from the west following the transit (083°) between Selkäsaari to the south and Kojukallio to the north (2·4m). If approaching from the south (10m deep water channel) past the commercial harbour to the west of the Ajos peninsula, follow the well-buoyed channel towards the marina. The final approach (011°) has a transit (church spire and Mansikkanokka light). The well-sheltered *gästhamn* provides 15 bows-to berths with stern buoys in 2·4m which are ahead of you when you enter the harbour.

The local yacht clubs with their restaurants, saunas and other services provide visitors with every facility and coast guides welcome visiting yachts during the high season.

Waste disposal, toilet pumping facilities, electricity, mast crane, boat ramp, liquid gas, fuel (only diesel), recycling, toilets, sauna, showers, drinking water, laundry room, restaurant, cafeteria, playground, campfire pits, guiding services.

Many more shops and restaurants are to be found in the town centre about 1km away.

Vatunginnokka

65°33′N 25°06′·7E (south mole)
Distance Kemi 26M
Charts G851, 853 and 58, 59
SH Bottenhavet *109* **FMA** *1938*
www.ii.fi
www.visitsaaristo.net

This is a safe harbour on an exposed coast, and is easily identified by the surrounding wind turbines. Straightforward entrance from the west-southwest with a lit transit (78°).

Approach from the west, leaving Samulinmatala to the south. Beware of the fish farms in the area. The channel leading to the marina has a depth of 2·2m.

The small harbour has 10 finger pontoons in 2–4m, with good facilities, provided by the power company Vapo, and shared with the caravan site. Café and good walks. It may be possible to buy fish from the fish farm on the south side. Fuel, showers, sauna, washing machine, water and electricity.

254   THE BALTIC SEA AND APPROACHES

1. BAY OF BOTHNIA: TORNIO TO RAAHE

Röyttä

65°16'·2N 25°13'E (south mole)
Distance Vatunginnokka 22M, Marjaniemi 32M
Charts G847, 850, 57 and 58
SH Bottenhavet 108 **FMA** 1927
http://ports.com/finland/port-of-roytta
www.visitsaaristo.net

Popular excursion island and nature reserve. The substantial stone walls give excellent shelter in all winds.

Röyttä was a loading port for the timber trade until 1960. The deepest approach is from the west, between Satakari and Röyttä through a well-buoyed channel. The marina has 40 visitor berths in 2–3m with stern buoys. Water and electricity on the pontoon. Several yacht clubhouses, one of which offers a sauna and hot water. Limited facilities and no supplies but good walks on a very attractive island. It can become very crowded during Midsummer and harvest festivals.

There is a narrow-gauge track along the top of the southeast wall which is now used to trolley luggage to the many holiday homes.

Oulu (Uleåborg)

65°00'·9N 25°27'·5E (harbour mole, Market Square (Meritulli))
Distance Li Röyttä 20M
Charts G846 and 57
SH Bottenhavet 99 **FMA** 1914
Communications
www.oulunliikekeskus.fi/meritulli_marina
www.visitsaaristo.net

Oulu, the capital of northern Finland, is the fifth biggest town in Finland and the largest town in the region with a population of 200,000. It was founded in 1605, by King Charles IX of Sweden, after a peace settlement with Russia. In 1822, a major fire destroyed much of the city. It was rebuilt according to the neoclassical plans of Carl Ludvig Engel. The attractive wooden buildings on the south side of the market are all that remain of the once important wood-tar trading and salmon markets. Oulu cathedral was completed in 1844.

There are two universities, the University of Oulu and the University for Applied Sciences. Prominent industries include wood refining, chemicals, pharmaceuticals, paper and steel.

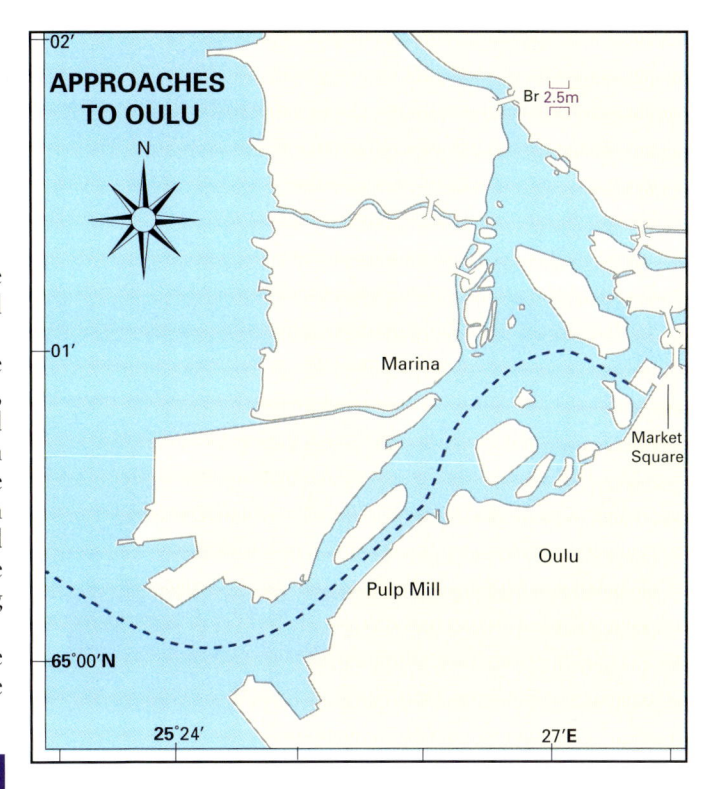

Approach and facilities

Although there are several marinas around the picturesque Oulu delta, the best and most convenient harbour is right in the city centre.

The approach is from the northwest. Follow the deep water channel 10m or approach from the north leaving Kraaseli to the west (note that this approach has 1·8m depth). Once in the commercial harbour follow the very well-buoyed channel and three sets of transits to the Meritulli harbour. Close by is the striking art centre and the market square where there are some excellent restaurants and cafés, and a very attractive covered food hall.

There are 11 bows-to berths from stern buoys in 2·3m. Water and electricity on the pontoons. The showers, sauna, toilet facilities and washing machine are in a café at the corner of the Market Square, the Kahvilamakasiini (red granary), where you collect the key (against a deposit of €20). Convenient diesel pump (24h) on the quay (credit cards only). Pump out station.

Airport with several flights a day to Helsinki.

Oulu M. Strobel

THE BALTIC SEA AND APPROACHES

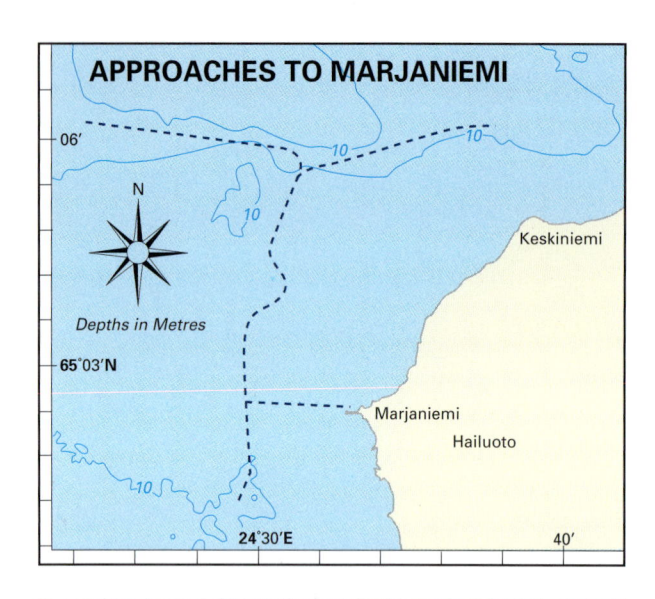

4A. THE FINNISH COAST OF THE GULF OF BOTHNIA

Sandy walks at Marjaniemi M. Strobel

Marjaniemi, Hailuoto

65°02′·4N 24°32′·8E (south mole, Hailuoto)
Distance Oulu 33M, Kemi 58M, Li Röyttä 32M
Charts G844, 56 and 57
SH Bottenhavet *94* **FMA** *1900*
Communications
www.hailuototourism.fi
www.visitsaaristo.net

A safe harbour, protected by a mole, on the west coast of Hailuoto island, west of Oulu, this is the largest island in the Bay of Bothnia.

The island is a popular holiday destination known for its extensive sandy beaches and attractive walks through the dunes and pine forests. The prominent lighthouse (25m high) and pilot station on Marjaniemi were built in 1871. Three wind turbines on the southern mole are visible from a long way off.

Marjaniemi is now a small fishing harbour with an active pilot station, campsite and *gästhamn* of up to 50 berths. Moor bows-to from stern buoys or alongside pontoons in 4·1m. Water and power available 100m away, otherwise good facilities with a hotel Luotsihotelli and campsite kiosk. It is sometimes possible to buy fish from the local processing shed.

There are good walks along the foreshore but the turnstones will protest if you stray a little too close to their nesting grounds. This is an excellent departure point for Sweden.

The approach is straightforward from the north–south coastal channel 4·2m past the island. When the wind turbines bear 275°, approach carefully watching your depth 2·6m.

Raahe (Brahestad)

64°41′·1N 24° 27′·7E (south mole Terässatama guest harbour)
Distance Oulu 41M, Marjaniemi 26M
Charts G839, 841 and 55
SH Bottenhavet *91, 92* **FMA** *1876, 1868*
Communications
www.raahe.fi
www.visitraahe.fi
www.visitsaaristo.net

Raahe has a great maritime history. Count Pehr Brahe, Queen Kristina's governor general in Finland, discovered Raahe harbour and founded the town with the name Salo in 1649. In the year of 1652 the name was changed to Brahestad and later to Raahe. Like many other wooden towns, Raahe was devastated by fire in 1810, and was rebuilt to new

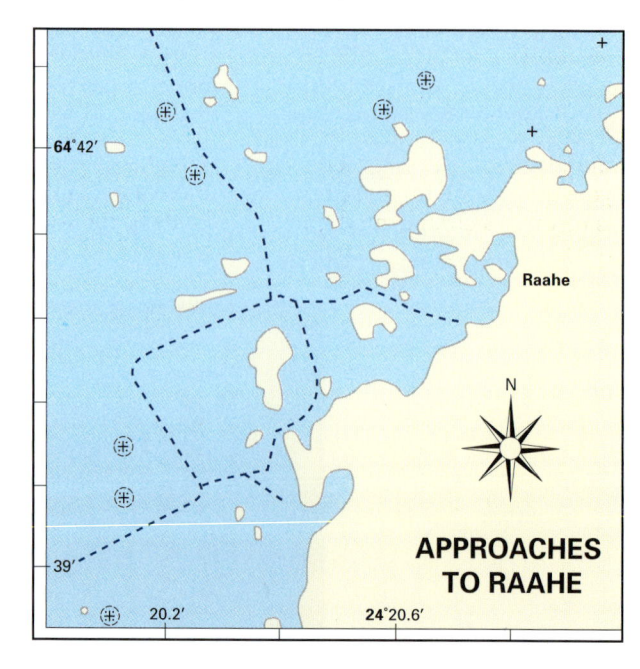

Wind-turbines near Marjaniemi M. Strobel

256 THE BALTIC SEA AND APPROACHES

2. THE KVARKEN: KOKKOLA TO VAASA

Raahe, Ruiskuhuone *M. Strobel*

Count Pehr Brahe, founder of many towns in Finland *M. Strobel*

design principles with a rectilinear town plan featuring an unusual central square (known as Pekkatori).

The Old Town of Raahe is one of the best-preserved wooden towns in Finland.

Trade and shipping were the main sources of income before the establishment of Rautaruukki steelworks in early 1960s.

Approach
The approach is either from the northwest 2·4m or the west past the commercial port. Whichever route you choose, the final approach to the town of Raahe is through a complicated group of islands to the west of the town. The channels are well buoyed (2·1m) and should be followed carefully.

There is a visitors' harbour (Terässatama) to port just before you enter the basin in front of the town centre (see the information on the website above). It is a 3km walk to the town. Services include a dry dock crane (5 tons). The other harbour is the Ruiskuhuone pier at the Museum Quay, right in front of the town.

There are 13 berths bows-to from stern buoys in 2·4m or moor alongside the town quay near the Pakkahuoneen museum. Water, electricity, showers, supermarket, restaurants, pharmacy.

2. The Kvarken: Kokkola to Vaasa

Distances Raahe to Kokkola 75M, Kokkola to Vaasa 75M
Charts Merikarttasarjat – F, Merenkurkku, Kvarken Rannikkokartat 48 to 54
www.visitfinland.fi

The Finnish side of the Kvarken (Quark(en))

This covers a vast archipelago of attractive islands stretching from Kokkola (Karleby) to Kaskinen (Kasko). This narrow strait lies in the middle of the Gulf of Bothnia. It separates the Bay of Bothnia (Bottenviken) in the north and the Sea of Bothnia (Bottenhavet) in the south. At its narrowest, the minimum distance from the outermost islands in the archipelago to the Swedish mainland is 25M and the depth is only 25m.

The Kvarken archipelago is a World Heritage Site.
  The archipelago is continuously rising from the sea in a process of rapid glacio-isostatic uplift, whereby the land, previously weighed down under the weight of a glacier, lifts at rates that are among the highest in the world. As a consequence islands appear and unite, peninsulas expand, and lakes evolve from bays and develop into marshes and peat fens. (whc.unesco.org)

There are well-buoyed routes inshore of many of the islands. These, together with their minimum associated depths are all well marked on the charts. Excellent transit marks make this much easier to cover than the charts might suggest. The thriving cities of Kokkola, Pietarsaari and Vaasa contrast with the abundance of natural anchorages.

THE BALTIC SEA AND APPROACHES

4. FINLAND

4A. THE FINNISH COAST OF THE GULF OF BOTHNIA

Tankar M. Strobel

Tankar

63°56'·9N 22°51'·1E (west mole)
Distances: Kokkola (Mustakari) 9M
Charts F833, 833.1 and 52
SH Bottenhavet *78* **FMA** *1752*
www.kokkola.fi
www.visitsaaristo.net

Tankar is a very attractive small island 9M northwest of Kokkola. It is a popular holiday destination. It has a very prominent lighthouse, built in 1888, which is 27·5m high and the light element, which originally came from Henry Lepautre's factory in Paris, was the most powerful of its time (13M). Today it is still one of the brightest lighthouses in Finland. Tankar is a pilot station.

It is worth visiting the sealing museum, which describes Tankar's historic way of life. The tiny church is booked throughout the summer for the celebration of weddings. The café and restaurant offers very good fresh food. There are fish-smoking boxes near the pontoon and a sauna.

Leave the charted route which passes very close to the eastern shore of the island when the entrance bears 252°. Make sure that you leave the E-cardinal buoy to port. 8–10 visitors moorings, bows-to from stern anchor or buoys.

Kokkola (Karleby), Mustakari

63°51·8'N 23°06'·8'E (south mole)
Distances Raahe 66M, Pietarsaari (Jakobstad) 28M
Charts F833, 834.1 and 52
SH Bottenhavet *77* **FMA** *1768*
Communications
www.kokkola.fi
www.mustakari.fi/hamnen-satama/gaesthamn-vierassatama
www.visitsaaristo.net

This is the largest harbour for visitors on the stretch of coast between Raahe and Pietarsaari.

Mustakari lies in the northeastern corner of Kokkola. It is home to one of the oldest sailing clubs in the Gulf of Bothnia, the Gamlakarleby Segelförening (GSF) founded in 1871. There is a very good restaurant in the beautifully-maintained wooden clubhouse. There are moorings for visiting yachts in the southern part of the marina. The approach can be tricky in onshore winds. Facilities include showers, sauna, washing machine, pump out station, fuel. The town is around a 30-minute walk away.

Kokkola, Mustakari M. Strobel

258   THE BALTIC SEA AND APPROACHES

2. THE KVARKEN: KOKKOLA TO VAASA

Approach

From the Kokkola light (Kokkolan Majakka 63°59'·8N 22°51'·7E, Fl(2)WRG.10s23m12M (Racon T)) follow the main buoyed channel southeast towards the chimneys of the town before branching east just before reaching the island of Repskär (fairway buoys K8 and K9) towards the northern tip of Trullevi (63°55'N 23°04'·3E) to join the channel parallel to the Trullevi peninsula (three sets of transits) that leads southeast towards Mustakari. The channel is very shallow (2·5m) and great care is needed. Mustakari *gästhamn* has 50 berths bows-to from stern buoys in 2·5m.

During the Crimean War Kokkola was involved in a fight known as the 'Skirmish of Halkokari' in 1854, during which the Royal Marines from HMS Vulture and HMS Odin tried to come ashore and were repelled by the local population supported by Finnish troops and Russian military. One of the British gunboats fell into the hands of the local defenders. This boat can still be seen in Kokkola's English Park. The British Treasury pays for the maintenance of the graves of the nine Royal Marines who lost their lives.

Pietarsaari (Jakobstad)

63°41'·4N 22°41'·5E (north quay, Smultrongrundet SSJ YC)

Distances Kokkola 28M, Vaasa 70M
Charts F831, 832 and 51
SH Bottenhavet *67, 68* FMA *1700, 1704*
Communications
www.jakobstad.fi
www.ssj.nu
www.visitsaaristo.net

Pietarsaari lies 28M southwest of Kokkola, inside a very dense and at times shallow archipelago. There are two recommended routes through the skerries. The main channel from the west 9m leads from Pietarsaaren Majakka light (63°44'·6N 22° 31'·8E, Fl) to the commercial port of Alholmen Leppäluoto. The alternative approach towards the commercial port is to leave the coastal channel (3m) 9M north of Alholmen and follow the inner lead (1·8m) through the archipelago north of Pietarsaari.

From Alholmen, the channel leading to the town is shallow (1·8–3m) and narrow. It leads directly to the SSJ, Segelsällskapet i Jakobstad yacht club where there are 30 bows-to moorings with stern buoys in 1·8–3m. This visitor harbour is only open from 15 June–15 Aug. All these routes are very well buoyed.

All the usual services are on hand and the yacht club has a good restaurant but it is 1km north of the town.

Although there are still many old wooden houses around the city centre, considerable late 20th-century development has transformed the shopping area where every facility is available.

Pietarsaari is well known amongst sailing enthusiasts for being home of Nautor Swan and Baltic yachts.

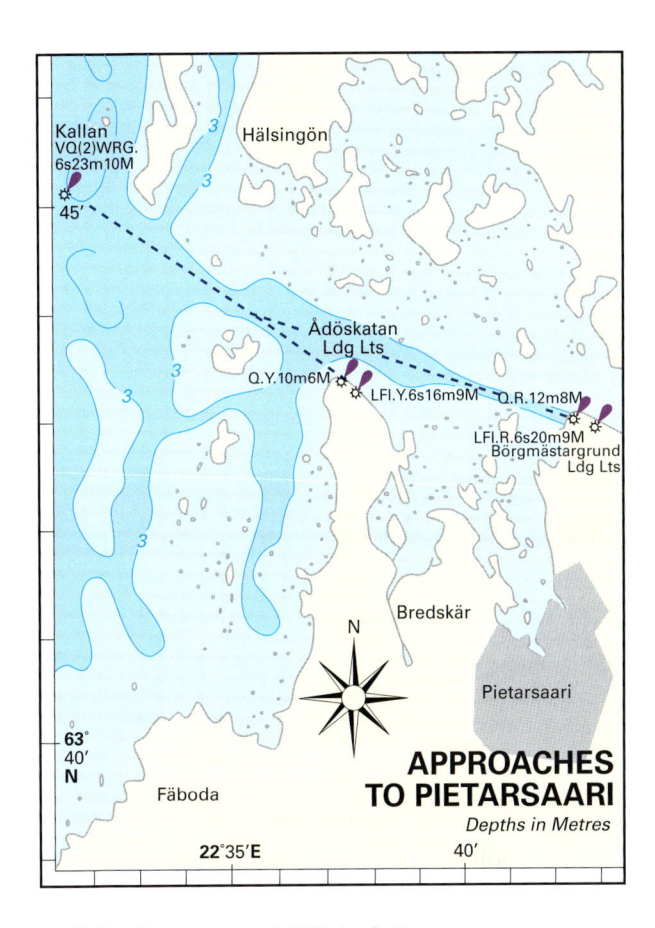

Mikkelinsaaret / Mickelsörarna, Kummelskäret

63° 27'·6N 21° 46'·4E (south mole, Mickelsörarna)
Distance Vaasa 25M
Charts F826, 826.1 and 49
SH Bottenhavet *59* FMA *1608*
www.kvarkenguide.org/mickelsen.html
www.visitsaaristo.net

If you intend to explore some of the many islands of the Kvarken, there is a route that leads around the Mickelsörarna archipelago which is made up of almost 300 islands, reefs and islets. Large and small forested islands are surrounded by relatively deep water with fewer underwater rocks than in many other parts of the Kvarken area, as well as rocky reefs and heath-covered islands. The many ancient ruins bear witness to the fact that humans have roamed these islands for a long time. The former coastguard station at Kummelskäret now serves as a harbour for excursions and also houses a nature centre (kvarkenguide.org). It has 10 moorings, bow-to from stern anchor or buoys, or alongside. Most of the islands south of Kummelskäret are a nature reserve.

The circular route leaves the main coastal channel and heads north, east of the Krokskäret/Villskär archipelago (3m). It leads to Kummelskäret harbour. The western route leads between the Krokskäret archipelago to the east and the Mickelsörarna archipelago to the west, a well-buoyed route (2·4m) which joins the main channel in the south. You can also approach Kummelskäret from the west and the open sea.

4A. THE FINNISH COAST OF THE GULF OF BOTHNIA

Djupkastet

63°18'·2N 21°37'·7E (transit on land)
Distance 21M, Kokkola 62M, Pietarsaari 47M
Charts F825, 825.1 and 49

Excellent safe anchorage just 0·7M off the main channel. Approach from the west, leaving Kvargrund Island to port.

The entrance is well marked with buoys and a transit. Good holding.

There is a small pontoon with stern buoys, which can be used with prior agreement from the WSF (Vaasa sailing club, see Vaasa). Floating pump out station in the middle of the anchorage.

Vaasa (Vasa), Vaskiluoto (WSF)

63°05'·7N 21°35'·2E (north mole, Wasa Segelförening)
Distances Pietarsaari 65M, Kristiinankaupunki 80M
Charts F819, 819.1 and 48
SH Bottenhavet 46 **FMA** 1536 (Vaskiluoto/Vasklot)
Communications
www.visitvaasa.fi
http://wasasegelforening.fi/klubbinfo/kontaktuppgifter.html
www.visitsaaristo.net

Completely sheltered harbour in a modern industrial town.

Wasa Segelforening Yacht Club (WSF) M. Strobel

There are various well-charted and buoyed routes from the Vaasan Majakka light (63° 14'·35N 20° 55'·6E, Fl(2)WRG.10s, Racon (T)) west of Vallgrund island towards Vaasa. This is the main approach from the open sea when crossing from Sweden. The shipping channel leads straight to the commercial harbour on the western shore of Vaskiluoto/Vasklot island. There are three marinas next to each other on the northeastern side of the island, which is connected to the city via a low bridge (about a 20-minute walk). The Wasa Segelförening Yacht Club (WSF), the southernmost marina, is a Swedish-speaking club.

It is well run with good facilities and a very good restaurant in the handsome wooden clubhouse.

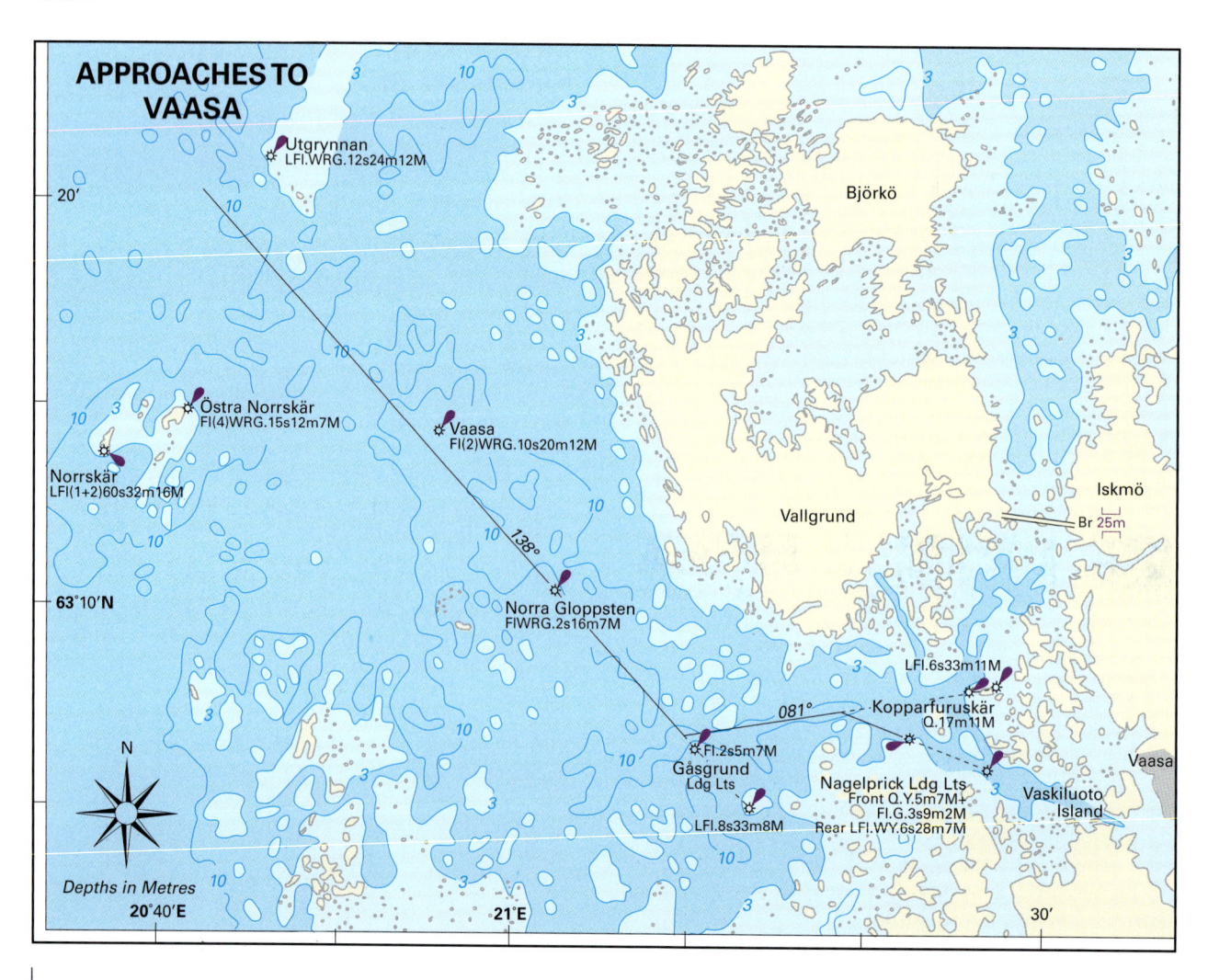

260 THE BALTIC SEA AND APPROACHES

3. SEA OF BOTHNIA: KASKINEN (KASKÖ) TO UUSIKAUPUNKI (NYSTAD)

Bicycles can be borrowed from the yacht club for shopping. There are also buses into town. Fuel is available from the jetty between the yacht clubs but it has only 2m of water alongside. There are 20 visitor moorings bows-to from stern buoys in 3–3·5m.

It is possible to anchor off or berth alongside the town quay which is convenient for shopping but short of facilities.

Approach

You can only approach the eastern side of Vaskiluoto island and Vaasa from the northwest as the south side of the island is blocked by two low bridges. On the final approach, even if depth allows you to go straight towards the yacht clubs on the east side. Beware of the overhead power cables. On chart 819.1 the height east of the pylon is shown as being 19m but on the base of the pylon there is a sign indicating 17m. If in doubt follow the indicated channel towards the town quay (where the height of the power cables is 32m) and only turn east when you have passed the central pylon.

Today, Vaasa has a population of 66,581, and is the regional capital of Ostrobothnia.

This is a busy sailing centre with first-class shopping in the Remell Centre, hotels, restaurants, museums and Fantoy chandlers 1km away. Heavy industries provide employment; there are three power stations and three universities.

3. Sea of Bothnia: Kaskinen (Kaskö) to Uusikaupunki (Nystad)

Distances Vaasa to Kaskinen (Kaskö) 62M
Vaasa to Kristiinankaupunki 76M
Kristiinanaupunki to Uusikaupunki 127M

Charts Merikarttasajat – E / F and Rannikkokarten 40 to 44

Once you leave the vast archipelago of the Finnish Kvarken (Quark(en)), the coast south of Vaasa becomes progressively more exposed to the west and the shoreline shallower. There are not many harbours and anchorages to choose from. Kaskinen (Kaskö), Kristiinankaupunki (Kristinestad), Reposaari, Rauma and Uusikaupunki (Nystad) are larger harbours that are deep enough for most sailing boats.

Kaskinen (Kaskö)

62° 23'·1N 21° 13'·2E (pier)
Distances Vaasa 62M, Kristiinankaupunki (Kristinestad) 14M, Reposaari 53M
Charts F812, 813.3 and 44
SH Bottenhavet *31, 32* FMA *1440*
Communications
http://visitkaskinen.fi   www.visitsaaristo.net

Kaskinen is a small, idyllic town situated on an island just off the mainland only 10M north-northwest of Kristinestad. The town has a unique plan of wooden houses with large green spaces giving a garden village effect in the summer.

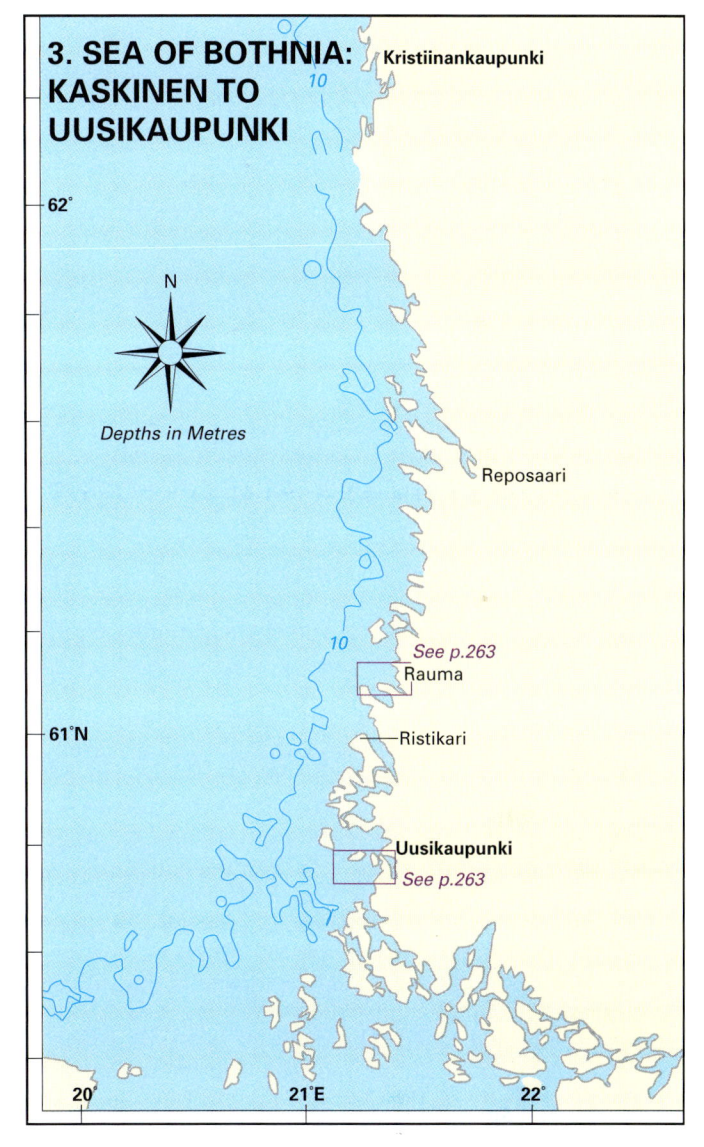

There are two possible ways to approach the town, either from the north via an approach channel, 3.4m, through the Järvöfjärden or from the south following the shipping channel, 9m, past the commercial harbour. Kaskinen is also an entry port. Moor at the town quay. There are 50 spaces alongside or bows-to from stern buoys in 3·5m. Facilities include water, electricity, showers, washing machine, sauna and all the other amenities of a town of 1,400 inhabitants.

Kristiinankaupunki (Kristinestad)

62°16'·3N 21°23'·1E (pier)
Distances Vaasa 76M, Merikarvia (Sastmola) 31M, Reposaari 54M, Uusikaupunki (Nystad) 127M
Charts F812, 812.2 and 44
SH Bottenhavet *27, 28* FMA *1432, 1433*
Communications www.visitkristinestad.fi

Kristinestad on the island of Koppö was founded in 1649 by Count Peter Brahe who noted the excellent conditions for a port. Kristinestad has a centuries old tradition as a marketing and trading town, and a distinguished history of ship and boatbuilding. The

THE BALTIC SEA AND APPROACHES   **261**

4A. THE FINNISH COAST OF THE GULF OF BOTHNIA

Kristiinankaupunki *M. Strobel*

beautiful town hall was built in 1856 and now Kristinestad is one of Scandinavia's best-preserved wooden towns. The authentic and picturesque buildings with their wooden fences stem from the 18th and 19th centuries.

Today the centre of the little town of 8,000 inhabitants has changed its face somewhat, but in the narrow alleys you can travel back hundreds of years in time.

The only approach to the town is from the south, either cutting through the skerries south of Furuviken (1·8m) following the buoyed channel (Chart 812.2) or taking the the deeper approach which involves leaving the main coastal channel (4–5m) 4M south of Kristiinankaupunki and turning north at Härkmeri island. The approach channel is well buoyed (5m) all the way to Östra sidan, the commercial harbour. From then on, the last 0·5M to the bridge in the town centre has to be navigated carefully as it gets very shallow towards the sides. Stay in the middle until you have reached hotel Kristina to starboard. There are 30 spaces bows-to from stern buoys in 3m and two further spaces at the town centre on the west side in only 1·4m depth.

Facilities include water, electricity, sauna, showers, washing machine, fuel and all amenities associated with a town of this size.

Reposaari (Räfsö)

61°37'N 21°26'·6E

Distances Kristiinankaupunki (Kristinestad) 54M, Uusikaupunki (Nystad) 73M
Charts E807, 808, 809 and 42
SH Bottenhavet *17* **FMA** *1362*
Communications
www.maisa.fi/en/reposaari
www.visitsaaristo.net

Reposaari is the deep-water harbour for Pori (Björneborg). It is situated on an island connected to the mainland by many bridges and railway lines. The whole area is industrial mainly to the southeast of Reposaari at Mäntyluoto and the northwest at Tahkoluoto. The tanks, chimneys and wind turbines can be seen from a distance. Yet Reposaari is a good, sheltered stopover.

The approach is straightforward. Leave the main coastal channel (3·4m) and approach the harbour through the commercial shipping channel (10m) (51°) towards the industrial harbour. Once through the breakwaters, turn to port following the transit and buoys (3·6m) that lead to the northwestern side of Reposaari and to the 60-berth visitor harbour. Moor alongside or bows-to from stern buoys in 2–2·5m. Good shelter. There is a wide range of facilities available. While the municipal centre of Pori, 22km away, can be reached by dredged channel (1·5m) it is probably best visited by bus or rail.

Rauma (Raumo)

61° 08'·1N 21°28'·1.4E (Syväraumanlahti, NW tip)
Distances Reposaari 37M, Uusikaupunki (Nystad) 36M
Charts E804, 804.1 and 41
SH Bottenhavet *4, 5, 6* **FMA** *1327, 1331, 1333*
Communications
www.rauma.fi
www.visitsaaristo.net

Rauma is a World Heritage Site and shipbuilding centre. It is also an entry port.

Rauma is one of the oldest harbours in Finland. Built around a Franciscan monastery, where the mid-15th-century Holy Cross Church still stands, it is an outstanding example of an old Nordic city

18th century interior in a patrician house in Kristiinankaupunki *M. Strobel*

3. SEA OF BOTHNIA: KASKINEN (KASKÖ) TO UUSIKAUPUNKI (NYSTAD)

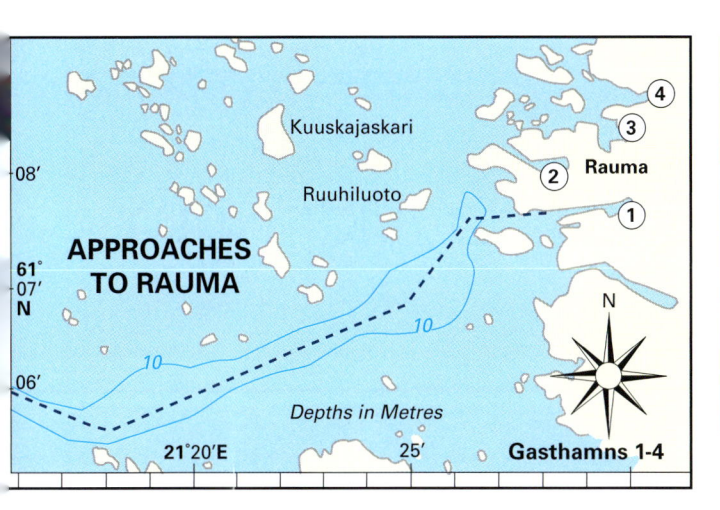

Pakkahuone gasthamn, Uusikaupunki M. Strobel

constructed in wood. Although ravaged by fire in the late 17th century, it has preserved its ancient vernacular architecture. The very well-preserved wooden houses have been sensitively adapted for modern use and merit the World Heritage Site status which is bringing tourism and new prosperity to the town (whc.unesco.org). Cycling is a good way to get about.

The very well-marked main deep-water channels from the northwest and southwest (amongst other shallower ones) lead to the commercial harbour of Ulko-Petäjäs. From here you can access a service harbour and two visitor harbours. Careful study of the large scale chart (804.1) is necessary before entering these harbours.

Petäjäs (61°07'·9N 21°27'·4E) is a fully-serviced shipyard with fuel, chandlery, boat ramp, engine and other services (not for overnight staying) with 5 berths in 2m. Another two visitor harbours are located on the north side of the town: Poroholma (61°08'·1N 21°28'·1E) with 15 berths bows-to from stern buoys in 1.9m, and Syväraumanlahti (61°08'·4N 21°28'·4E) with a visitor pontoon at the entrance to the 400-berth marina. This harbour is quite a distance away from the town centre. The outside berths here are in 3·8m but you will be lucky to find much more than 2m in the approach to both *gästhamns*. Most facilities nearby but fuel and chandlery only at Petäjäs.

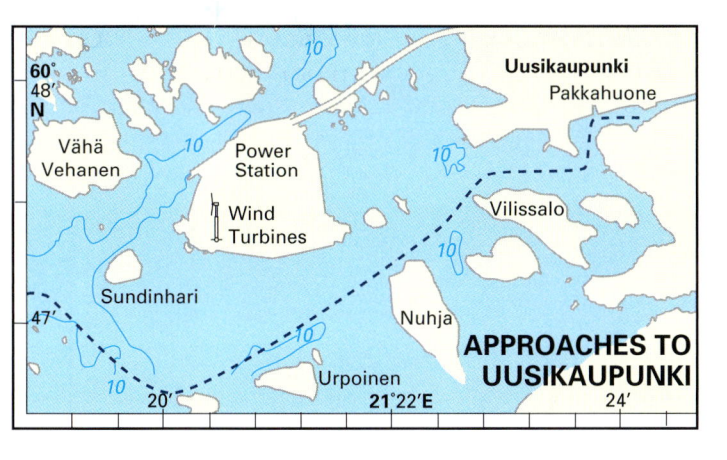

Uusikaupunki (Nystad)

60°47'·9N 21°24'·3E (Pakkahuone)
Distances Rauma 36M, Turku 55M approx.
Charts E735, 801, 802 and 40
SH1 *126* **FMA** *1060, 1072*
Communications
www.uusikaupunki.fi
www.visitsaaristo.net

Situated between the Sea of Bothnia and the Archipelago Sea, Uusikaupunki is a major sailing centre and attractive but large and industrialised town. Like most towns up and down the Gulf of Bothnia and the Åbo Archipelago, Uusikaupunki also has some very well-preserved wooden houses from the 17th and 18th centuries.

There are three main approach channels: from north, west and south, all of which are well marked and converge just northwest of Urpoinen island at 60°46'·8N 21°20'E (see chart 802.1). Then follow the fairway (and transit) south of the fertiliser plant and wind turbines on the island of Hanko and turn to starboard northwest of Vilissalo island and enter the very narrow (2·5m) channel which leads northwards to the inner harbour. After a sharp turn to starboard the fully-sheltered and award winning Pakkahuone *gästhamn* with up to 80 berths from stern buoys lies ahead and to port.

Up to 3m is claimed but this shoals to 1.5m beyond the café. Very good facilities and two chandlers, boatyards, extensive shopping and services. Fuel available from a prominent jetty to port. Salmeri is a very good service harbour to the south east of Sorvakko (60°47'·6N 21°23'·9E), which can deal with any repairs and engine troubles. However, it is about a 30-minute walk to the town centre.

Bus and rail services are good to Turku (Åbo) about 40km to the southeast where the international airport makes Uusikaupunki useful for crew changes.

THE BALTIC SEA AND APPROACHES 263

4. FINLAND

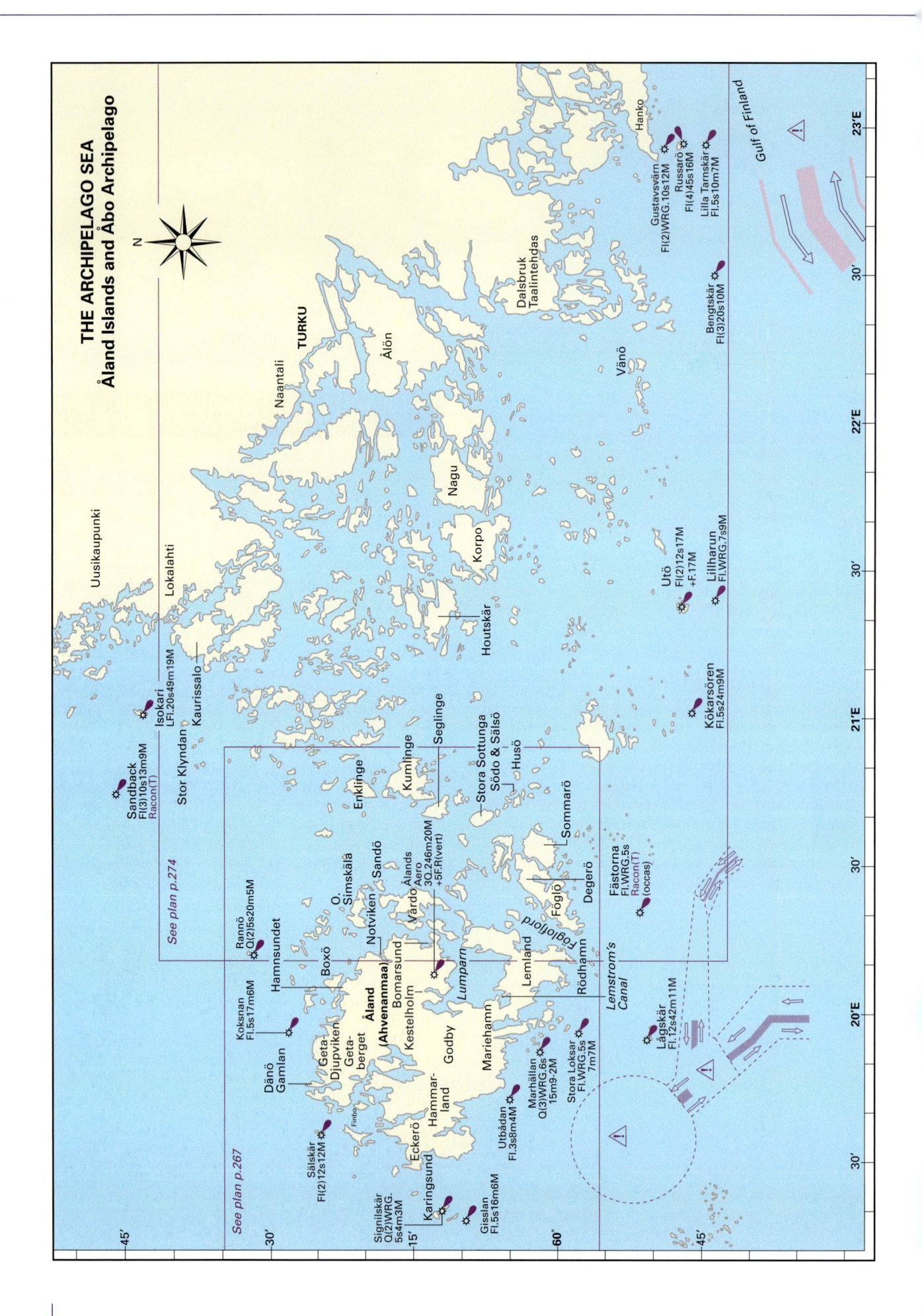

4B. THE ARCHIPELAGO SEA

4b. The Archipelago Sea: Åland Islands and Åbo Archipelago

The following section covers the complex area which includes the Åland Islands (Ahvenanmaa in Finnish and Åland in Swedish) and the Finnish Archipelago (Turun Saaristo in Finnish and Åbo *Skärgård* in Swedish), also known as Southwest Finland. The combined areas form the Archipelago Sea.

Most yachts sailing from Sweden towards Finland would probably cross from the Stockholm archipelago to the Åland Islands, particularly if they are short of time.

This section is therefore structured to reflect travel from west to east, from Åland to Hanko, leading to the Gulf of Finland.

Introduction

The Archipelago Sea, (Saaristomeri in Finnish, *Skärgård*shavet in Swedish) is part of the Baltic Sea between the Gulf of Bothnia, the Gulf of Finland and the Sea of Åland, within Finnish territorial waters. By some definitions it is the largest archipelago in the world by the number of islands, although many of these are very small and close together. The main ports in this area are Turku on the mainland and Mariehamn on the Åland Islands.

The islands are divided between the region of Southwest Finland (also known as Finland proper) and the autonomous region of Åland. The border between the regions runs along the (sea of) Skiftet (*Kihti* in Finnish), a long and narrow sound, only a mile wide in the northern part of the Archipelago Sea but relatively open in the south, which runs north–south roughly along longitude 21°07′E.

The larger islands are inhabited and are linked by ferries and bridges. The Åland Islands, the largest islands in the region, form an autonomous area within Finland. Although the Åland Islands are within the EU they remain outside its tax area. This exception allows for maintained tax-free sales on the ferries between Sweden and Finland, provided they stop at Mariehamn or Långnäs, and at the airport. It also means that Åland is a different tax-zone, which means that tariffs must be levied on goods brought to the islands. It has its own parliament, police and flag (a red cross on a broader yellow cross on a blue background), prints its own stamps, registers its own ships, is a member of the Nordic Council and enjoys a large measure of autonomy. It is legally a demilitarized zone, and its citizens are therefore exempt from military service.

The Archipelago Sea covers a roughly triangular area with the cities of Mariehamn (60°06′N 19°57′E), Uusikaupunki (60°47′·9N 21°24′·3E), and Hanko (59°49′·1N 22°58′·1E) at the corners. The archipelago can be divided into inner and outer archipelagos, with the outer archipelago consisting mainly of smaller, uninhabited islands. The total surface area is 8,300 square kilometers, of which 2,000 square kilometers is land.

The islands east of the Skiftet are part of the province of Southwest Finland.

There are 257 larger islands of over one square kilometer within the Archipelago Sea and about 17,700 smaller islets. A good estimate of the smallest uninhabitable rocks and skerries is about 50,000. It would require an entire summer to explore the whole archipelago and a lifetime to sample all the secluded anchorages or 'natural harbours'.

The islands began to emerge from the sea shortly after the last Ice Age 10,000 years ago. Due to post-glacial rebound the process is still going on with new skerries and islands being slowly created and old ones growing and even merging. The current rate of rebound is about 4mm a year. Because the islands are made of mainly granite and gneiss, two very hard types of rock, erosion is slow and due to its southerly location, the effect of post-glacial rebound is smaller than for example in the Kvarken (about 10mm) (Kvarken in Swedish, Merenkurkku in Finnish) further north in the Gulf of Finland.

The sea area is shallow, with a mean depth of 23m. Most of the channels are not navigable for large ships.

Administration, demographics and culture

Based on the languages spoken the archipelago can be divided into three parts. The Åland archipelago in the west is almost completely Swedish speaking, the Åboland archipelago in the south is mostly Swedish speaking and the northern archipelago is Finnish speaking. In many cases, place names are shown on the chart in both languages – usage here following that of the Merikarttasarjat chartbook series.

There are a number of small private islands in the Archipelago Sea and although these are not shown as such on the chart, the owners normally fly a national flag when at home. It is polite to recognise their privacy by not anchoring within sight of buildings or venturing ashore uninvited. Visiting yachts are strongly recommended to follow the 'everyman's right'. www.nationalparks.fi

Busy ferry traffic between Sweden and Finland *M. Strobel*

4B. THE ARCHIPELAGO SEA

The number of permanent residents on the islands is roughly 60,000, with 27,000 of them living in Åland.

Many Finns have summer residences on the islands in the area, known for its natural beauty. Due to this, the population of many islands can double or more during the summer.

The Archipelago Sea is a paradise for sailing with children. The innumerable islands are surrounded by waters which are sheltered and crystal clear. A short day sail will bring fresh adventures with each new anchorage.

Because Christianity spread to the islands before reaching the mainland, the churches on the major islands are relatively old; dating from the 13th, 14th and 15th centuries, with the oldest ones in Åland. About 75% of Finns are members of the Evangelical Lutheran Church of Finland, and this proportion is even higher in the archipelago – the area doesn't have an Orthodox or Catholic parish.

Communications

The islands are linked by bridges and ferries, also called *lossi* in Finnish and *färja* in Swedish. Pedestrians travel free on the numerous inter-island ferries. There are also large commercially-operated cruise ferries connecting the Finnish cities of Turku and Helsinki to Åland and Sweden. There is an airport in Mariehamn and a grass strip on Kumlinge. During cold winters official ice roads are established between some islands and it is sometimes possible to drive across the ice from the mainland. However, during spring and autumn the ice is too thin even for walking, but too thick for boating. This can leave some islands isolated for days or weeks and access is only maintained by hydrocopter, hovercraft or helicopter.

Crossing the the Gulf of Finland in winter *J. Langdon*

Acknowledgement
Partly adapted from: Wikipedia®
Text is available under the Creative Commons Attribution-ShareAlike License; additional terms may apply. By using this site, we agree to the Terms of Use and Privacy Policy. Wikipedia® is a registered trademark of the Wikimedia Foundation, Inc., a non-profit organization.

Navigational charts – Harbour guides

Chart folios
C-Ahvenanmaa/Åland, D-Turunmaan saaristo/Åbolands skärgård (scale 1:50,000)

Harbour guides
Stora Hamnboken Vol.1 Turun Saaristo/Åbo Skärgård (**SH1** *xxx*) and *Stora Hamnboken Vol.2 Ahvenanmaa/Åland* (**SH2** *xxx*)

Käyntisatamat/Besökshamnar guide to 511 harbours on the Finnish coast (the numbers of the harbours in the book correlate with the numbers in the chart folios - **FMA** *xxx*).

See also
Navigational charts – Finland and Åland and Harbour books and literature p.247 (general introduction to Finland).

Suggested cruising routes

Cruising through the Archipelago Sea can take any number of routes, criss-crossing the Archipelago Sea depending on time constraints, final destination and personal interest. The suggested routes in this chapter, together with the harbours and anchorages listed below are just that – suggestions. Finnish charts are excellent and if the recommended routes in the chart folios (which also indicate the minimum depth that could be encountered along them) are followed closely, the danger of hitting a rock or running aground are minimised. Of course, one can wander between them too – at your own risk. It is also possible to sail from Mariehamn direct to Hanko without stopping, but then one would be missing some of the best *skärgård* sailing in the entire Baltic.

Route 1 Circumnavigation of the main island of Åland, Rödhamn and Degerby

Route 2 A northern route through the Archipelago Sea

  2a: from Degerby to the northern Åbo archipelago and the Gulf of Bothnia

  2b: from Torsholma towards Turku or Hanko

Route 3 From Degerby towards Hanko – a central route

Route 4 From Degerby towards Hanko – a southern route

ROUTE 1 ÅLAND, RÖDHAMN AND DEGERBY

Route 1 Circumnavigation of the main islands of Åland, Rödhamn and Degerby

A cruise around the main island of Åland is strongly recommended for anyone who does not have the time to venture further east. There are many beautiful, peaceful and remarkably unfrequented anchorages to be discovered, together with a cross-section of cultural and historical sights. A fair insight into Åland will be gained even with this limited visit. The route begins in Eckerö, heads southeast towards Mariehamn (Maarianhamina), enters Lumparn through the Lemström's Canal, exits Lumparn via the Prästösundet, and finally skirts the northeast and northwest coasts of Åland before returning to Eckerö.

Käringsund (Käringsundet), Eckerö

60°14'·05N 19°32'·15E (Käringsundet lighthouse)
Charts C761, 34
SH2 35 **FMA** 1275
Communications
www.visitaland.com
www.visitsaaristo.net
www.karingsund.ax

This is a landlocked fishing harbour on the west coast of Eckerö accessed through a very narrow entrance which presents no difficulty in ordinary weather. The approach routes are both well buoyed. A small lighthouse with a sector light (Q.WRG) is located on the southern headland at the entrance to the pool. Inside the harbour there is a patch of rocks just above water. Pass north of these rocks, and then turn starboard towards the wooden jetty. Alternatively after entering the pool immediately turn to starboard between the rocks to port and close to the headland. There is a large wooden jetty to the east of the village, with room for about 80 yachts, bows-to from stern buoys. It is also possible to anchor between the rocks and the jetty. Käringsund has been developed as a summer resort and can become crowded but it is still attractive and comfortable. A large former post house is located about a mile south of the harbour entrance and is very conspicuous. There is an interesting fishing museum as well. It is only 25 miles to Arholma (Sweden) and the entrance to the Stockholm archipelago. Therefore it is a handy port of departure to and from Sweden. A ferry to Sweden departs from the L-shaped quay about ten minutes walk from the yacht harbour. Käringsund is a convenient place for crew changes. Facilities include fuel, showers, sauna, restaurant, WiFi, electricity, water (20m), pump-out station.

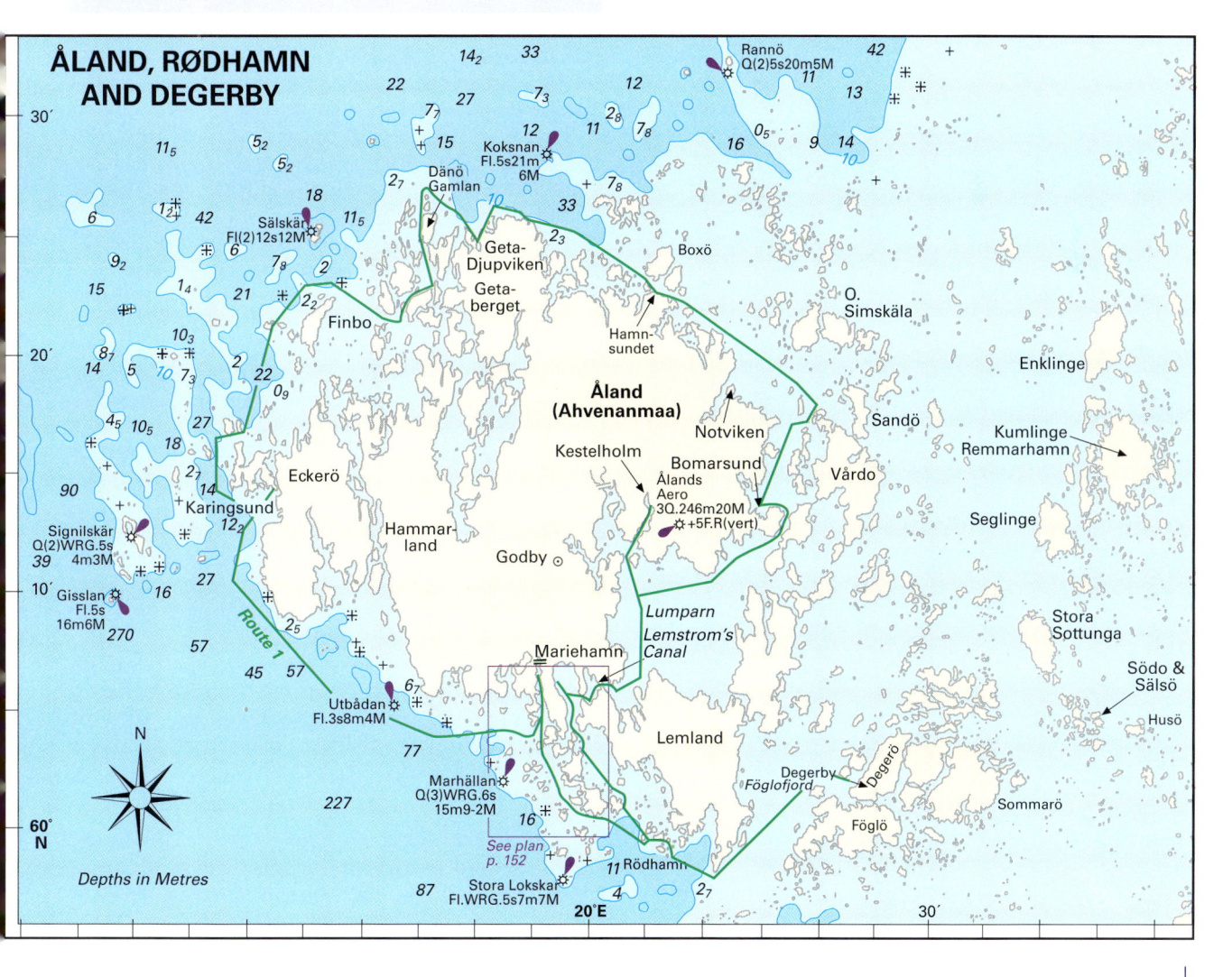

THE BALTIC SEA AND APPROACHES

4B. THE ARCHIPELAGO SEA

Mariehamn (Maarianhamina)

60°06′N 19°56′E (Länsisatama)

Distances
Stockholm 70M, Hanko 105M, Turku 75M

Charts and guides
Merikarttasarjat – Ahvenanmaa / C Åland, Rannikkokarten 22–34
Stora Hamnboken Vol. 2

Lights
Marhällan 60°01′·9N 19°52′·5E Q(3)WRG.6s15-9M 007°-W-120°-R-175°-G-219°-W-244°-R-333°-G-007° Round red tower, black bands. Floodlit
Tvibenan 60°02′·4N 19°53′·3E Q.WRG.6m4M 184°-G-210°-W-212°-R-273·5°-G-330°-W-341·5°-R-070° White rectangle
Ldg Lts 052° *Rear* 100m from front, LFl.G.6s21m11M 046°-vis-058° Red rectangle, yellow stripe
Korsö *Common front* 60°02′·4N 19°54′E Iso.WRG.7m8M 318°-G-003°-W-009°-R-032·5°-G-062·5°-W-075°-R-179·5° Racon Red rectangle, yellow stripe
Ldg Lts 066° *Rear* 180m from front, LFl.6s17m8M 062°-vis-070° Red rectangle, yellow stripe
Granö 60°03′·5N 19°55′·7E Q(2)WRG.5s6mW6M 146°-G-182°-W-185°-R-212°-G-332°-W-338°-R-006° Orange tower, white lantern
Lotsberget Ldg Lts 028° *Front* 60°05′N 19°56′·2E Iso.Y.2s31m10M 023°-vis-033°
Red rectangle, yellow stripe, on metal framework tower, white lantern
Rear 457m from front Iso.6s57m10M 023°-vis-033° Red rectangle, yellow stripe, on metal framework tower

Harbour communications
First Port of Entry
Mariehamn Port Authority ☏+358 18 531 470
VHF Ch 12, 16 (call *Mariehamn Port*)
http://port-authorities.com
www.noonsite.com
Passport control office ☏+358 20 410 7230, VHF Ch 74

Mariehamn has a year-round population of just under 11,500, though some 1·5 million tourists are estimated to pass through each year. It is the capital of the region of Åland.

It stands on a tongue of land separating two arms of the sea and has two yacht harbours, West Harbour (Västrahamnen) and East Harbour (Östrahamnen). Although less than a mile separates the two harbours by land, by sea it involves a detour of some 15M so that when coming from the south the decision as to which to head for must be made before passing Nyhamn light (59°57′·5N 19°57′·3E, sector light, Iso.R.2s, occas) see plan on page 267 (Åland, Rödhamn and Degerby, Route 1). The massive wind turbines around Nyhamn will be spotted a long way off. West Harbour is the deeper one and more easily reached by visiting yachts unfamiliar with the area, but is rather less sheltered than the East Harbour which is closer to the town centre.

Old wooden houses in Södragatan fringe wide tree-lined avenues, pedestrian areas full of small cafés, and a good shopping centre in this relaxed and spacious town.

Mariehamn is of particular interest to seafarers as the last home of square-rigged ships, and having been the port of registry for Captain Gustaf Erikson's famous 'Flying P' line. The four-masted barque *Pommern*, which last sailed commercially in 1939, is now a museum ship in the West Harbour and is well worth a visit, as is the nearby Åland Maritime Museum (note the north Atlantic chart on display, published by James Imray & Son in 1864).

The Maritime Quarter including museums, historic vessels and boatbuilding sheds can be found near the East Harbour. The 'Åland Sea Days', a five-day event held every July, is based in the Maritime Quarter and offers attractions for all ages including a busy programme for children.

Approach and entrance

Coming from Sweden and heading for the West Harbour, Mariehamn is usually approached either from the southwest or south.

Crossing from the Stockholm archipelago the most straightforward route will lead to the Marhällan light (60°01′·9N 19°52′·3E, Q(3)WRG.6s) which can be left to port or starboard. Two leading lights (marks), one in the white sector and the other in the green sector of Korsö light (60°01′·9N 19°53′·8E, Iso.WRG.2s, Racon (T)) will lead directly into the approach channel (leading lights on Lotsberget-028.1°) towards Mariehamn West Harbour. The marina lies to the north of the ferry docks and the barque *Pommern*.

There is also a well-buoyed (unlit) approach channel from the west, which provides a convenient short cut for yachts coming from the west coast of Åland. It enters the archipelago in the vicinity of 60°04′N 19°47′E and joins the two main routes 4M further east at 60°04′N 19°55′E.

Several other routes are possible (south or southeast), however, when approaching from the open sea entering the Åland archipelago can be very confusing – large scale charts are essential. The Finnish chart folios have many such special charts, 756.1 and 756.2 for Mariehamn.

The East Harbour is reached from the south or southeast, by way of several channels within the archipelago.

Coming from the southeast, south of Lemland, the East Harbour is reached via a well buoyed channel with a minimum depth of 3·7m, starting at Järsö just west of Rödhamn. Again, a large-scale chart (756.1) is a necessity.

Finally, if approaching from the east through Lumparn, follow the buoys to the Lemströms kanal, via the swing bridge, round Lembötе north of Lemland. From here, the most convenient marina is in the East Harbour.

Caution

It cannot be stressed too strongly that many of the channels used by the large ferries which ply from Stockholm to Turku via Mariehamn are narrow in the extreme. Ferries have priority AT ALL TIMES,

268 THE BALTIC SEA AND APPROACHES

ROUTE 1 ÅLAND, RÖDHAMN AND DEGERBY

APPROACHES TO MARIEHAMN (MAARIANHAMINA)

THE BALTIC SEA AND APPROACHES 269

4B. THE ARCHIPELAGO SEA

and yachts must keep well clear. They travel at speed, and it is necessary to keep a sharp look-out both ahead and behind as well as over the top of intervening islands.

Formalities

See page 248 for details. If in doubt contact the Border Guard
☎ +358 18 57055, aland.lsmv@raja.fi

There is a pontoon prominently marked PASSPORT CONTROL close to the south of the West Harbour marina where arriving yachts may be instructed to secure. When sailing in the Åland Island waters you fly (only) the Åland national flag and when entering Finland waters you change to the Finland national flag. Never fly the two flags together.

Anchorage

There are no special restrictions on anchoring in the area of Mariehamn, but there are only a few places to anchor including one that lies opposite the west harbour marina at 60°05'·8N 19°55'·1E. Here, as elsewhere, one must respect the private properties along the shoreline and keep well clear of the ferry routes.

Berthing

Mariehamn West Harbour (Länsisatama, Mariehamn Västra Hamnen) ÅSS

60°05'·8N 19°55'·4E (marina entrance)
Charts C756, 32
SH2 46 **FMA** 1220
www.visitsaaristo.net
www.visitaland.com
www.segel.ax
www.aland.com

ÅSS Marina with some 160 berths offers many services including sauna, showers and toilets (24h), waste disposal and laundry room. There are water and electricity outlets on all jetties. Next to the fuel station there is a pump-out station. WiFi is included in the harbour fee.

ÅSS Pavilion – the restaurant seats 80, both indoors and on a terrace – also has a small glassed-over pavilion for 35 guests. The restaurant is run by Björn Johansson and Jimmy Ström.
☎ +358 18 19141.
www.paviljongen.ax

Mariehamn East Harbour (Itäsatama/Mariehamn Östra Hamnen) MSF

60° 05'·9N 19° 56'·9E (southern mole)
Charts C756, 757, 32
SH2 45 **FMA** 1230
www.msf.ax
www.visitsaaristo.net
www.visitaland.com
www.aland.com

This is the largest marina in the Archipelago Sea, with approximately 340 berths. It is located two blocks away from the city centre and services are of a high standard and include showers, sauna and laundry which are open twenty-four hours a day.

Mariehamn, West harbor-ÅSS *M. Strobel*

The harbour shop offers basic food, coffee, sodas, ice cream, etc. There is lighting on the jetties and the harbour is guarded at night in July.

Services for yachts

Both marinas, ÅSS and MSF, provide water and electricity, and there are showers, sauna, laundry and toilet facilities ashore. There are diesel pontoons (West Harbour: 0800–2200, East Harbour: 0900–2100) where holding tanks can be emptied.

Finnish and Swedish propane bottles can be exchanged at both marinas and Camping Gaz is available at the STI fuel station near East Harbour.

Weather forecasts are posted daily.

There are small shops, cafés and restaurants near both marinas, plus a daily delivery of fresh bread every morning at around 0800.

Zetterströms Varv boatyard, about 0·75M upstream from the West Harbour, has long been a favourite spot for visiting yachts to have repairs carried out and to overwinter. There are two cranes capable of handling vessels up to 16 tonnes.
☎ +358 18 22855

THE BALTIC SEA AND APPROACHES

Sail repairs can be arranged at the West Harbour.

The Kalmers chandlery, is situated at Vikingagrand, about 3km north of Mariehamn (open 0800–1700 Monday–Saturday, 0800–1300 Sunday). A free minibus to the chandlery leaves the West Harbour at 1000 and 1200 calling at East Harbour 15 minutes later. The stock held is impressive, including general chandlery, rope, paint, electronics, etc.
☏ +358 18 12012
www.kalmers.com/marin

A few local charts are on sale at the West Harbour marina office, but for a full range of Swedish and Finnish charts and guides visit Lisco at Skarpansvägen 25.
☏ +358 18 17177
bok@lisco.ax www.lisco.fi

More limited stocks are available from Mariehamns Bokhandel, as well as the nearby Britas Bok & Papper (both in Mariehamn's pedestrian area).

General facilities

The main shopping centre lies on the east side of the peninsula, close to the East Harbour. Mariehamn offers all the facilities of a medium-sized town, including food stores, Alko, banks, restaurants and hotels, together with an excellent tourist information office and library. Parents with children aboard are recommended to visit the latter, which has an excellent children's area and play section with toys, books, CDs in English, storytelling and craft activities during July.

Communications and travel

Mail can be sent to both marinas – c/o ÅSS Marina, Strandpromenaden, Postbox 135, 22101 Mariehamn, Åland, Finland or c/o Mariehamns Seglarförening, Postbox 155, 22101 Mariehamn, Åland, Finland.

There are regular flights and ferries from Mariehamn to Stockholm, Turku and Helsinki. An inter-island ferry serves the archipelago, and all the islands can be reached from Mariehamn without difficulty.

Car hire is readily available, however, Mariehamn might have been designed for the cyclist, having almost no hills and little traffic. Bicycles can be hired from both marinas, with a wider choice including tandems and children's bicycles available from a store opposite the ferry dock on the west.

Lemströmin Kanava (Lemströms Kanal)

60°05.8′N 20°01′E
Chart C756, 757

The canal was built in 1880 to facilitate traffic between Lumparn and Slemmern (eastern Mariehamn).

The Lemströms Canal is in a beautiful setting, built in red granite and with a swing-bridge. This bridge is opened every full hour on the hour for a period of 10 minutes. One needs to be at or near the bridge, visible to the guard/control building, before

Kastelholm *Anthony Fawcett*

the full hour. It also opens 10 minutes before the hour for the final opening of the day and can be opened at other times, on payment of a fee, by contacting the operator on ☏ +358 18 33731. For opening times see
www.visitaland.com

Kastelholm

60°13′·4N 20°05′·07E (deep pool opposite golf club)
Marina (N 60°13′·7N 20°04′·8E)
Charts C757, 33
SH2 *27* FMA *1250*
www.visitsaaristo.net
www.visitaland.com
www.kastelholm.ax

Situated on the main island of Åland, Kastelholm lies only 12·5M northeast of Mariehamn. The southerly approach is from Lumparn, a relatively deep pool between Åland, Lemland and Lumparland. From Rödko light (60°09′·6N 20°04′E, Fl.WRG.3s) follow the buoyed channel northwards to W of Tingön island. Holmsudden is the narrow sound that opens up to the NE of Tingön. The river setting, with cows and sheep grazing down to the water's edge, is a contrast to the rocky coast. The overhead cable has a clearance of 22m. The large marina is quite near the castle. Facilities include water, electricity, pump out station, fuel, showers and sauna. There is a small but well-stocked shop and café on site and an excellent bakery nearby. Anchoring is possible opposite the marina in 3-4m. Anchoring in the pool at the end of the channel is now forbidden near the castle.

The Smakbyn restaurant opened in 2013, with master chef Michael Bjorklund, is very popular (reservations ☏ +358 18 43 666, www.smakbyn.ax).

Kastelholm castle (open 1000–1700) has an open-air museum showing a village in the nineteenth century.

This is an excellent place to spend Midsummer and watch the ceremony of raising the pole. All the locals are dressed in national costume.

4B. THE ARCHIPELAGO SEA

Bomarsund *Bindy Wollen*

Bomarsund
60°13·1'N 20°13·9'E (pontoon)
Charts C752, 32, 33
SH2 *3* **FMA** *1190*
www.visitsaaristo.net
http://bomarsund.ax
http://en.wikipedia.org/wiki/Battle_of_Bomarsund

The bridge between Bomarsund and the island of Prästö has a clearance of only 3m and therefore you can only access Bomarsund from the north. From Lumparn sail anticlockwise around Prästö leaving the islet of Slätskär to port before entering the small bay of Notviken. Bomarsund/Notviken offers good anchorage secure from all winds except northerlies. There are 26 spaces, bows-to from stern buoys (or anchor) to the wooden quay on the east side (1.9m). In the middle of the bay the water is very deep (9m). At Puttes Camping, 200m, showers, toilets and a restaurant are available. A small fee is charged at this jetty which also provides electricity.

This anchorage was a favourite of Tsar Alexander III; there are Russian characters to be seen on the cliffs at the entrance. It is possible to berth alongside the cliff face for climbers to ascend.

The ruins of the Bomarsund Fortress, bombarded and captured by the Anglo-French fleet during the Crimean War in 1854, are still plainly visible. A 800m walk through the campsite leads to the fortifications.

There is a small museum near the bridge, open 4 May to 30 June 1000–1500 and 1 July to 15 August 1000–17.00 which sells a booklet in English.

Delvik
60°14·8'N 20°12·8'E

Anchorage in Delvik, north of Storholm is a good alternative in northerly winds.

Anchor at the head of the bay or in good holding in the inlet to the NE (3–5m). This bay combines scenery with solitude.

Hamnsundet
60°22'·5N 20°05'·2E (pontoon)
Charts C751, 751.1, 759, 33
SH2 *18* **FMA** *1180*
www.visitsaaristo.net
www.visitaland.com

Conveniently situated in the sound, between the islands of Boxö, Boxö-ön and Åland, on the remote northern shore, Hamnsundet lies just off the main route around the island. It is a small service harbour and coastguard station offering good shelter except from the northeast and east. There are 15 visitors' berths, bows to pontoons from stern buoys (or anchor) and alongside the quay. Facilities include all normal guest harbour services including fuel. Power is only available with a 100m lead and water can be found on the fuel berth. There is a kiosk during the short sailing season.

Havsvidden, Geta
60° 25'·3N 19° 54'·7E (harbour mole)
Charts C759, 33
SH2 *19* **FMA** *1263*
www.visitsaaristo.net
www.visitaland.com

This is a small and rather shallow marina attached to the HavsVidden hotel and conference centre (2·5–1·5m), located on the exposed and remote northern shore of Åland called Geta. There are many submerged rocks towards the northwest of the small inlet and the approach has to be from the east-northeast, very close to the eastern shore, following the transit. The marina is exposed to the north. There are 25 places on the pontoon, bows-to from stern buoys. It tends to become crowded in the summer, so a reservation might be advisable.

Havsvidden marina and entrance *A. Fawcett*

ROUTE 1 ÅLAND, RÖDHAMN AND DEGERBY

Djupviken, Geta
60°24′N 19°50′E (anchorage)
Charts C759, 33
SH2 9

A long narrow inlet with an excellent anchorage at its head. Very good shelter, even from the north. From this anchorage it is possible to climb along a marked path to the second highest hill Geta berget in Åland (275m). There is a wooden tower at the top from which a good view can be obtained on a fine day – where there also is a coffee shop. An excellent place to appreciate the natural beauty of Åland.

Heading east from Mariehamn
Most of the vessels and ferry traffic between Mariehamn and Helsinki passes this way.

The route starts in Mariehamn, heads southeast into Rödhamnsfjärden and then north of Ledskär (59°58′N 20°10′E) to Degerby (60°02′N 20°23′E).

Rödhamn
59° 59′·1N 20° 06′·1E (marina)
Charts 753, 754, 756, 32
SH2 51 **FMA** 1205
Communications
www.visitsaaristo.net
www.hamneguiden.ax/rodhamn

An excellent landlocked harbour, which is a good place to wait for a fair wind for Sweden. Enter from the northwest or southeast.

The beautiful old harbour of Rödhamn ('red harbour') was an important anchorage for sailing ships en route from Sweden to Finland, as ships would sometimes lie for weeks waiting for favourable winds to carry them across the Åland Sea. A pilot station was built in 1818 and remained in use until the 1920s. In the late 1980s the building was recreated using building plans from 1858. There is

Rödhamn Bindy Wollen

also a small museum depicting the history of the radio beacon, in use from 1937 until 1970.

In addition to the *gästhamn*, the Åland Yacht Club (ÅSS) has a marina and premises on the island including a café offering fresh bread and freshly smoked fish, a sauna, and a boatshed which doubles as an art gallery.

Degerby
60° 01′·8N 20° 23′·2E (pontoon Degerby Lotsudden)
Charts C745, 32
SH2 8 **FMA** 1155, 1160
Communications
www.visitaland.com
www.visitsaaristo.net

Degerby lies on the west coast of Degerö island. It is considered to be the central point of the Föglö archipelago. There are two *gästhamns* with excellent facilities including shopping, restaurants and fuel, and everything is within walking distance. Both are

Degerby T. Fooks

THE BALTIC SEA AND APPROACHES   273

4. FINLAND

4B. THE ARCHIPELAGO SEA

open from the southwest to the northeast. One is next to the ferry landing and has 30 places on a pontoon pier, bows-to from stern buoys. There is a small supermarket, post office, bank, telephone, showers, sauna and laundry.

The other is Degerby, Lotsudden (60°01'·8N, 20°23'E), just 0·3M south of the ferry landing. The pontoon has 45 places, bows-to from stern buoys. Seagrams Restaurant and Hotel is next to the harbour. The keys to the community's modern indoor swimming pool (unheated in the summer) are held at the restaurant overlooking the harbour. The north *gästhamn*, although closer to the services, is more disturbed by ferries.

Route 2
A Northern route through the Archipelago Sea

Route 2a Leading to the northern Åbo archipelago and the Gulf of Bothnia

The northeastern part of the Åland archipelago has some of the most fascinating and least frequented waters, not least because they are off the beaten track from Mariehamn to Hanko and Helsinki. These northern waters can be approached from the west, from Vårdö (East of Åland) after crossing Lumparn or from the southwest, from Degerby. The northern route wanders northeast through the communities of Kumlinge and Brändö, which comprise many small islands and skerries. It also leads towards Uusikaupunki, the northern part of the Åbo (Turun) archipelago and the Gulf of Bothnia through the Kihti (Skiftet), the deep water sound that separates the Åland Islands from Southwest Finland. (See plan below.)

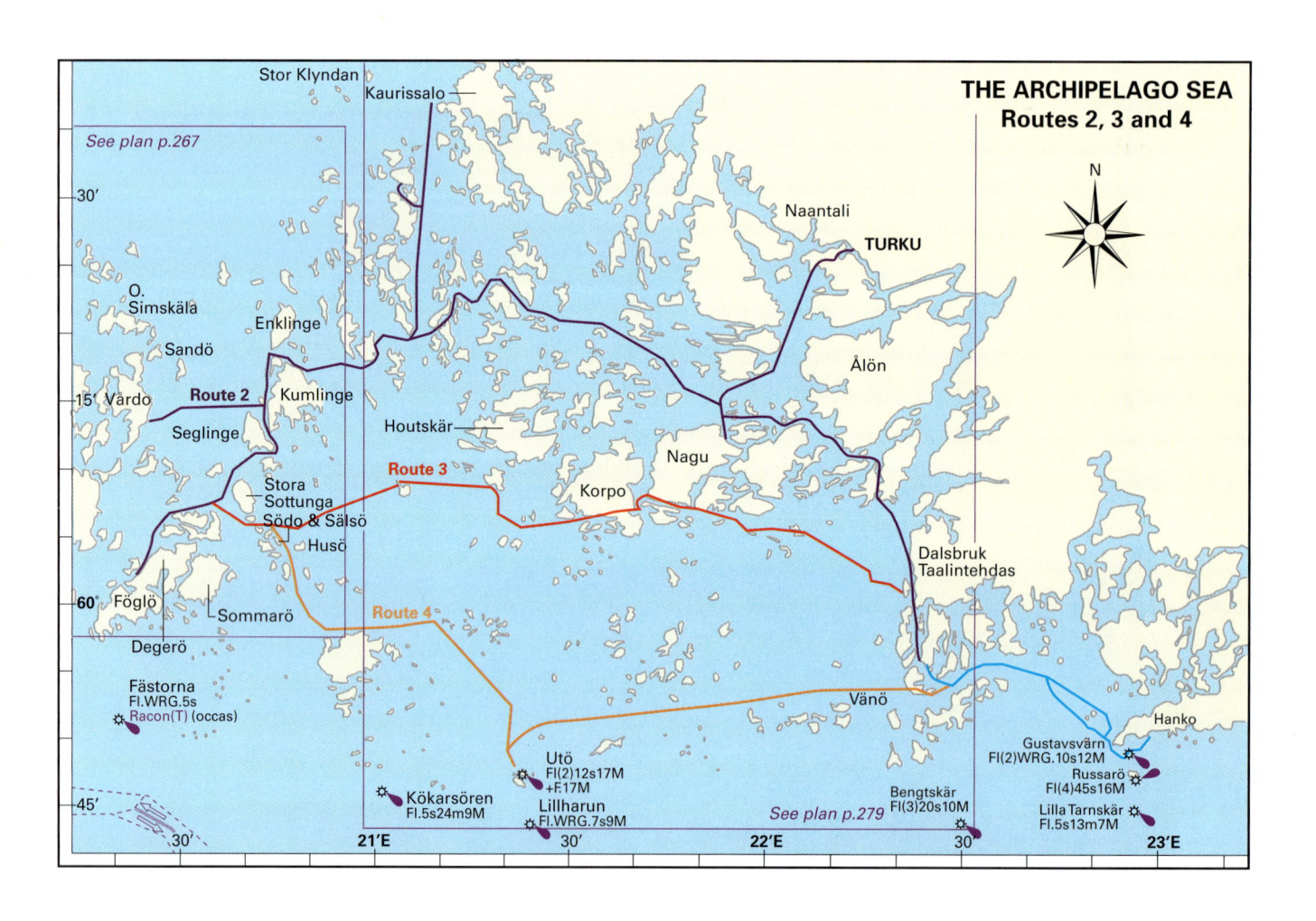

274   THE BALTIC SEA AND APPROACHES

ROUTE 2 NORTHERN ROUTE

Seglinge E, Finnhälla

60°12'·7N 20°42'·5E (wooden pontoon)
Charts C739, 747, 28, 30
SH2 52 **FMA** 1120
www.visitsaaristo.net

This is a quiet and secluded harbour on the east side of the island of Seglinge, in the narrow sound between the islands of Synderstö and Snäckö, and Seglinge. Coming from the northwest or southeast, follow the leading marks to enter the harbour, passing just north of two northerly cardinal buoys. Enter the pool in mid-channel, between Seglinge and Yttre Holmen. There is a frequent ferry between the south point of Snäckö and Seglinge. Moor alongside in 2·2–4m to a wooden jetty 200m past the ferry landing stage or further along, bows-to from stern buoys (30 spaces). Very rural with old fishing huts and boathouses. Well-stocked small shop 500m up the road. Water from a pump at the top of the track on the right. Electricity. Forest walking trails leading to a disused windmill (2km) and the famous Stangnäs cauldrons – deep hollows in the rocks where it is said that offerings were made for better fishing – with excellent views of surrounding islands.

Remmarhamn, Kumlinge

60°15'·4N 20°44'·2E (wooden pontoon)
Charts C738, 739, 747, 30
SH2 50 **FMA** 1115
www.visitaland.com

Remmarhamn is located just 2·5M further north in the sound from Seglinge, following the west shore of Snäckö. This is the largest guest harbour on the island. It is exposed to the southwest and there is also a strong current from under the road bridge to the east.

The marina is situated in the bay south of Ljugarsholm (Näset). Moor bows-to from stern buoys or finger pontoons (3·5m) (45 spaces). Fuel and gas (cheaper than Mariehamn), electricity, water, laundry, showers, sauna, pump-out station. Bicycle rental at the café. The village is 3km away and has a large well-stocked supermarket, post office and banks.

St Anna's church, less than 4km northeast of the harbour is well worth a visit with its distinctive wall paintings from around 1500, a style not seen elsewhere in Finland. Scenic walks over the rocky plateau.

In strong southwest to west wind it is better to use the marina on the north shore of the island in Kumlinge, Torsholm, which is also a safe anchorage in all but northerly to northeasterly winds.

Bärö, seen from the watch tower *M. Strobel*

Bärö

60°18'·2N 20°44'·6E (northern mole)
Charts 738, 30
SH2 7 **FMA** 1105
www.visitsaaristo.net
www.visitaland.com

Bärö is an island to the northwest of Kumlinge. The small harbour, a former coastguard station is situated on its north shore close to the southern tip of Enklinge island. It is open from the north to northeast. The former coastguard station has been leased and transformed into a very good restaurant, Glada Laxen, open only in the summer from mid-June through August. Reservations ☎ +358 400 108 800.

There are 20 spaces alongside or bows-to from buoys or anchor in 2·5–3m.

There are not many paths on the island because it essentially consists of rocks, but climbing up the 40m high watch tower gives a magnificent view of the archipelago.

4. FINLAND

THE BALTIC SEA AND APPROACHES

4B. THE ARCHIPELAGO SEA

Lappo
60°18'·9N 20°59'·7'E (pontoon)
Charts C732, 738, 29, 30
SH2 *40* **FMA** *1000*
www.visitsaaristo.net
www.visitaland.com

This sheltered and picturesque guest harbour is surrounded by traditional boathouses and has good facilities nearby. Approach from the northeast, following the transit, leaving the small island of Basthom to port. Moor bows-to from stern buoys or tie alongside to the pontoon (1·5–4m) (90 spaces). There are several good walks leading to a sandy beach and a bird reserve west of the jetty. The Archipelago Museum contains fine examples of traditional boats. Lappo also has good services, a sauna, washing machine, water, electricity, supermarket, pump-out station, fuel, fishmonger, and a restaurant.

Jurmo, Brändö
60°30'·9N 21°04'·5E
Charts C733, 29
SH2 *26* **FMA** *1025*
www.visitsaaristo.net
www.visitaland.com

The island of Jurmo, in the northeastern part of the Åland Islands can be reached either from the southeast coming from the Skiftet or directly from Kumlinge or Bärö from the west, sailing in a northeasterly direction. This western route through the archipelago is a very scenic and intricate one (see charts 738 and 737) but can only be attempted by yachts with a draught of not more than 2·1m.

The Jurmo guest harbour is located to the south of the island and is exposed to the west, southwest and east. The final approach is from the south, between Mjöholm and Tällholmen following transits and fairway buoys. Moor bows-to from stern anchor to the pontoon (2·4m) or alternatively anchor off the village (7–12m) with a line ashore on Tällholmen.

Jurmo is a very pretty guest harbour with many traditional wooden houses and boat sheds. Facilities include water, electricity, fuel, sauna, washing machine, shower, fuel, shop, fishmonger and a restaurant. There are several very interesting forest walks on the island. Jurmo prides itself for raising a herd of Highland cattle and for bringing Icelandic horses onto the island for the summer.

Route 2b From Lappo or Torsholma towards Turku or Hanko

To sail towards Turku or Hanko taking the northern route through the Finnish archipelago, leave Torsholma or Lappo and head east across the Skiftet (Kihti) sound. (See plan page 279.)

Iniö
60°23'·8N 21°23'·4E (Norrby)
Charts D725, 29
SH1 *43* **FMA** *958, 954*
www.visitsaaristo.net

Norrby lies to the east of the island of Iniö in a sheltered basin formed by a cluster of islands, Iniö, Kolko, Hepmo and Jumo. Approach either from the southwest, leaving the main channel (3·5m) and entering between Kupmo and Iniö or the southeast from Perkala fjärden leaving Kolko to starboard and the islets of Bergholm, Grisselholm, Hästholm and Jeppörarna to port. Kolko sound is well marked by cardinal buoys. Turn sharp around Jeppörarna to enter the approach channel (2·4m) that leads to the landing following the transit on Likholmen.

Jurmo, exposed to the W
M. Strobel

276 THE BALTIC SEA AND APPROACHES

ROUTE 2 NORTHERN ROUTE

There are two harbours on Iniö:

Norrby
Situated close to the village and is very shallow and cramped (1·5–2m).

Bruddalsviken
Only 0.5M further to the northwest (60°24'·3N 21°22'·6E), although further away from the village, has more space and is deeper (2·5–3m). Both have water, electricity, showers, sauna, post office, restaurant, shop, cashpoint in the village.

Pähkinäinen
60°19'·7N 21°41'·7E
Charts D719, 26
SH1 96 **FMA** 858
www.visitsaaristo.net

This is an almost landlocked small guest harbour and anchorage on the island of Pähkinäinen. Enter the lagoon from the east, leaving the islets of Mäntykari, Kalliokari, and Pikku Viljakari to port, and the shoals and Mustaluoto to starboard. There are two pontoons 1·5M from the entrance to port with bows-to from stern buoys (or anchor); there are 50 spaces. The pontoon on the right hand side is private or reserved for the ferry. The facilities are very limited. There is a floating pump-out station to the east of the pontoon. There is plenty of space to anchor in the lagoon, all the way to the southwest corner at Varsalahti (60°19'·8N 21°40'·8E). Beware of the submerged rock to the north of Varsalahti. This is a very popular weekend destination and owned by the city of Åbo (Turku).

Näsby, Houtskasi
60°13'·5N 21°22'·0E
Charts D727, 28, 29
FMA 970
www.visitsaaristo.net

Näsby harbor is located on the northern part of Houtskär. Approach from the west along the 3m route between Houtskär and Benskär. At Roslaxnäs turn starboard and westwards into the bay. Moor bows-to from stern buoys at the pontoon with place for 50 boats. Electricity, water, fuel, restaurant, sauna, shower, toilet, WiFi, washing machine.

Näsby village is 200m inland. There you find a well-stocked supermarket, bank and cafe. The wooden well-preserved church is from 1703. A culture path with 10 stops describes the history of the island.

Nauvo (Nagu) at Midsummer M. Strobel

Nauvo/Nagu, Kyrkbacken
60°11'·6N 21°54'·6.E
Charts D708, 25
SH1 79 **FMA** 746
www.visitsaaristo.net

A naturally sheltered bay, fringed by sand and pine trees on the northeast coast of the island of Nagu (Nauvo). This has become the attractive setting for a marina. The approach channels from the northwest and the east are well marked. Enter the harbour from the northeast, leaving two east cardinal buoys to starboard. There are 120 berths on pontoons, some finger pontoons, some bows-to with stern buoys, and some spaces alongside. Pump-out points on each pontoon. Excellent toilets, sauna and laundry block.

This marina gets very crowded during the summer, particularly during Midsummer.

There are fish and bread shops in separate little wooden cabins along the beach: the wonderful hot-smoked rainbow trout is not to be missed – the fish is smoked on site behind the kiosk. Very good restaurants, cafés and hotels. Fuel station with propane gas (butane), stores, post office, pharmacy, banks and supermarket are only a short walk away. This is a very useful stop to provision and fuel up. Usually very quiet; night silence 2300–0700 is observed, apart from Midsummer!

4B. THE ARCHIPELAGO SEA

Turku (Åbo)

60°25'·9N 22°13'·6E (mouth of the Aura river)

Distances
Mariehamn 75M, Hanko 65M

Charts and guides
UKHO 2297, 3439, 3440
Finnish D706, 26; (**SH1** *125*) (**FMA** *688, 689*)
Merikarttasarja D
Stora Hamnboken Vol.I

Lights
Lillharun 59°43'·6N 21°24'·2E Fl.WRG.7s17m8M 262°-G-340°-W-045°-R-101°-G-148°-W-156°-R-172° Racon Black concrete tower Wind generator
Utö 59°46'·9N 21°22'·3E Fl(2)12s40m18M 235°-vis-100° Auxiliary F.38m10M 163°-vis-253° Square white granite tower, red stripes 24m. In centre of island
Bokullankivi 59°50'·8N 21°25'·4E Fl.WRG.5s9m9M 009°-G-050°-W-054°-R-165°-G-232·5°-W-236·5°-R-009° Racon White tower, black band Wind generator
Lövskär 60°13'·2N 21°43'·6E VQ(5)WRG.6s7m7M 197°-G-254°-W-258°-R-000°-W-197° Framework tower
Petäis 60°14'·3N 21°48'·1E Fl.WRG.3s6m4M 030°-G-051°-W-055°-R-130°-G-209°-W-230°-R-240° Black concrete base, white lantern
Orhisaari 60°16'·5N 22°00'E Q(2)WRG.6s18m10M 019°-G-073°-W-158°-G-210°-W-217°-R-232°-G-246°-W-266°-R-284° White metal framework tower, concrete base
Rajakari 60°22'·7N 22°06'E Fl.WRG.4s13m11M 166°-G-171°-W-173°-R-194°-G-203·5°-W-205°-R-257°-G-016°-W-024·5°-R-031° Red and white round concrete tower

Harbour communications
Turku Port Authority ☎ +358 02 2674 122
VHF Ch 12,16, 71 (call Turku Port Control)
turkuport@port.turku.fi
www.visitsaaristo.net for Turku Aurajoki (west shore)
www.visitturku.fi

Turku, Aura river *M. Strobel*

Approach and entrance

The approach is from the southwest through the main commercial shipping channel (13m). Fork towards the northeast (c. 25°) when you reach Rajakari lighthouse (60°22'·6N 22°05'·8E, Fl.WRG.4s). This leads straight into the narrow, well-buoyed and deep approach channel towards Turku, between Ruissalo and Iso-Pukki regularly used by large ships. There is an alternative channel to the east of Iso-Pukki (3m). Both channels join at Kalkkiniemi (Oc.WRG.3s). Follow the channel to Turku docks, turn to starboard past the passenger and commercial port, and then to port up the Aura river past the shipbuilding yards and the three-masted Suomen Joutsen.

Formalities

The Finnish Customs Board has closed down the customer service desk in Turku. Customers will only be served electronically from 2016.

Berthing

There are several well-equipped marinas outside Turku, but visiting yachts will undoubtedly find it most convenient to moor at the city-run guest harbour, Aura å västra (FMA *688*), situated on the west bank of the Aura river, just downstream from the foot ferry. The marina office (open 0800–2200 in season) doubles as a café, both occupying a small grey kiosk, which also sells a few basic groceries. It has free internet access.

Designated the European Capital of Culture for 2011, Turku is well worth the detour from the open sea. Turku, the capital of Finland until the early 19th century, is the country's sixth largest city, with a population of more than 190,000. It is also one of the most important ports in Finland, handling oil, containers and other freight, together with frequent ferry services to Stockholm and Mariehamn. Its shipyards have constructed some of the world's largest cruise liners.

The modern city, built on a grid pattern, was rebuilt in 1827 after the old town was virtually wiped out by fire. The 13th-century cathedral, gutted by the fire, has been completely restored. Turku Castle, which stands near the mouth of the Aura river, also dates back to the 13th century and now houses an interesting museum. There is also an excellent maritime museum, the Forum Marinum, with exhibits both ashore and afloat.
www.forum-marinum.fi

Turku city centre *M. Strobel*

ROUTE 2 NORTHERN ROUTE

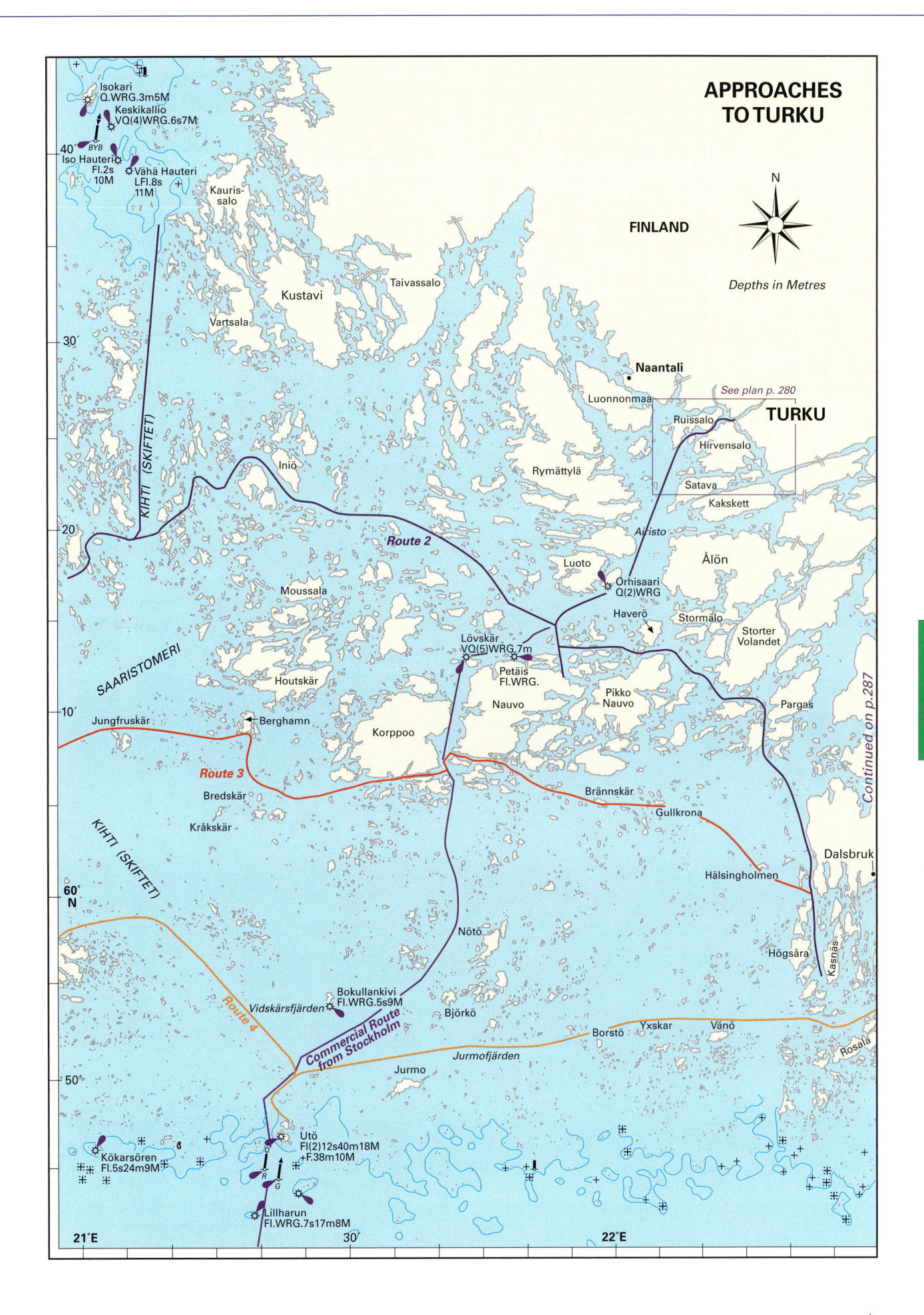

APPROACHES TO TURKU

FINLAND

Depths in Metres

THE BALTIC SEA AND APPROACHES

4B. THE ARCHIPELAGO SEA

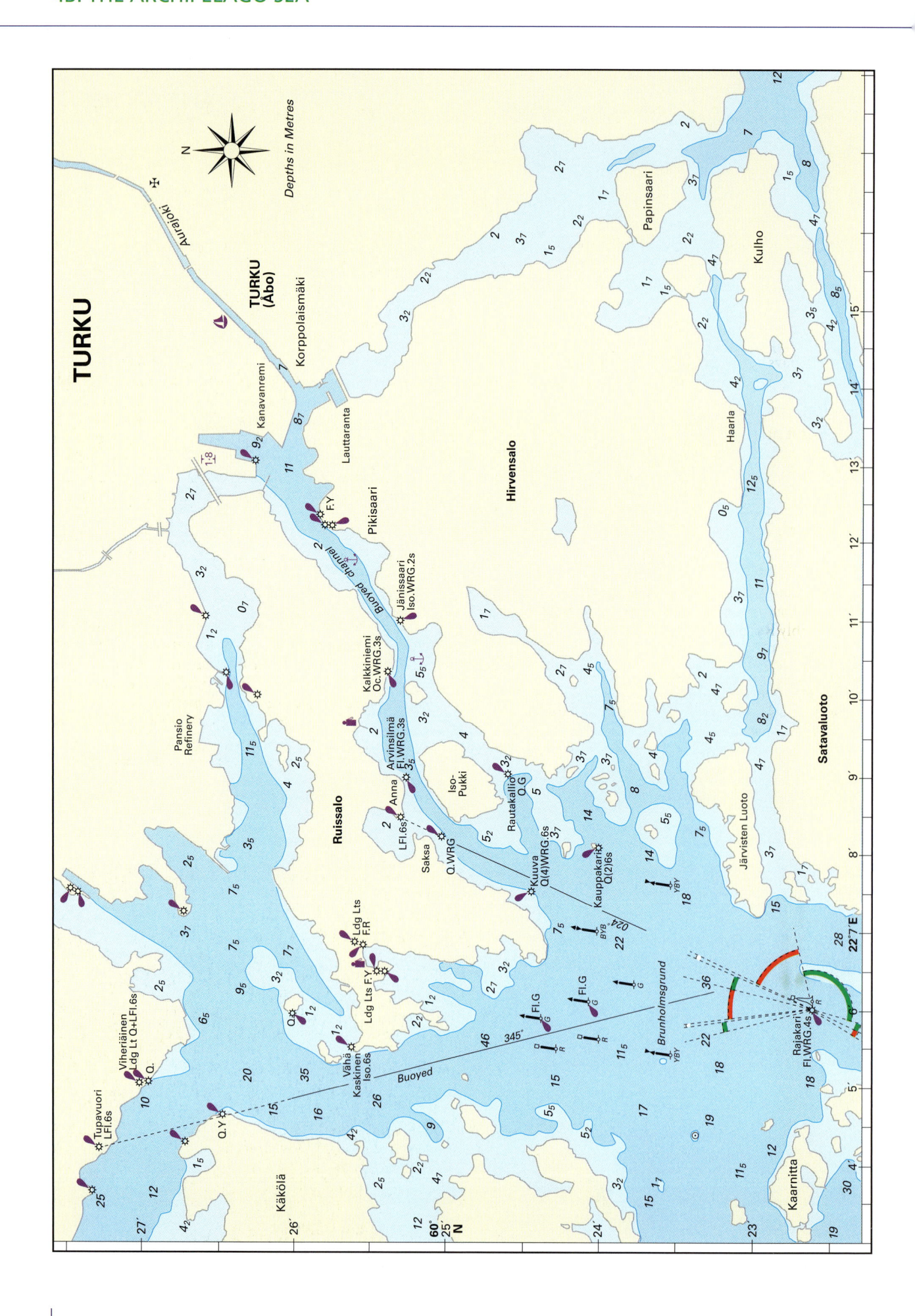

ROUTE 2 NORTHERN ROUTE

Among the 70 berths are several suitable for yachts of up to 3·5m beam and 2m draught, with larger yachts (up to 5m beam) berthing further downstream. Berthing is between posts, so check the width! Considerable disturbance is caused by wash from the many passing tourist boats. If there is no room on the west side, there are many spaces alongside the quay on the east bank, below the foot ferry at Aura å östra (FMA 689).

The guest harbour is often full to capacity from mid-June to mid-July, but it may be possible to lie alongside one of the charter vessels moored along the quayside.

Masted yachts are prevented from continuing up the river by a fixed bridge, but there are several public quays and landing places further up the river where a dinghy might be secured for short periods.

Services for yachts

The guest harbour has water and electricity on the pontoons (though washing boats down with fresh water is forbidden) with toilets, showers, sauna and laundry facilities in a block just across the road. Fresh rolls can be ordered at the marina office for morning collection.

Fuel is available from both Esso and Shell jetties on the west bank of the river in the dock area. Alternatively it may be found more convenient to call at one of the marinas in the approach – possibly Ruissalo's Santalanlahti (60°25'·5N 22°06'·4E) (FMA *702*).

For chandlery of all kinds visit Meredin-Ulkoiluaitta Oy at Puolalankatu 6, claiming to be one of the best chandleries in Finland. Amongst the items on offer are Finnish, Swedish and Estonian charts, electronics, clothing and shoes, and many leading international brands of hardware.
☎ +358 2 275 275
Meredin@meredin.fi

Winter storage and yacht repairs are available at Veneveistämö Janne Pettersson Oy . Located in the north-eastern part of Ruissalo, Hevoskarintie 23 20100 TURKU
☎ +358 40 5267701
www.venepuuseppa.fi

Boat repairs at Satavan Venepalvelu
☎ +358 20 735 1414
svp@satavanvenepalvelu.fi
www.satavanvenepalvelu.fi

Sail maker and repairs at Purjeneulomo Niiniranta Oy
☎ +358 2 247 1000
www.fi.northsails.com

General facilities

The yacht harbour is about 20 minutes' walk along the riverside to the town centre, where all normal shopping needs can be met. There are excellent outdoor and covered markets and various supermarkets, including one in the basement of a shopping mall. There is the usual range of cafés, restaurants and hotels, many overlooking the water and several on historic vessels moored on the river itself.

Several enormous out-of-town shopping centres lie to the north of the town on the bus route to Naantali.

Communications and travel

There is a bus stop behind the marina, one way leading to the maritime museum, castle and docks, the other to the city centre and the airport. Ferries leave the docks daily for the Åland Islands, Stockholm and Mariehamn.

Direct charter flights operate from Turku to the UK; Helsinki airport is easily reached by train, bus or plane. Turku is an excellent stop for crew changes.

Airristo marina *M. Strobel*

Airisto, Stormälö

60°15'·1N 22°06'·4E (pier)
Charts D707, 708, 26
SH1 *3* FMA *738*
www.visitsaaristo.net

This old harbour was used in the 19th century by the Tsarist navy with deep water all around the bay. There is a marina situated on the west side of the island of Stormälö. It is part of a holiday hotel development and can accommodate 100 boats. Yachts moor bows-to from stern buoys, alongside or in berths. There is space for several larger yachts alongside the outer pontoon. The marina has water, electricity, fuel, gas, WiFi connection and a pump-out station. Marina charge includes showers, toilet and sauna. There is also a restaurant and a kiosk with smoked fish and fresh vegetables.

Paraisten Portti, Parainen

60°09'N 22° 17'·1E (pier)
Charts D703, B649, 25
SH1 *88* FMA *638*
www.visitsaaristo.net

Located on the southern peninsula of the larger island of Attu, Paraisten Portti is a convenient service harbour in the sound between the islands of Attu, Jermo, Tammo and Sorpo. However, it is exposed to the north and wash from passing boats. It has room for 30 boats in 2–2·3m, bows-to from stern buoys. It has a good restaurant and the facilities include fuel, electricity, shop, sauna and pump-out station.

An alternative in northerly winds is a good anchorage, just 1M further north, in 10m in a large bay east of Dirholmen (Digerholm) (60°10'N 22°16'·6E) at the north end of Sorpo (Käringholm). It is open to the east and southeast.

Hamnholmen

60°01'N 22°21'·4E
Charts D702, 25
SH1 *31*
www.visitturku.fi

The anchorage of Hamnholmen lies within the Archipelago National Park and therefore care should be taken to respect the rules and regulations (see website above). It is located west of Purunpää and north of Noströ and Högsåra with good sheltered anchorage on the eastern side of the island. Access is easy from the main channel (4·2m). Approach either from the south, leaving all the islets and rocks at the entrance to port or from the north rounding the easterly-cardinal buoy just off Judasholm. Anchor in the north or south (3·5m) part of the pool. Note that there are many submerged rocks around Dömmaskärsgrunden south of Gåshalsen (see chartlet 702.4).

Kejsarhamnen, Högsåra

59° 57'·7N 22° 21'9E
Charts B647, B648, D701, D702, 25
SH1 *54* FMA *620*
www.visitsaaristo.net

Kejsarhamnen is a bay on the north side of the island of Högsåra on the west side of Jungfrusund. It affords excellent anchorage for large and small yachts. The bay can be entered from the north, between Nämanön and North- and South- Furuholm or from the east. The latter can be easily identified by the white cairn on the northern tip of Killingholm. The holding ground in the southern part of the bay is not good. However, there is a guest pontoon with electricity on the south shore just off Killingholm with 30 spaces, bows-to from stern anchor). There is a floating pump-out station just off the pontoon. Limited facilities ashore include a shower, sauna and a kiosk. The guest pontoon is open to north winds. The bay is called after Tsar Alexander III who used to anchor here in the royal yacht Standart. The nearby beach makes this a popular harbour for boats with young families. Fuel is obtainable at the village of Högsåra. An alternative well-sheltered anchorage with muddy bottom is located half a mile further north in Norrfladan off Nämanön, tucked behind the islands of North and South Furuholm. Anchor in 4m towards the northwestern end of the lagoon.

Byviken, Högsåra

59° 57'·1.2N 22° 22'·1E
Charts B645, B647, B648, D701, D702, 22, 25
SH1 *41* FMA *597*
www.visitsaaristo.net

This harbour on the island of Högsara, situated on the west side of the Jungfrusund, has a long history of providing pilotage services: as far back as the 16th century its tenant farmers piloted ships owned by the Swedish royal navy through the island's rocky waters. The island's pilotage services continued right up to 1985, and a visit to the local museum in the main harbour (Byviken) is worthwhile. The resident population has dwindled from about 100 in the 1950s to about 40 today, and the remaining inhabitants now depend on tourism and forestry for their living. The island's main employer is the Maritime Administration's shipping route station. The island has two guest pontoons, Byviken is on the southern side of the main harbour. This is a new *gästhamn* and can accommodate up to 40 boats, bows-to from stern buoys. A small ferry from Svartnäs calls in at the harbour, making the pontoon is susceptible to passing wash; it is also open to the east. The village is famous for Farmors (Granny's) Café, which sells mouth-watering pastries, snacks, coffee and bread. Lunch and dinner are also available.

ROUTE 3 CENTRAL ROUTE

Route 3
A central route through the Archipelago Sea leading from Degerby towards Hanko

From Degerby follow the main northeasterly route as for route 2 until you reach Skarpskär (60°06'·7N 20°28'·4E). From there, follow the transits eastwards until you have reached Enskär lighthouse (60°07'·4N 20°34'·9E, Fl.WRG.3s). The central route leads in a southeasterly direction past Sottunga and eastwards through the Archipelago Sea. From Sottunga, the central route continues past Husö, Jungfruskär, south of the large island of Korppoo (Korpo), then north of Ängsö and Bergö. From there it continues east-southeast and passes south of Brännskär and close south of Gullkrona. The final leg is southeasterly via Helsingholmen and through the Jungfrusund, between Högsåra and Kasnäslandet where the central and northern routes meet to join the southern route north of Rosala (see plan p.274).

Alternatively, starting from Degerby in the northeasterly direction, at Sandön (60°04'·1N 20°26'·3E) turn eastwards on the route with the name Ämbarsunden. Note the minimum depth of 1·8m! This route is beautiful, narrow at places and you can see a lot of wildlife. The route ends at Sälsö, just east of Husö, to join the central route.

Sottunga/Sottungalandet

60°06'·5N 20°40'9E (pier)
Charts C746, 740.1, 28
SH2 56 **FMA** 1165
www.visitsaaristo.net
www.sottunga.ax
www.visitaland.com

A small service harbour at the southern end of the island, north of the islets of Hamnklobb, Snackö and Hamnklobb. Tjurgrund light (60°06'·56N 20°41'·8E, Q(2)WRG.6s) has three white sectors from the west, south and southeast for the approach to the harbour; there is a transit as well. There are 30 to 35 spaces, bows-to from stern buoys (or anchor) to the pontoon near the ferry landing (2–3m) or alongside at the quay. Water and fuel in the inner harbour; shop and bank at the centre of the island. The small ferries to Sottunga and Snäckö berth just west of the harbour. There is a beautiful 15th century wooden church built in 1661 and dedicated to Mary Magdalene, 300m down the road, and several interesting walks around the island.

Bänö-ön

60°04·8'N 20°35·4'E
Charts C746, 32 (**SH2** 6)

Anchorage

A large and much indented bay affording anchorage sheltered from all winds. Enter between Bänö-ön and Gåsholm, the island E of it, or between Gåsholm and the two small skerries northwest of it to port and Bänö/Söderön to starboard. Anchor at the mouth of the Bänö-ön eastern (Söderklobba) bay with good holding, or in easterly winds in the bay on west side of Gåsholm (clay bottom); or in the bay Ålviken between Bänö and the islands immediately west of it. Many opportunities to moor to the shore, bows-to from stern anchor. Popular and very pleasant, remote and big enough to feel deserted.

Jungfruskär

60°08.3'N 21°04.2'E (pontoon)
Charts C, D731, 28
SH2 25 **FMA** 995
www.visitsaaristo.net

This is a beautiful inhabited group of islands, the largest ones being Jungfruskär, Nölstö and Hamnö. They are situated in the centre of the Archipelago Sea, remote from civilisation, softer and more tranquil than one might expect from their appearance from a distance. Enter from the north or the southwest and anchor anywhere in the sound between Hamnö and Jungfruskär, taking care to avoid the submerged rock close to the northeastern tip of Hamnö and the submerged power cable close by. Alternatively you might prefer to moor bows-to from stern anchor to the small guest pontoon on Jungfruskär (2–2·8m at the end of the pontoon) or bows-to with stern anchor to the shore just south of the pontoon. The other piers are private. Jungfruskär is open to the north.

Berghamn, Storlandet

60°09'N 21°19'E
Charts D728, 728.1, 28
SH1 8

Anchorage

A perfect landlocked harbour, wilder and grander than Jungfruskär, and secure from all winds. It is approached through two narrow channels, one from the south, between Röstholm and Hamnholm, the other from the southwest, through the Hamnholms sound between Hamnholm and Berghamn. Anchor anywhere in the middle of the lagoon, south of the W-card. Buoy, in order to keep clear of the two small ferry piers on the south tip of Berghamn and Lukholm. Alternatively, moor bows-to the shore from stern anchor on the east side of Hamnholmen immediately to port after the Röstholm and Hamnholm entrance.

Korpoström

60°06.6'N 21°36'E
Charts D717, 717.1, 25; (**SH1** 60 **FMA** 838)
www.visitsaaristo.net

The guest harbour is situated to the south of the large island of Korpo in the narrow straight between the main island and the offshore island of Kait. It has two visitors' pontoons with 70 spaces, bows-to from stern buoys just east of the fuel pontoon (1·5–2m). The marina has a smart hotel and wooden promenade with a high class restaurant overlooking

THE BALTIC SEA AND APPROACHES

4B. THE ARCHIPELAGO SEA

Kopoström *J. Langdon*

Helsingholm *J. Hörhammer*

the harbour. Services include fuel, pump-out station, water, electricity, showers, sauna, washing machine, bike hire, store, restaurant, café and tourist office. Korpoström is known for the big naval battle between the Swedes and the Russians in 1743 that took place in the narrow straight and ended with the defeat of the Swedish navy. There is a monument to the history of Korpoström nearby. As an alternative, a good anchorage in the channel is located 1.5M to the east (Norrsund) with private homes and a public jetty at Rumar (60°06'·7N 21°38'·7E) in 2·5–3m.

Stenskär and Birsskär

60°04'·3N 22°02'·9E and 60°04'·3N 22°02'·7E
Charts D709, 709.1, 25
SH1 109 **FMA** 762, 766
www.visitsaaristo.net

(60°04'N 22°03'E) A well-protected, landlocked harbour between Stenskär, Birsskär and Gråsö. A wonderfully scenic and sheltered anchorage, just S of Gullkrona. Enter from N or SW, following buoyed channel. Berth either bow to jetty with stern buoy in E corner (Stenskär 15 places), or alongside new pier running E from Birsskär Island (25 places). Good anchorage between the islands. Both guest harbours provide electricity, drinking water, waste disposal, toilet, shower, sauna, nature trail, and fresh fish for sale. The blue buoys are private.

Helsingholm

60°01'·8N 22°16'·9E
Charts D702, 702.1, B648, 25
SH1 30 **FMA** 626
www.visitsaaristo.net
www.helsingholm.fi

Anchor in the open bay to the N of the island or moor bows to wooden jetty (40 places, depth 1·5–2·5m). Protected from S with very attractive view to N. Smoked fish available in season. There is a sand bar between Helsingholm and Sandö, but a buoyed channel across it. Helsingholm is very popular, partly because of its beautiful location but also due to the warm welcome afforded by the host family Andersson.

Route 4
A southern route through the Archipelago Sea leading from Degerby towards Hanko

From Degerby follow the main northeasterly route as for routes 2 and 3 until you reach Skarpskär (60°06'·7N 20°28'·4E). From there, follow the transits eastwards until you reach Enskär lighthouse (60°07'·4N 20°34'·9E, Fl.WRG.3s). The southern route leads in a southeasterly direction past Sottunga (see above) and continues southwards to Husö and Kyrkogårdsö, passing north of Kökar before heading southeast towards Utö.

From Utö, Route 4 continues eastwards to Jurmo and Borstö (possibly with a diversion north to visit Björkö and Nötö in the Archipelago Sea National Park), east past Yxskar to Vänö, and finally north of Rosala and Hiittinen (Hitis) for the final leg southeast to Hanko. See plan page 274.

The total distance from Mariehamn's West Harbour to Hanko's East Harbour by Routes 3 and 4 is approximately 122M.

Husö

60° 03'·9N 20° 48'·2E
Chart C740

Anchorage

A small anchorage in the southwest corner of the island. Enter from the southeast, between Varpskär and Husö södra näset making sure to leave the east-cardinal buoy, and shortly after that a rock awash (marked by an iron post), to port. Beware of the overhead power cable between Småholmarna and the village of Södholm to the west of Varpskär. Anchor in the pool east of Södholm. The small ferry to other Åland destinations runs from the southern point of the island. It has many holiday cottages and is worth a visit. Very attractive rock formations and good bird watching.

A biological station is situated on Husö which is a part of the Environmental and Marine Biology Department at Åbo Akademi University. The station functions as the base for aquatic studies, but also botanical, mycological and entomological studies are conducted. The station provides space and equipment for experimental aquatic ecology, laboratory analysis, biological sampling as well as field investigations of coastal areas and lakes.

Kökar
59°57'N 20°54'E (northern approach)
www.visitsaaristo.net

Kökar comprises Karlby, Finnö and Helsö villages, and is both Åland and Finland's most southerly community.

Kökar, Sandvik
59°56'·3N 20°53'E
Chart C741, 27, 28
SH2 39 **FMA** 1140

This is one of the most interesting of the Åland villages. Sandvik is the best of the three yacht harbours for visitors – an excellent natural harbour on the north coast of Karlbylandet, affording secure shelter from all winds. The approaches are well marked by transits as well as by buoys. The guest harbour is situated on the south side of Hamnösund, the deep bay to the southeast of Hamnö. Berth bows-to from stern buoys; 50 spaces in 2–3m. These are too close to the pontoons for any yacht much over 40–45', but there is also good anchoring in the middle of the bay. The shop at the end of the marina stocks food essentials and also bakes delicious cinnamon buns and fresh bread. Bikes for hire to explore Kökar where any place is within a 10 km distance. Take a walk and visit the church of St. Anne, distance 2km. A 17th-century church built on the site of an old Franciscan monastery, founded in Hamnö in the 15th century and a Bronze Age settlement. Possible crew change via ferry.

Kökar, Karlby
59°55'·6N 20°54'·7E
Chart C741, 27, 28
SH2 37 **FMA** 1145

This is the principal village in the Kökar group of islands. It is all fairly shallow and yachts with more than 2m draught should take great care. The approach is from the southern tip of Kökar. The entrance to the very narrow and rocky passage is from the west side of Karlbylandet, between Klobbkläppen (on which there is a cairn) and Inre Jusskär (see charts C743 and C741.2). It is easily identifiable by a disused pilot station on the island of Aspskär, to the east of Inre Jusskär. Pass between Bässkär (which has a cairn on top) to port and Utterskär (which also has a cairn at its tip) to starboard. Follow three pairs of white transits bearing roughly southeast, east and northeast. When close to the third pair (on Amborsö) turn north-northwest and pass through a narrow gap between the two islands of Stenholm and Halsholm; there is a cairn on Halsholm and another white transit. The depth in this gap is about 2·5m. When past the narrows, turn to port and follow the buoyed channel to the marina at the head of the inlet (see plan SH2 37). Berth bows to the quay from posts, stern anchors or alongside (2–2·5m). All usual marina services, including fuel. Hotel and restaurant overlooking the harbour.

Kökar, Helsö
59°57'N 20°55'·4E
Chart C741, 27, 28
SH2 36 **FMA** 1135

Northeast of the island of Kökar. A small marina (50 spaces) with saunas and showers, fuel jetty and an excellent restaurant with a lovely 360° view. Electricity with long lead. Small but well-stocked shop and card phone 1km away. The marina gets very crowded in the season but if it is full drop a stern anchor and run to the end of the pontoon (3m). Bikes for hire and 6 km to Karlby.

Utö
59°46'·9N 21°22'·2E (end of the pier)
Charts C/D714, D713, 27
SH2 63 **SH1** 127 **FMA** 797, 798
www.visitsaaristo.net
www.parainen.fi

Utö is a pilot station and military area affording good shelter in any weather conditions. The harbour is well protected by the surrounding islands and is almost landlocked. The main approach from the northwest is intricate but every well marked as it is the main approach channel from the Gulf of Finland to the Archipelago Sea. Pass between Finnskär and Ormskär. Alternatively, if coming from the open sea, there is a shortcut through a very narrow entrance between Finnskär and Utö (3m). Follow the buoyed approach channel closely as the harbour tends to shoal very quickly towards the east. Anchor in the bay or moor bows-to from a stern anchor to the eastern side of the main pontoon (the western side is reserved for local fishing boats, a ferry and the pilot boat).

Utö itself is isolated and barren but has rather interesting scenery with bare rocks and no trees. The landscape is littered with bunkers and all sorts of remnants of its Russian history. The modern military installations are out of bounds. The lighthouse on

Utö M. Strobel

4B. THE ARCHIPELAGO SEA

Utö (Utön Lisäloisto, F.W.) is the oldest in Finland; the original tower was built in 1753 and the current tower in 1814. It has a chapel on the second floor. Basic facilities on the island include two small shops and a café, but fuel is not available. Just a few hundred meters to the north there is a hotel (Havshotel), which provides water and electricity, showers, washing machine, sauna and a restaurant. Moor bows-to from stern buoys to the guest pontoon (4m).

Jurmo
59°49'·6N 21°34'·9E (southern breakwater)
Charts D715, 24
SH1 *48* **FMA** *802*
www.visitsaaristo.net
www.parainen.fi

Interesting deserted low-lying and exposed island geologically different from the others. Much of it is a bird sanctuary but there are walking trails and a small church of interest. The island is known for its stone circles and mazes, some of which may date back to the Bronze Age. Their original purpose is unknown.

Very attractive anchorage in 4m just west of the leading line. A well-marked approach into the marina. Moor bows-to from stern buoys in the small harbour (1·8–3·8m). Manoeuvring in strong southwesterly wind can be very tricky in the confined marina. Basic shopping facilities. No fuel.

Björkö
59°54'·5N 21° 40'·8E
Charts D715, 24
SH1 *13* **FMA** *806*
www.visitsaaristo.net

A beautiful bay on the southwestern side of the island. Enter between the southwest tip of Björkö and the high rocky skerry of Yngerskär (1.8m). The passage is marked by a west-cardinal buoy. Anchor in 5–7m at the head of the bay; the water elsewhere is deep. Alternatively moor bows to the shore from a stern anchor. A highly recommended anchorage for swimming in the beautiful pool and for the view over the surrounding islands. Very popular with the Finns, especially on weekends. No facilities but there is a pump-out station and a small ferry.

Nötö
59°57'·2N 21°45'·4E
Charts D 711, 716, 716.2, 24
FMA *794*
www.visitsaaristo.net
www.noto.fi

Nötö is located in the southern archipelago of Nagu, and it is one of the largest islands in the Archipelago National Park. In the centre of the village there is a windmill, and a few minutes away from the village harbour there is a chapel, inaugurated in 1757. During the summer season, there is a cafeteria in the old primary school building, where e.g. various art exhibitions are held. Shop sells groceries, fuel, drinking water and gas. Shower, sauna and laundry facilities can be reserved. Well marked approach to the harbour. Pontoon with buoys, 10 places. Anchorage in the smal bay just west of the pontoon, Finnvik.

Nötö M. Strobel

Borstö
59°51'·6N 21°58'·1E
Charts D711, 24
SH1 *16* **FMA** *782*
www.visitsaaristo.net

The sheltered harbour is on the southeast side of the island surrounded by skerries. Approach from a position about mile northeast of the island and identify the transit boards on the islet of Bredskär (southeast of Borstö). Turn to starboard once you have passed Basskär and follow the next transit (west-southwest) on the southern tip of Borstö. Anchor off the jetty or moor bows-to from stern buoys to the guest pontoon (2·5–3m). A delightful fishing hamlet with a special variety of flat fish which is smoked in a shed by the harbour. Telephone, post box by ferry jetty, toilets. Walk to the Borstö Gumma (Borstö Lady), an old ship's figurehead on the hill.

Vänö
59°52'·1N 22°11'·5E
Charts D701, 701.1, 24
SH1 *132* **FMA** *608*
www.visitsaaristo.net

An interesting island, very beautiful in fine weather. The easiest approach is from the northeast, between Inre Bosskär and Hemören following the transit marks on Ölonskär and then to a second set of transit marks on Skinnarskär. The final approach is from the southeast. It is also possible to approach from the northwest, but this is not recommended unless familiar with the skerries. Moor bows-to from stern buoys (2·7–3·6m) to the pontoon (30–40 spaces). There is a small grocery shop and an indoor/outdoor cafe on the waterfront. An old chapel is a pleasant 1·5km walk. Facilities include water, electricity, sauna, pump-out station, a shop, café and a fishmonger.

4C. GULF OF FINLAND - WESTERN PART

All routes

Kasnäs
59°55'·3N 22°24'·6E
Chart B 645, 647, D701, 22
FMA 591
www.visitsaaristo.net
www.kasnas.com

Kasnäs is located at a crossroad. The routes north and northwest, west and east meet at Kasnäs. A large marina well protected from all winds with place for 100 boats.

The harbour offers everything that a boater needs and wishes. A sheltered guest harbour, a spa with its versatile services, sauna, a washhouse, a childcare room. Restaurant with good food, a local shop and a summer marketplace. Fuel around-the-clock, electricity, water and WiFi. The Nature Centre Blåmusslan and geological nature path are of interest to all age groups. An excellent place for crew changes. Bus connection to Turku and Helsinki.

4c. Gulf of Finland - western part

Routes between Hanko and Helsinki

There are two main routes along the southern coast of Finland from Hanko towards Helsinki. They converge in several places and, therefore, it is possible to 'mix and match' along the way. Up-to-date, large-scale Finnish charts are a necessity when cruising this area. East of Hanko the routes meander through a national park, the Ekenäs *Skärgård*s Nationalpark (Tammisaaren Saariston Kansallispuisto) which is home to elk, white-tailed deer and many bird species.

Between 23°20'E and 23°45'E the northern route passes north of Skärlandet, Torsö and Växär. This is a pretty, peaceful, easily followed route with some summer houses and many places to anchor. Fuel is available at several points. In rough weather it provides a welcome alternative to the more interesting, though exposed, southern route. The southern route passes south of Älgö and north of Busö, has some beautiful anchorages and is certainly the more popular of the two. Both converge at 59°55'N 23°45'·5E.

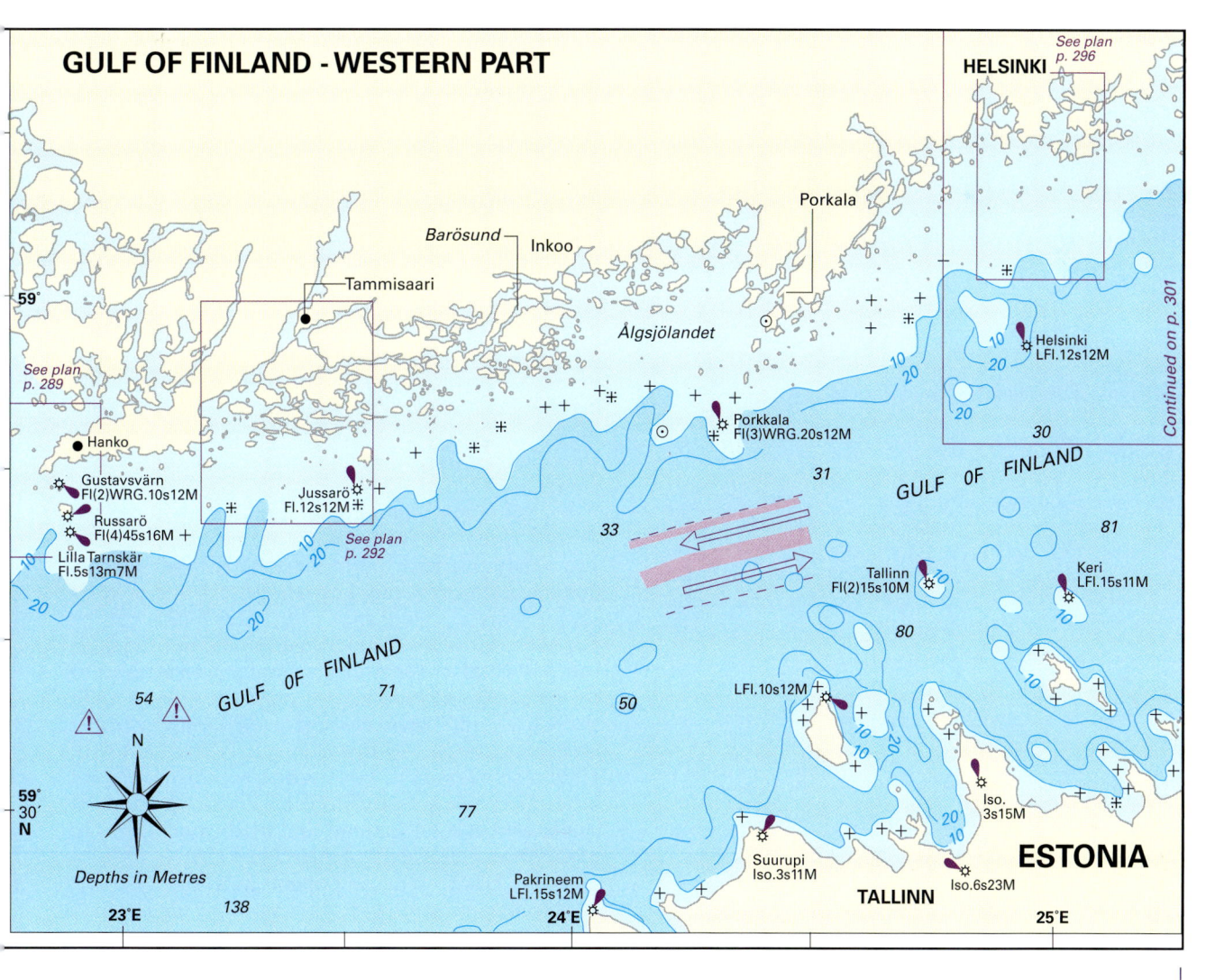

THE BALTIC SEA AND APPROACHES

4C. GULF OF FINLAND – WESTERN PART

Between 23°45'E and 24°24'E the northern route leads through Barösund, a relatively straight, well buoyed and lit sound between Orslandet and Barölandet.

The southern route winds and twists between many small islands, and is sometimes open to the Gulf of Finland in the south. It is very enjoyable from both the pilotage and scenic points of view. Both channels cross the Porkalafjärden (Porkkalanselkä) and converge just off Porkkala.

From here, the coastal route which is usually followed presents no difficulty. It can be exposed to swell in places.

Navigational charts – harbour guides

Planning chart

F952 (Gulf of Finland – West, 1:250 000)

Chart folios

B-Helsinki-Parainen/Helsingfors-Pargas (scale 1:50,000)

Harbour guides

Stora Hamnboken Vol.3-Suomenlahti/Finska Viken (**SH3** *xxx*)

Käyntisatamat/Besökshamnar guide to 511 harbours on the Finnish coast (the numbers of the harbours in the book correlate with the numbers on the charts - **FMA** *xxx*).

See also

Navigational charts – Finland and Åland, and harbour books and literature p.247 (general introduction to Finland).

A non-profit association, Föreningen Nylands Friluftsområden, Southern Finland Recreation Areas, has a number of places along the Gulf of Finland which are suited as yacht harbours. See link at:
www.uudenmaanvirkistysalueyhdistys.fi/se.php?k=13418

Hanko (Hangö)

59°48'36N 22°57'E

Distances

Turku 65M, Mariehamn 105M, Lehtma 50M, Haapsalu 55M, Tallinn 60M, Helsinki 70M

Charts and guides

UKHO 2241, 2614, 3832, 3437
Finnish B 636, 638, 21, 22 (**SH3** *33* **FMA** *516, 513*)
Merikarttasarja B
Stora Hamnboken Vol.3

Lights

Fläckgrund 59°52'·4N 22°50'·4E Q(2)WRG.3s6m9M 112°-W-115°-R-119°-G-170°-R-270°-G-307°-W-314°-R-020°-G-112° Red rectangle, yellow stripe
Bengtskär 59°43'·4N 22°30'·1E Fl(3)20s51m10M Round granite tower and building 46m Wind generator
Hanko No.1 59°44'·1N 23°02'·6E VQ(3)5s12m6M ♦ on black beacon, yellow band
Russarö 59°46'N 22°57'·1E Fl(4)45s34m16M 174°-vis-115° Red octagonal tower 21m
Djubkobben Ldg Lts 327° *Front* 59°48'·4N 22°58'·2E Fl.3s8m11M 324·5°-vis-329·5°
By day 8M 321·5°-vis- 332·5° Red rectangle, yellow stripe, on framework tower
Rear 59°49'·1N 22°57'·2E Iso.12s22m14M 324·5°-vis-329·5° *By day* 9M 321·5°-vis-332·5°
Red rectangle, yellow stripe, on framework tower
Hankoniemi Pohjoinen Ldg Lts 319° *Front* 59°49'·3N 22°55'·6E FFl.Y.1s16m7M 315°-vis-323°
Red rectangle, yellow stripe, on framework tower
Rear 59°49'·4N 22°55'·4E FlFl.Y.6s26m9M 315°-vis-323°
Red rectangle, yellow stripe, on framework tower

Harbour communications

Hanko Port Authority ① +358 19 2203 801
VHF Ch 12, 13, 14, 16, port@hanko.fi
www.visitsaaristo.net for Itämeren Portti, Smultrongrundet
www.hanko.fi
www.histdoc.net/history/hanko.html

The pleasant bilingual town of Hanko, population 9,000, was founded in 1874 and quickly developed as a spa town popular with the Russian ruling classes. A number of majestic 19th-century Finnish/Russian-style wooden villas are located to the northeast of the harbour amidst parks and tennis courts.

It has always been a useful destination, known to sailors since the 15th century and its continued prosperity has been mainly due to the fact that its commercial port – the West Harbour – is closed by ice for shorter periods than most other Finnish ports. For some 50 years around the beginning of the 20th century Hanko was a major point of embarkation for Finns leaving their native country for new lives in the USA and Canada – up to 370,000 by some estimates. In the Moscow Peace Treaty in 1940, Hanko was leased to the Soviet Union as a military base. This role was replaced by Porkkala after the armistice between Finland and the Soviet Union in 1944. It was returned to Finland in 1956.

Today Hanko remains popular as a holiday resort and tourist centre with two marinas in its East

HANKO

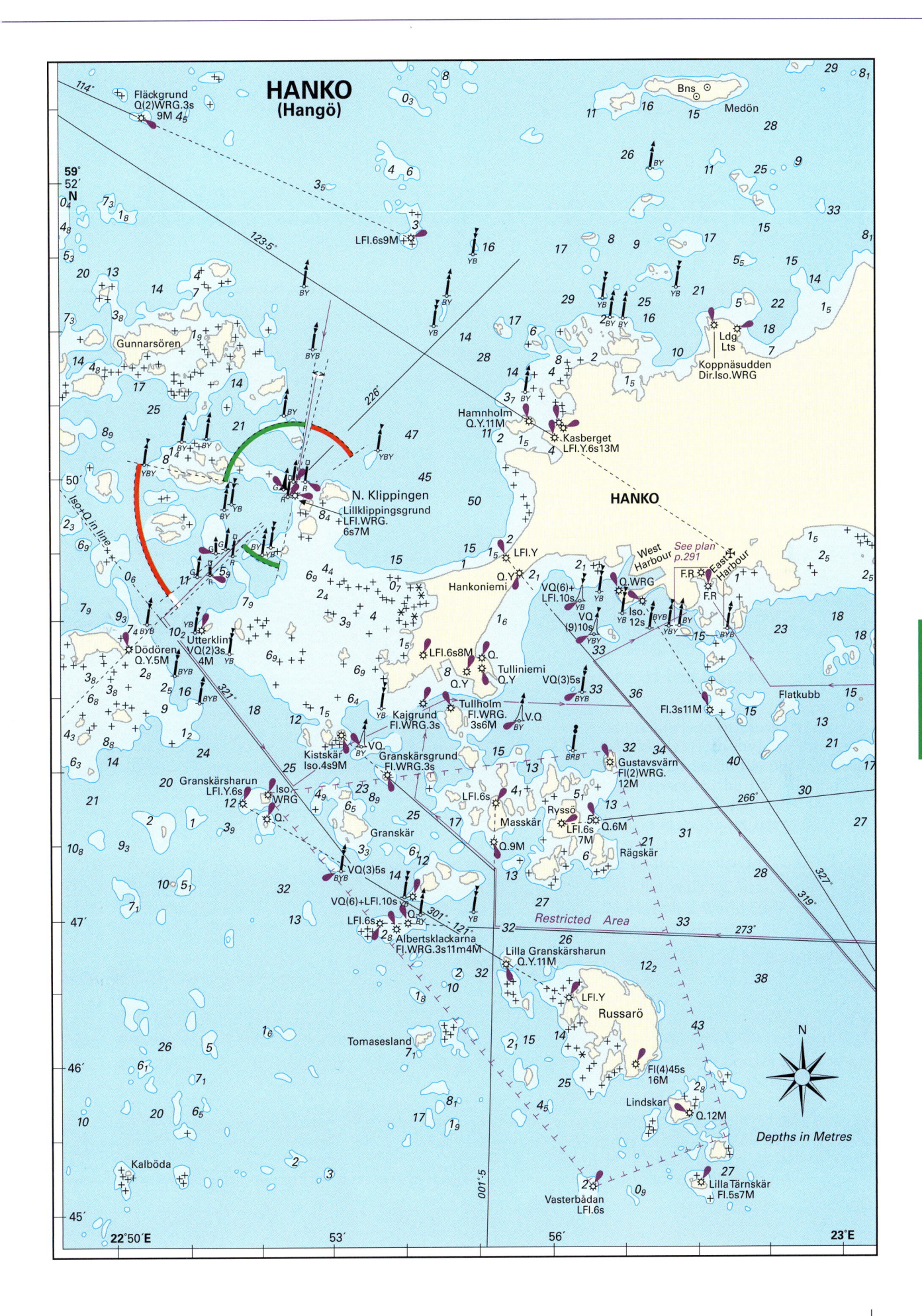

HANKO (Hangö)

THE BALTIC SEA AND APPROACHES   289

4. FINLAND

Depths in Metres

4C. GULF OF FINLAND – WESTERN PART

Hanko regatta *M. Strobel*

Harbour, both of which welcome visiting yachts. From the cruiser's point of view Hanko is a convenient port of call since it involves practically no detour from the main coastal fairway. Nowadays the Hangon Regatta is one of the major summer fixtures in the national and international sailing calendar, however, as with all these social events, it also attracts crowds of young people who come to party and drink.

Facilities for children are particularly good with playgrounds, beaches and plenty of open areas of rocks and short springy grass. Some visitors have likened the smooth, pinkish rocks to parts of northern Brittany.

Both Finnish and Swedish are spoken on a ratio of around 53:46 percent (the odd few per cent presumably speaking both with equal fluency).

Approach and entrance

The waters surrounding Hanko contain many hazards. However, the area is well marked with transits, buoys and beacons. Using a large-scale chart, navigation in daylight is a great deal easier than appears at first sight. Entry by night should not be attempted unless familiar with the area.

From the northwest, coming from the Archipelago Sea (see routes 2, 3 and 4, plan p.274-275), the route leading to Hanko either follows an open yet rocky channel (2·5m) through the national park between Finnharugrundet (59°53·7'N 22°42·8'E) and south of Uddskatan (59°48·5'N 22°53·4'E). This should not to be attempted in rough weather or poor visibility. Alternatively, pass close south of Fläckgrund lighthouse (59°52'·4N 22°50'·2E, Q(2)WRG.3s) and follow a somewhat circuitous path through a

Hanko, with Itämaren Portti marina in centre *Nigel Wollen*

290   THE BALTIC SEA AND APPROACHES

HANKO

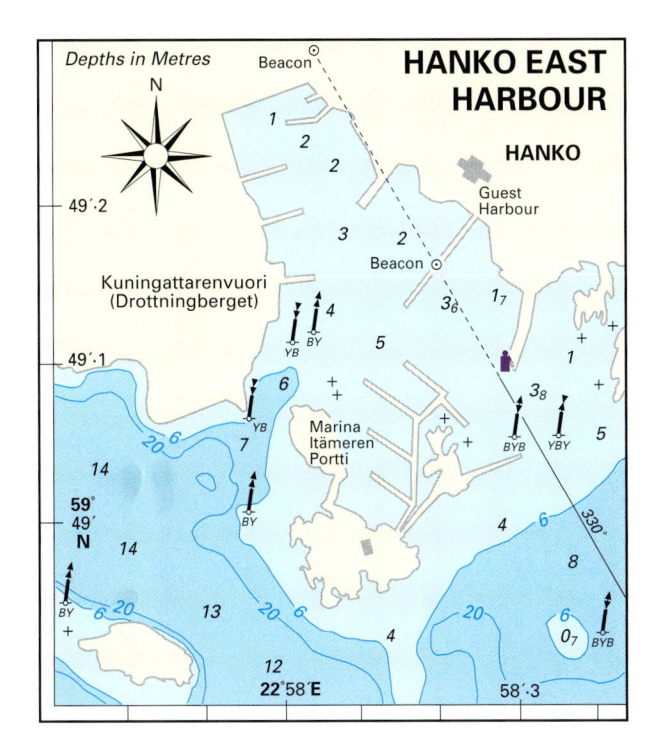

number of well-marked deep commercial channels around the western end of the Hanko peninsula. Approach the harbour passing north of Högskär (see chart plan 637.1). Continue in a northeasterly direction to the harbour entrance (see chart plan 637.1A).

From the southeast and the open sea, approach from Hanko No. 1 E-card buoy (59°44'·1N 23°02'·4E). The channel is wide and all hazards are well marked.

In the vicinity of 59°48'·7N 22°56'·4E, head east-northeast towards the marina. Enter the harbour from the southwest, immediately south of the Kuningattarenvuori (Drottningberget) peninsula. Although very narrow, the entrance is well marked by cardinal marks. Incoming vessels may be met by a reception boat. The channel has been dredged and changed. A chart printed after 2005 is needed.

From the east, the beautiful inshore passage between Helsinki and Hanko (see page 287) passes close north of the islands of Mulan and Andalskär (59°48'·5N 23°00'·8E), and leads directly to the well-marked southeastern entrance (course 330°T). Follow the leading marks into the marina.

Formalities

Hanko is a port of entry (See page 248 for details of formalities). The Finnish Customs Board has closed down the customer service desk in Hanko. Customers will only be served electronically from 2016 onwards.

Anchorage

Although there are few restrictions on anchoring, the depth of the water and the nature of the bottom make it impractical to anchor off in the vicinity of the town.

Berthing

Although there are other possibilities around the Hanko peninsula, visiting yachts without local knowledge are recommended to use the East Harbour where there are two good-sized marinas, both of which have good facilities and excellent shelter. Hanko is a very suitable place to leave a yacht whilst returning home or changing crew.

Hanko, Itäsatama/Hangö, Östra hamnen (59°49'·1N 22°58'·1E), open to the southwest, is located on the east side of the harbour basin and has some 180 visitors berths in depths of up to 3m. Mooring is bows-to from stern buoys, finger pontoons or alongside. However, the depth shoals quickly towards the shore (1·5m or less). If not met by a reception boat on arrival, take any suitable vacant berth and visit the marina office (open 0800–2400 in high season) as soon as possible.

Hanko, Itämeren Portti (Gateway to the Baltic), Smultrongrundet (59°49'·1N 22°58'E) just opposite, welcomes visiting yachts. It is built astride several small islands in the southwestern part of the harbour and has a further 150 berths, most equipped with finger pontoons. Depths range from 2m–3·5m or more. Berthing fees are in the upper band.

A regular ferry (free to berth-holders) runs between the marina and the shore.

Services for yachts

Both marinas have water and electricity on the pontoons with toilets, showers, saunas, laundry facilities and restaurants ashore.

There is a fuelling point at the end of the eastern mole which forms the starboard side of the southeast entrance where holding tanks can be emptied, and bottled gas (Finnish and Swedish cylinders only) and a few charts are available. It may be worth refuelling on arrival if there is no queue, as there can be a long wait on summer mornings. There is a Volvo Penta service centre nearby.

There is no boatyard at the East Harbour itself, but there are several in the wider Hanko area including Granströms Båtvarv, Galeasgatan 1A, 10900 Hanko, on the west coast of the peninsula.
ⓘ +358 19 248 6419

Ranmarina Oy, Ranmarinantie 120 , 25500 Perniö, Finland is located at 60°07'·7N 23°01'·6E.
ⓘ +358 50 328 7327

Sail repairs can be carried out by Stig Sandberg, on Kapteeninkatu, about 2km northeast of the harbour.
ⓘ +358 19 248 6292

Finnish charts (together with some English paperbacks) are stocked by Tias Bok at Vuorikatu 10 Berggatan, some 600m north of the harbour.
ⓘ +358 19 248 6060

A daily weather forecast in Finnish and Swedish is posted outside the harbour office.

4C. GULF OF FINLAND – WESTERN PART

General facilities
General provisions may be bought from a small mobile shop at the Itäsatamat (open 0800–2100 weekdays, 0900–1900 weekends) or from the wide variety of shops and supermarkets in the town centre, approximately 1km away, where there is also an outdoor market. In addition the town centre has the usual banks, post office, tourist office, hotels and restaurants. Shopping trolleys can be borrowed from the guest harbour office against a deposit and bicycles can be hired.

Communications and travel
Letters for visiting yachts can be sent c/o Itäsatama/Satamatoimisto, 10900 Hanko, Finland.

There are good rail connections in Hanko, and international air travel is possible via Helsinki or Turku. Car ferries run to Rostock in Germany. For more local exploration, bicycles and mopeds can be hired from several places around the harbour, including the fuel pontoon.

Tammisaari (Ekenäs)

59°58'·6N 23°25'·6E

Charts B634, 21
SH3 122 **FMA** 453

Communications
www.visitsaaristo.net   www.visitraseborg.com

Tammisaari, population 15,000, is a delightful, leafy town with many traditional wooden houses and a small guest harbour able to take around 120 yachts. There is a particularly appealing beach just south of the marina, backed by a children's playground, making Tammisaari an excellent port of call for those with young aboard.

Although the channel leading to the town is 12M from the Gulf of Finland, the approach is deep, well marked and presents no difficulty. On reaching the guest harbour, near the road bridge (H3·1m), it is impossible to miss the ornate building which houses the Knipan restaurant – built on stilts in the harbour at a time when only one licensed premises was permitted 'on the soil of the town'.

Visitors' berths are on the east side of the main jetty (to which the restaurant is attached). The pontoons either side of the fuel berth (1·6m) are private, though if the owner is away a green sign may be left at the berth to show it is free. Depths shoal quickly towards the land to 1·5m. There are 100 spaces bows-to from stern buoys, piles or you can anchor in the marina. The marina office occupies a small building near the fuel berth which doubles as a café.

Berths on the main quay have access to water and electricity (though some berths require long hoses and leads), and there are toilets, showers, sauna and laundry facilities ashore. A weather forecast (in Finnish and Swedish) is posted at the marina office and is updated daily. There is a small chandlery, Marinboden, on Norra Strandgatan 2, by the bridge.

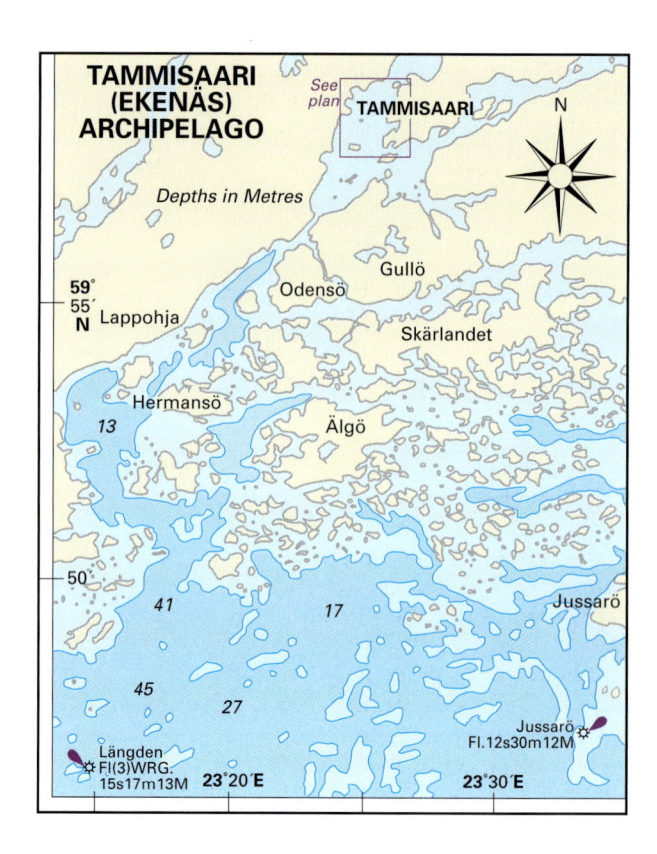

Directly across the bay, and clearly visible from the marina, is a large boatyard, Eke-Marin Oy (open 0830–1700 weekdays, Sat 1000–1700), which also stocks a wide range of chandlery. Although it mostly deals with motorboats, the yard can handle yachts of up to 20 tonnes and 13·5m LOA and undertake repairs in all materials. There are engineers and electricians on site. There is extensive undercover storage and this would be a definite possibility for over-wintering if booked well in advance. ☎ +358 19 241 2670, telakka@eke-marin.fi

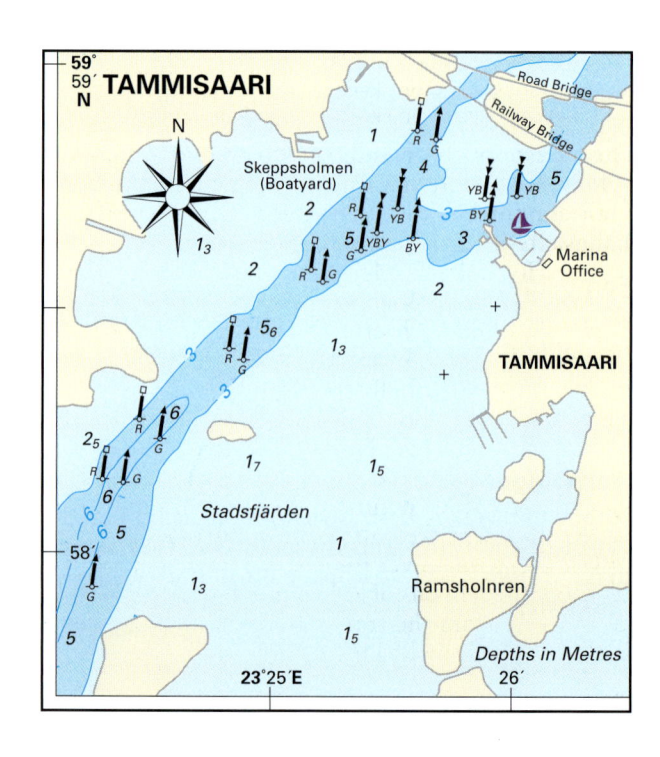

292   THE BALTIC SEA AND APPROACHES

There is good shopping of all kinds in Tammisaari, with a market on Wednesday and Saturday mornings. Bicycles can be hired from the marina office, and the town is linked to Helsinki and elsewhere by rail.

Ekenäs Archipelago

www.nationalparks.fi/en/ekenasarchipelagonp
www.nationalparks.fi/en/ekenasnaturecentre

Heading south from Tammisaari, the Ekenäs archipelago stretches from the inner archipelago to the open sea. It forms part of the Ekenäs Archipelago National Park. Almost 90 per cent of the park consists of watery areas and so the park conserves nature both above as well as under water.

During the summer, the Ekenäs archipelago is popular with sailors and motor boaters, as well as canoeists. The islands Fladalandet, Modermagan, Älgö and Jussarö are the most popular destinations for hikers.

The most significant attraction of the national park is its diverse natural habitats. The big islands of the inner archipelago conceal wilderness lakes, lush forests and beaches backed by cliffs. Elk and white-tailed deer can be seen on the islands. As for the outer archipelago, thousands of sea birds such as scaup, gulls and eider duck nest on the islets. In the southern parts of the park you can even see grey and ringed seals.

In the Ekenäs Archipelago National Park, visiting yachts can stay overnight in Modermagan, Fladalandet, Rödjan in Älgö, and Jussarö provided visitors follow the 'everyman's rights'.
www.nationalparks.fi/en/hikinginfinland

Älgö, Rödjan

59°51'·8N 23°23'·4E (Älgö, Rödjan) (southwestern entrance)
Charts B635, 21
SH3 *103* FMA *483* (Älgö, Rödjan 486k Norrklobbarna)
www.visitsaaristo.net
www.nationalparks.fi/en/ekenasarchipelagonp
www.nationalparks.fi/en/ekenasnaturecentre

The safest approach is from the channel that cuts across the southern Ekenäs archipelago south of Älgö. Approach from the southeast. Pass between Långskärsklobben and Modermagan (see B635.3), leaving Horsholmen, Mejholmen and all the rocks to starboard, and Fanklobben to port. Rödjan lies on Älgö to starboard. There are a few mooring spaces (bows to the shore from stern anchor) in 1–2m, or anchor in the pool. Rödjan's former fisherman's farm and cottage on Älgö, the largest island in Ekenäs Archipelago National Park, houses an exhibition depicting the life and history of Rödjan. A two-kilometer-long nature trail starts from the farm, leading to Storträsket lake and an observation tower with a great view over the entire National Park. In addition, the remains of a dugout from World War II can be seen from the trail. The farm manager sells self-caught and smoked fish.

Älgö, Norrklobbarna

59° 51'·7N 23° 22'·9E
Charts B635, 635.3, 21

Anchorage

When you reach the southwestern tip of Skedö (Västerudden) from the southwest, look out for leading marks on Norrklobbarna. These will lead you towards a very narrow passage between Norrklobbarna and Skedö. Once inside the pool, turn to port. Take care to avoid the rock at the northwestern tip of the islet to starboard. Anchor anywhere in the pool (2–10m). This is a very beautiful spot with a spectacular entrance. If it's crowded, there is an alternative secluded anchorage in Skedöfladan, a kilometer-long lagoon approached from the east, south of Fanklobben, opposite Horsholmen. The tall stands of birch and conifer give protection from all quarters. Anchor in 12m (or less, depending on the wind direction). Note that the soundings in Fanklobben are approximate and are highlighted in red.

Groplandet, Gropen

59° 51'·5N 23° 25'·8E
Chart B635, 20, 21
FMA *480*
www.visitsaaristo.net

Anchorage

Approach between Långskärsklobben and Modermagan (see B635.3), leaving Horsholmen to port. Sail into the pool to starboard, leaving the private N-cardinal buoy/marker to starboard. The Gropen pool provides excellent anchorage (5–9m) in all winds. It is possible to moor to the shore in the south west corner of the Gropen pool. On the north shore is a Merikarhut/Sea Bears private harbour (for members only).

Jussarö

59°49'·8N 23°34'·3E
Charts B633, B635, 20, 21
SH3 *39* FMA *445*
www.visitsaaristo.net
www.visitraseborg.com
www.nationalparks.fi/en/ekenasarchipelagonp

This small harbour lies to the north of the island between Lilla Jussarö and Jussarö. There are transits to guide you into the harbour. The single pontoon can accommodate up to 20 boats in 2·5–5·5m, bows-to from stern buoys. It is open to the northwest.

The island, in the Ekenäs Archipelago National Park, lies right at the edge of the open sea. It has been well-known to seafarers for more than 700 years. Jussarö's history is one of mining, fishing, seafaring and the defence of the Gulf of Finland. The island was under the control of the Finnish Defence Forces until 2005. Today it is open to the public.

4C. GULF OF FINLAND – WESTERN PART

There is a café (Café Ön) next to the guest marina. There is also a barbecue area and a new sauna. For swimming, head out to the Iron Beach that lies amongst red rocks. You can learn about the fascinating history of the island on guided walks.

From Lotssuberget tower, where pilots once kept a lookout for ships, and the old disused lighthouse towards the southeast end of the island, there are spectacular views of the open sea.

Limited facilities include water, electricity, sauna and a floating pump-out station.

Långön, Tammisaari

59°56'·4N 23°43'·7E
Charts B633, 20
SH3 *71*
www.visitsaaristo.net (Sandnäsudd)

Anchorage

This useful anchorage is 1·8M north of Fjärdskär lighthouse on the narrow northern route between Hanko and Helsinki. It lies opposite the small harbour of Sandnäsudd (SH3 *99*, FMA *434*), where there is a small shop and fuel. Anchor very close to the southwestern shore of the island of Långön in 2·5m or around the corner on the southeastern tip in 1·5–2·5m. Note the rock indicated on the sketch 431 (see web link above). The anchorage is open to the south.

Flakholmen

59°55'·76 N 23°46'·8E
Charts B633, 20
SH3 *22*

Anchorage

On the northern route leading towards Barösund there is a good small natural harbour at Flakholm. Anchor in the bay on the eastern side or moor to the shore. An alternative is to anchor north of Flakholm, a perfect landlocked pool secure from all winds. Anchor anywhere in the middle of the lagoon. Along the north shore there are many private summer houses.

Barösund

59°58'·6N 23°52'·8E (Orslandet)
Charts B632, 20
SH3 *4* **FMA** *422, 425*
www.visitsaaristo.net Barölandet / Orslandet
www.barosund.fi

The Finns are justly proud of Barösund, with its narrow and high rocky sides. It boasts a small shop, one of the few between Hanko and Helsinki not to involve a considerable detour, together with many summer homes and hence a lot of small motorboat traffic.

There is a good, strong jetty on the south side of the route to tie up to, a small supermarket with most essentials, fuel, post office and card phone in Barösund, Orslandet.

Barösund, Barölandet, on the opposite (north) side, is a service harbour with a fuel pump and not much else. There are limited facilities and the pontoon is exposed to the wash from the intense summer traffic of motorboats, the wind and the current in the sound. Alternatively, anchor north or northwest of Sparrholm (0·6M) towards the northeast end of the sound. Mörholmen island is private.

Älgsjö, Elisaari

59°58'·7N 23° 54'·6E
Charts B632, 20
SH3 *133* **FMA** *419*
www.visitsaaristo.net

An outstanding City of Helsinki Island Park marina, only 40km west of the capital. The entrance is at the northeastern corner of Mörholmen through a 20' wide channel running south between Mörholmen and Bråtaholmen. Its depth is 2·2–3m. The charted depth of 1m is incorrect, as are soundings further along the sound which has a minimum depth of 2·3m between Älgsjölandet and Orslandet. Moor to the solid wooden staging, bows-to from stern buoys, anchor or lie alongside (130 spaces). It gets very crowded on Midsummer's Night. There is a beautiful nature trail, campground, a small kiosk and two classic wood-fired saunas. Facilities include a restaurant, electricity, water and a pump-out station.

Vormö

60°00'·4N 24°11'·5E (Hamnholmen)
Charts B630, 19
SH3 *131* **FMA** *408s* Stickellandet

Anchorage

Between Barösund and Porkkala, the coast becomes exposed with no good sheltered harbours or anchorages.

Anchor off the village on Vormö at the southwestern end of the island in 4m between the southeastern side of Hamnholmen and Vormö, or secure to a tree from stern anchor (good holding). The easiest way in is from the northwest, between Hamnholmen and Furuholmen. If entering from the north, hug the west coast of Vormö and beware of the submerged rocks in mid-channel just south of the northwest tip of Vormö (see plan B, SH3 *131*). It is open to the southwest. An attractive spot amidst many summer houses.

Vormö, Stickellandet is considered to be an emergency anchorage which can be used in bad weather, depending on the direction of the wind. It is protected from the southwest but open to the northwest and north. It lies directly on the northern coastal channel (60°01'N 24°14'E). Enter the anchorage from the north, close to the shore of the small islet to the northeast of Vormö, Stickellandet. Anchor in 2–3m, bows-to from stern anchor to the northern tip of the islet. It is located just inside the firing exercise danger area of Porkkala (see notes page 249 on restricted areas in the general introduction to Finland).

Porkkala, Dragesviken

59°59'N 24°25'·4E
Charts B629, 629.1, 19
SH3 *88* **FMA** *403*
www.visitsaaristo.net
www.porkkala.net

Porkkala is a peninsula in the Gulf of Finland situated just 20M west-southwest of Helsinki. It has always had great military strategic value. At the end of World War II the Soviet Union leased and established a naval base in Porkkala, thus replacing it with the one they occupied until the end of WWII in Hanko and returning it to Finland in 1956.

Porkkala is a border crossing point and coastguard station ☏ +358 295 42 6100. Passport control and customs are situated at the southern tip of the peninsula at Tullandet (see page 248 Formalities in the general introduction to Finland).

From the coastal route, the approach channel is very short and straightforward. Enter the very narrow sound through a well buoyed channel passing east of Högholmen (2·4m) or pass west and north of Högholmen (1·5m). There are several places to moor or anchor. Berth alongside the eastern jetty of the customs and coastguard station on Tullandet in 4m (in an emergency only or if clearing customs). In strong easterlies there is a good anchorage 300m to the east by Kyrkogårdsön island, shallow but sheltered and with good holding.

Porkkala, Dragesviken in the northeastern corner (59°59'N 24°25'·4E) is the guest marina. Follow the narrow sound between Tullandet and Kyrkogårdsön, actual depth in channel is 2·1m. If approaching from the southeast leave the coastal channel at 59°58'·2N 24°26'E, turn northwestwards, leaving S cardinal and W cardinal buoys to starboard before turning north to enter the well-marked entrance to the basin. Moor to the northern side of the first pontoon. The third pontoon is a fuel dock. Facilities include fuel, water, electricity, shop, restaurant, washing machine, sauna and pump-out station.

Fine anchorage can be found north of the marina at the head of the basin. Good holding.

This is a popular birdwatching area, particularly during the migration of Arctic geese and waterfowl. It is a useful place to leave for Tallinn which is only 34M away to the south.

Stora Brändö

60°02'·6N 24°35'·6E
Charts B629, 629.3, 19
SH3 *108*
www.visitsaaristo.net

The south shore of Stora Brändö together with the outlying islets form part of a bird sanctuary where landing is prohibited between 1 April and 31 July. It is best approached from the southwest by way of the main coastal channel. There is a transit for commercial shipping on the islets south of Stora Brändö. Leave the channel following the transit and approach the west shore of Stora Brändö. Fairway markers guide you in. There are several possibilities for anchoring or to secure a boat to the shore from a stern anchor. The western shore is open to the west and southwest. There are a few mooring buoys on the northeastern side of the island as well. However, it is strewn with rocks and care must be taken in approaching these and the pontoon ashore (1·8m).

4C. GULF OF FINLAND – WESTERN PART

Helsinki (Helsingfors)

60°08'7N 24°58'·1E

Distances
Hanko 70M, Tallinn 45M, Porvoo 35M, Loviisa 60M, Kotka 75M, Haapasaari Island 80M, Vyborg 130M, St Petersburg 175M

Charts and guides
UKHO 2218, 2248, 3818
Finnish A+B626, 18; (SH3 35 FMA 356, 336, 324, 325, 345, 289, 307, 339)
Merikarttasarja A: Viipuri - Helsinki/Viborg - Helsingfors
Merikarttasarja B: Helsinki - Parainen/Helsingbois - Pargas
Stora Hamnboken Vol.3

Lights
Helsinki 59°56'·9N 24°55'·7E LFl.12s25m12M Racon White round tower, upper part red, three galleries, aluminium lantern 25m. Helipad
Gråskärsbådan 60°02'·2N 24°53'·6E Fl.WRG.3s12m7M 153°-G-175°-W-180°-R-153° Red concrete column
Flathällgrundet 60°05'N 24°58'·1E VQ(3)5s12m4M Black diamond on black metal structure, yellow band, on piles (East cardinal)
Harmaja Ldg Lts 007° Front 60°06'·3N 24°58'·7E Oc.WRG.6s24m15M 004·5°-W-010·5°-R-168°-G-187°-W-193°-R-212°-W-250°-R-260°-W-312°-G-004·5° Racon Red round tower, white band, square base
Suomenlinna Church Rear, 60°08'·9N 24°59'·4E (2·6M from front) Fl(4)15s54m20M Racon Cupola on church tower
Särkkä 60°09'·1N 24°58'·2E Fl.WRG.2s2m6M 175°-G-186°-W-191°-R-280° White lantern, red band
Valkosaari (Luoto) Ldg Lts 356·5° Front 60°09'·6N 24°58'·2E Q.R.2m6M 286°-vis-018° White lantern, red band
Valkosaari Rear 240m from front, Iso.WRG.4s7m7M 135°-W-213°-G-137°-W-260°-R-271°-G-283°-W-293°-R-006° White lantern, red band

Principal harbours
www.visitsaaristo.net
Helsingfors Segelklubb (HSK), Lauttasaari
Blekholmen, NJK, www.njk.fi
Pohjoissatama/Helsingfors, Norra hamnen (Helsingin Moottorivenekerho (HMVK)
Katajanokka/Skatudden
Liuskasaari/Skifferholmen (Helsingfors Segelsällskap (HSS)
Suomenlinna/Sveaborg

Harbour communications
Helsinki Port Authority ☏ +358 9173 331
port.helsinki@hel.fi
www.portofhelsinki.fi
Helsinki Vessel Traffic Service
www.portofhelsinki.fi/ahips/vessel_traffic_service
Use relevant VHF channel according to sector (all vessels more than 24m in length must maintain a listening watch on the relevant VTS channel). From E to W:
  VTS Sector 1: VHF Ch 71
  VTS Sector 2: VHF Ch 9
Helsinki VTS, Master's Guide:
  www.liikennevirasto.fi/documents/21386/143357/HKI_MG_en.pdf
www.visithelsinki.fi

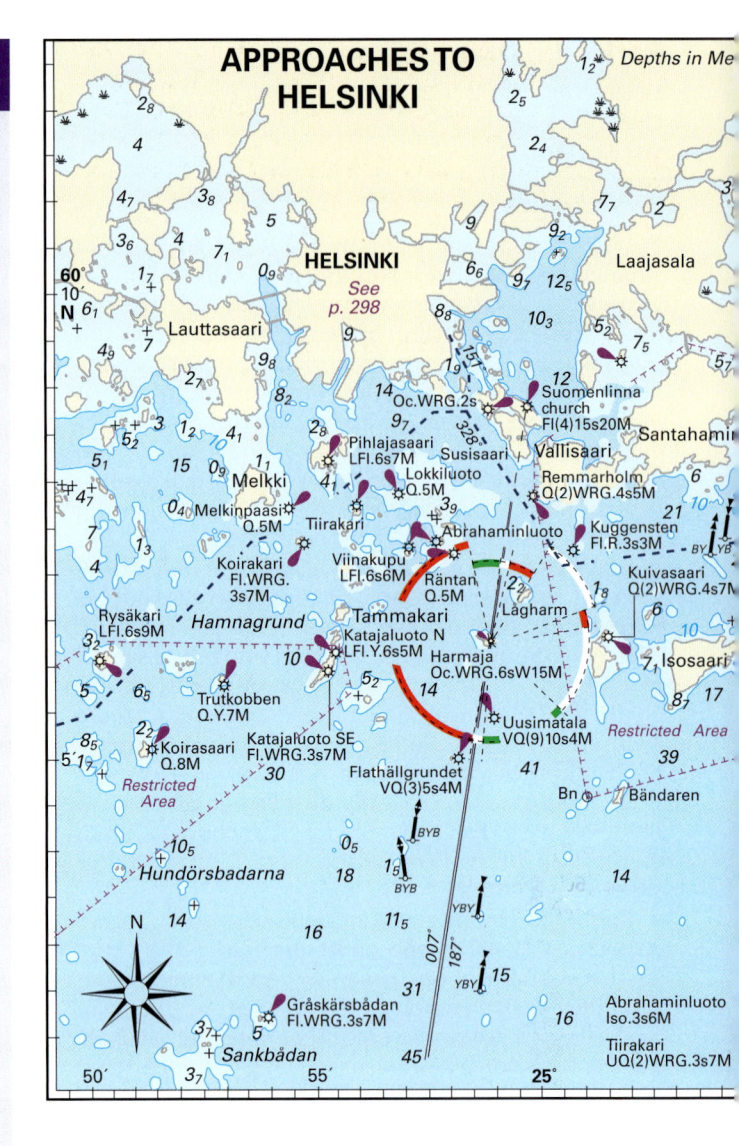

Helsinki, the capital of Finland, has a population of over 630,000 (urban population 1·2 million). It is Finland's major political, educational, financial, cultural and research centre as well as one of northern Europe's major cities.

It was founded in 1550 by the Swedish king Gustav Vasa and became the Finnish capital in 1812, taking over from Turku at a time of Russian domination. It is a prosperous and pleasant city with the relaxed and friendly atmosphere typical of most major Scandinavian capitals. Nearly everyone speaks fluent English and the standard of living is high.

The historic buildings, in particular both the Lutheran and Russian Orthodox (Uspenski) cathedrals and the university in the old part of the city, are important aesthetic and historic landmarks. The South Harbour (Eteläsatama/Södra Hamnen), the main harbour for passenger ships and yachts (Blekholmen (NJK), see website above), is conveniently close to the city centre.

The offshore fortress of Suomenlinna (Sveaborg) or 'fortress of Finland', built in the mid-18th century, lies just 1·5M to the southeast of the South Harbour.

It is a UNESCO World Heritage Site on five connected islands and is well worth a visit for its museum, galleries, heavily-built stone walls and beautiful buildings. It has a small guest harbour (see website above) and is the site of the Helsinki Frontier Guard station, where clearance is obtained. It can also be reached by ferry from Helsinki's South Harbour.

Approach and entrance
Helsinki is surrounded by water on three sides, and there are many possible approaches through the hundreds of nearby islands. However, although local yachtsmen appear to sail where they wish, the visitor is advised to use only the main routes indicated, at least until familiar with local hazards (of which there are many). Whichever approach is used, it is essential to be equipped with detailed charts.

Approach from the south
This is the main approach from the open sea and is heavily used by shipping, including cruise liners and fast ferries. A good watch must therefore be kept at all times. From Helsinki light (white round tower, upper part red, three galleries, aluminium lantern, 50°56'·95N 24°55'·6E, LFl.W.12s25m12M, Racon(T), helicopter platform), the channel runs slightly east of north with Harmaja lighthouse (60°06'·3N 24°58'·5E, Oc.WRG.6s24m14M, Racon(/)) in line with Suomenlinnan Kirkko (church) light (60°08'·87N 24°59'·2E, Fl(4)W.15s54m20M, Racon (M)). It passes close east of Harmaja light, but yachts should leave the main shipping channel before it continues northeast between the islands of Susisaari and Vallisaari.

Yachts are better advised to keep west of Susisaari island and to enter the South Harbour by the southern entrance, between the islands of Särkkä Långören and Länsi Mustasaari, the northwestern island that forms part of Suomenlinna.

Approach from the southwest
The inshore passage through the islands from the southwest passes between Rysäkari island (60°06'N 24°50'E) and Rysäkivi light (VQ(3)Y.3s), following three sets of transits and the well-buoyed channels in a northeasterly direction to converge with the southern approach west of Länsi Mustasaari. It is clearly marked, but it is easy to become confused by the plethora of beacons, lights and leading marks. It is advisable to consult chart B626.1 carefully. The tower of Suomenlinna church is a useful landmark throughout.

Approach from the east
The deep-water channel for vessels using the inshore route from the east passes south of the islands of Santahamina and Vallisaari, and joins the main channel from the south approximately one mile north of the Harmaja light. However, a slightly shorter but more interesting route, that carries (2·4m), passes north of Santahamina (see chart 626.2) through the swing bridge at Hevossalmi, operating at HR+00 and HR-30.

Formalities
See Formalities in Key information, page 248. If clearance is required there is a Frontier Guard station at the western end of Suomenlinna (Sveaborg) via the narrow entrance between Susisaari and Länsi Mustasaari.

Anchorage
Although there are few official restrictions on anchoring in the Helsinki area, in practice it is almost impossible to find a spot which does not involve landing on private property.

Berthing
There are at least 15 yacht harbours and clubs in the immediate vicinity of Helsinki, but the visitor will normally find it most convenient to use one of the marinas near the city centre. All the websites for these marinas (including contacts, services and information) are listed at www.visitsaaristo.net.

If heading for the Helsingfors Segelsällskap (HSS), Liuskasaari marina (FMA *345*), turn sharp to port north of Särkkä island. It lies further away from the city centre – though it is near a tram route – but its berths are undoubtedly quieter than those at the NJK.

Alternatively, continue to the Nylandska Jaktklubben (NJK) (FMA *336*) pontoons on Blekholmen (Valkosaari) island following the buoyed channel west of Luoto island into the South Harbour.

The NJK is the oldest yacht club in Finland and has an imposing and beautiful clubhouse on Blekholmen island, though the sailing activities of the club are now situated some distance from the city centre on the island of Koivusaari, Björkholmen (60°09'·7N 24°51'E). At Blekholmen there are some 25 visitors' berths in 3m depth. All moorings are bows-to from stern buoys. Berths marked 'P' are available for visitors. Berthing fees are in the mid cost band.

The surroundings are very scenic and visitors are made most welcome, but it is not particularly peaceful since large ferries pass and dock very close by. A two-minute ferry journey (every 20 minutes

NJK Clubhouse, Blekholmen, Helsinki *J. Langdon*

4C. GULF OF FINLAND – WESTERN PART

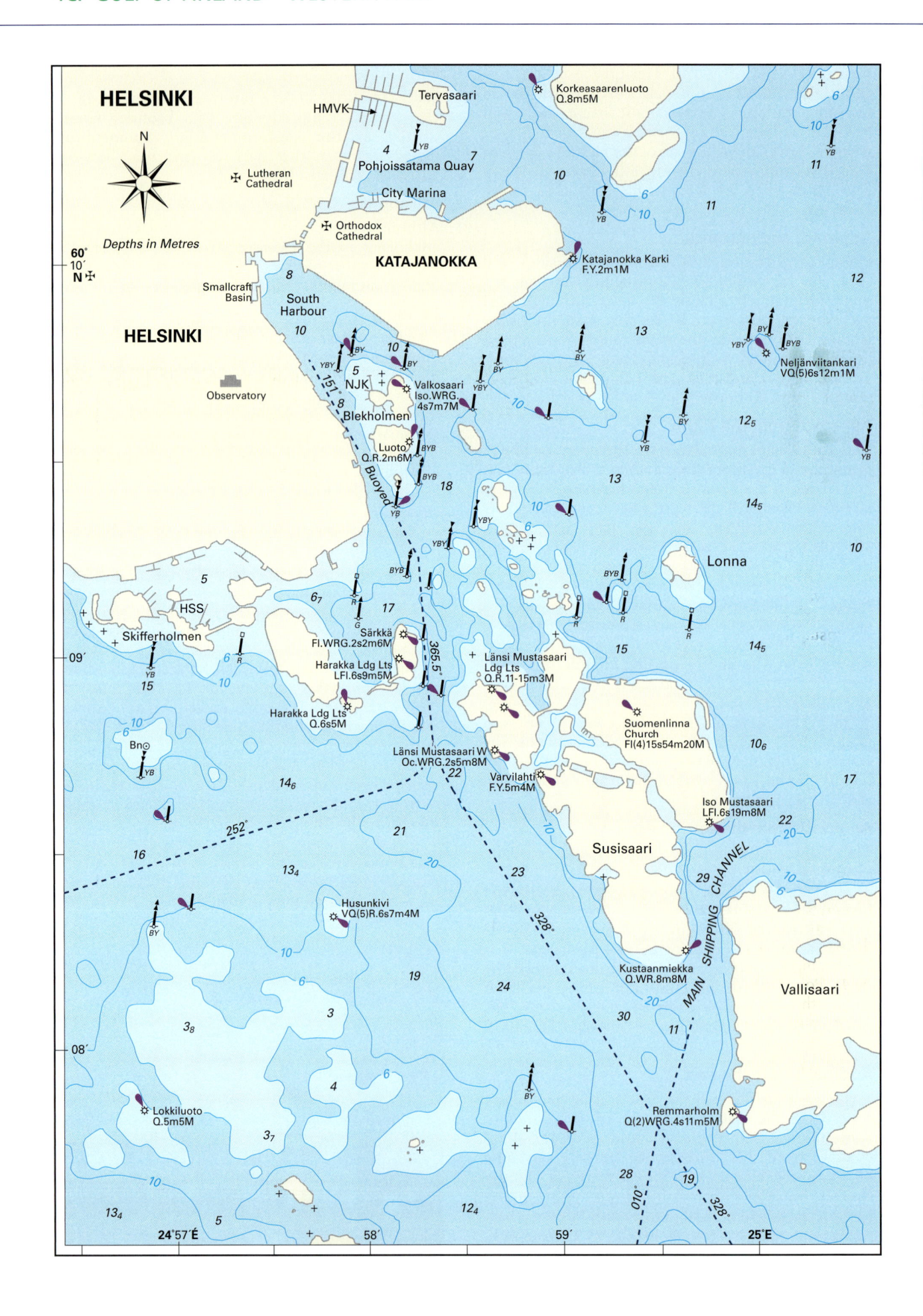

298 THE BALTIC SEA AND APPROACHES

Helsinki, from the South Harbour *M. Strobel*

from 0800 until late in the evening) connects Blekholmen with the shore, from where it is only a short walk into the city centre.

For any of the marinas north of the Katajanokka peninsula adjacent to the downtown area, Katajanokka or Pohjoisranta marinas, pass between Luoto and Ryssänsaari.

The city-run Katajanokka marina (FMA 325) on the north side of the Katajanokka peninsula (the site of the magnificent Orthodox cathedral) is the closest to the city of all Helsinki's marinas. It occupies the westernmost pontoon on the north side of the Katajanokka peninsula – the two to the east are private – and offers berthing for 120 yachts in depths of 4m or more, some alongside, some on finger pontoons and some with stern buoys. There is little wash to contend with, and security is good in the more expensive parts of the marina, but there is continuous noise from the nearby road. Berthing fees are in either the middle or upper bands depending on the berth.

Helsingin Moottorivenekerho (HMVK) (FMA 324), Pohjoisranta-Tervasaari just to the north on the south side of the causeway to Tervasaari island, north of Katajanokka, has around 400 berths, all of them between piles (some of which are rather narrow) in 2–4·5m. The visitors' pontoon is the one nearest to the shore; alongside mooring is mostly for bigger boats. There are a few boxes 15m by 5m and more boxes 13m by 4m.

Berths are available in July and the first half of August if permanent berth holders are away. The marina is peaceful and secure, if rather less picturesque than the two island marinas, and is convenient for the city. Berthing fees are in the lower band.

Larger, traditional yachts may find a welcome alongside the Pohjoissatama quay between the Katajanokka and HMVK marinas, but should contact the Port Authority before arrival. The marina on the north side of the Tervasaari causeway does not accept visitors. There is a small boat pool close to the covered market in the northwest corner of South Harbour where a yacht or dinghy might be left during a shopping trip (subject to the two-hour time limit).

Services for yachts

All four marinas have water and electricity at their berths with toilets and showers ashore and a station at which holding tanks can be pumped out. The Blekholmen (NJK), Liuskasaari (HSS) and Pohjoissatama (HMVK) marinas provide laundry facilities, while the NJK and HSS also have saunas on their islands, as well as first-class restaurants. Fuel is available at the HSS and HMVK, but not at the Katajanokka or NJK marinas. It might be possible to exchange propane gas cylinders at these clubs. Free WiFi is available at NJK Blekholmen marina.

Helsinki and its surrounding area has many boatyards able to carry out work of almost any description, in addition to winter lay-up. The advice of a club secretary or marina manager should be sought as to which to approach first.

For a very wide range of chandlery it is worth taking the bus to Lauttasaari island towards the west of the city, where three good-sized chandleries stand close together on Veneentekijäntie, near to the Helsingbors Segelklubb (HSK) (FMA 356).

The largest of these is Maritim Oy, which stocks an enormous range of paint, hardware, electronics, pilot books and charts. Nearby are the somewhat smaller chandleries, ProSailor and the Captain's Shop

☏ +358 10 2740 310
info@maritimshop.fi
www.maritim.fi (mainly in Finnish)

4D. GULF OF FINLAND – EASTERN PART

For worldwide charts visit John Nurminen Marine Ltd, which stocks charts for all the Baltic countries, including Russia, together with a wide selection of pilot books for Baltic waters, some of them in English. The staff are particularly helpful.
Veneentekijäntie 8
✆ +358 9 682 3180
marine@johnnurminen.com
www.johnnurminenmarine.com

Elvstrøm Sails, Veneentekijantie 5, also close by can carry out all kinds of sail repairs.
✆ + 358 404142545
rob@elvstromsails.com

Sailtex, also on Veneentekijäntie, mainly handles yacht upholstery work but will undertake some sail repairs.
✆ +358 9 682 2283

General facilities

Helsinki has excellent shops of all kinds, as expected in a capital city.

The open-air and covered markets overlooking South Harbour are excellent, mainly for their wide variety of fish, fresh vegetables and fruit. The small delicatessens in the covered market – the 'Vanha Kauppahalli' or 'Gamla Saluhallen' – to the west are particularly tempting but far from cheap.

There are many excellent supermarkets in the main shopping centre, a few minutes' walk from the harbour, and there are others beneath the main railway station. The large Akateeminen Kirjakauppa bookshop on Pohjoisesplanadi 39 stocks books, magazines and newspapers in many languages including English.

There is a tourist information office near the harbour, and many excellent (but expensive) restaurants in addition to those at the Nylandska Jaktklubben and the Helsingfors Segelsällskap.

Communications and travel

Mail for visiting yachts can be sent c/o the Nylandska Jaktklubben, Blekholmen, 00140 Helsingfors, Finland; and the Helsingfors Segelsällskap, Skifferholmen, 00130 Helsingfors, Finland.

Internet access is available at a number of places in the city including all public libraries – enquire at the marina office for the nearest.

There are good rail, air and coach services between Helsinki and all major European cities, plus regular ferries to Tallin and Stockholm, the latter via Mariehamn. There are regular ferry, as well as train services, from Helsinki to St Petersburg. (When travelling by ferry, no visa is required).

4d. Gulf of Finland – eastern part

Heading east from Helsinki, the choice of routes diminishes as you approach the Russian border. The skerries become less dense. The main northern route hugs the mainland and passes close to the bigger towns and harbours such as Porvoo/Borgå, Loviisa/Lovisa, Kotka, Hamina, ending in Virolahti on the border with Russia. The approach to these towns is still quite a long way inland from the main route. The southern route passes south of Emäsalo/Emsalö, Suur-Pellinki/Stor-Pellinge, Kejvsalö islands and comes closer and closer to the main route near Kotka, where the routes branch. If heading to St Petersburg, take the route southeast towards Haapasaari island, the border control point near the Russian border. The northern route continues eastwards and passes close to Santio island, the second border control point with Russia. If heading towards Vyborg/Viipuri and the Saimaa Canal and lakes, you have to clear customs and border formalities at Santio. See chapter 4e page 313.

Navigational charts – Harbour guides

Planning chart
F951 (Gulf of Finland – East, 1:250 000)

Chart folio
A-Viipuri-Helsinki/Viborg-Helsongfors (scale 1:50,000)
Stora Hamnboken Vol.3-Suomenlahti/Finska Viken (**SH3** *xxx*)
Käyntisatamat/Besökshamnar guide to 511 harbours on the Finnish coast (the numbers of the harbours in the book correlate with the numbers on the charts, **FMA** *xxx*).

See also
Navigational charts – Finland and Åland, and harbour books and literature page 247 (general introduction to Finland).

Havsudden, Emsalö

60°13'N 25°36'·9E
Charts A621, 622, 17
SH3 *34*

Anchorage

Situated at the southern end of the island of Emäsalo/Emsalö, just off the main commercial channel when approaching from the open sea and heading towards the oil refinery at Sköldvik and Porvoo, Havsudden is a small bay on the southwest coast of Emsalö.

A delightful anchorage in the southeast corner of the bay in 6m. Well sheltered except from north to northwest. Surrounded by trees and a few summer houses. There are two private pontoons on either side at Neste and Meriniemi and a few private moorings. Keep clear of these.

PORVOO

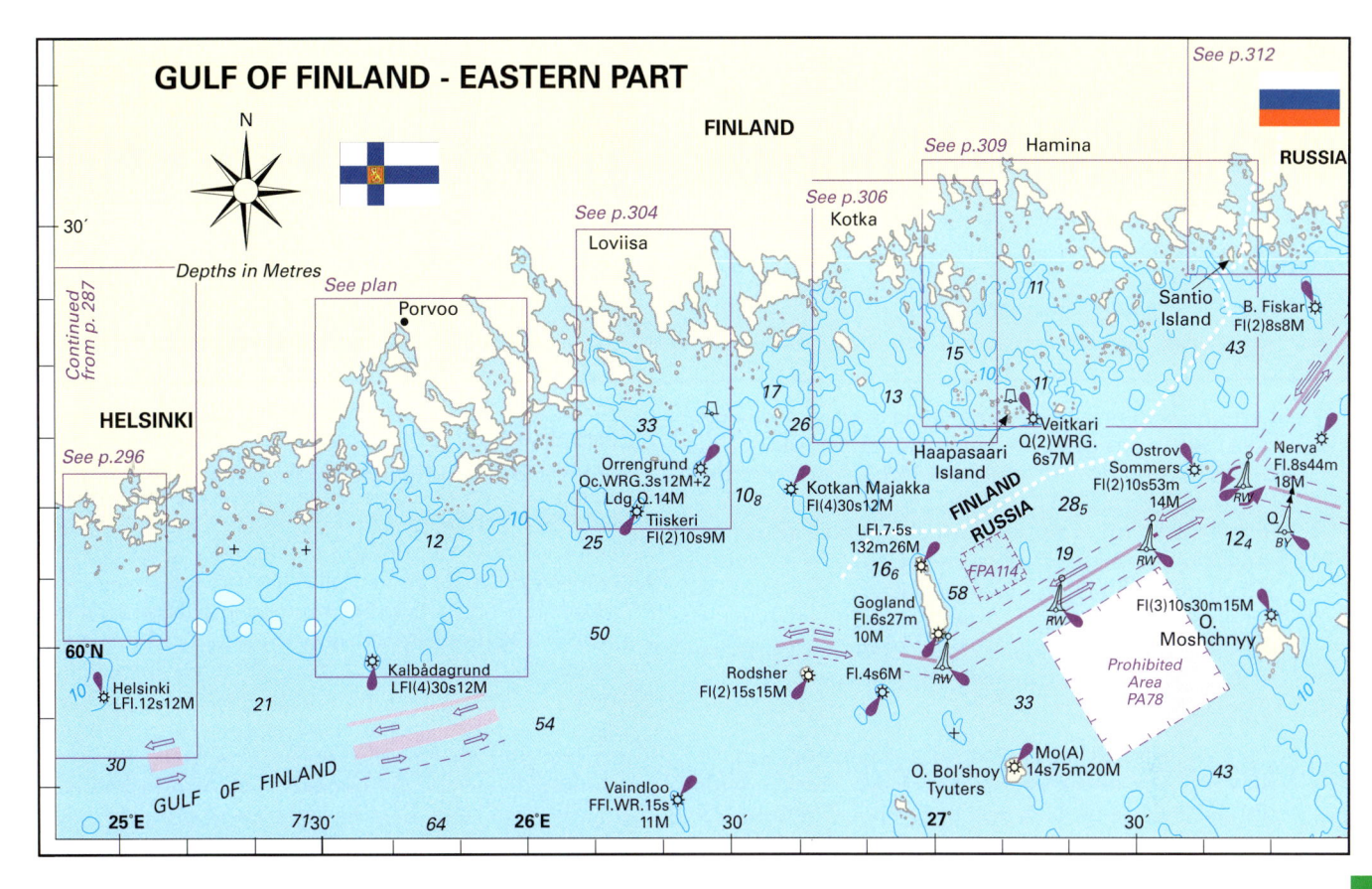

Porvoo (Borgå)

60°23'·3N 25°39'·9'E

Distances

Helsinki 65 km, Tallinn 105km, Loviisa 65km, Haapasaari Island 105km

Charts and guides

UKHO 2248, 3817
Finnish B622,17; (**SH3** *89* **FMA** *250*)
Merikarttasarja A: Viipuri - Helsinki/Viborg - Helsingfors
Stora Hamnboken Vol.3

Lights

Kalbådgrund 59°59'·1N 25°36'·1E LFl(4)30s27m12M 195°-vis-180° Racon Red concrete tower, white stripe 25m Helipad
Porvoon Majakka Ldg Lts 016° *Front* 60°05'·6N 25°36'E Fl.WRG.2s10m6M
004°-W-027°-R-105°-G-229°-W-237°-R-285°-G-004°
Racon Red tower, black band 10m
Rear **Larsskär** 60°08'·7N 25°37'·8E LFl.8s36m9M 014°-vis-018° Red rectangle, yellow stripe
Havsudden Ldg Lts 012° *Front* 310m from rear, Q.R.18m10M 007·5°-vis-015·5°
Red rectangle, yellow stripe
Varlaxudden Ldg Lts 340·5° *Front* 1570m from rear, Q.Y.15m12M 331°-vis-351°
Red rectangle, yellow stripe
Common rear 60°12'·9N 25°37'·1E Q.R.28m12M 001·5°-vis-021·5°+LFl.Y.6s33m12M 331°-vis-351°
Red rectangle, yellow stripe

Harbour communications

Porvoo Guest Harbour ☎ +358 19 584 727
www.visitsaaristo.net
www.porvoo.fi

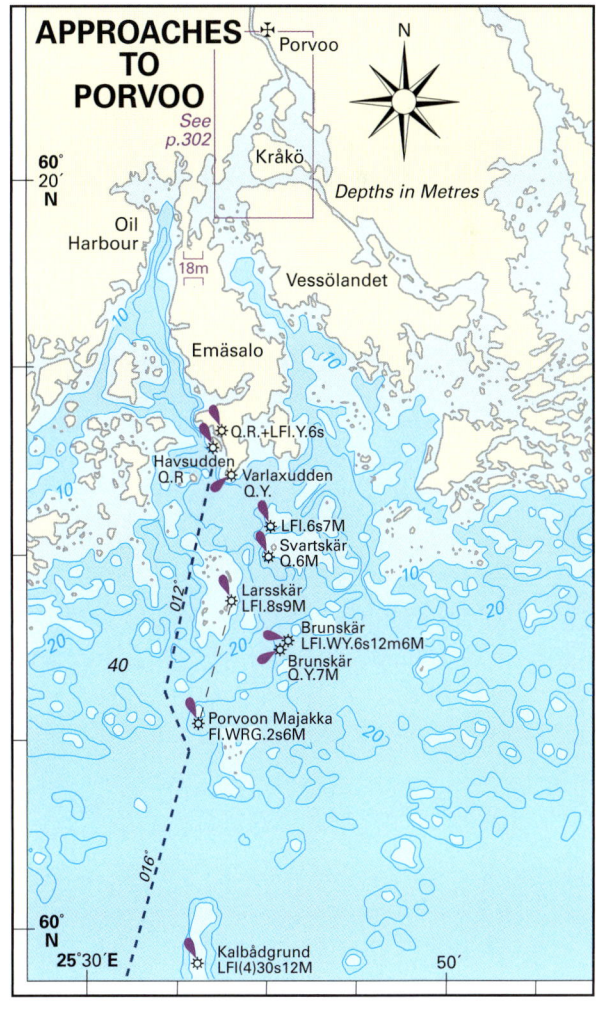

THE BALTIC SEA AND APPROACHES 301

4. FINLAND

4D. GULF OF FINLAND – EASTERN PART

Porvoo is the second oldest town in Finland, established in 1346. Its 15th-century cathedral overlooks the town, and there are numerous museums and art galleries. It is worth rowing upriver beyond the bridge to admire a most attractive row of fishermens' houses. If it is not possible to visit by yacht – and the harbour is shallow – it would make an interesting day out from Helsinki by either ferry or coach. There is no rail connection except for an occasional tourist steam train.

Approach and entrance

Porvoo lies some 12M north from the open sea. The harbour is approached from either south-southwest or south-southeast, leaving the large island of Emäsalo (Emsalö) either side. Approaching from the southwest, larger yachts are restricted by a bridge on the northern tip of Emsalö, which has a clearance of only 18m. Some 4M south of the town of Porvoo, the channel shoals to (1·9m) in places. The narrow channel is well marked throughout. The harbour is completely sheltered and has no vessel traffic other than yachts and the occasional tourist boat.

Berthing

Porvoo guest harbour, occupies a single pontoon on the east bank of the river and is clearly marked with the usual white-on-blue anchor symbol. There are 23 spaces in finger berths and a 66m quay to moor alongside in 2·5m. Water and electricity are supplied on the pontoon. The marina office is located in the small blue café slightly upstream. The services – which include laundry facilities and even a small kitchen in addition to the usual showers and toilets – are at the rear of the pink building directly opposite the pontoon walkway, the front of which is occupied by the customs office. A daily weather forecast is displayed at the marina office (Finnish and Swedish only). Fuel can be obtained at Hamari (Hammars) (60°21'·4N 25°38'·5E) (FMA 247) about 2M downstream.

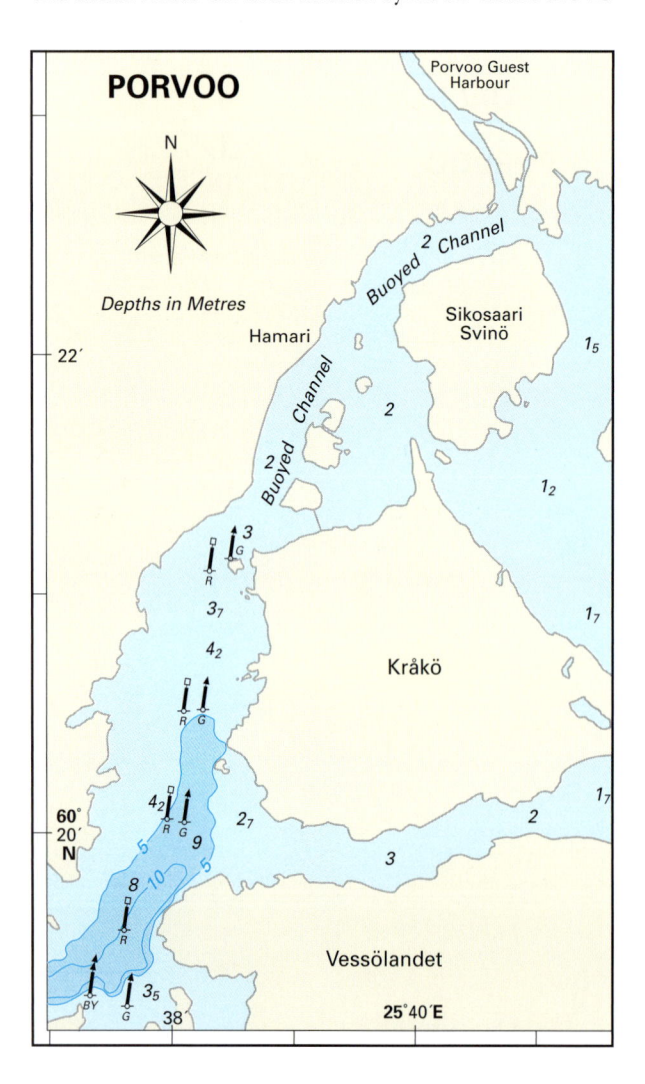

Formalities

See Formalities in Key information, page 248.

Services for yachts

Fuel can be obtained at Hamari (Hammars) (60°21'·4N 25°38'·5E) about 2M downstream.

Holding tanks can be pumped out at a facility about 0·5M downstream on the east side. There are several boatyards in the vicinity where repairs can be carried out and where it might be possible to lay-up. There is a variety of marine engineers and other services: the marina office produces a useful booklet detailing local services, but this is printed in Finnish and Swedish only. Familiar brands of clothing and chandlery are available from Meripuoti-Havsboden at Pernajank 23. ✆ +358 19 585 808

General facilities

Porvoo has good shopping, including a small outdoor market, within a short walk of the guest harbour.

Communications and travel

Porvoo is linked to Helsinki by bus and the occasional tourist steam train.

Sandholmsudden, Pellinki

60°14'·1N 25°52'·2E
Chart A619, 620, 16
SH3 98 **FMA** 232
www.visitsaaristo.net
www.pellinge.net/benitascafe/

The northern coastal channel (3m) that runs north of the island of Pellinki, 1·1M west of Sunisundet is Benitas Café and the pontoon harbour with 15 places. A good mooring in southwesterly winds when Sunisundet is quite windy. Nice café with some light food, fuel sales and free WiFi.

Suninsalmi (Sunisundet)

60°14'·7N 25°53'·8E
Chart A619, 620, 16
SH3 114 **FMA** 229
www.visitsaaristo.net

The northern coastal channel (3m) that runs north of the island of Pellinki passes through Sunisundet, the sound between Tirmo on the mainland and the island of Sundön. West from the ferry that connects Sundön with the mainland is the guest harbour of Sunnisund. It is open to the southwest and west.

PORVOO

There are 30 spaces, bows-to from stern buoys, on finger pontoons or alongside in 1·8–2·5m. This is the main shopping point for the Pellinki group of islands with a convenient jetty and a modest supermarket. Fuel (only 1·5m of water at the fuel jetty), gas and provisions can also be purchased here. There is a good anchorage with excellent holding in the bay on the opposite side of the channel.

Northeast from the harbour (1·5M) there is a good fish shop with a jetty – Nyholms Fisk – at Fölisöudden (60°15·5′N 25°56·0E) (FMA 228) – easily approached from the main coastal channel.

Bockholmen

60°12′N 25°54′·8E
Chart A620, 16
SH3 7

Anchorage

Just off the southern route between Helsinki and Kotka (9m), Bockholmen is a well sheltered and attractive anchorage surrounded by islands and almost landlocked. Good holding ground. Approach from the south, leaving Bockholmen lighthouse to starboard. Turn east as soon as you reach the lagoon and pass north of Tällholmen island. The anchorage is situated on the eastern side of Tällholmen in 4–5m. Beware of the rock awash 0·1M to the northeast of Tällholmen.

Bockhamn (Byön)

60°16·1′N 25°59′·8E
Charts A618, 619, 16
SH3 6   FMA 217
www.visitsaaristo.net

The island of Byön, south of Sarvisalo lies just off the northern route (2·4m) towards Loviisa. The lagoon is situated to the southeast of the island. It is owned by Föreningen Nylands Friluftsområden and opens to everyone. Enter from the southeast just over a cable east of a white stone cairn off the buoyed channel. Keep to the center of the very narrow entrance channel (2·7m). Anchor in the center of the lagoon (clay bottom) or bows-to from a stern buoy or anchor either east or west of the entrance to the pool (15–20 spaces) in 2m. The anchorage is almost landlocked and safe in all winds. There are just a few small summer houses and a farm nearby. It can get very crowded during the summer.

Sävtäktet, looking E *M. Strobel*

Sävtäktet

60°17′·1N 26°08′·3E
Chart A 618, 16
SH3 119

Anchorage

Very attractive anchorage between Helsinki and Kotka. It lies amidst a cluster of islands in Grundfjärden to the east of the island of Hästön. Situated roughly equidistant from the northern and the southern routes, it can be approached either from the south or the northeast.

From the south

From the south-cardinal buoy south of Risholmen leading mark, head towards the west of Risholmen island, past the narrow entrance between Skogshället, Lilla Risholmen to port and Risholmen to starboard. The archipelago widens at this point. Continue in a northerly direction (0·4M) until you have passed between Stora Andholmen (with a cairn) to starboard and Träskesholmen to port and anchor anywhere in the pool (7–8m). There are three red fairway buoys to guide you in.

From the north

Leave the main channel at the top of Kejvsalö island and head southwards entering the pool at the southeastern corner of Våtskär island.

Bockholmen anchorage *M. Strobel*

THE BALTIC SEA AND APPROACHES

4. FINLAND

4D. GULF OF FINLAND – EASTERN PART

Loviisa

60°27′N 26°14′E

Distances
Helsinki 55M, Porvoo 40M, Kotka 35M, Haapasaari Island 40M, Santio 56M

Charts and guides
UKHO 2248, 3814
Finnish A615,15,16 (SH3 *68* FMA *200, 201*)
Merikarttasarja A: Viipuri – Helsinki/Viborg – Helsingfors

Lights
Tiiskeri 60°09′·7N 26°15′·8E Fl(2)10s16m9M Racon Black concrete tower and lantern
Tainio 60°012′·7N 26°24′·7E VQ(5)6s17m6M Racon White round concrete tower, black top, red lantern 17m
Orrengrund, W end 60°16′·4N 26°26′·3E
Oc.WRG.3s13m12M 019°-R-082°-G-128°-W-138°-R-151°-obsd-184°-G-197°-W-203°-R-212°-obsd-288°-G-355°-W-019° White concrete tower, black lantern. Floodlit
Orrengrund Ldg Lts 023·1° *Front* 60°16′·4N 26°27′·1E
Q.13m13M 013°-vis-033° Racon
Red rectangle, yellow stripe
Rear 520m from front LFl.6s25m14M
019°-vis-026·5° Red rectangle, yellow stripe
Skarven 60°17′·8N 26°20′·91E Fl.WRG.3s7m4M 051°-G-064·5°-W-068·5°-R-159°-G-241°-W-267°-R-310° Racon Black concrete tower

Harbour communications
Loviisa Harbourmaster ☎ +358 19 515 163
VHF Ch 12, 13, 14, 16
www.visitsaaristo.net
www.visitloviisa.fi

Loviisa is a small and interesting town at the head of a long, peaceful inlet. It has a population of around 16,000. Loviisa is best known for its fortifications, the wooden houses of its old town and the Strömfors Iron Works. Loviisa was a thriving port during the 19th century and a resort town for the Russian nobility prior to 1914. Overlooking the guest harbour there is the Museum of Seafaring which has a fine collection of models and old photographs.

Finland's greatest composer, Jean Sibelius, spent his childhood summers in Loviisa, and the house, just beyond the church is open during the tourist season. A Sibelius Festival is held in the town each summer.

About 4.5M to the south, on the narrow approach to the town, stands the fortified island of Svartholm. It is well worth visiting (see harbour information above). It played an important role and was bombarded by the British fleet during the Crimean War.

Approach and entrance

Loviisa is situated some 12M north from the open sea. The nuclear power station on Hästholmen (60°22′N 26°21′E) is a very conspicuous landmark from afar. The approach from the southeast is straightforward, leaving Lilla Hudö and Hudö to port and Yttre Täktarn to starboard. Though narrow where it passes between Hudö and some offlying islets, the channel is well marked with transits, beacons and buoys. This is the approach route for the industrial port at Valko. Further north, past the industrial docks, the channel shoals progressively to 2·7m and widens before reaching the town. The final stretch is well marked with lateral buoys and Loviisan Kivi light (60°26′·23N 26°15′·7E, Q.WRG.).

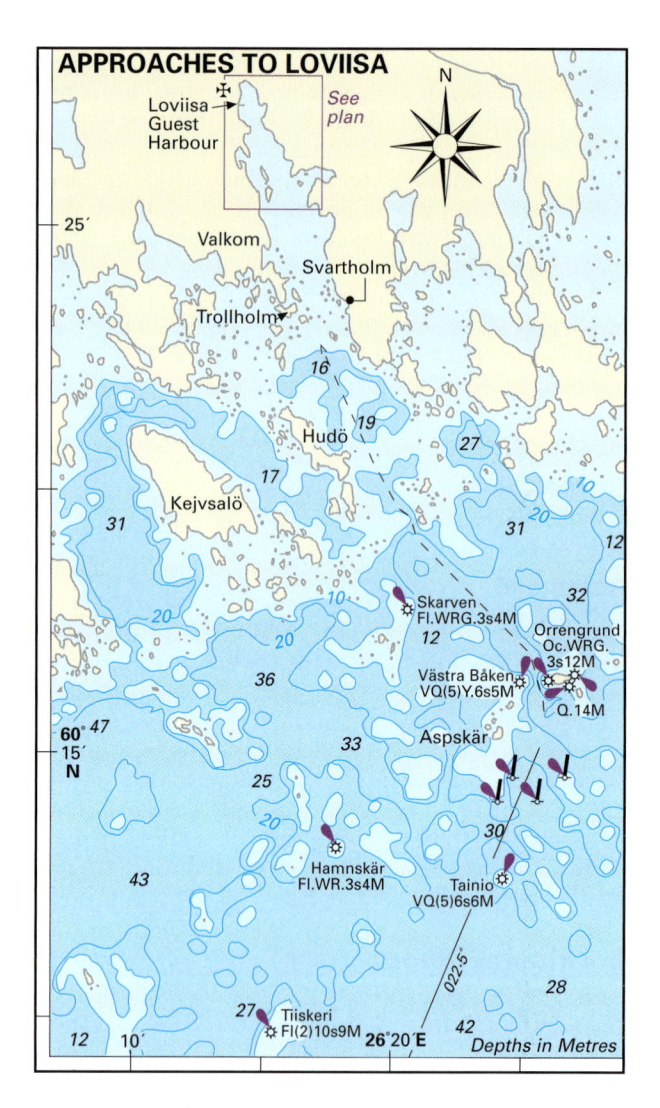

Approaching from the west, there is a shortcut that passes through the skerries north of Stor Hudö and joins the main shipping channel south of Svartholmen.

Formalities

See Formalities in Key information, page 248.
Harbour office ☎ +358 19 555 731.

Berthing

Loviisa Laivasilta (Skeppsbron) marina (FMA *201*) lies southeast of the town centre amid pleasant, park-like surroundings. There is a new visitors pontoon, bows-to from stern buoys in 2–2·5m. It is the longest pontoon as you approach the harbour. Deeper yachts can moor to a jetty at Tullisilta, about 0·4M further south, where there is a single pontoon with 15 berths in up to 3m (on the outside). It lies directly on the fairway, is subject to swell from passing boats and lies some distance from the town centre.

304   THE BALTIC SEA AND APPROACHES

LOVIISA

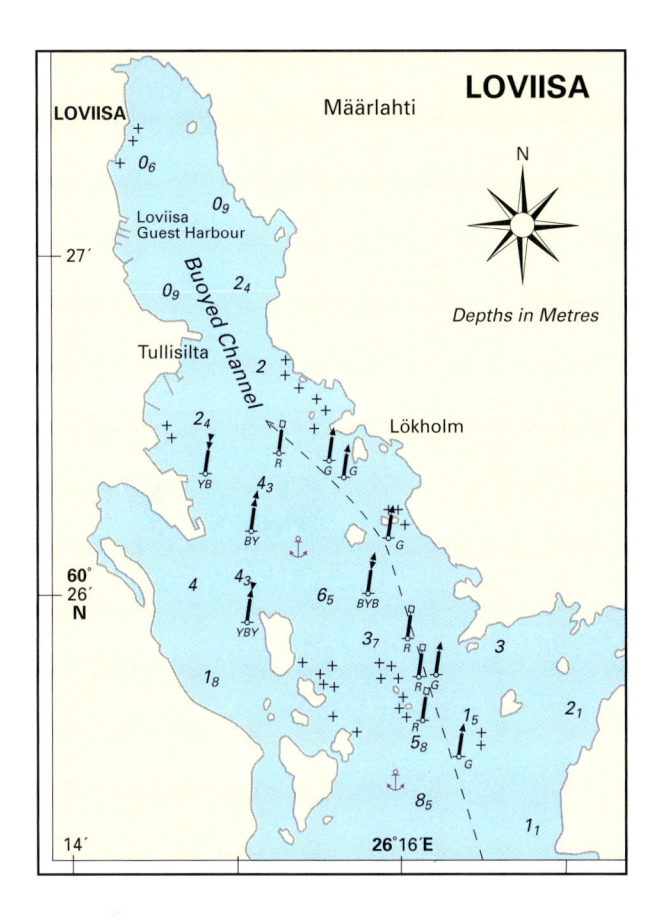

The harbour office at Laivasilta occupies a small kiosk near the fuel berth. At Tullisilta harbour dues are paid at the tourist information office.

Services for yachts
The guest harbour has all the usual facilities including showers, toilets, sauna and launderette, with cafés and restaurants nearby. Fuel is available at the service dock close south of the long visitors pontoon, where holding tanks can also be pumped out. The jetty at Tullisilta has toilets, showers and a small shop.

There are several boatyards in the area, and mechanical and other work can be carried out by a variety of local companies – seek advice at the marina office. Limited chandlery is available at the Varvet marina shop (☎ +358 19 535 149), near the town centre. Sails-Dynamic Oy, handle sailmaking and repairs of all kinds.

General facilities
All normal shopping needs can be met in Loviisa town centre, a pleasant 750m walk from the guest harbour, where there are also the usual banks, cafés, restaurants, etc.

Communications and travel
Loviisa is on the railway network, though travelling to Helsinki would require several changes. Buses run to Helsinki and Vantaa airport.

Svartholm
60°22'·8N 26°18'1E
Charts A615, 15, 16
SH3 *117* **FMA** *194*
www.visitsaaristo.net
www.cafesvartholm.fi/

Approach from the east from the fairway leading to Loviisa. Follow the marked fairway towards the service dock, located on the northern bank, or to the guest pontoons located on the northeastern corner of the island. Pontoons with stern buoys (4m). Open to the southeast and northwest-north winds.

Svartholm castle and island is a great destination for the whole family. In the castle there is an exhibition, which introduces the island's history. There are also guided walks that can be arranged and adventures for children.

There is a tourist boat going from Loviisa to Svartholm several times a day. This is a convenient way to do some shopping and sightseeing and return later in the day to Svartholm where you have left your yacht.

Kaunissaari/Pyttis Fagerö
60°20'·6N 26°46'·5E (south mole)
Charts A611, 611.2, 612, 14, 15
SH3 *47* **FMA** *172*
www.visitsaaristo.net
www.kaunissaari.fi

Situated on the southern tip of the island of Kaunissaari, the marina has a very narrow, rocky, and shallow (2·5m) entrance not to be attempted in strong southerly winds. The final approach is well buoyed with leading marks on Piktäniemi, but seems rather confusing at the entrance of the marina with several cardinal buoys marking the spit. Make sure that you leave two south- and one west-cardinal buoys to starboard, and the port-hand mark and one east-cardinal buoy to port before you enter the marina. The guest pontoons are immediately to port as you enter. There is little room to manoeuver in the

Kaunissaari *M. Strobel*

THE BALTIC SEA AND APPROACHES

4D. GULF OF FINLAND – EASTERN PART

marina and the stern buoys are too short for yachts over 10m (in which case take the stern buoy alongside). There are 20 spaces, bows-to from stern buoys in 1·9–2·4m. Kaunissaari is an attractive working village, well worth a visit. It can become very crowded with day-trippers from Kotka during the summer. A small well-stocked shop, smoked fish, and post box are located close to the marina. There is also a very interesting maritime curio museum nearby and a nice restaurant with several fish dishes.

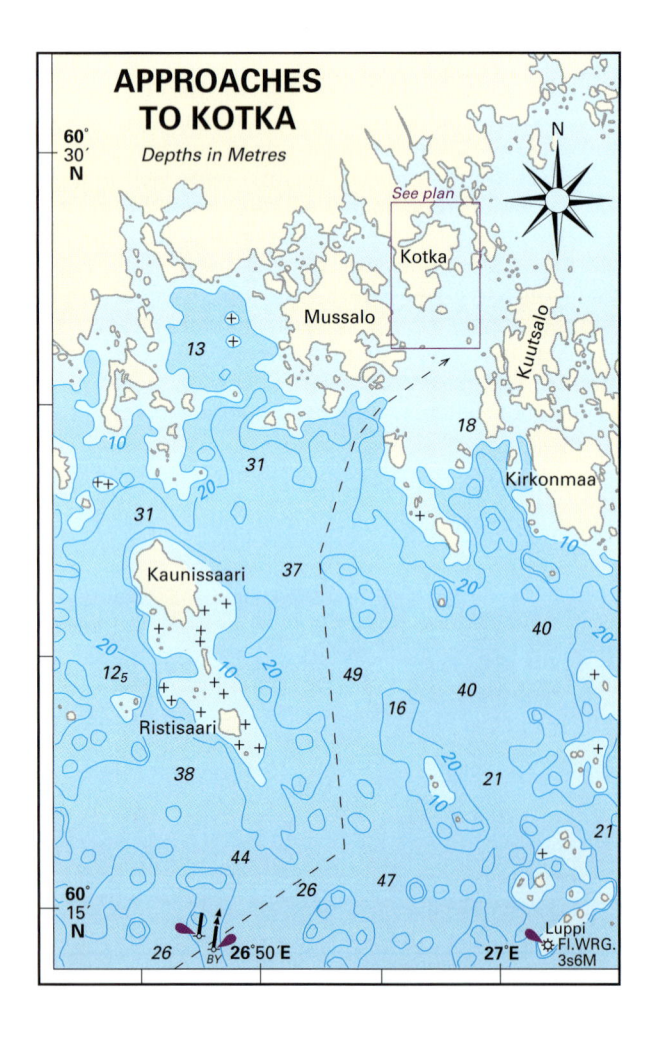

Kotka

60°27'·5N 26°57'·2E (Sapokanlahti)

Distances
Helsinki 75M, Loviisa 35M, Haapasaari Island 15M, Hamina 20M, Santio Island 30M, Vyborg 65M, St Petersburg 110M

Charts and guides
UKHO 2248, 2260, 2264, 3813
Finnish A609, 610,14 (**SH3** 55 **FMA** *149, 146*)
Merikarttasarja A: Viipuri – Helsinki/Viborg – Helsingfors

Lights
Kotkan Majakka 60°10'·3N 26°39'·2E Fl(4)30s23m12M Racon Yellow metal column, blue band Helipad
Luppi 60°14'·3N 27°01'·8E Fl.WRG.3s8m6M 247°-G-274°-W-048·5°-R-074°
Rankin Kivikari (Patricia) 60°21'·2N 26°57'·4E UQ(5)6s10m3M Racon White metal post, red band
Rankki 60°21'·9N 26°58'·3E Fl(3)WRG.10s11m6M 225·5°-G-288°-W-295°-R-048°-G-096°-W-101°-R-127° Black round concrete tower on reef
Lelleri 60°24'N 26°58'·5E Fl(2)WRG.5s5m7M 144°-G-167°-W-174°-R-244°-G-330·5°-W-336°-R-354° Yellow round tower, black top
Pirköyri 60°27'·5N 26°58'·6E Fl.WRG.3s6m5M 000°-G-163°-W-166°-R-178° Red lantern on white concrete base

Harbour communications
Kotka Port Authority ☎ +358 20 790 8800
  VHF Ch 16, 11, 13, 14
Kotka Vessel Traffic Service ☎ +358 204 485 391
  VHF Ch 67 (all vessels more than 12m in length must maintain a listening watch while in the fairways of the Kotka pilotage area)
Kotka Guest Harbour ☎ +358 5 218 1417
New Port Kotka ☎ +358 5 225 0074
  www.kotkayachtstore.fi
www.kotkanpursiseura.fi/meriniemi (for Sapokanlahti Yacht Club KPS)
www.kotka.fi
www.portofkotka.fi (commercial port)

With a population of more than 55,000, Kotka is the largest city between Helsinki and the Russian border, and is an important port mostly handling timber. Originally it occupied only the island of Kotkansaari but over the years has spread inland and to the adjacent islands. It is a useful point of departure from Finland to Vyborg or St Petersburg. Another reason for coming to Kotka is to visit the fishing lodge, built in 1889 for Tsar Alexander III. It lies by the rapids at Langinkoski about 5km northwest of the town and is easily reached by bus. It is intriguing and well worth visiting.

The Kotka Maritime Festival is held annually in early August – details on the Kotka city website (see above).

The stunning Maritime Museum of Finland and Maritime Centre Vellamo, opened in 2008, is situated near the docks on the north side of the island.

On the northwest side of Kotkansaari island, north of the pontoons, is the Maretarium (aquarium) and an impressive water garden with pleasant walks.

306   THE BALTIC SEA AND APPROACHES

KOTKA

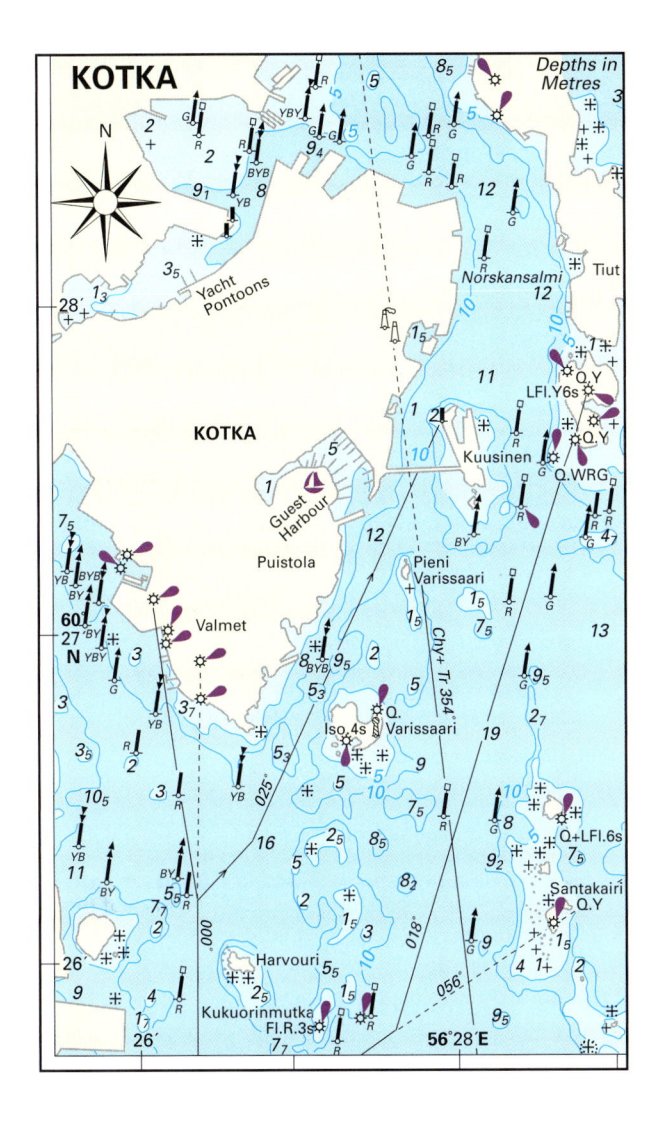

Approach and entrance

From the open sea, Kotka (Finnish for 'eagle') lies 6M to the north. The approach channel from Helsinki passes north of the island of Kaunissaari, follows three sets of leading marks to pass between Mussalo, the commencial port of Kotka and Viikarinsaari island, between Varissaari island and Kukouri fort, and finally northwest to the harbour entrance.

Approaching from the southeast, one of several approaches is between the islands of Kirkonmaa to starboard and Rankki to port towards Lelleri light (60°24'·02N 26°58'·32E, Fl(2)WRG.5s), leaving Lehmäsaari to starboard, where the route joins the main approach.

Formalities

See Formalities in Key information, page 248. Kotka is a Foreign Port of Call (Marina Cafe Pier) ☎ +358 44 2399 915. Frontier Guard posts at Haapasaari and Santio islands are about 21km and 48km away respectively.

Berthing

Kotka, Sapokanlahti on Meriniemi has 50 berths and is situated on the southeast shore of the Kotkansaari peninsula. It is run by the city's yacht club – the Kotkan Pursiseura KPS/KSS. The Marina Café Laituri (Winger) (see above) manages guest boat services. The Yacht Club also has a very good restaurant, the Ravintola Meriniemi, a stunning wooden building and excellent food, overlooking the harbour.

Visitors are normally berthed on the second pontoon on the left after entering the harbour (clearly identified with the usual white-on-blue anchor), which can take yachts up to 14m, bows-to from stern buoys in 2·5–5m.

Larger yachts may be able to berth north of the town at New Port Kotka (Centralhamnen västra), a service harbour (see above), beyond the old icebreaker Tarmo (built in Newcastle in 1907 and now a museum ship). It is operated by Kotka Yacht Store Oy. It is a large modern marina, which can take up to 30 visitors (4m), alongside or on finger pontoons. Most of the spaces are reserved for permanent berth holders and it would be wise to phone in advance (see details above). The area is a former passenger wharf and the water is deep.

Services for yachts.

Sapokanlahti (KPS/KSS) has water and electricity on the pontoon, with toilets and showers ashore. Laundry facilities are located in the marina yacht club building. The fuelling berth (where holding tanks can also be emptied) is at the end of the long, tree-shaded central mole, and also sells charts and a small amount of chandlery. Finnish propane gas cylinders can be exchanged there.

Kotka Yacht Store Oy (☎ +358 52 109 585), located in New Port Kotka, has a very large under cover facility and specialises in the laying-up and storage of boats. Other services include servicing, refitting and yacht transport. Veleiro Oy (☎ +358 52 109 555), just north of Kotkansaari, in the Puolanlaituri district past the docks, also offers winter storage and all kinds of boat repairs (including Volvo Penta spare parts) and a chandlery.

General facilities

The shopping centre is about 15 minutes' walk from the yacht harbour. There is also an outdoor market, as well as banks, restaurants and hotels in the town.
Communications and travel
Good coach services to Helsinki, Hamina and St Petersburg. The train to Helsinki involves a change at Kouvola. Bicycles can be hired at the marina office.

THE BALTIC SEA AND APPROACHES

4. FINLAND

4D. GULF OF FINLAND – EASTERN PART

Nuokko, Nuokot
60°27′N 27°13′4E
Charts A607, 607.1, 609, 610, 14
SH3 *80* **FMA** *128*

Anchorage
Ulko-Nuokko and Sisä-Nuokko are two islands east of Suuri-Musta island, due south of Hamina. The natural harbour is a landlocked lagoon with a very narrow entrance. The approach is from the south and the main southern route. It can't be easily approached from the northern inshore route without a considerable detour. This is due to extensive skerries stretching 8M southeast of Hamina. Enter from the south between Ulko-Nuokko and Sisä-Nuokko, and hug the Ulko-Nuokko shore until the lagoon opens up. There are rocks extending out (0·1M) south of both islands. Anchor in the southern half of the pool in 5m or take a line ashore from a stern anchor. This is a very beautiful and strongly recommended anchorage but it is popular with local boats at weekends.

There are several pontoon and places with mooring to the shore possibilities. On the islands you will find fireplaces and planned natural walk around the islands.

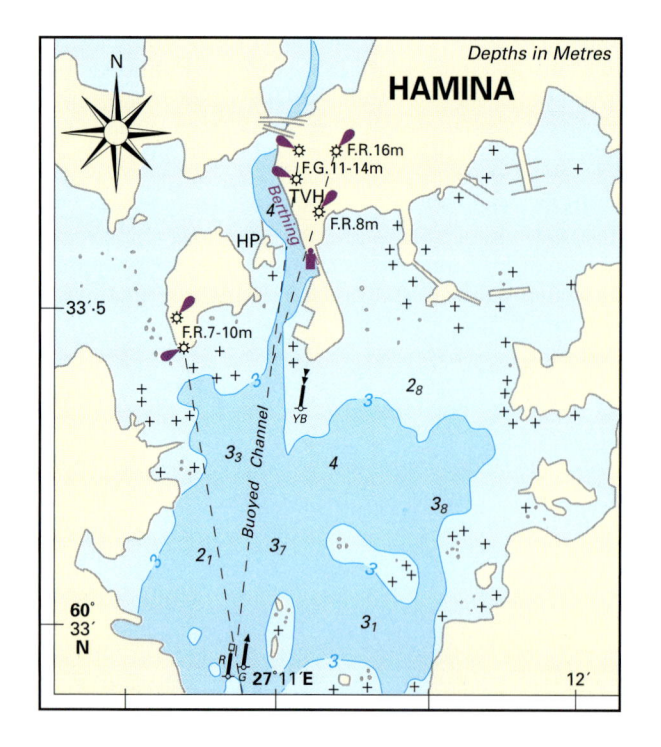

Hamina (Fredrikshamn)
60°33′·4N 27°10′·9E (Rampsinkari (south))

Distances
Kotka 20M, Haapasaari Island 15M, Santio Island 20M

Charts and guides
UKHO 2260, 2264, 3813
Finnish 609, 14 (SH3 *32* FMA *137, 138*)
Merikarttasarja A: Viipuri – Helsinki/Viborg – Helsingfors
Stora Hamnboken Vol.3

Lights
Haapasaari 60°17′·4N 27°12′·3E VQ(10)Y.6s4m3M 133°-vis-310° Grey round tower
Kivikari 60°17′·5N 27°12′·5E Q.WRG.8m7M 054°-G-154°-W-188°-R-205°-G-213°-W-217°-R-301° White lantern, white base
Kaurakari 60°30′·8N 27°10′·5E VQ(5)6s4m4M
Ulkokari 60°31′·5N 27°11′·3E VQ(2)Y.3s4m2M Column
Norskari 60°31′·8N 27°11′·5E VQ.6s5m3M White post, red band
Suviluoto 60°32′·3N 27°11′·8E Fl.WRG.3s3m5M 324°-G-005·5°-W-009·5°-R-027°-G-049·5°-W-056°-R-065°-G-078°-W-084°-R-105°
Yellow rectangle, red stripe, on post

Harbour communications
Hamina Port Authority ☎ +358 5 225 5400
 VHF Ch 12, 13, 16
 office@portofhamina.fi (Rampsinkari)
Tervasaari Visitors' Harbour ☎ +358 5 344 4828
Haminan Pursiseura Harbourmaster ☎ +358 5 572 1142
 uutela.jarmo@hotmail.com
www.visitsaaristo.net
www.visithamina.fi
www.portofhamina.fi

Just 40km west of the Russian border, Hamina is a pretty, spacious town with an unusual ground plan. Eight roads radiate from the old town centre, with others forming concentric circles around them so that, from the air, it resembles a giant spider's web. Designed to fit inside a vast rampart, Hamina has been a garrison town for most of its 360 years' existence. It was founded in 1653 by Count Per Brahe, who designed many beautiful towns around the coast of Finland. Its commercial port, which is 2·5M downstream, handles mainly container traffic and timber.

Approach and entrance
From the open sea Hamina can be approached either from the southeast or southwest, either side of Suuri-Musta and Majasaari, or from the northern inshore route, along well-marked channels towards the commercial port of Hamina. From there, the final approach shoals progressively to 4m and has a clearly marked fairway.

Formalities
See Formalities in Key information, page 248.

308 THE BALTIC SEA AND APPROACHES

HAMINA

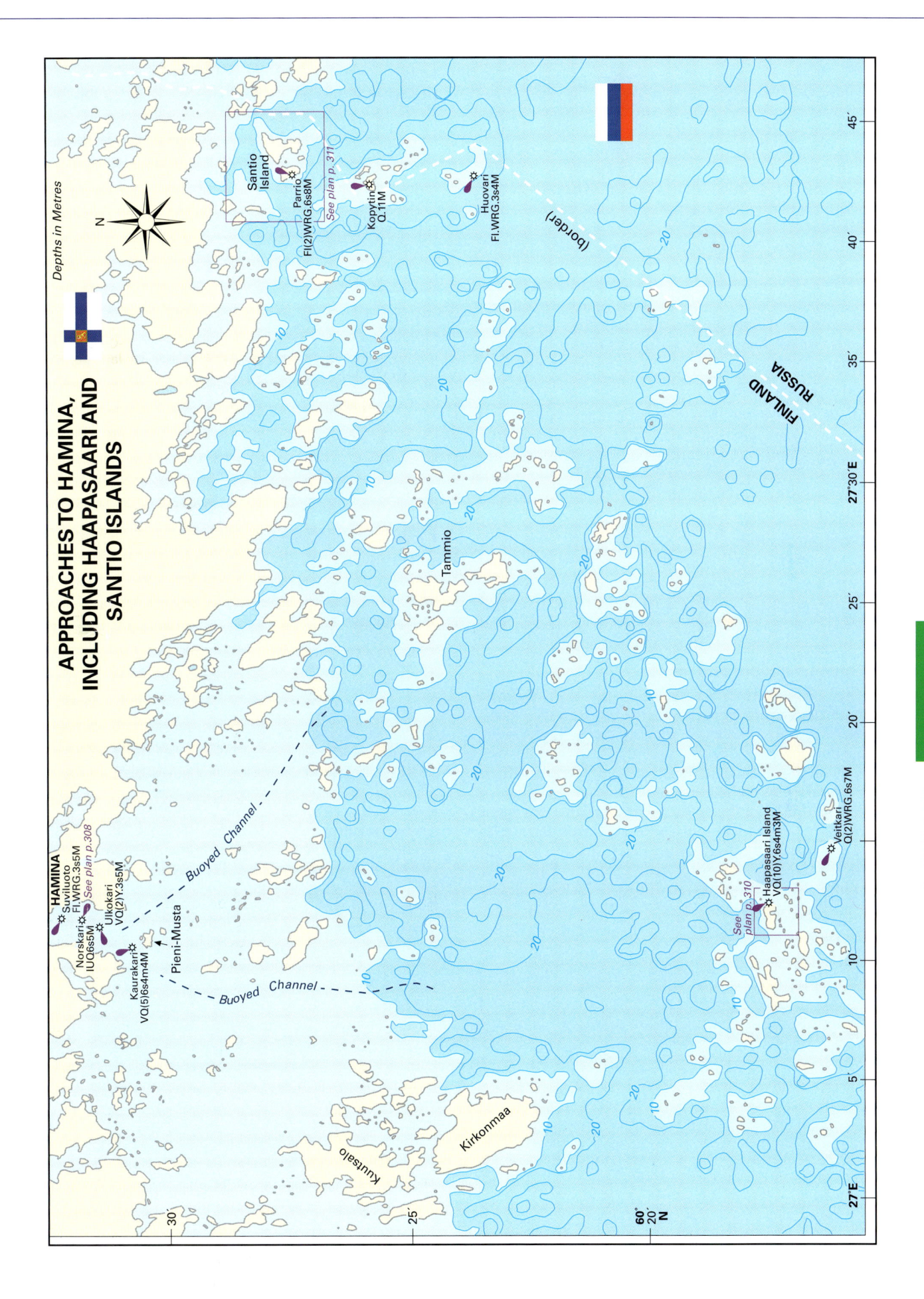

APPROACHES TO HAMINA, INCLUDING HAAPASAARI AND SANTIO ISLANDS

Depths in Metres

- Santio Island — Parrio Fl(2)WRG.6s8M — *See plan p. 311*
- Kopytin Q.11M
- Huovari Fl.WRG.3s4M
- (border) FINLAND / RUSSIA
- Tammio
- HAMINA — *See plan p.308*
  - Suviluoto Fl.WRG.3s5M
  - Norskari IUQ.6s5M
  - Ulkokari VQ(2)Y.3s5M
  - Kaurakari VQ(5)6s4m4M
  - Pieni-Musta
- Buoyed Channel
- Haapasaari Island VQ(10)Y.6s4m3M — *See plan p. 310*
- Veitkari Q(2)WRG.6s7M
- Kuutsalo
- Kirkonmaa

4. FINLAND

THE BALTIC SEA AND APPROACHES 309

4D. GULF OF FINLAND – EASTERN PART

Berthing
There are two guest harbours on either side of the fairway before you reach the bridges.

Hamina, Rampsinkari, on the east bank has space for 35 yachts in 4m alongside the quay near the café and restaurant, with another 15 berths in 2·2m or less further south. The harbour office is at the southern end of the quay (in the bar), near the fuel berth.

Haminan Pursiseura (Hamina Yacht Club), occupies the small island of Pieni Vuohisaari, directly opposite Rampsinkari, and accepts visiting yachts on the southern of its two pontoons, space permitting, bows-to from stern buoys in 2m. It has a restaurant and a small ferry between the yacht club and the town.

Services for yachts
Diesel and a pump-out station are available at Rampsinkari. Both marinas offer electricity, water, showers and sauna, but otherwise facilities are limited. There are several boatyards and other marine businesses in the locality, but Hamina is not a place to have major works carried out.

General facilities
Several cafés and restaurants overlook the harbour, and there is a good supermarket nearby. The town centre, which is about a 15-minute walk from the guest harbour, is well provided with shops and banks, and there is a large outdoor market.

Communications and travel
The railway runs down the west bank of the estuary, some distance from the town; the bus station is much closer to the town centre. Bicycles can be hired at the harbour office.

Hamina Tattoo, the International Military Music Festival is arranged annually in early August in Hamina. During the event week, you can enjoy great free concerts in Kesäpuisto Park, Tattoo Parade at the Town Hall Square, and the stalls and musical performances of the Tattoo Street. The week culminates with the March Shows in the event arena Hamina Bastion.

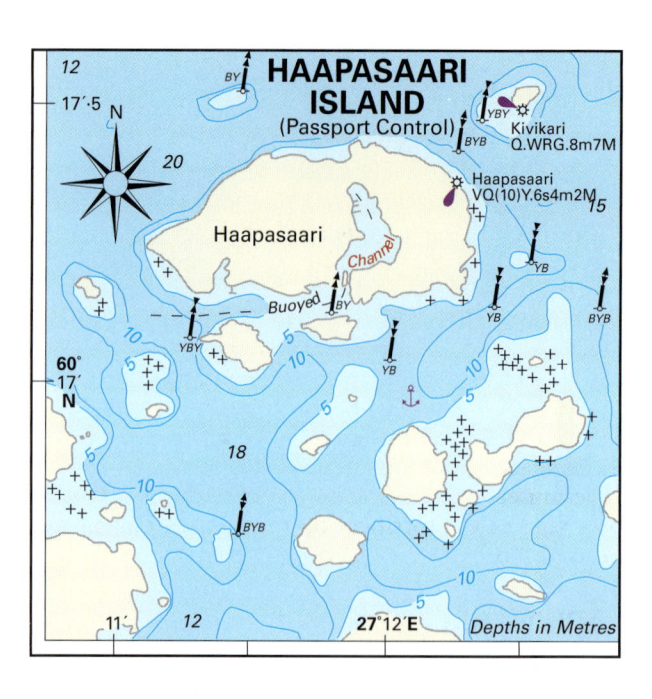

Haapasaari/Aspö Island

60°17'·3N 27°11'·7E
Charts A608, 608.1, 14
SH3 *29* **FMA** *134*
Communications
www.visitsaaristo.net
www.raja.fi/guidelines/border_crossing
www.raja.fi/guidelines/advice_to_boaters/border_checks_on_pleasure_craft

The most obvious reason to visit Haapasaari is to get Frontier Guard clearance to or from St Petersburg some 95M to the east. However, it is an attractive, unspoilt island with well-kept wooden houses and cobbled streets, and well worth visiting in its own right.

The Frontier Guard station ☎ +358 295 426 350 occupy the smaller inlet near the western end of the island, where yachts can berth whilst clearance is being arranged, either alongside on the outer quay in 4·5m on inside the bay in 2·5m as directed. See above for more information.

The small guest harbour is located in the larger inlet which almost bisects the island from south to north. Approach can be made via well-marked channels either from the west or east. The entrance into the lagoon is no more than 12m wide and 3·5m deep. It is well marked with cardinal buoys at the entrance and fairway buoys into the pool. Berthing is bow-to from stern anchor onto the pontoon in the northeastern corner in 1·5–2·2m. There is a fuel berth and a pump-out station on the west side of pool, near the well-stocked shop.

The island ferry from Kotka uses the western pier near the Frontier Guard station.

SANTIO ISLAND

Ulko-Tammio

60°21'N 27°27'2E
Charts A606, 606.2, 13
SH3 *127* **FMA** *122*
www.visitsaaristo.net

From deep-water commercial channel going east-west, turn southeast (130°) at approx 60°23·5'N 27°19·5'E. Pass east of Lammasaari and Rääntiö to the north west bay of Ulko-Tammio. A pontoon is located on the south shore.

Ulko-Tammio is the pearl of the national park of the Gulf of Finland. Its beatiful nature with its harsh cliffs and exuberant groves is impressive. Ulko-Tammio is an excellent destination for birdwatchers. The museum with its cannons and the cave, which was part of the fortification of the area during the Second World War is an interesting place to visit.

Lapurinsalmi

60°28'·3N 27°35'·1E
Charts A605, 13
SH3 *65*

Anchorage

This is a small natural harbour only a few miles away from Santio Frontier Guard station situated on the southwestern shore of Siikasaari, between Lapuri island and the mainland. Approach from the west. Anchor in 9m in the first third of the pool. The water becomes shallow after that and there are some rocks on the north side. This could be a good anchorage in which to wait before or after clearing immigration at Santio, though it is open to the east and west.

Santio Island

60°27'·4N 27°43'·2E
Charts A604, 605, 12, 13
SH3 *101*
Communications
www.raja.fi/guidelines/border_crossing
www.raja.fi/guidelines/advice_to_boaters/border_checks_on_pleasure_craft

Santio is a Frontier Guard station (see above) right on the border with Russia. Heading to or from Vyborg, or to the Saimaa Canal and Lakes, you must check in and out of Finnish/Russian waters at Santio Island. Vyborg and the Saimaa Canal are some 40M to the northeast. The formalities and how to approach the Saimaa Canal will be described in the next section. Moor to the solid pontoon (2–4m) (the inner side is well sheltered in strong winds) and yachts may be allowed to lie alongside overnight before a dawn departure – lie alongside the pontoon and await attention. There is no fuel available and few facilities other than rubbish bins, toilets and a barbecue, and though the island appears attractive, visitors are not permitted to leave the harbour area.

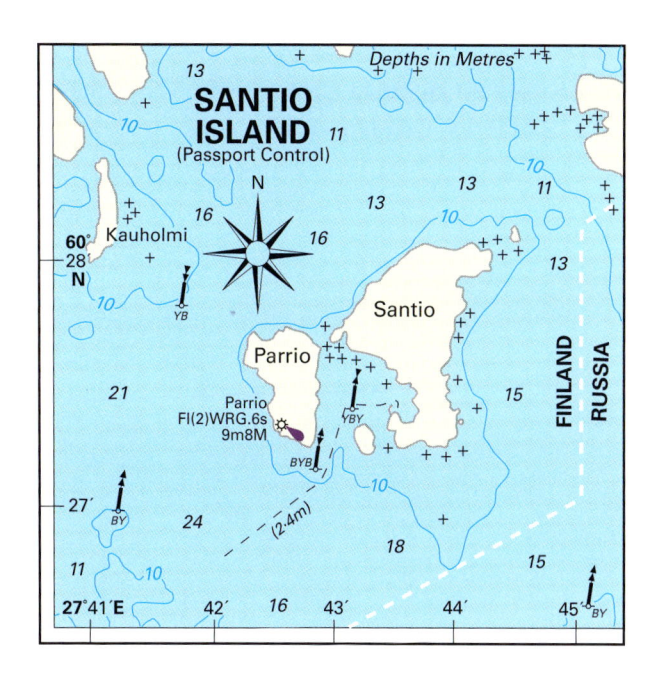

See *4e. The Russian Channel, Saimaa Canal and Lakes* for Frontier Guard station and crossing procedures.

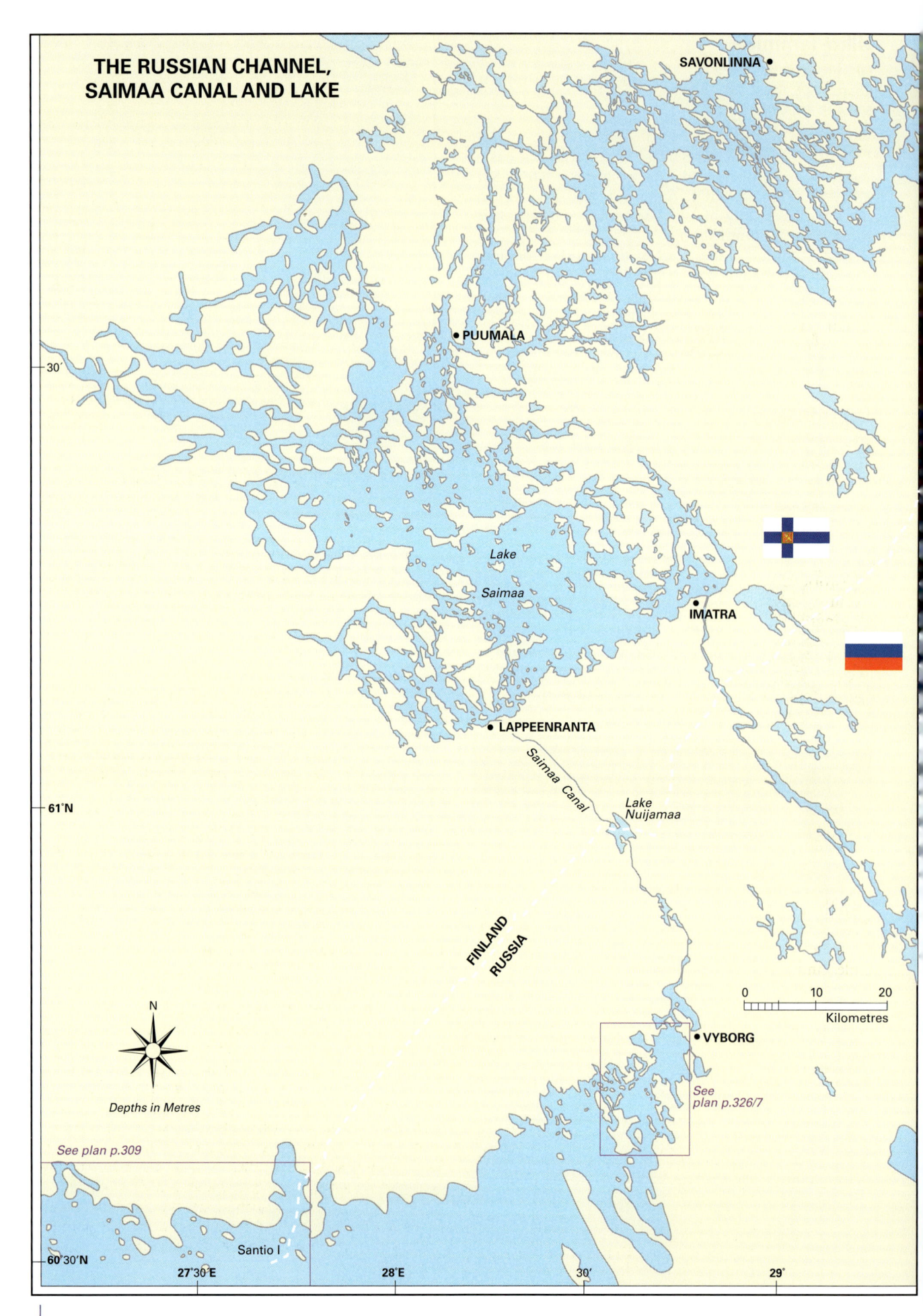

4E. THE RUSSIAN CHANNEL, SAIMAA CANAL AND LAKE

312 THE BALTIC SEA AND APPROACHES

4e. The Russian Channel, Saimaa Canal and Lake

The beautiful Saimaa Lake area is reached via the 23M (43km) Saimaa Canal.

Inaugurated in 1856, at the time when Finland was part of Russia as an autonomous Grand Duchy, the Saimaa Canal connected the enormous area of inland waterways, comprising more than 120 lakes in the south-central part of Finland, to the sea. The canal was built between Lappeenranta and Vyborg (now part of Russia).

When Finland became independent in 1917 the Karelian Isthmus, the stretch of land between the Gulf of Finland and Lake Ladoga, remained Finnish. After the Winter War, fought between the Soviet Union and Finland between 1939 and 1940 which left many thousands of soldiers dead during an attempted invasion of Finland, the Saimaa Lake was effectively cut off from the Gulf of Finland. During this conflict, the Soviet Union sought to claim parts of Finnish territory, demanding – amongst other concessions – that Finland cede substantial border territories in exchange for land elsewhere, claiming security reasons and the defense of the approaches to Leningrad (St Petersburg). When the Moscow Treaty was signed in 1940, some parts of Finland were ceded to the Soviet Union, including the southeastern Karelian Isthmus, including Vyborg and its approaches. In 1963, the USSR leased the Soviet section of the Saimaa Canal and its approach channel to Finland for 50 years. In 2008 negotiations took place to secure the lease for another 50 years starting in 2013 (with a rent of 1.22 million euros a year).

Approach
The shortest way to reach the Saimaa Canal is from the Frontier Guard station at Santio Island (see page 311) through the relatively narrow regulated passage leased from Russia by the Finns, leading through Russian waters. When travelling to and from the Saimaa Canal, provided that you conform to all the rules and regulations governing this passage you do not require a visa for Russia. Not having a valid visa restricts you to keeping strictly to this channel until you have reached the Finnish Border in Nuijamaa (50M), half way through the Saimaa Canal. The total distance between Santio Island and the entrance of the Saimaa Lake is 62·5M.

It is imperative that you read the information issued by the Finnish Ministry of Transport and Communications in the Saimaa Canal Pleasure Craft Guide and that you consult the Finnish Maritime Agency website before you leave.
www.liikennevirasto.fi

The Finnish Maritime Agency lists the forms required for the border crossings. You can also download them from their website. From these you will find all the necessary contact details, procedures to follow, papers required, forms to complete and formalities to observe at the border crossings.

Pleasure craft have been exempt from fees for use of the Saimaa Canal since the beginning of 2012. It may all look very complicated and you might even wonder whether it is worth the effort but if you follow everything to the letter, your passage to and from the Saimaa Lake should be smooth and truly enjoyable.

One piece of advice: it would be wise to keep your original registration documents on board but make sure you have a copy for the border guards in Russia. This might speed up the clearance procedure considerably.

Outward clearance from Finland must be obtained at the Frontier Guard station at either Haapasaari or Santio islands, although Santio might be the more straightforward option. When arriving at Santio or Haapasaari, the boat must follow the official navigational fairways, or the so-called customs fairway. The master of the boat must report to the border crossing point one hour before arrival. To Santio calls are made by VHF 68 or ☏ +358 295 426 110, and to Haapasaari by VHF 68 or ☏ +358 295 426 130.

At the inspection, the skipper hands in the 'Vessel's Report' form and makes a 'leisure boat inspection notification' to the customs. All leisure cruising through the Saimaa Canal is regarded as traffic across the EU's external borders in respect of border inspections.

Finnish entry/exit checks on leisure craft arriving at Lake Saimaa from the sea through the canal or leaving Lake Saimaa are carried out at the customs quay in Nuijamaa, the border crossing in the canal. Leisure boats not exceeding 24m in length may sail without a pilot, provided that there is a VHF radio telephone on board, tuned to VHF 11 for the duration of the entire passage; the skipper has a document certifying that he/she owns the boat and/or has the right to navigate it; and that there is a person on board with English or Russian skills to take care of communications.

In the territorial waters of Russia near Santio, a Russian guard vessel often keeps watch from a nearby buoy. When approaching or leaving Santio, leisure boats are requested to navigate close to the Russian guard vessel and to slow down so that the identification marks of the boat can be seen. Signals given by a guard vessel must be observed at all times.

The Russian border officials have the right to check that the documents of a boat and its crew are in order. Leisure boats may sail only during daylight hours, between 0800 and 2000 Moscow (UTC +3) time. If you leave Santio Island at 0600 (summer time), you might just make it to the Finnish border at Nuijamaa by 1800. Once in the canal, the locks and opening of the bridges operate like clockwork. Eight locks – at Brusnitchnoe, Iskrovka, Cvetotchnoe, Ilistoe, Pälli, Soskua, Mustola and Mälkiä – handle 76m difference in water level between the Baltic and Saimaa Lake.

4E. THE RUSSIAN CHANNEL, SAIMAA CANAL AND LAKE

Lock in the Saimaa Canal *M. Strobel*

Charts 600A and 600B (1:100 000) of the chart folio A – Vyborg – Helsinki show the regulated passage permitted for vessels in accordance with the treaties on Saimaa Canal. More detailed Russian large-scale charts of the area surrounding Vyborg are recommended (see below). There are two approach channels, one to the town of Vyborg (not part of the treaties on the Saimaa Canal, so a visa is required) and the regulated passage to the canal. Large-scale charts will avoid confusion.

Both plans on pages 326 and 327 in the Russia chapter illustrate this.

Navigational charts – harbour guides

Planning chart

F951 (Gulf of Finland – East, 1:250 000)

Chart folios

- A   Viipuri-Helsinki/Viborg-Helsongfors (scale 1:50 000)
- S   Saimaan kanava (1:10 000)
- L   Lappeenranta – Savonlinna (1:40 000)
- M   Savonlinna – Kuopio (1:20 000)
- V   Savonlinna – Joensuu (1:40 000)

Russian charts

28007 (INT 1257) (1:25 000)
Approaches to Vysotsk and Vyborg

28008 (INT 1258 (1:10 000)
Povorotnyy Lighthouse to Ostrov Malyy Vysotskiy

28010 (INT 1259) (1:12 500)
Dubovyy Light-Beacon to Ostrov Lavola

Harbour guide

Saimaan Käyntisatamat, ja kanavat, published annually, also give instructions for small boat traffic in the Saimaa Canal in several languages, including English. The numbers of the harbours in the book correlate with the numbers on the charts (**SKS** *xxx*).

Each lock is 85m long and 13·2m wide. There are also seven opening bridges and six fixed ones (minimum clearance 24·5m), and transit normally takes between six and eight hours.

No fuel is available on the canal – i.e. until reaching Lappeenranta – and skippers should ensure that they have plenty for the transit.

Provided you maintain a steady speed, the passage through the locks will be very smooth. The cruising speed limit in the canal is set at 6·5 knots (12km/h) for pleasure craft. Russian Customs control is at Brusnit noe (lock No. 1) and passport control is at Pälli (lock No. 5). If the voyage has already begun and delays occur during it (such as an engine failure), the authorities must be notified of this in order to avoid unnecessary searches and enquiries. You should inform, for example, the coastguard or Saimaa VTS, and they will forward the notification. If necessary, you can ask the Russian authorities to forward your notification to the Finnish authorities.

If you have a visa for a later visit to St Petersburg or Kaliningrad, ensure that it is not stamped in the Canal.

Lake Saimaa

Charts F921 (1:250,000)
Folios Merikarttasarja L, M and V (1:40,000)
www.visitfinland.com

Glacial melting at the end of the last Ice Age formed the south-central lakes of Finland, including the Saimaa Lake. Major towns on its shores include Lappeenranta, Imatra, Savonlinna, Joensuu and Kuopio. The deep channels covering some 500M are mainly used to transport commercial goods such as wood, minerals, metals and pulp. Both lakes and canal are major transport routes for the timber trade. Log rafts, consisting of felled timber piled on the ice during the winter and cleared from the south as the ice melts are frequently encountered as they are moved under tow at an unstoppable 1–2 knots. A yacht may encounter random logs floating in the water and even in the canal.

It is hard to describe the fascination of sailing in the fourth largest natural freshwater lake in Europe. The lake is navigable for deep-draught yachts with fixed masts for some 200M, as far as Joensuu

LAPPEENRANTA

Darkest part of midsummer night J. Langdon

(62°35′N 29°45′E) (Chart folio V/ Savonlinna-Joensuu) and Kuopio (62°50′N 27°40′E) (Chart folio M/ Savonlinna-Kuopio). The channels described locally as 'deep' (815km) are at least 4·2m, the 'main' channels (1,560km) at least 2·4m.

The water is very clean throughout and it warms very quickly to a swimming temperature of +20°C. It is strictly forbidden to drop any waste or empty holding tanks into the lake and therefore all harbours are equipped with pump-out stations. Winds are light and die at night. Due to the long hours of daylight during the summer, it is possible to navigate day and night.

People using the waterways may anchor, or moor and go ashore, under 'everyman's right' except where it is expressly prohibited, for example nature reserves during the nesting season .
www.nationalparks.fi/en/hikinginfinland/

The Saimaa Lake is dotted with 14,000 islands and narrow passages, which divide the lake into many parts – it feels like sailing through a forest maze. There is good sailing on the larger bodies of water and there are many sheltered but often tortuous channels. Like everywhere else in Finnish waters, the routes through the Saimaa Lake are very well marked with transits and buoys, and the charts are as detailed as the coastal ones (chart folios L, M and V). For planning purposes, the small scale planning chart (1:300,000) at the beginning of each chart folio shows the general area plan with all possible cruising routes including minimum depth, and clearance of bridges and overhead cables. When choosing a route, make sure that you check all the bridges and overhead cables beforehand.

For the scope of this pilot book, only the harbours of Lappeenranta, Imatra, Puumala and Savonlinna will be described. There are about 100 further harbours and anchorages classified in the Saimaan Käyntisatamat harbour guide and on the website.
www.gosaimaa.com

If you intend to sail towards Joensuu or Kuopio, which mark the limit of the navigable waterways for yachts with fixed masts, consult chart folios:

M – Savonlinna – Kuopio (1:20 000) and
V Savonlinna – Joensuu (1:40 000)

Distances
Joensuu – Lappeenranta 153M
Joensuu – Savonlinna 75M
Kuopio – Lappeenranta 164M
Kuopio – Savonlinna 90M

Lappeenranta

61°04′·1N 28°11′·2E (north mole, Rapasaari)
Distances Imatra 22M, Puumala 40M, Savonlinna 78M
Charts Folio L201, 200.1
SKS *4030*
Communications
www.satamapaikka.com
(marina spaces can be booked in advance)
www.gosaimaa.com
www.visitlappeenranta.fi
www.lappeenranta.fi

Following completion of the Saimaa Canal in 1856, Lappeenranta became the largest inland port in Finland. It remains a centre for the timber processing industry and is a thriving city with some 72,000 inhabitants. The cosmopolitan university has 15,000 students. It is a friendly town, popular with both Finnish and Russian tourists. The large paper mill is a prominent landmark on the approach from the canal with large wood ponds either side of the fairway. The old military area of Linnoitus on a hill overlooking the harbour has a good museum. It was successively a Swedish, then a Russian fortification and finally has been a Finnish prison and barracks

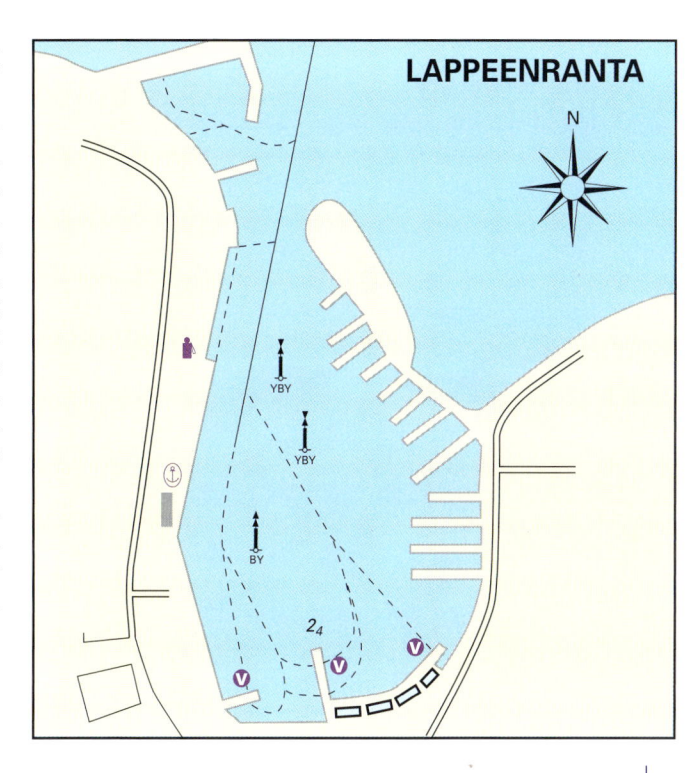

THE BALTIC SEA AND APPROACHES

4E. THE RUSSIAN CHANNEL, SAIMAA CANAL AND LAKE

since 1809. Lappeenranta also boasts the largest sand castle in Finland. It is built yearly and is open from June to September.

Approach and entrance
Lappeenranta lies to the west of the canal entrance. Pass between Hyötiönsaari and the mainland, under a bridge with 24·5m clearance. This leads into the extensive wood processing area, with log ponds and a timber wharf.

Further west, when you have reached the northwestern tip of Pappilanniemi, providing your clearance is less than 18m, turn sharp southwest between the Pappilanniemi and Akkasaari E, underneath the power cable. If not sure, it is safer to make a detour (1M) in a northwesterly direction to go around the island of Pieni Kaijansaari. The way into the marina is very well buoyed with plenty of cardinal buoys (though these can be confusing).

Berthing
Guest harbours in the Lappeenranta area are all located near the town centre. Guest harbours in Linnoitusniemi and Kasinonranta are suitable for small and medium-sized boats.

Vessels over 15m long can be moored at the fortification quay.

Linnoitusniemi sometimes referred to as Rapasaari, offers 20 visitors berths on the west side of the bay near the entrance, all bows-to from stern buoys.

Linnoituksen laituri, a little further south is a new facility, a 220m long quay intended for boats of more than 15m.

Maalaistenlaituri, in the southwest corner of the bay, has 10 visitors berths and some additional space for short (maximum four-hour) visits, particularly convenient as it is the closest to the shopping centre. Kasinonranta, in the southeast corner, is the largest facility with 50 visitors berths, some alongside and some bows-to from stern buoys, in 2·5m.

Services for yachts
All four berthing areas have water and electricity, with toilets, showers and sauna ashore. Fuel is available at Linnoitusniemi, where holding tanks can be emptied and there is also a small chandlery and a grocery store.

General facilities
Good shopping and several lively markets in the town centre as well as cafés at Linnoitusniemi and several good restaurants. There are also two 'boat restaurants' at Maalaistenlaituri.

Communications and travel
The airport lies about 3km outside the city, while mainline trains and express coaches run to Helsinki and elsewhere.

Imatra
61°12'·6N 28°43'·3E
Charts Folio L202, 202.1
SKS *4081*
www.gosaimaa.com

Imatra is a small town about 20M east-northeast of Lappeenranta. The town centre is on the west bank of the Vuoski River, the only river which flows from the southern Saimaa Lake into Lake Ladoga, over the border in Russia, which is only 13km away. The Vuoski River was a major defensive line against the Soviet advance during the Winter War (1939–1940). Before the Karelian Isthmus became part of Russia, it had been an important route for trade. There are spectacular rapids south of the town and the hydroelectric station built in 1929 helps control the lake levels.

There is a well-protected visitors marina on the west side of Imatra, between Lammassaari island and the mainland, owned by the nearby Imatra Spa Hotel. Mooring is bows-to from stern buoys in 4m. All berths have water and electricity, with toilets and showers in the hotel, where fees are also paid.

Basic food items are available at the hotel shop, otherwise the town can provide for most needs. Fuel is available at the marina at the south end of the bay. The marina lies 8km from the town centre. Bus No. 3 runs between the central station and the hotel. Distance to Lappeenranta airport is 37km.

Log processing plant Lappeenranta *M. Strobel*

Lappeenranta *M. Strobel*

SAVONLINNA

Puumala marina M. Strobel

Puumala

61°31'·2N 28°10'·6E
Charts Folio L213, 213.1
SKS *4407*
www.visitsaaristo.net www.puumala.fi

Puumala, 40M north of Lappeenranta, lies half way between Lappeenranta and Savonlinna. It is an attractive small town on the northern bank of the narrows through which larger traffic must pass en route from the southern and northern sections of the lake. A road bridge spans the channel (28·5m).

There is a municipal quay, also used by cruise and tourist boats, plus a guest harbour with all the usual facilities including fuel, both close to the bridge in 3m or more. A good supermarket is situated five minutes' walk up the hill, where there is also a bank and other small shops. It is a convenient stop on the way north.

Savonlinna

61°52'N 28°54'E
Charts Folio L218, 218.1
SKS *4528, 4529, 4536*
http://visitsavonlinna.fi

Savonlinna is situated 80M to the northeast of the canal entrance. It is a town of 36,000 inhabitants and is very popular with tourists. It is world famous for its opera festival, held in July each year in the imposing setting of the Olavinlinna castle.

Olavinlinna was built on a small island in 1475 to protect and control the border between the Kingdom of Sweden and Russia. The town itself straddles several islands and literally forms a bridge across the Saimaa Lake.

Savonlinna is also home to many old steam boats still in use today and which, although now converted from steam to diesel, lend a certain grace to the scene.

Approach and entrance

Savonlinna lies on one of the lakes' deep (4·2m) channels and the southerly approach is straightforward. If your intention is to continue sailing north, you have to have one railway and two road bridges opened. You need to announce your intention in advance and get an estimated time of opening for the bridges, which do not necessarily open at the same time. The telephone number to call is displayed on the bank as you approach the railway bridge.

Berthing

There are three possibilities for mooring on the south side of Savonlinna that don't require the opening of bridges. There are two on either side of Haislahti, straight ahead as you approach the town from the south. Haislahti läntinen (west) (61°52'N 28°52'·3E) has 20–25 mooring spaces and limited facilities. However it is very conveniently situated for the Citymarket shopping centre. V-S Marin (61°52'N 28°52'·4E), just across the water to the east, is near the town centre. Fuel is available and the holding tank can be emptied there. The boatyard has a ramp, can service engines and carry out some repairs. It also has 15 mooring spaces. Facilities include a café, small chandlery, showers and sauna, water and electricity. It is located very near the Kauppalinna shopping mall.

The biggest and most peaceful guest marina is Törninpyörä (61°51'·8N 28°53'·4E) with 60 guest spaces, bows-to from stern buoys. There is water and electricity on the pontoons but, apart from that, facilities are rather limited. The pontoons belong to the Perhehotelli Hospitz, just across the park. There you can have a shower and a sauna. The hotel has a nice veranda and a restaurant.

Communications and travel

Savonlinna has an airport that connects it to Helsinki (335km). There are also good train and express coach services to the capital, making Savonlinna by far the best city in the northern lake area for crew changes. There is also a regular ferry to Lappeenranta.

Approaches to Savonlinna M. Strobel

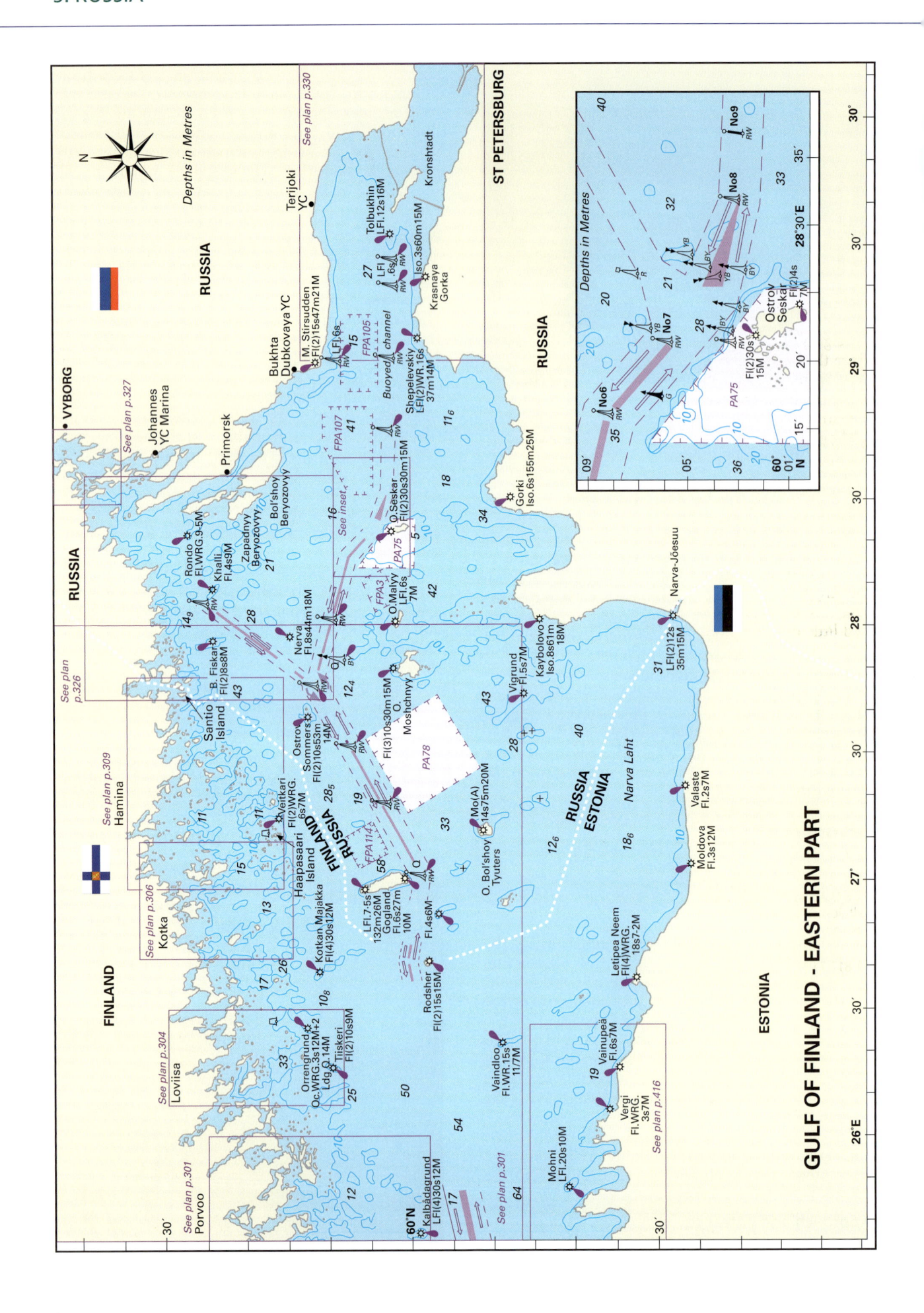

5. RUSSIA

5. Russia

Foreign yachts have been made welcome in Russia since the break-up of the Soviet Union in 1991 and have visited in ever increasing numbers, even though the formalities are complex and facilities for yachts are still somewhat limited by western standards. Although there are continuing uncertainties as to Russia's relationship with the West, the general consensus is that it remains a very rewarding destination, and that facilities are likely to continue to improve.

That part of Russia which borders the far east of the Baltic Sea is almost entirely low-lying and backed by extensive marshes and lakes. The delta of the River Neva was an uninhabited swamp until the founding of St Petersburg in the early 18th century, and little of the city stands more than 5m above sea level. The 200m contour lies several hundred kilometres inland.

The seas in the eastern part of the Gulf of Finland are as shallow as the land is low, with the 10m contour running well to the northwest of Kronshtadt and much of the Nevskaya Guba has depths 5m or less, other than where dredged. This may partly explain Russia's desire to retain Vyborg, close to the Finnish border, the approaches to which carry considerably greater depths.

Despite this, St Petersburg is home to a wide range of major industries – steel works, shipbuilding, mechanical equipment and heavy electrical engineering – as well as lighter industry such as timber processing, textiles and electrical goods. With minor exceptions, its only local fuel is some oil shale and peat, and its only mineral bauxite. The surrounding land grows timber and flax and not much else – nearly all fuel, food and other raw materials have to be brought in from outside.

Key information

Rescue and safety services
Emergency ☏ 112
Rescue at sea
VHF Ch16 working channels 71, 72, call sign *St.Petersburg Rescue Coordination Centre*
☏ +7 812 3274147, +7 812 4958995, +7 812 7188995

Charts and pilot books
British Admiralty and Russian charts cover the area, the latter more detailed and in many cases to a larger scale. Russian charts are essential if planning to take any short cuts across the Nevskaya Guba between Kronshtadt and St Petersburg.

See Appendix page 430 for details of Russian chart coverage.

The Baltic Pilot Volume II (NP 19) More suited to the needs of ships than of yachts.

Cruising Guide to Baltic Russia, Vladimir Ivankiv, Graham and Fay Cattell. Available from the Cruising Association and major suppliers in Scandinavia.

Time
St Petersburg and its environs are on Moscow time - UT+3 all year round.

Money
The Russian currency is the rouble (divided into 100 kopeks), the only legal tender even though Euro and US dollars are highly popular.

Banks and other authorised exchange offices (in hotels, restaurants and some shops) are widespread, and cash advances can also be drawn on most major credit cards, though subject to the usual commission. Roubles can be obtained from ATMs.

Public holidays
Public holidays are flexible, but may occur on:

1 January, 7 January (Russian Orthodox Christmas), 23 February (Defenders of the Motherland, or Men's Day), 8 March (International Women's Day), Easter Sunday (note that Orthodox Easter may not be on the same date as Easter in the West), 1–2 May (International Labour Day), 9 May (Victory Day 1945), 27 May (City Day – St Petersburg only), 12 June (Russian Independence Day), the last 10 days of June (St Petersburg's White Nights – a festival rather than a public holiday), 7 November (Russian Unity Day), 12 December (Russian Constitution Day), 31 December.

Communications
The Russian telephone system is generally good, and mobile phone coverage very good in the St Petersburg area though charges are high. Internet access in the city is available at the Central Telephone Office, as well as at practically all hotels, restaurants and cybercafés.

Card telephones with international dialling are now widely available in St Petersburg. All accept prepaid cards, which can be bought locally, and some also accept Visa or Mastercard.

International calls can usually be made during office hours from the two major yacht clubs, or from the tourist hotels though at much greater cost. To obtain

5. RUSSIA

an international line dial 8, wait for the dial tone, then dial 10 followed by the country code, area code (omitting any initial 0) and number.

The country code for Russia is 7, the city code for St Petersburg and the surrounding area, including Vyborg, is 812 (if dialling from abroad the initial 0 should be omitted).

✈ Travel

St Petersburg and its environs are well served by air, train, coach and ship.

St Petersburg's airport is known as Pulkovo and handles both international and domestic flights. It is located some 17km south of the city. There are direct flights to/from many European cities, including London.

A mainline **railway** connects St Petersburg with Helsinki four times daily using Allegro train taking 3½ hours. Coaches depart several times each day. There is also a direct coach service to Tallinn, Estonia, with four or five departures daily.

Taxis are available everywhere, but taxi drivers are well attuned to the presence of foreign tourists and for major journeys it is as well to arrange a taxi through the yacht club to avoid being charged excessive prices.

🖥 Websites

www.saint-petersburg.com
www.vyborg.ru Very professional Vyborg city homepage

📻 Radio communications

VHF radio is much used for marine communications. See details of requirements under sections on approach and individual harbours.

☁ Weather information

Radio **Navtex** broadcast from Tallinn (identification Station U) is the most reliable means of getting weather information.

No weather bulletins or navigational warnings are currently broadcast for the area via VHF. However it may be possible to obtain a forecast for the St Petersburg Harbour area from the pilot station on VHF Ch 16, 09 and 20.

📄 Formalities

Visas

All visitors require a visa. Most visitors will apply for a tourist visa which can be single or double entry (if wishing to visit both Kaliningrad and St Petersburg, a double entry visa is necessary). Visas are valid for 30 days. NB Passports must have a validity of six months beyond the expected date of departure from Russia and must have at least two blank pages to accommodate the Russian visa. Visas have to be obtained in one's country of residence (thus for example a British citizen permanently living in Sweden may obtain a visa in Sweden or an American citizen permanently living in London may obtain a visa in UK and so on). To obtain a visa it is first necessary to obtain two documents from Russia – a voucher and confirmation, for which a fee has to be paid. These documents are best obtained via an experienced local representative. One such who has acted for visiting yachtsmen over many years is Vladimir Ivankiv ☎ +7 812 510 7602 *Mobile* +7 921 932 5831, email vladimir@sailrussia.spb.ru or vladimirivankiv@yahoo.com (the latter is a reserve address which may not be checked regularly, but could nevertheless be useful if the primary one 'goes down' for any reason).

To obtain a voucher and confirmation (separate documents needed for each visitor) send the following information to the local representative:
- name of yacht
- full name (surname first), date of birth, nationality, passport number and expiry date

- earliest date of arrival
- latest date of departure
- port of arrival and cities to be visited
- email address for return of documents

The skipper must also apply for a berthing reservation.

Having received the voucher and confirmation, the next step is the visa application. In UK, although visas are issued by the Consular Section of the Russian Embassy, applications are handled by the VFS Global Agency. As regulations are subject to change, refer to their website http://ru.vfsglobal.co.uk/ for latest information. A visa application form and guidance are available on this site but note that it is necessary for each individual applicant to visit the agency in person to have their fingerprints taken when delivering their visa application. Passports/visas can be collected by a third party (London and Edinburgh only) or returned by post. Address in London: 15-27 Gee Street, Barbican, London EC1V 3RD. Address in Edinburgh: 64 Albion Road (back entrance), Edinburgh, EH7 5QZ. There is also an address in Manchester (see website).

For citizens of other countries visa application must be made to the Russian Embassy in their country of residence.

Persons staying in the country more than a week + an extra weekend (i.e. 9 days) should register visas with the immigration department. In practice this is not strictly enforced as far as those arriving and departing by yacht are concerned. It does however apply to those leaving by other means of transport e.g. plane, train or ferry.

The British Consulate in St Petersburg is located at PL Proletarskoy Diktatury 5, Smolinskiy Raion, 191124, St Petersburg, ☎ +7 812 320 3200, Fax +7 812 320 3211 ('00' for international calls is not used in Russia) www.gov.uk/government/world/russia. It is open during normal business hours only.

Details of other countries' representation are listed on www.russianembassy.net.

Information required about the boat

The following information about the boat is also required. This should be presented on arrival at Customs and Immigration or, preferably, sent to the local representative so that paperwork can be prepared in advance.
- Boat name
- Manufacturer and model
- LOA, beam, draught (m)
- Registration No.
- Year built
- Flag (ie country of registration)
- Colour of hull
- Sail number (if applicable)
- VHF call sign
- Engine type
- Engine make
- Engine number
- Engine – rated horsepower (hp)
- Home port
- Number of people on board
- Itinerary
- ETA

THE BALTIC SEA AND APPROACHES

In the case of boats overwintered a long distance from the skipper, some information e.g. engine number, may not be immediately available. In such cases, send what information is available to the representative and email the remainder as soon as possible. It would be useful if you could send a scanned copy of the Boat's Certificate of Registry to the representative via email.

Information required about skipper and crew

A quantity of crew lists will be needed. These should contain registration details of the boat, name of captain with date of birth, nationality, passport number and address. Each crew member should be listed with name, date of birth, nationality and passport number. If intending a crew change in St Petersburg list both incoming and outgoing crew. Be aware that a change of skipper is not permitted without serious reason.

Documentation required on arrival

- 3 copies of Crew List
- Passports with visas
- Proof of ownership of the boat (it can be either a Boat's Certificate of Registry or any other document with your name and the name of the boat in it).
- 3 copies of Skipper's Passport (page with photograph and details as well as page with Russian visa)
- 3 copies of the Boat's Certificate of Registry
- General Declaration (this form will be handed to the skipper on arrival).

Other documents which should be carried

- VHF licence and operators' certificate
- Yachtmaster Certificate/International Certificate of Competence

The Skipper is required to declare the following on behalf of all on board:

- the amount of currency (cash, cheques, travellers' cheques) carried (by country if the amount exceeds 10,000 US$ or equivalent)
- spirits, wine, beer, perfumes, cigars, cigarettes and tobacco
- number of baggage items
- certify they are not carrying drugs or firearms – see "Prohibited items".

Prohibited items

The list of substances prohibited for Russia is available on www.erowid.org/psychoactives/law/countries/russia/law_russia_schedules.shtml

Great care should be exercised regarding medicines carried and the contents of medicine chests. Before signing declarations, those on board should show Customs Officers the pills and medicines they hold and enquire if any are banned in Russia. A copy of the prescription or a letter from a doctor should be carried in the case of prescribed medicines.

Note that caviar and plants and flowers in soil are not permitted.

General comments regarding contact with officials

Surveillance is maintained over both foreign and Russian yachts, and most yachts will from time to time be called up on VHF (most likely on Ch 10, 11 or 16) or visited by a patrol boat. Normally a patrol vessel will approach to within 50m or so and ask on VHF for the name and nationality of the yacht, the number of people on board and the last and next ports of call. The first time this happens can be frightening, especially if the patrol vessel approaches without lights on a dark night and, without warning, focuses a powerful searchlight on the yacht. However, given the language problems, patrol vessel captains are not usually aggressive unless they believe that the yacht is being unco-operative.

The customs and immigration procedures on arrival are normally straightforward, provided all paperwork is correct. Yachts are generally boarded by two or three officials and sometimes an agent (if any) who tend to be concerned more with the appropriate forms than with inspecting the boat. Their main concerns are drugs, weapons and illegal migrants.

There are no specific rules restricting the temporary importation of yachts for wintering or repairs but one would be expected to prove the need for repairs to extend the temporary importation period if necessary.

Russian regulations stipulate that an 'agent' must notify the Vyborg Pilot Station or, the Customs Control Post at St Petersburg, or the St Petersburg Coast Information Post at least 24 hours before the yacht's arrival. Vladimir Ivankiv will make the necessary notifications.

Security

This is often a primary concern for those considering a visit to Russia, whether by yacht or conventionally. However modern sources maintain that St Petersburg is no more dangerous than any other large city, even though petty theft such as pocket-picking is rife. All sensible precautions should be taken – avoid carrying large amounts of money, conceal cameras etc inside nondescript, closed bags, be politely wary of over-friendly strangers, etc – but this would be equally true of most of the world's major cities.

Tales of mafia and other business-related crimes are undoubtedly true, but violence is invariably confined to others of the same ilk. A foreign visitor would have to be very unlucky – or unwise – to become caught in the crossfire. Yacht clubs provide 24 hour security and thefts from foreign yachts are extremely rare.

A few guidelines aimed at avoiding complications or embarrassments

- A lost Customs declaration is not replaceable – without it you are allowed to leave Russia with US$3,000, but everything else is subject to confiscation
- Do not take unmarked taxis unless you are with a Russian friend
- Avoid making acquaintances without a Russian friend as intermediary
- Do not visit strangers' homes.

5. RUSSIA

History

Russia as a nation was founded in the 9th century by Swedish Vikings who traded along its rivers to the Black Sea and Constantinople (or Byzantium, now Istanbul). *Rus* is thought to be the Viking word for an oar or oarsman. The Viking leader Rurik founded a base at Novgorod near the Baltic coast in 862AD. Oleg, his successor, moved their capital to Kiev further south, and came to rule a huge Slavic area known then as Kiev-Rus. It was strongly modelled on Constantinople, the capital of the surviving eastern Roman Empire. In 998 Kiev-Rus converted from paganism to Orthodox Christianity, which until 1057 still included the Roman Church.

Between 1223 and 1240 Ghengis Khan's Mongol Horde conquered all of Kiev-Rus up to Novgorod, which was now part of the Hanseatic League. It was still the Golden Age of Islamic civilisation and, as was the Moslem custom, once the ferocious fighting was over, the Mongols educated, and delegated much administrative power, to local rulers of their vassal states. The Russian Prince Alexander Nevsky was thus allowed to recruit an army to halt the Catholic Northern Crusades into Russia. (Rome now saw pagans and Orthodox Christians as equally legitimate targets.)

The centre of Russian power had been pushed northwards from Kiev to Moscow. During the 14th century, when Mongol control of eastern Europe began to decline, Moscow regained more and more of its earlier territory, particularly under Ivan III the Great. His son Ivan IV the Terrible consolidated this autocratic control and declared himself the first Tsar (Caesar) of all the Russians.

The death of Ivan's childless son in 1598 finally brought Rurik's dynasty to an end. There followed a leaderless 'Time of Troubles' when the Polish-Lithuanian Commonwealth from the east and Swedish Gustavus Adolphus from the north made huge inroads into Russian territory. Then in 1613 an assembly of Russian cities elected Michael Romanov, son of the Patriarch of Moscow, to become Tsar, thereby starting the second and final Russian dynasty, which lasted until the Revolution of 1917.

During the 17th century the Romanovs steadily regained much lost ground in the west and new territory in the east. By the beginning of Peter the Great's reign (1672-1725), Russian territory reached the Pacific Ocean, making Russia the largest country in the world, although much of it was unproductive and very under-populated. Russia's only port in the west, however, was Archangel in the Arctic. Peter made a secret alliance with Poland-Lithuania and Denmark to start the Northern War against Sweden, which still controlled most of the Baltic coasts. The outcome was to give Peter both the east and the south of the Gulf of Finland. Russia now replaced Sweden as the dominant power in the Baltic. Peter built St Petersburg as his new capital on the marshes of the Neva River, modelling it on the canals of Amsterdam.

On Peter's death, a series of Tsars and Tsarinas down to Catherine II the Great (1762-96) allowed a degree of liberalism to the nobles and gentry, but the lives of serfs became even worse. Catherine was regarded as an enlightened despot, enthusiastically promoting the arts, the sciences and her liking for handsome young guardsmen, while further restricting the power and wealth of the Orthodox Church and the freedoms of the serfs. In the Wars of Partition, Russia, Austria and Prussia destroyed the huge state of Poland-Lithuania. Russia gained much of central Europe while both Poland and Lithuania ceased to be independent states for over a century.

During the Napoleonic wars Tsar Alexander I changed sides four times. In the process he gained all of Finland from Sweden in 1809. Then after Napoleon's invasion of 1812 he drove Napoleon from Moscow, right back to Paris. Russia was now seen as the Saviour of Europe.

As the 19th century industrial revolution got under way in the rest of Europe, Russia was clearly falling badly behind. There were some reforms, notably the abolition of serfdom in 1861, but any attempt to speed up the process was ruthlessly crushed, leaving bureaucracy and incompetent leadership everywhere. Then in 1917 the communist revolution replaced the old order with one where all the means of production were to be managed by the state on behalf of everybody. The Russian Empire was now the Union of Soviet Socialist Republics. For

Church on the Spilled Blood, St Petersburg *V. Ivankiv*

The Winter Palace,
St Petersburg
V. Ivankiv

all its high ideals, however, communism proved no more effective than the tsars, and perhaps for the same reasons.

In WWII Hitler replayed Napoleon's 1812 invasion with the same outcome. The Nazi war machine was defeated in the east by Soviet troops, while the allies in the west defeated the rest. As the main victor, Russia now imposed communism on the nine subject countries in eastern Europe that it had captured, with corresponding damage to their economies. The whole Soviet communist system finally collapsed in 1991 and the Soviet Union was dissolved.

The people, the church and the language

Within the borders of what is now Russia there are many groups with customs, habits and languages quite different from those of the northwestern Russian. The Russian Federation contains, for instance, sixteen autonomous republics, five autonomous regions and ten autonomous areas, all based on ethnic differences. St Petersburg in particular is a cosmopolitan city where members of these groups may be encountered at any time, together with nationals of republics lying outside the Russian Federation.

With the abolition of communism as the state orthodoxy, the Russian Orthodox Church has enjoyed a major revival and now has more than 17,000 priests and 450 monasteries throughout the country as a whole. Churches and cathedrals are amongst the finest buildings in all Russia's Baltic cities, though many suffered vandalism during the Soviet era.

Cruising information

The attractions of a cruise to Baltic Russia have traditionally been principally concerned with St Petersburg, but there are several other possibilities, particularly since foreign vessels are now permitted to visit specified harbours on the north coast of the Gulf of Finland, albeit under strict conditions. The major condition is that checking in and out of Russia is permitted only at Vyborg, St Petersburg and, for those wishing to visit the Saimaa Lakes, at Brusnitchnoe. If wishing to visit any of the seven harbours on the way east to St Petersburg, the yacht must have checked in at Vyborg on the way. To visit on the way back west, do not check out when leaving St Petersburg but do so at Vyborg after visiting the harbours. In all cases ensure that the Russian Coast Guard is fully aware of intentions (this is best done via Vladimir Ivankiv - see contact details on page 320). Note that yachts are not permitted to stop at any harbours other than those listed.

Restricted areas

Currently there are three Prohibited Areas (PA) which must not be entered at any time. These are Nos. 75 and 78 marked on the plan on page 318 and No. 110 NE of the St Peterburgskiy buoy marked on the plan on page 330. All are outside official channels so should not prove a problem.

There are also four Firing Practice Areas (FPA) where firing times are announced on NAVTEX and VHF Ch 16. These are Nos. 3, 105, 107 and 114 each of which is marked on the plan on page 318.

All these Areas are shown on current charts and can be verified by Vladimir Ivankiv in advance or by VHF Ch 16 on entering Russian waters.

Firing range 107
Southeast of Bjorkesund Strait
60°10'.00N 28°45'.0E
60°07'.00N 28°34'.0E
60°04'.00N 28°34'.0E
60°04'.00N 28°55'.0E
60°10'.00N 28°55'.0E

Firing range 105
Southeast of Bjorkesund Strait
60°03'.5N 29°00'.00E
60°03'.5N 29°15'.00E
60°08'.0N 29°15'.00E
60°08'.0N 29°00'.00E

Firing range 114
East of Gogland Island
60°06'.3N 27°02'.5E
60°07'.5N 27° 07'.0E
60°03'.5N 27°11'.0E
60°02'.0N 27°06'.5E

5. RUSSIA

Caution
When sailing in the eastern Baltic, and particularly the shallow Nevskaya Guba, it is important to be aware that although the area has no daily tidal rise and fall, depths can vary considerably from those charted as a result of sustained strong winds from west or east. Changes of more than a metre in a few hours are not unusual. In addition to this, prolonged high pressure may result in a further decrease of up to 0·5m on charted depths.

Yacht services and chandlery
In St Petersburg there are several chandleries, sail lofts and workshops where general repairs can be carried out. The Central River Yacht Club in St Petersburg (CRYC) has facilities for sailmaking and general repairs (though electronic skills are limited); there is also a chandlers, mostly selling imported equipment.

Holding tanks
As yet there are no requirements for holding tanks and there are no pump out stations.

Gas
Gas bottles are unobtainable and refilling is also not possible.

Diesel
Diesel is available at CRYC very much cheaper than elsewhere in the Baltic.

Shopping
Current EU sanctions have strongly affected what is available in the shops. Imported goods including food are scarce or non existent and local producers have raised their prices.

Many shops now accept credit cards, though this should never be assumed. Shopping falls into several categories:

- Western shops, though only a few are actually run by Western companies. Almost anything is available, though prices are expensive in line with Scandinavia as a whole. Credit cards are generally welcome.
- Local super (and hyper)markets which carry good quality food at reasonable prices, clothes shops and boutiques and European-type hardware stores sometimes with a chandlery section. Most still accept cash (roubles) only, though an increasing number accept credit cards. All hypermarkets and most supermarkets accept credit cards as well as cash (roubles only) but some checkouts may not have card terminals available so check before choosing a particular checkout.
- Kiosks by the thousand, with tempting prices but often poor quality (check for sell-by dates). Alcohol in particular should NEVER be bought at a kiosk. However, if looking for a souvenir, the selection of nesting matryoshka dolls is immense and some bartering is generally acceptable.
- Markets sell meat, fruit, vegetables etc, usually of acceptable quality. Prices are often adjusted upwards when foreigners appear, so again it may be possible to bargain – always assuming that the language barrier can be overcome. Bags may not be provided.

There are several large DIY chains where tools and general hardware items can be purchased.

Alcohol
Alcohol is easily available in shops and supermarkets. The alcohol limit for those in charge of a leisure craft is 16mg.

Yacht clubs
In Russia most clubs remain owned by organisations such as town councils, local business enterprises, trade unions or the military, though others are being privatised. They employ full-time staff for administrative and technical work, frequently have their own boatyard facilities including sailmaking, and often have round the clock security.

Approach to Russia
Baltic Russia can be reached from Estonia or from Finland.

If coming from or returning to Estonia
Because Russian rules dictate that vessels sailing from Estonia must join the shipping lane which starts south east of Gogland Island, this route is less favoured. It also means that there is no point in sailing further east along the Estonian coast than Vergi. However, it is recommended to clear out at either Tallinn (No 12 border post) or Vergi. These posts are not permanently manned so arrangements for clearance need to be made in advance – it is recommended to call the Estonian Police and Border Guard helpdesk on ☏ +372 612 3000 or +372 637 7440.

If coming from or returning to Finland
Here there is a choice of routes – from Helsinki, Haapasaari or Santio:

From Helsinki clear out with Customs and Immigration, follow the coastline and join the shipping lane south of Gogland Island.

From Haapasaari, clear out with the Finnish Border Guards, cross the buoyed border between buoys 15 and 16, go south of Sommers Island to join the shipping lane.

From Santio (most useful if visiting Vyborg and the other harbours and/or wishing to sail via Bjorkesund). Cross the border between Kozlinyj and Kopytin Islands to join the Saimaa Channel. For Vyborg, continue with the Saimaa Channel. For St Petersburg leave the Viipuriin Light to port and head for Bjorkesund. Leaving Bjorkesund head for the main shipping lane and proceed to Kronshtadt. Contact Primorsk Traffic on VHF Ch 68 when entering and leaving Bjorkesund.

VYBORG (VIIPURI)

Vyborg (Finnish: Viipuri)

60°42'·58N 28°43'·73E centre of final approach channel

Distances
Helsinki 130M, Kotka 65M, Haapasaari Island 60M, Santio Island 40M, Kronshtadt 95M, St Petersburg 110M

Charts
UKHO 2264, 2259, 2260, 3813
For Russian and Finnish charts see diagrams, Appendix page 430

Lights
Ostrov Khalli 60°24'·2N 28°08'·3E Fl.4s16m9M
   Red metal framework tower, concrete base 12m
Ostrov Rondo 60°27'·4N 28°21'·6E Fl.WRG.1·5s14m9–5M
   063°-G-068°-W-077°-R-128°-G-162°-W-183°-R-201°-G-214°-W-234°-R-252°-W-063° White rectangle, black stripe, on red framework tower 10m
Vyborgskiy 60°31'·6N 28°22'·7E Fl(2)8s14m10M Whis
   White octagonal tower, red bands 10m
Lotsmanskiy lightbuoy 60°34'·5N 27°24'·5E LFl.6s Red and white pillar buoy, • topmark
Povorotnyy, N point 60°34'·5N 28°25'·6E
   Fl.WRG.1·5s18m7–2M shore-G-359°-W-009°-R-020°-G-029°-W-231° 239°-G-249°-W-255°-R-270° White octagonal tower, red lantern 13m
Ostrov Igrivyy buoy 60°35'N 28°28'·75E Q(6)+LFl.15s
   South cardinal lightbuoy Yellow and black pillar
Vysotskiy-Yuzhnyy breakwater head 60°36'·7N 28°33'·2E
   Fl(2)6·5s8m3M Green tower, white band
Leading lights Five sets of leading lights plus many lit buoys guide a vessel through the Vysotsk narrows into the Vyborgskiy Morskoy Kanal, the buoyed channel leading to the junction of the Saimaa canal approach with the Vyborg final approach (see plan)
Dybovyy 60°40'·2N 28°38'·9E
   Fl.G.2s6m2M Green column 3m
Saymenskiy 60°41'·9N 28°42'·8E Iso.Y.2s8m3M White column, red stripe 4m
Vyborg Severnyy 60°42'·6N 28°44'·1E Oc.R.3s23m4M
   White rectangle, red stripe, on white round concrete tower 9m
Many more lights and lit buoys exist in the approaches and harbour area.

Communications
Vyborg VTS Controller ☎ +7 812 789 3244
   VHF Ch 12 (call *Vyborg Radio 5*)
Vyborg Pilot Service ☎ +7 812 783 3449/93266
   VHF Ch 10, 74 (call *Vyborg Pilots*)
Vyborg Harbourmaster ☎ +7 812 782 0477/789 9650
   VHF Ch 12, 16
Vyborg Radio VHF Ch 02, 16, 24

General

For centuries Vyborg was Finland's second most important town and cultural centre. Already a trading centre in the 12th century, it later became a port of the Hanseatic League and was attacked by Russia at least four times during the 14th and 15th centuries. By the 18th century it was held by Peter the Great as part of his programme to consolidate his grip on St Petersburg. In 1812 it became part of Finland, then under Russian control, and benefited greatly from the opening of the Saimaa Canal in 1856. The port still handles timber, agricultural products, minerals and ironware.

Vyborg reverted to Russia following fierce fighting – and major damage – during the Second World War. Almost all the Finnish population were evacuated and the city resettled by Russians from elsewhere in the country, with a current population of around 80,000. Both the castle and the large and attractive Park Monrepo Reserve, beyond the bridge, are worth exploring.

Approach

All foreign vessels, including yachts, are required to inform Vyborg at least two hours before entering Russian waters. Details of the necessary telephone numbers and/or VHF channels should be obtainable from a number of sources including the Finnish Frontier Guard, the Board of Management of the Saimaa Canal (see page 313), or Vladimir Ivankiv (page 320). Russian visas are not required if only visiting the Saimaa Lakes but are required for a visit to Vyborg. Leaving the Saimaa Channel the final approach is via the main Vyborg fairway on course 24.8° turning to port to enter the port and proceed towards the castle. It is recommended to use the engine. The Immigration and Customs control berth is quay 2 (60°42'·79N 28°43'·67E).

Berthing

There are three possibilities in Vyborg all with the Favorit Yacht Club.

General facilities

Vyborg is reported to have several restaurants where good meals can be had for very reasonable prices. Maps of the city and surrounding area are available from the bookstore at Pr Lenina 6.

Vyborg Favorit YC with Customs Quay in background
Vladimir Ivankiv

THE BALTIC SEA AND APPROACHES

5. RUSSIA

OUTER APPROACHES TO VYBORG

VYBORG

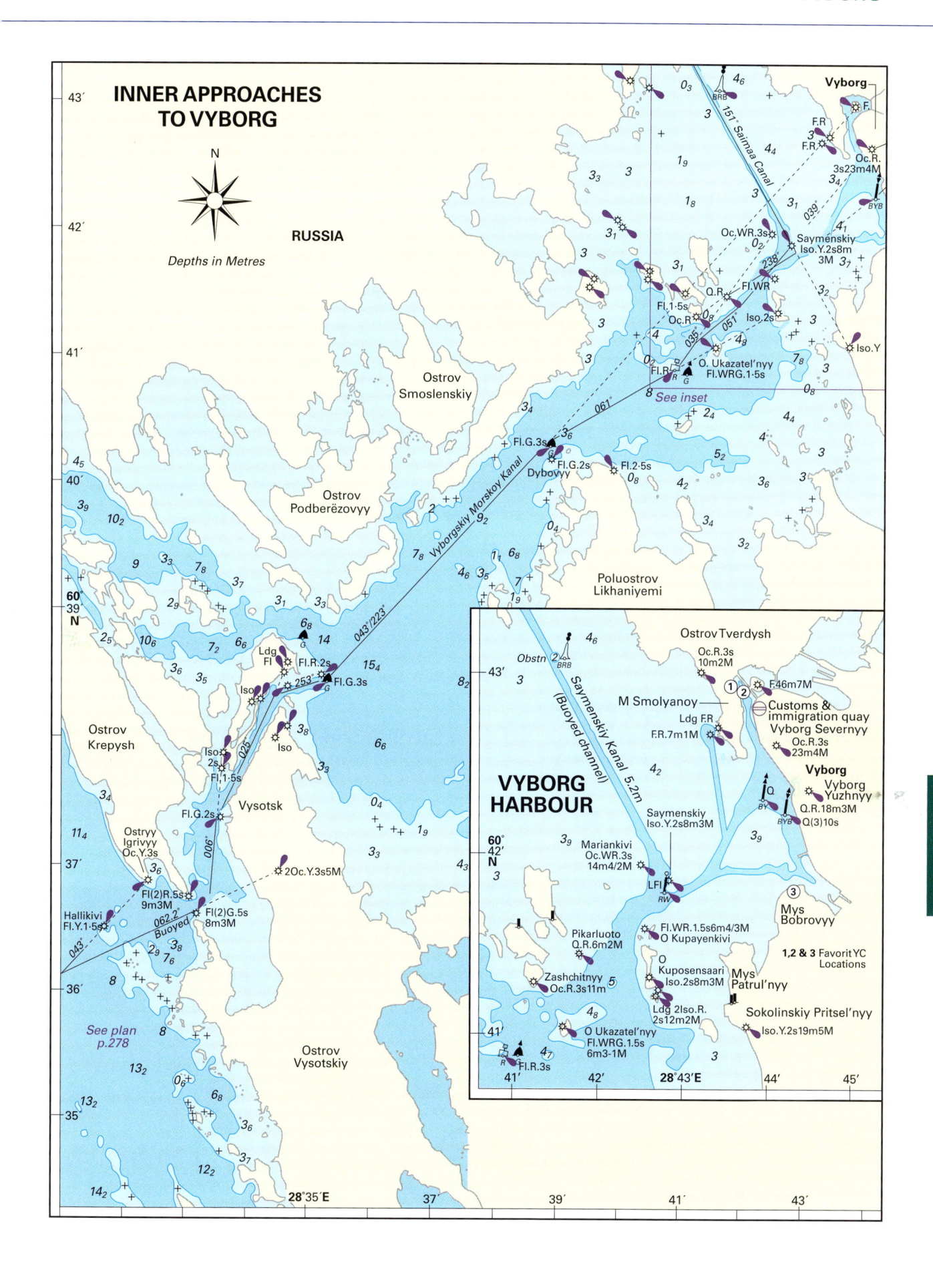

INNER APPROACHES TO VYBORG

VYBORG HARBOUR

5. RUSSIA

Vyborg, 2 Favorit YC left, Customs Quay middle, and 1 Favorit YC right *Vladimir Ivankiv*

Communications and travel

Vyborg is on the mainline railway between Helsinki and St Petersburg, and also on the principal coach and bus route. Trains to St Petersburg depart nearly every hour, taking about three hours for the journey.

1 & 2. Favorit YC (formerly the Vyborg Sea Yacht Club)

60°42'·90N 28°43'·62E general location of moorings
☎ +7 (813) 782 4536

There are mooring places both to port and starboard within the harbour (berthing 1 and 2). The starboard moorings below the castle are nearest to the city but have less facilities and security. Berthing reservation required.

3. Favorit YC (Mys Bobovyy)

60°41'·85N 28°44'·17E yacht moorings
☎ +7 (813) 789 9708

This is an exposed pontoon, some 2km from the city thus less attractive to visitors. Berthing reservation required.

Lavola Yacht Club Harbour

60°46'·33N 28°41'·97E
☎ +7 (931) 210 3832

This harbour is of most use for anyone going to check out in the Saimaa Canal. It is not possible to check in or out at Lavola – this harbour cannot be visited unless the yacht is already checked into Russia.

Lavola *Vladimir Ivankiv*

HARBOURS BETWEEN VYBORG AND ST PETERSBURG

Approaching Primorsk Yacht Pier Vladimir Ivankiv

Permitted harbours between Vyborg and St Petersburg

Johannes Marina
60°31'·53N 28°39'·34E
HM *mobile* +7 (911) 000 7531
Watchman ☎ +7 (911) 923 7330
http://johannes-port.ru/maps/23--johannes-info-map.html

It is necessary to call up the harbourmaster or watchman before arrival. A modern development close to the town of Sovetskij and reached by a circuitous route from Bjorkesund.

Primorsk Yacht Pier 29a
60°21'·81N 28°36'·64E
☎ +7 (911) 119 0287 or +7 (911) 002 2092.

Caution 2m draught limitation at the yacht berths. It is necessary to call in advance.

Bukhta Dubkovaya Yacht Club
60°14'·07N 28°59'·66E
HM ☎ +7(911) 928 0868

Berth reservation is required well in advance. Also call up when approaching the harbour. If the harbourmaster is not available call the hotel on ☎ +7(901) 300 4560. Modern development with usual facilities and restaurant.

Approaching Bukhta Dubkovaya Vladimir Ivankiv

Terijoki Yacht Club
60°11'·21N 29°42'·17E
☎ +7 (812) 611 0300 or +7 921 942 3845
VHF Ch 16, 72
www.yct.ru

Terijoki is the Finnish name for the town now called Zelenogorsk.

Vessels are required to be under engine in both approach channel and harbour.

On approach contact Harbourmaster on VHF Ch 16, 72 for permission to enter harbour. Usual facilities and access to fitness centre. Culture park with cafés, restaurants.

Primorsk yacht moorings Vladimir Ivankiv

Terijoki Yacht Club Vladimir Ivankiv

5. RUSSIA

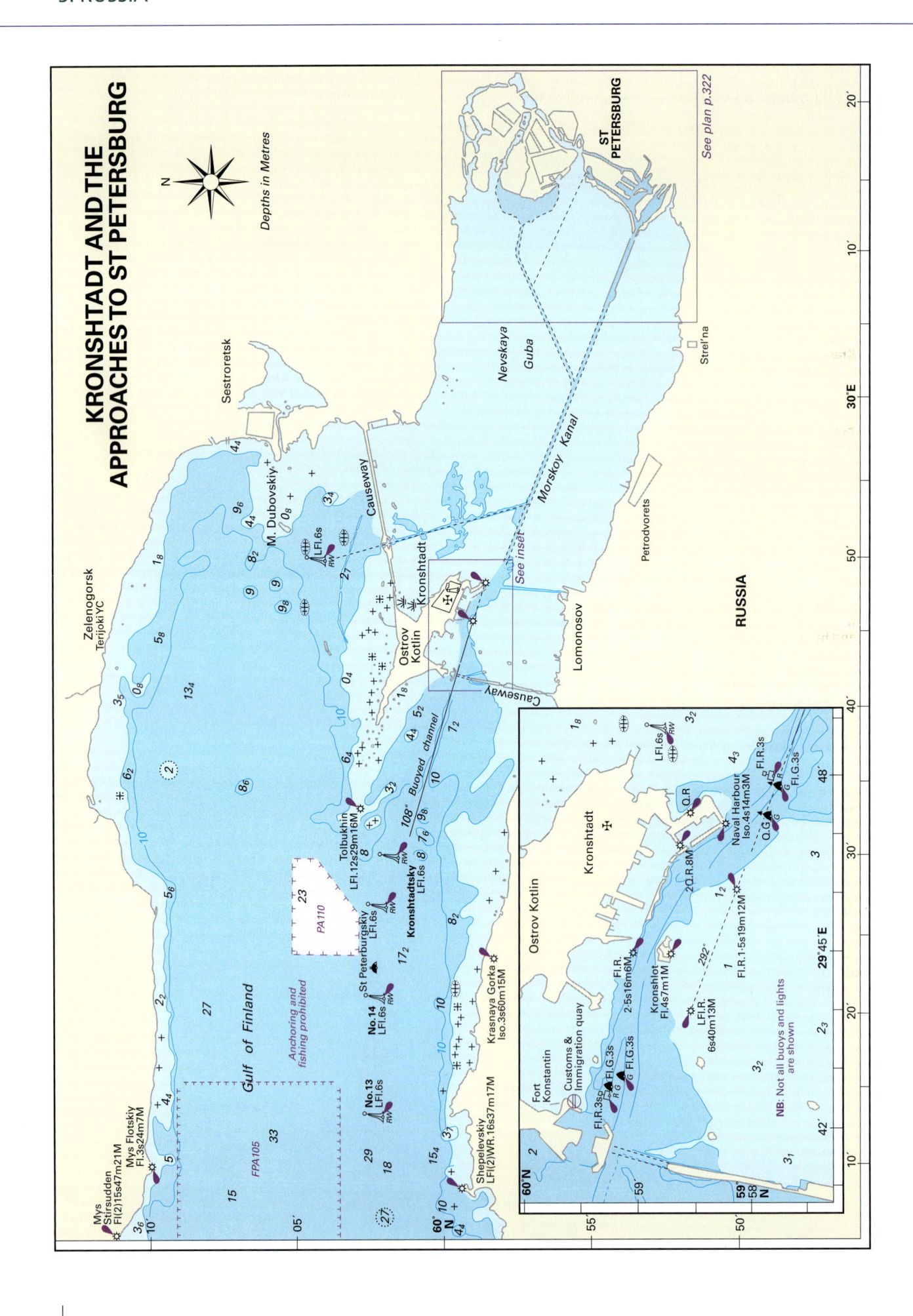

KRONSHTADT AND THE APPROACHES TO ST PETERSBURG

330 THE BALTIC SEA AND APPROACHES

ST PETERSBURG

St Petersburg

59°59'·55N 29°41'·33E centre of entrance through causeway at Fort Konstantin

Distances
Helsinki 175M, Tallinn 185M, Haapasaari Island 95M, Santio Island 85M, Vyborg 110M

Charts
UKHO 2264, 2395
For Russian and Finnish charts see the diagrams on page 430

Lights
Shepelevskiy 59°59'·5N 29°08'E LFl(2)WR.16s37m14M Round white stone tower, red bands. 053°-R-100°-W-265°-R-280°
Krasnaya Gorka 59°58'·4N 29°23'·2E Iso.3s60m15M Red rectangle, white stripe on red metal framework tower 38m
Buoy Sankt Peterburgskiy 60°01'·5N 29°29'·8E LFl.6s Red and white pillar buoy, B topmark
Tolbukhin 60°02'·5N 29°32'·7E LFl.12s29m16M Round white stone tower and building.
Kronshtadt Naval Harbour, south elbow 59°58'·2N 29°47'·3E Iso.4s14m3M 218°-vis-150° Red framework tower 12m
Severnaya Damba (north breakwater) 59°54'·3N 30°05'·7E Fl.R.1·5s11m3M White column, red bands, on base 9m
Yuzhnaya Damba (south breakwater) 59°54'·1N 30°05'·9E Fl.G.1·5s11m3M White column, red bands, on base 9m. There are Leading Lts on 108° through the barrier at Kronshtadt
Many more lights and lit buoys exist in the approaches and harbour area

Communications
St Petersburg Port Traffic Control Centre
 ☏ +7 812 251 0290, VHF Ch 09
St Petersburg Radar Guidance System (RASKAT)
 VHF Ch 12
St Petersburg Vessel Movements Control System
 VHF Ch 16, 78
St Petersburg Customs and Border Control
 VHF Ch 06 (call *Granit*). Call when in the vicinity of the Sankt Peterburgskiy lightbuoy, giving ETA St Petersburg
St Petersburg Port Authority ☏ +7 812 118 8951
 VHF Ch 09, 16, 26

General

St Petersburg, with an estimated 5.2 million inhabitants, is the second largest city in Russia. It is built on a complex of waterways, and is a grand and spacious city. It is justifiably recognised as the cultural capital of Russia – few cities in the world have art galleries, concert halls, museums and theatres which can compare with those of St Petersburg.

No visitor should miss the Hermitage (the Winter Palace), which undoubtedly contains one of the world's greatest collections of art treasures, nor the Russian Museum, actually an art gallery. The Peter and Paul Fortress, the cruiser Aurora, St Isaac's Cathedral, the Admiralty, Chesma Church, Kazanski Cathedral, Smolny Cathedral, the St Petersburg Philharmonia and the Kirov Theatre, to name a few, are very special and deserve a visit. A pocket guidebook such as St Petersburg in the Lonely Planet series will prove invaluable. A few miles outside the city are the resplendent Peterhof summer palace with its wonderful fountains and gilded statuary and Tsarskoye Selo, Catherine's Palace with its world famous Amber Room.

Peterhof can be reached by hydrofoil from behind the Hermitage while Tsarskoye Selo can be reached either by local train from Vitebski Station or by shuttle buses 342, 287, 347a from 'Moskovskaya' Metro Station (Blue Line).

Foreign yachtsmen, especially yachtsmen from Western Europe, are still few and far between. In consequence they receive a warm welcome, and the facilities at the Central River Yacht Club are now much improved.

Approach and entrance

Approach from the Gulf of Finland, either via Bjorkesund or the main shipping channel. For route via Bjorkesund see Approach to Russia page 324.

For approach via the main shipping channel - approach south of Ostrov Gogland via the Sommers big ship channel 'roundabout' at 60°11'·5N 27°46'·00E and Ostrov Seskar 60°04'·00N 28°20'·00E observing traffic separation lanes throughout (see plan page 318). A well-buoyed channel leads past the Sankt Peterburgskiy Landfall buoy and thence south of Ostrov Kotlin, at the eastern end of which lies the city of Kronshtadt. The route is fringed by various prohibited and restricted areas, and care should be taken to remain within the buoyed channel.

When approaching Kronshtadt yachts should contact the local Coastguard Post on VHF Ch 6, callsign *Granit* (pronounced Graneeet), to inform them of the name of the boat and the destination, St Petersburg, even though the boat's agent will have already informed the coastguard.

A pilot vessel, St Petersburg, is often stationed off the Sankt Peterburgskiy lightbuoy but Port Regulations do not require yachts to take a pilot at any stage of the approach detailed here.

Customs and Immigration procedures are carried out at Fort Konstantin on Kotlin Island. The naval port city of Kronshtadt is also located on Kotlin Island.

Kotlin Island lies just off the entrance to the Nevskaya Guba which could be described as a large bay with St Petersburg situated at its head. The island is now joined to the mainland by two causeways which, with the island, form a protective barrier to the city. There is only one entrance through the causeway, close to Fort Konstantin (see plan page 330.

Note that the Customs and Immigration post at the Passenger Terminal is now regarded as an auxiliary post for yachts and can be used if the authorities so decide. However, unless instructed to go elsewhere, all yachts should report to Fort Konstantin.

After clearance, it is possible to berth in the harbour at Fort Konstantin if wishing to explore Kronshtadt.

THE BALTIC SEA AND APPROACHES

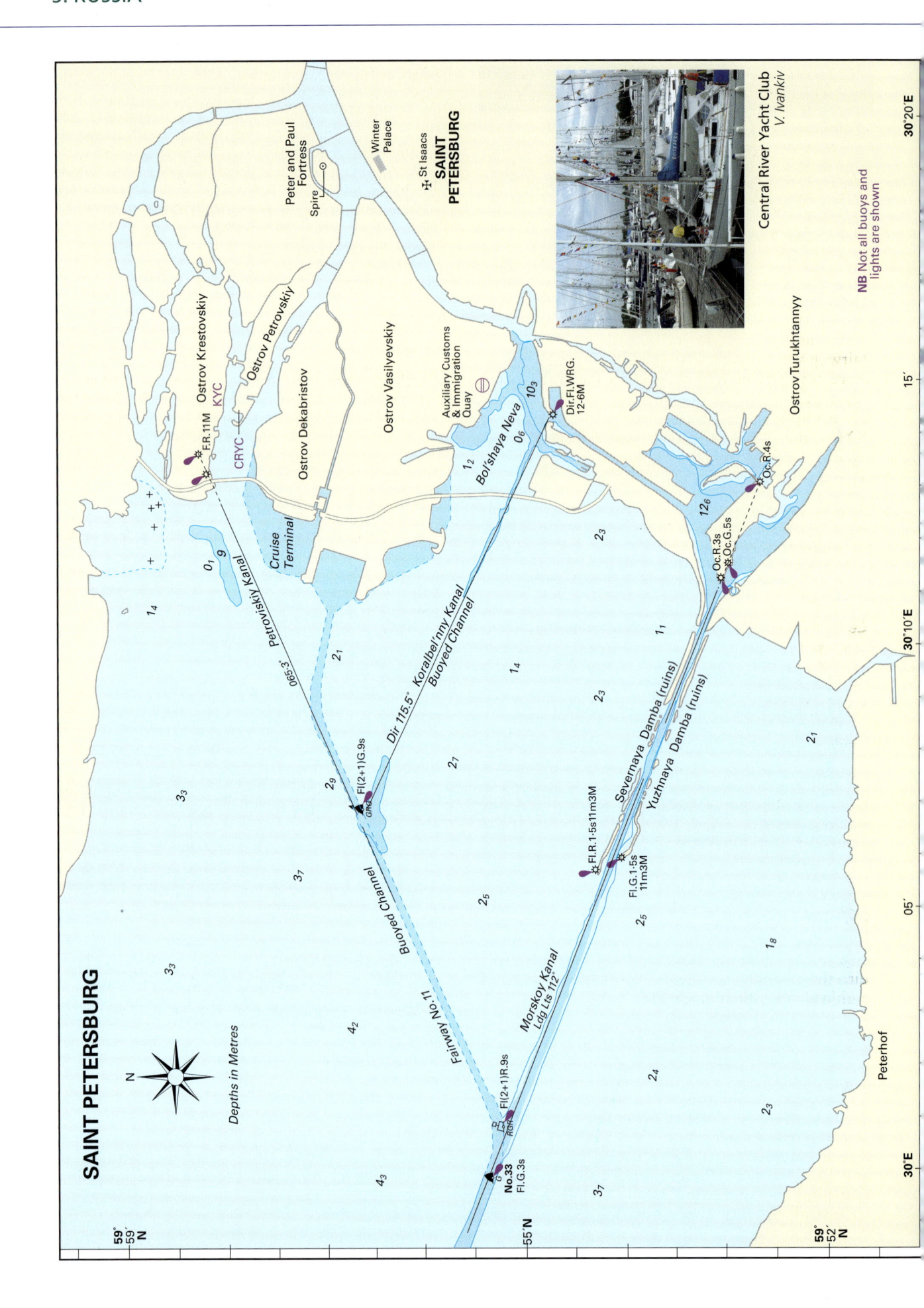

5. RUSSIA

SAINT PETERSBURG

Central River Yacht Club
V. Ivankiv

NB Not all buoys and lights are shown

ST PETERSBURG

In theory, yachts are permitted to berth at any of the St Petersburg yacht clubs but in practice many are not suitable due to their location distant from the sights, inaccessibility to masted craft because of bridges or possible lack of facilities. Central River Yacht Club (CRYC) and Krestovski Yacht Club (KYC) are considered the most suitable and most visiting yachts berth at one or the other.

From Kronshtadt to CRYC and KYC

Once past Kronshtadt take the Deep Sea Channel (Morskoy Kanal) to buoy 33 at **59°55'·17 30°00'·60E**, then change course to 65·3° (two fixed red Ldg Lts in line) to the GRG buoy at **59°56'·7N 30°06'·6E**. Continue on the same course to the end of the fairway when a direct course can be set along the more northerly buoyed channel for the north-facing entrance of the CRYC avoiding the sandbanks created by the Neva River. Alternatively, head for the KYC which is located on the opposite bank of the Malaya Neva.

Anchorage

Anchoring is not prohibited outside the port area, the buoyed channels and the military areas around Kronshtadt. However there are no viable anchorages.

Berthing

Central River Yacht Club (CRYC)

59°57'·96N 30°14'·27E centre of entrance
Petrovskaya Kosa 9, St Petersburg 197110
☎ +7 812 235 6636
yachtclubspb@gmail.com
http://spbryc.ru/ (In Russian, open with Google Translate)

Situated on the western part of Ostrov Petrovskiy. The CRYC is largest yacht club in St Petersburg and one of the largest in Russia, with seven pontoons of up to 50m in length in its main harbour, a southern work harbour, and a separate guest harbour at the western tip of the island, next to which stands the easily identified clubhouse. The approach is straightforward. Depths are normally around 3m, and the guest harbour pontoons have water and electricity, with toilets and showers ashore, plus a kiosk and restaurant. There is good access to the city, including a nearby trolleybus which runs directly to the Nevsky Prospekt, and a metro station within about a 20 minute walk.

Krestovski Yacht Club (KYC)

59°57'·97N 30°14'·78E yacht moorings

This yacht club is located east of CRYC on the opposite bank of the Malaya Neva. Good facilities. Restaurants within a short walk. Access to the city by metro – nearest metro station about 10 min walk. Only disadvantage is the nearby disco club which can be rather vibrant. Berth reservation required, particularly for craft over 20m long.

Visitors are recommended not to drink tap water without boiling it first – arrive with tanks full of Finnish or Estonian water, or buy bottled. This also applies to tooth brushing.

General facilities

St Petersburg offers cafés and restaurants at all levels, as well as street stalls selling blinis (pancakes) and all kinds of breads and pastries. City tours and guided visits to the many museums, art galleries and churches can usually be arranged for modest fees through the yacht clubs, or consult Vladimir Ivankiv. Tickets for the Kirov Theatre are extremely difficult to obtain through official channels, but are often obtainable outside the theatre immediately before the performance. Performances at the famous Philharmonia and other concert halls can usually be booked at the box office.

For medical care try:
American Medical Centre ☎ +7 (495) 933 7700
American Cardiovascular Centre ☎ +7 812 558 8797
Euromed Clinic ☎ +7 812 327 0301
International Clinic ☎ +7 812 320 3870

Krestovski YC, Central River YC in background *V. Ivankiv*

The Central River Yacht Club entrance *T. Gunnersen*

THE BALTIC SEA AND APPROACHES   333

6. Poland

The Polish coastline, which stretches for some 180 miles, is largely low lying with few features but there are harbours suitable for yachts every 30 to 50 miles and the unspoilt country is interesting. There are two regions of particular appeal to the cruising yachtsman – the inland 'Zalew Szczeciński' area between Świnoujście, Szczecin and Dziwnów, adjacent to the German border, and the Gdańsk/Gdynia area in the extreme east, just short of the border with Russian Kaliningrad.

The inland seas between and around Świnoujście and Szczecin provide areas of sheltered-water sailing. There are a number of attractive fishing harbours and several yacht harbours, many of which have been considerably upgraded. It is possible to cross the border from (or into) Germany via the Peenestrom.

In contrast, Gdynia is a major city and container port and has a well-equipped yacht harbour with some of the best facilities – and certainly the best chandleries – in Poland. Between these two areas lie some half dozen small harbours, several of which have either fully-fledged marinas or at least some provision for visiting yachts. The jewel in the crown, however, is Gdańsk. Nothing can beat berthing in the centre of this lovely UNESCO city beneath the impressive black crane, having wound your way down the canals of the 'Solidarnosc' shipyards.

There has been massive investment in infrastructure and Poland can now lay claim to being a Baltic cruising ground with excellent marinas in its own right rather than simply a curiosity for a few intrepid yachtsmen. German, Scandinavians, and occasionally British yachtsmen are cruising in Poland in increasing numbers. The Poles themselves have started to embrace yachting and indeed have begun to fill their own marinas with local boats, which can leave visitors short of space.

However, it remains a tricky coastline. Several ports have very narrow entrances which have been channelled through the adjacent beach and are prone to silting. Surprisingly large ships can suddenly emerge in these narrow canal entrances and therefore calling the port prior to entry is not only advised but is sometimes obligatory. Winds above F4 with any northing in them can make some entrances untenable. Strong cross winds can also make some of these artificial entrances tricky with a strong set across the entrance for which the helm must make allowance. Breakwaters have been extended and marinas much improved, but surge and groundswell can be a major issue, both at the entrance and in the marinas. You should be prepared to divert if necessary. Rønne on Bornholm is the Polish sailors' favoured port for diversion. The ubiquitous and jolly 'pirate ships' which take day trippers out to sea in clement conditions are a useful indicator that the entrance is tenable.

On looking at charts of the north coast one sees quite large areas of inland water adjacent to the coast but all of them apart from the Zalew Szczeciński are too shallow for vessels drawing more than half a metre.

There are military ranges along the coast, as well as offshore exercise areas which are restricted when in use – dates and times are broadcast on VHF and are also available from the local harbour authorities.

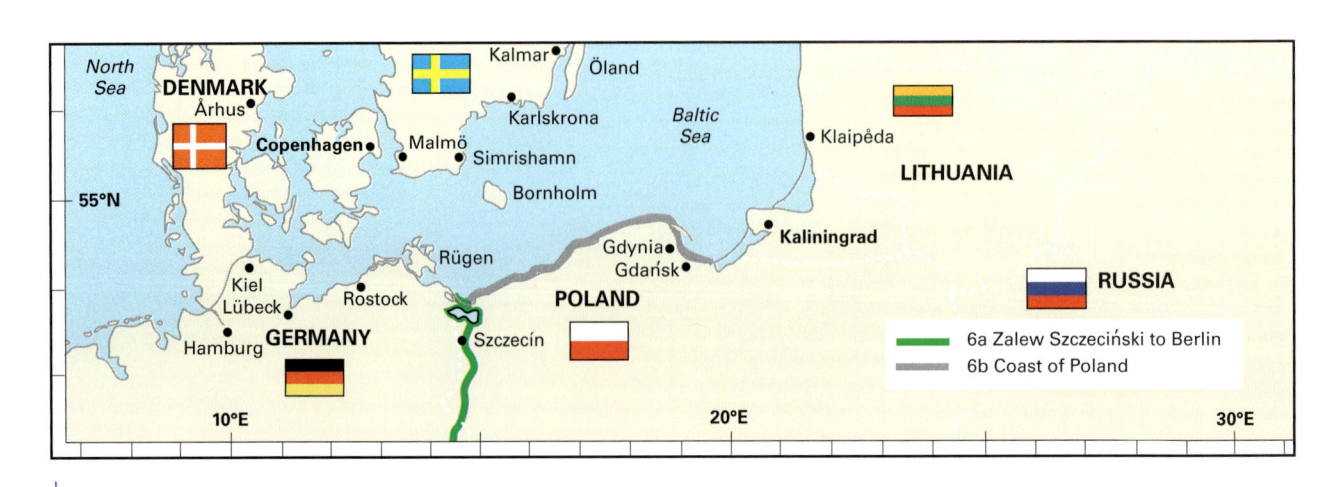

334 THE BALTIC SEA AND APPROACHES

POLAND - KEY INFORMATION

Key information

⚑ Rescue/Safety services

Emergency ☎ 112 (This is the emergency number for all EU countries)

Rescue SAR and Lifeboat stations monitor VHF Ch16. CH 11 is the SAR working channel

⊕ 📖 Charts, pilots and cruising guides

UKHO and Polish charts cover the coast adequately for passage making but it will be necessary to obtain Polish or German charts for detailed coverage of the smaller harbours. Those charts which are specific to an area or harbour are listed under individual harbour details. See the Appendix, page 419, for sources.

UKHO charts may be obtained from Smart Co Ltd, ☎ +48 91 488 33 79, Gdynia & Szczecin offices. Szczecin@smart.gda.pl, www.smart.gda.pl

Polish charts and other nautical publications can be obtained from Biuro Hydrograficzne Marynarki wojenej in Gdynia. ☎ +48 58 626 3283 sprzedaz.wydawnictw@bhmw.mw.mil.pl http://hopn.mw.mil.pl

The German Hydrographic Office (BSH) *Small Craft Pack 3020* is very useful for navigation of the Zalew Szczeciński from Świnoujście to Dziwnów and up the Odra River to Szczecin, and Pack 3021 covers the rest of Poland from Świnoujście to Gdańsk. Pack 3007 covers the western German part Zalew Szczeciński and the approach to it through the Peenestrom which are not covered by an UKHO chart. These can be obtained (with other nautical publications) from Sail-Ho who have a shop in Gdynia marina www.sklep.sail-ho.pl ☎ +48 609 105 163

Mapa Zeglarska (full name Mapa Zeglarska Zalewu Szczecińskiego, Kamienskiego i J Dabie) – a useful and detailed chart on a scale of 1: 85,000 which covers western Polish waters as far east as Dziwnów. Also contains information on customs and immigration, buoyage, VHF channels and telephone numbers, plus some photographs. In Polish, with English and German translations

Baltic Pilot Volume II (NP 19) – the British Admiralty pilot book for this area in English, but written with big ships in mind rather than yachts.

Cruising Guide to Poland 2015 by Nicholas Hill, published by the Cruising Association.

Küstenhandbuch Polen und Litauen by Jörn Heindrich, published by Delius Klasing.

The Sejlerens marina guide, No. 5 See www.sejlerens.com

Hafenhandbuch Polen, DSV, Delius Klasing

The Cruising Almanac Imray/Cruising Association www.imray.com

⌚ Time

Poland uses UT+1 in winter and UT+2 in summer (from the last Sunday in March until the Saturday before the last Sunday in September).

zł Money

The Polish unit of currency is the złoty, divided into 100 groszy. Currency can be readily exchanged at most banks or at bureaux de change (*kantor* in Polish) within the major shopping areas, and ATMs (cash dispensers) are also widely available. Now that Poland has joined the EU there is talk of her joining the Euro but it has not happened yet (2017).

📄 Formalities

Poland is a member of the EU and of the Schengen Area (see main Introduction page 7 for details of Schengen requirements).

Visas are not required for EU passport holders, nor for citizens of the USA.

Yachts coming from a non-Schengen area country (or if there are people on board who hold non-EU passports) should report to a passport office. In practice this means only the larger ports which have ferry services from other Baltic countries. Arriving yachts may be hailed by an official asking for their last port of call.

The yachts registration papers, radio licence, insurance documents, and International Certificate of Competence (or equivalent) are required..

The Polish flag is equal parts of white over red.

Polish Embassy, London
47 Portland Place, London W1B 1JH
☎ 0207 291 3520
London@mfa.gov.pl
http://london.polemb.net/

Polish Helpdesk
Informacja Celna-Ministerstwo Finansów
ul. Świętokrzyska 12, 00-916, Warszawa, Poland ☎ +48 (22)6943194,6943091
Informacja.Celna@mofnet.gov.pl

The Polish Visa Section, 10 Bouverie Street, London EC4Y 8AX, ☎ 0207 8228 900.

The British Embassy in Warsaw can be contacted on ☎ +48 22 311 0000
www.gov.uk/government/world/poland

☼ Public holidays

1 January, Easter Monday, 1 May (Labour Day), 3 May (Constitution Day), Ascension Day, Corpus Christi (60 days after Easter), 15 August (Assumption Day), 1 November (All Saints Day), 11 November (Independence Day), 25 and 26 December (Christmas Day and Boxing Day)

Peak summer holiday time is July to mid-August

☎ Communications

The country's telephone code is (00)48. Great strides have been made during the past decade in modernising the telephone system. Mobile phone and 3G coverage is also good, and internet access is now widely available. National and international calls can be made from public call boxes, requiring cards available from shops or the post office (poczta). To obtain an international line, dial 00 followed by the country code, area code (omitting any initial 0) and number. When dialling within Poland all calls require the 2-digit area code.

Marinas often prefer mobile phones for communication since VHF certificates are expensive for staff to acquire.

✈ Travel

Major **airports** serve Warsaw, Gdańsk and Kraków, with smaller airports near Poznan, Szczecin, Katowice and Wrocław. Whizz Air and Ryanair have cheap direct flights to the coast, LOT and BA use Warsaw. The airport is 30 minutes by taxi from the marina in Gdańsk city centre.

Railways connect most cities and towns. Schedules are posted on large boards showing times, express services and track numbers. Some journeys need reservations, book at the station.

Bus and trams require tickets purchased in advance at a newsagent (Ruch kiosk) which you then validate in the machine on the bus

💻 Websites

Poland's presence on the web is growing steadily, and as of 2017 there is more information about marinas, many of which have their own websites which are listed under the communications section of each harbour. Some sites are available with an English translation, (but Polish accented letters get corrupted on transcription, and some sites have given up the struggle!)

www.poland.pl The official Polish website, with some useful links.

THE BALTIC SEA AND APPROACHES   335

6. POLAND

6. POLAND

www.artmedialab.com The website of the Polish National Tourist Office in New York.

www.hopn.mw.mil.pl The official website of the Polish Hydrographic Office.

www.szczecin.eu/en/sczecin_na_fali/mariny Lists marinas and contact details

www.władysławowo.pl Website of the Władysławowo region, which encompasses some eight towns and villages. Interesting, but very little about the harbour.

www.gdynia.pl Gdynia city website, including brief information about the yacht harbour in the tourism section.

www.en.gdansk.pl Gdańsk city website, with English translation but no particular relevance to yachts and, surprisingly, no town plan.

www.noonsite.com/Countries/Poland tips on Poland for cruising sailors by cruising sailors.

www.polandforvisitors.com

www.inourpocket.com Polish cities including Gdynia and Gdańsk.

www.lonelyplanet.com/poland

Radio communications

VHF Ch 16 for SAR and Ch 11 is their working channel.

Ch 06, and Ch 10 are the preferred Ship to Ship channels for yachts (Ch 06 should not be used in Gdańsk Bay, and Ch 10 should not be used around Władysławowo and Hel as these are used for port operations)

VHF stations
Swinoujście Ch25; Kołowo, Ch24; Barzowice CH25; Rozewie Ch 24; Kyrnica Morska Ch25; Grzywacz Ch26, Kołobrzeg Ch 24; Rowokol Ch26; Oksywie Ch 26.

Weather information

Sea areas are: Western, Southern, South-eastern, Central, Northern Baltic and Polish coastal waters. Wind speed is given as m/sec (metres per second) – to convert (approximately) to knots, double the reading, and to convert to Beaufort halve the reading. Weather forecasts in Polish and English are broadcast by Witowo (pronounced *vitovo*) Radio on VHF Channels 24, 25 and 26 first announced on Ch 16. The English version is transmitted at 0133, 0733, 0933 1333, 1933 UTC. Witovo Radio can be contacted on MMSI 002610210. In the of Gulf of Gdańsk weather bulletins and navigational warnings in English are announced by VTS-Zakota (MMSI 0026 11400) on Ch 16 and 71 and then transmitted on Ch 66 at 0105, 0805, 1405 and 2005 LT.

Weather Bulletins for all sea areas in the Baltic are transmitted on NAVTEX twice daily. See Appendix page 426.

Meteorological information can also be obtained by telephoning offices at Gdynia ☎ +48 58 620 5493 (H24) or Szczecin ☎ +48 91 434 2012 (H24).

Polish sailors also refer to www.icm.edu.pl for a numerical forecast with an English version available.

The country

From the quiet anchorages and small marinas of the Bay of Pomerania in the west to the Amber Coast and Bay of Gdańsk in the east, the shoreline is mainly low-lying with few features. This terrain is the result of the last glacial period when much clay, sand and other small debris was deposited, and is characterised by beaches, national parks and small protected harbours. The national parks have preserved large forested regions, though agricultural land begins not far inland, much of it growing cereals and still in the hands of small farmers.

There are extensive inland lakes and several navigable inland seas, including two major routes to Berlin. The eastern coastal area is known as the Amber Coast due to the large quantities of amber (petrified tree resin from some 40 million years ago) which are still washed onto the beaches following winter's northwesterly gales.

Poland's major industries include coal, copper and steel production, engineering, chemicals, shipbuilding, fishing and forestry. Almost all the previously state-owned industries have been privatised, and the most recent investments in Poland have centred on technology, automotive and industrial equipment, manufacturing, electronics, computers and banking. In addition to being a major hub of ship builders and repairers, Poland is one of Europe's biggest moulders of GRP yacht hulls. The Poles also have skilled metal workers and produce high quality steel and aluminium yacht hulls.

POLAND - HISTORY

Gdańsk pirate ship *Miranda Delmar-Morgan*

Language

Polish words are often difficult to pronounce because of unfamiliar consonant groups. However, people in Poland are helpful and friendly to foreigners and language is seldom a problem. At most shops, hotels and customs offices and marinas some of the staff will be able to assist with at least basic English. English is now taught in schools instead of Russian so, for asking directions in the street for instance, a young person is likely to be more helpful than someone older. In the west, especially near Świnoujośie or Szczecin, both German and English are likely to be understood since there are many visiting German yachts. As always, slow, careful pronunciation and basic vocabulary will aid communication.

Some useful phrases are: *dzień dobry* pronounced 'jin-dobry' (good morning); *dziękuję* pronounced 'jin-ku-yea' (thank you); *prosze* pronounced 'pro-sheh' (please); przepraszam pronounced 'pseh-pra-sham' (excuse me); *tak* (yes), *nie* (no), and *toaleta* (toilet). (One point regarding the latter is that the symbols WC and a circle indicate women, with a triangle for men. Showers use the international visual symbol or the words *natryski* or *prysznice*.) At harbours, the word port is used, the harbourmaster is the *kapitan* working in the harbour office or *kapitanat*. The marina manager is the *bosman* (from the English bo's'un).

History

Poland is historically a land of transition between east and west, where different peoples and cultures have existed side by side. The Slavs, including the Polanians who gave the country their name, migrated north to the region which was then inhabited by the Balts and the Finns. These earliest cultures formed city-states with regional leaders, thus establishing from the 9th century onwards the dynasties which were to rule Poland. From the 10th century the Catholic religion provided a further unifying force. In the 14th century the Piast dynasty united the Polish city-states, codified the common law, established the university in Kraków, built roads and fortified castles. The Golden Age continued following the Polish victory over the Teutonic Order in 1410.

During the Jagiellonian dynasty (1382–1572) the crowns of Poland and Lithuania were combined and the economy flourished, while intellectual and artistic growth were exemplified by the contributions to astronomy of Nicolaus Copernicus. At the end of the 18th century three successive partitions by Russia, Prussia, and Austria imposed outside rule on the country, but although foreign political rule dominated the geographical region, the Polish culture strengthened internally giving rise to figures such as the composer Frederic Chopin. As a legacy of her diverse history, the cruising yachtsman can detect Pomeranian influence in the western port of Szczecin, admire the medieval fortifications in Kołobrzeg, and see the Prussian influence most clearly within the restored old city of Gdańsk.

Following the end of World War I in 1918 Poland regained her freedom, but in 1939 the invasion of the country by Germany, in co-operation with the USSR, signalled the beginning of World War II. Following the end of the war Poland came under the influence of the Soviet Union, and during the post-war period a Communist regime was imposed. The Polish people were frustrated by the government, the economy deteriorated, and strikes became increasingly frequent. This led to the founding of the independent trade union Solidarity (Solidarność).

With Solidarity, hope for democratic reforms strengthened. Another new factor for the regime was the increased influence of the Catholic Church headed by Polish Pope John Paul II. Unrest continued and the persistence of Polish citizens eventually forced the Soviets to negotiate in 1989. Following this meeting, democratic elections were held in Poland and Solidarity won 99% of the seats in the Senate. Changes following the election quickly re-established a free-market economy and social reform. This transition, although painful, has been fairly rapid. Poland has experienced economic growth since 1989, sometimes in partnership with foreign investors, and is receptive to new ideas. Poland joined NATO in 1999 and became a member of the European Union in 2004. Funding from several sources has been used to upgrade wharfs, roads and rail networks, to build new marinas and repair ancient buildings. Poland is being transformed and has excellent facilities for visiting sailors.

THE BALTIC SEA AND APPROACHES

6. POLAND

Practicalities

Shopping
Every town has its shopping area, usually in the centre where rows of shops offer a variety of goods. Large supermarkets are located at the edges of the towns, and there are also many open markets where fresh food and other products are available at prices lower than those in the shops. Bakery goods can be bought at a *piekarnia*, sweet rolls and cakes from a *cukiernia* – try *sernik* (cheese cake).

Hotels and restaurants
Most towns, especially seaside tourist resorts, have a range of hotels varying widely in quality and price.

Restaurants are similarly diverse, from high-priced speciality restaurants to pavement cafés and fast food outlets. If visiting one of those serving Polish food consider sampling *barszcz* (beetroot soup), *bigos* (a stew made with sauerkraut and a variety of meats,) or *pierogi* (large dumplings usually stuffed with white cheese and potatoes, meat or fruit). In summer open air snack bars spring up selling grilled fish, sausage or other kinds of meat served with fresh bread and pickles – and of course there are the ubiquitous American burger and pizza chains.

Cafés (*kawiarnia*) serve rich desserts and a variety of drinks. Tea, Turkish, expresso and even iced coffee are popular, Polish beer is good (try Bosman, Żywiec or Warka) and imported wine plentiful. Vodka can be bought in a variety of forms and flavours including *wioniówka* (sweet or dry cherry) and Żubrówka (flavoured with bison grass found only in one region of the country). Polish cognac is known as *winiak*. *Miód* (mead) is a delicious liqueur made from honey.

Medical matters
The EHIC card is needed for reciprocal EU care. The Polish National Health Fund is marked as NFZ. Clinics operate a normal 5-day week, otherwise go to the nearest hospital. For an ambulance dial 999 from a landline or 112 from a mobile phone. NFZ registered dentists offer basic care. www.nfz.gov.pl

Yacht services and chandlery
Drinking water is always readily available as are showers and toilets. However, an electrical connection may be some distance away and require a long lead and not always with the 3-pin EU connector. A continental 2-pin adaptor can be useful. Fuelling berths are becoming more frequent but in an emergency a nearby filling station selling diesel can generally be found, (a few 20 litre containers may prove useful, and it is believed that Polish diesel is free from biofuel). Fill up when you can! Fuel still often has to be paid for in cash. Polish propane gas bottles can sometimes be exchanged or refilled at the larger filling stations such as Shell and BP, but Calor Gas is not available and Camping Gaz is rare. It is prudent to stock up before entering the country.

The widest selection of chandlery is available in Gdynia – see page 363 – with more limited stocks at Świnoujście, Szczecin, Kołobrzeg, Władysławowo and Gdańsk. Elsewhere chandleries can be a bit thin on the ground. In the Szczecin area facilities for yachts are improving with marinas, boatyards, sailmakers and chandleries.

Fruit stall Władysławowo *Miranda Delmar-Morgan*

338 THE BALTIC SEA AND APPROACHES

POLAND - PRACTICALITIES

Gdańsk waterfront *Miranda Delmar-Morgan*

There are reasonable boatyards at Szczecin, Kołobrzeg, Łeba and Górki, and it is possible to lay up ashore in Gdynia, Górki, Łeba, Kołobrzeg and Szczecin though obtaining a cradle could be a problem. A lot of yacht building takes place at Górki, where there are overwintering facilities and six yacht clubs, but little transport and no shops.

Firing ranges

These are a particular problem between Darłowo and Ustka (Area 6) and less so off the Hel peninsula (Areas 10 and 11). There are also three small areas where navigation is forbidden at any time (Areas 3, and 15 north of Gdynia and Area 14 west of Hel). Firing times are broadcast by Witowo Radio VHF Chs 24, 25, and 26 at 0133, 0533, 0933, 1333, 1733, 2133hrs UT along with the weather forecast and other navigational warnings, after first being announced on VHF Ch 16. Słupsk Radio maintains a 24hr watch on Ch 16, and 2182kHz, and issues warnings and weather on Ch 71 at 0715, 1245, and 1845hrs LT. There are other less frequently used ranges as well and all must be allowed for. See diagrams of ranges on pages 340 and 360.

Up-to-date information can be obtained by phoning the Polish Navy 8th Coastal Defence Flotilla Operations Officer ☏ +48 661 417 339. Firing times and other navigational warnings for the northwest coast are also broadcast by Radio Słupsk on VHF Ch 71 at 0715, 1245, and 1845 LT after first being announced on VHF Ch 16 or ☏ +48 59 814 4889 (H24). NAVTEX also carries information.

See also the plan on page 367 and note on page 370 about Regulated Area 117.

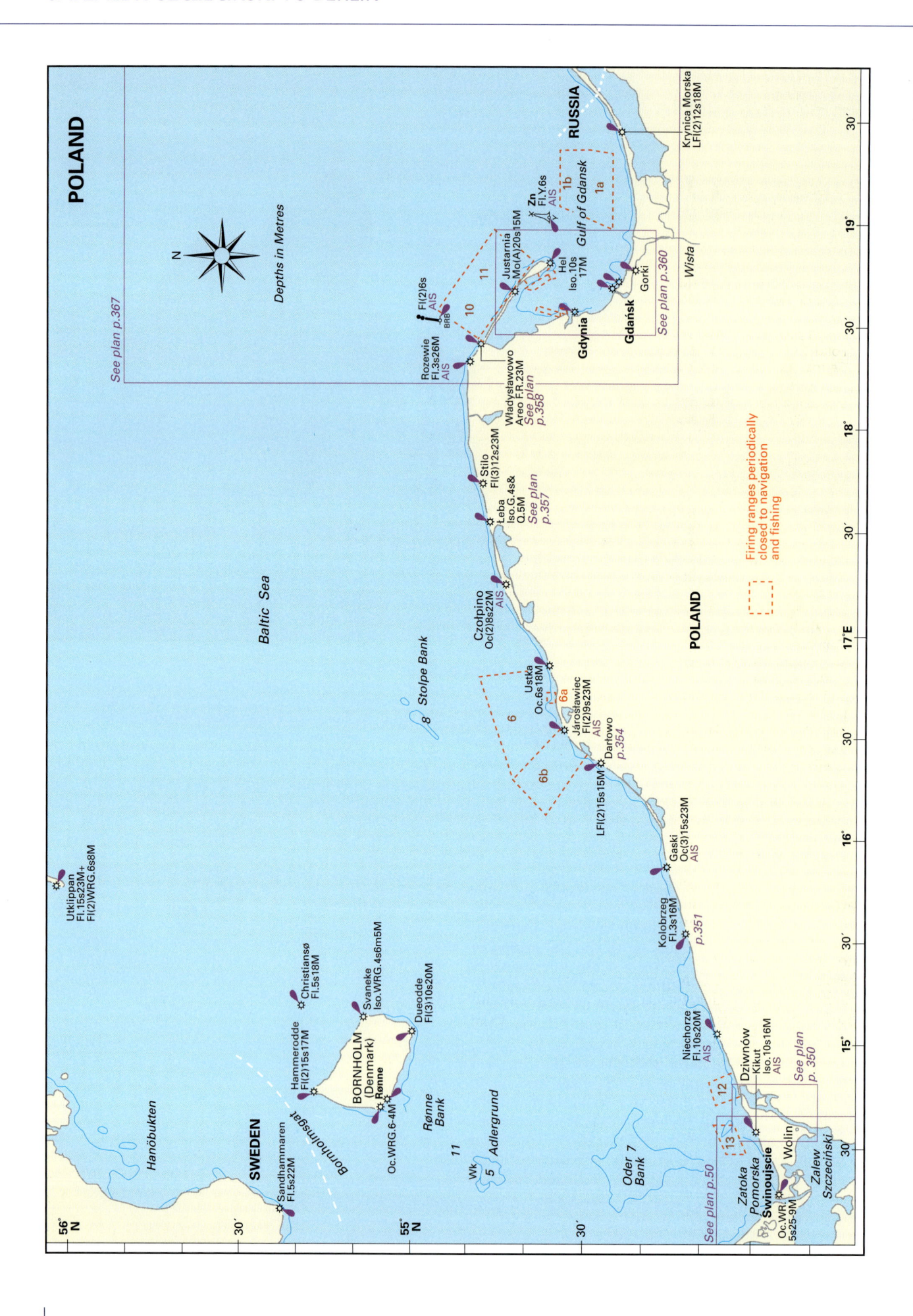

6A. ZALEW SZCZECINSKI TO BERLIN

340 THE BALTIC SEA AND APPROACHES

6a. Zalew Szczeciński to Berlin

Świnoujście

53°55′N 14°17′E

Distances
Stralsund 50M, Rønne 72M, Trzebież 15M, Szczecin 35M, Dziwnów 20M, Gdynia 190M

Charts
UKHO 2676, 2677, 2678, 2679
Polish 252, 154, 75, 74, 15, 302
German 151, NV Serie 4, DK Satz 2, 13

Lights
Świnoujście 53°55′N 14°17′·1E
 Oc.WR.5s65m25/9M 029°-R-057°-W-280° Yellow round tower on red building 65m
Landfall buoy 54°14′·7N 14°11′E Iso.10s Red and white pillar buoy
Kikut 53°59′N 14°34′·9E Iso.10s91m16M 063°-vis-241° Grey round stone tower, white lantern 18m
Outer Ldg Lts 170·2° *Front* Mlyny (west breakwater) 53°55′·6N 14°16′·6E Oc.10s11m17M White beacon resembling windmill 11m
 Rear Galeriowa 520m from front, Oc.10s23m17M White triangle on white round tower, three galleries 24m
East breakwater 53°55′·9N 14°16′·8E Oc.WR.6s13m2M Red tower

Communications
Świnoujście Harbourmaster ☎ +48 91 321 3662 (0730–1500 LT)
Świnoujście Port Control and VTS ☎ +48 91 321 6203 VHF Ch 12, 16, 71
Basen Stoczniowy (Basen Północny) Marina
 ☎ +48 91 321 9177, VHF Ch 12
 Mobile +48 502 443 954 www.osir.uznam.net.pl

General

Świnoujście (pronounced *Sfeen-o-weesh-chey*) is the outer port of Szczecin. It lies at the mouth of the Odra River, which separates Usedom and Wolin islands, just east of the Polish/German border. It is a holiday resort with an esplanade and a blue flag beach as well as a commercial, fishing and naval harbour. A considerable amount of commercial traffic passes through the harbour en route to Szczecin, via the Odra River.

Approach and entrance
53°56.2′N 14°16.8′E north mole

The main shipping channel is 14m deep and is well buoyed on a bearing of 170° from the landfall buoy (some 20M offshore) to the breakwaters. Yachts can safely take their own route but avoiding a shoal which extends 1M offshore close west of the entrance. Entrance is said to be safe in up to Force 9 onshore winds. A large new outer breakwater has been built on the eastern side to protect ships associated with a gas terminal.

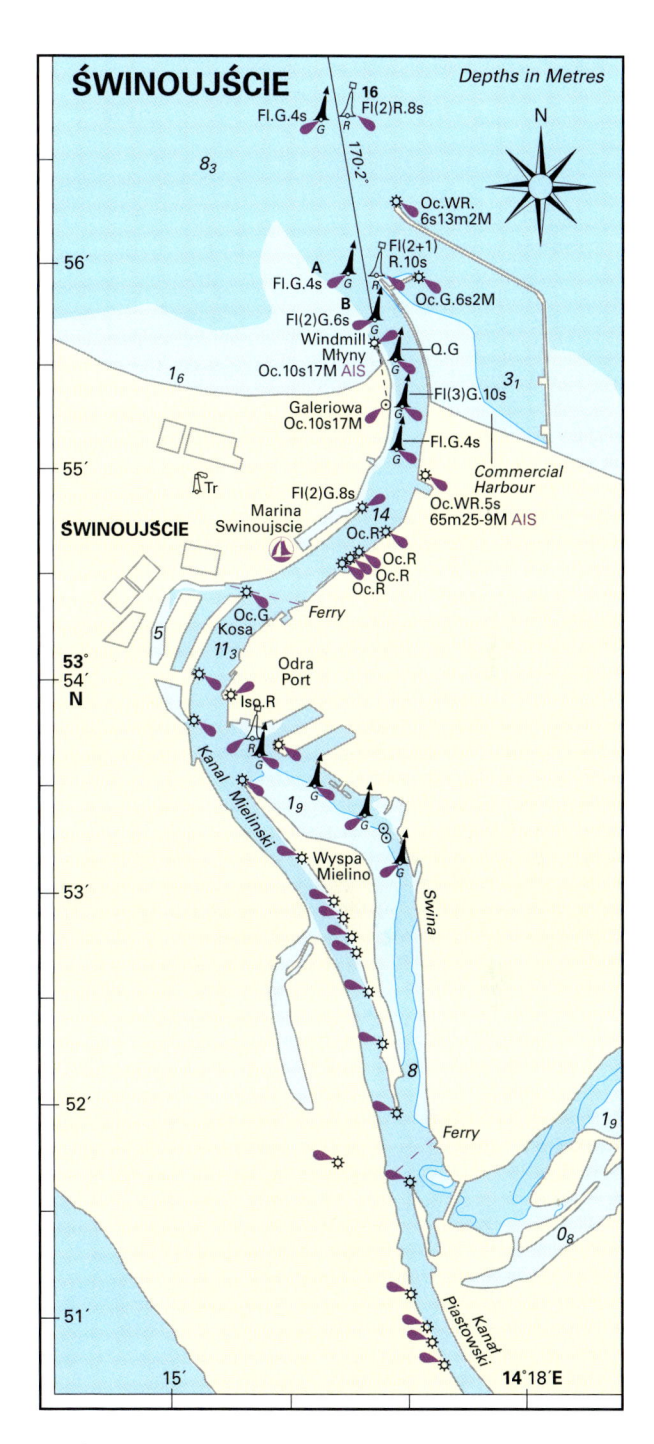

The inner eastern breakwater, the lighthouse, and the harbour control tower are all conspicuous from well offshore. The entrance itself is obvious, well marked and free from obstructions. There can be currents across and into the entrance of up to two knots or an outflow current of up to four knots depending on the strength and direction of the wind.

Świnoujście can also be approached from the south via the Kanals Piastowski and Mielenski from the Zalew Szczeciński.

6A. ZALEW SZCZECIŃSKI TO BERLIN

ŚWINOUJŚCIE

Świnoujście approach *Miranda Delmar-Morgan*

Outer leading mark, Świnoujście
J. Mottram

Anchorage
There is no anchorage within Świnoujście itself – continue some 10M southeast to the lake and island area of Zalew Szczeciński.

Berthing
The municipal marina (Marina Świnoujście) in Basen Północny (Stoczniowy) is on the west side of the harbour 1M south of the entrance. The brick water tower beyond the SW end of the basin is conspicuous and there is a SAR centre at the marina entrance. It is safe and comfortable and about 1km from the town centre. Limited berthing may also be available alongside in the town centre by arrangement with the harbourmaster. But there are no facilities and there can be wash from passing traffic.

Facilities
Basen Północny has been greatly improved. Facilities are good with showers and toilets now on both sides of the basin, new pontoons, and alongside berthing in 4m depths. Fuel berth (0800-1000 and 1600-1800), water and electric via a card system. There is also a bar/café, and sailmaker, laundry. WiFi if you are within range.

There is a small chandlery in the town centre which is about 1km from the marina along the harbourside. It stocks charts together with a reasonable selection of standard chandlery.

Bus, train and ferry services to Szczecin where there are connections to Poznan and Berlin. There are also regular ferry services to Sweden via Rønne on Bornholm and to Copenhagen.

The Kanał Mieleński and Zalew Szczeciński

Leading southeast from Świnoujście is the Kanał Mieleński, which then becomes the Kanal Piastowski before opening into the wide Zalew Szczeciński. Both the canal and the buoyed channel across the Zalew Szczeciński are dredged to 10m, and there are 5m depths across most of the remainder of the area. The main channel is well buoyed and lit, with 25m towers at 2M intervals. The surrounding area is heavily forested and offers many quiet and scenic anchorages, though yachts venturing outside the fairway should keep a sharp watch for the many fishing nets, marked by stakes with red and white diamonds; the red side indicating danger and the white pointing to safe passage.

The Zalew Szczeciński can also be accessed from both west and east – the former from Stralsund through the Greifswalder Bodden and the Peenestrom (see pages 63-4), and the latter from the Baltic east of Świnoujście via Dziwnów, Kamien Pomorski and Wolin (see page 350).

Świnoujście marina *Miranda Delmar-Morgan*

THE BALTIC SEA AND APPROACHES 343

6A. ZALEW SZCZECIŃSKI TO BERLIN

Trzebież

53°40′N 14°31′E

Distances
Świnoujście 17M, Szczecin 15M, Ueckermünde 20M, Karnin (at S end of Peenestrom) 26M

Charts
UKHO 2678, 2677
Polish 15, 48, 75, 3020
German folios DK Satz 13, NV Serie 4

Lights
From NW
Brama Tower No. 3 53°39′·92N 14°32′E Iso.2s25m7M Red tower with two galleries
Brama Tower No. 4 53°39′·83N 14°31′·83E Iso.2s25m7M Green tower with two galleries
N Landfall Buoy TN-A 53°40′·85N 14°29′·85E Fl.G.2s G buoy
Ldg Lights 150·2° *Front* 53°39′·6N 14°31′·1E Oc.4s11m7M Red oblong shape on white framework tower *Rear* 433m from front Oc.4s22m7M Red oblong shape on framework tower
From SE
Ldg Lts 301·2° *Front* 53°39′·8N 14°30′·9E Oc.Y.4s11m4M Yellow square shape on white framework tower *Rear* 380m from front Oc.Y.4s18m4M Orange inverted triangle on white framework tower

Communications
Harbourmaster ☏ +48 913 128 516
Marina Manager ☏ +48 913 128 294 or +48 535 500 362 VHF Ch 69 www.coz.com.pl

General

At the southern neck of the Zalew Szczeciński, on the western shore, lies Trzebież (pronounced *Cheh-byeh*), an attractive small yacht and fishing harbour with berthing for approximately 60 yachts moored bows to the quay with stern buoys in two basins. The northern basin carries depths of 2·5–3m and the southern one 1–1·5m. It can be approached either from the north or the south by buoyed channels off the main channel to Szczecin. Both channels have leading lights.

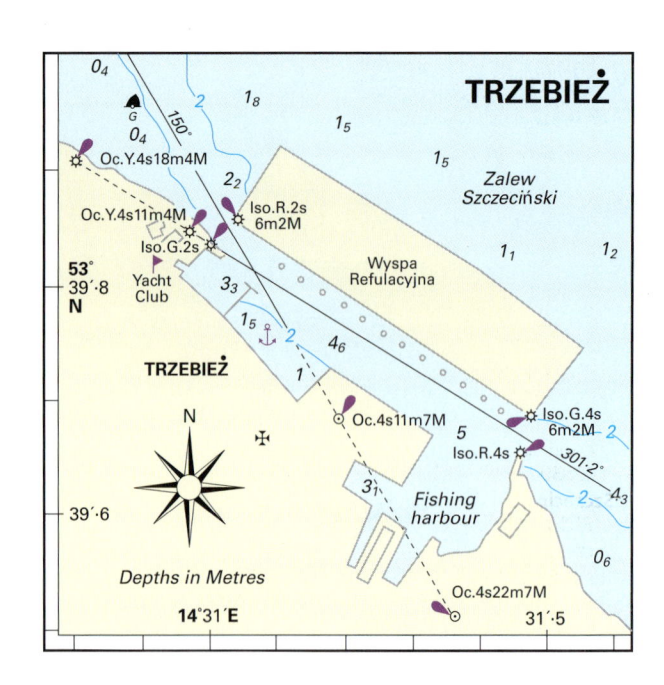

Facilities

Facilities include water, diesel, electricity, showers, WCs, and a café/bar but limited shopping. There is a Customs office. The marina (COZ) is the headquarters of the Polish Sailing Association and the café/bar serves as a club when the fleet is in. There is a 30 tonne hoist and some maintenance services. Yachts are also welcomed at alongside berths in the more sheltered fishing harbour where there are facilities similar to the yacht harbour. Both harbours are subject to surge from onshore winds and passing ships. Train to Szczecin.

Trzebież harbour *Miranda Delmar-Morgan*

Szczecin

53°25′N 14°33′E

Distances
Stralsund via the Peenestrom 85M, Świnoujście 35M, Trzebież 15M

Charts
UKHO 2678, 2676
Polish 15, 48, 75, 3020

Lights
Night approach not recommended – the latter part is narrow and unlit.

Communications
Szczecin Harbourmaster ☎ +48 91 433 6657/440 3596 (0830–1500 LT Monday–Friday)
Szczecin Port Control and VTS ☎ +48 91 433 0697/ 440 3510, VHF Ch 16, 69
Szczecin Customs ☎ +48 91 440 6500
NorthEast Marina Szczecin ☎ +48 91 311 15 21 or +48 91 311 15 21, VHF Ch 65
Mobile +48 539 924 222
port@zegluga.szn.pl
Marina Gocław ☎ +48 91 423 5031
Mobile +49 73 002 3666 or + 48 91 4230 656
Pogon Marina (Zielona Marina)
☎ +48 91 462 4657 or +48 602 808 280
Marina Porta Hotele ☎ +48 91 812 80 45, +48 601 989 718 or +48 461 4350 www.marina-club.pl
Yacht Club AZS Szczecin (Academic Yacht Club)
☎ +48 91 461 2734 www.azs.szczecin.pl
Centrum Zeglarski ☎ +48 91 460 0844 or +48 91 460 0845
www.zentrumzeglarskie.pl
Camping Marina ☎ +48 91 460 11 65
www.campingmarina.pl

General

Szczecin (pronounced *Sheh-chen-chin*) was a Slavic fishing and trading port from the 9th century, and today is the seventh largest city in Poland. In spite of its distance from the sea it remains one of Poland's major ports and is an important shipbuilding and ship repair centre. It has extensive waterways bordered by trees and fields and there are historic monuments dating from the 14th century, although the city was very severely damaged during the Second World War.

Approach

Waypoint 53°42′N 14°29′·1E

From the Zalew Szczeciński and Trzebież the ship channel follows the Odra River south to Szczecin. It is clearly marked and dredged to a minimum of 10m. Although some areas outside the fairway have adequate depths, shoal areas also exist just close to the main channel.

The Jezioro Dąbie, which has depths of 2·3–3·5m and where three of Szczecin's four marinas are located, can either be entered from the north at Mewia Island or from the south via the Regalica Mienia. To reach the southern marinas, continue south along the River Odra past Marina Gocław (see below) and at Okrętowa island take the eastern channel, Przekop Mieleński. Large vessels signal their intentions at the junction with Kanał Grabowski. Continue along Przekop Mieleński

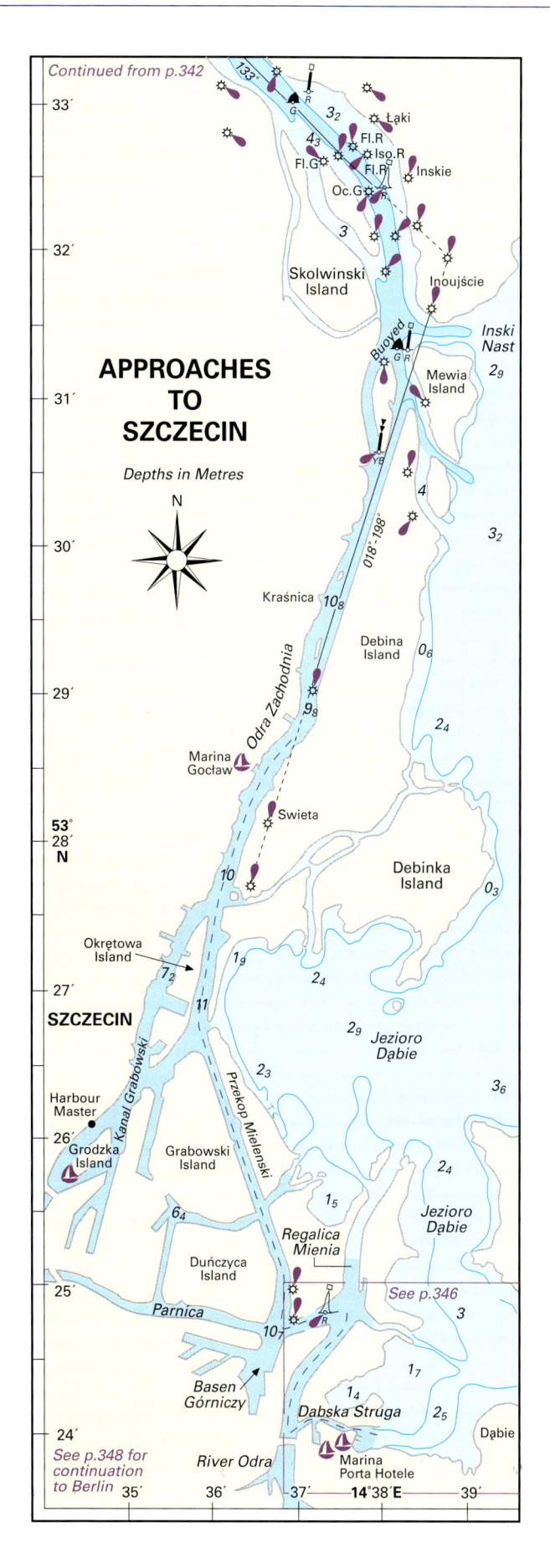

6A. ZALEW SZCZECIŃSKI TO BERLIN

Szczecin panorama *Miranda Delmar-Morgan*

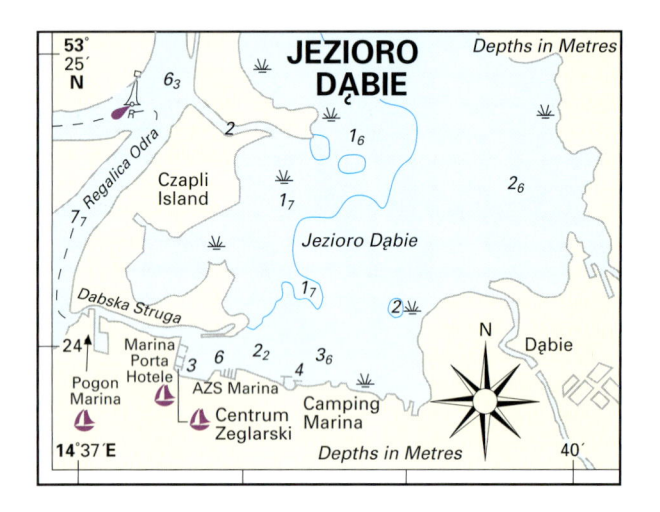

across its intersection with the Dunczyca and past Mielenski island until, some 0·8M further on, there is a four-way junction – the Parnica to the west, the Basen Górniczy (a dead end) ahead and the Regalica Mienia to the east. Northwards the Regalica Mienia leads directly into the Jezioro Dąbie, but by turning south at the first opportunity into the Regalica Odra yachts reach the Dąbska Struga, the canal serving Pogon Marina, Marina Porta Hotele, the Centrum Zeglarski and the AZS Yacht Club (see below). The entrance to the canal is distinctively marked on the starboard hand by the bridge superstructure of a large ship set on dry land, but beware the long spit which extends 20m into the river on the northern side of the entrance.

Anchorage
Anchoring is prohibited in the fairways, but the many creeks and harbours of the Jezioro Dąbie offer countless attractive anchorages.

Berthing
All of the marinas listed below are at the southern end of the Dąbie Lake and can be approached via the lake, but it is littered with stakes and very shallow, so the canals provide easier access. They are some distance from town but well served by buses.

NorthEast Szczecin Marina
53°25·6′N 14°34′·2E

A brand new marina opened in 2015 on Grodzka island, opposite the town, just below the fixed bridge. This is much more handy than the more established marinas and is closer to town than those in the Dąbie Lake.

Depths of 2·5-5m depths. There is a bus service into town and great view of the city. WiFi. Reported to have most facilities in place, including pump-out station, but no diesel. 25 visitors' berths.

The town quayside has excellent shower, toilet and laundry facilities behind the Tourist Office. The quayside is quite busy with ferry traffic which causes wash.

Marina Gocław
53°28′·45N 14°36′E

A pleasant yacht harbour situated at Gocław, on the west bank of the main channel about 2M north of the city centre and 20 minutes away by bus or tram. Mooring is bows to the quayside and stern to a buoy in about 4m. The marina is quiet and totally

Szczecin city wharf *Miranda Delmar-Morgan*

346   THE BALTIC SEA AND APPROACHES

SZCZECIN

Gocław Marina entrance Miranda Delmar-Morgan

Gocław Marina, Szczecin Miranda Delmar-Morgan

sheltered but facilities are limited. Some food is available in the hotel, part of the marina building, and there is a small shop across the road. Water and electricity on the quayside and showers ashore. It is possible to arrange for diesel to be delivered in containers. It has a crane for stepping and unstepping masts, much used by German yachts exiting or entering the German canal system. There is a boatyard (with no marina facilities) a short distance to the south.

Pogon Marina
53°24′N 14°37′·2E

Lies on the south side of the Dąbska Struga near its junction with the Regalica Odra and about 500m west of the Marina Porta Hotele. It is not as large as its neighbour, with fewer facilities but in equally pleasant surroundings, and is better suited to smaller yachts.

Marina Porta Hotele
54°24′N 14°37′·2E

The most expensive, is situated in pleasant surroundings at the southern end of the Jezioro Dąbie. It is reached via the Dąbska Struga, passing the Pogon Marina en route. New pontoons, with approx depths of 2·5-4m. Marina Porta Hotele has all facilities except, contrary to their advertising, laundry, but it does have a fuel berth. There is a crane suitable for stepping and unstepping masts.

YC AZS Marina

A most welcoming marina in the two basins adjacent to Marina Porta Hotele. Depths are 2–2·5m in the northern basin and 1·5–2m in the southern one. Berths outside the basins carry depths of 3–5m.

Services for yachts

Centrum Zeglarskie has an enormous Dornier Flying Boat hanger dating from the 1920s which provides winter storage, and slippage and craneage. There is a sailmaker and a well-stocked chandlery.

Pogon Marina has the usual facilities, sells Camping Gaz and has a marine electronics outlet.

AZS Marina (Academic Yacht Club) has the usual facilities as well as a Taverna type bar/restaurant.

Camping Marina allows sailors from adjacent marinas to use their laundry facilities. Berths are exposed to the fetch of the Dąbie Lake.

For Admiralty and local charts there is a Smart chandlery and Aquarius Marine Services in Szczecin.

General facilities

Szczecin has all the facilities of a major city, including some good shops, banks and restaurants. There is a hotel of that name at the Marina Porta Hotele, which also has a restaurant, and there is a good supermarket in Dąbie, a short (2km) bus ride east of the marina.

Communications and travel

Transport to the city centre, about 4km by road, involves a change from bus to tram at Basen Górniczy where tickets for both the bus and the tram are sold. There are good train services to all parts of Poland and, via Berlin, to the rest of Europe.

The airport for Szczecin is at Goleniow, 45km north. Direct flights from UK with Whizz Air, Ryanair, and LOT.

Caution

Within the port area, yachts and other small craft must always yield to ship movements. *The Baltic Pilot Volume II* (NP 19) includes extensive instructions for these areas and the ship turning basins. Finally, top up your diesel here, the next yacht bunker station is 125M away, at Łeba.

Wały Chrobrego embankment, Szczecin
Miranda Delmar-Morgan

THE BALTIC SEA AND APPROACHES **347**

6. POLAND

6A. ZALEW SZCZECIŃSKI TO BERLIN

River and canal passage Szczecin to Berlin

NV Map/guides cover the passage. These are obtainable from Imray www.imray.com, www.hansenautic.de or www.sklep.sail-ho.pl at Gdynia

Many German yachts unstep their masts to make this trip twice a year, between their winter moorings near Berlin and their summer sailing ground of the Baltic. The usual route is by the West Oder and the Oder-Havel Kanal which then gives access to the German canal system.

Pilotage notes

Draught Passage may be made by either the West Oder (Odra) or the East Oder. The West Odra has much less current, and its recommended draught is officially 1·8 metres, though up to two metres is thought to be safe. There is a connection between the two rivers about 25 miles south of Sczcecin which can provide a compromise, as the limiting section of the West Oder is the dredged section approaching the locks at Oder-Havel Kanal. There may be more depth in the East Oder, which is the main river, but as such is faster flowing and more subject to depth/current variations according to the weather further inland.

Advice should be sought before leaving Sczcecin. There is lock access to the canal from either Oder.

Air draught The official recommendation is four metres, but a motor yacht with an air draught of 4·2m is known to have made safe passage in August 2008, reporting a minimum clearance of 30cm. This is despite markings of 3·45m and 3·75m on the first two bridges in central Sczcecin, which is thought to refer to winter flood conditions. Any vessel contemplating passage should check the current conditions with the Sczcecin harbourmaster before departure.

Distance and Time

106M (GPS distance) should take about four days cruising at 5½–6 knots.

Formalities

None, both countries being part of the Schengen area. 10M south of Szczecin is the now abandoned Polish/German border crossing where it is possible to stop overnight. There are no facilities.

Moorings and facilities

Hohensaaten Lock is 35M from Szczecin where you leave the West Oder River and join the Oder-Havel Kanal.

4M past the lock is Marina Oderberg ☎ +49 (0) 33369 75540 www.marina-oderberg.de. Draught is restricted to 1·8m. Full facilities including a good restaurant. Overnight dues €1.20/m. The town of Oderberg is 1½ miles further on, with basic shops and small supermarket.

6M beyond the marina is the ship lift at Niederfinow. This huge piece of canal engineering, built to replace a series of four conventional locks, is one of the biggest in Europe, lifting vessels something over 30 metres. Air draught is 4·4 metres with little prospect of ever increasing. Shortly after this there is a one-way section of canal which changes traffic direction at set times during the day. Leisure craft do not appear to be required to comply, the canal being wide enough to permit a yacht to pass an on-coming barge with care.

Near the town of Oranienburg there is an anchorage in the lake immediately south of the Schleuse Lehnitz lock in 3·5 metres. This is suitable for an overnight stop.

Leave the Oder-Havel canal after Henningsdorf and enter the lake area west of Berlin. One lock, then via a short canal to the River Spree. There is a wide choice of places to moor, some free, in and around Berlin. The central ones, though free and convenient, have no facilities and are subject to continual disturbance from passing river traffic. Generally more remote places are preferable, and most have readily available public transport to the city centre.

348   THE BALTIC SEA AND APPROACHES

DZIWNÓW

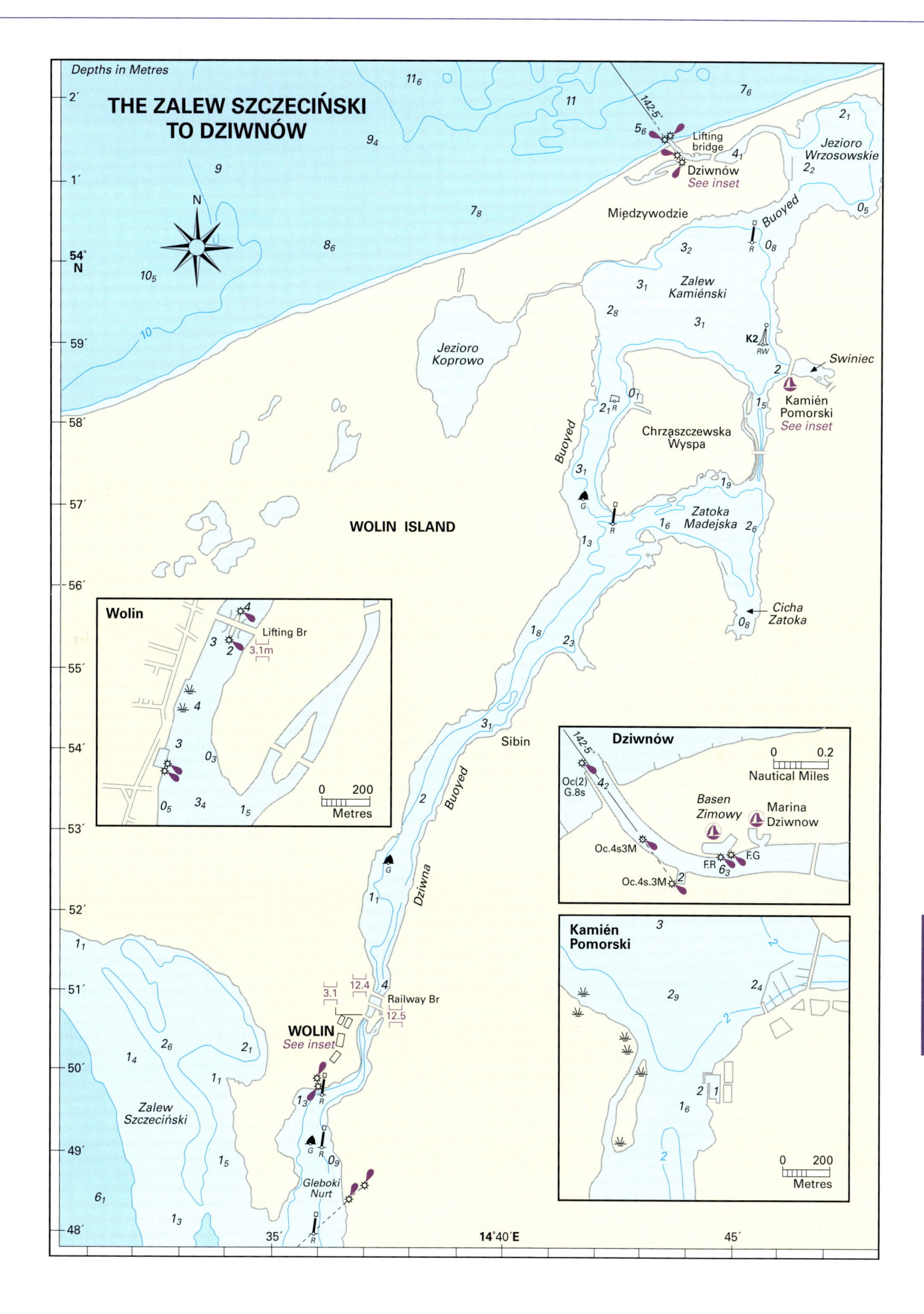

THE ZALEW SZCZECIŃSKI TO DZIWNÓW

Depths in Metres

THE BALTIC SEA AND APPROACHES 349

6. POLAND

6B. COAST OF POLAND

The Zalew Szczeciński to Dziwnów

Yachts with limited water and air draughts can take the inland route from the Zalew Szczeciński to Dziwnów via Wolin and Kamien Pomorski. The marked channel carries a minimum depth of 1·7m, but two fixed bridges at Wolin limit height to 12·4m thus preventing a circumnavigation of the island by larger yachts. The lower road bridge opens twice daily Monday to Friday (0900 and 1600) and once daily on Saturday (1000), Sunday and feast days (1300).

Wolin
53°51′N 14°37′E

A small town and minor port with no specific facilities for yachts but there is a waiting quay on both sides of the bridge on the west side of the river.

Kamien Pomorski
53°58′N 14°46′E
☎ +48 661 213 391, +48 91 382 0882 or
Mobile +48 601 724 494.

A lovely town, accessible from Dziwnów. There is a new 250 berth marina with depths of up to 2m in attractive surroundings. The approach is well marked but very shallow. There is long quay backed by parkland overlooking a castle. General supplies are available.

Entrance to Dziwnów marina Miranda Delmar-Morgan

6b. Coast of Poland

Dziwnów

54°01′N 14°44′E

Distances
Świnoujście 20M, Kołobrzeg 30M

Charts
UKHO 2679
Polish 39, 74, 75, 154, 252, 3020
German 1301, NV Serie 6 and Serie 4

Lights
Świnoujście 53°55′N 14°17′·1E
  Oc.WR.5s65m25/9M 029°-R-057°-W-280°
  Yellow round tower on red building 65m
Kikut 53°59′N 14°34′·9E Iso.10s91m16M
  063°-vis-241° Grey round stone tower,
  white lantern 18m
Niechorze 54°05′·8N 15°03′·9E Fl.10s63m20M Grey
  octagonal tower and red building
Ldg Lts 142·5° *Front* 54°01′·2N 14°43′·8E Oc.4s8m3M
  White diamond on white metal framework tower
  Rear 130m from front, Oc.4s13m3M
  White rectangle on red and white framework tower
West breakwater 54°01′·4N 14°43′·5E Oc(2)G.8s10m7M
  Column
East breakwater 54°01′·5N 14°43′·6E Oc(2)R.8s10m7M
  Column Horn Mo(A)60s

Communications
Dziwnów Harbourmaster ☎ +48 91 3813 754
  VHF Ch 10, 71
Dziwnów Port Control ☎ +48 91 381 3754/3642
  VHF Ch 12, 16, 71
Opening bridge ☎ +48 91 381 3711, VHF Ch 10
Marina Bosman ☎ +48 91 381 1235
Polmax marina ☎ +48 91 381 3634
  www.polmax.com.pl/tour/marina.htm

General

Dziwnów (pronounced *Jiv-noof*) set amongst trees, is an attractive small fishing and holiday resort at the mouth of the Dziwnów River, which links to the Jezioro Wrzosowskie and Zalew Kamienski lakes and thence to the Zalew Szczeciński. To the west lies Wolin island and to the east the Polish mainland.

Approach
54°01·4′N 14°43·5′·8E western molehead

The coastline on either side consists of low forested hills and sandy beaches, with no off-lying dangers. Entrance is straightforward using the 142·5° leading line although the leading marks can be difficult to see because of trees. Depths are 4·2m in the entrance and 5m inside.

Warning In winds over Force 5 from the west or northwest the entrance can be dangerous and should not be attempted. About 0·6M inside the entrance (beyond the yacht berths) lies a bridge which operates on request (see Berthing).

Berthing

On the starboard hand close inside the entrance lies the small Polmax marina, It has a maximum depth of 2·5m. It is some distance from the village and

350 THE BALTIC SEA AND APPROACHES

KOŁOBRZEG

much less used. Opposite is the Border Control checkpoint. Yachts may be hailed by an official ashore asking for their last port of call. There is a major new development around Basen Zimowy but this is for fishing boats only and not intended for visiting yachts.

The new Dziwnów Marina just beyond, opened in 2014 with all facilities. It has finger pontoons but space is quite tight, and it soon fills up. Yachts can raft onto the outside moles up to about three deep but after that, and for yachts over 12m it is best to go through the bridge and find a berth on the quay east of the excursion boats, or anchor off Wolin Island, good holding in mud. There is a small yacht club with some new pontoons opposite the town but they too soon fill and may be uncomfortable in strong S to SE winds owing to the fetch from Jezioro Wrzosowskie. Preliminary contact may be made on VHF Ch 12. The bridge (VHF Ch 10) opens on demand on the even hours. Call with estimated time of arrival (24hr). It remains closed in winds of F6 and above.

Facilities

The new marina, with depths of 3.5m, is excellent. Clubhouse with bar, good shelter. Supermarket 200m. Laundry facilities in town. WiFi. Very helpful staff will organize bike hire. There is a bunker station to port beyond the bridge. General supplies, banks and small restaurants are available in the town.

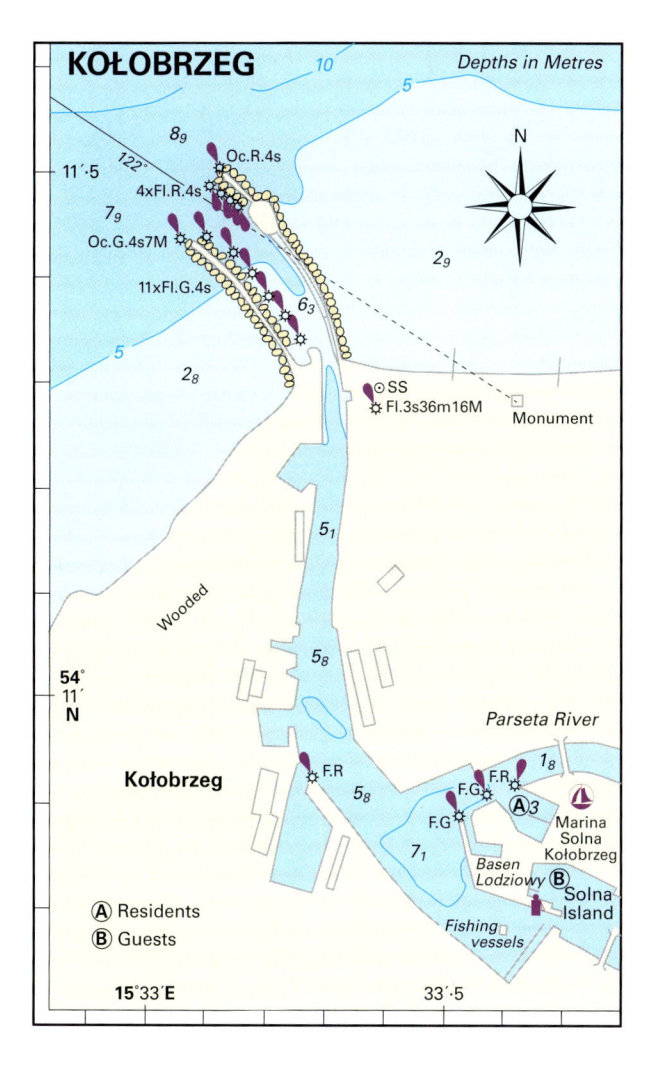

Kołobrzeg

54°11'N 15°33'E east mole head

Distances
Świnoujście 50M, Dziwnów 30M, Darłowo 30M

Charts
Polish 57, 153, 252

Lights
Niechorze 54°05'·8N 15°03'·9E Fl.10s63m20M
  Grey octagonal tower and red building
Dźwirzyno 54°09'·6N 15°23'·4E Oc.R.4s7m6M
  Red post
Kołobrzeg 54°11'·3N 15°33'·4E Fl.3s36m16M
  Red round tower, black cupola
Koł light buoy 54°13'·5N 15°30'·6E LFl.10s
  Red and white pillar buoy, • topmark
West breakwater 54°11'·4N 15°33'·2E Oc.G.4s11m7M
  Green round column, two galleries
East breakwater 54°11'·5N 15°33'·2E Oc.R.4s
  Red round column, two galleries Horn Mo(K)60s
Gaski 54°14'·7N 15°52'·5E Oc(3)15s50m23M Red round tower, gallery and cupola

Harbour communications
Kołobrzeg harbourmaster ☏ +48 94 352 2703
  (0730–1530 LT Monday–Friday)
Port Control ☏ +48 94 352 2799, VHF Ch 12, 16
Solna Marina ☏ +48 94 354 4301 or +48 94 351 6765
  Mobile +48 785 882 842
  www.zpm.portkolobrzeg.pl

General

Kołobrzeg (pronounced *Co-wob-jeck*) is a tourist resort and commercial and fishing harbour, the largest on the long stretch of coast between Świnoujście and Gdynia. The harbour entrance has a boardwalk, popular with tourists who gather to watch the maritime activities, and a long seafront promenade with shops and cafés. Near the marina stand parts of the walls of a fort built in 1774, where there is now a café and bar and music is played on summer evenings. It is a busy place with an industrial port. Rail links to Szczecin. Customs point.

Approach

The approach channel lies on a bearing of 148° from the Koł landfall buoy, though the surrounding coast is clear of off-lying hazards. Two curved concrete moles extend from the entrance, the red structure on the port hand one being particularly prominent. When the eastern molehead is abeam to port turn on to 122° between the piers with the needle-like monument 'Marriage to the Sea' directly on that bearing. The large brick lighthouse can also be seen from well offshore. Vessels up to 85m use the port and the canal is very narrow, it is essential to call Port Control (VHF Ch 12) in advance. The entrance itself is narrow and is subject to swell from west through northwest. It can also be affected by strong cross-currents, depending on wind strength and direction. Extensive alterations and bright yellow baffles have been added to the moles to improve safety. Depths are 5–6m in the entrance and harbour, decreasing to 3m in the marina basin.

THE BALTIC SEA AND APPROACHES   351

6B. COAST OF POLAND

Approach to Kołobrzeg Miranda Delmar-Morgan

Kołobrzeg from the canal Miranda Delmar-Morgan

View of Kołobrzeg residents' marina from the bridge Miranda Delmar-Morgan

Do not confuse the illuminated pleasure pier 800m to the east with the entrance.

There also tourist 'pirate ships' which are busy in summer. Beware of fishing nets anywhere along the adjacent coast where there are small fishing villages. They can be found well out at sea.

Warning In west or northwest winds over Force 5 the entrance is dangerous and should not be attempted.

Berthing
Kołobrzeg Marina (Marina Solna) lies 0·6M inside the entrance at the northwest end of Solna island. It is now for residents only. A new basin with 150 visitor berths has been excavated to the south of Marina Solna and small signs labeled '*goście*' (guests) direct you onwards to the new basin. Yachts requiring depths greater than 3m can lie on the outside of the Basen Lodziowy quay.

Facilities
Facilities in the smaller Marina Solna are excellent, and the staff are multi-lingual. It is likely that the new basin will be run to the same standard. It has its own HM office and ablutions. Finger pontoons are quite long and well spaced. There is a bar/restaurant at Marina Solna and in the redoubt. The attractive town is a short distance away and has open air cafes and good shops. There is a sailmaker and chandlery and yachts can be slipped and repairs carried out. Diesel is available 0800–1200.

352   THE BALTIC SEA AND APPROACHES

DARŁOWO

Darłowo

54°26'·5N 16°22'·5E west mole head

Distances
Kołobrzeg 32M, Ustka 22M

Charts
UKHO 2014, 2015, 2018, 2040
Polish 56, 152, 153, 252

Lights
Gaski 54°14'·7N 15°52'·5E Oc(3)15s50m23M
　Red round tower with gallery and cupola
E. Mole near root 54°26'·4N 16°22'·7E LFl(2)15s20m15M
　Red square tower with white gallery and dome
Jaroslawiec 54°32'·3N 16°32'·6E Fl(2)9s50m23M
　Red round tower with white dome

Communications
Harbourmaster ☏ +48 94 314 2683 or + 48 94 314 2485
　VHF Ch 6, 12, 14, 16, 71
Marina Manager ☏ +48 94 314 5185,
　Mobile +48 509 462 214
Opening Bridge ☏ +48 94 314 2976 VHF Ch 12
Radio Słupsk ☏ +48 59 814 4889
　SAR VHF Ch 11, 16 ☏ +48 505 050 975

General
Darłowo port is a 10 minute ferry ride from the town, which is attractive, with well-preserved historical sites, and well worth a visit. King Eric, who was the last king of Scandinavia, was married to a daughter of Henry V of England and made Darłowo his base for piratical raids on Scandinavia after he was deposed and banished, hence all the pirate ships. It is a popular holiday resort with an outdoor sea pool and lots of restaurants.

Approach
In fair conditions the approach is straightforward, but the entrance itself is narrow and curved. Depths are around 4m, but an uncomfortable surge can enter in strong winds from between west and north.

A retracting bridge 0·5M inside the entrance opens on the hour (24 hours) when craft are waiting, and by special arrangement. Commercial ships use this port and the canal is very narrow. Permission to enter or leave must be sought on VHF Ch 12. Yachts awaiting a bridge opening can lie on the seaward wharfside but will be uncomfortable in onshore winds when a bad scend will build.

Warnings The entrance is dangerous in onshore winds over Force 5 and susceptible to cross currents. There are firing ranges, Areas 6, 6a and 6b between Darłowo and Ustka. See under Ustka for details.

Berthing
Darłowo has new marina facilities and a new clubhouse, with finger pontoons in the Basen Rybacki, which was the fishing harbour. Commercial repairs take place on the NE side of the basin and fishing boats share this basin. New wharves have been built the entire navigable length of the north side of the River Wieprza with electrical points in one or two places, exercise machines, but no facilities except for two portaloos beside the quay in 2015. In severe conditions if a *scend* is entering the marina then this may provide more shelter.

Basen Zimowy on the west side of the canal has been excavated and has pontoons, and by summer 2017 it should have water and electricity.

Facilities
New clubhouse with excellent facilities. WiFi. No fuel berth. Strong winds might carry dust and grit from the shipyard across the marina. Very nice staff who will greet you late at night. The marina is popular with local boats and is busy in high season. Small chandler will refill gas bottles if given notice. Customs. Basic supplies can be obtained in the port area and across the foot bridge. The interesting town can be reached by the ferry or the riverside walk and has plenty of shops and hardware stores.

Retracting bridge at Darłowo *Miranda Delmar-Morgan*

THE BALTIC SEA AND APPROACHES

6B. COAST OF POLAND

PORT DARŁOWO

N

Depths in Metres

Chart annotations:
- 8₅, 5₈, 5₈, 5₆, 5₂, 3₃, 3₃, 2₈ — soundings
- Iso.R.4s10m6M
- Iso.G.4s10m6M
- Q.G.6m5M
- Q.G.6m 5M
- Darłowo LFl(2)15s20m15M
- Falochron Wschodni
- Falochron Zachodni
- 26.5'
- Ferry to Darłowo
- Retracting bridge opens on the hour
- Shipyard
- Basen Rybacki
- Basen Zimowy Darłowo
- 54°26'
- Wieprza
- Darłowo
- 25.5'
- 22.5' 16°23'E 23.5' 24'

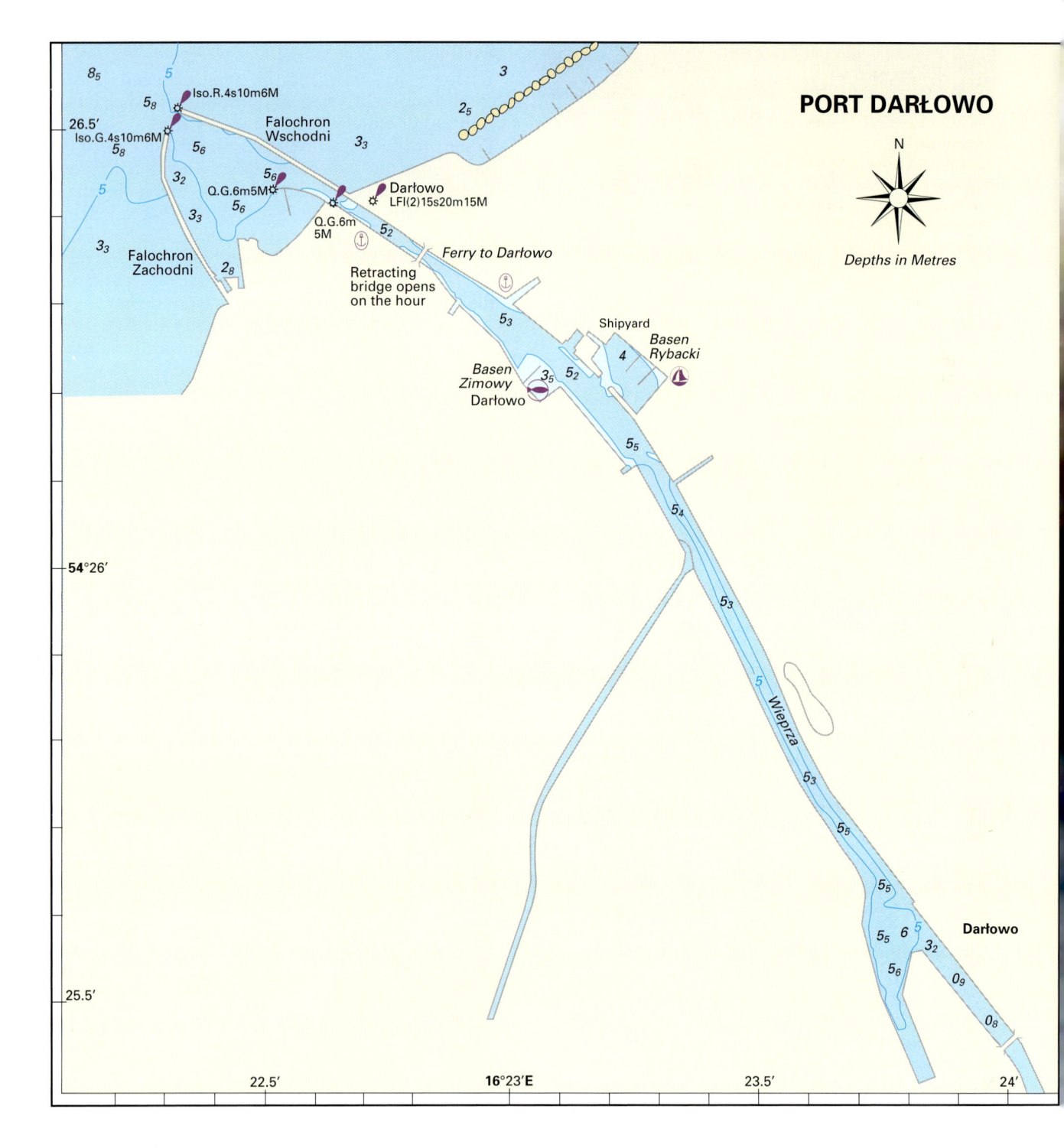

Ustka with footbridge
Nicholas Hill

354   THE BALTIC SEA AND APPROACHES

Ustka

54°35'·50N 16°51'·0E west mole head

Distances
Darłowo 20M, Łeba 30M

Charts
UKHO 2014, 2015, 2018, 2040, 2369,
Polish 54, 55, 152, 153, 252

Lights
Jaroslawiec 54°32'·3N 16°32'·6E Fl(2)9s50m23M
 Red round tower, white dome
Port Ustka 54°35'·3N 16°51'·3E Oc.6s22m8M
 Red octagonal tower, white cupola.
Rowy 54°40'·1N 17°03'·1E Iso.Y.6s10m2M
Czołpino 54°43'·1N 17°14'·5E Oc(2)8s75m22M
 Round brick tower, black cupola

Communications
Harbourmaster ☎ +48 59 814 4430, +48 59 815 4356 or
 Mobile +48 885 515 415
Port Control (Bosmanat) ☎ +48 59 814 4533, VHF Ch 12, 16
Radio Słupsk ☎ +48 59 814 4889
 Medical help ☎ +48 59 814 6011
 www.umsl.gov.pl

Approach

The approach to Ustka is straightforward on a bearing of 150° on the lighthouse or harbour entrance. The entrance carries 5–6m, with 4–5m inside the harbour. A new footbridge has been built across the canal entrance. The bridge closes on the hour for 20 minutes. There is no waiting facility on the seaward side of the wharves, so if you have missed the opening it is best to wait outside. The harbourmaster's office, clearly marked Kapitanat Portu Ustka, is situated on the east pier – dues are paid at the office on the top floor. Also on the first floor are the offices of Radio Słupsk where the staff are helpful with enquiries about the firing ranges.

Warnings Entry is dangerous in winds over Force 5 from southwest through north to east. And beware of cross currents.

There are firing ranges (Areas 6, 6a and 6b) between Ustka (pronounced *Oostka*) and Darłowo where passage may be prohibited – dates and times are broadcast on VHF accompanying the weather forecasts and navigational warnings. See page 339 for details. In general firing takes place every day from 0500 until 0200 the next day except on Sundays, Mondays and public holidays. It may be necessary to make a long diversion out to sea. Patrol craft are in attendance.

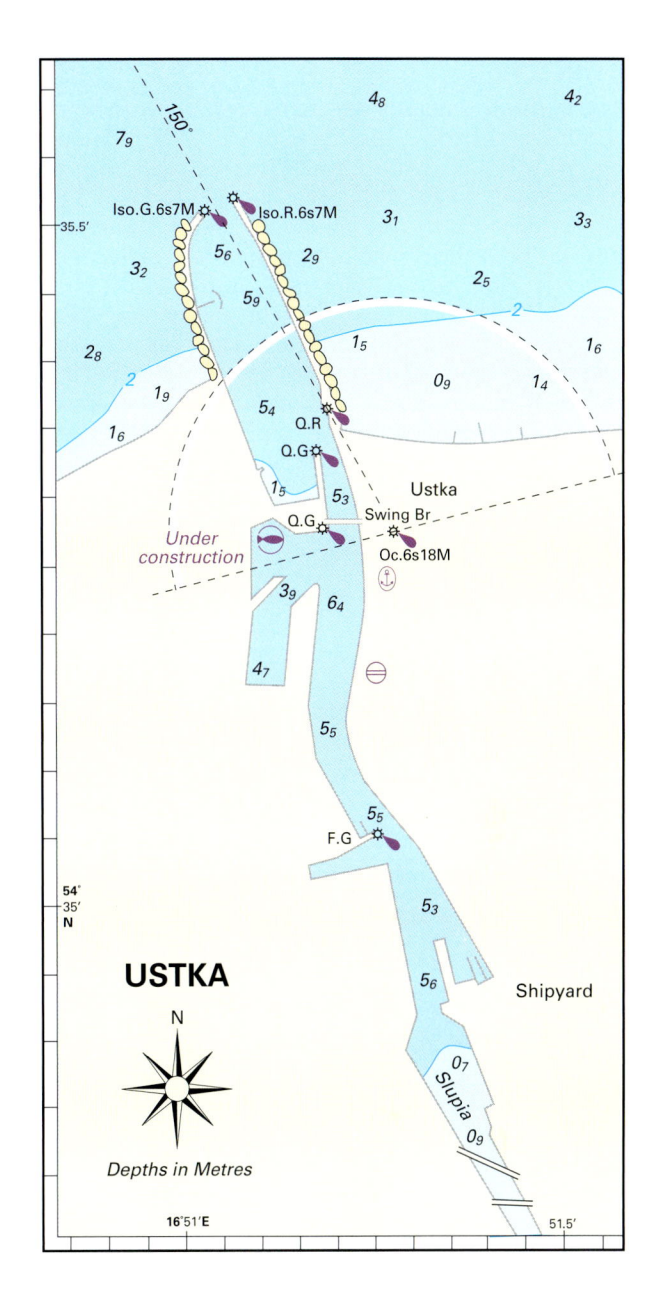

Ustka Marina Nicholas Hill

6B. COAST OF POLAND

Berth
The harbour is mainly devoted to fishing, with some commercial traffic, and is also a popular holiday resort. There are now (2017) two basins immediately beyond the bridge to starboard. The northern one is for fishing vessels and the southern one has been developed as a marina for yachts. The pontoon fingers are quite small and soon fill with local yachts but it is possible to lie on the quaysides. Larger yachts can also berth alongside on the quay on the east side of the harbour clear of a crane and the SAR vessel. Swell may enter the harbour in strong northerlies and the canal and basins are subject to severe surge in adverse conditions.

Facilities
Showers and toilets are in a block resembling a portacabin, for use by sailors and fishermen. There is a good selection of shops in town. Customs point.

Łeba

54°47'·11N 17°33'·80E safe water RW buoy

Distances
Kołobrzeg 85M, Darłowo 55M, Ustka 30M, Władysławowo 30M, Gdynia 65M

Charts
Admiralty 2014, 2015, 2018, 2040
Polish 53, 251, 252, 152

Lights
Czołpino 54°43'·3N 17°14'·6E Oc(2)8s75m22M Round brick tower, black cupola 25m
Dir Lt 203° 54°46'·1N 17°33'N Dir.WRG.7m8–6M 197°-Fl.G.3s-198°-F.G-201°-Al.WG-202°-F.W-204°-Al.WR-205°-F.R-208°-Fl.R.3s-209°
GW buoy **Łeba** 54°47'·2N 17°32'·5E LFl.10s Red and white pillar buoy, ● topmark
West breakwater 54°46'·2N 17°33'E Q.10m5M 025°-vis-180°+Iso.G.4s5M 180°–vis-025°
Marina breakwater 54°45'·9N 17°33'E F.G.
Stilo 54°47'·3N 17°44'·2E Fl(3)12s75m23M 050·5°-vis-290·5° Red, white and black banded tower 33m

Communications
Łeba Harbourmaster ☎ +48 59 866 2973 (0730–1530 LT)
Łeba Port Control (Bosmanat) ☎ +48 59 866 1530/8 VHF Ch 12,
Łeba Marina ☎ +48 59 866 1735
    mobile +48 605 668 427, VHF Ch 12,16 and 17
    http://port.leba.eu/pl/yacht-port

General
Łeba (pronounced *Weh-ba*) is a popular tourist resort with a small commercial and fishing harbour. The relatively new yacht marina with all facilities is on the starboard hand just inside the entrance. Łeba is close to the Slowinski National Park, a UNESCO Biosphere Reserve with forests, lakes and close to the beautiful shimmering sand dunes.

Approach
Between Ustka and Łeba the Traffic Separation Scheme (TSS) Słupska Bank East has an inshore traffic zone for vessels less than 20m. Czolpino lighthouse to the west is obscured by trees apart from the lantern.

The suggested approach is made on a bearing of 203° from the Łeba light buoy, heading for the leading light tower which is on a white column on

Approach to Łeba Miranda Delmar-Morgan

ŁEBA

Request permission to enter or leave from Port Control on VHF Ch 12. There is a very tall white column on the east mole supporting radar. Port Control will provide guidance in poor visibility.

Warning The entrance shoals and although it gets dredged regularly it is dangerous in winds over Force 5 from west to northeast through north. Also beware of cross currents and there can be an outflow of up to two knots from Lake Lebsko.

Berthing

Łeba Marina has 150 berths inside a long eastern wall which blocks swell entering from the main harbour entrance, however it still suffers from surge. Mooring is alongside thin finger pontoons, with stern buoys, and yachts of up to 18m can be accommodated in depths of 2·3–3m. Berths towards the north side of the marina appear to be silting and are shallower. Larger yachts berth in the southwest corner. The marina office is clearly marked in English and staff will assist with mooring.

Facilities

Water and electricity on the marina pontoons, with showers, and laundry facilities. WiFi. Diesel berth in the marina. There is a boatyard nearby, and a winter storage facility is planned for the marina site, but as yet no chandlery. The marina and its facilities are notably well maintained and the staff, who speak English and German, will assist with information about the harbour and town. There is a bar/restaurant in the marina complex, and some overnight accommodation on the upper floor. Shopping, banks etc are to be found in the town. There is an ATM 500m to the south near the bridge and a Polo supermarket across the bridge. Bicycles can be hired for exploration of the National Park. Customs point.

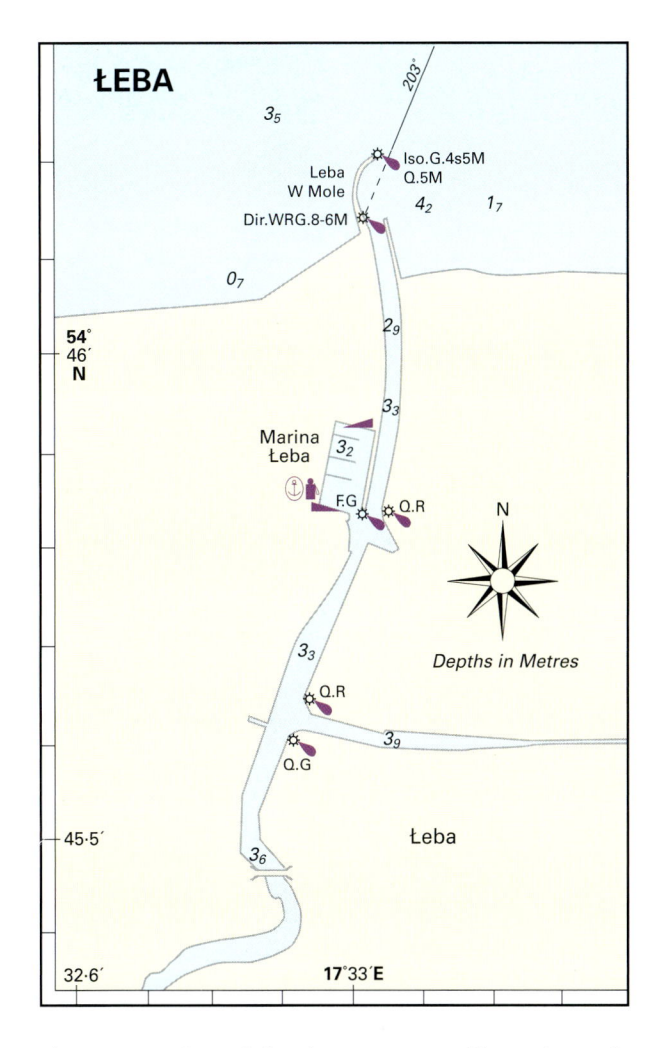

the west mole. Whilst there are no offlying hazards the adjacent depths are very shoal. Entry is made between two curved concrete breakwaters – it is both shallow (2·5m to sometimes as little as 2m after storms) and narrow. A signal mast is on the port hand close to the entrance and shows Traffic Safety Signals. The marina is just beyond it to starboard and needs a sharp starboard turn to enter. The Port Control Office is on the eastern side in a bungalow.

Łeba marina entrance Nicholas Hill

THE BALTIC SEA AND APPROACHES 357

6B. COAST OF POLAND

Władysławowo

58°47'·87N 18°26'·53E safe water mark

Distances
Kołobrzeg 115M, Ustka 60M, Łeba 30M, Hel 22M, Gdynia 30M, Gdańsk 32M

Charts
UKHO 2014, 2015, 2018, 2040, 2288, 2688
Polish 251, 151, 152, 73, 35, 3022

Lights
Rozewie 54°49'·8N 18°20'·2E Fl.3s83m26M
　Red round tower, red top, two galleries
Landfall buoy 54°47'·8N 18°26'·5E LFl.10sRW buoy
Ldg Lts 260° *Front* E Breakwater 54°47'·7N 18°25'·2E
　Oc.R.6s14m4M Yellow framework tower
　Rear Ldg Lt 245m from front Oc.R.6s22m4M
　On roof of building
Jastarnia 54°42'N 18°40'·9E Mo(A)20s22m15M
　White round tower, red bands, gallery

Communications
Harbourmaster ☎ +48 58 674 0486
　Bosmanat ☎ +48 58 674 02 64
Port Control ☎ +48 58 674 0066, VHF Ch 10, 16
www.szkuner.pl

General
Władysławowo (pronounced *Vwah-dih-swa-vo-vo*) is an artificial harbour near the root of the Mierzeja Helska (Hel peninsula) and some 4M SE of Rozewie Point, a prominent headland which forms Poland's northernmost extremity. This is Poland's largest fishing port, landing between 25–35,000 tons of fish annually, but has some facilities for a small number of yachts. It is also a popular holiday resort.

Approach
Just to the north west of Rozewie Lighthouse is an area marked as 'entry forbidden' on the chart for reasons unknown, and although there are no physical marks it is probably best to comply.

Straightforward approach and entrance on 260° from the landfall buoy with the front leading mark, which is a column on the east breakwater, 100m back from the east molehead, in line with the tall Dom Rybaka tower, (see plan) though care must be taken not to stray north of the approach line on closing the north breakwater. Keep an eye on the depth sounder during the approach as the sandbanks shift. There is a small green unlit buoy on the approach, and a red pillar buoy 300m east of the eastern end of the breakwater.

Władysławowo leading marks Miranda Delmar-Morgan

Warnings
The approach is dangerous in winds over Force 5 from the north and east because of sand banks.

Between Władysławowo and the eastern end of the Hel peninsula are two firing ranges (Areas 10 and 11) firing up to 10M out to sea. Firing times will need to be checked. See under firing ranges and navigational warnings on page 339.

Berth
Berth on the yacht pontoons with thin fingers and stern buoys in the extreme west of the harbour clearly marked 'For Yachts Only'. Yachts can also lie on the SW harbour wall, against tyres, or alongside

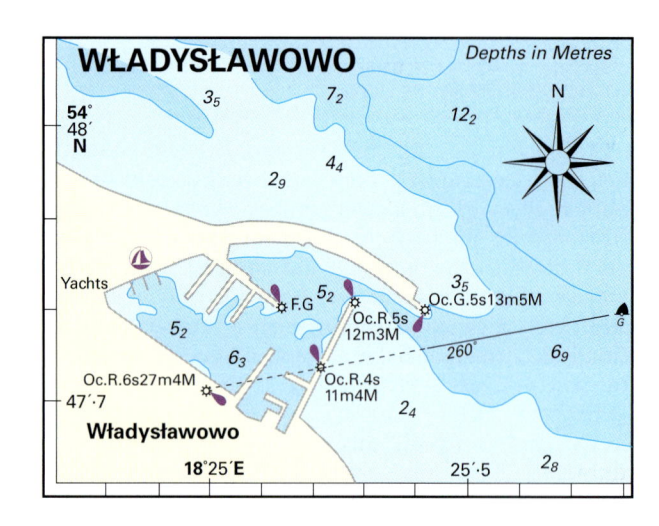

Yacht berths at Władysławowo Miranda Delmar-Morgan

358　THE BALTIC SEA AND APPROACHES

the breakwater in the outer basin, but this berth is much less protected from swell and there are no facilities. The harbour carries a depth of 5m almost throughout.

Facilities
Water/electricity on the pontoons. Independently run showers/toilets near the shipyard/marina entrance opposite the harbourmaster's office, with a key from the security guard on the gate if the office is closed. Diesel for yachts available, via the harbourmaster.

Shops/restaurants in town 1km to northwest of shipyard gate. Shipyard with mechanical and electronic workshops. Trains to Hel, Gdynia and Gdańsk.

Hel

54°36'N 18°48'E

Distances
Łeba 52M, Władysławowo 22M, Gdynia 10M, Gdańsk 15M, Kaliningrad 30M, Klaipėda 105M

Charts
UKHO 2014, 2015, 2018, 2040, 2688
Polish 12, 44, 45, 73, 151, 251

Lights
Jastarnia 54°42'N 18°40'·2E Mo(A)20s22m15M
   White round tower, red bands and gallery
HL-S SCM 54°35'·3N 18°48'E Q(6)+LFl.15s
Hel 54°36'N 18°48'·75E Iso.10s39m17M Red octagonal masonry tower with gallery vis 151°-102°

Communications
Marina ☎ +48 58 675 01 50
Port office +48 58 675 08 08
   porthel@home.pl www.porthel.home.pl
Harbourmaster ☎ +48 58 675 0618
Port Control ☎ +48 58 675 0624, VHF Ch 10, 16, 71
Marina Manager ☎ +48 58 675 0618
www.hel-miasto.pl www.hel.pl

General
This busy and popular family holiday resort has a small and pleasant fishing port. Hel is just inside the tip and on the southwest side of the Hel peninsula (Mierzeja Helska) which extends for 18M in a northwest/southeast direction, a line of wooded dunes no higher than 30m, and in places no more than 250m wide and quite steep-to. It carries road and rail links.

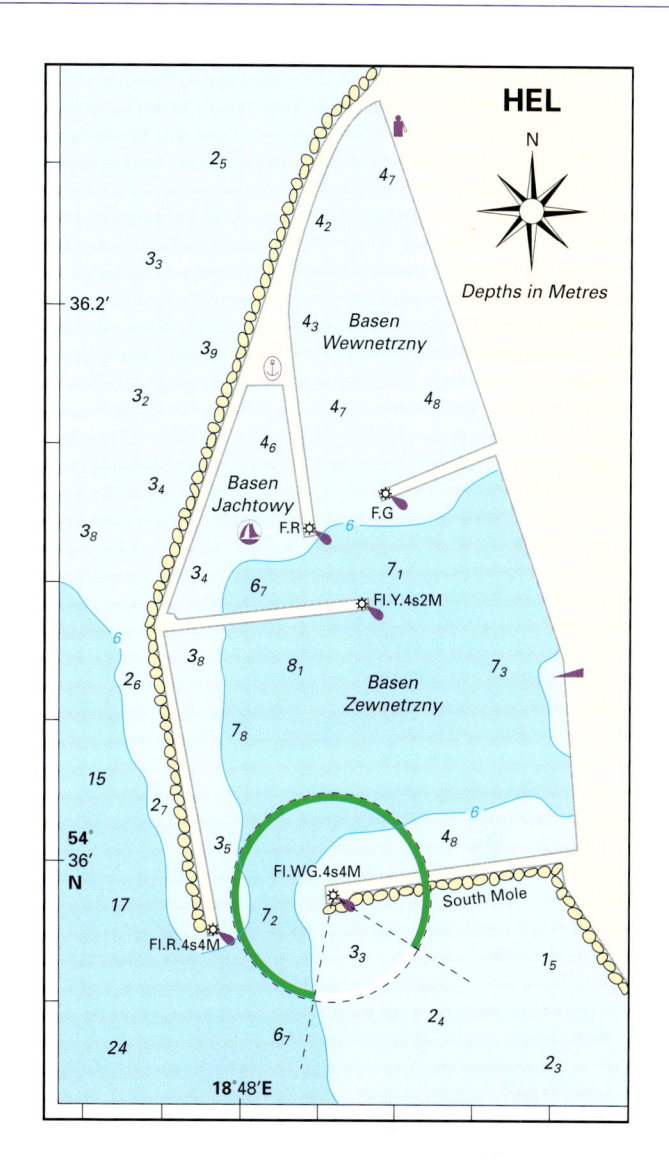

Warning Between the eastern end of the Hel Peninsula and Władysławowo are two firing ranges (Areas 10 and 11) firing up to 10M out to sea. Firing times will need to be checked. See page 339.

Approach
54°35'·97N 18°47'·98E west mole
54°35'·30N 18°47'·90E HL-S south cardinal buoy

Approach from the south is straightforward but do not confuse the entrance with that of the naval harbour 1M to the northwest where entry is prohibited.

Hel Marina approach *Miranda Delmar-Morgan*

6B. COAST OF POLAND

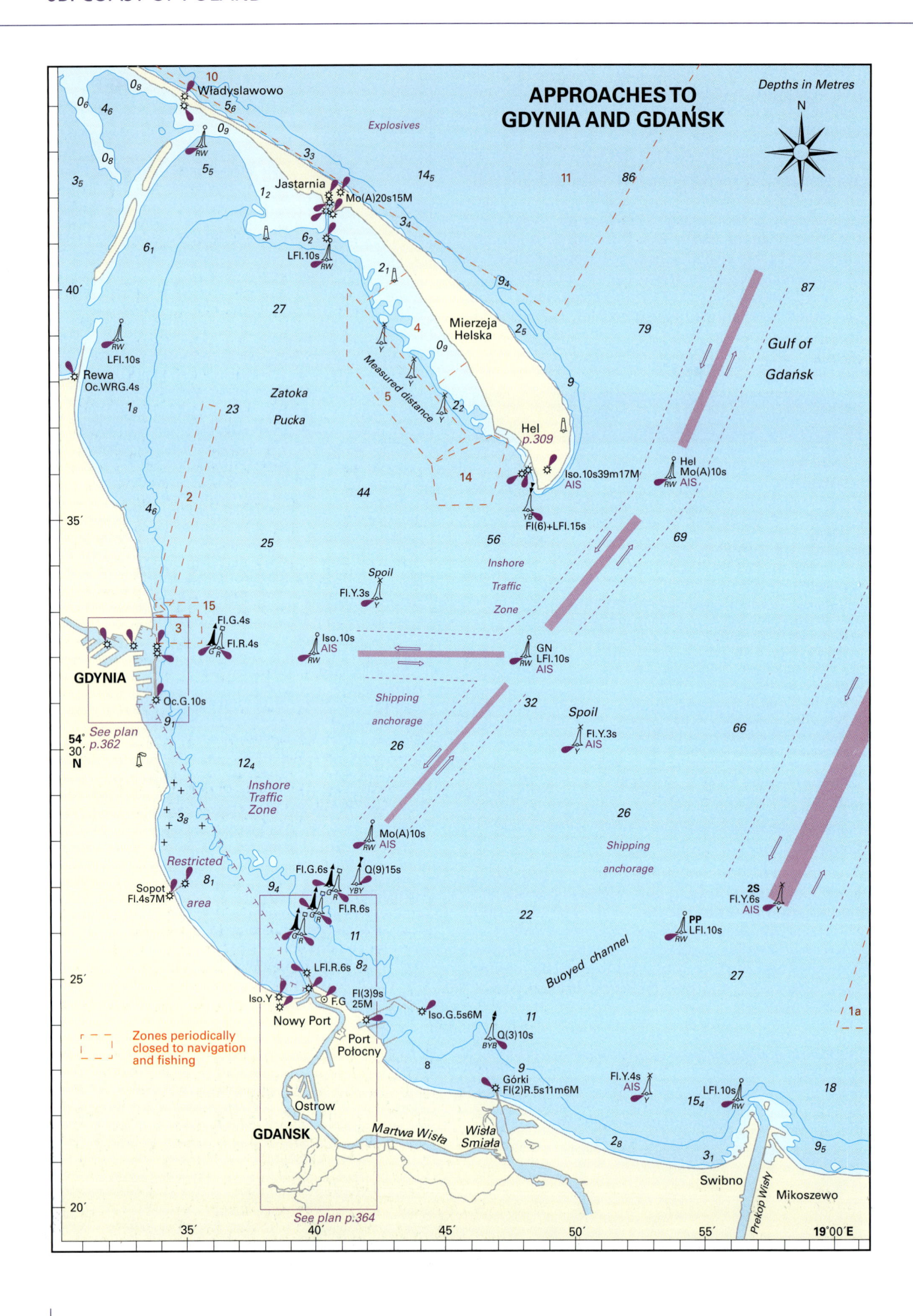

APPROACHES TO GDYNIA AND GDAŃSK

Depths in Metres

GDYNIA

Approach from the north involves rounding the South cardinal mark at the end of a very shallow spit running out from the tip of the peninsula. Unlit nets are a real menace over the whole area, on both sides.

Commercial shipping in the area is moderately heavy, but yachts using the inshore traffic zone to Gdynia remain clear of the major separation scheme for the ports of Gdynia and Gdańsk.

Berth

In the yacht basin on the west side of the harbour. Moor to pontoons or alongside in depths from 2·5–4·0m. Good shelter in north and westerlies, but subject to surge in strong winds with southing in them, and pontoons can be noisy chafing against the piles.

Facilities

Water on the quay and electricity on the pontoon. Showers/toilets are in portacabins behind the onion domed building on the breakwater. Diesel in the fishing harbour. Workshops and mobile crane on harbourside. Shops and restaurants (including an Admiral Nelson and a Captain Morgan where there are menus in English) in the main street close to the harbour. Maritime Museum and a Baltic Seal aquarium. Trains to Gdynia and Gdańsk. Passport control and Customs.

Gdynia

54°32′N 18°33′E

Distances
Władysławowo 35M, Łeba 70M, Kołobrzeg 155M, Gdańsk 10M, Kaliningrad 45M, Klaipėda 115M

Charts
UKHO 2369, 2288, 2688, 2680
Polish 12, 44, 45, 73, 151, 251, 3022

Lights
Rozewie 54°49′·9N 18°20′·3E Fl.3s83m26M
  Red round tower, red top, two galleries
Władysławowo 57°47′·8N 18°24′·6E
  Aero F.R.78m23M Tower
Jastarnia 54°42′N 18°40′·9E Mo(A)20s22m15M
  White round tower, red bands and gallery
Hel 54°36′·1N 18°48′·9E Iso.10s39m17M
  130°-vis-080°+F.R Red octagonal tower with gallery
Ldg Lts 271·5° *Front* 54°32′·2N 18°32′·9E Oc.Y.5s15m8M
  White metal framework tower 15m
  Rear 0·57M from front Oc.Y.5s30m8M
  White metal framework tower, black stripe 24m
South detached breakwater, north end
  (main entrance) 54°32′·1N 18°34′·8E Iso.R.4s15m10M
  Round concrete tower with gallery and dome
South detached breakwater, south end
  54°31′N 18°33′·7E Oc.G.10s12m9M
  Concrete tower with glass cupola
Basen żeglarski (yacht basin), east wall 54°31′N 18°33′·2E
  F.G.6m2M Green concrete column
Basen żeglarski (yacht basin), south wall 54°31′N
  18°33′·2E F.R.5m2M Red concrete column on hut
Port Północny (Gdańsk) 54°24′N 18°41′·8E Fl(3)9s61m25M
  Blue square tower with white gallery
Note Lights for the central (main) and north entrances are not described

Communications
Gdynia Harbourmaster ☏ +48 58 621 0705/7983
  VHF Ch 12
Gdynia Port Control ☏ +48 58 621 6636, VHF Ch 12, 16
  (Yachts are required to monitor VHF Ch 12 and request permission to leave or enter the marina)
Gdynia Yacht Club Marina *Mobile* +48 785 174 719
  VHF Ch 12 www.marinagdynia.pl
  www.gdynia.pl

General

The Gulf of Gdańsk has two Traffic Separation Schemes running across it from the Hel Peninsula to the Gdynia and Gdańsk approaches. There are two prohibited areas to the north of Gdynia and several yellow buoys marking one of them. It also has further nets to avoid, and numerous sailing clubs

Gdynia approach Miranda Delmar-Morgan

THE BALTIC SEA AND APPROACHES 361

6B. COAST OF POLAND

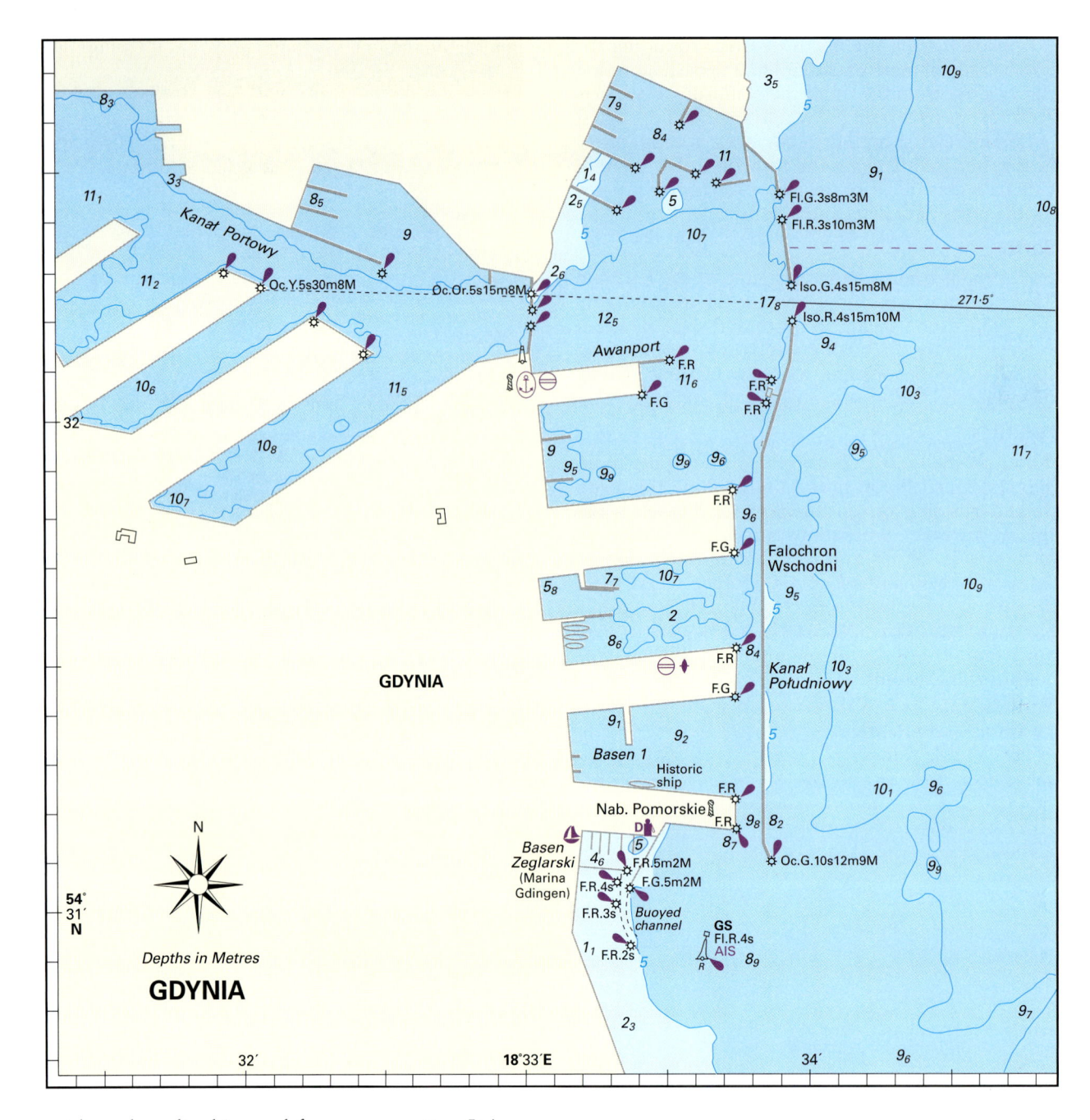

with yachts, dinghies and frequent regattas. It is a very busy place. Gdynia (pronounced *Guh-din-ya*) is a major commercial and shipbuilding port. Most container traffic for Poland passes through Gdynia. The secure yacht harbour lies south of the main port entrance.

South of the city lies a popular beach area with pavement cafés, bars and local shops lining the seafront and main avenue. South again, by some 9km, is the highly fashionable city of Sopot (see opposite) where cultural events, concerts and seaside recreation are popular.

Approach and entrance
54°30'·95N 18°33·20'E south mole

Gdynia is protected by north-south detached breakwaters more than 1·5M in length, pierced by three entrances. The leading lights direct shipping through the main (central) entrance and should be ignored by yachts.

Staying clear of the TSS which begins 2M east of the Hel Peninsula, yachts should steer for the south end of the eastern detached breakwater. On rounding the outer breakwater the marina's east wall will be seen about 550m ahead, with a green column marking the entrance.

The entrance channel to the yacht basin (Basen Zeglarski) is narrow and the approach is very close to the beach. After a tight turn to starboard around the harbour wall there are two port hand buoys

Gdynia marina *Miranda Delmar-Morgan*

marking the 2m contour. This entrance could be dangerous in strong onshore winds.

The Polish Naval Yacht Club Kotwica uses the berths to port immediately inside the entrance. These berths use long floating polypropylene lines. Visiting yachts should call in advance on VHF Ch 12 for permission to leave and enter, and to ensure/request a berth. The marina can fill with yachting events. The *Dar Pomorza* square rigger is conspicuous on an adjacent quay.

It should be noted that a restricted area extends southwards from a point approximately 100m south of this, due E of Orłowo.

Berthing
The marina master's office is at the marina entrance and staff will direct an incoming yacht to a vacant berth. There are about 50 visitors' berths. Maximum length 20m and maximum draught 2·8m in the entrance. In season berths are often in short supply. Shower tokens from an attendant.

Facilities
Water and electricity on the pontoons. Toilets and showers at the marina office (shower tokens from an attendant). Fuel is available in the eastern corner of the basin.

Gdynia undoubtedly has the best chandleries in Poland. They include SMART, an Admiralty chart agent and Sail-Ho, an agent for Imray, NV-Verlag and Delius Klasing publications.

There is a three tonne crane for masts and small craft and a larger one can be arranged if required. Engineers and boatbuilders are also available. The nearest sailmaker is at Gdańsk. Winter storage outside can be arranged although a cradle may be difficult to find. Free WiFi throughout the city.

Good shopping is available on the main avenue leading from the marina with further shops, including smaller speciality shops, along the main walkway. An open-air market is located adjacent to the multi-level Batory shopping centre, about 10 minutes' walk up the avenue. For major provisioning it may be worth visiting the major Real superstore development approximately 20 minutes by taxi west of the city centre.

The railway station is about 15 minutes' walk from the marina. There is a frequent service to Gdańsk, 20km and about 25 minutes to the southeast, and good links with Szczecin and Berlin.

Sopot

54°26'·80N 13°34'·76E outer mole, south eastern end

Distances
Gdańsk 3·3M, Gdynia 4·5M, Hel 12·5M

Charts
UKHO 2014, 2015, 2018, 2040, 2288, 2636, 2637, 2688
Polish 12, 44, 45, 151, 251, 73, 12, 3022

Lights
Safe water RW buoy 54°26'·7N 18°34'·8E LFl.10s
South end of outer mole, stbd hand 54°26'·8N 18°34'·7E Fl.G.6s4M
NE tip of pier 54°26'·9N 18°34'·7E Fl.Y.5s4M
NE tip of inner mole 54°26·8'N 18°34'·7E Fl.R.6s4M

Communications
☎ + 49 500 696 588, VHF Ch 63
www.sopot-marina.pl/english

Sopot, which lies half way between Gdynia and Gdańsk, is the most expensive marina in Poland. It is Swedish run and part of the Promarina chain. Set at the foot of the long pier, this is an interesting and highly fashionable resort with all the associated entertainments, shops and restaurants. Good facilities but limited toilets and showers. Exposed to southeasterlies.

6B. COAST OF POLAND

Gdańsk

54°21′N 18°39′E

Distances
Łeba 80M, Gdynia 10M, Kaliningrad 45M, Klaipėda 110M

Charts
UKHO 2014, 2015, 2018, 2040, 2288, 2636, 2637, 2688
Polish 41, 44, 71, 251, 151, 73, 12, 500, 3022

Lights
Hel 54°36′·1N 18°48′·9E Iso.10s39m17M 130°-vis-080°
 F.R Red octagonal tower with gallery
Port Północny 54°24′N 18°41′·8E Fl(3)9s61m25M
 Blue square tower with white gallery
Outer Ldg Lts 196° *Front* 54°24′·5N 18°38′·4E
 Iso.Y.5s23m13M White triangle with red border, on white metal framework tower 24m
 Rear 330m from front Iso.Y.5s31m13M Triangle on black metal framework tower 36m
Inner Ldg Lts 147·7° *Front* 54°24′·6N 18°39′·8E
 Oc.G.5s23m8M Two white triangles with red borders, on white beacon 20m
 Rear 370m from front, Oc.G.5s35m8M Black triangle on dark grey beacon 32m
East breakwater 54°25′N 18°39′·5E LFl.R.6s13m7M
 Red tower 13m
West molehead 54°24′·7N 18°39′·6E LFl.G.6s13m7M
 Green framework tower
Górki 54°22′·5N 18°46′·9N Fl(2)R.5s11m6M
 Red round tower with gallery
Krynica Morska 54°23′·1N 19°27′E
 LFl(2)12s53m18M Red round tower, white lantern

Harbour communications
Gdańsk Harbourmaster ☎ +48 58 343 0610
 VHF Ch 14
Gdańsk Port Control ☎ +48 58 343 0710
 VHF Ch 14, 16
Gdańsk Marina *Mobile* +48 695 56 48 48
 or +48 58 301 3378
 www.marinagdansk.pl www.sailgdansk.pl

General

The historic city of Gdańsk (pronounced *Guh-dansk*), and the Nowy (pronounced *Novv-I*) Port is situated at the mouth of the Wisła River, the largest river in Poland. At a strategic location on the old Amber Road, the city has long been a fortified trading settlement. It was a stronghold of the Teutonic Knights, and later a formidable member of the Hanseatic League. Prussian influence is strongly seen in the old waterfront buildings, especially the Crane Gate, constructed in 1440, the largest goods lift of the 15th century. The Stare Miasto (old town), originally built with much Dutch influence, has been carefully restored since the Second World War when 80% of the city was destroyed. It is now the site of cultural events and outdoor festivals during the summer, as well as numerous shops and cafés. The three week festival of St Dominic's Fair takes place in late July/early August and claims to be the largest trade and cultural event in Europe, attracting large numbers of visitors.

Amber is available from local artisans, and the National Museum houses an excellent collection of art, including a collection of Polish and Flemish paintings, relief panels and sculpture.

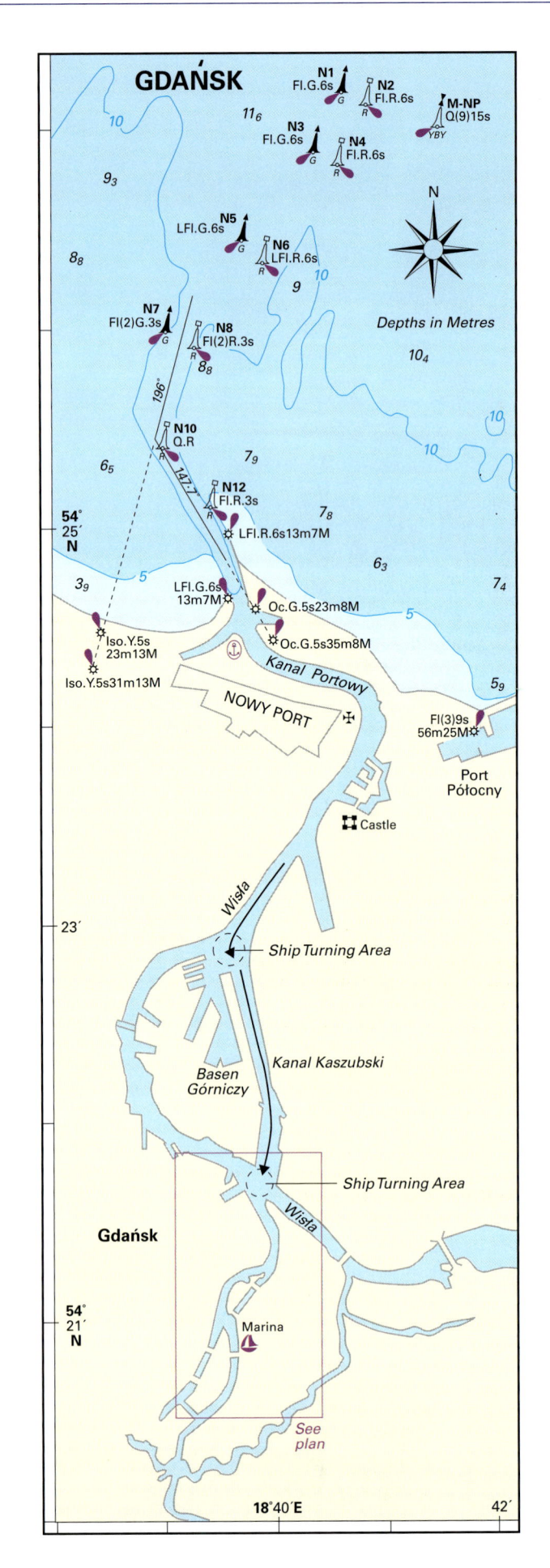

GDAŃSK

Gdańsk concert hall *Miranda Delmar-Morgan*

Gdańsk city centre *Miranda Delmar-Morgan*

The local shipyards were the birthplace of Solidarity (Solidarność), the union movement which eventually led to the demise of Soviet control in Poland, and are now a World Heritage Site. The ship-building and bulk-shipping areas are to the north and east of the old town.

Approach and entrance

The approach from within the Gulf of Gdańsk is straightforward and can be taken in all but the severest of onshore weather conditions. Yachts should stay well clear of the TSS which begins 2M east of the tip of the Hel peninsula. The outer and inner leading lines can be followed, although yachts can safely cut the corner and head directly for the eastern (outer) breakwater head.

Permission to enter (or leave) must be sought from Gdańsk Nowy Port Control on VHF Ch 14.

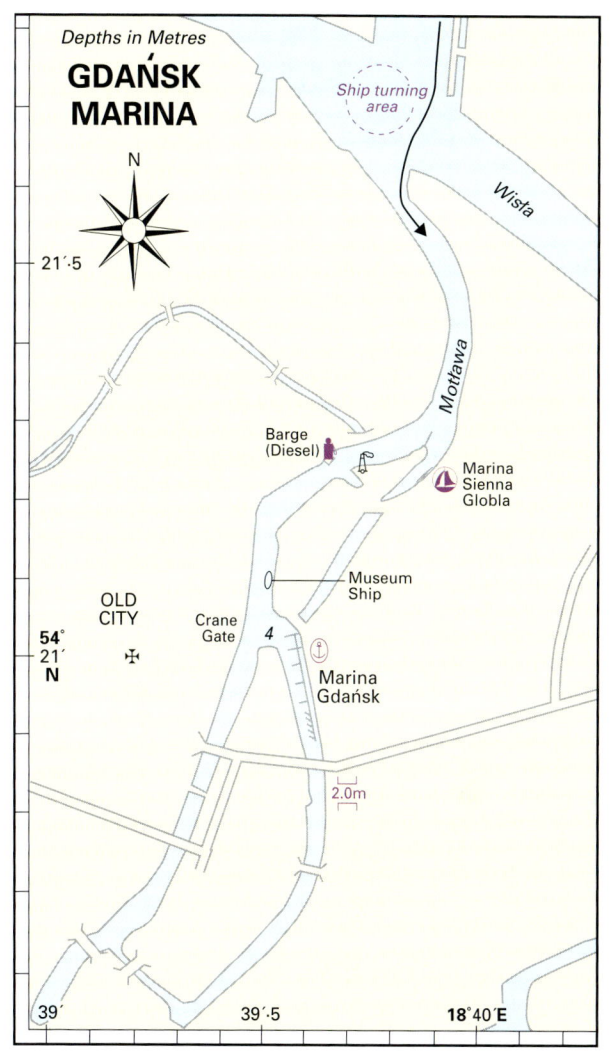

Gdańsk entrance *Miranda Delmar-Morgan*

Just inside the entrance, on the east side, there is a large monument commemorating the men who died when the first shots of the Second World War were fired, by a German battleship, at the barracks on Westerplatte. It is customary to hold one's ensign at the dip when passing it.

The channel follows the Kanal Portowy and Wisła River for 3·7M through the commercial port and shipyards. At the ship turning area, north of Basen Gorniczy (54°23'N) follow the eastern channel, the Kanal Kaszubski. At the next ship turning area (54°21'·7N 18°40'E) follow the small channel directly

THE BALTIC SEA AND APPROACHES

6B. COAST OF POLAND

Gdańsk marina approach *Miranda Delmar-Morgan*

ahead – the Motława River – which leads to the marina in the heart of the old city directly opposite the historic Crane Gate (54°21′N 18°39′E).

Berthing
Gdańsk marina has 70 berths. There are 2·8m depths in the main area but somewhat less near the bridge where smaller vessels are berthed. Staff, who speak good English, are on duty around the clock during summer and will direct visitors to an empty berth. The manager prefers to be contacted by mobile. A yacht could safely be left here for several weeks.

Facilities
The new marina office across the street has excellent facilities and laundry and WiFi. Water and electricity are provided on the pontoons. There is a Lotos fuel barge in the Motława Canal near the Raduni Canal junction, just NE of the opera house. There is a small chandlery with limited stock about 100m from the marina where Polish Hydrographic Charts are available. The excellent hardware store, Metalzbyt, near the Sienna Grobla 11 basin, just north of Gdańsk marina, has a huge range of chandlery and other goods. The Martwa Wisła has a variety of services, marine electricians, sailmakers, overwintering facilties etc., but has to be approached via the Wisła Smiala owing to the fixed bridges across the Martwa Wisła.

Gdańsk has all the facilities of a long-established city. Restaurants, cafés and small shops will be found along the waterfront and in the Stare Miasto (old town) area. There is a small grocery near the marina, but it is necessary to travel further for major shopping.

Transport
Gdańsk Airport has international and national connections, and there are also good train services to Szczecin and Berlin. Marina staff can assist in arranging taxis to the airport or station if requested.

Górki Zachodnie
54°22′N 18°47′E
Charts
UKHO 2369, 2288, 2688, 2680
Polish 11, 73, 151, 251, 3022

The harbour of Górki (pronounced Gor-key) is located 5M to the east of the main entrance of Gdańsk, at the mouth of one of the channels which form the Wisła delta. See plan on page 360. The entrance is protected by breakwaters but they are on a shoal area of sand. There is no internal route from Gdańsk owing to fixed bridges mentioned above.

Warning Sand banks make the approach particularly dangerous in onshore winds and it is probably best not entered in onshore winds over F5.

This a major centre for yacht building and home to around six yacht clubs, including the National Sailing Centre. There are several big yards here: Alu International specialise in aluminium; the Conrad Shipyard built the *Malcolm Miller*; Galeon shipyard has a 200-ton travel lift. Delphia Yachts, and a Yamaha agent are also here. Overwinter storage is available and there is a good choice for yacht and ship repairs and good boatyard facilities, but there is not much in the way of shops or transport. Customs. SAR.

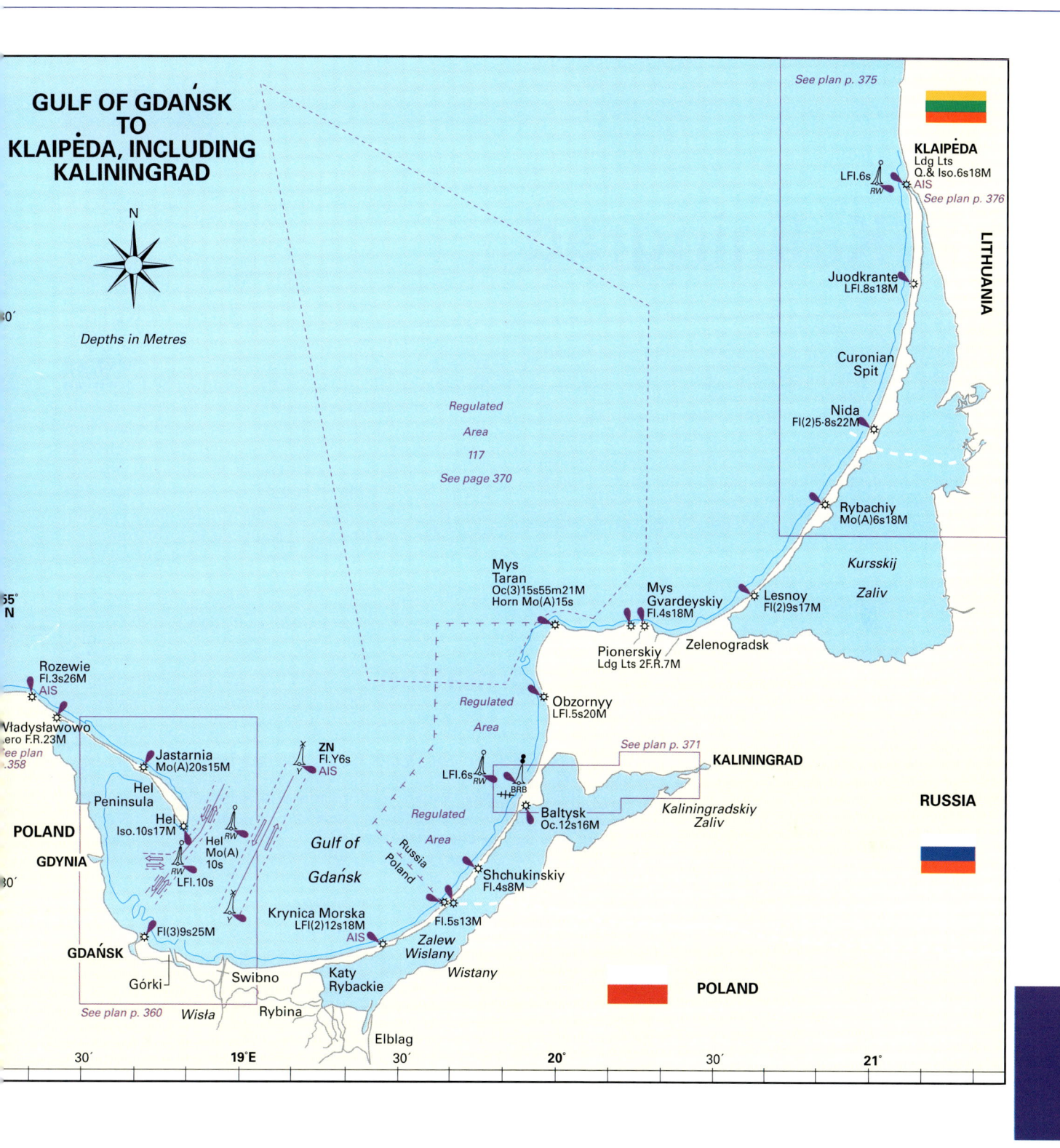

GÓRKI ZACHODNIE

GULF OF GDAŃSK TO KLAIPĖDA, INCLUDING KALININGRAD

Depths in Metres

Regulated Area 117
See page 370

LITHUANIA

KLAIPĖDA
Ldg Lts Q.& Iso.6s18M
LFl.6s
AIS
See plan p. 375
See plan p. 376

Juodkrante
LFl.8s18M

Curonian Spit

Nida
Fl(2)5·8s22M

Rybachiy
Mo(A)6s18M

Kursskij Zaliv

Mys Taran
Oc(3)15s55m21M
Horn Mo(A)15s

Mys Gvardeyskiy
Fl.4s18M

Lesnoy
Fl(2)9s17M

Pionerskiy
Ldg Lts 2F.R.7M

Zelenogradsk

Rozewie
Fl.3s26M
AIS

Władysławowo
aero F.R.23M
See plan p.358

Jastarnia
Mo(A)20s15M

Hel Peninsula

Hel
Iso.10s17M

Hel RW
Mo(A) 10s
LFl.10s RW

ZN
Fl.Y6s
AIS

Obzornyy
LFl.5s20M

LFl.6s RW

See plan p. 371
KALININGRAD

Baltysk
Oc.12s16M

Kaliningradskiy Zaliv

RUSSIA

POLAND

GDYNIA

Gulf of Gdańsk

Russia
Poland

Shchukinskiy
Fl.4s8M

Krynica Morska
LFl(2)12s18M
AIS

Fl.5s13M
Zalew Wiślany

POLAND

Fl(3)9s25M

GDAŃSK
Górki
See plan p. 360

Świbno
Wisła
Rybina

Katy Rybackie

Wistany

Elbląg

30′ | 19°E | 30′ | 20° | 30′ | 21°

THE BALTIC SEA AND APPROACHES   367

6. POLAND

7. Kaliningrad

See location plan page 334

There are two main reasons for visiting Kaliningrad. The first is practical in that Baltiysk, at the seaward end of the approach channel, could serve as a harbour of refuge on an otherwise rather bleak part of the Baltic coast(but to arrive in Kaliningrad without a visa would land you in serious trouble, and should not be contemplated save 'in extremis'). The second is cultural, in that it is a part of Russia easily accessible from the west which retains much from the Stalinist era.

The Kaliningrad oblast (region) is part of Russia, retained after the disintegration of the Soviet Union in order to provide ice-free access to the Baltic Sea throughout the year. It lies sandwiched between Poland and Lithuania, and is isolated from the bulk of Russia by Belarus. The city itself is well inland and approached via a long sea canal from Baltiysk. Shallow-draught boats used to be able to cross the border into Poland through the Zalew Wislany but unmarked nets now make this impossible. There are also inland waterways to Klaipėda in Lithuania.

Key information

Rescue/Safety services

Emergency ☎ 112
MRCC Kaliningrad GMDSS Area A1. VHF Ch 16 and VHF DSC Ch 70. Ch 3 and 7 call sign *Kaliningrad-1*.
☎ +7 4012 538 470.

Charts and pilot books

Russian charts See Russian chart diagrams Appendix page 430.
Baltic Pilot Volume II (NP 19)
Cruising Guide to Baltic Russia, Vladimir Ivankiv, Graham and Fay Cattell available from the Cruising Association and chart agents in Scandinavia

Time

Kaliningrad is on UT+2 all year.

Money

The rouble (divided into 100 kopecks) is the official currency. ATMs accepting credit cards can be found in the city centre where there are also exchange offices. Tips should always be made in roubles.

Formalities

Formalities are as described in the Section on Russia.– see pages 320–321. Vladimir Ivankiv can assist with obtaining visas but will arrange for someone local to provide on the spot support after arrival – see contact details for Vladimir on pages 320.

Notice of arrival – including all the information in the list on page 320 – must be submitted to the Customs Post at Kaliningrad at least 72 hours prior to the yacht's arrival by the host yacht club or agent. Passport Control and Customs are located at the furthest north-eastern corner of Basin No 3 (Quay 81). Working hours are generally between 0800 and 2000 only so arrival and departure have to be timed accordingly. Inward and outward clearance are both mandatory and both may take several hours.

As in St Petersburg persons staying in the country more than a week + an extra weekend (i.e. 9 days) should register visas with the immigration department. In practice this is not strictly enforced as far as those arriving and departing by yacht are concerned. It does however apply to those leaving by other means of transport e.g. plane, train or ferry.

Public holidays

As for Russia – see page 319.

Communications

Public call boxes, either coin or card operated, are widespread. To obtain an international line dial 8, wait for the dial tone, then 10 followed by the country code, area code (omitting any initial 0) and number. If dialling from abroad the country code for Russia is 7 and the area code for Baltiysk and Kaliningrad is 4012.

VHF Ch 16 and/or 74 should be monitored on approach.

Travel

There are road and rail links to the surrounding countries, and ferry services to Gdynia with the Polish line Zegluga Gdańsk and to St Petersburg. Kaliningrad airport lies some 18km distant with regular flights to Moscow, Copenhagen and destinations in Germany. Taxis are inexpensive and readily available for the journey from yacht harbour to city centre.

Websites

marinakaliningrad.ru/engservices.html Marina Kaliningrad website (in English) with charts and advice on navigation and formalities.

www.inyourpocket.com/kaliningrad Tourist information

Radio communications

VHF Ch 16 should be monitored at all times.
Baltiysk Traffic VHF Ch 16, 74. Call Sign *Baltiysk Traffic*

KALININGRAD - KEY INFORMATION

Kaliningrad Port Control VHF Ch 67 call sign *Kaliningrad Port Control*
Border Guard VHF Ch 74 call *IMPULS*
Customs Control VHF Ch 74 call *MECH*
Pilots VHF Ch 67 call *Kaliningrad 11*
See also detail regarding reporting in Formalities above.

Weather information

Navtex and the internet are the best way of obtaining weather information. Kaliningrad Radio broadcasts warnings and weather forecasts, in Russian, on VHF Ch 07 on receipt and at 0533 and 1333 UT.

History

Kaliningrad was named after Mikhail Kalinin, Stalin's inconsequential chairman of the USSR Praesidium, when the area was captured at the end of WWII. The whole Kaliningrad *oblast*, or region, is only 120km by 300km, with its capital in Kaliningrad City, formerly Königsberg.

In the Middle Ages Kaliningrad was part of east Prussia, northeast of Poland. Prussia still consisted of pagan tribal lands that Poland had failed to subdue, so in 1226 they invited the Teutonic Knights to conquer and convert the area to Christianity. Although nominally a Polish fiefdom, after much slaughter Prussia became populated by immigrant Germans who owned the land while the locals had to work as serfs. Then in the Reformation, the Knights' Grand Master secularised the order and made Prussia a Grand Duchy, building Königsberg (now Kaliningrad city) as its capital. As Prussia expanded, Berlin became its new capital, but Königsberg continued to be a major German cultural centre until the end of the Second World War, having been home to such people as the philosopher Immanuel Kant.

Towards the end of WWII, Soviet troops advancing on Germany captured the area and it was later annexed to the Russian Soviet. Huge numbers of Germans were killed or fled westwards, while the rest were used as forced labour.

Kaliningrad was the only Soviet port to remain ice-free all year round, so in the 1950s Stalin used it as the military base for his Baltic fleet. The land route to the Russian Soviet goes through Lithuania and Belarus. Nonetheless, it remained part of the Russian Soviet partly because Lithuania didn't want such a large Russian military base on its territory and also because Russia was happy to keep direct control of a base that separated the Baltic States further from the West.

Following the break up of the Soviet Union in 1990, Kaliningrad remained part of the new Russian Federation, although surrounded by the newly independent states of Poland and Lithuania, both of whom also became members of NATO and the EU. We now know that Russia once offered to sell it back to Germany, but they refused.

Kaliningrad remains a military base. The number of military personnel has been much reduced, initially with a bad effect on the economy, but it has subsequently been more than made up for by tax breaks and investment from foreign manufacturing companies. One in three Russian televisions, for example, is now made in Kaliningrad.

Cruising information

Yacht services

Marina Kaliningrad in Kaliningrad City Harbour offers basic yacht services (see below under Kaliningrad for details).

Kaliningrad Yacht Club Harbour has very limited services.

Chandlery

Seek advice from Marina Kaliningrad.

Holding tanks

There are no laws requiring holding tanks and there are no pump out facilities.

Gas

It is most unlikely that bottles can be refilled and visitors would be advised to carry sufficient for the duration of their visit.

Diesel

Available at Marina Kaliningrad.

Shopping

All supplies can be obtained.

Alcohol

As in the rest of Russia, alcohol supplies are unrestricted.

Caution

The situation in all Russian ports is always subject to change and every effort should be made to check current requirements while the cruise is still at the planning stage.

The security of both yacht and crew is plainly of great importance and all sensible precautions should be taken – see page 321.

THE BALTIC SEA AND APPROACHES

7. KALININGRAD

Kaliningrad

54°38'·88N 19°52'·02E centre of harbour entrance

Distances
Gdynia 45M, Gdańsk 45M, Klaipėda 80M

Charts
UKHO 2288
Russian See chart diagram, Appendix p.430

Lights
Shchukinskiy 54°31'·6N 19°44'·5E Fl.4s50m8M
  Black and white metal framework tower 29m
Baltiysk Fairway rear light, 54°38'·4N 19°53'·7E
  Oc.12s30m16M Round white tower, red top,
  two galleries 32m
Obzornyy 54°49'·7N 19°57'·3E LFl.5s54m20M Triangle on
  orange round tower, white bands 22m
Mys Taran 54°57'·6N 19°58'·9E Oc(3)15s55m21M
  Emergency light Iso.4s13M Red octagonal tower on
  building 30m Horn Mo(A)15s13m Red metal mast
  4m120m NW of light
Baltiysk Fairway Ldg Lts 122·1° Front 54°38'·6N 19°53'·1E
  Oc.12s12m12M 116°-vis-128°
  Two white rectangles with black stripes on red metal
  framework tower 21m
  Rear 770m from front Oc.12s30m16M
Fairway No.1 buoy 54°41'·3N 19°45'·1E LFl.6s Red and
  white pillar buoy
North mole 54°39'N 19°52'·3E Fl.R.2·5s3M
South mole 54°38'·8N 19°52'·1E Fl.G.4s1M
Many more lights and lit buoys mark the Kaliningradskiy
Morskoy Kanal

Harbour communications
See Key information section above.

Approach and entrance

Beware of the Navy firing ranges to the north and northwest of the port of Baltiysk and the cape of Taran.

Particular attention should be paid to Regulated Area 117. See plan on page 367. It is important to monitor VHF Ch 16 when sailing in or close to Russian waters so as to be able to respond to instructions as all vessels will be on their radar. Details of any closure of regulated areas are posted on Navtex with five days warning and can also be found on the website of the Swedish Maritime Administration www.sjofartsverket.se – NAVTEX – south-eastern Baltic.

Approach is made from the Gulf of Gdańsk (see plan page 367). Though depths are generally good within 1M of the coast it would nevertheless be wise to keep well offshore until able to approach via the designated channel on 122°, passing Fairway Buoy No. 1 en route. Contact should be made with Baltiysk Traffic (land based border guard call sign Vyshka or coast guard ship call sign Velbot). Required information is name of vessel, last port, port of arrival, purpose of entering territorial waters, number of persons on board. Reporting is mandatory, and contact should be made when more than 7M (or one hour) from the entrance. An escort vessel may approach the yacht to check credentials and escort her in. Night approach should be avoided as immigration and customs working hours are generally between 0800 and 2000.

Final entry is straightforward, with the Passport Control and Customs berth on the north side of the channel 2M from the entrance in the northeast corner of Basin No. 3 (quay 81) (54°38'·19N 19°55'·29E). From Baltiysk the well-buoyed Kaliningradskiy Morskoy Kanal runs some 22M (41km) between low-lying banks to the commercial port and city of Kaliningrad. Depths are dredged to a nominal 9m throughout its length, but shoal steeply on either side.

For Marina Kaliningrad follow the Morskoy Kanal all the way into the city. Marina Kaliningrad is situated on the northern bank of the River Pregolya just before the railway bridge which cannot be passed by masted craft.

For the Kaliningrad Yacht Club harbour in the southeastern corner of the Kaliningradskiy Zaliv (the large inland sea traversed by the Kaliningradskiy

Kaliningrad Marina Channel and berthing, showing industrial backdrop Photos kindly supplied by Marina Kaliningrad

KALININGRAD

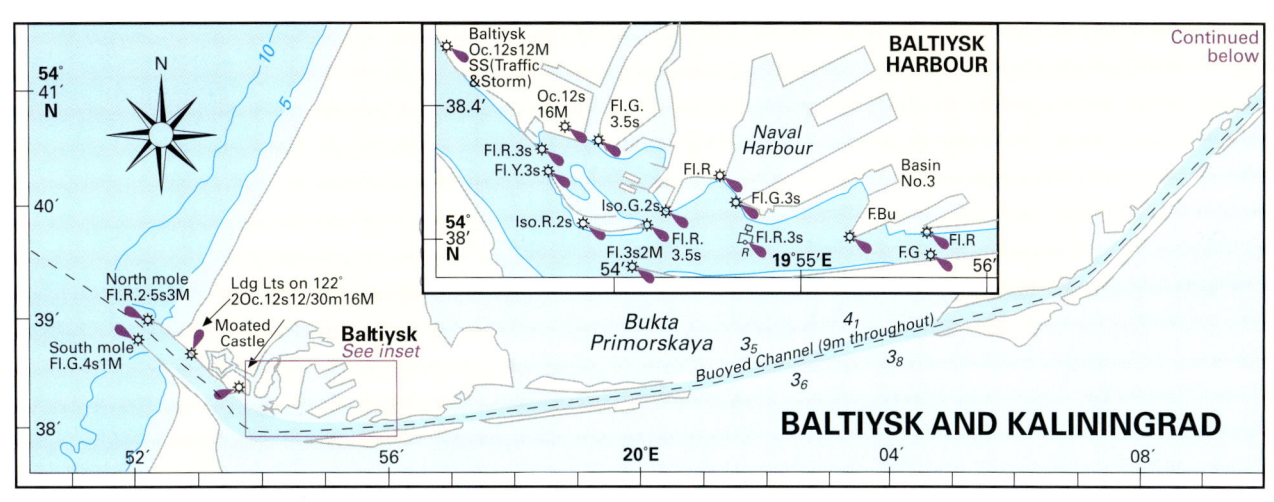

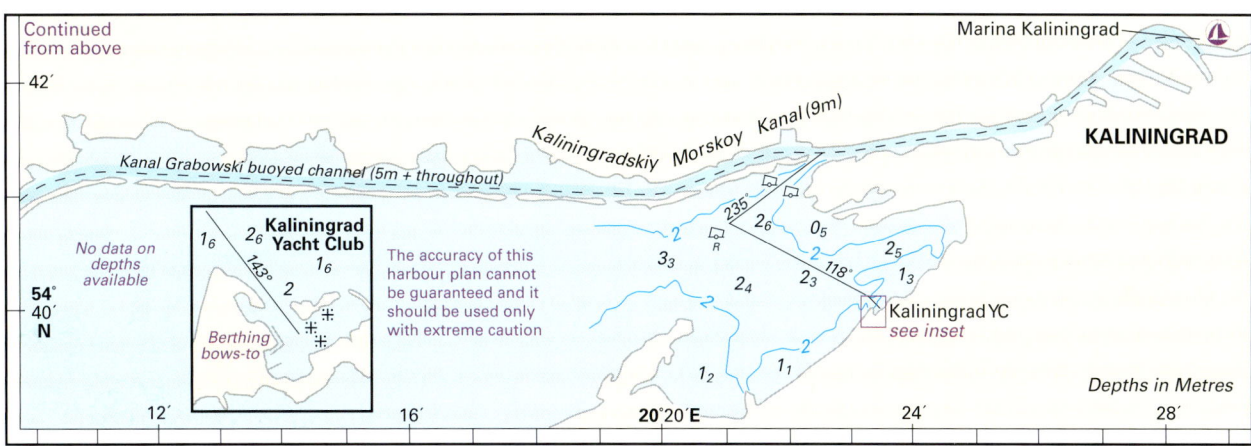

Morskoy Kanal) the main channel is followed as far as light beacon No. 30 (54°41'·40N 20°22'·40E). From there a course of 235° is followed for 1M, before swinging onto 118° towards the harbour and buildings of the Kaliningrad Yacht Club and 143° for the final approach. Parts of the route are shallow – less than 2m – though the bottom is soft. Do not stray as there are unmarked fishing nets and wrecks in the Kaliningradskiy Zaliv.

At least four hours should be allowed between the Passport Control berth and the yacht harbour.

Berthing

Baltiysk
Although there is a yacht harbour within the Naval Base area this is not available for foreign leisure craft.

Marina Kaliningrad
54°42'·28N 20°28'·76E yacht moorings
Anton Pavloski ① +7 921 269 52 16 (24h), +7 (4012) 52 33 62
http://marinakaliningrad.ru/engservices.html

Developed in Kaliningrad City harbour and currently the best option for visiting yachts. Foreign visitors are welcome but advance reservation of a berth is recommended, as most berths are occupied by locals. Contact Anton Pavlovski (website in English with charts and advice on navigation and formalities). Facilities include finger pontoons, water (not drinking quality) and electricity, one toilet and one shower (both in containers), fuel, repairs, crane, et al. The marina and boat yard has a 24 hour security guard. The managers speak English, but the guards do not. The marina is just 1.5 km from the city centre. Nearest bus stop is about 1 km. No shops or restaurants nearby. During the day there is some wash from excursion boats on the river.

Kaliningrad Yacht Club
54°39'·93N 20°23'·26E
① +7 4012 466 331

Located on the SE coast of the Kaliningradskiy Zaliv has berthing for about 10 visiting yachts moored bows-to in 2·5m depth. Its members are most welcoming to visitors. Public transport 1·5km. City centre 15km.

Yachts with a draught of over 2m should berth at Marina Kaliningrad.

Note Pionerskiy has been omitted from this edition as it is now closed to yachts.

THE BALTIC SEA AND APPROACHES 371

8. Lithuania

Lithuania has only the one Baltic Sea port of Klaipėda, although it is possible to explore the Curonian Lagoon as far as Nida, using well-marked channels. Small former fishing harbours such as Mingė have facilities for yachts.

South of Lithuania lies the Russian enclave of Kaliningrad, for which visas are required.

Regulated Area 117

If sailing from Gdańsk to Klaipėda or vice versa the direct route is through this area. See plan on page 367 and details on page 370.

Key information

Rescue/Safety services

Emergency 112

National SAR agency MRCC Klaipėda, DSC MMSI 002770330. +370 46 391257 or +370 46 391258. *Email* mrcc@mil.lt. Within 6NM from shore it is possible to call 112 and ask to be connected to SAR.

Charts and pilot books

British Admiralty and Lithuanian Maritime Safety Administration charts cover the coast. Those charts which are specific to an area or harbour are listed under individual harbour details. See the Appendix, page 419 for sources.

Lithuanian Maritime Safety Administration 7 sheet charts covering the coast in the approaches to Klaipėda.

Lithuanian Inland Waterways Authority Curonian Lagoon and the Nemunas Delta.

Latvian chart 1253

Baltic Pilot Volume II (NP 19)

Harbours of the Baltic States, F & G Cattell, available through the Cruising Association and major nautical suppliers in Scandinavia.

Sailing Guide Kuršių marios

Kaliningradskiy Zaliv 2007 Guide to harbours in the Curonian Lagoon as well as Kaliningrad, Baltiysk and the Kaliningradskiy Zaliv (lagoon south of Kaliningrad between Russia and Poland). In English.

Time

Lithuania is in the Eastern European time zone (UT+2 in winter/UT+3 in summer). Summer time starts and ends on the same dates as the rest of the EU.

Money

Lithuania adopted the Euro in 2015. Cash is easily obtained from banks or ATMs and credit cards are widely accepted although harbour fees have to be paid in cash.

Formalities

Lithuania is a member of the EU and the Schengen Area. (see Main Introduction page 7 for details of Schengen formalities). EU passport holders do not require visas. If a visa is needed contact the Lithuanian Consulate at Lithuania House, 2 Bessborough Gardens, London SW1V 2JE 0207 592 2840, amb.uk@urm.lt http://uk.mfa.lt. The British Embassy in Vilnius can be contacted on +370 5 246 2900, be-vilnius@britain.lt, www.gov.uk/government/world/lithuania

Formal reporting is not required for passages between Lithuania and another Schengen country. Klaipėda Port Immigration/Coastguard may call up yachts on VHF 73 when about 6M off to enquire as to last port of call and number of persons aboard. Alternatively Immigration may visit to check boats after arrival.

To prevent possible difficulties entering harbour at the same time as a large cargo vessel is moving, it is recommended to call VTS on VHF Ch 9 call sign *Radio 5* when approaching the harbour entrance. When departing it is similarly advisable to call the Coastguard on VHF Ch 73 call sign *Impuls 3* to report flag state, number of persons aboard, nationality, previous port and port of destination. Vessels arriving from or departing to a non-Schengen country, such as Russia, must complete immigration procedures and should contact the authorities on arrival and departure.

372 THE BALTIC SEA AND APPROACHES

Although nationals are required to have a boat driving licence, this does not apply to skippers of foreign flagged vessels. In practice, skippers and crew would be advised to carry any certificates of competence wherever they are sailing.

All craft, regardless of flag state, are required to carry pyrotechnics appropriate to the category of vessel.

☼ Public holidays

Major public holidays occur on:
1 January, 16 February (Independence Day), 11 March (Restoration of Independence), Easter Sunday and Monday,1 May (Labour Day), 24 June (St John's Day), 6 July (Statehood Day), 15 August (Feast of the Assumption), 1 November and 24–26 December. There are also many 'commemorative days' on which most shops and offices remain open.

☽ Communications

There are efficient telephone and mail systems and full coverage of mobile phone networks. Internet access is widely available with many free WiFi points.

To obtain an international line dial 00, followed by the country code, area code (omitting any initial 0) and number. Lithuanian phone numbers now begin with a figure 8 but this is not always necessary. If difficulties are experienced the advice is to replace the 8 with the international code for Lithuania +370.

Calling from one landline to another in Lithuania dial 8 + city code + the number. Calling from one Lithuanian mobile (i.e. if using a local simcard) to another dial +370 + the number (omitting the figure 8). Calling from a Lithuanian mobile to a Lithuanian landline dial +370 + city code + the number. A useful website is www.teo.lt.

The country code for Lithuania is 370.

Public WiFi is available at Klaipėda harbour charged by credit or debit card to obtain an enabling code. Internet access is available at both the public library and the telephone office.

✈ Travel

Taxis and minibuses provide local transport, and Klaipėda is served by international bus and rail networks.

There are international **airports** at Vilnius, Kaunas and Palanga. Palanga is more suitably located for crew changes in Klaipėda. Airline services change frequently so it is best to check availability when required.

Comprehensive **bus** and **rail** network with trains running from Vilnius to Warsaw, Berlin, Budapest, Prague and Sofia. As of 2015 ferries run from Klaipėda to Germany and Sweden.

Note substantial freight traffic between Russia and the EU operated via Klaipėda. Due to the current EU sanctions against Russia, freight traffic is severely reduced and some ferry lines no longer operate.

💻 Websites

www.portofklaipeda.lt/the-port-of-klaipeda Port of Klaipėda

www.msa.lt/en/home-page.html The Lithuanian Maritime Safety Administration

http://kariuomene.kam.it/en/structure_1469/naval_force/units_of_the_naval_force/maritime_rescue_coordination_center.html MRSS

www.yacht.lt/Klaipeda%20Castle%20Harbour.html Klaipėda Old Castle Harbour

📻 Radio communications

Details of the above, including Search & Rescue, GMDSS, Coast Radio Stations, Weather Bulletins and Navigational Warnings, NAVTEX and Weatherfax transmissions, weather forecasts on the internet and Firing Practice areas will be found in the Appendix.

Navigational and other information is broadcast on request by Klaip da Traffic on VHF Ch 09.

☁ Weather information

www.meteo.lt

Also call Klaipėda VTS on VHF 9, call sign *Radio 5*.

The country

Lithuania has a total area of 65,300km², the majority a flat plain but with a few hills in the south and west. To the east and southeast the Baltic Highlands rise, the highest point being Mount Juoapine at 292m. There are many lakes, particularly in the northeast, and meandering rivers. Marshes and swamps are prevalent. The 99km coastline has sandy beaches backed by sand dunes and pine forest, while in the southwest the long Curonian sand spit almost encloses the Curonian Lagoon. South of Klaipėda lie the famous amber mines.

Lithuania's economy became one of the fastest growing in Europe post independence and was the largest economy of the Baltic States. Industry accounts for just over 25% of GDP, oil transit activity between Russia and Europe 12% and services 60%. Food processing, shipbuilding, electronics, machine tools and furniture are the main industries whilst IT is also developing. Main foreign trade is with Russia, Germany, Latvia and Poland. About 50% of land is arable though the agricultural sector now employs only 8% of the workforce. Mineral oils and fuels, foodstuffs, machinery and mechanical appliances, electrical equipment and chemicals form the major exports.

Highlights
The Curonian Spit is a UNESCO World Heritage Site.

The people, the church and the language

Of a total population of some 2.95 million, 84.2% are Lithuanians, 6.6% are Poles and 5.8% are Russians. The remaining 3.4% is made up of small numbers from Belarus, Ukraine, Germany and Latvia, as well as Jews and Tartars. 67% of the population is urban. Visitors to Lithuania can be assured of a warm and friendly welcome.

The majority of believers (approx 77%) follow the Catholic faith, but there are also large numbers of Russian Orthodox, Evangelical Lutherans and Baptists.

8. LITHUANIA

The Curonian Spit looking northeast over Nida *E. Redfern*

The national language is Lithuanian, in modern times similar only to Latvian but also said to bear a resemblance to ancient Sanskrit. There is still a strong Polish influence in much of the country – the capital, Vilnius, was a Polish city for many centuries – and the language is widely understood. The generations educated in Soviet times have fluent Russian whereas younger generations have fluent English. German is a good alternative with the older generation.

History

The Lithuanian people together with the Latvians are descended from the Balts, the earliest Indo-European settlers still living in the Baltic. They seem to have been peaceful people and by the Middle Ages were being raided first by Vikings and then by Russians from Kiev-Rus and Novgorod. From the mid 12th century, however, the main tribes were becoming united and started to fight back. Duke Mindaugas of Lithuania eventually quashed his rivals, converted to Christianity to get the Teutonic Knights on side, captured much of Russian Novgorod and was crowned King of Lithuania in 1253. Subsequent rulers had the title of Grand Duke, however, and by 1560 had reverted to paganism to keep the support of the Samogitian tribe.

In the course of the 13th and 14th centuries Lithuania continued to make territorial gains in Russia, while fighting off the Teutonic Knights from Prussia and Latvia. The disruption caused by Ghengis Khan's armies helped Lithuania to win more and more Russian territory, sometimes helped and sometimes opposed by the Mongols.

In 1377 when Jogailla became Grand Duke, he now ruled most of modern Belarus and Ukraine. Lithuania relied heavily on its Russian territories for resources and manpower. They were allowed to keep their old administrative structures and their Orthodox Christian religion, now regarded by Rome as heresy. Lithuania itself was a mixture of pagans and Orthodox, as well as Jews and some Moslems. There were clear advantages in joining Catholic western Europe, however, so in 1386 Jogailla converted to Catholicism and married the young Queen of Poland, thereby starting the highly successful union with Poland that was to last for four centuries and is outlined in the section on Poland.

Towards the end of the 18th century, the huge extent of Poland-Lithuania's territory lead to the wars of Partition, at the end of which 90% of Lithuania was controlled by Tsarina Catherine the Great and the rest became part of Prussia.

During the 19th century there was a period of intense "Russification" of Lithuania by Tsar Alexander, but this only intensified the growing nationalist movement defined by the Lithuanian language and its traditions from before the union with Poland. During WWI, Lithuania was occupied by Germany until its defeat in the west in 1918. Then the newly formed Red Army tried to take both Lithuania and Poland. It was not until 1924, when Klaipėda was retaken from Germany, as Lithuania's only Baltic port, that all fighting ended and Lithuania could start to build a united independent nation.

During WWII Lithuania was occupied first by the Soviet Union, then Germany, and then by the Soviet Union again. After the war Lithuania was made a Soviet within the USSR. Soviet Union rule was fiercely resisted and more Lithuanians were killed in the years following the war than during it. Then eventually in 1990, following Gorbachev's reforms,

LITHUANIA - CRUISING INFORMATION

Lithuania became the first Soviet to declare its independence. USSR troops promptly captured the Vilnius broadcasting tower, killing 14 civilians and wounding many more, but amateur radio operators were able to broadcast to the world what was going on. Then, when the coup in Moscow against Gorbachev failed, the Soviet system collapsed and Soviet troops withdrew. Lithuania became a member of the UN in 1991, of the EU and NATO in 2004 and signed the Schengen agreement at the end of 2007.

Cruising information

Yacht services
See under Klaipėda, page 376.

Sailing is popular both at Klaipėda and on the inland lakes. Although many yachts are privately owned, some still belong to yacht clubs. The Lithuanian Yachting Union is very active and organises training and regattas.

Chandlery
Limited chandlery in garage opposite the harbour office in Klaipėda. Most local yachtsmen buy from online chandlers. Winter storage and repairs are possible.

Holding tanks
See main introduction page 8 for general information. Holding tanks are not yet mandatory although desirable. Currently there is only one pump out station in Lithuania, located at Smiltynė Yacht Harbour.

Gas
See main introduction page 8 for general information. Exchange Camping Gaz cylinders are not available.

Diesel
See main introduction page 9 for general information. All diesel contains a 6% bio component There is a fuelling berth at Klaipėda.

Shopping
Well stocked shops and supermarkets can be found in Klaipėda and other towns.

Alcohol
Alcohol can be purchased from shops and supermarkets without restriction.
 The alcohol limit at sea for leisure boats is 0.4/ml but in case of an accident charges may be brought even if under this limit.

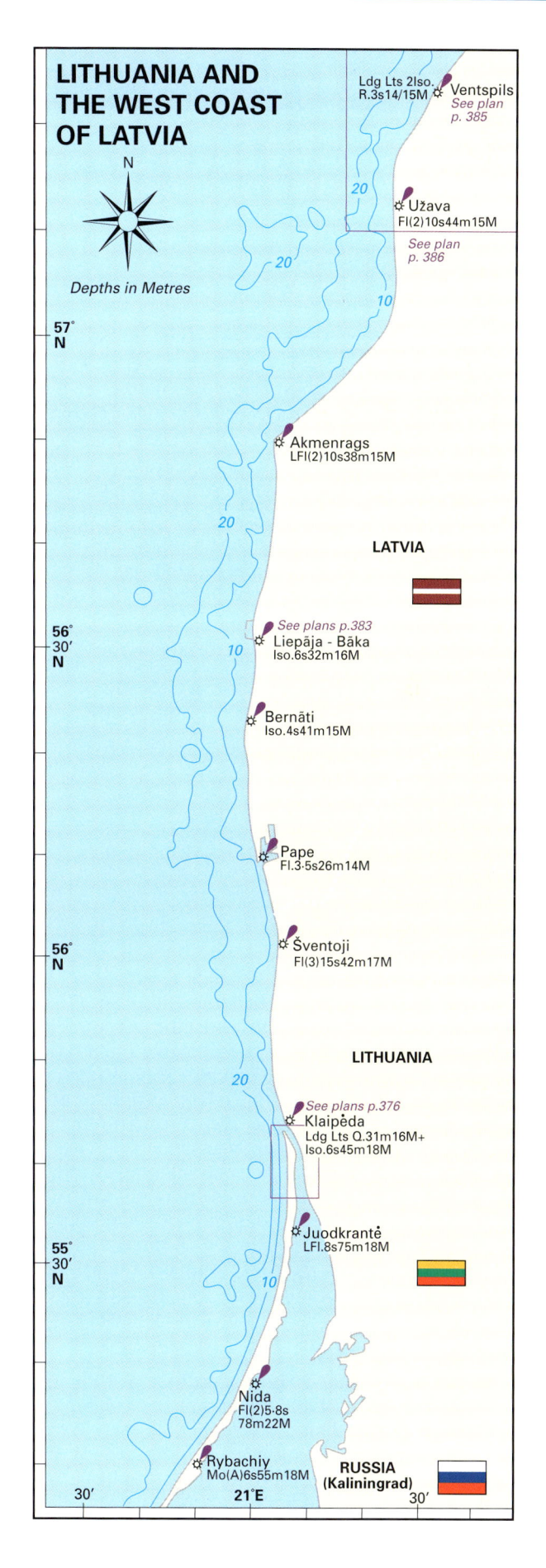

THE BALTIC SEA AND APPROACHES

8. LITHUANIA

Klaipėda

55°43'·6N 21°04'·5E

Distances
Gdynia 115M, Gdańsk 110M, Kaliningrad 80M, Liepāja 50M

Charts
See charts diagram for Lithuana, Appendix p.433
UKHO 2288, 2276
Latvian 1253

Lights
Juodkrantė (if coming from S) 55°33'·39N 21°06'·95E
LFl.W.8s75m18M White rectangle on black square metal framework tower with viewing platform 20m

Šventoji (if coming from N) 56°01'·51N 21°04'·93E
Fl(3)W.15s42m17M Red rectangle with white band on red square metal framework tower with balcony and lantern room 39m

Klaipėda Ldg Lts 092.5° *Front* 55°43'·67N 21°05'·47E
Q.W.31m16M White rectangle with black stripe and white diamond above on red metal framework tower 29m
Rear 285m from front Iso.W.6s45m18M 000°-vis-180° White round concrete tower, black bands and black stripe with balcony and lantern room 37m

Klaipėda North breakwater 55°43'·76N 21°04'·65E
Fl.R.3s16m5M White square with red borders marked '2 B' on black metal cylindrical column with a viewing platform 12m

Klaipėda South breakwater 55°43'·62N 21°04'·61E
Fl.G.3s16m5M White triangle with green borders marked '1 B'
on black metal cylindrical column with viewing platform 16m

Communications
Klaipėda Port Control ☎ +370 46 499 799
    Yacht Harbourmaster ☎ +370 46 490 975
Klaipėda VTS VHF Ch 09, 16 call sign *Klaipėda Radio 5*

General

Klaipėda was founded in 1252 and taken over by the Teutonic Knights who fortified it in 1404. Since then its ownership has been in constant dispute. Its industry was established by the Germans and it has a large port and shipbuilding complex. The waterway leads to the Curonian Lagoon, a large inland, mostly shallow, expanse of water separated from the sea by the narrow, sandy Curonian Spit.

There is an interesting maritime museum and an aquarium on the west bank of the river not far from Smiltynė. An old three-master, now a restaurant, is moored near the centre of town. Amber is mined locally, and amber jewellery and ornaments are readily available. Small pieces can sometimes be found on the beach following onshore winds.

Approach and entry

The town and the harbour entrance are clearly visible from seaward and the entrance, heavily used by commercial shipping, is well marked for entry at any time, though it would become hazardous for small craft in strong onshore (westerly) winds.

From the safe water light buoy No. 1 (55°43'·82N 20°59'·63E) follow the leading line on 092·5°.

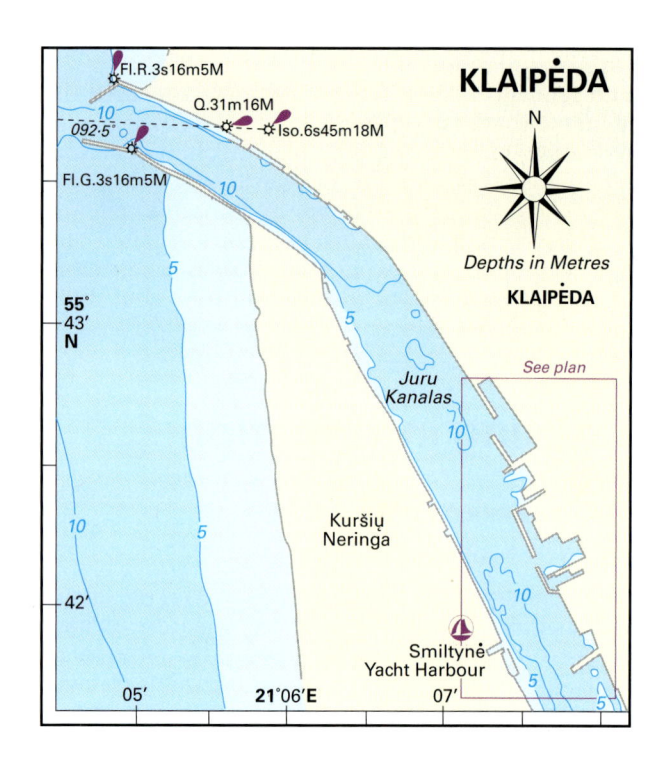

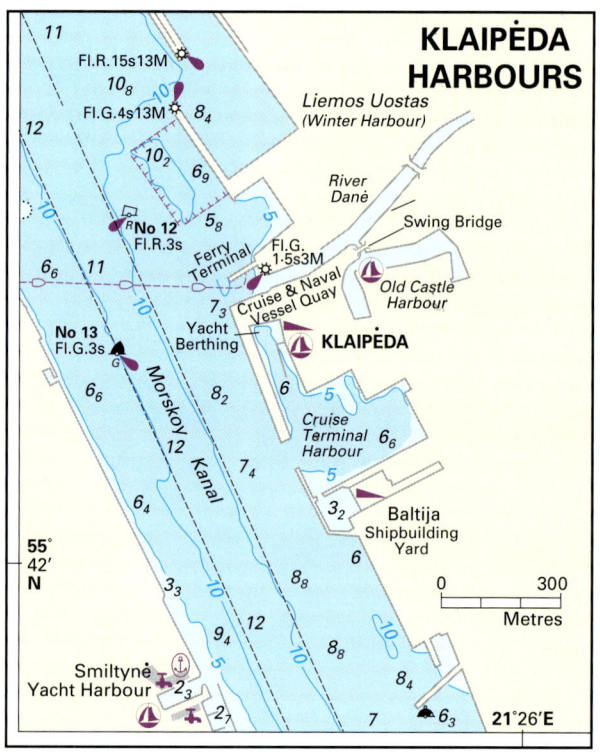

Berthing

With the need for many berths due to the massive expansion in local yachting, the yacht harbours of Klaipėda have been reconstructed. Visitors should berth in Old Castle Harbour on the town side of the Curonian Lagoon – the Harbourmaster uses every endeavour to find space for all visitors although on occasion it may be necessary to tie up alongside in the entrance to the River Danė. Access to Old Castle Harbour is via an opening bridge from the River Danė. This harbour offers good shelter and facilities. It is also convenient for the town. The Cruise

KLAIPĖDA

Old Castle Harbour visitors' moorings *F. and G. Cattell*

Terminal Harbour is usually reserved for residents. On the opposite side of the Curonian Lagoon there is a further reconstructed facility for yachts at Smiltynė – see below for more information.

Klaipėda Harbour is a commercial waterway and anchoring is not permitted.

Old Castle Harbour and Cruise Terminal Harbour

55°42'·35N 21°07'·32E centre of entrance to Danė river
55°42'·14N 21°07'·42E centre of entrance to Cruise Terminal Harbour for fuel berth

Water and electricity are available in both harbours with toilets and showers in a facilities building which also houses the harbour office. Access with a keycard. Washing and drying machines also available as well as a fuel berth. Good repair and craning facilities.

Access to Old Castle Harbour is via an opening bridge.

Smiltynė Yacht Harbour

55°41'·85N 21°07'·27E yacht harbour entrance, midway between moles

Smiltynė YH has undergone a complete overhaul and the reconstructed harbour was open in 2016.

Water and electricity are available on the quay, with toilets and showers in the club building. Repairs and craning can be organised through the harbour captain, but the availability of parts and equipment is likely to be limited. Facilities and spares would be better at the Old Castle Harbour side. Pump out station at Smiltynė. This harbour has two basins and is well equipped.

Whilst the Smiltynė harbour is thought to be safe in all weathers, strong onshore winds can send enough swell along the two miles of river to make the berths uncomfortable.

General facilities

The town centre is very close to Old Castle and the Cruise Terminal harbours but on the opposite side of the river from Smiltynė (ferry a short walk from the harbour). Shops are well stocked and there is a good indoor/outdoor market. There are several restaurants in the town.

Nida

55°18'·11N 21°00'·65E yacht harbour entrance, midway between moles

Nida, some 30M from Klaipėda, is set among attractive surroundings on the sandspit which separates the Curonian Lagoon from the Baltic Sea. Nida is accessible by bus or taxi as well as water. The harbour consists of two basins, the southern for yachts and the northern for fishermen.

Note Passage through the Curonian Lagoon should be made only within the marked channel. Outside the channel the waters are very shallow.

Nida Harbour *F. and G. Cattell*

Smiltynė Harbour under reconstruction *F. and G. Cattell*

THE BALTIC SEA AND APPROACHES

9. Latvia

The Latvian coastline stretches from Ainaži in the eastern part of the Gulf of Rīga to Pape on the Baltic Sea coast. It provides an attractive cruising ground with a combination of interesting harbours and places of great historic interest. Visiting yachtsmen can be sure of a warm welcome.

Particular care should be taken when transiting the Irbensky Strait due to extensive shoals outside the buoyed channels. There are few suitable places to anchor with the possible exception of the River Lielupe.

Key information

Rescue/Safety services

Emergency ☏ 112

Maritime Rescue Coordination Centre (MRCC Rīga) www.mrcc.lv

Coast Guard
Emergency phone ☏ +371 67 323 103, +371 29 476 101, +371 67 082 070

Rīga Rescue Radio permanently monitors MF 2182 kHz, VHF channel 16, DSC MMSI number 002750100 on MF 2187.5 kHz and VHF channel 70.

Charts, pilot books and cruising guides

UKHO Admiralty and Latvian Hydrographic Service charts cover the coast. UKHO Admiralty charts are useful for passage planning but for detailed navigation the Latvian charts must be used. Those charts which are specific to an area or harbour are listed under individual harbour details. See the Appendix, page 419, for sources.

The Folio of Charts of Latvia for Yachts is recommended (covering the coast from just south of Klaipėda (Lithuania) to the southern end of Moon Sound including southern coast of Saaremaa (Estonia). This also includes detailed harbour charts for all Latvian ports).

Harbours of the Baltic States
F & G Cattell, available through the Cruising Association and major nautical suppliers in Scandinavia.

Baltic Pilot Volume II (NP 19) Pilot of Baltic Sea, Latvian Coast. Maritime Administration of Latvia. Updated by Notices to Mariners at www.lhd.lv/ATONLV/?gnotice=1 Click on flag for English. Ignore username and password – click on Notices to Mariners.

Time

Latvia is in the Eastern European time zone (UT+2 in winter/UT+3 in summer). Summer time starts and ends on the same dates as the rest of the EU.

€ Money

The Euro. All major currencies can be readily exchanged at banks or exchange booths, and cash is easily obtained from ATMs. Credit cards are widely used, but payment of harbour fees in most harbours must be made in cash.

Formalities

Latvia is a member of the EU and of the Schengen Area (see Main Introduction page 7 for details of Schengen formalities). EU passport holders do not require a visa. The website of the **Latvian Embassy** www.mfa.gov.lv/en/london lists countries whose citizens do not need visas.

If a visa is needed contact the Consular Office of the Latvian Embassy at Grove House, 248A Marylebone Road NW1 6JZ, ☏ 0207 312 0040, consulate.uk@mfa.gov.lv.

The British Embassy in Rīga can be contacted on ☏ +371 6777 4700, britishembassy.riga@fco.gov.uk, www.gov.uk/government/world/latvia

Formal reporting is not required for passages between Latvia and another Schengen country. Vessels arriving from or departing to a non-Schengen country, such as Russia, must complete immigration procedures and should contact the authorities on arrival or before departure.

Within the country, it is a requirement for yachts to report arrival and departures to the coastguard at each port visited. Calls should be made on Ch 16 giving name of vessel, number of persons on board, intended destination and flag state. This is not an immigration formality but a matter of maritime safety. In practice most reporting is done by the harbour office.

Latvian Border guards are on duty in some harbours and perform a role as coastguards. In some harbours (Pāvilosta and Liepāja) a yacht declaration form (essentially a crew list) has to be completed at the harbour office and this information is subsequently forwarded to the border guards.

378 THE BALTIC SEA AND APPROACHES

LATVIA - THE COUNTRY

Although nationals are required to have a 'boat driving licence', this does not apply to skippers of foreign flagged vessels. In practice, skippers and crew would be advised to carry any certificates of competence wherever they are sailing.

☼ Public holidays

Public holidays occur on:

1 January, Good Friday, Easter Sunday and Monday, 1 May (Labour Day), 4 May (Declaration of Independence), the second Sunday in May (Mothers' Day), 23 June (Ligo, the midsummer festival), 24 June (St John's Day), 18 November (Independence or National Day), 25–26 December, 31 December. There are, in addition, Remembrance Days on which some services may not be open.

☾ Communications

Public telephone, mobile phones and the mail system all function efficiently. WiFi and internet access is available in most ports in Latvia.

National and international calls may be made from the few remaining public phone boxes. These operate on cards obtainable from shops or street kiosks.

To ring abroad from Latvia dial 00 followed by the country code, area code (omitting any initial 0) and number.

The country code for Latvia is 371 followed by the 8 digits which comprise Latvian telephone numbers (this includes the area code).

Mobile numbers begin with a 2 and landlines with a 6.

✈ Travel

Rīga has an international **airport** with direct flights to many European and Scandinavian cities. Rīga can be reached by bus and train from cities all across Europe. There is also a good internal network for **bus** travel but the internal **train** network is limited.

As of 2017 **ferries** sail from Rīga to Stockholm (Sweden), from Liepāja to Travemunde (Germany), from Ventspils to Travemunde (Germany) and Nynashamn (Sweden). However routes and operating companies change frequently and the current situation should be checked before any plans are made. Useful website for ferry information www.ferrylines.com.

💻 Websites

www.latviatravel.com Contains much practical information for visitors plus other useful links

www.inyourpocket.com The homepage of inyourpocket – search for Latvia

www.rigathisweek.lv The homepage of the Rīga This Week guide

www.lja.lv/en/ The Maritime Administration of Latvia, including the Latvian Hydrographic Service and current chart catalogue

📻 Radio communications

VHF Ch 16 should be monitored while on passage. The coastguard at Pape and Kolka lights may call up passing craft including yachts. Details of VHF channels and call signs will be found under each harbour heading.

☔ Weather information

General details of Weather Bulletins and Navigational Warnings, NAVTEX and Weatherfax transmissions, weather forecasts on the internet and Firing Practice areas will be found in the Appendix.

Weather forecasts and navigational warnings are broadcast in the Liepeja area on Ch 11 at 0805 and 2005 LT, by Rīga Rescue Radio (MRCC Rīga) on Ch 71 at 0703 and 1503 LT. Rīga Traffic and Ventspils Traffic give weather information on request.

The country

Latvia's total area of 64,589km² consists mostly of a low lying plain, though to the east the country becomes hilly. The land is crossed by a number of rivers, many of which drain into the Gulf of Rīga. The largest of these is the Daugava which rises in Russia. There are also numerous lakes, streams, marshes and bogs. Forest covers 43% of the country and peat bogs account for a further 10%. Nearly half the land is agricultural, with small farms and fields often tucked away in forest clearings. The coastline extends some 500km along the Baltic Sea and the Gulf of Rīga, and is lined with sandy beaches, mostly backed by dunes and pine forest.

Latvia's harbours all lie in river mouths and in former times served fishing fleets and canning factories. With the demise of the Soviet Union the market for processed fish disappeared. At the same time fish stocks diminished and EU quotas came into force, all contributing to a loss of work for the fishing fleets. This has given some of the harbours opportunities to develop facilities for yachting. The major harbours Liepāja, Ventspils (which also has an oil terminal) and Rīga are ice-free ports and have commercial import/export work.

Services account for 71% of GDP and industry for about 25%. Major products are synthetic fibres, agricultural machinery, textiles, electronics, processed foods and timber. Agriculture is now of lesser importance but combined with forestry still provides about 15% of employment compared with 25% for industry and 60% for services. Forestry provides important exports such as paper and sawn timber, and both major and minor harbours export timber in all its forms. 78% of trade is with the EU and major exports comprise machinery, electrical equipment, wood, metal and mineral products.

Highlights

Rīga Old Town. Villas from Tsarist times and beach at Majori, Jurmala. Rundāles and Mežotne Palaces. Europe's widest waterfall – the Rumba at Kuldiga. Sigulda and the cable car crossing the Gauja river.

9A. LATVIA – BALTIC SEA COAST

The Rumba, Europe's widest waterfall at Kuldiga
F. and G. Cattell

The people, the church and the language

The total population of some 1.99 million is made up of 61% Latvians and 26% Russians, the remainder being Belorussians, Ukrainians, Poles and Lithuanians. Now 86% of the population have the status of 'citizen', which is dependent upon both residency and proficiency in Latvian.

The majority of Christians are Lutherans, but many follow the Orthodox faith and in the east of the country there is a predominance of Catholics. The national language is Latvian. Some of the ethnic Russian population speak only Russian. The generations educated in Soviet times have fluent Russian, whereas younger generations have fluent English. German is a good alternative with the older generation.

History

The Latvian people, like the Lithuanians, are descended from the Balts, Indo-European tribes who arrived around 3,000BC. The Daugava River through Rīga had been one of the trading routes of the Amber Road to the Mediterranean and Black seas since ancient times. In the 12th century, the Hanseatic League set up a trading centre on the river near modern Rīga.

Present day Latvia devolves from the major tribes whose names live on in the regions – Kurzeme, Zemgale, Vidzeme and Latgale. The Couronians in the west were fighting folk, known as Baltic Vikings, while the tribes to the south and east were prosperous and peaceful farmers. In between, around the Gulf of Rīga, were Livonian fishermen and traders.

Latvian peoples were still mainly pagan, although some were members of the Russian Orthodox Church. Then the Pope declared the Northern Crusade. Bishop Albrecht arrived in Rīga in 1202 with 300 boatloads of soldiers, the 'Livonian Brothers of the Sword', to convert everybody. The Livonian Order made steady progress conquering much of Latvia and then southern Estonia, but was routed when they attacked Lithuania in 1236. The Pope assigned the survivors to the Teutonic Order, a more disciplined and even more ruthless crusading army, brought in by Poland to subjugate pagan Prussia to the southwest.

Once Latvia and southern Estonia were defeated, German immigrants formed a ruling elite of landowners and merchants, while the local people were reduced to serfs. The name 'Livonia' was used to describe the whole conquered area, which later included all the rest of Estonia as well. Over the coming years Livonia was fought over by Denmark, Sweden, Russia and the Polish-Lithuanian Commonwealth. By the end of the 16th century Livonia was a Duchy within Poland-Lithuania. Then Gustavus Adolphus of Sweden won it in 1621. Under his control, serfs were liberated and offered education and large private estates were broken up.

In 1700 came the Great Northern War, when Denmark, Poland-Lithuania and Russia sought to break up the huge Swedish empire in the Baltic. In 1710 Peter the Great secured Swedish Livonia for Russia. Then at the end of the century, a similar alliance broke up Poland-Lithuania, and Russia gained the rest of Livonia. Gustavus Adolphus's reforms were reversed as Russia used the German landowners of Livonia to run the Duchy.

In the 19th century Latvian nationalism developed, centred on the Latvian language, just as similar movements in Estonia and Lithuania centred on their respective languages. Tsar Alexander III's efforts to Russify all three were correspondingly counter-productive. Poverty led to a growth of socialist revolutionary movements. During the attempted Russian revolution of 1905, a thousand armed conflicts were registered in Latvia, between peasants and the German nobility.

During WWI, Germany occupied Latvia until 1918 when Latvia declared itself an independent democracy within its current ethnographic borders. There were three more years of fighting before Latvia had cleared both German and Soviet forces. Land reforms were then introduced whereby traditional landlords were allowed only fifty hectares, the rest being shared amongst the Latvian peasantry. Soon more land was under cultivation than ever before and Latvian prosperity continued to grow until WWII.

During the Second World War Latvia suffered the same fate as Estonia and Lithuania: first Soviet occupation, then Nazi and then Soviet again. After the war Latvia was made a Soviet within the Soviet Union, with large numbers being deported to Siberia and replaced by Russians. The Soviet authorities did, however, see the potential of Latvia and set up some of its most advanced chemical and manufacturing facilities alongside the existing farming and food processing. As in the other Baltic States, passive

LATVIA - CRUISING INFORMATION

resistance grew in the later 1980s. On August 23 1989, to mark 50th anniversary of the signing of the infamous Molotov-Ribbentrop Pact, two million Lithuanians, Latvians and Estonians formed the 'Baltic Way', a human chain 675km long that linked their three capital cities. Independence at last returned with the collapse of the Soviet Union in 1991.

Latvia is now a democratic member of NATO, the UN, the EU and signed the Schengen Agreement in 2007.

Cruising information

Yacht services

Advice regarding craning and repair facilities should be sought from the local yacht club or harbour captain, but other than in Rīga the availability of parts and equipment is likely to be limited.

Local yachts are taken ashore during winter and a few foreign yachts have overwintered. Anyone planning to overwinter should check the options early in the season and ensure that their insurers are agreeable. There may be a problem finding suitable cradles although it is sometimes possible to have a local cradle adapted. Twin keeled craft can easily be accommodated. There are over-wintering facilities on both banks of the river at Pavilosta.

Yachts clubs are run as businesses and own a number of yachts but private yacht ownership continues to increase.

Chandlery

Other than in Rīga there are no specific chandlers. Spare parts may be available elsewhere and advice should be sought from the harbourmaster. Most local boatowners make purchases online. In Rīga the chandlers Regate has a small shop at Andrejosta harbour.

Holding tanks

Holding tanks are not yet mandatory although desirable. Currently there is only one pump out station in Latvia, located at Rīga City Marina (known locally as Kipsala).

Gas

Regate, the chandlers at Andrejosta harbour, Rīga, stock exchange Camping Gaz cylinders.

Diesel

Latvian diesel contains 5% bio component. There are fuelling berths in the River Daugava 5M north of Rīga (57°02'·30N 24°03'·74E), at Andrejosta Yacht Centre and at Pāvilosta. Non-masted craft can also obtain fuel beyond the bridges in the Daugava River. Elsewhere fuel can generally be obtained either through special delivery organised by a yacht club or harbour captain, or by cans carried from the nearest filling station.

Shopping

Well stocked shops and supermarkets can be found in all towns.

Alcohol

Alcohol can be purchased from shops and supermarkets without restriction.

There is a limit of 50mg in inland waterways. At sea this applies to professional seamen on commercial ships but it is considered that the same regulation could be applied to leisure sailors in the case of an accident.

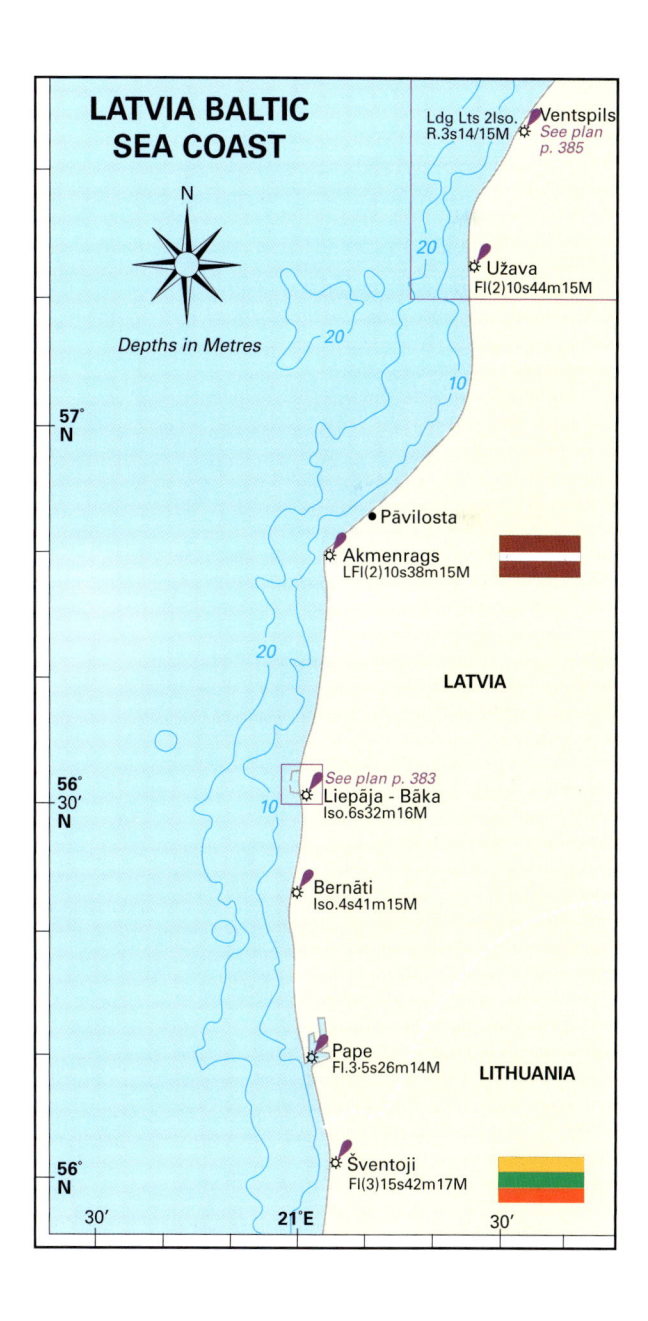

THE BALTIC SEA AND APPROACHES

9a. Baltic Sea coast Latvia

Liepāja

56°30'·76N 21°00'·74E yacht moorings

Distances
Klaipėda 50M, South Gotland 80M, Ventspils 55M

Charts
UKHO 2288, 2292, 2231, 2289
Latvian See chart diagram, Appendix p.433 plus Set of Charts of Latvia for Yachts (small craft folio)

Lights
Bernāti 56°22'·9N 20°58'·9E Iso.W.4s41m15M Red planking on metal framework tower 21m
Liepāja-Bāka 56°31'·0N 20°59'·5E Iso.W.6s32m16M 000°-vis-180° Round tower, red and white bands 30m
Akmenrags 56°49'·9N 21°03'·4E LFl(2)W.10s38m15M Red round stone tower 37m
Central entrance, Ldg Lts 067·7° *Front* 56°32'·7N 20°59'·9E Iso.R.3s21m12M 064°-vis-072° White rectangle, black vertical stripe on white framework tower 20m
Rear, 984m from front, Iso.R.3s33m14M Red trapezium, white vertical stripe on red framework tower 30m
Central entrance, north side 56°32'·3N 20°57'·9E Iso.R.4s10m3M Red round column with platform 5m
Central entrance, south side 56°32'·2N 20°57'·9E Iso.G.4s15m2M Green round column with platform 5m
South entrance, Ldg Lts 112·4° *Front* 56°31'·4N 20°59'·7E Iso.G.2s33m9M White rectangle, black stripe on framework tower 30m
Rear 422m from front Iso.G.2s49m9M White rectangle, black stripe on framework tower 45m Both lights visible on leading line only
South entrance, north side 56°31'·8N 20°58'·1E Iso.R.2s9m3M Red round column with platform 5m
South entrance, south side 56°31'·7N 20°58'·1E Iso.G.2s11m2M Green round column with platform 5m

Communications
Liepāja-1/Liepāja Traffic Control VHF Ch 11, 16
Harbour ☎ +371 634 83801

General
Liepāja (pronounced *Leea-pie-ya*) is Latvia's third major port, handling mainly grain and timber but also with a shipyard, naval base and fishing harbour. Under the Soviet system the city had many factories and was a centre for the manufacture of ladies' underwear, but most now lie idle and unemployment is high. The town centre, which has been refurbished, straddles the canal which connects Lake Liepāja to the Baltic Sea.

Approach and entry
56°30'·39N 20°49'·78E safe water buoy

The approaches to Liepāja harbour are shallow and should be regarded as unsafe in bad weather. Either the southern or the central entrances should be used, although in 2017 it is reported that the northern entrance is passable. From the fairway the leading line to the southern entrance is 112·4° and to the central entrance 067·7°.

The outer harbour, enclosed by the breakwaters, has numerous wrecks and is very shallow, particularly at the southern end. It is thus imperative to follow the buoyage and leading marks, and not to stray outside the marked channel.

For the yacht harbour, follow the Tirdzniecības channel for about 1·5km towards the first bridge.

Anchoring is not permitted.

Permission is required to leave harbour in adverse weather conditions - F7 and above.

Berthing
The yacht harbour is located on the starboard side of the channel just below the first bridge, with berthing alongside wooden staging or a concrete quay. It may be necessary to raft up, depending on the space available.

Liepāja harbour visitors' pontoon F. and G. Cattell

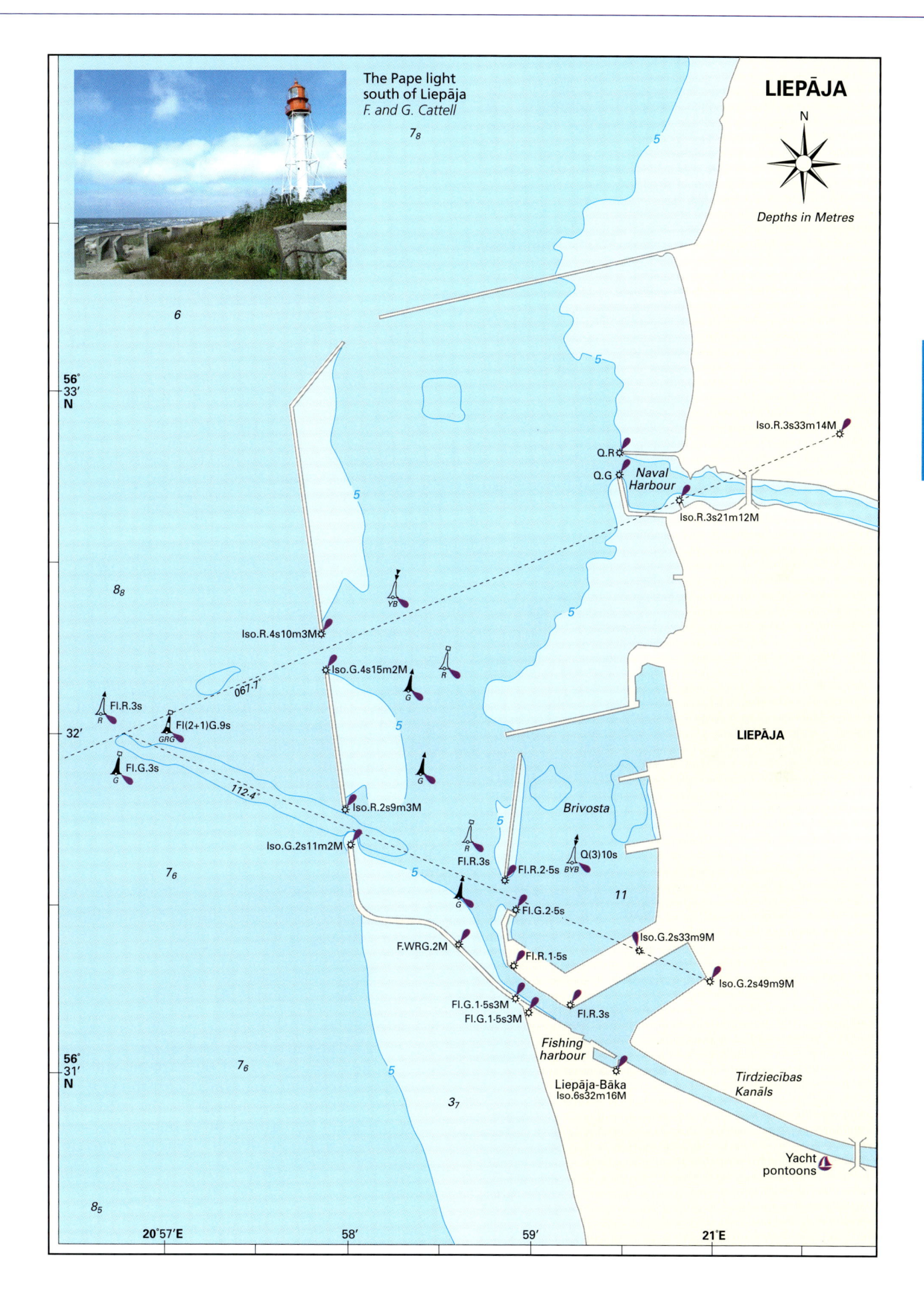

LIEPĀJA

LIEPĀJA

The Pape light south of Liepāja
F. and G. Cattell

Depths in Metres

Iso.R.3s33m14M
Q.R
Q.G
Naval Harbour
Iso.R.3s21m12M

Iso.R.4s10m3M
Iso.G.4s15m2M
067·7°
Fl.R.3s
Fl(2+1)G.9s GRG
Fl.G.3s
112·4°
Iso.R.2s9m3M
Iso.G.2s11m2M
Fl.R.3s
Fl.R.2·5s
Q(3)10s BYB
Brivosta
LIEPĀJA
Fl.G.2·5s
Iso.G.2s33m9M
F.WRG.2M
Fl.R.1·5s
Iso.G.2s49m9M
Fl.G.1·5s3M
Fl.G.1·5s3M
Fl.R.3s
Fishing harbour
Liepāja-Bāka
Iso.6s32m16M
Tirdziecības Kanāls
Yacht pontoons

56°33'N
56°31'N
20°57'E · 58' · 59' · 21°E

9. LATVIA

THE BALTIC SEA AND APPROACHES 383

9A. BALTIC SEA COAST (LATVIA)

Services for yachts

The yacht harbour no longer belongs to the Promenade Hotel (2017). Water and electricity are available on the quay. In late 2016, use of toilets, showers and other facilities was temporarily transferred to the Fontaine Hotel. From 2019 season full facilities will be available at the newly constructed marina. The fuel berth beside the river is only for commercial craft. The Harbourmaster can arrange for fuel to be collected from a nearby filling station. For repair facilities consult the HM.

General facilities

Post Office, banks, restaurants and supermarket are all conveniently located in nearby streets. The shops are well stocked and the open air and indoor markets are full of excellent fresh produce.

Communications and travel

Card-operated phones in the town, internet access at the public library.

Trains and buses run to Rīga, buses to Ventspils. Ferries to Germany. Domestic airport at Liepāja. See Travel, page 379.

Pāvilosta

56°54′·34N 21°08′·94E safe water buoy
56°53′·53N 21°10′·03E centre of harbour entrance
Latvian charts - see chart diagram on Appendix p.433
plus Set of Charts of Latvia for Yachts (small craft folio)

A small port at the mouth of the River Saka on the Baltic Sea coast. Entry and exit considered dangerous in winds over F5 (20 knots). Purpose built yacht harbours on both sides of the river. Pāvilosta Marina on starboard side/Pāvilosta Port Authority on port (village) side. Alongside berthing at the marina – finger berths at Port Authority. Toilets, showers, washing and drying machine in harbour building at Pāvilosta Marina - in harbour building at Pavilosta Port Authority. WiFi. Fuel berth just upriver on starboard side. (www.pavilostamarina.lv and www.pavilostaport.lv)

Small supermarket and restaurant in village. Winter storage and repairs at Boatpark (www.boatpark.lv)

Pāvilosta looking towards entrance from the fuel pontoon
F. and G. Cattell

Ventspils

57°24′·40N 21°31′·53E centre of harbour entrance
57°23′·73N 21°32′·38E centre of entrance to Fish Dock

Distances
Liepāja 55M, South Gotland 95M, Fårösund 85M, Roomassaare 65M, Roja 70M, Rīga 115M

Charts
UKHO 2059, 2288, 2226, 2277, 2716
Latvian See chart diagram, Appendix p.433 plus Set of Charts of Latvia for Yachts (small craft folio)

Lights
Užava 57°12′·6N 21°24′·9E Fl(2)W.10s44m15M 178° -vis-18° Racon White round stone tower with balcony 19m
Ldg Lts 143·7° *Front* 57°23′·7N 21°32′·5E Iso.R.3s28m14M 136° -vis-152° Red rectangle, white stripe, on framework tower 25m
Rear 0·5M from front, Iso.R.3s45m15M 128° -vis-160° Red rectangle, white stripe, on framework tower 35m
Oviši 57°34′·1N 21°43′·0E LFl.W.7.5s38m15M 204°-vis-076° Racon White round stone tower 37m
North breakwater 57°24′·5N 21°31′·6E Fl(2)R.3s14m4M White round concrete tower, red lantern 11m
South breakwater 57°24′·3N 21°31′·5E Fl(2)G.3s14m3M White round concrete tower, green lantern 11m

Harbour communications
Port Control VHF 9, 16, 67 call *Ventspils Vessel Traffic* for clearance on entry or departure
Yacht Harbour ☎ +371 636 20151
Mobile +371 292 87670

General

Founded in 1343 but with a castle dating from 1290, Ventspils is a substantial commercial port and oil terminal providing excellent shelter. It is the nearest Latvian port to Gotland.

The town is attractive with wide, tree-lined streets and parks and has all the normal facilities. If time permits take a bus to the charming small town of Kuldiga, which has the widest waterfall in Europe.

Approach and entry

From north: fairway buoy 57°28′·52N 21°25′·91E
From south: fairway buoy 57°26′·28N 21°24′·67E

The approach is via a straight, buoyed channel to the harbour entrance. It would be unwise to stray from the channel due to a number of dangerous wrecks in the vicinity. Entry is straightforward by day or night, although a detailed chart is necessary for the latter.

Berthing

Yachts berth at the western end of the fish dock. Keep to the starboard side of the harbour, and head for a large grey/white building. Turn to starboard just before the building and moor at the head of the basin in front of the harbour office building, bows to staging and stern to a buoy. Anchoring is not permitted.

VENTSPILS

Services for yachts
Electricity and water is available on the quayside and showers, sauna and laundry facilities in harbour building. Fuel can be delivered in cans by arrangement with the harbour office. The harbour staff may also be able to assist with limited repair facilities.

General facilities
Bar in the harbour building, and small general store outside the dock gates. For shops, banks and restaurants, plus indoor and open air markets, it is necessary to go into the town some 2·5km away.

Communications/travel
WiFi at the harbour. Card-operated phones, and internet access at the public library and internet cafes. From Ventspils it is possible to travel by bus or train all over Latvia, or across Europe, via Rīga. Car hire can be arranged via the harbour office. Ferries to Nynashamn (Sweden) and Travemünde (Germany).

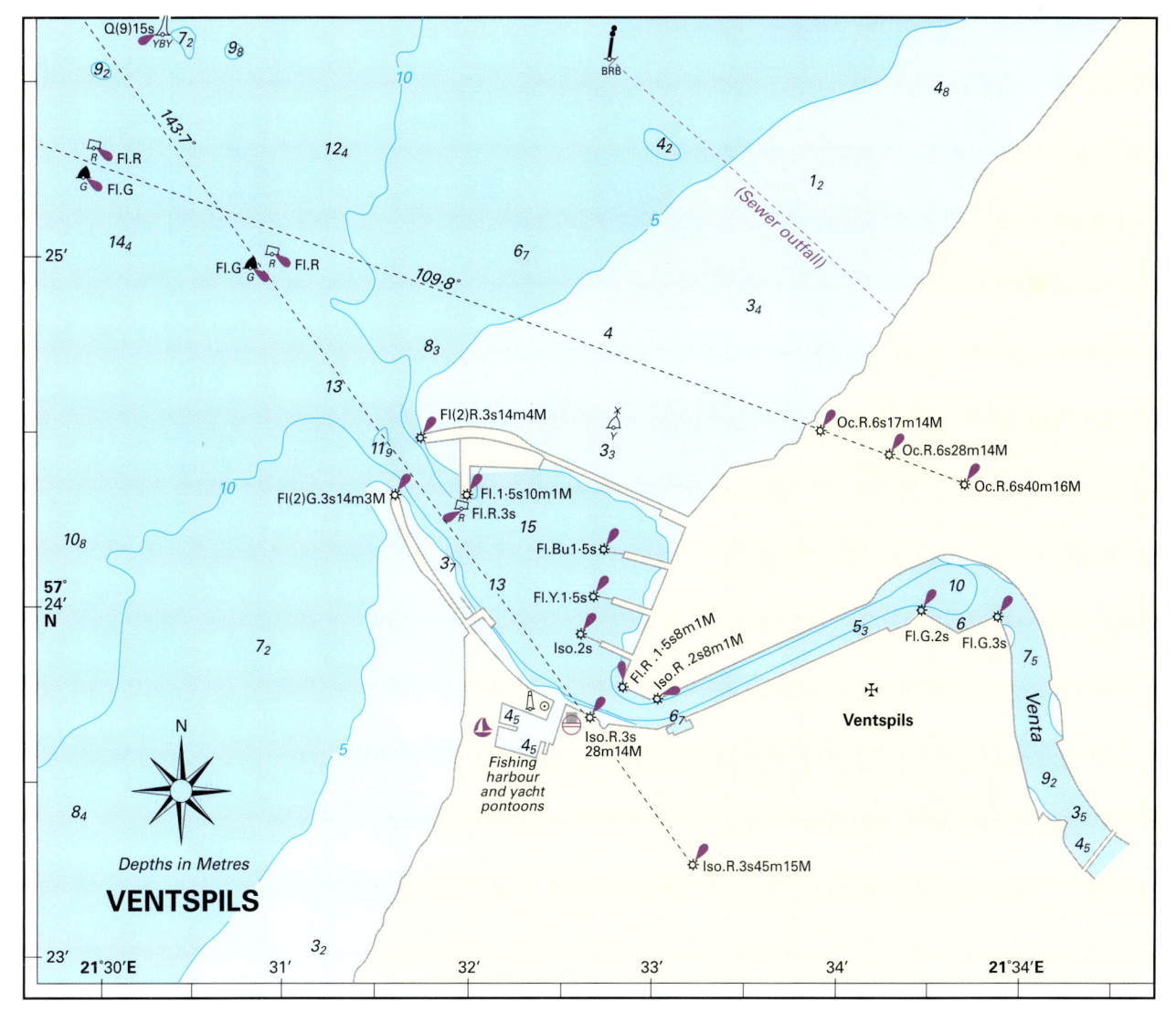

Above Ventspils yacht moorings in Fish Dock
Right Ventspils Castle
F. and G. Cattell

THE BALTIC SEA AND APPROACHES 385

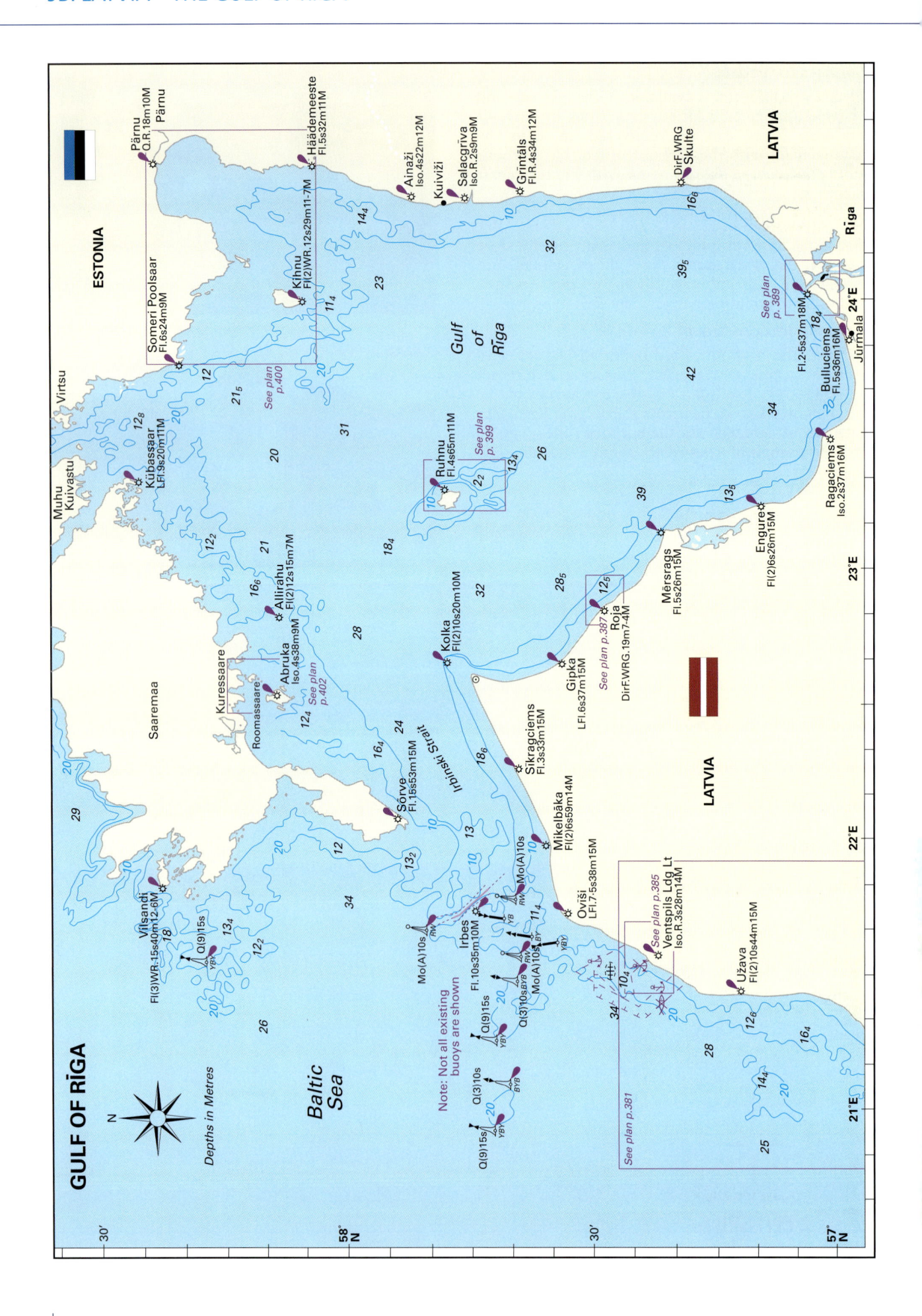

9B. LATVIA – THE GULF OF RĪGA

9b. The Gulf of Rīga

Roja

57°30'·64N 22°48'·79E centre of entrance to outer harbour

Distances
Ventspils 70M, Roomassaare 45M, Rīga 50M, Pärnu 75M

Charts
UKHO 2215, 2226
Latvian See chart diagram, Appendix p.433 plus Set of Charts of Latvia for Yachts (small craft folio)
Estonian 519

Lights
Kolka 57°48'·0N 22°38'·0E Fl(2)10s20m10M
  Red round tower with balcony and lantern room 21m
  Racon (K)
Gipka 57°34'·2N 22°39'·5E LFl.W.6s37m15M
  Two red rectangles over white square on metal framework tower 30m
Dir Lt. 215° 57°30'·5N 22°48'·6E F Sectored
  DirF.WRG.19m7-4M Red triangular tower 19·5m
Northwest mole 57°30'·7N 22°48'·7E Fl.G.3s6m2M
  White round column 3m
Southeast mole 57°30'·6N 22°48'·8E Fl.R.3s6m2M
  Red round column 3m

Harbour communications
Rojas Osta (Port Authority) ☎ +371 632 69957
  VHF 10, 16 *Roja 1*

General

A commercial and fishing harbour (pronounced *Roy ya*) in the entrance to the Roja River with facilities for yachts. Its location makes it useful if on passage between Ventspils and Rīga, or Rīga and Ruhnu or Saaremaa. The town is small but has adequate facilities.

Roja visitors' pontoons *F. and G. Cattell*

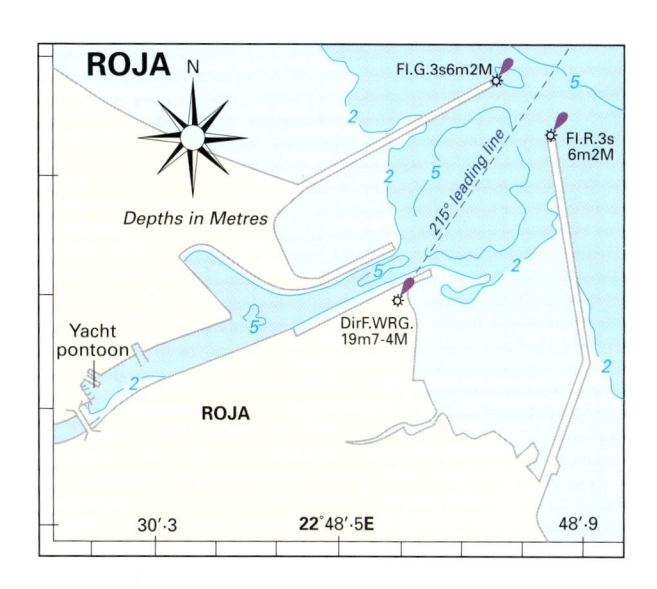

Approach and entry

Follow the sectored light F.WRG on leading line 215°. Once inside the outer harbour it is essential to keep to the marked channel, as depths outside it shoal rapidly. Pass between the inner moles and continue past the fishing vessel berths to the yacht pontoons at the head of harbour.

Berthing

Yachts berth to finger pontoons or alongside pontoons just below the road bridge. Anchoring is not permitted. If mooring on the south side, dues are paid to the Mare Hotel.

Services for yachts

Electricity and water on the pontoons. Showers and toilets in facilities building or hotel. Diesel can be supplied by arrangement with the harbour captain, whose advice should be sought for any matters relating to repairs etc.

General facilities

Adequate food and general shops within a short distance of the harbour. Bars and restaurants at the Roja and Mare hotels.

Communications and travel

Internet access at hotels. Bus services to Rīga and elsewhere.

Mersrags

57°20'·95N 23°11'·92E safe water buoy
Approach via lateral red/green buoyed channel.
57°20'·08N 23°08'·47E centre of harbour entrance
57°20'·09N 23°07'·57E yacht moorings
See chart diagram, Appendix p.433 plus Set of Charts of Latvia for Yachts (small craft folio)

A commercial/fishing port on the western shore of the Gulf of Rīga, open to the east. Entrance is straightforward. Yacht berths at pontoon at head of harbour before the road bridge. Shops and cafés will be found ashore. WiFi at harbour.

THE BALTIC SEA AND APPROACHES

9B. LATVIA – THE GULF OF RĪGA

Engures Ezers, lake behind Mersrags
F. and G. Cattell

The shallow entrance to Jurmala with the River Bullupe on the right   *F. and G. Cattell*

Engure

This small harbour south of Mersrags has been omitted due to shifting entry channel and current lack of facilities within the harbour.

Jūrmala

57°01'·51N 23°55'·42E safe water waypoint (entrance to River Lielupe)
Approach by buoyed channel and leading marks. Note this has been dredged in recent times but is prone to silting. Caution advised - seek local advice. Entry dangerous in strong onshore winds.
56°58'·86N 23°52'·71E yacht moorings
Latvian charts - see chart diagram Appendix p.433 plus Set of Charts of Latvia for Yachts (small craft folio)

Jūrmala is the collective name for a number of famous holiday resorts/health spas situated along a narrow strip of land between the Lielupe River and the Gulf of Rīga.

A number of small private marinas and yacht clubs lie on the bank of the River Lielupe. Enter the Lielupe from the Gulf of Rīga or for unmasted craft via the River Bullupe from the River Daugava. Anchoring in the river may be possible.

Rīga

56°57'·56N 24°05'·81E visitors' pontoon Andrejosta
56° 57'·20N 24°05'·30E yacht moorings Rīga City Marina

Distances
Roja 50M, Roomassaare 85M, Salacgriva 45M, Pärnu 80M

Charts
UKHO 2816, 2817, 2215, 2239, 2859, 2973, 3004, 3007
Latvian See chart diagram, Appendix p.433 plus Set of Charts of Latvia for Yachts (small craft folio)

Lights
Ragaciems 57°02'·1N 23°29'·2E Iso.W.2s37m16M 095°-vis-330° Red slatted daymark and skeletal mast on square framework tower 30m
Bulluciems 56°59'·6N 23°53'·2E Fl.W.5s36m16M Red and white planking on a framework tower 28m
Daugavgrīva 57°03'·6N 24°01'·3E Fl.W.2.5s37m18M 035°-vis-245° Racon Round white concrete tower, black bands, balcony 35m
Ldg Lts 141° *Front* 57°03'·6N 24°01'·3E Iso.R.5s20m11M White daymark, red stripe, on red framework tower 15m
Rear 549m from front Iso.R.5s29m11M White rectangle, red stripe, on square red metal framework 26m. Both lights visible on leading line only
West breakwater 57°03'·9N 24°00'·6E Fl.G.3s11m2M White concrete tower 7m
East breakwater 57°04'·1N 24°00'·9E Fl.R.3s11m4M Round red metal tower with balcony 11·5m

Harbour communications
Rīga Traffic VHF Ch 09, 16 ☏ +371 6708 2000 or +371 6708 2035
Andrejosta Yacht Centre ☏ +371 2921 9427 or +371 2644 4012

General

Rīga is the capital city of Latvia, with a population of about 800,000, and lies on the River Daugava about 8M from the sea. There is a busy port along the banks of the river between the city centre and the sea and a considerable amount of industry outside the central area. The old town is extremely picturesque and the newer city centre is spaciously laid out with tree-lined streets and parks.

The old town with its Hanseatic connections has many buildings of interest particularly the castle, Swedish Gate, the Powder Tower, the Dome Cathedral, St Peter's Church (take a lift to the top for

Rīga canal. Modern building in the park *F. and G. Cattell*

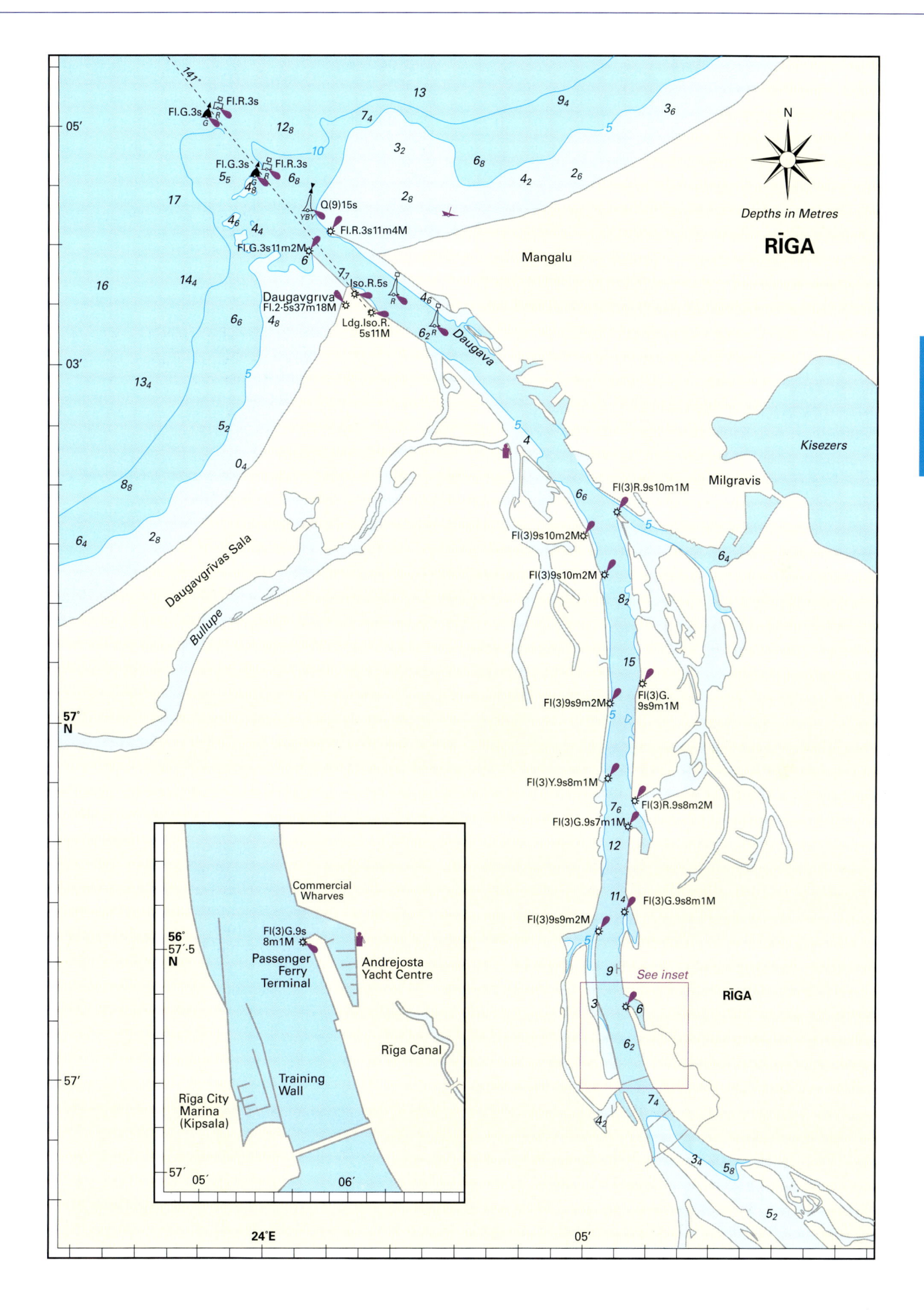

RĪGA

Depths in Metres

RĪGA

9B. LATVIA – THE GULF OF RĪGA

Andrejosta Yacht Harbour, Rīga F. and G. Cattell

a view over the entire city) and the restored House of the Blackheads. There are various museums including the Museum of the Occupation. An excellent way to see the beauty of the parks and city is via a Rīga Canal Boat – these run from the Passenger Terminal side of Andrejosta Basin opposite the yacht harbour with several stopping places en route through the park. Rīga has many fine examples of Art Nouveau architecture.

Approach and entry

57° 06'.50N 23° 56'.94E safe water buoy
Approach via lateral red/green buoyed channel
57° 04'.02N 24° 00'.76'E centre of harbour entrance

The wide river mouth with its powerful leading lights on 141° presents no problems at any time of the day or night. The river itself is wide and well marked, and normally has an outgoing current of around 2 knots.

Berthing

There are several yacht harbours along the river but foreign yachts normally stay at the Andrejosta Yacht Centre, which is located in a basin behind the passenger ferry terminal and just below the cable bridge. The harbour has long pontoons, most with individual finger berths. It is sometimes possible for larger craft to lie alongside. Andrejosta YC owns the pontoons on the town side of the basin. There are other pontoons on the passenger terminal side but without adequate facilities and at higher cost.

Other possibilities are the more recently developed Rīga City Marina at Kipsala on the opposite side of the Daugava River but this is less convenient for the city. Anchoring is not permitted.

Services for yachts

At both Andrejosta and Rīga City Marina water and electricity are provided on the pontoons. At Andrejosta toilets, showers and washing machine are located to the rear of the former clubhouse (now an expensive restaurant). Fuel berth at harbour or from the fuel berth at Latvijas Jahta (Pildne) about 5 miles down river. The Harbourmaster can arrange for repairs. Camping gaz bottles can be exchanged at Regate, the chandlers at the harbour. Rīga City Marina (across the river) has a pump out facility (the only one in Latvia as at 2016).

The Jana Seta Map Shop is the largest chart supplier in the country and will despatch orders abroad. Most major credit cards are accepted.
85a Elizabetes iela, Block 2, Rīga LV–1050, ☏ +371 6724 0894, veikals@kartes.lv, www.mapshop.lv

General facilities

Rīga itself has all the facilities of a major city – many shops, a choice of restaurants, banks, post office etc. Currency exchange is readily available in hotels and kiosks and cash can be obtained from ATMs. The

Vanšu Tilts (bridge) and Rīga skyline from Rīga City Marina F. and G. Cattell

Rīga City Marina from Vanšu Tilts (bridge)   F. and G. Cattell

390 THE BALTIC SEA AND APPROACHES

market, which takes place in four ex-Zeppelin hangars, is one of the largest in Europe and can provide almost anything edible and much more besides.

Communications and travel
Card-operated telephones, WiFi at the harbour and internet access at the public library and internet cafés.

International airport, railway and bus services within Latvia and to cities all over Europe, taxis and hire cars. Ferries to Stockholm (Sweden) but routes are subject to constant change and availability should be checked in advance if necessary.

Skulte
57°19'·20N 24°21'·81E safe water buoy
Sectored approach light flashing W/R/G.
57°19'·02N 24°23'·97E centre of harbour entrance
57°19'·06N 24°24'·68E yacht moorings
UKHO chart 2215
Latvian charts - see chart diagram on Appendix p.433
    plus Set of Charts of Latvia for Yachts (small craft folio)

A small commercial harbour on the eastern shore of the Gulf of Rīga, open to the west. There is a small general store close by but little else. A pontoon with finger berths has been established well into the harbour giving good shelter. Water and electricity.

Salacgrīva

57°45'·35N 24°21'·49E yacht moorings

Distances
Rīga 45M, Roomassaare 65M, Pärnu 40M

Charts
UKHO 2215, 2817
Latvian See chart diagram, Appendix p.433 plus Set of Charts of Latvia for Yachts (small craft folio)

Lights
Ldg Lts 072·3° *Front* 57°45'·4N 24°21'·2E Iso.R.2s9m9M
    White rectangle, black stripe, on framework tower.
    6.4m Visible on leading line only
    Rear 207m from front Iso.R.4s24m9M
    000° -vis-170° White rectangle, black stripe, on framework tower 18m

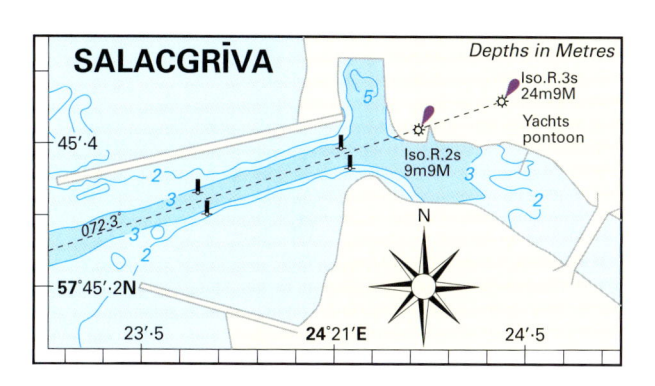

Harbour communications
Salacgriva 52 (Port Authority) VHF Ch 12, 16
    call *Port control*
    ☏ +371 2201 6399

Salacgrīva yacht moorings *F. and G. Cattell*

General
A small commercial port conveniently located midway between Rīga and Pärnu.

Approach and entry
57°44'·80N 24°17'·78E safe water buoy
Approach via lateral red/green buoyed channel
57°45'·26N 24°20'·40E centre of harbour entrance

The harbour entrance is well marked with buoys and leading marks on 072·3°, but becomes rough in onshore (westerly) winds. Entry/exit is restricted in winds over Force 7 (30 knots).

Berthing
There is a small pontoon for yachts with stern buoys. Anchoring is not permitted.

Services for yachts
Toilets and showers in facilities building. Shops and restaurants in the village. Water and electricity. Pontoon protected by security coded gate.

General facilities
Bar and restaurant at the harbour, with shops and cafés in the nearby village. Internet access at the information bureau on the south side of the river.

Communications and travel
Buses to Rīga and elsewhere.

Kuiviži
57°47'·34N 24°20'·57E centre of harbour entrance
57°47'·29N 24°21'·03E yacht moorings
Latvian charts - see chart diagram on Appendix p.433
    plus Set of Charts of Latvia for Yachts (small craft folio)

Redeveloped fishing harbour with separate and well sheltered facilities for yachts. Shallow and narrow entrance recommended to enter only in daylight with good visibility but not in strong onshore winds. Small shop. WiFi at harbour hotel. Restaurant, toilets, showers, sauna.

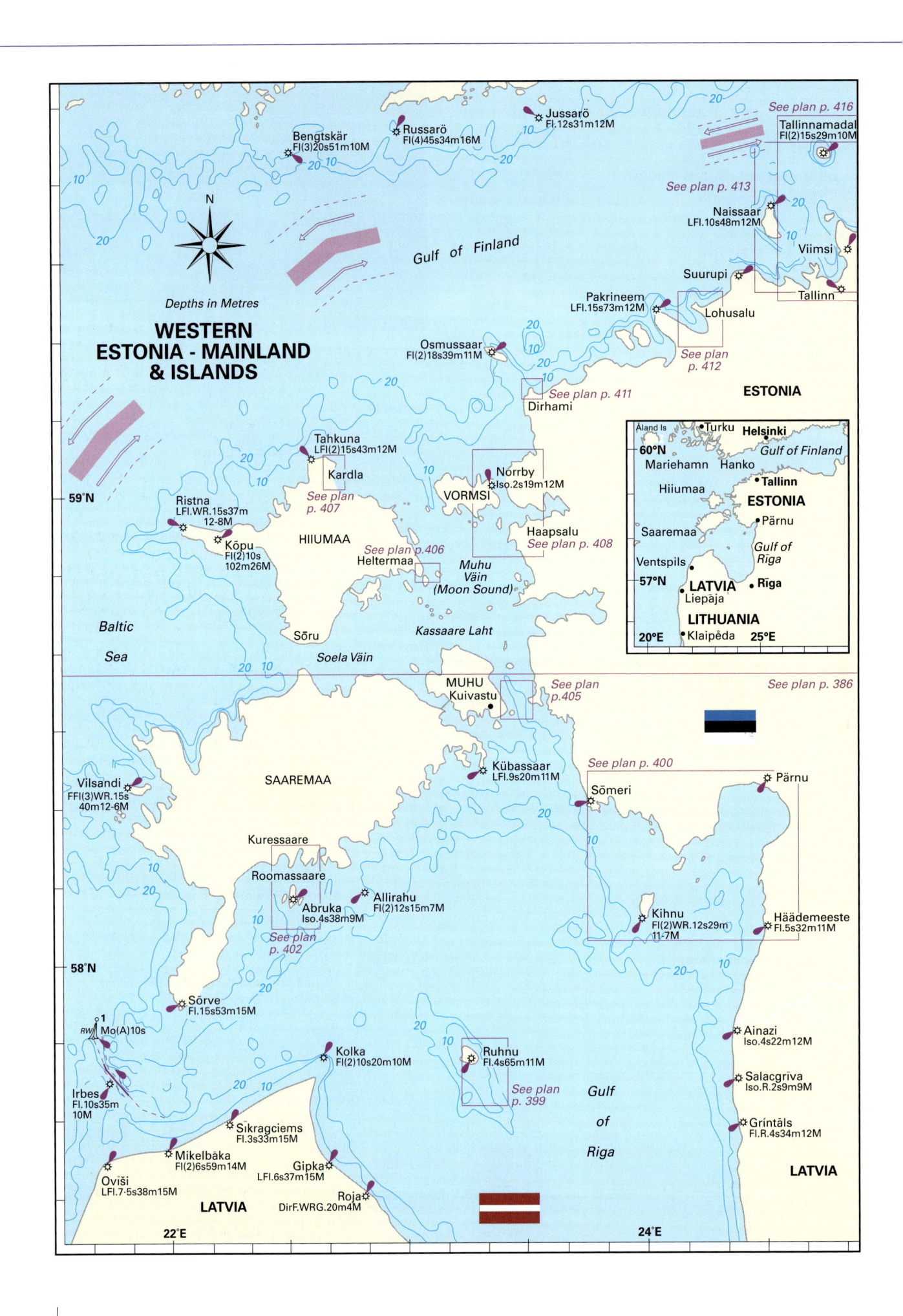

WESTERN ESTONIA - MAINLAND & ISLANDS

Depths in Metres

Lights and landmarks

- Bengtskär Fl(3)20s51m10M
- Russarö Fl(4)45s34m16M
- Jussarö Fl.12s31m12M
- Tallinnamadal Fl(2)15s29m10M
- Naissaar LFl.10s48m12M
- Viimsi
- Suurupi
- Tallinn
- Pakrineem LFl.15s73m12M
- Lohusalu
- Osmussaar Fl(2)18s39m11M
- Dirhami
- Tahkuna LFl(2)15s43m12M
- Kärdla
- Norrby Iso.2s19m12M
- VORMSI
- Haapsalu
- Ristna LFl.WR.15s37m 12-8M
- Kõpu Fl(2)10s 102m26M
- HIIUMAA
- Heltermaa
- Muhu Väin (Moon Sound)
- Sõru
- Kassaare Laht
- Soela Väin
- MUHU Kuivastu
- SAAREMAA
- Kübassaar LFl.9s20m11M
- Sõmeri
- Pärnu
- Vilsandi FFl(3)WR.15s 40m12-6M
- Kuressaare
- Roomassaare
- Abruka Iso.4s38m9M
- Allirahu Fl(2)12s15m7M
- Kihnu Fl(2)WR.12s29m 11-7M
- Häädemeeste Fl.5s32m11M
- Sõrve Fl.15s53m15M
- Ainazi Iso.4s22m12M
- Kolka Fl(2)10s20m10M
- Ruhnu Fl.4s65m11M
- Salacgrīva Iso.R.2s9m9M
- Irbes Fl.10s35m 10M
- Sīkragciems Fl.3s33m15M
- Mikelbāka Fl(2)6s59m14M
- Gipka LFl.6s37m15M
- Grīntāls Fl.R.4s34m12M
- Ovīši LFl.7·5s38m15M
- Roja DirF.WRG.20m4M

Gulf of Finland

Baltic Sea

Gulf of Riga

ESTONIA

LATVIA

See plan p. 416
See plan p. 413
See plan p. 412
See plan p. 411
See plan p. 407
See plan p. 406
See plan p. 408
See plan p. 405
See plan p. 386
See plan p. 400
See plan p. 402
See plan p. 399

Inset
- Åland Is
- Turku
- Helsinki
- Gulf of Finland
- Mariehamn
- Hanko
- Hiiumaa
- Tallinn
- ESTONIA
- Pärnu
- Saaremaa
- Gulf of Riga
- Ventspils
- LATVIA
- Rīga
- Liepāja
- LITHUANIA
- Klaipėda

392 THE BALTIC SEA AND APPROACHES

10. Estonia

Estonia is a most attractive destination for the cruising yachtsman, with good facilities and interesting towns and cities, as well as some intricate pilotage.

The Estonian Maritime Authority has encouraged the building of new yacht harbours, firstly in Western Estonia (mainland and islands), and this has encouraged a growth in the number of visiting yachts. Many improvements to existing harbours have also been carried out in conjunction with rebuilding of the ports used by ferries to the islands. These harbours belong to the State-owned company Saarte Liinid which administers them under the name of SL Marinas. Those included in this book are identified as such. SL Marinas operate a discount card system - purchase an SL Marinas Client or Discount card. A Client card lasts for a whole season whereas a Discount card covers four nights. The latter is probably more appropriate for the cruising sailor making passage through Estonia. Prices depend on length of vessel. See www.slmarinas.ee for full details.

Attention is now focussed on improving the harbours on the north coast but thus far developments are mostly of very small and shallow harbours.

The most popular route for visiting yachts on passage between the Gulf of Rīga and the north coast of Estonia or Gulf of Finland is via Moon Sound, which runs between the mainland and the larger Estonian islands. Notwithstanding Arthur Ransome's well known 1923 voyage from Rīga to Helsinki described in *Racundra's First Cruise*, passage through Moon Sound should not be attempted without large-scale local charts, as in places the navigable channels are narrow and the waters on either side are shallow and rock strewn. This applies particularly to the northern part of the passage between Vormsi and the mainland. The route is well marked with transit beacons and buoys where necessary, but it is dangerous to venture outside the channel. Since the establishment of good harbours at Heltermaa and Kärdla on Hiiumaa, the route between Vormsi and Hiiumaa is increasingly used particularly for yachts transiting to or from the Hanko peninsula in Finland. The complete coastline is covered by Estonian sheet charts but there are three small craft portfolios which cover the whole of Estonia and these are ideally suited for the cruising yachtsman.

Other than the major ports, caution should be exercised if approaching in darkness.

Sorve Lighthouse, Saaremaa *F. and G. Cattell*

10. ESTONIA

Key information

Rescue/Safety services

Emergency ☏ 112

Rescue and Coordination Centre JRCC Tallinn ☏ +372 619 1224, call-sign (VHF 16 and 69) *Tallinn RESCUE*.

Charts and pilot books

British UKHO Admiralty and Estonian charts cover the coast. British UKHO Admiralty charts are useful for passage planning but for detailed navigation the Estonian charts must be used. Those charts which are specific to an area or harbour are listed under individual harbour details. See the Appendix, page 419, for sources. The Estonian charts are as follows:

Charts of Estonia Vol. 1 Gulf of Finland – Suurupi Peninsula to Narva

Charts of Estonia Vol. 2 Vainameri - Suurupi Peninsula to Saaremaa.

Charts of Estonia Vol. 3 From Saaremaa to Ruhnu

A series of small craft plans giving the recommended routes and contact information for Tallinn Bay, Haapsalu Bay, Pärnu Bay and Suur Katel Bay (Kuressaare area) have been produced and are downloadable from the Estonian Maritime Administration website www.vta.ee. Follow link to Recreational Craft.

Harbours of the Baltic States, F & G Cattell, available through the Cruising Association and major nautical suppliers in Scandinavia.

Baltic Pilot Volume II & III (NP 19)

Sailing Directions for Estonian Waters. Estonian Maritime Administration. Updated by Notices to Mariners.

Time

Estonia is in the Eastern European time zone (UT+2 in winter/UT+3 in summer). Summer time starts and ends on the same dates as the rest of the EU.

Money

The Euro. Cash is easily obtained from ATMs. Credit cards are widely accepted but most harbours expect to be paid in cash.

Formalities

Estonia is a member of the EU and of the Schengen Area (see main Introduction page 7 for details of Schengen formalities). EU passport holders do not require visas. The website of the Foreign Ministry (www.vm.ee) lists countries whose citizens do not need visas. If a visa is needed, contact the Estonian Consulate at 44 Queens Gate Terrace, London SW7 5PJ ☏ 0207 838 5388, london@mfa.ee, http://london.vm.ee /

The British Embassy in Tallinn can be contacted on ☏ +372 667 4700, infotallinn@fco.gov.uk, www.gov.uk/government/world/estonia

Formal reporting is no longer required for passages between Estonia and another Schengen country and yachts may arrive or depart from any Estonian harbour. Vessels arriving from or departing to a non-Schengen country, such as Russia, should telephone the Border Guards on ☏ +372 619 1260 and +372 612 3000 for guidance on clearance.

According to the Estonian regulation *Requirements for Operating Recreational Craft* skippers of recreational craft flying the Estonian flag (and skippers of foreign flagged craft whose flag state requires such) require a registration certificate and a certificate of a skipper of a recreational craft. For British-flagged craft there is no legal requirement to have such certificates when sailing in Estonian waters as there is no requirement for such under British law. In practice, skippers and crew would be advised to carry any certificates of competence wherever they are sailing.

Public holidays

Public holidays occur on:

1 January, 24 February (Independence Day), Good Friday, Easter Sunday, 1 May (May Day), Pentecost, 23 June (Victory Day), 24 June (St John's Day), 20 August (Restoration of Independence Day) and 24, 25, 26 December.

Communications

There are efficient telephone and mail systems and full coverage of mobile phone networks. Internet access is widely available with many free WiFi points.

National and international calls may be made from the few remaining public phone boxes which operate on cards obtainable from shops or street kiosks. To obtain an international line, dial 00 followed by the country code, area code (omitting any initial 0) and number. Dialling within Estonia only the 7 digit number is required. There are no longer area codes nor an initial 0. All mobile numbers start with 5. The country code for Estonia is 372.

Travel

Tallinn has an international **airport** only 3km from the city centre, with domestic airports at Pärnu and on the islands of Hiiumaa (Kärdla) and Saaremaa (Roomassaare). The country is served by a network of **buses** and **trains**, while **Eurolines** provides a link all the way from St Petersburg to cities in most European countries.

Tallinn has **ferries** to Helsinki and Stockholm. Other international ferries run from Paldiski to Kapellskär (Sweden). Internal ferries run between Rohuküla and Heltermaa (Hiiumaa) and Vormsi island; between Virtsu and Kuivastu (Muhu) and thence to Saaremaa; between Triigi (Saaremaa) and Sõru (Hiiumaa); and between Roomassaare (Saaremaa) and the small offlying island of Abruka.

Websites

A great deal of information about Estonia is available on the internet, much of it in English. However it should be remembered that not all sites are updated regularly.

www.tourism.ee The Estonian Tourist Board. Well presented website with many useful links.

www.inyourpocket.com Tourist information.

www.estonica.org An interesting site containing well-written articles on Estonia's history, culture and nature.

www.marinas.nautilus.ee The Estonian Cruising Association

www.vta.ee The Estonian Maritime Administration

Radio communications

Details of the above, including Search & Rescue, GMDSS, Coast Radio Stations, Weather Bulletins and Navigational Warnings, NAVTEX and Weatherfax transmissions and weather forecasts on the internet will be found in the Appendix.

VHF radio is much used for marine communications - details of channels and call signs will be found under each harbour heading.

VHF Ch 16 should be monitored while on passage e.g. the coastguard station at Paldiski may call up passing craft including yachts.

Weather information

Weather bulletins and navigational warnings are broadcast at 0633 and 1533 LT on VHF Ch 1, 3, 5, 7, 20, 26 and 27 by Tallinn Radio, in English and Estonian. See page 428 for full details.

ESTONIA – THE COUNTRY

The country

Estonia consists for the most part of a low lying plain with higher ground towards the east. There are numerous streams and lakes including one of Europe's largest, Lake Peipsi, lying on the border with Russia. The coast is also low lying and, particularly to the west, is fringed by islands which make up nearly 10% of Estonian land. The surrounding seas to the south and west are shallow. About a quarter of the country is forested.

Highlights
Haapsalu castle, Kuressaare Castle, two Swedish churches on Ruhnu, Kaali crater on Saaremaa, Tallinn old town

The people, the church and the language

Estonians are of the same race as the Finns and share a similar language. In the 20th century great numbers of the native population emigrated, and today Estonia has a total population of just over 1.3 million and an ethnic mix of which about 68% are Estonian and 26% Russian, the balance being made up of Ukrainians, Belorussians, Finns, Jews and Latvians. About 70% live in urban areas, nearly 30% about 408,000 live in Tallinn alone.

The official language is Estonian – a Finno-Ugric language – but most speak or understand Russian. Finnish and German are commonly understood and many younger people are delighted to communicate in excellent English. Estonia suffered badly from the Soviet policy of 'Russification', and since independence the government has introduced laws concerning not only citizenship requirements but also language ability for employment. Some of the ethnic Russian population speak only Russian. The generations educated in Soviet times have fluent Russian, whereas younger generations have fluent English. German is a good alternative with the older generation.

Estonians often describe themselves as pagan. Forcibly converted to Christianity by the Teutonic Knights, the majority of those still practising are split between the Lutheran and Orthodox churches with a smaller number adhering to the Catholic faith.

Visitors, whether they come by sea, air or land, can be assured of a warm welcome.

Estonia monument and lighthouse at Tahkuna, Hiiumaa. The ferry *Estonia* sank while on overnight passage from Tallinn to Stockholm on 28 September 1994. Tahkuna is the nearest part of Estonia to where the ship was lost. The monument is a bell suspended from a specially designed framework in such a way that it will toll when the wind direction and speed (SW 15-20m/s F7-8) are the same as at the time of the tragedy.
F. and G. Cattell

History

Estonia's border with Latvia is now set by language. The Estonian language, like Finnish, is part of the Finno-Ungrian family, while Latvian is Indo-European. Nonetheless, both countries have shared much of their history over the past few centuries.

In the late Middle Ages, Estonia was made up of eight 'counties', but still had no central ruler. Raids and counter raids with its neighbours were graduating into battles and invasions as the evolving nations of Denmark, Sweden, Russia, Prussia and Poland recognised the strategic importance of Estonia's coast.

In 1193 Pope Celestine declared the Northern Crusades, thereby telling the foreign invaders that they now had God on their side - except the Russian Christians, now that Rome broke had broken with the Orthodox Church. By 1227 the Danes had conquered north Estonia by sea, while the south was defeated by the Brothers of the Sword following their conquest of Latvia. Reval (now Tallinn) became a Hanseatic port. A century and a half later, the Danish king decided to move out of Estonia and sold his part to the Teutonic Knights, who now included the Brothers of the Sword, to add to Livonia, as they called their conquered territories. The whole of Estonia and Latvia were now managed by immigrant German landlords and merchants.

During the Reformation the Grand Master of the Teutonic Knights became a Lutheran and Livonia did the same. To meet the Lutheran rule that everyone should be able to read the Bible in their own language, literacy and education were now provided to the locals.

10. ESTONIA

Meteorite crater at Kaali, Saaremaa F. and G. Cattell

Later in the 16th century, the rivalries between Denmark, Sweden, Ivan the Terrible's Russia and the Polish-Lithuanian Union lead to the Livonian War. In 1561, Sweden took over north Estonia, while southern Estonia and north Latvia became Polish Livonia in the 1580s. Then Gustavus Adolphus became king of Sweden. He conquered most of the Baltic coastal regions and in 1625 Livonia became Swedish. Gustavus Adolphus did much to improve the lot of the indigenous peasantry, but then came the Great Northern War to destroy the Swedish Empire. Under the Treaty of Nystad in 1710, Estonia became part of the Russian Empire, which ruled them through their existing Germanic authorities. As in Latvia and Lithuania, pride in their language and traditions began to develop, particularly during the 19th century.

With the 1917 Russian Revolution, the Bolsheviks allowed north and south Estonia to unite, and the modern borders between Estonia and Latvia were more or less established. Both countries still had to fight for their independence, however, as first Germany and then the Red Army tried to re-assert control. At last in 1920 the Soviet Union accepted Estonia's independence.

During the interwar years, the large estates were broken up and redistributed, the Estonian language replaced German and Russian in schools and Estonian art began to flourish. Then came the Second World War with invasion by first the Soviets, then the Nazis and then the Soviets again. Despite fierce resistance, Estonia became one of Stalin's Soviets. Huge numbers of Estonians were executed or deported, being replaced by Russians as the new elite.

Hope was kept alive across the nation through traditional Estonian songs. Since Stalin's days the authorities had tried to hijack the national singing festival by making everyone sing songs about the joys of Soviet communism. 1969 was the centenary of the festival, so the authorities brought in several extra brass bands to drown out any attempts to sing nationalist songs, but to no avail.

Restrictions began to ease from 1985 under Gorbachev's reforms. Estonians were able to watch Finnish TV to see how the rest of the world was living and to hear the news without any Soviet bias. Then in 1988 passive resistance turned into the 'Singing Revolution'. A series of public concerts were lead with patriotic songs by Estonian rock bands, with up to 300,000 Estonians participating - a quarter of the population. The old Estonian three coloured flags had been banned so they flew them in three separate pieces. More and more of the Estonian authorities began to support them, or at least to bow to the inevitable. Estonia finally regained its independence on 20 August 1991, with full recognition by Yeltsin's Russia.

Estonia is now well established as a free-market democracy, a member of both the EU and the Euro zone.

In the years since independence the pace of change has been fast, progress rapid and Estonia has made great strides towards updating facilities and services.

Estonia orientates itself firmly towards the West and joined both the EU and NATO in 2004, signing the Schengen agreement in 2007.

Cruising

Yacht services
Yachting, both sail and motor, has become increasingly popular with Estonians. Many harbours have a yacht club but these are mostly owned by groups of businessmen and run as businesses, often with a hotel and restaurant open for tourists or conferences as part of the complex. The clubs may own a small fleet of racing yachts but many boats – including expensive motor yachts – are privately owned.

Chandlery
Chandlery and charts can be obtained at some harbours, but it is wise to obtain charts before arrival as stocks may be limited.

Holding tanks
Holding tanks are to become obligatory for new Estonian boats. Although not obligatory for others, it is illegal to discharge toilets or grey water within 5M of the coast. It is intended that Estonian harbours provide pump-out facilities but so far only the more modern or reconstructed harbours have such facilities alongside.

Gas
Local gas refills are available in some harbours and Camping Gaz is available in Pärnu and Tallinn.
www.campingaz.com

Diesel
Fuelling berths are available in Pärnu, Roomassaare, Kuressaare, Kuivastu, Kärdla, Haapsalu, Dirhami, Lohusalu, Tallinn (Pirita and Old City Marina) and Vergi. Elsewhere fuel can be obtained by arrangement with the yacht club or Harbourmaster. There is a 5% bio-component added.

Shopping
Well stocked shops and supermarkets can be found in all towns.

Alcohol
Alcohol can be purchased from shops and supermarkets without restriction. There are large alcohol outlets adjoining the ferry terminal in Tallinn.

The alcohol limit at sea for leisure boats is 0.5mg alcohol in 1g of blood (i.e. 0.5/ml) or 0.25mg alcohol in 1l of breath.

Windmills at Angla, Saaremaa *F. and G. Cattell*

10. ESTONIA

Direction of travel

The general direction of travel in Estonia in this chapter is from south to north, starting with the island of Ruhnu and proceeding via Kihnu to Pärnu thence to the island of Saaremaa, through Moon Sound and the islands of Hiiumaa and Vormsi, returning to the mainland at Haapsalu. The direction follows the coast northwards and eastwards to Tallinn and Vergi including some islands as appropriate.

Ruhnu

57°46'·90N 23°16'·20E yacht moorings
57°46'·80N 23°16'·32 centre of harbour entrance
57°46'·62N 23°17'·39 safe water buoy (normally on station May-October)

Charts
UKHO 2215
Estonian charts see diagram Appendix p.431-2
Charts of Estonia Vol. 3 (small craft folio)

Lights
Ruhnu Lighthouse 57°48'·08N 23°15'·6E Fl.W.4s65m11M
Dark brown metal tower with supporting pillars, balcony and lantern 40m

An SL Marinas harbour

A small island with Swedish cultural interest in the Gulf of Rīga. Ringsu harbour on the SE point provides good shelter (in the inner portion) with individual finger berths. Additional alongside berthing inside the west mole in the outer harbour has less shelter from south and east and becomes untenable in strong southeasterly weather. The village is about 3km distant. Limited shopping, post office, bar, museum. No banks but most currencies accepted by harbour office. Leading line for approach 286·6°. Entry recommended in good visibility and moderate weather only. Ruhnu is a useful and convenient staging point on passages between Latvia and Estonia.

Kihnu

58°08'.49N 24°01'.17E yacht moorings
58°08'.50N 24°02'.76E safe water buoy
UKHO chart 2215
Estonian charts see diagram, Appendix p.431
    plus Charts of Estonia Vol. 3 (small craft folio)
Sailor Infopage Shipping Routes of Parnu Bay
An SL Marinas harbour.
See plan on next page.

A small island in the approaches to Pärnu surrounded by shoals up to 2M offshore. If approaching from the south keep at least 2M offshore leaving east cardinal mark to port and on reaching leading line sail in on 273°. (See *Estonian Small Craft Chart Vol. 3*). If approaching from north or east, well-buoyed channels lead in to join the leading line.

There is a fishing/ferry harbour with pontoons and stern buoys for yachts. Facilities include bars and a shop. The island has a very small permanent population. Ferries to Pärnu and Munalaid.

Right Kihnu lighthouse

Below Kihnu Harbour
F. and G. Cattell

Ruhnu outer harbour mooring pontoon *F. and G. Cattell*

398 THE BALTIC SEA AND APPROACHES

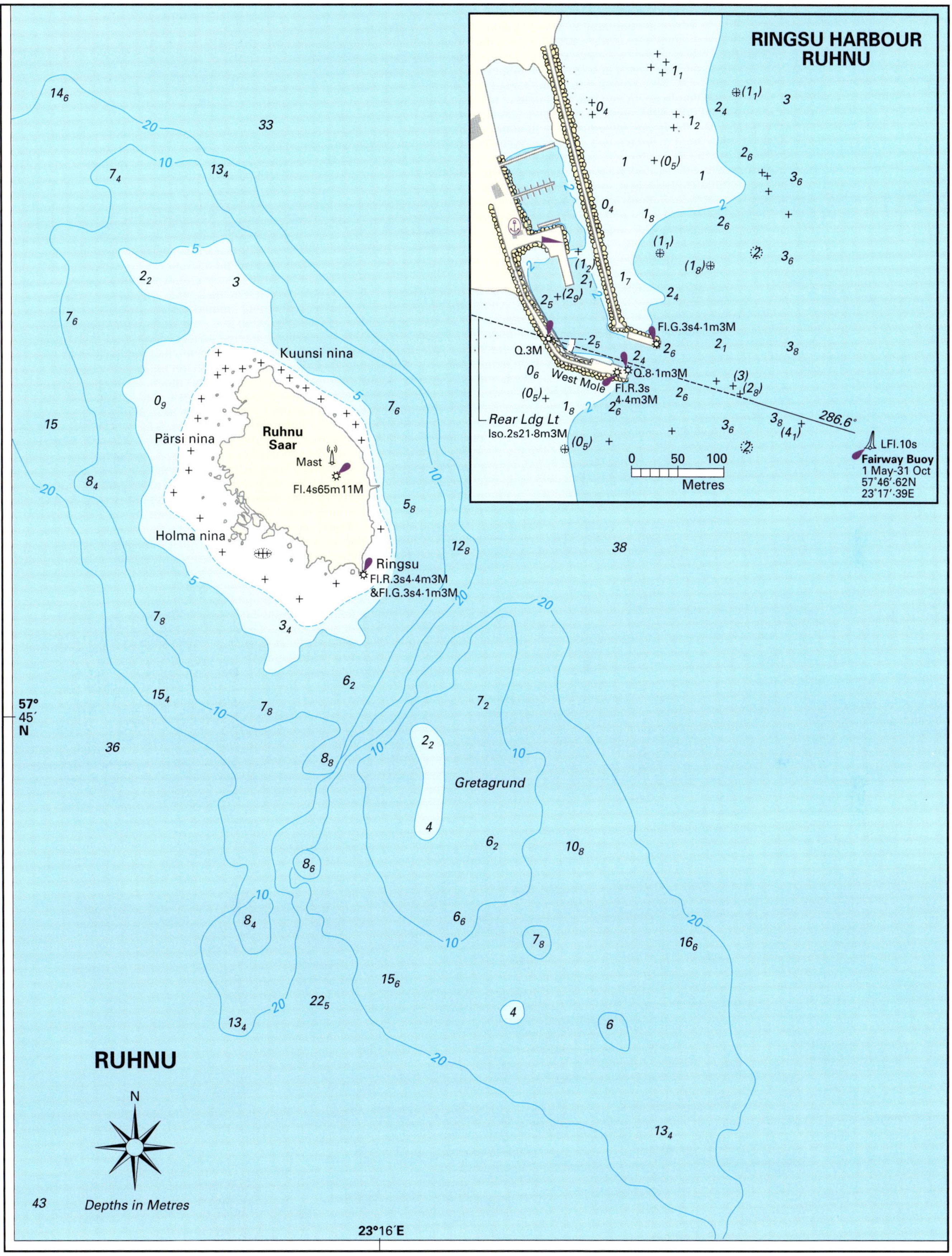
RINGSU HARBOUR
RUHNU
Fl.G.3s4·1m3M
Q.3M
West Mole
Q.8·1m3M
Fl.R.3s
4·4m3M
Rear Ldg Lt
Iso.2s21·8m3M
286.6°
LFl.10s
Fairway Buoy
1 May-31 Oct
57°46′·62N
23°17′·39E
0 50 100
Metres
Kuunsi nina
Ruhnu
Saar
Mast
Fl.4s65m11M
Pärsi nina
Holma nina
Ringsu
Fl.R.3s4·4m3M
&Fl.G.3s4·1m3M
Gretagrund
57°
45′
N
23°16′E
RUHNU
N
Depths in Metres

10. ESTONIA

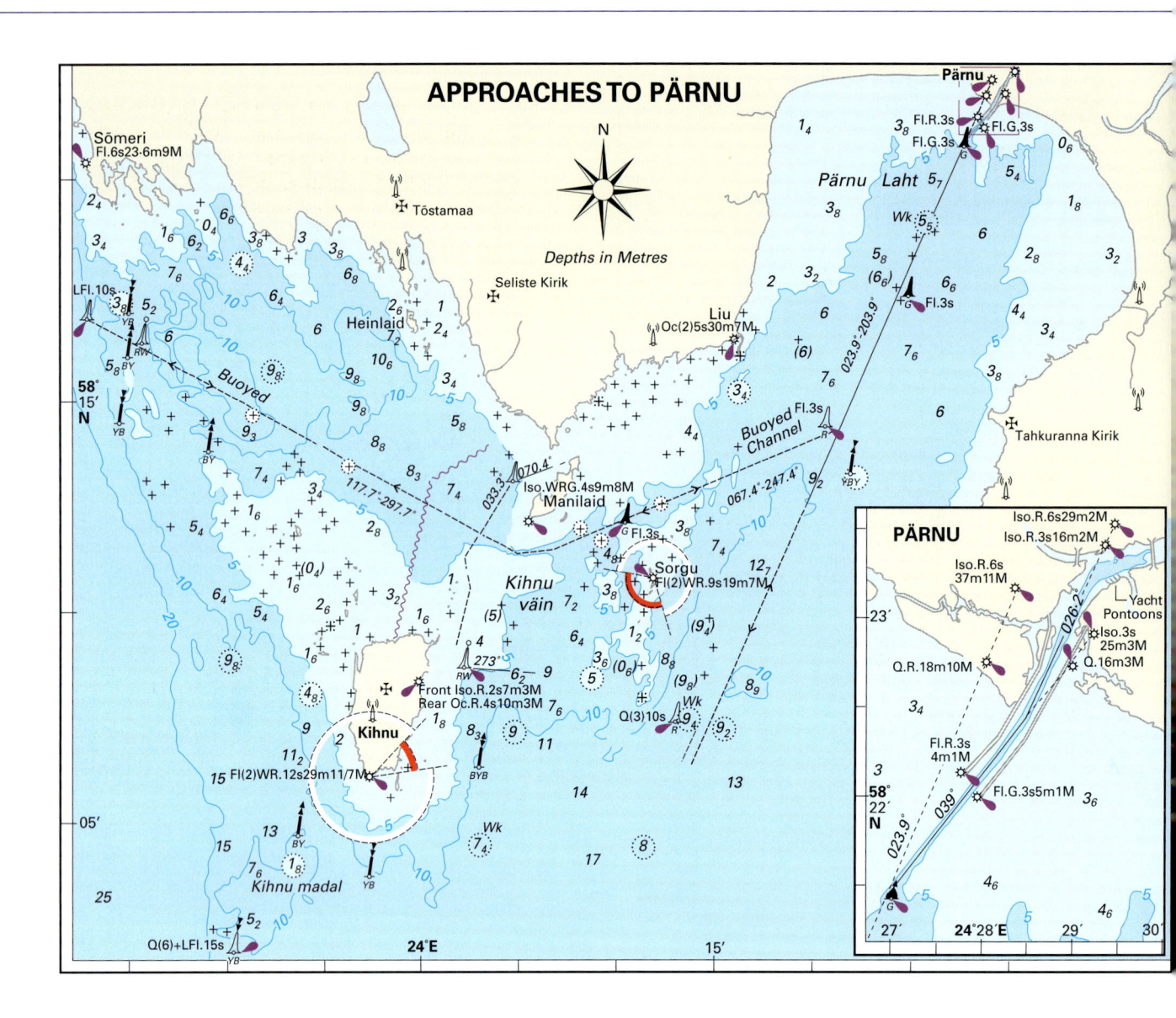

Pärnu Yacht Club Moorings *F. and G. Cattell*

THE BALTIC SEA AND APPROACHES

PÄRNU

Pärnu

58°23'·17N 24°29'·22E

Distances
Rīga 80M, Salacgriva 40M, Roomassaare 75M, Virtsu (inside Kihnu) 50M, Virtsu (outside Kihnu) 60M

Charts
UKHO 2215, 2816, 2817
Estonian charts see diagram Appendix p.431-2
Charts of Estonia Vol. 3 (small craft folio)
Latvian charts 1251, 1011
Sailor Infopage Shipping Routes of Parnu Bay

Lights
Kihnu 58°05'·8N 23°58'·3E Fl(2)W.R.12s29m11–7M 262° -W-225° -R- 262° Round white metal tower with balcony 28m
Häädemeeste 58°04'·4N 24°29'·2E Fl.W.5s32m11M White square metal framework tower 28m
Sorgu Saar 58°10'·7N 24°12'·00E Fl(2)WR.9s19m7M 101° -W-342° -R-101° Round red brick tower with balcony 16m
Liu Light Beacon 58°16'·6N 24°15'·9E Oc(2)5s30m7M White planking on metal framework tower 28m
Pärnu Ldg Lts 023.9° *Front* 58°22'·7N 24°27'·9E Q.R.17·6m10M White rectangle, black stripe, on red round metal tower 22m. Visible on leading line only *Rear* 821m from front, Iso.R.6s37m11M White rectangle, black stripe, on metal framework tower 34m
East breakwater 58°22'N 24°28'E Fl.G.3s5m1M White metal column, green band, concrete base 3m
West breakwater 58°22'·1N 24°27'·7E Fl.R.3s4m1M White metal column, red band, on concrete base 3m

Communications
Pärnu Jahtklubi Marina ☎ +372 44 71750
Pärnu Port VHF Ch 16 call *Parnu Sadam*

General

Pärnu, an attractive small town and holiday resort in the extreme northeast corner of the Gulf of Rīga, is known as Estonia's Summer Capital. Timber is exported and there is a small amount of fishing. It is surrounded by beautiful sandy beaches – one of which is reserved for ladies only. The orthodox church is worth visiting.

Approach and entry

58°22.04N 24°27.76E centre of harbour entrance

Straightforward approach on 023·9°, following the leading marks.

Berthing

Berth at Pärnu Yacht Club on the east bank of the river just round a bend. Mooring is bows-to pontoon and stern line to buoy or stern anchor in 2·5–3m depths in reasonable shelter. Visitors should use the first pontoon if possible, or otherwise tie up where space allows and seek advice at the yacht club. Anchoring is not advised as the waterway is used by commercial shipping.

Services for yachts

Water and electricity on the pontoons, showers and toilets at the yacht club (which also has a bar and a restaurant). There is a fuel berth beyond the yacht club pontoons and a chandlery.

General facilities

The small town is about a mile from the yacht club and has all facilities including shops, post office, banks and restaurants.

Communications and travel

Buses to Tallinn, Rīga and elsewhere. Airport for domestic flights. Ferries to Ruhnu and Kihnu.

WiFi at the sailing club and internet cafés in the town.

Pärnu, looking NE towards town bridge *F. and G. Cattell*

10. ESTONIA

THE BALTIC SEA AND APPROACHES 401

10. ESTONIA

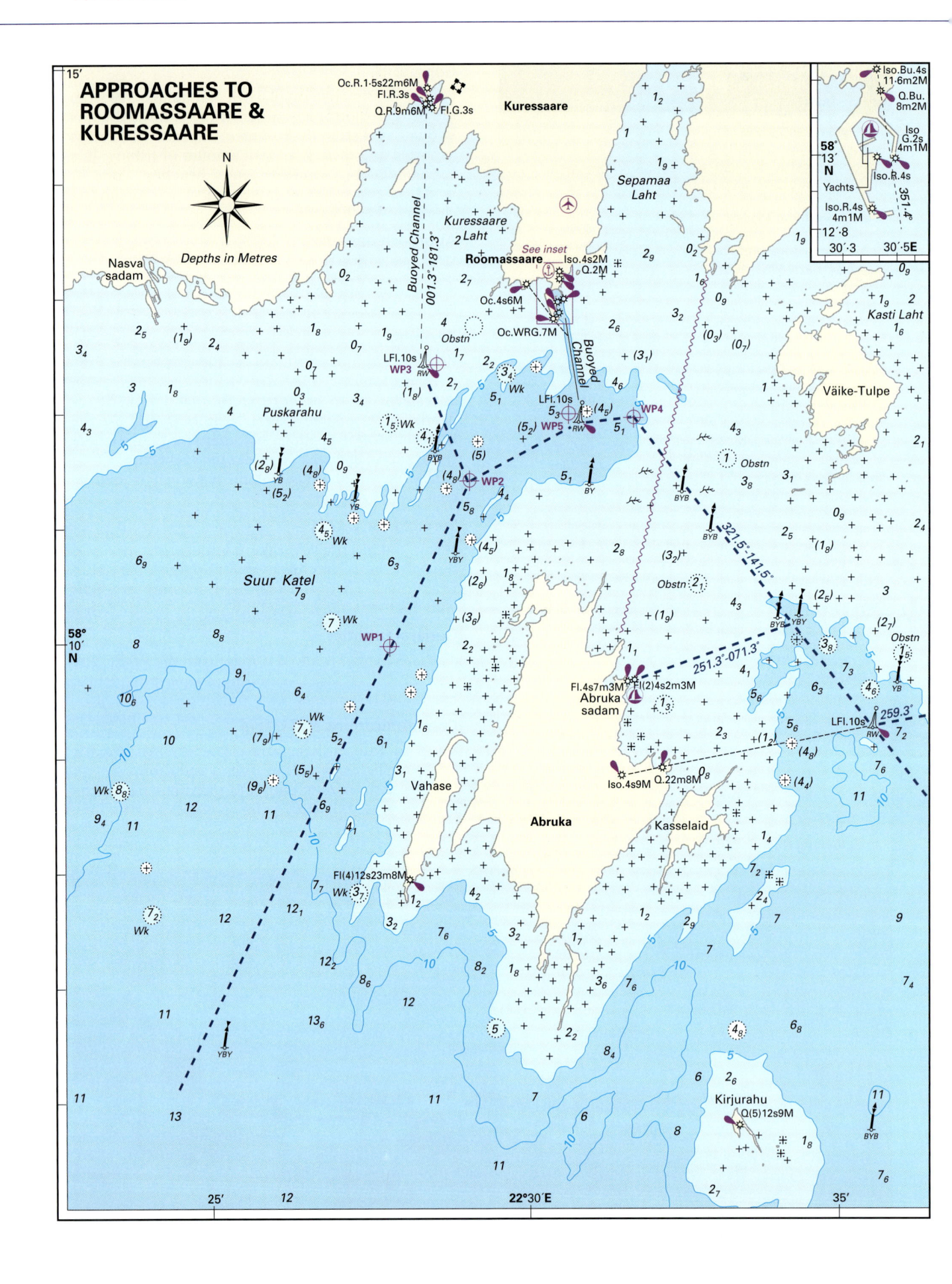

APPROACHES TO ROOMASSAARE & KURESSAARE

KURESSAARE

Kuressaare (Saaremaa)

58°13'·02N 22°30'·34E yacht moorings
58°14'·63N 22°28'·32E centre of harbour entrance

Distances
Ventspils 65M, Roja 45M, Rīga 85M, Kuivastu 50M, Pärnu 75M

Charts
UKHO 2059, 2215
Estonian charts see diagram Appendix p.431-2
Charts of Estonia Vol. 3 (small craft folio)
Latvian charts 1251, 1013
Sailor Infopage Recommended Routes for Recreational Craft on Suur Katel Bay

Lights
Abruka safe water buoy 58°09'·34N 22°35'·58E LFl.10s3M
Abruka 58°08'·9N 22°31'·5E
  Iso.W.4s38m9M White round concrete tower, black bands 36m
Allirahu 58°09'·7N 22°47'·2E
  Fl(2)W.12s14·9m7M Metal framework tower with orange planking on all sides 9·8m
Kuressaare Fairway buoy 58°12'·5N 22°28'·14E
  LFl.W.10s3M
Kuressaare Ldg Lts 1.3° *Front* 58°14'·65N 22°28'·23E
  Q.R.9m6M White rectangle with red stripe on red metal cylinder 7m
  Rear 240m from front Oc.R.1·5s22m6M
  White rectangle with red strip on building – height above building 3m

Communications
VHF Ch 11 & 16 call sign *Tori Sadam*
Harbourmaster ☏ +372 453 3450

The harbours of Kuressaare and Roomassaare on the southern shore of Saaremaa are located close together and are both based on the town of Kuressaare. Kuressaare harbour has the advantage of being within the town whereas Roomassaare, which has the advantage of a better location for onward passages, is some 4km to the east.

Kuressaare is the capital of Saaremaa, the largest of the Estonian islands and the second largest island in the entire Baltic Sea. The island has one of the highest standards of living in Estonia and is highly popular with tourists. Kuressaare has many attractive buildings and a superb moated castle complete with large museum (it is claimed that the castle is the best-preserved medieval fortress in the Baltic) plus reasonable shops and many cafés and restaurants. Other places of interest on Saaremaa include Panga Pank, the windmills at Angla and the meteorite crater at Kaali.

Approach and entry

Approaching from SW in Suur Katel bay
From SW
Waypoint 1 58°10'·00N 22°27'·00E
Waypoint 2 58°11'·90N 22°29'·40E
Waypoint 3 Kuressaare safe water buoy 58°12'·5N 22°28'·14E to join leading line of 01·3°

Approaching from southeast (east of Abruka)
Head for the Abruka safe water buoy 58°09'·34N 22°35'·58E. Follow the outer leading line for Roomassaare 321·5° until Waypoint 4 58°11'·90N 22°31'·70E is reached then proceed to Roomassaare safe water buoy 58°11'·97N 22°30'·78E (Waypoint 5) then follow a course to Waypoints 2 and 3 as above.

The approach is by a long, buoyed and dredged channel on a leading line of 01·3° from the fairway buoy. Channel said to be dredged to 2·5m but weed can give false depth readings.

Berthing
Kuressaare harbour is located very close to the small town. Berthing is to stern buoys and bows to pontoon with limited alongside berthing. There is no shelter to be obtained outside the harbour and the water is shallow outside the channel so anchoring off is not possible. Anchoring within the harbour would not be permitted.

Services for yachts
Water and electricity on pontoon, toilets, showers, sauna and laundry facilities in the harbour office building. Fuel berth and holding tank pump-out facilities. For repairs etc seek the advice of the Harbourmaster.

General facilities
Restaurant at harbour. Charts for sale at harbour office. All facilities – shops, banks, post office, restaurants, outdoor market, car hire and tourist office in the town.

Communications and travel
Bus and ferry to Tallinn etc. Airport for domestic flights at Roomassaare (4km distant). WiFi and internet access.

Kuressaare harbour
F. and G. Cattell

10. ESTONIA

Roomassaare (Saaremaa)

58°13'·02N 22°30'·34E yacht moorings
An SL Marinas harbour
See plan on page 402

Distances
Ventspils 65M, Roja 45M, Rīga 85M, Kuivastu 50M, Pärnu 75M

Charts
UKHO 2059, 2215
Estonian see diagram, Appendix p.431-2
Charts of Estonia Vol. 3 (small craft folio)
Latvian charts 1251, 1013
Sailor Infopage Recommended Routes for Recreational Craft on Suur Katel Bay

Lights
Abruka 58°08'·9N 22°31'·5E Iso.W.4s38m9M
   White round concrete tower, black bands 36m
Allirahu 58°09'·7N 22°47'·2E Fl(2)W.12s14·9·8m7M
   Metal framework tower with orange planking on all sides 8m
Outer Ldg Lts 321·5° *Front* 58°12'·82N 22°30'·35E
   Oc.WRG.4s14m7/6M 276·5°-W-6·5° 15° -G-24° -W-30° -R-39° Black rectangle, white stripe, on red framework tower 12m
   Rear 721m from front Oc.W.4s33m6M
   Black rectangle, white stripe, on metal framework tower 30m
Fairway buoy 58°11'·97N 22°30'·78E LFl.W.10s3M
Inner Ldg Lts 351·1° *Front* 58°13'·17N 22°30'·43E
   Q.Bu.8m2M Black rectangle, white stripe, on red metal post 7m
   Rear 107m from front, Iso.Bu.4s11.2M Black rectangle, white stripe, on red metal post 9·7m
Yacht harbour West mole 58°12'·97N 22°30'·42E
   Iso.R.4s4m1M Red metal post 2m
Yacht harbour East mole 58°12'·96N 22°30'·48E
   Iso.G.2s4m1M Green metal post 2m

Communications
Roomassaare Port Control ☎ +372 5335 8313
   VHF Ch 14, 16 call *Roomassaare sadam*

Approach and entry

Approaching from southwest in Suur Katel bay
Waypoint 1 58°10'·00N 22°27'·00E
Waypoint 2 58°11'·90N 22°29'·40E
Waypoint 5 (Roomassaare safe water buoy) 58°11'·97N 22°30'·78E to join leading line 351·4° to enter harbour

Roomassaare harbour from Yacht Club Tower
F. and G. Cattell

Approaching from southeast (east of Abruka)
58°12'·97N 22°30'·45E centre of harbour entrance

Head for the Abruka safe water buoy 58°09'·34N 22°35'·58E. Follow the outer leading line on a course of 321·5° until Waypoint 4 58°11'·90N 22°31'·70E is reached then follow a course to Waypoint 5 Roomassaare safe water buoy 58°11'·97N 22°30'.78E to join leading line 351·4° to enter harbour.

Berthing
Roomassaare has a small modern marina in the inner basin, beyond the commercial harbour. Berths are alongside individual finger pontoons in 2·5-3m. There is no shelter to be obtained outside the harbour, so anchoring off is not possible.

Services for yachts
Water and electricity on pontoon, toilets, showers and sauna in the harbour office building. Fuel berth which also has holding tank pump-out facilities. For repairs etc seek the advice of the Harbourmaster.

General facilities
Bar, restaurant and small shop in the harbour area. All facilities – shops, banks, post office, restaurants, outdoor market, car hire and tourist office – in Kuressaare.

Communications and travel
Bus to Kuressaare from outside the marina, and thence bus and ferry to Tallinn etc. The island also has an airport handling domestic flights.

Roomassaare harbour *F. and G. Cattell*

KUIVASTU

Kuivastu

58°34'·36N 23°23'·58E yacht moorings
An SL Marinas harbour

Distances
Roomassaare 50M, Pärnu (inside Kihnu) 50M, Pärnu (outside Kihnu) 60M, Haapsalu 30M

Charts
UKHO 2215, 2816, 2817
Estonian charts see diagram, Appendix p.431-2
Charts of Estonia Vol. 2 & 3 (small craft folio)
Latvian charts 1251, 1013

Lights
Kübassaare 58°25'·70N 23°17'·99E LFl.W.9s20m11M 228°-vis-048° Round concrete tower, black upper white lower with balcony and lantern 18m
Pöörilaid 58°27'·68N 23°37'·78E Fl(4)WRG.18s14m7M 007°-W-141°-R-160°-W-220·5°-340·5°-G-007° White round concrete tower with balcony and lantern 13m
Viirelaid 58°32'·69N 23°26'·58E Fl.WR.8s15m9–7M 163°-W-349°-R-163° Red round concrete tower with balcony and lantern 11m
Virtsu 58°34'·03N 23°30'·10E Fl.W.5s19m11M Red upper and white lower – square concrete tower 18m
Kuivastu Ldg Lts 267·7° *Front* 58°34'·42N 23°23'·39E Q.W.11m6M W 265·7°-269·7° White rectangle, red stripe, on red metal framework 8m
Rear 320m from front Iso.W.3s17m6M W 265·7°-269·7° White rectangle, red stripe, on red metal framework 12m
Kuivastu Yacht Harbour Lt beacon 58°34'·32N 23°23'·58E Fl.G.5s4m3M Green concrete column 3m
Kuivastu Pier Lt beacon 58°34'·42N 23°23'·79E Q.R.8m2M Red concrete column with balcony 5m

Communications
Kuivastu Port Control ① +372 5400 4131, VHF Ch 14 call sign *Kuivastu harbour*

General

Kuivastu is the harbour for ferries between the Estonian mainland and Muhu (for Saaremaa) and has a purpose-built yacht harbour adjacent to the ferry terminal. There is no town but Kuivastu offers an excellent stopover on the journey through Moon Sound. The 'Old Russian Inn' visited by Arthur Ransome is a short distance along the road, but sadly is no longer an Inn!

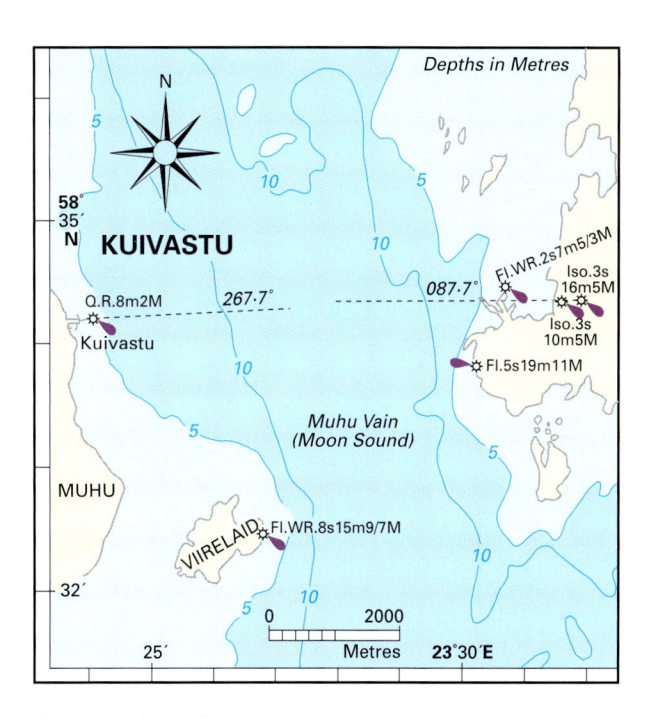

Approach and entry

58°34'·33N 23°23'·57E centre of harbour entrance
Approach on leading line used by ferries 267·7° (front beacon Q.W.11m6M, rear Iso.W.3s17m6M) towards ferry quay to enter dredged entrance channel south of ferry quay between a pair of lateral buoys. Turn to starboard at final port hand buoy.

Berthing

Finger pontoons. Larger vessels lie alongside quays.

Services for yachts and general facilities

Water, electricity on quays. Toilets, showers, sauna, washing machine in harbour building. Fuel berth, pump out facility (sewage and bilge water). Small shop and restaurant. WiFi.

Communications and travel

Buses to Saaremaa and Estonian mainland (for Tallinn). Car hire via HM office.

Virtsu

Virtsu lies on the opposite (mainland) side of the Sound but is now for local craft only and has been omitted from this edition.

Kuivastu Harbour looking east F. and G. Cattell

THE BALTIC SEA AND APPROACHES

10. ESTONIA

Sõru Harbour entrance F. and G. Cattell

Sõru (Hiiumaa)

58°41'·45N 22°31'·33E centre of harbour entrance
Estonian charts see diagram, Appendix p.431-2
Charts of Estonia Vol. 2 & 3 (small craft folio)
Approach waypoint 58°41'·30N 22°31'·30E in dredged channel
An SL Marinas harbour

Note It is important to follow the channels marked on the chart as the area is very shallow.

Harbour used by ferries from Triigi (Saaremaa) with limited facilities and good shelter for yachts in inner harbour. Limited facilities ashore but useful as an arrival or departure point for Sweden.

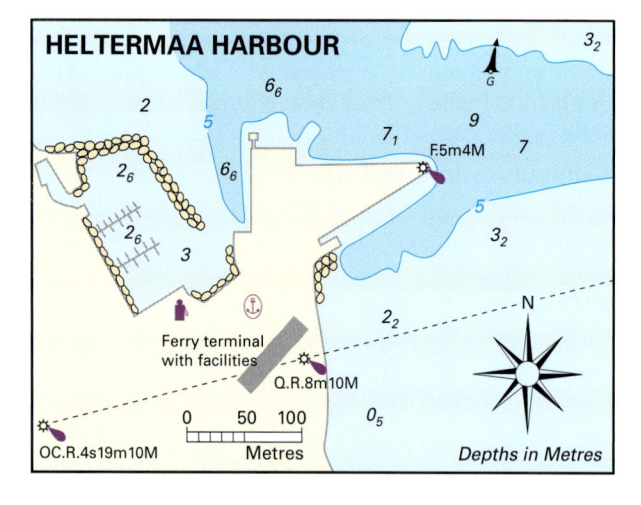

Heltermaa (Hiiumaa)

58°51'·99N 23°02'·69E yacht moorings
An SL Marinas Harbour

Distances
Roomassaare 72M, Kardla 24M, Haapsalu 17M

Charts
UKHO 2817
Estonian charts see diagram, Appendix p.432-1 plus
Charts of Estonia Vol. 2 & 3 (small craft folio)

Lights
Heltermaa Ldg Lts 254.7° *Front* 58°51'·93N 23°02'·86E
Q.R.8m10M R251·8°-257·8° White diamond with black stripe on metal framework 12m
Rear 315m from front, Oc.R.4s19m10M 251·8°-257·8° White diamond with black stripe on metal framework 18m
Heltermaa Pier Lt beacon 58°52'·02N 23°02'·97E
F.W.5m4M grey metal column 3m

Harbour communications
Heltermaa Harbour ☎ +372 523 7633
VHF Ch 16 call *Heltermaa harbour*

General
Heltermaa is the harbour for ferries between the Estonian mainland at Rohukula and Hiiumaa and has a purpose-built yacht harbour close to the ferry terminal. There is no town.

Approach and entry
58°51'·99N 23°02'·78E centre of harbour entrance

Approach on leading line 254.8° and turn to starboard before reaching the ferry quay. Yacht harbour is west of the ferry quay.

Berthing
Finger pontoons.

Services for yachts and general facilities
Water, electricity on pontoons. Toilets, showers, sauna in passenger terminal building. Fuel pump. Small shop and café/bar.

Communications and travel
WiFi. Buses around the island. Ferry to mainland thence bus to Tallinn etc. Domestic airport at Kärdla.

Heltermaa Harbour from Ferry Dock F. and G. Cattell

406 THE BALTIC SEA AND APPROACHES

KÄRDLA

Kärdla (Hiiumaa)

59°00'·56N 22°45'·19E yacht moorings

Distances
Roomassaare 89M, Heltermaa 24M, Haapsalu 30M

Charts
UKHO 2241, 2817
Estonian charts see diagram, Appendix p.431-2 plus
Charts of Estonia Vol.2 & 3 (small craft folio)

Lights
Kõpu lighthouse 58°54'·96N 22°11'·98E Fl(2)10s102m26M
  White square stone tower, balcony, red lantern 36m
Takhuna lighthouse 59°05'·48N 22°35'·17E
  LFl(2)15s43m12M 95·0°-W-253·5° White conical metal tower, balcony, lantern 43m
Kärdla Ldg Lts 162·2° *Front* 59°00'·62N 22°45'·26E
  Fl.WG.2s5/2M 160·2°-W-164·2°-G-160·2°
  White rectangle with green stripe on green metal cylinder 5m
  Rear 556m from front Fl.2s5M 160·2°-W-164·2°
  White rectangle with green stripe on grey metal framework 17m
East mole Lt beacon Fl(2)R.4s2M 204·2°-R-142·2°
  Red metal cylinder 2·7m
North mole beacon is Kärdla Front Ldg Lt 162·2°

Harbour communications
Kardle Marina ☎ +372 5328 5218
  VHF Ch 16 call *Kärdla Marina*

General

Kärdla is the capital of Hiiumaa and the main small town on the island. Purpose-built yacht harbour on site of former small fishing/commercial harbour.

Approach and entry

From Waypoint 1 (59°03'.70N 22°43'.35E) steer to Waypoint 2 (59°00'.73N 22°45'.19E) then to Waypoint 3 (59°00'.63N 22°45'.30E).
59°00'·61N 22°45'·27E centre of harbour entrance

Approach on Kärdla leading line 162·2°. Enter around N mole.

It is dangerous to enter or leave the harbour in strong north to easterly winds

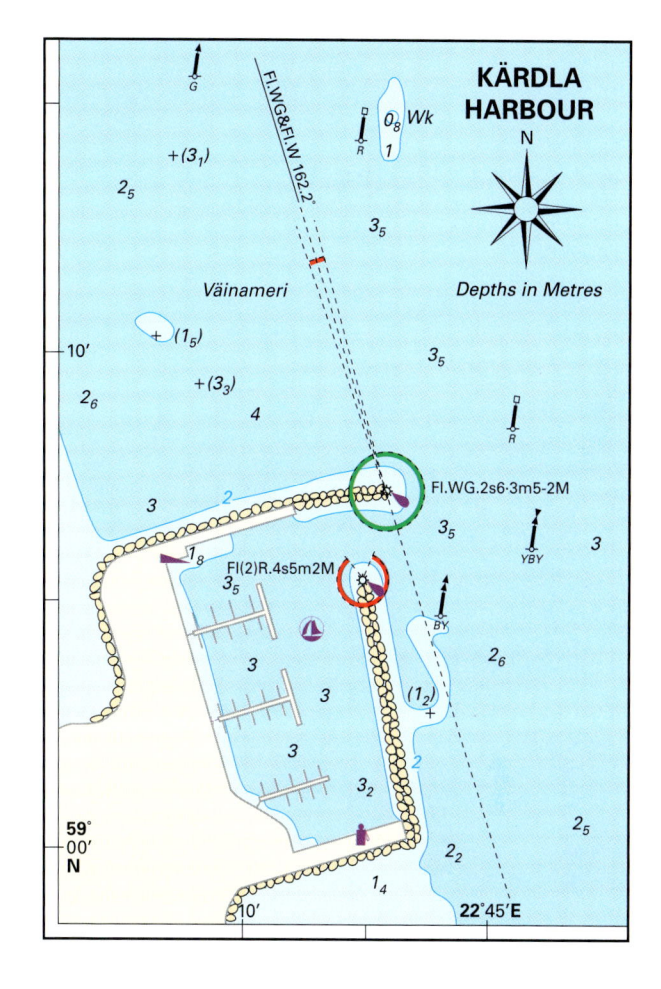

Coastal boulder at Kärdla with heights of the sea in the great storms of 1893 and 1967
F. and G. Cattell

Kärdla Harbour wooden carvings *F. and G. Cattell*

Kärdla Harbour *F. and G. Cattell*

THE BALTIC SEA AND APPROACHES 407

10. ESTONIA

10. ESTONIA

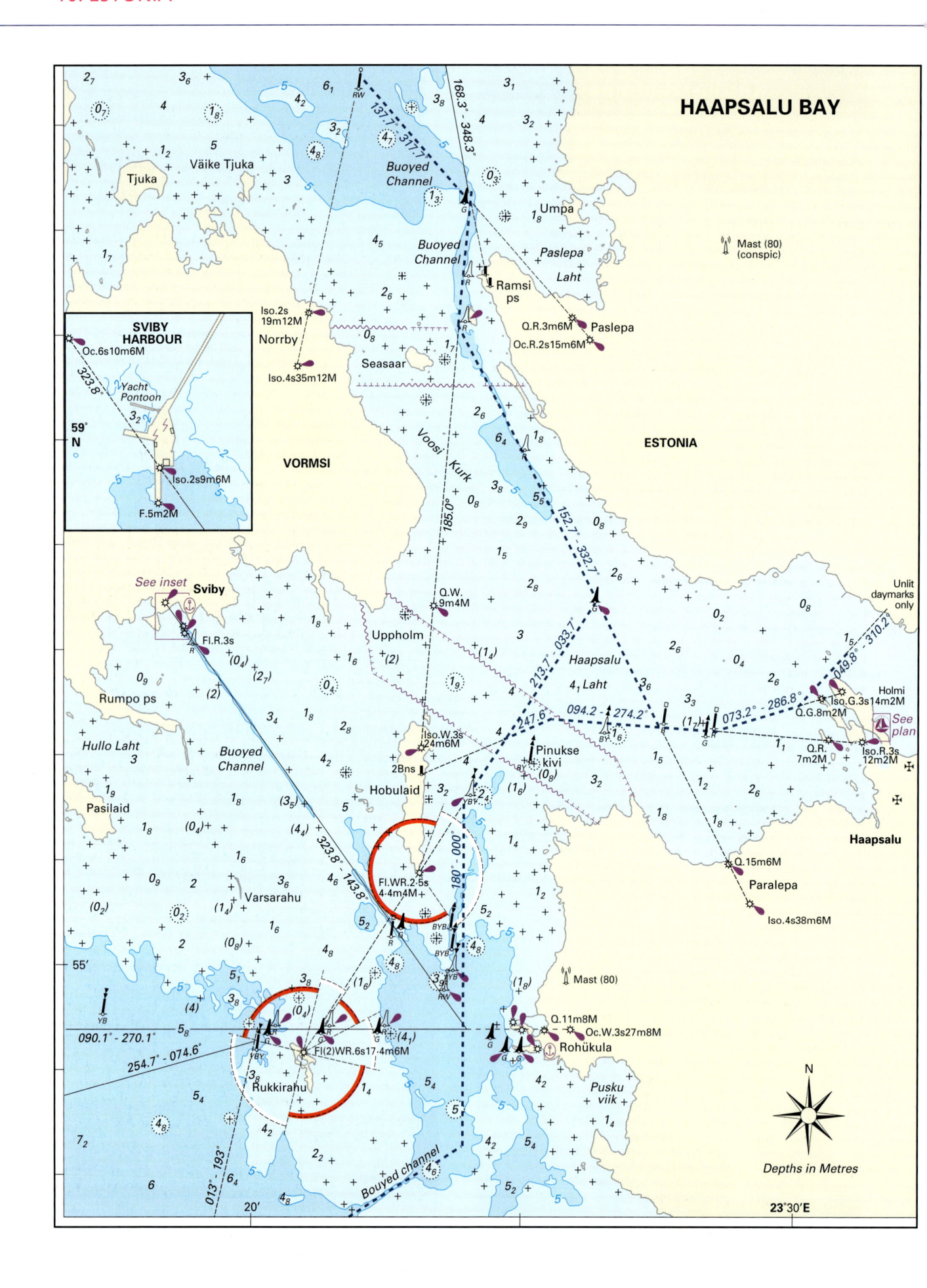

HAAPSALU BAY

HAAPSALU

Berthing
Finger pontoons. Good shelter but avoid first line of pontoon berths in strong north to easterly winds.

Services for yachts and general facilities
Water, electricity on pontoons. Toilets, showers, sauna, washing machine in harbour building. Fuel berth, pump out facility. Small shop and restaurant. Small chandlers and repairs. Winter storage. Banks, shops in Kärdla about 1km distant.

Communications and travel
WiFi. Buses around island. Bus to Selver supermarket in season. Ferry to mainland from Heltermaa. Domestic airport.

Lehtma
This harbour has been omitted from the current edition. With the opening of the relatively close Kärdla harbour, Lehtma is no longer used by yachts.

Sviby (Vormsi)
58°58'·20N 23°18'·70E
UKHO chart 2241
Estonian charts see diagram, Appendix p.431-2, *Charts of Estonia Vol. 2*
Sailor infopage for Haapsalu Bay. Recommended routes for recreational craft on Haapsalu Bay.
An SL Marinas harbour.

Harbour for ferries from Rohuküla on the mainland. Two pontoons for yachts on north west side of the jetty. Limited facilities. The island is interesting as there are many remains from the time when it was inhabited by Swedes.

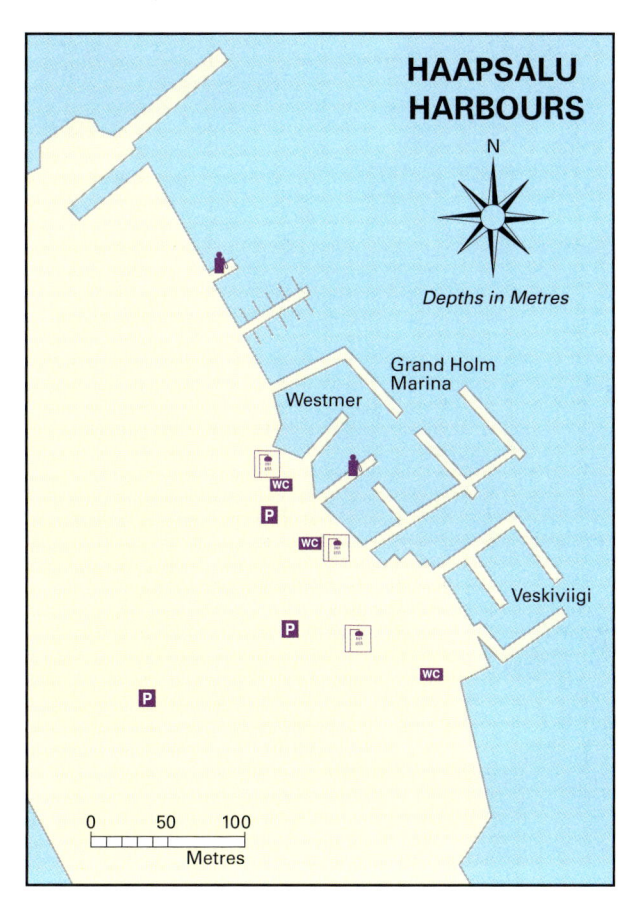

HAAPSALU HARBOURS
N
Depths in Metres
Grand Holm Marina
Westmer
Veskiviigi
0 50 100 Metres

Haapsalu
58°57'·50N 23°31'·61E yacht harbours

Distances
Kuivastu 30M, Kardla 30M, Hanko 55M, Lohusalu 45M, Tallinn 65M

Charts
UKHO 2241, 2817
Estonian see diagram on p.431-2 plus *Charts of Estonia Vol. 2 & 3* (small craft folio)
Sailor infopage for Haapsalu Bay. Recommended routes for recreational craft on Haapsalu Bay.

Lights
Paralepa Ldg Lts 152·7° *Front* 58°56'·04N 23°28'·97E
  Q.15·5m6M White round concrete tower with balcony and lantern 16m
  Rear 800m from front, Iso.4s38m6M Round white tower, black bands on upper part. Balcony, black lantern 34m
Kajakarahu Ldg Lts 094·2° *Front* 58°57'·19N 23°30'·83E
  Q.R.7m2M Orange triangle, yellow stripe, on metal column 8m
  Rear 600m from front Iso.R.3s12m2M Orange triangle, yellow stripe, on metal framework yellow disk on top 13m
Holmi Ldg Lts 073·2° *Front* 58°57'·59N 23°30'·67E
  Q.G.8m2M White rectangle, black stripe on metal framework 7m
  Rear 390m from front Iso.G.3s14m2M White rectangle, black stripe on metal framework 12m
Tahu (now unlit) Daymarks only in Line 049·8° *Front* 58°58'·40N 23°32'·14E White rectangle, black stripe on metal framework 6m
  Rear 233m from front White rectangle, black stripe on concrete post 9m
Note All three pairs of lights visible on leading lines only

Harbour communication
VHF Ch 12 *Grand Holm* ℡ +372 565 2887
Haapsalu Yacht Club ℡ +372 524 7533 VHF Ch 10
Westmer ℡ +372 530 39129 VHF Ch 16 *Westmer*

General
Haapsalu lies on a small peninsula, on which also stand the ruins of an old castle with a high tower. It is a pleasant old town of about 15,000 inhabitants with medieval roots. At the end of the 19th century it was a popular resort for the wealthy of St Petersburg and their grand wooden villas dominate the scenery – it is still a health spa famous for mud baths. There are several museums, including the restored railway station which is now a museum and tourist office. There are three possibilities for berthing. Side by side along the waterfront are Westmer with excellent facilities (reflected in the price), next is Grand Holm Marina and, lastly, the yacht club Veskiviigi, all with good facilities. A dredged channel allows access to all three facilities but note that outside the channel the water is shallow.

Approach and entry
Approach waypoint in Haapsalu Laht (Bay) 58°57'·30N 23°27'·70E on leading line.

Whether coming from south or north it is essential to have detailed plans of the approach. Consult either *Charts of Estonia, Vol 2*; *Harbours of the Baltic*

10. ESTONIA

THE BALTIC SEA AND APPROACHES   409

10. ESTONIA

States or *Recommended Routes for Recreational Craft on Haapsalu Bay*, for the buoyage and leading lines. Provided the latter are followed closely a vessel with 2m draught can approach Haapsalu without problem. The final approach to the harbour has been dredged to 2·5m in 2016.

Berthing

At Westmer mooring is to finger pontoons. Grand Holm Marina has a mixture of stern buoys and finger pontoons. Veskiivgi yacht club has finger pontoons and stern buoys. The harbour has no shelter from the east or northeast and in strong wind conditions all berths can become very uncomfortable.

Depths either side of the channel and in the harbour surroundings are extremely shallow and anchoring should not be attempted.

Services for yachts

Water and electricity available on quay or pontoon. Showers, toilets and all facilities including restaurant at each harbour. Fuel berth in outer harbour.

Local gas cylinders are available in the town. For repair facilities, sailmaker etc, enquire with the harbourmaster where berthed.

General facilities

The harbour is located about 2·5km from the town. Take the bus from the end of the short lane leading from the yacht club gate. Haapsalu has all the usual facilities of a major town; banks, post office, shops, restaurants etc.

Communications and travel

WiFi at all harbours. Regular bus service to Tallinn and other Estonian towns, but no rail connection. Hire cars can be arranged either through the yacht club or the tourist office.

Haapsalu - typical leading mark
F. and G. Cattell

Haapsalu castle *F. and G. Cattell*

Haapsalu - showing Grand Holm and Westmer yacht moorings *F. and G. Cattell*

LOHUSALU

Dirhami

59°12'·58N 23°29'·97E yacht moorings
UKHO chart 2241
Estonian charts 302, 509, 614, *Charts of Estonia Vol. 2*

A commercial/fishing harbour with dedicated berthing facilities for yachts on pontoons or alongside the pier. Entry/exit dangerous in strong northwesterly winds but sheltered inside harbour. A useful point of arrival/departure for Finland. Toilets and showers available. Fuel berth. Small shop nearby. Internet at harbour office.

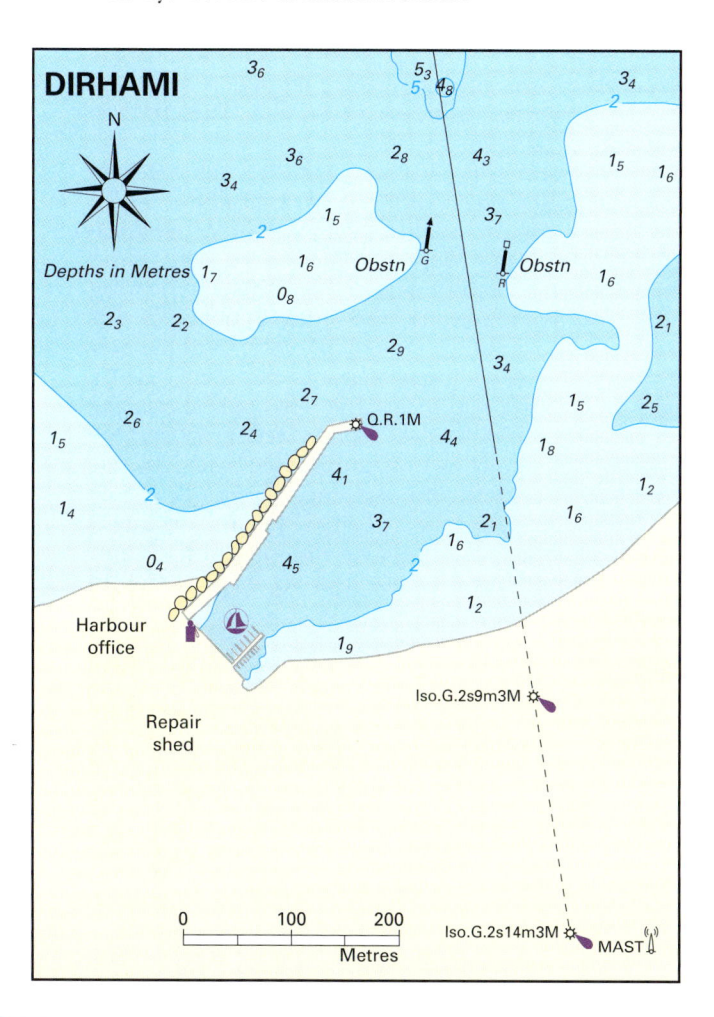

Paldiski Nord

Omitted from this edition as available only in emergency.

Lohusalu

59°24'·16N 24°12'·28E yacht moorings

Distances
Kardla 52M, Haapsalu 45M, Hanko 45M, Tallinn 25M

Charts
UKHO 2241, 2248
Estonian see diagram, Appendix p.431-2 plus *Charts of Estonia Vol. 1* (small craft folio)

Lights
Pakri Lighthouse 59°23'·24N 24°02'·26E LFl.W.15s73m12M 011° -vis-243° Red round brick tower with balcony 52m
Suurupi 59°27'·81N 24°22'·82E Oc(2)15s68m12M 056° – vis – 261·5° (vis 15M) 250·5°–W–242·5° (vis 12M) White round stone tower with balcony and black lantern 22m
Ldg Lts 233·3° *Front* 59°24'·15N 24°12'·39E Iso.R.2s5m6M White rectangle, red stripe on metal post 3·5m *Rear* 134m from front, Iso.R.4s8m6M White rectangle, red stripe on white metal post 5m

Harbour communications
Lohusalu Port Control ☎ +372 677 1640
VHF Ch 10, 16 call *Lohusalu marina*

General
A small, modern yacht harbour with very few spaces for visitors, surrounded by forest and superb beaches.

Approach and entry
The leading line on 233·3° is marked with two boards.

Berthing
Visitors may berth in the southern part of the harbour bows to the quay and stern to a buoy if space available. Anchoring outside the harbour is not advised, due to fishing nets and lack of shelter.

Dirhami Harbour viewed from near the pier head
F. and G. Cattell

The small harbour at Lohusalu *F. and G. Cattell*

10. ESTONIA

THE BALTIC SEA AND APPROACHES 411

10. ESTONIA

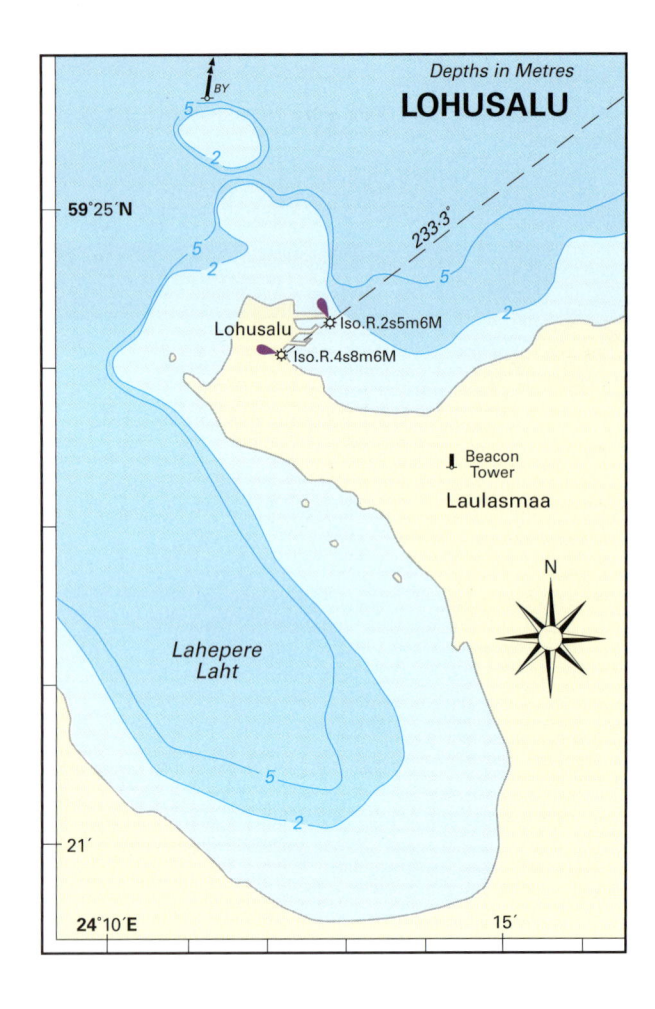

Services for yachts
Water, electricity, showers, toilets, sauna, laundry facilities, pump out facilities. The fuel berth at the head of harbour has only 1·5m depth. For other services seek advice at the harbour office.

General facilities
Restaurant at the yacht club, plus a small rural café. Shops in the town of Laulasmaa, about 5km distant.

Communications and travel
WiFi at harbour. Buses to Tallinn and elsewhere.

Naissaar
59°33'·43N 24°33'·22E yacht moorings

Estonian charts see diagram, Appendix p.431 plus *Charts of Estonia Vol.1* (small craft folio)

Sailor Infopage Recommended Routes for Recreational Craft on Tallinn Bay

An SL Marinas harbour.

Island lying north west of Tallinn Bay. Essential to use Estonian chart. Convenient stopover when sailing between Tallinn and Finland or worth a visit for its own interest. Formerly inhabited by people of Swedish descent. Later a source of aggregate and a store and workshop for mines during Soviet times. Finger berths or alongside. Few facilities. Harbour belongs to Saarte Liinid and is used for the ferry from Tallinn.

Tallinn

Distances
Haapsalu 65M, Lohusalu 25M, Hanko 60M, Helsinki 45M, Vergi 55M

Charts
UKHO 2241, 2248, 2227

Estonian charts see diagram, Appendix p.431-2 plus *Charts of Estonia Vol. 1* (small craft folio)

Sailor Infopage *Recommended Routes for Recreational Craft on Tallinn Bay*

Tallinn, the capital of Estonia, has about 408,000 inhabitants and is a busy commercial harbour and industrial centre. It was part of the Hanseatic league from the 13th century and has the oldest surviving Gothic town hall in northern Europe. The city was fought over and badly damaged by both the Russians and the Germans but the old town in particular has been skilfully and tastefully restored. There are three possibilities for berthing based on Tallinn (Old City Marina, Noblessner/Lennusadam and Pirita). Old City Marina is located beside the city and is, therefore, the most convenient for sightseeing, public transport etc. Noblessner/Lennusadam is a short distance to the northwest by bus or walking and located in a former submarine dock. Pirita is 6km east of the city, built for the yachting Olympics in 1980 and subsequently became Tallinn's main centre for yachting.

Tallinn has an international airport, frequent ferries to Stockholm and Helsinki, and rail and bus links throughout Estonia and to many cities in Europe via Eurolines.

Red roofs of Tallinn viewed from Toompea *F. and G. Cattell*

412 THE BALTIC SEA AND APPROACHES

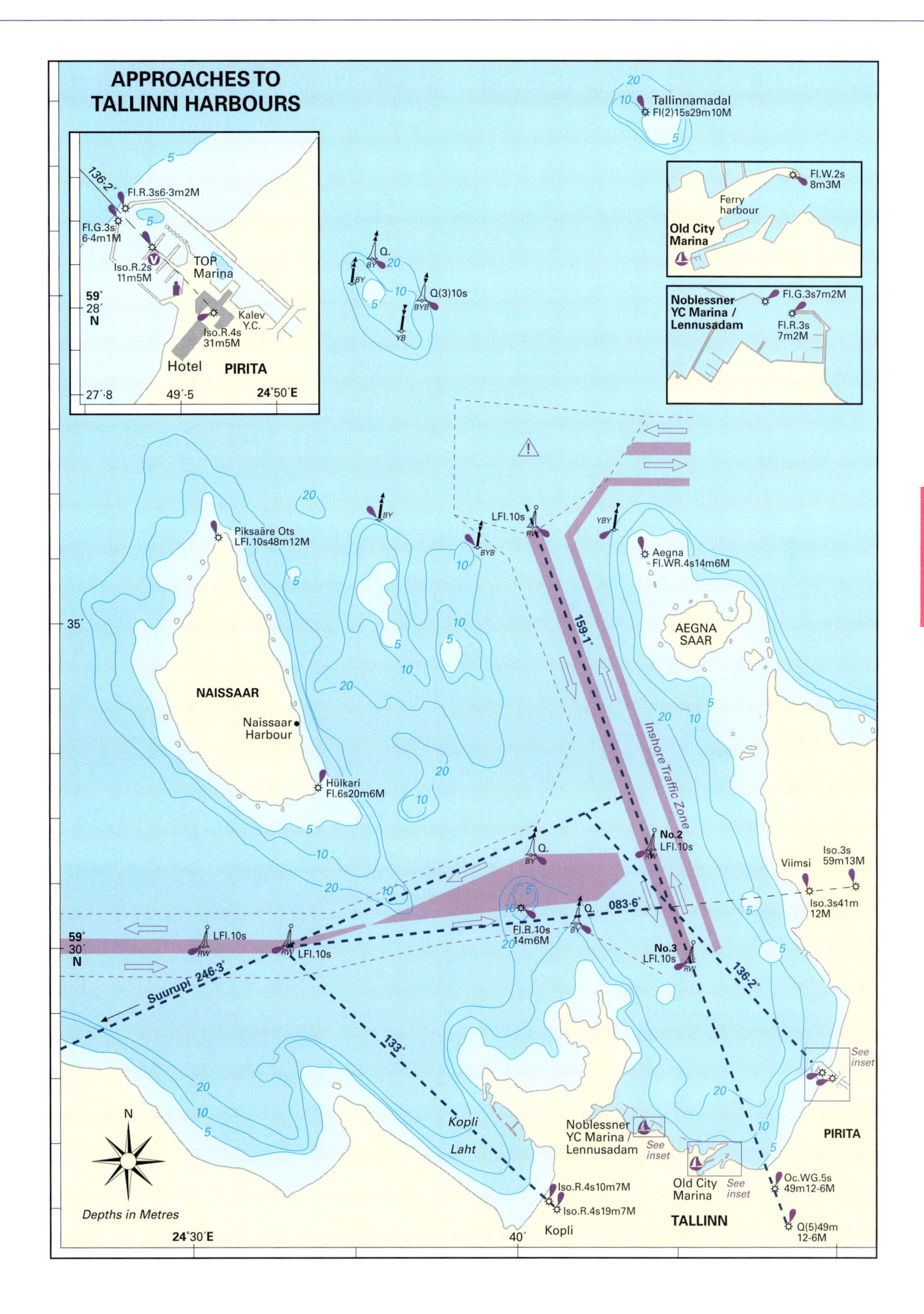

TALLINN

APPROACHES TO TALLINN HARBOURS

PIRITA (inset)
- 136.2°
- Fl.R.3s6·3m2M
- Fl.G.3s 6·4m1M
- Iso.R.2s 11m5M
- TOP Marina
- Kalev Y.C.
- Iso.R.4s 31m5M
- Hotel
- 59°28'N
- 27'·8 49'·5 24°50'E

Old City Marina (inset)
- Ferry harbour
- Fl.W.2s 8m3M

Noblessner YC Marina / Lennusadam (inset)
- Fl.G.3s7m2M
- Fl.R.3s 7m2M

Main Chart

- Tallinnamadal Fl(2)15s29m10M
- Q. BY
- Q(3)10s BYB
- BY
- LFl.10s RW
- BYB
- YBY
- Piksaäre Ots LFl.10s48m12M
- Aegna Fl.WR.4s14m6M
- AEGNA SAAR
- 159.1°
- Inshore Traffic Zone
- NAISSAAR
- Naissaar Harbour
- Hülkari Fl.6s20m6M
- No.2 LFl.10s RW
- Viimsi Iso.3s 59m13M
- Iso.3s41m 12M
- Q. BY
- Fl.R.10s 14m6M
- Q. BY
- 083·6°
- 59°30'N
- LFl.10s RW
- LFl.10s RW
- No.3 LFl.10s RW
- 136.2°
- Suurupi 246·3°
- 133°
- Kopli Laht
- See inset
- Noblessner YC Marina / Lennusadam — See inset
- Old City Marina — See inset
- PIRITA
- Iso.R.4s10m7M
- Iso.R.4s19m7M
- Kopli
- Oc.WG.5s 49m12-6M
- Q(5)49m 12-6M
- TALLINN

N

Depths in Metres

24°30'E   40'

10. ESTONIA

THE BALTIC SEA AND APPROACHES   413

10. ESTONIA

Tallinn Noblessner/Lennusadam

59°27'·21N 24°43'·88E yacht moorings

Lights
Naissaar Lighthouse 59°36'·22N 24°30'·64E
  LFl.W.10s48m12M 025° -vis-335° Octagonal white conical concrete tower, red top and balcony 45m
Aegna 59°36'·04N 24°43'·8E Fl.WR.4s14m6M 053·5° -R-101° -W-053·5° Yellow rectangle on red metal post 12m
Vahemadal 59°30'·61N 24°39'·97E Fl.R.10s14m6M Octagonal truncated pyramid with white upper and red lower part 13m
Tallinnamadal 59°42'·72N 24°43'·89E Fl(2)W.15s29m10M Racon Red round metal tower, yellow top, black base, with three galleries 31m
Noblessner/Lennusadam East mole Lt beacon 59°27'·31N 24°44'·22E Fl.R.3s7m2M Red metal column with balcony 5m
Noblessner/Lennusadam West mole Lt beacon 59°27'·34N 24°44'·12E Fl.G.3s7m2M Green metal column 3m

Communications
VHF Ch 9 and 16 call *Port Noblessner*
  Mobile +372 513 6726

Approach and entry
Located in Peetri harbour. Straightforward approach from Tallinn Bay.

Berthing
Finger pontoons – note that some are reserved for resident yachts. Caveat: although work has been carried out on the outer breakwater, washes from passing ferries still cause disturbance making the berths very uncomfortable at times.

Services for yachts
Water and electricity on pontoons. Toilets and showers in portacabins.

General facilities
Restaurant at harbour. Seaplane Harbour Maritime Museum is worth a visit. Other facilities as for Old City Marina.

Communications and travel
WiFi. Tallinn city centre can be reached by bus no. 3 from Noblessner and bus no.73 from Lennusadam. to Tallinn centre.

Noblessner YC Marina *F. and G. Cattell*

Tallinn Old City Marina

59°26'·54N 24°45'·50E yacht moorings

Lights
Naissaar Lighthouse 59°36'·22N 24°30'·64E
  LFl.W.10s48m12M 025° -vis-335° Octagonal white conical concrete tower, red top and balcony 45m
Aegna 59°36'·04N 24°43'·8E Fl.WR.4s14m6M 053·5° -R-101° -W-053·5° Yellow rectangle on red metal post 12m
Vahemadal 59°30'·61N 24°39'·97E Fl.R.10s14m6M Octagonal truncated pyramid with white upper and red lower part 13m
Tallinnamadal 59°42'·72N 24°43'·89E Fl(2)W.15s29m10M Racon Red round metal tower, yellow top, black base, with three galleries 31m
Tallinna Ldg Lts 159.1° *Front* 59°26'·24N 24°47'·91E Oc.WG.5s49m12/6M 154·5°-W-165·0° 143°-G-154.5° Red conical tower on a house 18m
  Rear 1·1km from front Q(5)W.5s80m12M 139·0°-W-154·5°-W-163·5°-W-187·5° White round stone tower, black top with balcony and lantern 40m
Vanasadam North mole Lt beacon 59°26'·95N 24°46'·54E Fl.W.2s8m3M Green metal construction 5m

Communications
Port Control *Radio 5* VHF Ch 14 (or *Mobile* +372 510 3360) before entry.

Approach and entry
Located in old Admiralty Basin. Straightforward approach from Tallinn Bay. Essential to call Port Control for permission to enter. Observe two sets of traffic lights controlling entry.

Berthing
Individual finger pontoons. Tends to get very full during the holiday season and at weekends, but the friendly staff make every effort to find a space.

Services for yachts
Water and electricity at all berths. Toilets beside security gate. Showers and sauna in yacht club. Washing machine, dryer, pump out facilities, fuel berth.

General facilities
All facilities – banks, post office, restaurants, tourist office and souvenirs available in Tallinn.

Yacht berths at Old City Marina *F. and G. Cattell*

414 THE BALTIC SEA AND APPROACHES

TALLINN

Entrance to Old City Marina with Tallinn Old Town in the background *F. and G. Cattell*

Communications and travel
WiFi. Local, national and international buses. Local trams. Airport for domestic and international flights.

Tallinn (Pirita)

59°28'·22N 24°49'·07E centre of harbour entrance

Lights
Naissaar Lighthouse 59°36'·22N 24°30'·64E
LFl.10s48m12M 025° -vis-335° Octagonal white conical concrete tower, red top and balcony 45m
Aegna 59°36'·04N 24°43'·8E Fl.WR.4s14m6M 053·5° -R-101° -W-053·5° Yellow rectangle on red metal post 12m
Vahemadal 59°30'·61N 24°39'·97E Fl.R.10s14m6M Octagonal truncated pyramid with white upper and red lower part 13m
Tallinnamadal 59°42'·72N 24°43'·89E Fl(2)W.15s29m10M Racon Red round metal tower, yellow top, black base, with three galleries 31m
Tallinna Ldg Lts 159.1° *Front* 59°26'·24N 24°47'·91E Oc.WG.5s49m12/6M 154·5°-W-165·0° 143°-G-154.5° Red conical tower on a house 18m
Rear 1·1km from front Q(5)W.5s80m12M 139·0°-W-154·5°-W-163·5°-W-187·5° White round stone tower, black top with balcony and lantern 40m
Pirita Ldg Lts 136·2° *Front* 59°28'·13N 24°49'·24E Iso.R.2s11m5M Orange round concrete tower, three white balconies 9m
Rear 400m from front Iso.R.4s31m5M White square concrete tower 28m
Pirita northeast breakwater 59°28'·23N 24°49'·10E Fl.R.3s7m2M Orange metal cylinder with balcony 5m
Pirita southwest breakwater 59°28'·20N 24°49'·05E Fl.G.3s7m1M Green metal column with balcony 5m

Communications
Pirita Port Control and Marina ✆ +372 639 8800
No VHF
Kalev Jahtklubi Marina ✆ +372 623 9158
VHF Ch 11 call Kalev Marina

Approach and entry
The approach is straightforward, with the television tower visible from many miles offshore and the gable end of the convent ruins coming into view on closer approach. The harbour entrance with its double breakwater is conspicuous and there are no offlying hazards.

Berthing
Yachts may berth at either TOP Marina or further in at the Kalev Yacht Club. For the TOP visitors' area, on entering harbour turn to starboard and berth in the area bounded by the first two quays. Berthing at Kalev Yacht Club is limited but if space is available, access is by turning to port on entering the harbour and proceeding towards the road bridge. Kalev Yacht Club is on the starboard side before the bridge.

Services for yachts
Water and electricity at all berths and plenty of rubbish skips, with toilets and showers at both TOP Marina and Kalev Yacht Club.

Fuel is available from the fuel berth close to the museum ships at the head of the western basin, where local gas bottles can also be exchanged and the pump out station is situated.

There is a boatyard beside the marina and the Kalev Yacht Club has skilled shipwrights and well-equipped workshops where repairs can be carried out, as well as a small sail-loft. There is a chandlery within the complex.

Weather forecasts are displayed at the harbour office.

General facilities
Good restaurant at the Club plus a snack bar next to the small general shop. Other facilities, including an ATM and small post office, in the foyer of the Pirita TOP Spa Hotel.

The large Selver supermarket (on the opposite side of the main road a few hundred metres southwest), stocks most items, and there are other shops and kiosks in the vicinity. All facilities – banks, post office, restaurants, tourist office and souvenirs – are available in Tallinn itself.

There is a good beach beyond the river east of the harbour, with the impressive and well preserved ruins of St Birgitta's convent just inland.

THE BALTIC SEA AND APPROACHES

10. ESTONIA

10. ESTONIA

Pirita visitors' berths
F. and G. Cattell

Communications and travel

WiFi is available in the area of the harbour but does not extend to the visitors' area. Internet access is available at the harbour office and the hotel.

Local buses run along the main road behind the harbour. It is necessary to purchase tickets in the local kiosk before boarding.

Prangli (Kelnase harbour)

59°38'·23N 25°00'·75E yacht moorings
Estonian charts see diagram, Appendix p.431-2
    plus *Charts of Estonia Vol. 1* (small craft folio)

Small island off Muuga Bay, northeast of Tallinn, with approximately 100 inhabitants. Harbour used by passenger ferry to Leppneeme. There are dangerous rocks in the approach – essential to use good scale Estonian Chart. Approach and entry should be made only in daylight and calm conditions. Alongside berthing, few facilities.

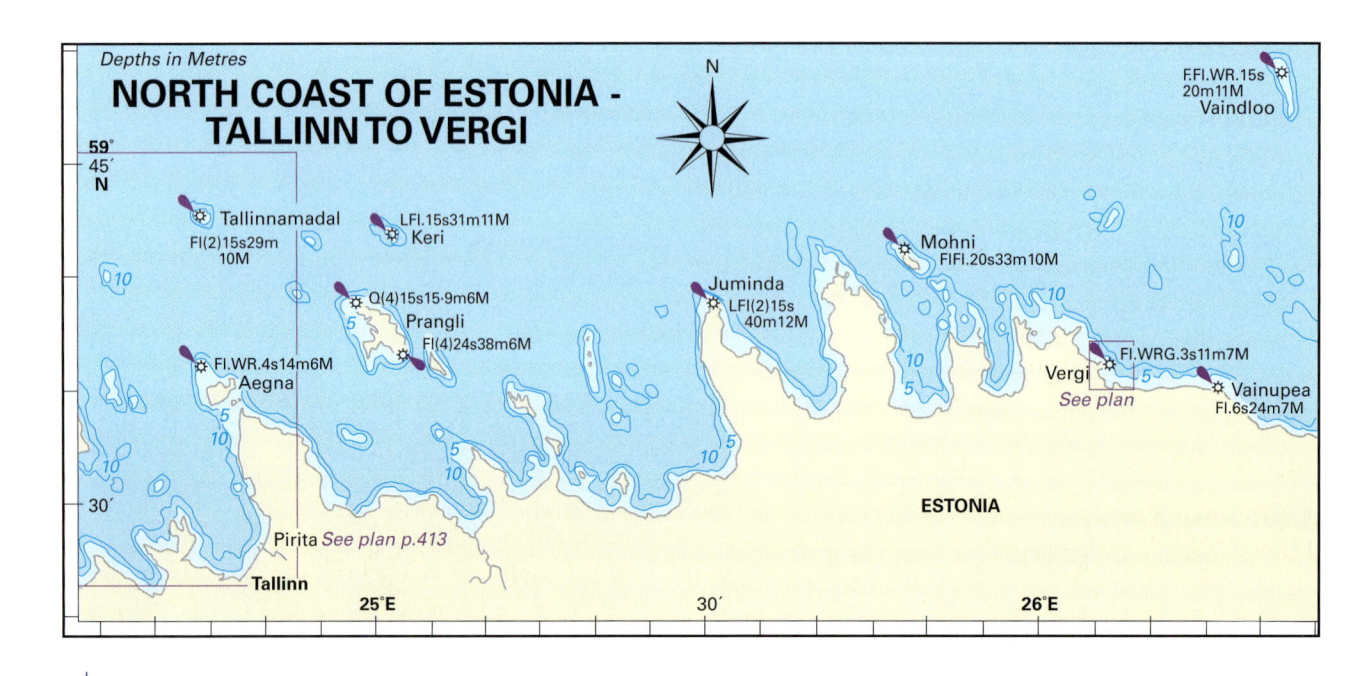

416 THE BALTIC SEA AND APPROACHES

VERGI

Vergi

59°35'·99N 26°06'·03E

Distances
Tallinn 55M, Helsinki 50M, Kotka 60M,
  St Petersburg 145M

Charts
UKHO 2248
Estonian charts see diagram, Appendix p.431-2
plus *Charts of Estonia Vol. 1* (small craft folio)

Lights
Vergi light beacon 59°36'·09N 26°06'·05E
  Fl.WRG.3s11m7M 120°-G-167°-W-267°-R-356° White
  round concrete tower with balcony 10m
Ldg Line 261·8° Daymarks only

Harbour communications
Vergi Port Control VHF Ch 10, 16 call Vergi 32
  Mobile +372 55 567 349.

General
A small former fishing harbour. Due to the Russian requirement that yachts follow the shipping lane into St Petersburg, Vergi has effectively replaced Narva–Jõesuu as the port of departure and return for yachts travelling between Estonia and St Petersburg.

Approach and entry
Approach from east-northeast on 261·8°, curving somewhat south before reaching the breakwater end to avoid a shoal patch. Do not attempt to close the harbour in darkness.

Berthing
Yachts berth at finger pontoons or occasionally alongside. Anchoring is not an option due to rocks and shallows.

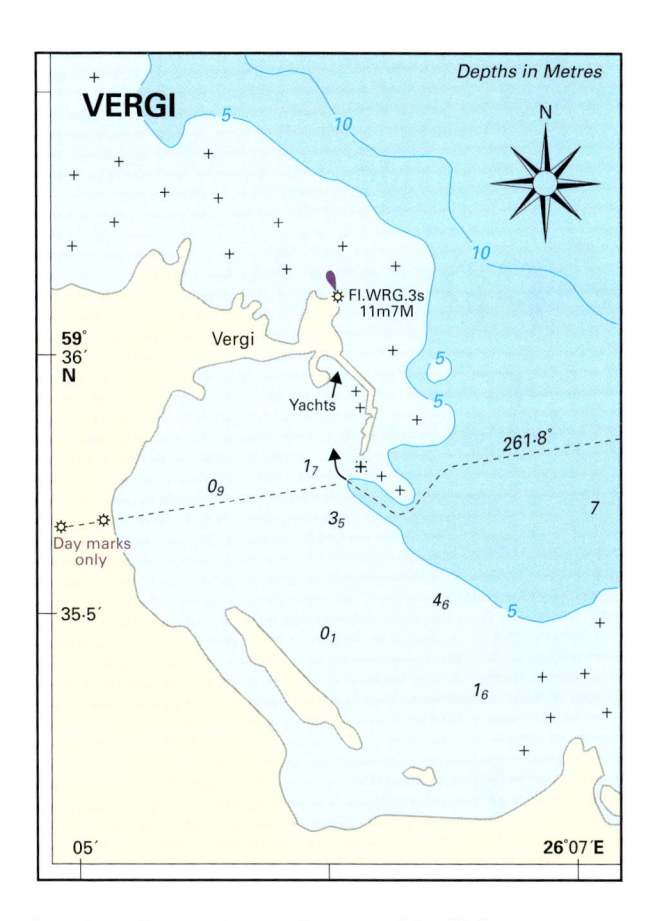

Services for yachts and general facilities
Water and electricity on the pontoon, toilets and showers in the harbour building where there is also a small restaurant. Fuel pump on the quay. Seek the advice of the harbourmaster if repair or other services are necessary.

Communications and travel
Buses to Tallinn and elsewhere in Estonia. WiFi at harbour.

Vergi harbour *F. and G. Cattell*

THE BALTIC SEA AND APPROACHES

10. ESTONIA

Appendix

I. Suppliers of charts and publications

British Admiralty charts are excellent for passage-making, but as a major part of the attraction of the Baltic is exploring the coastal islands and navigating through inshore channels, detailed local charts or chart packs/books are necessary, as listed in the text.

Many yachtsmen prefer to leave home already equipped with all the charts and other publications which they expect to need, either by ordering through one of the British suppliers listed below or arranging for charts to be shipped from a supplier in the country of origin. Others prefer to buy their charts on reaching the area, possibly from Nautischer Dienst (Kapitän Stegmann) in Kiel or Nautic Center in Göteborg.

Most of the charts and publications listed in the introductory section of each country are available through Imray (below) whose staff are able to advise on availability and and local agents.

UNITED KINGDOM

Imray Laurie Norie & Wilson Ltd
Wych House, St Ives,
Cambridgeshire PE27 5BT
☏ +44 (0)1480 462114
ilnw@imray.com
www.imray.com

ChartCo Ltd (Bookharbour)
Digital House
Kemps Quay
Quayside Road
Southampton
SO18 1AD
☏ +44 (0)2380 714300
www.bookharbour.com

United Kingdom Hydrographic Office
www.ukho.gov.uk – homepage of the United Kingdom Hydrographic Office, including free, downloadable weekly Notices to Mariners and the entire Admiralty Chart Catalogue. Orders for UKHO charts and publications must be placed with official agents.

GERMANY

Nautischer Dienst
Kapitän Stegmann, Makler Strasse 8
Postfach 80, D–24159 Kiel
☏ +49 (0)431 331772/332353
naudi@t-online.de

HanseNautic
Herrengraben 31, D 20459 Hamburg
☏ +49(0)40 374842-0
www.hansenautic.de

German Hydrographic Office
www.bsh.de/ includes a complete listing of German charts and official publications. English translation.

NV-Verlag
Carlshöhe 75, Eckernförde 24340, Germany
☏ +49 (0)4351 860 990
www.nautische-veroeffentlichung.de

Delius Klasing
Siekerwall 21, D-33602 Bielefeld
☏ +49 (0)521 - 55 90
www.delius-klasing.de

DENMARK

Iver Weilbach & Co A/S
Toldbodgade 35,
DK 1253 København K
☏ +45 33 34 35 60
sales@weilbach.dk
www.weilbach.dk

Danish Geodata Agency
www.gst.dk - Geodatastyrelsen – homepage of the national mapping and charting agency. Includes pilotage corrections to Danish charts and the entire map and chart catalogue.

SWEDEN

www.sjofartsverket.se – homepage of the Swedish Maritime Administration, which is responsible for the country's hydrographic service

Nautiska Magasinet AB
Shop address: Slussplan 5, Gamla Stan,
Box 15410, 104 65 Stockholm
☏ +46 (0)8 677 0000
nautiska@nautiska.com
www.nautiska.com

Nautic Center
Klangfärgsgatan 16
SE-426 52 Västra Frölunda
☏ +46 (0)31 100885
office@nautic-center.se
www.nautic-center.se

Svenska Kryssarklubben
Augustendalsvägen 54, S–13127 Nacka Strand,
Box 1189, Stockholm
☏ +46 (0)8 448 2880
info@sxk.se
www.sxk.se
(The Svenska Kryssarklubben (SKK) – Swedish Cruising Club – sells a wide range of Swedish charts, guides and other yachting publications)

FINLAND

www.fma.fi – homepage of the Finnish Maritime Administration.

Nautical charts are published by the Hydrography and Waterways Department of the Finnish Maritime Administration. John Nurminen Marine Oy are exclusive agents for the sale and nautical charts. Other publications can be purchased direct from the Hydrography.

Finnish Transport Agency
Hydrography, P.O. BOX 185
FIN-00101 Helsinki
☏ +358 (0)20 637 373
Email karttamyynti@liikennevirasto.fi

John Nurminen Marine Oy
Veneentekijänte 8, FI – 00210 Helsinki
Finland
☏ +358 9 682 3180
www.johnnurminenmarine.com
(Also stocks Russian, Latvian and Estonian charts, amongst others)

RUSSIA

Morintech Ltd
6 Prospekt Kima,
199155 Saint Petersburg
☏ +7 812 3254048
☏ +7 812 3238528
support@morintech.ru
www.dkart.com/ & www.morintech.spb.su

POLAND

Polskie Biuro Hydrograficzne Marynarki Wojennej w Gdyni
ul. Jana z Kolna 4–6
81 – 912 Gdynia
☏ +48 (0)58 620 7472/626 6208
(Polish charts can be ordered direct from the Polish Hydrographic Office, which currently has no website)

SMART Sp. z o.o.
Al Zjednoczenia 7, 81 – 345 Gdynia
skr. poczt. 224
☏ +48 (0)58 661 1751/661 1752/620 4567
digital@smart.gda.pl
www.smart.gda.pl

LITHUANIA
Lithuanian sheet charts can be obtained from

The Lithuanian Maritime Safety Administration
J. Janonio St. 24, 92251 Klaipėda, Lithuania. www.msa.lt.

Chart of Curonian Lagoon available from:

The Jana Seta Map Shop
85a Elizabetes iela. Rīga LV-1050, Latvia
☏ +371 6724 0894, veikals@kartes.lv, www.mapshop.lv.

LATVIA

Maritime Administration of Latvia
Responsible for hydrography. Website features the current chart catalogue www.jurasadministracija.lv

The Jana Seta Map Shop
The largest chart supplier in the country and will despatch orders abroad. Most major credit cards are accepted.
85a Elizabetes iela. Rīga LV-1050, Latvia
☏ +371 6724 0894, veikals@kartes.lv www.mapshop.lv. is

ESTONIA

Gotta Port Services and GT Baltic Charts
Lootsi 11, 10151 Tallinn, Estonia
☏ +372 646 0650
chart@gotta.ee
www.gotta.ee

II. Abbreviations used on Russian charts

IALA System A	МАМС
List of Lights	список маяков
Light	свет/огонь

Structures

Lighthouse	маяк (Мк)
Light vessel	пл. Мк
Radiobeacon (RC)	РМк
Beacon	зн
Column	колонна
Framework tower	ажурная установка ферма
House	дом
Building	здание, домик
Hut	будка
Mast	мачта
Post	столб
Tower	башня (бня)
Concrete	бетон(ный)
Iron	желез(ный)
Metal	металл(ический)
Stone	камен(ный)
Wooden	дерев(янный)
Band	горизонтальная полоса
Stripe	вертикальная полоса
Destroyed	разруш(енный)
Occasional	случ(айный)

Lights

Temporary	времен(ный)
Extinguished	погаш(енный)
F	П
Oc	Зтм
Iso	Изо
Fl	Пр
Q	Ч. Пр
IQ	прер. Ч. Пр
Al	пер
Oc(…)	Гр. Зтм
Fl(…)	Гр. Пр
F.Fl	П. Пр
FlFl(…)	П. Гр. Пр
LFl	Дл. Пр
Sec	С
Leading light	Ств.

Examples

Fl.7s8M	Пр 7С 8М
Iso.7M	Изо 7М
Fl(3)WR.15s12/10M	Пр(3)15С12/10М
Q.5M	Ч. Пр5М
Leading light, Q	Ств Ч. Пр
Leading light, Iso	Ств Изо

APPENDIX

Supplementary information

Whistle	(Рев)
Horn	(Н)
Gong	(гонг)
Bell	(К)
Explosive	(В)
Cannon	(П)
Reed	(Г)
Siren	(С)

Colours

Black	чр.
Violet	фл.
Blue	сн.
Green	зл.
Orange	ор.
Red	кр.
White	бл.
Yellow	жл.
Brown	кч.
Grey	ср.
Pale blue	гл.

Or abbreviated as in:

Black/red/black	ч к ч
Black/yellow/black	ч ж ч
Yellow/black/yellow	ж ч ж
Red/white	к б

Bottom

Bottom	грунт
Broken, cracked	б
Pebbles, shingle	гк
Clay	гл
Gravel, sand with small stones	гр
Mud, silt, sludge	И
Clay, mud, silt	гл. И
Lime	Изв
Stone	К
Small stones	мК
Large stone, boulders	кК
Shallow	м
Soft	мг
Coarse	к
Hard, firm	т
Sand	П
Fine sand	мП
Coarse sand	кП
Plate, slab	Пл
Shells	Р
Cliff, rock face	С
Medium, average	с
Weed	вд
Firm, fine sand and mud	тмПИ
Magnetic variation	Магн. скл
(former) spoil dumping ground	(бывшая) свалка грунта

III. Firing practice areas

Military firing takes place in the waters adjoining Denmark, Sweden, Finland, Poland and Russia:

Denmark

A Danish list of Firing Practice Areas is issued by Danish Maritime Authority, Carl Jacobsens Vej 31, DK 2500 Valby.
☏ +45 (0) 91 37 60 00
sfs@dma.dk, www.soefartsstyrelsen.dk.

Sweden

Firing practice takes place in seven areas around the Swedish coast, as well as on Lake Vättern. Information is available from:

Ringenäs (56°40'·8N 12°41'·1E) ☏ +46 (0) 3169 2600
Kabusa (55°25'N 14°00'E) ☏ +46 (0) 411 522 180/550 652, VHF Ch 16 (call *Kabusa skjufält*)
Ravlunda (55°46'N 14°20'E) ☏ +46 (0) 4147 4180, VHF Ch 16 (call *Ravlunda skjutfält*)
Landsort/Utlängan (58°45'N 19°10'E – 58°15'N 18°10'E, the area joining Landsort, Utö and Huvudskär), ☏ +46 (0) 850 261 823
Utlängan/Falsterborev ☏ +46 (0) 45 586 880
Utö southeastward (58°57'N 18°15'·8E), ☏ +46 (0) 850 157 045 (24 hour recorded information), VHF Ch 16 (call *Utö skjufält*)
Tåme (64°59'N 21°21'E) ☏ +46 (0) 912 43036; VHF Ch 16 (call *Tåme skjufält*)
Junkön (65°26'N 22°21'E), ☏ +46 (0) 920 258 013.

Finland

Finland has only one firing practice area, in the vicinity of 60°06'N 24°55'E. Information is available from the Katajaluoto Safety Office, ☏ +46 (0) 9 1814 5173, *Mobile* 040 503 5570 (no VHF contact).

Poland

There are six areas in regular use and a further eight used occasionally (see pages 291, 292 and 308).

Firing times are announced on NAVTEX and VHF Ch 16 followed by Chs 24, 25 or 26.

Phone the Polish Navy ☏ +48 91 324 2080 or for the northwest coast Radio Słupsk ☏ +48 59 814 4889 for full details.

Radio Słupsk also broadcasts details on VHF Ch 16 followed by Chs 71 at 0715, 1245 and 1845.

The Baltic States and Kaliningrad

While there are no firing practice areas along the coasts of the Baltic States Regulated Area 117 off Kaliningrad should be noted. See page 318 and the plan on page 315.

Russia

There are seven Prohibited Areas (PA) or Firing Practice Areas (FPA) in Russian waters approaching St Petersburg. Further details are given on page 275 and plans on pages 274 and 282 as well as current charts.

THE BALTIC SEA AND APPROACHES

IV. Search and rescue

Germany
National SAR Agency German Sea Rescue Service
Communicate via MRCC Bremen, VHF DSC MMSI 002111240
☏ +49 (0)421 53 6870 (124 124 for Mobiles within German network coverage).

Denmark
National SAR Agency Ministry of Defence
Communicate via the three centres controlled by Århus
☏ +45 (0)89 433203, or coast radio stations controlled by Lyngby Radio, VHF DSC MMSI 002191000
☏ +45 (0)45 6663 4800

Sweden
National SAR Agency Swedish Maritime Administration
Communicate via MRCC Göteborg, VHF DSC MMSI 002653000
☏ +46 (0)31 699080
(emergency) ☏ +46 (0)31 699050
(ship) mrccgbg@amrcc.sjofartsverket.se
Inmarsat–C (581) 426 590 010; or
Stockholm SJD, VHF DSC MMSI 002652000,
☏ +46 (0)8 601 7906
maritime@stockholmradio.se

Finland
National SAR Agency Finnish Frontier Guard Headquarters, SAR Branch. The National Alarm number ☏ +358 (0) 204 1000 always connects to the nearest MRCC or MRSC.
Communicate via:
MRSC Vaasa, VHF DSC MMSI 002303000,
☏ +358 (0)204 1003 (emergency)
☏ +358 (0)718 720300
mrsc.vaasa@raja.fi
MRCC Turku, VHF DSC MMSI 002301000
☏ +358 (0)204 1000 (emergency)
☏ +358 (0)204 107070, mrcc@smmv.rvl.fi,
Inmarsat–C (581) 423 002 211
MRSC Helsinki (Gulf of Finland CG District), VHF DSC MMSI 002302000
☏ +358 (0)204 1002 (emergency)
☏ +358 (0)718 720200
mrsc.helsinki@slmv.rvl.fi.

Russia (Gulf of Finland)
National SAR Agency MRCC Moskva
Communicate via MRCC Saint Petersburg, VHF DSC MMSI 002733700
☏ +7 (0)812 327 4146/718 8995
Telex 121512RCC.RU
mrcc@mail.pasp.ru
Inmarsat–C (581) 492 509 012, Inmarsat Mini–M 761 319 893.

Poland
National SAR Agency Polish Ship Salvage Company
Communicate via:
MRCC Gdynia, VHF DSC
☏ +48 (0)58 6205 551/6216 811/6610 196;
polratok.1@sar.gov.pl
MRSC Świnoujście, ☏ +48 (0)91 3215 929/
☏ +48 (0)91 3214 917
polratok.2@sar.gov.pl
Witowo (SPS), VHF DSC MMSI 002610210,
☏ +48 (0)59 8109 425
radio.witowo@emitel.pl

Russia (Kaliningrad)
National SAR Agency MRCC Moscva
Communicate via MRCC Kaliningrad, DSC MMSI 002734417
☏ +7 (0)4012 538470
mrsc@mapkld.ru
Inmarsat Mini–M 762 830 387.

Lithuania
National SAR Agency MRCC Klaipėda
Communicate via MRCC Klaipėda, DSC MMSI 002770330
☏ +370 46 491015/019 (maritime medical centre)
☏ +370 391257/258.

Latvia
National SAR Agency Sea Search and Rescue Service, Maritime Administration of Latvia
Communicate via MRCC Rīga VHF DSC MMSI 002750100
☏ +371 673 23103 (emergency)/
☏ +371 294 76101/+371 670 82070 (mobile)
sar@mrcc.lv
Inmarsat–C 581–427518510.

Estonia
National SAR Agency Estonian Border Guard and Ministry of Transport and Communication
Communicate via JRCC Tallinn, VHF DSC MMSI 002761000
☏ +372 6 692222/6925000 (MRCC Tallinn)
ncc_estonia@pohja.pv.ee
Inmarsat–C (AOR-E) 492480040.

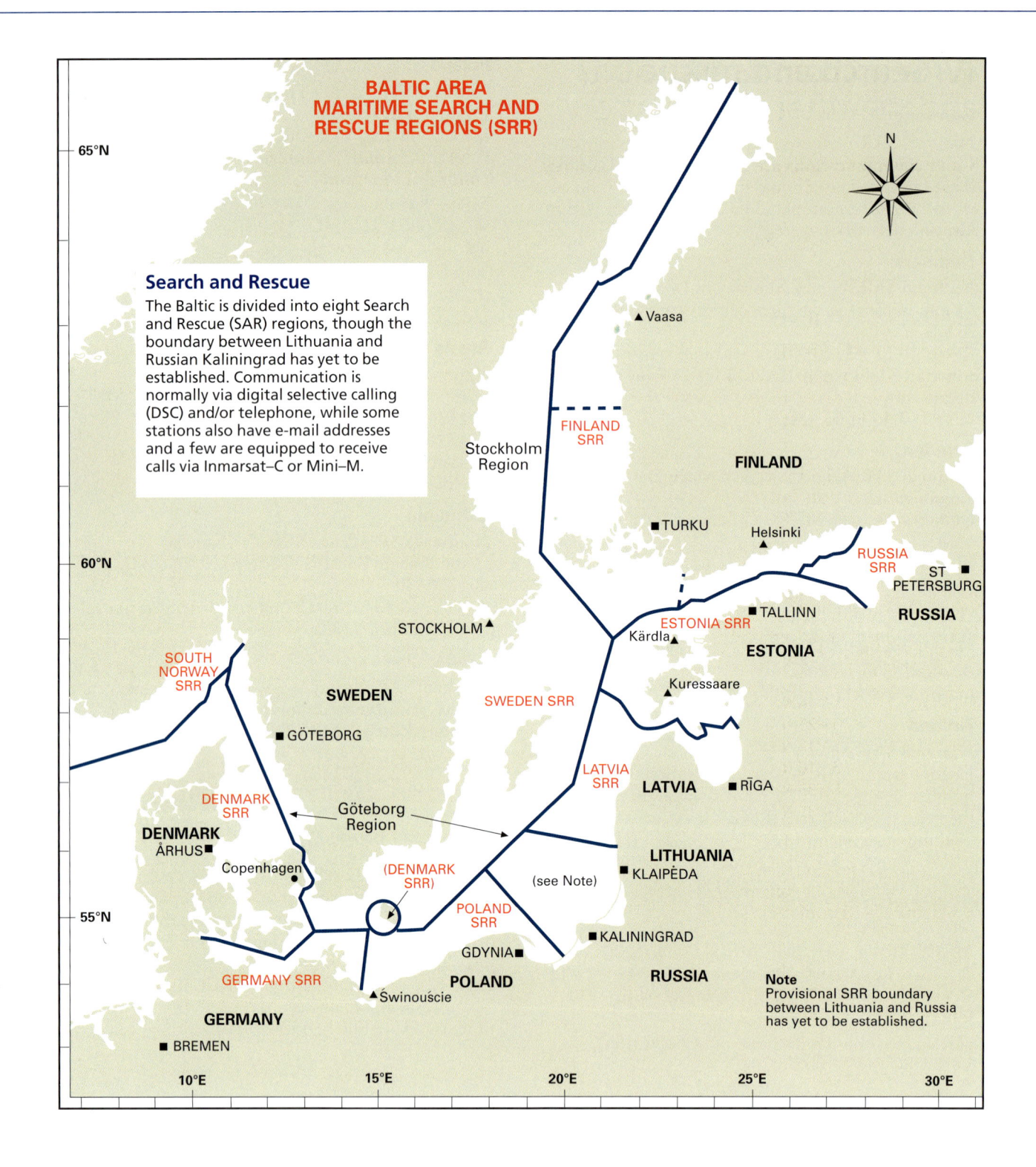

APPENDIX

BALTIC AREA MARITIME SEARCH AND RESCUE REGIONS (SRR)

Search and Rescue

The Baltic is divided into eight Search and Rescue (SAR) regions, though the boundary between Lithuania and Russian Kaliningrad has yet to be established. Communication is normally via digital selective calling (DSC) and/or telephone, while some stations also have e-mail addresses and a few are equipped to receive calls via Inmarsat–C or Mini–M.

Note
Provisional SRR boundary between Lithuania and Russia has yet to be established.

422 THE BALTIC SEA AND APPROACHES

V. Radio communications and weather information

Radio communications are detailed under a number of section headings. Should further detail be required the reader is recommended to obtain the current edition of NP 291, *Admiralty Maritime Communications – United Kingdom and the Baltic*. All times are given in UT unless stated.

GMDSS, Coast Radio Stations, weather bulletins and navigational warnings

Boundaries of forecast areas are shown on page 369. Details of port or harbour radio services on VHF will be found in the text relating to that harbour.

Note Some forecasts give wind speed in metres per second – multiply by two for the approximate equivalent in knots and divide by two for the approximate figure in Beaufort.

Germany

Bremen (MRCC) (53°05'N 8°48'E) (24 hours)
VHF DSC MMSI 002111240
VHF antennas and remotely controlled stations accepting VHF DSC are situated at:

		VHF Ch
Flensburg	54°44'N 09°30'E	*16, 27*
Kiel	54°25'N 10°11'E	*16, 23*
Lübeck	54°13'N 10°43'E	*16, 24*
Rostock	54°10'N 12°06'E	*16, 60*
Arkona	54°33'N 13°35'E	*16, 66*
Rügen	54°35'N 13°40'E	*16*

Navigational warnings

Important navigational warnings are broadcast on Ch 16 by all stations, on receipt and repeated every H+00 and H+30 until cancelled.

Traffic centres

Storm warnings, weather bulletins, visibility and, when appropriate, ice reports are broadcast from the following Traffic Centres:

	VHF Ch	
Kiel Canal (east-going)	02	Every H+15 and H+45
Kiel Canal (west-going)	03	Every H+20 and H+50
Travemünde Traffic	13	Every 3 hours from 0600–2100 LT
Wismar Traffic	12	0230, 0630, 0930, 1230, 1530, 1830 and 2130 LT
Warnemünde Traffic	73	0115 then every odd H+15 from 0515–2115 LT
Stralsund Traffic	67	0235 then every even H+35 from 0635–2235 LT
Sassnitz Traffic	13	0230 then every even H+30 from 0630–2230 LT
Wolgast Traffic	09	0115 then every odd H+15 from 0515–2115 LT

Offenbach (Main)/Pinneberg

Offenbach/Pinneberg broadcasts detailed weather bulletins and navigational warnings in English on 4583, 7646 and 10100·8kHz. Full details are given in NP 291 *Admiralty Maritime Communications, United Kingdom and the Baltic*, which the owners of yachts with suitable receivers may wish to carry.

Other sources of German weather information

Weather bulletins and navigational warnings are broadcast by Deutschlandradio (Berlin), Deutschlandfunk (Köln), and Norddeutscher Rundfunk, in German only. Full details will be found in NP 291 *Admiralty Marititme Communications, United Kingdom and the Baltic*.

VHF transmission five times a day, provides a very comprehensive forecast in deliberately slow German. For times and frequencies see www.see-wetter.de/seefunk.

The website www.dwd.de is excellent for Baltic Sea areas

German Weather Service – Marine Weather

Strong wind and storm warnings (in excess of Force 6/22 knots) for the German North Sea and Baltic coasts are available on ☏ +49 (0) 40 6690 1209. When no warning is in operation a forecast is given.

Worldwide meteorological and routing advice via phone and/or modem is also available – for further information contact: German Weather Service – Shipping Department, PO Box 301190, 20304 Hamburg, Germany, ☏ +49 40 6690 1852.

Ice Reports

Ice information is available from the German Ice Report Service from late November until early June.
☏ +49 (0) 3814563787
ice@bsh.de
www.bsh.de or www.bsis-ice.de

Denmark

Lyngby (56°22'N 10°44'E) (24 hours)
☏ +45 666 34800
www.sarcontacts.info
VHF DSC MMSI 002191000
VHF Call Lyngby Radio. When traffic on hand, ship will be called by radio, DSC or satellite. Weather bulletins and navigational warnings as detailed below, both on working channels (bold type). Antennas and remotely controlled stations accepting VHF DSC are situated at:

		VHF Ch	
Karleby	54°52'N 11°12'E	16, 28, 61, 63	Areas 4, 5
Møn (Mern)	55°03'N 11°59'E	16, 02, 64	Areas 2, 3, 4
Åarsballe (Bornholm)	55°09'N 11°53'E	16, 04, 07	Areas 1, 2, 3
København	55°41'N 12°37'E	16, 03, 26,	Areas 3, 4, 5
Røsnæs	55°44'N 10°55'E	16, 04, 23	Areas 4, 5
Vejby	56°05'N 12°08'E	16, 83	Areas 4, 5
Fornæs	56°27'N 10°57'E	16, 05	Areas 3, 4
Anholt	56°43'N 11°31'E	16, 07	Areas 4, 5
Læsø	57°17'N 11°03'E	16, 64	Area 5
Skagen	57°44'N 10°35'E	16, 04	Area 5

APPENDIX

Weather bulletins
Gale and storm warnings are broadcast on the working channel on receipt, in Danish and English, for the area(s) indicated on page 369. Gale warnings are repeated, in English, on request.

Navigational warnings
Navigational and Mine warnings are broadcast at the end of the first silence period after receipt (0133, 0533, 0933, 1333, 1733 and 2133), in Danish and English. Ice reports are broadcast at 1305 and on request in English.

Other sources of Danish weather information
Weather bulletins and navigational warnings are also broadcast by Danmarks Radio, in Danish only. www.dmi.dk Denmarks Meteorologiske Institute for forecasts and sejladsudsigt.dk, maritime weather for Denmark as an app displaying forecasts for wind, wave, currents temperature and salinity.

Sweden

Göteborg (57°28'N 11°56'E) (24 hours)
VHF DSC MMSI 002653000. For remotely controlled stations see under Stockholm.

Stockholm (59°17'N 18°43'E) (24 hours)
VHF DSC MMSI 002652000
VHF Calling vessels should give the name of the station and the channel number. An audible pulse is transmitted every 10 seconds to indicate that a working channel is occupied. Traffic lists are broadcast on working frequencies only at: 0200, 0600, 1000, 1400, 1800 and 2200.
Those stations which also accept remotely controlled VHF DSC traffic for Göteborg (see above) are indicated thus*. Antennas are situated at:

West coast (plus many others)		VHF Ch
Göteborg*	57°42'N 12°03'E	16, 24
Göta Canal and Lakes		
Trollhättan	58°17'N 12°17'E	16, 25
Kinnekulle*	58°36'N 13°25'E	16, 01
East coast		
Kivik*	55°40'N 14°10'E	16, 21
Karlshamn (Hörvik)	56°14'N 14°47'E	16, 25
Karlskrona*	56°10'N 15°36'E	16, 81
Ölands Södra Udde*	56°14'N 16°27'E	16, 27
Västervik*	57°43'N 16°26'E	16, 23
Hoburgen (Gotland)*	56°56'N 18°13'E	16, 24
Visby (Gotland)*	57°36'N 18°22'E	16, 25
Fårö (Gotland)*	57°52'N 19°02'E	16, 28
Gotska Sandön*	58°22'N 19°14'E	16, 65
Norrköping*	58°41'N 16°28'E	16, 64
Torö*	58°49'N 17°50'E	16, 24
Södertälje*	59°13'N 17°37'E	16, 66
Nacka (Stockholm)*	59°18'N 18°10'E	16, 03, 23, 26
Svenska Högarna*	59°27'N 19°30'E	16, 84
Väddö*	59°58'N 18°50'E	16, 78
Gävle*	60°38'N 17°08'E	16, 23
Hudiksvall*	61°42'N 16°51'E	16, 25
Sundsvall*	62°24'N 17°27'E	16, 24
Härnösand*	62°37'N 17°58'E	16, 23
Kramfors	62°57'N 17°57'E	16, 84
Mjällom*	62°59'N 18°24'E	16, 64
Örnsköldsvik	63°18'N 18°40'E	16, 28
Umeå*	63°50'N 19°49'E	16, 26
Skellefteå*	64°46'N 20°57'E	16, 23
Luleå*	65°36'N 21°56'E	16, 25
Mälaren		
Västerås*	59°39'N 16°24'E	16, 25
Hjälmaren	59°06'N 15°50'E	16, 81

Weather bulletins
24 hour forecast and synopsis for areas 1–15 are broadcast in Swedish and English on VHF working channels at 0600 and 1800 (see page 369).

WIND SCALES

Beaufort	Wind Description	Effect on Sea	Effect on Land	Wind speed (knots)	m/sec
0	Calm	Sea like a mirror	Smoke rises vertically	<1	–
1	Light air	Ripples like scales, no crests	Direction of wind shown by smoke	1–3	2
2	Light breeze	Small wavelets, crests do not break	Wind felt on face, leaves rustle	4–6	2–3
3	Gentle breeze	Large wavelets, some crests break	Wind extends light flags	7–10	3–5
4	Moderate breeze	Small waves, frequent white horses	Small branches move	11–16	5–8
5	Fresh breeze	Moderate waves, many white horses	Small trees sway	17–21	8–11
6	Strong breeze	Large waves form, white crests	Large branches move	22–27	11–14
7	Near gale	Sea heaps up, white foam from breaking waves	Whole trees in motion	28–33	14–17
8	Gale	Moderately high waves some spindrift. Foam blown with wind	Twigs break from trees, difficult to walk	34–40	17–20
9	Strong gale	High waves, dense foam, wave crests topple, spray may affect visibility	Slight structural damage	41–47	20–24
10	Storm	Very high waves, sea appears white, visibility affected	Trees uprooted, structural damage	48–55	24–27
11	Violent storm	Exceptionally high waves, long white patches of foam, crests blown into froth	Widespread damage	56–63	28–31
12	Hurricane	The air is filled with foam, visibility very seriously affected	Widespread structural damage	64+	32–

V. RADIO COMMUNICATIONS AND WEATHER INFORMATION

VHF RADIO STATIONS IN THE BALTIC

More detailed information is given in the text for individual countries

NORWAY

SWEDEN

FINLAND

Turku Radio
MMSI: 002300230

Stockholm Radio
MMSI: 002652000

St Petersburg Radio
MMSI: 002733700

Tallinn Radio
MMSI: 002761000

ESTONIA

LATVIA

(MRCC Göteborg)
MMSI: 002653000

Riga Radio
MMSI: 002750100

Klaipeda Radio
MMSI: 002770330

LITHUANIA

Lyngby Radio
MMSI: 002191000

DENMARK

Kaliningrad Radio
MMSI: 002734417

RUSSIA

Witowo Radio
MMSI: 002610210

Szczecin Radio
MMSI: 002610110

Gdynia Radio
MMSI: 002610310

RUSSIA

Bremen Radio
MMSI: 002111240

GERMANY

POLAND

APPENDIX

THE BALTIC SEA AND APPROACHES 425

APPENDIX

Navigational warnings
Navigational warnings for all areas are broadcast in Swedish and English on VHF working channels at 0200, 0600, 1000, 1400, 1800 and 2200.

Ice reports
Reports for all areas are broadcast at 1400 and on request, in English.

Other sources of Swedish weather information
Swedish Meteorological and Hydrological Institute Weather bulletins and ice reports in Swedish and English are available on request (though at a charge) from the SMHI marine forecasting service at Norrköping, ☎ +46 11 495 8400/8532/8533/8535.

Finland
Turku (60°10′N 21°43′E) (24 hours)
VHF DSC MMSI 002300230
All stations are remotely controlled from Turku. Weather bulletins and navigational warnings are broadcast on working channels by all stations

Those stations which accept remotely controlled VHF DSC traffic are indicated thus* and grouped according to Marine Rescue Co-ordination Centre – Vaasa, Turku and Helsinki. Antennas are situated at:

MRSC Vaasa (MMSI 002303000)

		VHF Ch
Kemi*	65°47′N 24°33′E	26
Hailuoto*	65°02′N 24°35′E	27
Kalajoki*	64°18′N 24°11′E	84
Kokkola*	63°50′N 23°09′E	28
Raippaluoto*	63°18′N 21°10′E	25

MRCC Turku (MMSI 002301000)

Kristiinankaupunki*	62°16′N 21°24′E	24
Pori*	61°37′N 21°27′E	26
Rauma*	61°07′N 21°31′E	28
Uusikaupunki*	60°49′N 21°26′E	01
Turku (MRCC)*	60°27′N 22°20′E	02, 26
Brändo*	60°25′N 21°03′E	86
Geta*	60°23′N 19°53′E	05
Korpoo*	60°10′N 21°33′E	23
Turku Radio	60°09′N 21°42′E	02, 26
Järsö*	60°01′N 20°00′E	25

MRSC Helsinki (MMSI 002302000)

Utö*	59°47′N 21°22′E	24
Hanko*	59°50′N 22°56′E	03
Porkkala*	59°59′N 24°26′E	04
Helsinki*	60°09′N 25°02′E	05
Sondby (Porvoo)*	60°16′N 25°51′E	01
Kotka*	60°29′N 26°52′E	25
Virolahti*	60°36′N 27°50′E	24

Weather bulletins
Gale warnings are broadcast on receipt and at 0233, 0633, 1033, 1433, 1833 and 2223 in English, for Areas 1–5 and 7 (see page 427). Weather forecasts, including wave heights, are broadcast at 0633 and 1833, in English, for the same areas.

Navigational warnings
Local and coastal warnings in English for the Gulf of Finland are broadcast on receipt and at 0233, 0633, 1033, 1433, 1833 and 2233. Ice reports are broadcast, in English, at 1033 and 1833.

Other sources of Finnish weather information
Weather bulletins and navigational warnings are also broadcast by Radio Vega and Radio Suomi, in Swedish and Finnish respectively.

Ice reports
Ice reports in Finnish, Swedish or English are available from the Finnish Institute of Marine Research (FIMR), ☎ +358 9 685 7659
ice_info@fimr.fi
Services from www.iceservice.fi are charged for.

Russia (Gulf of Finland)
Vyborg (60°42′N 28°46′E) (24 hours)
VHF DSC MMSI 002734415 (60°42′N 28°43′E)
VHF Ch 02, 16
Saint Petersburg (MRCC) (59°33′N 30°13′E) (24 hours)
VHF DSC MMSI 002733700
VHF Ch 09, 16, 24, 27, 67, 71 (other channels may be used on request)
While some weather bulletins and navigational warnings are broadcast in Russian, the area is well covered by the English VHF broadcasts from Finland and Sweden.

Poland
Świnoujście (MRSC 53°55′N 14°17′E) (Ch 11, 16, 74 operates 24 hours)
VHF Call Szczecin Radio. Both stations also accept remotely controlled VHF DSC traffic for Szczecin. Antennas are situated at:

		VHF Ch
Zatoka Pomorska	53°57′N 14°16′E	16, 25, 26, 27
Szczecin	53°28′N 14°35′E	16, 24, 28

Weather bulletins
Weather bulletins in English and Polish are broadcast by Zatoka Pomorska at 0705, 1305 and 1905. Coastal warnings are broadcast in English and Polish by both stations at 0200, 0600, 1000, 1400, 1800 and 2200. Ice reports are broadcast when relevant.

Navigational warnings
Witowo Radio (SPS) (54°33′N 16°32′E) (24 hours)
VHF DSC MMSI 002610210.
VHF Call Witowo Radio. All three stations also accept remotely controlled VHF DSC traffic for Witowo. Antennas are situated at:

		VHF Ch
Kolobrzeg	54°11′N 15°33′E	16, 24
Barzowice	54°28′N 16°30′E	16, 25
Rowokól	54°39′N 17°13′E	16, 26

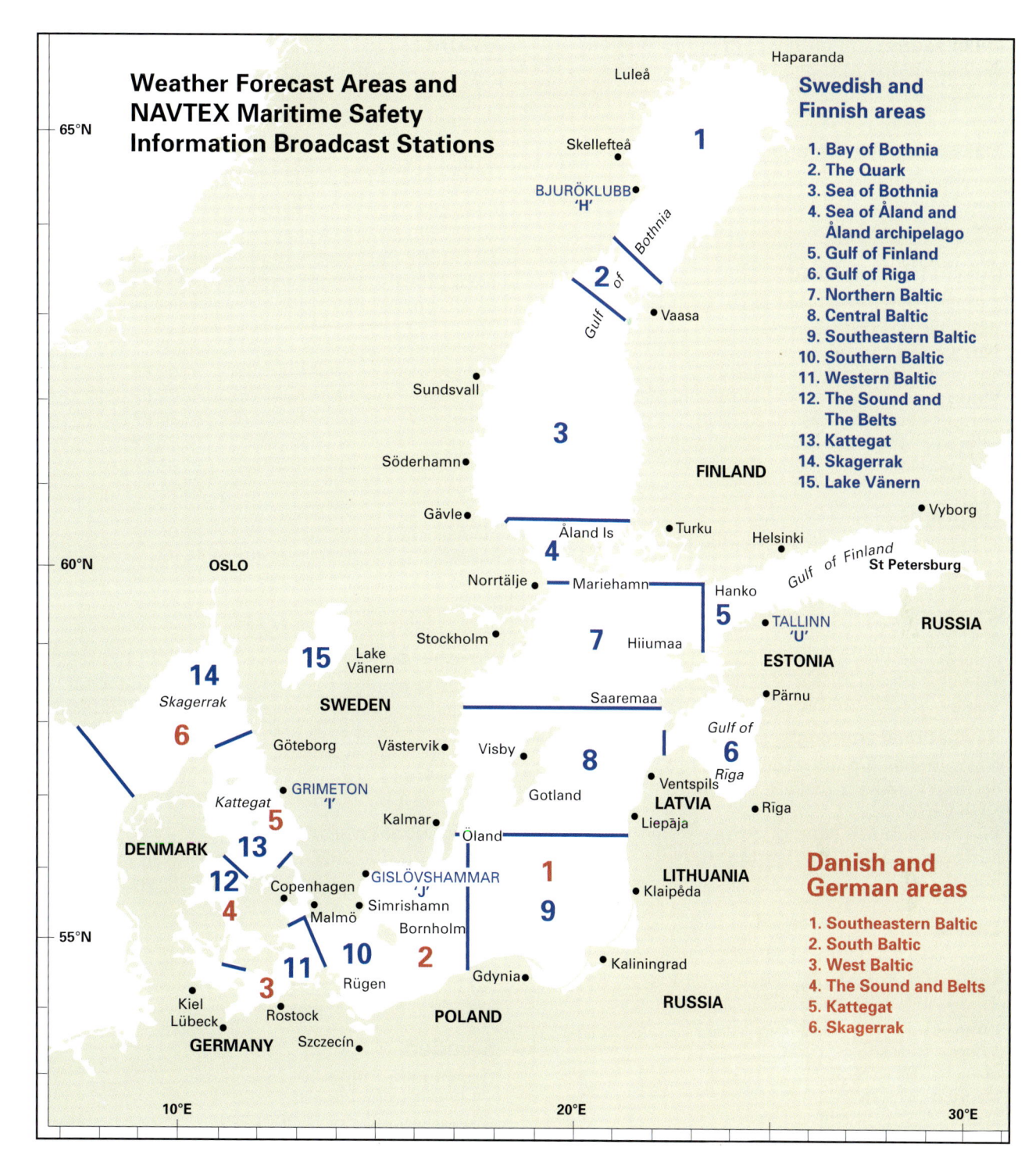

V. RADIO COMMUNICATIONS AND WEATHER INFORMATION

Weather Forecast Areas and NAVTEX Maritime Safety Information Broadcast Stations

Swedish and Finnish areas
1. Bay of Bothnia
2. The Quark
3. Sea of Bothnia
4. Sea of Åland and Åland archipelago
5. Gulf of Finland
6. Gulf of Riga
7. Northern Baltic
8. Central Baltic
9. Southeastern Baltic
10. Southern Baltic
11. Western Baltic
12. The Sound and The Belts
13. Kattegat
14. Skagerrak
15. Lake Vänern

Danish and German areas
1. Southeastern Baltic
2. South Baltic
3. West Baltic
4. The Sound and Belts
5. Kattegat
6. Skagerrak

Gdynia Radio (MRCC) (54°33′N 18°32′E) (24 hours)
VHF DSC MMSI 002610310
VHF Call Gydnia Radio. All three stations also accept remotely controlled VHF DSC traffic for Witowo (SPS). Antennas are situated at:

		VHF Ch
Rozewie	54°50′N 18°20′E	16, 24
Oksywie	54°33′N 18°32′E	16, 26, 27
Krynica Morska	54°23′N 19°27′E	16, 25

Weather bulletins
Weather bulletins are broadcast on VHF working channels at 0135, 0735, 1335 and 1935, in Polish and English, for Areas 7–11 (see page 369).

Navigational warnings
Coastal warnings are broadcast on receipt and at 0133, 0533, 0933, 1333, 1733 and 2133, in Polish and English. Ice reports, when relevant, are broadcast at 1035 and 1335 in Polish and English.

THE BALTIC SEA AND APPROACHES

APPENDIX

Other sources of Polish weather information
Weather bulletins and navigational warnings are broadcast by Polish (Polskie) Radio SA, in Polish only.

Marine Weather Telephone Service
Current condition reports and forecasts are available from Gdynia, ☎ 058 6203 422, and Szczecin, ☎ 091 4342 012.

Russia (Kaliningrad)
Kaliningrad (UIW) (54°42'N 20°30'E) (24 hours)
VHF DSC MMSI 002734417
VHF Ch 07, 16
Kaliningrad Radio-1 VHF Ch 07
While some weather bulletins and navigational warnings are broadcast in Russian, the area is well covered by the English VHF broadcasts from Finland and Sweden.

Lithuania
Klaipėda (MRCC) (55°43'N 21°06'E) (24 hours)
VHF DSC MMSI 002770330
Call Klaipėda Rescue Radio. Antennas are situated at:

		VHF Ch
Klaipėda	55°43'N 21°06'E	16
Nida	55°18'N 20°59'E	16
Šventoji	56°01'N 21°05'E	16

Navigational warnings
Navigational and other information is broadcast as necessary and on request by Klaipėda Traffic on VHF Ch 09.
JSC Navigation Center of Service Radio Centre of Klaipėda (Radio 5) (VTS) (55°43'N 21°06'E) (24 hours).

Latvia
Rīga (MRCC) (57°02'N 24°05'E) (24 hours)
VHF DSC MMSI 002750100. Call *Rīga Rescue Radio* (VHF Ch 71). Antennas are situated at:

Uzava	57°13'N 21°26'E
Jenupe	57°32'N 21°41'E
Kolka	57°45'N 22°35'E
Mersrags	57°22'N 23°07'E
Rīga	57°02'N 24°05'E
Vitrupe	57°36'N 24°23'E

Rīga (57°02'N 24°05'E) (24 hours)
VHF 70
Liepāja Radio (56°30'N 21°00'E) (24 hours).

Other sources of Latvian weather information
Gale warnings and local forecasts are broadcast by:

		VHF Ch
MRCC Rīga	0703, 1503 LT	71

Estonia
Kuressaare (MRSC) (58°15'N 22°29'E)
VHF DSC MMSI 002760120
Pärnu (ESP) (58°23'N 24°29'E) (24 hours)
VHF Ch 16, 10
Tallinn (MRCC) (59°24'N 24°40'E) and Tallinn (ESA) (59°28'N 24°21'E) (both 24 hours)
VHF DSC MMSI 002761000.
VHF All stations accept remotely controlled VHF DSC traffic on VHF Ch 70. Weather bulletins and navigational warnings are broadcast on VHF Ch 69 by all stations after prior announcement on VHF Ch 16.

		VHF Ch
Ruhnu	57°48'N 23°15'N	16, 03, 69
Tõstamaa	58°18'N 24°00'E	16, 01, 69
Torgu	57°59'N 22°05'E	16, 26, 69
Undva	58°31'N 21°56'E	16, 01, 69
Orissaare	58°34'N 23°04'E	16, 27, 69
Kõpu	58°55'N 22°12'E	16, 03, 69
Dirhami	59°12'N 23°31'E	16, 26, 69
Suurupi	59°28'N 24°23'E	16, 01, 69
Tallinn	59°24'N 24°40'E	16, 03, 27
Aabla	59°35'N 25°31'E	16, 27, 69
Eisma	59°34'N 26°17'E	16, 03, 69
Toila	59°25'N 27°32'E	16, 26, 69

Weather bulletins
Storm warnings for the Baltic Sea and Gulf of Finland are broadcast on receipt and at 0233, 0633, 1033, 1433, 1833 and 2233, in English and Estonian. Gale warnings, synopsis, and 24/48 hour weather and sea state forecasts are broadcast at 0433 and 1333 in English and Estonian.

Navigational warnings
Navigational warnings are broadcast on receipt and at 0233, 0633, 1033, 1433, 1833 and 2233 in English and Estonian.

Navtex
All broadcasts are in English. Boundaries of forecast areas are shown on page 369.

Sweden
Grimeton (57°06'N 12°23'E) Range 300M.
  Identification letter I
  Weather bulletins 0520, 1720.
  Navigational warnings 0120, 0520, 0920, 1320, 1720 and 2120
  Ice reports 1320
Gislövshammar (55°29'N 14°19'E) Range 300M.
  Identification letter J
  Weather bulletins 0520, 1730
  Navigational warnings 0130, 0530, 0930, 1330, 1730, 2130
  Ice reports 1330, 1730
Bjuröklubb (64°28'N 21°36'E) Range 300M.
  Identification letter H. (This station appears to broadcast only full gale warnings and ice reports).
  Weather bulletins 0510, 1710

THE BALTIC SEA AND APPROACHES

V. RADIO COMMUNICATIONS AND WEATHER INFORMATION

Navigational warnings 0110, 0510, 0910, 1310, 1710, 2110
Ice reports 1310.

Estonia
Tallinn (59°30′N 24°30′E) Range 300M.
  Identification letter U.
  Weather bulletins 0720, 1920 for Areas 1–15
  Navigational and near gale warnings 0320, 0720, 1120, 1520, 1920, 2320 for Areas 4–8.
  Ice reports 1120, 1520 for Areas 1–15. (See page 369).

Weatherfax
A number of weatherfax transmissions cover the Baltic Sea, including those from Northwood (UK) and Offenbach (Main)/Pinneberg (DDH) (DDK) (Germany). Full details are given in NP 291, *Admiralty Maritime Communications – United Kingdom and the Baltic*, which the owners of all yachts equipped with weatherfax receivers are strongly advised to carry.

Northwood transmits on 2618·5, 4610, 8040, 11086·5kHz, with a schedule at 0236 and 1424, 24 hour forecasts at 0524, 0800, 1000, 1300, 1736, 2200, and gale warnings at 0348, 0600, 0700, 1148, 1548 and 1900. Coverage extends from the US East Coast across the North Atlantic as far as Russia.

Offenbach/Pinneberg transmits on 4583, 7646 and 10100·8kHz, Notices at 1110; outlook and 2-day forecast at 0905, 2105; outlook and 5-day forecast at 0330, 1505; marine weather reports at 0020, 0320, 0550, 0850, 1150, 1450, 1750 and 2050. Coverage varies from transmission to transmission.

Weather forecasts on the internet
An ever-increasing amount of weather-related information can be found on the internet. The following sites may be useful, though some information is duplicated at least once. Further investigation immediately before departure would be worthwhile, as new sites are coming online all the time.

www.cnn.com/WEATHER – worldwide weather coverage from CNN, with charts, satellite imagery and three day forecasts for principal cities. Cluttered with unrelated advertisements

www.ecmwf.int – the homepage of the European Centre for Medium-Range Weather Forecasts with links to almost every national met office in Europe. Fast and user-friendly

http://weather.mailasail.com/Franks-Weather/Home – a very interesting private site run by yachtsman and ex Met Office employee Frank Singleton. Particularly useful section (with links) devoted to Baltic Weather Forecasts

www.greatweather.co.uk – private site compiled by Ant Veal with hundreds of useful meteorological links for the UK and Europe, plus bookshop etc

www.metoffice.com – the homepage of the UK Met Office, with worldwide coverage in addition to the UK. Some services are subscription-based

www.sat.dundee.ac.uk – images from orbiting and geostationary satellites courtesy of Dundee University's satellite receiving station. Available free on completion of a registration form

www.foreca.se 5-day Swedish forecasts

http://weather.noaa.gov/ – site of the US National Weather Service, including highly detailed 24 hour weather reports (not forecasts) for many towns in Europe and beyond

http://weather.yahoo.com/ – Yahoo! Weather, an easy site to navigate (though with too many irritating advertisements) giving tourist-type weather information worldwide

www.wmo.ch – website of the World Meteorological Organization (a United Nations Specialized Agency) with information from many national met offices throughout the world. Text in English, French and Spanish

www.smhi.se – Swedish website providing forecasts in English for all areas of the Baltic Sea

APPENDIX

VI. Chart coverage in Russia, Estonia, Latvia and Lithuania

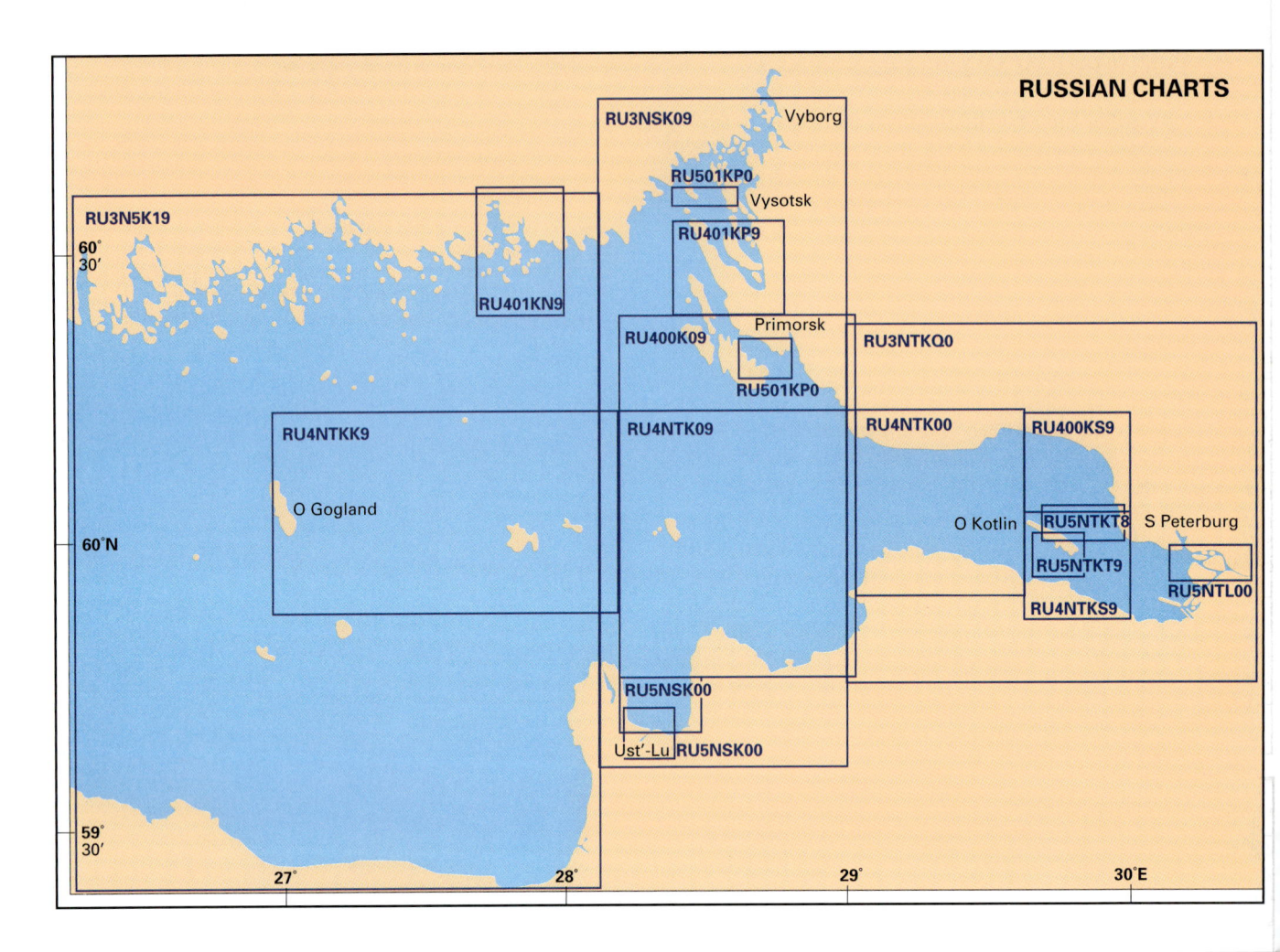

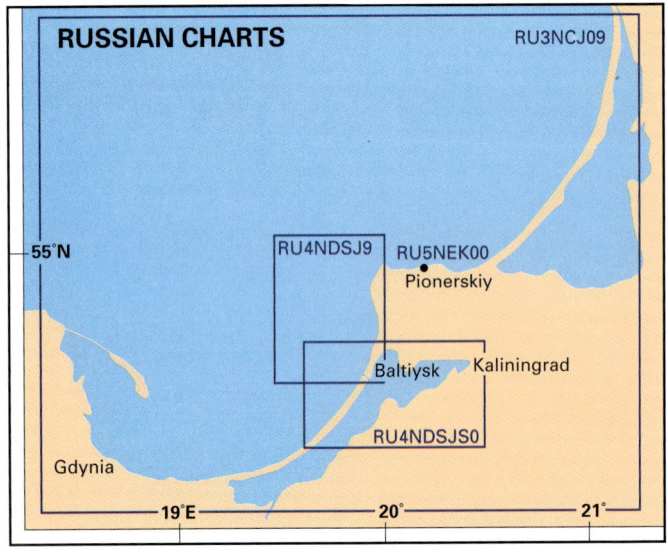

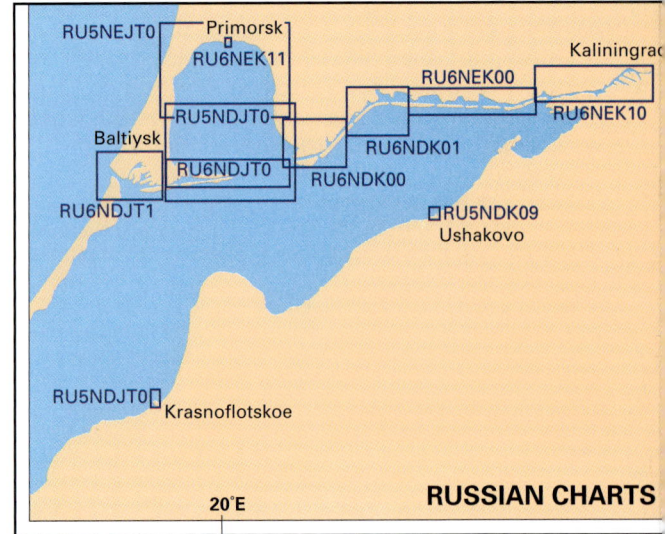

430 THE BALTIC SEA AND APPROACHES

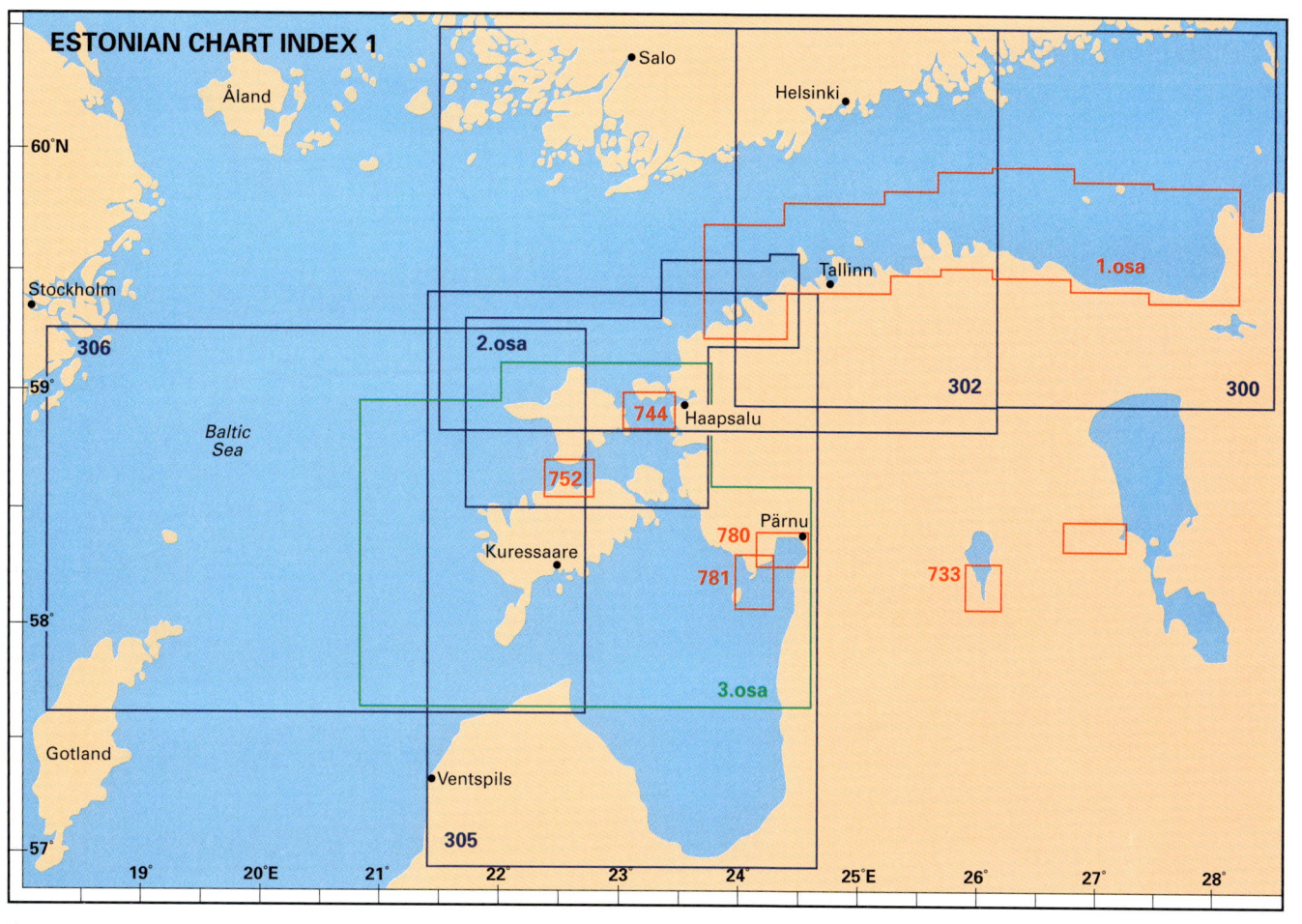

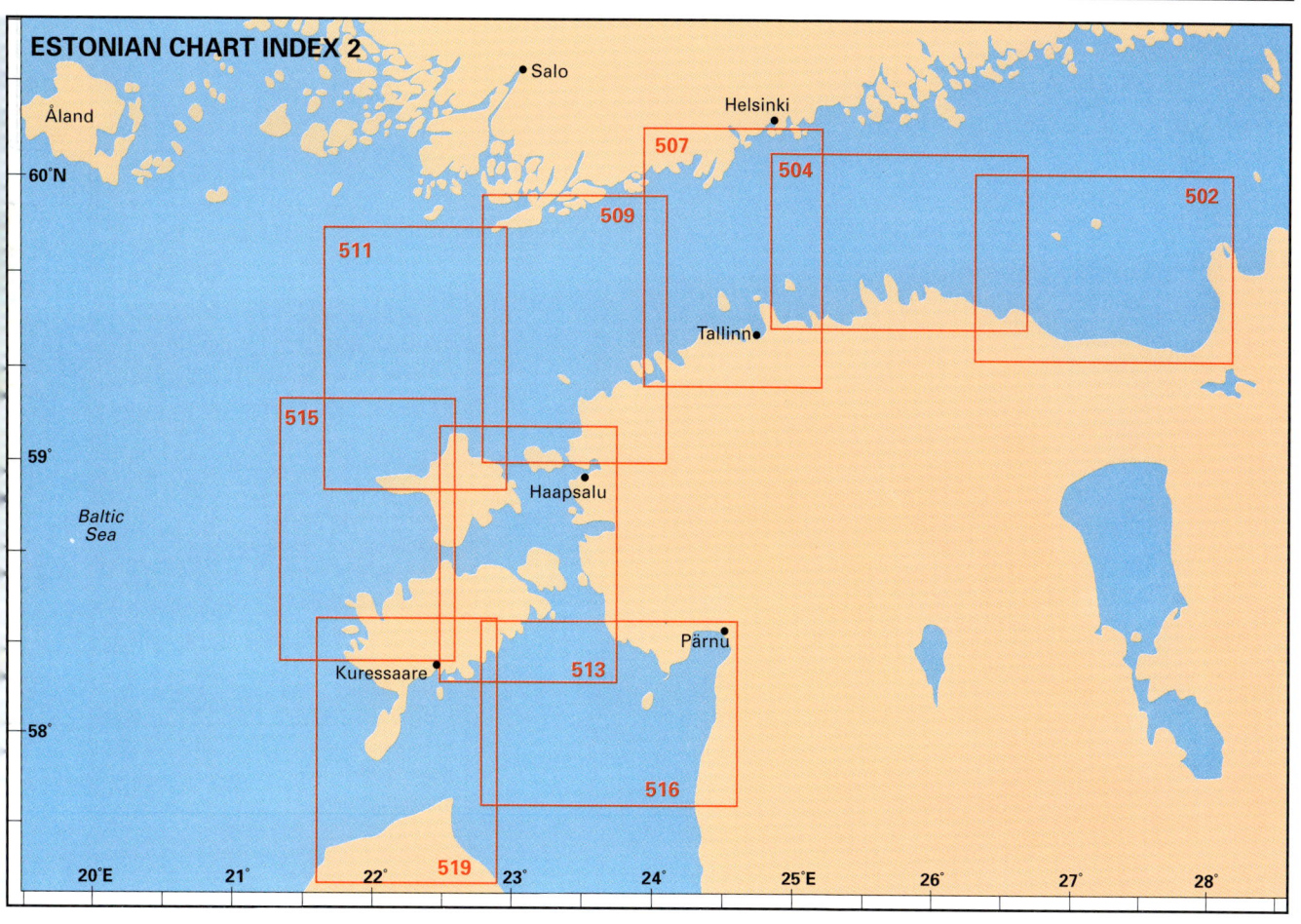

VI. CHART COVERAGE

ESTONIAN CHART INDEX 1

ESTONIAN CHART INDEX 2

THE BALTIC SEA AND APPROACHES 431

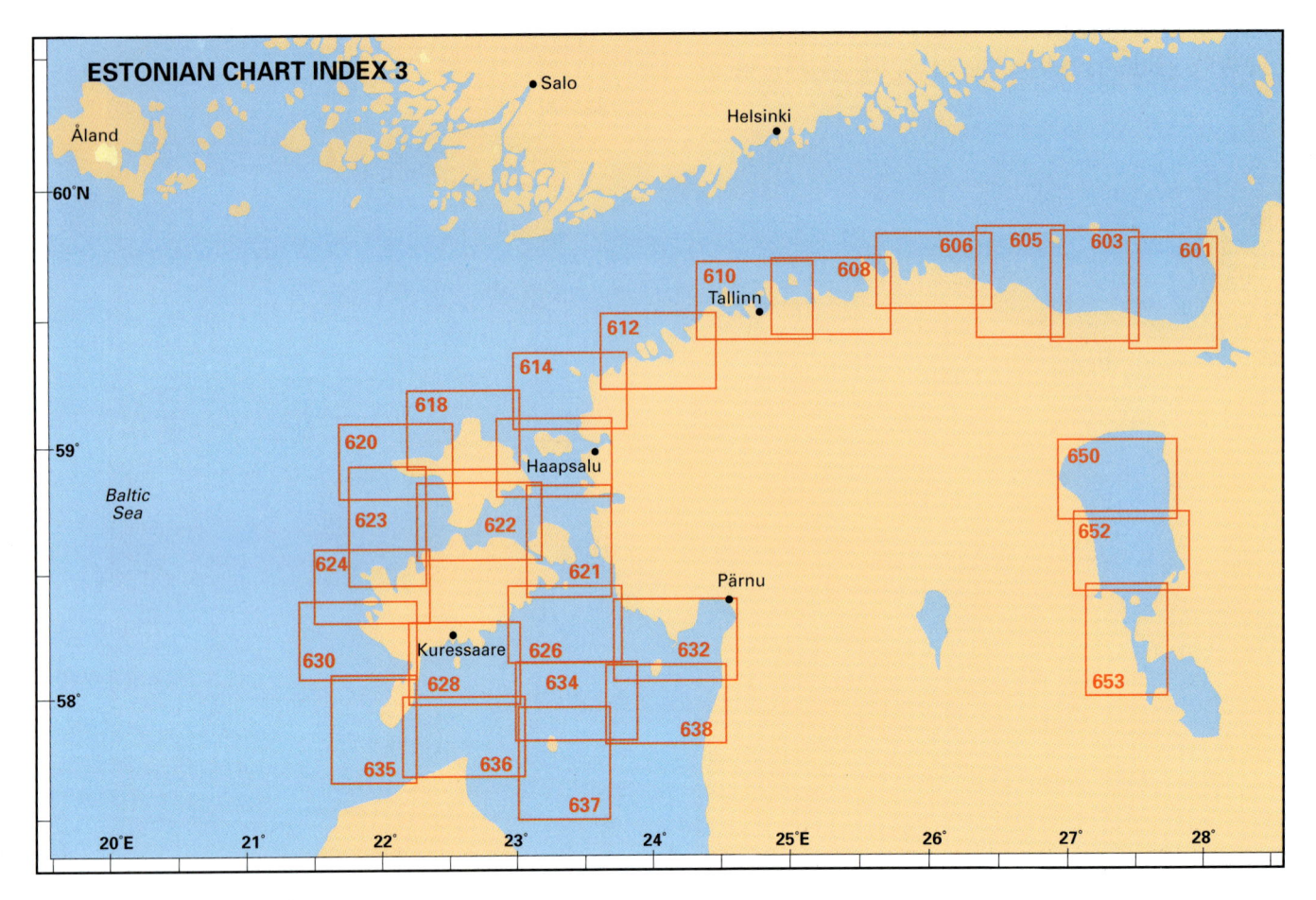

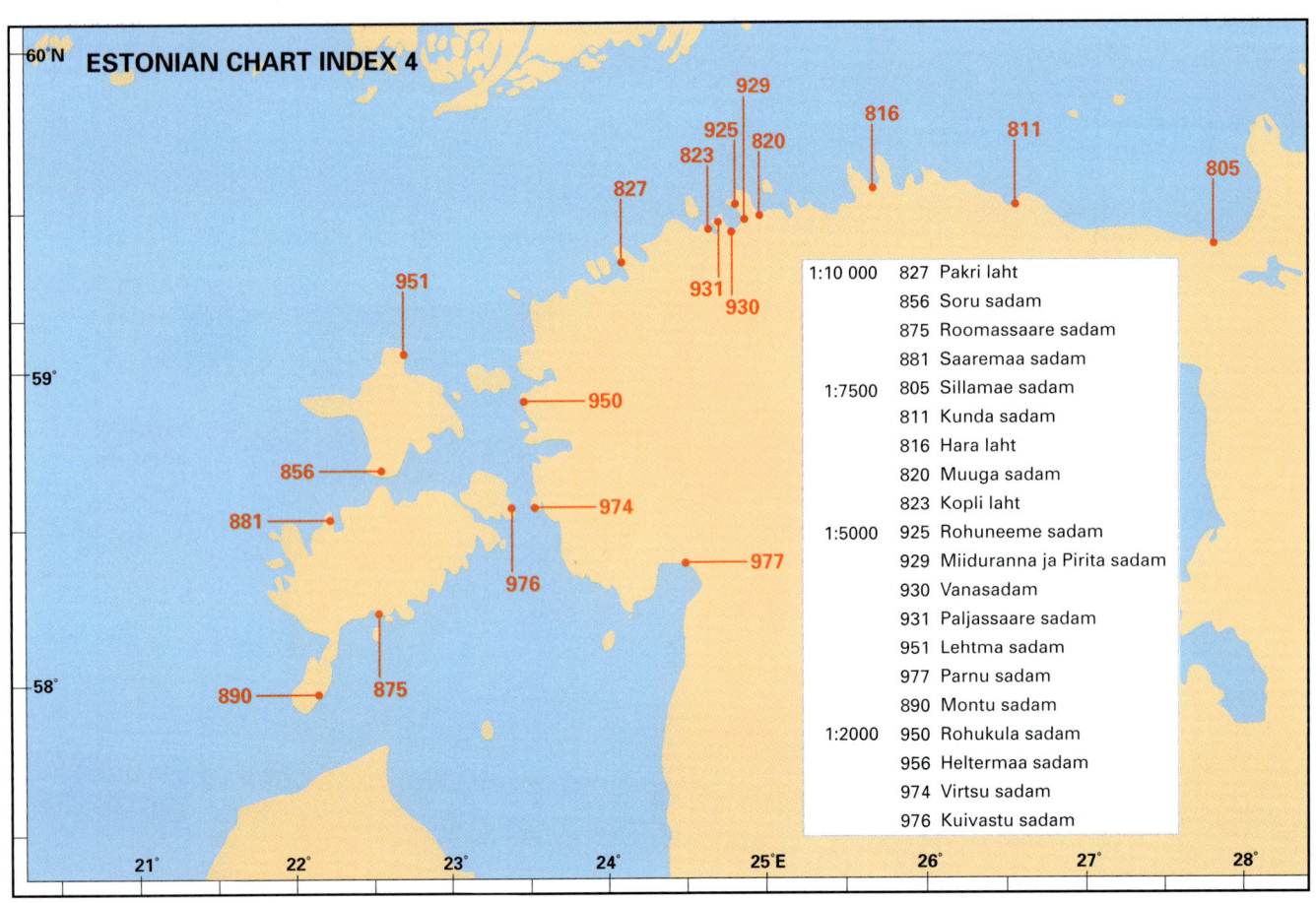

APPENDIX

ESTONIAN CHART INDEX 3

ESTONIAN CHART INDEX 4

1:10 000	827	Pakri laht
	856	Soru sadam
	875	Roomassaare sadam
	881	Saaremaa sadam
1:7500	805	Sillamae sadam
	811	Kunda sadam
	816	Hara laht
	820	Muuga sadam
	823	Kopli laht
1:5000	925	Rohuneeme sadam
	929	Miiduranna ja Pirita sadam
	930	Vanasadam
	931	Paljassaare sadam
	951	Lehtma sadam
	977	Parnu sadam
	890	Montu sadam
1:2000	950	Rohukula sadam
	956	Heltermaa sadam
	974	Virtsu sadam
	976	Kuivastu sadam

432 THE BALTIC SEA AND APPROACHES

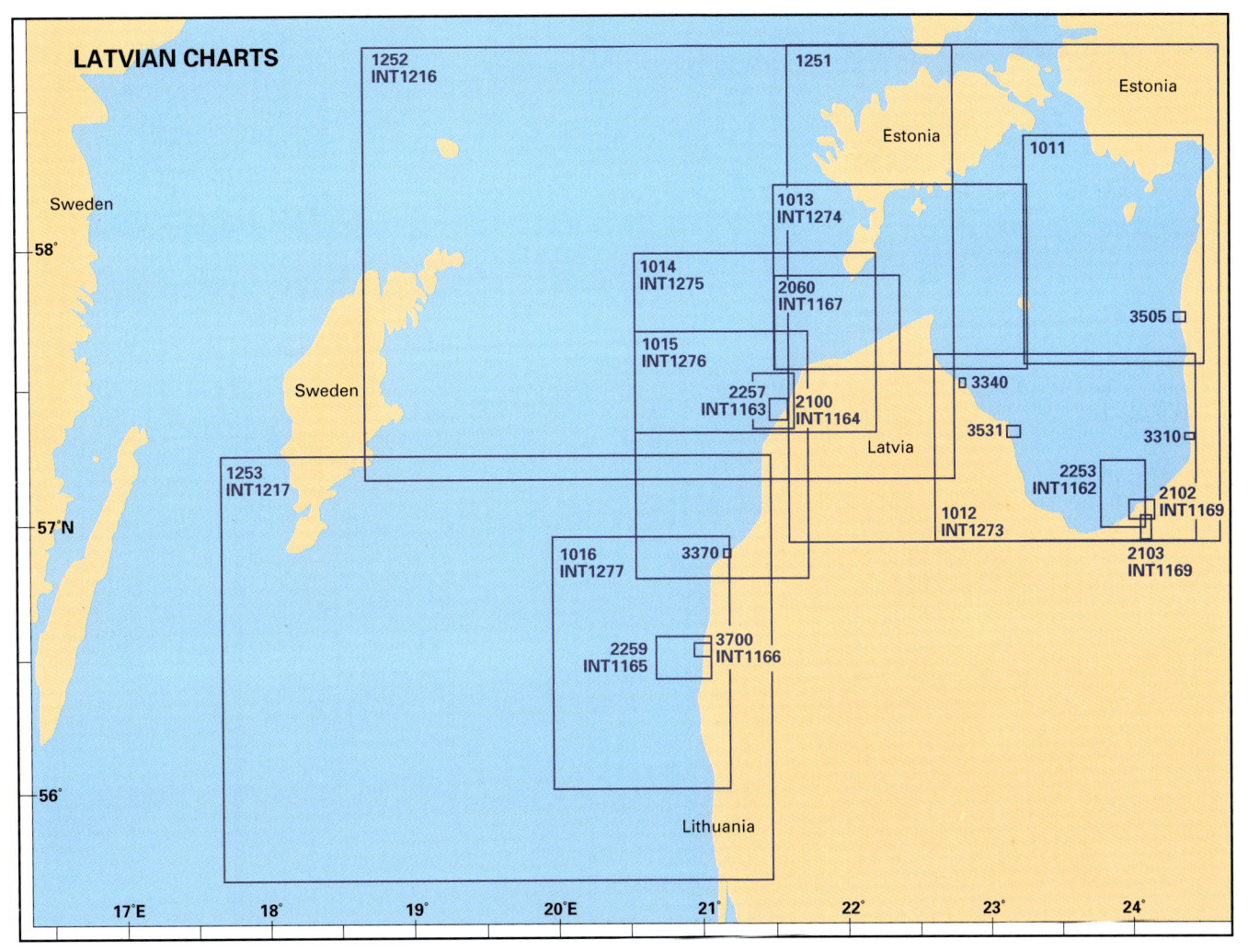

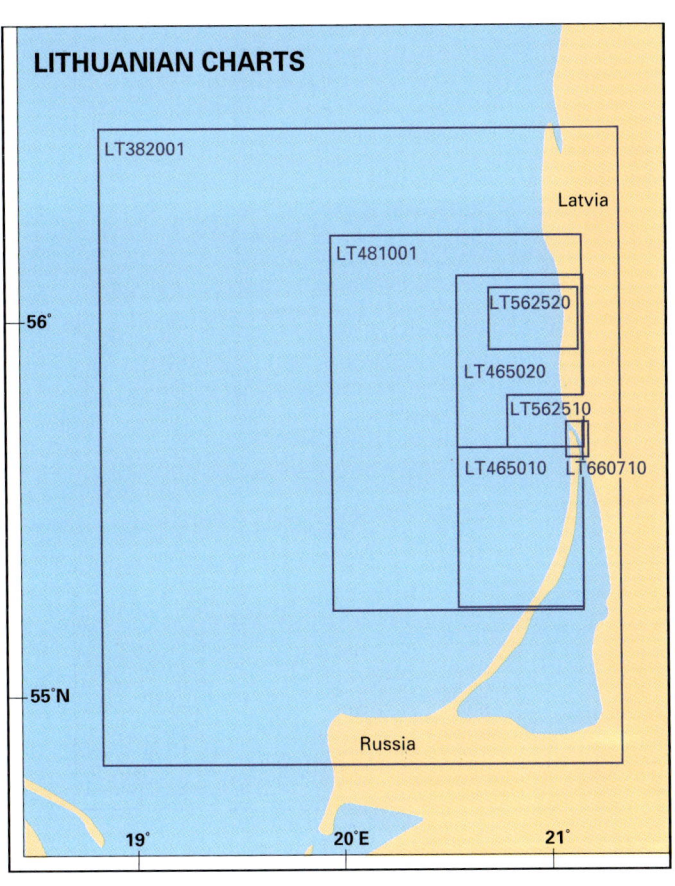

VI. CHART COVERAGE

LATVIAN CHARTS

LITHUANIAN CHARTS

THE BALTIC SEA AND APPROACHES

Index

Åbo (Turku), 278-81
Åbo *Skärgård*, 264, 265, 278, 287-8
Abruka, 403, 404
Achterwasser, 63
Ærøskøbing, 109-110
Ägnofjärden, 215
Agön, 229
Åhus, 177
Ahvenanmaa (Åland Islands), 7, 245-6, 264-76, 287
Ainaži, 378
air travel, 5, see also start of each chapter
Airisto, 281, 282
Åkerssjö, 169
Åland (Ahvenanmaa), 7, 245-6, 264-76, 287
Åland Sea, 213, 219, 245
Ålborg, 90-91
alcohol, 9-10, see also start of each chapter
algae, 8
Algkobb, 219
Algö, 287, 293
Älgsjö, 294
Alholmen, 259
Allemansrätten (Right of Public Access), 137, 251
Allinge, 128
Ålö, 212
Als Fjord, 113-15
Ålviken, 283
Åmål, 172
Åmbarsunden, 283
amber, 3, 336, 364, 373, 376, 380
anchoring, 12, 13
Ancora Marina (Neustadt), 39
Andrejosta Yacht Centre (Riga), 381, 389, 390
Ängsö, 283
Anholt, 99
Antnäs-Börskä, 240
Archipelago Sea, 246, 265, 266, 276-87
Arctic Circle, 240, 245
Area 117, 370, 372
Arholma, 217, 226
Århus, 102-3
Arkösund, 194, 200, 201-2
Arvika Canal, 172
Askeröfjorden, 160
Askfatshamnen, 217
Aspö Island, 310
Augustenborg, 113, 114
Axmar, 228
AZS (YC) Marina, 347

Bäckviken (Ven), 143-4
Bad Doberan, 46, 51
Bagenkop, 123
Baggensstäket, 213, 214, 215, 243
Ballen, 116
Baltic Bay, Marina, 31
Baltic Canal, 5

Baltiysk, 368, 370, 371
Banö-ön, 283
Barhöft, 51, 53, 54
Bärö, 275
Barölandet, 294
Barösund, 288, 294
Barth, 53
Barther Bodden, 52, 53
Båtskärnäs, 242
Bay of Bothnia (Perämeri; Bottviken), 238-43, 252-7
Beaufort wind scale, 424
Berg, 174, 175
Berg Kanal, 173
Berghamn (Storlandet), 283
Bergkvara, 188
Berlin, 348
berthing, 10-12, see also start of each chapter
Birka (Björkö, Lake Mälaren), 209
Birsskär, 284
Bjorkesund, 324, 331
Björkö (Archipelago Sea), 284, 286
Bjorkö (Lake Mälaren), 209
Bjørnø (Fåborg Fjord), 107
Björskärs, 219
Bjuröklubb, 237
Blå Jungfrun (Blue Maiden), 191
Blå Kusten (Blue Coast), 194-202
Blankaholm, 194
Blidösund, 219
Blue Coast (Blå Kusten), 194-202
Blue Maiden (Blå Jungfrun), 191
boat & equipment, 8-10
boatyards, 10
Bock, 54
Bockhamn (Byön), 303
Bockholmen, 303
The Boddens, 19-20, 52-61
Bodstetter Bodden, 52, 53
Bøgestrøm, 123
Bohuslän, 131, 156-66
Bomarsund, 272
Bondön, 239
Bönhamn, 232
books & guides see start of each chapter
booms, 12, 13
Borensberg, 174, 175
Borenshult, 175
Borgå (Porvoo), 301-2
Borgstedter See, 22, 24
Bornholm, 1, 126-9, 178, 179, 334
Bornholmsgat TSS, 179
Borstö, 284, 286
bottled gas, 8-9
Bottviken *see* Bay of Bothnia
Brädholmen Marina (Oskarshamn), 191
Brahe, Tycho, 143, 144
Brahestad (Raahe), 252, 256-7
Brändö, 274
Brannø, 152

Brännskär, 283
Brinkebergskulle, 169
British Kiel Yacht Club (BKYC), 30
Brödstycket, 217
Brommö (Lake Vänern), 171, 172
Bruddalsviken, 277
Brunsbüttel, 21, 23, 24
Brusnitchnoe, 313, 314, 323
Bukhta Dubkovaya YC, 329
Bullandö, 213, 217, 221
Bullupe River, 388
buoyage, 6, see also start of each chapter
Burger See, 37
Burgstaaken, 37
Burgtiefe, 37
Busö, 287
Byön, 303
Byviken (Hogsara), 282
Byviken (Holmön), 236
Byxelkrok, 193

Central River YC (St Petersburg), 324, 331, 332, 333
certificates of competence, 4, 7
chandlery, 9, see also start of each chapter
chartplotters, 6
charts, 6
  abbreviations on Russian charts, 419-20
  chart coverage in Russia, Estonia, Latvia & Lithuania, 430-33
  chart suppliers, 418-19
  see also start of each chapter
Christianshavns Kanal (Copenhagen), 81-2
Christiansø, 126-7, 129
climate & weather services, 1, 6, 423-429, see also start of each chapter
coast radio stations, 423-8
communications, 6, 8, see also start of each chapter
conservation areas see start of each chapter
consulates see start of each chapter
Copenhagen, 79-83
cruise planning, 5
cruising areas & guides see start of each chapter
Cruising Association, 4, 5, 10
Curonian Lagoon & Spit, 372, 373, 374, 376-7
currency see start of each chapter
currents, 1, 6
customs & immigration, 7, see also start of each chapter
cycling see start of each chapter

Dąbska Struga, 346, 347
Dalarö, 216, 217
Dalbergsa, 169
Dalbosjön, 171
Dalslands Canal, 171-2
Danė River, 376
Dänholm, 55, 57

434   THE BALTIC SEA AND APPROACHES

INDEX

Darłowo, 353-4, 355
Darss, 52
Darsser Ort, 20, 51, 52, 53
Dassower See, 40, 41
Daugava River, 379, 380, 388, 390
Degerby, 273-4, 283, 284
Degerö, 273-4
Delvik, 272
Denmark, 1, 66-129
Die Schlei, 31-4
diesel, 9
Dirhami, 396, 411
Dirholmen (Digerholm), 282
Djäknesundet, 174
Djupkastet, 262
Djupviken (Geta), 273
Djurö (Lake Vänern), 172
Djuro (Värmdö), 217
Donsø, 151, 152
Dragesviken, 295
Dragør (Copenhagen), 82-3
Dragsö Yacht Harbour, 184-5
driving, 5
Drottningholm, 210
Dückerswisch Siding, 24
Düsternbrook, 28, 31
Dyvig Anchorage, 113-14
Dziwnów, 334, 343, 349-50

Ebeltoft, 100-102
Eckerö, 267
Egense, 96-8
Eider River, 22, 25-7
Eiderdamm, 26
Eidersperrwerk, 25, 27
Ekenäs Archipelago, 293
Ekenäs *Skärgårds* Nationalpark (Tammisaaren Saariston Kansallispuisto), 287, 293
Ekenäs (Tammisaari), 292
Ekens *skärgård* (Lake Vänern), 169, 172
electricity, 9
electronic chartplotters, 6
Elisaari, 294
Ellös, 160
email access, 8
embassies see start of each chapter
emergency phone numbers, 6
emergency services see start of each chapter
Emsalö (Emäsalo), 300, 302
Engure, 388
environment, 1-2
Ernemar Marina (Oskarshamn), 191
Esterson, 241
Estonia, 324, 392-417
Ettersundet, 201
European Health Insurance Card, 7
European Union, 4, 7, see also start of each chapter
Everyman's Right (Public Access), 137, 251

Fåborg, 107-8
Fågelö, 171
Falkenberg, 146, 148, 149
Falsterbo Kanal, 140-41
Favorit YC (Vyborg & Mys Bobovyy), 328
Fehmarn Island, 37
Fehmarnsund, 37, 39-40, 41
Fejø, 123
Femø, 123
ferries, 5
Finland, 244-317

Finnhälla, 275
Finnish Archipelago, 264, 265, 278, 287-8
firing practice areas, 420, see also start of each chapter
Fjuk, 173
Fjukson, 241
Fladalandet, 293
flags & ensigns, 7, see also start of each chapter
Flakholmen, 294
Flemhuder See, 24, 25
Flensburg, 19, 35-6
Flensburg Förde, 35-6
Fliskar, 227, 228
Föglö, 273
food & drink, 2
formalities, 7, see also start of each chapter
Forsvik, 173
Frederikshavn (Kattegat), 93-4
Fredrikshamn (Hamina), 300, 308-310
Fredrikstad (Norway), 166
Friedrichsort, 30
Friedrichstadt, 25, 26, 27
fuel, 8-9, see also start of each chapter
Furusund, 219
Fyrudden, 199

Gager, 59
Gammelstad Church Village, 240
gas, 8-9, see also start of each chapter
Gåsholm, 283
Gauja River, 379
Gävle, 227-8
Gävleborg, 226
Gdańsk, 334, 339, 360, 361
Gdańsk Nowy Port, 364, 365
Gdynia, 334, 360-63
Gedser, 48, 72, 73-4
Gehlsdorf, 49
Gellenstrom, 20, 54
geology, 2
Germany, 14-65
Geta, 272-3
Getholmen, 219
Getteron, 149, 150
Gieselau Kanal, 22, 24, 25
Gilleleje, 84-5
Gillinge, 219
Gimo, 227
Gislövs Läge, 177-8
Glommen, 149
GMDSS, 6, 7, 423
Gocław, 345, 346-7
Gogland Island, 324
Goleniow, 347
Górki Zachodnie, 339, 366
Göta Älv, 167, 168, 169
Göta Kanal, 5, 155, 167-75, 187, 194, 202
Göteborg (Gothenburg), 133, 146, 152-5
skärgård, 131, 152, 157
Gotland, 187, 192-4
Gotska Sanden, 187
Grabow, 52, 53
Grabowski Kanal, 345
Gräddö, 226
Grand Holm Marina (Haapsalu), 409, 410
Gränsö Slott, 196
Gråsö, 284
Greifswald, 60-61
Greifswald Wieck, 60
Greifswalder Bodden, 20, 54, 58, 59-61, 343

Greifswalder Oie, 20, 61
Grenå, 100
Grindafjärden, 217
Grodzka Island, 346
Gröneborg, 210
Grønsund, 123, 125
Gropen, 293
Groplandet, 293
Gudhjem South, 128, 129
Gulf of Bothnia, 131
 Finland, 244, 245, 252-63
 Sweden, 131, 225-43
Gulf of Finland
 Estonia, 318, 324, 393, 411-17
 Finland, 287-317
 Russia, 312-14, 318-33
Gulf of Gdańsk, 334, 360-66
 TSS, 360, 361, 362, 365
Gulf of Rīga
 Estonia, 392, 398-404
 Latvia, 378, 379, 386-91
Gullholmen, 160, 161
Gullkrona, 283, 284

Haapasaari, 300, 310, 313, 324
Haapsalu, 395, 396, 408, 409-410
Hadsund, 98
Hailuoto, 256
Hajstorp, 173
Hakefjord, 160
Halden, 166
Hallands Väderö, 148
Halmstad, 146, 147, 148
Hals, 96-8
Halsefjorden, 160
Hälsingland, 229
Hamari (Hammars), 302
Hamburgsund, 164-5
Hamina (Fredrikshamn), 300, 308-310
Hammarbyleden, 209, 223
Hammars (Hamari), 302
Hammerhavn, 128
Hamnholmen, 282
Hamnklobb, 283
Hamnö, 283, 285
Hamnsundet, 272
Hanko (Hangö), 245, 284, 287, 288-92, 392
routes to/from Helsinki, 287-95
Hanö, 181, 182
Haparanda, 225, 242
Haparandahamn, 225, 242
Haraholmen, 239
Härnösand, 225, 229, 230-31
Hasle, 128
Hasselkobben, 219
Hästholmen, 151, 217, 219, 221
Hästö, 202
Havstensfjorden, 160
Havsvidden (Geta), 272
health insurance, 7
health risks, 8
Heiligendamm, 46
Heiligenhafen, 37-9
Hel, 359-61
Hel peninsula (Mierzeja Helska), 358, 359, 360, 361
Hellerup (Copenhagen), 80, 81, 82
Helsingborg, 144, 145
Helsingfors *see* Helsinki
Helsingholm, 284
Helsingør, 83-4

THE BALTIC SEA AND APPROACHES 435

INDEX

Helsinki (Helsingfors), 296-300, 324
  approaches, 296-7
  routes to/from Hanko, 287-95
Helsö, 285
Heltermaa, 392, 406
Henän, 160
Henningsdorf, 348
Herreninsel, 43
Hiddensee, 19, 20, 54, 59
High Coast (Höga Kusten), 131, 226, 232-4
Hiittinen (Hitis), 284
Hiiumaa, 397, 406-9
Himmerfjärden, 205
history, 1-4, *see also start of each chapter*
Hitis (Hiittinen), 284
Hobro, 98
Höga Kusten (High Coast), 131, 226, 232-4
Höganäs, 146
Högsåra, 282, 283
Högskär, 219
Hohensaaten lock, 348
holding tanks, 8
Hölick, 229, 230
holidays, public see start of each chapter
Höllviken, 141
Holmön, 236
Holmsund, 236
Holtenau, 21, 23, 28, 29, 30
Horsholm (Arkösund), 202
Horslandet, 230
Hotellbryggan (Dalarö), 217
Hötterskär, 219
Houtskär, 277
Hudiksvall, 225, 229, 230
Hundested, 85
Hundskärsknuv, 219
Hunnebostrand, 164, 165
Husö, 283, 284-5
Husum, 235
Huvön, 219
Huvudskär, 217

ice reports, 423-8
Imatra, 314, 315, 316
immigration, 7, *see also start of each chapter*
Iniö, 276-7
Inston, 160
insurance, 7
International Certificate of Competence, 7
internet, 4, 8, 429, *see also start of each chapter*
iPads, 6
Irbensky Strait, 378
Ivankiv, Vladimir, 323, 325, 333

Jakobstad (Pietarsaari), 252, 257, 259
Jarlehusudde, 169
Järnäsklubb, 235
Jättholmarna, 230
Jezioro Dabie, 345, 346
Jezioro Wrzosowskie, 349
Joensuu, 314, 315
Johannes Marina, 329
Juelsminde, 104
Jungfruskär, 283
Jungfrusund, 283
Junkon, 241
Jūrmala, 388
Jurmo, 276, 284, 286
Jussarö, 293-4

Kaali, 395, 396
Kait, 283
Kaliningrad, 314, 367, 368-71
Kaliningrad Regulated Area 117, 370, 372
Kaliningradskiy Morskoy Kanal, 370, 371
Kaliningradskiy Zaliv, 367, 368-71
Kalkebrænderihavnen (Copenhagen), 80
Kallandsö, 169
Källö-Knippla, 158
Källön, 160
Kalmar, 131, 133, 187, 188-90, 243
Kalmarn, 235
Kalmarsund, 181, 187-8, 194
Kalundborg, 116-17
Kamién Pomorski, 343, 350, 351
Kanal Grabowski, 345
Kanal Mielenski, 341, 343
Kanal Piastowski, 341, 343
Kanholmsfjärden, 219
Kappeln, 31, 33
Kappelshamn, 194
Kärdla, 392, 407-409396
Karelian Isthmus, 313, 316
Käringholm, 282
Käringsund(et), 267
Karlby (Kökar), 285
Karleby (Kokkola), 252, 257, 258-9
Karlsborg, 168, 173
Karlshagen, 61
Karlskrona, 131, 133, 182, 183-5
Karlstad, 172
Karnin, 63
Kasinonranta, 316
Kaskinen (Kaskö), 261
Kasnäs, 287
Kasnäslandet, 283
Kastelholm, 271
Kattegat, 5
  approach through Limfjord, 87-91
  Danish coast, 92-105
  Swedish coast, 146-55
Kaunissaari (Pyttis Fagerö), 305-6
Kavlön, 217
Kejarshamnen, 282
Kelnase Harbour (Prangli), 416
Kemi, 252, 253-4
Kerteminde, 118
Kiel, 29
Kiel Kanal (Nord-Ostsee Kanal), 5, 21-4
Kieler Förde, 29-31
Kieler Hafen, 21, 29-31
Kieler YC (Düsternbrook), 31
Kihnu, 398
Kihti (Skiftet), 245, 274, 276
Kinnekulle, 169
Kipsala, 390
Kirchdorf, 44
Kiuasletto, 253
Klaipėda, 367, 368, 372, 374, 376-7
Klintholm, 76, 77
Kloster, 54
København (Copenhagen), 79-83
Koivuluodonletto, 253
Kökar, 284, 285
Kokkola (Karleby), 252, 257, 258-9
Kolobrzeg, 351-2
Königsberg, 369
Koön, 160
Köpmannebro, 171
Koppö, 261-2
Korpoström, 283-4
Korppoo (Korpö), 283
Korsö, 219

Korsør, 121-2
Kotka, 300, 306-7
Krakesund, 194
Krestovski YC, 333
Kristiinankaupunki (Kristinestad), 252, 261-2
Kristinehamn, 172
Krokskäret, 259
Kronshtadt, 319, 324, 331-3
Kröslin, 61
Kühlungsborn, 46, 47
Kuivastu, 396, 405
Kuiviži, 391
Kuldiga, 379, 380, 384
Kullen, 131, 146, 147
Kumlinge, 274, 275
Kummelskäret, 259
Kungälv, 169
Kungl Svenska Segel Sallskapet (KSSS), 214, 215, 220
Kungshamn, 163, 164, 213, 214
Kuopio, 314, 315
Kuressaare, 395, 396, 402, 403
Kurjoviken, 238
Kusör, 228
Kvarken (Quark(en)), 226, 235, 246, 257-61
Kyrkbacken (Nauvo/Nagu), 277
Kyrkbacken (Ven), 143
Kyrkogårdsö, 284

Laboe, 28, 31
Läckö, 171
Læsø, 95-6
Lagnnöviken bay, 205
Laholmsbukten, 147
Lake Asplången, 175
Lake Boren, 175
Lake Ladoga, 316
Lake Liepaja, 382
Lake Mälaren, 131, 187, 204, 205, 208, 209-210, 222
Lake Peipsi, 395
Lake Roxen, 175
Lake Saimaa, 246, 312, 313, 314-17
Lake Vänern, 131, 167, 168, 169-71, 169-72
Lake Vättern, 131, 167, 173-4
Lake Viken, 172, 173
Landskrona, 143
Landsort, 204, 213
Långbäling, 212
Langeland, 122, 123
Langelinie (Copenhagen), 80, 81
Långh, 219
Långön, 294
Länsi Mustasaari, 297
Lapland, 246, 250
Lappeenranta, 313, 314, 315-16
Lappo, 276
Latvia, 378-91
Laulasmaa, 412
laundry, 9
Lauterbach, 59-60
Lauterhorn, 194
Lavola YC Harbour, 328
laying-up, 10, *see also start of each chapter*
lazy lines, 12
Łeba, 356-7
Lehnitz lock, 348
Lehtma, 409
Lemströmin Kanava (Lemströms Kanal), 268, 271

INDEX

Lemvig, 89
Leppäluoto, 259
Leppaniemi, 241-2
Leppneeme, 416
Lerkil, 151
Lervik, 191
Libben, 20, 54
Lickershamn, 194
Lielupe River, 378, 388
Liepāja, 379, 382-4
Likskarët, 240
Lilla Edet, 169
Lille Bælt, 106-115
Lille Melskär, 219
Limfjord, 5, 86, 87-91, 96, 97
Limön, 227
Lindalssundet, 217
Lindöfjarden, 202
Linnoitusniemi, 316
Liss Lindö, 202
Lithuania, 372-7
Livonia, 380, 395
Ljugarsholm, 275
Ljusne, 229
Loftahammar, 194, 199
Lohals, 122
Lohusalu, 396, 411-12
Lökholmen, 220
Lotsudden, 274
Loviisa (Lovisa), 300, 304-5
Lübeck, 19, 40, 41, 43
Luleå, 225, 240
Lumparn, 268, 271, 274
Lundeborg Havn, 121
Lurö skärgård (Lake Vänern), 171
Lusärnafjärden, 196, 197
Lyme disease, 8
Lynæs, 85
Lyrestad, 168, 173
Lysekil, 157, 160, 162

Maalaistenlaituri, 316
Maarianhamina *see* Mariehamn
Maasholm, 33
Malmö, 133, 141-4
Malö, 151
Malören, 241
Marbäling, 212
Margretheholm (Copenhagen), 81
Mariager Fjord, 98, 99
Mariefred, 210
Mariehamn (Maarianhamina), 226, 265, 268-71
Mariestad, 169, 171
marine environment, 1-2, 8
Marjaniemi, 256
Marstrand, 157, 158
Masnedsund, 123, 124, 125
Måsskär, 219
Mecklenburg Lake District, 19, 44, 46
Mecklenburger Bucht TSS, 51
Medelpad, 229
medical matters, 8
Mellanfjärden, 230
Mellerston, 239
Mem, 168, 174, 175, 202
Memar Marina (Oskarshamn), 191
Mērsrags, 387, 388
Mickelsörarna, 259
Middelfart, 106-7
Mieleński Kanal, 341, 343

Mierzeja Helska (Hel peninsula), 358, 359, 360, 361
MiFi, 8
Mikkelinsaaret, 259
military restrictions, 420, see also start of each chapter
Minge, 372
Mjältön, 233
mobile phones, 6, 8
Modermagan, 293
Mollösund, 161
Moltenört, 28
money see start of each chapter
Mönster, 151
Moon Sound, 392, 405-410
mooring, 10-13
Mörholmen, 294
Morsken, 219
Morskoy Kanal (Kaliningrad), 370, 371
Morskoy Kanal (St Petersburg), 332, 333
Mörtö, 219
Mörtöklubb, 219
mosquitoes, 8
Motala, 168, 173, 174
motor/sailing cone, 8
Mottawa River, 366
Muhu, 393, 405
Mustakari, 258-9
Muuga Bay, 416

Nagu (Nauvo), 277
Naissaar, 412
Nämdö, 217
Narva-Jõesuu, 417
Näsby, 277
Näset, 275
Nåttarö, 212
nature harbours, 136-7
Nauvo (Nagu), 277
navigation, 6
navigational warnings, 423-8
Neu Mukran, 57, 59
Neuendorf Marina, 65
Neustadt (Ancora Marina), 39
Nevskaya Guba, 319, 324
New Port Kotka, 307
Nexø, 128-9
Nida, 372, 374, 377
Niederfinow ship lift, 348
Nölstö, 283
Norbotten, 238-40
Nord-Ostsee Kanal (Kiel Kanal), 5, 21-4
Norra Kvarken, 235-7
Norra Västkusten, 156-66
Norrby, 276, 277
Norrbyskär, 235
Norreborg (Ven), 143
Nørrekås (Rønne), 127
Norrfällsviken, 233
Norrklobbarna, 293
Norrsund, 284
Norrsundet, 228
Norsholm, 168, 174
Nortälje, 226
Norway, 157, 166
Notholmen, 198
Nötö, 284, 286
Nötviken, 272
Nowy Port (Gdańsk), 364, 365
Nuijamaa, 313
Nuokko (Nuokot), 308

Nyborg (Fyn), 120-21
Nyhavn (Copenhagen), 81
Nykøbing (Mors), 89
Nyköping, 202, 204
Nynäshamn, 195, 204, 211-12, 213, 217, 219
Nystad (Uusikaupunki), 252, 261, 263

Obereidersee, 22
Odden, 85
Oddesund Bridge, 89-90
Oder Havel Kanal, 348
Oderberg, 348
Odra (Oder) River, 341, 345, 348
Öland, 181, 187
Öland TSS, 187
Ölands Bridge, 187, 188, 189
Old Castle Harbour (Klaipėda), 376, 377
Oldenbüttel Siding, 24
Olpenitz Marina, 32
Olympiahafen Schilksee Marina (Strande), 31
Orana, 227
Oranienburg, 348
Öregrund, 226, 227
Öregrund TSS, 226
Øresund (The Sound)
    Bridge, 78, 139
    Denmark, 78-85
    Sweden, 131, 138, 139-46
TSSs, 78
Ornö, 212
Örnsköldsvik, 226, 234
Orrön, 219
Orslandet, 294
Orth, 37
Orust, 160, 161
Oskarshamn, 191, 194
Oslo Fjord, 166
Østerby, 96
Ostrov Seskar, 318
Oulu (Uleåborg), 252, 255
Oxelösund, 202, 203

Pähkinäinen, 277
Paldiski Nord, 411
Pälli, 313, 314
Pape, 378, 383
paperwork, 7, see also start of each chapter
Paraisten Portti (Parainen), 282
Pärnu, 391, 396, 400, 401
passports, 7, see also start of each chapter
Patholmsviken YC, 236
Pāvilosta, 381, 384
Peenemünde, 61
Peenestrom, 20, 54, 59, 61-5, 334, 343
Peetri (Tallinn), 414
Pellinki (Sandholmsudden), 302
Perämeri *see* Bay of Bothnia
Petäjäs, 263
Piastowski Kanal, 341, 343
Pietarsaari (Jakobstad), 252, 257, 259
pilots & cruising guides, 4, 6, 418-19, see also start of each chapter
Pionerskiy, 371
Pirita, 412, 413, 415
Pite-Rönnskär, 238-9
Piteå, 226, 239
Pitsundet, 239
Poel, 44
Pogon Marina, 347

INDEX

Poland, 334-67
pollution, 8
Pomorski, Kamién, 343, 350, 351
Pori, 252, 262
Porkkala, 288, 295
Poroholma, 263
Port Darłowo, 353-4, 355
Port Olpenitz Marina, 32
Porta Hotele, Marina, 347
Porvoo (Borgå), 301-2
Potenitzer Wiek, 40
Prangli (Kelnase Harbour), 416
Prästö, 272
Prerow, 51
Primorsk Yacht Pier 29a, 329
provisioning, 9-10, *see also start of each chapter*
Przekop Mielenski, 345-6
public holidays see *start of each chapter*
Putbus, 54
Puumala, 315, 317
Pyttis Fagerö (Kaunissaari), 305-6

Quark(en) (Kvarken), 226, 235, 246, 257-61

Råå, 144
Raahe, 252, 256-7
radio communications, 421-8, see also *start of each chapter*
radio operators' certificates, 4, 7
Räfsö (Reposaari), 261, 262
Ränö, 212
Ransome, Arthur, 392, 405
Rapasaari, 316
Ratan, 237
Rataskärr, 237
Rauma (Raumo), 252, 261, 262-3
RCC Pilotage Foundation, 5
Regalica Mienia, 345, 346
Regalica Odra, 346
Regulated Area 117, 370, 372
Remmarhamn, 275
Rendsburg, 21, 22, 24, 25
repairs, 9, *see also start of each chapter*
Reposaari (Räfsö), 261, 262
Resarö, 217, 221
rescue/safety services see *start of each chapter*
Resö, 165
restricted areas see *start of each chapter*
Rīga, 379, 385, 388-91
Right of Public Access, 137, 251
Ringsu, 398-9
rock mooring, 12, 13
Rødbyhavn, 72-3
Rödhamn, 273
Rödhamnsfjärden, 273
Rödjan, 293
Rødvig, 77
Rohuküla, 406
Roja, 387
Romans, 3
Rønne, 127, 334
Rönnskär, 238-9
Roomassaare, 396, 402, 403, 404
Rørvig, 85
Rosala, 283, 284
Rostock, 47, 49-51
routes to the Baltic, 5
Royal Swedish YC (KSSS), 214, 215, 220

Royal Yachting Association, 4
Röyttä, 255
Rozewie Point, 358
Ruden, 61
Rügen, 19, 20, 56, 57, 59-60
Ruhnu, 387, 395, 398-9
Ruiskahuone, 257
Rumar, 284
Runmarö, 217, 219
Russia, 319-33
　abbreviations on Russian charts, 419-20
　approaches, 301, 312-14, 318, 323, 324, 325, 331-3
　see also Kaliningrad
Russian Channel (Finland), 312-17
Rysäkari, 297

Saaler Bodden, 52, 53
Saaremaa, 387, 393, 395, 396, 397, 402-4
Sæby, 94-5
safety/rescue services see *start of each chapter*
Säffle, 172
Saimaa Canal, 246, 313-14, 324, 325, 328
Saimaa Lakes, 246, 312, 313, 314-17
St Petersburg, 5, 310, 314, 319-24, 331-3
　approaches, 330-33, 417
Saka River, 384
Salacgrīva, 391
Salmeri, 263
Sälsö, 283
Saltholmen, 151
Saltsjöbaden, 213, 214-15
Samsø, 116
Sandhamn (S of Kalmar), 188
Sandhamn (Stockholm *skärgård*), 213, 217, 219-20
Sandholmsudden (Pellinki), 302
Sandöfjärden, 217
Sandön (Archipelago Sea), 283
Sandön (Luleå), 240
Sandön (Sandhamn), 219, 220
Sandvik (Kökar), 285
Sanneboviken, 169
Santahamina, 297
Santio, 300, 313, 324
SAR (Search & Rescue), 6, 421-2, see also *start of each chapter*
Särkkä, 297
Sassnitz, 54, 59
saunas, 4
Savonlinna, 246, 314, 315, 317
Sävtäktet, 303
Schaprode, 59
Schaproder Bodden, 54, 59
Schengen area, 7
Die Schlei, 19, 31-4
Schleimünde, 32-3
Schleswig, 33-4
Schlutup, 43
Schwerin, 44
Schweriner See, 44
sea travel, 5
search & rescue (SAR), 6, 421-422, see also *start of each chapter*
Seedorf, 60
Seglinge, 275
Sejerø, 116
Seskaro, 241-2
sewage disposal, 8, *see also start of each chapter*

ship's papers, 7
shopping, 9-10, *see also start of each chapter*
Sigulda, 379
Sikeå, 237
Sikhamn, 191
Sikhjälma, 227
Silk, 40
Simrishamn, 131, 177, 179, 180-81
Sjötorp, 168, 169, 171, 173
Skagen, 92-3
Skaggerak, 5, 157
Skälderviken, 147
Skallahamn, 151
Skanör, 140
skärgårds, 131, 136
　Lake Vänern, 169-72
　saaristo (Finland), 246, 287-95, 300-311
　Stockhölm & NE, 131, 136, 152, 205, 213-21
　Sweden East Coast S of Stockholm, 187-8, 194-204
　Sweden West Coast, 131, 151-2
Skärlandet, 287
Skarpskär, 283, 284
Skellefteå, 225, 238
Skelleftehamn, 238
Skeppsbrofjarden, 196, 197, 198
Skiftet (Kihti), 245, 274, 276
Skillinge, 181
Skulte, 391
Slätbaken, 174, 175, 202
Slemmern, 271
Slupska Bank East TSS, 356
Smålandsfarvandet, 123
smart phones, 6, 8
Smiltynė Yacht Harbour, 377
Smögen, 162, 163
Smörasken, 219
Snäckö, 275, 283
Söderarm, 219
Söderhamn, 226, 229
Söderklobba, 283
Söderköping, 168, 174, 175
Södermöja, 219
Södertälje, 205-7
Södertälje Kanal, 204, 205-8, 209, 213
Södholm, 284
Sodra Västkusten, 146-55
Södra Vaxlet, 219
Solberg Udde, 196
Sønderborg, 113, 114-15
Sopot, 361
Sorpo, 282
Sõru, 406
Sorvakko, 263
Sotekanalen, 162, 164
Sottunga, 283, 284
Sottungalandet, 283
The Sound *see* Øresund
Soviet Union, 4
Sovietskij, 329
Sparrholm, 294
Spiken, 171
Spikön, 169
Spodsbjerg Turistbådhavn, 122
Spree River, 348
Stegeborg, 201
Stenskär (Archipelago Sea), 284
Stenskäret (Gulf of Bothnia), 239
stern anchor, 12

438　THE BALTIC SEA AND APPROACHES

INDEX

stern buoy, 11
Stettiner Haff, 20, 54, 59, 63, 64-5, *see also* Zalew Szczeciński
Stickellandet, 294
Stickenhörn Marina, 28, 30
Stockholm, 131, 133, 208, 211, 217, 222-4
    approaches, 205, 213-15, 221
    routes within skärgård, 213-21
Stor-Pellinge (Suur-Pellinki), 300
Stora Brändö, 295
Stora Hästskär, 219
Stora Melskär, 219
Stora Möja, 219
Stora Nasset, 219
Stora Skärgården, 219
Store Bælt, 116-26
Store Bælt Bridge, 119, 120
Storjungfrun, 229
Stormälö, 281, 282
Storstrøm, 123, 124
Strägnäs, 210
Stralsund, 20, 53, 54-7, 343
Strande, 31
Strelasund, 20, 53-7
Strömstad, 157, 165, 166
Stubbekøbing, 75, 76, 123
Styrsø, 152
Sundsvall, 225, 226, 229, 230, 231
Suninsalmi (Sunisundet), 302-3
Sunna Holme, 160
Sunnisund, 302-3
Suomenlinna (Sveaborg), 296-7
Susisaari, 297
Suur Katel Bay, 403, 404
Suur-Pellinki (Stor-Pellinge), 300
Svaneke, 128
Svannemølle (Copenhagen), 81, 82
Svartholm, 305
Svartklubben, 226
Sveaborg (Suomenlinna), 296-7
Svendborg, 110-112
Svenska Kryssarklubben (Swedish Cruising Club), 224
Sviby, 408, 409
Sweden, 1, 131-243
Swinoujscie, 59, 178, 334, 341-3
Syväraumanlahti, 263
Szczecin, 334, 341, 345-7, 348

Tallholmen, 303
Tallinn, 324, 395, 396, 412-16
Tammisaaren Saariston Kansallispuisto (Ekenäs *Skärgårds* Nationalpark), 287, 293
Tammisaari (Ekenäs), 292, 294
Tankar, 258
Taran, 370
Tåtorp, 173
TBE *(tick-borne encephalitis)*, 8
telephones, 6, 8, *see also start of each chapter*
Terijoki YC, 329
Thurø Bund, 112
Thyborøn, 88-9
ticks, 8
tides & tidal streams, 1, 6, *see also start of each chapter*
Tiessenkai, 23, 30
time see *start of each chapter*
Tjärven, 213, 217, 219
Tjen, 128

Tjörn, 160
Tjuvholmsundet Canal, 240
Tönning, 25, 26, 27
Töre, 225, 241
Töreboda, 168, 173
Törehamn, 241
Torekov, 147-8
Tornio, 252, 253
Torsholm, 275
Torsö (Lake Vanern), 169
Torsö (W Gulf of Finland), 287
Tösse *skärgård* (Lake Vänern), 172
traffic separation schemes (TSSs), 6, 51, 78, 179, 187, 226, 356, *see also* Gulf of Gdańsk
Trälhavet, 219
Träslövsläge, 149
Trave, River, 43
travel, 5, *see also start of each chapter*
Travemünde, 19, 40-43, 385
Trelleborg, 48, 177, 178
Triigi, 406
Troense, 112
Trollhätte Kanal, 167, 168, 169
Trosa, 205
Trysunda, 233-4
Trzebież, 344
Tuborg Marina (Copenhagen), 82
Tullandet, 295
Tullisilta, 304, 305
Turku (Åbo), 278-81
Turun Saaristo, 264, 265, 278, 287-8
Tylösand, 148

Uddevalla, 157, 160
Ueckermünde, 65
Uleåborg (Oulu), 252, 255
Ulko-Petäjäs, 263
Ulvesund, 123
Ulvöhamn, 233
Umeå, 225, 236
Uppsala, 210
Ursvikens SC, 238
Usedom, 19, 20, 64
Ustka, 354, 355-6
Utklippan, 181, 185
Utlangan, 185, 187
Utö (Archipelago Sea), 284, 285-6
Utö (Nynäshamn), 212, 217
Uusikaupunki, 252, 261, 263, 274

Vaasa (Vasa), 252, 257, 260-61
Väddö Canal, 226
Vadstena, 173-4
Vallisaari, 297
Vallvik, 229
Vänersborg, 169
Vänö, 284, 286
Varberg, 146, 149-51
Vårdö, 274
Vårholma, 217
Värmlandssjön, 172
Varsalahti, 277
Vasa (Vaasa), 252, 257, 260-61
Vaskiluoto (WSF), 260-61
Vassbacken, 173
Västerås, 210
Västerbotten, 235-7
Västerholmen, 217
Västernorrland, 232
Västervik, 194, 195, 196-8

VAT, 4, 7
Vatunginnokka, 254
Växär, 287
Vaxholm, 213, 217, 219, 221, 243
Vejle, 105
Vejrø, 123
Ven Island, 143-4
Ventspils, 48, 212, 379, 384-5
Vergi, 324, 396, 417
Veskiviigi (Haapsalu), 409, 410
Vesterø, 95-6
Viipuri see Vyborg
Vikings, 3
Viksberg, 205
Villskär, 259
Vilnius, 374
Vindö (Orust), 160, 161
Vindö (Stockholm *skärgård*), 217, 219
Virolahti, 300
Virtsu, 405
visas, 7
Visby, 187, 193-4
Vitte, 19, 54
Vladimir Ivankiv, 323, 325, 333
Vordingborg, 124-5
Vormö, 294
Vormsi, 392, 409
Vrangö, 152
Vyborg (Viipuri), 319, 323, 325-8
    approaches, 300, 314, 324, 325

Warnemünde, 47-8, 49
waste disposal, 8
water, 9, *see also start of each chapter*
waypoints/positions, 6
weather & weather services, 1, 6, 423-9, *see also start of each chapter*
weatherfax, 429
websites, 4, *see also start of each chapter*
Westerviks Segelsällskap Wikingarna YC, 198
Westmer (Haapsalu), 409, 410
White Sea, 5
Wieck, 60
Wieprza River, 353
WiFi, 8
wind scales, 424
wind speeds, 6
Wisła River, 364, 365, 366
Wislany, Zalew, 368
Wismar, 44-6
Wismar Bucht, 45
Władyslawowo, 338, 358-9
Wolgast, 20, 61, 62, 63
Wolin, 251, 349, 350

yacht clubs see *start of each chapter*
yacht services & chandlery, 8-10, *see also start of each chapter*
Yngerskar, 286
Ystad, 178-9
Yxlan, 219
Yxskar, 284

Zalew Kamienski, 349
Zalew Szczeciński, 334, 342, 343-5, 349, *see also* Stettiner Haff
Zalew Wislany, 368
Zecherin Bridge, 63
Zelenogorsk, 329
Zingst, 52

THE BALTIC SEA AND APPROACHES